Lecture Notes in Computer Science 16556

Formal Methods

Subline of Lecture Notes in Computer Science

More information about this series at https://link.springer.com/bookseries/558

Augusto Sampaio · Marielle Stoelinga
Editors

Formal Methods

27th International Symposium, FM 2026
Tokyo, Japan, May 18–22, 2026
Proceedings, Part I

Editors
Augusto Sampaio
Universidade Federal de Pernambuco
Recife, Brazil

Marielle Stoelinga
University of Twente
Enschede, The Netherlands

ISSN 0302-9743 ISSN 1611-3349 (electronic)
Lecture Notes in Computer Science
ISBN 978-3-032-26203-5 ISBN 978-3-032-26204-2 (eBook)
https://doi.org/10.1007/978-3-032-26204-2

This Springer imprint is published by the registered company Springer Nature Switzerland AG
The registered company address is: Gewerbestrasse 11, 6330 Cham, Switzerland

Preface

We proudly present two volumes with the papers accepted for publication and presented at the 27th International Symposium on Formal Methods (FM 2026), in Tokyo, Japan, from May 18–22, 2026.

FM 2026 is the 27th edition of the symposium series organized by Formal Methods Europe (FME), an independent association that promotes the effective use of formal methods in system development. The FM symposia serve as a forum for researchers and practitioners from academia, industry, and government to present new results, report on experience, and explore emerging directions. FM 2026 continues this role, supporting interaction across different parts of the community.

Tracks. The current two LNCS volumes contain the papers presented in four different tracks at FM 2026:

- *The Main track,* co-chaired by us, Augusto Sampaio (Universidade Federal de Pernambuco, Brazil) and Marielle Stoelinga (University of Twente & Radboud University, The Netherlands),
- *The Tests and Proofs (TAP) track,* co-chaired by Achim Brucker (University of Exeter, UK) and Marie-Christine Jakobs (Ludwig-Maximilians-Universität München, Germany),
- *Industry Day,* co-chaired by Jeroen Keiren (Eindhoven University of Technology, The Netherlands) and Naoto Sato (Hitachi, Japan), and
- *The Tutorials track,* co-chaired by Kazuhiro Ogata (Japan Advanced Institute of Science and Technology, Japan) and Neeraj Kumar Singh (University of Toulouse, France).

In addition, the FM program features several tracks published at other venues:

- *Journal First Track,* chaired by Anne Haxthausen (Technical University of Denmark),
- Doctoral Symposium, co-chaired by Toshiaki Aoki (JAIST, Japan) and Cyrille Artho (KTH Royal Institute of Technology, Sweden),
- International Conference on Rigorous State-Based Methods (ABZ, co-chaired by Elvinia Riccobene, Università degli Studi di Milano, Italy) and Yamine Ait-Ameur (University of Toulouse, France).
- *Workshops:* AIPV, FMTea, Overture, and Rodin.

Keynotes. FM 2026 featured four keynotes by internationally renowned researchers,

- Cristian Cadar (Imperial College London, UK)
- Daniel Kroening (Amazon Web Services, AWS, USA)
- Ichiro Hasuo (National Institute of Informatics, Japan)
- Ruzica Piskac (Yale University, USA).

Submission numbers. FM 2026 again received a record number of submissions, namely, **239** submissions for the Main and TAP tracks. Each submission underwent review by at least three reviewers, followed by a discussion within the program committee. The Main and TAP tracks accepted **49 papers** (43 papers in the Main track and 6 papers in the TAP track), resulting in an acceptance rate of **21%.** Furthermore, 16 tutorials were submitted, of which 8 were accepted for publication. The Industry Day received 17 submissions and accepted 9.

Artifact evaluations. The authors of all accepted regular papers were strongly encouraged to submit an artifact: additional material, such as software, datasets, log files, machine-checkable proofs, etc., that substantiates the claims made in the paper. Ideally, artifacts allow for the full reproduction of all results in the corresponding paper by providing details on all relevant steps, inputs, configurations, and parameters used. For tools, an artifact typically includes the source code or a binary of the tool and corresponding documentation on how to use, reuse, and possibly extend it.

Artifacts were evaluated by an Artifact Evaluation Committee (AEC), chaired by Étienne André (Nantes Université, France) and Masaki Waga (Kyoto University, Japan). After a short quick-check phase, at least two and, for most artifacts, three AEC members reviewed each artifact in terms of consistency with and reproducibility of results presented in the paper, completeness, documentation, and ease of (re)use, and availability in an online repository with a DOI.

The authors of the accepted tutorial papers were also invited to the artifact evaluation. Although the quick-check phase was skipped due to timing constraints, the tutorial artifacts were evaluated under the same criteria as the regular papers' artifacts by two AEC members.

Based on these reviews, and in strict adherence to the EAPLS artifact badging guidelines, artifacts were awarded a badge in the following categories:

- **Available.** Artifacts that are publicly archived permanently with a DOI that are in some way "*relevant to*" *and* "*add value beyond the text in the article*" were awarded the available badge.
- **Functional.** Artifacts that are documented (containing at least an inventory and "*sufficient description to allow artifacts to be exercised*"), consistent (i.e., "relevant to the associated paper and significantly contribute to the generation of its main results"), complete ("as far as possible") and exercisable, received the functional badge.
- **Reusable.** Functional and available artifacts that are "*very carefully documented and well-structured to the extent that reuse and repurposing is facilitated*" received the reusable badge instead.

Of the **33 submitted artifacts**, 2 received the available badge, 21 were functional, and 10 were awarded the (functional and) reusable badge.

Thank you! We thank all who contributed to FM 2026. We are especially grateful to the FME board for their support and prompt responses to all our questions. We are grateful to the general chair Fuyuki Ishikawa (National Institute of Informatics, Japan) and his team for the smooth organization. We thank the program committees and all reviewers for their careful work, and the organizers of the various tracks and co-located events. Finally, a big thanks to the authors of all submissions.

March 2026

Augusto Sampaio
Marielle Stoelinga

Organization

Program Committees

Main Track and TAP Track

Augusto Sampaio (Co-chair Main Track)	Federal University of Pernambuco, Brazil
Marielle Stoelinga (Co-chair Main Track)	University of Twente, Netherlands
Achim D. Brucker (Co-chair TAP)	University of Exeter, UK
Marie-Christine Jakobs (Co-chair TAP)	LMU Munich, Germany
Erika Abraham	RWTH Aachen University, Germany
Wolfgang Ahrendt	Chalmers University of Technology, Sweden
Bernhard Aichernig	Institute for Formal Models and Verification, Johannes Kepler University Linz, Austria
Alessandro Aldini	University of Urbino "Carlo Bo", Italy
Oana Andrei	University of Glasgow, UK
Pedro Antonino	The Blockhouse Technology Limited, UK
Toshiaki Aoki	JAIST, Japan
Alessandro Armando	University of Genova & Fondazione Bruno Kessler, Italy
Christel Baier	TU Dresden, Germany
Clark Barrett	Stanford University, USA
Ezio Bartocci	TU Wien, Austria
Gustavo Betarte	InCo, Universidad de la República, Uruguay, Uruguay
Mohamed Bettaz	Czech Technical University in Prague, Czechia
Dirk Beyer	LMU Munich, Germany
Roderick Bloem	Graz University of Technology, Austria
Patricia Bouyer	CNRS, France
Gustavo Carvalho	Universidade Federal de Pernambuco, Brazil
Darion Cassel	Amazon Web Services, USA
Valentina Castiglioni	Eindhoven University of Technology, Netherlands
Ana Cavalcanti	University of York, UK
Milan Ceska	Brno University of Technology, Czechia
Yu-Fang Chen	Academia Sinica, Taiwan

Pedro R. D'Argenio	Universidad Nacional de Córdoba, CONICET, Argentina
Nancy Day	University of Waterloo, Canada
Frank de Boer	Centrum Wiskunde & Informatica, Netherlands
Jin Song Dong	National University of Singapore, Singapore
Brijesh Dongol	University of Surrey, UK
Catherine Dubois	ENSIIE-Samovar, France
João F. Ferreira	University of Porto, Portugal
Marco Faella	Università di Napoli "Federico II", Italy
Marie Farrell	The University of Manchester, UK
Natasha Fernandes	Macquarie University, Australia
Carla Ferreira	Universidade NOVA de Lisboa, Portugal
Wan Fokkink	Vrije Universiteit Amsterdam, Netherlands
Jose Fragoso Santos	INESC-ID/IST, Portugal
Carlo A. Furia	USI - Università della Svizzera italiana, Switzerland
Mario Gleirscher	University of Bremen, Germany
Jan Friso Groote	Eindhoven University of Technology, Netherlands
Ernst Moritz Hahn	University of Twente, Netherlands
Ichiro Hasuo	National Institute of Informatics, Japan
Paula Herber	University of Münster, Germany
Falk Howar	TU Clausthal/IPSSE, Germany
Marieke Huisman	University of Twente, Netherlands
Reiner Hähnle	TU Darmstadt, Germany
Atsushi Igarashi	Kyoto University, Japan
Einar Broch Johnsen	University of Oslo, Norway
Sun Jun	Singapore Management University, Singapore
Jeroen Keiren	Eindhoven University of Technology, Netherlands
Alexander Knapp	Universität Augsburg, Germany
Tsutomu Kobayashi	Japan Aerospace Exploration Agency, Japan
Nikolai Kosmatov	Thales Research & Technology, France
Laura Kovács	TU Wien, Austria
Juneyoung Lee	Amazon Web Services, USA
Zhiming Liu	Southwest University, China
Nuno Macedo	University of Porto & INESC TEC, Portugal
Diego Marmsoler	University of Exeter, UK
Mieke Massink	CNR-ISTI, Pisa, Italy
Anastasia Mavridou	KBR/NASA Ames Research Center, USA
Annabelle McIver	Macquarie University, Australia
Hernan Melgratti	Universidad de Buenos Aires, Argentina
Alexandra Mendes	University of Porto, Portugal
Carroll Morgan	The University of New South Wales, Australia

Alexandre Mota	Universidade Federal de Pernambuco, Brazil
Mohammad Reza Mousavi	King's College London, UK
David Naumann	Stevens Institute of Technology, USA
Daniel Neider	TU Dortmund University, Germany
Gethin Norman	University of Glasgow, UK
Kazuhiro Ogata	JAIST, Japan
Jose Oliveira	University of Minho, Portugal
Luigia Petre	Åbo Akademi University, Finland
Laure Petrucci	Université Paris 13, France
Jean-Francois Raskin	Université libre de Bruxelles, Belgium
Matteo Rossi	Politecnico di Milano, Italy
Marco Roveri	University of Trento, Italy
Pierluigi San Pietro	Politecnico di Milano, Italy
Gerardo Schneider	Chalmers University of Technology and University of Gothenburg, Sweden
Daniel Schoepe	Amazon, USA
Cristina Seceleanu	Mälardalen University, Sweden
Emil Sekerinski	McMaster University, Canada
Adenilso Simao	ICMC/USP, Brazil
Graeme Smith	The University of Queensland, Australia
Ana Sokolova	University of Salzburg, Austria
Silvia Lizeth Tapia Tarifa	University of Oslo, Norway
Maurice ter Beek	CNR, Italy
Jan Tretmans	TNO - Embedded Systems Innovation, Netherlands
Mattias Ulbrich	Karlsruhe Institute of Technology, Germany
Frits Vaandrager	Radboud University, Netherlands
Jaco van de Pol	Aarhus University, Denmark
Matthias Volk	Eindhoven University of Technology, Netherlands
Heike Wehrheim	University of Oldenburg, Germany
Kirsten Winter	The University of Queensland, Australia
Burkhart Wolff	University Paris-Saclay, France
Jim Woodcock	University of York, UK
Naijun Zhan	Institute of Software, Chinese Academy of Sciences, China
Min Zhang	East China Normal University, China
Zhenya Zhang	Kyushu University, Japan

Tutorials

Kazuhiro Ogata (Co-chair)	JAIST, Japan
Neeraj Kumar Singh (Co-chair)	INPT-ENSEEIHT/IRIT, University of Toulouse, France
Erika Abraham	RWTH Aachen University, Germany
Toshiaki Aoki	JAIST, Japan
Nikolaj Bjørner	Microsoft, USA
Sylvie Boldo	Inria and Université Paris-Saclay, France
Michael Butler	University of Southampton, UK
Ana Cavalcanti	University of York, UK
Yunja Choi	Kyungpook National University, South Korea
Alcino Cunha	University of Minho, Portugal
Deepak D'Souza	Indian Institute of Science, India
Thi Thu Ha Doan	Japan Advanced Institute of Science and Technology, Japan
Brijesh Dongol	University of Surrey, UK
Catherine Dubois	ENSIIE-Samovar, France
Marie Farrell	The University of Manchester, UK
Leo Freitas	Newcastle University, UK
Kim Guldstrand Larsen	Aalborg University, Denmark
Raju Halder	IIT, Patna, India
Marieke Huisman	University of Twente, Netherlands
Fuyuki Ishikawa	National Institute of Informatics, Japan
Sun Jun	Singapore Management University, Singapore
Regine Laleau	Paris Est Creteil University, France
Thierry Lecomte	CLEARSY, France
Michael Leuschel	University of Düsseldorf, Germany
Stephan Merz	Inria Nancy, France
Canh Minh Do	Japan Advanced Institute of Science and Technology, Japan
Antoine Miné	LIP6, UPMC, France
Rosemary Monahan	Maynooth University, Ireland
Cesar Munoz	NASA, USA
Fumiko Nagoya	Nihon University, Japan
Masaki Nakamura	Toyama Prefectural University, Japan
Anh Nguyen	Japan Advanced Institute of Science and Technology, Japan
S. Ramesh	General Motors R&D, India
Elvinia Riccobene	University of Milan, Italy
Graeme Smith	The University of Queensland, Australia
Tsubasa Takagi	Japan Advanced Institute of Science and Technology, Japan

Carolyn Talcott	SRI International, USA
Maurice ter Beek	CNR, Italy
Tatsuhiro Tsuchiya	The University of Osaka, Japan
Laurent Voisin	Systerel, France
Tim Willemse	Eindhoven University of Technology, Netherlands

Artifact Evaluation

Étienne André (Co-chair)	Université de Nantes, France
Masaki Waga (Co-chair)	Kyoto University, Japan
Augustin Albert	LIX, France
Ricardo Almeida	University of Glasgow, UK
Thom Badings	University of Oxford, UK
Lydia Bakiri	Université Sorbonne Paris Nord, France
Hugo Bazille	LRE, France
Laura Bussi	University of Amsterdam, Netherlands
Shaowei Cai	Institute of Software, Chinese Academy of Sciences, China
Juan Diego Campo	Universidad de la República, Uruguay
Agnishom Chattopadhyay	Imiron, Japan
Po-Chun Chien	LMU Munich, Germany
Susmoy Das	University of Glasgow, India
Sarah Dépernet	Inria Nancy, Université de Lorraine, Loria, France
Yanni Dong	University of Twente, Netherlands
Daniel Drodt	TU Darmstadt, Germany
Paul Eichler	CISPA - Helmholtz Center for Information Security, Germany
Mohamed Elwakil	United States Coast Guard Academy, USA
Eduardo Fernandes	University of Southern Denmark, Denmark
Chao Gao	Kyoto University, Japan
Gloria Gori	University of Florence, Italy
Matthias Güdemann	UAS Munich, Germany
Amit Gurung	UPES, Dehradun, India
Niklas Heidler	Technical University Darmstadt, Germany
Hsi-Ming Ho	University of Sussex, UK
Chiao Hsieh	Kyoto University, Japan
Noa Izsak	CISPA Helmholtz Center for Information Security, Germany
Philipp Kern	KIT, Germany
Elvis Gerardin Konjoh Selabi	Gran Sasso Science Institute & University of Camerino, Italy
Marian Lingsch-Rosenfeld	LMU Munich, Germany

Tianhai Liu	ITI KIT, Germany
Wei Liu	Concordia University, Canada
Deyun Lyu	National Institute of Informatics, Japan
Dara MacConville	Maynooth University, Ireland
Misato Nakabayashi	NTT Social Informatics Laboratories, Japan
Tiago Oliveira	University of Minho, Portugal
Rémi Parrot	École Centrale de Nantes, LS2N, France
Samuel Pastva	Masaryk University, Slovakia
Reuven Peleg	Hebrew University of Jerusalem Israel
Bram Pellen	Radboud University, Netherlands
Kittiphon Phalakarn	National Institute of Informatics, Japan
Tephilla Prince	Indian Institute of Technology, Dharwad, India
Lisa Pühl	RWTH Aachen University, Germany
Robert Rubbens	University of Twente, Netherlands
Sota Sato	Kyoto University, Japan
Rohith Kumar Shanmuganathan	Fraunhofer IEM, Germany
Fabien Siron	Université Paris-Saclay, CEA, List, France
Soaibuzzaman	Bauhaus University Weimar, Germany
Reza Soltani	University of Twente, Netherlands
Gaëtan Staquet	École Centrale Nantes, France
Amy Stell	University of Exeter, UK
Han Su	National Institute of Informatics, Japan
Takashi Suwa	Graduate School of Informatics, Kyoto University, and National Institute of Informatics, Japan
Landon Taylor	Utah State University, USA
Benjamin von Berg	IST, Graz University of Technology, Austria
Masaki Waga	Kyoto University, Japan
Ryo Wakizaka	Kyoto University, Japan
Yilong Yang	Beihang University, China
Shenghao Yuan	Nanjing University of Aeronautics and Astronautics (NUAA), China
Guanqin Zhang	University of New South Wales, Australia
Lei Zhang	University of Maryland, Baltimore County, USA
Zicen Zhao	Kyushu University, Japan
Kevin Zhou	National Institute of Informatics, Japan

Industry Day Track

Jeroen Keiren (Co-chair)	Eindhoven University of Technology, Netherlands
Naoto Sato (Co-chair)	Hitachi, Ltd., Japan
Klaus Havelund	Jet Propulsion Laboratory, California Institute of Technology, USA

Peter Höfner	Australian National University, Australia
Joseph Kiniry	Galois, Inc., USA
Nikolai Kosmatov	Thales Research & Technology, France
Cong Liu	Collins Aerospace, USA
Cristina Seceleanu	Mälardalen University, Sweden

Doctoral Symposium

Toshiaki Aoki (Co-chair)	Japan Advanced Institute of Science and Technology, Japan
Cyrille Artho (Co-chair)	KTH Royal Institute of Technology, Sweden
Kyungmin Bae	Pohang University of Science and Technology (POSTECH), South Korea
Alcino Cunha	University of Minho, Portugal
Guillaume Dupont	Institut de Recherche en Informatique de Toulouse, France
Dimitra Giannakopoulou	AWS, USA
Daisuke Ishii	Japan Advanced Institute of Science and Technology, Japan
Yi Li	Nanyang Technological University, Singapore
Shaoying Liu	East China Normal University, China
Peter Ölveczky	University of Oslo, Norway
Elvinia Riccobene	University of Milan, Italy
Kristin Yvonne Rozier	Iowa State University, USA
Gerardo Schneider	Chalmers University of Technology and University of Gothenburg, Sweden
Martina Seidl	Johannes Kepler University Linz, Austria
Masaki Waga	Kyoto University, Japan

Journal First Track

Anne Haxthausen (Chair)	Technical University of Denmark, Denmark
Jeannette Wing	Columbia University, USA
Cliff Jones	Newcastle University, UK
Michael Butler	University of Southampton, UK

FME Board

Ana Cavalcanti	University of York, UK
Maurice ter Beek	CNR, Italy
Nico Plat	Thanos, Netherlands
Lars-Henrik Eriksson	Uppsala University, Sweden

Einar Broch Johnsen	University of Oslo, Norway

Organization Committee

General Chair

Fuyuki Ishikawa	National Institute of Informatics, Japan

Financial Chair

Paolo Arcaini	National Institute of Informatics, Japan

Publicity Chair

Tsutomu Kobayashi	Japan Aerospace Exploration Agency (JAXA), Japan

Web Chair

Deyun Lyu	National Institute of Informatics, Japan

Workshop Chairs

Elena Troubitsyna	KTH, Sweden
Tomoyuki Yokogawa	Okayama Prefectural University, Japan

Additional Reviewers

Aadithya Srinivasan Anand
Alex Ozdemir
Alexander Stekelenburg
Alexander Weigl
Alexandre Moine
Alvaro Miyazawa
Álvaro Silva
Álvaro Tasistro
Amir Goharshady
Andrea Esposito
Andrea Manini
Andreas Bremer
Anirban Majumdar
Anna Stramaglia
Armando Tacchella
Arnaud Grivet Sébert
B. Srivathsan
Benjamin Lucien Kaminski
Benjamin von Berg
Benoît Delahaye
Bharti Chimdyalwar
Bohua Zhan

Boutheina Bannour
Bram Pellen
Calvin Chau
Carlos Tavares
Caroline Lemke
Ciaran Dunne
Clemens Eisenhofer
Daisuke Ishii
Daniel Baier
Daniel Daniel
Daniel Drodt
Daniel Luick
David Lidell
David Pape
Davide Basile
Dejan Nickovic
Delphine Longuet
Diego Latella
Dirk Pattinson
Dominik Haneberg
Dominik Mascherbauer
Dominik Schmidt
Dorde Žikelić
Duong Dinh Tran
Eduard Kamburjan
Emilio Tuosto
Fabian Vu
Fabio Mogavero
Fang Yan
Fang-Yi Lo
Federico Olmedo
Felix Gigler
Felix Wallner
Filip Macák
Filipe Arruda
Florian Sextl
Francesca Randone
Francesco Girardello
François Bobot
Franziska Alber
Gabriele Costa
Gaëtan Staquet
George Granberry
Gerhard Schellhorn
Giorgio Delzanno
Giovanni Bacci
Harshit Jitendra Motwani
Hengjun Zhao
Henrik Wachowitz
Hubert Garavel
Jacques-Henri Jourdan
Jakob Piribauer
Jie An
João Pascoal Faria
Johanna Schwartzentruber
Johannes Schoisswohl
Jonas Becker-Kupczok
Jorge Sousa Pinto
José Proença
Juan García-Garland
Julius Adelt
Juraj Síč
Kais Klai
Kevin van de Glind
Lara Bargmann
Laurent Fuchs
Leandro Buss Becker
Leopoldo Teixeira
Livia Lestingi
Lorenz Winkler
Luca Di Stefano
Luca Marzari
Luca Verderame
Ludovico Fusco
Luigi D. C. Soares
Luigi Sauro
Lukas Grätz
Lukas Holik
Lukas Panneke
Malte Lochau
Marco Scaletta
Marek Jankola
María Belén Rodríguez
Maria João Frade
Marian Lingsch-Rosenfeld
Mario Carneiro
Mark van Wijk
Martim Afonso
Martín Pedemonte
Martin Tappler

Massimo Benerecetti
Matthias Kettl
Michele Chiari
Mihaela-Larisa Clement
Mingyue Zhang
Moamin Abughazala
Mohammad Kakooei
Nazareno Aguirre
Nestan Tsiskaridze
Nicholas Smallbone
Nicola Thoben
Nicolas Berthier
Nuno Rodrigues
Ondřej Lengál
Pauline Blohm
Pedro Carrott
Peixin Wang
Peter Riviere
Philip Tasche
Philipp Kern
Philipp Wendler
Philippe Heim
Po-Chun Chien
Prince Mathew
Renato Neves
Richard Bubel
Richard Stewing
Robert J. Colvin
Robert Mensing
Robert Rubbens
Robin Coutelier
Rocio Aldeco-Perez
Rohit Kumar Shanmuganathan
Roman Andriushchenko
S. Akshay
Saina Sunny
Samuel Teuber
Sascha Klüppelholz
Sebastián Betancourt
Shuling Wang
Simon Foster
Simon Jantsch
Simone Tini
Stéphane Demri
Takashi Tomita
Teofil Sidoruk
Terru Stübinger
Thom Badings
Thomas Hader
Thomas Lemberger
Tianhai Liu
Till Schallau
Tobias Nießen
Valentin Promies
Vincenzo Ciancia
Wanwei Liu
Wasim Essbai
Wei-Lun Tsai
Wolfram Pfeifer
Xiong Xu
Yicheng Qian
Zhenbang Chen
Zhixuan Yang
Ziggy Attala

Invited Papers

The Industrial Perspective on GenAI for Formal Methods

Daniel Kroening

Amazon, Inc.,, Seattle, USA
dkr@amazon.com

Abstract. We explore opportunities for delivering robust, formal guarantees for hardware and software systems using generative AI. Neural networks offer the opportunity to significantly improve the heuristic search in both formal verifiers and synthesis engines that implement *guess-and-check*. The neural engine delivers a guess, which is then checked formally using a sound, trusted symbolic verifier. Any counterexample is then passed back to the neural engine, and we iterate until we obtain an answer that satisfies the formal engine. We present an instance of this approach used at AWS for verifying LTL properties of synchronous hardware circuits and liveness properties of software [1, 3, 4].

We refine this approach by considering large language models (LLMs) and their ability to deliver mathematical proof to obtain formal proof for hardware and software designs [3]. Finally, we discuss the potential of using the contextual knowledge of LLMs to refine design intent, by translating informal specifications into formal ones and by disambiguating and completing the given requirements and environment assumptions.

STLts-Div: Diversified Trace Synthesis from STL Specifications Using MILP

Martin Jouve-Genty[1,2], Han Su[2], Sota Sato[2,5], Jie An[3], Zhenya Zhang[2,4], and Ichiro Hasuo[2,5,6]

[1] Département Informatique, ENS de Lyon, Lyon, France
martin.jouve-genty@ens-lyon.fr
[2] National Institute of Informatics, Tokyo, Japan
{suhan,sotasato,hasuo}@nii.ac.jp, zhang@ait.kyushu-u.ac.jp
[3] Institute of Software, Chinese Academy of Sciences, Beijing, China
anjie@iscas.ac.cn
[4] Kyushu University, Fukuoka, Japan
[5] SOKENDAI (The Graduate University for Advanced Studies), Tokyo, Japan
[6] Imiron Co., Ltd., Tokyo, Japan

Abstract. Modern cyber–physical systems are complex, and requirements are often written in Signal Temporal Logic (STL). Writing the right STL is difficult in practice; engineers benefit from concrete executions that illustrate what a specification actually admits. Trace synthesis addresses this need, but a single witness rarely suffices to understand intent or explore edge cases—diverse satisfying behaviors are far more informative. We introduce diversified trace synthesis: the automatic generation of sets of behaviorally diverse traces that satisfy a given STL formula. Building on a MILP encoding of STL and system model, we formalize three complementary diversification objectives—Boolean distance, random Boolean distance, and value distance—all captured by an objective function and solved iteratively. We implement these ideas in STLts-Div, a lightweight Python tool that integrates with Gurobi.

References

1. Giacobbe, M., Kroening, D., Pal, A., Tautschnig, M.: Neural model checking. In: Advances in Neural Information Processing Systems, vol. 38 (NeurIPS) (2024)

M. Jouve-Genty, H. Su: Equal contribution.

The authors are supported by JST ASPIRE Grant No. JPMJAP2301. Jie An is supported by the CAS Project for Young Scientists in Basic Research Grant No. YSBR-123. Zhenya Zhang is supported by JST BOOST Grant No. JPMJBY24D7 and JSPS Grant No. JP25K21179. The work was done during M.J.'s internship at National Inst. of Inform., Japan.

2. Giacobbe, M., Kroening, D., Pal, A., Tautschnig, M.: Let a neural network be your invariant. In: Advances in Neural Information Processing Systems, vol. 39 (NeurIPS) (2025)
3. Peled, R., Kroening, D., Tautschnig, M., Vizel, Y.: Large lemma miners: Can LLMs do induction proofs for hardware? CoRR abs/2511.02521 (2025)
4. Yang, A.Z.H., Takashima, Y., Paulsen, B., Dodds, J., Kroening, D.: VERT: polyglot verified equivalent Rust transpilation with large language models. In: Automated Software Engineering, ASE, pp. 1453–1463. IEEE (2025)

Towards Privacy-Preserving Verification

Timos Antonopoulos[1], Ning Luo[2], and Ruzica Piskac[1]

[1] Yale University, New Haven, USA
{timos.antonopoulos,ruzica.piskac}@yale.edu
[2] University of Illinois Urbana-Champaign, Illinois, USA
nl27@illinois.edu

Abstract. Program verification provides stronger guarantees of correctness than standard testing. The verification process takes a program as input and derives a mathematical formula. Proving that a program is correct then reduces to establishing that this derived formula is unsatisfiable. Traditionally, automated reasoning tools can be used to determine unsatisfiability automatically. Furthermore, modern solvers can also produce a proof of unsatisfiability. However, these techniques typically rely on the proof and the underlying code being publicly available, which may not be desirable for certain applications.

This work shows how to address this problem. Our team initially developed a protocol for validating the unsatisfiability of Boolean formulas in privacy-preserving settings. Building on these initial results, we devised ZKSMT, a virtual machine for validating unsatisfiability results produced by SMT solvers in zero-knowledge settings. In this paper we describe the theoretical foundations of such virtual machines and demonstrate how they can be applied to the theories of uninterpreted functions and linear integer arithmetic, two of the most widely used theories in verification.

We conclude by outlining how the full formal verification workflow can be adapted to operate in privacy-preserving settings.

Testing and Analysis in the AI Era

Cristian Cadar

Imperial College London, UK
c.cadar@imperial.ac.uk

Abstract. Software development is undergoing a profound transformation, with developers increasingly relying on AI assistants and incorporating AI-generated code. These are seismic changes: software systems are evolving faster than ever before, and the core activity of software developers is shifting more and more from writing code to reviewing and validating it.

However, human-scale code review and validation cannot keep up with the speed and volume of AI-driven development. As a result, automated software analysis methods—ranging from fuzzing to symbolic execution to formal verification—are becoming critical safeguards in this AI era. To remain effective, these methods must scale along multiple dimensions: they must handle larger codebases, keep up with increasingly rapid development cycles, operate across a growing diversity of programming languages and system architectures, and infer and reason about higher-level semantic properties.

In this talk, I argue that testing and analysis techniques can themselves take advantage of AI. I will present our recent research efforts in this direction, including our work on designing an agentic concolic executor, an agentic hybrid fuzzer, and an LLM-based technique for inferring the intent of software patches. These systems build on traditional analysis techniques but leverage large language models and agentic AI frameworks to extend their capabilities along the dimensions discussed above. I end the talk by reflecting on the comparative strengths and weaknesses of traditional and AI-based testing and analysis techniques and what this means for building trustworthy software in an era increasingly shaped by AI-generated code.

Contents

Invited Papers

STLts-Div: Diversified Trace Synthesis from STL Specifications Using MILP 3
Martin Jouve-Genty, Han Su, Sota Sato, Jie An, Zhenya Zhang, and Ichiro Hasuo

Towards Privacy-Preserving Verification 21
Timos Antonopoulos, Ning Luo, and Ruzica Piskac

Main Track (1)

A Formal Framework for Predicting Distributed System Performance Under Faults 47
Ziwei Zhou, Si Liu, Zhou Zhou, Peixin Wang, and Min Zhang

Mining Verdict Boundaries for Neural Network Verification 67
Jiawei Ren, Guanqin Zhang, Zhenya Zhang, and Yulei Sui

FastLEC: Parallel Datapath Equivalence Checking with Hybrid Engines 89
Xindi Zhang, Furong Ye, Zhihan Chen, and Shaowei Cai

Towards Proving Liveness on Weak Memory 109
Lara Bargmann and Heike Wehrheim

Test Coverage of Automated Robotic Systems in Open World Environments 130
Lukas Westhofen, Till Schallau, Dominik Schmid, Stefan Naujokat, Falk Howar, and Daniel Neider

SAPSE-Synergy: Balancing Formal Soundness and Empirical Coverage in Neural Theorem Proving 151
Minrui Chen, Huidong Jiang, and Hiroto Saigo

Certifying Constraints in Hardware Model Checking 170
Nils Froleyks, Emily Yu, Armin Biere, and Keijo Heljanko

Tools and Algorithms for Sound Multi-objective Probabilistic Model Checking (Long Tool Paper) 189
Arnd Hartmanns, Tim Quatmann, and Mark van Wijk

ModelWisdom: An Integrated Toolkit for TLA$^+$ Model Visualization, Digest and Repair (Short Tool Paper) ... 211
Zhiyong Chen, Jialun Cao, Chang Xu, and Shing-Chi Cheung

SAT-Based Syndrome Decoding and Low-Weight Codewords ... 220
Carl Berton, Sami Cherif, and Claire Delaplace

Accelerating Kind Realizability: A Multi-stage Incremental Realizability Checking Framework ... 240
Sirui Liu and Wei Dong

Verifying Sampling Algorithms via Distributional Invariants ... 259
Daniel Zilken, Kevin Batz, Joost-Pieter Katoen, and Tobias Winkler

Validating Formal Specifications with LLM-Generated Test Cases ... 279
Alcino Cunha and Nuno Macedo

BDD-Based Deadlock Avoidance for Automated Guided Vehicles in Warehouse Logistics (Case Study Paper) ... 298
Benjamin von Berg, Bernhard K. Aichernig, and Fabian Wedenik

Automatic Memory Management for Dataflows ... 317
Michael Lienhardt

Hybrid Spatiotemporal Logic for Automotive Applications: Modeling and Model-Checking ... 337
Radu-Florin Tulcan, Rose Bohrer, Yoàv Montacute, Kevin Zhou, Yusuke Kawamoto, and Ichiro Hasuo

RustyDL: A Program Logic for Rust ... 357
Daniel Drodt and Reiner Hähnle

Generating Rely-Guarantee Conditions with the Conditional-Writes Domain ... 378
James Tobler and Graeme Smith

Array-Carrying Symbolic Execution for Function Contract Generation ... 397
Weijie Lu, Jingyu Ke, Hongfei Fu, Zhouyue Sun, Yi Zhou, Guoqiang Li, and Haokun Li

Incremental Synthesis of Safe Controller Guided by Learning-Enabled Barrier Certificates with Efficient LP Verification ... 419
Niuniu Qi, Hanrui Zhao, Zhengfeng Yang, Xia Zeng, Mengxin Ren, Chao Peng, and Zhiming Liu

Specializing Anti-unification for Interaction Models Composition via Gate Connections 440
Joel Nguetoum, Boutheina Bannour, Pascale Le Gall, and Erwan Mahe

Differential Verification of Information Flow in SEAndroid Policies 461
Lorenzo Ceragioli, Letterio Galletta, and Edoardo Lunati

Formal Reasoning About Confidence and Automated Verification of Neural Networks 480
Mohammad Afzal, S. Akshay, Blaise Genest, and Ashutosh Gupta

A Refined Ordering Consistency Theory: Full Sequential Consistency and Generalized Preventive Reasoning 500
Zhiheng Cai, Zhihang Sun, and Fei He

Error-Awareness Accelerates Active Automata Learning 520
Loes Kruger, Sebastian Junges, and Jurriaan Rot

History-Constrained Systems 541
Louwe B. Kuijer, David Purser, Henry Sinclair-Banks, and Patrick Totzke

Highly Incremental: A Simple Programmatic Approach for Many Objectives 559
Philipp Schröer and Joost-Pieter Katoen

QSeqSim: A Symbolic Simulator for Qiskit While Loops Using Sequential Quantum Circuits (Long Tool Paper) 578
Zihao Li, Ji Guan, and Mingsheng Ying

Reachability-Guided Abstraction Refinement 599
Pierre Ganty, Nicolas Manini, and Francesco Ranzato

Towards Language Model Guided TLA$^+$ Proof Automation 619
Yuhao Zhou and Stavros Tripakis

Exact Verification of Graph Neural Networks with Incremental Constraint Solving 641
Minghao Liu, Chia-Hsuan Lu, and Marta Kwiatkowska

Author Index 663

Invited Papers

STLts-Div: Diversified Trace Synthesis from STL Specifications Using MILP

Martin Jouve-Genty[1,2], Han Su[2], Sota Sato[2,5], Jie An[3], Zhenya Zhang[2,4], and Ichiro Hasuo[2,5,6](✉)

[1] Département Informatique, ENS de Lyon, Lyon, France
suhan@nii.ac.jp
[2] National Institute of Informatics, Tokyo, Japan
sotasato@nii.ac.jp, anjie@iscas.ac.cn
[3] Institute of Software, Chinese Academy of Sciences, Beijing, China
zhang@ait.kyushu-u.ac.jp
[4] Kyushu University, Fukuoka, Japan
hasuo@nii.ac.jp
[5] SOKENDAI (The Graduate University for Advanced Studies), Tokyo, Japan
[6] Imiron Co., Ltd, Tokyo, Japan

Abstract. Modern cyber-physical systems are complex, and requirements are often written in Signal Temporal Logic (STL). Writing the right STL is difficult in practice; engineers benefit from concrete executions that illustrate what a specification actually admits. Trace synthesis addresses this need, but a single witness rarely suffices to understand intent or explore edge cases—diverse satisfying behaviors are far more informative. We introduce diversified trace synthesis: the automatic generation of sets of behaviorally diverse traces that satisfy a given STL formula. Building on a MILP encoding of STL and system model, we formalize three complementary diversification objectives—Boolean distance, random Boolean distance, and value distance—all captured by an objective function and solved iteratively. We implement these ideas in STLts-Div, a lightweight Python tool that integrates with Gurobi.

Keywords: Cyber-Physical Systems · Signal Temporal Logic · Trace Synthesis

1 Introduction

Cyber-physical systems (CPS) underpin safety-critical applications such as aircraft collision-avoidance protocols [23], aerospace [2], and pacemakers [24].

M. Jouve-Genty, H. Su: Equal contribution.
The authors are supported by JST ASPIRE Grant No. JPMJAP2301. Jie An is supported by the CAS Project for Young Scientists in Basic Research Grant No. YSBR-123. Zhenya Zhang is supported by JST BOOST Grant No. JPMJBY24D7 and JSPS Grant No. JP25K21179. The work was done during M.J.'s internship at National Inst. of Inform., Japan.

A. Sampaio and M. Stoelinga (Eds.): FM 2026, LNCS 16556, pp. 3–20, 2026.
https://doi.org/10.1007/978-3-032-26204-2_1

Ensuring their reliability is essential, yet formal verification is challenging due to hybrid/nonlinear dynamics, continuous state spaces, and environmental uncertainty. As a result, full verification is often infeasible in practice.

Trace synthesis offers a pragmatic alternative: instead of proving properties for all behaviors, it constructs concrete executions that satisfy (or violate) a given temporal specification, providing actionable artifacts for testing and analysis. As a dual to model checking [20], trace synthesis has been realized via SMT encodings [3], optimization-based falsification [8], and—more recently—mixed-integer linear programming (MILP) encodings that capture both *Signal Temporal Logic (STL)* constraints and plant dynamics [20]. These approaches generate informative scenarios and counterexamples while interfacing naturally with simulators and models.

However, a single satisfying trace is often insufficient—for example, when validating whether an STL requirement truly captures the intent of the engineer. A *set* of behaviorally diverse traces that illuminate different ways the specification can be met is required. In this work we study *diversified trace synthesis* from STL, aiming to generate traces that satisfy the specification while exhibiting sufficient diversity.

We address this problem with STLts-Div, a tool that synthesizes sets of diverse traces for a given system model $\mathcal{M}$ and STL specification φ. STLts-Div builds on the MILP-based synthesis framework of [20]. We introduce three complementary diversity objectives—Boolean distance (BD), randomized Boolean distance (RBD), and value distance (VD)—and encode them as MILP objectives. We adopt the MILP setting because its numeric decision variables allow these objectives to be integrated directly, whereas propositional SMT encodings do not readily support summing/counting of truth assignments (see Remark 2).

Contributions and Organization. We summarize our contributions as below.

- We formulate the problem of diversified trace synthesis for STL.
- We propose three diversity objectives (BD, RBD, VD) and provide MILP objective function encodings compatible with [20].
- We implement these ideas in STLts-Div, a Python package, and evaluate them on benchmark suites, demonstrating substantially higher diversity than a solution-pool baseline.

Section 2 reviews STL preliminaries and states the problem. Section 3 recaps the MILP encoding of [20], which underpins our approach. Section 4 formalizes three diversity objectives and presents our MILP-based synthesis procedures. Section 5 demonstrates the STLts-Div tool. Section 6 reports experiments evaluating effectiveness and efficiency. We conclude in Sect. 7.

Related Work. Signal Temporal Logic is widely used for specifying CPS behaviors. Prior work spans controller synthesis [6,17,18,21], runtime/online monitoring [22,25], and trace synthesis/falsification [3,20], among others. The choice of technique depends on the task: for continuous-time control, Lyapunov/barrier-based methods synthesize controllers that enforce STL constraints [13]; for bounded model checking, SMT encodings search for a time partition witnessing satisfaction [3]; and recent MILP encodings support trace synthesis by jointly searching over signal values and a δ-stable partition (see Sect. 3) [20]. Existing approaches, however, typically return one satisfying execution. In contrast, we target the multi-trace setting and synthesize sets of behaviorally diverse traces for a fixed model and STL formula.

2 Preliminaries

Let $\mathbb{N}$, $\mathbb{R}$, and $\mathbb{R}_{\geq 0}$ denote the sets of natural numbers, real numbers, and non-negative real numbers, respectively. Let $\mathbb{B} = \{\top, \bot\}$ denote the Boolean domain. For a set X, we write $\wp(X)$ for its power set and $|X|$ for its cardinality. An *interval* is any subset of $\mathbb{R}_{\geq 0}$ of the form $(a, b), (a, b], [a, b)$, or $[a, c]$, where $a < b$ and $a \leq c$.

Signal. Let $T > 0$ and V be a finite set of variables. A *signal* over V with time horizon T is a function $\sigma\colon [0, T] \to \mathbb{R}^{|V|}$. We let $\mathbf{Signal}_V^T$ denote the set of all such signals; when T is clear from the context we write $\mathbf{Signal}_V$. For $v \in V$ we write $\sigma(t)(v)$ for the value of the variable v in σ at time t. We extend any $\sigma \in \mathbf{Signal}_V^T$ to $t > T$ by setting $\sigma(t) := \sigma(T)$ for all $t > T$.

For a signal σ and $t \geq 0$, the *t-postfix* is the signal σ^t defined by $\sigma^t(t') := \sigma(t + t')$. The *t-postfix* is the basis for defining the STL semantics (see [11]).

System model. Let V' and V be the input and output variable sets. A *system model* $\mathcal{M}$ from V' to V with a time horizon T is a (possibly nondeterministic) map $\mathcal{M}\colon \mathbf{Signal}_{V'}^T \to \wp(\mathbf{Signal}_V^T)$. The trace set of $\mathcal{M}$ is $\mathcal{L}(\mathcal{M}) := \bigcup_{\tau \in \mathbf{Signal}_{V'}^T} \mathcal{M}(\tau)$, i.e., the set of all output signals under any input τ.

Example 1 (Single-lane car). Consider a car moving in a single lane whose dynamics are given by the ordinary differential equation (ODE)

$$\dot{x} = v, \qquad \dot{v} = a, \tag{1}$$

where x, v and a denote position, velocity and acceleration, respectively.

We formalize this system as $\mathcal{M}_{\text{car}}$ with input variables $V' = \{a, v^{\text{init}}, x^{\text{init}}\}$ and output variables $V = \{a, v, x\}$. Here, the acceleration a changes over time; the initial velocity and position $v^{\text{init}}, x^{\text{init}}$ change as well but only their initial values $\tau(0)(v^{\text{init}}), \tau(0)(x^{\text{init}})$ matter. Given an input signal τ, the model yields $\mathcal{M}_{\text{car}}(\tau) = \{\sigma\}$, where σ is determined by Eq. (1): $\sigma(t)(a) = \tau(t)(a)$, $\sigma(t)(v) = \tau(0)(v^{\text{init}}) + \int_0^t \tau(\theta)(a)\mathrm{d}\theta$, $\sigma(t)(x) = \tau(0)(x^{\text{init}}) + \int_0^t \sigma(\theta)(v)\mathrm{d}\theta$.

2.1 Signal Temporal Logic (STL)

We use the standard syntax and semantics of STL [14,20]. We present some basic definitions for the record.

In STL, an *atomic proposition* over a variable set V is represented as $p :\equiv (\pi_p(\vec{w}) \geq 0)$, where $\pi_p : \mathbb{R}^{|V|} \to \mathbb{R}$ maps a valuation $\vec{w} \in \mathbb{R}^{|V|}$ of variables in

V to a real value. In this work, we restrict attention to *linear* (affine) atomic propositions, i.e., $\pi_p(\vec{w}) = a^\top \vec{w} + c$ with $a \in \mathbb{R}^{|V|}$ and $c \in \mathbb{R}$. This syntactic restriction enables an MILP encoding of STL formulas.

Any STL formula has an equivalent *negation normal form* (NNF) [9], in which negations appear only adjacent to atomic propositions. We assume all STL formulas are in NNF in this work. The syntax of STL is as follows:

$$\varphi :\equiv \top \mid p \mid \neg p \mid \varphi_1 \wedge \varphi_2 \mid \varphi_1 \vee \varphi_2 \mid \varphi_1 \,\mathcal{U}_I\, \varphi_2 \mid \varphi_1 \,\mathcal{R}_I\, \varphi_2,$$

where I is a nonsingular closed time interval, and $\mathcal{U}_I$ and $\mathcal{R}_I$ are temporal operators *until* and *release*, respectively. The *eventually* and *always* operators are syntactic sugars defined as $\Diamond_I \varphi = \top \,\mathcal{U}_I\, \varphi$, $\Box_I \varphi = \bot \,\mathcal{R}_I\, \varphi$. The set of all subformulas of φ is denoted by $\mathrm{Sub}(\varphi)$.

The Boolean semantics $\sigma \models \varphi$ and robust semantics $[\![\sigma, \varphi]\!] \in \mathbb{R} \cup \{+\infty, -\infty\}$ of STL are standard. Details can be found in the Appendix A of [11].

2.2 Finite Variability

Finite variability is a standard assumption used to make STL model checking and synthesis tractable in practice (see, e.g., [12,15]). In particular, without such a restriction the full (unbounded) STL model-checking problem is EXPSPACE-complete [1]; adopting finite variability permits efficient bounded analyses, which we also assume in this work.

Definition 1 (finite variability [16]). *A Boolean signal $q : \mathbb{R}_{\geq 0} \to \mathbb{B}$ has* N-bounded variability *if there exists a collection $\mathcal{P} = \{J_i\}_{i=1}^N$ of nonempty, pairwise disjoint intervals with $\bigcup_{i=1}^N J_i = \mathbb{R}_{\geq 0}$ such that q is constant on every $J_i \in \mathcal{P}$.*

Intuitively, N-bounded variability means that the Boolean signal can change its value at most $N-1$ times over $\mathbb{R}_{\geq 0}$. We say that a signal σ has N-bounded variability *with respect to* an STL formula φ if the Boolean signal $t \mapsto (\sigma^t \models \varphi)$ has the N-bounded variability. Moreover, σ has *hereditary N-bounded variability* (abbreviated N-HBV) with respect to φ if σ has N-bounded variability with respect to every subformula $\psi \in \mathrm{Sub}(\varphi)$.

We recall the bounded STL trace synthesis problem from [20]:

Problem 1. Given an STL formula φ (over V), a system model $\mathcal{M}$ (from V' to V) with time horizon T, and a variability bound $N \in \mathbb{N}$, find a trace $\sigma \in \mathcal{L}(\mathcal{M})$ such that i) σ has the N-HBV with respect to φ and ii) $\sigma \models \varphi$ holds, or prove such σ does not exist.

In this paper we study a *diversity-aware* variant of the above problem: instead of returning an arbitrary satisfying trace, we generate a set of traces that are mutually diverse, i.e., sufficiently distinct under a suitable notion of difference.

Formalizing diversity is nontrivial: it can be quantified in multiple, fundamentally different ways. In Sect. 4 we discuss this issue and present three distinct methods for measuring and enforcing diversity in MILP-based synthesis.

3 MILP-Based Trace Synthesis

We recall the MILP-based trace synthesis workflow in [20]. The key idea, originally from [3], is to *partition* the time horizon into time intervals, with respect to the truth values of relevant STL formulas. The partition should be such that

- it ensures *interval-wise constancy*: the truth value of each subformula $\psi \in \mathrm{Sub}(\varphi)$ remains constant on each interval;
- it is *MILP-encodable*: it avoids strict inequalities ($<$), since MILP solvers cannot distinguish $<$ from $\leq$ and only support non-strict ones ($\leq$) [10].

The original SMT-based approach [3] partitions the horizon into alternating singleton and open intervals, i.e., $\dots, (\gamma_{i-1}, \gamma_i), \{\gamma_i\}, (\gamma_i, \gamma_{i+1}), \dots$. However, this scheme requires $<$ to distinguish open and closed intervals and is therefore not MILP-encodable. To address this, we use closed intervals $\dots, [\gamma_{i-1}, \gamma_i], [\gamma_i, \gamma_{i+1}], \dots$ to partition the horizon.

Closed intervals can be expressed only using $\leq$; but they have overlaps (at γ_i). This overlap creates ambiguity for the previous notion of interval-wise constancy, which requires that a subformula is either "constantly true" or "never true" on an interval. The technique of *δ-stable partition* [20] avoids this ambiguity via introducing the *δ-tightening* of a STL formula with some $\delta > 0$ (Def. 4).

Definition 2 (time sequence, time state sequence [20]). *A* time sequence *over* $[0,T]$ *is a sequence* $\Gamma = (0 = \gamma_0 < \cdots < \gamma_N = T)$. *The same construct is often denoted by* $\Gamma = ([\gamma_{i-1}, \gamma_i])_{i=1}^{N}$, *using the corresponding partition of* $[0,T]$ *into closed intervals with singular overlaps. We write* Γ_i *for* $[\gamma_{i-1}, \gamma_i]$.

Given a time sequence, a time state sequence *over* V *is a sequence* $\varsigma = ((x_0, \gamma_0), \dots, (x_N, \gamma_N))$, *where* $x_0, \dots, x_N$ *in* $\mathbb{R}^{|V|}$.

Definition 3 (piecewise-linear signal [20]). *Given a timed state sequence* $\varsigma = ((x_0, \gamma_0), \dots, (x_N, \gamma_N))$, *the piecewise-linear signal* $\varsigma^{\mathrm{pwl}} \colon [0, \gamma_N] \to \mathbb{R}^{|V|}$ *is defined by the following linear interpolation:* $\varsigma^{\mathrm{pwl}} := (1-\lambda)x_{i-1} + \lambda x_i$ *if* $\gamma_{i-1} \leq t \leq \gamma_i$ *(where* $\lambda = \frac{1}{\gamma_i - \gamma_{i-1}}(t - \gamma_{i-1})$*).*

Definition 4 (δ-tightening of STL formulas in NNF [20]). *Let* φ *be an STL formula in NNF whose atomic propositions are linear predicates of the form* $(c^\top x + b \geq 0)$. *Given* $\delta > 0$, *the* δ-tightening φ^δ *is obtained from* φ *by i) replacing every occurrence of* $(c^\top x + b \geq 0)$ *with* $(c^\top x + b \geq \delta)$, *and ii) replacing every occurrence of* $\neg(c^\top x + b \geq 0)$ *with* $(-c^\top x - b \geq \delta)$. *All Boolean connectives and temporal connectives (with the time intervals therein) are left unchanged.*

Note that φ^δ is stronger than φ, i.e., $(\sigma \models \varphi^\delta) \Rightarrow (\sigma \models \varphi)$ for all signals σ. Using this notion, a δ-stable partition defined below classifies each subformula on each closed interval as either i) always true, or ii) never *robustly* true.

Definition 5 (δ-stability [20]). *Let* φ *be an STL formula over* V *in NNF,* $\sigma \in \mathbf{Signal}_V^T$ *be a signal, and* $\Gamma = (\gamma_0, \dots, \gamma_N)$ *be a time sequence (Def. 2) with* $\gamma_N = T$. *We say* Γ *is* δ-stable *for* σ *and* φ *if, for each* $i = 1, \dots, N$ *and each subformula* $\psi \in \mathrm{Sub}(\varphi)$, *either of the following holds: i)* $\sigma^t \models \psi$ *for each* $t \in \Gamma_i$, *or ii)* $\sigma^t \not\models \psi^\delta$ *for each* $t \in \Gamma_i$.

Finding a δ-stable partition Γ for a signal σ and formula φ, so that $\sigma^t \models \varphi$ holds for $t \in \Gamma_1$, is a sufficient method to prove $\sigma \models \varphi$. Recall that $\Gamma_1 = [\gamma_0, \gamma_1]$ with $\gamma_0 = 0$ (see Def. 2). As shown in [20], this search can be encoded as an MILP when σ is piecewise-linear (Def. 3).

Definition 6 (conservative valuation [20]). *Let φ be an STL formula in NNF, and $\Gamma = (\gamma_0, \ldots, \gamma_N)$ be a time sequence. A* valuation *of φ in Γ is a function $\Theta\colon \mathrm{Sub}(\varphi) \times \{1, \ldots, N\} \to \mathbb{B}$ that assigns, to each subformula and index of the intervals of Γ, a Boolean truth value. Let σ be a signal with a time horizon $T = \gamma_N$. We say that Θ is a* conservative valuation *of φ in Γ on σ (up to δ) if i) $\Theta(\psi, i) = \top$ implies that, for each $t \in \Gamma_i$, $\sigma^t \models \psi$ holds; and ii) $\Theta(\psi, i) = \bot$ implies, for each $t \in \Gamma_i$, $\sigma^t \not\models \psi^\delta$.*

Lemma 1 ([20]). *Suppose there is a conservative valuation Θ of an STL formula φ in a time sequence Γ on σ up to δ. Then Γ is δ-stable for σ and φ.*

We simply write $\langle\psi\rangle_i$ for $\Theta(\psi, i)$ when Θ is clear from context. The MILP problem therefore searches for i) a partition $\Gamma = ([\gamma_{i-1}, \gamma_i])_{i=1}^N$ (see Def. 2), and ii) a conservative valuation Θ (see Def. 6), such that:

- the truth values assigned to subformulas comply with the STL semantics (Sect. 2.1), e.g., for a subformula $(\psi_1 \wedge \psi_2) \in \mathrm{Sub}(\varphi)$ and $i \in \{1, \ldots, N\}$, $\langle\psi_1 \wedge \psi_2\rangle_i = \langle\psi_1\rangle_i \wedge \langle\psi_2\rangle_i$;
- Θ assigns $\top$ to the top-level formula φ in Γ_1; and
- there is a piecewise-linear trace $\sigma \in \mathcal{L}(\mathcal{M})$ of $\mathcal{M}$ that yields Θ.

The entities Γ, Θ we search for are expressed as MILP variables, and the above three conditions are expressed as MILP constraints. The variables can be classified into four types, where $N \in \mathbb{N}$ is a constant for variability bound (Prob. 1).

- Real-valued variables $\gamma_0, \ldots, \gamma_N$ specifying the time sequence Γ.
- Boolean variables $\{\langle\psi\rangle_i \mid 1 \le i \le N, \psi \in \mathrm{Sub}(\varphi)\}$ for the value $\Theta(\psi, i)$ of a valuation Θ that we search for.
- Real-valued variables $\{x_{i,v} \mid 0 \le i \le N, v \in V\}$ for the values of a piecewise-linear trace $\sigma \in \mathcal{L}(\mathcal{M})$.
- Auxiliary variables (real or binary) used to encode big-M constraints—a common technique in LP—and the temporal/satisfaction encodings.

We omit the MILP details here; see [20] for the full encoding.

4 Diversity-Aware Synthesis

This section presents methods to synthesize mutually diverse traces. Although modern MILP solvers such as Gurobi [10] can return multiple solutions from the solution pool of a single instance, those solutions are typically very similar (see Sect. 6 for an empirical demonstration).

To overcome this limitation, we propose three diversity measures that quantify how "different" one trace is from another. Each measure is encoded as an MILP objective to promote diverse solutions. We do not claim that the three methods presented here are the only possible approaches. However, given the practical need to generate diverse example traces, it is important to provide methods that work.

4.1 Boolean Distance Method (BD)

As flipping the truth value of a subformula may induce substantial changes in the underlying signal variables, an initial attempt to diversify traces is to bias the truth valuations of subformulas in each trace. We quantify the resulting diversity using a Boolean distance between traces.

Definition 7 (Boolean distance). *Let σ_1, σ_2 be two traces found by an MILP solver that i) have N-HBV (see Prob. 1) and ii) satisfy the same STL formula φ.*

Let Γ^{σ_1} (resp. Γ^{σ_2}) be the δ-stable partition for σ_1 (resp. σ_2) and φ. Let $\langle\psi\rangle_i^{\sigma_j}$ denote the Boolean valuation of $\psi \in \mathrm{Sub}(\varphi)$ over the interval $\Gamma_i^{\sigma_j}$ of the partition Γ^{σ_j}, where $i \in \{1, \ldots, N\}$ and $j \in \{1, 2\}$. The Boolean distance *between σ_1 and σ_2 is*

$$d_{\mathrm{B}}(\sigma_1, \sigma_2) := \sum_{i=1}^{N} \sum_{\psi \in \mathsf{Sub}(\varphi)} |\langle\psi\rangle_i^{\sigma_1} - \langle\psi\rangle_i^{\sigma_2}|. \tag{2}$$

By construction, $d_{\mathrm{B}}(\sigma_1, \sigma_2)$ is equal to the number of pairs (i, ψ) on which the two traces assign different truth values. Hence, a larger Boolean distance indicates greater diversity, in the sense of satisfaction of subformulas.

Remark 1. In Eq. (2), if the Boolean value of $\langle\psi\rangle_i^{\sigma_1}$ is fixed for $i \in \{1, \ldots, N\}$ (which is the case in our usage), the absolute value can be rewritten as

$$|\langle\psi\rangle_i^{\sigma_1} - \langle\psi\rangle_i^{\sigma_2}| = \begin{cases} \langle\psi\rangle_i^{\sigma_2} & \text{if } \langle\psi\rangle_i^{\sigma_1} = 0, \\ 1 - \langle\psi\rangle_i^{\sigma_2} & \text{if } \langle\psi\rangle_i^{\sigma_1} = 1, \end{cases}$$

$$\text{or equivalently,} \quad |\langle\psi\rangle_i^{\sigma_1} - \langle\psi\rangle_i^{\sigma_2}| = (1 - 2\langle\psi\rangle_i^{\sigma_1})\,\langle\psi\rangle_i^{\sigma_2} + \langle\psi\rangle_i^{\sigma_1}.$$

Note that the last expression is affine in $\langle\psi\rangle_i^{\sigma_2}$ ($\langle\psi\rangle_i^{\sigma_1}$ is a constant). Applying this rule to Eq. (2), we obtain an affine expression over variables $\langle\psi\rangle_i^{\sigma_2}$.

Given a fixed variability bound $N \in \mathbb{N}$, we incorporate the Boolean distance of traces into the MILP objective while keeping the original constraints from Sect. 3 unchanged. This MILP problem is then solved iteratively, for $m = 1, 2, \ldots$, to synthesize a trace σ_m that is maximally distinct (in terms of Boolean distance) from the previously synthesized traces $\sigma_1, \ldots, \sigma_{m-1}$. The objective in each iteration is defined as follows.

- **Initialization** ($m = 1$). Maximize $f_1 := 0$.
- **Iteration** ($m > 1$). Let σ_m denote the trace to be synthesized at the current iteration (this gives decision variables). Given the previously obtained traces $\{\sigma_i\}_{i=1}^{m-1}$ (which are constants in MILP), maximize

$$f_m := \sum_{i=1}^{m-1} d_{\mathrm{B}}(\sigma_m, \sigma_i). \tag{3}$$

By Remark 1, f_m is an affine function of the Boolean decision variables of the trace σ_m, with coefficients determined by the constants for $\{\sigma_i\}_{i=1}^{m-1}$.

Remark 2. The above diversification method is possible due to our use of MILP. A similar method in SMT is nontrivial. The key difference is that, in MILP, truth values are encoded as integer variables and they can be summed up (as in Eq. (3)), whereas in SMT they are propositional variables and cannot be summed. Counting the number of subformulas with different truth values across models would require techniques such as MaxSMT or model counting, which we leave for future work.

4.2 Randomized Boolean Distance Method (RBD)

This subsection introduces a randomized variant of the Boolean distance. It promotes diversity by evaluating each candidate trace against an independently sampled reference, thereby decoupling the current solution from all previous ones.

Specifically, for a fixed variability bound N, the valuation of all $\psi \in \mathrm{Sub}(\varphi)$ across the intervals $(\Gamma_i)_{i=1}^{N}$ form an $N|\mathrm{Sub}(\varphi)|$-dimensional Boolean vector. We sample a *reference valuation* σ_{ref} from the uniform distribution in $\mathbb{B}^{N|\mathrm{Sub}(\varphi)|}$ and solve an MILP problem that maximizes the Boolean distance between σ_{ref} and the candidate trace. Let σ denote the candidate trace, the objective is

$$f := d_{\mathrm{B}}(\sigma, \sigma_{\mathrm{ref}}),$$

which yields a trace that is as far as possible, in Boolean distance, from the reference valuation. By Remark 1, f is affine in the decision variables of trace σ.

Remark 3. The choice between maximization and minimization is immaterial: for any reference valuation $\sigma_{\mathrm{ref}} \in \mathbb{B}^{N\,|\mathrm{Sub}(\varphi)|}$,

$$d_{\mathrm{B}}(\sigma, \sigma_{\mathrm{ref}}) = N\,|\mathrm{Sub}(\varphi)| - d_{\mathrm{B}}(\sigma, \bar{\sigma}_{\mathrm{ref}}),$$

where $\bar{\sigma}_{\mathrm{ref}}$ denotes the bitwise complement of σ_{ref}. Hence, maximizing distance from σ_{ref} is equivalent to minimizing distance to $\bar{\sigma}_{\mathrm{ref}}$.

The following proposition provides a quantitative guarantee that the probability of generating identical reference traces is small, which supports the diversity of traces. The proof can be found in Appendix B of [11].

Proposition 1. *For a δ-stable partition $\Gamma = (\gamma_0, \cdots, \gamma_N)$ of the time horizon for a formula φ, let $d := N\,|\mathrm{Sub}(\varphi)|$. Suppose $m \geq 2$ reference valuations $\sigma^1_{\mathrm{ref}}, \ldots, \sigma^m_{\mathrm{ref}}$ are drawn independently and uniformly from $\mathbb{B}^d$. Let p denote the probability that at least two references coincide. Then*

$$p = 1 - \frac{2^d!}{(2^d - m)!\, 2^{md}},$$

and the following upper bound holds:

$$p \leq \frac{m(m-1)}{2^{d+1}}.$$

4.3 Value Distance Method (VD)

Although the Boolean distance can serve as a metric for diversification, we also consider a more direct metric: the distance between the trace values. For two piecewise-linear traces that share the same time sequence, their *value distance* is defined as follows.

Definition 8. *Let ς_1, ς_2 be two time state sequences (Def. 2) with the same time sequence $\Gamma = (\gamma_0, \ldots, \gamma_N)$. Let V be a set of signal variables. For two piecewise-linear traces $\sigma_1, \sigma_2 : [\gamma_0, \gamma_N] \to \mathbb{R}^{|V|}$ generated from ς_1, ς_2, respectively, their* value distance *is defined by*

$$d_{\mathrm{V}}(\sigma_1, \sigma_2) := \sum_{i=0}^{N} \|\sigma_1(\gamma_i) - \sigma_2(\gamma_i)\|_1 = \sum_{i=0}^{N} \sum_{v \in V} |\sigma_1(\gamma_i)(v) - \sigma_2(\gamma_i)(v)|.$$

Here $\|\cdot\|_1$ denotes the ℓ_1-norm on $\mathbb{R}^{|V|}$.

Essentially, the value distance is the cumulative distance between traces at $(\gamma_i)_{i=0}^N$ of the time sequence Γ.

Remark 4. Note that, although the time partitions Γ may vary across traces for BD and RBD (i.e., Γ^{σ_i} may differ from Γ^{σ_j}), they are fixed for VD. This is because allowing variable partitions in VD may reduce meaningful diversity: two identical signals could appear artificially distant if compared at different time instants.

The diversified trace synthesis procedure is iterative: at each step it maximizes the value distance between the candidate trace and all previously generated traces, subject to the constraint that all traces share the same time sequences. Let σ_m denote the piecewise-linear signal produced at iteration m, and let $(\gamma_0^{(m)}, \ldots, \gamma_N^{(m)})$ be the corresponding δ-stable partition at iteration m. The iterative synthesis procedure is as follows.

- **Initialization** ($m = 1$). Solve the original MILP problem with objective $f_1 := 0$.

- **Iteration** ($m > 1$). Let $\mathcal{C}$ denote the original MILP constraints from Sect. 3. Solve the following MILP:

$$\text{maximize} \sum_{k=1}^{m-1} \sum_{i=0}^{N} \sum_{v \in V} Z_{k,i,v}, \tag{4}$$

subject to $(\mathcal{C})$,

$$\begin{aligned} \gamma_i &= \gamma_i^{(m-1)} && 0 \le i \le N, \\ Z_{k,i,v} &= \texttt{abs}(Y_{k,i,v}) && 1 \le k \le m-1, 0 \le i \le N, v \in V, \\ Y_{k,i,v} &= x_{i,v} - \sigma_k(\gamma_i)(v) && 1 \le k \le m-1, 0 \le i \le N, v \in V. \end{aligned}$$

Here, $x_{i,v}$ is the MILP decision variable representing the value of signal variable $v \in V$ on the interval $[\gamma_{i-1}, \gamma_i]$.

At iteration $m > 1$, to i) ensure that synthesized traces share the same δ-stable partition, and ii) simplify the encoding of absolute values in the objective, we augment $\mathcal{C}$ with the constraints above. The relations $Z_{k,i,v} = \texttt{abs}(Y_{k,i,v})$ are implemented by standard MILP linearization (introducing auxiliary variables and linear inequalities), so the resulting problem remains an MILP.

Remark 5. Due to the use of absolute-value terms in the constraints, the MILP complexity increases with each iteration. Specifically, at iteration m, new variables $Y_{m,i,v}$ and $Z_{m,i,v}$ are introduced for every $i = 0, \dots, N$ and $v \in V$, adding $2(N+1)|V|$ variables per iteration. Consequently, the overall complexity of generating m solutions grows faster than linearly with respect to the size of the individual MILP problem.

Nevertheless, the value distance method is substantially faster than the two Boolean distance approaches when synthesizing a small number of traces. The value distance objective sums over signal variables, whereas the Boolean distance objective sums over subformulas. Since $|V|$ is typically much smaller than $|\text{Sub}(\varphi)|$ for realistic STL formulas, the value distance objective contains far fewer terms and is therefore cheaper to optimize. See Sect. 6 for experimental results.

5 Demonstration of STLts-Div

STLts-Div is a Python package for MILP-based diversified trace synthesis from STL. It can be installed by i) ensuring a working Gurobi installation, and ii) running `pip install stltspref`. We use the name `stltspref` for the pip package to accommodate future extensions incorporating preference-based trace synthesis methods.

The procedure to run STLts-Div is shown in Fig. 1. The user must provide the following input.

```
import gurobipy as gp
from stltspref.problem import create_stl_milp_problem

bound = 10                              # variability bound (see Problem 1)
milp = gp.Model()                                   # Gurobi model
prob = create_stl_milp_problem(milp,N=bound) # initialize the MILP problem
```

(a) Create the MILP problem `prob`.

```
# Define system model and its continuous states
car = prob.create_system_model()
car.add_state('x', 0, 40)               # position x in [0,40]
car.add_state('v', -5, 5)               # velocity v in [-5,5]
car.add_state('a', -3, 3)               # acceleration in [-3,3]

# Set initial state and dynamics (double-integrator model)
car.set_initial_state(x=(0,0), v=(0,0), a=(0,0))    # initial value ranges
car.add_dynamics('a', -3, 3, constant=True)
car.add_double_integrator_dynamics('x', 'v', 'a')
```

(b) Define the system model $\dot{x} = v,\ \dot{v} = a,\ a \in [-3, 3]$, and add it to `prob`.

```
from stltspref.linear_expression import LinearExpression as L
from stltspref.stl import Atomic, BoundedAlw, Ev

danger = Atomic(L.unit('x') <= 10)    # atomic proposition
stl_spec = Ev(BoundedAlw([0, 5], danger))            # STL specification

prob.initialize_milp_formulation(stl_spec)           # add the spec to MILP
```

(c) Specify the STL formula $\Diamond\left(\Box_{[0,5]}\, x \leq 10\right)$ and add it to `prob`.

```
from stltspref.preferential_synthesis import diversity_finder

diversity_method = 'RBD'     # random Boolean distance method
trace_num = 5              # synthesis 5 diverse traces

diversity_finder(prob, diversity_method, bound, trace_num)
```

(d) Solve `prob` to synthesize diverse traces.

Fig. 1. Workflow for MILP-based trace synthesis using STLts-Div.

- A system model. STLts-Div supports models such as *double-integrator dynamics* and *rectangular hybrid automata* (RHA) (cf. [20] for details); see Fig. 1a.
- An STL formula (encoded in a DSL style); see Fig. 1c;
- A diversification method: SP (Gurobi solution pool [10]), BD (Boolean distance; Sect. 4.1), RBD (randomized Boolean distance; Sec. 4.2), or VD (value difference; Sect. 4.3); see Fig. 1d;
- The desired number of traces to synthesize (a positive integer); see Fig. 1d.

6 Experimental Analysis

In this section, we evaluate our tool across different benchmarks and STL specifications to assess the efficiency and effectiveness of each diversification method. As a baseline, we also include the standard approach that extracts traces directly from the solution pool of Gurobi.

6.1 Experiment Setting

Benchmarks. To evaluate the efficiency of our diversification tool, we used benchmarks from four categories: *Danger-then-Stop* (DSTOP), *Rear-End Near Collision* (RNC), *Navigation* (NAV), and *Disturbance Scenarios in ISO 34502* (ISO). Each category shares the same system model but includes several distinct STL specifications, resulting in a total of 13 benchmarks.

Danger then stop (DSTOP) Consider two cars in a single lane, where the rear car $\mathrm{Car_r}$ repeatedly approaches the front car $\mathrm{Car_f}$ too closely, creating a potentially dangerous situation. Eventually, one of the cars comes to a stop. The system dynamics are given by $\dot{x}_\mathrm{r} = v_\mathrm{r}$, $\dot{v}_\mathrm{r} = a_\mathrm{r}$, $\dot{x}_\mathrm{f} = v_\mathrm{f}$, $\dot{v}_\mathrm{f} = a_\mathrm{f}$, with $a_\mathrm{r}, a_\mathrm{f} \in [-3, 3]$. The STL specification DSTOP is defined as follows:

$$\begin{aligned}&\texttt{lead} :\equiv x_\mathrm{f} - x_\mathrm{r} \geq 0, \qquad \texttt{close} :\equiv x_\mathrm{f} - x_\mathrm{r} \leq 10, \qquad \texttt{far} :\equiv x_\mathrm{f} - x_\mathrm{r} \geq 40,\\ &\texttt{DSTOP} :\equiv (\Box\ \texttt{lead}) \wedge (\Box_{[0,2]}\,\texttt{far}) \wedge \Big[(\Diamond_{[0,10]}\,\texttt{close})\,\mathcal{U}_{[10,15]}\,(v_\mathrm{f} \leq 0 \vee v_\mathrm{r} \leq 0)\Big]\,.\end{aligned}$$

Rear-End Near Collision (RNC1–3) The system model for RNC1–3 is identical to that of DSTOP. These benchmarks describe driving scenarios in which the rear car $\mathrm{Car_r}$ approaches the front car $\mathrm{Car_f}$ too closely. The corresponding STL specifications, RNC1, RNC2, and RNC3, are defined as follows:

$$\begin{aligned}\texttt{danger} &:\equiv x_\mathrm{f} - x_\mathrm{r} \leq 10,\\ \texttt{dyn\_inv} &:\equiv x_\mathrm{f} - x_\mathrm{r} \geq 0 \wedge 2 \leq v_\mathrm{f} \leq 27 \wedge 2 \leq v_\mathrm{r} \leq 27,\\ \texttt{trimming} &:\equiv (\Diamond\,\texttt{danger}) \Rightarrow \big((\Box_{[0,0.2]}\,a_\mathrm{r} \geq 0.5)\,\mathcal{U}\,\texttt{danger}\big),\\ \texttt{trimming2} &:\equiv (\Diamond\texttt{danger}) \Rightarrow \big((\Box_{[0,1]}a_\mathrm{r} \geq 1)\,\mathcal{U}\,\texttt{danger}\big),\\ \texttt{RNC1} &:\equiv \Box(\texttt{dyn\_inv} \wedge \texttt{trimming}) \wedge \Diamond_{[0,9]}\,\Box_{[0,1]}\,\texttt{danger},\\ \texttt{RNC2} &:\equiv \big(\Box(x_\mathrm{f} - x_\mathrm{r} \geq 0)\big)\wedge\\ &\quad\ \Diamond_{[0,9]}\big((\Box_{[0,1]}\texttt{danger}) \wedge (\Box_{[0,1]}a_\mathrm{r} \geq 1) \wedge (\Diamond_{[1,5]}\neg\texttt{danger})\big),\\ \texttt{RNC3} &:\equiv \Box(\texttt{dyn\_inv} \wedge \texttt{trimming2}) \wedge \Diamond_{[0,9]}\Box_{[0,1]}\texttt{danger}.\end{aligned}$$

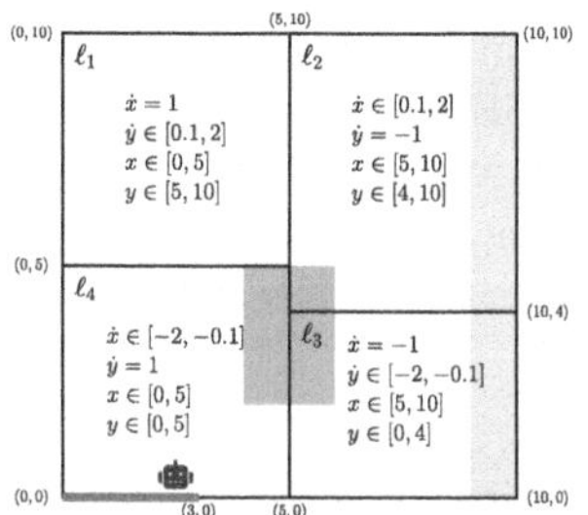

Fig. 2. The NAV1–2 RHA

Navigation (NAV1–2) The system model for NAV1–2 is adapted from [7], a standard example of a rectangular hybrid automaton (RHA) widely used in prior work (e.g., [4,20]). The model describes the motion of a robot on a grid consisting of four rectangular regions $\ell_1, \ldots, \ell_4$. Each region has its own dynamics (see Fig. 2). The environment includes an unsafe region `unsafeR` (red) and a goal region `goalR` (green). The robot starts from an initial position (x_0, y_0) where $x_0 \in [0,3]$ and $y_0 = 0$ (blue line). The STL specifications are $\texttt{NAV1} :\equiv \Diamond(\Box_{[0,3]}((x,y) \in \texttt{goalR})) \wedge \Box(x \notin \texttt{unsafeR})$
and $\texttt{NAV2} \equiv \Box((x,y) \in \ell_3 \Rightarrow \Diamond_{[0,3]}(x,y) \in \ell_4)$. Here, `NAV1` specifies a reach-avoid property, while `NAV2` requires that whenever the robot enters region ℓ_3, it must reach region ℓ_4 within three seconds.

Disturbance Scenarios in ISO 34502 (ISO1, ISO3, ..., ISO8) ISO 34502 is an international standard for testing autonomous vehicles. The system model is similar to that of RNC1–3, and the specifications $\texttt{ISO1}, \texttt{ISO3}, \ldots, \texttt{ISO8}$ are obtained in [19]. ISO2 is omitted because it involves three vehicles. Each spec $\texttt{ISO}i$ follows the general structure defined in [19]:

$$\begin{aligned} \texttt{ISO}i &:\equiv \texttt{initSafe} \wedge \texttt{disturb}_i, \\ \texttt{disturb}_i &:\equiv \texttt{initialCondition}_i \wedge \texttt{behaviourSV}_i \wedge \texttt{behaviourPOV}_i, \end{aligned}$$

where SV denotes the subject ("ego") vehicle and POV the principal other vehicle. The subformulas $\texttt{initialCondition}_i$, $\texttt{behaviourSV}_i$, and $\texttt{behaviourPOV}_i$ vary across scenarios (indexed by i). Their detailed definitions are beyond the scope of this paper; please refer to [19] for full descriptions.

Experiment design. We evaluate four diversification strategies implemented in our tool—SP (solution pool), BD (Boolean distance), RBD (randomized Boolean distance), and VD (value distance)—for synthesizing diverse traces. For each benchmark and each method, we generate 8 traces. We set the variability bound as 10 uniformly for each benchmark. While measuring diversity via coverage metrics over the space of all possible traces would provide a comprehensive quantification of diversity, the infinite nature of the trace space (since signals evolve in continuous time) makes such an approach computationally intractable. Investigating tractable approximations is left for future work. Instead, we quantify diversity using the aggregate pairwise Euclidean distance (APED) over time, a common choice in the literature [5]:

$$D_{\mathrm{E}} := \sum_{i<j} \int_0^T \left\|\sigma_i(t) - \sigma_j(t)\right\|_2 \mathrm{d}t,$$

where i and j index the traces ($i, j \in \{1, \ldots, 8\}$ in our experiments) and T is the time horizon. The synthesized traces are resampled over $[0, T]$ with a time step of 0.02, and the integral is computed numerically in Python.

Our experiments were conducted on an Amazon EC2 c5.2xlarge instance (3.00 GHz Intel Xeon Platinum 8275CL, 16 GB RAM) running Ubuntu Server 20.04 LTS.

6.2 Evaluation

We evaluate our tool along from *effectiveness* and *efficiency.*

Effectiveness. Table 1a reports APED for each method and benchmark under a 6-minute per-trace timeout; a dash "—" indicates that no feasible trace was found within the timeout. Across benchmarks, our diversification methods (BD, RBD, VD) consistently achieve substantially higher diversity than the baseline (SP)—typically about an order of magnitude larger APED.

Occasionally the baseline attains APED > 0, reflecting that some specifications are relatively permissive for the given system model: multiple distinct MILP assignments can satisfy φ while respecting the dynamics, yielding non-identical traces. The `DSTOP`, `IS05`, and `IS08` exhibit this behaviour.

Efficiency. Table 1a reports the total time required to generate the full set of traces. For `NAV1` and `NAV2` no feasible trace was found within our setting; this matches [20], which reports that `NAV1` and `NAV2` becomes solvable only with a much larger variability bound (e.g. $N = 17$ for `NAV1`, versus our uniform bound N=10).

Because our diversification is posed as an optimization problem, a solver timeout *does not* necessarily imply infeasibility—it may simply return a suboptimal or low-quality solution. To assess sensitivity to the time budget, we repeated the experiments with a reduced per-trace timeout of 60 seconds; results appear in Table 1b.

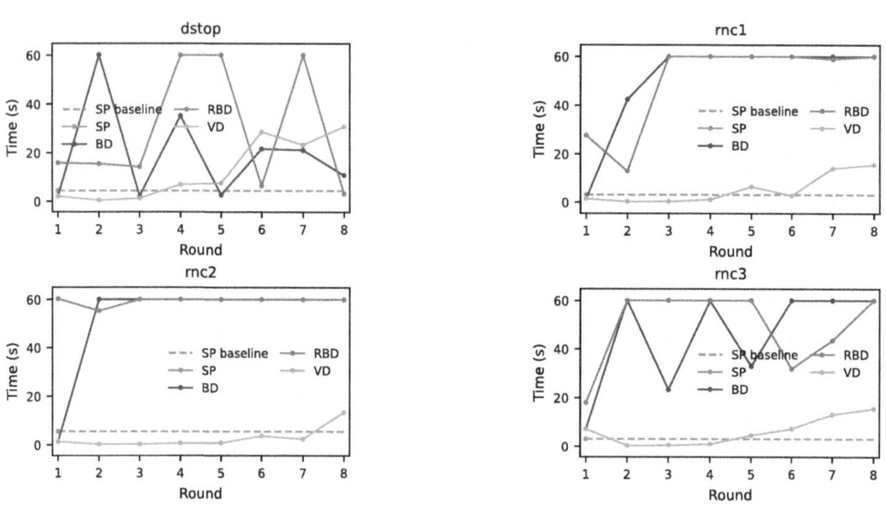

Fig. 3. Round time of `DSTOP`, `RNC1`, `RNC2`, `RNC3`.

For relatively simple benchmarks (e.g., `DSTOP`, `RNC1`, `RNC2`), reducing the timeout has little effect on diversity for any method. In particular, RBD requires

Table 1. Aggregated pairwise Euclidean distance under two timeout settings.

(a) Timeout per trace: 360 s.

Benchmarks	SP	BD	RBD	VD
DSTOP	~129k (4.62 s)	~1.6M (200 s)	~934k (1178 s)	~3M (107 s)
RNC1	0(3.11 s)	~1.3M (2207 s)	~1.5M (1881 s)	~1.6M (44.0 s)
RNC2	0(5.87 s)	~2.8M (2523 s)	~2.2M (1867 s)	~4.8M (25.4 s)
RNC3	0(3.13 s)	~1.7M (1473 s)	~1.3M (158 s)	~1.5M (53.0 s)
NAV1	—	—	—	—
NAV2	—	—	—	—
ISO1	~18 (95.9 s)	~466k (2529 s)	~403k (2882 s)	~1.5M (2529 s)
ISO3	~153 (63.8 s)	~701k (2527 s)	~71k (2882 s)	~792k (2528 s)
ISO4	~772 (29.6 s)	~633k (2526 s)	~174k (2881 s)	~598k (2526 s)
ISO5	~34k (266 s)	~1M (2561 s)	~32k (2882 s)	~1.7M (2361 s)
ISO6	~122 (19.1 s)	~413k (2529 s)	—	~1.6M (1653 s)
ISO7	—	~230k (2556 s)	—	~911k (2555 s)
ISO8	~1.2k (66.8 s)	~447k (2527 s)	~291k (2882 s)	~896k (2444 s)

(b) Timeout per trace: 60 s

Benchmarks	SP	BD	RBD	VD
DSTOP	~130k (4.33 s)	~1.6M (157 s)	~1M (237 s)	~3M (102 s)
RNC1	0(3.03 s)	~1.3M (405 s)	~1.4M (401 s)	~1.6M (42 s)
RNC2	0(5.52 s)	~2.4M (423 s)	~2.3M (477 s)	~4.8M (24.4 s)
RNC3	0(3.05 s)	~1.7M (365 s)	~1.2M (395 s)	~1.6M (50.6 s)
NAV1	—	—	—	—
NAV2	—	—	—	—
ISO1	—	~79k (429 s)	—	~1.4M (429 s)
ISO3	—	0(428 s)	—	~133k (426 s)
ISO4	~772 (32.1 s)	~177k (426 s)	—	~256k (425 s)
ISO5	—	0(464 s)	—	~1.5M (464 s)
ISO6	~122 (21.2 s)	0(429 s)	—	~1.6M (389 s)
ISO7	—	0(457 s)	—	~271k (458 s)
ISO8	—	~88k (427 s)	0(480 s)	~431k (426 s)

Entries show APED; parentheses give the total time to produce 8 traces (in seconds); '—' indicates that no feasible traces were produced within the timeout; numbers use suffixes $k = 10^3$ and $M = 10^6$;

significantly less time while producing nearly the same APED. This suggests that, with a larger time budget (i.e., 360s per trace), the optimization process may spend most of its time attempting to approach the optimal solution without reaching it before the timeout. In practice, however, a near-optimal solution already provides sufficient diversity, which explains the similar APED values observed under both timeout settings.

By contrast, on more challenging benchmarks (e.g., `ISO1`, `ISO8`, `ISO4`), performance diverges: RBD often fails to produce feasible traces, and BD frequently returns only trivial repeats after the first iteration (APED = 0). VD is the most robust under tight time limits: it continues to produce nontrivial, diverse traces even with the shorter timeout.

To study how per-iteration runtime (i.e., the time to synthesize one trace) evolves with the iteration index, we record the runtime at each iteration for `DSTOP`, `RNC1`, `RNC2`, and `RNC3` and plot the results in Fig. 3. For VD, the per-iteration time increases steadily, consistent with our analysis in Sect. 4.3 that each round enlarges the MILP problem (additional auxiliary variables). In contrast, BD and RBD show fluctuating runtimes with no clear trend: BD changes the coefficients of the accumulated objective each round, and RBD re-samples the reference, both of which alter the search landscape and lead to non-monotonic solver times.

Table 2. Comparison of diversification methods

Criteria	**SP**	**BD**	**RBD**	**VD**
Total runtime	●1–100	◔Varying with timeout setting	◔Varying with timeout setting	⦿Varying with timeout setting
Stable per-trace time	-	⦿ Varying across iterations	⦿ Varying across iterations	◔ Time increase per iteration
Diversity	◔	●	●	●
Compatibility with other tools	● Support all MILP-based formulations	⦿ Compatible only with full Boolean-variable formulations	⦿ Compatible only with full Boolean-variable formulations	◔ Limited compatibility
Deterministic	✓	✓	✗	✓

● = good; ⦿ = moderate; ◔ = poor; - = not applicable.

Summary. Table 2 contrasts the three diversification strategies. Achieving diversity incurs extra runtime for all of them. The ideas behind BD and RBD are broadly portable: for problems with only Boolean decision variables, adding (possibly randomized) Boolean distance terms can produce multiple diverse solutions. By contrast, VD depends on continuous state variables and absolute-value linearization, which enlarges the MILP problem and makes the approach less directly compatible with other tools or settings.

7 Conclusion

We introduced diversification into MILP-based STL trace synthesis. We formulated several complementary objectives—e.g., Boolean distance, randomized Boolean distance, and value distance—that promote dissimilarity by maximizing an appropriate distance between the candidate trace and previously generated ones. We implemented these objectives in STLts-Div and evaluated effectiveness and efficiency on a suite of benchmarks, showing clear improvements over a solution-pool baseline.

A complete MILP encoding of robust semantics remains open. Such an encoding could enable richer preference objectives and stronger guarantees, including true corner-case synthesis (robustness exactly 0) and additional forms of preferential synthesis.

References

1. Alur, R., Feder, T., Henzinger, T.A.: The benefits of relaxing punctuality. Journal of the ACM (JACM) **43**(1), 116–146 (1996)
2. Atkins, E.M., Bradley, J.M.: Aerospace cyber-physical systems education. In: AIAA Infotech@ Aerospace (I@ A) Conference. p. 4809 (2013)
3. Bae, K., Lee, J.: Bounded model checking of signal temporal logic properties using syntactic separation. Proceedings of the ACM on Programming Languages **3**(POPL), 1–30 (2019)
4. Bu, L., Frehse, G., Kundu, A., Ray, R., Shi, Y., Zaffanella, E., et al.: Arch-comp22 category report: Hybrid systems with piecewise constant dynamics and bounded model checking. In: Proceedings of 9th International Workshop on Applied Verification of Continuous and Hybrid Systems (ARCH22). EPiC Series in Computing vol. 90, pp. 44–57 (2022)
5. Cheng, M., Zhou, Y., Xie, X.: Behavexplor: Behavior diversity guided testing for autonomous driving systems. In: Proceedings of the 32nd ACM SIGSOFT International Symposium on Software Testing and Analysis. pp. 488–500 (2023)
6. Donzé, A., Raman, V., Frehse, G., Althoff, M.: Blustl: Controller synthesis from signal temporal logic specifications. ARCH@ CPSWeek **34**, 160–8 (2015)
7. Duggirala, P.S., Mitra, S.: Abstraction refinement for stability. In: 2011 IEEE/ACM Second International Conference on Cyber-Physical Systems. pp. 22–31. IEEE (2011)
8. Ernst, G., Arcaini, P., Bennani, I., Chandratre, A., Donzé, A., Fainekos, G., Frehse, G., Gaaloul, K., Inoue, J., Khandait, T., et al.: Arch-comp 2021 category report: Falsification with validation of results. In: ARCH@ ADHS. pp. 133–152 (2021)
9. Fainekos, G.E., Pappas, G.J.: Robustness of temporal logic specifications for continuous-time signals. Theoret. Comput. Sci. **410**(42), 4262–4291 (Sep2009). 10.1016/j.tcs.2009.06.021, http://dx.doi.org/10.1016/j.tcs.2009.06.021
10. Gurobi Optimization, LLC: Gurobi Optimizer Reference Manual (2024), https://www.gurobi.com
11. Jouve-Genty, M., Su, H., Sato, S., An, J., Zhang, Z., Hasuo, I.: STLts-Div: Diversified trace synthesis from STL specifications using MILP (Extended Version) (2025), available on arXiv
12. Lee, J., Yu, G., Bae, K.: Efficient smt-based model checking for signal temporal logic. In: 2021 36th IEEE/ACM international conference on automated software engineering (ASE). pp. 343–354. IEEE (2021)
13. Lindemann, L., Dimarogonas, D.V.: Control barrier functions for signal temporal logic tasks. IEEE control systems letters **3**(1), 96–101 (2018)
14. Maler, O., Nickovic, D.: Monitoring Temporal Properties of Continuous Signals, p. 152–166. Springer Berlin Heidelberg (2004https://doi.org/10.1007/978-3-540-30206-3_12, http://dx.doi.org/10.1007/978-3-540-30206-3_12

15. Prabhakar, P., Lal, R., Kapinski, J.: Automatic trace generation for signal temporal logic. In: 2018 IEEE Real-Time Systems Symposium (RTSS). pp. 208–217. IEEE (2018)
16. Rabinovich, A.M.: On the decidability of continuous time specification formalisms. J. Log. Comput. **8**(5), 669–678 (1998)
17. Raman, V., Donzé, A., Sadigh, D., Murray, R.M., Seshia, S.A.: Reactive synthesis from signal temporal logic specifications. In: Proceedings of the 18th international conference on hybrid systems: Computation and control. pp. 239–248 (2015)
18. Raman, V., Maasoumy, M., Donzé, A.: Model predictive control from signal temporal logic specifications: A case study. In: Proceedings of the 4th ACM SIGBED international workshop on design, modeling, and evaluation of cyber-physical systems. pp. 52–55 (2014)
19. Reimann, J., Mansion, N., Haydon, J., Bray, B., Chattopadhyay, A., Sato, S., Waga, M., André, É., Hasuo, I., Ueda, N., et al.: Temporal logic formalisation of iso 34502 critical scenarios: modular construction with the rss safety distance. In: Proceedings of the 39th ACM/SIGAPP Symposium on Applied Computing. pp. 186–195 (2024)
20. Sato, S., An, J., Zhang, Z., Hasuo, I.: Optimization-Based Model Checking and Trace Synthesis for Complex STL Specifications, p. 282–306. Springer Nature Switzerland (202https://doi.org/10.1007/978-3-031-65633-0_13, http://dx.doi.org/10.1007/978-3-031-65633-0_13
21. Su, H., Feng, S., Zhan, S., Zhan, N.: Switching controller synthesis for hybrid systems against stl formulas. In: International Symposium on Formal Methods. pp. 229–247. Springer (2024)
22. Su, H., Shankar, S., Pinisetty, S., Roop, P.S., Zhan, N.: Runtime enforcement of cps against signal temporal logic. In: Proceedings of the 28th ACM International Conference on Hybrid Systems: Computation and Control. pp. 1–11 (2025)
23. Tomlin, C.J., Lygeros, J., Sastry, S.S.: A game theoretic approach to controller design for hybrid systems. Proc. IEEE **88**(7), 949–970 (2000)
24. Ye, P., Entcheva, E., Smolka, S.A., Grosu, R.: Modelling excitable cells using cycle-linear hybrid automata. IET Syst. Biol. **2**(1), 24–32 (2008)
25. Zhang, Z., An, J., Arcaini, P., Hasuo, I.: Online causation monitoring of signal temporal logic. In: International Conference on Computer Aided Verification. pp. 62–84. Springer (2023)

Towards Privacy-Preserving Verification

Timos Antonopoulos[1], Ning Luo[2], and Ruzica Piskac[1(✉)]

[1] Yale University, New Haven, USA
{timos.antonopoulos,ruzica.piskac}@yale.edu
[2] University of Illinois Urbana-Champaign, Illinois, USA
nl27@illinois.edu

Abstract. Program verification provides stronger guarantees of correctness than standard testing. The verification process takes a program as input and derives a mathematical formula. Proving that a program is correct then reduces to establishing that this derived formula is unsatisfiable. Traditionally, automated reasoning tools can be used to determine unsatisfiability automatically. Furthermore, modern solvers can also produce a proof of unsatisfiability. However, these techniques typically rely on the proof and the underlying code being publicly available, which may not be desirable for certain applications.

This work shows how to address this problem. Our team initially developed a protocol for validating the unsatisfiability of Boolean formulas in privacy-preserving settings. Building on these initial results, we devised ZKSMT, a virtual machine for validating unsatisfiability results produced by SMT solvers in zero-knowledge settings. In this paper we describe the theoretical foundations of such virtual machines and demonstrate how they can be applied to the theories of uninterpreted functions and linear integer arithmetic, two of the most widely used theories in verification.

We conclude by outlining how the full formal verification workflow can be adapted to operate in privacy-preserving settings.

1 Introduction

Conventional approaches to verifying software take for granted that the code under scrutiny can be freely inspected. A verifier is given both the program and a formal description of how it ought to behave, and then works to establish that the program lives up to that description. Open-source projects lend themselves naturally to this paradigm, as do proprietary systems in which the organization performing the verification has full access to the underlying codebase.

Reality, however, presents cases that fall outside this comfortable assumption of code accessibility. There are often circumstances in which the very party that needs reassurance about a piece of software is also the one that should be kept away from the software source code. A company's IP may reside in its codebase, proprietary methods, hard-won algorithms, and competitive secrets, making it impossible to hand over that code to an outside organization for auditing, even

A. Sampaio and M. Stoelinga (Eds.): FM 2026, LNCS 16556, pp. 21–43, 2026.
https://doi.org/10.1007/978-3-032-26204-2_2

if the organization constantly runs the software in some encrypted or obfuscated form. In this setting, verification must be delegated to a trusted third party—one granted access to the code for inspection, yet equally bound to preserve its confidentiality.

Privacy-preserving verification tools have been proposed to eliminate this dependence on a trusted intermediary entirely. By integrating cryptographic techniques into formal verification methods, such tools enable an untrusted party to verify the correctness of a confidential program without learning anything about its internals. In privacy-preserving verification setting, two mutually distrusting parties interact: the program owner and the verifier. The program owner wishes to convince the verifier that her code satisfies some desired property, such as safety or soundness, without exposing the code itself. The verifier, for his part, wants a guarantee that the program behaves exactly as the owner claims. Each party can act maliciously: a dishonest program owner might cheat about her program, for instance by implementing only a subset of the functionality the verifier expects, while a dishonest verifier might attempt to extract information about the program from the verification process itself.

Drawing inspiration from classical program verification, privacy-preserving verification builds on the same logical foundation that underlies most modern verification tools: automated reasoning and formula solving. In the standard, non-private setting, the claim a program owner establishes is that the program cannot violate a given property under any circumstances. When the program and its specification are encoded as logical formulas, this reduces to showing that a certain formula is *unsatisfiable*. When these formulae are indeed unsatisfiable, the certificate that asserts the formula's unsatisfiability, also known as the refutation proof, can be output by the formula solvers. Privacy-preserving verification lifts this foundation into a private setting. Rather than handing over the formula or its refutation proof, the program owner proves to the verifiers that a formula is unsatisfiable, without revealing any information on formulae or proofs.

Proving the unsatisfiability of a formula in a privacy-preserving setting is achieved via *zero-knowledge proof* (ZKP) [20, 22]. ZKP is a cryptographic protocol between a prover and a verifier in which the prover convinces the verifier that a statement, which can contain confidential components, is true without revealing any information beyond the truth of the statement itself. In our setting, the statement is that a valid refutation proof for a private formula exists; the prover establishes this fact without disclosing the formula, the proof, or anything else about the program under verification.

The logical formalisms employed in program verification differ in expressive power. This paper explains the ZKP of refutation for the three principal automated-reasoning formalisms employed in software verification: Boolean unsatisfiability (SAT/UNSAT), Satisfiability Modulo Theories (SMT), and Quantified Boolean Formulas (QBF). In this paper, we survey these recent lines of work that collectively establish a coherent methodology for privacy-preserving automated reasoning.

1. **Verifying UNSAT of propositional Boolean formulae.** Luo et al. [34] introduced the first practical ZKP for proving propositional unsatisfiability, addressing a problem that had resisted practical treatment despite the theoretical existence of ZK proofs for all of PSPACE. The key insight is to prove, in ZKP, the validity of a resolution refutation proof. Clauses are encoded as low-degree polynomials over a finite field, where the roots correspond to the field-element encodings of the clause's literals. This polynomial representation is compatible with a wide class of efficient ZKP backends. The resolution rule then translates naturally into an arithmetic divisibility check over the committed polynomials.
2. **Verifying unsatisfiability of SMT formulae.** Luick et al. [33] extended this approach to the full SMT setting, which is the language in which realistic program verification tools actually operate. The central challenge is that SMT refutation proofs employ dozens of theory-specific inference rules beyond resolution, such as Farkas' lemma certificates, congruence closure steps, and others, making the proof objects far more complex than their purely propositional counterparts and rendering the machinery of ZKUNSAT inapplicable. ZKSMT overcomes this by introducing a tailored zero-knowledge virtual machine (ZKVM) modeled on the Von Neumann architecture. Theory-specific proof rules are compiled into VM instructions, and the main checker performs step-by-step proof validation in ZKP. Instantiated with the theories of equality and linear integer arithmetic and evaluated on Boogie-generated verification benchmarks, the system achieves a three-order-of-magnitude speedup over a general-purpose ZKP baseline.
3. **ZK proofs for unsatisfiability of QBF (PSPACE).** Karthikeyan et al. [27] push the frontier further, presenting the first *practical* ZK protocols for PSPACE-complete statements by targeting QBF evaluation. The core idea is to validate *quantified resolution* (Q-Res) proofs in ZKP, extending the polynomial encoding of [34] to handle universal and existential quantifier alternation. The work also introduces a complementary protocol for proving knowledge of a *winning strategy* for a QBF game, which is often the object of interest in hardware synthesis and reactive verification. Evaluated on QBFEVAL benchmarks, the system verifies 72% of instances via Q-Res proof and 82% of instances' winning strategies within 100 s.

2 Background

In deductive verification, the verification process typically involves proving the validity of a logical implication of the form $F \Rightarrow G$, where F represents the program semantics and G denotes the desired safety or correctness properties. To prove this validity, automated solvers typically demonstrate that the negation of the implication, $F \wedge \neg G$, is unsatisfiable (UNSAT). This section provides the necessary background for privacy-preserving automated reasoning, specifically focusing on resolution proofs, proofs of unsatisfiability, and zero-knowledge proofs.

2.1 Automated Reasoning and Proofs of Unsatifiability

The ability to automatically determine the satisfiability of a given formula, either by finding a satisfying assignment or providing a proof of its non-existence, remains a fundamental challenge in computer science. A significant milestone in this domain was the development of SAT solvers and the DPLL (Davis-Putnam-Logemann-Loveland) algorithm [15]. A SAT solver accepts a Boolean formula, typically in Conjunctive Normal Form (CNF), and determines if a satisfying assignment exists. While SAT solvers operate within the bounds of decidable propositional logic, first-order theorem provers extend these capabilities to tackle formulas expressed in first-order logic, which offers greater expressivity but introduces undecidability in the general case [43].

Despite the inherent undecidability of first-order logic, resolution-based first-order theorem provers have been highly effective in proving formulas coming from mathematics and formal verification [42]. All these systems are based on the resolution rule [38], which defines a refutationally complete calculus for first-order logic. In its simplest propositional form, the resolution rule is defined as:

$$\frac{A \vee B \quad \neg A \vee C}{B \vee C}$$

In the first-order case, this rule is also combined with unification to handle variables.

The refutational completeness of the resolution calculus means that for every unsatisfiable formula, a proof of its unsatisfiability can be systematically derived [3]. These resolution-based derivations serve as the foundational framework for a wide variety of modern proof formats. In the context of SAT solvers, for instance, the DRAT (Deletion Resolution Asymmetric Tautology) format has become the de facto standard for certifying solver outputs [46].

However, reasoning algorithms for first-order theories, in particular those used in SMT solvers, is often not purely resolution-based. SMT solvers employ specialized decision procedures to handle specific theories such as linear arithmetic, bit-vectors, or uninterpreted functions. Consequently, generating and verifying proofs in SMT is a significantly more intricate task than in propositional logic, as the proof must encapsulate the interactions between the SAT engine and multiple theory-specific solvers. Typical proof formats used by modern SMT solvers to address this complexity include LFSC (Logical Framework with Side Conditions) [41] and the Alethe proof format [39].

While standard SMT and resolution proofs are designed for public verifiability, where the verifier has full access to the formula and its derivation, certain industrial applications require privacy-preserving automated reasoning. In such scenarios, a prover must demonstrate that a formula is unsatisfiable (or satisfiable) without revealing the internal structure of the program F, the specific properties G, or the intermediate steps of the proof derivation process. This requirement leads to the integration of zero-knowledge proofs into the automated reasoning pipeline.

2.2 Zero Knowledge Proof

A standard interactive Zero-Knowledge Proof (ZKP) [20,22] protocol involves two parties: the *prover* and the *verifier*. It is important to stress that these two terms have slightly different meanings in the cryptography and formal verification communities, which can occasionally lead to misunderstanding. In automated reasoning, a "prover" typically refers to the algorithmic engine (such as a SAT or SMT solver) that searches for a proof. In the context of ZKPs, however, the prover is a party that already possesses a witness (a resolution proof or a satisfying assignment) and has to convince the verifier of a statement's validity. In these settings, the witness remains strictly private. The goal of the protocol is for the prover to demonstrate the correctness of the statement, while maintaining that the verifier learns nothing about the underlying witness, specific axioms, or intermediate resolution steps used to derive the result, other than the fact that the statement itself is indeed true.

Formally, a ZKP is defined as follows: given a public predicate P and a public input x, a prover must convince a verifier that it holds a private input w such that $P(w, x) = 1$, while revealing no additional information about w. Both prover and verifier may behave maliciously: the prover may not possess a valid witness w satisfying the predicate, and the verifier may attempt to extract information about the prover's private input. A secure ZKP must satisfy two properties *Soundness* ensures that a malicious prover cannot convince the verifier of a false statement. *Zero-knowledge* ensures that a malicious verifier learns nothing about the private input w beyond the fact that the statement is true.

The soundness and zero-knowledge properties of ZKP make them a natural cryptographic foundation for privacy-preserving verification. Soundness plays the role of a trust anchor for the verifier: it guarantees that no matter how a dishonest program owner constructs the proof, the prover cannot convince the verifier that an incorrect or unsafe program satisfies the specification. Zero-knowledge, on the other hand, protects the program owner: the verifier learns nothing about the program, its specification, or the intermediate steps of the verification beyond the single bit of information that the program is correct. There have been many lines of work designing practically efficient and secure ZK protocols under different settings and assumptions [21,23–25].

We next describe a widely adopted ZKP paradigm known as *commit-and-prove* [9], which underlies all of the privacy-preserving verification protocols surveyed in this paper.

Commit and Prove. In the commit-and-prove ZKP, the interaction between the prover and verifier is split into two phases. In the *commitment phase*, the prover cryptographically commits to its private witness, using a binding and hiding commitment scheme. In our setting, the witness consists of the formula and the refutation proof. Binding ensures that the prover cannot alter the committed values after the fact. Hiding ensures that the commitments reveal nothing about the underlying witness to the verifier. Conceptually, commitment can be understood as a process where the prover encrypts and "locks" the proof. This ensures that the proof cannot be altered during the protocol, while its contents remain hidden from the verifier. We use $[\![\cdot]\!]$ to denote a committed value.

In the *proving phase*, the prover demonstrates to the verifier that the committed values satisfy the desired predicate, for instance, that the committed proof is a valid refutation of the committed formula. Crucially, all interaction occurs only through the commitments: the underlying values are never revealed to the verifier at any point during the protocol.

The commit-and-prove ZKP can be applied, in principle, on any predicate P. Therefore, we apply it to validate refutation proofs for program verification. The protocol begins with the prover *committing* to the entire proof (for example, a resolution proof), via a cryptographic commitment scheme. After this commitment phase, the prover and verifier engage in a protocol to validate each step of the committed proof. Proof steps, such as resolution or redundancy checks, are individually checked without revealing the actual clauses or literals involved. By applying a zero-knowledge protocol to each proof step, the prover can demonstrate that a specific resolvent $B \vee C$ follows logically from its committed parents $A \vee B$ and $\neg A \vee C$, or that a clause meets the criteria for a DRAT-style deletion. This granular verification ensures that the verifier is convinced of the overall proof's validity while the underlying logic, axioms, and intermediate lemmas remain entirely private.

Despite the theoretical feasibility, the cost of verifying each proof step in ZK can be prohibitive without careful design. To make commit-and-prove ZKP practical for refutation proof, the proof must first be *arithmetized*, i.e. translated from its logical form into an algebraic one, so that each proof step reduces to a relation over committed field elements that a ZKP backend can verify efficiently. The central challenge and the primary technical contribution of the protocols surveyed in this paper is to find arithmetizations that are simultaneously faithful to the logical semantics of the underlying proof system and amenable to the algebraic operations supported by ZKP backends. In what follows, we describe the key arithmetization techniques and algebraic relations that have been developed and exploited in privacy-preserving verification.

Polynomial Equivalence in ZKP. A polynomial is committed by committing all its coefficients. Given two committed polynomials, denoted by $[\![P(X)]\!]$ and $[\![Q(X)]\!]$, the prover can convince the verifier that $P(X) = Q(X)$ without revealing the polynomials themselves. The key tool is the *Schwartz–Zippel lemma* [40]: if P and Q are distinct polynomials of degree at most d over a finite field $\mathbb{F}$, then they agree on at most d points. Consequently, if both polynomials evaluate, using their commitments, to the same value at a uniformly random point $r \in \mathbb{F}$ chosen by the verifier, then $P = Q$ holds with overwhelming probability when $|\mathbb{F}| \gg d$. This reduces a global structural equality between two polynomials to a single field equality checking, making it exceptionally cheap to verify in ZK.

More generally, given committed polynomials $[\![P(X)]\!]$, $[\![Q(X)]\!]$, and $[\![R(X)]\!]$, the prover can demonstrate that $[\![P(X) \cdot Q(X)]\!] = [\![R(X)]\!]$ by again invoking the Schwartz–Zippel lemma at a random evaluation point. This primitive is particularly useful in privacy-preserving verification because many structural properties of proofs, such as clause containment and resolution steps, reduce naturally to divisibility relations between polynomials, which in turn reduce to product checks.

Encoding logical objects, such as resolution proofs, as polynomials and reducing logical relations to polynomial relations verified in ZK via Schwartz–Zippel, is the arithmetization backbone shared by ZKUNSAT, ZKSMT, and the QBF protocols described in this paper. It enables the prover to commit once to the entire proof structure and then discharge each proof step with a small, constant number of field operations, yielding the practical efficiency that makes privacy-preserving verification feasible at scale.

3 Proving Unsatisfiability of Propositional Boolean Formulae in Privacy Preserving Settings

In program verification, the assertion that a program is *safe* reduces precisely to the unsatisfiability of the formula encoding the program together with the negation of the safety property. An efficient ZKP for UNSAT is therefore a direct cryptographic primitive for privacy-preserving program verification. However, most ZKP systems focus on the converse proving knowledge of a satisfying assignment to a Boolean formula, circuit, or program. Luo et al. [34]'s work provides the first practical ZKP for proving UNSAT of propositional Boolean formulae. Formally, to prove unsatisfiability, the statement to be proved in ZK is:

$$\exists \pi \; : \; \pi \text{ is a valid resolution refutation of } \varphi, \tag{1}$$

where φ is a CNF formula known only to the formula or program owner.

3.1 Polynomial Encoding of Clauses

The central technical contribution of [34] is an algebraic encoding that represents clauses as low-degree polynomials over a finite field, enabling resolution steps to be validated via arithmetic checks that are amenable to zero-knowledge proof.

The literal encoding $\phi : \mathit{Lits} \to \mathbb{F}$ satisfies the negation constraint

$$\phi(x) + \phi(\neg x) = 1_{\mathbb{F}}, \tag{2}$$

so that a literal and its negation sum to the field identity. This is required to enable efficient ZK operations.

A clause $C = \ell_1 \vee \cdots \vee \ell_k$ is then encoded as the polynomial

$$\gamma(C)(X) = \prod_{j=1}^{k} \big(X - \phi(\ell_j)\big) \;\in\; \mathbb{F}[X], \tag{3}$$

whose roots are exactly the field-element encodings of the clause's literals. For example, the clause $C = x_1 \vee \neg x_2 \vee \neg x_3$ is encoded as:

$$\gamma(C)(X) = \big(X - \phi(x_1)\big)\big(X - \phi(\neg x_2)\big)\big(X - \phi(\neg x_3)\big). \tag{4}$$

The degree of $\gamma(C)$ equals the width of C, so for a proof of width w, all polynomials have degree at most w.

We now explain the intuition behind the polynomial encoding. A clause is a disjunction of literals, and as such it can be viewed as a *set* of literals with no inherent ordering. Under the literal encoding ϕ, this set of literals corresponds to a set of field elements in $\mathbb{F}$. A finite set of field elements is uniquely represented, up to a scalar factor, by the monic univariate polynomial whose roots are exactly those elements. This is precisely the clause encoding γ in (3): the polynomial $\gamma(C)$ has as its roots the field-element images $\phi(\ell)$ of the literals $\ell \in C$.

The key observation is that the central operation over clauses, namely, resolution relation, translates cleanly into this polynomial representation. Recall that resolution derives a new clause C_r from two premise clauses C_0 and C_1 by canceling a complementary pivot literal pair. At the set level, this corresponds to taking the union of the two literal sets after removing the pivot literal and its negation. At the polynomial level, this set-theoretic relationship is captured by the divisibility relations, which we explain in detail next.

3.2 Algebraic Characterization of Resolution

Lemma 1 (Implication as Divisibility [34]**).** *For clauses C and C', $C \to C'$ if and only if $\gamma(C) \mid \gamma(C')$ in $\mathbb{F}[X]$.*

This follows immediately from the fact that $C \subseteq C'$ implies every root of $\gamma(C)$ is a root of $\gamma(C')$, so the linear factors of $\gamma(C)$ divide $\gamma(C')$.

Weak Resolution. Rather than checking standard resolution directly, ZKUNSAT introduces *weak resolution*, which relaxes the standard rule while remaining sound and complete for refutation. A non-tautology clause C_r is a *weak resolvent* of C_0 and C_1 on pivot variable x if

$$C_0 \to C_r \vee x \qquad \text{and} \qquad C_1 \to C_r \vee \neg x. \tag{5}$$

mmmmmmm Standard resolution is the special case in which C_r is the smallest such clause.

Weak resolution improves the efficiency of verifying unsatisfiability in ZK without sacrificing the soundness. In standard resolution, the resolvent C_r must be *exactly* the clause obtained by merging the two premises and removing the pivot literal pair. Enforcing such equivalence in ZK is expensive. Weak resolution drops the exactness requirement and replaces it with a one-sided check: the "resolvent" C_r is allowed to contain more literals than the standard resolvent, i.e., it is only required to be a superset of the standard resolvent. This reduces the verification condition to a pure subset relation, which at the polynomial level corresponds to the two divisibility relations. Last, as established by Lemma 1, this relaxation preserves soundness: a formula is unsatisfiable if and only if it admits a weak resolution proof. A weak resolution proof mirrors a standard resolution proof, except that each resolution step is replaced by weak resolution

To verify a weak resolution step in zero knowledge, the prover commits to the polynomial encodings $q_0 = \gamma(C_0)$, $q_1 = \gamma(C_1)$, $q_r = \gamma(C_r)$, together with linear pivot polynomials $\rho(X) = X - \phi(x)$ and $\bar{\rho}(X) = X - \phi(\neg x)$. The *weak resolution test* asserts:

$$q_0 | q_r \cdot \rho, \tag{6}$$

$$q_1 | q_r \cdot \bar{\rho}, \tag{7}$$

$$\rho(X) + \bar{\rho}(1_{\mathbb{F}} - X) = 0. \tag{8}$$

Equation (6) encodes $C_0 \rightarrow C_r \vee x$ as polynomial divisibility: $q_0 \mid q_r \cdot \rho$, with w_0 the explicit quotient. Equation (7) encodes $C_1 \rightarrow C_r \vee \neg x$ analogously. Equation (8) enforces the negation consistency (2) between ρ and $\bar{\rho}$, ensuring that the two pivot polynomials genuinely encode complementary literals. All three equations are checked probabilistically via the Schwartz–Zippel lemma by evaluating at a random field point.

3.3 The ZKUNSAT Protocol

Setup. The prover holds a CNF formula $\varphi = C_1 \wedge \cdots \wedge C_m$ over n variables, together with a weak resolution refutation $\pi = (D_1, \ldots, D_\ell)$ of width w and length ℓ. Each D_j is either an input clause $C_i \in \varphi$ or a weak resolvent of two earlier clauses D_a and D_b in π on some pivot variable x, and the final clause $D_\ell = \bot$ is the empty clause. The verifier knows only the claimed dimensions (m, n, w, ℓ) of the formula and the proof.

Commit Phase. The prover encodes every input clause C_i and every derived clause D_j as a polynomial via (3), and commits to each polynomial using a commitment scheme. We denote them as $[\![\gamma(C]\!]$ for the committed polynomial of clause C. The prover also commits to additional quotient polynomials $w_0^{(j)}, w_1^{(j)}$ and the linear pivot polynomials $\rho^{(j)}, \bar{\rho}^{(j)}$ for each resolution step j.

Proving Phase. The prover convinces the verifier of the following three conditions, each checked in ZKP over the commitments.

1. *Resolution correctness.* For each derivation step $D_j = \text{Res}(D_a, D_b, x)$, the committed polynomials satisfy the weak resolution test (6)–(8):

$$[\![w_0^{(j)}]\!] \cdot [\![D_a]\!] = [\![D_j]\!] \cdot [\![\rho^{(j)}]\!],$$

$$[\![w_1^{(j)}]\!] \cdot [\![D_b]\!] = [\![D_j]\!] \cdot [\![\bar{\rho}^{(j)}]\!],$$

$$[\![\rho^{(j)}(X)]\!] + [\![\bar{\rho}^{(j)}(1_{\mathbb{F}} - X)]\!] = 0.$$

   Each check reduces to a polynomial product equality verified via the Schwartz-Zippel lemma at a single random evaluation point, as we explained in Sect. 3.2 making the per-step cost essentially a constant number of field operations.

2. *Contradiction.* The final derived clause D_ℓ encodes the empty clause, i.e., $\gamma(D_\ell) = 1_{\mathbb{F}}$, the constant polynomial with no roots. The prover demonstrates that the committed polynomial $[\![D_\ell]\!]$ evaluates to $1_{\mathbb{F}}$ at every point, confirming that the derivation terminates in a contradiction.

Random-Access Memory. A central challenge in the proof phase is that each resolution step $D_j = \mathrm{Res}(D_a, D_b, x)$ may reference arbitrary earlier steps D_a and D_b at non-consecutive positions in π, requiring random access to the committed clause table. The protocol handles this using a *zero-knowledge random-access memory* (ZK-RAM) [18], which allows the prover to demonstrate, in zero knowledge, that the polynomial retrieved at a given index is consistent with the committed table, without revealing the index or the contents of the table. The ZK-RAM argument contributes a $O(\ell \log \ell)$ overhead to the proof size, which in practice is dominated by the $O(\ell \cdot w)$ cost of the resolution checks.

Security. Soundness follows from the binding property of the commitment scheme and Lemma 1: if the weak resolution test passes at a random evaluation point, the committed polynomials decode via p^* to a valid weak resolution step with overwhelming probability by the Schwartz–Zippel lemma. Zero-knowledge follows from the hiding property of the commitment scheme: the verifier's view consists entirely of commitments and polynomial evaluations at a single verifier-chosen random point, from which no information about φ, π, or the program they encode can be extracted. The only information revealed is the dimensions (m, n, w, ℓ) of the formula and the proof, which the verifier must know to bound its own verification cost.

4 Proving First-Order Unsatisfiability in Privacy-Preserving Settings

The propositional setting covered in Sect. 3 provides an approach to proving unsatisfiability of propositional Boolean formulae, but practical program verification rarely operates at the level of pure Boolean logic. Modern verification toolchains, such as Boogie [5], CBMC [10], Dafny [31], and their relatives, reduce program correctness to the unsatisfiability of *Satisfiability Modulo Theories* (SMT) formulas: Boolean combinations of atoms drawn from rich first-order theories such as equality with uninterpreted functions (EUF) and linear integer arithmetic (LIA). Extending the ZKUNSAT approach to this setting is the goal of ZKSMT [33].

The central difficulty is that SMT refutation proofs are structurally far more complex than their propositional counterparts. A resolution refutation of a CNF formula applies a single, uniform rule at every step, which is why the polynomial encoding of Sect. 3 suffices: every step reduces to the same divisibility check. An SMT refutation proof, by contrast, may invoke dozens of theory-specific inference rules: congruence closure, Farkas' lemma certificates, arithmetic normalization steps, and many others, each with its own side conditions, and the number and shape of its premises.

ZKSMT overcomes this challenge by introducing a purpose-built *zero-knowledge virtual machine* (ZKVM) whose instruction set is precisely the set of SMT proof rules required to validate a given refutation. We describe its architecture and its instantiation on the theories of propositional logic, EUF, and LIA below.

4.1 The ZKSMT Virtual Machine

An SMT refutation proof can be viewed as a sequence of *proof steps*, each consisting of a rule identifier, a list of premises (references to earlier steps), and a conclusion formula. This sequential structure closely mirrors the execution model of a Von Neumann processor: rules correspond to instructions, proof steps correspond to program statements, and the formula being refuted corresponds to the program input. ZKSMT exploits this analogy directly.

Encoding Formulas: The Expression Table. Every formula that appears anywhere in the proof is stored, in abstract syntax tree (AST) form, in a read-only table M_e called the *expression table*. Each row of M_e represents one AST node and contains three fields: a *NodeID* identifying the operator (e.g., `Eq`, `Lt`, `And`), an *immediate address list* `ImmAddr` for constants and variable names, and an *indirect address list* `IndAddr` holding indices into M_e for the node's children. Sharing is explicit: if the same subformula t appears in ten different formulas, M_e contains exactly one entry for t, and all ten formulas reference it by index. This sharing is crucial for efficiency in the ZK setting, since equality of two subformulas reduces to equality of their indices, a single field comparison rather than a full structural traversal.

Encoding Proofs: The Step Table. The proof steps themselves are stored in a second read-only table M_p. Each row of M_p records a *StepID* (the logical ordering of the step), a *RuleID* (identifying the theory and the rule applied), a *Result* (an index into M_e for the conclusion formula), and a list of *Premises* (StepIDs of the proof steps whose conclusions are used as premises). The size of the machine is parameterized by π (the maximum number of proof steps), χ (the number of expressions in M_e), μ (the maximum number of premises in any rule), α (the maximum argument list length of any expression), and ρ (the number of distinct rules used).

Machine Execution. The main verification loop iterates over all π proof steps. For each step, the machine (i) fetches the rule identifier and the conclusion from M_p and M_e, (ii) fetches the conclusion expressions of each listed premise by reading the corresponding entries of M_p and M_e, (iii) dispatches to the *checking instruction* for the given `RuleID`, which asserts that the conclusion is a valid consequence of the premises under that rule, and (iv) records the step's `StepID` in an append-only array D. After the loop, a permutation check confirms that D

is a permutation of $\{0, 1, \ldots, \pi - 1\}$, ensuring that every proof step was validated exactly once. The acyclicity of the proof graph is enforced by requiring that the `StepID` of every premise is strictly smaller than the `StepID` of the step that uses it.

This architecture is both *complete* and *sound*. Any valid SMT refutation proof can be verified by some ZKSMT instance with appropriate size parameters. Any proof accepted by the machine corresponds to a valid derivation in the underlying theory. These properties are proved formally in [33].

4.2 Theory Instantiations

To make the ZKVM useful in practice, one must supply a checking instruction for each inference rule of each theory. We describe the most significant examples.

Propositional Rules. Simple tautology rules, such as the law of the excluded middle $(a \vee \neg a)$, require only pattern-matching on the structure of the conclusion node: the checking instruction confirms that the `NodeID` is `Or`, retrieves its two children from M_e, and verifies that one is the negation of the other by comparing indices. The Resolution rule is more involved: its checking instruction must verify that the multiset of literals in one premise, minus the pivot literal p, is contained in the conclusion's literal multiset, and similarly for the other premise and the negation $\neg p$ of the pivot. The natural language of these conditions is that of *multiset containment*.

Equality with Uninterpreted Functions (EUF). The congruence rule, which derives $f(a_1, \ldots, a_n) = f(b_1, \ldots, b_n)$ from pairwise equalities $a_i = b_i$, is checked by ZKSMT in an alternative but logically equivalent formulation: a disjunction is derived from no premises, asserting that either the two function applications are equal or some argument pair is not. The checking instruction confirms that the conclusion has the correct disjunctive structure, identifies the pair of function applications, and verifies that the remaining disjuncts match the corresponding argument pairs by index comparison in M_e.

Linear Integer Arithmetic (LIA). The two most important LIA rules are multiplication distribution (MulDist) and Farkas' lemma. The MulDist checking instruction validates the identity $c \cdot (\sum_i d_i \cdot x_i) = \sum_i (c \cdot d_i) \cdot x_i$ by iterating over the children of the sum nodes in lockstep, verifying that scaling factors combine correctly and that child expressions match by index. Farkas' lemma is a linear arithmetic rule that derives a strict inequality from a collection of hypotheses; its checking instruction confirms the structural pattern of the premise and conclusion and verifies that the coefficients satisfy the required non-negativity conditions.

4.3 Zero-Knowledge Instantiation

Running the ZKSMT machine in zero knowledge requires hiding the contents of M_e and M_p, that is, the formula and the proof, while still allowing the verifier to be convinced that every step was correctly executed. ZKSMT is instantiated using the VOLE-based ZK backend of [6,45], which supports efficient polynomial operations and read-only memory accesses.

Committing the Proof. Every integer field of every entry in M_e and M_p is committed bit-by-bit using the VOLE commitment scheme. To avoid leaking the `NodeID` of an expression from the sizes of its argument lists, all `ImmAddr` and `IndAddr` lists are padded to the uniform maximum length α.

Group Checking. A naive implementation would, at each step, multiplex over all ρ possible checking instructions—executing all of them and selecting the result corresponding to the private `RuleID`. This incurs a ρ-fold overhead. ZKSMT instead uses *group checking*: all steps that use the same rule are verified consecutively, invoking only that rule's checking instruction. The verifier therefore learns how many times each rule is applied—the *rule histogram*—but nothing about which specific steps use which rule. This is the primary privacy–efficiency trade-off in ZKSMT: revealing the rule histogram enables SIMD-style batch optimizations (verifying many instances of the same rule in a single amortized pass) at the cost of leaking aggregate rule usage counts.

Multiset Checks via Polynomial Arithmetic. Many checking instructions reduce to verifying multiset containment relations among the argument lists of the relevant M_e entries—as seen in the Resolution and DeDup rules above. ZKSMT encodes multisets as univariate polynomials over a finite field $\mathbb{F}$: a multiset $\{\ell_0, \ldots, \ell_d\}$ is represented as $\prod_i (X - \psi(\ell_i))$, where ψ is an injective encoding of expression indices into $\mathbb{F}$. Multiset containment $A \subseteq B$ then corresponds to polynomial divisibility, and the verifier can check this at a single random evaluation point via the Schwartz–Zippel lemma. A more refined relation, containment of distinct elements, ignoring multiplicity, written $A \subseteq_d B$, is checked using a bivariate polynomial protocol from [37]. Together, these two relations suffice to implement the checking instructions for all propositional, EUF, and LIA rules in ZKSMT.

Read-Only Memory Accesses. Fetching entries from M_e and M_p by committed (private) index requires a ZK read-only memory (ROM) protocol. ZKSMT uses the constant-overhead ZK-RAM construction of [19], which provides amortized $O(1)$ cost per access. In practice, memory accesses dominate the cost of rules like Farkas' lemma (which must read every argument of its premise and conclusion to match their structure), while arithmetic operations dominate for rules like Resolution and Consolidate (which perform multiset checks but can work directly with expression indices without reading full node data).

5 Privacy-Preserving Reasoning for Other Formalisms

The protocols described in Sects. 3 and 4 establish that the unsatisfiability of propositional and SMT formulas can be certified in ZK with practical efficiency.

Many problems of genuine interest in formal verification lie strictly in PSPACE, beyond the complexity class within which both ZKUNSAT and ZKSMT operate. Hardware synthesis, reactive controller, and planning under uncertainty all give rise to PSPACE-complete decision problems.

The classical result IP = PSPACE ensures that zero-knowledge proofs exist for all PSPACE-complete problems, but the generic construction based on the sumcheck protocol requires evaluating high-degree multivariate polynomials over large fields, with degree scaling linearly in the number of variables. This renders it impractical for real-world instances. Karthikeyan et al. [27] bridge this gap by presenting the first practical ZK protocols for PSPACE-complete statements, targeting the evaluation of Quantified Boolean Formulas (QBFs).

5.1 Q-Resolution Proofs

A QBF in prenex conjunctive normal form (PCNF) has the structure

$$\Psi = Q_1 X_1 \; Q_2 X_2 \cdots Q_k X_k.\; \psi(x_1, \ldots, x_n),$$

where each $Q_i \in \{\forall, \exists\}$ is a quantifier, each X_i is a block of Boolean variables, and ψ is a propositional CNF formula over those variables. QBF evaluation is PSPACE-complete, and many practically important problems reduce to it naturally.

The Q-resolution (Q-Res) proof system provides a complete and practical certificate format for establishing that a QBF is *false*. A Q-Res proof is a sequence of clauses derived from the matrix ψ by two inference rules, terminating in the empty clause $\bot$.

Universal Reduction ($\forall$*-Red).* Let y be the innermost existential literal in a clause C. Any universal literal $x_i \in C$ that appears *after* y in the quantifier prefix (i.e., $y \prec x_i$) can be safely removed from C without affecting the truth value of Ψ. Intuitively, the universal player's choice of x_i can always be made after observing the existential choice of y, so x_i provides no additional power to make the clause false.

Existential Resolution ($\exists$*-Res).* Given two clauses C_a and C_b and an existential variable $y \in X_\exists$ such that $y \in C_a$ and $\neg y \in C_b$, the Q-resolvent is $C_r = (C_a \cup C_b) \setminus \{y, \neg y\}$, provided C_r is non-tautological. This is standard propositional resolution restricted to existentially quantified pivot variables.

A complete Q-Res proof derives the empty clause by interleaving $\forall$-Red and $\exists$-Res steps. The soundness and completeness of Q-Res is classical: a closed PCNF formula is unsatisfiable if and only if a Q-Res proof exists [4,36].

5.2 Polynomial Encoding for Q-Res

The polynomial clause encoding introduced for propositional UNSAT (Sect. 3) extends to the QBF setting, but with a key augmentation: literals must carry quantifier-order information to enable checking of $\forall$-Red. The encoding of a literal ℓ is the concatenation of two binary strings,

$$\varepsilon(\ell) = \mathrm{order}(\ell)_{\mathbf{B}} \parallel \mathrm{sign}(\ell),$$

where $\text{sign}(\ell) \in \{0, 1\}$ indicates the polarity of the literal and $\text{order}(\ell)$ is the position of its variable in the quantifier prefix. This encoding is interpreted both as a finite field element (enabling polynomial clause encoding) and as a natural number (enabling comparison of quantifier levels). The same injective negation constraint $\varphi(\ell) + \varphi(\neg\ell) = 1_{\mathbb{F}}$ required for resolution checks continues to hold under this encoding. Two public sets $L_\forall$ and $L_\exists$ record the literals of universally and existentially quantified variables respectively, and their membership can be checked in ZK using standard set-argument protocols.

Checking ∃-Res. An existential resolution step is a standard (propositional) resolution step with the additional requirement that the pivot literal ℓ_p is existentially quantified. The pivot membership check $\ell_p \in L_\exists$ is appended to the resolution check from [34], adding negligible overhead.

Checking ∀-Red. A valid universal reduction step on clause C producing clause C_r is characterized by four conditions: the removed literals W_{rem} must all be universally quantified; they must all appear after the innermost existential literal w_ℓ in the prefix; the retained literals W_{res} must all appear before w_ℓ; and C decomposes as $W_{\text{res}} \cup W_{\text{rem}} \cup \{w_\ell\}$ while $C_r = W_{\text{res}} \cup \{w_\ell\}$. The prover commits all four components as extended witnesses. Quantifier membership is checked via $L_\forall$ and $L_\exists$; quantifier order comparisons exploit the integer interpretation of the literal encoding, checked via a range-proof gadget; and the clause decomposition is verified using the polynomial equality operations already needed for ∃-Res. Together, these checks add a small, fixed overhead per proof step relative to a propositional resolution step.

Protocol Structure. Both parties agree publicly on the proof length R, the maximum clause width w, and the maximum number of literals removed in any single ∀-Red step. The prover commits all clauses, both input clauses from ψ and derived clauses, via the polynomial encoding, stores them in a ZK append-only array (as in ZKUNSAT [34]), and iterates through each Q-Res step, invoking the ∃-Res and ∀-Red checks. After all R steps, the verifier confirms that the final derived clause is the empty clause. The ZKQRES protocol is proven to be a ZKP of knowledge for QBF falsification.

5.3 Winning Strategies in Zero Knowledge

Beyond certifying the evaluation of a QBF, the prover may wish to demonstrate possession of a concrete *winning strategy.* For a false QBF, this is a Herbrand strategy: a set of Boolean functions $H = \{g_x : \text{Pred}_\exists(x) \to \{0, 1\} \mid x \in X_\forall\}$ that assign values to universally quantified variables based on the existential variables preceding them in the prefix, in a way that forces the formula to be false regardless of the existential player's choices. Formally, substituting each universal variable x with its Herbrand function g_x in ψ yields a propositional formula ψ_H, the Herbrandization, that is unsatisfiable. Symmetrically, for a true QBF, a Skolem strategy assigns values to existential variables as functions of preceding universal variables, yielding a Skolemization ψ_S that is a tautology.

The ZKWS protocol in [33] verifies a winning strategy in zero knowledge by decomposing the task into three sub-problems. First, the Herbrand (or Skolem) function must be *well-formed*: each universal variable is defined exactly once, the dependency graph is acyclic, and each variable depends only on literals that precede it in the quantifier prefix. Second, the propositional formula ψ_H produced by applying the strategy must be a correct Tseitin CNF encoding of the Herbrand function. Third, ψ_H must be unsatisfiable, which is handled by invoking ZKUNSAT [34] as a sub-protocol.

The Herbrand function is represented as a list of triples $\{(x_i, \ell_i^a, \ell_i^b)\}$ encoding gates $x_i \Leftrightarrow \ell_i^a \wedge \ell_i^b$, committed as an And-Inverter Graph (AIG). Well-formedness is verified in ZK by checking uniqueness of output variables via set operations, acyclicity by confirming that each input literal refers to an earlier-indexed variable (leveraging the append-only array), and prefix-consistency by checking that the dependency level of each defined variable does not exceed its quantifier-prefix position, using the integer interpretation of literal encodings. Substitution correctness is verified by checking that the Tseitin clauses of ψ_H are consistent with the committed AIG gates, using the literal membership primitives of the clause commitment scheme.

Efficiency Advantage. When the prover is willing to reveal the size of the winning strategy, the ZKP for PSPACE reduces to ZKP for UNSAT with only a small overhead for well-formedness and substitution checks. On instances where compact winning strategies exist, this yields dramatic savings compared to Q-Res proof checking: the paper reports reductions in proving time of up to 200× on individual benchmarks.

ZKUNSAT Optimization. A practical complication arises when running ZKUNSAT on ψ_H: all clauses must be padded to the width of the widest clause, and the Herbrandization often produces many narrow clauses alongside a few wide ones. To mitigate this, the protocol introduces a *clause bucketing* scheme that partitions the proof into groups of clauses with similar width, running a separate ZKUNSAT instance per bucket. This exposes the bucket-width histogram (a mild leakage) but reduces padding waste substantially, yielding approximately a 2× runtime improvement in practice.

5.4 ZKPs for Regular Expression Equivalence

Proving that a QBF instance is unsatisfiable is a PSPACE-complete problem, and we have developed other frameworks that target problems in the same complexity class, namely, regular expression equivalence. More specifically, party A can convince party B that two private regular expressions are equivalent, or more generally that the language of one is contained in the language of the other, without revealing either expression unless explicitly chosen to do so [29]. A naïve approach would be to convert the regular expressions into finite automata and prove the existence of a simulation relation between them, which would require separate ZK protocols for the conversion step and for the simulation relation itself, resulting in a more complex pipeline with longer proofs. Instead, our approach operates directly on regular expressions via a custom, sound and complete calculus of proof rules based on Brzozowski derivatives and coinduction, keeping individual proof step checking to constant or linear time and avoiding the overhead of validating format conversions. Intuitively, this approach fuses the automaton construction and the simulation argument into a single coinductive proof over the regular expressions themselves.

6 Challenges and Future Directions

The privacy-preserving verification techniques described above establish a strong foundation, but they leave open a number of important challenges. Some concern the broader verification pipeline: ensuring that the chain of trust extends from the logical formula all the way to the running binary. Others are foundational: extending the scope of what can be verified privately, from standard safety properties to richer relational and hyperproperties, and from propositional and first-order reasoning to problems in higher complexity classes. In this section we look at some of these challenges and outline directions for future work, including ongoing work from our group that begins to address some of them.

6.1 Completing the Verification Pipeline

Once a piece of code has been proved correct using the privacy-preserving techniques surveyed above, several further aspects of the deployment pipeline still require trust. The techniques described so far establish that a combined formula is unsatisfiable: that is, the formula encoding the program, conjoined with the negation of the specification, admits no satisfying assignment. This is precisely the statement that the program cannot violate the specification. However, this guarantee is only as strong as the chain of transformations that produced the formula in the first place. There are still many layers and sublayers that need to be handled:

Formalization Layer: One still needs to trust that the conversion from program source code to a logical formula was done faithfully. In real-world verification pipelines this is achieved by tools such as Boogie [5], CBMC [10], and Frama-C [13], among others. This is not simply a syntactic translation, but involves deeper verification condition generation: computing weakest preconditions, handling loops via invariants, and encoding memory models and heap reasoning into the formula. In order for the private program to be trusted, this transformation needs to be performed under the same Zero-Knowledge guarantees.

Deployment Layer: Even more importantly, once one is convinced that a particular piece of source code satisfies a given property, there remains a significant deployment gap: how can they be sure that the program actually being executed corresponds to the verified source code?

- **Compilation sublayer:** First, one needs to trust that the compiler preserves the semantics established at the source level, and moreover that this preservation can be attested to under zero-knowledge guarantees: one must be able to prove that a correct compilation took place without revealing the source. Certified compilation [30,32] addresses the first requirement but not the second.
- **Execution sublayer:** Second, even given a trustworthy and privacy-preserving compilation step, one needs assurance about the execution environment: specifically, that the binary being run is indeed the one produced from the verified source, and not a modified or substituted version. This second aspect requires some form of attestation from the execution environment, provided in practice either by hardware-based trusted execution environments (TEEs) such as Intel SGX [12] or AMD SEV [26], or by zkVM-based execution proofs [2,8].

Even assuming all three layers of the deployment pipeline are addressed, a more fundamental challenge remains. Consider a network equipment vendor that proves, using the privacy-preserving techniques described above, that their router firmware satisfies a given security property, compiles it under zero-knowledge guarantees to a binary, and deploys it with zkVM or TEE-based execution attestation. A customer receiving these proofs might reasonably ask how they can be certain that the program actually processing their network traffic is the one for which all these proofs were produced. Nothing in the proof chain prevents the vendor from running two separate instances: a verified one that produces attestations on a designated stream, and an unverified one that actually handles customer data. All proofs would remain valid, and the customer would have no cryptographic means of detecting the discrepancy. This is what we call the *binding problem*: the proofs establish correctness of an execution in the abstract, but they do not bind that execution to any specific interaction.

What is needed to address this challenge is a guarantee that this *particular execution*, processing this *particular input*, is the one for which the proof was produced. Establishing this requires orthogonal mechanisms from outside the proof-theoretic framework, such as network-level monitoring, hardware integrity guarantees, and auditability requirements.

6.2 Specifications

The type of users of such a system who can tolerate the higher costs of privacy-preserving verification is often more interested in security properties of the software under analysis. As a typical example, they may be interested in knowing that the output of the software will always be independent of its input, especially any secret inputs. Expressing such properties requires reasoning about more than one execution of the given program. There are many such properties, often called hyperproperties or relational properties, which strictly subsume the standard non-relational ones. These properties often quantify over the inputs or executions of the program, with arbitrary quantifier complexity. The simplest, termed hypersafety properties, are those where all executions are universally quantified; therefore, refuting those properties requires only a finite collection of traces. The example above, *observational determinism*, is one such property: for any two executions π_1 and π_2 of the program, if the former results from feeding in secret input s_1 and public input p, and the latter results from feeding in secret input s_2 but the same public input p, then their public outputs, *i.e.*,what can be observed by a third party, are the same.

Existing tools geared towards non-relational properties are insufficient to support this richer formalism. Hypersafety properties can be reduced to non-relational ones via self-composition, where two or more copies of the program are stitched together to simulate tuples of executions. However, verifying such properties through this translation is often significantly harder in practice than reasoning about them natively, with an analysis designed with relational reasoning in mind. A natural next challenge then is to extend the privacy-preserving formula satisfiability and unsatisfiability approaches described above towards supporting such richer reasoning. Formalisms such as Relational Hoare Logic [7], HyperLTL [11], BiKAT [1], and Hyper Hoare Logic [14] are designed precisely for this purpose, offering native support for relational reasoning without the overhead of self-composition. The challenge is to lift the privacy-preserving verification machinery to operate within such formalisms, while retaining the efficiency and soundness guarantees established in the non-relational setting. With the ultimate goal of exploring Hyper Hoare Logic and BiKAT in a privacy-preserving setting, we have developed the protocol, briefly discussed at the end of Sect. 5, allowing one party to convince another that two (private) regular expressions are equivalent, in Zero Knowledge [29].

Verification of Machine Learning Systems: A further compelling direction concerns the formal verification of privacy guarantees for machine learning systems. The verification of neural network properties such as robustness and safety has seen substantial recent progress, with a growing ecosystem of tools including $\alpha\beta$-CROWN [44], NeuralSAT [16,17], and Marabou [28], and an annual competition (VNN-COMP) benchmarking their performance. Furthermore, a central tension is that ML models are most powerful when trained on large, representative datasets, yet such datasets frequently contain sensitive or proprietary records whose custodians are unwilling to release without assurances. The risk is not merely that the raw data is exposed during training: models can memorize their training data in subtle ways, making it possible for adversaries to recover sensitive information through inference attacks on the deployed model. What is needed is a way for model developers to give verifiable, cryptographic assurances that such leakage is bounded or impossible, without themselves having to reveal the model architecture, weights, or training corpus. This connects naturally to the relational and hyperproperty verification challenges discussed above, since the relevant properties, such as various notions of non-leakage, are inherently statements about a model's behavior on different types of contents of its training set. Extending the privacy-preserving verification machinery of this paper to reason about such properties in a zero-knowledge setting, so that a model developer can convince a third party of a neural network property without revealing the model itself, is a significant open challenge.

Acknowledgments. The work presented in this paper provides an overview of results previously published in [27,29,33–35]. We acknowledge all co-authors of these works for their contributions and for the collaborations that significantly shaped the results reported here. The authors of this paper were partially supported by NSF awards CCF-2106845, CCF-2131476, CCF-2219995, CCF-2318974, and CNS-2245344 as well as by a grant from Google. We gratefully acknowledge this support.

References

1. Antonopoulos, T., Koskinen, E., Le, T.C., Nagasamudram, R., Naumann, D.A., Ngo, M.: An algebra of alignment for relational verification. Proc. ACM Program. Lang. **7**(POPL), 573–603 (2023)
2. Arun, A., Setty, S.T.V., Thaler, J.: Jolt: snarks for virtual machines via lookups. In: Joye, M., Leander, G. (eds.) Advances in Cryptology - EUROCRYPT 2024 - 43rd Annual International Conference on the Theory and Applications of Cryptographic Techniques, Zurich, Switzerland, 26–30 May 2024, Proceedings, Part VI. LNCS, pp. 3–33. Springer (2024)
3. Bachmair, L., Ganzinger, H.: Resolution theorem proving. In: Robinson, J.A., Voronkov, A. (eds.) Handbook of Automated Reasoning (in 2 volumes), pages 19–99. Elsevier and MIT Press (2001)
4. Balabanov, V., Jiang, J.-H.R.: Resolution proofs and Skolem functions in QBF evaluation and applications. In: Gopalakrishnan, G., Qadeer, S. (eds.) CAV 2011. LNCS, vol. 6806, pp. 149–164. Springer, Heidelberg (2011). https://doi.org/10.1007/978-3-642-22110-1_12
5. Barnett, M., Chang, B.-Y.E., DeLine, R., Jacobs, B., Leino, K.R.M.: Boogie: a modular reusable verifier for object-oriented programs. In: de Boer, F.S., Bonsangue, M.M., Graf, S., de Roever, W.-P. (eds.) FMCO 2005. LNCS, vol. 4111, pp. 364–387. Springer, Heidelberg (2006). https://doi.org/10.1007/11804192_17
6. Baum, C., Malozemoff, A.J., Rosen, M.B., Scholl, P.: Mac'n'cheese: zero-knowledge proofs for Boolean and arithmetic circuits with nested disjunctions, pp. 92–122 (2021)
7. Benton, N.: Simple relational correctness proofs for static analyses and program transformations. In: Jones, N.D., Leroy, X. (eds.) Proceedings of the 31st ACM SIGPLAN-SIGACT Symposium on Principles of Programming Languages, POPL 2004, Venice, Italy, 14–16 January 2004, pp. 14–25. ACM (2004)
8. Bruestle, J., Gafni, P., The RISC Zero Team: RISC zero zkVM: scalable, transparent arguments of RISC-V integrity. Technical report

9. Canetti, R.: Universally composable security: a new paradigm for cryptographic protocols. In: Proceedings 42nd IEEE Symposium on Foundations of Computer Science, pp. 136–145. IEEE (2001)
10. Clarke, E., Kroening, D., Lerda, F.: A tool for checking ANSI-C programs. In: Jensen, K., Podelski, A. (eds.) TACAS 2004. LNCS, vol. 2988, pp. 168–176. Springer, Heidelberg (2004). https://doi.org/10.1007/978-3-540-24730-2_15
11. Clarkson, M.R., Finkbeiner, B., Koleini, M., Micinski, K.K., Rabe, M.N., Sánchez, C.: Temporal logics for hyperproperties. In: Abadi, M., Kremer, S. (eds.) POST 2014. LNCS, vol. 8414, pp. 265–284. Springer, Heidelberg (2014). https://doi.org/10.1007/978-3-642-54792-8_15
12. Costan, V., Devadas, S.: Intel SGX explained. IACR Cryptol. ePrint Arch. **2016**, 86 (2016)
13. Cuoq, P., Kirchner, F., Kosmatov, N., Prevosto, V., Signoles, J., Yakobowski, B.: Frama-C - a software analysis perspective. In: Eleftherakis, G., Hinchey, M., Holcombe, M. (eds.) SEFM 2012. LNCS, vol. 7504, pp. 233–247. Springer, Heidelberg (2012). https://doi.org/10.1007/978-3-642-33826-7_16
14. Dardinier, T., Müller, P.: Hyper hoare logic: (dis-)proving program hyperproperties. Proc. ACM Program. Lang. **8**(PLDI), 1485–1509 (2024)
15. Davis, M., Logemann, G., Loveland, D.: A machine program for theorem-proving. Commun. ACM **5**(7), 394–397 (1962)
16. Duong, H., Nguyen, T., Dwyer, M.: A DPLL(T) framework for verifying deep neural networks (2024)
17. Duong, H., Xu, D., Nguyen, T., Dwyer, M.B.: Harnessing neuron stability to improve DNN verification. Proc. ACM Softw. Eng. **1**(FSE) (2024)
18. Franzese, N., Katz, J., Lu, S., Ostrovsky, R., Wang, Weng, C.: Constant-overhead zero-knowledge for ram programs. In: Proceedings of the 2021 ACM SIGSAC Conference on Computer and Communications Security, pp. 178–191 (2021)
19. Franzese, N., Katz, J., Lu, S., Ostrovsky, R., Wang, X., Weng, C.: Constant-overhead zero-knowledge for RAM programs, pp. 178–191 (2021)
20. Goldreich, O., Micali, S., Wigderson, A.: Proofs that yield nothing but their validity or all languages in NP have zero-knowledge proof systems. J. ACM **38**(3), 691–729 (1991)
21. Goldwasser, S., Kalai, Y.T., Rothblum, G.N.: Delegating computation: interactive proofs for muggles, pp. 113–122 (2008)
22. Goldwasser, S., Micali, S., Rackoff, C.: The knowledge complexity of interactive proof-systems (extended abstract), pp. 291–304 (1985)
23. Groth, J.: Short pairing-based non-interactive zero-knowledge arguments, pp. 321–340 (2010)
24. Ishai, Y., Kushilevitz, E., Ostrovsky, R., Sahai, A.: Zero-knowledge from secure multiparty computation, pp. 21–30 (2007)
25. Jawurek, M., Kerschbaum, F., Orlandi, C.: Zero-knowledge using garbled circuits: how to prove non-algebraic statements efficiently, pp. 955–966 (2013)
26. Kaplan, D., Powell, J., Woller, T.: AMD SEV-SNP: strengthening vm isolation-with integrity protection and more. White Paper, Advanced Micro Devices Inc, 65 (2020)
27. Karthikeyan, A., Liu, H., Meel, K.S., Luo, N.: Towards practical zero-knowledge proof for PSPACE. arXiv preprint arXiv:2511.15071 (2025)
28. Katz, G., et al.: The Marabou framework for verification and analysis of deep neural networks. In: Dillig, I., Tasiran, S. (eds.) CAV 2019. LNCS, vol. 11561, pp. 443–452. Springer, Cham (2019). https://doi.org/10.1007/978-3-030-25540-4_26

29. Kolesar, J.C., Ali, S., Antonopoulos, T., Piskac, R.: Coinductive proofs of regular expression equivalence in zero knowledge. Proc. ACM Program. Lang. **9**(OOPSLA2), 357–385 (2025)
30. Kumar, R., Myreen, M.O., Norrish, M., Owens, S.: CakeML: a verified implementation of ML. In: Jagannathan, S., Sewell, P. (eds.) The 41st Annual ACM SIGPLAN-SIGACT Symposium on Principles of Programming Languages, POPL 2014, San Diego, CA, USA, 20–21 January 2014, pp. 179–192. ACM (2014)
31. Leino, K.R.M.: Dafny: an automatic program verifier for functional correctness. In: Clarke, E.M., Voronkov, A. (eds.) LPAR 2010. LNCS (LNAI), vol. 6355, pp. 348–370. Springer, Heidelberg (2010). https://doi.org/10.1007/978-3-642-17511-4_20
32. Leroy, X.: Formal certification of a compiler back-end or: programming a compiler with a proof assistant. In: Gregory Morrisett, J., Jones, S.L.P. (eds.) Proceedings of the 33rd ACM SIGPLAN-SIGACT Symposium on Principles of Programming Languages, POPL 2006, Charleston, South Carolina, USA, 11–13 January 2006, pp. 42–54. ACM (2006)
33. Luick, D., et al.: ZKSMT: a VM for proving SMT theorems in zero knowledge. In: 33rd USENIX Security Symposium (USENIX Security 2024), pp. 3837–3845 (2024)
34. Luo, N., Antonopoulos, T., Harris, W.R., Piskac, R., Tromer, E., Wang, X.: Proving unsat in zero knowledge. In: Proceedings of the 2022 ACM SIGSAC Conference on Computer and Communications Security, pp. 2203–2217 (2022)
35. Luo, N., Judson, S., Antonopoulos, T., Piskac, R., Wang, X.: {ppSAT}: towards {Two-Party} private {SAT} solving. In: 31st USENIX Security Symposium (USENIX Security 2022), pp. 2983–3000 (2022)
36. Niemetz, A., Preiner, M., Lonsing, F., Seidl, M., Biere, A.: Resolution-based certificate extraction for QBF. In: Cimatti, A., Sebastiani, R. (eds.) SAT 2012. LNCS, vol. 7317, pp. 430–435. Springer, Heidelberg (2012). https://doi.org/10.1007/978-3-642-31612-8_33
37. Pearson, L., Fitzgerald, J., Ardévol, H.M., Muñoz, M.B., Tapia, J.L.M.: Reconciling plonk with plookup, Plonkup (2022)
38. Robinson, J.A.: A machine-oriented logic based on the resolution principle. J. ACM **12**(1), 23–41 (1965)
39. Schurr, H.-J., Fleury, M., Barbosa, H., Fontaine, P.: Alethe: towards a generic SMT proof format (extended abstract). In: Keller, C., Fleury, M. (eds.) Proceedings Seventh Workshop on Proof eXchange for Theorem Proving, PxTP 2021, Pittsburg, PA, USA, 11 July 2021, vol. 336. EPTCS, pp. 49–54 (2021)
40. Schwartz, J.T.: Fast probabilistic algorithms for verification of polynomial identities. J. ACM (JACM) **27**(4), 701–717 (1980)
41. Stump, A.: Proof checking technology for satisfiability modulo theories. In: Abel, A., Urban, C. (eds.) Proceedings of the International Workshop on Logical Frameworks and Metalanguages: Theory and Practice, LFMTP@LICS 2008, Pittsburgh, PA, USA, 23 June 2008. Electronic Notes in Theoretical Computer Science, vol. 228, pp. 121–133. Elsevier (2008)
42. Sutcliffe, G.: The TPTP problem library and associated infrastructure - from CNF to th0, TPTP v6.4.0. J. Autom. Reason. **59**(4), 483–502 (2017)
43. Turing, A.M.: On computable numbers, with an application to the Entscheidungsproblem. Proc. Lond. Math. Soc. **42**(1), 230–265 (1936). Published 1936–37

44. Wang, S., et al.: Beta-crown: efficient bound propagation with per-neuron split constraints for neural network robustness verification. In: Ranzato, M.A., Beygelzimer, A., Dauphin, Y.N., Liang, P., Vaughan, J.W. (eds.) Advances in Neural Information Processing Systems 34: Annual Conference on Neural Information Processing Systems 2021, NeurIPS 2021, 6–14 December 2021, Virtual, pp. 29909–29921 (2021)
45. Weng, C., Yang, K., Katz, J., Wang, X.: Wolverine: fast, scalable, and communication-efficient zero-knowledge proofs for boolean and arithmetic circuits, pp. 1074–1091 (2021)
46. Wetzler, N., Heule, M.J.H., Hunt, W.A.: DRAT-trim: efficient checking and trimming using expressive clausal proofs. In: Sinz, C., Egly, U. (eds.) SAT 2014. LNCS, vol. 8561, pp. 422–429. Springer, Cham (2014). https://doi.org/10.1007/978-3-319-09284-3_31

Main Track (1)

A Formal Framework for Predicting Distributed System Performance Under Faults

Ziwei Zhou[1], Si Liu[2], Zhou Zhou[1], Peixin Wang[1], and Min Zhang[1](✉)

[1] Shanghai Key Laboratory of Trustworthy Computing, East China Normal University, Shanghai, China
zhangmin@sei.ecnu.edu.cn

[2] Texas A&M University, College Station, USA
si.liu@tamu.edu

Abstract. Today's distributed systems operate in complex environments that inevitably involve faults and even adversarial behaviors. Predicting their performance under such environments directly from formal designs remains a long-standing challenge. We present the first formal framework that systematically enables performance prediction of distributed systems across diverse faulty scenarios. Our framework features a fault injector together with a wide range of faults, reusable as a library, and model compositions that integrate the system and the fault injector into a unified model suitable for statistical analysis of performance properties such as throughput and latency. We formalize the framework in Maude and implement it as an automated tool, PERF. Applied to representative distributed systems, PERF accurately predicts system performance under varying fault settings, with estimations from formal designs consistent with evaluations on real deployments.

1 Introduction

Distributed systems, such as cloud databases and blockchains, form the backbone of today's digital infrastructure. Formal methods have proven highly effective in verifying the correctness of their designs [34,48]. *Performance, however, is equally critical.* The need to predict a system's performance (e.g., throughput and latency) in realistic distributed environments, ideally before its implementation and deployment, has long been recognized by both academia [9,14] and industry [20,24,50]. Such environments inevitably involve faults, including network partitions, message delays, and even Byzantine behaviors [45,55]. In particular, Amazon Web Services has been seeking, for over a decade, a feasible way to model distributed systems and predict their performance degradation [15,50].

State-of-the-Art. Despite attempts to address this long-standing challenge, it remains largely unresolved. First, most quantitative formal analyses of distributed systems assume a fault-free environment [14,35,37,39–43,53,56]. Yet

Ziwei Zhou and Si Liu are the joint first authors with equal contribution.

A. Sampaio and M. Stoelinga (Eds.): FM 2026, LNCS 16556, pp. 47–66, 2026.
https://doi.org/10.1007/978-3-032-26204-2_3

ignoring faults can introduce a significant gap between model-based predictions and observed system performance. For instance, two distributed transaction protocols that appear competitive under a recent fault-free analysis [40] diverge sharply once message loss is introduced (see Sect. 6). Second, approaches that incorporate faults are often *ad hoc* [7,8,25,38,57], manually intertwining fault behaviors with system semantics. This hinders reuse, e.g., applying the same fault to a different protocol requires rebuilding the entire model from scratch. Third, all of these approaches consider only a few isolated fault types, whereas systems in practice often experience a wide range of faults that may also coexist, e.g., network partitions coinciding with malicious attacks. Therefore, existing analyses capture only a narrow fragment of the overall system performance space.

All of these limitations call for a systematic formal framework that (i) provides *comprehensive fault coverage* across diverse faults encountered in practice; (ii) ensures *modularity* by decoupling individual fault modeling from system modeling to support composition, reuse, and extensibility; and (iii) enables *automatic* generation of fault-injected system models and quantitative analysis of performance properties, e.g., using statistical verifiers.

Our Solution. We present the *first* formal framework that realizes these goals. At its core lies *a library of faults* covering a wide range, including both benign faults (e.g., message loss and network partitions) and Byzantine faults (e.g., tampering and equivocation). We model each fault as a message-passing *actor system* [3], a design choice that is motivated by our two insights. First, virtually all distributed systems can be specified as actor systems, where nodes, such as clients and servers, communicate via asynchronous message exchanges. Modeling faults as actors allows their effects on a system to be naturally captured by message-triggered interactions between the fault injector and system actors. Second, most practically relevant faults in distributed systems can be commonly viewed as manipulations of messages between actors. For instance, a node crash corresponds to dropping all of the messages sent to a specific actor; a network partition can be seen as discarding all of the messages between two actor sets, while preserving communication within each set. This unified view not only simplifies the modeling of individual faults but also allows different fault behaviors to be seamlessly integrated into the framework for performance analysis.

How do faults, then, interact with the distributed system under analysis? We realize this interaction through *model composition.* Specifically, our framework takes as input a system model and a fault injector incorporating one or more faults, and constructs an integrated model that preserves the original system semantics while enriching it with relevant fault behaviors. To account for realistic environments in which multiple faults may arise simultaneously (e.g., a network partition alongside equivocation), we introduce *fault-behavior priority levels* for fine-grained control over their interactions. This avoids semantic inconsistencies such as delivering an equivocated message across partitions. Moreover, we design the model composition to also preserve the *absence of nondeterminism* property [4], thereby supporting *statistical model checking* analysis, a formal approach that offers stronger guarantees for quantitative results than pure simulation and scales to large distributed systems [5,54]. To facilitate exploring performance space, our framework also allows users to configure which faults to inject and when to inject them and provides a monitor that records events of interest at runtime, based on which users can readily define performance properties. All of these features are integrated into our automated tool PerF.

Our approach is formalism-independent. In this work, we instantiate it in the Maude specification language and tool [21] that has been successfully applied to a wide range of distributed systems [40,46]. Specifically, both the distributed system under analysis and the faults are formalized as *probabilistic rewrite theories* [4]. Since performance properties, such as throughput and latency, intrinsically involve time, probabilities are primarily used to model message delays, which are sampled from certain probability distributions. The model compositions are then realized as compositions of rewrite theories.

Contributions. Overall, this work makes the following contributions:

- At the conceptual level, we address the long-standing challenge of predicting the performance of distributed systems under realistic faulty environments directly from their formal designs.
- At the technical level, we develop an actor-based formal framework in Maude, featuring a reusable library of practically relevant faults. We design a model composition that integrates the system and the fault injector managing these fault behaviors into a unified model amenable to quantitative analysis.
- At the practical level, we implement our framework as an automated tool, called PerF, that supports configurable fault injection and end-to-end performance prediction through statistical model checking.

We apply PerF to six representative distributed systems of different kinds. Experimental results demonstrate that it can accurately predict system performance under various types and combinations of faults, with model-based estimations aligning closely with empirical evaluations on real deployments (Sect. 6).

This work also complements long-established, *post hoc* fault-injection efforts on distributed system deployments by offering *proactive* insight into system dynamics under faults, already at the design stage. See Sect. 7 for a discussion.

2 Preliminaries

Maude. As an executable formal specification language and analysis tool, Maude [21] has been successfully applied to a broad spectrum of distributed systems. A Maude module specifies a *rewrite theory* [47] $\mathcal{R} = (\Sigma, E, L, R)$, where:

- Σ is an algebraic *signature*, i.e., a set of *sorts*, *subsorts*, and *function symbols*;
- (Σ, E) is an *order-sorted equational logic theory* [27] specifying the system's data types, where E is a set of (possibly conditional) equations and axioms;
- L is a set of rule *labels*; and
- R is a collection of *labeled conditional rewrite rules* $[l] : t \longrightarrow t' \; if \; cond$, with t, t' Σ-terms and $l \in L$. These rules specify the system's local transitions.

We summarize the fragment of Maude syntax used in this paper and refer the reader to [21] for details. Operators are declared by `op` f : $s_1 \ldots s_n$ `->` s and may have user-defined syntax, where '_' denotes argument positions, as in `_+_`. (Unconditional and conditional) equations and rewrite rules are introduced with the keywords `eq` and `ceq`, and `rl` and `crl`, respectively. Modules can be imported as submodules, e.g., by using the keyword `inc`. Comments start with '***'.

Actors. We follow Agha's message-passing *actor* paradigm [3] to specify systems. In Maude, a declaration `class` C — $att_1 : s_1, \ldots, att_n : s_n$ declares an actor (or object) class C with attributes att_1 to att_n of sorts s_1 to s_n. An instance of class C is a term `<` $o : C$ `|` $att_1 : val_1, \ldots, att_n : val_n$ `>` , where o (of sort `Oid`) is the object's identifier, and val_1 to val_n are the values of the attributes. Messages exchanged between objects are terms of sort `Msg`. A system state is modeled as a term of sort `Config` and is structured as a *multiset* of objects and messages, formed via the (juxtaposition) multiset union operator `__`.

The dynamic behavior of a system is axiomatized by specifying each of its transition patterns through a rewrite rule. For instance, the rule labeled `[reply]`

```
rl [reply] :  (read(KEY) from O' to O)    < O : Server | database: DB >
          =>  < O : Server | >    (<KEY, DB[KEY]> from O to O') .
```

defines a family of transitions in which a message `read(KEY) from O' to O` sent by the client object `O'` is consumed by the server object `O`. The server then looks up its database and replies with the corresponding key-value pair via the message `<KEY, DB[KEY]> from O to O'`. Note that attributes whose values do not change, such as `database`, can be omitted in the right-hand side of a rule. We provide a Maude specification of the Two-Phase Commit protocol in [61, Appendix A], which we use to illustrate our framework and tool.

Probabilistic Rewrite Theories. Extending the original rewrite theories, *probabilistic rewrite theories* [4] can specify a broader class of systems with probabilistic behavior. In our framework, probabilities arise from message delays sampled from probability distributions *and* from probabilistic choices during fault injection, e.g., the likelihood of dropping a message. Probabilistic behavior can be modeled with rules of the form

$$[l] : t(\overrightarrow{x}) \longrightarrow t'(\overrightarrow{x}, \overrightarrow{y}) \ \ if \ cond(\overrightarrow{x}) \ \ with \ probability \ \overrightarrow{y} := \pi(\overrightarrow{x})$$

where the term t' has new variables $\overrightarrow{y}$ disjoint from the variables $\overrightarrow{x}$ in t. The probabilistic nature of the rule stems from the probability distribution $\pi(\overrightarrow{x})$, which depends on the matching instance of $\overrightarrow{x}$, and governs the probabilistic choice of the instance of $\overrightarrow{y}$ in the term $t'(\overrightarrow{x}, \overrightarrow{y})$ according to $\pi(\overrightarrow{x})$.

Statistical Model Checking (SMC). This is a formal method for analyzing probabilistic systems against temporal logic properties, which scales to large distributed systems [5,54]. SMC verifies whether a property, expressed in a stochastic temporal logic like QuaTEx [4], holds with a user-specified statistical confidence by performing Monte Carlo simulations of the system model. The expected value of the property is iteratively evaluated with respect to two parameters α (confidence level) and δ (error margin) until a value $\bar{v}$ is obtained such that with $(1-\alpha)$ statistical confidence, the expected value lies in the interval $[\bar{v}-\frac{\delta}{2}, \bar{v}+\frac{\delta}{2}]$.

A Maude model is suitable for SMC analysis only if it satisfies the *absence of nondeterminism* (AND) property [4]. Intuitively, this property requires that, for any given system state, the subsequent transition is uniquely determined, without any nondeterministic branching. We establish that the model composition, as well as the model transformation (Sect. 5), satisfies this guarantee. Our framework then integrates the PVeStA tool [6] for end-to-end statistical model checking of system performance properties expressed in QuaTEx formulas. See [61, Appendix A] for an example QuaTEx formula for average latency.

3 Framework Overview

Our formal framework composes a distributed system model with a fault injector that includes a library of fault behaviors. This yields an integrated model in which the system interacts with the faults through message passing.

Fault Library. Seven representative faults are currently included in the fault library: *message loss*, *duplication*, *delay*, *tampering*, *equivocation*, *node crash*, and *network partition*. These cover both benign and Byzantine fault behaviors commonly observed in realistic distributed environments and widely exercised in deployment-level fault-injection analyses in industrial practice [2,11,32,49].

Each fault is modeled as an actor, referred to as a *fault handler* (see below and Sect. 4.3). This design choice is motivated by our two insights. First, modeling faults as actors allows their effects to be captured through message-triggered interactions with the system, whose nodes themselves communicate via asynchronous message passing. Second, all of these faults can be viewed as manipulations of messages exchanged between actors. For example, message loss, duplication, delay, tampering, and equivocation operate on individual messages: loss drops a message between two nodes; duplication creates a copy; delay injects an abnormal latency (due to network congestion or adversarial interference); tampering modifies the message content; equivocation sends different message copies to different recipients. Other faults operate on *sets* of messages. Crashing a node can be represented as dropping all of the messages destined for it; a network partition corresponds to dropping all of the messages between two disjoint node sets, while preserving communication within each set.

This unified view not only simplifies the modeling of individual faults but also provides a common "interface" for extending the library with new faults.

Fault Injection. Injecting faults is carried out through the cooperation of three components within the fault injector: the *scheduler*, the *fault controller*, and the *fault handlers*. All interactions among these components occur internally and are thus transparent to the system. In other words, the system continues to evolve according to its original semantics; the injector merely intercepts and manipulates in-transit messages without altering the system's transition rules.

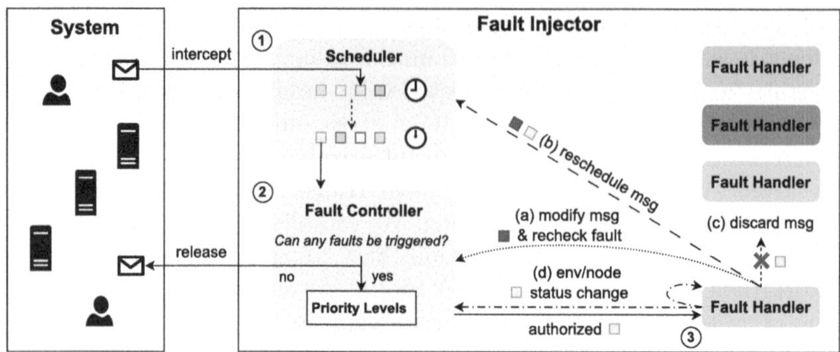

Fig. 1. The workflow of our fault-injection framework. Arrows of different types in (a)–(d) represent the possible outcomes after a fault handler executes its designated operation to the message (Step ③).

The overall workflow of our framework is as follows (also illustrated in Fig. 1):

① **Message Interception and Scheduling.** Fault injection begins when the scheduler intercepts an outgoing message *msg* from a sender node in the system, e.g., the server's reply in the example of Sect. 2. It then augments the message into the form $[\mathtt{gt} + \mathtt{md}, msg, l]$, where $gt + md$ denotes the message's expected arrival time, with gt the current global time maintained by the scheduler and md a message delay sampled from a predefined probability distribution (e.g., lognormal [12]), and l is the label of the rewrite rule that produced the message.[1]

The scheduler maintains an ordered list of all in-transit messages, sorted by their expected arrival times. When a message reaches the head of the list, the global clock is advanced to its expected arrival time. Rather than delivering the message directly to the destination node, the scheduler hands it over to the fault controller for potential fault injection. See Sect. 4.1 for details.

② **Fault Control.** Upon receiving the message, the fault controller determines if any fault conditions are triggered based on its metadata (e.g., its destination, content, and source rule label). If a condition holds, the controller authorizes the corresponding fault behavior *fbhv* and passes the message to the appropriate handler via $\mathtt{auth}([\mathtt{gt} + \mathtt{md}, msg, l], fbhv)$. For instance, under a network partition, *fbhv* may be `part-drop` that discards the message sent across partitions.

If multiple conditions hold simultaneously, the controller selects which fault behavior to authorize first according to a predefined *fault priority* (Sect. 4.2). Note that, in our framework, fault control is designed to be *fine-grained*: a single fault type may encompass multiple distinct fault behaviors. For example, network partition also includes behaviors such as `part-msg`, where partitions are triggered by a specific message that marks an "interesting" moment in the system execution (e.g., right before a leader is selected in consensus protocols).

[1] More precisely, a preprocessing step annotates each outgoing message with the corresponding rule label prior to interception; see Sect. 5.

Otherwise, the fault controller releases the message directly into the system configuration. Note that the delivered message may differ from the original one if it has been modified by a fault handler, as explained below.

③ **Fault Handling.** Once a fault behavior is authorized, the corresponding handler applies its designated operation to the message. This results in one of the following four outcomes (see Sect. 4.3 for details):

(a) The handler modifies the message and sends it back to the fault controller for rechecking, which may authorize another fault behavior to be injected. This arises in faults such as message tampering and equivocation.
(b) The handler produces one or more messages that must be rescheduled. For example, a delay fault adds an additional abnormal delay to the message.
(c) The handler discards the message, which may result from a message-loss fault, a network partition, or delivery to a crashed node.
(d) The message remains unchanged and is rechecked for other faults, while the environment (e.g., a network partition or recovery) or the node's status (e.g., a crash or reboot) is altered.

4 Formalizing Fault Injection

In this section, we formalize the three components within the fault injector, namely the scheduler, the fault controller, and the fault handlers, together with their interactions.[2]

4.1 Scheduler

The scheduler maintains a message queue `msgQueue`, sorted by the messages' expected arrival times, and a global clock, `clock`, which is advanced based on these times. The Maude module `SCHEDULER` below presents its declaration as an actor class, along with its key operation (corresponding to Step ① in Fig. 1):[3]

```
mod SCHEDULER is
  ...   *** omitted variable declarations and module importations

  class Scheduler | clock: Float, msgQueue: List{Msg} .

  *** intercept and schedule an outgoing msg
  eq [MSG, L]  < sch : Scheduler | clock: GT, msgQueue: MS >
   = < sch : Scheduler | msgQueue: insert(MS, [GT + md, MSG, L]) > .
  *** tick global clock
  eq tick(< sch : Scheduler | clock: GT, msgQueue: [GT',MSG,L] ; MS >  OBJS)
   = < sch : Scheduler | clock: GT', msgQueue: MS >  OBJS  [GT',MSG,L] .
endm
```

[2] The entire Maude specification is available at [62].

[3] For brevity, we omit variable declarations while following the Maude convention that variables are written in capital letters.

The first equation (lines 7–8) inserts an outgoing message `MSG` into the scheduler's queue with its expected arrival time `GT + md`, where `md` is sampled at runtime from a certain probability distribution. Note that the source rule label `L` has been captured by a preprocessing step (Sect. 5). The second equation (lines 10–11) advances the global clock to the corresponding time `GT'` when the message is forwarded to the fault controller for potential manipulation.

4.2 Fault Controller

Table 1. Priority levels of fault behaviors. Level 1: time-triggered behaviors; Level 2: message-modification behaviors; Level 3: message-induced behaviors.

Behavior	Description	Level 1	Level 2	Level 3
`msg-loss`	drop an in-transit message		•	
`tampering`	modify the message content		•	
`equivocation`	send different message copies to different receivers		•	
`part-time`	network is partitioned when the global time reaches a specific point	•		
`part-msg`	partition the network right before delivering a specific message			•
`part-drop`	drop a message across partitions		•	
`recover-time`	partition is recovered when the global time reaches a specific point	•		
`recover-msg`	recover the partition right before delivering a specific message			•
`crash-time`	a node crashes when the global time reaches a specific point	•		
`crash-msg`	crash a node right before delivering a specific message			•
`crash-drop`	drop a message destined for the crashed node		•	
`reboot-time`	a node is rebooted when the global time reaches a specific point	•		
`reboot-msg`	reboot a crashed node right before delivering a specific message			•
`duplication`	create extra copies of the message			•
`abnormal-delay`	add an extra delay to the message			•

Fault control is complex as our framework incorporates a wide range of faults, some of which encompass multiple behaviors. This complexity is further amplified when several behaviors become applicable simultaneously, making it hard for the controller to determine when and how they should be injected effectively.

Prioritizing Fault Behaviors. We introduce a set of fault-behavior priority levels to enable fine-grained control over these behaviors. Based on the precondition required to trigger each behavior (see below), we organize all fault behaviors into three levels, where Level i has higher priority than Level j for $i < j$; therefore, behaviors at Level i are always triggered before those at Level j at runtime. If multiple fault behaviors at the same level become simultaneously applicable, the controller uniformly selects one to trigger, with the remaining behaviors considered in subsequent iterations. Table 1 summarizes these behaviors, along with their descriptions and assigned priority levels.

Level 1: Time-Triggered Behaviors. These behaviors are triggered purely by time.[4] As the global clock may be advanced by messages whose expected arrival times go beyond the scheduled times of these behaviors, all pending ones at this level must be applied before processing any behaviors of other levels. For example, consider a network partition (`part-time`) scheduled to occur at time t_1, but the global time has already been advanced to t_2 by a cross-partition message m, where $t_2 > t_1$. If the partition is not triggered first, m would be delivered to its destination, which is semantically incorrect, as no message should be delivered across partitions once the network partition has taken effect.

Level 2: Message-Modification Behaviors. These behaviors operate on a message while it is still mutable, i.e., modifiable or removable, assuming that all Level 1 behaviors have already been resolved. They directly alter the message's content (the behaviors `tampering` and `equivocation`) or existence (the behaviors `msg-loss`, `part-drop`, and `crash-drop`).

Level 3: Message-Induced Behaviors. These behaviors require the message to be stable, i.e., its content and destination have been finalized, and they act based on this finalized message without modifying it. Such behaviors may create new message copies (`duplication`), add an extra delay (`abnormal-delay`), or trigger message-induced changes to the system or environment (e.g., `part-msg` for partitioning the network and `reboot-msg` for rebooting a crashed node).

Formalizing Fault Control. The module `CONTROLLER` specifies the fault controller, as shown below. It imports all predefined fault handlers (Sect. 4.3) relevant to the user-specified faults (line 2). Here, we use message loss and network partition to illustrate how the controller operates (referring to Step ②).

```
1  mod CONTROLLER is
2    inc MSG-LOSS + PARTITION .   *** imported according to the user config
3
4    class Controller | fbhvs : List{Bhv}, priority : Map{Bhv, Nat} .
5
6    ceq [GT, MSG, L]  < ml : MsgLoss | >  < pt : Partition | >
7        < ctrl : Controller | fbhvs: BS, priority: P >
8      = < ml : MsgLoss | >  < pt : Partition | >  < ctrl : Controller | >
9        (if isSatisfied(BS,[GT,MSG,L], < ml : MsgLoss | > < pt : Partition
         | >)
10           then auth([GT, MSG, L], B)  *** fault behavior authorized
11           else MSG fi)  *** msg released into the system config
12     if B := topBhv(BS,P,[GT,MSG,L],< ml : MsgLoss | > < pt : Partition |
        >) .
13
14   *** check whether message loss can be triggered
15   eq isSatisfied(msg-loss, [GT, CONTENT from O to O', L],
16        < ml : MsgLoss | lossReceivers: OS, lossRules: LS, lossRate: R >
       HDLS)
17    = O' in OS and L in LS and rand < R .
18
19   *** check whether network partition can be triggered by time
20   eq isSatisfied(part-time, [GT, MSG, L],
```

[4] Our framework allows users to specify the time points at which these behaviors are triggered; see [61, Appendix A].

```
21         < pt : Partition | status: S, occurTime: T > HDLS)
22     = GT >= T and S == healthy .
23     ...
24 endm
```

The controller is modeled as an actor class with two attributes (line 4): **fbhvs**, which specifies the list of all fault behaviors to be injected, and **priority**, which maps each fault behavior to a natural number indicating its priority level. Both attributes are initialized according to the user configuration; see [61, Appendix A] for an example with the message-loss and network-partition fault behaviors.

The controller's operation is defined by a conditional equation (lines 6–12), where the controller evaluates all fault behaviors in **fbhvs** via the predicate **isSatisfied** to determine which behaviors are eligible for triggering (line 9). For example, the **msg-loss** behavior is eligible when the receiver `O'` belongs to the designated set of receivers `OS` whose incoming messages may be dropped, the source rule label matches (by the predicate `L in LS`), which identifies a specific execution point relevant to that receiver, and a probabilistic draw, denoted by the random number **rand**, falls below the user-specified loss rate `R` (lines 15–17). The **part-time** behavior becomes eligible when the global time exceeds the configured trigger time of the network partition (i.e., `GT >= T`) and the current status of the network is **healthy** (lines 20–22).

When multiple behaviors are eligible, the controller selects the highest-priority one based on the predefined levels `P` via the function **topBhv** (line 12). For instance, **part-time** is chosen over **msg-loss** when both apply. The controller then forwards the message, along with the selected behavior to the corresponding handler (line 10), or releases it into the system configuration otherwise (line 11).

4.3 Fault Handlers

A fault handler is the component for executing the designated fault behavior once it has been authorized by the controller. All handlers are modeled as actors, each with its operation defined in its own module. Depending on the specific behavior, a handler may produce one of the four outcomes, as described in Step ③.

The module `PARTITION` below exemplifies how the fault handler manages three network-partition behaviors of different levels. For brevity, only the attributes of the `Partition` class that are relevant to these behaviors are shown.

```
mod PARTITION is
  class Partition | status : NetworkStatus, allNodes : Set{Oid},
                    parts : Partitions, occurTime : Float, ...

  *** Level 1: a network partition is triggered by a specific time
  eq auth([GT, MSG, L], part-time)
     < pt : Partition | status: healthy, parts: [OS1 | OS2], allNodes:
     OS >
   = < pt : Partition | status: partitioned,
           parts: (if OS1 == empty then randomPart(OS) else [OS1 | OS2]
     fi) >
     [GT, MSG, L] .

  *** Level 2: a message is dropped across partitions
```

```
13   eq auth([GT,MSG,L],part-drop) < pt : Partition | > = < pt : Partition
       | > .
14
15   *** Level 3: a network partition is triggered by a specific message
16   eq auth([GT, MSG, L], part-msg)
17      < pt : Partition | status: healthy, occurTime: T,
18                         allNodes: OS, parts: [OS1 | OS2] >
19    = < pt : Partition | status: partitioned, occurTime: GT,
20            parts: (if OS1 == empty then randomPart(OS) else [OS1 | OS2]
       fi) >
21      [GT, MSG, L] .
22   ...
23 endm
```

The network is partitioned either at a specific time point (lines 6–10) or upon the arrival of a designated message (lines 17–22). A partition is created by switching the network status from `healthy` to `partitioned`. The partition sets are either preconfigured, e.g., `[OS1 | OS2]` denotes two disjoint node sets `OS1` and `OS2` that are instantiated in the initial state, or generated probabilistically via the function `randomPart`. Once the partition is applied, the message is returned to the controller for further fault processing, as discussed earlier. This corresponds to the outcome (d) in Step ③.

During a network partition, any message sent across the two partitions is dropped. This is signaled by `part-drop` and realized by the equation at line 13, corresponding to the outcome (c) in Step ③.

4.4 Fault Injector

The fault injector is formed by importing the two modules `SCHEDULER` and `CONTROLLER` introduced earlier, with the latter also importing all user-specified fault handlers such as `MSG-LOSS` and `PARTITION`.

```
mod FAULT-INJECTOR is    inc SCHEDULER + CONTROLLER .    endm
```

As we will see in the next section, our framework automates the fault injection for quantitative performance analysis, including statistical model checking (SMC). To ensure that the composed system model with the fault injector is suitable for SMC, we prove that it satisfies the *absence of nondeterminism* (AND) property [4] (see also Sect. 2).

Theorem 1. *The composed system model with fault injection guarantees AND.*

Intuitively, AND holds throughout the entire reachable state space: it holds in the initial state (base case) and is preserved by every rewrite (inductive step), and thus cannot be violated along any execution of the composed system. A detailed proof is given in [61, Appendix B].

5 Automating Fault-Injection Analysis

We have implemented our fault-injection framework in Maude and incorporated several additional components into an automated tool, called PerF (available

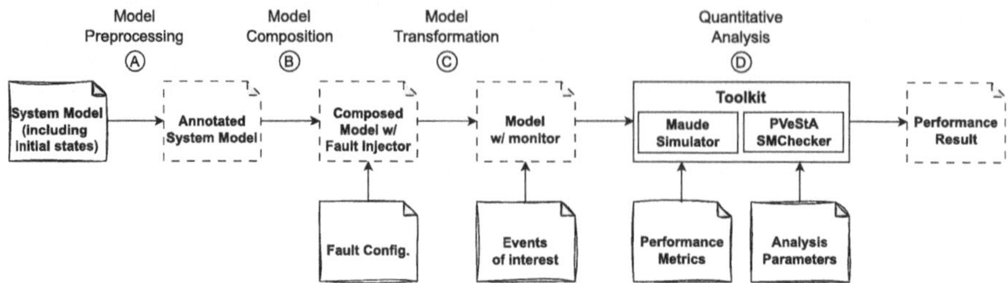

Fig. 2. The pipeline of PERF. Sketched files are provided by users, while dashed files are generated automatically by the tool. The composed model with the fault injector in Step Ⓑ corresponds to Fig. 1.

at [62]), to enable end-to-end performance prediction. The overall tool pipeline comprises four steps, as shown in Fig. 2:

Ⓐ **Model Preprocessing.** The tool annotates the user-provided system model, typically nondeterministic and untimed, by attaching to each outgoing message *msg* the label l of the rule that generates it, yielding `[msg,`l`]`.

Ⓑ **Model Composition.** This step corresponds to the discussion in Sect. 4, where the annotated system model is composed with the fault injector that consists of the scheduler, the fault controller, and the relevant fault handlers. Before injecting any faults, the scheduler augments each message with a normal delay that is sampled at runtime from a user-specified probability distribution. Our tool provides a collection of network latency distributions, including lognormal, Weibull, and exponential, that reflect the characteristics of real data centers [12]. It also offers an interface through which users can specify both the types of faults to inject (e.g., message loss) and their injection parameters (e.g., a 10% loss rate for acknowledgments from followers to the leader).

Ⓒ **Model Transformation.** The composed model is then transformed into one equipped with a monitor that timestamps events during execution, e.g., the times at which a transaction is issued and committed. We realize this monitoring mechanism by extending the approach introduced in [40] to support logging multiple events of interest, allowing users to readily define and compute performance metrics such as throughput and abort rate over these events.

Ⓓ **Quantitative Analysis.** The toolkit performs quantitative analysis using either Maude's built-in simulator or the PVeStA statistical model checker [6]. In both modes, simulations are produced by executing the transformed model from the initial state. For statistical model checking, users additionally provide performance properties expressed as QuaTEx formulas, along with experimental parameters (e.g., the statistical confidence level). The analysis output is either the raw simulation result or the expected value of a given QuaTEx formula.

We illustrate these steps using the Two-Phase Commit protocol, which is deferred to [61, Appendix A]. Note that, in addition to Theorem 1, we prove that the model transformation in Step © also preserves AND, making the resulting model suitable for SMC analysis. The proof is given in [61, Appendix B].

6 Case Studies

We apply PERF to six distributed systems of different kinds: (1) the widely used atomic commitment protocol 2PC, which integrates the Cooperative Termination Protocol (CTP) [13] to mitigate its blocking issues during failures; (2) the consensus protocol Raft [51], which achieves fault-tolerant log replication; (3) the authoritative DNS server PowerDNS [52], which is widely deployed in production networks to ensure reliable name resolution; (4) the quorum-based consistency protocol of Apache Cassandra [1], which balances data consistency and availability via read/write quorums; (5) the RAMP distributed transaction protocol [10], along with its optimization, which has been layered atop Facebook's TAO [19]; and (6) the Byzantine fault-tolerant consensus protocol Fast-HotStuff [30], which improves the classical HotStuff design for low-latency agreement.

Table 2 summarizes these case studies, including the system types, modeling and implementation efforts, and the injected faults considered in our analysis.

Table 2. Summary of case studies. †: Maude specifications obtained from the public repositories; ‡: implementations developed in this work.

System	Kind	Model LoC	Impl. LoC	Injected Fault	Deployment Platform
2PC with CTP	atomic commitment	314	354‡	message loss	CloudLab Utah (d6515)
Raft	consensus	536	1400	node crash	CloudLab Utah (xl170)
PowerDNS	name resolution	2200†	4887	delayed messages	DNS testbed [38]
Cassandra Quorum	consistency	465	1402‡	network partition	CloudLab Clemson
RAMP & OPW	concurrency control	2523†	7977	message loss	Tencent Cloud
Fast-HotStuff	Byzantine consensus	304	4247	equiv. & network part.	Emulab

6.1 Experimental Setup and Rationale

Setup. We predict system performance from the formal models under different network latency distributions, including lognormal and exponential. We employ a cluster of Emulab machines [58] to parallelize the PVeStA analysis, each with a 2.4 GHz quad-core Xeon processor and 12 GB of RAM. The statistical confidence level α is set to 95%, and the error margin δ to 0.01. All three steps prior to SMC are performed on a single machine, each completing instantly.

We deploy the actual systems across multiple platforms (see Table 2), including CloudLab (and its different clusters) and Tencent Cloud, each exhibiting distinct characteristics of real-world distributed environments. For each system, we implement dedicated fault injectors that correspond to our model-based analysis.

Evaluation Rationale. Our evaluation rationale follows prior work [40,44]: we consider a model-based prediction as accurate if it closely mirrors the observed behaviors in the deployment evaluation in terms of overall curve trends, up to a certain scaling factor. This criterion is motivated by the fact that model-based predictions seldom align numerically with empirical results.[5] In a probabilistic model, quantitative values are inherently tied to an abstract unit of time. This unit only approximates the real timing observed in deployed systems, and the corresponding scaling factor remains unknown at the design stage.

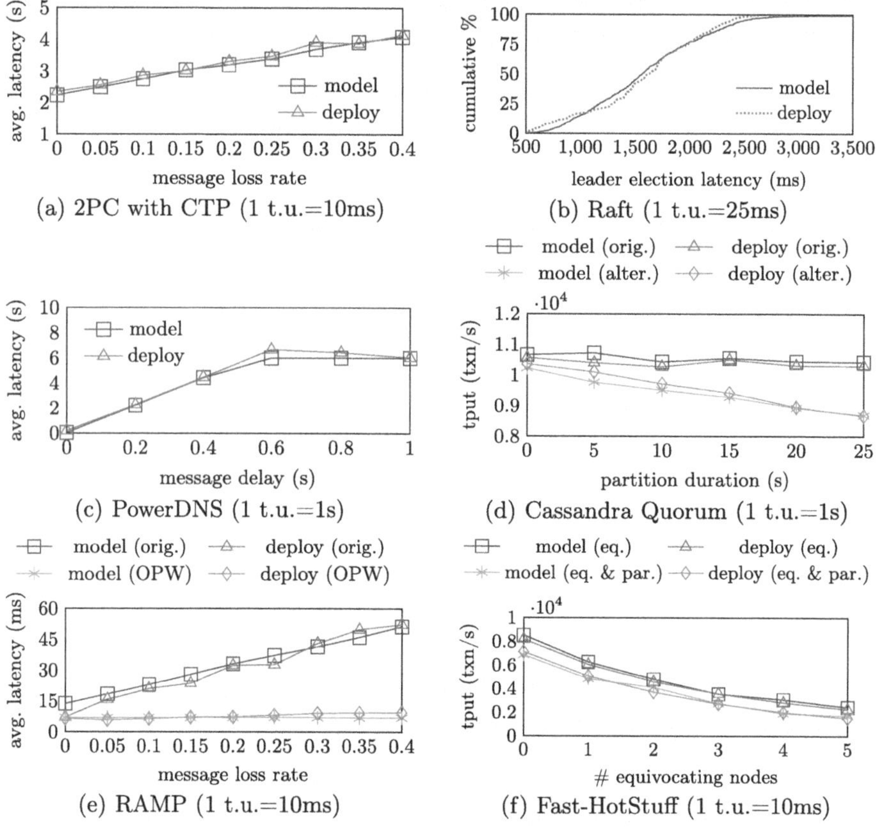

(a) 2PC with CTP (1 t.u.=10ms)

(b) Raft (1 t.u.=25ms)

(c) PowerDNS (1 t.u.=1s)

(d) Cassandra Quorum (1 t.u.=1s)

(e) RAMP (1 t.u.=10ms)

(f) Fast-HotStuff (1 t.u.=10ms)

Fig. 3. Model-based performance predictions vs. deployment-level evaluations across six distributed systems and their variants. The scaling factor 1 t.u.= T ms means that one time unit in the model corresponds to T ms in the deployment.

[5] Even the same implementation evaluated on different platforms rarely yields numerically identical results due to factors like distinct network latency distributions [40].

6.2 Experimental Results

Summary. Our experimental results are shown in Fig. 3. Overall, across all six case studies, we demonstrate the predictive power of our framework by showing that the model-based performance estimations, specifically throughput and latency, align closely with evaluations of the deployed systems under various types of faults. These include message loss (Fig. 3(a) and (e)), node crashes (Fig. 3(b)), delayed messages (Fig. 3(c)), network partitions (Fig. 3(d)), and equivocation combined with network partitions (Fig. 3(f)).

In particular, our analysis reveals that although some systems were previously deemed competitive with their variants, substantial performance degradation can occur in either the original design or its optimization once faults are introduced. This highlights the strength of PERF: it enables the exploration of a much broader spectrum of system behaviors already at the design stage. We discuss one such case, namely RAMP and its optimization, along with a mixed-fault analysis of Fast-HotStuff; the remaining ones are deferred to [61, Appendix C].

RAMP. The Read Atomic Multi-Partition (RAMP) system [10] delivers performant transactions and the read atomicity isolation through efficient concurrency control. In addition to the original design, its developers introduced a faster variant with one-phase writes (OPW) that relaxes certain consistency guarantees

A recent study [40] found both designs competitive, with the original design incurring only marginally higher latency. However, this conclusion holds only under fault-free conditions. Using PERF, we reveal that as message loss increases, the original design exhibits significantly higher latency than the optimization OPW. Deployment-level results corroborate our model-based predictions, as shown in Fig. 3(e). Since message loss is inevitable in practical deployments and often intensifies under high network contention, this finding can help practitioners make more informed choices between alternative designs.

Fast-HotStuff. Byzantine fault-tolerant consensus plays a pivotal role in modern blockchain systems. The recently proposed Fast-HotStuff consensus protocol [30] offers improved performance and greater robustness against forking attacks compared to the state of the art.

We use PERF to predict how Fast-HotStuff behaves under equivocation attacks [11,29], where adversaries propose conflicting blocks that cause ambiguity among participants, leading to forks and delayed consensus progress. As shown in Fig. 3(f), increasing the number of equivocating nodes causes throughput to decline. Moreover, we assess Fast-HotStuff's performance when equivocation and (benign yet prevalent) network partitions coexist. The results indicate a moderate decrease in throughput, an expected yet reassuring outcome, as the degradation remains limited. All our model-based predictions align closely with deployment-level evaluations conducted on a real cluster.

Notably, this mixed-fault experiment extends beyond the evaluations performed in the original study [30], providing a more comprehensive understanding of Fast-HotStuff's behavior under more realistic scenarios. Additionally, this case study demonstrates the modularity of our framework, which enables rapid exploration of a system's performance space under complex fault combinations.

7 Related Work

Formal Quantitative Analysis. We have already discussed in Sect. 1 the limitations of existing approaches to predicting distributed system performance from formal designs. They either ignore faults entirely, couple them directly with system semantics, or examine only a few isolated fault types. All of these works are based on Maude [21] or TLA+ [34], which is largely because both formalisms provide high expressiveness for modeling large-scale distributed systems. On the other hand, a number of automata-based quantitative frameworks, such as UPPAAL-SMC [16], PRISM [33], and MODEST [28], support statistical or probabilistic model checking over timed or stochastic automata. Nevertheless, applying these frameworks to our setting remains highly challenging, as certain system characteristics are difficult to capture within automata-based models, e.g., the dynamic creation of actors or messages that can lead to an unbounded population of such components. Yet this is common in both normal (e.g., the joining of new nodes) and faulty scenarios (e.g., message duplication).

PERFORMAL [60] advances the formal verification of distributed system performance by providing worst-case latency bounds; yet such bounds are generally unattainable, e.g., in the presence of Byzantine behaviors. Network calculus [23] provides a mathematical foundation for reasoning about networked system performance and has been applied to establish latency guarantees [31,36]. These approaches address an orthogonal problem; we aim instead to capture the concrete system dynamics under faults, covering a wide range of quantitative metrics beyond latency, e.g., those expressible in QuaTEx (see examples in [4,40]).

Posterior Fault Injection. Recent years have witnessed a growing number of deployment-level fault injectors for assessing the reliability and resilience of distributed systems. Academic advances include CoFI [17] for exposing network-partition failures, Chronos [18] for detecting timeout bugs, CrashFuzz [26] for uncovering crash-recovery bugs, and ByzzFuzz [59] for triggering Byzantine consensus bugs. Fault-injection techniques have also been widely adopted in production, exemplified by Jepsen [32], Netflix's Chaos Monkey [49], AWS's FIS [2], and Facebook's Twins [11].

Compared with these approaches, our framework enables early and proactive performance exploration during the design stage, rather than being reactive and applicable only after system implementation. Moreover, our work focuses on system performance, quantifying how systems behave under diverse faults, whereas most existing approaches concentrate on correctness and reliability issues and on how to trigger them. It is also worth noting that, although various benchmarks exist across different domains for evaluating system performance, e.g., YCSB [22] for cloud database systems, they do not incorporate faults and therefore can only explore a limited portion of the overall performance space.

8 Conclusion

We have presented a formal framework and tool for predicting distributed system performance under fault conditions. Built on Maude, our framework introduces semantics-preserving model compositions that seamlessly integrate system and fault models into a unified representation suitable for statistical analysis. Case studies demonstrate that the framework accurately captures the performance impact of diverse and co-existing faults, aligning with empirical observations.

This work paves the way for rapid and comprehensive exploration of the system performance space at an early design stage. When paired with deployment-level fault injection, it offers a complementary means to better understand and improve the performance robustness of future distributed systems.

Acknowledgments. We thank the anonymous reviewers for their valuable feedback. Min Zhang was funded by the NSFC Project (No. 62372176) and Shanghai Trusted Industry Internet Software Collaborative Innovation Center. Peixin Wang was sponsored by the NSFC project (No. 92582108) and the CCF-Huawei Populus Grove Fund. Si Liu and Min Zhang are the corresponding authors.

References

1. Apache Cassandra: Open Source NoSQL Database (Nov 2025). https://cassandra.apache.org/
2. AWS Fault Injection Service (Nov 2025). https://aws.amazon.com/fis/
3. Agha, G.: Actors: A Model of Concurrent Computation in Distributed Systems. MIT Press, Cambridge, MA, USA (1986)
4. Agha, G., Meseguer, J., Sen, K.: PMaude: Rewrite-based specification language for probabilistic object systems. Electr. Notes Theor. Comput. Sci. **153**(2) (2006)
5. Agha, G., Palmskog, K.: A survey of statistical model checking. ACM Trans. Model. Comput. Simul. **28**(1) (2018)
6. AlTurki, M., Meseguer, J.: PVeStA: a parallel statistical model checking and quantitative analysis tool. In: Corradini, A., Klin, B., Cîrstea, C. (eds.) CALCO 2011. LNCS, vol. 6859, pp. 386–392. Springer, Heidelberg (2011). https://doi.org/10.1007/978-3-642-22944-2_28
7. AlTurki, M.A., Kanovich, M.I., Kirigin, T.B., Nigam, V., Scedrov, A., Talcott, C.L.: Statistical model checking of distance fraud attacks on the Hancke-Kuhn family of protocols. In: CPS-SPC@CCS 2018, pp. 60–71. ACM (2018)
8. Alturki, M.A., Roşu, G.: Statistical model checking of RANDAO's resilience to pre-computed reveal strategies. In: Sekerinski, E., et al. (eds.) FM 2019. LNCS, vol. 12232, pp. 337–349. Springer, Cham (2020). https://doi.org/10.1007/978-3-030-54994-7_25
9. Alur, R., Henzinger, T.A., Vardi, M.Y.: Theory in practice for system design and verification. ACM SIGLOG News **2**(1) (2015)
10. Bailis, P., Fekete, A., Ghodsi, A., Hellerstein, J.M., Stoica, I.: Scalable atomic visibility with RAMP transactions. ACM Trans. Database Syst. **41**(3), 15:1–15:45 (2016)

11. Bano, S., Sonnino, A., Chursin, A., Perelman, D., Li, Z., Ching, A., Malkhi, D.: Twins: BFT systems made robust. In: OPODIS 2021. Leibniz International Proceedings in Informatics (LIPIcs), vol. 217, pp. 7:1–7:29 (2022)
12. Benson, T., Akella, A., Maltz, D.A.: Network traffic characteristics of data centers in the wild. In: IMC 2010, pp. 267–280. ACM (2010)
13. Bernstein, P.A., Hadzilacos, V., Goodman, N.: Concurrency Control and Recovery in Database Systems. Addison-Wesley (1987)
14. Bobba, R., Grov, J., Gupta, I., Liu, S., Meseguer, J., Ölveczky, P.C., Skeirik, S.: Survivability: design, formal modeling, and validation of cloud storage systems using Maude. Assured Cloud Comput., 10–48 (2018)
15. Brooker, M.: Fifteen years of formal methods at AWS. TLA+ Conference (2024). https://conf.tlapl.us/2024/MarcBrooker-FifteenYearsOfTLAPlus.pdf
16. Bulychev, P.E., David, A., Larsen, K.G., Mikucionis, M., Poulsen, D.B., Legay, A., Wang, Z.: UPPAAL-SMC: statistical model checking for priced timed automata. In: QAPL 2012. EPTCS, vol. 85, pp. 1–16 (2012)
17. Chen, H., Dou, W., Wang, D., Qin, F.: CoFI: consistency-guided fault injection for cloud systems. In: ASE 2020, pp. 536–547 (2020)
18. Chen, Y., Ma, F., Zhou, Y., Gu, M., Liao, Q., Jiang, Y.: Chronos: finding timeout bugs in practical distributed systems by deep-priority fuzzing with transient delay. In: IEEE Symposium on Security and Privacy (SP), IEEE Computer Society (2024)
19. Cheng, A., et al.: RAMP-TAO: layering atomic transactions on facebook's online TAO data store. Proc. VLDB Endow. **14**(12), 3014–3027 (2021)
20. Chuat, L., Legner, M., Basin, D.A., Hausheer, D., Hitz, S., Müller, P., Perrig, A.: The Complete Guide to SCION - From Design Principles to Formal Verification. Springer, Information Security and Cryptography (2022). https://doi.org/10.1007/978-3-031-05288-0
21. Clavel, M., et al.: All About Maude, LNCS, vol. 4350. Springer (2007)
22. Cooper, B.F., Silberstein, A., Tam, E., Ramakrishnan, R., Sears, R.: Benchmarking cloud serving systems with YCSB. In: SoCC 2010, pp. 143–154. ACM (2010)
23. Cruz, R.L.: A calculus for network delay, part II: network analysis. IEEE Trans. Inf. Theory **37**(1), 132–141 (1991)
24. Davis, A.J.J.: Are we serious about using TLA+ for statistical properties? TLA+ Community Event (2025). https://conf.tlapl.us/2025-etaps/davis-slides.pdf
25. Eckhardt, J., Mühlbauer, T., AlTurki, M., Meseguer, J., Wirsing, M.: Stable availability under denial of service attacks through formal patterns. In: de Lara, J., Zisman, A. (eds.) FASE 2012. LNCS, vol. 7212, pp. 78–93. Springer, Heidelberg (2012). https://doi.org/10.1007/978-3-642-28872-2_6
26. Gao, Y., Dou, W., Wang, D., Feng, W., Wei, J., Zhong, H., Huang, T.: Coverage guided fault injection for cloud systems. In: 2023 IEEE/ACM 45th International Conference on Software Engineering (ICSE), pp. 2211–2223 (2023)
27. Goguen, J.A., Meseguer, J.: Order-sorted algebra I: equational deduction for multiple inheritance, overloading, exceptions and partial operations. Theor. Comput. Sci. **105**(2), 217–273 (1992)
28. Hartmanns, A., Hermanns, H.: The modest toolset: an integrated environment for quantitative modelling and verification. In: Ábrahám, E., Havelund, K. (eds.) TACAS 2014. LNCS, vol. 8413, pp. 593–598. Springer, Heidelberg (2014). https://doi.org/10.1007/978-3-642-54862-8_51
29. Jaffe, A., Moscibroda, T., Sen, S.: On the price of equivocation in byzantine agreement. In: PODC 2012, pp. 309–318. ACM (2012)
30. Jalalzai, M.M., Niu, J., Feng, C., Gai, F.: Fast-HotStuff: a fast and robust BFT protocol for blockchains. IEEE Trans. Dependable Sec. Comput., 1–17 (2023)

31. Jang, K., Sherry, J., Ballani, H., Moncaster, T.: Silo: predictable message latency in the cloud. In: SIGCOMM 2015, pp. 435–448. ACM (2015)
32. Jepsen: A framework for distributed systems verification, with fault injection (Nov 2025). http://jepsen.io/
33. Kwiatkowska, M., Norman, G., Parker, D.: PRISM 4.0: verification of probabilistic real-time systems. In: Gopalakrishnan, G., Qadeer, S. (eds.) CAV 2011. LNCS, vol. 6806, pp. 585–591. Springer, Heidelberg (2011). https://doi.org/10.1007/978-3-642-22110-1_47
34. Lamport, L.: Specifying Systems. The TLA+ Language and Tools for Hardware and Software Engineers. Addison-Wesley (2002)
35. Liang, L., Liu, S.: Exploring design alternatives for replicated RAMP transactions using Maude. In: TASE 2021, pp. 111–118. IEEE (2021)
36. Liebeherr, J., Burchard, A., Ciucu, F.: Delay bounds in communication networks with heavy-tailed and self-similar traffic. IEEE Trans. Inf. Theory **58**(2), 1010–1024 (2012)
37. Liu, S.: All in one: Design, verification, and implementation of SNOW-optimal read atomic transactions. ACM Trans. Softw. Eng. Methodol. **31**(3) (2022)
38. Liu, S., Duan, H., Heimes, L., Bearzi, M., Vieli, J., Basin, D., Perrig, A.: A formal framework for end-to-end DNS resolution. In: SIGCOMM 2023, pp. 932–949. ACM (2023)
39. Liu, S., Ganhotra, J., Rahman, M.R., Nguyen, S., Gupta, I., Meseguer, J.: Quantitative analysis of consistency in NoSQL key-value stores. Leibniz Trans. Embed. Syst. **4**(1), 03:1–03:26 (2017)
40. Liu, S., Meseguer, J., Ölveczky, P.C., Zhang, M., Basin, D.A.: Bridging the semantic gap between qualitative and quantitative models of distributed systems. Proc. ACM Program. Lang. **6**(OOPSLA2), 315–344 (2022)
41. Liu, S., Ölveczky, P.C., Ganhotra, J., Gupta, I., Meseguer, J.: Exploring design alternatives for ramp transactions through statistical model checking. In: Duan, Z., Ong, L. (eds.) ICFEM 2017. LNCS, vol. 10610, pp. 298–314. Springer, Cham (2017). https://doi.org/10.1007/978-3-319-68690-5_18
42. Liu, S., Ölveczky, P.C., Wang, Q., Gupta, I., Meseguer, J.: Read atomic transactions with prevention of lost updates: ROLA and its formal analysis. Formal Aspects Comput. **31**(5), 503–540 (2019)
43. Liu, S., Ölveczky, P.C., Wang, Q., Meseguer, J.: Formal modeling and analysis of the walter transactional data store. In: Rusu, V. (ed.) WRLA 2018. LNCS, vol. 11152, pp. 136–152. Springer, Cham (2018). https://doi.org/10.1007/978-3-319-99840-4_8
44. Liu, S., Sandur, A., Meseguer, J., Ölveczky, P.C., Wang, Q.: Generating correct-by-construction distributed implementations from formal maude designs. In: Lee, R., Jha, S., Mavridou, A., Giannakopoulou, D. (eds.) NFM 2020. LNCS, vol. 12229, pp. 22–40. Springer, Cham (2020). https://doi.org/10.1007/978-3-030-55754-6_2
45. Lynch, N.A.: Distributed Algorithms. Morgan Kaufmann (1996)
46. Maude: Applications (Nov 2025). https://maude.cs.illinois.edu/wiki/Applications
47. Meseguer, J.: Conditioned rewriting logic as a united model of concurrency. Theor. Comput. Sci. **96**(1), 73–155 (1992)
48. Meseguer, J.: Capturing system designs with formal executable specifications. In: FASE 2025, LNCS, vol. 15693, pp. 1–32. Springer (2025). https://doi.org/10.1007/978-3-031-90900-9_1
49. Netflix: Chaos Monkey (Nov 2025). https://netflix.github.io/chaosmonkey/
50. Newcombe, C., Rath, T., Zhang, F., Munteanu, B., Brooker, M., Deardeuff, M.: How Amazon Web Services uses formal methods. Commun. ACM (2015)

51. Ongaro, D., Ousterhout, J.: In search of an understandable consensus algorithm. In: USENIX ATC 2014, pp. 305–320. USENIX Association (2014)
52. PowerDNS: PowerDNS: a faster, safer, and more secure internet (Nov 2025). https://www.powerdns.com/
53. Rubio, R., Martí-Oliet, N., Pita, I., Verdejo, A.: QMaude: quantitative specification and verification in rewriting logic. In: FM 2023. LNCS, vol. 14000, pp. 240–259. Springer (2023). https://doi.org/10.1007/978-3-031-27481-7_15
54. Sen, K., Viswanathan, M., Agha, G.: On statistical model checking of stochastic systems. In: Etessami, K., Rajamani, S.K. (eds.) CAV 2005. LNCS, vol. 3576, pp. 266–280. Springer, Heidelberg (2005). https://doi.org/10.1007/11513988_26
55. Tanenbaum, A.S., van Steen, M.: Distributed systems - principles and paradigms, 2nd Edition. Pearson Education (2007)
56. Vanlightly, J., Kuppe, M.: Obtaining statistical properties via TLC simulation. TLA+ Conference (2022). https://conf.tlapl.us/2022/JackMarkusTLA+Statistics.pdf
57. Weghorn, T., Liu, S., Sprenger, C., Perrig, A., Basin, D.A.: N-Tube: formally verified secure bandwidth reservation in path-aware Internet architectures. In: CSF 2022, pp. 147–162. IEEE (2022)
58. White, B., et al.: An integrated experimental environment for distributed systems and networks. In: OSDI 2002. USENIX Association (2002)
59. Winter, L.N., Buse, F., de Graaf, D., von Gleissenthall, K., Ozkan, B.K.: Randomized testing of Byzantine fault tolerant algorithms. Proc. ACM Program. Lang. **7**(OOPSLA1), 757–788 (2023)
60. Zhang, T.N., Sharma, U., Kapritsos, M.: Performal: formal verification of latency properties for distributed systems. Proc. ACM Program. Lang. **7**(PLDI) (2023)
61. Zhou, Z., Liu, S., Zhou, Z., Wang, P., Zhang, M.: A Formal Framework for Predicting Distributed System Performance under Faults (Extended Version). Tech. rep. (2026). https://arxiv.org/abs/2602.19088
62. Zhou, Z., Liu, S., Zhou, Z., Wang, P., Zhang, M.: Artifact for "A Formal Framework for Predicting Distributed System Performance under Faults (2026). https://doi.org/10.5281/zenodo.18619604

Mining Verdict Boundaries for Neural Network Verification

Jiawei Ren[1(✉)], Guanqin Zhang[1], Zhenya Zhang[2,3], and Yulei Sui[1]

[1] University of New South Wales, Sydney, Australia
{jiawei.ren,guanqin.zhang,y.sui}@unsw.edu.au
[2] Kyushu University, Fukuoka, Japan
zhang@ait.kyushu-u.ac.jp
[3] National Institute of Informatics, Tokyo, Japan

Abstract. Branch and Bound (BaB) aims to achieve complete verification of neural networks by adaptively partitioning the problem and applying off-the-shelf verifiers to subproblems. Its problem-splitting history can be represented as a tree, where each subproblem corresponds to a child node. A key problem of BaB lies in searching for the *verdict boundaries* across all the paths that divide the verified and unverified subproblems. We observe that the existing BaB approach tackles this problem by solving each expensive subproblem sequentially along the tree path as its depth increases, requiring costly bounds propagation at every visited BaB tree node (i.e., subproblem), which is inefficient. To address this issue, we propose effective search approaches that leverage the monotonicity of each path to efficiently and precisely locate the verdict boundary by simultaneously splitting multiple activation functions (e.g., ReLU), rather than processing them one at a time as in the classical approach. Our approach performs an effective exponential search along each path, allowing us to skip many boundary-unrelated subproblems when identifying the verdict boundary. The enhanced version further improves this process by estimating the boundary's position using quantitative information obtained from subproblem solving. We perform experimental evaluation on commonly-used benchmarks to assess our proposed techniques, and compare them with recent BaB-based approaches.

1 Introduction

The rapid adoption of neural networks in safety-critical settings, such as autonomous driving, makes unexpected model failures potentially severe. Their susceptibility to adversarial perturbations [12,22] underscores the need for rigorous assurance. Neural network verification offers provable guarantees of safety and robustness under specified input conditions [15,21,23] and has therefore become a rapidly growing area within formal verification research.

Existing Efforts. Typical neural network verification approaches include completeness-driven constraint solving with a timeout budget [19,31] and

A. Sampaio and M. Stoelinga (Eds.): FM 2026, LNCS 16556, pp. 67–88, 2026.
https://doi.org/10.1007/978-3-032-26204-2_4

approximation-based methods [28,29,32]. While the former aims to compute exact bounds, the latter trades precision for efficiency. To mitigate the incompleteness of approximation-based methods, *Branch and Bound* (BaB) [5] has emerged as the state-of-the-art abstraction refinement approach. Given a specification, BaB employs an efficient approximation-based verifier to compute a distance $\hat{p}$ that signifies *how much* the network satisfies the specification; if $\hat{p}$ is negative, it splits the problem into subproblems (e.g., on input intervals [33] or ReLU phases [4]). It repeats this process on each subproblem, which can yield a tighter approximation and hence a greater $\hat{p}$, for each subproblem, until all the subproblems are verified (i.e., $\hat{p} > 0$) [34].

Motivation and Insights. In BaB, the iterative problem splitting process can be structured as a tree, where each node identifies a subproblem. The objective is to confirm that each tree path ends with a verified node, which is a necessary condition to verify the original problem. Moreover, since problem splitting reduces approximation error, $\hat{p}$, which measures how much the over-approximation satisfies the specification ($\hat{p} > 0$ implies satisfaction), often exhibits a high degree of monotonicity along each path as the node depth increases. We empirically confirm this behavior using a state-of-the-art BaB approach [34]. Because of this, there must exist a *boundary point* (regardless of special cases, such as when the problem is verified at the root) in each path that divides the verified nodes and the unverified nodes, which require no further problem splitting. BaB essentially needs to find such a verdict boundary for each path of the tree.

However, existing BaB approaches, e.g., [5,34], identify the verdict boundary in each path by calling an approximated verifier on each node *one by one* along the path, to locate the boundary point. Since each visit of a node involves a non-trivial problem-solving process by approximated verifiers, this introduces significant time costs. On the other hand, due to the monotonicity of $\hat{p}$ in each path, the problem of finding the boundary point in each path boils down to a search problem for a value in a nearly sorted array. To this end, we can devise more efficient approaches to find the verdict boundary.

Our Solution. In this paper, we propose a new verification approach, BMINER, which performs efficient per-path boundary mining within the BaB tree. By exploiting the monotonicity of $\hat{p}$ in each tree path, BMINER formulates the location of the verdict boundary as a search problem in a nearly sorted array and thereby devises two efficient search approaches that, instead of visiting each tree node one-by-one, skip significant node visits in each tree path.

The first approach BMINER$_\mathsf{E}$ adapts the classic *exponential search* [1]. Given a path, BMINER$_\mathsf{E}$ involves two phases to locate the boundary point: first, it identifies a range that contains the verdict boundary point, by progressively sliding and expanding the range with an exponentially increasing size; after fixing such a range, it locates the exact boundary point position by binary search.

While BMINER$_\mathsf{E}$ can reduce the number of node visits compared to classic BaB, it may still need too many node visits to identify the range that contains the boundary point in a path. To further improve this, we devise BMINER$_\mathsf{G}$, which leverages the quantitative $\hat{p}$ of nodes to estimate its *gradient* (more precisely, its changing rate) in a path, by which it predicts the position of the boundary point. While the prediction may not be precise, by checking the node at the predicted position, we can efficiently update the gradient information and continue our search until we find the boundary point.

We compare with two state-of-the-art tools as our baselines, on 500 verification problem instances from the widely used `MNIST` and `CIFAR-10` datasets. The evaluation results demonstrate that our proposed approach can reduce the average verification time cost by 17% – 30%, with a maximum reduction of 44.7% across five neural networks.

2 Preliminaries

2.1 Neural Network Verification Problem

We define feed-forward neural networks following standard literature [5,19,29].

Definition 1 (Neural networks). A (feed-forward) neural network $N : \mathbb{R}^n \rightarrow \mathbb{R}^m$ consists of alternating affine transformations and nonlinear activations σ. Let $\boldsymbol{x}_0$ be the input. For each layer i ($i \in \{1, \ldots, L\}$), $\boldsymbol{x}_i = \sigma(W_i \boldsymbol{x}_{i-1} + B_i)$, where W_i, B_i are the weights and biases. The dimension of $\boldsymbol{x}_i$ equals the number of neurons in layer i. Following established works [20], we adopt ReLU in our neural networks, defined as $\mathsf{ReLU}(x) = \max(0, x)$.

Specifications are used to formalize desired properties of neural networks. We adopt the notation in Definition 2 as our specification formalism, which is sufficiently expressive for commonly-used properties, such as *local robustness* [12].

Definition 2 (Specification). We define a *specification* for a neural network as a pair (Φ, Ψ) that includes an input specification Φ and an output specification Ψ. The *input specification* Φ is a predicate over the input region, and the output specification Ψ is a predicate over the output of the neural network. Specifically, we represent the output specification Ψ as $f(N(\boldsymbol{x})) > 0$, where $f \colon \mathbb{R}^m \rightarrow \mathbb{R}$ is a function that maps an m-dimensional vector to a real number.

Definition 3 (Verification problem). Given a neural network N and a specification (Φ, Ψ), a verification problem aims to answer the question whether $\Psi(N(\boldsymbol{x}))$ holds, for any input $\boldsymbol{x}$ that holds $\Phi(\boldsymbol{x})$. A verifier is a tool designed to solve this problem. It either returns true, certifying that N satisfies the specification, or returns false with a counterexample.

We now demonstrate how our notations formalize a verification problem as in Definition 3 against local robustness, a property frequently studied in image classification. Local robustness requires that a neural network classifier consistently assigns the same label to two images, $\boldsymbol{x}$ and $\boldsymbol{x}_0$, where $\boldsymbol{x}$ is derived from $\boldsymbol{x}_0$ by applying small perturbations. Formally, given a reference input $\boldsymbol{x}_0$, the input specification $\Phi(\boldsymbol{x})$ enforces that $\boldsymbol{x}$ should hold that $\|\boldsymbol{x} - \boldsymbol{x}_0\|_\infty \leq \epsilon$, where $\|\cdot\|_\infty$ is the ℓ^∞-norm distance metric, and ϵ is a small positive real. The output specification $\Psi(N(\boldsymbol{x}))$ requires that $\min_{1 \leq i \leq m, i \neq i_0}(N(\boldsymbol{x})_{i_0} - N(\boldsymbol{x})_i) > 0$ where $N(\boldsymbol{x})_i$ denotes the i-th component of the output vector $N(\boldsymbol{x})$, and i_0 is the label assigned to $\boldsymbol{x}_0$ by the neural network, i.e., $i_0 = \arg\max_{1 \leq i \leq m} N(\boldsymbol{x}_0)_i$.

2.2 Verification by Branch-and-Bound (BaB)

BaB [5] serves as the backbone for several advanced verification tools, such as $\alpha\beta$-Crown [34]. Essentially, it is a *"divide-and-conquer"* strategy that adaptively splits a verification problem into its subproblems and leverages off-the-shelf approximated verifiers to tackle the resulting subproblems. Since approximated verifiers can yield tighter over-approximations on subproblems, BaB mitigates their completeness limitations when applied directly to the original problem.

Algorithm 1. Branch and Bound [5]

Require: A neural network N, an input specification Φ, an output specification Ψ, an approximated verifier $\mathtt{AppVer}(\cdot)$, and a ReLU selection heuristic $\mathsf{H}(\cdot)$.
Ensure: A *verdict* $\in \{\mathsf{true}, \mathsf{false}\}$.

```
Q ← {⊤}, T ← ∅
BaB(Q)
function BaB(Q)
    if Empty(Q) then
        return true
    Γ ← Pop(Q)
    p̂ ← AppVer(N, Φ, Ψ, Γ)
    T ← T ∪ {⟨Γ, p̂⟩}
    if p̂ < 0 then
        if |Γ| = K then
            return false
        else
            {r_i^+, r_i^-} ← H(Γ)
            for a ∈ {r_i^+, r_i^-} do
                Q ← Q ∪ {Γ ∧ a}
    return BaB(Q)
```

Approximated Verifiers. Various techniques have been proposed to construct over-approximation, e.g., linear relaxation by *DeepPoly* [29] that uses linear constraints to bound each ReLU's output (see Fig. 1). Notably, BaB is orthogonal to these approaches, i.e., it works with any of the selected ones. For a verification problem, an approximated verifier AppVer returns a quantity $\hat{p} \in \mathbb{R}$ called a *verifier assessment* [41], computed by $\hat{p} = \min_{\boldsymbol{y} \in \hat{\Omega}} f(\boldsymbol{y})$, where $\hat{\Omega}$ is the over-approximated region of the neural network output, and f is the function in output specification as defined in Definition 2. Here $\hat{p}$ indicates *how much* the over-approximation satisfies the specification: If $\hat{p}$ is positive, the original output satisfies the specification, thereby certifying the neural network.

Definition 4 (ReLU specification). Let N be a neural network with K neurons, and $\hat{x}_i \in \mathbb{R}$ $(i \in \{1, \dots, K\})$ be the input for the ReLU function in the i-th neuron. Introduce two literals $r_i^+ := (\hat{x}_i \geq 0)$, $r_i^- := (\hat{x}_i < 0)$. A *ReLU specification* is a conjunction of literals that fixes the activation sign of a (possibly empty) set of distinct neurons: $\Gamma = \bigwedge_{i \in I} \ell_i$, where $I \subseteq \{1, \dots, K\}$ and $\ell_i \in \{r_i^+, r_i^-\}$. The length of the specification is defined as $|\Gamma| = |I|$. When $I = \varnothing$, we write $\Gamma = \top$ and call it an empty specification.

Given a neuron i, w.r.t the sign of its pre-activation value, r_i^+ and r_i^- can be derived to split the ReLU function into two linear functions. By adding each proposition as an additional constraint, the verification problem can be divided into two subproblems. If both subproblems are verified, since r_i^+

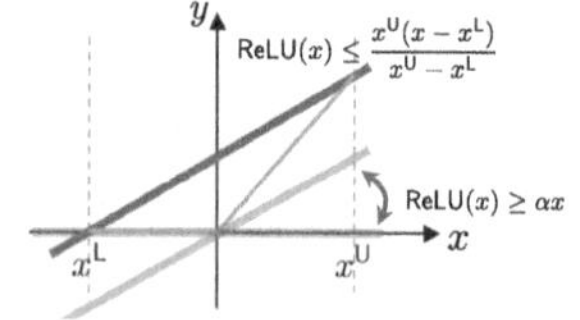

Fig. 1. Linear relaxation of ReLU function.

and r_i^- cover all possible cases of the ReLU input, the original problem is also verified.

The BaB algorithm is presented in Algorithm 1. In addition to input/output specification, we allow AppVer to take an additional argument, i.e., a ReLU specification Γ, which identifies a subproblem obtained by adding Γ (i.e., the conjunction of a number of propositions about ReLU inputs) as a constraint to the original problem. Algorithm 1 uses a queue Q to maintain the (sub)problems to be solved, which is initialized as a set that contains only $\top$, i.e., the original problem. The algorithm starts with a call of function BAB with the initial Q (Line 2).

i) First, BaB applies AppVer to the original problem (Line 7): if AppVer returns a positive $\hat{p}$, it implies that the original problem is verified and so the verification can be terminated with true returned;
ii) In the case the problem cannot be verified (i.e., $\hat{p} < 0$), it splits the problem into two subproblems. This is achieved by selecting a ReLU in the neural network according to a pre-defined ReLU selection heuristic H that returns two propositions $\{r_i^+, r_i^-\}$ about the input of the selected ReLU, based on a given ReLU specification Γ (Line 13; details are introduced later). The selected ReLU i derives two subproblems, identified by $\Gamma \wedge r_i^+$ and $\Gamma \wedge r_i^-$ respectively, which are pushed into Q;
iii) Then, the function BAB is called recursively with the updated Q (Line 16), so it can apply AppVer to the new subproblems. For each subproblem, it goes through a similar process with the original problem: the subproblem can be verified if $\hat{p} > 0$; otherwise, it needs to be further split;
iv) The original problem (identified by $\top$) can be verified if all of the subproblems are verified, in which case Q will be empty (Line 5).

BaB needs a ReLU selection heuristic H that orders neurons and selects the next ReLU according to the specification. Existing strategies such as DeepSplit [14] and FSB [8] can be integrated, as our method is orthogonal to them. Following an existing neural network verification approach [34], we adopt and extend the state-of-the-art ReLU selection strategy [8] (detailed in Sect. 5).

3 Verdict Boundary Insight and Formulation

We introduce a formulation that models BaB-based verification as a search problem. Strictly, this formulation should be on the premise of the near-monotonicity of $\hat{p}$ when problem splitting happens, but this may not always hold for some recent implementations of BaB, such as $\alpha\beta$-Crown [34]. Our empirical study shows that such non-monotonic splitting is rare, and even when it occurs, it is typically local and does not change the overall monotonic trend of $\hat{p}$; thus, it does not affect the effectiveness of our approach, as confirmed experimentally.

3.1 Near-monotonic Behaviour in BaB Tree Paths

The BaB approach (Algorithm 1.) produces a binary tree, called the BaB tree.

Definition 5. (BaBtree) In BaB, a binary tree $\mathcal{T}$, called a BaB tree, is used to record the (sub)problems produced during the execution of BaB. Each node is denoted as a tuple $\langle \Gamma, \hat{p} \rangle$, which consists of a ReLU specification Γ that identifies a (sub)problem, and a verifier assessment $\hat{p}$ that indicates the verification result of the (sub)problem by applying AppVer.

In general, as a *divide-and-conquer* approach, BaB aims to continuously refine the approximation to increase $\hat{p}$, i.e., the distance between the over-approximated output region $\hat{\Omega}$ and the negation of the specification, via a sequence of problem splitting in different paths. In other words, during a sequence of problem splitting, $\hat{p}$ is expected to keep monotonically increasing until it becomes positive at some point, which signifies a successful verification of the subproblem.

However, problem splitting may not always produce an increased $\hat{p}$, depending on the adopted approximated verifier. For example, BaB with Planet [9] as the verifier, holds such monotonicity, because every problem splitting can lead the over-approximation $\hat{\Omega}$ to a subset $\hat{\Omega}^{\dagger} \subseteq \hat{\Omega}$. In recent approaches, e.g., $\alpha\beta$-Crown [34], this monotonicity may be broken. Instead of using a fixed linear bound for ReLU, they search for an optimal lower bound by varying α (i.e., the slope of the linear constraints in Fig. 1). This may lead to the situation where the over-approximation $\hat{\Omega}^{\dagger}$ after problem splitting is not necessarily a subset of $\hat{\Omega}$ before the splitting. Consequently, $\hat{p}$ may decrease. To understand how frequently this can happen, we perform an empirical study for $\alpha\beta$-Crown.

Empirical Evidence on. $\alpha\beta$-Crown. We adopt the same set of benchmarks used in our experimental evaluation (see Table 2). We apply $\alpha\beta$-Crown to solve each problem, and record the resulting BaB tree.

Figure 2 shows a box plot of the distribution of the ratio of the monotonic paths over all the paths in each BaB tree. By a monotonic path, we mean the paths in which $\hat{p}$ never decreases in a node against its parent. We annotate the relevant statistical data, including the average ratio and the number of trees whose ratio is below 95%. By Fig. 2, we can find that, for many BaB trees, all their paths are monotonic, as evidenced by the very narrow distance between the lower and upper quartiles. Even if there are some trees in which non-monotonic paths exist, the number of such trees is not very large in most models. The notable exception is $\texttt{MNIST}_{\texttt{L4}}$, for which there is a considerable number of trees whose monotonic path ratio is relatively low. This could be attributed to

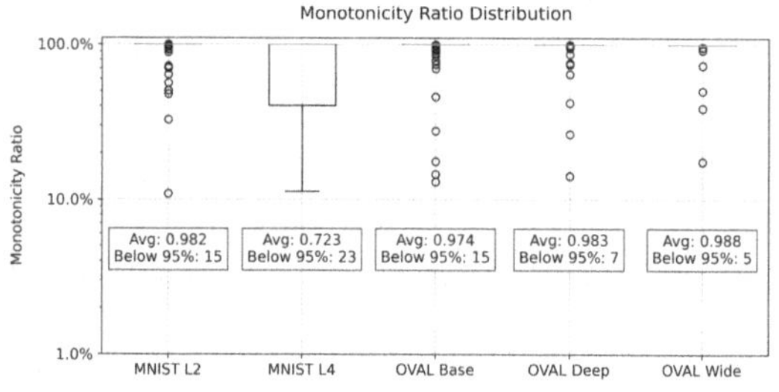

Fig. 2. Distribution of ratio of monotone paths

our way of counting, i.e., as long as there exists a non-monotonic node, we count the path as non-monotonic; because of this, if a non-monotonic node occurs at a location close to the root, it affects all the paths in its sub-trees, so it can make the ratio very low.

Note that the metric used in Fig. 2, i.e., the ratio of monotonic paths, is relatively strong, because monotonicity of the whole path requires that there does not exist even a single pair of nodes that breaks the monotonicity. Therefore, the metric used in Fig. 2 is a relatively strong one, and is subject to the positions of such non-monotonic pairs of tree nodes. In Table 1, we further analyze the impact of these pairs on the whole paths.

- First, the column "Path$^{\texttt{mono}}$" shows the overall ratio of the monotonic paths over all the paths of all the trees in the tasks of each model. This confirms that most of the paths hold monotonicity;
- Second, the column "Pair$^{\texttt{mono}}$" shows how many pairs are non-monotonic, over all the pairs in the trees. We find that, the ratios are all greater than those in "Path$^{\texttt{mono}}$", showing that mostly the non-monotonicity of paths happens, due to some individual pairs in the paths;
- Third, the column "Triple$^{\texttt{mono}}$" records that, among the non-monotonic pairs in "Pair$^{\texttt{mono}}$", how many of them hold that, $\hat{p}$ in the subsequent node after the pair is increased compared to the first node in the pair, namely, this metric implies that how many non-monotonic pairs only happen locally and do not have a significant impact on the whole paths.

The results indicate that, while some BaB implementations may not hold monotonicity, such violations do not happen frequently. Moreover, the impact on the whole path mostly remains local. By this, we proceed to our formulation that deems BaB verification as a search problem.

Table 1. Monotonicity Statistics.

Model	Tree size	Path$^{\texttt{mono}}$	Pair$^{\texttt{mono}}$	Triple$^{\texttt{mono}}$
MNIST$_{\text{L2}}$	163	98.1%	99.8%	69.1%
MNIST$_{\text{L4}}$	2535	72.3%	96.6%	74.7%
OVAL21$_{\text{BASE}}$	896	97.4%	99.7%	95.8%
OVAL21$_{\text{DEEP}}$	366	98.3%	99.8%	97.3%
OVAL21$_{\text{WIDE}}$	877	98.8%	99.9%	99.7%

3.2 Verdict Boundary

We first introduce the notion of verdict boundary in Definition 6. Later, we show the connection between this notion and the objective of BaB-based verification.

Definition 6 (Verdict boundary). Given a BaB tree that has n paths, a *verdict boundary* is an n-tuple $\langle b_1, \dots, b_n \rangle$, where each $b_i \in \mathbb{N}_{\geq 0}$ $(i \in \{1, \dots, n\})$ is called a *boundary point* such that, for each node $\langle \Gamma, \hat{p} \rangle$ in the i-th path, if $|\Gamma| \geq b_i$, then $\hat{p} \geq 0$; otherwise if $|\Gamma| < b_i$, then $\hat{p} < 0$. Specifically, $b_i = 0$ if the root node of the BaB tree is verified; $b_i = K + 1$ (K is the total number of ReLUs) if none of the nodes is verified in the i-th path.

Intuitively, each element b_i in a verdict boundary is a position in a tree path that divides the nodes respectively decided as verified and unverified by approximated verifiers. As $\hat{p}$ is *mostly* monotonic in each path, the nodes preceding

b_i are most likely to be unverified, and the nodes succeeding (including) b_i are most likely to be verified. Example 1 visualizes a verdict boundary in a BaB tree.

Example 1. Figure 3a depicts a BaB tree, in which the verifier assessment $\hat{p}$ of each node is annotated in each node. In this example, the BaB algorithm finally verifies the problem because all the subproblems are verified (i.e., $\hat{p} > 0$ for all the leaf nodes). We depict the verdict boundary in this BaB tree, which is $\langle 3, 3, 2, 3, 3, 2 \rangle$, as illustrated by the blue line.

Recall the objective of BaB in Sect. 2.2. To verify a problem, it needs to exhaustively check all the paths in a BaB tree, until it finds that every path ends with a verified leaf node (in which case, the queue Q used in Algorithm 1 will be empty so it can return true in Line 5). As shown in Fig. 3a, this is equivalent to finding the verdict boundary in a BaB tree, because 1) the verdict boundary covers all the paths; 2) the verdict boundary signifies the shifts from unverified nodes to verified ones, and due to the monotonicity of $\hat{p}$ in each path, the nodes succeeding the boundary point are all verified. Therefore, for verification, the objective of BaB can be deemed to be deciding the verdict boundary in the tree.

Motivation and Benefits for Fast Boundary Mining. We first look at how existing BaB (Algorithm 1) finds the verdict boundary. It essentially performs a *linear search* in each path, i.e., it checks each node one by one along a path, as visualized in Fig. 3a. Note that this way of checking is independent of how Q in Algorithm 1 works. Specifically, regardless of whether Q is *first-in-first-out* or *first-in-last-out*, for a given path, the existing BaB checks the nodes one by one.

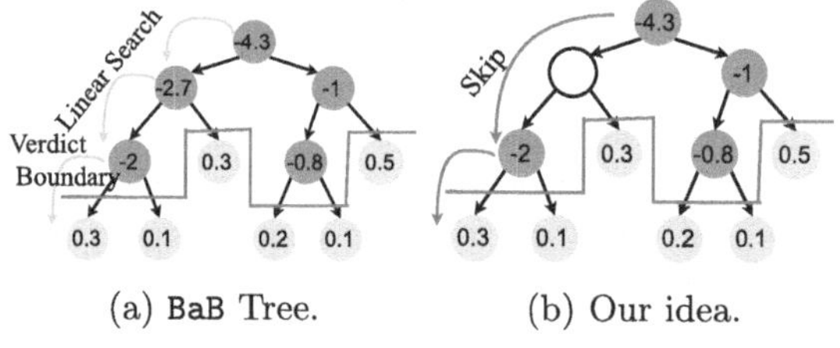

(a) BaB Tree. (b) Our idea.

Fig. 3. Verdict boundary and our idea.

On the other hand, due to the trend of $\hat{p}$ in each path, we can treat each path as a nearly sorted array, in which each element (i.e., each node) has a value $\hat{p}$, and consequently, the problem of deciding the boundary point for a given path can be translated to a *search problem* for the position of *the first positive value* in the array. Note that, to deal with such a problem, linear search, as classic BaB does, is often known as inefficient. Instead, thanks to nearly monotonic trend of $\hat{p}$, we do not need to check the node one by one. For example, Fig. 3b shows how to locate the boundary point by skipping the second node. We can devise more efficient approaches that reduce the number of node visits, hence significantly reducing the number of calls to approximate verifiers for bounds propagation.

4 Our Proposed Approaches

Taking the insights from Sect. 3, in this section, we propose two novel approaches that tackle the problem of deciding the verdict boundary in a BaB tree.

4.1 Exponential Search Approach for Verdict Boundaries

As mentioned in Sect. 3.2, the BaB-based verification can be considered as a problem that aims to find the verdict boundary, and in each path of a BaB tree, finding the boundary point involves a search problem for the position of a specific value 0 in a nearly ascending array. While existing BaB adopts linear search (see Fig. 3a), there are some other methods, such as exponential search [1], that are known to be more efficient than linear search in handling this problem. In this section, we present our proposed approach based on exponential search.

Exponential search, originally proposed in [1], is an algorithm that tackles the search problem in a sorted array. Compared to other search methods, such as binary search, it can outperform if the search target is relatively close to the beginning of the array. In our case, as neural networks typically consist of a large number of neurons, as long as the position of the boundary point is not too deep in a path, this method should be suited for our purpose.

Algorithm Details. Our proposed algorithm is presented in Algorithm 2. It consists of two phases to decide the boundary point for each path: first, it identifies a range that contains the boundary point, by progressively sliding and expanding the range whose size increases exponentially; given such a range, it searches for the exact position of the boundary point by a binary search.

Algorithm 2 uses a queue Q to maintain the paths to be checked, which is initialized to contain Γ only, i.e., the original verification problem. The algorithm starts with a call of the function ExpSearchBaB with the initial Q (Line 2), and then in function ExpSearchBaB, with a ReLU specification Γ (i.e., a node) popped from Q (Line 6), it goes through the two phases of exponential search:

- The first phase (Line 7 – Line 14) aims to identify a range $[i_l, i_r]$ that contains the boundary point, which is initialized to be $[|\Gamma|, K]$ in Line 7. To achieve high efficiency, unlike existing BaB that checks the nodes sequentially, it skips nodes with an exponentially increasing step size (Line 8). For each selected node $\Gamma \wedge a_0 \wedge a_1 \wedge \ldots \wedge a_l$, it applies AppVer to obtain $\hat{p}$ of the node (Line 9): if $\hat{p} < 0$ (i.e., the node is not verified), the lower bound i_l of the range is updated to be the current l (Line 11) and the search proceeds to the next l; otherwise, the upper bound i_r is updated (Line 13), and this phase can be terminated (Line 14), because at this point, i_l identifies an unverified node and i_r identifies a verified node, so the boundary point must be within $[i_l, i_r]$.
- The second phase (Line 19 – Line 24) performs a binary search to exactly find the boundary point. Here, it iteratively checks the node in the middle of $[i_l, i_r]$ (Line 21, 22) to obtain $\hat{p}$, and updates i_l or i_r according to the sign of $\hat{p}$ to further shrink the range. On the termination of this phase, the node identified by i_l is unverified and the node identified by i_r is verified; by Definition 6, i_r can be returned as the boundary point for this path.

After finding the boundary point i_r, Algorithm 2 pushes to Q all the unsolved paths resulted from the path $\Gamma \wedge a_0 \wedge a_1 \wedge \ldots \wedge a_{i_r - |\Gamma|}$ that has just been checked.

Algorithm 2. Our proposed exponential search approach

Require: A neural network N with K neurons, an input specification Φ, an output specification Ψ, an approximated verifier $\texttt{AppVer}(\cdot)$, a ReLU selection heuristic $\mathsf{H}(\cdot)$.
Ensure: A *verdict* $\in \{\mathsf{true}, \mathsf{false}\}$.

1: $\mathrm{Q} \leftarrow \{\top\}$ ▷ initialize Q with the original problem
2: ExpSearchBaB(Q) ▷ start the process

3: **function** ExpSearchBaB(Q)
4: **if** Empty(Q) **then**
5: **return** true ▷ manage to verify the problem
6: $\Gamma \leftarrow$ Pop(Q)
7: $i_l \leftarrow |\Gamma|, i_r \leftarrow K$ ▷ initialize search range $[i_l, i_r]$
8: **for** $l \in \{0, 2^0, \ldots, 2^{\lfloor \log (K-|\Gamma|) \rfloor}, K-|\Gamma|\}$ **do** ▷ exponentially select nodes
9: $\hat{p} \leftarrow \texttt{AppVer}(N, \Phi, \Psi, \Gamma \wedge a_0 \wedge \ldots \wedge a_l)$
where $a_0 \equiv \top$, $a_j \in \mathsf{H}(\Gamma \wedge a_0 \wedge \ldots \wedge a_{j-1})$ for $j \in \{1, \ldots, l\}$
10: **if** $\hat{p} < 0$ **then** ▷ the subproblem is not verified
11: $\begin{cases} \textbf{return } \mathsf{false} & \text{if } l+|\Gamma| = K \\ i_l \leftarrow l+|\Gamma| & \text{otherwise} \end{cases}$ ▷ update i_l or return false
12: **else**
13: $i_r \leftarrow l+|\Gamma|$ ▷ update i_r
14: **break** ▷ the range $[i_l, i_r]$ is decided
15: $i_r \leftarrow$ BinarySearch(Γ, i_l, i_r)
16: **for** $k \in \{1, \ldots, i_r-|\Gamma|\}$ **do**
17: $\mathrm{Q} \leftarrow \mathrm{Q} \cup \{\Gamma \wedge a_0 \wedge \ldots \wedge a_{k-1} \wedge \neg a_k\}$ ▷ add unsolved paths to Q
18: **return** ExpSearchBaB(Q) ▷ recursive call with updated Q

19: **function** BinarySearch(Γ, i_l, i_r)
20: **while** $i_r - i_l > 1$ **do**
21: $m \leftarrow \lceil \frac{i_l+i_r}{2} \rceil$ ▷ take the mid of $[i_l, i_r]$
22: $\hat{p} \leftarrow \texttt{AppVer}(N, \Phi, \Psi, \Gamma \wedge a_0 \wedge \ldots \wedge a_{m-|\Gamma|})$ ▷ obtain $\hat{p}$
23: $\begin{cases} i_l \leftarrow m & \text{if } \hat{p} < 0 \\ i_r \leftarrow m & \text{otherwise} \end{cases}$ ▷ update i_l or i_r accordingly
24: **return** i_r

One such unsolved path can be obtained by concatenating a prefix of the checked path with the negation of the last node, i.e., $\Gamma \wedge a_0 \wedge a_1 \wedge \ldots \wedge a_{k-1} \wedge \neg a_k$, for each $k \in \{1, \ldots, i_r - |\Gamma|\}$, in Line 17. Then, Algorithm 2 recursively calls function ExpSearchBaB with the updated Q to process the subsequent unsolved paths.

Algorithm 2 can be terminated if Q is empty (Line 4), in which case the verdict boundary for each path of the BaB tree has been found, and so , Algorithm 2 can return true, signifying that the problem can be verified (Line 5).

4.2 Gradient-Based Approach for Verdict Boundaries

The exponential search approach in Sect. 4.1 allows skipping boundary-unrelated subproblems (hence avoid redundant calling to approximated verifiers) compared to linear search in classic BaB, however, it may still require a large number of visits of tree nodes before identifying the range that contains the boundary point, as it ignores the quantitative information about the change of $\hat{p}$ of the nodes in a path. To bridge this gap, we propose a *gradient*-based search approach that leverages quantitative information about the ascending rate of nodes, allowing us to identify the verdict boundary with much fewer node visits.

In this approach, by treating the absolute value $|\hat{p}|$ of $\hat{p}$ of each node in a path as the objective function, we can transform the problem of deciding the verdict boundary in that path, into an optimization problem that minimizes $|\hat{p}|$. Specifically, the optimization problem aims to identify the local minimum, namely, the position of the node for which $|\hat{p}| = 0$.

To solve this problem, our approach iteratively estimates the position of the local minimum, by leveraging the *"gradient"* of the nodes in the path. The gradient can be estimated by exploiting the quantitative $\hat{p}$ of the nodes that have been visited, i.e., given two nodes Γ_1 and Γ_2 with verifier assessments $\hat{p}_1$ and $\hat{p}_2$ respectively, we can estimate the gradient by $\frac{\hat{p}_2 - \hat{p}_1}{|\Gamma_2| - |\Gamma_1|}$. While this may not be precise and so our estimated local optimum can be deviated, we continue our search using the updated gradient information obtained by checking the node in the estimated position, until we find the verdict boundary.

Algorithm Details. Our proposed algorithm is presented in Algorithm 3. Similarly to exponential search, Algorithm 3 also consists of two phases to identify the boundary point. First, it identifies a range $[i_l, i_r]$ that contains the boundary point by leveraging the gradient information; after having such a range, the second phase applies binary search to exactly locate the boundary point, similarly to Algorithm 2 .

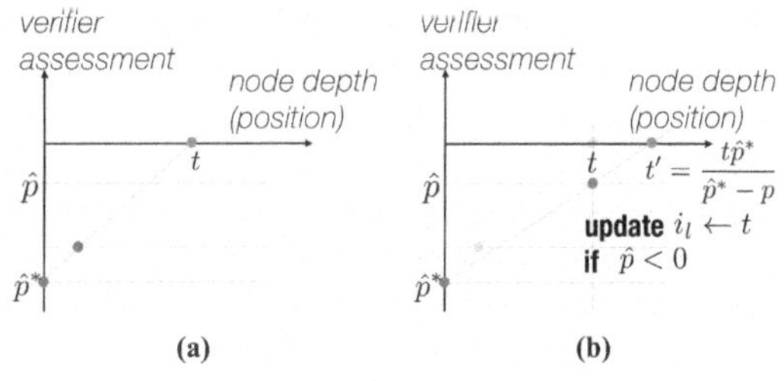

Fig. 4. Gradient-based search approach.

Algorithm 3 uses a queue Q to maintain the paths to be checked. At the beginning of Algorithm 3, it checks the original problem by applying AppVer and obtains its verifier assessment $\hat{p}^*$ (Line 1). If this node is not verified, Algorithm 3 pushes its children into Q (Line 5), and then calls GradSearchBaB with Q to search for the verdict boundary in the BaB tree (Line 6).

The function GradSearchBaB includes the two phases of searching for the boundary point in a specific path. We first elaborate on the first phase (Line 11 – Line 21). This phase involves two `while` loops which iteratively update the upper bound i_r and the lower bound i_l of the range $[i_l, i_r]$ that contains the boundary point, by iteratively checking the position where $\hat{p}$ is estimated to be 0. This process is visualized in Fig. 4, and described as follows:

- In the first loop, t is the estimated position of boundary point, which is computed by taking the minimum between $\lceil \frac{t \cdot \hat{p}^*}{\hat{p}^* - \hat{p}} \rceil$ and K (Line 15), as

Algorithm 3. Our proposed gradient-based search approach

Require: A neural network N with K neurons, an input specification Φ, an output specification Ψ, an approximated verifier $\texttt{AppVer}(\cdot)$, a ReLU selection heuristic $\mathsf{H}(\cdot)$.
Ensure: A *verdict* $\in \{\mathsf{true}, \mathsf{false}\}$.

1: $\hat{p}^* \leftarrow \texttt{AppVer}(N, \Phi, \Psi, \top)$ ▷ check the original problem and record $\hat{p}^*$
2: **if** $\hat{p} > 0$ **then**
3:     **return** true ▷ verify the problem if $\hat{p} > 0$
4: **else**
5:     $\mathrm{Q} \leftarrow \mathrm{Q} \cup \{a\}$, for $a \in \mathsf{H}(\top)$ ▷ add children to Q
6: GradSearchBaB(Q) ▷ start the search process

7: **function** GradSearchBaB(Q)
8:     **if** Empty(Q) **then**
9:         **return** true ▷ manage to verify the problem
10:     $\Gamma \leftarrow \mathrm{Pop}(\mathrm{Q})$
11:     $i_l \leftarrow |\Gamma|, i_r \leftarrow K, t \leftarrow |\Gamma|$ ▷ initialize $[i_l, i_r]$ and estimation t
12:     $\hat{p} \leftarrow \texttt{AppVer}(N, \Phi, \Psi, \Gamma)$ ▷ check the node Γ
13:     **while** $\hat{p} < 0$ **do**
14:         $\begin{cases} \textbf{return}\ \mathsf{false} & \text{if } t = K \\ i_l \leftarrow t & \text{otherwise} \end{cases}$ ▷ update i_l or return false
15:         $t \leftarrow \min\left(\lceil \frac{t \cdot \hat{p}^*}{\hat{p}^* - \hat{p}} \rceil, K\right)$ ▷ estimate t based on updated information
16:         $\hat{p} \leftarrow \texttt{AppVer}(N, \Phi, \Psi, \Gamma \wedge a_0 \wedge \ldots \wedge a_{t-|\Gamma|})$ ▷ check node at t
            where $a_0 \equiv \top$,
                $a_j \in \mathsf{H}(\Gamma \wedge a_0 \wedge \ldots \wedge a_{j-1})$, for $j \in \{1, \ldots, t - |\Gamma|\}$
17:     **while** $\hat{p} > 0$ **do**
18:         $i_r \leftarrow t$ ▷ update i_r if $\hat{p} > 0$ at t
19:         $t \leftarrow \max\left(\lceil \frac{t \cdot \hat{p}^*}{\hat{p}^* - \hat{p}} \rceil, i_l\right)$ ▷ estimate t based on updated information
20:         $\hat{p} \leftarrow \texttt{AppVer}(N, \Phi, \Psi, \Gamma \wedge a_0 \wedge \ldots \wedge a_{t-|\Gamma|})$ ▷ check node t
21:     $i_l \leftarrow t$ ▷ update i_l if $t < i_l$
22:     $i_r \leftarrow$ BinarySearch(Γ, i_l, i_r)
23:     **for** $k \in \{1, \ldots, i_r - |\Gamma|\}$ **do**
24:         $\mathrm{Q} \leftarrow \mathrm{Q} \cup \{\Gamma \wedge a_0 \wedge \ldots \wedge a_{k-1} \wedge \neg a_k\}$ ▷ collect unsolved paths
25:     **return** GradSearchBaB(Q) ▷ recursive call with updated Q

shown in Fig. 4a. This loop applies `AppVer` to check the $\hat{p}$ of the node at t (Line 16), and if $\hat{p}$ is negative, it updates the lower bound i_l to be t (Line 14), and re-estimates t based on the updated $\hat{p}$ of the node at t (Line 15). The loop is terminated if $\hat{p}$ is positive at the estimated position, signifying that i_l cannot be further refined to a greater position where $\hat{p}$ is still negative;

- The second loop is similar to the first loop, but the purpose is to refine i_r to be a smaller position where $\hat{p}$ is still positive. It uses a similar method to estimate the boundary point position t, by taking the maximum between $\lceil \frac{t \cdot \hat{p}^*}{\hat{p}^* - \hat{p}} \rceil$ and i_l (Line 15), as shown in Fig. 4b. This loop applies `AppVer` to check the $\hat{p}$ of the node at t (Line 16), and if $\hat{p}$ is positive, it updates the upper bound i_r to be t (Line 14), and re-estimates t based on the updated $\hat{p}$ of the node at t (Line 15). The loop is terminated if $\hat{p}$ is negative at the estimated position, signifying that i_r cannot be further refined to be a smaller position.

Note that, during the loop, it is possible to encounter the situation that $\hat{p}$ does not monotonically increase as discussed in Sect. 3.1; in this case, as we show that such monotonicity often happens locally, we just skip such a non-monotonic node and use the next one. After the loop, if t is greater than i_l, i_l will be updated to be t to further shrink the range (Line 21). This range $[i_l, i_r]$ then serves as the inputs of the binary search (Line 19) of Algorithm 2 in the second phase to exactly locate the boundary point.

While the second phase (Line 22) of Algorithm 3 also uses binary search, its input range $[i_l, i_r]$ can be much narrower than in Algorithm 2. This is because the exponential search in Algorithm 2 expands the range exponentially, whereas our loops can produce a relatively smaller range. The binary search in Algorithm 3 can be more efficient to locate the boundary.

5 Experimental Evaluation

We present the experimental setup, results, and analysis. Our implementation and data are available at [26].

Benchmarks. We adopt widely-used benchmarks from the neural network verification community [3] and five neural network models relevant to two common datasets MNIST and CIFAR-10 adopted in VNN-COMP series [3].

Table 2. Benchmark details.

#Problem	Network	Architecture	Dataset	#ReLU
100	MNIST_{L2}	2 × 256 linear	MNIST	512
100	MNIST_{L4}	4 × 256 linear	MNIST	1024
100	$\text{OVAL21}_{\text{BASE}}$	2 Conv, 2 linear	CIFAR-10	3172
100	$\text{OVAL21}_{\text{WIDE}}$	2 Conv, 2 linear	CIFAR-10	6244
100	$\text{OVAL21}_{\text{DEEP}}$	4 Conv, 2 linear	CIFAR-10	6756

- For MNIST, we use two fully connected networks, MNIST_{L2} and MNIST_{L4}.
- For CIFAR-10, we adopt $\text{OVAL21}_{\text{BASE}}$, $\text{OVAL21}_{\text{WIDE}}$ and $\text{OVAL21}_{\text{DEEP}}$.

We call each pair that consists of a neural network and a specification to be a verification problem. As shown in Table 2, we have a total of 500 problems that concern the five neural networks and different specifications.

Baseline. To assess BMINER, we compare with existing tools as our baselines:

- $\alpha\beta$-Crown [34] is the winner of VNN-COMP [3] that adopts classic BaB with an approximated verifier that is not monotonic under problem splitting;
- Oliva [41] is a meta-heuristic BaB falsifier that aggressively guides the tree search toward rejecting unsafe verification instances as fast as possible.

Extension of ReLU Selection Strategy. Our approaches adopt the same ReLU selection strategy as baselines to ensure the fairness of comparison. As the ReLU selection strategy is not the primary focus of this work, we make an extension of existing methods to integrate into our framework. Commonly used ReLU selection strategies, such as DeepSplit [14], BaBSR [5] and FSB [8], generally follow a two-step procedure:

(1) each neuron is assigned a score based on its potential abstractionrefinement gain and its estimated impact on the final network output
(2) the neuron with the highest score (Top-1) is selected for splitting.

In our approach, we adopt and extend the state-of-the-art ReLU selection strategy [8]. While Step (1) remains unchanged, we extend Step (2) by selecting the Top-k neurons to split simultaneously, where k corresponds to the number of neurons skipped by our method. This extension allows our verification approach to retain compatibility with existing selection heuristics while improving efficiency through parallel refinement of multiple high-impact neurons.

This extension further inspires the development of novel ReLU selection heuristics incorporating abstractionrefinement prediction mechanisms, which could better complement our BMINER. As designing such strategies is non-trivial, we leave this as future work.

Evaluation Metrics. In our experiments, to compare the performances of different approaches, we apply both the baseline approaches and our proposed approaches BMINER$_\mathsf{E}$, BMINER$_\mathsf{G}$, to all the verification problems. For each problem, we set 1,000 s as the timeout. We adopt the following metrics:

- *Verification result*: It indicates whether an approach can solve a problem (i.e., it returns either true or false for the problem) within the given time budget;
- *Time cost*: In this case, if an approach successfully solves a problem, we record the time taken as an indicator of its efficiency.

Experiment Environment. The experiments were conducted on AWS EC2 instance with 32GB memory and 8-core CPUs.

5.1 Evaluation Results

RQ1 *Are our proposed approaches more efficient than the baseline approach?*

Comparison with Baselines. Table 3 reports the number of verification instances. For certified instances (C), $\alpha\beta$-Crown serves as a strong baseline, certifying more instances than Oliva. Our approaches, BMINER$_\mathsf{E}$ and BMINER$_\mathsf{G}$, consistently surpass Oliva, certifying more instances than it, while matching or slightly exceeding $\alpha\beta$-Crown. This demonstrates the strengths of our approaches. On the other hand, Oliva maintains an advantage in falsification (F), consistently identifying more counterexamples due to its design, which focuses on rapid falsification rather than exhaustive proof.

Table 3. RQ1 – Performance comparison on certified (C) and falsified (F) counts.

Model	Oliva		αβ-Crown		BMiner$_E$		BMiner$_G$	
	C	F	C	F	C	F	C	F
MNIST$_{L2}$	72	7	89	4	89	4	89	7
MNIST$_{L4}$	39	10	51	2	51	2	51	2
OVAL21$_{BASE}$	69	10	83	0	85	1	85	1
OVAL21$_{DEEP}$	53	8	71	0	71	0	76	1
OVAL21$_{WIDE}$	51	9	70	1	70	1	72	1

Efficiency Comparison Relative to αβ-Crown. To further highlight the benefits of our approaches, Table 4 reports the relative change in verification time compared to αβ-Crown. Notably, BMiner$_G$ achieves substantial time savings, with average reductions of 17.0%–29.2% and up to 44.7% in best-case scenarios, thanks to the gradient-based estimation strategy that skips redundant computations. BMiner$_E$ provides a smaller but consistent average improvement of about 4%. In worst-case scenarios, the aggressive search strategy can introduce overhead (up to 16.7%), caused by backtracking when the initial estimation overshoots the verdict boundary (Lines 18–20 in Algorithm 3). Overall, these results demonstrate that, compared to αβ-Crown, our approaches bring an evident improvement in terms of verification efficiency.

Table 4. RQ1 – Average, best, and worst-case time comparison w.r.t. αβ-Crown.

	BMiner$_E$			BMiner$_G$		
	AVG	BC	WC	AVG	BC	WC
MNIST$_{L2}$	-4.5%	-12.9%	+5.6%	-29.2%	-44.7%	+13.0%
MNIST$_{L4}$	-4.7%	-11.5%	+5.1%	-17.9%	-34.2%	+16.7%
OVAL21$_{BASE}$	-4.0%	-13.8%	+4.1%	-17.9%	-35.8%	+8.4%
OVAL21$_{DEEP}$	-3.9%	-13.2%	+5.8%	-18.1%	-34.5%	+8.4%
OVAL21$_{WIDE}$	-4.5%	-10.5%	+3.0%	-17.0%	-26.9%	+5.8%

Impact of Non-monotonicity. Since non-monotonicity does not affect the soundness of our approach, we mainly demonstrate our hypothesis that it does not hinder our performance. We present an analysis of the performance comparison of our approaches for monotonic paths and non-monotonic paths, by which we can see that the impact of non-monotonicity is not significant.

To evaluate the impact of non-monotonicity on the efficiency of our verification strategies, we compare the runtime performance between monotonic and non-monotonic paths across different benchmark networks. We exclude MNIST$_{L2}$ from the results because it does not generate a meaningful number of non-monotonic paths. Specifically, we recorded the execution time and monotonicity status of all analyzed paths. For both monotonic and non-monotonic paths, we computed the time reduction ratio, defined as the running time of linear search divided by the running time of our proposed methods BMiner$_E$ and BMiner$_G$, respectively. We further conduct experiments on MNIST and OVAL21 models.

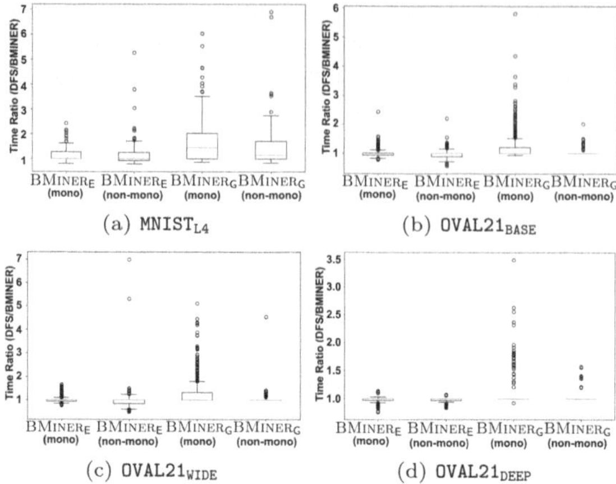

Fig. 5. Comparison of time ratios between monotonic and non-monotonic paths for BMINER$_E$ and BMINER$_G$.

The distribution of time ratio (for comparison, we compared each approach with a naive baseline that explores a BaB tree by depth first search (DFS)) in Fig. 5 shows the consistency between monotonic and non-monotonic paths:

- **Analysis of** BMINER$_E$: Comparing on MNIST$_{L4}$ and OVAL21$_{BASE}$ in Fig. 5a and Fig. 5b, both monotonic and non-monotonic groups exhibit a similar median time ratio, indicating that BMINER$_E$ achieves consistent speedup over DFS regardless of path monotonicity. The interquartile range and outliers are slightly smaller in the non-monotonic group, further supporting the robustness of BMINER$_E$ in handling non-monotonic paths.
- **Analysis of** BMINER$_G$: Comparing on OVAL21$_{WIDE}$ and OVAL21$_{DEEP}$ in Fig. 5c and Fig. 5d, the median time ratio for both groups is around 1.0, indicating that BMINER$_G$ consistently improves efficiency over DFS across both path types. However, the monotonic group exhibits a wider interquartile range and more high-value outliers (some exceeding 5), whereas the non-monotonic group shows a narrower spread with almost no extreme outliers. This suggests that non-monotonicity does not hinder—and may even contribute to—more stable and predictable performance under BMINER$_G$.

In conclusion, this supports our hypothesis that the non-monotonicity of certain paths has little impact on the effectiveness of our techniques.

RQ2 *Which factors affect the performance of our approaches?*

We look into the verification processes of our two approaches to understand the reasons behind performance advantages. To that end, we select 3 problems, and show how our performance advantages (in terms of the number of skipped node visits, compared to $\alpha\beta$-Crown) evolve throughout a verification process.

Our experimental results are shown in Fig. 6. In each sub-figure, y-axis denotes the number of skipped nodes, compared to the hypothetical number

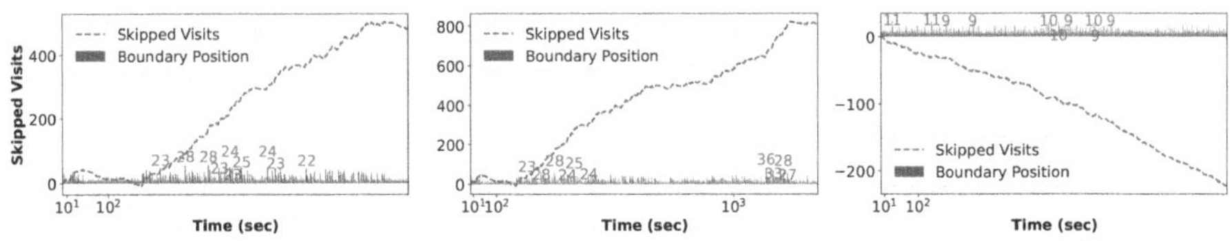

Fig. 6. RQ2 – Our performance advantage throughout verification processes.

of visits by $\alpha\beta$-Crown for covering the same tree nodes. By the results, in the problems where BMINER outperforms $\alpha\beta$-Crown, the number of skipped node visits keeps increasing in most cases. This result implies that, our strategies are indeed helpful to save subproblem solving/visits in verification.

Moreover, we also annotate the position of a boundary point in each path, i.e., the search goal of our approaches. By observing this, we find that our performance advantages stem from the ability of our approach in handling long paths, because when such a long path occurs, the improvement rate will often increase. Over the verification process, there are many paths where the boundary point is small, for which the naive linear search in BaB-baseline can also work well; for this reason, our improvement rate can decrease as the verification process evolves. This can also explain when our approaches cannot perform well, as in the last sub-figure: it happens when there is almost no long path in the BaB tree.

RQ3 *What causes performance differences between* BMINER$_E$ *and* BMINER$_G$*?*

In this RQ, we compare the search strategies used in BMINER$_E$ and BMINER$_G$ to locate the boundary point in a path. We select two verification problems for which BMINER$_G$ outperforms BMINER$_E$, and we look into the number of node visits consumed by BMINER$_E$ and BMINER$_G$ for each path during each verification process, to understand the performance advantage of BMINER$_G$.

Table 5 shows the total number of visits for paths with different lengths. We find that BMINER$_G$ has advantages in handling long paths. For example, in the first problem, for paths with length 16–40, BMINER$_G$ takes an average of 6.3 visits to locate the boundary, while BMINER$_E$ requires 11.2 visits. These results demonstrate the usefulness of our estimation strategy in BMINER$_G$, and explain why BMINER$_G$ can outperform BMINER$_E$. Moreover, by observing the detailed node visits for Phase 1 and Phase 2 in each approach, BMINER$_E$ in Phase 1 can take fewer visits for shorter paths than BMINER$_G$, but it takes more visits for longer paths. In Phase 2, BMINER$_G$ generally requires fewer visits than BMINER$_E$, particularly on long paths (e.g., 1640 in the second problem), as our effective boundary estimation yields a much narrower search range.

6 Related Work

Neural network verification has been extensively studied [2,7,9,16–20,24,25,27–30,35–40,43,44]. Notably, the combined use of BaB [5] with approximated methods is both efficient and complete, and has been adopted by many advanced tools

Table 5. RQ3 – Node visits by BMiner$_E$ and BMiner$_G$. # denotes the number of paths with a specific length. Each value shows the average number of visits.

len.	#	BMiner$_E$			BMiner$_G$			len.	#	BMiner$_E$			BMiner$_G$		
		Ph1	Ph2	Total	Ph1	Ph2	Total			Ph1	Ph2	Total	Ph1	Ph2	Total
0-7	70	4.2	1.4	5.6	5.2	1.9	7.1	0-7	1151	3.2	0.5	3.7	5.5	0.6	6.1
8-15	26	6.0	3.0	9.0	4.5	2.3	6.8	8-15	441	5.9	2.9	8.8	6.6	0.8	7.4
16-40	8	7.1	4.1	11.2	3.3	3.0	6.3	16-40	367	7.0	4.0	11.0	5.3	0.8	6.1

such as $\alpha\beta$-Crown [34]. There has been a rich body of literature [6,8,11,14,42] that aims to improve BaB, but mostly they focus on issues such as splitting strategy [33], selection of ReLU functions [8,14], counterexample-guided falsification [10,13,41]. In contrast to the classical one-by-one processing, our contribution is a new per-path formulation that jointly splits multiple activation functions to speed up BaB-based certification-centric verification.

7 Conclusion and Future Work

This paper introduces BMiner, which reformulates BaB-based verification as verdict boundary mining via exponential and gradient-based searches. BMiner exploits the near-monotonic nature of verification assessments to skip redundant subproblems computations, which outperforms state-of-the-art verification approaches and reduces the average verification time by 17% to 30%, with a maximum time reduction of 44.7%. As future work, we aim to further improve the efficiency by considering GPU parallelization, meta-heuristic falsification, and the order of checking different paths in verdict boundary mining, which can affect the efficiency of our approaches.

Acknowledgements. We thank the anonymous reviewers for their comments and suggestions. This research is supported by the Australian Research Grant DP250101396, the JST BOOST Grant No. JPMJBY24D7 and the JSPS Grant No. JP25K21179.

References

1. Bentley, J.L., Yao, A.C.C.: An almost optimal algorithm for unbounded searching. Inform. Process. Lett. **5**(SLAC-PUB-1679) (1976). https://doi.org/10.1016/0020-0190(76)90071-5
2. Boudardara, F., Boussif, A., Meyer, P.J., Ghazel, M.: A review of abstraction methods toward verifying neural networks. ACM Trans. Embedded Comput. Syst. **23**(4), 1–19 (2024). https://doi.org/10.1145/3617508
3. Brix, C., Bak, S., Liu, C., Johnson, T.T.: 4th int. verification of neural networks competition (vnn-comp 2023): Summary and results. arXiv preprint arXiv:2312.16760 (2023)

4. Bunel, R., et al.: Lagrangian decomposition for neural network verification. In: Conference on Uncertainty in Artificial Intelligence, pp. 370–379. PMLR (2020). http://proceedings.mlr.press/v124/bunel20a.html
5. Bunel, R., Mudigonda, P., Turkaslan, I., Torr, P., Lu, J., Kohli, P.: Branch and bound for piecewise linear neural network verification. J. Mach. Learn. Res. **21**(2020) (2020), https://jmlr.org/papers/v21/19-468.html
6. Cohen, E., Elboher, Y.Y., Barrett, C., Katz, G.: Tighter abstract queries in neural network verification. arXiv preprint arXiv:2210.12871 (2022)
7. Dalrymple, D., et al.: Towards guaranteed safe ai: A framework for ensuring robust and reliable ai systems. arXiv preprint arXiv:2405.06624 (2024)
8. De Palma, A., et al.: Improved branch and bound for neural network verification via lagrangian decomposition. arXiv preprint arXiv:2104.06718 (2021)
9. Ehlers, R.: Formal verification of piece-wise linear feed-forward neural networks. In: D'Souza, D., Narayan Kumar, K. (eds.) ATVA 2017. LNCS, vol. 10482, pp. 269–286. Springer, Cham (2017). https://doi.org/10.1007/978-3-319-68167-2_19
10. Fukuda, K., Zhang, G., Zhang, Z., Sui, Y., Zhao, J.: Adaptive branch-and-bound tree exploration for neural network verification. In: 2025 Design, Automation & Test in Europe Conference (DATE), pp. 1–7 (2025). https://doi.org/10.23919/DATE64628.2025.10992738
11. Geng, C., Le, N., Xu, X., Wang, Z., Gurfinkel, A., Si, X.: Towards reliable neural specifications. In: International Conference on Machine Learning, pp. 11196–11212. PMLR (2023). https://proceedings.mlr.press/v202/geng23a.html
12. Goodfellow, I.J., Shlens, J., Szegedy, C.: Explaining and harnessing adversarial examples. In: 3rd Int. Conf. on Learning Representations (ICLR 2015). Int. Conf. on Learning Representations, ICLR, San Diego, CA, United States (2015). https://doi.org/10.48550/arXiv.1412.6572
13. Guo, X., Wan, W., Zhang, Z., Zhang, M., Song, F., Wen, X.: Eager falsification for accelerating robustness verification of deep neural networks. In: 2021 IEEE 32nd Int. Symp. on Software Reliability Engineering (ISSRE), pp. 345–356. IEEE (2021). https://doi.org/10.1109/ISSRE52982.2021.00044
14. Henriksen, P., Lomuscio, A.: Deepsplit: an efficient splitting method for neural network verification via indirect effect analysis. In: IJCAI, pp. 2549–2555 (2021). https://doi.org/10.24963/ijcai.2021/351
15. Henzinger, T.A., Lukina, A., Schilling, C.: Outside the box: abstraction-based monitoring of neural networks. In: ECAI 2020, pp. 2433–2440. IOS Press (2020). https://doi.org/10.48550/arXiv.1911.09032
16. Huang, P., Wu, H., Yang, Y., Daukantas, I., Wu, M., Zhang, Y., Barrett, C.: Towards efficient verification of quantized neural networks. In: Proceedings of the AAAI Conference on Artificial Intelligence, vol. 38, pp. 21152–21160 (2024). https://doi.org/10.1609/aaai.v38i19.30108
17. Huang, X., Kwiatkowska, M., Wang, S., Wu, M.: Safety verification of deep neural networks. In: Majumdar, R., Kunčak, V. (eds.) CAV 2017. LNCS, vol. 10426, pp. 3–29. Springer, Cham (2017). https://doi.org/10.1007/978-3-319-63387-9_1
18. Isac, O., Zohar, Y., Barrett, C., Katz, G.: Dnn verification, reachability, and the exponential function problem. arXiv preprint arXiv:2305.06064 (2023)
19. Katz, G., Barrett, C., Dill, D.L., Julian, K., Kochenderfer, M.J.: Reluplex: an efficient SMT solver for verifying deep neural networks. In: Majumdar, R., Kunčak, V. (eds.) CAV 2017. LNCS, vol. 10426, pp. 97–117. Springer, Cham (2017). https://doi.org/10.1007/978-3-319-63387-9_5
20. Liu, C., et al.: Algorithms for verifying deep neural networks. Foundat. Trends® Optimizat. **4**(3-4), 244–404 (2021). https://doi.org/10.1561/2400000035

21. Lukina, A., Schilling, C., Henzinger, T.A.: Into the unknown: active monitoring of neural networks. In: Feng, L., Fisman, D. (eds.) RV 2021. LNCS, vol. 12974, pp. 42–61. Springer, Cham (2021). https://doi.org/10.1007/978-3-030-88494-9_3
22. Madry, A., Makelov, A., Schmidt, L., Tsipras, D., Vladu, A.: Towards deep learning models resistant to adversarial attacks. In: 6th Int. Conf. on Learning Representations (ICLR 2018), Vancouver, Canada (2018). https://doi.org/10.48550/arXiv.1706.06083
23. Mandal, U., et al.: Formally verifying deep reinforcement learning controllers with lyapunov barrier certificates. arXiv preprint arXiv:2405.14058 (2024)
24. Mitra, S., et al.: Formal verification techniques for vision-based autonomous systems–a survey. In: Principles of Verification: Cycling the Probabilistic Landscape: Essays Dedicated to Joost-Pieter Katoen on the Occasion of His 60th Birthday, Part III, pp. 89–108. Springer (2024). https://doi.org/10.1007/978-3-031-75778-5_5
25. Ostrovsky, M., Barrett, C., Katz, G.: An abstraction-refinement approach to verifying convolutional neural networks. In: International Symposium on Automated Technology for Verification and Analysis, pp. 391–396. Springer (2022). https://doi.org/10.1007/978-3-031-19992-9_25
26. Ren, J.: Artifact: "mining verdict boundaries for neural network verification". GitHub (2026). https://github.com/jiawei-95/BMiner
27. Shi, Z., Wang, Y., Zhang, H., Kolter, J.Z., Hsieh, C.J.: Efficiently computing local lipschitz constants of neural networks via bound propagation. Adv. Neural Inform. Process. Syst. **35**, 2350–2364 (2022). http://papers.nips.cc/paper_files/paper/2022/hash/0ff54b4ec4f70b3ae12c8621ca8a49f4-Abstract-Conference.html
28. Singh, G., Gehr, T., Mirman, M., Püschel, M., Vechev, M.: Fast and effective robustness certification. Adv. Neural Inform. Process. Syst. **31** (2018). https://proceedings.neurips.cc/paper/2018/hash/f2f446980d8e971ef3da97af089481c3-Abstract.html
29. Singh, G., Gehr, T., Püschel, M., Vechev, M.: An abstract domain for certifying neural networks. ACM Program. Lang. **3**(POPL), 1–30 (2019). https://doi.org/10.1145/3290354
30. Strong, C.A., et al.: Global optimization of objective functions represented by relu networks. Mach. Learn. **112**(10), 3685–3712 (2023). https://doi.org/10.1007/s10994-021-06050-2
31. Tjeng, V., Xiao, K.Y., Tedrake, R.: Evaluating robustness of neural networks with mixed integer programming. In: Int. Conf. on Learning Representations (2018). https://openreview.net/forum?id=HyGIdiRqtm
32. Wang, S., Pei, K., Whitehouse, J., Yang, J., Jana, S.: Efficient formal safety analysis of neural networks. Adv. Neural Inform. Process, Syst. **31** (2018), https://proceedings.neurips.cc/paper/2018/hash/2ecd2bd94734e5dd392d8678bc64cdab-Abstract.html
33. Wang, S., Pei, K., Whitehouse, J., Yang, J., Jana, S.: Formal security analysis of neural networks using symbolic intervals. In: 27th USENIX Security Symp. (USENIX Security 2018), pp. 1599–1614 (2018). https://www.usenix.org/conference/usenixsecurity18/presentation/wang-shiqi
34. Wang, S., et al.: Beta-crown: efficient bound propagation with per-neuron split constraints for neural network robustness verification. Adv. Neural Inform. Process. Syst. **34**, 29909–29921 (2021). https://proceedings.neurips.cc/paper/2021/hash/fac7fead96dafceaf80c1daffeae82a4-Abstract.html

35. Wei, D., Wu, H., Wu, M., Chen, P.Y., Barrett, C., Farchi, E.: Convex bounds on the softmax function with applications to robustness verification. In: International Conference on Artificial Intelligence and Statistics, pp. 6853–6878. PMLR (2023). https://proceedings.mlr.press/v206/wei23c.html
36. Wu, H., et al.: Marabou 2.0: a versatile formal analyzer of neural networks. In: Gurfinkel, A., Ganesh, V. (eds.) Computer Aided Verification. pp. 249–264. Springer Nature Switzerland, Cham (2024). https://doi.org/10.1007/978-3-031-65630-9_13
37. Wu, H., et al.: Toward certified robustness against real-world distribution shifts. In: 2023 IEEE Conference on Secure and Trustworthy Machine Learning (SaTML), pp. 537–553. IEEE (2023). https://doi.org/10.1109/SaTML54575.2023.00042
38. Wu, M., Wu, H., Barrett, C.: Verix: towards verified explainability of deep neural networks. Adv. Neural Inform. Process. Syst. **36** (2024). http://papers.nips.cc/paper_files/paper/2023/hash/46907c2ff9fafd618095161d76461842-Abstract-Conference.html
39. Xie, X., Kersting, K., Neider, D.: Neuro-symbolic verification of deep neural networks. In: Raedt, L.D. (ed.) Proceedings of the Thirty-First International Joint Conference on Artificial Intelligence, IJCAI 2022, pp. 3622–3628. International Joint Conferences on Artificial Intelligence Organization (7 2022). https://doi.org/10.24963/ijcai.2022/503, main Track
40. Zelazny, T., Wu, H., Barrett, C., Katz, G.: On optimizing back-substitution methods for neural network verification. In: 2022 Formal Methods in Computer-Aided Design (FMCAD), pp. 17–26. IEEE (2022). https://doi.org/10.34727/2022/isbn.978-3-85448-053-2_7
41. Zhang, G., et al.: Efficient neural network verification via order leading exploration of branch-and-bound trees. In: 39th European Conference on Object-Oriented Programming (ECOOP 2025), vol. 333, pp. 36:1–36:29 (2025). https://doi.org/10.4230/LIPIcs.ECOOP.2025.36
42. Zhang, H., Shinn, M., Gupta, A., Gurfinkel, A., Le, N., Narodytska, N.: Verification of recurrent neural networks for cognitive tasks via reachability analysis. In: ECAI 2020, pp. 1690–1697. IOS Press (2020). https://doi.org/10.3233/FAIA200281
43. Zhang, R., Sun, J.: Certified robust accuracy of neural networks are bounded due to bayes errors. In: Gurfinkel, A., Ganesh, V. (eds.) Computer Aided Verification. pp. 352–376. Springer Nature Switzerland, Cham (2024). https://doi.org/10.1007/978-3-031-65630-9_18
44. Zhang, Y., Chen, G., Song, F., Sun, J., Dong, J.S.L: Certified quantization strategy synthesis for neural networks. In: Platzer, A., Rozier, K.Y., Pradella, M., Rossi, M. (eds.) FM 2024. LNCS, vol. 14933. Springer, Cham . (2025). https://doi.org/10.1007/978-3-031-71162-6_18

FastLEC: Parallel Datapath Equivalence Checking with Hybrid Engines

Xindi Zhang[2,3], Furong Ye[4], Zhihan Chen[2,3], and Shaowei Cai[1,2,3(✉)]

[1] School of Software, Beihang University, Beijing 100191, China
[2] Key Laboratory of System Software (CAS), ISCAS, Beijing, China
shaoweicai.cs@gmail.com
[3] School of Computer Science and Technology, University of Chinese Academy of Science, Beijing, China
[4] LIACS, Leiden University, Leiden, The Netherlands
f.ye@liacs.leidenuniv.nl

Abstract. Combinational equivalence checking (CEC) remains a challenge EDA task in the formal verification of datapath circuits due to their complex arithmetic structures and the limited capability or scalability of SAT, BDD, and exact-simulation (ES) based techniques when used independently. This work presents FastLEC, a hybrid prover that unifies these three formal reasoning engines and introduces three strategies that substantially enhance verification efficiency. First, a regression-based engine-scheduling heuristic predicts solver effectiveness, enabling more accurate and balanced allocation of computational resources. Second, datapath-structure-aware partitioning strategies, along with a dynamic divide-and-conquer SAT prover, exploit the regularity of arithmetic designs while preserving completeness. Third, the memory overhead of ES is significantly reduced through address-reference-count tracking, and simulation is further accelerated through a GPU-enabled backend. FastLEC is evaluated across 368 datapath circuits. Using 32 CPU cores, it proves 5.07× more circuits than the widely used ABC &cec tool. Compared with the latest best datapath-oriented serial and parallel CEC provers, FastLEC outperforms them by 3.33× and 2.67× in PAR-2 time, demonstrating an improvement of 74 newly solved circuits. With the addition of a single GPU, it achieves a further 4.07× improvement. The prover also demonstrates excellent scalability.

Keywords: Combinational Equivalence Checking · Parallel · Algorithm Scheduling · GPU · Divide-and-Conquer

1 Introduction

Combinational Equivalence Checking (CEC) is a fundamental formal verification technique used to determine whether two combinational netlists compute the same Boolean function. It plays a critical role in modern Electronic Design Automation (EDA) flows and is widely employed during logic synthesis, optimization, and circuit formal verification and testing [11,21,31]. The predominant industrial paradigm is the SAT-sweeping framework; tools such as the &cec engine in Berkeley ABC [23] are based on this methodology.

A. Sampaio and M. Stoelinga (Eds.): FM 2026, LNCS 16556, pp. 89–108, 2026.
https://doi.org/10.1007/978-3-032-26204-2_5

Despite their success on control-oriented logic, SAT-sweeping techniques exhibit inherent limitations on arithmetic-intensive datapath circuits [26]. Structured arithmetic components, e.g., compressor trees, Booth encoders, partial-product networks, create dense XOR dependencies [8,18], while synthesis-induced divergence [12] further disrupts structural matching [14]. Formally, high XOR depth and long carry chains suppress CDCL propagation, yielding branching-sensitive and unstable SAT runtimes. Conversely, BDDs suffer exponential blow-up when wide adder or multiplier cones enlarge the PI-cut, causing decision-diagram widths to exceed memory despite dynamic reordering. Datapath CEC thus remains a class of instances where neither SAT nor BDD provides robust worst-case behavior.

Several recent efforts have proposed enhanced reasoning engines for datapath CEC. Exact simulation (ES) complements SAT by efficiently handling difficult node pairs, enabling hybrid frameworks such as HybridCEC. Parallelization has been explored through CPU/GPU collaboration [3], partitioning [24], while more recent approaches such as pHCEC [6] and PDP-CEC [36] extend HybridCEC using parallel reasoning engines or metis-based [13] graph partitioning. Although these techniques offer substantial improvements, many equivalence pairs in large datapath circuits remain hard to prove, and the scalability of existing methods is still insufficient for increasingly complex industrial designs.

At the core of our approach is the observation that no single reasoning paradigm, whether SAT, BDD, or exact simulation (ES), scales uniformly across all datapath structures. Each engine exhibits complementary strengths that can be exploited if orchestrated intelligently.

Building on this insight, we introduce FastLEC, a unified hybrid CEC framework that integrates SAT solving, BDD reasoning, and ES into a coordinated verification workflow. The framework leverages datapath-aware structural information, adaptive engine scheduling, and resource-conscious simulation strategies to systematically reduce the complexity of hard-to-prove equivalence pairs while preserving soundness and completeness.

Our contributions are as follows:

1. **A hybrid verification framework with predictive engine scheduling.** We integrate SAT solving, exact simulation (ES), and binary decision diagram (BDD) reasoning into a single coordinated CEC framework. A regression-based predictor estimates engine effectiveness on demand, enabling informed and balanced scheduling among heterogeneous solvers and significantly improving resource efficiency.
2. **A memory-efficient, GPU-accelerated exact-simulation backend.** We reduce ES memory consumption through address-reference-count tracking and further accelerate simulation using a GPU-enabled backend, yielding substantial throughput improvements for arithmetic-heavy designs.
3. **A datapath-aware partitioning strategy combined with a parallel divide-and-conquer SAT engine.** By exploiting the structural regularity of arithmetic datapath circuits, we design partitioning techniques tailored to arithmetic topologies and couple them with a parallel SAT-based decomposi-

tion procedure that preserves completeness while reducing the complexity of hard equivalence pairs.

We use a benchmark suite of 368 datapath miters to evaluate FastLEC against the widely used CEC prover ABC &cec [23], the leading datapath-oriented solver HybridCEC [5], and a recent parallel datapath prover PDP-CEC [36]. Under a 32-core configuration, FastLEC solves 74 more instances than the best existing competitor. In terms of PAR-2 performance, it achieves speedups of 7.73×, 3.33×, and 2.67× over ABC &cec, HybridCEC, and PDP-CEC, respectively.

FastLEC also exhibits substantial scalability. The 128-thread configuration verifies 44.88% more instances than the sequential version. Notably, the 32-thread solver attains speedups of 100×, 500×, and 1000× on **33**, **19**, and **14** miters, respectively. Furthermore, augmenting the 32-thread version with a single NVIDIA 4090 GPU provides an additional 4.07× speedup.

2 Preliminaries

2.1 Combinational Equivalence Checking

Combinational Equivalence Checking (CEC) is the task of determining whether two combinational circuits compute the same Boolean function.

Datapath circuits, prevalent in microprocessor design, contain dense arithmetic logic (e.g., multipliers, adders, and multiplexers) with high XOR density, making equivalence checking particularly difficult [7,20]. In this work, circuits are represented as latch-free *And-Inverter Graphs* (AIGs), where each primary input (PI) and gate output is mapped to a Boolean variable. For ease of algorithm design and evaluation, this paper converts the AIG into a more compact XOR-AND (inverter) Graphs (XAGs) representation. The *transitive fan-in cone* (TFI) of a node g includes all nodes that have a path leading to g.

To check equivalence, a *miter* circuit is built by XOR-ing corresponding primary outputs (PO) of the two circuits and OR-ing the results; the circuits are equivalent iff the miter output is identically zero for all inputs.

2.2 Proof Engines

Several complete methods have been employed to verify the output constant-zero property for given miters. Boolean Satisfiability (SAT) solvers [15], Binary Decision Diagram (BDD) compilers [16], Exact Simulation (ES) provers [32], and their hybrid methods [7,16] are among the most commonly used approaches.

SAT Solving. Given Boolean variables $V = \{v_1, \ldots, v_n\}$, a *literal* is a variable or its negation, a *clause* is a disjunction ($\vee$) of literals, and a *Conjunctive Normal Form (CNF)* formula is a conjunction ($\wedge$) of clauses. The satisfiability (SAT) problem asks whether there exists an assignment to V that satisfies the CNF.

AIGs and XAGs can be translated into CNF via Tseitin transformation [29], with miter checking encoded by adding a clause asserting the output is zero.

Modern SAT solvers are based on the conflict-driven clause learning (CDCL) framework, a systematic search algorithm equipped with powerful reasoning techniques. Parallel solving typically follows two paradigms: clause-sharing portfolios, which run diversified solvers concurrently [25,34], and partitioning-based methods like cube-and-conquer [10], which split the CNF into many subproblems solved in parallel—particularly effective for hard combinatorial instances [9].

Exact Simulation *(ES).* It is a method for enumerating all the possible assignments of PI and checking the corresponding output of the miter.

A straightforward approach is to explicitly enumerate all Boolean assignments (0/1) for each primary input (PI). Meanwhile, more efficient methods exploit SIMD-style propagation or probability-based simulation [1,33].

Meanwhile, alternative methods based on floating-point number propagation exploit the principles of Single Instruction, Multiple Data (SIMD) to accelerate the evaluation process. The runtime or memory usage of an ES engine proposed by [33] is exponentially related to the number of PIs N and linearly related to the number of gates.

Binary Decision Diagram *(BDD).* The miter's output function can be encoded as a BDD. If the compiled BDD reduces to the constant-zero terminal, then the two circuits are equivalent. Otherwise, any non-zero path corresponds to a distinguishing input pattern. BDD-based checking is exact and efficient for small or structured circuits, but suffers from exponential growth on datapath logic [16]. CUDD [28] and Sylvan [30] are representative sequential and parallel BDD packages, respectively.

2.3 Standard Sweeping Flow

A typical sweeping flow for CEC is presented in Fig. 1. To check equivalence, a miter is constructed and simplified using logic synthesis [2,16,22], then refined via a sweeping flow [15,16]. The process includes: (1) logic simulation to identify potentially equivalent (PE) node pairs; (2) localized checking of PE pairs using SAT, BDD, or ES; and (3) circuit simplification by merging proven pairs.

Recent work [7] shows that exact simulation (ES) excels on small-input, XOR-heavy cones, complementing SAT. An XOR-density score is used to guide engine selection, improving performance on datapath circuits. This heuristic remains effective in recent parallel datapath CEC solvers [5,36].

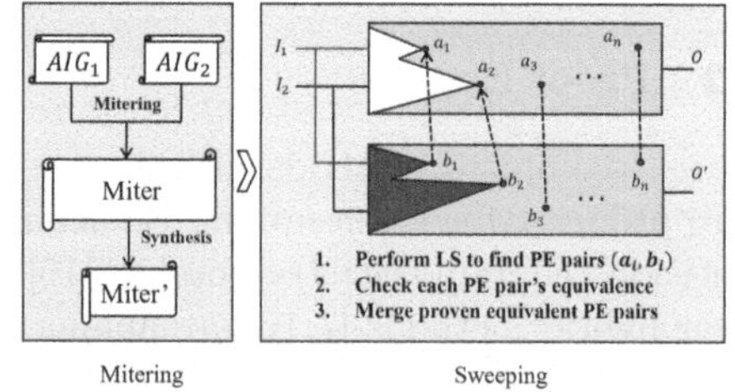

Fig. 1. Overviewing Sweeping Flow.

2.4 Regression Models and Hyperparameter Optimization

The Gradient-boosted regression trees (GBRT) framework has been widely used in *supervised learning* due to its efficiency in capturing non-linear dependencies and supporting heterogeneous features. Its well-known and optimized implementation in XGBOOST [4] has been widely adopted across various applications and has been a top contender in Kaggle competitions. This competitive performance and its mechanism for handling heterogeneous features make XGBoost well-suited for predicting solver performance on structured inputs.

While the performance of machine learning models, including XGBoost, is known to be sensitive to their hyperparameter settings, various hyperparameter optimization techniques have been proposed. Among them, SMAC3 [17], which is based on Bayesian Optimization, has emerged as a standard tool for tuning machine learning models and optimizers such as SAT solvers.

3 Hybrid Scheduling–Based CEC Framework

3.1 Motivation: Absence of a Dominant Reasoning Engine

SAT solvers are generally effective on most miter circuits and large synthesized logic [24]; however, their performance often becomes unstable when handling datapath circuits with strong arithmetic regularities, where arithmetic regularities and dense XOR interactions can lead to severe slowdowns. Table 1 provides empirical evidence that, in such cases, BDD/ES-based approaches consistently outperform SAT. BDDs perform well on small unsynthesized datapath cones but experience abrupt blow-ups once structural complexity increases due to synthesis. ES exhibits far more stable behavior and strong parallel scalability. Table 2 shows that ES can solve many instances that defeat both SAT and BDD with the aid of CPU or GPU parallelism; the techniques will be discussed later.

These complementary yet non-overlapping strengths give rise to the `No-Gold Selection Phenomenon`: no single engine dominates across all datapath structures, motivating an adaptive and instance-aware hybrid scheduling framework.

Table 1. Runtime (s) of SAT, ES, and BDD on multiplier miters.

Miter	SAT	CPU-ES				GPU-ES	BDD
		1T	32T	64T	128T		
8*8	0.45	< 0.01	< 0.01	< 0.01	< 0.01	< 0.01	< 0.01
9*9	2.40	< 0.01	< 0.01	< 0.01	< 0.01	0.01	< 0.01
10*10	22.79	< 0.01	< 0.01	< 0.01	< 0.01	0.01	< 0.01
11*11	85.75	< 0.01	< 0.01	< 0.01	< 0.01	0.01	0.01
12*12	434.88	0.10	< 0.01	< 0.01	< 0.01	0.01	0.66
13*13	NA	1.94	< 0.01	< 0.01	< 0.01	0.01	2.70
14*14	NA	10.23	0.17	< 0.01	< 0.01	0.05	7.53
15*15	NA	52.23	1.58	0.88	0.37	0.29	25.11
16*16	NA	229.37	6.58	4.36	2.41	2.06	85.80
17*17	NA	1029.06	34.42	18.00	9.63	10.57	257.90
18*18	NA	NA	139.64	77.75	39.07	46.93	783.67
19*19	NA	NA	690.54	347.43	174.53	215.89	NA
20*20	NA	NA	2779.61	1535.40	790.08	983.99	NA

Table 2. Runtime comparison on representative hard cases.

Miter	Instance	SAT	GPU-ES	BDD
11*11	17_29_9	27.58	**0.01**	1.24
11*11	14_22_8	35.47	**0.01**	NA
12*12	21_19_10	135.27	**0.01**	10.13
12*12	17_17_0	NA	**0.01**	NA
13*13	13_25_25	121.53	**0.01**	261.73
13*13	15_14_13	883.17	**0.01**	NA
14*14	29_18_2	NA	**0.06**	NA
15*15	17_18_17	NA	**0.28**	NA
16*16	17_29_4	NA	**1.98**	NA
16*16	15_20_4	NA	**2.03**	NA
17*17	17_32_53	NA	**9.61**	NA
18*18	17_12_7	NA	**41.54**	NA

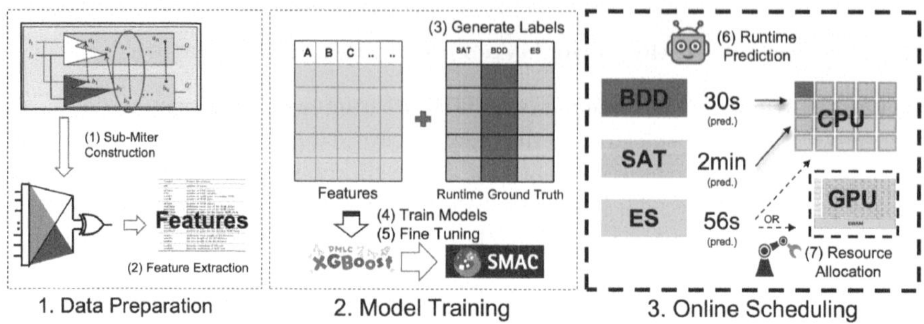

Fig. 2. The Scheduling Framework of FastLEC.

3.2 The Hybrid Scheduling Framework

Overview. Figure 2 overviews the organization of our hybrid-engine scheduling method. The key objective is to exploit the complementary algorithmic strengths of three verification back-ends, SAT, ES, and BDD, while avoiding the pathological behaviors that each engine can exhibit on specific circuit structures. To achieve this, our approach is divided into three stages: *data preparation*, *offline model training*, and *online scheduling*. The offline stages construct a learned cost model that predicts the runtime of each engine on a given sub-miter; the online stage uses these predictions to drive a resource-aware scheduling policy on heterogeneous compute hardware.

Data Features Preparation. Given a miter circuit, we generate a set of *sub-miters* by virtually simulating a sweeping pass. Each target signal pair is isolated by retaining only its fanin cones and aggressively merging topologically preceding nodes, thereby encoding localized equivalence obligations and producing compact subcircuits comparable to those obtained through standard sweeping.

For every sub-miter, we extract a compact feature vector describing its structural, logical, and arithmetic characteristics. The features include:

(i) Structural Indicators such as XAG features (No. 1–4), CNF features (No. 5–7), distances to any input, the output, and their sum (No. 16–22), and fanout degrees (No. 23–24);
(ii) Datapath descriptors capturing XORs (No. 8–15). Two XOR gates are in the same *XOR block* if they are directly connected; In this paper, two gates are in the same *XOR chain* if they are connected by an XOR gate;
(iii) Cost Estimations for SAT and ES, the same method as [7] (No. 25–26). $\texttt{cost\_ES} = 2^{\texttt{num\_PIs}}$; $\texttt{cost\_SAT} = \sum_{b \in \texttt{XOR\_Blocks}} 2^{|b|}$;
(iv) Logic Simulation-based Characteristics (No. 27–32). `Stability` measures the signal bias of each node from random simulation, where signals whose values remain consistent across all simulation rounds are considered maximally stable, while `entropy` quantifies information uncertainty using Shannon entropy (higher values indicate greater uncertainty) (Table 3).

These features collectively form a heterogeneous representation that captures the behaviors most relevant to the three verification engines.

Table 3. Feature List for XAG Analysis (32 features)

No.	Features
1–4	num_PIs, num_gates, num_XOR_gates, num_AND_gates (basic XAG statistics)
5–7	num_CNF_vars, num_CNF_clauses, num_CNF_lits (CNF characteristics)
8–11	min/max/avg/geo_mean_XOR_block (XOR block statistics)
12–15	min/max/avg/geo_mean_XOR_chain (XOR chain statistics)
16–22	max/avg_idis (distance to inputs), max/avg_odis (distance to outputs), max/min/avg_sum_dis (combined distance)
23–24	max/avg_out_degree (out-degree statistics)
25–26	cost_SAT, cost_ES (solver costs estimate heuristic as in [7])
27–29	min/max/avg_stability (stability of simulation)
30–32	min/max/avg_entropy (entropy during simulation)

Table 4. Parameters for XGBoost

Parameter	Min	Max
learning rate	0.01	0.30
max depth	3	10
subsample	0.50	1.00
colsample	0.50	1.00
lambda	0.00	10.00
alpha	0.00	5.00
number of trees	50	500

Model Training. To obtain supervised learning targets, we execute all three engines on the training set under controlled time (20 min) and record their actual runtimes. This produces a ground-truth runtime matrix indexed by (sub-miter, engine), forming a dataset of triples (features, engine, runtime).

We use XGBoost [4] to train regression models that predict the one-core CPU time of SAT and BDD on a given sub-miter. The models are trained on 7,892 sub-miters, obtained by sampling 10% from the original 179,478 PE pairs and discarding instances with num_PIs $\leq$ 22. Each sub-miter is represented by 32 extracted features.

Using 10-fold cross-validation with each fold trained on 80% of the dataset and tested on the remaining 20%, our predictors, i.e., regression models, achieved Mean Squared Errors (MSEs)[1] of 1,462 for SAT and 49,684 for BDD, which are largely inflated by capped runtimes. Restricting to samples with SAT/BDD CPU times below 1,200 s can reduce the MSEs to 463 and 14,550. The pronounced disparity indicates that SAT runtimes are substantially more predictable from the given features, likely reflecting its more stable behavior across instances. Note that all reported results are obtained with the predictors in which hyperparameters were fine-tuned by SMAC3 [17] with a budget of 500 trials (Table 4). This hyperparameter optimization process yielded a 10% (1,601 to 1,462) MSE improvement for SAT and 25% (62,202 to 49,684) MSE improvement for BDD.

Runtime Prediction and Scheduling Method. During verification, each sub-miter is featurized and evaluated by the trained models to estimate its one-core costs for SAT and BDD, denoted as $\hat{t}_{\text{SAT}}$ and $\hat{t}_{\text{BDD}}$, respectively.

Unlike the NP-hard and highly variable SAT/BDD runtimes, ES runtime is deterministically governed by circuit size and input space. It depends linearly on the number of gates and exponentially on the number of primary inputs, and is thus readily predictable. We model it as $\hat{t}_{\text{ES}} = \alpha \cdot \texttt{num\_gates} \cdot 2^{(\texttt{num\_PI}-\beta)}$, with coefficients fitted from the training data.[2]

These runtime predictions are consumed by a scheduling module that distributes the n available cores across engines according to the following principles:

[1] MSE is the average squared error between predictions and true values; both ground-truth and predicted CPU times are capped at 1,200 s.

[2] In the Sect. 4.1 setting, the best-fit parameters are $\alpha = 0.0003$ and $\beta = 23$.

- *Engine feasibility.* SAT is always enabled when $n \geq 2$; Enable ES when $\hat{t}_{\mathsf{ES}}/n \leq \gamma \cdot \mathsf{cutoff}$, where $\gamma = 1.5$[3] serves as a safety margin against prediction error; BDD is enabled only when $\hat{t}_{\mathsf{BDD}} < \varphi \cdot \hat{t}_{\mathsf{SAT}}$, where the safety margin is $\varphi = 0.8$ and at least two threads are available.
- *CPU scheduling.* The BDD engine, when enabled, receives at most one thread[4], while still offering useful complementarity on certain large, unsynthesized circuits. To determine the SAT–ES split, we evaluate the ratio $\rho = \hat{t}_{\mathsf{SAT}}/n \cdot \hat{t}_{\mathsf{ES}}$.[5] Ideally, all resources should be devoted to the engine with the smallest predicted cost; however, due to inherent prediction noise, we introduce a margin that treats runtimes within a bounded range as equivalent.

(i) When $\rho < 1/2$, SAT is predicted to be more promising; thus ES and BDD each receive one thread, and all remaining threads are assigned to SAT;
(ii) When $\rho \in [1/2, 2]$, the engines are potentially complementary, so threads are divided evenly between SAT and ES, with at most one SAT thread reallocated to BDD;
(iii) When $\rho > 2$, ES is predicted to be more promising; thus SAT and BDD each receive one thread, and all remaining threads are assigned to ES.

- *GPU-accelerated scheduling.* GPU-based ES is modeled as 128 CPU threads and enabled when its predicted time exceeds 0.1 s. When enabled, ES is offloaded to the GPU, one CPU thread is assigned to BDD, and the remaining threads to SAT; otherwise, the scheduler reverts to the CPU-only allocation.
- *Special-case handling.* For easy instances $\hat{t}_{\mathsf{ES}}/n \leq 0.1$ s, only ES is enabled. When $n = 1$, only SAT and ES are enabled with the selection heuristic according to $score_{XOR} = cost_{SAT}/cost_{ES}$, same as [7].

By integrating this hybrid engine selection method, a CEC prover named FastLEC has been developed.

Scheduling Never Degrades Correctness. The scheduling policy affects only how engines are invoked, not the semantics of the proof procedures. SAT, BDD, and ES remain individually sound and complete, and scheduling neither alters the miter nor modifies any inference rule. In particular, the parallel SAT

[3] Safety marjins in this paper are tuned in [0.5–2]× which is empirically robust, since variations of this scale fall within normal prediction noise and therefore do not materially affect performance while preventing mis-allocation.

[4] Although Sylvan [30] supports parallel BDD execution, additional threads incur significant memory and synchronization overhead and offer limited speedup; moreover, Sylvan lacks explicit support for external interruption, which motivates restricting the BDD engine to a single thread.

[5] We use the n-thread ES cost as it reflects the expected parallel runtime; when predictions are noisy and speedups non-linear, enabling additional engines yields risk without guaranteed benefit. In contrast, our parallel SAT scheme preserves the root task on its original thread, ensuring that parallelization rarely degrades the single-thread baseline if ignoring memory and system overheads.

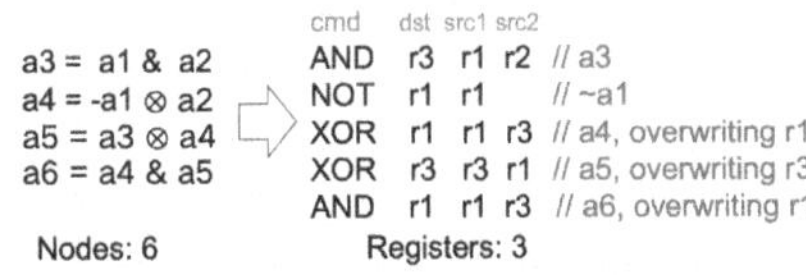

Fig. 3. Instructionalized Example.

Table 5. Compression achieved by instructionalization on multiplier miters.

Multiplier Miter	Vars (Before)	Instrs (After)	Compression Ratio
8×8	1463	61	4.16%
12×12	3647	99	2.71%
16×16	6822	143	2.09%
24×24	16178	234	1.44%
32×32	29553	309	1.04%

engine always retains the unsplit root CNF on its original thread, ensuring that all partitioned tasks are conservative refinements. Thus, mispredictions may impact runtime but cannot compromise soundness or completeness.

3.3 GPU-Accelerated Exact Simulation Engine

Instructionalized ES. To make exhaustive simulation feasible on GPUs, the circuit is compiled into a compact, branch-free instruction stream, with registers aggressively reused under reference-count guidance. This transformation reduces memory footprint to the minimal cut of the circuit rather than its full structural size, enabling GPU execution even for large datapath miters. As illustrated in Fig. 3, reference-count guided register reuse can shrink a six-node circuit to only three registers. This compression is essential because the key limitation of GPU execution is the extremely small amount of on-chip memory available per SM. For larger datapath circuits, the effect becomes even stronger. As reported in Table 5, the number of instructions grows much more slowly than the total gate count, since it is governed by the minimal cut of the circuit rather than by its full structural size.

During simulation, the instruction stream is stored in the constant cache of each SM and all bit-vector registers of a thread reside in shared memory. The kernel then executes a simple sequence of bitwise operations without branching or pointer lookup. CPU-based ES typically propagates 2^{14} input vectors in parallel, as suggested by our preliminary experiments, whereas, in this paper, each GPU thread processes only 32 due to its limited per-thread on-chip memory. Through this combination of structural compression and highly regular parallel execution, exhaustive evaluation becomes efficient even for large multiplier miters that would otherwise overwhelm GPU resources.

Effectiveness. The combination of structural compression and branch-free SIMD execution yields orders-of-magnitude acceleration on large multipliers. As shown in Table 1, a single GPU delivers throughput comparable to roughly one hundred CPU cores. Nevertheless, profiling reveals that the dominant performance bottleneck remains global-memory traffic, indicating that further speedups hinge primarily on reducing memory reads and writes rather than on additional computation parallelism.

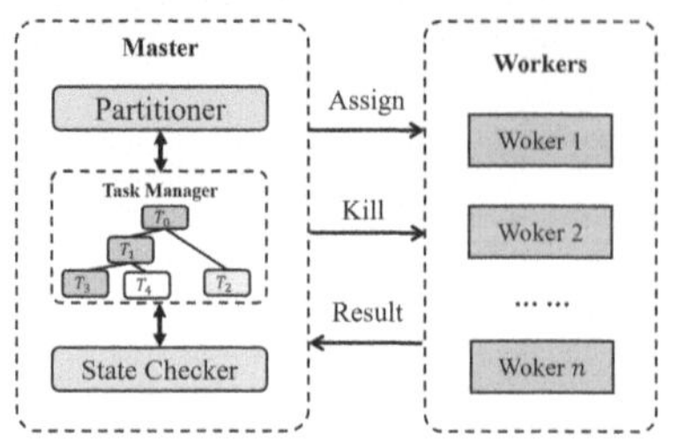

Fig. 4. Parallel SAT Framework for Structure-Aware Partitioning

Algorithm 1: Structural Scoring for Partition

Input: XAG netlist N, a cube L
Output: Variables scores $sc(v)$

$N' \leftarrow$ `propagate_and_preprocess`(N, L);
$chains \leftarrow$ `extract_XOR_Chains`(N');
$\mathtt{dis}_I, \mathtt{dis}_O \leftarrow$ `compute_distance`(N');
for c *in* ***XOR_chains*** **do**
  $S \leftarrow$ `compute_cut_points`(N', c);
  for v *in* c **do**
    $d \leftarrow \alpha \cdot \mathtt{dis}_O[v] + (1 - \alpha) \cdot \mathtt{dis}_I[v] + 1.0$;
    $sc[v] \leftarrow |c|^2 / d$;
    if v *in* S **then** $bump(v)$

$sc \leftarrow$ `score_propagte`$(sc, factor, round)$;
return sc;

3.4 Structure-Aware Parallel SAT Engine

For circuits with a relatively large number of primary inputs, ES-based and BDD-based methods become ineffective, while Boolean SAT solving remains the most viable approach. Therefore, enhancing SAT techniques specifically designed for datapath circuits is of vital importance.

This subsection presents a parallel divide-and-conquer framework, equipped with a structure-aware partitioning heuristic, for efficient equivalence checking of datapath circuits.

Dynamic SAT Partitioning Framework. As illustrated in Fig. 4, FastLEC adopts a classical *master–worker* execution model [35]. Worker threads carry out sub-tasks and report their results, whereas the master handles task generation, dependency tracking, and global state deduction.

- *Partitioner.* Selects an unsplit, long-running, and unsolved sub-task, chooses a splitting variable, and generates two child tasks, which are further simplified through Boolean propagation.
- *Task Manager.* Maintains the task hierarchy (dependencies, liveness, scheduling) and dispatches ready tasks to idle workers, ensuring that no worker receives a task that has already been solved.
- *State Checker.* A `SAT` result immediately certifies non-equivalence and halts the procedure. A sub-task proven `UNSAT` invalidates all its descendants; if all siblings are `UNSAT`, the parent is also marked `UNSAT`, enabling upstream propagation and early pruning of the task tree.

Structural Aware Boolean Partitioning

Observations and Explanations. FastLEC provides a toolkit for analyzing partitioning variables, measuring their actual acceleration effect under specific task states and supporting visual interpretation. Preliminary experiments show that, in XOR-dominated regions, variables nearer the primary outputs are often effective partition points, as they naturally decompose the region into more balanced smaller components.

Since strict XOR-block detection is overly rigid, we approximate such structures using XOR chains, their structural cuts, and the minimum distances to one PI and the PO ($\texttt{dis}_I$, $\texttt{dis}_O$).

Long XOR chains dominate datapath dependencies; fixing a variable near the chain's output cuts the largest portion of this structure. Distance terms approximate this reduction, so high-scoring variables yield the greatest collapse of XOR depth and, therefore, the most effective SAT decomposition.

Partition Heuristics. The task to be split is chosen as the unsolved leaf with the longest runtime, prioritizing computational bottlenecks; each task is represented by a cube (a conjunction of literals). The scoring algorithm for selecting the splitting variable is shown in Algorithm 1. We first extract XOR gates and construct an XOR–AND Graph (XAG), whose node indices can be aligned with CNF variables after redundant intermediate nodes are removed.

Algorithm 1 simplifies the netlist (line 1), extracts XOR chains (line 2), and computes input/output distances (line 3). For each chain c, it identifies structural cut points and increases their scores (lines 5 and 9). Each node receives a score proportional to $|c|^2$ and inversely scaled by its topological distance (line 8), with a bias toward nodes nearer the outputs ($\alpha = 0.6$). Consequently, longer XOR chains contribute more prominently to the scoring.

We refine the variable scores through a propagation mechanism that diffuses scores across the circuit structure. Each variable's score is updated by averaging with its neighboring variables' scores, weighted by a self-influence factor. This process is abstracted in line 10, where factor controls the self-weight and round specifies the number of propagation iterations.

4 Experimental Evaluation

This section evaluates FastLEC against state-of-the-art CEC provers, examines the effectiveness of its core techniques, and provides further analysis.

- FastLEC is *open-sourced* at https://github.com/dezhangxd/fastLEC.

Settings and Competitors. All experiments run on a cluster with 1 TB RAM, two AMD EPYC 9754 CPUs (128 physical cores), and one NVIDIA GeForce RTX 4090 (24G) graphics card under Ubuntu 20.04; We use 32 cores as the default following prior SAT and EC papers [34,36], while also reporting results up to 128 cores. FastLEC is implemented in C++17/C11, relies on XGBoost,

AIGER, and KISSAT, and is compiled with g++ 9.4.0 using -O3. All competing CEC provers are written in C/C++ and compiled in the same environment.

The competitors being considered are:

- **ABC &CEC**: A sequential SAT-sweeping CEC prover in Berkeley-ABC [23], targeting general benchmarks.
- **HYBRIDCEC** [7]: A strong datapath-oriented prover that integrates exact simulation with SAT sweeping, effective on XOR-dense circuits.
- **&SPLITPROVE**: A parallel divide-and-conquer CEC tool built in ABC [23].
- **PHCEC** [5]: Parallelizing HYBRIDCEC by replacing its SAT solver with PRS [34] and parallelizing ES, often achieving super-linear speedups.
- **PDP-CEC** [36]: A parallel datapath prover inspired by HYBRIDCEC, using graph partitioning and solving many cases beyond HYBRIDCEC.

Benchmarks. The benchmarks used in this paper originate from the latest datapath EC track of the Integrated Circuit EDA Elite Challenge[6]. The suite consists of 368 single-output equivalence miters derived from real-world datapath designs, and the full collection is available in the FASTLEC repository. It represents a superset of the benchmarks used in prior studies, such as [7,36], as provided by the competition organizers. For evaluation, the benchmarks are divided into three difficulty classes: easy (127), medium (120), and hard (121).

Metrics. The wall-clock timeout for each prover is set to `1 h`. To evaluate overall performance, we use the penalized average runtime (`PAR2` (in sec.)), a standard metric in formal methods competitions, where each unsolved miter is assigned twice the cutoff time, i.e., 2 h.

4.1 Comparasions with State-of-the-Arts

Table 6 compares FASTLEC with two sequential CEC provers (ABC &CEC and HYBRIDCEC) and three parallel provers (&SPLITPROVE, PDP-CEC, and the parallel configuration of PHCEC).

All parallel tools are evaluated with 32 threads, and a suffix (n`t` or GPU) indicates the number of CPU threads or the use of a GPU. For each solver, we report the number of solved instances (`#Proved`), the PAR2 score (PAR2), and the number of miters solved monolithically (`Mono`).

The results in Table 6 demonstrate the strong performance of FASTLEC. Relative to the best sequential prover, HYBRIDCEC, our solver achieves substantial improvements: FASTLEC is at least 5×, 10×, and 32× faster on 97, 70, and 33 instances, respectively.

FASTLEC also surpasses the latest parallel datapath-oriented CEC prover PDP-CEC presented at DAC'25. Overall, FASTLEC solves 74 more instances (27.82%) than PDP-CEC, and on the most challenging hard-miter category, it

6 https://eda.icisc.cn/.

Table 6. Comparing FASTLEC with Top Sequential and Parallel CEC Provers.

Class	Prover	#Proved	PAR2	Mono	Class	Prover	#Proved	PAR2	Mono
Easy (127)	FASTLEC (32t+GPU)	127	8.66	0	Medium (120)	FASTLEC (32t+GPU)	120	11.88	32
	FASTLEC (32t)	**127**	14.4	0		FASTLEC (32t)	**120**	**62.11**	**32**
	PDP-CEC (32t)	126	71.26	0		PDP-CEC (32t)	88	1930.22	0
	PHCEC (32t)	**127**	**6.15**	0		PHCEC (32t)	87	1981.85	0
	&SPLITPROVE (32t)	23	5897.08	0		&SPLITPROVE (32t)	0	7200.0	0
	HYBRIDCEC	125	115.61	0		HYBRIDCEC	88	2259.1	0
	ABC &CEC	67	3412.27	0		ABC &CEC	0	7200.0	0
Hard (121)	FASTLEC (32t+GPU)	121	401.68	69	All (368)	FASTLEC (32t+GPU)	368	138.94	101
	FASTLEC (32t)	**93**	**2241.89**	**41**		FASTLEC (32t)	**340**	**762.36**	**73**
	PDP-CEC (32t)	52	4203.61	0		PDP-CEC (32t)	266	2036.18	0
	PHCEC (32t)	52	4120.75	0		PHCEC (32t)	266	2003.29	0
	&SPLITPROVE (32t)	0	7200.0	0		&SPLITPROVE (32t)	23	6750.35	0
	HYBRIDCEC	38	5368.01	0		HYBRIDCEC	251	2541.58	0
	ABC &CEC	0	7200.0	0		ABC &CEC	67	5892.82	0

verifies 41 additional miters (78.85%), highlighting its superiority on structurally difficult arithmetic circuits.

For relatively easy instances, the runtime may appear slightly longer. This overhead arises from feature extraction, model prediction, and latency introduced by the engine timeout callback mechanism.

To convey overall trends without listing per-instance results, Fig. 5 presents the cumulative distribution function (CDF) of solved miters, where steeper curves indicate higher efficiency. Hybrid-engine approaches (HYBRIDCEC, PDP-CEC, PHCEC, and FASTLEC) solve many benchmarks quickly, but their progress slows on harder cases when strategy choices or engine capabilities become limiting. Overall, FASTLEC achieves the best combined proving power and scalability among all evaluated solvers. The knee point around 250 s marks the transition from structurally easy equivalence pairs to deep arithmetic cones, where solver performance begins to diverge across engines.

Moreover, with the help of a single GPU, FASTLEC (32t+GPU) achieves the strongest performance across all difficulty levels: it maintains full coverage on Easy and Medium cases while reducing PAR2 by roughly 72.8%, and increases solved Hard instances from 93 to a full 121. Overall, these results show that GPU-accelerated ES effectively cuts deep search costs and substantially strengthens the solver's total proving capacity.

While GPU-based ES can yield substantial acceleration, its efficiency is mainly bounded by GPU-side parallelism and memory bandwidth. In particular, throughput depends on the available thread-level parallelism and clock frequency; the circuit's maximum cut determines the register footprint required by ES; and the total gate count affects how often intermediate states must be copied or materialized. Since GPU ES is fundamentally memory-access intensive, memory traffic typically becomes the dominant bottleneck.

4.2 Speedup Analysis for *FastLEC*

Speedup is an important metric for evaluating the scalability of a parallel algorithm. The *t-thread speedup* for a parallel algorithm is defined as the single-core runtime $\eta(1)$ divided by the t multi-core runtime $\eta(t)$.

Table 7 presents the performance of FastLEC across various core configurations, including 1, 2, 4, 8, 16, 32, 64, and 128 cores. Beside arithmetic mean PAR2 speedup (`Mean`), we also provide the maximum (`Max`), minimum (`Min`), and geometric mean (`Geo`) of the speedup for each category. Noting that the significant improvement in the 2-threading speedup column, which can be attributed to the introduction of the portfolio approach. This strategy effectively assigns hard-to-prove pairs to the most suitable engine, leading to enhanced performance. Thus, we should focus more on the PAR2 and Geo metric.

From the CDF plot in Fig. 6, we observe that FastLEC demonstrates strong speedup performance. As complexity increases, the PAR2 score decreases more significantly. Meanwhile, FastLEC exhibits substantial enhancement with the deployment of more than 8 CPU cores.

4.3 Effectiveness of Engine Scheduling

To assess the effectiveness of our scheduling engine, we evaluate two FastLEC variants: V_1 (only selection, no scheduling), which replaces the scheduling policy with the heuristic used in HybridCEC/pHCEC/PDP-CEC, and V_2 (poor scheduling strategy), a basic portfolio that splits threads evenly between ES and SAT and shares 1 thread from SAT to BDD. The 32-thread results are summarized in Table 8. #P denotes #Proved; Δ denotes the change.

The scheduling mechanism significantly improves performance, particularly on harder instances, by selecting the appropriate engine and distributing resources effectively. On easy cases, however, its overhead becomes noticeable,

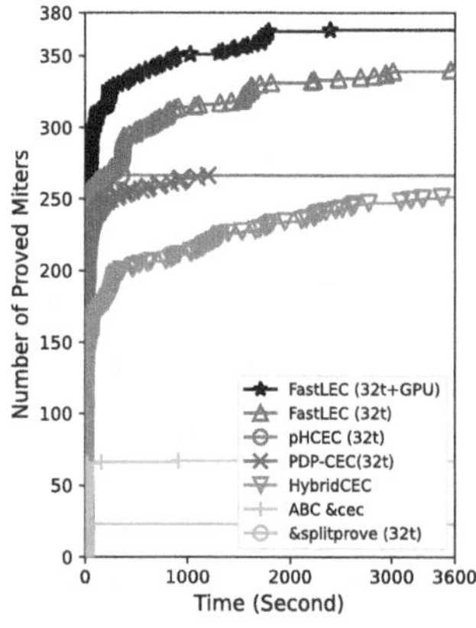

Fig. 5. Comparing with SOTA.

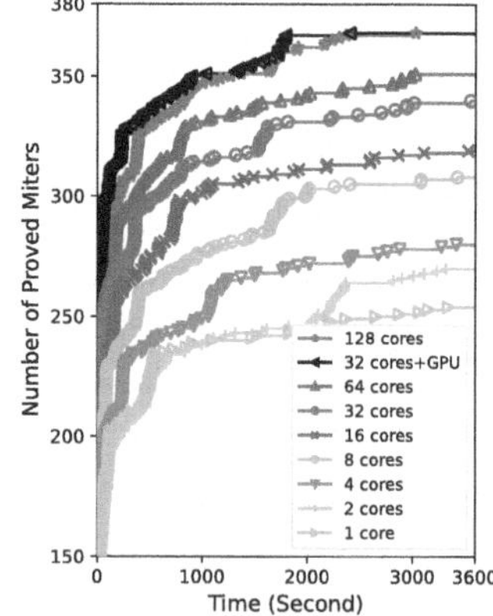

Fig. 6. With different resources.

Table 7. Performance of FastLEC under various CPU cores

Class	Metric	1t	2t	4t	8t	16t	32t	64t	128t
Easy (127)	# Proved	127	127	127	127	127	127	127	127
	PAR2	14.47	27.40	15.15	14.52	13.89	14.40	13.57	13.00
	Max	1.00	1.15	1.27	1.26	1.37	1.44	1.61	1.59
	Min	1.00	0.03	0.30	0.33	0.36	0.42	0.48	0.52
	Mean	1.00	0.53	0.96	1.00	1.04	1.01	1.07	1.11
	Geo	1.00	0.21	0.46	0.47	0.53	0.58	0.69	0.80
Medium (120)	# Proved	88	104	108	120	120	120	120	120
	PAR2	2042.67	1370.06	992.19	270.87	123.05	62.11	33.43	18.55
	Max	1.00	1.42	2.31	6.43	13.69	25.60	45.66	80.87
	Min	1.00	0.07	0.58	0.64	0.74	0.87	1.12	1.16
	Mean	1.00	1.49	2.06	7.54	16.60	32.89	61.10	110.12
	Geo	1.00	0.59	1.33	2.46	3.79	5.14	6.87	8.97
Hard (121)	# Proved	39	39	45	61	72	93	104	121
	PAR2	5208.29	5235.80	4838.12	3972.17	3338.35	2241.89	1551.44	537.12
	Max	1.00	1.08	2.11	6.22	12.58	24.01	46.31	85.80
	Min	1.00	0.21	1.12	1.28	1.32	1.38	1.47	1.44
	Mean	1.00	0.99	1.08	1.31	1.56	2.32	3.36	9.70
	Geo	1.00	0.83	1.68	3.27	5.13	7.16	8.97	11.57
ALL (368)	# Proved	254	270	280	308	319	340	351	368
	PAR2	2383.59	2177.77	1919.56	1399.40	1142.59	762.36	525.71	187.15
	Max	1.00	1.42	2.31	6.43	13.69	25.60	46.31	85.80
	Min	1.00	0.03	0.30	0.33	0.36	0.42	0.48	0.52
	Mean	1.00	1.09	1.24	1.70	2.09	3.13	4.53	12.74
	Geo	1.00	0.37	0.81	1.12	1.49	1.83	2.28	2.79

and V_1 achieves lower PAR2. For easy classes, the portfolio approach (V_2) performs well, even better than FastLEC, because SAT, BDD, and ES offer strong complementarity, and engine choice dominates runtime. For hard instances, both engine selection and resource allocation are critical, and the scheduling method enables FastLEC to outperform both variants.

4.4 Effectiveness of Structure-Aware SAT Partitioning

To obtain a clean measurement of SAT scalability, ES and BDD are disabled, and only the SAT engine is evaluated under the structure aware partitioning framework. We select ten XOR intensive sub-mitters that $\hat{t}_{\mathsf{SAT}} < \hat{t}_{\mathsf{BDD}}$ and the 1-thread runtime for SAT $t^{1t}_{SAT} > 500$ s to avoid confounding influence. Table 9 reports the averaged PAR2 scores and speedup (arithmetic mean) over thread

Table 8. Performance of the two variants of FastLEC.

Prover	Easy (127)		Medium (120)		Hard (121)		All (368)	
	#P (Δ)	PAR2 (Δ)	#P (Δ)	PAR2 (Δ)	#P (Δ)	PAR2 (Δ)	#P (Δ)	PAR2 (Δ)
FastLEC (32t)	127	14.40	120	62.11	93	2241.89	340	762.36
V_1(32t)	127 (0)	5.35 (−62.85%)	88 (−32)	1927.55 (3003.68%)	52 (−41)	4179.91 (86.45%)	267 (−73)	2004.77 (162.97%)
V_2(32t)	127 (0)	15.33 (6.45%)	120 (0)	120.63 (94.24%)	81 (−12)	2999.52 (33.79%)	328 (−12)	1030.88 (35.22%)

counts from 1 to 128, revealing the intrinsic asymptotic behavior of the SAT component and confirming its monotonic scalability.

Table 9. Performance Analysis for the Structure-Aware Partitioning SAT Solver

ID	num_vars	1t	2t	4t	8t	16t	32t	64t	128t
1	1349	632.28	415	227.49	116.56	60.16	50.75	33.9	18.84
2	1359	593.96	446.78	234.96	123.55	62.09	73.28	28.68	17.64
3	1364	534.04	303.7	181.73	106.84	55.68	64.06	34.97	21.94
4	1594	–	3188.45	1630.19	792.21	480.34	310.77	188.99	87.86
5	1603	–	–	1449.07	924.43	582.93	343.54	199.89	131.81
6	1603	–	2856.8	1358.31	892.7	605.84	385.9	143.43	101.94
7	1842	–	–	–	–	–	–	1130.47	567.04
8	2287	2278.79	1732.17	999.92	464.62	212.59	146.11	94.27	31.18
9	2973	–	–	–	–	–	–	2108.05	1394.81
10	3005	–	3152.65	1775.62	698.1	400.07	219.2	128.74	101.73
PAR2		4723.91	3369.55	2225.73	1851.9	1685.97	1599.36	409.14	247.48
Geo Mean		3022.69	2004.15	1111.14	665.00	416.09	332.05	148.82	85.79
Speedup(PAR2)		–	1.40x	2.12x	2.55x	2.80x	2.95x	11.55x	19.09x
Speedup(Geo)		–	1.51x	2.72x	4.55x	7.26x	9.10x	20.31x	35.23x

4.5 Feature Contribution to the Prediction

We present in Fig. 7 each feature's marginal contributions to the models' prediction using the SHAP package [19], which explains the output of machine learning models based on the classic Shapley values [27] from game theory. Shapley values fairly attribute credit to individual features for their contributions to the model's overall prediction. Computing exact Shapley values can be computationally intensive. We refer readers to the previous work [19] for detailed definitions and implementations of Shapley values. Figure 7 presents the SHAP values of the top 9 features that most influence the prediction of the regression model, highlighting the most important properties of miters.

The prediction models for SAT and BDD performance share only three common features as shown in Fig. 7, including `max_out_degree`, `num_XOR_gates`,

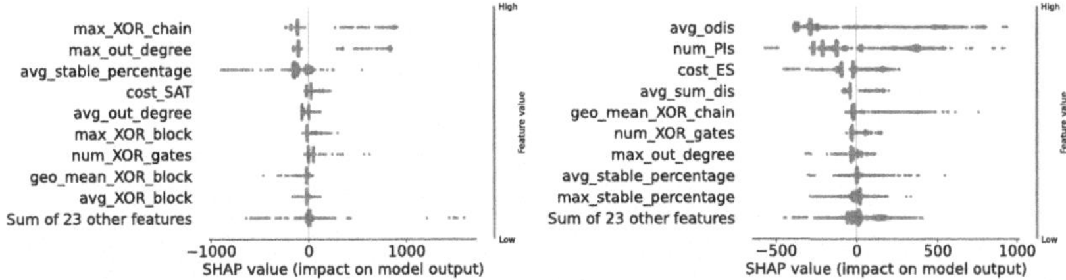

Fig. 7. The left and right panels depict results for SAT and BDD, respectively. Each dot represents the SHAP value of a feature for one sample, with color indicating its original value. Positive SHAP values contribute to an increase in the predicted runtime.

and `avg_stable_percentage`. For SAT, `max_XOR_chain`, `max_out_degree`, and `avg_stable_percentage` emerge as the most influential predictors. This is consistent with the operational principles of CDCL solving, where shorter XOR dependencies and easier structural elements facilitate localized propagation and effective conflict-driven learning, thereby reducing search divergence.

For BDDs, the leading contributors are `avg_odis`, `num_PIs`, and `cost_ES`. These features characterize the global connectivity that drives decision diagram growth. Higher `avg_odis` reflects stronger inter-node interactions that enlarge intermediate BDDs, while `num_PIs` determines the dimensionality of the decision space and `cost_ES` serves as a proxy for the underlying structural complexity. Unlike SAT, whose behavior is shaped largely by local conflict reasoning, BDD performance is driven by global structural dependencies, often leading to significant variation in diagram size and runtime.

5 Conclusion

We presented FastLEC, a learned, hybrid CEC framework that coordinates SAT, BDD, and CPU/GPU ES through predictive scheduling and datapath-aware decomposition. The resulting prover achieves substantial gains over existing sequential and parallel tools, with marked improvements in scalability and coverage. Looking forward, we plan to extend FastLEC toward distributed, multi-node verification, enabling heterogeneous engines to cooperate at cluster scale for even larger industrial datapath designs.

Acknowledgement. This work is supported by NSFC 62532014 and NSFC 62502507.

References

1. Agrawal, V.D., Lee, D.: Characteristic polynomial method for verification and test of combinational circuits. In: Proceedings of 9th International Conference on VLSI Design, pp. 341–342. IEEE (1996)

2. Bjesse, P., Boralv, A.: Dag-aware circuit compression for formal verification. In: IEEE/ACM International Conference on Computer Aided Design, 2004, ICCAD-2004, pp. 42–49. IEEE (2004)
3. Chatterjee, D., Bertacco, V.: EQUIPE: parallel equivalence checking with GP-GPUs. In: 2010 IEEE International Conference on Computer Design, pp. 486–493. IEEE (2010)
4. Chen, T., Guestrin, C.: XGBoost: a scalable tree boosting system. In: Proceedings of the 22nd ACM SIGKDD International Conference on Knowledge Discovery and Data Mining, pp. 785–794 (2016)
5. Chen, Z., Zhang, X., Qian, Y., Cai, S.: Datapath combinational equivalence checking with hybrid sweeping engines and parallelization. arXiv preprint arXiv:2501.14740 (2024)
6. Chen, Z., Zhang, X., Qian, Y., Cai, S.: Datapath combinational equivalence checking with hybrid sweeping engines and parallelization. ACM Trans. Des. Autom. Electron. Syst. **31**(1), 1–27 (2025)
7. Chen, Z., Zhang, X., Qian, Y., Xu, Q., Cai, S.: Integrating exact simulation into sweeping for datapath combinational equivalence checking. In: 2023 IEEE/ACM International Conference on Computer Aided Design (ICCAD), pp. 1–9. IEEE (2023)
8. Chowdhary, A., Kale, S., Saripella, P.K., Sehgal, N.K., Gupta, R.K.: Extraction of functional regularity in datapath circuits. IEEE Trans. Comput. Aided Des. Integr. Circuits Syst. **18**(9), 1279–1296 (1999)
9. Heule, M.J.H., Kullmann, O., Marek, V.W.: Solving and verifying the Boolean Pythagorean triples problem via cube-and-conquer. In: Creignou, N., Le Berre, D. (eds.) SAT 2016. LNCS, vol. 9710, pp. 228–245. Springer, Cham (2016). https://doi.org/10.1007/978-3-319-40970-2_15
10. Heule, M.J.H., Kullmann, O., Wieringa, S., Biere, A.: Cube and conquer: guiding CDCL SAT solvers by lookaheads. In: Eder, K., Lourenço, J., Shehory, O. (eds.) HVC 2011. LNCS, vol. 7261, pp. 50–65. Springer, Heidelberg (2012). https://doi.org/10.1007/978-3-642-34188-5_8
11. Jarratt, T., Eckert, C.M., Caldwell, N.H., Clarkson, P.J.: Engineering change: an overview and perspective on the literature. Res. Eng. Design **22**, 103–124 (2011)
12. Kamaraju, M., Kishore, K.L., Tilak, A.: Power optimized ALU for efficient datapath. Int. J. Comput. Appl. **11**(11), 39–43 (2010)
13. Karypis, G., Kumar, V.: Metis: A software package for partitioning unstructured graphs, partitioning meshes, and computing fill-reducing orderings of sparse matrices (1997)
14. Kaufmann, D., Biere, A., Kauers, M.: Incremental column-wise verification of arithmetic circuits using computer algebra. Formal Methods Syst. Des. **56**(1), 22–54 (2020)
15. Kuehlmann, A.: Dynamic transition relation simplification for bounded property checking. In: IEEE/ACM International Conference on Computer Aided Design, 2004. ICCAD-2004, pp. 50–57. IEEE (2004)
16. Kuehlmann, A., Paruthi, V., Krohm, F., Ganai, M.K.: Robust boolean reasoning for equivalence checking and functional property verification. IEEE Trans. Comput. Aided Des. Integr. Circuits Syst. **21**(12), 1377–1394 (2002)
17. Lindauer, M., et al.: SMAC3: a versatile Bayesian optimization package for hyperparameter optimization. J. Mach. Learn. Res. **23**(54), 1–9 (2022). http://jmlr.org/papers/v23/21-0888.html
18. Long, J., Brayton, R.K., Case, M.: LEC: learning-driven data-path equivalence checking. In: Program Proceedings, p. 9 (2013)

19. Lundberg, S.M., et al.: From local explanations to global understanding with explainable AI for trees. Nat. Mach. Intell. **2**(1), 56–67 (2020)
20. Lv, J., Kalla, P.: Formal verification of Galois field multipliers using computer algebra techniques. In: 2012 25th International Conference on VLSI Design, pp. 388–393. IEEE (2012)
21. Mishchenko, A., Case, M., Brayton, R., Jang, S.: Scalable and scalably-verifiable sequential synthesis. In: 2008 IEEE/ACM International Conference on Computer-Aided Design, pp. 234–241. IEEE (2008)
22. Mishchenko, A., Chatterjee, S., Jiang, R., Brayton, R.K.: FRAIGs: a unifying representation for logic synthesis and verification. Technical report, ERL Technical Report (2005)
23. Mishchenko, A., et al.: ABC: a system for sequential synthesis and verification **17** (2007). http://www.eecs.berkeley.edu/alanmi/abc
24. Possani, V.N., Mishchenko, A., Ribas, R.P., Reis, A.I.: Parallel combinational equivalence checking. IEEE Trans. Comput. Aided Des. Integr. Circuits Syst. **39**(10), 3081–3092 (2019)
25. Schreiber, D., Sanders, P.: MallobSat:: scalable sat solving by clause sharing. J. Artif. Intell. Res. **80** (2024)
26. Seger, C.-J.H.: Formal verification of complex data paths: an industrial experience. In: Huisman, M., Păsăreanu, C., Zhan, N. (eds.) FM 2021. LNCS, vol. 13047, pp. 697–716. Springer, Cham (2021). https://doi.org/10.1007/978-3-030-90870-6_38
27. Shapley, L.S., et al.: A value for n-person games (1953)
28. Somenzi, F.: CUDD: CU decision diagram package release 2.3. 0. University of Colorado at Boulder **621** (1998)
29. Tseitin, G.S.: On the complexity of derivation in propositional calculus. In: Siekmann, J.H., Wrightson, G. (eds.) Automation of Reasoning: 2: Classical Papers on Computational Logic 1967–1970, pp. 466–483. Springer, Heidelberg (1983). https://doi.org/10.1007/978-3-642-81955-1_28d
30. van Dijk, T., van de Pol, J.: Sylvan: multi-core decision diagrams. In: Baier, C., Tinelli, C. (eds.) TACAS 2015. LNCS, vol. 9035, pp. 677–691. Springer, Heidelberg (2015). https://doi.org/10.1007/978-3-662-46681-0_60
31. Vasicek, Z.: Relaxed equivalence checking: a new challenge in logic synthesis. In: 2017 IEEE 20th International Symposium on Design and Diagnostics of Electronic Circuits & Systems (DDECS), pp. 1–6. IEEE (2017)
32. Wu, S.C., Wang, C.Y., Chen, Y.C.: Novel probabilistic combinational equivalence checking. IEEE Trans. Very Large Scale Integr. (VLSI) Syst. **16**(4), 365–375 (2008)
33. Wu, S.C., Wang, C.Y., Hsieh, J.A.: The potential and limitation of probability-based combinational equivalence checking. In: 2006 15th Asian Test Symposium, pp. 103–108. IEEE (2006)
34. Zhang, X., Chen, Z., Cai, S.: Parkissat: random shuffle based and pre-processing extended parallel solvers with clause sharing. In: SAT COMPETITION 2022, p. 51 (2022)
35. Zhao, M., Cai, S., Qian, Y.: Distributed SMT solving based on dynamic variable-level partitioning. In: Gurfinkel, A., Ganesh, V. (eds.) Computer Aided Verification - 36th International Conference, CAV 2024, Montreal, QC, Canada, 24–27 July 2024, Proceedings, Part I. LNCS, vol. 14681, pp. 68–88. Springer (2024). https://doi.org/10.1007/978-3-031-65627-9_4
36. Zhou, S., Zhang, W., Zhang, X., Jiang, Z., Cai, S., You, H.: DPCEC: a dynamic partitioning combinational equivalence checking parallel engine. In: 2025 62th ACM/IEEE Design Automation Conference (DAC), pp. 1–6. IEEE (2025)

Towards Proving Liveness on Weak Memory

Lara Bargmann(✉) and Heike Wehrheim

Carl von Ossietzky Universität Oldenburg, Oldenburg, Germany
{lara.bargmann,heike.wehrheim}@uol.de

Abstract. Reasoning about concurrent programs executed on weak memory models is an inherently complex task. So far, existing proof calculi for weak memory models only cover *safety* properties. In this paper, we provide the first proof calculus for reasoning about *liveness*. Our proof calculus is based on Manna and Pnueli's proof rules for response under weak fairness, formulated in linear temporal logic. Our extension includes the incorporation of *memory fairness* into rules as well as the usage of *ranking functions* defined over weak memory state. We have applied our reasoning technique to the Ticket lock algorithm and have proved it to guarantee starvation freedom under memory models Release-Acquire and Strong Coherence for any number of concurrent threads.

Keywords: concurrency · weak memory models · liveness · proof calculus

1 Introduction

Verification of concurrent programs is inherently complex due to the fine-grained interleavings of program steps. This complexity is further increased when *weak memory models* of multiprocessor hardware architectures or modern programming languages need to be taken into account. As existing reasoning techniques often assume *sequential consistency* (SC, [23]), they cannot directly be applied in a setting with weak memory.

Recent years have thus seen numerous approaches transferring verification techniques for concurrent programs to weak memory models. These approaches – automatic and deductive – almost exclusively concentrate on *safety* proofs. Program termination or more generally *liveness* has only recently been considered when studying *fairness* in weak memory: Both Lahav et al. [21] and Abdulla et al. [1,2] provide notions of fairness for weak memory that specifically incorporate effects arising in weak memory models.

Here, we develop the first *proof calculus* for reasoning about liveness properties of concurrent programs on weak memory models. More specifically, we start

Bargmann and Wehrheim are supported by the German Research Council DFG (project no. 467386514).

A. Sampaio and M. Stoelinga (Eds.): FM 2026, LNCS 16556, pp. 109–129, 2026.
https://doi.org/10.1007/978-3-032-26204-2_6

with Manna and Pnueli's (MP's) proof rules for response properties specified in linear temporal logic (LTL). These rules involve a notion of (weak) fairness with respect to program steps. Our first extension of the rules is the incorporation of Lahav et al.'s [21] notion of *memory fairness*. In particular, we allow for giving memory model internal steps as "helpful transitions" (in Manna and Pnueli terminology) to be treated fairly. Our second extension is the usage of *ranking functions* defined over weak memory state. Ranking functions are typically employed in liveness or termination proofs to measure the distance to a target (e.g., end of program).

values	$v \in \mathsf{Val} = \{0, 1, \ldots\}$	*locations*	$x, y \in \mathsf{Loc} = \{\mathtt{x}, \mathtt{y}, \ldots\}$
local registers	$a \in \mathsf{Reg} = \{\mathsf{a}, \mathsf{b}, \ldots\}$	*thread identifiers*	$\tau \in \mathsf{Tid} = \{\mathtt{T}_0, \mathtt{T}_1, \ldots\}$
program counters	$l \in \mathsf{PC} = \{\mathtt{l}_0, \mathtt{l}_1, \mathtt{m}_0, \ldots\}$		

$$
\begin{aligned}
e &::= a \mid v \mid e+e \mid e=e \mid e>e \mid \neg e \mid e \wedge e \mid e \vee e \mid \ldots \\
c &::= a := e \mid \mathsf{STORE}(x, e) \mid a := \mathsf{LOAD}(x) \mid a := \mathsf{FADD}(x, e) \\
C &::= l : \mathsf{SKIP} \mid l : c \mid C \,;\, C \mid l : \mathsf{if}\ e\ \mathsf{then}\ C\ \mathsf{else}\ C \mid l : \mathsf{while}\ e\ \mathsf{do}\ C
\end{aligned}
$$

Fig. 1. Program syntax.

Instead of defining proof rules for *one* fixed memory model, we build on the generic approach of Bargmann et al. [4], allowing for proofs (potentially) valid in multiple memory models. This approach employs the semantic domain of *potentials* for weak memory state, and the logic Piccolo of Lahav et al. [20] to specify assertions over potentials. We extend Piccolo with further concepts and proof rules to allow reasoning about liveness. The thus constructed liveness proofs are then valid for all memory models in which the employed proof rules are sound. To determine rule soundness, the semantic domains of specific memory models need to be mapped onto potentials. Here, we provide such mappings and soundness results for the memory models *Release-Acquire* (RA, [18,21]) and Strong Coherence[1] (StrCOH, [21]).

Using our Piccolo extension, the adapted Manna-Pnueli proof rules (in particular rule WELL-JP for *parameterized programs*) and our soundness results for proof rules in weak memory models, we prove starvation freedom of the Ticket lock algorithm [26] on StrCOH and RA for any number of concurrent threads.

2 Program Syntax and Semantics

We start by giving the syntax and semantics of concurrent programs on weak memory models. We consider concurrent programs with top-level parallelism only. Sequential programs (defined in Fig. 1) contain standard programming constructs with named program positions (from a set of program counter values PC,

[1] Strong Coherence is discussed in the extended version of this paper [5].

disjoint between threads). A mapping $\mathcal{C}$ from thread identifiers to sequential programs describes a concurrent program, where $\mathcal{C}(\tau)$ is the sequential program of thread τ in $\mathcal{C}$. Threads use disjoint local registers in Reg and shared locations in Loc. Both take values out of a set Val. In Fig. 1, we see statements for storing to and loading from shared locations (write and read instructions), as well as a read-modify-write instruction (RMW) called fetch-and-add (FADD).

An example program[2] using this syntax is given in Fig. 2. Here, thread $\mathtt{T}_1$ frees a lock (by writing to `free`) and then sends a signal to potentially waiting threads (by writing to `sig`). Thread $\mathtt{T}_2$ is one such thread and loads the values of both shared locations into local registers. If the lock is not free ($\mathtt{u} \neq 1$), $\mathtt{T}_2$ enters its while loop and waits for the signal. More specifically, thread $\mathtt{T}_2$ waits for the signal *to change* by repeatedly reading it and comparing it to `s1`.

Thread $\mathtt{T}_1$	**Thread** $\mathtt{T}_2$
$\mathtt{l}_0$: STORE(free, 1);	$\mathtt{m}_0$: s1 := LOAD(sig);
$\mathtt{l}_1$: STORE(sig, 1)	$\mathtt{m}_1$: u := LOAD(free);
$\mathtt{l}_2$:	$\mathtt{m}_2$: if (u ≠ 1) then
	$\mathtt{m}_3$: s2 := LOAD(sig);
	$\mathtt{m}_4$: while (s2 = s1) do
	$\mathtt{m}_5$: s2 := LOAD(sig)
	$\mathtt{m}_6$:

$$\Box(\mathsf{at\_m}_0 \rightarrow \Diamond \mathsf{at\_m}_6)$$

Fig. 2. Concurrent program `Waiting`; property at the end specifying thread $\mathtt{T}_2$ to terminate.

As the semantics of such programs on weak memory models, we give labelled transition systems (LTS) which are constructed in three steps.

Local semantics. We first give a *local* semantics (program semantics without the memory model) in Fig. 3. Therein, *labels* (of type $\mathsf{Lab} = \{\mathtt{R}(x, v_\mathtt{R}), \mathtt{W}(x, v_\mathtt{W}), \mathtt{RMW}(x, v_\mathtt{R}, v_\mathtt{W}) \mid x \in \mathsf{Loc}, v_\mathtt{R}, v_\mathtt{W} \in \mathsf{Val}\}$) for each action (read/write/read-modify-write) associated with each command are fixed. Assignments to local registers lead to transitions labelled with ε. The semantics tracks a local register store $\gamma \in \mathsf{Reg} \rightarrow \mathsf{Val}$. Initially, all values of registers are 0. Note that in the read rules of Fig. 3 (LOAD and FADD), the value read is arbitrary. In the combined program semantics, this value will be fixed by the memory model semantics.

Figure 3 only details the semantics of simple commands c. The extended version [5] gives the operational semantics of sequential and concurrent programs using the transitions of commands c ($c \gg \gamma \xrightarrow{\ell_\varepsilon} \gamma'$) as derived in the rules of Fig. 3 ($\ell_\varepsilon \in \mathsf{Lab} \cup \{\varepsilon\}$). Therein, the state of programs also includes a program counter map $pc \in \mathsf{Tid} \rightarrow \mathsf{PC}$ (initially being the first program position for every thread). The map pc is used for building assertions over program positions (like $\mathsf{at\_m}_0$ occurring in the property of Fig. 2). We assume a function next giving us

[2] Pointed to us by Thomas Haas.

the position of the next program instruction. Altogether, the local semantics fixes an LTS for a concurrent program $\mathcal{C}_0$ with states of the form $\langle \mathcal{C}, (\gamma, pc)\rangle \in \mathcal{C}_0.\mathsf{Q}$ (remaining concurrent program $\mathcal{C}$ plus register and program counter map), initial states $\mathcal{C}_0.\mathsf{Q}_0 = \{\langle \mathcal{C}_0, (\gamma_0, pc_0)\rangle\}$ and the transitions $\rightarrow$ of [5].

Weak memory semantics. The semantics of weak memory models is also an LTS, $\mathcal{M}$, with a set of states denoted by $\mathcal{M}.\mathsf{Q}$, initial states $\mathcal{M}.\mathsf{Q}_0$, and transitions $\rightarrow_{\mathcal{M}}$. Transition labels of $\mathcal{M}$ consist of observable program transition labels (elements of $\mathsf{Tid} \times (\mathsf{Lab} \cup \{\varepsilon\})$) and a (disjoint) set $\mathcal{M}.\mathbf{\Theta}$ of unobservable *internal* memory labels. As an example, we present the SC memory model below. The RA model is presented in Fig. 12 and the StrCOH model in [5].

*Example 1 (*SC*memory model).* The memory model SC simply tracks the most recent value written to each variable (plus the id of the writing thread), i.e., $\mathsf{SC.Q} \triangleq \mathsf{Loc} \rightarrow (\mathsf{Val} \times \mathsf{Tid})$. SC has no internal memory steps (i.e., $\mathsf{SC}.\mathbf{\Theta} \triangleq \emptyset$), and the initial state is defined by $\mathsf{SC.Q}_0 \triangleq \{\lambda x.\ \langle 0, \mathrm{T}_0\rangle\}$ (storing initial value plus T_0 as the initializing thread), and transitions are given by:

$$\text{WRITE}\ \frac{\ell = \mathtt{W}(x, v_{\mathtt{W}}) \qquad q' = q[x \mapsto \langle v_{\mathtt{W}}, \tau\rangle]}{q \xrightarrow{\tau,\ell}_{\mathsf{SC}} q'} \qquad \text{READ}\ \frac{\ell = \mathtt{R}(x, v_{\mathtt{R}}) \qquad q(x) = \langle v_{\mathtt{R}}, \cdot\rangle}{q \xrightarrow{\tau,\ell}_{\mathsf{SC}} q}$$

The semantics of the read-modify-write corresponds to a read and a write in one atomic step.

Combined program semantics. The two semantics are combined into a joint semantics $\overline{\mathcal{M}}$ using the three rules below for steps corresponding to (1) joint executions of reads, writes and RMWs, (2) steps of the program only and (3) internal steps of the memory model $\mathcal{M}$ only:

$$(1)\ \frac{\begin{array}{c}\langle \mathcal{C}, (\gamma, pc)\rangle \xrightarrow{\tau,\ell,l} \langle \mathcal{C}', (\gamma', pc')\rangle \\ \ell \in \mathsf{Lab}\ \ q \xrightarrow{\tau,\ell}_{\mathcal{M}} q'\end{array}}{\langle \mathcal{C}, (\gamma, pc), q\rangle \xrightarrow{\tau,\ell,l}_{\overline{\mathcal{M}}} \langle \mathcal{C}', (\gamma', pc'), q'\rangle} \qquad (2)\ \frac{\langle \mathcal{C}, (\gamma, pc)\rangle \xrightarrow{\tau,\varepsilon,l} \langle \mathcal{C}', (\gamma', pc')\rangle}{\langle \mathcal{C}, (\gamma, pc), q\rangle \xrightarrow{\tau,\varepsilon,l}_{\overline{\mathcal{M}}} \langle \mathcal{C}', (\gamma', pc'), q\rangle}$$

$$(3)\ \frac{\iota \in \mathcal{M}.\mathbf{\Theta} \qquad q \xrightarrow{\iota}_{\mathcal{M}} q'}{\langle \mathcal{C}, (\gamma, pc), q\rangle \xrightarrow{\iota}_{\overline{\mathcal{M}}} \langle \mathcal{C}, (\gamma, pc), q'\rangle}$$

In summary, for a given concurrent program $\mathcal{C}_0$ and memory model $\mathcal{M}$, we thus get an LTS $\overline{\mathcal{M}} = (\mathsf{Q}, \mathsf{OLab}, \mathbf{\Theta}, \mathsf{Q}_0, \mathsf{T})$ of states $\mathsf{Q} = \mathcal{C}_0.\mathsf{Q} \times \mathcal{M}.\mathsf{Q}$, observable labels $\mathsf{OLab} = \mathsf{Tid} \times (\mathsf{Lab} \cup \{\varepsilon\}) \times \mathsf{PC}$ and unobservable labels $\mathbf{\Theta} = \mathcal{M}.\mathbf{\Theta}$, initial states $\mathsf{Q}_0 = \mathcal{C}_0.\mathsf{Q}_0 \times \mathcal{M}.\mathsf{Q}_0$, and transitions $\mathsf{T} = \rightarrow_{\overline{\mathcal{M}}}$ (out of $\mathsf{Q} \times (\mathsf{OLab} \cup \mathbf{\Theta}) \times \mathsf{Q}$) defined by the rules (1), (2) and (3).

$$\frac{\gamma' = \gamma[a \mapsto \gamma(e)]}{a := e \gg \gamma \xrightarrow{\varepsilon} \gamma'} \quad \frac{\ell = \mathtt{W}(x, \gamma(e))}{\mathsf{STORE}(x, e) \gg \gamma \xrightarrow{\ell} \gamma} \quad \frac{\ell = \mathtt{R}(x, v_\mathtt{R}) \quad \gamma' = \gamma[a \mapsto v_\mathtt{R}]}{a := \mathsf{LOAD}(x) \gg \gamma \xrightarrow{\ell} \gamma'} \quad \frac{\ell = \mathtt{RMW}(x, v_\mathtt{R}, v_\mathtt{R} + \gamma(e)) \quad \gamma' = \gamma[a \mapsto v_\mathtt{R}]}{a := \mathsf{FADD}(x, e) \gg \gamma \xrightarrow{\ell} \gamma'}$$

Fig. 3. Local semantics of commands ($\ell \in \mathsf{Lab}$); missing cases to be found in ??.

3 Fairness, Linear Temporal Logic and a Response Rule

We employ linear temporal logic (LTL) for the specification of liveness properties. LTL formulae are typically interpreted over infinite sequences of states. Thus, we assume all states in our LTS to have successors, i.e., for every state $\mathsf{q} \in \mathsf{Q}$ there has to be a transition $\mu \in \mathsf{T}$ with $\mu = (\mathsf{q}, \cdot, \cdot) \in \mathsf{T}$[3].

Fairness. Fairness is defined on runs of LTS'. A *run* π of an LTS $T = (\mathsf{Q}, \mathsf{OLab}, \boldsymbol{\Theta}, \mathsf{Q}_0, \mathsf{T})$ is an infinite sequence of transitions $(\mathsf{q}_0, \alpha_0, \mathsf{q}_1)(\mathsf{q}_1, \alpha_1, \mathsf{q}_2)\ldots$ such that $\mathsf{q}_0 \in \mathsf{Q}_0$ and $(\mathsf{q}_i, \alpha_i, \mathsf{q}_{i+1}) \in \mathsf{T}$, $i \geq 0$. The *computation* σ of a run $\pi = (\mathsf{q}_0, \alpha_0, \mathsf{q}_1)(\mathsf{q}_1, \alpha_1, \mathsf{q}_2)\ldots$ is the infinite sequence of states $\sigma = \mathsf{q}_0\mathsf{q}_1\mathsf{q}_2\ldots$. A transition $\mu = (\mathsf{q}, \alpha, \mathsf{q}')$ is *enabled at position* k in π if $\pi[k] = (\mathsf{q}, \cdot, \cdot)$, and μ is *continuously enabled from position* k *on* if μ is enabled at all positions $i \geq k$. A transition $\mu \in \mathsf{T}$ is *taken at position* k in a run π if $\pi[k] = \mu$.

Definition 1. *Let* $T = (\mathsf{Q}, \mathsf{OLab}, \boldsymbol{\Theta}, \mathsf{Q}_0, \mathsf{T})$ *be a labeled transition system,* $\mathcal{J} \subseteq \mathsf{T}$ *a set of transitions (the* just *transitions). A run* π *of* T *is* $\mathcal{J}$-fair *if every transition* $\mu \in \mathcal{J}$ *which is continuously enabled from a position* k *on is taken at some position* $i \geq k$*.*

In the sequel, we identify transitions of program commands by their positions $l \in \mathsf{PC}$, i.e., we will also say that a command at position l is enabled or taken when a transition $\mu = (\cdot, (\tau, \ell, l), \cdot)$ for some τ and $\alpha = (\tau, \ell, l)$ is enabled or taken. In particular, a command of thread τ at position l is enabled, $En(l)$, if $pc(\tau) = l$. Note that besides program transitions, we also have *internal* transition of the memory model in an LTS. These memory internal transitions are transitions with labels $\iota \in \boldsymbol{\Theta}$ (and we identify them with their label ι). By allowing them to be part of just sets $\mathcal{J}$, we can express *memory fairness*, i.e., define runs being fair wrt. internal memory transitions.

Linear Temporal Logic. For LTL, we assume to have a logic at hand for specifying *atomic propositions* (i.e., predicates) φ describing sets of states. In Sect. 4, we will introduce the logic Piccolo for this purpose. Its interpretation fixes the meaning of $\mathsf{q} \models \varphi$ for states q. On top of Piccolo, we build linear temporal logic formulae using operators $\Box$ (always) and $\Diamond$ (eventually). In our proof rules, we only consider formulae of the form $\Box(\varphi \rightarrow \Diamond\psi)$ (*response* properties) where φ and ψ are state formulae in Piccolo.

Definition 2. *Let* π *be a run of an LTS* T *and* σ *its corresponding computation. For LTL formula* Ψ *and* Piccolo *formula* φ*, we define* $(\sigma, k) \models \Psi$ *as follows:*

[3] When the semantics of programs derives states without successors, we add an idling transition $(\mathsf{q}, \varepsilon, \mathsf{q})$ to T.

- $(\sigma, k) \models \varphi$ *(φ an atomic propositions) iff* $\sigma[k] \models \varphi$ *(see Definition 5),*
- $(\sigma, k) \models \Box\, \Psi$ *iff* $(\sigma, i) \models \Psi$ *for all* $i \geq k$,
- $(\sigma, k) \models \Diamond\Psi$ *iff* $(\sigma, i) \models \Psi$ *for some* $i \geq k$.

An LTS T satisfies Ψ, $T \models \Psi$, *if* $(\sigma, 0) \models \Psi$ *for all computations* σ *of runs of* T*;* T fairly satisfies Ψ *with respect to some set of just transitions* $\mathcal{J}$ *if* $(\sigma, 0) \models \Psi$ *for all computations* σ *of* $\mathcal{J}$*-fair runs of* T.

The property given at the end of the program in Fig. 2 is a response formula specifying that thread $\mathtt{T}_2$ will eventually reach position $\mathtt{at\_m}_6$, i.e., will terminate.

$$\frac{\begin{array}{l}\textbf{JW1}.\ \varphi \rightarrow \bigvee_{j=0}^{m} \varphi_j \\ \textbf{JW2}.\ \{\varphi_i \wedge \delta_i = z_i\}\ \mu\ \{(\bigvee_{j=0}^{m}(\varphi_j \wedge z_i \succ \delta_j)\ ) \vee (\varphi_i \wedge z_i = \delta_i)\} \\ \textbf{JW3}.\ \{\varphi_i \wedge \delta_i = z_i\}\ \mu_i\ \{\bigvee_{j=0}^{m}(\varphi_j \wedge z_i \succ \delta_j)\} \\ \textbf{JW4}.\ \varphi_i \rightarrow En(\mu_i)\end{array}}{\Box(\varphi \rightarrow \Diamond\psi)}$$

Fig. 4. Rule WELL-J with assertions $\varphi, \psi, \varphi_0, \ldots, \varphi_m$ ($\varphi_0 = \psi$), $\mu \in \mathsf{T}$ any transition, helpful transitions $\mu_1, \ldots, \mu_m \in \mathcal{J}$, ranking functions $\delta_0, \ldots, \delta_m$, z_i meta variables for elements in $\mathcal{A}$ and i ranging over $1, \ldots, m$.

A Proof Rule for Response. Manna and Pnueli introduce a number of proof rules for response formulae. Here, we employ the rule WELL-J (for well-founded response under justice) in which all premises of the rule are non-temporal (see Fig. 4). We give the premises **JW2** and **JW3** in the form of *Hoare triples* [16]. The rule WELL-J builds on a *well-founded domain* $(\mathcal{A}, \succ)$: $\mathcal{A}$ is a set and $\succ$ is a transitive and irreflexive relation such that no infinitely descending sequences of elements $a_1 \succ a_2 \succ a_3 \succ \ldots$ exist. We often employ well-founded domains which are *products* of other well-founded domains, then using a lexicographic ordering. For measuring distance to targets, rule WELL-J uses *ranking functions* $\delta_i : \mathsf{Q} \rightarrow \mathcal{A}$. While trying to reach the target, the program might pass through a number of intermediate states, represented by state assertions $\varphi_0, \ldots, \varphi_m$. Progress towards the target is achieved by executing *helpful transitions* $\mu_1, \ldots, \mu_m$ which need to be in the justice set $\mathcal{J}$. More specifically, rule WELL-J in Fig. 4 has four premises (for proving $\Box(\varphi \rightarrow \Diamond\psi)$):

JW1 states that the "start" property φ of the response formula implies one of the intermediate assertions φ_j.

JW2 states that for all intermediate assertions φ_i and all transitions $\mu \in \mathsf{T}$, the execution of μ either leads to states satisfying some φ_j, thereby decreasing the ranking function, or stays inside φ_i and keeps the value of δ_i.

JW3 states executions of helpful transitions μ_i to definitely decrease ranking functions.

JW4 requires showing that helpful transition μ_i is enabled in states satisfying intermediate assertion φ_i.

This proof rule is sound, i.e., if all four premises hold, an LTS fairly satisfies the response property with respect to $\mathcal{J}$.

Lemma 1 (Manna and Pnueli [25]). *Rule WELL-J is sound.*

We can employ this rule to prove the response property in program `Waiting` (Fig. 2) under SC, i.e., prove termination of thread $\mathtt{T}_2$. We see that $\mathtt{T}_2$ either terminates when it does not enter the "then"-branch of the if statement at all ($\mathtt{u} = 1$), or when the while loop terminates ($\mathtt{s1} \neq \mathtt{s2}$). One of these situations will occur in `Waiting` since $\mathtt{sig} \neq 0 \Rightarrow \mathtt{free} = 1$ is an invariant. We employ this invariant when defining the intermediate assertions for WELL-J. More specifically, we need different intermediate assertions for each position of thread $\mathtt{T}_2$ ($\mathsf{at\_m}_0$, $\mathsf{at\_m}_1$, $\mathsf{at\_m}_2$, $\mathsf{at\_m}_3$, $\mathsf{at\_m}_4$, $\mathsf{at\_m}_5$, and $\mathsf{at\_m}_6$), each with their related helpful transition in $\mathtt{T}_2$. For example, the assertion $\mathsf{at\_m}_1 \wedge (\mathtt{s1} = 0 \vee \mathtt{free} = 1)$ has the helpful transition $\mathtt{m}_1$. Additionally, while $\mathtt{T}_2$ is in its while loop ($\mathsf{at\_m}_{4,5}$), we track the progress of $\mathtt{T}_1$ to ensure that we will eventually leave the loop. This leads to a total of nine state assertions φ_i with ranking functions $\delta_i : (i, 1 - \mathtt{sig}, 1 - \mathtt{s2})$, where i tracks the progress of $\mathtt{T}_2$ to enter and leave its loop, $1 - \mathtt{sig}$ tracks the progress of $\mathtt{T}_1$ writing to `sig` and $1 - \mathtt{s2}$ tracks whether $\mathtt{T}_2$ has read the necessary value to leave its loop. Basically, all transitions are helpful here since they participate in achieving the progress of $\mathtt{T}_2$.

This proof, however, does not hold for programs under weak memory, as threads then might not see the *same* values of shared locations like `free` at the same time. This, in particular, means that state assertions like $\mathtt{sig} \neq 0 \Rightarrow \mathtt{free} = 1$ are not well defined. Nevertheless, rule WELL-J is sound in such a setting, as we still simply work on LTS of programs, albeit with "unusual" state and "unusual" memory model internal steps. What we need to properly employ this rule in our setting is a way of defining (1) intermediate assertions as well as (2) ranking functions in terms of weak memory state.

4 Potentials and the Piccolo Logic

For sequential consistency, we use predicates on locations and registers for specifying state assertions. This is different when we consider weak memory models, in particular when constructing proofs that are potentially valid for multiple memory models. Here, we employ Piccolo [4,20] for this purpose. Piccolo is an interval-based logic for weak memory formalized using a notion of *potentials*.

Notation. For sets S and lists L, we write $\#S$ and $\#L$ for the size and length of S, L, respectively; $L[i]$, $1 \leq i \leq \#L$, is the i-th element in L; $L_1 \cdot L_2$ is the concatenation of lists.

Potential Domain. Potentials [19,20] reflect the phenomenon of weak memory models that threads might still see *stale* values of shared locations and thus may read from several possible writes to a location, stale ones and more recent ones.

Potentials reflect this by describing *views* of threads which – contrary to SC – differ between threads. Weak memory models typically have memory model internal steps (like flushes) which *advance* these views. For liveness proofs, we need to be able to reason about such view advancements. For example, for termination in program `Waiting` it is crucial that thread $\mathtt{T}_2$ eventually sees the latest values of `free` and `sig` which thread $\mathtt{T}_1$ has written.

Technically, a potential store is a mapping from locations to tuples of values, thread IDs (of the writer), *covered flags* (needed for RMWs), plus some auxiliary information required by specific memory models. This auxiliary information differs between memory models: SC requires no additional auxiliary information, while RA and StrCOH keep track of *timestamps* (see Sect. 6 and [5]).

Definition 3. *A* potential store *is a function* $\beta : \mathsf{Loc} \to \mathsf{Val} \times \mathsf{Tid} \times \{T, F\} \times \mathsf{Aux}$, *where* Aux *captures the auxiliary information.*

We use $\beta(x)$`.val`, $\beta(x)$`.tid`, $\beta(x)$`.flag` and (potentially) $\beta(x)$`.ts` to retrieve the value, thread id, covered flag, and auxiliary timestamp of $\beta(x)$, respectively.

Potentials are then sequences (lists) of potential stores.

Definition 4. *A* potential *is a non-empty set of lists of potential stores. We let $\mathcal{L}$ be the set of all potentials. A* potential mapping *is a partial function* $\mathcal{B}$: $\mathsf{Tid} \to \mathcal{L}$ *that maps thread identifiers to potentials such that all lists agree on the last store.*

Example 2. Consider the following two lists of potential stores

$$L_1 = \begin{bmatrix} \mathtt{free} \mapsto \langle 0, \mathtt{T}_0, T\rangle \\ \mathtt{sig} \mapsto \langle 0, \mathtt{T}_0, T\rangle \end{bmatrix} \cdot \begin{bmatrix} \mathtt{free} \mapsto \langle 1, \mathtt{T}_1, T\rangle \\ \mathtt{sig} \mapsto \langle 0, \mathtt{T}_0, T\rangle \end{bmatrix} \qquad L_2 = \begin{bmatrix} \mathtt{free} \mapsto \langle 1, \mathtt{T}_1, T\rangle \\ \mathtt{sig} \mapsto \langle 0, \mathtt{T}_0, T\rangle \end{bmatrix}$$

and the program `Waiting` in Fig. 2. In the program, the initialization of locations to value 0 is done by a specific thread $\mathtt{T}_0$. After executing instruction $\mathtt{l}_0$ of $\mathtt{T}_1$, thread $\mathtt{T}_2$ could have the potential $\mathcal{B}(\mathtt{T}_2) = \{L_1\}$. In this, $\mathtt{T}_2$ currently sees the *stale* value 0 of `free` and value 0 of `sig`. The potential, however, also includes the latest values of `free`, as represented by the second potential store in the list.

In the future (e.g., after some memory model internal steps), $\mathtt{T}_2$'s potential might only include the list L_2 in which it will see `free` to be 1 while `sig` is still 0. Note that the covered flag T is only relevant for programs containing RMWs and can therefore be ignored here.

extended expr.	$E ::= e \mid x \mid \vec{x} \mid E + E \mid E - E \mid \neg E \mid E \wedge E \mid \dots$
interval assertions	$I ::= [E] \mid I \,;\, I$
assertions	$\varphi ::= \tau \ltimes I \mid \mathsf{C}(x) \mid \mathsf{dist}(\tau, x) = n \mid \mathsf{at}\_l \mid e \mid \varphi \wedge \varphi \mid \dots$

Fig. 5. Assertions of Piccolo (excerpt)

Logic Piccolo. The logic Piccolo (given in Fig. 5[4]) is interpreted over potentials. The key concept of Piccolo are *interval assertions*: a potential list fulfills an

[4] We have elided constructs occurring in [4] which are not needed here.

interval assertion $[E]$ when all elements in the list satisfy E, and a list L satisfies $[I_1];[I_2]$ (where ; is the *chop* operator [7,27]) if L can be split into lists L_1 and L_2 such that L_1 satisfies $[I_1]$ and L_2 satisfies $[I_2]$. This allows us to write assertions on values of shared locations currently seen by a thread as well as seen in the future.

Here, we build on the version of Piccolo in [4] and extend it with three constructs: (a) we introduce the *current* (most recent/last) value $\boldsymbol{x}$ of a location x, (b) introduce the distance function dist to describe the distance in the potential to the most recently written value of a location, and (c) introduce the *covered* predicate $\mathsf{C}(x)$ for reasoning about RMWs. Intuitively, locations are covered when an RMW has to read from the most recent value of a location.

We use $\tau \uparrow x$ as a shorthand for $\mathsf{dist}(\tau, x) = 0$ to stand for *view maximality*, specifying a thread τ to only see the most recent value of a location x. Note that we can thereby also state *negated* view-maximality (by writing $\mathsf{dist}(\tau, x) = n$ for some $n \neq 0$). In prior works, such negations have been disallowed because they impact the *stability* of assertions: An assertion is said to be stable if its validity cannot be changed by memory model internal steps. This is of key importance for safety proofs where we only reason about program steps. For liveness, this is different: here, we want to explicitly reason about memory model internal steps and specify that their execution changes properties, namely the distance of a thread towards observing the most recent value of a shared location.

Next, we define the interpretation of Piccolo on the domain of potentials.

Definition 5. *Let γ be a register store, pc a program counter map, β a potential store, L a store list, and $\mathcal{B}$ a potential mapping. For an expression e, we let $[\![e]\!]_{\langle(\gamma,pc),\beta,L\rangle} \triangleq \gamma(e)$, $[\![x]\!]_{\langle(\gamma,pc),\beta,L\rangle} \triangleq \beta(x).\mathtt{val}$ and $[\![\boldsymbol{x}]\!]_{\langle(\gamma,pc),\beta,L\rangle} \triangleq L[\#L](x)$[5]. The extension of this notation to any extended expression E is standard. The validity of state assertions φ in $\langle(\gamma,pc),\mathcal{B}\rangle$, denoted by $\langle(\gamma,pc),\mathcal{B}\rangle \models \varphi$, is defined as follows:*

1. $\langle(\gamma,pc),L\rangle \models [E]$ *if* $[\![E]\!]_{\langle(\gamma,pc),\beta,L\rangle} = \mathit{true}$ *for every* $\beta \in L$.
2. $\langle(\gamma,pc),L\rangle \models I_1 ; I_2$ *if* $\langle(\gamma,pc),L_1\rangle \models I_1$ *and* $\langle(\gamma,pc),L_2\rangle \models I_2$ *for some (possibly empty)* L_1 *and* L_2 *such that* $L = L_1 \cdot L_2$.
3. $\langle(\gamma,pc),\mathcal{B}\rangle \models \tau \ltimes I$ *if* $\langle(\gamma,pc),L\rangle \models I$ *for every* $L \in \mathcal{B}(\tau)$.
4. $\langle(\gamma,pc),\mathcal{B}\rangle \models \mathsf{C}(x)$ *if* $L[i](x).\mathtt{flag} = T$ *for every* $L \in \mathcal{B}(\tau), \tau \in \mathsf{Tid}, 1 \leq i \leq \#L$.
5. $\langle(\gamma,pc),\mathcal{B}\rangle \models \mathsf{dist}(\tau,x) = n$ *if* $\max\{k \mid k = \#\{L[i](x) \mid L[i](x) \neq L[\#L](x)\}, L \in \mathcal{B}(\tau)\} = n$.
6. $\langle(\gamma,pc),\mathcal{B}\rangle \models \mathsf{at\_}l$ *if* $pc(\tau) = l$ *for some* $\tau \in \mathsf{Tid}$[6], *and* $\langle(\gamma,pc),\mathcal{B}\rangle \models e$ *if* $\gamma(e) = \mathit{true}$.
7. $\langle(\gamma,pc),\mathcal{B}\rangle \models \varphi_1 \wedge \varphi_2$ *if* $\langle(\gamma,pc),\mathcal{B}\rangle \models \varphi_1$ *and* $\langle(\gamma,pc),\mathcal{B}\rangle \models \varphi_2$.

[5] Note again that in potential domains all lists have to agree on the very last store.

[6] Note that program positions are disjoint between threads so that there is at most one such thread here.

Example 3. In Example 2 we had the following list of potential stores of thread $\mathtt{T}_2$:

$$L_1 = \begin{bmatrix} \texttt{free} \mapsto \langle 0, \mathtt{T}_0, T \rangle \\ \texttt{sig} \mapsto \langle 0, \mathtt{T}_0, T \rangle \end{bmatrix} \cdot \begin{bmatrix} \texttt{free} \mapsto \langle 1, \mathtt{T}_1, T \rangle \\ \texttt{sig} \mapsto \langle 0, \mathtt{T}_0, T \rangle \end{bmatrix}$$

Assuming this to be the only list in $\mathcal{B}(\mathtt{T}_2)$, this state satisfies $\mathsf{dist}(\mathtt{T}_2, \texttt{free}) = 1$, $\mathtt{T}_2 \ltimes [\texttt{free} = 0] ; [\texttt{free} = 1]$, $\mathtt{T}_2 \ltimes [\texttt{sig} = 0]$, $\neg(\mathtt{T}_2 \uparrow \texttt{free})$ and $\mathsf{C}(\texttt{free})$. The value of $\overrightarrow{\texttt{free}}$ is 1.

Proof Rules. Piccolo already comes with a set of base proof rules for Hoare triples [16]. So far, these have been used to build Owicki-Gries-like proof outlines [29] for safety proofs. Here, we employ the Hoare triples to show (part of) the premises of rule WELL-J. Figure 6 gives some proof rules needed for our examples; further rules, in particular about interval formulae, can be found in [4]. We use the following notation: For an assertion φ, we let $fv(\varphi) \subseteq \mathsf{Reg} \cup \mathsf{Loc}$ be the set of registers and locations occurring in φ, and we use $\psi \notin \varphi$ to say that formula ψ is not occurring as a subterm in φ. We will shortly discuss all the rules.

Assumption	Pre	Command	Post	Reference
$x \notin fv(\varphi), \mathsf{at\_}l \notin \varphi$	$\{\varphi\}$	$\tau \mapsto l : \mathsf{STORE}(x, e)$	$\{\varphi\}$	STBL-ST
$x, a \notin fv(\varphi)$, $\mathsf{at\_}l \notin \varphi$, $\forall y : \neg(\tau \uparrow y) \notin \varphi$	$\{\varphi\}$	$\tau \mapsto l : a := \mathsf{FADD}(x, e)$	$\{\varphi\}$	STBL-RMW
$a \notin fv(\varphi), \mathsf{at\_}l \notin \varphi$, $\forall y : \neg(\tau \uparrow y) \notin \varphi$	$\{\varphi\}$	$\tau \mapsto l : a := \mathsf{LOAD}(x)$	$\{\varphi\}$	STBL-LD
$\mathsf{at\_}l \notin \varphi$	$\{\varphi(a := e)\}$	$\tau \mapsto l : a := e$	$\{\varphi\}$	SUB
	$\{\mathsf{at\_}l\}$	$\tau \mapsto l : C$	$\{\mathsf{at\_next}(l)\}$	PC
	$\{\tau \uparrow x\}$	$\tau \mapsto l : \mathsf{STORE}(x, e)$	$\left\{\begin{array}{l}\tau \uparrow x \wedge \tau \ltimes [x = e] \wedge \\ \vec{x} = e\end{array}\right\}$	ST
$\eta \neq \tau,\ x \notin fv(I_\tau)$	$\{\tau \ltimes I_\tau \wedge \eta \ltimes I ; I_\tau\}$	$\tau \mapsto l : \mathsf{STORE}(x, e)$	$\{\eta \ltimes I ; I_\tau\}$	ST-OTHER
	$\left\{\begin{array}{l}\mathsf{C}(x) \wedge \\ \vec{x} = e_1\end{array}\right\}$	$\tau \mapsto l : a := \mathsf{FADD}(x, e_2)$	$\left\{\begin{array}{l}\mathsf{C}(x) \wedge \vec{x} = e_1 + e_2 \wedge \\ \tau \ltimes [x = e_1 + e_2]\end{array}\right\}$	RMW
	$\{\tau \uparrow x \wedge e(a := \vec{x})\}$	$\tau \mapsto l : a := \mathsf{LOAD}(x)$	$\{e\}$	LD
P	$\{\tau \ltimes [e(a := x)]; I\}$	$\tau \mapsto l : a := \mathsf{LOAD}(x)$	$\{e \vee \psi\}$	LD-SH

Fig. 6. Piccolo proof rules ($\varphi(a := e)$ means replacement of a by e in φ and τ is the executing thread and $P \triangleq \{\tau \ltimes I\} \tau \mapsto a := \mathsf{LOAD}(x) \{\psi\}$, P is thus a Hoare triple).

- The rules for stability, STBL-ST, STBL-RMW, and STBL-LD, state that Piccolo formulae not referring to specific registers and locations, program counters, or negated view maximality, are not affected by load and store instructions.
- Rule SUB states the standard axiom of assignment of Hoare logic, which is here only defined with respect to registers and local expressions. Rule PC is solely used to reason about program counter values.

- Rule ST describes the changes a store has on the potential of the writing thread, namely, if a thread is view-maximal, the only value it can see for location x after the store is its own value. Furthermore, this value is the most recent value for x. Rule RMW describes a similar effect but requires the location to be covered, $\mathtt{C}(x)$, so that the RMW cannot read from a stale value. This means in particular, that locations on which only RMWs are executed are always covered.
- Finally, the rules LD and LD-SH describe the loading of values of shared locations into registers, where LD covers the case in which the reading thread is view maximal.

Note that all of these proof rules are entirely syntactic: we have no semantics of store and load instructions on the level of potentials. Hence, such proof rules cannot be proven sound on this level. However, when deriving potentials from weak memory states (as we do in Sect. 6), we can show soundness of rules within specific memory models.

5 Liveness Proofs

Next, we apply the proof rule WELL-J together with Piccolo and its proof rules to two example programs. We in particular illustrate how Piccolo allows us to write ranking functions over weak memory state and why we need memory internal steps as helpful transitions.

5.1 Program Waiting

In Fig. 7, we see an overview of the state assertions $\varphi_9, \ldots, \varphi_0$ and their helpful transitions μ_i necessary for applying the WELL-J rule to our Waiting program.

$$
\begin{array}{ll}
\varphi_9 : \mathsf{at\_m}_0 \wedge \mathcal{I} & \mu_9 : \mathtt{m}_0 \\
\varphi_8 : \mathsf{at\_m}_1 \wedge (\mathtt{s1} = 0 \vee \mathrm{T}_2 \ltimes [\mathtt{free} = 1]) \wedge \mathcal{I} & \mu_8 : \mathtt{m}_1 \\
\varphi_7 : \mathsf{at\_m}_2 \wedge (\mathtt{s1} = 0 \vee \mathtt{u} = 1) \wedge \mathcal{I} & \mu_7 : \mathtt{m}_2 \\
\varphi_6 : \mathsf{at\_m}_3 \wedge \mathtt{s1} = 0 \wedge \mathcal{I} & \mu_6 : \mathtt{m}_3 \\
\varphi_5 : \mathsf{at\_m}_{4,5} \wedge \mathsf{at\_l}_0 \wedge \mathtt{s1} = 0 \wedge \mathcal{I} & \mu_5 : \mathtt{l}_0 \\
\varphi_4 : \mathsf{at\_m}_{4,5} \wedge \mathsf{at\_l}_1 \wedge \mathtt{s1} = 0 \wedge \mathcal{I} & \mu_4 : \mathtt{l}_1 \\
\varphi_3 : \mathsf{at\_m}_{4,5} \wedge \mathsf{at\_l}_2 \wedge \mathtt{s1} = 0 \wedge \neg \mathrm{T}_2 \!\uparrow\! \mathtt{sig} \wedge \mathrm{T}_1 \ltimes [\mathtt{sig} = 1] \wedge \mathcal{I} & \mu_3 : \iota \\
\varphi_2 : \mathsf{at\_m}_4 \wedge \mathsf{at\_l}_2 \wedge \mathtt{s1} = 0 \wedge \mathrm{T}_2 \!\uparrow\! \mathtt{sig} \wedge \mathrm{T}_1 \ltimes [\mathtt{sig} = 1] \wedge \mathcal{I} & \mu_2 : \mathtt{m}_4 \\
\varphi_1 : \mathsf{at\_m}_5 \wedge \mathsf{at\_l}_2 \wedge \mathtt{s1} = 0 \wedge \mathrm{T}_2 \!\uparrow\! \mathtt{sig} \wedge \mathrm{T}_1 \ltimes [\mathtt{sig} = 1] \wedge \mathcal{I} & \mu_1 : \mathtt{m}_5 \\
\varphi_0 : \mathsf{at\_m}_6 &
\end{array}
$$

Fig. 7. State assertions and helpful transitions for program Waiting.

During all executions of Waiting the following invariant $\mathcal{I}$ holds:

$$\mathcal{I} : \mathrm{T}_2 \ltimes [\mathtt{sig} = 0]; [\mathtt{free} = 1] \wedge \mathrm{T}_2 \ltimes [\mathtt{sig} = 0]; [\mathtt{sig} = 1] \wedge \mathrm{T}_1 \!\uparrow\! \mathtt{sig}$$

We need this invariant (more specifically $\mathtt{T}_2 \ltimes [\mathtt{sig} = 0]; [\mathtt{free} = 1]$) for example to show that transition $\mathtt{m}_0$ brings us from φ_9 to φ_8. For this, we use the rules PC and LD-SH. $\mathtt{T}_2 \ltimes [\mathtt{sig} = 0]; [\mathtt{free} = 1]$ holds throughout the entire program because of the STBL rules and ST-OTHER.

Note that this proof has an additional assertion (φ_3) compared to the SC proof in Sect. 3, and assertions regarding locations are now written in Piccolo. After $\mathtt{T}_1$ has finished, this is necessary to differentiate between the states where $\mathtt{T}_2$ can only read the newest value 1 of sig and where it could still read 0. As helpful transitions of φ_3, we need memory internal transitions ι, since in this state, only view advancement will bring the program nearer to termination. This is possible in our setting since (memory) fairness allows us to include internal transitions ι into the just set $\mathcal{J}$.

To apply rule WELL-J, we also need ranking functions for every state assertion. In this proof, they use the well-founded domain $\mathbb{N} \times \mathbb{N} \times \mathbb{N} \times \mathbb{N}$ and are defined as

$$\delta_i : (i, 1 - \overrightarrow{\mathtt{sig}}, \mathsf{dist}(\mathtt{T}_2, \mathtt{sig}), 1 - \mathtt{s2})$$

for $0 \leq i \leq 9$. In contrast to the SC proof, our ranking functions here need to include $\mathsf{dist}(\mathtt{T}_2, \mathtt{sig})$, measuring the distance of $\mathtt{T}_2$ towards seeing the latest value of sig. This helps us to ensure **JW3** holds for φ_3 (we still make progress with its helpful transition) even if $\mathtt{T}_2$ is not directly view maximal after executing ι.

Next, we will look at a further case study showing starvation freedom of the Ticket lock algorithm, using a variant of WELL-J for parameterized programs.

5.2 Ticket Lock

```
Thread T1                              ||     ||  Thread Tn
l10 : nxt[1] := FADD(next, 1);         ||     ||  ln0 : nxt[n] := FADD(next, 1);
l11 : while (s[1] ≠ nxt[1]) do         ||     ||  ln1 : while (s[n] ≠ nxt[n]) do
      l12 : s[1] := LOAD(srv)          || ... ||        ln2 : s[n] := LOAD(srv)
l13 : FADD(srv, 1)                     ||     ||  ln3 : FADD(srv, 1)
l14 :                                  ||     ||  ln4 :
```

$$\forall k : \Box(\mathsf{at\_l}_{k0} \rightarrow \Diamond \mathsf{at\_l}_{k4})$$

Fig. 8. The Ticket Lock algorithm Ticket for n threads; property stating starvation freedom for all threads $\mathtt{T}_k$, $k = 1, \ldots, n$.

The Ticket lock algorithm [26] given in Fig. 8 is a synchronization mechanism employed to achieve mutual exclusion. In ticket locks, threads take tickets in the order of their arrival (stored in the register $\mathtt{nxt}[k]$ for thread $\mathtt{T}_k$). The thread currently served is the one whose nxt is equal to the shared variable srv. The "critical section" for which mutual exclusion should be achieved is the position $\mathsf{at\_l}_{k3}$; after that srv is incremented and the next thread is served. The property we are interested in here is *starvation freedom*: every thread wanting to be served is eventually served, i.e., reaches its (empty) critical section.

Here, we assume to have a finite number n of threads running the ticket lock. We thus employ a version of WELL-J for parameterized programs (called WELL-JP), i.e., concurrent programs in which all threads execute the same code[7]. In this rule, intermediate assertions and helpful transitions can be parameterized (with parameters ranging over thread identifiers). Figure 9 gives the rule WELL-JP.

$$\frac{\begin{array}{l}\text{JW1. } \varphi \rightarrow \bigvee_{j=0}^{m} \bigvee_{\tau \in \mathsf{Tid}} \varphi_j[\tau] \\ \text{JW2. } \{\varphi_i[\tau] \wedge \delta_i[\tau] = z_i\}\ \mu\ \{(\bigvee_{j=0}^{m}(\bigvee_{\tau' \in \mathsf{Tid}} \varphi_j[\tau'] \wedge z_i \succ \delta_j[\tau'])\ ) \vee (\varphi_i[\tau] \wedge z_i = \delta_i[\tau])\} \\ \text{JW3. } \{\varphi_i[\tau] \wedge \delta_i[\tau] = z_i\}\ \mu_i[\tau]\ \{\bigvee_{j=0}^{m}(\bigvee_{\tau' \in \mathsf{Tid}} \varphi_j[\tau'] \wedge z_i \succ \delta_j[\tau'])\} \\ \text{JW4. } \varphi_i[\tau] \rightarrow En(\mu_i[\tau])\end{array}}{\Box(\varphi \rightarrow \Diamond\psi)}$$

Fig. 9. Rule WELL-JP with assertions $\varphi, \psi, \varphi_0, \varphi_1[\tau], \ldots, \varphi_m[\tau]$ ($\varphi_0 = \psi$), $\mu \in \mathsf{T}$ any transition, helpful transitions $\mu_1[\tau], \ldots, \mu_m[\tau] \in \mathcal{J}$, ranking functions $\delta_0, \ldots, \delta_m$, z_i meta variables for elements in A and $i = 1, \ldots, m$.

Intermediate assertions and helping transitions for `Ticket` are as follows. We let $hT(k) \equiv \mathsf{at\_l}_{k1}, \mathtt{l}_{k2}, \mathtt{l}_{k3}$ to describe program positions in which $\mathtt{T}_k$ has taken a Ticket. We prove the property of starvation freedom for all threads by showing it for some arbitrarily chosen thread called $\mathtt{T}_{\mathsf{ego}}$. Figure 10 gives intermediate assertions and helpful transitions.

$\varphi_5:$	$\mathsf{at\_l}_{\mathsf{ego0}}$	$\mu_5: \ \mathtt{l}_{\mathsf{ego0}}$
$\varphi_4[\mathtt{T}_k]:$	$\mathsf{at\_l}_{k1}, \mathtt{l}_{k2} \wedge hT(\mathsf{ego}) \wedge \mathtt{nxt}[k] = \overrightarrow{\mathtt{srv}} \wedge \neg(\mathtt{T}_k \uparrow \mathtt{srv}) \wedge$ $\mathtt{T}_k \ltimes [\mathtt{srv} = 0]\,; \ldots; [\mathtt{srv} = \overrightarrow{\mathtt{srv}}] \wedge \mathtt{s}[k] \leq \overrightarrow{\mathtt{srv}}$	$\mu_4[\mathtt{T}_k]: \iota$
$\varphi_3[\mathtt{T}_k]:$	$\mathsf{at\_l}_{k1} \wedge hT(\mathsf{ego}) \wedge \mathtt{nxt}[k] = \overrightarrow{\mathtt{srv}} \wedge \mathtt{T}_k \uparrow \mathtt{srv} \wedge \mathtt{s}[k] \leq \overrightarrow{\mathtt{srv}}$	$\mu_3[\mathtt{T}_k]: \mathtt{l}_{k1}$
$\varphi_2[\mathtt{T}_k]:$	$\mathsf{at\_l}_{k2} \wedge hT(\mathsf{ego}) \wedge \mathtt{nxt}[k] = \overrightarrow{\mathtt{srv}} \wedge \mathtt{T}_k \uparrow \mathtt{srv} \wedge \mathtt{s}[k] < \overrightarrow{\mathtt{srv}}$	$\mu_2[\mathtt{T}_k]: \mathtt{l}_{k2}$
$\varphi_1[\mathtt{T}_k]:$	$\mathsf{at\_l}_{k3} \wedge hT(\mathsf{ego}) \wedge \mathtt{nxt}[k] = \overrightarrow{\mathtt{srv}} \wedge \mathtt{T}_k \uparrow \mathtt{srv} \wedge \mathtt{s}[k] = \mathtt{nxt}[k]$	$\mu_1[\mathtt{T}_k]: \mathtt{l}_{k3}$
$\varphi_0:$	$\mathsf{at\_l}_{\mathsf{ego4}}$	

Fig. 10. State assertions and helpful transitions for program `Ticket`.

The ranking functions use the well-founded domain $(\mathbb{N} \cup \{\infty\}) \times (\mathbb{N} \cup \{\infty\}) \times \{0,1,2,3,4,5\} \times (\mathbb{N} \cup \{\infty\})$ and are defined as $\delta_5 : (\infty, \infty, 5, \infty)$, $\delta_0 : (0,0,0,0)$ and $\delta_i[\mathtt{T}_k] : (\mathtt{nxt}[\mathsf{ego}] - \overrightarrow{\mathtt{srv}}, \mathtt{nxt}[k] - \mathtt{s}[k], i, \mathsf{dist}(\mathtt{T}_k, \mathtt{srv}))$, for $i \in \{1,2,3,4\}$.

The assertions and ranking functions basically state that some thread has a ticket in `nxt` which is equal to the most recent value of `srv`, and this thread makes progress towards observing $\overrightarrow{\mathtt{srv}}$ (via some helpful transition ι) as well as towards reading this value and checking it to be the same as its `nxt`. By executing $\mathtt{l}_{k3}$, this thread will then increment `srv`, thus decreasing the distance

[7] In our example, the threads' code differs only in the (indices of) names of local registers.

for ego to have its own ticket in nxt[ego] become the same as $\overrightarrow{\texttt{srv}}$. To be able to show all the premises, we need some further invariants about program `Ticket`, e.g., $0 \leq \overrightarrow{\texttt{srv}} \leq \overrightarrow{\texttt{next}}$ and in particular $\mathsf{C}(\texttt{next})$.

Note that we need the read-modify-write instruction FADD in both positions $\texttt{l}_{k0}$ and $\texttt{l}_{k3}$. Without them (i.e., with a plain LOAD followed by a STORE), the executing thread might read a stale value for `next` (so that multiple threads have the same `nxt` then) or for `srv` (so that the most recent value for `srv` is not incremented). Fairness wrt. memory model internal steps does not help in that case as the instructions are not repeatedly executed.

6 Lifting Memory Models to **Piccolo** Proofs

Our liveness proofs of `Waiting` and the ticket lock are so far completely independent of a concrete memory model. We, however, ultimately want to be able to say whether this proof is valid for a specific memory model. To this end, we need to fix how we interpret Piccolo on a memory model $\mathcal{M}$.

Definition 6. *A function* $map_{\mathcal{M}} : \mathcal{M}.\mathsf{Q} \to (\mathsf{Tid} \to \mathcal{L})$ *is a* lifting function *of* $\mathcal{M}$ *if* $map_{\mathcal{M}}$ *fulfills the following property for all initial states* $q \in \mathcal{M}.\mathsf{Q}_0$*:*

$$\langle(\gamma, pc), map_{\mathcal{M}}(q)\rangle \models \forall \tau \in \mathsf{Tid}\ \forall x \in \mathsf{Loc} : \tau \uparrow x \wedge \mathsf{C}(x) \wedge \tau \ltimes [x = 0] \qquad (\text{INIT})$$

A lifting function thus maps memory states to potential mappings, and in particular maps initial states of a memory model to "initial" states in the potential domain. Such lifting functions can be employed for interpreting Piccolo formulae on states $\mathsf{q} = \langle \mathcal{C}, (\gamma, pc), q\rangle$ of the combined semantics by defining $\mathsf{q} \models \varphi$ to be $\langle(\gamma, pc), map_{\mathcal{M}}(q)\rangle \models \varphi$.

Assumption	Pre	Command	Post	Reference
$\forall\tau\forall x\forall n > 0$: $\mathsf{dist}(\tau, x) = n \notin \varphi$	$\{\varphi\}$	ι	$\{\varphi\}$	STBL-INT
	$\{\mathsf{dist}(\tau, x) = n \wedge n > 0\}$	ι	$\{\mathsf{dist}(\tau, x) = m \wedge m < n\}$	DIST

Fig. 11. Piccolo proof rules for memory internal transitions labelled $\iota \in \mathcal{M}.\Theta$.

With this in mind, we define what it means for a memory model to fulfill a Piccolo proof rule.

Definition 7. *The* Piccolo *proof rule* $\{\varphi\}\ \tau \mapsto l : c\ \{\psi\}$ *is* sound *in a memory model* $\mathcal{M}$ *if for every LTS* $\overline{\mathcal{M}} = (\mathsf{Q}, \mathsf{OLab}, \Theta, \mathsf{Q}_0, \mathsf{T})$ *we have*

$$\forall \mathsf{q}, \mathsf{q}' \in \mathsf{Q} : \mathsf{q} \models \varphi \wedge \mathsf{q} \xrightarrow{\tau, lab(c), l} \mathsf{q}' \Rightarrow \mathsf{q}' \models \psi$$

where $lab(c)$ *maps each command* c *to its respective labels in* Lab_ε*. Similarly, we define* $\{\varphi\}\ \iota\ \{\psi\}$ *for* $\iota \in \Theta$*.*

For achieving validity of liveness proofs for memory models, the following basic healthiness conditions furthermore need to be satisfied by a memory model.

Definition 8. *We say that a lifting function* $map_{\mathcal{M}}$ *of a memory model* $\mathcal{M}$ *guarantees* view advancement of internal transitions, *if the following conditions hold for all internal labels* $\iota \in \mathcal{M}.\Theta$ *and states* $q \in \mathcal{M}.Q$*:*

1. $\langle(\gamma, pc), map_{\mathcal{M}}(q)\rangle \models (\exists\tau\exists x : \mathsf{dist}(\tau, x) \neq 0) \Rightarrow En(\iota)$, *and*
2. *the rules in Fig. 11 are sound for* ι*-labelled transitions.*

Recall $\mathsf{dist}(\tau, x) \neq 0$ implies that thread τ cannot see the newest value for x at the moment (its distance to this value is not zero). For liveness proofs via rule WELL-J, we want a helpful transition to decrease this distance such that we eventually reach a state where $\mathsf{dist}(\tau, x) = 0$ and τ therefore sees the newest value of x. Definition 8 guarantees that we can use *memory*internal transitions as helpful transitions, since a ι-labelled transition is enabled when the distance is not zero (condition 1) and it decreases dist (condition 2).

$$\frac{\ell = \mathtt{R}(x, v_\mathtt{R}) \qquad \langle x : v_\mathtt{R}@t, \tau, V\rangle \in q.M \qquad q.\nu(\tau)(x) = t}{q \xrightarrow{\tau,\ell}_{\mathsf{RA}} q}$$

$$\frac{\ell = \mathtt{W}(x, v_\mathtt{W}) \qquad \neg\exists m \in q.M_{|x} : m.\mathtt{ts} = t \qquad q.\nu(\tau)(x) < t}{q \xrightarrow{\tau,\ell}_{\mathsf{RA}} \langle q.M \cup \{\langle x : v_\mathtt{W}@t, \tau, q.\nu(\tau)[x \mapsto t]\rangle\}, q.\nu[\tau \mapsto q.\nu(\tau)[x \mapsto t]]\rangle}$$

$$\frac{\begin{array}{ccc}\ell = \mathtt{RMW}(x, v_\mathtt{R}, v_\mathtt{W}) & \ell_1 = \mathtt{R}(x, v_\mathtt{R}) & \ell_2 = \mathtt{W}(x, v_\mathtt{W}) \\ q'.\nu(\tau)(x) = q.\nu(\tau)(x) + 1 & & q \xrightarrow{\tau,\ell_1}_{\mathsf{RA}} q \xrightarrow{\tau,\ell_2}_{\mathsf{RA}} q'\end{array}}{q \xrightarrow{\tau,\ell}_{\mathsf{RA}} q'}$$

$$\frac{\ell = \mathsf{prop} \qquad m \in q.M \qquad \exists\tau \in \mathsf{Tid} : \nu(\tau)(m.\mathtt{loc}) < m.\mathtt{ts}}{q \xrightarrow{\ell}_{\mathsf{RA}} \langle q.M, q.\nu[\tau \mapsto q.\nu(\tau) \sqcup m.\mathtt{view}]\rangle}$$

Fig. 12. Operational semantics of RA using colors to highlight the updated memory and view components; $M_{|x} \subseteq M$ is the set of messages m with $m.\mathtt{loc} = x$.

Memory Model Release-Acquire. As an example of a concrete memory model and its lifting to potentials, we consider the Release-Acquire memory model RA, following the semantics of [21][8]. For RA, we get the following components of the LTS:

- The set of memory model internal labels is $\mathsf{RA}.\Theta \triangleq \{\mathsf{prop}\}$.
- Each state $q = \langle M, \nu\rangle \in \mathsf{RA.Q}$ consists of a set M of *messages* and a *view* ν per thread. A view is a mapping from locations to timestamps (here, $\mathbb{N}$), i.e., $\mathsf{View} \triangleq \mathsf{Loc} \rightarrow \mathbb{N}$. We use $\sqcup$ on views for the point-wise maximum on

[8] We slightly deviate from [21] as to separate reads and view advancements.

timestamps. Messages $m \in M$ record the previously executed writes and store location x, written value v, and timestamp t (denoted $x : v@t$) plus the writing thread and the view of the thread when writing, i.e., messages have the type $(\mathsf{Loc} \times \mathsf{Val} \times \mathbb{N}) \times \mathsf{Tid} \times \mathsf{View}$. The view $\nu : \mathsf{Tid} \to \mathsf{View}$ maps each thread to a timestamp for each location. Thus, $\mathsf{RA.Q} \triangleq \mathcal{P}(\mathsf{Loc} \times \mathsf{Val} \times \mathbb{N} \times \mathsf{Tid} \times \mathsf{View}) \times (\mathsf{Tid} \to \mathsf{View})$.

- The set of initial states is $\mathsf{RA.Q}_0 \triangleq \{\langle M_0, \nu_0 \rangle\}$. In this, the memory M_0 contains one message $\langle x : 0@0, \mathtt{T}_0, V_0 \rangle$ where $V_0(x) = 0$ for each location x and $\nu_0(\tau) = V_0$ for each thread τ.
- The transition relation $\rightarrow_{\mathsf{RA}}$ is given in Fig. 12. For a given location x, the read transition chooses the message $m \in M_{|x}$ to read from with a timestamp equal to the thread's view on x. The write transition adds a new message to memory. Its timestamp t has to be greater than the current view of the thread on x, which then gets updated to t. The RMW transition simply first executes a read and after that a write transition. To ensure that no thread can write between the written message m_w and the one read from, m_r, the timestamp is set to $m_w.\mathtt{ts} = m_r.\mathtt{ts} + 1$. Finally, the propagate transition updates the view of a thread τ to the maximum of its current view and the view of a message m. For this, the timestamp of m needs to be greater than the view of τ on m's location.

Lifting of RA States. When lifting RA states to the potential domain, the auxiliary information Aux we need are *timestamps*, i.e., we have $\mathsf{Aux} = \mathbb{N}$. An RA state determines multiple potential store lists per thread. Each such list $L \in \mathcal{B}(\tau)$ starts with the same potential store

$$\begin{aligned} \Delta_\tau(q) : \mathsf{Loc} &\to (\mathsf{Val} \times \mathsf{Tid} \times \mathbb{N}) \times \{T, F\} \\ x &\mapsto \langle m_\tau.\mathtt{val}, m_\tau.\mathtt{tid}, m_\tau.\mathtt{ts}, cov_q(m_\tau) \rangle \end{aligned}$$

where m_τ is the message in $q.M_{|x}$ with $m_\tau.\mathtt{ts} = q.\nu(\tau)(x)$ and

$$\begin{aligned} cov_q(m_\tau) \triangleq \textbf{ if } & m_\tau.\mathtt{ts} = \max\{t \mid t = m'.\mathtt{ts} \wedge m' \in q.M_{|x}\} \\ & \vee \exists m' \in q.M_{|x} : m'.\mathtt{ts} = m_\tau.\mathtt{ts} + 1 \textbf{ then } T \textbf{ else } F\ . \end{aligned}$$

Note that this definition is well-defined since for every RA state there exists exactly one such $m_\tau \in M$ for each thread τ. If $cov_q(m_\tau) = T$ for all threads τ, then the message of a new write to x automatically receives the highest timestamp with respect to x and is therefore the latest one. This leads us to the lifting map $map_{\mathsf{RA}} : \mathsf{RA.Q} \to \mathcal{B}$, where

$$map_{\mathsf{RA}}(q)(\tau) \triangleq \Delta_\tau(q) \cdot \bigcup_{q' \text{ s.t. } q \xrightarrow{\mathsf{prop}}_{\mathsf{RA}} q'} map_{\mathsf{RA}}(q')(\tau)$$

Here, we let $e \cdot \mathsf{L} \triangleq \{\langle e \rangle \cdot L \mid L \in \mathsf{L}\}$. Since timestamps are unique for every write to a given location x in an RA-state q, and propagates have to increase a thread's view, every list in each $map_{\mathsf{RA}}(q)(\tau)$ ends with the same potential store. Hence, map_{RA} is a potential according to Definition 4.

Soundness of Rules in RA. With the lifting for RA at hand, we can formally study the soundness of Piccolo proof rules in RA.

Theorem 1. *All* Piccolo *proof rules in Fig. 6 are sound for* RA.

All soundness proofs can be found in the extended version of this paper [5]. Finally, we have to look at the memory model internal steps.

Lemma 2. *The lifting function* map_{RA} *guarantees view advancement of* RA*s internal transitions.*

As a corollary, we get the following.

Corollary 1. *The liveness proofs of the programs* `Waiting` *in Fig. 7 and* `Ticket` *in Fig. 10 are valid under the memory model* RA.

Other Memory Models. Besides RA, all rules of Figs. 6 and 11 are also sound in memory models SC and TSO [28,31]. The extended version [5] furthermore contains a definition of StrCOH and soundness proofs. Memory model StrCOH does, however, not satisfy rule ST-OTHER[9]. In the liveness proof of program `Waiting`, this rule is used to show that the invariant $\mathtt{T}_2 \ltimes [\mathtt{sig} = 0]; [\mathtt{free} = 1]$ (which guarantees the order in which $\mathtt{T}_2$ can read something) holds throughout the entire program, especially after executing $\mathtt{l}_1$. Under StrCOH, Thread $\mathtt{T}_2$ of `Waiting` can see the write to `sig` before it sees the write to `free` and hence might not terminate, namely when reading `free` to be 0, `sig` to be 1 and then not seeing any changes to `sig` anymore. Since the liveness proof of the Ticket Lock algorithm does not need the ST-OTHER rule, it is valid for StrCOH.

For SC and TSO, on the other hand, both proofs are valid.

7 Conclusions and Related Work

In this paper, we have proposed a method for deductively verifying liveness properties of concurrent programs on weak memory models. Our method includes a program logic and associated *syntactic* proof rules, thereby making reasoning generic and proofs valid for multiple memory models, namely for all models in which the employed proof rules are sound.

As future work, we intend to look into other memory models, e.g., Partial Store Ordering. Furthermore, we will study strong fairness (compassion in the terminology of [25]) and Manna and Pnueli's rules for response under justice and compassion.

[9] This rule describes the message passing ability: If a thread sees another thread's write, it will also see that thread's earlier writes.

Safety in Weak Memory. A number of works have proposed program logics and proof calculi for reasoning about concurrent programs on weak memory with respect to safety properties (e.g., [4,6,10,13,18,20,22]). Some of them also use Piccolo [4,13,20]. For example, [13] have also employed a notion of "latest value".

Liveness for SC. Numerous works have studied general liveness properties or total correctness for concurrent programs wrt. sequential consistency. Owicki and Gries [29] were the first to introduce termination proofs within Hoare-like proof calculi, later corrected by Apt et al. [3]. Similar proof calculi for total correctness are also studied within rely-guarantee reasoning [17,33]. Cook et al. [9] propose automatic techniques for proving termination by incrementally constructing and eliminating possible interferences by threads.

These approaches only provide a proof strategy for total correctness where the threads *in isolation* terminate (plus their termination proofs fulfill non-interference). Manna and Pnueli [24,25] provide temporal logic proof calculi for general response properties based on fairness. Podelski et al. [30] also employ fairness and provide a technique that constructs abstract transition programs on which fair termination can be checked. Concurrent separation logic was used in an automatic technique by D'Osualdo et al. [14].

Liveness in Weak Memory. Only a few works have considered progress properties for concurrent programs on weak memory. The only one based on proof calculi is from Colvin et al. [8]. They use rely-guarantee reasoning on weak memory, which, as mentioned above, can only prove thread-wise termination. For decidability, Wang et al. [32] prove the liveness properties lock-freedom, wait-freedom, deadlock-freedom, and starvation-freedom to be undecidable for TSO. Lahav et al. introduce the notion of memory fairness [21] and provide a theorem (Theorem 5.3) allowing to reduce the checks for (the absence of) infinite computation to executions in which read statements finally read from writes being maximal wrt. the modification order in execution graphs. The tool Dartagnan [11,12] performs termination checks for axiomatic memory models based on insights of [21]. In [15], it is extended to prove non-termination for any given fairness assumptions. Abdulla et al. [1,2] develop fairness notions and show that liveness can be reduced to control state reachability under their notion of fairness.

References

1. Abdulla, P.A., Atig, M.F., Godbole, A., Krishna, S.N., Vahanwala, M.: Fairness and liveness under weak consistency. In: Kiefer, S., Křetínský, J., Kučera, A. (eds.) Taming the Infinities of Concurrency. LNCS, vol. 14660, pp. 1–21. Springer, Cham (2024). https://doi.org/10.1007/978-3-031-56222-8_1
2. Abdulla, P.A., Atig, M.F., Godbole, A., Krishna, S., Vahanwala, M.: Overcoming memory weakness with unified fairness. In: Enea, C., Lal, A. (eds.) CAV 2023. LNCS, vol. 13964, pp. 184–205. Springer, Cham (2023). https://doi.org/10.1007/978-3-031-37706-8_10

3. Apt, K.R., de Boer, F.S., Olderog, E.-R.: Proving Termination of Parallel Programs, pp. 1–6. Springer, New York (1990). https://doi.org/10.1007/978-1-4612-4476-9_1
4. Bargmann, L., Dongol, B., Wehrheim, H.: Unifying weak memory verification using potentials. In: Platzer, A., Rozier, K.Y., Pradella, M., Rossi, M. (eds.) FM 2024. LNCS, vol. 14933, pp. 519–537. Springer, Cham (2024). https://doi.org/10.1007/978-3-031-71162-6_27
5. Bargmann, L., Wehrheim, H.: Towards proving liveness on weak memory (extended version) (2026). https://doi.org/10.48550/arXiv.2602.19609
6. Bila, E.V., Dongol, B., Lahav, O., Raad, A., Wickerson, J.: View-based Owicki-Gries reasoning for persistent x86-TSO. In: Sergey, I. (ed.) ESOP 2022. LNCS, vol. 13240, pp. 234–261. Springer, Cham (2022). https://doi.org/10.1007/978-3-030-99336-8_9
7. Chaochen, Z., Hoare, C.A.R., Ravn, A.P.: A calculus of durations. Inf. Process. Lett. **40**(5), 269–276 (1991). https://doi.org/10.1016/0020-0190(91)90122-X
8. Colvin, R.J., Hayes, I.J., Heiner, S., Höfner, P., Meinicke, L., Su, R.C.: Practical rely/guarantee verification of an efficient lock for seL4 on multicore architectures. In: Cavalcanti, A., Baxter, J. (eds.) The Practice of Formal Methods. LNCS, vol. 14780, pp. 65–87. Springer, Cham (2024). https://doi.org/10.1007/978-3-031-66676-6_4
9. Cook, B., Podelski, A., Rybalchenko, A.: Proving thread termination. In: PLDI, pp. 320–330. ACM (2007). https://doi.org/10.1145/1250734.1250771
10. Dalvandi, S., Doherty, S., Dongol, B., Wehrheim, H.: Owicki-Gries reasoning for C11 RAR. In: Hirschfeld, R., Pape, T. (eds.) ECOOP, LIPIcs, pp. 11:1–11:26. Schloss Dagstuhl - Leibniz-Zentrum für Informatik (2020). https://doi.org/10.4230/LIPIcs.ECOOP.2020.11
11. Ponce-de-León, H., Furbach, F., Heljanko, K., Meyer, R.: DARTAGNAN: bounded model checking for weak memory models (competition contribution). In: TACAS 2020. LNCS, vol. 12079, pp. 378–382. Springer, Cham (2020). https://doi.org/10.1007/978-3-030-45237-7_24
12. Ponce-de-León, H., Haas, T., Meyer, R.: DARTAGNAN: leveraging compiler optimizations and the price of precision (competition contribution). In: TACAS 2021. LNCS, vol. 12652, pp. 428–432. Springer, Cham (2021). https://doi.org/10.1007/978-3-030-72013-1_26
13. Dongol, B., Lahav, O., Wehrheim, H.: A rely-guarantee framework for proving deadlock freedom under causal consistency. In: Cavalcanti, A., Baxter, J. (eds.) The Practice of Formal Methods. LNCS, vol. 14780, pp. 88–108. Springer, Cham (2024). https://doi.org/10.1007/978-3-031-66676-6_5
14. D'Osualdo, E., Sutherland, J., Farzan, A., Gardner, P.: Tada live: compositional reasoning for termination of fine-grained concurrent programs. ACM Trans. Program. Lang. Syst. **43**(4), 16:1–16:134 (2021). https://doi.org/10.1145/3477082
15. Haas, T., Meyer, R., de León, H.P., Garduño, A.L.: Recurrence sets for proving fair non-termination under axiomatic memory consistency models. Proc. ACM Program. Lang. **10**(POPL), 1296–1325 (2026). https://doi.org/10.1145/3776687
16. Hoare, C.A.R.: An axiomatic basis for computer programming. Commun. ACM **12**(10), 576–580 (1969). https://doi.org/10.1145/363235.363259
17. Jones, C.B.: Tentative steps toward a development method for interfering programs. ACM Trans. Program. Lang. Syst. **5**(4), 596–619 (1983). https://doi.org/10.1145/69575.69577

18. Kaiser, J.-O., Dang, H.-H., Dreyer, D., Lahav, O., Vafeiadis, V.: Strong logic for weak memory: reasoning about release-acquire consistency in iris. In: Müller, P. (ed.) ECOOP. LIPIcs, vol. 74, pp. 17:1–17:29. Schloss Dagstuhl - Leibniz-Zentrum für Informatik (2017). https://doi.org/10.4230/LIPICS.ECOOP.2017.17
19. Lahav, O., Boker, U.: What's decidable about causally consistent shared memory? ACM Trans. Program. Lang. Syst. **44**(2), 8:1–8:55 (2022). https://doi.org/10.1145/3505273
20. Lahav, O., Dongol, B., Wehrheim, H.: Rely-guarantee reasoning for causally consistent shared memory. In: Enea, C., Lal, A. (eds.) CAV 2023. LNCS, vol. 13964, pp. 206–229. Springer, Cham (2023). https://doi.org/10.1007/978-3-031-37706-8_11
21. Lahav, O., Namakonov, E., Oberhauser, J., Podkopaev, A., Vafeiadis, V.: Making weak memory models fair. Proc. ACM Program. Lang. **5**(OOPSLA), 1–27 (2021). https://doi.org/10.1145/3485475
22. Lahav, O., Vafeiadis, V.: Owicki-Gries reasoning for weak memory models. In: Halldórsson, M.M., Iwama, K., Kobayashi, N., Speckmann, B. (eds.) ICALP 2015. LNCS, vol. 9135, pp. 311–323. Springer, Heidelberg (2015). https://doi.org/10.1007/978-3-662-47666-6_25
23. Lamport, L.: How to make a multiprocessor computer that correctly executes multiprocess programs. IEEE Trans. Comput. **28**(9), 690–691 (1979). https://doi.org/10.1109/TC.1979.1675439
24. Manna, Z., Pnueli, A.: Completing the temporal picture. Theor. Comput. Sci. **83**(1), 91–130 (1991). https://doi.org/10.1016/0304-3975(91)90041-Y
25. Manna, Z., Pnueli, A.: Temporal verification of reactive systems: response. In: Manna, Z., Peled, D.A. (eds.) Time for Verification. LNCS, vol. 6200, pp. 279–361. Springer, Heidelberg (2010). https://doi.org/10.1007/978-3-642-13754-9_13
26. Mellor-Crummey, J.M., Scott, M.L.: Algorithms for scalable synchronization on shared-memory multiprocessors. ACM Trans. Comput. Syst. **9**(1), 21–65 (1991). https://doi.org/10.1145/103727.103729
27. Moszkowski, B.C.: A complete axiom system for propositional interval temporal logic with infinite time. Log. Methods Comput. Sci. **8**(3) (2012). https://doi.org/10.2168/LMCS-8(3:10)2012
28. Owens, S., Sarkar, S., Sewell, P.: A better x86 memory model: x86-TSO. In: Berghofer, S., Nipkow, T., Urban, C., Wenzel, M. (eds.) TPHOLs 2009. LNCS, vol. 5674, pp. 391–407. Springer, Heidelberg (2009). https://doi.org/10.1007/978-3-642-03359-9_27
29. Owicki, S.S., Gries, D.: An axiomatic proof technique for parallel programs I. Acta Inf. **6**, 319–340 (1976). https://doi.org/10.1007/BF00268134
30. Podelski, A., Rybalchenko, A.: Transition predicate abstraction and fair termination. ACM Trans. Program. Lang. Syst. **29**(3), 15 (2007). https://doi.org/10.1145/1232420.1232422
31. Sewell, P., Sarkar, S., Owens, S., Nardelli, F.Z., Myreen, M.O.: x86-TSO: a rigorous and usable programmer's model for x86 multiprocessors. Commun. ACM **53**(7), 89–97 (2010). https://doi.org/10.1145/1785414.1785443
32. Wang, C., Petri, G., Lv, Y., Long, T., Liu, Z.: Decidability of liveness for concurrent objects on the TSO memory model. In: Dong, W., Talpin, J.P. (eds.) SETTA 2022. LNCS, vol. 13649, pp. 149–165. Springer, Cham (2022). https://doi.org/10.1007/978-3-031-21213-0_10
33. Qiwen, X., de Roever, W.P., He, J.: The rely-guarantee method for verifying shared variable concurrent programs. Formal Asp. Comput. **9**(2), 149–174 (1997). https://doi.org/10.1007/BF01211617

Test Coverage of Automated Robotic Systems in Open World Environments

Lukas Westhofen[1(✉)], Till Schallau[2], Dominik Schmid[2], Stefan Naujokat[2], Falk Howar[2,3], and Daniel Neider[2,4]

[1] German Aerospace Center, Institute of Systems Engineering for Future Mobility, Oldenburg, Germany
lukas.westhofen@dlr.de

[2] TU Dortmund University, Dortmund, Germany

[3] Fraunhofer Institute for Software and Systems Engineering, Dortmund, Germany

[4] Center for Trustworthy Data Science and Security, Dortmund, Germany

Abstract. Automated robotic systems operating in real-world environments require thorough test campaigns before deployment, in which engineers assess whether the system is actually exposed to critical scenarios. A well-established way to judge the efficacy of test campaigns in controlled environments is scenario coverage: It quantifies the quality of recorded data from test campaigns w.r.t. a set of (critical) scenario classes of interest. Challenges arise when transferring coverage from controlled to open environments, as it may no longer be exactly determined to which scenario class the recorded test data belongs to: sensors offer limited observability, e.g., by occlusions or hardware failures, and specifications might be inherently vague, e.g., via imprecise traffic regulations. We leverage the Open World Assumption to formally extend scenario coverage to such ambiguous test data and present algorithms for computing guaranteed lower and upper bounds on coverage. Whereas deciding the lower bound problem is D^p-complete, the upper bound can be computed in polynomial time. We extend an existing coverage software tool with two approaches for incorporating the Open World Assumption, grounded in LTL_f. Our evaluation shows that meaningful statements on scenario coverage are feasible, even under intricacies of the real world.

Keywords: Testing · Robotics · Safety · Automated Driving · Scenario Coverage · Temporal Logics

1 Introduction

Verification of highly automated robotic system relies heavily on testing due to complex and uncontrolled operating environments. This forces manufacturers to test in the intended operating domain already during development. The collected data are then used to evaluate system performance. Prominent examples are the large-scale test campaigns by automated driving companies, such as Waymo.

When testing, a central question arises: Did the observed test runs actually expose the system to critical situations? An effective way to quantify this

A. Sampaio and M. Stoelinga (Eds.): FM 2026, LNCS 16556, pp. 130–150, 2026.
https://doi.org/10.1007/978-3-032-26204-2_7

question is through scenario coverage [15, Section 3.3], in which engineers specify a set of scenario classes to cover the space of relevant, e.g., safety-critical, environmental inputs to the system, as mandated by ISO 21448 [20]. In Germany, this is even legally required for automated driving (which will act as an example use case throughout this work): "test cases must provide sufficient test coverage for all scenarios, test parameters, and environmental influences. The coverage must be justified [...]" [11]. Coverage of scenario classes, i.e., particularly interesting type of test inputs, by a recorded data set then refers to the proportion of the scenario classes for which at least one instance was observed. The goal is to identify testing gaps, which can then be re-tested more exhaustively. Recent approaches have examined scenario coverage in environments with almost-perfect knowledge, such as bird-eye simulations or drone data [13,29].

In this paper, we push coverage from laboratory to real-world settings. This presents a challenge: both data and specifications might be incomplete. Under these assumptions, the scenario class of a recording cannot always be exactly determined: First, there is no perfect ground truth, i.e., the recorded data is incomplete. This can be caused by perception characteristics such as occlusions, sensor failures, and lossy post-processing. Second, even if all relevant information is available, there might be incomplete specifications of scenario classes due to complexity and vagueness. Causes include intentionally fuzzy definitions in legal texts (such as safety distances) [10,30] and partial knowledge of engineers.

To account for both incomplete data and knowledge, this work incorporates the Open World Assumption (OWA) into scenario coverage. Intuitively, the OWA states that we cannot infer the truth of a statement from the absence of knowledge about the inverse statement [22], e.g., we cannot state that no vehicle is present from not knowing about any vehicle. This leads to situations in which neither a statement nor its inverse hold, representing absence of knowledge about the actual truth. We can use this OWA to propagate both incomplete data – by not inferring from the absence of data – and incomplete knowledge – by allowing for "gray zones" in specifications – into coverage. Observed scenarios can then possibly belong to one of multiple scenario classes. For example, we might observe a record where it is unknown if a passed vehicle is parking. It must be either parking or not parking; however, based on the available data and specification, it can be impossible to determine exactly its state.

The main contribution of this paper is to extend the classic coverage problem (introduced in Sect. 2) by an OWA: Instead of unambiguous assignments to scenario classes, we now also allow for gray zones. Since coverage cannot be exactly determined anymore, we update the classic problem to now yield lower and upper approximations in Sect. 3. Naïve algorithms fail for both bounds. We hence analyze computational complexity and present efficient algorithms. In Sect. 4, we contribute two ways of incorporating the OWA in a temporal logic for scenario class specification. The first is based on standard propositional logic, while the second uses Description Logics (DLs). An implementation of both approaches allows an evaluation of OWA coverage on practically relevant configurations in Sect. 5. As we delineate in Sect. 6, this contribution is novel in the sense that, to the best knowledge, all related works make the Closed World Assumption (CWA), i.e., assuming the available knowledge to be complete. While limitations of our OWA integration remain, we conclude in Sect. 7 that the approach is efficient and useful in real-world settings.

2 Preliminaries

We are faced with recorded results of test runs of the robotic system as a list of finite data traces $(d_1, \ldots, d_n)$. Each data trace d_i consists of data points that contain environment information, e.g., road infrastructure, as well as dynamic properties, e.g., positions and speeds of actors. Formally, $d_i = (\mathfrak{D}^i_1, \ldots, \mathfrak{D}^i_m)$, where $\mathfrak{D}^i_j \in \mathbb{D}$ is the recorded data at timestamp j for a (for now not further specified) set $\mathbb{D}$ of all possible data points (Sect. 4 gives two realizations of $\mathbb{D}$).

Based on the ISO 34504 terminology, our *scenario classes* correspond to *scenario categories* defined by sets of tags [21]. We model each tag as a Boolean predicate over a recorded test run, so class membership follows ISO's tag-inclusion semantics (conjunction of tag predicates). Coverage metrics therefore rely on an explicit abstraction that maps continuous, high-dimensional data traces to a finite tag vocabulary. This abstraction is a standard and necessary precondition of coverage analysis: it makes coverage computation and gap identification tractable, but it introduces the usual trade-off that overly abstract tags may hide relevant differences while overly fine-grained tags can reduce interpretability and scalability. Accordingly, any coverage statement is conditional on the chosen tags and the tag-assignment method. In this paper, we treat the tag vocabulary and classifiers as given engineering inputs and focus on making coverage robust when data or specifications are incomplete.

It is envisioned that the system is put under comparable challenging conditions in each instance of a scenario class – such as encountering a pedestrian at parking vehicles. To represent this formally, we use a finite set of tags T and a finite set of possible values V_t for each tag $t \in T$. The set of all values is $V = \bigcup_{t \in T} V_t$. This results in a list of *scenarios* $(s_1, \ldots, s_n)$ corresponding to the given test runs, where each s_i is a function from T to V.

As a running example, consider four tags $T = \{t_1, \ldots, t_4\}$. For simplicity, $V = \{0, 1\}$, where 0 encodes the absence and 1 presence of the tag in the data:

$\mathbf{t_1}$ denotes whether a violation of the safety distance to a lead vehicle was observed.

$\mathbf{t_2}$ holds if a pedestrian or bicycle is present.

$\mathbf{t_3}$ addresses passing of parking vehicles (as opening doors or occluded pedestrians can be critical).

$\mathbf{t_4}$ specifies a condition where cameras are susceptible to glare: The system drives towards a low sun for a considerable amount of time.

An example scenario $s_1 : t_1 \mapsto 0, t_2 \mapsto 0, t_3 \mapsto 0, t_4 \mapsto 1$ encodes no safety distance violation, present pedestrian or bicycle, or passing of parking vehicles, while the system drives towards a low sun.

For deriving s_i from a recorded data trace d_i, we assume a function from the set of all data traces of finite lengths to tag evaluations: $\Lambda_{T,V} : \bigcup_{h>0} \mathbb{D}^h \rightarrow V^T$ for tags T and values V, where $V^T = \{f : T \rightarrow V\}$. As we operate on data traces, we can apply temporal logics for classification. For now, we will not put further constraints on $\Lambda_{T,V}$ and assume that $\Lambda_{T,V}(d_i)$ was evaluated on all data traces. Section 4 gives possible implementations of $\Lambda_{T,V}$.

When running test campaigns, engineers are typically interested in how exhaustive the system has been tested after the data has been assigned to the predefined scenario classes. A possible way to assess the exhaustiveness is *scenario class coverage* (SCC). It has been examined under the Closed World Assumption (CWA) [29]. The CWA implies that the data are given as a perfect ground truth and no ambiguities exist in the specification. SCC is defined as the ratio of observed and all possible scenario classes for a list of scenarios $(s_1, \ldots, s_n)$:

$$\mathrm{SCC}(\mathbb{T}, V, s_1, \ldots, s_n) = \frac{|\{s_i \mid i \in \{1, \ldots, n\}\}|}{|\mathbb{T}|}, \tag{1}$$

where $\mathbb{T}$ is the space of all possible options. In the simplest case, $\mathbb{T} = V^T$ (which we assume in this work). Equation 1 allows quantifying the gap in which the system has not yet been tested and gives valuable feedback to engineers and authorities.

3 Coverage Under the Open World Assumption

The main contribution of our work is to extend scenario class coverage to the OWA, as the CWA is not always applicable, especially when testing robotic systems in real-world environments. The OWA can alleviate this problem by allowing the value of some tags to be unknown due to two reasons: The behavior of robotic systems is often hard to specify completely. Additionally, their perception is naturally limited due to sensor technology capabilities. As an example, consider the tag t_1 (safety distance violation). While several rules of thumb and approximating formulae exist, a gray area will always remain in the specification. Hence, t_1 must be considered under the OWA.

To formalize this, for each tag, we allow adding a unique symbol $*$ to V_t, where $s_i(t) = *$ indicates that $s_i(t)$ is not known and might take any value from the original tag values $V_t \setminus \{*\}$. In our example, we extend the values for the first tag, V_{t_1}, from $\{0, 1\}$ to $\{0, 1, *\}$ with $*$ encoding no observation of a safety distance violation. This can happen due to perception insufficiencies or fuzzy specifications. A similar reasoning can be applied to t_2 (presence of a pedestrian or bicycle) and t_3 (passing of parking vehicles). These tags will serve as our running example. For instance, in Sect. 5, we analyze their value distributions on a real-world dataset. Note that not all tags must be given the $*$ option, thus allowing to still partially rely on the CWA, e.g., if perfect information can be assumed, such as positioning and time for t_4. For tags with an "unknown" option, i.e., t where $* \in V_t$, on the other hand, $s_i(t) = *$ induces the set $V_t \setminus \{*\}$ as possible options, from which only one could have been true. We are thus confronted with a set of possible options for a scenario s_i. This set contains all functions representing possible resolutions of $*$-entries of a tag t to some value in $V_t \setminus \{*\}$, and otherwise respecting the non-$*$-entries of s_i:

$$\mathsf{O}(s_i) = \left\{ o : T \to V \middle| \begin{array}{c} \forall t \in T.\ s_i(t) \neq * \to o(t) = s_i(t) \wedge \\ s_i(t) = * \to o(t) \in V_t \setminus \{*\} \end{array} \right\}.$$

In what follows, we operate directly on $\mathsf{O}(s_i)$ instead of s_i, which means that we use a list $S = (S_1, \ldots, S_n) = (\mathsf{O}(s_1), \ldots, \mathsf{O}(s_n))$ instead of $(s_1, \ldots, s_n)$. This translation creates, in the worst case, $|V|^{|T|}$ many entries for each observed scenario and is therefore exponential. Hence, all examined problems would directly be exponential as well. Assuming a constant tag size on the other hand allows us to uncover subtleties in the theoretical data complexity [34] of computing coverage under an OWA.

3.1 Definition of Lower and Upper Coverage Bounds

We can now update the definition of coverage under the CWA as given in Eq. 1 to our formalized OWA framework. This is not straightforward: due to the missing information, the numerator of the SCC cannot be determined exactly. However, it is still possible to identify correct lower and upper approximations to the unknown numerator of the SCC by appropriately selecting one of the possible options. For the lower bound, the goal is to select the options such that as many duplicates (i.e. identical scenario classifications) as achievable are created to calculate a pessimistic coverage guarantee. The upper bound on coverage, on the other hand, maximizes the diversity of the scenarios by avoiding duplicates to emulate the best possible bound, if possible. The idea of optimally selecting scenarios from the set of options is formally captured by the following two problems, representing the lower and upper bound, respectively.

Definition 1 (MinCover). *For a list of non-empty finite sets* $S = (S_1, \ldots, S_n)$ *over the universe* $U = \bigcup_{i \in \{1,\ldots,n\}} S_i$*, find* k_{min} *which is the smallest* $k \leq n$ *s.t. there is a function* π *with* $|Im(\pi)| = k$ *assigning each index* i *an element of* S_i*, i.e.,* $\pi : \{1, \ldots, n\} \to U$ *where* $\pi(i) \in S_i$ *for all* $i \in \{1, \ldots, n\}$.

Definition 2 (MaxCover). *For a list of non-empty finite sets* $S = (S_1, \ldots, S_n)$ *over the universe* $U = \bigcup_{i \in \{1,\ldots,n\}} S_i$*, find* k_{max} *which is the largest* $k \leq n$ *s.t. there is a function* π *with* $|Im(\pi)| = k$ *assigning each index* i *an element of* S_i*, i.e.,* $\pi : \{1, \ldots, n\} \to U$ *where* $\pi(i) \in S_i$ *for all* $i \in \{1, \ldots, n\}$.

Here, $\mathrm{Im}(\pi)$ refers to the image of π. Both problems require selecting exactly one element from each set S_i s.t. the number of unique, overall selected elements is minimal or maximal, respectively. The corresponding decision problems IsMinCover and IsMaxCover ask if $k \in \mathbb{N}$ is equivalent to k_{min} or k_{max}, respectively.

Consider our running example, where t_1 to t_3 are interpreted under the OWA. The following examples represent the i-th scenario as $(s_i(t_1), \ldots, s_i(t_4))$, e.g., $(1, 0, 0, 1)$, and, for ease of presentation, also refers to its list of tags with value

1, e.g., (t_1, t_4). Assume four recorded scenarios $s_1 = (0,0,0,1)$, $s_2 = (1,0,0,1)$, $s_3 = (*,0,0,1)$, and $s_4 = (*,*,0,1)$. To determine both approximations, we derive all possibilities and compute coverage for all combinations (explicated values are marked bold):

$$\mathsf{O}(s_1) = \{s_1\} = \{(0,0,0,1)\} = \{(t_4)\} \quad \mathsf{O}(s_2) = \{s_2\} = \{(1,0,0,1)\} = \{(t_1,t_4)\}$$

$$\mathsf{O}(s_3) = \left\{ \begin{matrix} (\mathbf{0},0,0,1) = (t_4), \\ (\mathbf{1},0,0,1) = (t_1,t_4) \end{matrix} \right\} \qquad \mathsf{O}(s_4) = \left\{ \begin{matrix} (\mathbf{0},\mathbf{0},0,1) = (t_4), \\ (\mathbf{0},\mathbf{1},0,1) = (t_2,t_4), \\ (\mathbf{1},\mathbf{0},0,1) = (t_1,t_4), \\ (\mathbf{1},\mathbf{1},0,1) = (t_1,t_2,t_4) \end{matrix} \right\}$$

The worst case assigns s_3 and s_4 the same scenario as s_1 or s_2. The corresponding function π of Definition 1 can, e.g., assign $\pi(1) = \pi(3) = \pi(4) = s_1$ and $\pi(2) = s_2$, and hence $k_{min} = |Im(\pi)| = 2$. The best case assigns s_4 a unique scenario. However, s_3 must always be an existing scenario, as $s_1, s_2 \in \mathsf{O}(s_3)$. We can hence set $\pi(1) = \pi(3) = s_1$, $\pi(2) = s_2$, $\pi(4) = (t_1, t_2, t_4)$, and $k_{max} = |Im(\pi)| = 3$.

The values k_{min} and k_{max} can be used as a replacement of the numerator in Eq. 1. This allows us to give lower and upper approximations on the (indeterminable) SCC when given a list of observed scenarios $(S_1, \ldots, S_n)$ under the OWA:

$$\frac{k_{min}}{|\mathbb{T}|} \leq \mathrm{SCC}(\mathbb{T}, (s'_1, \ldots, s'_n)) \leq \frac{k_{max}}{|\mathbb{T}|},$$

where $s'_i \in S_i$ is the "real" ground truth of the i-th scenario that could not be determined. The computation of the denominator does not change under the OWA, i.e., we still require computing the size of the option space $|\mathbb{T}|$.

When testing robotic systems, the lower and upper bound can inform test engineers and approval authorities about the current test coverage state, even under incomplete specifications or imperfect perception. There are, however, practical differences between both bounds, and MinCover (k_{min}) might be argued as more relevant in practice than MaxCover (k_{max}). MinCover reports the minimum amount of scenarios possibly seen in the test run, and hence can be used for proving coverage against approval authorities. In Germany, such a coverage demonstration is required for a permit to operate an automated driving system, as argued in the introduction [11]. Contrarily, a low MaxCover can indicate a required increase in efforts to engineers during testing since it reports the best coverage possible when assuming maximum diversity in the observed scenarios. If it is known that the best case coverage is still below the designated target value, the tests will provably not suffice for a system release. While this is valuable input to guide the engineers' decisions, it is of a rather informative nature compared to the approval-enabling capabilities of the lower bound.

3.2 Computing the Lower and Upper Bound

We now analyze the complexity of computing both bounds. From a practical perspective, this especially allows understanding how the required computational efforts depend on the data, which can grow extremely large as the test campaigns progress. As we will see, handling extensive test data is not a small feat.

A naïve algorithm is to compute coverage for all possible explicated combinations, which has a worst-case exponential complexity of $\mathcal{O}(|V|^{|T|\cdot n})$. Even if $|T|$ is constant, this is not a viable solution as n typically grows as the test campaign progresses, resulting in a complexity of $\mathcal{O}(2^n)$ already for binary tags. Preliminary experiments show that this brute-force algorithm is infeasible on small data: it did not terminate within one hour on 10^2 scenarios on standard consumer hardware for three OWA and four CWA tags (with equal probabilities for 0 and 1, and 10% probability for $*$-entries). Even a more sophisticated method involving highly efficient Satisfiability Modulo Theories (SMT) solving fails the same setup for 10^3 scenarios (more details are given online [41]).

The main finding of this work is that we can devise algorithms that perform theoretically *and* practically better than both brute force and SMT solving. We will see that IsMinCover is, in fact, not easily solvable: It is D^p-complete, where $D^p = \{L_1 \cap L_2 \mid L_1 \in \text{NP}, L_2 \in \text{coNP}\}$, i.e., the intersection of an NP- and coNP-problem. Contrarily, IsMaxCover can be computed in polynomial time. Hence, from a theoretical viewpoint, both the brute-force and SMT-based approach are suboptimal for computing the upper approximation. For the lower approximation, we show that – from a practical perspective – there is a problem in which the bound computation can be encoded more naturally than SMT, yielding practical improvements.

MinCover. IsMinCover is D^p-complete: First, note that it is the intersection of an NP-problem (checking whether there is a function with the mentioned constraints) and a coNP-problem (checking whether there is no such smaller function). Leveraging this duality, hardness follows by reduction from SAT-UNSAT, a classical D^p-complete problem [26]. A full proof is given in the online material [41].

Our computation of MinCover leverages analogies to finding minimal hitting sets, which is typically solved by unweighted partial MaxSAT. Let $X = \{x_1, \ldots, x_u\}$ be a set of variables and $\overline{X} = \{\neg x \mid x \in X\}$ their negations. A Conjunctive Normal Form (CNF) is a set of clauses $C = \{C_1, \ldots, C_v\}$ where each clause is a finite set of literals from $X \cup \overline{X}$. A solution to a CNF C is a function that satisfies all of its clauses, i.e., $\alpha : X \to \{0, 1\}$ where for all $C_j \in C$ there is some $l \in C_j$ s.t. $\alpha(l) = 1$ if $l \in X$ or $\alpha(x) = 0$ if $l \in \overline{X}$. In unweighted partial MaxSAT, we are given two CNFs C_h (hard clauses) and C_s (soft clauses, which have an implicit weight 1). The task is to find a solution to C_h which additionally satisfies a maximal number of clauses in C_s.

To solve MinCover via a MaxSAT solver, we set $C_h = S$. To ensure that the identified solution is minimal, soft clauses $C_s = \{\{\neg s\} \mid s \in U\}$ are added. This enforces solutions which maximize the number of excluded elements of U but still (due to the hard clause) hit each set at least once. The desired k_{min} is then the number of satisfied variables, i.e., $k_{min} = |\{s \in U \mid \alpha(s) = 1\}|$. Correctness is shown in the online material [41]. While MaxSAT is NP-hard (more specifically, OptP-complete [23]), optimized algorithms exist and current approaches can offer a worst-case complexity $\mathcal{O}^*(1.2886^n)$ on our setting [42]. An exponential dependency on the data remains, yet this reflects a substantial improvement over $\mathcal{O}(2^n)$ required by the naïve brute-force approach. For our running example, we encode the four scenarios in S by the following CNFs:

$$C_h = \{\{(t_4)\}, \{(t_1, t_4)\}, \{(t_4), (t_1, t_4)\}, \{(t_4), (t_2, t_4), (t_1, t_4), (t_1, t_2, t_4)\}\},$$
$$C_s = \{\{\neg(t_4)\}, \{\neg(t_1, t_4)\}, \{\neg(t_2, t_4)\}, \{\neg(t_1, t_2, t_4)\}\},$$

The resulting maximal solution is indeed $\alpha((t_4)) = \alpha((t_1, t_4)) = 1$ and $\alpha((t_2, t_4)) = \alpha((t_1, t_2, t_4)) = 0$ (satisfying two of the four soft clauses), confirming $k_{min} = 2$.

MaxCover. Contrary to MinCover, MaxCover can be computed in polynomial time. For this, we reduce MaxCover to finding the maximum matching in bipartite graphs [19] (which we call MaxMatch). An undirected graph $G = (V, E)$ with $E \subseteq \{\{v_1, v_2\} \mid v_1, v_2 \in V\}$ is bipartite if there is a partition of V into V_1 and V_2 s.t. $E = \{\{v_1, v_2\} \mid v_1 \in V_1, v_2 \in V_2\}$. For a bipartite graph $G = (V, E)$, a maximum matching is a maximal set of edges $E_{max} \subseteq E$ s.t. for all $\{v_1, v_2\}, \{v_3, v_4\} \in E_{max}$ with $\{v_1, v_2\} \neq \{v_3, v_4\}$ it holds that $v_1 \neq v_3$ and $v_2 \neq v_4$. This problem can be solved in polynomial time, specifically, $\mathcal{O}(\sqrt{V}E)$ [19], and recently, even more optimized algorithms were proposed [7].

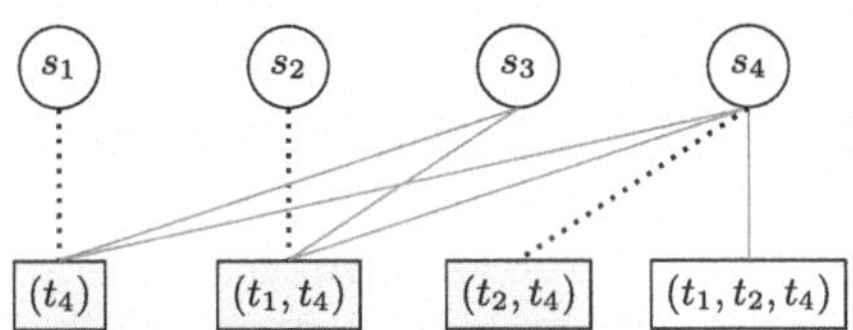

Fig. 1. G_S for the running example; the maximum cardinality matching is dotted.

To reduce MaxCover for $S = (S_1, \ldots S_n)$ over a universe U to MaxMatch, we define a graph $G_S = (\{s_1, \ldots, s_n\} \cup U, \{\{s_i, s\} \mid i \in \{1, \ldots, n\}, s \in S_i\})$ over the partitions $\{s_1, \ldots, s_n\}$ and U. Then, $k_{max} = |E_{max}|$, i.e., the cardinality of a maximum matching of G_S. The proof is available online [41]. In terms of our original inputs, this computation translates to a complexity of $\mathcal{O}(\sqrt{n + |U|} \sum_{S_i \in S} |S_i|)$, improving on the naïve and SMT-based approaches. This also implies the corresponding decision problem IsMaxCover to be in P. For the running example, the resulting graph is given in Fig. 1.

4 Realizing Open World Scenario Classification

In Sect. 3, we simply assumed unknown scenario information in the scenario data, accounting for the OWA required when analyzing test data from robotic systems operating in complex contexts. We have not yet explained how we derive from the data $d = (\mathfrak{D}_1, \ldots, \mathfrak{D}_m)$ a scenario possibly containing unknown information, i.e., implementing a (partial) function $\Lambda_{T,V\cup\{*\}} : \bigcup_{h>0} \mathbb{D}^h \rightarrow (V \cup \{*\})^T$. Recall that this function assigns a given data trace its tag values. To implement $\Lambda_{T,V\cup\{*\}}$, the idea is to use formulae of a Boolean logic to decide the value of a tag for a given data trace. More specifically, we employ *two* formulae, one representing certainty about the tag value being 0, and the other formalizing the case where a tag value of 1 must hold. In the gray zone between both formulae (where none is true), the tag value $*$ is assigned to the data trace.

Formally, we assume to have some Boolean logic L with semantics $d \models \psi$ for $\psi \in \mathsf{L}$, indicating that formula ψ to hold given the data d. We can then define the tag value for a given data trace under an OWA via two formulae $\psi_t^+, \psi_t^- \in \mathsf{L}$ for safe satisfaction and violation of some tag $t \in T$, respectively:

$$\Lambda_{T,V\cup\{*\}}(d) \quad = \quad t \mapsto \begin{cases} 1, \text{ if } d \models \psi_t^+ \text{ and } d \not\models \psi_t^-, \\ 0, \text{ if } d \not\models \psi_t^+ \text{ and } d \models \psi_t^-, \\ *, \text{ if } d \not\models \psi_t^+ \text{ and } d \not\models \psi_t^-. \end{cases} \tag{2}$$

If both formulae hold, a modeling error is present and no value can be identified (hence the function being partial). If both formulae do not hold, no decision on the tag's value can be made and $*$ is assigned.

It remains to instantiate L, for which temporal logics lend themselves naturally due to their ability to reason over finite, discrete temporal data. They were successfully applied, albeit under a CWA [9,18,24,29], as also delineated in Sect. 6. In what follows, we show two such temporal logics, both based on Linear Temporal Logic over Finite Traces (LTL_f) [8]. For some language of atoms $\mathcal{A}$, $\text{LTL}_\text{f}^\mathcal{A}$ syntax is defined by the grammar $\psi ::= \mathcal{A} \mid \neg\psi \mid \psi \wedge \psi \mid \psi\, \mathcal{U}\, \psi \mid \bigcirc\, \psi$, where we allow for atoms from $\mathcal{A}$, the usual Boolean operators ($\wedge$ and $\neg$), as well as until ($\mathcal{U}$) and next ($\bigcirc$). $\mathcal{A}$ is intentionally left open: Whereas our first proposal assumes $\mathcal{A}$ as propositions, the second one uses model-theoretic semantics and defines $\mathcal{A}$ as Conjunctive Queries (CQs) over DLs.

4.1 Propositional Logic

In standard LTL_f [8], data are sequences of propositions $\mathcal{P}$, i.e., $\mathbb{D} = 2^\mathcal{P}$. A formula $\psi \in \text{LTL}_\text{f}^\mathcal{P}$ is satisfied by a data trace $d = (\mathfrak{D}_1, \ldots, \mathfrak{D}_m)$, written $d \models \psi$, if $d, 1 \models \psi$, where

$d, i \models P$, for $P \in \mathcal{P}$, iff $P \in \mathfrak{D}_i$,
$d, i \models \neg\psi$ iff $d, i \not\models \psi$,
$d, i \models \psi_1 \wedge \psi_2$ iff $d, i \models \psi_1$ and $d, i \models \psi_2$,
$d, i \models \bigcirc\, \psi$ iff $i < m$ and $d, i+1 \models \psi$, and
$d, i \models \psi_1\, \mathcal{U}\, \psi_2$ iff ex. a $k \in [i, m]$ s.t. $d, k \models \psi_2$ and $d, j \models \psi_1$ for all $j \in [i, k)$.

Typical syntactical definitions apply, e.g., $\Diamond\ \psi\ = \mathsf{true}\, \mathcal{U}\, \psi$. As propositional logics are interpreted under a CWA, it remains to use ψ_t^+ and ψ_t^- for modeling an OWA, i.e., by Eq. 2, the gray zone is present iff both conditions are false. For a meaningful OWA, users must carefully model the conditions ψ_t^+ and ψ_t^-.

Consider the example t_1 (whether a safety distance violation is present), for which we use, for the sake of the example, the half-speed rule as an over-approximation. To under-approximate, we use the distance requirements specified in for Automated Lane Keeping Systems in the UNECE Regulation No. 157 [33]. Both rules span the gray zone sketched in Fig. 2. With corresponding propositions, we can define inclusion and exclusion conditions for t_1:

- Inclusion ($\psi_{t_1}^+$): The requirements of the UNECE R157 were violated; $\Diamond\,(\texttt{lead\_vehicle} \land \neg\texttt{safety\_distance}_{\texttt{R157}})$.
- Exclusion ($\psi_{t_1}^-$): The half-speed rule was always adhered to; $\Box\,\neg(\texttt{lead\_vehicle} \land \neg\texttt{safety\_distance}_{\frac{1}{2}})$.

This approach adds the OWA only at the very end of the specification side (meaning the determination of the tag's value), while $\mathrm{LTL}_\mathrm{f}^\mathcal{P}$ formulae are interpreted under the CWA. This has the advantage of enabling efficient computation, as the word problem (deciding membership of a data trace to the language of a formula) in $\mathrm{LTL}_\mathrm{f}^\mathcal{P}$ can be decided in polynomial time [5], however, to the detriment of a fully integrated OWA. In our example, $\psi_{t_1}^+$ itself is interpreted under a CWA, i.e., if $\psi_{t_1}^+$ is not present in the data, $\neg\psi_{t_1}^+$ is assumed to hold.

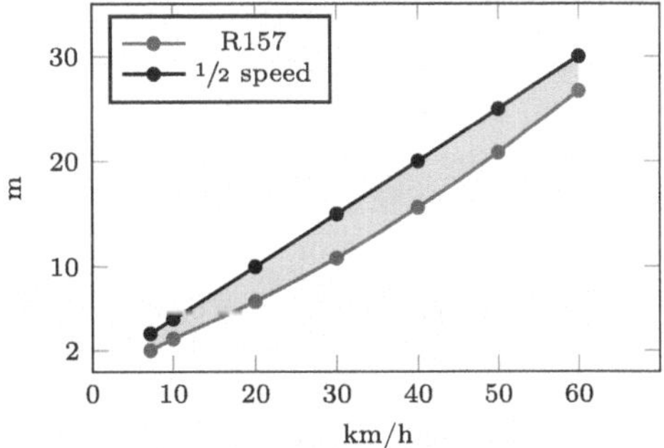

Fig. 2. Distance regulations.

4.2 Description Logics

DLs, a decidable fragment of first order logic, inherently make the OWA, contrary to propositional logic. They are a popular choice for augmenting data by background knowledge [3] which can then be queried by CQs. The temporal logic $\mathrm{LTL}_\mathrm{f}^\mathrm{CQ}$ uses CQs as its atom language [39].

We model data over so-called individuals (observable entities) that can be classified by means of concepts and roles. For this, we assume name supplies $\mathsf{N_C}$ (concepts), $\mathsf{N_R}$ (roles), and $\mathsf{N_I}$ (individuals). Examples are `Walkway` or `Vehicle` as concepts and `v` as an individual. Data axioms are assignments of individuals to concepts and roles, and of the form $\mathtt{C}(\mathtt{i}_1)$ and $\mathtt{r}(\mathtt{i}_1, \mathtt{i}_2)$ a concept $\mathtt{C} \in \mathsf{N_C}$, role $\mathtt{r} \in \mathsf{N_R}$, and individuals $\mathtt{i}_1, \mathtt{i}_2 \in \mathsf{N_I}$. For example, `NonMovingVehicle(v)` adds the individual `v` to the concept `NonMovingVehicle`. $\mathbb{D}$ is then the set of all data axiom sets, allowing to represent a finite data trace d as a sequence data axioms, i.e., $d = (\mathfrak{D}_1, \ldots, \mathfrak{D}_m)$ with $\mathfrak{D}_i \in \mathbb{D}$. Example temporal data are $d_{ex} = (\{\texttt{NonMovingVehicle(v)}, \texttt{intersects(v,w)}, \texttt{Walkway(w)}\}, \emptyset)$, asserting `v` to be a non-moving vehicle intersecting a walkway first, followed by no observation.

The data are interpreted over an ontology $\mathcal{O}$, which is a set of axioms describing background knowledge of the form $C \sqsubseteq D$ (a concept D subsumes C), allowing to infer additional facts from the observed data. In the expressive DL $\mathcal{ALC}$, concepts can be composed of concept names ($\mathsf{N_C}$), intersections ($C \sqcap D$), unions ($C \sqcup D$), negations ($\neg C$), universal role restrictions ($\forall \mathtt{r}.C$), and existential role restrictions ($\exists \mathtt{r}.C$), for concepts C, D and a role $\mathtt{r} \in \mathsf{N_R}$. An example $\mathcal{ALC}$-ontology $\mathcal{O}_{ex} = \{\mathtt{NonMovingVehicle} \sqcap \exists \mathtt{interects.ParkingSpot} \sqsubseteq \mathtt{ParkingVehicle}, \mathtt{Walkway} \sqsubseteq \mathtt{ParkingSpot}\}$ states that non-moving vehicles on parking spots, which include walkways, are parking.

DLs employ model-theoretic semantics by using temporal interpretations $\mathfrak{I}$, which are sequences $(\mathcal{I}_i)_{i \in \{1,\dots,m\}}$ of $\mathcal{ALC}$-interpretations $\mathcal{I} = (\Delta^{\mathcal{I}}, \cdot^{\mathcal{I}})$. Here, $\Delta^{\mathcal{I}}$ is a shared interpretation domain and $\cdot^{\mathcal{I}}$ maps concepts, roles, and individuals to its elements. Any model $\mathcal{I}$ of an $\mathcal{ALC}$-ontology and data axioms $(\mathcal{O}, \mathfrak{D})$ – we write $\mathcal{I} \models (\mathcal{O}, \mathfrak{D})$ – must respect its constraints. For brevity, we omit formal details on DL semantics here and refer the reader to the literature [3,39]. In our example, in any model $\mathcal{I}$ of $\mathcal{O}_{ex}$ it must hold that $\mathtt{Walkway}^{\mathcal{I}} \subseteq \mathtt{ParkingSpot}^{\mathcal{I}}$. Hence, for the ontology and data, it follows that in all its temporal models $\mathfrak{I}$, $\mathtt{v}$ must be parking in $\mathcal{I}_0$. No inferences on $\mathtt{v}$ can be made for the second timestamp (it might be parking or not parking), and it can belong to any concept in $\mathcal{I}_1$.

We now define $\mathrm{LTL}_\mathrm{f}^\mathrm{CQ}$, which incorporates DL semantics into LTL_f by using Boolean CQs as its atomic expressions $\mathcal{A}$ [39]. A Boolean CQ φ is a finite conjunction of data axioms, but additionally allows existentially quantified variables in place of individuals. We say that φ is entailed by some interpretation $\mathcal{I}$ ($\mathcal{I} \models \varphi$) if the query's constraints are reflected in the interpretation under a suitable mapping of the variables into the interpretation domain. For example, the Boolean CQ $\exists x.\mathtt{ParkingVehicle}(x)$ is entailed by any model $\mathcal{I}$ of $(\mathcal{O}_{ex}, (d_{ex})_1)$, as x can be assigned $\mathrm{v}^{\mathcal{I}}$. We lift entailment from CQs to $\mathrm{LTL}_\mathrm{f}^\mathrm{CQ}$ formulae ψ:

$\mathfrak{I}, i \models \varphi$ iff $\mathcal{I}_i \models \varphi$ (for a Boolean CQ φ),
$\mathfrak{I}, i \models \neg\psi$ iff $\mathfrak{I}, i \not\models \psi$,
$\mathfrak{I}, i \models \psi_1 \wedge \psi_2$ iff $\mathfrak{I}, i \models \psi_1$ and $\mathfrak{I}, i \models \psi_2$,
$\mathfrak{I}, i \models \bigcirc\, \psi$ iff $i < m$ and $\mathfrak{I}, i+1 \models \psi$, and
$\mathfrak{I}, i \models \psi_1 \,\mathcal{U}\, \psi_2$ iff ex. a $k \in [i, m]$ s.t. $\mathfrak{I}, k \models \psi_2$ and $d, j \models \psi_1$ for all $j \in [i, k)$.

Then, ψ is entailed by an ontology and data trace $(\mathcal{O}, d)$, written $(\mathcal{O}, d) \models \psi$, if for *all* their models $\mathfrak{I}$ it holds that $\mathfrak{I}, 1 \models \psi$.

$\mathrm{LTL}_\mathrm{f}^\mathrm{CQ}$ makes the OWA through this model-based semantics. Specifically, from the non-entailment of a formula its negation does not follow: By definition, the negated universal quantification over all interpretations (non-entailment) implies solely the existence of a model consistent with the negated fact (satisfiability of the negation), which is not equivalent to entailment of the negation. For example, $(\mathcal{O}_{ex}, (d_{ex})_2) \not\models \mathtt{ParkingVehicle}(\mathtt{v})$ ($\mathtt{v}$ is not guaranteed to be parking in the second timestamp) does not imply $(\mathcal{O}, (d_{ex})_2) \models \neg\mathtt{ParkingVehicle}(\mathtt{v})$ ($\mathtt{v}$ is not parking); only in some but not all models $(\neg\mathtt{ParkingVehicle})(\mathtt{v})$ holds.

Similar to what is done for $\mathrm{LTL}_\mathrm{f}^\mathcal{P}$ above, we define a tag $t \in T$ via formulae $\psi_t^+, \psi_t^- \in \mathrm{LTL}_\mathrm{f}^\mathrm{CQ}$. In the simplest case, $\psi_t^- = \neg\psi_t^+$, as, under the OWA semantics, both formulae might be not entailed, enabling the desired gray zone. The example tag t_3 is a suitable candidate for formalization via DLs, since engineers can model their ontological knowledge on what encompasses parking vehicles, as exemplified by the $\mathcal{ALC}$-ontology $\mathcal{O}_{ex}$ above. A more involved ontology on parking vehicles is given in the reproducibility artifact [31]. We can then ask if at some point a parking vehicle v was passed by the system s: $\psi_{t_3}^{+} = \Box\, \mathtt{ParkingVehicle(v)} \wedge \Diamond \left(\mathtt{inProximity(s, v)} \wedge \mathtt{inFront(v, s)} \wedge \Diamond\, (\mathtt{inProximity(s, v)} \wedge \mathtt{behind(v, s)})\right)$, and set $\psi_{t_3}^{-} = \neg\psi_{t_3}^{+}$. If v is not explicitly modeled as parking in the data, we require interpreting d_{ex} under $\mathcal{O}_{ex}$ for additional inferences. While we can infer v to be parking for the first timestamp in d_{ex}, its second timestamp does not allow making any inferences in that regard. Hence, both ψ_{t_3} and $\neg\psi_{t_3}$ are not entailed on $(\mathcal{O}_{ex}, d_{ex})$, resulting in the tag value being $*$.

To summarize, DLs use the OWA *inherently* for reasoning over *all* axioms, adding gray zones also to all intermediate reasoning steps, e.g., determining whether ParkingVehicle(v) holds. This comes to the expense of complexity, as, in contrast to $\mathrm{LTL}_\mathrm{f}^{\mathcal{P}}$, the word problem of $\mathrm{LTL}_\mathrm{f}^{\mathrm{CQ}}$ is ExpTime-complete [39].

5 Evaluation

We implemented the algorithms of Sect. 3.2 for computing both bounds into STARS, a scenario coverage measurement framework [29]. For calculating MinCover, we use the Z3 solver[1]. For MaxCover, we allow using either Edmonds' blossom or the Hopcroft-Karp algorithm for maximum cardinality (bipartite) matching, as implemented in jgrapht[2].

For computing tag values for a given data trace, STARS provides, by default, CMFTBL, which can be seen as an extension of $\mathrm{LTL}_\mathrm{f}^{\mathcal{P}}$. Equation 2 allows users of STARS to specify two formulae for safe inclusion and exclusion of a tag. Additionally, we added a module to STARS that includes Topllet [40], a software that implements $\mathrm{LTL}_\mathrm{f}^{\mathrm{CQ}}$ [37,39]. The module acts as a drop-in replacement for CMFTBL [36]. In STARS, we allow tags to be interpreted either under the CWA or OWA, justified by the observation that information and specification can be sometimes assumed to be virtually perfect. We use our implementation for answering the following main research questions:

- Q1 What are grounded assumptions on the distribution of $*$-entries in real data?
- Q2 Do the lower and upper bound provide useful approximations on coverage under such $*$-distributions?
- Q3 Can both bounds be computed efficiently also on practically relevant data configurations, and how is performance impacted by different factors?

[1] https://github.com/Z3Prover/z3.

[2] https://jgrapht.org.

5.1 Tag Value Distributions on Real-World Data

For answering Q1, we again rely on the three example OWA tags t_1 to t_3. The first tag ("safety distance") can be implemented in a propositional fashion (cf. Sect. 4.1). Similarly, corresponding OWA predicates for t_2 ("presence of a pedestrian or bicycle") can be defined: We degrade any perceived bicycle with a speed over 12 m/s and pedestrian over 5 m/s as a not further identifiable vulnerable road user (there is a realistic chance that the bicycle was, in fact, a motorcycle, and the pedestrian was actually mounted on a vehicle), and assign $*$ in those cases. The third tag ("passing parking vehicle") lends itself for formalization in DLs, as seen in Sect. 4.2, for which we specified a corresponding query in the input language of Topllet.

For real-world data, we use the established inD data set, which contains roughly 7 500 scenarios from drone camera recordings of four intersections in Aachen, Germany [4]. The videos are post-processed by neural networks to extract trajectories and classify traffic participants, and also contain road network information. Each scenario represents one ego vehicle traversing an intersection. Based on these details, we determine values for our three example OWA tags t_1 to t_3. Since the drone data does not contain scenarios at low sun positions, the example tag t_4 was excluded from the analysis. The evaluation scripts are given in the reproduction artifact; unfortunately, an individual copy of the data must be obtained due to licensing.

Table 1 shows the resulting distributions of tag values. Whereas the first two tags, relating to safety distance fuzziness and vague perception classification, exhibit less than 10% $*$-entries, the third tag accumulates to roughly 14%. For t_3, it is certainly possible to reduce uncertainty by a more refined specification of parking vehicles. We draw upon these empirical observations to determine grounded probabilities for $*$-entries in the subsequently used synthetic data.

Table 1. Distributions for the OWA example tags on inD.

V_t \ t	t_1	t_2	t_3
0	73.03%	14.91%	46.43%
1	17.60%	78.95%	39.59%
$*$	9.37%	6.14%	13.98%

5.2 Quality and Runtime Analysis on Synthetic Data

For the remaining research questions, we require controlled data to assess quality and runtime under different configurations. This includes the numbers of tags, the split between OWA and CWA tags, and the distribution of $*$-entries. This level of control is unfortunately not present in real-world data, which is why we construct synthetic data for answering Q2 and Q3. The data are generated for all numbers $n_t \in [1, 15]$ of tags, where the number of OWA tags is $n_{\text{owa}} \in [1, n]$ and the number of CWA tags is $n_{\text{cwa}} = n_t - n_{\text{owa}}$, with different probabilities of $*$-entries $p_* \in \{5\%, 10\%, 15\%, 20\%\}$, derived from our practical experiences with inD. The data were created by first generating a "ground truth", i.e., records where each value is known, which are then made unknown by probabilistically overwriting entries with $*$-values. This allows for reporting "real" coverage values later on. The probability of all tags being either true or false is set to 50% each. We generate data in batches of scenarios and then compute coverage for all data. For efficiency reasons, we increase the batch size depending on the numbers of assessed tags to a maximum of 10 000 for $n_t \geq 13$. All subsequently presented computations were done single threaded on a `Intel Xeon Gold 6342 CPU` running Ubuntu 20 using docker. While the data were generated probabilistically, practical experience showed that results for different seeds did not differ meaningfully, and hence only a single run is executed per configuration. The results of all configurations are available in our replication artifact [31].

Coverage Approximation Quality. For Q2, we start by showcasing the progression of MaxCover, MinCover, and real coverage on the configuration $n_{\text{owa}} = 5$, $n_{\text{cwa}} = 10$, and $p_* = 10\%$ in Fig. 3. We additionally depict naïve lower and upper bounds. The upper bound is constructed by assuming for every $*$ that both options happened (which is impossible), and the lower bound by ignoring all scenarios containing $*$. Observe that the x-axis of Fig. 3 is scaled logarithmically, since coverage improvements degrade exponentially over time.

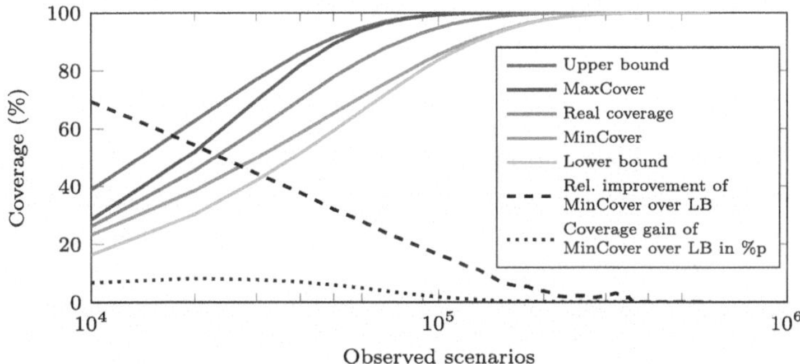

Fig. 3. Coverage and derived bounds for $n_{\text{owa}} = 5, n_{\text{cwa}} = 10, p_* = 10\%$.

In Fig. 3, we focus only on the performance gain of MinCover, due to its higher practical relevancy (as argued in Sect. 3) and for ease of presentation. Naturally, improvements are most immanent at the beginning, with up to 69% relative and 7% points absolute gain. For full coverage, all bounds nearly coincide – however, during short development cycles observed in practice, full coverage is likely an unrealistic goal. Rather, 80% appears as a more reasonable target in industrial settings, for which MinCover still reduces the error of the naïve lower bound to real coverage by 28% on the example. Over all conducted experiments with $n_t \geq 5$, we report a reduced error of MinCover over the lower bound of $30.61\% \pm 6.23\%$ at 80% real coverage. For the upper bound, error reduction becomes uninformative at 80% (since it approaches zero). We hence report it at 50% real coverage, where we achieve an error reduction of $35.73\% \pm 18.76\%$.

Runtime Analysis. In Q3 we ask whether coverage approximations can be computed on real-world settings. Figure 4 reports the gap between MinCover and MaxCover for $n_{\text{owa}} = 10$ and $n_{\text{cwa}} \in [0, 8]$ at $p_* = 5\%$ on a normalized scale (with 1 representing the sample at which the gap reached zero). Evidently, there is no influence of additional closed tags on the spread of the bounds, so we conduct this analysis on OWA tags only. For MaxCover, Edmonds' blossom and the Hopcroft-Karp algorithm yield comparably fast computation times (with the latter being slightly advantageous). We however omit those in the runtime analysis, as MinCover uses on average > 98% of the total runtime for $n_{\text{owa}} \geq 2$.

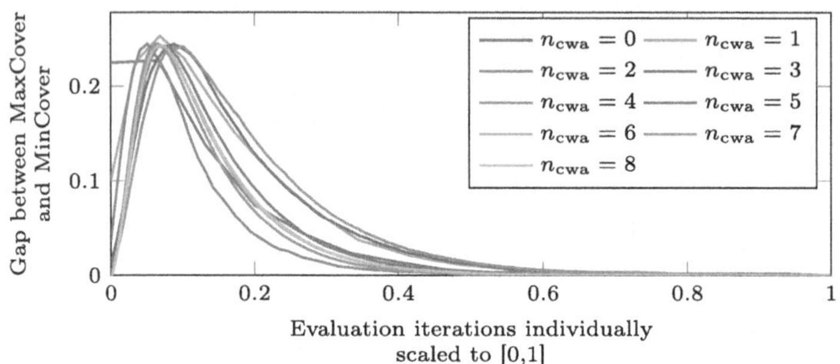

Fig. 4. Bound gap at $n_{\text{owa}} = 10$, $p_* = 5\%$ over added CWA tags n_{cwa}.

Figure 5 reports the runtime of MinCover for $n_{owa} = 13$ and $n_{cwa} = 0$ with varying p_*, where each point represents one computation of MinCover on the full dataset up the given amount of scenarios. The plot indicates a sublinear relationship between the number of scenarios and the required computation time, with spikes at the beginning most likely being due to solver initialization. Lower p_*-values reach 100% MinCover after fewer scenarios (due to lesser degrees of freedom in selecting a worst case), and their graphs therefore abort early in Fig. 5. This shows that coverage bounds can be computed timely even at realistic data sizes of 10^6 (recall that inD contains less than 10^4 scenarios). To assess the influence of different numbers of OWA tags on runtime, Fig. 6 compares the wall-clock time of MinCover for the last iteration, i.e., when the coverage hit 100%, of all examined configurations, to the amount of observed scenarios needed to achieve 100% coverage. The computations for $n_{\text{owa}} > 13$ at $p_* = 20\%$ and $n_{\text{owa}} > 15$ had to be terminated due to excessive runtime.

Our results show that for up to but excluding 15 OWA tags, MinCover can be successfully computed in 35 s or less at the last iteration (meaning on as many scenarios as required for 100% coverage). We also observe a direct correspondence of runtime to the number of scenarios required to obtain full coverage. Most likely, this behavior originates from adding for each new scenario its explicated options as a new hard clause. The solver must hence consider, at worst, 3^{n_t} different hard clauses. We remark that also adding CWA tags influences the overall runtime of the solver exponentially: For example, at

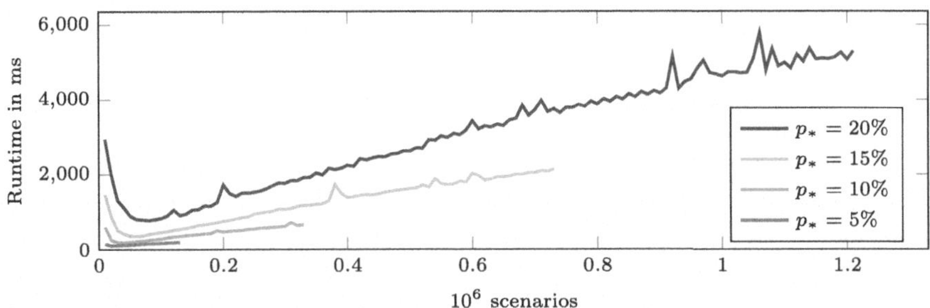

Fig. 5. Runtime of MinCover for $n_{\text{owa}} = 13, n_{cwa} = 0$ over the data size.

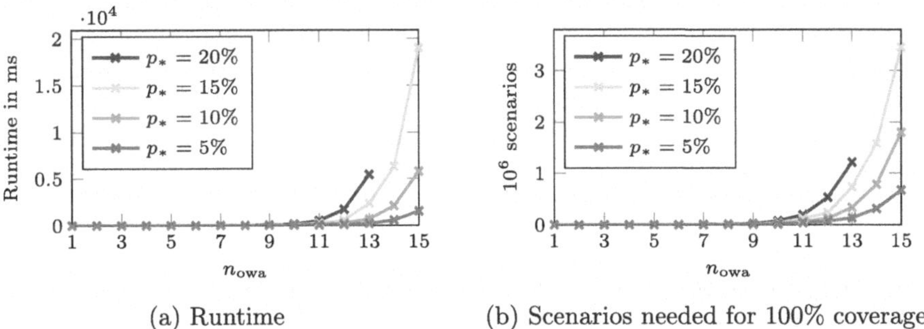

(a) Runtime

(b) Scenarios needed for 100% coverage

Fig. 6. Comparison of wall-clock time to compute last iteration of MinCover, and scenarios needed for 100% coverage across different amounts of OWA tags.

$n_{\text{cwa}} = 9, n_{\text{owa}} = 10, p_* = 5\%$, the calculation was terminated after exceeding 32 h wall-clock time. In practice, the number of tags and their definitions must thus be chosen carefully.

6 Related Work

We have above assumed that an input classification system is available for computing coverage. It must be methodically derived and specified, e.g., based on an ontology [14,38] or combinatorics [35]. Here, the general assumption is that the system shows equivalent behavior w.r.t. safety within a class [1]. Subsequently, recognizing the specified classes in data is required, e.g., by using classifiers trained on human reference behavior [28], trajectory matching [35], or comparing against sequences of events [16]. Another popular choice in automated driving are temporal logics, e.g., MTL or STL over discrete-time [18,24], LTL [9], and CMFTBL [29], which we also used as a foundation. These formalisms originally all make the CWA. This assumption has been extended in this work.

Once scenario classes are specified and recognized in test data, coverage can be computed. In software engineering, coverage (such as branch, statement, and MC/DC coverage) is well-established [43]. Transfer to the emerging domain of automated systems is ongoing [13], where it forms one of the fundamental safety challenges [25,27]. While arguments have been made against excessive dogmatic use of coverage in software engineering [12,17], it may be justified as an important component in testing automated systems if metrics exhibit certain qualities, such as tractability [1]. One of the most foundational metrics for automated robotic systems is tag-based coverage [13,29] – which has also been used in this paper as a canonical basis for demonstrating how the OWA can generally be integrated into coverage. Other metrics exist, including tree-based coverage (removing implausible combinations by constraints [29]), time-based coverage (the duration where no class applies [13]), probabilistically-bounded coverage (counting only combinations that are at least somewhat likely [1]), t-wise coverage (restricting to t-combinations, where the assumption is that many hazards are triggered by at most t classes [32]), quantitative k-projection coverage (a weighted, rule-based extension of t-wise coverage [6]), or concrete scenario coverage (where classification is omitted altogether [2]). Again, all these works make the CWA. We are not aware of any OWA work in our context. Thus, to the best of knowledge, our presented formalism is the first OWA framework in the field of test coverage.

7 Conclusion

In this work, we extended coverage from closed to open world environments, under which MinCover and MaxCover give lower and upper approximations on the actual coverage. Our novel formal framework enabled theoretical complexity analyses, where the corresponding decision problem is D^p-complete for MinCover and polynomially decidable for MaxCover. We presented two ways of relying on temporal logics for an open world scenario classification, one based on propositional and the other on DL semantics. Experiments with an implementation of our formal framework – based on MaxSAT and maximum cardinality matching algorithms – showed both bounds to be feasibly computable on realistic data, and also add value over naïve lower and upper bound computations.

Future work includes optimizing the MinCover computation, e.g., by catching certain cases to avoid running the solver, since our results showed that most of the time is spent solving MaxSAT. Additionally, we plan to assess real-world data from an ego-perspective to also include occlusion effects, which are a relevant source of unknowns not present in inD. To summarize, with this work, we aim at sparking interest in a challenging new field in test coverage analysis, motivated from practical demands while simultaneously offering surprising theoretical subtleties.

References

1. Alexander, R., Hawkins, H.R., Rae, A.J.: Situation coverage - a coverage criterion for testing autonomous robots. Report, The University of York (2015). https://eprints.whiterose.ac.uk/id/eprint/88736/

2. Amersbach, C., Winner, H.: Defining required and feasible test coverage for scenario-based validation of highly automated vehicles. In: 2019 IEEE Intelligent Transportation Systems Conference (ITSC), pp. 425–430. IEEE (2019). https://doi.org/10.1109/ITSC.2019.8917534
3. Baader, F., Calvanese, D., McGuinness, D.L., Nardi, D., Patel-Schneider, P.F.: The Description Logic Handbook: Theory, Implementation and Applications, 2 edn. Cambridge University Press (2007). https://doi.org/10.1017/cbo9780511711787
4. Bock, J., Krajewski, R., Moers, T., Runde, S., Vater, L., Eckstein, L.: The inD dataset: a drone dataset of naturalistic road user trajectories at German intersections. In: 2020 IEEE Intelligent Vehicles Symposium (IV), pp. 1929–1934. IEEE (2020). https://doi.org/10.1109/iv47402.2020.9304839
5. Bundala, D., Ouaknine, J.: On the complexity of temporal-logic path checking. In: Esparza, J., Fraigniaud, P., Husfeldt, T., Koutsoupias, E. (eds.) ICALP 2014. LNCS, vol. 8573, pp. 86–97. Springer, Heidelberg (2014). https://doi.org/10.1007/978-3-662-43951-7_8
6. Cheng, C.-H., Huang, C.-H., Yasuoka, H.: Quantitative projection coverage for testing ML-enabled autonomous systems. In: Lahiri, S.K., Wang, C. (eds.) ATVA 2018. LNCS, vol. 11138, pp. 126–142. Springer, Cham (2018). https://doi.org/10.1007/978-3-030-01090-4_8
7. Chuzhoy, J., Khanna, S.: A faster combinatorial algorithm for maximum bipartite matching. In: Proceedings of the 2024 Annual ACM-Siam Symposium on Discrete Algorithms (SODA), pp. 2185–2235. Society for Industrial and Applied Mathematics (2024). https://doi.org/10.1137/1.9781611977912.79
8. De Giacomo, G., Vardi, M.Y.: Linear temporal logic and linear dynamic logic on finite traces. In: Proceedings of the Twenty-Third International Joint Conference on Artificial Intelligence, IJCAI 2013, pp. 854–860. Association for Computing Machinery, New York, NY, USA (2013). https://dl.acm.org/doi/abs/10.5555/2540128.2540252
9. Esterle, K., Gressenbuch, L., Knoll, A.: Formalizing traffic rules for machine interpretability. In: 2020 IEEE 3rd Connected and Automated Vehicles Symposium (CAVS), pp. 1–7. IEEE (2020). https://doi.org/10.1109/CAVS51000.2020.9334599
10. Federal Ministry for Digital and Transport (Germany): Straßenverkehrs-Ordnung (StVO). Regulation BGBl. I S. 367, BMDV (2013). https://www.gesetze-im-internet.de/stvo_2013/
11. Federal Ministry for Digital and Transport (Germany): Verordnung zur Regelung des Betriebs von Kraftfahrzeugen mit automatisierter und autonomer Fahrfunktion und zur Änderung straßenverkehrsrechtlicher Vorschriften. Regulation 86/22, BMDV (2022). https://www.bundesrat.de/bv.html?id=0086-22
12. Gay, G., Staats, M., Whalen, M.W., Heimdahl, M.P.E.: Moving the goalposts: coverage satisfaction is not enough. In: Proceedings of the 7th International Workshop on Search-Based Software Testing (SBST), SBST 2014, pp. 19–22. Association for Computing Machinery, New York, NY, USA (2014). https://doi.org/10.1145/2593833.2593837
13. de Gelder, E., Buermann, M., ob den Camp, O.: Coverage metrics for a scenario database for the scenario-based assessment of automated driving systems. In: 2024 IEEE International Automated Vehicle Validation Conference (IAVVC), pp. 1–8. IEEE (2024). https://doi.org/10.1109/iavvc63304.2024.10786405
14. de Gelder, E., et al.: Towards an ontology for scenario definition for the assessment of automated vehicles: an object-oriented framework. IEEE Trans. Intell. Veh. **7**(2), 300–314 (2022). https://doi.org/10.1109/tiv.2022.3144803

15. de Gelder, E., Singh, T., Hadj-Selem, F., Vidal Bazan, S., Op den Camp, O.: Scenario metrics for the safety assurance framework of automated vehicles: a review of its application. Vehicles **7**(3), 100 (2025). https://doi.org/10.3390/vehicles7030100
16. de Gelder, E., Manders, J., Grappiolo, C., Paardekooper, J.P., ob den Camp, O., de Schutter, B.: Real-world scenario mining for the assessment of automated vehicles. In: 2020 IEEE 23rd International Conference on Intelligent Transportation Systems (ITSC), pp. 1–8. IEEE (2020). https://doi.org/10.1109/itsc45102.2020.9294652
17. Hamlet, D., Taylor, R.: Partition testing does not inspire confidence (program testing). IEEE Trans. Software Eng. **16**(12), 1402–1411 (1990). https://doi.org/10.1109/32.62448
18. Hekmatnejad, M., et al.: Encoding and monitoring responsibility sensitive safety rules for automated vehicles in signal temporal logic. In: Proceedings of the 17th ACM-IEEE International Conference on Formal Methods and Models for System Design, MEMOCODE 2019, pp. 1–11. Association for Computing Machinery, New York, NY, USA (2019). https://doi.org/10.1145/3359986.3361203
19. Hopcroft, J.E., Karp, R.M.: A N5/2 algorithm for maximum matchings in bipartite. In: 12th Annual Symposium on Switching and Automata Theory (SWAT 1971). IEEE (1971). https://doi.org/10.1109/swat.1971.1
20. International Organization for Standardization: Road vehicles — safety of the intended functionality. ISO Standard 21448:2022, ISO (2022). https://www.iso.org/standard/77490.html
21. International Organization for Standardization: Road vehicles — test scenarios for automated driving systems — scenario categorization. ISO Standard 34504:2024, ISO (2024). https://www.iso.org/standard/78953.html
22. Keet, C.M.: Open World Assumption, p. 1567. Springer New York, New York, NY (2013). https://doi.org/10.1007/978-1-4419-9863-7_734
23. Krentel, M.W.: The complexity of optimization problems. J. Comput. Syst. Sci. **36**(3), 490–509 (1988). https://doi.org/10.1016/0022-0000(88)90039-6
24. Maierhofer, S., Moosbrugger, P., Althoff, M.: Formalization of intersection traffic rules in temporal logic. In: 2022 IEEE Intelligent Vehicles Symposium (IV), pp. 1135–1144. IEEE (2022). https://doi.org/10.1109/IV51971.2022.9827153
25. Neurohr, C., Westhofen, L., Henning, T., de Graaff, T., Mohlmann, E., Bode, E.: Fundamental considerations around scenario-based testing for automated driving. In: 2020 IEEE Intelligent Vehicles Symposium (IV), pp. 121–127. IEEE (2020). https://doi.org/10.1109/iv47402.2020.9304823
26. Papadimitriou, C.H., Yannakakis, M.: The complexity of facets (and some facets of complexity). In: Proceedings of the Fourteenth Annual ACM Symposium on Theory of Computing - STOCK 1982, STOC 1982, pp. 255–260. Association for Computing Machinery, New York, NY, USA (1982). https://doi.org/10.1145/800070.802199
27. Riedmaier, S., Ponn, T., Ludwig, D., Schick, B., Diermeyer, F.: Survey on scenario-based safety assessment of automated vehicles. IEEE Access **8**, 87456–87477 (2020). https://doi.org/10.1109/ACCESS.2020.2993730
28. Roesener, C., Fahrenkrog, F., Uhlig, A., Eckstein, L.: A scenario-based assessment approach for automated driving by using time series classification of human-driving behaviour. In: 2016 IEEE 19th International Conference on Intelligent Transportation Systems (ITSC), pp. 1360–1365. IEEE (2016). https://doi.org/10.1109/itsc.2016.7795734
29. Schallau, T., Naujokat, S., Kullmann, F., Howar, F.: Tree-based scenario classification. In: Benz, N., Gopinath, D., Shi, N. (eds.) NASA Formal Methods. LNCS,

vol. 14627, pp. 259–278. Springer Nature Switzerland, Cham (2024). https://doi.org/10.1007/978-3-031-60698-4_15
30. Schmid, D., et al.: A qualitative analysis of the german road traffic regulations (StVO) for automated driving. In: 2025 IEEE International Automated Vehicle Validation Conference (IAVVC), pp. 1–8. IEEE (2025). https://doi.org/10.1109/IAVVC61942.2025.11219635
31. Schmid, D., Westhofen, L., Schallau, T.: Data from: test coverage of automated robotic systems in open world environments (2026). https://doi.org/10.5281/zenodo.17775279. Dataset
32. Sun, J., Zhang, H., Zhou, H., Yu, R., Tian, Y.: Scenario-based test automation for highly automated vehicles: a review and paving the way for systematic safety assurance. IEEE Trans. Intell. Transp. Syst. **23**(9), 14088–14103 (2022). https://doi.org/10.1109/TITS.2021.3136353
33. United Nations: Uniform provisions concerning the approval of vehicles with regard to automated lane keeping systems (ALKS). UN Regulation 157, United Nations (2021). https://documents.un.org/symbol-explorer?s=E/ECE/TRANS/505/REV.3/ADD.156, e/ECE/TRANS/505/Rev.3/Add.156
34. Vardi, M.Y.: The complexity of relational query languages (extended abstract). In: Proceedings of the Fourteenth Annual ACM Symposium on Theory of Computing - STOC 1982, STOC 1982, pp. 137–146. Association for Computing Machinery, New York, NY, USA (1982). https://doi.org/10.1145/800070.802186
35. Weber, H., Glasmacher, C., Schuldes, M., Wagener, N., Eckstein, L.: Holistic driving scenario concept for urban traffic. In: 2023 IEEE Intelligent Vehicles Symposium (IV). IEEE (2023). https://doi.org/10.1109/iv55152.2023.10186385
36. Westhofen, L.: STARS logic MTCQ (2025). https://doi.org/10.5281/zenodo.17791768. Software
37. Westhofen, L., Jung, J.C., Neider, D.: Temporal conjunctive query answering via rewriting. Proc. AAAI Conf. Artif. Intell. **39**(14), 15221–15229 (2025). https://doi.org/10.1609/aaai.v39i14.33670
38. Westhofen, L., Neurohr, C., Butz, M., Scholtes, M., Schuldes, M.: Using ontologies for the formalization and recognition of criticality for automated driving. IEEE Open J. Intell. Transp. Syst. **3**, 519–538 (2022). https://doi.org/10.1109/ojits.2022.3187247
39. Westhofen, L., Neurohr, C., Jung, J.C., Neider, D.: Answering temporal conjunctive queries over description logic ontologies for situation recognition in complex operational domains. In: Finkbeiner, B., Kovács, L. (eds.) Tools and Algorithms for the Construction and Analysis of Systems. LNCS, pp. 167–187. Springer Nature Switzerland, Cham (2024). https://doi.org/10.1007/978-3-031-57246-3_10
40. Westhofen, L., Neurohr, C., Jung, J.C., Neider, D.: Topllet: an optimized engine for answering metric temporal conjunctive queries. In: NASA Formal Methods, pp. 314–321. Springer Nature Switzerland, Cham (2024). https://doi.org/10.1007/978-3-031-60698-4_18
41. Westhofen, L., Schallau, T., Schmid, D., Naujokat, S., Howar, F., Neider, D.: Supplementary material to 'test coverage of automated robotic systems in open world environments'. Supplementary Mater. (2026). https://doi.org/10.5281/zenodo.18803837

42. Xiao, M.: An exact MaxSAT algorithm: further observations and further improvements. In: Proceedings of the Thirty-First International Joint Conference on Artificial Intelligence (IJCAI-22), IJCAI-2022, pp. 1887–1893. International Joint Conferences on Artificial Intelligence Organization (2022). https://doi.org/10.24963/ijcai.2022/262
43. Zhu, H., Hall, P.A.V., May, J.H.R.: Software unit test coverage and adequacy. ACM Comput. Surv. **29**(4), 366–427 (1997). https://doi.org/10.1145/267580.267590

SAPSE-Synergy: Balancing Formal Soundness and Empirical Coverage in Neural Theorem Proving

Minrui Chen[1], Huidong Jiang[2], and Hiroto Saigo[1(✉)]

[1] Kyushu University, Fukuoka, Japan
chen.minrui.978@s.kyushu-u.ac.jp, saigo@inf.kyushu-u.ac.jp
[2] Institute of Science Tokyo, Yokohama, Japan
jiang.h.af@m.titech.ac.jp

Abstract. Large language models (LLMs) can propose candidate lemmas, yet translating natural-language reasoning into verified Coq artifacts remains difficult due to semantic drift, missing abstractions, and weak type discipline. Most existing systems treat the prover as a black-box filter: as long as some candidates verify, little is known about which transformations are semantically safe, or how much coverage must be sacrificed to obtain formal guarantees.

We present Semantic Alignment for Proof Strategy Extraction (SAPSE), a retrieval-first framework that links natural-language proof steps with formal lemmas through dual-domain embeddings and type-aware abstraction. At its core, SAPSE introduces an abstract syntax tree (AST) sanitizer whose verified fragment, mechanized in Rocq 9.1.0 for a minimal calculus, consists of two concretely implemented transformations, require injection and equality canonicalization, together with a parametric binder-normalization schema that is currently instantiated as the identity on terms. For all admissible inputs in this calculus, these verified passes are proved to preserve both typing and logical equivalence under import-only context extension. A production sanitizer extends this core with unverified but practical passes: scope resolution, list parameterization, and formatting for complete Coq syntax, while reusing the same verified interface.

On top of this verified core, we develop an adaptive Synergy pipeline that first applies unverified heuristic repairs to maximize empirical coverage and then invokes the verified core under admissibility guards to enforce soundness. Rather than optimizing raw verification accuracy, Synergy exposes a reproducible safety-coverage frontier: on a 2,000-lemma real Coq benchmark, a retrieval-only baseline verifies 37.6% of generated candidates, while the Synergy configuration verifies 32.8% with zero unsafe rewrites among guarded repairs and comparable runtime. Fragment-coverage analysis shows that 98.1% of benchmark lemmas lie in the mechanized fragment and that every Synergy success falls inside this fragment, so the AST-level soundness theorem applies directly. A differential analysis of the 96 lemmas that the retrieval-only baseline verifies but Synergy fails on decomposes these "lost successes" by semantic category, structural complexity, and failure mode, turning the observed

A. Sampaio and M. Stoelinga (Eds.): FM 2026, LNCS 16556, pp. 151–169, 2026.
https://doi.org/10.1007/978-3-032-26204-2_8

performance gap into a diagnostic tool for future verified transformations.

Overall, SAPSE-Synergy provides a partially mechanized but practically effective bridge between probabilistic lemma generation and formally verified transformation. It quantifies, for the first time, how much empirical coverage must be traded for a small, compositional verified core that safely mediates heuristic repairs in neural theorem proving. (Source code and full experimental artifacts are publicly available at: https://github.com/leochenminrui/SAPSE-Synergy)

Keywords: Semantic alignment · Verified transformation · Type-safe lemma synthesis · Retrieval-augmented generation · Large language models · Coq

1 Introduction

Formal verification provides machine-checkable guarantees of correctness, but constructing verified proofs remains slow and expertise-intensive [1,10]. Recent advances in large language models (LLMs) have renewed the vision of automating this process by translating informal reasoning into verified formal artifacts [4,12]. Retrieval-augmented frameworks such as Strat2Rocq [2] and related systems [5,11,13,18] show that semantic embeddings can align natural-language reasoning with existing proof corpora, improving contextual selection and partial automation of lemma reuse.

However, simply asking an LLM to propose candidate lemmas and letting Coq filter them is not enough. Generated statements often deviate semantically from their intended meaning, lack the right level of abstraction for reuse, or violate typing constraints that make them unverifiable [9,16]. More importantly, most existing pipelines rely on heuristic repair passes whose correctness is not formalized: empirical verification rates may look healthy, yet there is no clear account of which transformations are semantically safe, which are merely convenient, and how much empirical coverage one must sacrifice to obtain a small, trusted core.

This work introduces Semantic Alignment for Proof Strategy Extraction (SAPSE), a framework that combines large-scale retrieval with structurally disciplined transformation, built around a Rocq-verified core. SAPSE embeds natural-language reasoning steps and formal lemmas into a shared semantic space, retrieves structurally similar examples, and synthesizes candidate statements through type-aware abstraction. It then applies an abstract-syntax-tree (AST) sanitizer that enforces syntactic and typing consistency. The sanitizer's core passes include require injection, a binder-normalization schema, and equality canonicalization, which are mechanically verified in Rocq 9.1.0 for a minimal calculus to preserve both typing and logical equivalence under import-only context extension. Practical binder elaboration, scope resolution, and other normalization steps for full Coq are realized by unverified utility passes in the production sanitizer and are deliberately kept outside the scope of the soundness theorem.

Beyond this static verified core, we introduce a Synergy execution mode: an adaptive two-stage sanitizer that first applies unverified utility passes to heuristically repair structural inconsistencies and then invokes the verified core under admissibility guards. This design explicitly trades off empirical coverage against formal guarantees. On the one hand, heuristic normalization can fix many issues that would otherwise trigger guard failures; on the other hand, it can also break goals that a retrieval-only baseline could have proved. Rather than hiding this trade-off, we make it the central object of study and show how Synergy exposes a *safety–coverage frontier* that is stable across Rocq random seeds.

Our empirical study evaluates SAPSE-Synergy on large, verified Coq developments from CompCert, coq-ext-lib, and Coq'Art. We construct a large lemma corpus (Sect. 5.2) and a 2,000-item real Coq benchmark of generated lemmas, and we compare four pipeline configurations: a retrieval-only baseline, a strictly guarded sanitizer, an unguarded fast mode, and the proposed Synergy mode. In a representative experiment, the baseline verifies 37.6% of candidates; Synergy verifies 32.8% with zero unsafe rewrites among guarded repairs and comparable runtime, while Strict and Fast anchor the extremes of maximal soundness and maximal heuristic coverage. Fragment-coverage, semantic-category, and structural-complexity breakdowns quantify where the verified core applies and which lemma families benefit from heuristic repair. A differential analysis of the 96 lemmas that the baseline can verify but Synergy fails on further clarifies how and where unverified utilities hurt coverage and how the verified core fails to repair these cases.

The contributions of this work are as follows:

1. **A Rocq-mechanized, compositional AST-level sanitization core.** We formalize a minimal calculus of terms, typing, and semantics in Rocq 9.1.0 and implement three transformations: require injection, a parametric binder-normalization schema, and equality canonicalization. In the current implementation, binder normalization is instantiated as the identity on terms; the modular soundness theorem is stated for any sequence of locally sound passes satisfying a local preservation lemma, so that future non-trivial binder elaborations can be plugged in without changing the statement. This makes explicit that all non-trivial rewriting in the present core arises only from the require-injection and equality-canonicalization passes.
2. **A retrieval and generation framework that connects neural and formal reasoning.** SAPSE aligns natural-language reasoning with verified Coq lemmas through embedding-based retrieval and type-aware abstraction, feeding into both the verified core and the production sanitizer. The generation layer relies on structured prompt templates and interface contracts that expose explicit, checkable header specifications to the sanitizer.
3. **A safety–coverage frontier for neural theorem proving.** We introduce a new experimental suite on a 2,000-lemma real Coq benchmark that compares Baseline-RAG, SAPSE-Strict, SAPSE-Fast, and SAPSE-Synergy, together with additional regex- and CoqHammer-only baselines. Rather than claiming a pure accuracy improvement, we show that Synergy quantifies a

reproducible safety–coverage trade-off: it loses 4.8% points of empirical coverage relative to the retrieval-only baseline but guarantees zero unsafe rewrites within the mechanized fragment, and this frontier is stable across Rocq random seeds.
4. **A differential analysis of lost successes and limits of mechanization.** We analyze the 96 lemmas that the retrieval-only baseline can verify but Synergy fails on, decomposing these "lost successes" by syntactic change, failure mode (type error, timeout, guard rejection, tactic failure), semantic category, and complexity band. This analysis turns the coverage gap into a diagnostic tool for future verified transformations and clarifies the limits of our current calculus, which deliberately omits advanced Coq features such as type classes, canonical structures, and ssreflect idioms.

SAPSE-Synergy does not primarily aim to increase raw verification rate; instead, it makes explicit and quantifiable the trade-off between empirical coverage and mechanized soundness in neural theorem proving. By inserting a small verified core between noisy neural generators and a deterministic prover, it offers a blueprint for building AI-assisted proof pipelines whose safety properties are grounded in formal reasoning rather than empirical success rates.

2 Related Work

2.1 Bridging Neural and Formal Reasoning

Efforts to connect natural-language reasoning with formal proofs have generally followed retrieval-augmented or generation-first paradigms. Early systems such as Strat2Rocq [2] and DRIFT [17] demonstrated that retrieving structurally similar lemmas can guide LLMs toward valid formalizations. However, these approaches remained empirical: they improved contextual relevance but lacked any formal guarantee that retrieved or rewritten statements would remain type-correct or logically equivalent to their intended meanings.

SAPSE advances this line of work by embedding natural-language reasoning and verified Coq lemmas into a shared semantic space and introducing a machine-checked transformation pipeline. Instead of relying only on heuristic repairs, the verified core of SAPSE is proved in Rocq to preserve typing and semantics for all admissible repairs over a minimal calculus. Our Synergy mode then composes this core with unverified utility passes to expand empirical coverage while keeping all accepted transformations within the scope of the soundness theorem. This explicitly connects neural retrieval to formal soundness, turning probabilistic alignment into type-safe lemma synthesis.

2.2 LLMs and Formal Verification Reliability

LLMs have recently shown the ability to assist theorem provers such as Coq, Lean, and Isabelle/HOL [4,9,12,16]. Most of these systems generate candidate proofs directly and depend on the prover to reject invalid outputs, offering no reliability beyond empirical success rates. As a result, neural generation can still produce ill-typed or semantically inconsistent statements even when the verification rate appears high. SAPSE reframes this process: between the stochastic LLM and the deterministic verifier, it inserts a formally verified sanitizer that enforces type safety and logical equivalence at the abstract-syntax-tree level. In Synergy mode, heuristic normalization is allowed to operate first, but its outputs are still subjected to the verified core and admissibility guards before they reach the prover. This design transforms verification from a post-hoc filter into a constructive guarantee, ensuring that only admissible, type-preserving repairs are ever passed to the prover.

2.3 Verified Transformations and Macro Systems

Formal verification has long relied on proven-correct transformations, exemplified by verified compilers such as CompCert [8], to guarantee that source and target programs are semantically equivalent. CompCert focuses on whole-program compilation and C semantics, with passes proven correct relative to a rich operational semantics. In contrast, macro and scripting frameworks in interactive theorem provers (e.g., ProofGeneral and tactic languages) allow users to script transformations on proof states and terms but typically offer no machine-checked soundness guarantees for these macros.

SAPSE occupies a different point in this design space. Its sanitizer targets localized AST-level repairs of Coq lemma statements produced by LLMs, rather than full programs, and its core transformations are mechanized in Rocq. Unlike ad-hoc macro systems, SAPSE provides a small, compositional trusted computing base (TCB) with explicit admissibility predicates, and integrates this TCB directly into a retrieval-augmented neural pipeline whose behavior is empirically characterized along a safety–coverage frontier.

3 Problem Formulation

We separate two layers: (i) an *empirical* retrieval model aligning natural-language steps to Coq lemmas via similarity, and (ii) a *mechanized* calculus specifying AST-level repairs and proving them sound in Rocq. Only (ii) is in the trusted computing base.

3.1 Empirical Retrieval Model

Let $\mathcal{S} = \{s_i\}_{i=1}^{N}$ be natural-language steps extracted from proof trajectories, and let $\mathcal{L}$ be a corpus of verified Coq lemmas. SAPSE assigns embeddings in a shared space:

$$E_{\mathrm{NL}} : \mathcal{S} \to \mathbb{R}^d, \qquad E_{\mathrm{Coq}} : \mathcal{L} \to \mathbb{R}^d,$$

and uses cosine similarity $\mathsf{Sim}(u, v) = \cos(u, v)$ to form candidates

$$\mathsf{Cand}_\tau(s) = \{\, L \in \mathcal{L} \mid \mathsf{Sim}(E_{\mathrm{NL}}(s), E_{\mathrm{Coq}}(L)) \geq \tau \,\}.$$

A verification-aware selector chooses the best-scoring candidate that type-checks:

$$\pi_{\text{ver}}(s, S) = \arg\max_{L \in S} \mathsf{Sim}(E_{\text{NL}}(s), E_{\text{Coq}}(L)) \quad \text{s.t.} \quad \Gamma \vdash L : \tau'.$$

Define $f_\theta(s) = \pi_{\text{ver}}(s, \mathsf{Cand}_\tau(s))$. All objects in this subsection are *external* to the Rocq development.

3.2 Formal Calculus and Typing (Mechanized Layer)

Let Σ be raw Coq ASTs (possibly missing imports/annotations), and

$$\mathcal{T}_\Gamma = \{t \in \Sigma \mid \exists \tau.\ \Gamma \vdash t : \tau\}$$

the well-typed subset under context Γ. For a well-typed lemma L, let $\mathsf{goal}(L)$ be the proposition extracted from its Coq type.

In Rocq we define a minimal syntax (for the sanitizer-relevant fragments), a typing judgment $\Gamma \vdash t : \tau$, and a denotational semantics $[\![t]\!]_\rho$ (environment ρ). All soundness claims below are proved solely in this mechanized layer and do not assume anything about retrieval.

3.3 Admissible Structural Repairs and Verified Core

Generated candidates may be incomplete/ill-typed. Let the sanitizer core be the Rocq-total function

$$\mathcal{R}_{\text{AST}} = \mathcal{R}_{\text{eq}} \circ \mathcal{R}_{\text{bind}} \circ \mathcal{R}_{\text{req}} : \Sigma \to \Sigma,$$

where the verified passes are: require injection ($\mathcal{R}_{\text{req}}$), a (parametric) binder-normalization schema ($\mathcal{R}_{\text{bind}}$), and equality canonicalization ($\mathcal{R}_{\text{eq}}$).

We write

$$L^* \rightsquigarrow_{\text{adm}} (\Gamma', L) \quad \text{iff} \quad L = \mathcal{R}_{\text{AST}}(L^*) \text{ and the structural preconditions hold.}$$

Admissibility is captured by:

$$\mathsf{AdmissibleSpec}(\Gamma_{\text{ext}}, \Gamma, t) \triangleq \begin{array}{l} \mathsf{WellFormedU}(t) \ \wedge\ \mathsf{disjoint\_ctx}(\Gamma_{\text{ext}}, \Gamma) \\ \wedge\ \exists \tau.\ \Gamma \vdash t : \tau \ \wedge\ (\forall \tau'.\ \Gamma \vdash t : \tau' \Rightarrow \tau' = \tau). \end{array}$$

Here $\mathsf{WellFormedU}$ and $\mathsf{disjoint\_ctx}$ denote the well-formedness and context-disjointness predicates used in the formalization.

Verified Core Definitions

The verified sanitizer is defined as:

$$(\Gamma', t') = \mathcal{R}_{\text{AST}}(\Gamma_{\text{ext}}, \Gamma, t)$$

subject to structural preconditions:

$$\text{Disjoint}(\Gamma_{\text{ext}}, \Gamma), \quad \text{WellFormedU}(t), \quad \Gamma \vdash t : \tau.$$

These predicates form the structural admissibility conditions enforced by the verified sanitizer.

3.4 Empirical Adequacy and Calibration

We relate retrieval to intended meaning via an empirical notion and a mechanized feasibility notion.

Semantic adequacy (empirical).

$$\mathsf{Adeq}(s, L) = \mathcal{I}_{\mathrm{NL}}(s) \models \mathcal{I}_{\mathrm{Coq}}(\mathsf{goal}(L)),$$

a statistical assumption used to guide retrieval (not mechanized).

Verifier feasibility (formal).

$$\mathsf{Feas}_{\Gamma}(L) = \Gamma \vdash L : \tau \ \wedge \ \mathsf{Verify}_{\Gamma}(L) = \textit{success},$$

which is checkable by Coq and underlies the trusted results.

We assume a monotone calibration that upper-bounds inadequacy by similarity.

Assumption 31. (Empirical calibration of similarity) *There exists a nonincreasing* $\psi : [-1, 1] \to [0, 1]$ *such that for all* $s \in \mathcal{S}$ *and* $L \in \mathcal{L}$,

$$\Pr[\neg\mathsf{Adeq}(s, L)] \leq \psi(\mathsf{Sim}(E_{\mathrm{NL}}(s), E_{\mathrm{Coq}}(L))).$$

Empirically fix τ_{safe} *satisfying*

$$\mathsf{SafeTau}(\tau) \triangleq \forall s, L.\ \mathsf{Sim}(E_{\mathrm{NL}}(s), E_{\mathrm{Coq}}(L)) \geq \tau \Rightarrow \mathsf{Adeq}(s, L).$$

Assumption 31 is never used inside Rocq; it only supports claims about meaning alignment.

3.5 Modular Soundness of the Sanitizer Core

We prove per-component soundness under AdmissibleSpec and then compose.

Definition 1 (Component soundness). *A transformation* $\mathcal{R} : \Sigma \to \Sigma$ *is sound if for all admissible* $(\Gamma_{\mathrm{ext}}, \Gamma, t)$,

$$\mathsf{AdmissibleSpec}(\Gamma_{\mathrm{ext}}, \Gamma, t) \Rightarrow \exists \Gamma', \tau.\ \Gamma \preceq \Gamma' \wedge \Gamma' \vdash \mathcal{R}(t) : \tau \wedge \forall \rho.\ [\![t]\!]_{\rho} \leftrightarrow [\![\mathcal{R}(t)]\!]_{\rho}.$$

Write Sound($\mathcal{R}$) *for this property.*

Theorem 1 (Modular soundness of compositional sanitizer). *If*

$$\mathrm{Sound}(\mathcal{R}_{\mathrm{req}}),\quad \mathrm{Sound}(\mathcal{R}_{\mathrm{bind}}),\quad \mathrm{Sound}(\mathcal{R}_{\mathrm{eq}})$$

hold under AdmissibleSpec, *then the composed sanitizer*

$$\mathcal{R}_{\mathrm{AST}} = \mathcal{R}_{\mathrm{eq}} \circ \mathcal{R}_{\mathrm{bind}} \circ \mathcal{R}_{\mathrm{req}}$$

is sound.

Our Rocq 9.1.0 development is fully mechanized with no `Admitted`; all results reported here are formally verified in Rocq. In the current version, $\mathcal{R}_{\text{bind}}$ is instantiated as the identity on terms; the theorem is stated for an arbitrary total $\mathcal{R}_{\text{bind}}$ satisfying the local soundness lemma, so stronger binder elaborations can be substituted later without changing Theorem 1.

3.6 AST-Level Soundness and Problem Statement

Theorem 2 (AST-level soundness). *If* $L^* \rightsquigarrow_{\text{adm}} (\Gamma', L)$ *via* $\mathcal{R}_{\text{AST}}$ *and* $\mathsf{AdmissibleSpec}(\Gamma_{\text{ext}}, \Gamma, L^*)$ *holds, then*

$$\Gamma \preceq \Gamma', \qquad \Gamma' \vdash L : \tau, \qquad \mathsf{goal}(L^*) \equiv \mathsf{goal}(L).$$

Thus, within the verified core, repairs preserve typing and goal semantics; if admissibility fails (e.g., missing imports, non-principal typings, or non-import-only extensions), $\mathcal{R}_{\text{AST}}$ abstains.

Overall Objective. Given $s \in \mathcal{S}$, find $L^\star \in \mathcal{L} \cup \Sigma$ and a realized lemma $L^\dagger$ such that

$$\text{(i)} \quad \mathsf{Sim}(E_{\text{NL}}(s), E_{\text{Coq}}(L^\dagger)) \geq \tau,$$
$$L^\dagger \text{ is retrieved or obtained via an admissible repair of } L^\star,$$

$$\text{(ii)} \quad \mathsf{Adeq}(s, L^\dagger) \quad \text{and} \quad \mathsf{Feas}_{\Gamma'}(L^\dagger).$$

For any raw lemma L^* with admissible repair $L^* \rightsquigarrow_{\text{adm}} (\Gamma', L)$, Theorem 2 yields

$$\Gamma \preceq \Gamma', \qquad \Gamma' \vdash L : \tau, \qquad \mathsf{goal}(L^*) \equiv \mathsf{goal}(L),$$

independently of Assumption 31. In short, the trusted layer guarantees *structural* soundness, while semantic adequacy remains an *empirical* assumption, keeping the boundary of the trusted core explicit.

4 Methodology

4.1 Workflow

SAPSE implements a retrieval-augmented, type-safe pipeline that maps natural-language reasoning steps to verified Coq lemmas (Fig. 1). Given a proof trajectory, SAPSE segments it into atomic steps, embeds both steps and existing Coq lemmas into a shared vector space, and performs similarity-based retrieval to obtain candidate reasoning patterns. Retrieved lemmas are abstracted into parameterized templates, which are instantiated into candidate Coq statements under explicit typing constraints. Each candidate is then type-checked and, if necessary, repaired by the Synergy sanitizer before being submitted to Coq.

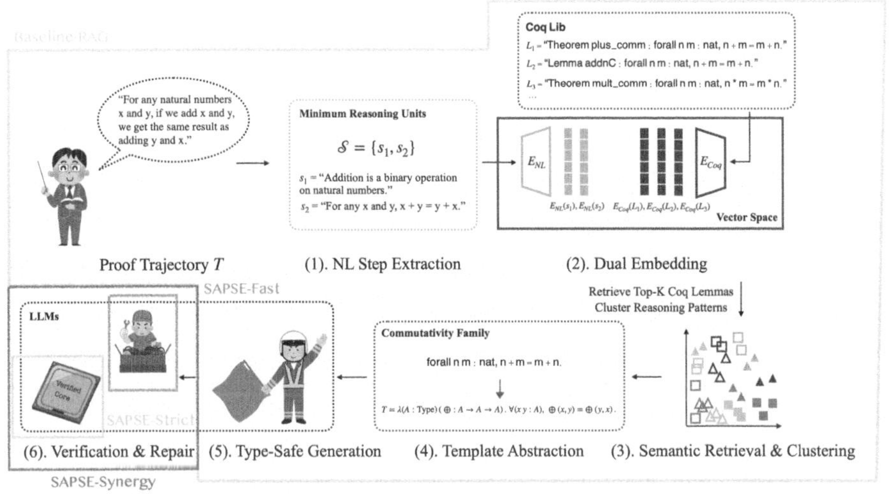

Fig. 1. Overview of the SAPSE pipeline, annotated with the four execution modes used in our evaluation. The outer yellow region corresponds to the **Baseline-RAG** setting, which uses only steps (1)–(5) and performs direct Coq verification without any sanitization. The red region marks **SAPSE-Fast**, which applies only unverified heuristic repairs. The small cyan region highlights **SAPSE-Strict**, which applies only the Rocq-verified sanitizer core under admissibility guards. The purple region denotes **SAPSE-Synergy**, which first applies unverified utilities and then routes candidates through the verified core before Coq checking. These regions visually separate the empirical retrieval–generation pipeline from the verified transformations that enforce soundness. (Color figure online)

4.2 Verified Sanitizer Formalization

The verified sanitizer consists of three mechanized modules—*require injection*, *binder normalization*, and *equality canonicalization*—composed as

$$\mathcal{R}_{\text{AST}} = \mathcal{R}_{\text{eq}} \circ \mathcal{R}_{\text{bind}} \circ \mathcal{R}_{\text{req}}.$$

All three transformations are implemented and proved in Rocq 9.1.0 to preserve typing and denotational semantics for inputs satisfying the admissibility predicate. The development is fully mechanized and is available in the accompanying artifact.

4.3 Execution Modes and Synergy

SAPSE exposes three operating modes. *Strict* applies only the verified core $\mathcal{R}_{\text{AST}}$, rejecting any input violating admissibility. *Fast* applies unverified utility passes for maximal empirical coverage. *Synergy* combines both: unverified passes heuristically repair candidates, after which the verified core enforces admissible structure before final Coq checking. These modes trace different points on the safety–coverage frontier discussed in Sect. 5.

4.4 Deduplication Scoring

Redundant lemmas are detected via cosine similarity:

$$\mathrm{sim}(L_p, L_q) = \frac{\langle E_{\mathrm{Coq}}(L_p), E_{\mathrm{Coq}}(L_q)\rangle}{\|E_{\mathrm{Coq}}(L_p)\|\|E_{\mathrm{Coq}}(L_q)\|}.$$

Lemmas with $\mathrm{sim} \geq 0.90$ are marked duplicates; those with $0.80 \leq \mathrm{sim} < 0.90$ are treated as parameterized variants.

4.5 Trusted Computing Base and Limits of Mechanization

Our Rocq development deliberately targets a minimal calculus that captures the core fragments exercised by the sanitizer. Higher-order Coq features such as type classes, canonical structures, and ssreflect-specific idioms are currently outside the mechanized model.

As a result, our soundness guarantees are relative to: (i) terms that fall inside the verified fragment (Sect. 5.5), and (ii) structural repairs that satisfy AdmissibleSpec. All unverified utility passes operate outside this TCB and are treated as best-effort heuristics, whose empirical effect is measured in Sect. 5 but not part of the formal soundness claims. A fragment-coverage experiment in Sect. 5.5 quantifies how often Synergy operates inside this verified fragment on real Coq benchmarks.

5 Experiments

5.1 Overview

We evaluate SAPSE on large, verified Coq corpora with a focus on how the sanitizer's execution mode shapes the trade-off between empirical coverage and formal soundness. Our primary study is a real Coq Synergy experiment on a 2,000-item dataset of generated lemmas, comparing four pipeline configurations: a retrieval-only baseline, a strictly guarded sanitizer, an unguarded fast mode, and the proposed Synergy pipeline. We report retrieval quality, verified-lemma conversion, abstention behavior, runtime, and unsafe-rewrite counts, and we visualize the resulting safety–coverage frontier. Unless otherwise stated, results are reported for a single 2,000-item run; we also repeat the experiment under four independent Rocq random seeds to assess reproducibility. Prompt templates, header contracts, and YAML configuration files specify the generation and sanitization pipeline of SAPSE.

5.2 Datasets

The corpus integrates natural-language reasoning traces and verified Coq lemmas from established repositories. In total, it comprises 7,218 proofs, 74,796 reasoning steps, 5,399 lemmas, and 2,946 theorems across 575 source files (16.4 MB). Lemmas are grouped into five semantic categories: arithmetic, boolean logic, list operations, inductive relations, and miscellaneous (Table 1).

Table 1. Corpus statistics for FAISS index construction. Domains include verified compiler semantics, reusable proof utilities, and textbook examples.

Corpus	Files	Lemmas	Theorems	Size	Notes
CompCert	253	4750	2327	13.0 MB	Verified C compiler corpus
coq-ext-lib	129	142	72	0.97 MB	Community extensions
Coq'Art	193	507	547	2.4 MB	Didactic examples
Total	575	5399	2946	16.4 MB	

5.3 Embedding and Indexing

Natural-language steps are encoded with E5 [14], and Coq statements with CodeBERT [3]. Embeddings are indexed in FAISS [7] using `FlatL2` search. Unless otherwise stated, retrieval uses top $k = 10$, similarity threshold $\tau \in [0.80, 0.85]$, and deduplication threshold $\delta = 0.95$.

Embedding-based retrieval is standard in modern neural theorem proving. LeanDojo [16] employs dense retrieval for premise selection, and earlier work on graph and representation learning similarly maps formal objects into vector spaces [15]. ProofBridge [6] further explores joint embeddings aligning natural-language and formal proofs. A broader overview is provided in [9].

Our use of off-the-shelf encoders follows this established paradigm. The contribution of SAPSE-Synergy lies not in the embedding mechanism itself, but in the Rocq-mechanized sanitizer that constrains how retrieved candidates are transformed and admitted.

5.4 Experimental Setup and Metrics

All experiments are conducted under Rocq 9.1.0 with a 30 s per-goal timeout, assisted by CoqHammer for hard cases. We fix the retrieval and prompting setup and vary only the sanitizer execution mode, yielding four pipeline configurations: (i) Baseline-RAG, which performs retrieval-augmented generation without any sanitizer; (ii) SAPSE-Strict, which applies only the verified core with all admissibility guards enabled; (iii) SAPSE-Fast, which applies unverified utility passes without guards and bypasses the verified core; and (iv) SAPSE-Synergy, which first applies unverified passes and then routes the result through the guarded verified core before Coq checking. This spectrum exposes the safety–coverage frontier, with Baseline-RAG providing an upper bound on raw retrieval performance and Strict representing the fully mechanized, guard-enforced setting.

Retrieval quality is reported using standard metrics such as Recall@k and MAP@k. Verification-related indicators include conversion rate (Conv), type-error rate (TER), CoqHammer rescue rate (HG), admissible rate (AR), sound repair success (SRS), and unsafe-rewrite count (URC). URC is measured only for configurations that pass candidates through the verified core.

Table 2. Fragment coverage of the mechanized calculus on the 2,000-item benchmark.

Scope	#Lemmas	InFrag (%)	Synergy verified in-frag	Synergy verified out-of-frag
All	2000	1962 (98.1%)	656	0

Table 3. Real Coq verification outcomes on 2,000 generated lemmas (single seed).

Configuration	Guards	Verified (%)	Abstained (%)	Avg Time (s)
Baseline-RAG	None	37.6 (752/2000)	0.0 (0/2000)	0.142
SAPSE-Strict	VC-Guarded	37.3 (746/2000)	5.3 (106/2000)	0.112
SAPSE-Fast	None	32.8 (656/2000)	0.0 (0/2000)	0.094
SAPSE-Synergy	UP→VC	32.8 (656/2000)	0.1 (1/2000)	0.092

5.5 Fragment Coverage of the Verified Core

Because the Rocq formalization targets a minimal calculus, we first quantify how often the Synergy pipeline operates inside this verified fragment on real Coq inputs.

We implement a static checker $\mathsf{InFrag} : \Sigma \rightarrow \{\mathsf{true}, \mathsf{false}\}$ that recognizes terms whose constructors are supported by the mechanized calculus (for example, universal quantification, arrows, and propositional equality) and that avoid features currently outside the model (such as type classes). For each candidate lemma in the 2,000-item benchmark, we record whether its final Coq statement falls inside the verified fragment.

Table 2 reports the aggregate fragment coverage and Synergy outcomes.

Overall, 1,962 out of 2,000 benchmark lemmas (98.1%) fall inside the verified fragment. All 656 lemmas that SAPSE-Synergy successfully verifies are in-fragment; we observe no Synergy successes on out-of-fragment lemmas in this experiment. Thus the soundness theorem for the sanitized AST applies directly to every Synergy success, while the remaining 38 out-of-fragment lemmas rely solely on Coq's type checker and are not covered by the current mechanized calculus. This highlights both the breadth of the fragment and the limits of our present formalization.

5.6 Safety–Coverage Frontier on Real Coq Benchmark

Real Coq Synergy Experiment (2,000 items). Table 3 reports results for the four configurations on the 2,000-item dataset of generated lemmas.

Safety–Coverage Trade-Off. The retrieval-only Baseline-RAG configuration verifies 37.6% of candidates and serves as an empirical upper bound in our study. Introducing the sanitizer in Strict mode maintains a comparable verified ratio (37.3%) but abstains on 5.3% of inputs, reflecting the conservativeness of the admissibility predicates.

Fast mode applies only unverified utility passes and verifies 32.8% of candidates. Although its overall average runtime (0.094 s) is lower than that of Baseline-RAG (0.142 s), this reduction is primarily attributable to early failures on modified goals rather than uniformly faster successful verifications. Fast frequently fails quickly after heuristic goal-shape changes, which reduces mean runtime but does not imply improved verification efficiency on successfully proven lemmas.

The Synergy configuration matches Fast in verified ratio (32.8%) and exhibits a negligible abstention rate (0.1%). Its runtime profile closely follows that of Fast, as both configurations share the same utility pipeline. However, Synergy additionally enforces that all accepted transformations pass through the Rocq-mechanized core and admissibility guards, thereby establishing a formally delimited transformation boundary.

Compared to the retrieval-only baseline, both Fast and Synergy lose 96 successfully verified lemmas (4.8% points of coverage). As analyzed in Sect. 5.8, these lost successes arise from heuristic goal-shape changes that degrade tactic effectiveness, rather than from abstention by the verified core. In its current form, Synergy does not improve coverage over Fast and reduces the empirical upper bound provided by the retrieval-only baseline, while making the safety boundary explicit and mechanically justified.

Abstention Behavior and Guards. The abstention behavior of Strict and Synergy illustrates the effect of admissibility guards. In Strict mode, 106 out of 2,000 candidates (5.3%) are rejected prior to transformation, typically due to unbound identifiers, missing principal types, or context extensions violating the import-only restriction. Synergy's additional unverified repairs reduce this to a single abstained case (0.1%), indicating that many guard failures can be eliminated by lightweight heuristic normalization. However, as the lost-success analysis shows, the same heuristic modifications may also render otherwise provable goals less amenable to existing tactics.

Crucially, all candidates that pass the guards and are transformed by the verified core satisfy the AST-level soundness theorem. Among these guarded transformations, we observe no unsafe rewrites (URC= 0).

Reproducibility Across Seeds. We repeat the Synergy experiment for four independent Rocq random seeds (3, 5, 7, 11), each with 2,000 generated lemmas and all four configurations. Across seeds, the verified and abstention ratios for each configuration vary by less than 0.3% points, and average runtimes vary by less than 0.02 s. The Synergy configuration consistently achieves 32.8% verified, approximately 0.1% abstained, and zero unsafe rewrites among candidates that pass the guards. This indicates that the observed safety–coverage trade-off and the 4.8% point gap to the baseline are structural properties of the current pipeline design rather than artifacts of a particular random initialization.

Table 4. Verification outcomes by semantic category on the 2,000-item benchmark (single seed). Percentages are with respect to the number of lemmas in each category.

Category	#Lemmas	Baseline-RAG	Strict	Fast	Synergy	Strict abstain
Arithmetic	334	29.0% (97)	29.0% (97)	22.5% (75)	22.5% (75)	7.2% (24)
Boolean	381	35.2% (134)	34.6% (132)	29.9% (114)	29.9% (114)	9.7% (37)
Inductive	129	31.0% (40)	31.0% (40)	28.7% (37)	28.7% (37)	3.1% (4)
List	71	42.3% (30)	42.3% (30)	36.6% (26)	36.6% (26)	2.8% (2)
Misc	1085	41.6% (451)	41.2% (447)	37.2% (404)	37.2% (404)	3.6% (39)
All	2000	37.6% (752)	37.3% (746)	32.8% (656)	32.8% (656)	5.3% (106)

5.7 Semantic Category and Structural Complexity Analysis

To understand which lemmas benefit most from the sanitizer and where coverage is lost, we analyze verification outcomes by semantic category and structural complexity.

Semantic categories. Table 4 reports verified and abstention ratios for each configuration broken down by the five semantic categories from Sect. 5.2.

Strict mode closely tracks Baseline-RAG in all categories: the verified counts are identical for Arithmetic, Inductive, and List lemmas, and differ only slightly for Boolean and Misc. This confirms that the verified core, together with admissibility guards, does not substantially harm coverage when run alone. In contrast, Fast and Synergy reduce verified ratios uniformly across categories, with the largest absolute losses in the Misc (47 lemmas) and Arithmetic (22 lemmas) categories. Section 5.8 shows that these losses correspond precisely to the 96 lemmas that Baseline-RAG can verify but both Fast and Synergy cannot.

Structural Complexity. Under our AST-based complexity measure, all 2,000 lemmas fall into the shallow band, with verification rates showing no meaningful complexity-related variation (Baseline-RAG: 37.6%, Strict: 37.3%, Fast/Synergy: 32.8%).

Consequently, we cannot yet distinguish behavior across structural bands on this dataset. We therefore focus our fine-grained analysis on semantic categories and on the lost-success subset (Sect. 5.8), leaving a more nuanced complexity stratification to future work and larger, more structurally diverse benchmarks.

5.8 Differential Analysis of Lost Successes

To understand the 4.8% point gap between Baseline-RAG (37.6%) and SAPSE-Synergy (32.8%), we examine the set of lemmas that the baseline verifies but Synergy does not. This *lost-success set* contains 96 lemmas, all of which are shallow under our structural-complexity measure. For every such lemma, Baseline-RAG verifies it, while both Fast and Synergy produce outright failures rather than abstentions. These losses arise entirely from unverified heuristic transformations that Synergy cannot repair with the current verified core. A full breakdown of semantic categories, representative patterns.

6 Discussion and Case Studies

The previous sections present SAPSE-Synergy mainly through formal definitions and aggregate statistics. In this section we switch to a more qualitative, design-level view. We first walk through a representative case where Synergy successfully repairs and verifies a neural candidate, making explicit which parts of the pipeline are heuristic and which are covered by the Rocq development. We then examine cases where Synergy hurts coverage relative to a retrieval-only baseline, and we discuss the safety–coverage frontier as a design knob rather than an incidental artifact. Finally, we outline threats to validity and limits of the current mechanization.

6.1 When Synergy Helps and When it Hurts

The real Coq experiment on 2,000 generated lemmas (Sect. 5) reveals that Synergy verifies 32.8% of candidates, compared to 37.6% for the retrieval-only baseline and 37.3% for the Strict configuration. At first glance this seems purely negative: a substantial loss in empirical coverage. However, closer analysis shows that Synergy occupies a qualitatively different point in the design space.

Synergy as a Conservative Extension of Fast. Numerically, SAPSE-Fast and SAPSE-Synergy achieve the same verification rate (32.8%), but their guarantees differ. Fast applies unverified utility passes without any admissibility checks and forwards whatever emerges directly to Coq. Synergy, in contrast, subjects the utilities' output to the guarded, Rocq-verified core. In our experiments, this guard never accepts an unsafe transformation: for all candidates that pass admissibility and are rewritten by $\mathcal{R}_{\text{AST}}$, we observe no counterexamples to the soundness theorem. Thus Synergy can be viewed as a conservative extension of Fast that prunes some candidates that utilities would otherwise send to Coq, without improving coverage yet.

Sources of Coverage Loss. Section 5.8 identifies 96 *lost successes*: lemmas that the baseline verifies but both Fast and Synergy fail on. Empirically, these lost successes are concentrated in three semantic families:

- arithmetic and bit-manipulation lemmas over nat and machine integers,
- boolean and conditional simplifications, and
- engineering-style invariants in ValueDomain, Bounds, and related modules.

All of them fall in the shallow structural band according to our AST complexity measure, which indicates that the failures are not due to intrinsically hard higher-order structure. Instead, heuristic repairs sometimes change the shape of goals in ways that degrade the effectiveness of existing tactics. The verified core, instantiated with an identity-like binder schema and a simple equality transformer, currently cannot undo these harmful changes, and therefore Synergy inherits Fast's lost successes.

Interpreting the Safety–Coverage Frontier. Viewed from this angle, the safety–coverage frontier measured in Table 3 is not an immutable property of SAPSE-Synergy but a function of three independent design choices:

1. the expressiveness of the mechanized calculus (which determines the fragment in which the soundness theorem applies),
2. the strength of the verified transformations (currently very conservative), and
3. the aggressiveness of the unverified utilities (currently tuned for coverage rather than reversibility).

Pushing the frontier outward—for example, by recovering some of the 96 lost successes without sacrificing soundness—requires co-design across all three axes. A richer calculus can express more of Coq's idioms; stronger verified passes can perform meaning-preserving rewrites that directly help proofs; and better-behaved utilities can avoid transformations that are unlikely to be recoverable by the core.

6.2 Threats to Validity and Limitations

SAPSE-Synergy combines empirical retrieval with a formally verified core, and its guarantees therefore come with several important limitations.

- **Fragment mismatch.** The verified core operates in a small calculus that covers most (98.1%) of our benchmark lemmas but omits many Gallina features (e.g., type classes, canonical structures, ssreflect idioms).
- **Dependence on retrieval.** The system inherits all errors from embedding-based retrieval; the sanitizer can repair structure but cannot recover mathematical intent absent from the retrieved candidates.
- **Tactic sensitivity.** Verification outcomes reflect interaction with our specific tactic stack (including CoqHammer), and different proof-search configurations could shift the safety–coverage frontier.
- **Admissibility checking.** While the admissibility predicate is mechanized, the implementation-side checker is unverified and thus part of the trusted computing base.
- **Scope of formal guarantees.** The soundness theorem covers only the three verified sanitizer passes and not retrieval, generation, utility rewrites, or Coq's proof search.

Despite these limitations, our results show that even a small verified core can act as an effective safety gate for thousands of neural candidates, with the empirical cost of this gate made explicit and measurable.

6.3 Practical Deployment Considerations

The choice between Baseline-RAG and SAPSE-Synergy should be understood as a deployment-level decision rather than a purely numerical comparison of verification rates.

Baseline-RAG achieves higher empirical coverage (37.6%) but applies heuristic AST rewrites without formally verified admissibility conditions. In contrast, SAPSE-Synergy verifies slightly fewer candidates (32.8%) but guarantees that every accepted transformation lies within the Rocq-mechanized fragment and satisfies the soundness theorem under import-only context extension.

In risk-sensitive environments—such as certified libraries, proof-carrying code, or formally audited developments—the cost of admitting a semantically unsound transformation may outweigh the benefit of marginally higher coverage. In such contexts, Synergy provides a principled safety gate whose empirical cost is explicit and measurable.

Conversely, in exploratory or interactive proof development, where suggestions are subject to human inspection and rapid iteration is preferred, higher coverage may be more valuable than formal guarantees on intermediate rewrites. In such settings, Baseline-RAG may constitute an appropriate choice.

Therefore, Synergy is most appropriate when soundness guarantees are non-negotiable, whereas Baseline-RAG may be preferable when maximizing empirical success is the primary objective.

7 Conclusion

SAPSE-Synergy links neural reasoning with formal verification through a lightweight, fully mechanized sanitizer. The system shows that even a very small verified core can act as an effective filter for neural candidates: it accepts only transformations justified by mechanized proofs, yet still verifies a substantial portion of generated lemmas.

Experiments on large verified corpora and a 2,000-lemma benchmark confirm this behavior. A retrieval-only baseline verifies 37.6% of candidates, while Synergy verifies 32.8% with no unsafe transformations. This difference makes the cost of formal guarantees explicit and provides a concrete measure of how neural generation interacts with verified repair.

The broader contribution is a shift in perspective. Instead of maximizing raw accuracy, SAPSE-Synergy highlights the importance of understanding and quantifying the role of mechanized guarantees inside neural proof pipelines. Future work will expand the verified calculus, strengthen binder handling, and integrate search methods that work in concert with the sanitizer. Together, these steps aim toward proof assistants where learning and verification reinforce each other in a principled and transparent way.

References

1. Barras, B., Bertot, Y., et al.: The coq proof assistant—reference manual. INRIA (2015)
2. Fang, J., Sun, Y., Xiong, Y.: Proof strategy extraction from LLMs for enhancing symbolic provers. arXiv preprint arXiv:2510.10131 (2025)
3. Feng, Z., et al.: CodeBERT: a pre-trained model for programming and natural languages. In: Findings of the Association for Computational Linguistics: EMNLP (2020). https://arxiv.org/abs/2002.08155, arXiv preprint arXiv:2002.08155
4. First, E., Piotrowski, B., Thakur, A., et al.: Baldur: whole-proof generation and repair with large language models. arXiv preprint arXiv:2303.04910 (2023)
5. Han, J.M., Zhao, Z., Polu, S.: Learning to prove theorems via interacting with proof assistants. In: International Conference on Machine Learning (ICML) (2022)
6. Jana, P., Kale, K., Tanriverdi, A.E., Song, C., Vishwanath, S., Ganesh, V.: Proofbridge: auto-formalization of natural language proofs in lean via joint embeddings. arXiv preprint arXiv:2510.15681 (2025)
7. Johnson, J., Douze, M., Jégou, H.: Billion-scale similarity search with GPUs. IEEE Trans. Big Data **7**(3), 535–547 (2019)
8. Leroy, X., Blazy, S., Kästner, D., Schommer, B., Pister, M., Ferdinand, C.: Compcert-a formally verified optimizing compiler. In: 8th European Congress, ERTS 2016: Embedded Real Time Software and Systems (2016)
9. Li, Y., Yang, K., Wang, H., Zhang, M.: A survey on deep learning for theorem proving. OpenReview (2024)
10. Paulson, L.C.: Isabelle: the next 700 theorem provers. Logic J. IGPL **27**(1), 67–93 (2019)
11. Polu, S., Han, J.M., Sutskever, I.: Minif2f: a cross-domain benchmark for formal theorem proving. In: International Conference on Learning Representations (ICLR) (2022)
12. Thakur, A., First, E., Chalamala, R., et al.: An in-context learning agent for formal theorem proving. arXiv preprint arXiv:2310.04353 (2023)
13. Wang, H., et al.: Lego-prover: neural theorem proving with growing libraries. In: International Conference on Learning Representations (ICLR) (2024)
14. Wang, L., et al.: Text embeddings by weakly-supervised contrastive pre-training. arXiv preprint arXiv:2212.03533 (2022)
15. Wang, M., Tang, Y., Wang, J., Deng, J.: Premise selection for theorem proving by deep graph embedding. In: Advances in Neural Information Processing Systems, vol. 30 (2017)
16. Yang, K., Swope, A.M., Gu, A., Chalamala, R., Anandkumar, A.: Leandojo: theorem proving with retrieval-augmented language models. In: Advances in Neural Information Processing Systems (NeurIPS) (2023)
17. Zhang, M., Borchert, P., Gritta, M., Lampouras, G.: Drift: decompose, retrieve, illustrate, then formalize theorems. arXiv preprint arXiv:2510.10815 (2025)
18. Zhou, T., Xu, Y., Wang, R., Zhang, J., Liu, W., Xiong, Y.: Refactor: learning to extract theorems from proof trees. In: International Conference on Learning Representations (ICLR) (2024)

Certifying Constraints in Hardware Model Checking

Nils Froleyks[1(✉)], Emily Yu[2], Armin Biere[3], and Keijo Heljanko[4,5]

[1] KU Leuven, Leuven, Belgium
nfroleyks@gmail.com
[2] Leiden University, Leiden, Netherlands
[3] University of Freiburg, Freiburg, Germany
[4] University of Helsinki, Helsinki, Finland
[5] Helsinki Institute for Information Technology, Helsinki, Finland

Abstract. Model checking is a powerful automated reasoning technique for verifying hardware designs, ensuring that they function correctly before deployment. However, modern model checkers are complex software systems with hundreds of thousands of lines of code, making them prone to errors. To increase confidence in verification results, recent efforts in hardware verification focus on requiring model checkers to produce machine-checkable proofs according to a standardized format that can be independently validated. Yet, implementing proof generation across different verification algorithms presents a unique challenge. In hardware model checking, constraints play an essential role, as they encode assumptions about the environment and help simplify analysis. This paper addresses the challenge by developing a certification approach that ensures verification results remain trustworthy when constraints are present. We introduce certificate generation methods for three classes of constraints that can be extracted from the models. Furthermore, to support a broader range of constraints and more complex reset logic for industrial use, we also provide alternative Quantified Boolean Formula checks in the proof format with a single quantifier alternation. Lastly, we present a certificate generation method for k-induction with uniqueness constraints, an important model checking technique. We implement these in a certification toolkit, and provide empirical evaluation on competition benchmarks, demonstrating their effectiveness.

1 Introduction

Model checking is a widely used technique in hardware verification to ensure that hardware designs, such as processors or embedded circuits, operate correctly before they are manufactured. This automated process checks whether a design in the form of a gate-level netlist satisfies specific requirements by exploring all possible executions of the system. However, the automated reasoning tools that perform model checking, i.e., the model checkers, are complex, often consisting of hundreds of thousands of lines of code. This complexity introduces the risk of

A. Sampaio and M. Stoelinga (Eds.): FM 2026, LNCS 16556, pp. 170–188, 2026.
https://doi.org/10.1007/978-3-032-26204-2_9

errors within the tools themselves, raising questions about the reliability of their results. To address this, recent developments in hardware verification emphasize the generation of certificates, which are formal proofs that can be independently verified by another program to confirm the verdicts [1–5].

As in most industrial verification languages [6,7], following the assume-guarantee methodology [8], an essential feature of hardware model checking is the use of *constraints*, which represent assumptions about the environment in which the hardware operates. These assumptions simplify the verification task, improve computational efficiency, and allow model checking to tackle more complex designs. The AIGER format [9], a standard in hardware model checking competitions (HWMCCs) [10], explicitly incorporates constraints as part of its design description language. In the latest iteration, HWMCC'24, certification became mandatory [11], where all participating model checkers had to produce a machine-checkable certificate when confirming a design's correctness. The verification pipeline is illustrated in Fig. 1.

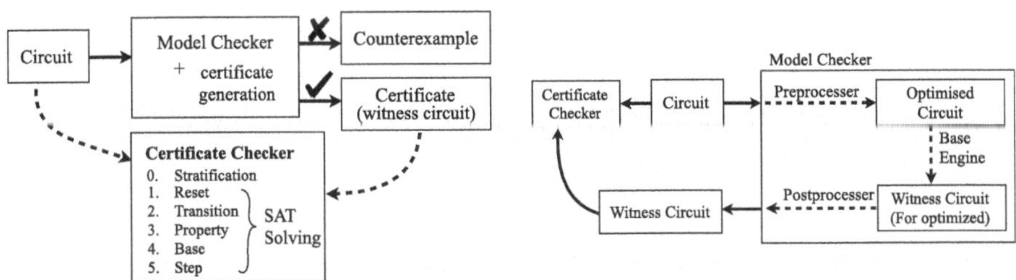

Fig. 1. An overview of the model checking certification process (left), and the certification flow when preprocessing is employed in a model checker (right).

The certificate format [11], in the form of a witness circuit, relies on five simple satisfiability (SAT) checks and a polynomial-time check for reset function acyclicity (called stratification [12]). This approach is efficient and compatible with most bit-level model checking algorithms. However, challenges arise when designs include complex reset logic, such as cyclic dependencies, which complicates certificate generation but are common in industrial practice [13–15]. To overcome this, we propose alternative checks using Quantified Boolean Formula (QBF) in the same format that are less restrictive. This relaxed format is easily adapted by the certificate checker CERTIFAIGER used in the HWMCC'24, and offers more flexibility for model checker developers while maintaining trust in the results.

Since commercial designs often require hundreds of constraints to accurately model their environments, verification tools must go beyond the explicit constraints provided in the design description. *Hidden constraints* can often be inferred from the model itself [16,17]. In fact, such constraint extraction is also implemented in the state-of-the-art model checker ABC [18], as documented in its official manual. Complementary efforts have also focused on the efficient synthesis of such constraints [19,20]. These constraints, identified through preprocessing, refine the verification problem by focusing only on parts of system states, while preserving the validity of the original property. While this simplification enhances efficiency, the resulting certificate from the model checker applies only to the reduced model, not the original. This thus adds additional challenges to certification.

Our Contribution. We address this challenge by presenting a certification approach that proves the correctness of the original design while accounting for extracted constraints. Furthermore, we consider k-induction [21], a powerful model checking technique based on inductive reasoning over sequences of states. For completeness, k-induction requires *uniqueness constraints*, which exclude cyclic transitions from consideration. Producing certificates when using such constraints is challenging [22], as soundness implicitly relies on a reachability analysis over the entire state space. In this paper we also demonstrate certificate generation for it. We summarize our main contributions as follows.

1. *Certification of extracted constraints.* We introduce a method for generating certificates that account for three classes of extracted constraints: *model constraints*, *inductive constraints*, and *property constraints*. The resulting certificates validate that the verification result holds for the original model, prior to constraint extraction.
2. *Relaxed certificate format.* To accommodate more complex encoding logic in modern model checking techniques, we propose alternative QBF-based certificate checks. These relaxations extend the certificate format used in HWMCCs and remain verifiable by an independent checker.
3. *Certification of uniqueness constraints in k-induction.* We present a certificate generation method for k-induction with uniqueness constraints.
4. *Empirical evaluation.* We evaluate our approach on a set of HWMCC benchmarks, demonstrating its practicality and effectiveness.

2 Background

In the rest of the paper, we employ the following notation: let $\mathcal{V}$ be a set of Boolean variables, we consider formulas over $\mathcal{V}$ with the Boolean operators $\neg$, $\vee$, $\wedge$, $\rightarrow$, $\leftrightarrow$. The last denotes equivalence and can have an infix negation $\not\leftrightarrow$. A (partial) assignment gives each variable in (a subset of) $\mathcal{V}$ the value *true*($\top$) or *false*($\bot$). Applying a function f to an assignment s, denoted as $f(s)$, follows the usual semantics. If s is a total assignment, $f(s)$ yields a truth value; if s is partial, $f(s)$ results in a formula not dependent on any variables in s. By *dependent* we mean syntactically dependent, i.e. no variable v in s appears in $f(s)$. For a partial assignment, we use *extension* to refer to an assignment that assigns more variables and is otherwise the same. For sets of Boolean variables $\mathcal{U}$ and $\mathcal{V}$, we denote union as $\mathcal{U}, \mathcal{V}$ and as $\mathcal{U} \mathbin{\dot\cup} \mathcal{V}$ when we want to emphasize that $\mathcal{U}$ and $\mathcal{V}$ are disjoint. For next-state variables, we write $\mathcal{V}_1$ to denote a copy of

$\mathcal{V}$, and for symmetry we then refer to the original copy $\mathcal{V}$ as $\mathcal{V}_0$. We extend this notation to any number of transitions.

We consider hardware designs modeled as finite logical circuits [3]. Each circuit is associated with a safety property and an environment constraint encoded as Boolean formulas over input and latch variables. A state of the system is an assignment to inputs and latches satisfying the constraint. The values of the latches are initialized using their reset function and evolve according to the transition functions. At every timestamp, the values of latches are determined by the values of inputs and the previous latch values. The inputs can have arbitrary values and represent non-determinism.

Definition 1 (Circuit). *A circuit $M = (I, L, R, F, P, C)$ is defined as a tuple consisting of the following attributes:*

1. *I: a finite ordered set of Boolean input variables;*
2. *L: a finite ordered set of Boolean latch variables;*
3. *$R = \{r_l(I, L) \mid l \in L\}$, where $r_l(I, L)$ is a reset function for latch l;*
4. *$F = \{f_l(I, L) \mid l \in L\}$, where $f_l(I, L)$ is a transition function for latch l;*
5. *$P(I, L)$ represents the set of good states; and*
6. *$C(I, L)$ encodes the set of constrained states.*

In this paper, we focus on safety properties, which should hold in all reachable states. For circuits that do not come with explicitly given constraints, we simply consider $C(I, L) = \top$. For multiple constraints $c_0, c_1, \ldots$, we take their conjunction to form a single one $C(I, L) = \bigwedge_i c_i$. The set of initial states is defined by $R\{L\} = \bigwedge_{l \in L}(l \leftrightarrow r_l(I, L))$. The same notation is used for transitions $F_{0,1}\{L\} = \bigwedge_{\ell \in L}(\ell_1 \leftrightarrow f_\ell(I_0, L_0))$. Both are also used for subsets of L. The convention to use indices on formulas, while omitting explicit variable references, extends to other circuit components, e.g., C_0 stands for $C(I_0, L_0)$.

When designing a certificate format, one of the key objectives is to eliminate the need for quantifiers in certificate checking, allowing the process to fall within the co-NP complexity class and admits the use of SAT solvers. For this purpose, the authors of [12] introduced the concept of *stratified* reset functions, i.e., the reset functions of a circuit do not have cyclic dependencies. This entails that the formula $R\{L\}$ is always satisfiable.

A circuit is said to be safe if the property P holds in all states reachable from the initial states without violating the constraint. Therefore a counterexample is a path $s_0, s_1, \ldots, s_n$ from a reset state s_0 to a bad state s_n where all s_i satisfy the constraint:

$$R_0\{L\} \wedge \bigwedge_{i \in [0,n)} F_{i,i+1}\{L\} \wedge \bigwedge_{i \in [0,n]} C_i \wedge \neg P_n.$$

Example 1. A common problem in hardware design is to arbitrate the usage of shared resources. In the following, we illustrate with such an example, described in Fig. 2. Each user i can send a request for the shared resources by setting the

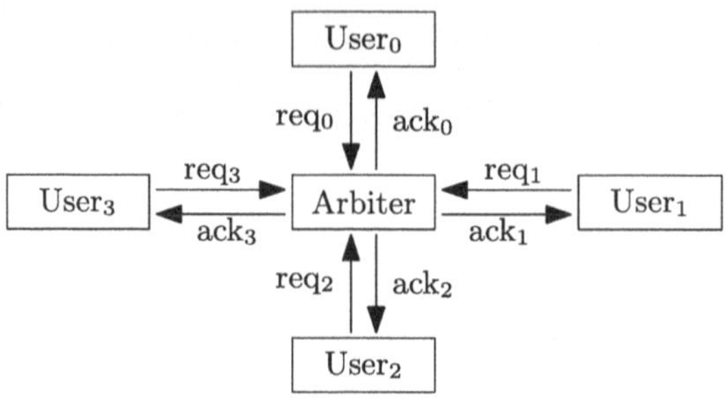

Fig. 2. An arbiter for four users.

input signal req_i and gains access from the acknowledge signal ack_i. The crucial property is that no two users get acknowledged at the same time. The internal design of the arbiter can be quite complex when additional properties, such as fairness, are considered. To make the model checking task easier, we specify the constraint as $C = \bigwedge_{i \neq j} \neg(ack_i \wedge ack_j)$. This constraint can either be extracted by the model checker in a preprocessing step (we later discuss this in Sect. 3), or it can be specified explicitly by the hardware designer. In both cases, the implementation details of the arbiter may be abstracted away from the design.

Counterexamples are witnesses for validating model checking failures. On the other hand, when model checking succeeds, we rely on a certificate, i.e., a witness circuit, which is the format used in the hardware model checking competition.

Definition 2 (Witness Circuit). *$W = (I', L', R', F', P', C')$ is a witness circuit of circuit $M = (I, L, R, F, P, C)$, both with constraints, if R' is stratified and for $K = L \cap L'$:*

1. *Reset:* $R\{K\} \wedge C \rightarrow R'\{K\} \wedge C'$;
2. *Transition:* $F_{0,1}\{K\} \wedge C_0 \wedge C_1 \wedge C'_0 \rightarrow F'_{0,1}\{K\} \wedge C'_1$;
3. *Property:* $(C \wedge C') \rightarrow (P' \rightarrow P)$;
4. *Base:* $R'\{L'\} \wedge C' \rightarrow P'$;
5. *Step:* $P'_0 \wedge F'_{0,1}\{L'\} \wedge C'_0 \wedge C'_1 \rightarrow P'_1$.

Each condition defined above is encoded as a SAT formula. Additionally, a polynomial-time check that R' is stratified [12] is needed, such that there are no cyclic dependencies among the reset functions.

3 Certifying Constraint Extraction

Constraint extraction is a effective preprocessing step that simplifies verification for any base model checking engine [16,17], such as k-induction. In this section, we address the challenge of certifying the hidden constraints uncovered by this process, as illustrated in Fig. 1. Because a witness circuit generated by the base engine only proves correctness on the preprocessed circuit, it does not immediately satisfy Def. 2. Consequently, postprocessing the witness circuit is necessary to produce a valid certificate for the original problem [23].

3.1 Model Constraints

The first type of constraints we consider is *model constraints*. Intuitively, they are those that hold in all reachable states, like a safety property. It is therefore evident that adding them does not change the set of reachable states in the model. In industrial practice, it is common to verify hundreds of properties for the same design, and it is beneficial for verification performance to add already proven properties as constraints [24,25].

Definition 3 (Model Constraint). *Given a circuit $M = (I, L, R, F, P, C)$, the formula $D(I, L)$ is said to be a model constraint if it holds in all reachable states, i.e., the following formula is unsatisfiable for any n:*

$$R_0\{L\} \wedge \bigwedge_{i\in[0,n)} F_{i,i+1}\{L\} \wedge \bigwedge_{i\in[0,n]} C_i \wedge \neg D_n.$$

By Definition 3, during model checking, the extracted model constraints can simply be appended to strengthen C to form a new constraint $C \wedge D$. A base model checker that uses for instance IC3/PDR [26] or k-induction can then be employed. Once verification is completed, the base engine provides a witness circuit. Next, we are going to show how to postprocess such a witness circuit to obtain one that certifies the safety of the original circuit. For that we are going to compose it with another witness circuit for the model constraint D.

In the following we assume inputs and latches not shared with the model to be unique to the respective witness circuits. Otherwise renaming is necessary.

Theorem 1. *Let $M = (I, L, R, F, P, C)$ be a model with constraint D, and let $M_P = (I, L, R, F, P, C \wedge D)$ be the constrained model with witness $W_P = (I^P, L^P, R^P, F^P, P^P, C^P)$. Let $W_D = (I^D, L^D, R^D, F^D, D^D, C^D)$ be a witness certifying that D is a model constraint, i.e., a witness for $M_D = (I, L, R, F, D, C)$. If the inputs and latches of W_P and W_D are disjoint except for those shared with M, then the combined witness circuit W defined as follows is a witness for M.*

$$W = (I^P \cup I^D,\ L^P \cup L^D,\ R^P \cup R^D,\ F^P \cup F^D,\ P^P \wedge P^D,\ C^P \wedge C^D \wedge D)$$

Proof. Before we show that W passes every check of Definition 2, we note that W_P and W_D not sharing any additional inputs or latches implies that $R^P \cup R^D$ is still stratified. Further, given the reset check for both W_P and W_D the reset states in W are simply: $(R^P \cup R^D)\{L^P \cup L^D\} = R^P\{L^P\} \wedge R^D\{L^D\}$. The same is true for encoding transitions. We begin with the reset check and show that the premise implies D by the witness relation between M_D and W_D:

$$R\{K\} \wedge C \Rightarrow R^D\{K\} \wedge C^D \Rightarrow R^D\{L^D\} \wedge C^D \Rightarrow P^D \Rightarrow D$$

Now the premise for the reset check for both W_P and W_D are met, and the conclusion of the reset check for W follows. The premise of the transition check of W gives us D_0, which by the transition check of W_D gives $F^D \wedge C_1^D$ and further

D_1 using the step check. Again the premises for the step check of both W_P and W_D are fulfilled. For the remaining three checks, no additional arguments are needed as the conclusions are the same as in the witness checks for W_P and W_D and the premises have only been strengthened.

Another interesting application of the described construction is the efficient certification of multi-property circuits. Consider a model $M = (I, L, R, F, P, C)$, where $P = \bigwedge_{i \in [0,n]} P^i$, and each P^i typically concerns only a sub-circuit of the original. A model checker may verify these properties individually and later compose the corresponding witness circuits using the same construction as above. In this case both witnesses are produced without the addition of an explicit model constraint and the D in the constraint definition of W is simply true. Any number of witness circuits may be composed through repeated application of the construction, corresponding to a union over all witnesses at each component.

3.2 Inductive Constraints

Inductive constraints [16] can be used to strengthen existing constraints in a model, partially motivated by their use in backward reachability [27].

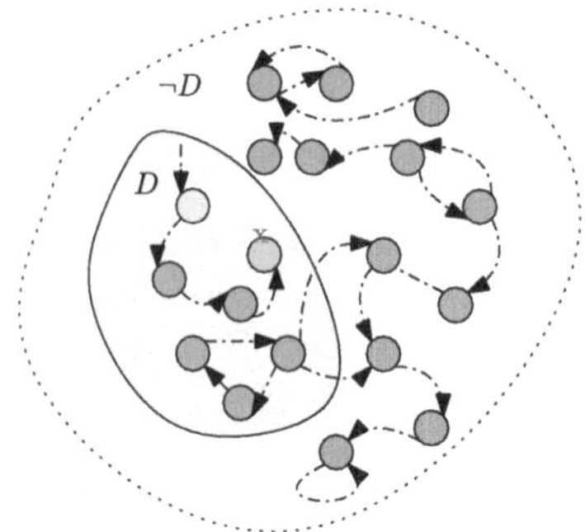

Fig. 3. An illustration of the state space for inductive constraints. The bad states are marked gray; and the initial state is marked yellow. The blue region is the set of states satisfying the constraint D. Note that D is of course not a subset of $\neg D$. (Color figure online)

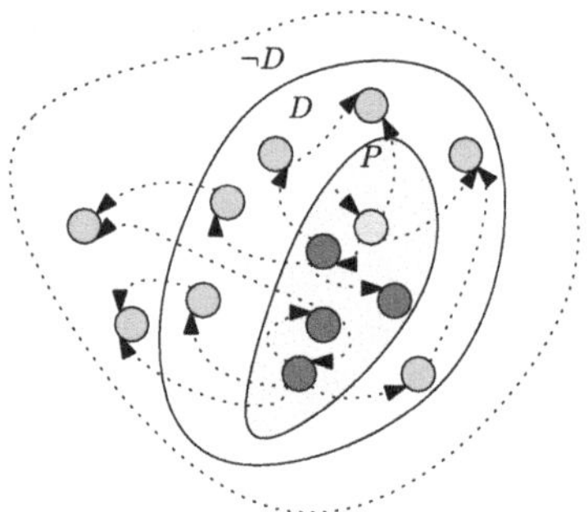

Fig. 4. An illustration of property constraints. Since the property constraints act as conditions in the transition function, outgoing transitions only take place in states that satisfy D. There is no transition from states in $\neg D$ to D.

Definition 4 (Inductive Constraint). *An inductive constraint $D(I, L)$ of a circuit $M = (I, L, R, F, P, C)$ satisfies: (1) $F_{0,1}\{L\} \wedge \neg D_0 \rightarrow \neg D_1$; and (2) $\neg D \rightarrow P$.*

We illustrate inductive constraints in Fig. 3. The soundness of adding inductive constraints follows from the fact that these constraints do not eliminate any bad traces of the original model; therefore, the safety property is preserved. Once a trace leaves D it cannot cross back, since $\neg D$ is inductive, and no bad state can be reached with $\neg D \rightarrow P$. Therefore the model checker only needs to ensure P holds in the states that satisfy D (i.e., the area marked blue). Note the slightly confusing naming of *inductive* constraints taken from [16]; it is the negation of D that is inductive, and moreover it is not an inductive invariant, as it does not necessarily hold in the reset states.

We now show how to produce witness circuits for models with added inductive constraints. The following theorem requires the constraint to also be inductive with respect to the transition function of the witness under constraint W_D. This does not impose a practical limitation, since D only depends on inputs and latches from the original circuit and witness circuits typically do not introduce additional transitions for original latches. If this does happen to be the case, F' can be restricted to the original transitions without changing the success of the transition or step check in Definition 2.

To simplify the presentation, we denote a modified set of reset and transition functions like this $R' \vee \neg D$ and $F' \vee \neg D_1$. This construction can be easily achieved by introducing a fresh input i_l for each latch l, and encoding the formula D over these inputs to obtain D_I. With this setup, the new reset function for each latch l is defined as: $\texttt{ite}(D_I, r'_l, i_l)$, which selects r'_l when D_I holds, and otherwise takes the value of i_l. The transition function $\texttt{ite}(D_I, f'_l, i_l)$, similarly allows to transition to any state violating D. Since R' is stratified and D_I depends only on inputs, the resulting reset function remains stratified.

We prove the correctness of our construction in the following theorem.

Theorem 2. *Given model $M = (I, L, R, F, P, C)$, the constrained model $M_D = (I, L, R, F, P, C \wedge D)$ with witness $W_D = (I', L', R', F', P', C')$, where D is an inductive constraint in M and $F' \wedge \neg D_0 \rightarrow \neg D_1$, the unconstrained witness $W = (I', L', R' \vee \neg D, F' \vee \neg D_1, P' \vee \neg D, C' \vee \neg D)$ is a witness for M.*

Proof. We consider an arbitrary assignment to the formula $L_0 \cup L'_0 \cup I \cup I' \cup L_1 \cup L'_1$. If it satisfies $\neg D$, then it also satisfies P and the property, reset and base check are trivially fulfilled. Similarly, with the assumption $\neg D_1$ the transition and step check hold. If D holds, any violation of the property, reset or base check would also be a violation for the witness relation of M_D and W_D. Since $\neg D$ is inductive under F and F', D_1 implies D_0 if the assignment violates either the transition or step check. In both cases, it would also contradict the witness relation of M_D and W_D.

3.3 Property Constraints

We now take a look at another class of constraints, namely property constraints, that can be generated from a model by a dedicated constraint mining algorithm. Intuitively, property constraints are implied by the property itself.

Definition 5 (Property Constraint). *A property constraint* $D(I, L)$ *of a circuit* $M = (I, L, R, F, P, C)$ *satisfies:* $P \rightarrow D$.

Once property constraints are extracted, their use differs from the previous two constraint types, as both model constraints and inductive constraints are directly appended to the explicit constraint, i.e., $C \wedge D$. Property constraints, on the other hand, need to be integrated into the transition functions.

Model Checking Under Property Constraints. Given a circuit $M = (I, L, R, F, P, C)$ with property constraint D. The circuit under the property constraint is $M_D = (I, L, R, F_D, P, C)$ where: $F_D = \{\texttt{ite}(D_0, f_l, l) \mid l \in L\}$.

This suggests that at every step, if the property constraint holds in the current state, then it follows the same transition as before, otherwise it stays in the current state. We illustrate in Fig. 4 that adding property constraints does not affect the model checking result. In other words, if the circuit under property constraints is proven to be safe, then this implies the original circuit is also safe. This can be validated by a certificate, constructed as follows.

Theorem 3. *Given model* $M = (I, L, R, F, P, C)$, *the model under property constraint* $M_D = (I, L, R, F_D, P, C)$ *with witness* $W_D = (I', L', R', F'_D, P', C'_D)$, *the witness circuit for property constraints* $W' = (I', L', R', F', P', C')$, *where* $F' = \{ite(D_0, f_l'^D, f_l) \mid l \in K\} \cup \{f_l'^D \mid l \in L' \setminus K\}$ *and* $C' = C'_D \wedge D$, *is a witness for* M.

Proof. Given the witness relation between M_D and W_D, we need to prove that W is a witness for M. First we conclude that D holds in any reset of M valid under the constraint:

$$R\{K\} \wedge C \Rightarrow R'\{K'\} \wedge C'_D \Rightarrow R'\{L'\} \wedge C'_D \Rightarrow P' \Rightarrow P \Rightarrow D$$

Now, we assume an assignment s to $L_0 \cup L'_0 \cup I \cup I' \cup L_1 \cup L'_1$ violating any of the witness checks outlined in Definition 2. If D_0 does not hold, the reset check is fulfilled by the above argument. The other checks are trivially fulfilled as C'_0 is false. If D_0 holds in s, the assignment will also violate the same check for the witness relation between M_D and W_D.

4 Relaxed Simulation

According to Definition 2, in order for the Reset and Transition checks to pass, the constraint C' needs to hold for all possible extensions generated by the reset and transition functions. One solution is to ensure that the constraint only contains variables shared between the two circuits, which is a natural assumption. For many model checking algorithms such as IC3/PDR, it is often the case that the certificate W is simply $W = (I, L, R, F, P', C)$ [28], where P' is the inductive strengthening generated by the algorithm itself, encoding an over-approximation of the reachable states, with the rest of the circuit unchanged from M.

However, for other algorithms where it is necessary to constrain new variables in the witness circuit as well as to allow cyclic reset definitions, the format in Definition 2 has to be relaxed to include quantifiers in the checks. We therefore present, in the following, a more general certificate format. While this generalized format is inherently more expensive to check due to the presence of quantifiers, we expect the certificate checker to fall back to the quantifier-free checks of Definition 2 whenever possible, in order to retain efficient certificate validation.

Definition 6 (Quantified Reset and Transition). *Consider the given circuit $M = (I, L, R, F, P, C)$, then the circuit W with $W = (I', L', R', F', P', C')$ is a witness circuit for the local witness variables $X' = (I' \cup L') \setminus (I \cup L)$ if it satisfies Definition 2, with the* Reset *and* Transition *conditions relaxed as follows:*

- *Reset$^\exists$:* $R\{L\} \wedge C \rightarrow \exists X' \, [R'\{L'\} \wedge C']$;
- *Transition$^\exists$:* $F_{0,1}\{L\} \wedge C_0 \wedge C_1 \wedge C'_0 \rightarrow \exists X'_1 \, [F'_{0,1}\{L'\} \wedge C'_1]$.

If Reset$^\exists$ is not used, R' has to be stratified.

If the reset functions of W are cyclic, it is necessary to use the Reset$^\exists$ check. Without this existential quantification, it is not sufficient to prove the soundness theorem of Definition 2: *if W is a witness circuit of M, then M is safe.* Proving this theorem requires establishing a simulation relation between M and W, which in turn requires every reset state in M to correspond to a reset state in W.

Since the Reset$^\exists$ condition directly guarantees that any reset state in M aligns with a reset state in W, we no longer need to impose the stratification requirement on W.

In the following, we formally prove the soundness of this format.

Theorem 4. *Given a circuit M and its witness circuit W that satisfies Definition 6, then M is safe.*

Proof. We assume that W is a witness circuit for M, and do a proof by contradiction. Suppose M is not safe. Then there is a bad trace of some finite length n in the form of an assignment to $n + 1$ copies of $I \cup L$ satisfying:

$$R_0\{L\} \wedge C_0 \wedge F_{0,1}\{L\} \wedge C_1 \dots C_{n-1} \wedge F_{n-1,n}\{L\} \wedge C_n \wedge \neg P_n.$$

We extend this assignment to each copy of the variables in X' that satisfies:

$$R'_0\{L'\} \wedge C'_0 \wedge F'_{0,1}\{L'\} \wedge C'_1 \dots C'_{n-1} \wedge F'_{n-1,n}\{L'\} \wedge C'_n \wedge \neg P'_n.$$

The Reset$^\exists$ and Transition$^\exists$ checks directly imply the existence of a reset state in W, respectively a successor state. Since the Transition$^\exists$ check only quantifies over the next-state version of the extension variables X'_1 the trace in W can be constructed iteratively from reset to bad state. Applying the same argument n times yields an assignment to $(X')^n$ satisfying $F'_{i,i+1}\{L\}$ for $i \in [0, n)$ and C_i for $i \in [0, n]$. Lastly, the property check guarantees $\neg P'_n$, giving us the desired assignment. However, the Base and Step check together ensure that the property P' holds on all reachable states of W, thus contradicting the initial assumption that a bad trace exists in M.

5 Extending Circuits with Oracles

The model checking technique k-induction checks (1) k consecutive states from any initial state are safe; and (2) if any k consecutive states are safe, then the subsequent $(k+1)$-th state is also safe. Even though certifying k-induction has been studied before [3,29–31], none of these works address *uniqueness constraints*, which requires in the second check that the sequence of k consecutive states to be unique. The main difficulty of certifying uniqueness constraints comes from the requirement of accounting for multiple possible execution paths for the inductiveness. It became neccessary for us to further relax the proof format definition. We therefore in the following define witness circuits with *oracles*. Oracles are just like inputs and can be assigned arbitrary values. However, we distinguish oracles from inputs so that they can be explicitly identified and correctly handled in the certificate checks.

Definition 7 (Step check with oracles). *Consider the circuit M with $M = (I, L, R, F, P, C)$, then the circuit W with $W = (I' \dot{\cup} O', L', R', F', P', C')$ where O' are the oracle inputs. W is a witness if R' and F' are independent of O' and the circuits satisfy the conditions in Definition 2, where the step check is relaxed to:*

$$\mathit{Step}^{\exists} : \forall O'_0\, [P'_0 \wedge F'_{0,1}\{L'\} \wedge C'_0] \wedge C'_1 \rightarrow P'_1$$

If R' or F' are dependent on O', we need additional quantifiers in the respective checks similar to Definition 6.

Definition 8 (Reset and Transition with oracles). *Given a circuit M, the circuit W, with $M = (I, L, R, F, P, C)$, $W = (I' \dot{\cup} O', L', R', F', P', C')$, and $X' = (I' \cup L') \setminus (I \cup L)$, is a witness circuit if it meets Definition 2, where the step check has been relaxed to $\mathit{Step}^{\exists}$ from Definition 7 and either or both reset and transition checks have been relaxed to:*

- *$\mathit{Reset}^{\exists\forall}$:* $R\{L\} \wedge C \rightarrow \exists X' \forall O'\, [R'\{L'\} \wedge C']$;
- *$\mathit{Transition}^{\exists\forall}$:* $F_{0,1}\{L\} \wedge C_0 \wedge C_1 \wedge C'_0 \rightarrow \exists X'_1 \forall O'_1\, [F'_{0,1}\{L'\} \wedge C'_1]$.

Theorem 5. *A witness circuit that satisfies the certificate format with oracles is a valid certificate.*

Proof. Since the oracles are only in the witness, the $\text{Reset}^{\exists\forall}$ and $\text{Transition}^{\exists\forall}$ conditions still allow us to construct the trace in W the same way as in the proof of Theorem 4. The same is true if R' or F' are syntactically independent of O' and the quantifier-free checks from Definition 2 are used. What is left to show is that no bad state is reachable in W. We will be considering the equivalence classes induced by O' on the state space of W, i.e., states only differing in O' are in the same equivalence class. Assume there exists a bad trace $s_0, \ldots, s_n$ in W. By the reset check, all states in the equivalence class of s_0 also satisfy R', and by the base check are guaranteed to be good. By applying the transition check to all states in the equivalence class of s_0, we know they each have a transition to all states in the equivalence class of s_1. This allows us to apply the step condition to all states in the equivalence class of s_1, concluding that they are all good. This argument can be applied n times to show that all states in the equivalence class of s_n are good, including s_n itself.

This more complex certificate is, in fact, hard for the second level of the polynomial hierarchy.

Theorem 6. *A closed formula $\forall A \exists E f$ is true exactly if the witness circuit $W = (I', L', R', F', P', C')$ passes the Step$^{\exists}$ check, where $I' = A$, $O' = E$, $L' = \{\ell\}$, $r'_\ell = \top$, $f'_\ell = \top$, $C' = \top$, and $P' = \neg f \wedge \neg \ell$.*

Proof. In the Step$^{\exists}$ check, F' is simply ℓ_1, which implies $\neg P'_1$. With C constant true, O'_0 quantifies over $\neg f_0 \wedge \neg \ell_0$. Since ℓ_0 is independent of O'_0, we can leave it behind when moving the rest to the other side of the implication. Omitting the universal quantifiers for unused variables, we are left with: $\forall \ell_0 \forall \ell_1 \forall A_0 \left[\neg \ell_0 \wedge \ell_1 \rightarrow \exists E_0 \left[f_0\right]\right]$, which is trivially true for all valuations of the first two quantifiers, except for one where it simplifies to $\forall A_0 \exists E_0 f_0$.

5.1 Uniqueness Constraints

In the following, we present certificate generation for uniqueness constraints. We begin by providing the definition of k-induction under uniqueness constraint.

Definition 9. *A property P of a given circuit $M = (I, L, R, F, P, C)$ is said to be k-inductive under uniqueness constraints iff the following holds:*

$$R_0\{L\} \wedge \big(\bigwedge_{i \in [0,k-1)} F_{i,i+1}\{L\}\big) \rightarrow \Big(\bigwedge_{i \in [0,k)} \big(\bigwedge_{j \in [0,i]} C_j\big) \rightarrow P_i\Big) \text{ and}$$

$$\big(\bigwedge_{i \in [0,k)} F_{i,i+1}\{L\}\big) \wedge \big(\bigwedge_{i \in [0,k)} C_i \wedge P_i\big) \wedge \mathit{unique}_k \rightarrow (C_k \rightarrow P_k),$$

$$\text{where } \mathit{unique}_k = \bigwedge_{0 \leq i < j < k} (I_i \not\leftrightarrow I_j) \vee (L_i \not\leftrightarrow L_j).$$

The first formula, called the initiation check, specifies that the property holds for k steps from the initial states. The second formula is an inductive check such that if the property holds for k steps then it also holds at the $(k+1)$-th step. The uniqueness constraint ensures that the inductive step only considers k consecutive states that are all distinct from one another.

Next we present our certificate construction for k-induction under uniqueness constraints. An example for an intuitive understanding of our certificate construction is in Fig. 5. The construction relies on the following idea. A k-inductive property can be strengthened to be inductive: for every bad state, all predecessors up to k steps back are labelled as bad states too.

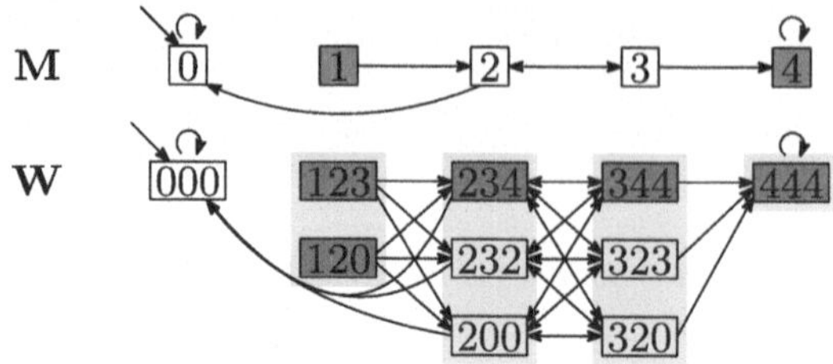

Fig. 5. Example of the k-witness construction for certifying k-induction under uniqueness constraints. The figure displays the state space of a circuit M, which is 3-inductive under uniqueness constraints, alongside its corresponding k-witness circuit W (Definition 10). Bad states are marked in red, state 0 is the only initial state. Witness states that differ only by the value of O' are grouped vertically. If at least one state in a group violates the property, the entire group is highlighted with a light red background.

Definition 10. *(**k -witness circuit under uniqueness constraints**) Given a circuit* $M = (I, L, R, F, P, C)$ *with* $k \in \mathbb{N}^+$. *The k-witness circuit under uniqueness constraints is defined as* $W = (I \dot{\cup} O', L, R, F, P', C)$, *where* $O' = \bigcup_{i \in [0,k)} I^i$ *and* $P' = \bigwedge_{i \in [0,k)} [v^i \rightarrow P(I^i, L^i)]$, *with* $v^0 = C(I, L)$, $v^i = v^{i-1} \wedge C(I^i, L^i)$, $L^0 = L$ *and* $L^{i+1} = \{f_l(I^i, L^i) \mid l \in L\}$.

In the above definition, $L^1, \ldots, L^{k-1}$ are not necessarily latches: we directly use the output of the transition functions, which are simply AND-gates in practice. The variables v^i keep track of the depth up to which the path along the L^i remains valid; that is, only traverses states satisfying the constraint. The latches are the same in the original and the k-witness circuit, however, the k-witness circuit has more bad states, as it requires all states reachable in $k-1$ steps to be good. Note that by construction the reset and transition functions are independent of the oracles, thus the Reset$^{\exists\forall}$ and Transition$^{\exists\forall}$ checks are not necessary and the quantifier-free versions should be used.

Even though Definition 10 is also a valid construction for k-induction *without* uniqueness constraints, it is expensive for the certificate checker to perform QBF checks. Hence in the case where uniqueness constraints are not required, the witness circuit construction should still follow the construction outlined in [12]. Their approach produces inductive witnesses by recording a history of k states rather than precomputing a possible future. While this method avoids the quantification, it would violate the transition check, since the witness is not allowed to transition to a state already in the history while the correctness of the construction relies on the model being inductive under uniqueness constraints.

Theorem 7. *Given a circuit* $M = (I, L, R, F, P, C)$ *with some* $k \in \mathbb{N}^+$, *and a k-witness circuit* $W = (I \dot{\cup} O', L, R, F, P', C)$. *If M is k-inductive under uniqueness constraints, then W is a valid witness circuit for M.*

Proof. Since L, R, F and C remain unchanged, the reset and transition conditions hold trivially. Given C, the new property P' clearly implies P, thus the

Table 1. The HWMCC set contains 39 multi-property benchmarks, split into 7 families, each with the same number of properties (B). The other columns display the number of and-gates (A), total time taken in seconds for checking individual witness circuits for a single property (Σ), and time taken for checking the composed witness circuit ($\cup$). Additionally, the table presents the time taken up just by the Property check for the individual witnesses (Σ_P) and the composed witness ($\cup_P$), which in both cases has to be done B times. As well as the Transition check, which has to be done for each individual witness (Σ_F) but only once for the composed witness ($\cup_F$). This is the same for every other check, but the transition check is the most complex on this set of benchmarks. Each row presents the mean over the benchmarks in the family (number given in parentheses). The mean over all benchmarks is presented at the top.

	A	O	Σ	$\cup$	Σ_P	$\cup_P$	Σ_F	$\cup_F$
Mean (39)	25411	64	777.20	37.18	36.23	30.77	660.37	4.15
picorv32 (8)	54042	201	3455.78	144.77	107.99	128.20	3037.94	14.89
mentor (1)	31613	36	505.96	38.70	23.40	25.53	440.87	12.37
dspfilters (17)	28397	49	120.07	9.45	29.66	7.58	58.22	1.22
sm98 (3)	5126	2	25.17	21.35	1.56	1.16	4.83	2.38
zipcpu (7)	2946	2	3.46	2.57	1.49	1.46	0.54	0.23
zipversa (3)	2775	3	5.92	3.44	2.17	2.13	0.70	0.26

property check is satisfied. For the base check we note that if an initial state of the witness violates P', a bad state in the original circuit can be reached in k steps or less. It is left to show that if the Step$^{\exists}$ check fails, the original circuit is not k-inductive. Assume two consecutive states u' and v' in C' for which the Step$^{\exists}$ check fails. Let u and v be the states in M induced by the assignment to L in u' and v' respectively. The shortest path from v to a bad state has exactly k states, all are different, satisfy the constraint, and all but the last are good. If the number of steps was less, P' would not hold in u', and if it was any more, P' would hold in v'. The other two claims follow from the path being the shortest. Since u is guaranteed to satisfy C and be different from the bad state, prepending the path with u yields a path in M consisting of k unique good states followed by a bad state, thus M is not k-inductive under uniqueness constraints.

6 Experimental Evaluation

We implemented the proposed certificate format in our certificate checker CERTIFAIGER[1], together with the relaxed checks that require quantifiers. Note that in all HWMCC benchmarks, all reset functions are stratified, as the standard AIGER format used in the competitions only supports stratified resets. We also extended the open-source k-induction-based model checker MCAIGER [32] to

[1] https://github.com/Froleyks/certifaiger.

generate k-witness circuits as defined in Definition 10 when uniqueness constraints are enabled. Additionally, we implement our tool AIGMERGE[2] that uses the construction described in Theorem 1 to compose arbitrary circuits.

CERTIFAIGER uses KISSAT [33] for SAT checks and QUABS [34] for quantified checks. All input circuits are in the AIGER 1.9 format. Each certificate check is generated as combinatorial circuits in either AIGER (for SAT checks) or QAIGER (for QBF checks) and is then translated to CNF or the circuit-based QCIR format [35].

Table 2. In the HWMCC'10 benchmark set, 8 additional instances are solved with uniqueness constraints. We list the model checking (t_{MC}) and certification time (t_{Cert}). The table also presents the portion of the certification time taken for the 4 SAT checks (t_{SAT}). The last three columns denote the inductive depth k, the number of input variables I, and gates A respectively.

	t_{MC} (s)	t_{Cert} (s)	t_{SAT} (s)	k	I	A
bobcount	426.68	26.86	2.40	76	3	77
eijks298	383.05	2192.33	9.77	138	3	225
pdtvispeterson	6.29	249.35	2.76	59	2	700
pdtvisvending00	14.25	to	2.37	35	2	959
pdtvisvending02	199.05	to	2.03	33	2	958
pdtvisvending05	3.13	26663.62	1.70	28	2	951
pdtvisvending07	3.41	22117.90	2.34	29	2	952
pdtvisvending08	117.81	to	2.07	33	2	950

The goal of our first experiment is to evaluate the certification method for composing witness circuits, which also provides insight into certifying extracted constraints. Although we could not find an open-source model checker that implements explicit constraint extraction, the concept of model constraints naturally arises in circuits where multiple properties are of interest. Therefore, we focus on multi-property benchmarks that are present in HWMCC'12 and HWMCC'19. We first ran our certifying model checker VOIRAIG for each property individually, which left us with one witness circuit per property that could be proven. We then used AIGMERGE to combine all the witness circuits for an individual model into one. Certificate checking for such a certificate proceeds as follows: verify the reset, transition, base, and step condition for the composed witness according to Definition 2. For each original property run the property check. We compare the total time of these checks to the total time it takes to

[2] AIGMERGE may eventually be added to the set of AIGER utilities at https://github.com/arminbiere/aiger.

certify the original witness circuits for each property individually. We present the results obtained in Table 1. As can be seen, directly verifying the composed witness circuit is significantly more efficient than verifying individual witness circuits for each property. Interestingly, the transition check appears to be the bottleneck during the certification process, which differs from the experimental results in [36], where the step check always takes significantly longer.

In the second experiment, we study the effectiveness of our certification method for k-induction under uniqueness constraints. We selected the benchmarks that require uniqueness constraints from HWMCC'10. Results are summarized in Table 2. We used a timeout of 50 000 s for certificate checking. Despite the QBF check creating a bottleneck in certification performance, our certifier successfully validated 5 out of 8 instances. The QBF solver QuAbs failed to complete the $\text{Step}^{\exists}$ checks for three instances within the time limit, whereas for the same instances the rest of the checks were solved in less than 10 s (see t_{SAT} in the table). While QBF solving is inherently more challenging than SAT solving, we attribute the substantial performance gap in part to recent advances in SAT solving, particularly the circuit-specific optimizations introduced in Kissat [37]. We believe that incorporating similar optimizations into QuAbs could significantly improve the efficiency of QBF-based certificate checking. Exploring such enhancements is an important direction for future work.

7 Conclusion

Recent hardware model checking competitions have employed a standardized certification approach, relying on simple SAT-based certificate validation. This approach has proven highly effective, with certification overhead constituting only a small fraction of the total verification effort. In this work, we introduce certification generation techniques tailored to both explicit and implicitly extracted constraints for three different constraint classes. Furthermore, we present alternative QBF-based checks to replace pure SAT checks in the certificate format, addressing the challenges of certificate generation posed by intricate reset logic and complex encodings in model checking. Extending this, we also demonstrate certification generation for k-induction under uniqueness constraints. The empirical evaluation, conducted on a range of competition benchmarks, demonstrates the effectiveness and practical relevance of our method. Looking forward, we plan to incorporate the remaining techniques in bit-level hardware model checking, such as retiming [38] and localization. Furthermore, we aim to broaden the scope of our certification method to infinite-state systems to support program verification as well as exploring the certification of security properties.

Acknowledgement. Partially funded by the European Union (ERC, CertiFOX, 101122653). Views and opinions expressed are however those of the author(s) only and do not necessarily reflect those of the European Union or the European Research Council. Neither the European Union nor the granting authority can be held responsible for them. Further funded by, the Research Council of Finland under the project 369068, and a gift from Intel Corporation.

References

1. Beyer, D., Dangl, M., Dietsch, D., Heizmann, M., Stahlbauer, A.: Witness validation and stepwise testification across software verifiers. In: Proceedings of the 2015 10th Joint Meeting on Foundations of Software Engineering, pp. 721–733 (2015)
2. Esparza, J., Lammich, P., Neumann, R., Nipkow, T., Schimpf, A., Smaus. J.-G.: A fully verified executable LTL model checker (2014)
3. Yu, E., Biere, A., Heljanko, K.: Progress in certifying hardware model checking results. In: Silva, A., Leino, K.R.M. (eds.) CAV 2021. LNCS, vol. 12760, pp. 363–386. Springer, Cham (2021). https://doi.org/10.1007/978-3-030-81688-9_17
4. Griggio, A., Roveri, M., Tonetta, S.: Certifying proofs for SAT-based model checking. Formal Methods Syst. Des. **57**(2), 178–210 (2021)
5. Namjoshi, K.S.: Certifying model checkers. In: Berry, G., Comon, H., Finkel, A. (eds.) CAV 2001. LNCS, vol. 2102, pp. 2–13. Springer, Heidelberg (2001). https://doi.org/10.1007/3-540-44585-4_2
6. Kaufman, M., Martin, A., Pixley, C.: Design constraints in symbolic model checking. In: Hu, A.J., Vardi, M.Y. (eds.) CAV 1998. LNCS, vol. 1427, pp. 477–487. Springer, Heidelberg (1998). https://doi.org/10.1007/BFb0028768
7. Hollander, Y., Morley, M., Noy, A.: The e language: a fresh separation of concerns. In: Proceedings Technology of Object-Oriented Languages and Systems. TOOLS, vol. 38, pp. 41–50. IEEE (2001)
8. Alur, R., Henzinger, T.A.: Reactive modules. Formal Methods Syst. Des. **15**, 7–48 (1999)
9. Biere, A., Heljanko, K., Wieringa, S.: AIGER 1.9 and beyond (2011)
10. Biere, A., Froleyks, N., Preiner, M.: Hardware model checking competition 2024. In: FMCAD, p. 7. TU Wien Academic Press (2024)
11. Froleyks, N., Yu, E., Preiner, M., Biere, A., Heljanko, K.: Introducing certificates to the hardware model checking competition. In: Piskac, R., Rakamarić, Z. (eds.) Computer Aided Verification. CAV 2025. Lecture Notes in Computer Science, vol. 15931, pp. 281–295. Springer, Cham (2025). https://doi.org/10.1007/978-3-031-98668-0_14
12. Yu, E., Froleyks, N., Biere, A., Heljanko, K.: Stratified certification for K-induction. In: FMCAD, pp. 59–64. IEEE (2022)
13. Malik, S.: Analysis of cyclic combinational circuits. IEEE Trans. Comput. Aided Des. Integr. Circuits Syst. **13**(7), 950–956 (1994)
14. Jiang, J-HR., Mishchenko, A., Brayton, R.K.: On breakable cyclic definitions. In: IEEE/ACM International Conference on Computer Aided Design, 2004. ICCAD-2004, pp. 411–418. IEEE (2004)
15. Riedel, M.D.: Cyclic combinational circuits. California Institute of Technology (2004)
16. Cabodi, G., Camurati, P., Garcia, L.A., Murciano, M., Nocco, S., Quer, S:. Speeding up model checking by exploiting explicit and hidden verification constraints. In: DATE, pp. 1686–1691. IEEE (2009)
17. Koen Claessen, K., Sörensson, N.: A liveness checking algorithm that counts. In: FMCAD, pp. 52–59. IEEE (2012)
18. Brayton, R., Mishchenko, A.: ABC: an academic industrial-strength verification tool. In: Touili, T., Cook, B., Jackson, P. (eds.) CAV 2010. LNCS, vol. 6174, pp. 24–40. Springer, Heidelberg (2010). https://doi.org/10.1007/978-3-642-14295-6_5

19. Jahanpour, M.S., and Mohamed, O.A.: Automatic generation of model checking properties and constraints from production based specification. In: The 2004 47th Midwest Symposium on Circuits and Systems, 2004. MWSCAS'04, vol. 3, pp. iii–435. IEEE (2004)
20. Yuan, J., Albin, K., Aziz, A., Pixley, C.: Constraint synthesis for environment modeling in functional verification. In: Proceedings of the 40th Annual Design Automation Conference, pp. 296–299 (2003)
21. Sheeran, M., Singh, S., Stålmarck, G.: Checking safety properties using induction and a sat-solver. In: Hunt, W.A., Johnson, S.D. (eds.) FMCAD 2000. LNCS, vol. 1954, pp. 127–144. Springer, Heidelberg (2000). https://doi.org/10.1007/3-540-40922-X_8
22. Yu, Z.E.: Certifying hardware model checking/submitted by Emily Zhengqi Yu (2023)
23. Yu, E., Froleyks, N., Biere, A., Heljanko, K.: Towards compositional hardware model checking certification. In: FMCAD, pp. 1–11. IEEE (2023)
24. Goldberg, E., Güdemann, M., Kroening, D., Mukherjee, R.: Efficient verification of multi-property designs (the benefit of wrong assumptions). In: 2018 Design, Automation & Test in Europe Conference & Exhibition (DATE), pp. 43–48 (2018)
25. Das, S., Hazra, A., Dasgupta, P., Kundu, S., Jain, H.: Purse: property ordering using runtime statistics for efficient multi - property verification. In: 2024 Design, Automation & Test in Europe Conference & Exhibition (DATE), pp. 1–6 (2024)
26. Bradley, A.R.: Understanding IC3. In: Cimatti, A., Sebastiani, R. (eds.) SAT 2012. LNCS, vol. 7317, pp. 1–14. Springer, Heidelberg (2012). https://doi.org/10.1007/978-3-642-31612-8_1
27. Bjesse, P., Claessen, K.: SAT-based verification without state space traversal. In: Hunt, W.A., Johnson, S.D. (eds.) FMCAD 2000. LNCS, vol. 1954, pp. 409–426. Springer, Heidelberg (2000). https://doi.org/10.1007/3-540-40922-X_23
28. Yu, Z., Biere, A., Heljanko, K.: Certifying hardware model checking results. In: Ait-Ameur, Y., Qin, S. (eds.) ICFEM 2019. LNCS, vol. 11852, pp. 498–502. Springer, Cham (2019). https://doi.org/10.1007/978-3-030-32409-4_32
29. Gurfinkel, A., Ivrii, A.: K-induction without unrolling. In: FMCAD, pp. 148–155. IEEE (2017)
30. Bjørner, N., Gurfinkel, A., McMillan, K., Rybalchenko, A.: Horn clause solvers for program verification. In: Beklemishev, L.D., Blass, A., Dershowitz, N., Finkbeiner, B., Schulte, W. (eds.) Fields of Logic and Computation II. LNCS, vol. 9300, pp. 24–51. Springer, Cham (2015). https://doi.org/10.1007/978-3-319-23534-9_2
31. Champion, A., Mebsout, A., Sticksel, C., Tinelli, C.: The kind 2 model checker. In: Chaudhuri, S., Farzan, A. (eds.) CAV 2016. LNCS, vol. 9780, pp. 510–517. Springer, Cham (2016). https://doi.org/10.1007/978-3-319-41540-6_29
32. Biere, A., Brummayer, R.: Consistency checking of all different constraints over bit-vectors within a SAT solver. In: 2008 Formal Methods in Computer-Aided Design, pp. 1–4. IEEE (2008)
33. Biere, A., Faller, T., Fazekas, K., Fleury, M., Froleyks, N., Pollitt, F.: CaDiCaL, Gimsatul, IsaSAT and Kissat entering the SAT Competition 2024. In: Heule, M., Iser, M., Järvisalo, M., Suda, M.(eds.) Proceedings of SAT Competition 2024 – Solver, Benchmark and Proof Checker Descriptions, vol. B-2024-1 of Department of Computer Science Report Series B, pp. 8–10. University of Helsinki (2024)
34. Tentrup, L.: CAQE and QuAbS: abstraction based QBF solvers. J. Satisfiability Boolean Model. Comput. **11**(1), 155–210 (2019)

35. Jordan, C., Klieber, W., Seidl, M.: Non-CNF QBF solving with QCIR. In: AAAI Workshop: Beyond NP, vol. WS-16-05 of AAAI Technical Report. AAAI Press (2016)
36. Froleyks, N., Yu, E., Biere, A., Heljanko, K.: Certifying phase abstraction. In: Benzmüller, C., Heule, M.J., Schmidt, R.A. (eds) Automated Reasoning. IJCAR 2024. Lecture Notes in Computer Science(), vol. 14739. Springer, Cham (2024). https://doi.org/10.1007/978-3-031-63498-7_17
37. Biere, A., Fazekas, K., Fleury, M., Froleyks, N.: Clausal congruence closure. In: 27th International Conference on Theory and Applications of Satisfiability Testing (SAT 2024). Schloss Dagstuhl–Leibniz-Zentrum für Informatik (2024)
38. Shenoy, N., Rudell, R.: Efficient implementation of retiming. The Best of ICCAD: 20 Years of Excellence in Computer-Aided Design, pp. 615–630 (2003)

Tools and Algorithms for Sound Multi-Objective Probabilistic Model Checking
(Long Tool Paper)

Arnd Hartmanns[1], Tim Quatmann[2], and Mark van Wijk[1](✉)

[1] University of Twente, Enschede, The Netherlands
{a.hartmanns,mark.vanwijk}@utwente.nl
[2] RWTH Aachen University, Aachen, Germany
tim.quatmann@cs.rwth-aachen.de

Abstract. Practical verification tasks often involve multiple goals, such as maximising an expected reward within a specified reliability threshold. Algorithms to solve such multi-objective probabilistic model checking (MO-PMC) problems were developed over a decade ago, and are implemented by multiple tools. However, the algorithms are *unsound* in general—at best delivering some underapproximation of the true result—and the implementations are unreliable, with different tools producing inconsistent results. In this paper, we present the first implementations of recently-developed *sound* MO-PMC algorithms that bound the true result from above *and* below, in two independent tools. We discuss ways to consistently treat infinite rewards and extend the algorithms with relative-error termination criteria. On the practical side, we add support for multi-objective properties to the Jani interchange format for tool interoperability, and extend the Quantitative Verification Benchmark Set with multi-objective problems. Based on the latter, we conduct an extensive experimental evaluation of the two tools' new sound MO-PMC capabilities, showing in particular that they produce consistent results.

1 Introduction

Scenarios involving decision-making under uncertainty can formally be modelled as Markov decision processes (MDPs) [10,32]: a state-transition model in which

The authors are ordered alphabetically. This work was supported by the European Union's Horizon 2020 research and innovation programme under Marie Skłodowska-Curie grant agreement 101008233 (MISSION), by the Interreg North Sea project STORM_SAFE, by the KI-Starter Project Verifying AI Systems under Partial Observability of the Ministry of Culture and Science of the German State of North Rhine-Westphalia, and by NWO VIDI grant VI.Vidi.223.110 (TruSTy). Experiments were performed with computing resources granted by RWTH Aachen University under project rwth1632.

A. Sampaio and M. Stoelinga (Eds.): FM 2026, LNCS 16556, pp. 189–210, 2026.
https://doi.org/10.1007/978-3-032-26204-2_10

the transition to take out of a state is chosen nondeterministically (in a controllable or adversarial manner) while the transition's target is a probability distribution over successor states. Probabilistic model checking (PMC) [2] can then compute the values of various kinds of properties ranging from reachability probabilities and expected rewards [25] over LTL [1, Sect. 5] and PCTL formulas [21] to quantiles [35,47] and risk measures [3,37].

Practical applications, however, often pose a *multi-objective* problem in which *one* strategy resolving the nondeterministic choices is sought that simultaneously optimises *many*, possibly conflicting, properties. Examples include maximising a satellite's expected utility with a low probability of depleting the battery [11] and balancing cost and comfort in heat-pump control [29]. Given an MDP and a multi-objective property of d individual properties, multi-objective PMC (MO-PMC) can compute the *achievable set*: the points in $\mathbb{R}^d$ in which the i-th coordinate is the value of the i-th property for the strategy associated with that point. The boundary of this set is the front of Pareto-optimal solutions.

The standard MO-PMC approaches, developed in the early 2010, are to use either linear programming (LP) [16] or value iteration (VI) [17]. However, value iteration is unsound in the single-objective case [19], i.e. its results may be arbitrarily far from the property's (unknown) true value, and this carries over to its multi-objective variant. Standard commercial and open-source LP solvers face the same problem [25]. The QComp 2023 competition [1] compared five MO-PMC tools—EPMC [18], MULTIGAIN [8,12], PRISM [39], PRISM-GAMES [38], and STORM [31]—and found that they reported inconsistent results [1, Sect. 6.2]. While some of the inconsistencies were due to bugs that have since been fixed [49, Sect. 4.3], we also found that different tools use different semantics when infinite rewards are involved. Most critically, however, none of these tools so far provided a *sound* MO-PMC implementation. In the single-objective case, a sound result is an interval of user-specified absolute or relative width that is guaranteed to contain the true value, and several sound variants of VI exist [20,26,43]. In MO-PMC, a sound result would be a pair of guaranteed under- and over approximations of the achievable set of user-specified absolute or relative width, for some appropriate notion of width.

In this tool paper, we present two tools for sound MO-PMC: MCSTA of the MODEST TOOLSET [23] and STORM. They independently implement the recently-developed sound MO-PMC algorithm of [41, Sect. 3.4], which lifts sound single-objective VI into the VI-based MO-PMC method of [17] in a way that guarantees sound bounds on the achievable set. STORM previously implemented only some parts of [41, Sect. 3.4], which resulted in its results not being sound unless run in `--exact` mode (which does not use VI and consequently does not scale). MCSTA previously did not implement MO-PMC at all.

In addition to the tools themselves (Sect. 5), we (1) classify the possible ways to treat infinite-reward cases in MO-PMC—which were the cause of previous semantic differences between tools—and make consistent choices in MCSTA and STORM; (2) fill in a missing proof for the correctness of the convergence check for absolute width of [41, Sect. 3.4]; and (3) extend the algorithm with a notion of relative-width convergence (Sect. 3). Furthermore, we extend the

JANI model exchange formalism [14] with support for multi-objective properties (Sect. 4.1), enabling MCSTA and STORM to work on the same input files. This also enables us to make the JANI-based Quantitative Verification Benchmark Set (QVBS) [27] multi-objective (Sect. 4.2) by (i) extending existing QVBS models with multi-objective properties, and (2) adding multi-objective models from the literature [1,25] not previously part of the QVBS to the benchmark set. Using these new benchmarks, we experimentally evaluate the two new implementations (Sect. 6), comparing their performance and showing that they produce consistent results in all cases.

Related Work. As mentioned above, MO-PMC was so far implemented in EPMC, MULTIGAIN, PRISM, PRISM-GAMES, and STORM. PRISM and EPMC use the unsound VI-based algorithm of [17]. PRISM-GAMES also uses an unsound VI-based approach [9], but works for stochastic games [45] instead of MDPs. PRISM also implements the LP-based approach of [16], while MULTIGAIN solves multi-objective combinations of LTL properties and long-run average rewards using an LP-based method [13,36]. However, LP-based approaches tend to not scale well in single-objective PMC, and standard (non-exact) LP solvers can be arbitrarily wrong [25]. Using LP thus leads to unsound results in general. Prior to this work, STORM offered a fast but unsound implementation of the sound algorithm of [41, Sect. 3.4] plus an exact but less scalable variant using infinite-precision rational arithmetic. For a more in-depth comparison of the features of (unsound) MO-PMC tools, we refer the reader to [1, Sect. 6].

Watanabe et al. [48] *use* MO-PMC within their approach for solving single-objective queries on string diagrams of MDPs. They claim to implement a sound algorithm based on [44] (where [44] is the basis of [41, Sect. 3.4]) for this purpose.

Approaches to produce certificates and witnesses for MO-PMC are presented in [4,5]. The obtained certificates can be checked independently to validate the correctness of the verification results whereas the witnesses provide further diagnostic information. However, the existing LP-based approaches are limited to small and medium-sized models.

2 Background

We introduce MDPs, single- and multi-objective properties, and concepts from geometry. See [41, Sect. 2] for further details. For countable set X, $Dist(X)$ is the set of all probability distributions $\mu\colon X \to [0,1]$ such that $\sum_{x\in X} \mu(x) = 1$.

Definition 1. *A* Markov decision process *(MDP) is a tuple* $\mathcal{M} = \langle \mathcal{S}, s_{init}, \mathcal{A}, \delta \rangle$ *consisting of finite sets* $\mathcal{S}$ *and* $\mathcal{A}$ *(the* state space *and* actions, *respectively),* initial state $s_{init} \in \mathcal{S}$, *and partial* transition function $\delta\colon \mathcal{S} \times \mathcal{A} \rightharpoonup Dist(\mathcal{S})$, *where for each* $s \in \mathcal{S}$, *there exists at least one* $\alpha \in \mathcal{A}$ *such that* $\delta(s,\alpha)$ *is defined. The* enabled actions *for state* $s \in \mathcal{S}$ *are* $\mathcal{A}(s) = \{\alpha \in \mathcal{A} \mid \delta(s,\alpha)$ *is defined*$\}$ *and a* transition *is* $\delta(s,a)$ *for* $a \in \mathcal{A}(s)$. *A reward structure is a function* $\mathcal{R}\colon \mathcal{S}\times\mathcal{A}\times\mathcal{S} \to \mathbb{R}$ *that provides rewards for the branches (i.e. successor states) of transitions.*

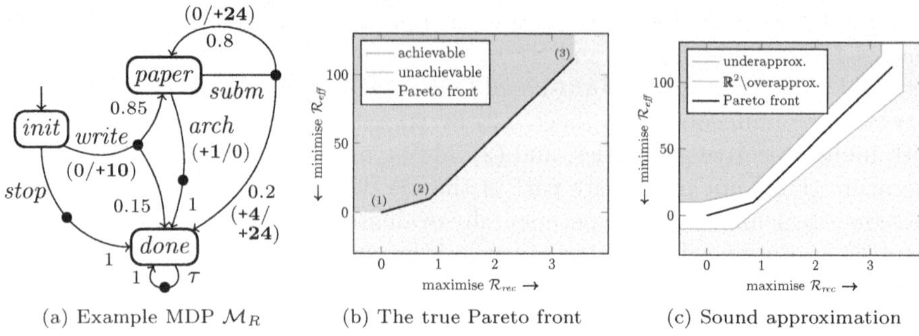

(a) Example MDP $\mathcal{M}_R$ (b) The true Pareto front (c) Sound approximation

Fig. 1. An example MDP and the corresponding expected-reward Pareto fronts. (Color figure online)

MDP $\mathcal{M}_R$ shown in Fig. 1a models a research process: We start with an idea in state *init*, which provides a choice between two actions: to *write* a paper, or to *stop*. If the paper was written successfully (0.85 probability), it can either be *subm*itted to a prestigious conference, or *arch*ived on arXiv. The conferences have a 20 % acceptance rate only, but if the paper gets rejected, it can be submitted to another prestigious conference. Reward structure $\mathcal{R}_{rec}$ represents the recognition for the paper, and $\mathcal{R}_{eff}$ the effort. We label each branch $\delta(s,a)(s')$ with $(\mathcal{R}_{rec}(s,a,s') \,/\, \mathcal{R}_{eff}(s,a,s'))$, omitting (0/0)s and labelling the transition instead if the rewards are the same for all its branches.

A *path* π is an infinite alternating sequence of states and actions $s_1 \xrightarrow{a_1} s_2 \xrightarrow{a_2} \ldots$ such that $s_1 = s_{init}$, $a_i \in \mathcal{A}(s_i)$ and $\delta(s_i,a_i)(s_{i+1}) > 0$ for all $s_i \in \mathcal{S}$. The *set of all paths* of MDP $\mathcal{M}$ is $\Pi_\mathcal{M}$. *Strategies* (also known as adversaries, policies, or schedulers) are used to resolve the nondeterminism in an MDP. A *(probabilistic) memoryless strategy* is a function $\sigma\colon \mathcal{S} \to \mathit{Dist}(\mathcal{A})$ such that $\sigma(s)(a) > 0$ implies $a \in \mathcal{A}(s)$ for all $s \in \mathcal{S}$. The *set of all probabilistic memoryless strategies* is $\mathit{Strat}_\mathcal{M}$. A memoryless strategy is *deterministic* iff all states map to Dirac distributions, i.e. $\sigma(s,\alpha)(s') = 1$ for some $s' \in \mathcal{S}$. The probability measure $\mathbb{P}^\sigma_\mathcal{M}\colon \Pi_\mathcal{M} \to \mathbb{R}_{\geq 0}$ over all paths by resolving the nondeterminism using strategy σ can be obtained via the standard cylinder set construction [6].

Single-objective properties. Typical PMC tasks are to check whether the minimum probability of reaching some goal state is above a given threshold, or to compute the maximum expected reward that can be accumulated. In general, such a *property* asks for the expected value of a random variable $X\colon \Pi_\mathcal{M} \to \overline{\mathbb{R}}$, where $\overline{\mathbb{R}} = \mathbb{R} \cup \{-\infty, +\infty\}$. Under a given strategy σ, the expected value is $\mathbb{E}^\sigma_\mathcal{M}(X) = \int_{\pi \in \Pi_\mathcal{M}} X(\pi) d\mathbb{P}^\sigma_\mathcal{M}$.[1] We focus on *total reward* properties, where a reward structure $\mathcal{R}$ induces $X^\mathcal{R}_{tot}(s_1 \xrightarrow{a_1} s_2 \xrightarrow{a_2} \ldots) = \sum_{i=1}^{\infty} \mathcal{R}(s_i,a_i,s_{i+1})$, i.e.

[1] $\mathbb{E}^\sigma_\mathcal{M}(X)$ is undefined if X is not measurable or evaluates to $-\infty$ and $+\infty$ both with positive probability (i.e. $\mathbb{P}^\sigma_\mathcal{M}\{\, X = -\infty \,\} > 0$ and $\mathbb{P}^\sigma_\mathcal{M}\{\, X = +\infty \,\} > 0$). We only consider properties for which $\mathbb{E}^\sigma_\mathcal{M}(X)$ is defined for all σ.

the total reward accumulated over the path. Memoryless strategies suffice for such properties [41, Sect. 3.4]. Several other types of properties can be reduced to expected total rewards, notably reachability probabilities [17, Prop. 2] and expected reachability rewards [41, Thm 4.1].

The *quantitative* single-objective properties are $E^{\mathcal{R}}_{\max} \stackrel{\text{def}}{=} \sup_\sigma \mathbb{E}^\sigma_{\mathcal{M}}(X^{\mathcal{R}}_{tot})$ and $E^{\mathcal{R}}_{\min} \stackrel{\text{def}}{=} \inf_\sigma \mathbb{E}^\sigma_{\mathcal{M}}(X^{\mathcal{R}}_{tot})$, the maximum and minimum total reward. They can be approximated by an interval $[\underline{E^{\mathcal{R}}_{\text{opt}}}, \overline{E^{\mathcal{R}}_{\text{opt}}}] \ni E^{\mathcal{R}}_{\text{opt}}$. *Qualitative* properties or *constraints* are of the form $E^{\mathcal{R}}_{\triangle c} \stackrel{\text{def}}{=} \exists \sigma \colon \mathbb{E}^\sigma_{\mathcal{M}}(X^{\mathcal{R}}_{tot}) \triangle c$, with $\triangle \in \{<, \leq, >, \geq\}$. We say property $E^{\mathcal{R}}_{\circ}$ is *maximising* iff $\circ \in \{\max, >c, \geq c\}$, else it is *minimising.*

Geometry. We fix a dimension $d \in \mathbb{N}_{>0}$. A *halfspace* is a subset of $\mathbb{R}^d$ containing all points $\boldsymbol{x} \in \mathbb{R}^d$ which satisfy $\boldsymbol{w} \cdot \boldsymbol{x} \leq c$ for a chosen vector $\boldsymbol{w} \in \mathbb{R}^d$ and $c \in \mathbb{R}$. The *convex hull* of a set of points $\{\boldsymbol{x_1}, \boldsymbol{x_2}, \ldots\} = X \subseteq \mathbb{R}^d$ is the set $conv(X) = \{\sum_{i=1}^{|X|} w_i \boldsymbol{x_i} \mid \boldsymbol{w} \in [0,1]^{|X|} \wedge \sum_{i=1}^{|X|} w_i = 1\}$. The *downward closure* under (partial) order $\preceq$ on $\mathbb{R}^d$ is $down_{\preceq}(X) = \{\boldsymbol{y} \in \mathbb{R}^d \mid \exists \boldsymbol{x} \in X \colon \boldsymbol{y} \preceq \boldsymbol{x}\}$.

Example 2. A halfspace in $\mathbb{R}^2$ is bounded by a line. In Fig. 2a, with $\mathcal{R}_{red}$ on the horizontal and $\mathcal{R}_{eff}$ on the vertical axis, $\mathbb{R}^2 \setminus$ overapprox. (the red area) is the halfspace $0 \cdot \mathcal{R}_{rec} + 1 \cdot \mathcal{R}_{eff} \leq -10$. The convex hull of points (1), (2), and (3) in Fig. 1b is the area of the triangle formed by connecting these three points; the downward closure of this convex hull under ascending order for $\mathcal{R}_{rec}$ and descending order for $\mathcal{R}_{eff}$ is the blue area.

Multi-objective properties. A list of d single-objective properties $E^{\mathcal{R}_1}_{\circ_1}, \ldots, E^{\mathcal{R}_d}_{\circ_d}$ gives rise to a *multi-objective property* $\boldsymbol{\phi} = multi(E^{\mathcal{R}_1}_{\circ_1}, \ldots, E^{\mathcal{R}_d}_{\circ_d})$ and a partial order $\leq_{\boldsymbol{\phi}}$ on $\mathbb{R}^d$ defined by $\boldsymbol{x} \leq_{\boldsymbol{\phi}} \boldsymbol{y} \Leftrightarrow \forall i \colon x_i \triangle_i y_i$, where $\triangle_i$ is $\leq$ if the i-th property is maximising and $\geq$ otherwise. The *achievable set* contains all points for which a solution exists that is at least as good. Formally: the achievable set is $Ach_{\mathcal{M}}(\boldsymbol{\phi}) = down_{\leq_{\boldsymbol{\phi}}}(conv(\{\langle E^{\mathcal{R}_1}_{\sigma}, \ldots, E^{\mathcal{R}_d}_{\sigma}\rangle \mid \sigma \in Strat_{\mathcal{M}}\}))$. The *Pareto front* is the set $Pareto_{\mathcal{M}}(\boldsymbol{\phi}) = \{\boldsymbol{x} \in Ach_{\mathcal{M}}(\boldsymbol{\phi}) \mid \forall \boldsymbol{y} \in \mathbb{R}^d \setminus \{\boldsymbol{x}\} \colon \boldsymbol{x} \leq_{\boldsymbol{\phi}} \boldsymbol{y} \rightarrow \boldsymbol{y} \notin Ach_{\mathcal{M}}(\boldsymbol{\phi})\}$, i.e. the subset of achievable points for which no property can be improved without sacrificing another. We distinguish three types of multi-objective properties based on the number of quantitative and constraint properties:

- *Pareto properties* consist only of (one or more) quantitative properties. An under- and over approximation of $\boldsymbol{\phi}$ is a tuple $\langle \underline{\boldsymbol{\phi}}, \overline{\boldsymbol{\phi}} \rangle$ s.t. $\underline{\boldsymbol{\phi}} \subseteq Ach_{\mathcal{M}}(\boldsymbol{\phi}) \subseteq \overline{\boldsymbol{\phi}}$.
- *Multi-objective quantitative properties* consist of one quantitative property followed by one or more constraints. Let $A = \{c \in \mathbb{R} \mid \langle c, c_2, \ldots, c_d\rangle \in Ach_{\mathcal{M}}(\boldsymbol{\phi})\}$. Then an approximation of $\boldsymbol{\phi} = multi(E^{\mathcal{R}_1}_{\square}, E^{\mathcal{R}_2}_{\triangle c_2}, \ldots, E^{\mathcal{R}_d}_{\triangle c_d})$ with $\square \in \{\max, \min\}$ is a range $[\underline{\boldsymbol{\phi}}, \overline{\boldsymbol{\phi}}] \ni opt A$ (with $opt = \sup$ if $\square = \max$ and $opt = \inf$ otherwise) if $A \neq \varnothing$ and $\perp$ otherwise, i.e. an interval around the best value for the quantitative property that satisfies all constraints.
- *Multi-objective achievability properties* consist of (one or more) constraints only. The value and approximation of $\boldsymbol{\phi}$ is $ach_{\mathcal{M}}(\boldsymbol{\phi}) \Leftrightarrow \langle c_1, \ldots c_d\rangle \in$

$Ach_{\mathcal{M}}(\phi)$, i.e. *true* iff there exists a strategy such that all constraints are satisfied.

Example 3. Consider $\mathcal{M}_R$ from Fig. 1a again. To minimise $\mathcal{R}_{\mathit{eff}}$ it would be optimal to *stop* immediately, but to maximise $\mathcal{R}_{rec}$ it is important to *write* and *submit* the paper. To find all tradeoffs between the two properties, we can use the Pareto property $\mathit{multi}(E_{\max}^{\mathcal{R}_{rec}}, E_{\min}^{\mathcal{R}_{\mathit{eff}}})$, as visualised in Fig. 1b. Point (1) corresponds to *stop*ping immediately, while (2) and (3) correspond to deciding to *write* first, and then to *arch*ive or to *subm*it, respectively. An under- and over approximation of the achievable set are shown in Fig. 1c. All probabilistic (or convex) combinations of strategies (1)-(3) are also achievable and thus on the Pareto front. The multi-objective quantitative property $\mathit{multi}(E_{\max}^{\mathcal{R}_{rec}}, E_{\leq 50}^{\mathcal{R}_{\mathit{eff}}})$ queries the maximum value for $\mathcal{R}_{rec}$ given that $\mathcal{R}_{\mathit{eff}}$ should be at most 50. An approximation based on Fig. 1c would be the intersections of the line $\mathcal{R}_{\mathit{eff}} = 50$ with the under- and over approximations, that is, the range $[1.95, 2.3]$. Finally, the multi-objective achievability property $\mathit{multi}(E_{\geq 3}^{\mathcal{R}_{rec}}, E_{\leq 50}^{\mathcal{R}_{\mathit{eff}}})$ queries whether the point $\langle 3, 50\rangle$ is in the achievable set, which is not the case in this example.

3 Sound Multi-objective PMC

The goal of *sound MO-PMC* is to approximate the achievable set with a user-specified maximum uncertainty. For Pareto properties, the uncertainty is typically the distance between the under- and over approximation, while for multi-objective quantitative properties, it is the width of the interval. The sound MO-PMC algorithm of [41, Sect. 3.4] extends the unsound VI-based approach [17] based on linear scalarisation [33,40]. On an abstract level, it works as follows:

To each property in $\phi = \mathit{multi}(E_{\circ_1}^{\mathcal{R}_1}, \ldots, E_{\circ_d}^{\mathcal{R}_d})$, it assigns a *weight* $w_i \in \mathbb{R}$ with $w_i \geq 0$ for a maximising and $w_i \leq 0$ for a minimising property. Via sound single-objective PMC with reward structure $\mathcal{R}_{\boldsymbol{w}} = \sum_{i=1}^{d} w_i \cdot \mathcal{R}_i$, it then finds an interval $[\underline{E_{\max}^{\mathcal{R}_{\boldsymbol{w}}}}, \overline{E_{\max}^{\mathcal{R}_{\boldsymbol{w}}}}]$. Now $\sum_{i=1}^{d} w_i \cdot E_{\sigma}^{\mathcal{R}_i} \leq \overline{E_{\max}^{\mathcal{R}_{\boldsymbol{w}}}}$ for all $\sigma \in \mathit{Strat}_{\mathcal{M}}$, providing an upper bound on the achievable set. This over approximation is iteratively refined by repeating the process with different *weight vectors* $\boldsymbol{w} = (w_1, \ldots, w_d)$. Similarly, the algorithm iteratively refines an underapproximation. For each $\boldsymbol{w}$, it computes an achievable point $\boldsymbol{p}_{\boldsymbol{w}}$ by fixing a strategy $\sigma_{\boldsymbol{w}}$ that induces $\underline{E_{\max}^{\mathcal{R}_{\boldsymbol{w}}}}$ from above. Sound single-objective PMC yields an interval $[\underline{E_{\sigma_{\boldsymbol{w}}}^{\mathcal{R}_i}}, \overline{E_{\sigma_{\boldsymbol{w}}}^{\mathcal{R}_i}}]$ for each $\mathcal{R}_i$. Then, point $\langle \underline{E_{\sigma_{\boldsymbol{w}}}^{\mathcal{R}_i}} \rangle_{i \in \{1, \ldots, d\}}$ is achievable by construction. For set $X \subseteq Ach_{\mathcal{M}}(\phi)$ it holds that $\mathit{down}_{\leq_\phi}(\mathit{conv}(X)) \subseteq Ach_{\mathcal{M}}(\phi)$. This way, the algorithm can at any time return a *sound* result, i.e. a correct over- *and* underapproximation.

Example 4. Consider the MDP $\mathcal{M}_R$ shown in Fig. 1a and Pareto property $\phi_R = \mathit{multi}(E_{\max}^{\mathcal{R}_{rec}}, E_{\min}^{\mathcal{R}_{\mathit{eff}}})$. As a first weight vector, we find an upper bound on $\mathcal{R}_{\mathit{eff}}$ by giving it weight -1 (minimising) and $\mathcal{R}_{rec}$ weight 0. This gives $\boldsymbol{w}_{(1)} = \langle 0, -1\rangle$, which means $\mathcal{R}_{\boldsymbol{w}_{(1)}} = -\mathcal{R}_{\mathit{eff}}$. Using sound single-objective PMC, we now find the approximation $E_{\max}^{\mathcal{R}_{w_{(1)}}} \in [-10, 10]$, which is achieved by any strategy $\sigma_{stop} \in Strat_{\mathcal{M}_R}$ that *stops* immediately. We can use σ_{stop} to find the achievable point $\langle -0.1, 10 \rangle$. Figure 2a shows the under- and over approximations after these steps. We repeat this process for $\boldsymbol{w}_{(2)} = \langle 1, 0 \rangle$ to find that $E_{\max}^{\mathcal{R}_{w_{(2)}}} \in [3.1, 3.6]$, which with $\langle 3.2, 120 \rangle \in Ach_{\mathcal{M}_R}(\phi_R)$ gives Fig. 2b. Finally, using $\boldsymbol{w}_{(3)} = \langle 100, -3 \rangle$ provides the under- and over approximations of Fig. 2c.

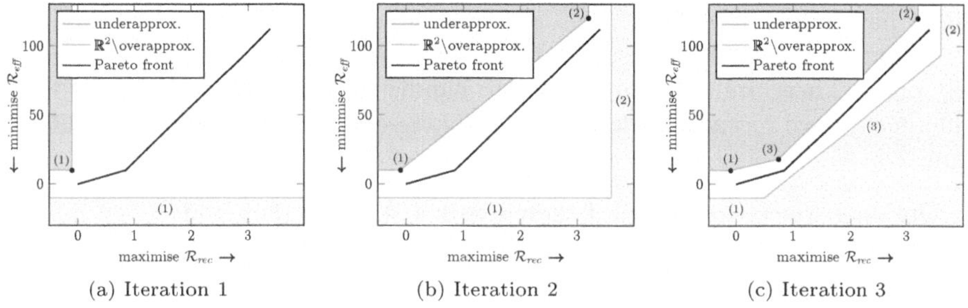

(a) Iteration 1 (b) Iteration 2 (c) Iteration 3

Fig. 2. Iterations of sound MO-PMC

3.1 Semantical Differences

In single-objective PMC there are differences in semantics for the same kind of property [46, Sect. 4.1]. In particular for reachability reward properties, which just like total reward properties use a reward-structure $\mathcal{R}$, but also require a goal set $G \subseteq \mathcal{S}$. The cumulative semantics for reachability rewards use a random variable over a path that cuts-off rewards when a goal state is reached:

$$X_{cum}^{\mathcal{R},G}(s_1 \xrightarrow{a_1} s_2 \xrightarrow{a_2} \dots) = \sum_{i=1}^{\infty} \begin{cases} \mathcal{R}(s_i, a_i, s_{i+1}) & \text{if } \forall j \leq i \colon s_j \notin G \\ 0 & \text{otherwise} \end{cases}$$

While the infinite semantics use a random variable that provides an infinite reward if the goal set is not reached—which can indicate a modelling error:

$$X_{inf}^{\mathcal{R},G}(s_1 \xrightarrow{a_1} s_2 \xrightarrow{a_2} \dots) = \begin{cases} X_{rr,cum}^{\mathcal{R}}(s_1 \xrightarrow{a_1} s_2 \xrightarrow{a_2} \dots) & \text{if } \exists i \colon s_i \in G \\ \infty & \text{otherwise} \end{cases}$$

So far, most PMC tools, including MCSTA and STORM have implemented reachability rewards using the infinite semantics for single-objective properties. Unfortunately both sound and unsound MO-PMC algorithms typically require all values to be finite, making the infinite semantics infeasible in the multi-objective case. To maintain consistency with single-objective PMC, MCSTA uses the infinite semantics, but rejects all reachability rewards for which the goal set might not be reached. STORM on the other hand uses the cumulative semantics

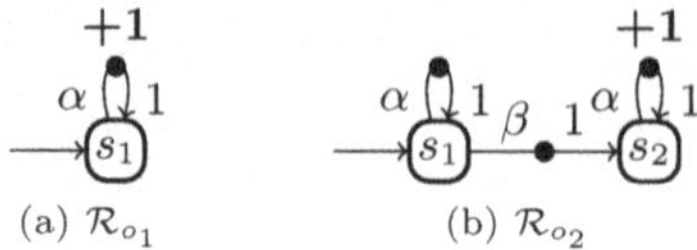

(a) $\mathcal{R}_{o_1}$ (b) $\mathcal{R}_{o_2}$

Fig. 3. MDPs with infinite total rewards

instead for MO-PMC which allows more models to be check, but ϕ and $multi(\phi)$ might have different values.

Infinite reward is also accumulated when a nonzero reward is reached infintely often. There are different options to handle these infinities and so far their differences have received little attention. There exist five such options in literature:

- Option 1: reject the model if there exists a strategy that leads to an infinite reward for at least one property [17, Condition (ii)];
- Option 2: reject the model if there exists a strategy that satisfies all constraints (of a certain form which we ignore for simplicity) and leads to an infinite reward for at least one property [16, Assumption 1];
- Option 3: only consider strategies that have finite rewards for all properties, reject the model if no such strategy exists [41, Assumption 3.1];
- Option 4: only consider strategies that are not infinite good (∞ for maximising properties and $-\infty$ for minimising ones), reject the model if no such strategy exists [41, Lemma 3.12];
- Option 5: consider all strategies, including ones with infinite rewards [41, Sec. 3.4.4].

Options 4 and 5 are the most lenient, but to the best of our knowledge no efficient way to handle infinities exists yet and thus no tool implements them. Options 1 and 2 maintain consistency with the single-objective case, while Option 3 and 4 can break this equivalence since it might not consider the optimal strategy. Option 1 can be checked using the same algorithms as in the single-objective case and are therefore implemented in PRISM, EPMC, and MCSTA. Linear programming solvers typically already check for Option 2, hence this option is feasible for linear programming based solutions. STORM uses Option 3, but gives a warning to inform its users that the results might differ from single-objective PMC.

Notice that the models supported by Option 1 are a strict subset of the models supported by Options 2, 3, 4, and 5. Option 2 can however support properties that Options 3 and 4 cannot and vice versa: in case the constraints cannot be satisfied Option 2 always works, whereas Options 3 and 4 can handle models containing strategies leading to infinite rewards as long as a strategy with a finite reward exists.

Example 5. To illustrate the different options, we use the MDPs shown in Fig. 3a and 3b with reward-structure $\mathcal{R}_1$ and $\mathcal{R}_2$ respectively. We show the results for a several properties in Table 1. Note in particular that for $multi(E_{\max}^{\mathcal{R}_{o2}})$ Option

Table 1. Infinity handling options examples

Property	Option 1	Option 2	Option 3	Option 4	Option 5
$multi(E_{\max}^{\mathcal{R}_{o1}})$	n/a	n/a	n/a	n/a	$+\infty$
$multi(E_{\min}^{\mathcal{R}_{o1}})$	n/a	n/a	n/a	$+\infty$	$+\infty$
$multi(E_{\max}^{\mathcal{R}_{o2}})$	n/a	n/a	0	0	$+\infty$
$multi(E_{\min}^{\mathcal{R}_{o2}})$	n/a	n/a	0	0	0
$multi(E_{\max}^{\mathcal{R}_{o2}}, E_{\leq 0}^{\mathcal{R}_{o2}})$	n/a	0	n/a	n/a	0

3 and 4 compute different results than Option 5. Hence, it is important to be aware of the Option used in a tool or algorithm to correctly interpret its results.

3.2 Termination Criteria

Since sound PMC algorithms iteratively shrink the difference between the under- and over approximation, a termination criterion is required to determine whether the approximations are sufficiently close. A common way to decide termination in single-objective PMC is whether the approximation $[\underline{\phi}, \overline{\phi}] \ni \phi$ for quantitative property ϕ satisfies $\overline{\phi} - \underline{\phi} \leq \epsilon$, known as the absolute termination criterion. However, when the value to be approximated is very large or small the order of magnitude of the difference between the under- and over approximation might be more relevant than the absolute difference. For that purpose, the relative termination criterion given by $\frac{\overline{\phi}-\underline{\phi}}{|\phi|} \leq \epsilon$ may be considered.[2] However, since ϕ is still unknown, the following inequality can be used:

$$\frac{\overline{\phi} - \underline{\phi}}{|\phi|} \leq \frac{\overline{\phi} - \underline{\phi}}{\inf_{x \in [\underline{\phi}, \overline{\phi}]} |x|} \leq \epsilon.$$

An equivalent under- and over approximation ($\underline{\phi} = \overline{\phi}$) is required if $\phi = 0$.

For MO-PMC termination criteria are required as well, which is typically done by finding the maximum distance between the under- and over approximation. Using a distance function $dist\colon \mathcal{P}(\mathbb{R}^d) \times \mathcal{P}(\mathbb{R}^d) \to \mathbb{R}_{\geq 0}$ and a Pareto property $\boldsymbol{\phi}$ with the current approximation $\langle \underline{\boldsymbol{\phi}}, \overline{\boldsymbol{\phi}} \rangle$, termination is allowed when:

$$\forall \boldsymbol{p} \in \underline{\boldsymbol{\phi}}, \exists \boldsymbol{q} \in \overline{\boldsymbol{\phi}}\colon dist(\boldsymbol{p}, \boldsymbol{q}) \leq \epsilon \quad \text{and} \quad \forall \boldsymbol{q} \in \overline{\boldsymbol{\phi}}, \exists \boldsymbol{p} \in \underline{\boldsymbol{\phi}}\colon dist(\boldsymbol{p}, \boldsymbol{q}) \leq \epsilon,$$

known as the Hausdorff metric [30].

The absolute termination criterion is lifted to higher dimensions by using the Hausdorff metric with Euclidean distance, i.e.

$$dist(\boldsymbol{p}, \boldsymbol{q}) = dist_{euclid}(\boldsymbol{p}, \boldsymbol{q}) = \sqrt{\sum_{i=1}^{d} |p_i - q_i|^2}.$$

[2] We define $\frac{0}{0} = 0$ and $\frac{|y|}{0} = \infty$ for $y \neq 0$.

```
1 function TermRel(down-closed Q ⊆ ℝ^d, down-closed P ⊆ Q, ε ∈ [0, 1])
2     Compute the set of halfspaces H_P such that ∩H_P = P;
3     δ ← ε/√d;
4     foreach h = { x | w · x ≤ b } ∈ H_P do
5         if Q ∩ { x | Σ_{i=1}^{d} w_i · a_i · x_i ≥ b, a_i ∈ { 1/(1+δ), 1 + δ } } ≠ ∅ then
6             return Continue
7     return Terminate
```

Algorithm 1: Determine relative termination for MO-PMC

Observe that if $d = 1$ this coincides with the single-objective absolute termination criterion. For the same reasons as for single-objective PMC we would like to have a relative termination criterion in MO-PMC, which to the best of our knowledge has not been defined before. Therefore we propose a relative termination criterion that satisfies the following three conditions: (1) the multi-objective case coincides with the single-objective case when using only one property, (2) the relative error is unaffected by scalar multiplication of any reward-structure, and (3) a similar structure to the multi-objective absolute termination criterion. This is achieved by using use the Hausdorff metric with:

$$dist(\boldsymbol{p}, \boldsymbol{q}) = dist_{rel}(\boldsymbol{p}, \boldsymbol{q}) = \sqrt{\sum_{i=1}^{d} \Big(\frac{|p_i - q_i|}{\inf_{r_i \in [\min(q_i, p_i), \max(q_i, p_i)]} |r_i|}\Big)^2}.$$

To determine whether the multi-objective termination criteria is satisfied is a non-trivial task. For the multi-objective absolute difference an approach is shown in [41], but it lacks a proof and relies on the triangle inequality. The triangle inequality however does not hold for relative distance, since already in the single-objective case: $dist_{rel}(\langle 1\rangle, \langle 2\rangle) + dist_{rel}(\langle 2\rangle, \langle 3\rangle) < dist_{rel}(\langle 1\rangle, \langle 3\rangle)$.

We therefore propose and prove Algorithm 1, which shows how to determine termination using a relative multi-objective termination criterion. For simplicity of the proofs it is assumed that all properties are maximising, since minimising properties can be converted in into a maximising counter-part [41, Lemma 2.8]. A set is called X *down-closed* if there exists a set $Y \subseteq X$ and property $\boldsymbol{\phi}$ consisting of only maximising properties such that $down_{\leq_{\boldsymbol{\phi}}}(Y) = X$.

The algorithm iterates over all halfspaces that bound the underapproximation and for each determine whether there is a point that is further away than ϵ, but is in Q. Line 2 can be implementing using a convex hull algorithm and [41, Lemma 2.3]. For line 5 a constraint solver suffices since Q can also be represented by the intersection of a set of halfspaces.

Theorem 1. *If Algorithm 1 returns 'Terminate' then the Hausdorff distance using* $dist(\boldsymbol{p}, \boldsymbol{q}) = dist_{rel}(\boldsymbol{p}, \boldsymbol{q})$ *between* P *and* Q *is less than* ϵ.

Proof. We need to show that $\forall \boldsymbol{p} \in P, \exists \boldsymbol{q} \in Q\colon dist_{rel}(\boldsymbol{p}, \boldsymbol{q}) \leq \epsilon$ *and* $\forall \boldsymbol{q} \in Q, \exists \boldsymbol{p} \in P\colon dist_{rel}(\boldsymbol{p}, \boldsymbol{q}) \leq \epsilon$. *Since* $P \subseteq Q$ *and* $dist_{rel}(\boldsymbol{x}, \boldsymbol{x}) = 0$ *for all* $\boldsymbol{x}$, *we get* $\forall \boldsymbol{p} \in$

$P, \exists \boldsymbol{q} \in Q$: $dist_{rel}(\mathbf{p}, \boldsymbol{q}) = 0 \leq \epsilon$. It therefore only remains to be shown that $\forall \boldsymbol{q} \in Q, \exists \mathbf{p} \in P$: $dist_{rel}(\mathbf{p}, \boldsymbol{q}) \leq \epsilon$.

Let $\boldsymbol{q} \in Q$ and consider $\mathbf{p} = \langle a_i \cdot q_i \rangle_{i \in \{1,\ldots,d\}}$ with $a_i = \frac{1}{1+\delta}$ if $q_i \geq 0$ and $a_i = 1+\delta$ otherwise, where $\delta = \frac{\epsilon}{\sqrt{d}}$. We show that for all $i \in \{1, \ldots, d\}$ it holds that $\frac{|p_i - q_i|}{\inf_{r_i \in [\min(p_i,q_i), \max(p_i,q_i)]} |r_i|} \leq \delta$ by cases:

- *Case $q_i > 0$: Then $0 < p_i = \frac{1}{1+\delta} \cdot q_i \leq q_i$. Therefore:*

$$\frac{|p_i - q_i|}{\inf_{r_i \in [\min(p_i,q_i), \max(p_i,q_i)]} |r_i|} = \frac{|p_i - q_i|}{|p_i|}$$
$$= \frac{|p_i - (1+\delta) \cdot p_i|}{|p_i|} = |1 - (1+\delta)| = \delta$$

- *Case $q_i < 0$: Then $0 > q_i \geq (1+\delta) q_i = p_i$. Therefore:*

$$\frac{|p_i - q_i|}{\inf_{r_i \in [\min(p_i,q_i), \max(p_i,q_i)]} |r_i|} = \frac{|p_i - q_i|}{|p_i|}$$
$$= \frac{|p_i - (1+\delta) \cdot p_i|}{|p_i|} = |1 - (1+\delta)| = \delta$$

- *Case $q_i = 0$: Then $p_i = \frac{1}{1+\delta} \cdot q_i = 0$. Therefore:*

$$\frac{|p_i - q_i|}{\inf_{r_i \in [\min(p_i,q_i), \max(p_i,q_i)]} |r_i|} = \frac{|0 - 0|}{|0|} = 0 \leq \delta.$$

Then we know that $dist_{rel}(\mathbf{p}, \boldsymbol{q}) = \sqrt{\sum_{i=1}^{d} \left(\frac{|p_i - q_i|}{\inf_{r_i \in [\min(p_i,q_i), \max(p_i,q_i)]} |r_i|}\right)^2} \leq \sqrt{\sum_{i=1}^{d} \delta^2} = \sqrt{\sum_{i=1}^{d} (\frac{\epsilon}{\sqrt{d}})^2} = \epsilon$.

Next we need to show that $\mathbf{p} \in P$. Let $h = \{\boldsymbol{x} \mid \boldsymbol{w} \cdot \boldsymbol{x} \leq b\} \in \mathcal{H}_P$ and consider the two cases:

- *Case $\boldsymbol{q} \in h$: since all values in $\boldsymbol{w}$ are positive [41, Lemma 2.3] and by construction for all i we have $p_i \leq q_i$ it must be that then $\mathbf{p} \in h$, and*
- *Case $\boldsymbol{q} \notin h$: now $\mathbf{p} \notin h$ is a contradiction since otherwise $\boldsymbol{w} \cdot \mathbf{p} = \sum_{i=1}^{d} w_i \cdot a_i \cdot q_i > b$ and since $\boldsymbol{q} \in Q$ and Q is down-closed we also have $\mathbf{p} \in Q$. Then $\mathbf{p} \in Q \cap \{\boldsymbol{x} \mid \sum_{i=1}^{d} w_i \cdot a_i \cdot x_i \geq b, a_i \in \{\frac{1}{1+\delta}, 1+\delta\}\}$, which means that 'Continue' should have been returned.*

Since when Algorithm 1 returns 'Terminate' we have $\mathbf{p} \in P$ and $dist_{rel}(\mathbf{p}, \boldsymbol{q}) \leq \epsilon$ and arbitrarily selected $\boldsymbol{q} \in Q$, it must also hold that:

$$\forall \boldsymbol{q} \in Q, \exists \mathbf{p} \in P\colon dist_{rel}(\mathbf{p}, \boldsymbol{q}) \leq \epsilon.$$

4 Modelling and Benchmarks

MDP with multi-objective properties could so far be specified in the language of the Prism tool[3], with e.g. $\phi_{50} = \mathit{multi}(E_{\max}^{\mathcal{R}_{rec}}, E_{\leq 50}^{\mathcal{R}_{eff}})$ from Ex. 3 written as

```
multi(R{"rec"}max=?[ C ], R{"eff"}<=50 [ C ]).
```

We are not aware of other higher-level modelling languages for MO-PMC problems. This means that access to MO-PMC benchmarks, such as those from QComp 2023, was so far limited to tools implementing the Prism language. To facilitate tool interoperability and establish a tool-independent benchmark set for MO-PMC, we extended the JSON-based Jani model interchange format with support for general multi-objective properties, and the QVBS.

4.1 Multi-Objective JANI

Using Jani's extension mechanism, we specify a `multi-objective-properties` extension[4] in which ϕ_{50} from above could be written as shown in Fig. 4 (assuming the reward structures' values are assigned to transient numeric variables `R_rec` and `R_eff` in the part of the model encoding the MDP). In addition to the multi-objective tradeoffs that we focus on in this paper, the extension also supports lexicographic objectives [15,50] (value `"lexicographic"` for `type`).

```
1 { "op": [ "Multi" ], "type": "tradeoff", "properties": [
2     { "opt": "max",
3       "exp": { "op": "Emax", "exp": R_rec,
4                "accumulate": [ "steps" ] } },
5     { "exp": { "op": "≤", "right": 50,
6                "left": { "op": "Emax", "exp": R_eff,
7                          "accumulate": [ "steps" ] } } }
8 ] }
```

Fig. 4. A Jani property expressing $\mathit{multi}(E_{\max}^{\mathcal{R}_{rec}}, E_{\leq 50}^{\mathcal{R}_{eff}})$

In our single-objective properties as well as in PCTL and Prism, constraints implicitly specify an optimisation over *all* strategies, with e.g. $E_{\leq 50}^{\mathcal{R}_{eff}}$ asking whether the supremum over all strategies is ≤ 50. In Jani, this is made explicit and flexible, with the encoding being rather like $E_{\max}^{\mathcal{R}_{eff}} \leq 50$ (see line 6 in Fig. 4). In multi-objective properties, however, the outer *multi* operator has the effect of the same strategy being subject to the optimisation directions and constraints of all of its individual properties (cf. p. 193), so quantifying over strategies within constraints no longer makes sense. We thus explicitly specify in our Jani extension that the `Multi` operator evaluates its individual properties *per strategy*,

[3] prismmodelchecker.org/manual/PropertySpecification/Multi-objectiveProperties

[4] The formal definition is in the Jani spec at docs.google.com, see also jani-spec.org.

with the result that nested minimisations and maximisations have no effect; for quantitative properties, the optimisation direction must be explicitly specified in the `opt` property.

4.2 A Multi-Objective Benchmark Set

The QVBS, available at qcomp.org, is a widely-used benchmark set for quantitative verification. Its models were originally specified in various modelling languages, and the QVBS provides a JANI version of each. In this way, every tool supporting JANI can be compared on one standardised benchmark set. By extending JANI with multi-objective properties, we also opened the door to extending the QVBS with multi-objective benchmarks.

First, we manually inspected all models already in the QVBS to find tradeoffs between their existing single-objective properties that make sense in the domain of the model, and added these as new Pareto properties. Moreover, we newly added the models from [25] that contained at least two properties to the QVBS. These are 3 out of the 20 models of [25], which we further extended with multi-objective properties. Finally, we also added the MO-PMC benchmarking models from QComp 2023 that were not yet in QVBS, which accounts for 7 more new models. We also considered adding models from [48], but these are specifically made for string diagrams of MDPs, which are not supported by JANI.

Overall, we established a new benchmark set for MO-PMC within the QVBS with 51 multi-objective properties (48 Pareto and 3 multi-objective quantitative properties) in 34 different models. As most of the models are parametrised, this gives rise to a large number of possible MO-PMC benchmark instances.

Table 2. Supported Properties

Property	MCSTA	STORM
Probabilistic reachability	yes	yes
Reachability reward	yes	yes
Total reward	yes	yes
Long-run averages	no	yes
Linear temporal logic	no	yes
Reward-bounded	no	yes

5 Tools for Sound MO-PMC

We show what models and properties can be analysed and which parameters can be tweaked. Moreover we discuss how rounding influences the soundness of our approaches.

5.1 Supported Models and Properties

Storm has developed MO-PMC over the course of several years and does therefore naturally support more than mcsta, for which this is the first version that contains MO-PMC.

Models. mcsta supports only MDPs, but also supports probabilistic timed automata via a digital clocks conversion. Storm supports the more general Markov automata (MA) [42], which extend MDPs by continuous time.

Properties. Besides total reward and reachability reward properties, several other types of single-objective properties exist that can be part of a multi-objective property.

- Long-run averages [13,44]: the average total reward obtained per time-unit (time in case of a MA, actions in an MDP);
- Linear temporal logic (LTL) [16,36]: the probability of satisfying a given LTL formula;
- Probabilistic reachability [17]: the probability of reaching any state in a given goal set while avoiding given states, and
- Reward-bounded [24]: the value of any property only evaluated on its longest prefix a given constraint is satisfied.

Table 2 shows which types of properties are supported by both tools. mcsta only supports probabilistic reachability, reachability rewards and total rewards, while Storm supports the other properties as well.

A notable difference between our tools and other MO-PMC tools is that both our implementations support arbitrarily long Pareto properties, whereas other tools typically restrict to 2 or 3 properties. For a more detailed comparison with other MO-PMC tools, we refer to [1, Table 4].

```
$ mcsta model.jani --alg IntervalIteration
    --mo-epsilon 0.01 --mo-gamma 0.5
$ storm --jani model.jani --janiproperty --sound
    --multiobjective:precision 0.01
    --multiobjective:approxtradeoff 0.5
```

Fig. 5. Commands to run *model.jani* using mcsta and Storm

5.2 Parameters

Precision. The precision parameters for both tools is equivalent to ϵ in Sect. 3.2. For mcsta the default value for this parameter is 10^{-6} and 10^{-3} for Storm.

Single-objective solver. To approximate single-objective properties both tools support multiple algorithms. MODEST supports value iteration [10] for unsound MO-PMC and iterval iteration [7] for sound MO-PMC. The architecture would in theory support any existing single-objective algorithm to be used, but since their current implementations currently only support nonnegative rewards they are not yet available for MO-PMC. STORM does allow all its single-objective algorithms to be used. It also has value iteration for the unsound approach, but for sound MO-PMC it supports interval iteration, sound value iteration [43], and optimistic value iteration [26] (default).

Gamma. To determine the precision for each individual single-objective approximation, a heuristic parameter $\gamma \in (0,1)$ is used. A lower value for γ requires each single-objective approximation to be more precise, which may lead to fewer single-objective approximation being required, at the cost of each single-objective approximation requiring more time. The default for both tools is $\gamma = 0.5$, we evaluate its practical implications in Sect. 6.

5.3 Floating-Point Errors

While the sound MO-PMC algorithm in theory always returns sound results, our implementations have a few sources of numerical imprecision which can invalidate soundness in corner cases. STORM and MCSTA use floating-point numbers, since this is typically faster than infinite-precision rational arithmetic, but also introduce rounding errors. To achieve "absolute" soundness without sacrificing performance, we plan to use directed rounding as in single-objective PMC [22,34] in the future.

Example 6. In Fig. 5 we show an example of how to run the model *model.jani* using MCSTA and STORM with sound MO-PMC using $\epsilon = 0.01$ and $\gamma = 0.5$.

6 Experimental Evaluation

Benchmarks and Setup. We evaluate *sound* multi-objective model checking implemented in MCSTA and STORM. Experiments with other (unsound) MO-PMC tools—including EPMC [18], MULTIGAIN [8], and PRISM [39]—can be found in [1, Sect. 6]. We employ our multi-objective extension of the QVBS from Sect. 4.2 and consider 261 concrete MO-PMC queries specified in JANI, out of which 140 are supported by MCSTA and 228 are supported by STORM.[5] We compare unsound value iteration (VI_{MCSTA}, VI_{STORM}) and sound interval iteration (II_{MCSTA}, II_{STORM}). Additionally, we consider STORM's exact mode using policy iteration ($\text{PI}^{\text{exact}}_{\text{STORM}}$). Unless stated otherwise, we consider an absolute termination criterion with precision $\epsilon = 10^{-3}$ and use $\gamma = 0.5$ for the approximation

[5] MCSTA only supports MDPs and objectives that reduce to (finite) expected total rewards. STORM does not support some PTA instances. STORM's exact mode additionally does not support long-run average and time-bounded reachability queries.

heuristic (see Sect. 5.2). All experiments were run on Rocky Linux 9.6 systems limited to 4 cores of an Intel Xeon 8468 Sapphire CPU @ 2.1 GHz and 16 GB of memory. We report on the wall-clock runtime of the corresponding tool and abort experiments after 2700 s. The results are presented in the form of comprehensive plots. Raw logfiles are provided in the supplemental material.

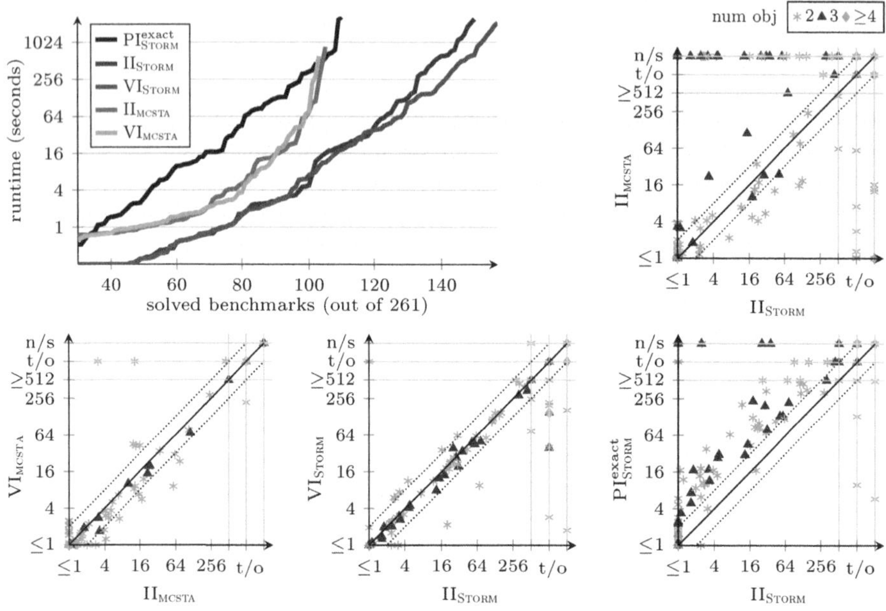

Fig. 6. Comparison of different single-objective solvers

Results. Figure 6 compares the performance of MCSTA and STORM for different underlying single-objective solvers. The quantile plot on the left of Fig. 6 provides an overview over all tool/solver configurations. A point (x, y) on the line of a solver indicates that there are x MO-PMC queries in the benchmark set that (individually) have been solved within y seconds. A flat line thus indicates faster runtimes. The remaining scatter plots directly compare the runtime two configurations, where a point (x, y) means that for one benchmark instance, the two configurations solved the instance in x and y seconds, respectively. A point above the diagonal thus means that the configuration on the horizontal axis was faster. Timeouts (t/o) and not supported instances (n/s) are indicated accordingly.

Discussion. $\mathrm{VI}_{\text{STORM}}$ solves the most instances (157) but is not sound. $\mathrm{II}_{\text{STORM}}$ is a viable sound alternative as it solves 150 instances—usually with only minor runtime overhead. Similar observations are made when comparing $\mathrm{VI}_{\text{MCSTA}}$ and

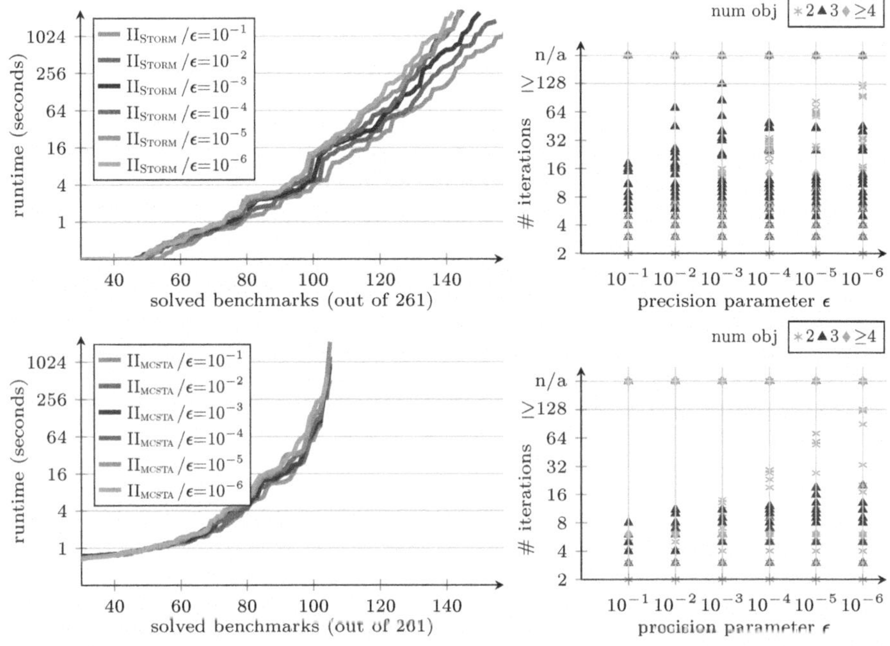

Fig. 7. Effect of precision parameter ϵ in STORM (top) and MCSTA (bottom)

II_{MCSTA} which solve 103 and 105 instances, respectively. $\text{PI}^{\text{exact}}_{\text{STORM}}$ results in significantly increased runtimes and only 110 out of the 174 supported instances are solved. As the scatter plot on the top right shows, the two implementations II_{MCSTA} and II_{STORM} have competitive performance, which is not visible in the quantile plot since MCSTA supports fewer instances.

Effect of Parameters. We empirically evaluate the effect of choosing different parameters $\epsilon > 0$ for the desired precision and $\gamma \in (0, 1)$ for the approximation heuristic. Figure 7 shows the obtained runtimes for II_{STORM} and II_{MCSTA} when varying ϵ while fixing $\gamma = 0.5$. The plots on the right show the different parameter values on the x-axis and the number of refinement iterations—i.e. single-objective solver calls—on the y-axis. As expected, requiring a more precise solution increases the runtime and decreases the number of instances solved within the time limit.

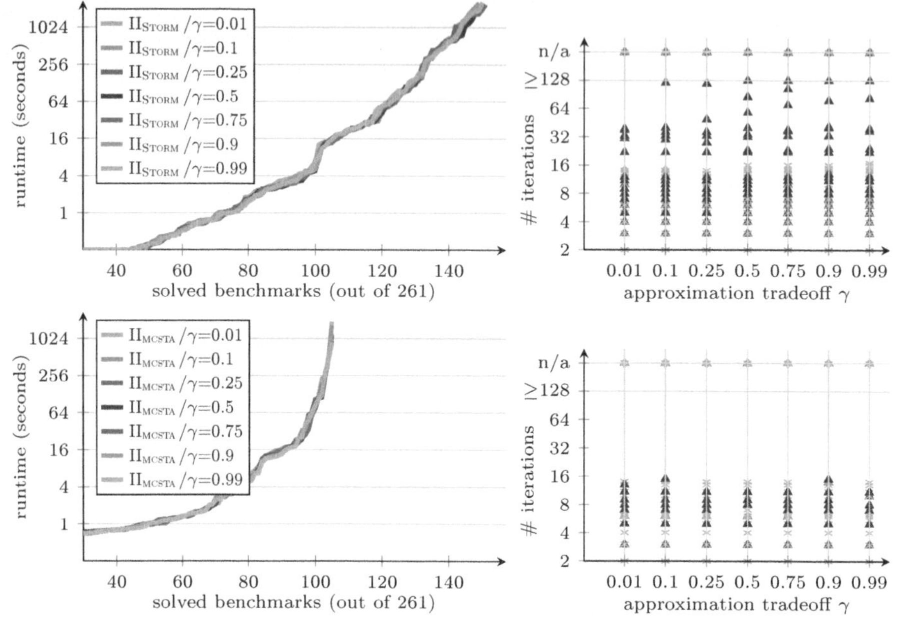

Fig. 8. Effect of heuristic parameter STORM (top) and MCSTA (bottom)

Figure 8 varies γ while fixing $\epsilon = 10^{-3}$. The heuristic parameter γ has almost no effect on the required runtime in our experiments. Both parameters affect the number of required iterations for some—but not all—benchmark instances.

7 Conclusion

This paper presents a scalable *and* sound framework for multi-objective probabilistic model checking implemented in the two state-of-the art model checkers MCSTA and STORM. The experiments indicate that the usage of sound algorithms result in an acceptable runtime overhead. Our extensions of the JANI model specification and the quantitative verification benchmark set provide a solid baseline for future tool and algorithm development.

Data Availability. The exercised versions of MCSTA and STORM, benchmarks, produced logfiles, and a docker environment are available on ZENODO [28].

References

1. Andriushchenko, R., et al.: Tools at the frontiers of quantitative verification – QComp 2023 competition report. In: Beyer, D., Hartmanns, A., Kordon, F. (eds.) TOOLympics Challenge 2023 – Updates, Results, Successes of the Formal-Methods Competitions (TOOLympics 2023). Lecture Notes in Computer Science, vol. 14550, pp. 90–146. Springer, Cham (2023). https://doi.org/10.1007/978-3-031-67695-6_4

2. Baier, C., de Alfaro, L., Forejt, V., Kwiatkowska, M.: Model checking probabilistic systems. In: Handbook of Model Checking, pp. 963–999. Springer, Cham (2018). https://doi.org/10.1007/978-3-319-10575-8_28
3. Baier, C., Chatterjee, K., Meggendorfer, T., Piribauer, J.: Entropic risk for turn-based stochastic games. Inf. Comput. **301**, 105214 (2024). https://doi.org/10.1016/J.IC.2024.105214
4. Baier, C., Chau, C., Drobitko, V., Jantsch, S., Klüppelholz, S.: Certificates and witnesses for multi-objective ømega-regular queries in Markov decision processes. In: Bianculli, D., Gómez-Martínez, E. (eds.) Software Engineering and Formal Methods - 23rd International Conference, SEFM 2025, Toledo, Spain, November 10-14, 2025, Proceedings. Lecture Notes in Computer Science, vol. 16192, pp. 129–147. Springer, Cham (2025). https://doi.org/10.1007/978-3-032-10444-1_8
5. Baier, C., Chau, C., Klüppelholz, S.: Certificates and witnesses for multi-objective queries in Markov decision processes. Perform. Eval. **168**, 102482 (2025). https://doi.org/10.1016/J.PEVA.2025.102482
6. Baier, C., Katoen, J.P.: Principles of Model Checking. The MIT Press, Cambridge (2008)
7. Baier, C., Klein, J., Leuschner, L., Parker, D., Wunderlich, S.: Ensuring the Reliability of Your Model Checker: interval iteration for Markov decision processes. In: Majumdar, R., Kunčak, V. (eds.) CAV 2017. LNCS, vol. 10426, pp. 160–180. Springer, Cham (2017). https://doi.org/10.1007/978-3-319-63387-9_8
8. Bals, S., Evangelidis, A., Křetínský, J., Waibel, J.: MULTIGAIN 2.0: MDP controller synthesis for multiple mean-payoff, LTL and steady-state constraints. In: Ábrahám, E., Jr., M.M. (eds.) Proceedings of the 27th ACM International Conference on Hybrid Systems: Computation and Control, HSCC 2024, Hong Kong SAR, China, May 14-16, 2024, pp. 24:1–24:7. ACM (2024). https://doi.org/10.1145/3641513.3650135
9. Basset, N., Kwiatkowska, M.Z., Topcu, U., Wiltsche, C.: Strategy synthesis for stochastic games with multiple long-run objectives. In: Baier, C., Tinelli, C. (eds.) Tools and Algorithms for the Construction and Analysis of Systems - 21st International Conference, TACAS 2015, Held as Part of the European Joint Conferences on Theory and Practice of Software, ETAPS 2015, London, UK, April 11-18, 2015. Proceedings. Lecture Notes in Computer Science, vol. 9035, pp. 256–271. Springer, Berlin, Heidelberg (2015). https://doi.org/10.1007/978-3-662-46681-0_22
10. Bellman, R.: A Markovian decision process. J. Math. Mech. **6**(5), 679–684 (1957)
11. Bisgaard, M., Gerhardt, D., Hermanns, H., Krcál, J., Nies, G., Stenger, M.: Battery-aware scheduling in low orbit: the GomX-3 case. Formal Aspects Comput. **31**(2), 261–285 (2019). https://doi.org/10.1007/S00165-018-0458-2
12. Brázdil, T., Chatterjee, K., Forejt, V., Kučera, A.: MultiGain: a controller synthesis tool for MDPs with multiple mean-payoff objectives. In: Baier, C., Tinelli, C. (eds.) TACAS 2015. LNCS, vol. 9035, pp. 181–187. Springer, Heidelberg (2015). https://doi.org/10.1007/978-3-662-46681-0_12
13. Brázdil, T., Brožek, V., Chatterjee, K., Forejt, V., Kučera, A.: Markov decision processes with multiple long-run average objectives. Log. Methods Comput. Sci. **10**(1) (2014). https://doi.org/10.2168/LMCS-10(1:13)2014
14. Budde, C.E., Dehnert, C., Hahn, E.M., Hartmanns, A., Junges, S., Turrini, A.: JANI: quantitative model and tool interaction. In: Legay, A., Margaria, T. (eds.) 23rd International Conference on Tools and Algorithms for the Construction and Analysis of Systems (TACAS 2017). Lecture Notes in Computer Science, vol. 10206, pp. 151–168 (2017). https://doi.org/10.1007/978-3-662-54580-5_9

15. Chatterjee, K., Katoen, J., Mohr, S., Weininger, M., Winkler, T.: Stochastic games with lexicographic objectives. Formal Methods Syst. Des. **63**(1), 40–80 (2024). https://doi.org/10.1007/S10703-023-00411-4
16. Forejt, V., Kwiatkowska, M., Norman, G., Parker, D., Qu, H.: Quantitative multi-objective verification for probabilistic systems. In: Abdulla, P.A., Leino, K.R.M. (eds.) TACAS 2011. LNCS, vol. 6605, pp. 112–127. Springer, Heidelberg (2011). https://doi.org/10.1007/978-3-642-19835-9_11
17. Forejt, V., Kwiatkowska, M., Parker, D.: Pareto curves for probabilistic model checking. In: Chakraborty, S., Mukund, M. (eds.) ATVA 2012. LNCS, pp. 317–332. Springer, Heidelberg (2012). https://doi.org/10.1007/978-3-642-33386-6_25
18. Fu, C., Hahn, E.M., Li, Y., Schewe, S., Sun, M., Turrini, A., Zhang, L.: EPMC gets knowledge in multi-agent systems. In: Finkbeiner, B., Wies, T. (eds.) VMCAI 2022. LNCS, vol. 13182, pp. 93–107. Springer, Cham (2022). https://doi.org/10.1007/978-3-030-94583-1_5
19. Haddad, S., Monmege, B.: Reachability in MDPs: refining convergence of value iteration. In: Ouaknine, J., Potapov, I., Worrell, J. (eds.) RP 2014. LNCS, vol. 8762, pp. 125–137. Springer, Cham (2014). https://doi.org/10.1007/978-3-319-11439-2_10
20. Haddad, S., Monmege, B.: Interval iteration algorithm for MDPs and IMDPs. Theor. Comput. Sci. **735**, 111–131 (2018). https://doi.org/10.1016/J.TCS.2016.12.003
21. Hansson, H., Jonsson, B.: A logic for reasoning about time and reliability. Formal Aspects Comput. **6**(5), 512–535 (1994). https://doi.org/10.1007/BF01211866
22. Hartmanns, A.: Correct probabilistic model checking with floating-point arithmetic. In: TACAS 2022. LNCS, vol. 13244, pp. 41–59. Springer, Cham (2022). https://doi.org/10.1007/978-3-030-99527-0_3
23. Hartmanns, A., Hermanns, H.: The Modest Toolset: an integrated environment for quantitative modelling and verification. In: Ábrahám, E., Havelund, K. (eds.) TACAS 2014. LNCS, vol. 8413, pp. 593–598. Springer, Heidelberg (2014). https://doi.org/10.1007/978-3-642-54862-8_51
24. Hartmanns, A., Junges, S., Katoen, J., Quatmann, T.: Multi-cost bounded tradeoff analysis in MDP. J. Autom. Reason. **64**(7), 1483–1522 (2020). https://doi.org/10.1007/S10817-020-09574-9
25. Hartmanns, A., Junges, S., Quatmann, T., Weininger, M.: A practitioner's guide to MDP model checking algorithms. In: Sankaranarayanan, S., Sharygina, N. (eds.) 29th International Conference on Tools and Algorithms for the Construction and Analysis of Systems (TACAS 2023). Lecture Notes in Computer Science, vol. 13993, pp. 469–488. Springer, Cham (2023). https://doi.org/10.1007/978-3-031-30823-9_24
26. Hartmanns, A., Kaminski, B.L.: Optimistic value iteration. In: Lahiri, S.K., Wang, C. (eds.) CAV 2020. LNCS, vol. 12225, pp. 488–511. Springer, Cham (2020). https://doi.org/10.1007/978-3-030-53291-8_26
27. Hartmanns, A., Klauck, M., Parker, D., Quatmann, T., Ruijters, E.: The quantitative verification benchmark set. In: Vojnar, T., Zhang, L. (eds.) TACAS 2019. LNCS, vol. 11427, pp. 344–350. Springer, Cham (2019). https://doi.org/10.1007/978-3-030-17462-0_20
28. Hartmanns, A., Quatmann, T., van Wijk, M.: Tools and algorithms for sound multi-objective probabilistic model checking (artifact) (2026). https://doi.org/10.5281/zenodo.18604533

29. Hasrat, I.R., Jensen, P.G., Larsen, K.G., Srba, J.: A toolchain for domestic heat-pump control using Uppaal Stratego. Sci. Comput. Program. **230**, 102987 (2023). https://doi.org/10.1016/J.SCICO.2023.102987
30. Hausdorff, F.: Grundzüge der Mengenlehre (1914)
31. Hensel, C., Junges, S., Katoen, J.P., Quatmann, T., Volk, M.: The probabilistic model checker Storm. Int. J. Softw. Tools Technol. Transf. **24**(4), 589–610 (2022). https://doi.org/10.1007/S10009-021-00633-Z
32. Howard, R.A.: Dynamic Programming and Markov Processes. MIT Press, Cambridge (1960)
33. Hwang, C.L., Masud, A.S.M.: Multiple Objective Decision Making – Methods and Applications. Lecture Notes in Economics and Mathematical Systems, Springer, Berlin, Heidelberg (1979). https://doi.org/10.1007/978-3-642-45511-7
34. Kohlen, B., Schäffeler, M., Abdulaziz, M., Hartmanns, A., Lammich, P.: A formally verified IEEE 754 floating-point implementation of interval iteration for MDPs. In: Piskac, R., Rakamaric, Z. (eds.) 37th International Conference on Computer Aided Verification (CAV 2025). Lecture Notes in Computer Science, vol. 15932, pp. 122–146. Springer, Cham (2025). https://doi.org/10.1007/978-3-031-98679-6_6
35. Krähmann, D., Schubert, J., Baier, C., Dubslaff, C.: Ratio and weight quantiles. In: Italiano, G.F., Pighizzini, G., Sannella, D. (eds.) 40th International Symposium on Mathematical Foundations of Computer Science 2015 (MFCS). Lecture Notes in Computer Science, vol. 9234, pp. 344–356. Springer, Berlin, Heidelberg (2015). https://doi.org/10.1007/978-3-662-48057-1_27
36. Kretínský, J.: LTL-constrained steady-state policy synthesis. In: Zhou, Z. (ed.) 30th International Joint Conference on Artificial Intelligence (IJCAI 2021), pp. 4104–4111. ijcai.org (2021). https://doi.org/10.24963/IJCAI.2021/565
37. Kretínský, J., Meggendorfer, T.: Conditional value-at-risk for reachability and mean payoff in Markov decision processes. In: Dawar, A., Grädel, E. (eds.) 33rd Annual ACM/IEEE Symposium on Logic in Computer Science (LICS), pp. 609–618. ACM (2018). https://doi.org/10.1145/3209108.3209176
38. Kwiatkowska, M., Norman, G., Parker, D., Santos, G.: PRISM-games 3.0: stochastic game verification with concurrency, equilibria and time. In: Lahiri, S.K., Wang, C. (eds.) CAV 2020. LNCS, vol. 12225, pp. 475–487. Springer, Cham (2020). https://doi.org/10.1007/978-3-030-53291-8_25
39. Kwiatkowska, M., Norman, G., Parker, D.: PRISM 4.0: verification of probabilistic real-time systems. In: Gopalakrishnan, G., Qadeer, S. (eds.) CAV 2011. LNCS, vol. 6806, pp. 585–591. Springer, Heidelberg (2011). https://doi.org/10.1007/978-3-642-22110-1_47
40. Moffaert, K.V., Drugan, M.M., Nowé, A.: Scalarized multi-objective reinforcement learning: novel design techniques. In: 2013 IEEE Symposium on Adaptive Dynamic Programming and Reinforcement Learning (ADPRL 2013), pp. 191–199. IEEE (2013). https://doi.org/10.1109/ADPRL.2013.6615007
41. Quatmann, T.: Verification of multi-objective Markov models. Ph.D. thesis, RWTH Aachen University (2023). https://doi.org/10.18154/RWTH-2023-09669
42. Quatmann, T., Junges, S., Katoen, J.: Markov automata with multiple objectives. Formal Methods Syst. Des. **60**(1), 33–86 (2022). https://doi.org/10.1007/S10703-021-00364-6
43. Quatmann, T., Katoen, J.-P.: Sound value iteration. In: Chockler, H., Weissenbacher, G. (eds.) CAV 2018. LNCS, vol. 10981, pp. 643–661. Springer, Cham (2018). https://doi.org/10.1007/978-3-319-96145-3_37

44. Quatmann, T., Katoen, J.P.: Multi-objective optimization of long-run average and total rewards. In: Groote, J.F., Larsen, K.G. (eds.) 27th International Conference on Tools and Algorithms for the Construction and Analysis of Systems (TACAS 2021). Lecture Notes in Computer Science, vol. 12651, pp. 230–249. Springer, Cham (2021). https://doi.org/10.1007/978-3-030-72016-2_13
45. Shapley, L.: Stochastic games. Proc. Natl. Acad. Sci. U.S.A. **39**(10), 1095–1100 (1953). https://doi.org/10.1073/pnas.39.10.1095
46. Simaitis, A.: Automatic verification of competitive stochastic systems. Ph.D. thesis, University of Oxford, UK (2014). http://ora.ox.ac.uk/objects/uuid:68b5e2d8-ba04-419f-8926-4cd542121e2d
47. Ummels, M., Baier, C.: Computing quantiles in Markov reward models. In: Pfenning, F. (ed.) FoSSaCS 2013. LNCS, vol. 7794, pp. 353–368. Springer, Heidelberg (2013). https://doi.org/10.1007/978-3-642-37075-5_23
48. Watanabe, K., van der Vegt, M., Hasuo, I., Rot, J., Junges, S.: Pareto curves for compositionally model checking string diagrams of MDPs. In: Finkbeiner, B., Kovács, L. (eds.) 30th International Conference on Tools and Algorithms for the Construction and Analysis of Systems (TACAS 2024). Lecture Notes in Computer Science, vol. 14571, pp. 279–298. Springer (2024). https://doi.org/10.1007/978-3-031-57249-4_14
49. van Wijk, M.: The State of Multi-objective Model Checking. Master's thesis, University of Twente (2024). https://purl.utwente.nl/essays/104622
50. Wray, K.H., Zilberstein, S., Mouaddib, A.: Multi-objective MDPs with conditional lexicographic reward preferences. In: Bonet, B., Koenig, S. (eds.) Proceedings of the Twenty-Ninth AAAI Conference on Artificial Intelligence, January 25-30, 2015, Austin, Texas, USA, pp. 3418–3424. AAAI Press (2015). https://doi.org/10.1609/AAAI.V29I1.9647

ModelWisdom: An Integrated Toolkit for TLA+ Model Visualization, Digest and Repair (Short Tool Paper)

Zhiyong Chen[1,2], Jialun Cao[3,4], Chang Xu[1,2(✉)], and Shing-Chi Cheung[3,4]

[1] State Key Laboratory for Novel Software Technology, Nanjing University, Nanjing, China
zhiyongchen@smail.nju.edu.cn
[2] School of Computer Science, Nanjing University, Nanjing, China
changxu@nju.edu.cn
[3] Department of Computer Science and Engineering, The Hong Kong University of Science and Technology, Hong Kong, China
jialuncao@ust.hk, scc@cse.ust.hk
[4] Guangzhou HKUST Fok Ying Tung Research Institute, Guangzhou, China

Abstract. Model checking in TLA+ provides strong correctness guarantees, yet practitioners continue to face significant challenges in interpreting counterexamples, understanding large state-transition graphs, and repairing faulty models. These difficulties stem from the limited explainability of raw model-checker output and the substantial manual effort required to trace violations back to source specifications. Although the TLA+ Toolbox includes a state diagram viewer, it offers only a static, fully expanded graph without folding, color highlighting, or semantic explanations, which limits its scalability and interpretability. We present ModelWisdom, an interactive environment that uses visualization and large language models to make TLA+ model checking more interpretable and actionable. ModelWisdom offers: (i) Model Visualization, with colorized violation highlighting, click-through links from transitions to TLA+ code, and mapping between violating states and broken properties; (ii) Graph Optimization, including tree-based structuring and node/edge folding to manage large models; (iii) Model Digest, which summarizes and explains subgraphs via large language models (LLMs) and performs preprocessing and partial explanations; and (iv) Model Repair, which extracts error information and supports iterative debugging. Together, these capabilities turn raw model-checker output into an interactive, explainable workflow, improving understanding and reducing debugging effort for nontrivial TLA+ specifications. This tool is available: https://github.com/ModelWisdom/ModelWisdom. A demonstrative video can be found at https://www.youtube.com/watch?v=plyZo30VShA.

Keywords: Model Checking · Large Language Model

Z. Chen and J. Cao—Contributed equally to this work.

A. Sampaio and M. Stoelinga (Eds.): FM 2026, LNCS 16556, pp. 211–219, 2026.
https://doi.org/10.1007/978-3-032-26204-2_11

1 Introduction

Model checking [3,10] in TLA+ [17,18,21] provides strong correctness guarantees, yet practitioners often struggle to interpret the large state-transition graphs and counterexamples produced by the model checker. While the TLA+ Toolbox [16] includes a built-in state diagram viewer, it displays graphs in a static, fully expanded form without node or edge folding, colorized violation cues, or semantic explanations. As a result, users need to sift through dense graphs manually, trace transitions back to the code, and connect violation states to the temporal properties they violate – tasks that become increasingly difficult as models grow in size and complexity.

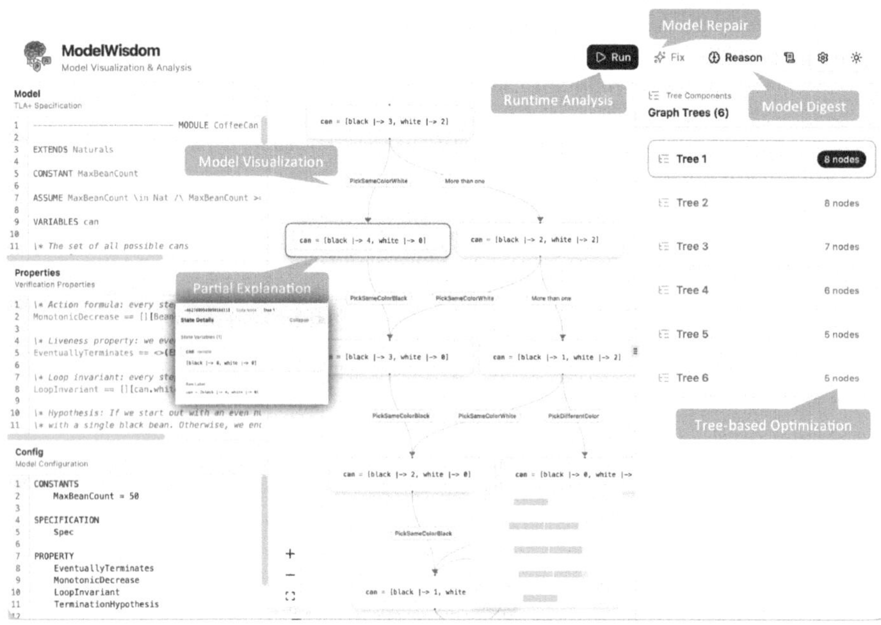

Fig. 1. Interface of ModelWisdom with Highlight Features

These challenges echo long-standing usability problems in model checking tools [11,12], where understanding diagnostic output often becomes harder than writing the specification itself. Meanwhile, recent advances in large language models (LLMs) open new opportunities to turn these verification artifacts into interactive, interpretable representations. While prior work has used LLMs for specification synthesis [1,7,14,20,24,26] or proof assistance [22,23,25], little attention has been given to enhancing the visibility, navigability, and explainability of model checking. Complementing algorithmic improvements, improving the humanâĂŞtool interface is increasingly recognized as a critical step toward broader industry adoption of formal verification.

To address these gaps, we present ModelWisdom, an LLM-assisted interactive environment that enhances the interpretability, explorability, and repairability of TLA+ model-checking results. ModelWisdom integrates visualization, structural abstraction, automated debugging support, and model summarization into a unified workflow. Its contributions are fourfold:

✔ **Model Visualization & Explainability**: Colorized violation nodes, click-to-navigate edges linking to source code, and direct mapping from violating states to broken properties.

✔ **Performance-Oriented Optimization**: Scalable exploration through tree-structured graph layouts, node and edge folding, and automated graph compaction, as well as support for identifying homogeneous node clusters that can guide parameterized verification [2,8,9,13,27].

✔ **Model Digest**: Graph summarization, preprocessing, and selective subgraph explanation using LLM-guided analysis.

✔ **Model Repair Assistance**: Structured extraction of error information, support for both single-pass and multi-pass repair strategies, and an interactive history panel that records intermediate fixes and enables systematic, traceable debugging of faulty specifications.

2 ModelWisdom

ModelWisdom is open source on Github (https://github.com/ModelWisdom/ModelWisdom), comprising approximately 7,000 lines of fully typed TypeScript and Python code. It consists of two main components: the primary web application and a server responsible for executing the TLC (i.e., TLA+ Checker). The supporting LLMs include GPT and Claude families (e.g., gpt-4 and Claude 3.7 Sonnet), and can be set on the website.

2.1 Model Visualizer

In this paper, we introduce ModelVisualizer, a tool designed to enhance both the visualization and performance of state transition graph analysis in the context of TLA+ verification. ModelVisualizer enables users to input a TLA+ model, specify properties, and configure parameters for verification via TLC. Upon completion, ModelVisualizer automatically collects the resulting state transition graph and tightly integrates it with the underlying TLA+ code.

One of our insights is to bridge model code and interactive exploration: ModelVisualizer highlights violation nodes with distinct colors, provides click-through navigation from transitions directly to the corresponding lines of TLA+ code, and offers a direct mapping between violating states and the specific properties they break. This approach allows users to quickly trace errors from state graph nodes to concrete model definitions. Similar visualization features are also supported by the TLA+ Toolkit [16] and UPPAAL [4–6,19], while ModelWisdom was empowered by LLMs, offering explaining and repairing features.

To address the challenge of visualizing large and complex state graphs without sacrificing performance, ModelVisualizer incorporates several graph optimization techniques. These include tree-based structuring for hierarchical clarity, node and edge folding to reduce visual clutter, and graph compaction for efficient rendering. The core idea behind these optimization strategies is lazy rendering, where only the currently interacted portions of the graph are generated and displayed on demand.

Demonstration 1. Figure 1 demonstrates the interface of ModelWisdom under the TLA+ official example of `CoffeeCan`[1]. The interactive state graph is visualized in the middle of the application after successful runtime analysis. Meanwhile, the ModelVisualizer only renders one tree at a time for performance, and the users can toggle the trees on the right-handle panel. Figure 2 demonstrates the node-folding technique, which can be utilized to track state transitions incrementally, or to collapse irrelevant paths for enhanced rendering efficiency. Figure 3a demonstrates the highlight of violated states and properties, where we deliberately modify the postcondition statement of the `PickSameColorWhite` action from `can' = [can EXCEPT !.black = @ + 1, !.white = @ - 2]` to `can' = [can EXCEPT !.black = @ + 1, !.white = @ - 1]`.

Fig. 2. Interface of ModelWisdom with node folding

[1] https://github.com/tlaplus/Examples/blob/master/specifications/CoffeeCan/CoffeeCan.tla.

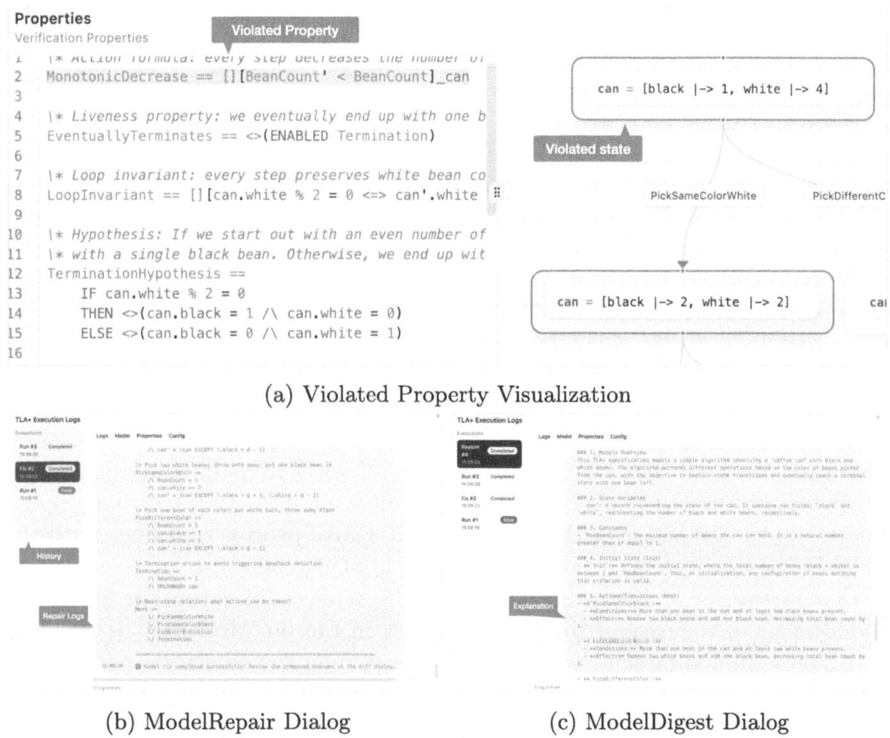

(a) Violated Property Visualization

(b) ModelRepair Dialog

(c) ModelDigest Dialog

Fig. 3. Interface of ModelWisdom with highlighting violated properties, ModelRepair, and ModelDigest

2.2 Model Digest

In this paper, we offer ModelDigest to explain TLA+ models as a whole or in part. ModelDigest enables users to highlight specific code segments of interest directly within the editor, facilitating targeted explanations. Prior to engaging LLMs, ModelDigest automatically extracts key structural information from the state graph, including initial and terminal states, cycles, and the most frequent transitions—to provide essential context. Leveraging this information, LLMs generate comprehensive explanations of the TLA+ model, covering aspects including the overall model structure, state variables, constants, actions, transitions, and invariants.

Demonstration 2. Figure 3c demonstrates the explanation of ModelDigest for the repaired model in Fig. 3a. ModelDigest provides LLMs with the complete TLA+ specification as well as a summary of the state graph, including the initial state (`can = [black |-> 0, white |-> 5]`) and the terminal state (`can = [black |-> 0, white |-> 1]`). Finally, ModelDigest's explanation includes the semantics of each action in natural language. For example, for the action `PickSameColorBlack`, the explanation is as follows: (1) Removes two black beans and adds one black bean back; (2) Preconditions: more than one bean in total and at least two black beans; (3) Postcondition: one black bean is removed.

2.3 Model Repair

In this paper, we propose ModelRepair. It is designed to facilitate the debugging and iterative repair of TLA+ models, inspired by the TLA+ debugger [15]. ModelRepair automatically extracts error messages generated during TLC checking and leverages LLMs to repair the TLA+ model when syntax errors or violations of properties are detected. The tool supports both single-pass and multi-pass repair workflows. In the single-pass repair mode, ModelRepair provides an interactive, one-shot repair experience, where the user can review and accept the suggested fix for a given error. In contrast, the multi-pass repair workflow enables iterative debugging by automatically engaging in multiple rounds of interaction between LLMs and TLC. During this process, ModelRepair maintains a history panel that records each repair attempt, allowing users to track changes and understand the evolution of the model. The iterative process continues until the model is free of errors or a predefined repair limit is reached.

Demonstration 3. Figure 3b illustrates the repair and execution history of ModelRepair in the case of the invalid models in Fig. 3a. ModelRepair provides the LLMs with comprehensive information regarding the incorrect specification as well as the extracted error message. Subsequently, ModelRepair successfully corrects the erroneous statement `!.white = @ - 1`, reverting it to the correct one `!.white = @ - 2`. On the right side, detailed logs are provided, including the specific content of the LLM-driven dialog as well as the repaired model.

3 Future Work

In future work, we plan to extend ModelWisdom beyond TLA+ to support a broader class of model checking languages and verification frameworks. Many of the challenges addressed by ModelWisdom, such as interpreting counterexamples, navigating large state-transition graphs, summarizing behaviors, and assisting with repair, are shared across specification languages like Promela, Alloy, NuSMV, and UPPAAL and other state-transition models. By generalizing our visualization pipeline, LLM-assisted summarization modules, and repair interfaces, we aim to create a unified, language-agnostic environment that brings explainability and interactive assistance to diverse verification ecosystems. This expansion will not only increase the tool's applicability but also deepen our understanding of how LLMs and visualization techniques can systematically enhance the broader practice of formal verification.

4 Conclusion

ModelWisdom enhances the usability and interpretability of TLA+ model checking by integrating scalable graph visualization, semantic summarization, and automated repair assistance. By combining interactive state-space exploration with LLM-driven explanations, the tool lowers the cognitive barrier to understanding counterexamples and accelerates the process of correcting faulty specifications. These capabilities go beyond the existing TLA+ Toolbox, offering colorized violation highlighting, collapsible graph structures, and property-aware diagnostics. Together, these features make ModelWisdom a practical and powerful companion for engineers and researchers working with complex TLA+ specifications.

Acknowledgments. We would like to thank the reviewers for their insightful comments. This work is supported by the National Natural Science Foundation of China (Grant No. 92582201), the Hong Kong SAR Research Grant Council/General Research Fund (Ref No. 16206524), and the Hong Kong SAR Research Grant Council/Theme-based Research Scheme (Ref No. T41-517/25-N). The authors would like to thank the support from the Collaborative Innovation Center of Novel Software Technology and Industrialization, Jiangsu, China.

References

1. Alhanahnah, M., Rashedul Hasan, M., Xu, L., Bagheri, H.: An empirical evaluation of pre-trained large language models for repairing declarative formal specifications. Empir. Softw. Eng. **30**(5), 149 (2025)
2. Arons, T., Pnueli, A., Ruah, S., Xu, Y., Zuck, L.: Parameterized verification with automatically computed inductive assertions? In: Berry, G., Comon, H., Finkel, A. (eds.) CAV 2001. LNCS, vol. 2102, pp. 221–234. Springer, Heidelberg (2001). https://doi.org/10.1007/3-540-44585-4_19
3. Baier, C., Katoen, J.P.: Principles of Model Checking. MIT Press (2008)
4. Behrmann, G., David, A., Larsen, K.G.: A tutorial on Uppaal. In: Bernardo, M., Corradini, F. (eds.) SFM-RT 2004. LNCS, vol. 3185, pp. 200–236. Springer, Heidelberg (2004). https://doi.org/10.1007/978-3-540-30080-9_7
5. Behrmann, G., David, A., Larsen, K.G.: A tutorial on uppaal 4.0. Department of computer science, Aalborg University **1**(1), 1–48 (2006)
6. Behrmann, G., et al.: UPPAAL 4.0. In: QEST, vol. 6, pp. 125–126 (2006)
7. Cao, J., et al.: From informal to formal – incorporating and evaluating LLMs on natural language requirements to verifiable formal proofs. In: Che, W., Nabende, J., Shutova, E., Pilehvar, M.T. (eds.) Proceedings of the 63rd Annual Meeting of the Association for Computational Linguistics (Volume 1: Long Papers), pp. 26984–27003. Association for Computational Linguistics, Vienna, Austria, July 2025. https://doi.org/10.18653/v1/2025.acl-long.1310. https://aclanthology.org/2025.acl-long.1310/
8. Chen, X., Gopalakrishnan, G.: A general compositional approach to verifying hierarchical cache coherence protocols. Technical report, Technical Report. UUCS-06-014, School of Computing, University of Utah (2006)
9. Chou, C.-T., Mannava, P.K., Park, S.: A simple method for parameterized verification of cache coherence protocols. In: Hu, A.J., Martin, A.K. (eds.) FMCAD 2004. LNCS, vol. 3312, pp. 382–398. Springer, Heidelberg (2004). https://doi.org/10.1007/978-3-540-30494-4_27

10. Clarke, E.M.: Model checking. In: Ramesh, S., Sivakumar, G. (eds.) FSTTCS 1997. LNCS, vol. 1346, pp. 54–56. Springer, Heidelberg (1997). https://doi.org/10.1007/BFb0058022
11. Havelund, K., Rosu, G.: Monitoring programs using rewriting. In: Proceedings 16th Annual International Conference on Automated Software Engineering (ASE 2001), pp. 135–143. IEEE (2001)
12. Holzmann, G.J.: The model checker spin. IEEE Trans. Software Eng. **23**(5), 279–295 (1997)
13. John, A., Konnov, I., Schmid, U., Veith, H., Widder, J.: Parameterized model checking of fault-tolerant distributed algorithms by abstraction. In: 2013 Formal Methods in Computer-Aided Design, pp. 201–209. IEEE (2013)
14. Kogler, P., Falkner, A., Sperl, S.: Reliable generation of formal specifications using large language models. In: SE 2024-Companion, pp. 141–153. Gesellschaft für Informatik eV (2024)
15. Kuppe, M.A.: The TLA+ debugger. In: International Conference on Software Engineering and Formal Methods, pp. 174–180. Springer (2022)
16. Kuppe, M.A., Lamport, L., Ricketts, D.: The TLA+ toolbox. arXiv preprint arXiv:1912.10633 (2019)
17. Lamport, L.: Specifying concurrent systems with TLA+. Calculational System Design, pp. 183–247 (1999)
18. Lamport, L.: Specifying systems (2002)
19. Larsen, K.G., Pettersson, P., Yi, W.: UPPAAL in a nutshell. Int. J. Softw. Tools Technol. Transfer **1**(1), 134–152 (1997)
20. Ma, L., Liu, S., Li, Y., Xie, X., Bu, L.: SpecGen: automated generation of formal program specifications via large language models. In: 2025 IEEE/ACM 47th International Conference on Software Engineering (ICSE), pp. 16–28. IEEE (2025)
21. Merz, S.: The specification language TLA^+. In: Bjørner, D., Henson, M.C. (eds.) Logics of Specification Languages. MTCSAES, pp. 401–451. Springer, Heidelberg (2008). https://doi.org/10.1007/978-3-540-74107-7_8
22. Qu, Y., Zhang, T., Garg, N., Kumar, A.: Recursive introspection: teaching language model agents how to self-improve. In: Advances in Neural Information Processing Systems, vol. 37, pp. 55249–55285 (2024)
23. Song, P., Yang, K., Anandkumar, A.: Towards large language models as copilots for theorem proving in lean. In: The 3rd Workshop on Mathematical Reasoning and AI at NeurIPS'23 (2023)
24. Wen, C., et al.: Enchanting program specification synthesis by large language models using static analysis and program verification. In: International Conference on Computer Aided Verification, pp. 302–328. Springer (2024)
25. Yang, K., et al.: LeanDojo: theorem proving with retrieval-augmented language models. In: Advances in Neural Information Processing Systems, vol. 36, pp. 21573–21612 (2023)
26. Zhao, M., Tao, R., Huang, Y., Shi, J., Qin, S., Yang, Y.: NL2CTL: automatic generation of formal requirements specifications via large language models. In: International Conference on Formal Engineering Methods, pp. 1–17. Springer (2024)
27. Zuck, L., Pnueli, A.: Model checking and abstraction to the aid of parameterized systems (a survey). Comput. Lang. Syst. Struct. **30**(3–4), 139–169 (2004)

SAT-Based Syndrome Decoding and Low-Weight Codewords

Carl Berton(✉), Sami Cherif, and Claire Delaplace

Laboratoire MIS UR 4290, Université de Picardie Jules Verne, Amiens, France
{carl.berton,sami.cherif,claire.delaplace}@u-picardie.fr

Abstract. The Syndrome Decoding Problem (SDP) for a binary linear code consists in finding a particular solution to an underdetermined linear system defined over the finite field of two elements, such that the Hamming weight of this solution is smaller than a given bound. In this paper, we explore several satisfiability-based models for solving this problem relying on XNF and classical CNF representations. We compare these approaches to assess their efficiency in solving SDP. Furthermore, we also introduce a Maximum Satisfiability (MaxSAT) model of the Low-Weight Codeword Problem (LWCP), which consists in finding a word with minimal Hamming weight in a given code. In particular, we introduce three MAX-SAT models for LWCP: an XNF model, which reuses the XOR constraints from the SDP formulations, and two CNF models, which are also based on the CNF formulations from SDP. For all three models, we add soft clauses to minimize the Hamming weight. Finally, we assess the models using state-of-the-art MaxSAT solvers, which apply different solving paradigms to compute optimal codeword weights.

Keywords: Satisfiability · Maximum Satisfiability · Cryptography · Syndrome Decoding · Low Weight Codeword Problem

1 Introduction

Information security has become a major strategic concern for states, businesses, and citizens, in a context where the multiplication of digital exchanges makes the use of cryptography essential to ensure the confidentiality, authenticity, and integrity of sensitive data. In this context, symmetric cryptography enables confidential communication between at least two parties who share a common secret key, using a symmetric encryption algorithm (such as AES [16]) to protect communications and enable secure key exchange or electronic signatures. However, the emergence of quantum computers challenges the robustness of classical schemes, leading the American National Institute of Standards and Technology (NIST) to launch a standardization process for post-quantum algorithms based on asymmetric schemes which rely on key pairs and hard problems, such as code-based decoding, to ensure robust security against both classical and quantum adversaries [11].

Meanwhile, automated reasoning tools have become powerful instruments for analysis and optimization in cryptography, particularly for refining attacks

A. Sampaio and M. Stoelinga (Eds.): FM 2026, LNCS 16556, pp. 220–239, 2026.
https://doi.org/10.1007/978-3-032-26204-2_12

against classical symmetric schemes [15,31]. Yet, many algorithms remain understudied from this perspective and the application of these tools to asymmetric and particularly quantum-resilient schemes remains limited despite the existence of problems that naturally lend themselves to such approaches. In this regard, the propositional satisfiability (SAT) problem stands out as a powerful automated reasoning tool capable of assisting in the analysis and exploration of quantum-resilient cryptographic constructions. SAT consists in determining whether there exists an assignment of variables that satisfies a given formula in Conjunctive Normal Form (CNF) [9]. As the first problem proven to be NP-complete [14], it is a fundamental decision paradigm in computer science and artificial intelligence, used to solve a wide range of applications in various fields such as cryptography [23,42,44], hardware and software verification [20], and planning [37]. Maximum Satisfiability (MaxSAT) is an optimization extension of the SAT problem which consists in finding an assignment of truth values to the variables that maximizes the number of satisfied clauses of a given CNF formula. MaxSAT has also been successfully applied to a wide range of real-world instances in various domains such as scheduling [13,17] and verification [12,38].

Some problems, particularly in cryptanalysis, are naturally expressed in another form called Algebraic Normal Form (ANF). While a conversion to CNF is always possible, it is known that such a conversion may lead to a combinatorial blow-up. A classical example is the encoding of parity constraints, where the well-known method of Jeroslow [22] explicitly eliminates all forbidden assignments: each assignment violating the parity constraint generates a clause that excludes it. To address this limitation, some solvers, such as CryptoMiniSat [42], use a hybrid formula structure that combines classical CNF clauses with XOR clauses, a format known as XOR-CNF (XNF) [33], potentially splitting long XORs into smaller ones (cutting) during internal conversions [40].

This work focuses on decoding problems. Cryptographers have been interested in them since the 1970s [28], when McEliece introduced the first public-key encryption scheme whose security relies on the difficulty of decoding a binary linear code. With the advent of post-quantum cryptography, code-based cryptography has become more popular than ever, as it enables the construction of schemes resistant against quantum adversaries. The last few years have particularly seen numerous efforts both in terms of constructions and attacks (e.g., [6,19,29,30,32]). A topic that interests cryptographers in this context is the Syndrome Decoding Problem (SDP), which consists in solving an underdetermined linear system (modulo 2) while ensuring that the solution has at most t non-zero coefficients, where t is known and small [4]. Another closely related problem, which is also of significant interest in cryptography, is the Low-Weight Codeword Problem (LWCP). This task amounts to searching for a non-zero vector of lowest weight in the kernel of the code's parity-check matrix. Both are known to be NP-hard [5].

In this paper, we first study two modeling approaches for SDP. The first approach relies on an XNF representation, which allows parity constraints to be directly expressed, and is complemented by classical clausal constraints to enforce the weight constraint on the error vector. The second approach consists in formulating the problem using a standard CNF format, by proposing two alternative models in which XOR constraints are rewritten in clausal form through the use of Pseudo-Boolean (PB) constraints. This latter approach has the advantage of integrating the error weight specification more naturally during the XOR reformulation and allowing to take advantage of the power of modern SAT solvers.

It is believed that classical clausal representations are generally less efficient than XNF representations for cryptographic problems (see e.g., [44]). Our objective is therefore to compare a standard XNF modeling with a CNF approach enriched with Pseudo-Boolean constraints, in order to evaluate their respective performance and determine whether a classical CNF representation can remain relevant for certain types of cryptographic problems, such as syndrome decoding. Surprisingly, our experimental results show that CNF-based models prove to be competitive with XNF for this problem. Furthermore, we introduce three MAX-SAT models for LWCP. The first model in XNF reuses the XOR constraints from the SDP formulations, while the other two are CNF models also derived from SDP. For all three models, we add soft clauses to minimize the weight of the error vector and a hard clause to forbid solutions consisting entirely of zeros. This approach allows us to explore the potential of CNF-based formulations within an optimization framework for solving related cryptographic problems and to compare them directly with the XNF modeling.

This paper is organised as follows. In Sect. 2, we introduce the fundamental concepts, including a review of the different clausal representations used in SAT and MaxSAT, followed by a detailed presentation of SDP and LWCP. In Sect. 3, we describe how these problems are modeled using both XNF and CNF formats for SDP, and using Partial MaxSAT for LWCP. Section 4 presents and analyzes the experimental results comparing the different approaches. Finally, Sect. 5 concludes the paper and outlines directions for future work.

2 Preliminaries

2.1 (Maximum) Satisfiability

Let $X = \{x_1, x_2, \ldots, x_n\}$ be a set of Boolean variables that may take the values *True* ($\top$ or 1) or *False* ($\bot$ or 0). A literal is either a variable $x \in X$ or its negation $\overline{x}$. A CNF formula ϕ is a conjunction of clauses $\phi = C_1 \wedge C_2 \wedge \cdots \wedge C_m$, where each clause C_j is a disjunction ($\vee$) of literals. An assignment $\alpha : X \rightarrow \{True, False\}$ is a function that maps each variable in X to a truth value. A clause is satisfied by an assignment α if at least one of its literals is satisfied by α. A CNF formula ϕ is satisfied by α if all of its clauses are satisfied by α. In this case, we say that the formula is satisfiable and that α is a model of ϕ.

The propositional satisfiability problem (SAT) consists in determining whether a given CNF formula is satisfiable. Modern SAT solvers are extremely powerful and can solve formulas with a very large number of variables and clauses in a remarkably short time, despite the theoretical hardness of the problem.

Indeed, these solvers are based on the CDCL (Conflict-Driven Clause Learning) algorithm [39] and thus employ powerful mechanisms such as clause learning, backjumping and dedicated branching heuristics, among many others [9].

Another form of representation particularly used for cryptographic problems in the context of satisfiability is the XNF format. Unlike classical CNF formulas, which only use clausal constraints with logical disjunction, XNF formulas also include clauses based on the XOR (exclusive disjunction) operator. An XNF formula is thus a conjunction of both CNF and XOR clauses, where each XOR clause is an exclusive disjunction of literals. A XOR clause is written as $C = l_1 \oplus l_2 \oplus \cdots \oplus l_k$, where each l_i is a literal and $\oplus$ denotes the XOR operator. It is also possible to include the constant $\top$ in a clause to indicate a literal that is always satisfied. A XOR clause is satisfied by an assignment α if and only if an odd number of its literals are satisfied. An XNF formula is satisfied by α if all of its CNF and XOR clauses are satisfied by α.

The Maximum Satisfiability (MaxSAT) problem is a natural optimization extension of SAT which consists in determining the maximum (resp. minimum) number of clauses satisfied (resp. falsified) by an assignment of a given CNF formula ϕ[1] [2]. More formally, to each assignment α we associate a cost, denoted $\text{cost}_\alpha(\phi)$, corresponding to the number of clauses falsified by α in ϕ. The objective of MaxSAT is therefore to find an assignment α that minimizes this cost, (i.e., $\text{opt}(\phi) = \min_\alpha \text{cost}_\alpha(\phi)$).

Several extensions of the MaxSAT problem have been proposed in the literature. Here, we focus on one of the most well-known variants, called Partial MaxSAT. In this variant, the formula is composed of two disjoint subsets of clauses: the hard clauses, which represent constraints that must be satisfied, and the soft clauses, which are constraints we seek to satisfy as much as possible. The classical MaxSAT problem can be seen as a special case of Partial MaxSAT in which all clauses are soft. More formally, a partial CNF formula is defined as a bipartite set of clauses $\phi = H \cup S$, where H denotes the set of hard clauses and S the set of soft clauses. Given such a formula, the goal of Partial MaxSAT is to find an assignment which maximizes (resp. minimizes) the number of satisfied (resp. falsified) clauses in S while satisfying all clauses in H.

In our models, we will also use Pseudo-Boolean (PB) constraints, which impose a bound on a weighted sum of literals under the form $\left(\sum_{i=1}^{h} a_i \times l_i\right) \bowtie \text{k}$, where $a_i, k \in \mathbb{N}$ and $\bowtie \in \{\leq, =, \geq\}$. In the specific case where all weights are equal to 1 (and may therefore be omitted), such constraints are more commonly referred to as cardinality constraints. PB and cardinality constraints are typically used by solvers to impose relevant bounds during search and can be encoded efficiently into clausal form [7]. It is important to note that, even when expressed in PB or cardinality form, these constraints are ultimately rewritten into standard CNF clauses using common encodings before being processed by (Max)SAT solvers.

[1] In MaxSAT, the CNF formula is treated as a multiset of clauses, with duplicate clauses being explicitly retained in the formula.

2.2 Decoding Problems

Let $\mathbb{F}_2$ be the finite field with two elements, and let n and k be integers such that $0 < k < n$. For any vector $v \in \mathbb{F}_2^n$, let $\mathrm{wt}(v)$ be its Hamming weight i.e., the number of non-zero entries in v. Given an $(n-k)$-by-n matrix H with coefficients in $\mathbb{F}_2$, the binary linear code C with parity-check matrix H is defined as the set of vectors v belonging to the right kernel of H. That is,

$$C = \{v \in \mathbb{F}_2^n : Hv = 0\} \tag{1}$$

We call minimum distance of C the parameter $0 < d < n - k$, such that $d = \min\{\mathrm{wt}(v + u) : (u, v) \in C \text{ and } u \neq v\}$. In short, d is the minimal Hamming distance between two distinct code words.

Note that for any vector $u \in \mathbb{F}_2^n$, u can be expressed as $u = v+e$, where $v \in C$ is a codeword and e is a short error vector. Typically, in the case of full-distance decoding, we have $wt(e) \leq d$. We call syndrome of u, the vector $s \in \mathbb{F}_2^{(n-k)}$ such that $Hu = s$. Since $v \in C$, we have $Hu = H(v + e) = Hv + He = He$. In other words, the syndrome of u is identical to that of e. We can therefore decode u by performing the following steps:

1. Compute the syndrome $s = Hu$.
2. Find a vector $e \in \mathbb{F}_2^n$ such that $He = s$ and $\mathrm{wt}(e) \leq t$.
3. Recover the corrected codeword $v = u + e$.

It is clear that the difficulty lies in step 2. Here, the task is to find a low Hamming weight solution to an underdetermined linear system, referred to as the *Syndrome Decoding Problem* (SDP). This problem is NP-hard [5] and can be formally defined as follows:

Definition 1 (Full-distance syndrome decoding). *Given a binary linear code C of parameters n, k, and d represented by its parity-check matrix $H \in \mathbb{F}_2^{(n-k)\times n}$, a parameter $t < d$ and a vector $s \in \mathbb{F}_2^{n-k}$, the syndrome decoding problem consists in finding $e \in \mathbb{F}_2^n$ such that $He = s$ and $wt(e) \leq t$.*

If we consider integer representatives on $\mathbb{Z}$ of the elements of $\mathbb{F}_2$, a syndrome decoding system, which we will call $Syndrome(k, n, t)$, can be written as:

$$He = s \mod 2 \tag{2a}$$

$$\sum_{i=0}^{n-1} e_i \leq t, \tag{2b}$$

where H is an $(n - k)$-by-n matrix with integer coefficients, and e and s are integer vectors of size n and $n - k$ respectively. Cryptographers are particularly interested in the case of random binary linear codes.

Example 1 (Syndrome Decoding). Let us consider a binary linear code with parameters $n = 5$, $k = 2$, and a maximum error weight $t = 1$. The parity-check matrix $H \in \mathbb{F}_2^{3\times 5}$ is defined in the systematic form $[I_3 \mid A]$ as follows:

$$H = \begin{pmatrix} 1\,0\,0\,1\,1 \\ 0\,1\,0\,1\,0 \\ 0\,0\,1\,0\,1 \end{pmatrix}$$

Suppose we receive the vector $u = (1, 0, 1, 1, 1)^\top$. To recover the original codeword v, we follow the decoding steps:

1. Compute the syndrome s: We calculate $s = Hu \pmod 2$:

$$s = \begin{pmatrix} 1\,0\,0\,1\,1 \\ 0\,1\,0\,1\,0 \\ 0\,0\,1\,0\,1 \end{pmatrix} \begin{pmatrix} 1 \\ 0 \\ 1 \\ 1 \\ 1 \end{pmatrix} = \begin{pmatrix} 3 \\ 1 \\ 2 \end{pmatrix} \equiv \begin{pmatrix} 1 \\ 1 \\ 0 \end{pmatrix} \pmod 2$$

2. Find the error vector e: We look for a vector $e \in \mathbb{F}_2^n$ with $\mathrm{wt}(e) \leq 1$ such that $He = s$. Since $\mathrm{wt}(e) \leq 1$, the vector e has at most one non-zero entry. In that case, the product He is equal to one column of H. Therefore, finding e amounts to identifying a column of H that is equal to the syndrome s.
   By comparing $s = (1, 1, 0)^\top$ with the columns of H, we observe that it coincides with the fourth column of H. Hence, the error occurred in position 4, and the corresponding error vector is

$$e = (0, 0, 0, 1, 0)^\top$$

3. Recover the codeword v:

$$v = u + e = (1, 0, 1, 1, 1)^\top + (0, 0, 0, 1, 0)^\top = (1, 0, 1, 0, 1)^\top$$

One can verify that $Hv = (0, 0, 0)^\top$, confirming that the corrected vector v belongs to the code C.

The Syndrome Decoding Problem plays a fundamental role in code-based cryptography and cryptanalysis. Since the early 1960s, a long line of combinatorial techniques, starting with Prange's seminal decoding algorithm [36] and later refined through the works of Lee and Brickell [24], Stern [43], and Dumer [18], have led to the family of Information Set Decoding (ISD) algorithms. More recent advances, such as the MMT algorithm [27] and the BJMM algorithm [3], further improve the asymptotic complexity, and form the basis of today's security estimates for code-based cryptography. Despite decades of progress, all known ISD variants still run in exponential time on random linear codes, making SDP a strong candidate assumption for post-quantum cryptography.

Another closely related problem is the Low Weight Codeword Problem (LWCP), which can be seen as an optimization variant of SDP, where the syndrome is fixed to zero. The goal thus shifts to finding a non-zero codeword of minimal Hamming weight that lies in the kernel of the parity-check matrix. More formally, given a binary linear code C of parameters n and k, represented by its full-rank parity-check matrix $H \in \mathbb{F}_2^{(n-k)\times n}$, LWCP consists in finding a non-zero vector $c \in \mathbb{F}_2^n$ such that $Hc = 0$ and $wt(c) = d$, where d is the (unknown) minimum distance of the code C.

3 Modeling of Syndromes

In this section, we focus on modeling both SDP and LWCP using propositional satisfiability. Specifically, we introduce models based on both XNF and CNF formats for SDP, as well as three partial Max-SAT models for the LWCP.

3.1 XNF Encodings for SDP

The syndrome decoding system can be modeled in XNF format using the XOR operator to verify the parity in the equations $E_i : \sum_{j=0}^{n-1}(H_{i,j} \cdot e_j) = s_i$ where $0 \le i \le n-k-1$ and $H_{i,j}$ denotes the coefficient in the i-th row and j-th column of the parity-check matrix H. To simplify notations, we denote $m = n - k - 1$, and V_{E_i} as the set of variable indices present in equation E_i. More formally, for every $i \in \{0, \dots, m\}$, we have $V_{E_i} = \{j \mid 0 \le j \le n-1 \text{ and } H_{i,j} = 1\}$. The system $Syndrome(k, n, t)$ can thus be written as follows:

$$\left(\bigoplus_{j \in V_{E_i}} e_j\right) \underset{s_i=0}{\oplus} \top, \quad \forall 0 \le i \le m, \tag{3a}$$

$$\sum_{j=0}^{n-1} e_j \le t \tag{3b}$$

The constant $\top$ is added to the XOR clauses whenever necessary to ensure the correct parity of the equations in the system[2]. We can also observe that when the size of a XOR clause exceeds the weight t, the solver must solely rely on the weight constraint (3b), which involves variables that may appear in other XOR clauses, to eliminate search subspaces where no solution can exist. To help the solver reason directly on the variables of a single XOR clause at a time, we can thus add the following redundant constraints:

$$\sum_{j \in V_{E_i}} e_j \le t, \qquad \forall 0 \le i \le m \text{ s. t. } |V_{E_i}| > t \tag{4}$$

These redundant constraints (4) are logically implied by the global weight constraint (3b). While they do not change the set of solutions, they allow the solver to perform earlier pruning of the search space by propagating the weight limit locally on each parity-check equation. This prevents the solver from exploring branches where a single XOR equation would already exceed the global weight threshold t. If we rely on an efficient encoding, such as Cardinality Network[3] [1], for translating cardinality constraints into CNF form, the complexity of our model is in $O(n \log^2 t)$ in terms of number of generated clauses, with an additional factor of n if we add the redundant constraints.

[2] Note that, in practice, this constant is usually represented by a single additional variable to the formula which is always set to true.

[3] This encoding enables to translate a cardinality constraints of the form $\sum_{i=1}^{h} l_i \le b$ using $O(h \log^2 b)$ clauses and auxiliary variables.

3.2 CNF Encodings for SDP

It is widely acknowledged that clausal representations (with classical disjunction) are less efficient for cryptographic problems than XNF representations, where clauses may contain exclusive disjunctions (XOR). Indeed, a straightforward conversion of a XOR clause into CNF format without introducing additional variables can have an exponential cost [22]. In our case, we aim to introduce CNF-based models specifically designed for SDP and compare them to the XNF representations introduced in the previous section. To this end, for $0 \leq i \leq m$, we define the following sets:

$$K_{E_i} = \{0 \leq j \leq \min(|V_{E_i}|, t) \mid j \mod 2 = s_i\},$$

which represent the possible values that the sums $\sum_{j \in V_{E_i}} e_j$ can take in a given equation E_i, depending on the parity indicated by s_i. It is important to note that these sets naturally take the weight bound t into account to eliminate sums that would not yield a feasible solution.

To represent the selection of possible values in these sums for the various equations, we introduce the variables $x_{i,v}$ for all $(i, v) \in \{0, \ldots, m\} \times K_{E_i}$, which are set to true if the sum of the variables in equation E_i is equal to v. More formally, $x_{i,v}$ is true if $\sum_{j \in V_{E_i}} e_j = v$. The system $Syndrome(k, n, t)$ can thus be rewritten as follows:

$$\sum_{j \in V_{E_i}} e_j + \sum_{v \in K_{E_i} \setminus \{0\}} v \cdot \overline{x}_{i,v} = \sum_{v \in K_{E_i}} v, \quad \forall 0 \leq i \leq m \tag{5a}$$

$$\sum_{v \in K_{E_i}} x_{i,v} = 1, \qquad \forall 0 \leq i \leq m \tag{5b}$$

$$\sum_{i=0}^{n-1} e_i \leq t \tag{5c}$$

Constraint (5a), expressed as a PB constraint, ensures that the sum of the variables in an equation equals one of the values consistent with its parity. It originates from the initial equality stating that the weighted sum of the error variables in equation E_i must exactly match the value selected by the one-hot variables $x_{i,v}$, and can be written as:

$$\sum_{j \in V_{E_i}} H_{i,j} \cdot \left(\sum_{c=1}^{Z-1} e_{j,c} \right) = \sum_{v \in K_{E_i}} v\, x_{i,v}$$

Constraint (5b) ensures that exactly one value is selected for a given equation. The last constraint enforces the weight bound t on the error vector variables.

It can also be noted that the elements of the set K_{E_i} can be determined by increments of 2, since we are reasoning on parity. To take advantage of this feature, we can adapt the semantic meaning of the variables $x_{i,v}$ to represent the fact that the sum of the variables in equation E_i is less than or equal to v.

More formally, $x_{i,v}$ is set to true if $\sum_{j \in V_{E_i}} e_j \leq v$. These variables will thus now enforce whether the last increment of 2 has been enforced to attain the value v. This allows us to reformulate the syndrome system as follows:

$$\sum_{j \in V_{E_i}} e_j + \sum_{v \in K_{E_i} \backslash \{0,1\}} 2 \cdot \overline{x}_{i,v} = \max\ K_{E_i}, \quad \forall 0 \leq i \leq m \tag{6a}$$

$$\overline{x}_{i,v} \vee x_{i,v-2} \qquad \forall 0 \leq i \leq m, v \in K_{E_i} \backslash \{0,1,2,3\} \tag{6b}$$

$$\sum_{i=0}^{n-1} e_i \leq t \tag{6c}$$

Constraint (6a) offers a more natural way to represent the parity of sums, making it particularly well-suited for integrating parity constraints into the CNF modeling of SDP. Its structure naturally lends itself to a PB formulation, where *max* denotes the usual operator that returns the maximum element of a given set. Through a simple rewriting of this constraint in the following form:

$$\sum_{j \in V_{E_i}} e_j = \sum_{v \in K_{E_i} \backslash \{0,1\}} 2 \cdot x_{i,v} + s_i\,,$$

we can observe that this formulation closely aligns with the natural mathematical representation of parity. Constraint (6b) ensures that the possible values of the sums are selected in a consistent and ordered manner, i.e., $x_{i,v} \rightarrow x_{i,v-2}$, respecting the increment by 2 imposed by the structure of the sets K_{E_i}, while the last constraint remains from previous models to enforce the error vector weight bound.

It is worth noting that the second representation is not only more natural but also enables to reduce the encoding complexity. Indeed, the complexity of encoding a PB constraint is generally governed by the number of literals to sum and the maximum weight of the literals. In our case, the number of literals to sum remains of the same order in both models. More formally, for $0 \leq i \leq m$, we observe that $|K_{E_i}| \leq |V_{E_i}| \leq n$, where n denotes the code length, and thus the number of summed literals is of the order of $O(n)$ in both CNF models. However, in the first CNF model, the maximum weight is $max\, K_{E_i}$, which can reach n, while the maximum weight in the second model is always fixed and equal to 2. More specifically, if we use an efficient encoding such as Binary Merger[4] [26] to encode these PB constraints (specifically constraints (5a) and (6a)) alongside Cardinality Network, the complexity of the first and second models would be in $O(n \log^3 n)$ and $O(n \log^2 n)$, respectively.

3.3 MaxSAT Encodings for LWCP

We can model the LWCP as a partial MaxSAT problem using both hard and soft clauses. To minimize the Hamming weight of the codeword (i.e., the sum

[4] This encoding enables to translate a PB constraint in $O(h \log^2 h \log W)$ clauses and auxiliary variables, where h denotes the number of literals in the sum and W the maximum weight.

of the error variables e_j), we add, for each variable e_j, a soft clause $\neg e_j$, whose violation (when $e_j = 1$) contributes to the total cost. Formally, these soft clauses are written as:

$$\bigwedge_{0 \leq j \leq n-1} \neg e_j \tag{7a}$$

We also ensure that the error vector is a non-zero vector by adding a single hard clause on the error variables in our model:

$$\bigvee_{0 \leq j \leq n-1} e_j \tag{7b}$$

Based on these constraints, we can now lift our previous SDP models to LWCP while ensuring that all syndrome equations are satisfied. To do so, we first preserve the XOR constraints in their native form, as described in (3a), and include them as hard clauses, yielding a MaxSAT model that we refer to as XNF. Alternatively, if we encode the XOR constraints using the CNF transformations from (5a)-(5b) and (6a)-(6b), we obtain two MaxSAT CNF models, which we refer to as CNF1 and CNF2.

4 Experimental Evaluation

4.1 Experimental Protocol

To evaluate the SDP models, we tested instances from the Decoding Challenge[5], with values of n ranging from 10 to 150. We refer to our models (3), (3-4), (5), and (6) as XNF1, XNF2, CNF1, and CNF2, respectively. The implementation of our models as well as the scripts used to generate the instances and run the experiments are available online[6]. For Jeroslow's model, we were only able to generate and test instances for n ranging from 10 to 50. Beyond this range, instance generation became infeasible due to the extremely large number of clauses.

We used the PySAT library[7] to encode our models with Cardinality Network (CardNetwork) and Binary Merger (BinMerge) encodings used respectively for cardinality and PB constraints. The experiments were conducted using the CryptoMiniSat [42] solver for XNF instances and CaDiCaL [8] for CNF instances. It is also worth noting that, even though modern cryptographic SAT solvers such as CryptoMiniSat integrate dedicated XOR-reasoning (e.g., Gauss-Jordan elimination), these mechanisms alone do not guarantee efficient solving of cryptographic instances. Such observations were showcased for instance in [10,44], showing that XOR-reasoning can perform poorly on certain families of asymmetric cryptographic problems. In addition, we also compared our models using

[5] https://decodingchallenge.org/syndrome.

[6] https://github.com/carlberton/sat-syndrome-decoding.git.

[7] https://pysathq.github.io/.

CP-SAT from OR-Tools[8], allowing us to assess the performance of a constraint-programming approach on the same instances.

For LWCP models introduced in Sect. 3.3, we generated instances with values of n ranging from 10 to 80 for each model. The solving was performed using five state-of-the-art Max-SAT solvers: the SAT-based solvers UWrMaxSAT [35] and RC2 [21], the ILP-based solver MaxHS [34], the Branch-and-Bound solver Max-CDCL [25], and GaussMaxHS [41], which extends MaxHS with XOR reasoning where XOR clauses are handled as hard constraints. All the classical MaxSAT solvers we used have won previous editions of the Max-SAT Evaluation[9]. In addition, we compared the performance of these solvers to the CP-SAT solver. To this end, we evaluated two configurations, CP1 and CP2, which are based on the CNF1 and CNF2 formulations respectively. This comparison allows us to explore the effectiveness of a constraint programming approach on these formulations.

All tests were performed on the MatriCS computing platform[10] on the bigmem partition, equipped with 12 dual-processor Intel Xeon E5-2680 v4 (2.40 GHz) servers, each with 512 GB of memory. The time limit was set to 3,600 s (1 h) per SDP instance and 7,200 s (2 h) per LWCP instance. Finally, for each value of n and each model, we generated 20 instances using different random seeds.

4.2 Performance on SDP

The results in terms of the number of solved instances and solving time are presented in Table 1. We evaluate our results using the Penalized Summed Runtime (PSR) score, which assigns the actual solving time to successful instances and the full time limit to those that remain unsolved within the timeout. XNF2 solves the highest number of instances (243), slightly ahead of CNF1 and CNF2, which solve 234 and 233 instances respectively, (i.e., 9 and 10 fewer). However, these two CNF-based models stand out with their better efficiency in terms of solving time, with improvements of approximately 44% for CNF1 and 67% for CNF2 compared to XNF2. The XNF1 model remains significantly less efficient, solving only 205 instances. It is also worth noting that CNF2 is around 38% faster than XNF1, while solving 28 additional instances. Overall, CNF2 appears to be an excellent compromise between the number of solved instances and solving time, as it achieves 41% gain in solving time performance compared to CNF1, while solving just one instance less. We also observe that XNF2 tends to be more robust in terms of the number of solved instances, particularly as instance difficulty increases. It particularly outperforms the CNF-based models for sizes $n = 120$, 130, and 140, solving respectively 16, 8, and 4 instances, compared to 12, 3, and 4 for CNF1, and 13, 4, and 0 for CNF2.

We classified the instances into three groups: easy (n from 10 to 50), intermediate (n from 60 to 100), and hard (n from 110 to 150), and computed the

[8] https://developers.google.com/optimization/cp/cp_solver.

[9] https://maxsat-evaluations.github.io/.

[10] https://www.matrics.u-picardie.fr/.

Table 1. Sum of solving times in seconds for the solved SDP instances for each size n and t, and PSR scores for each solver-model combination on the whole benchmark. If some instances were not solved within the timeout, the number of solved instances is indicated in parentheses '()'. The best results are marked in bold, first based on the number of solved instances, and in case of a tie, based on the solving time.

Instance		CryptoMiniSat		CaDiCaL		CP-SAT	
n	t	XNF1	XNF2	CNF1	CNF2	CP1	CP2
10	4	163.9	191.4	78.4	78.2	0.2	0.2
20	5	91.8	61.5	1.4	7.5	0.3	0.2
30	7	12.3	12.4	43.9	26	1.3	0.9
40	8	47.6	48.6	8.4	42.9	3.7	**3.3**
50	9	88.6	95.3	38.3	24.1	21.6	**12.1**
60	10	123.8	111.7	**31.1**	48.4	153.6	195.6
70	11	137.6	135.7	**81.3**	96.3	901.1	1562.6
80	12	1831.6	2314.1	752	**368.6**	7045.7	5128.4
90	13	10788.2 (17)	6859.9	3636.3	**2623.9**	17303.9 (19)	15320 (19)
100	14	16510.4 (11)	**21601.3 (18)**	11696.8 (15)	7479.8 (17)	18276.9 (10)	19205.6 (10)
110	16	13202.2 (9)	15629.8 (16)	13770.2 (18)	**10099.5 (18)**	17524.5 (11)	16335.3 (11)
120	17	392.6 (3)	**23613.9 (10)**	8323.6 (12)	7184 (13)	18445.8 (10)	12575 (7)
130	18	7118.1 (4)	**13741.3 (8)**	3962.5 (3)	2882.1 (4)	10493.4 (4)	4766.2 (2)
140	19	- (0)	9196.2 (4)	**8583.4 (4)**	- (0)	7285.3 (4)	5635.8 (2)
150	20	71.3 (1)	1536.5 (1)	**2304.4 (2)**	271.7 (1)	– (0)	– (0)
SUM		50580.7 (205)	**95150.4 (243)**	53312.6 (234)	31233.3 (233)	97457.8 (218)	80741.7 (211)
PSR		392580.7	300350.4	290912.6	**272433.3**	392657.8	401141.7

PSR score accordingly. For easy instances, all CNF models outperform their XNF counterparts. It is also worth noting that the Jeroslow model requires 179% more time than CNF1 and 166% than CNF2 to solve these instances. Both XNF1 and XNF2 are significantly slower than CNF1 and CNF2, with XNF1 being 137% and 127% slower, and XNF2 being 140% and 129% slower than CNF1 and CNF2, respectively. On intermediate instances, CNF2 was the fastest, with XNF2 taking approximately 78% more time than CNF2. For hard instances, XNF2 solved up to 9 more instances than CNF2, but CNF2 remained 60% faster on the ones it did solve. Overall, CNF2 is leading in terms of PSR score, showing a 6% improvement over CNF1 and 9% over XNF2.

In Fig. 1, we observe the evolution of solving times for each model on SDP instances. Three distinct groups of behavior can be identified. First, the XNF1 and CP models exhibit a rapid growth in solving time early on and solve comparatively fewer instances overall. By contrast, the XNF2 and CNF models, especially CNF2, demonstrate much greater overall performance. In particular, CNF2 displays a significantly slower increase in solving time for the vast majority of instances, highlighting its superior efficiency on most of the benchmark.

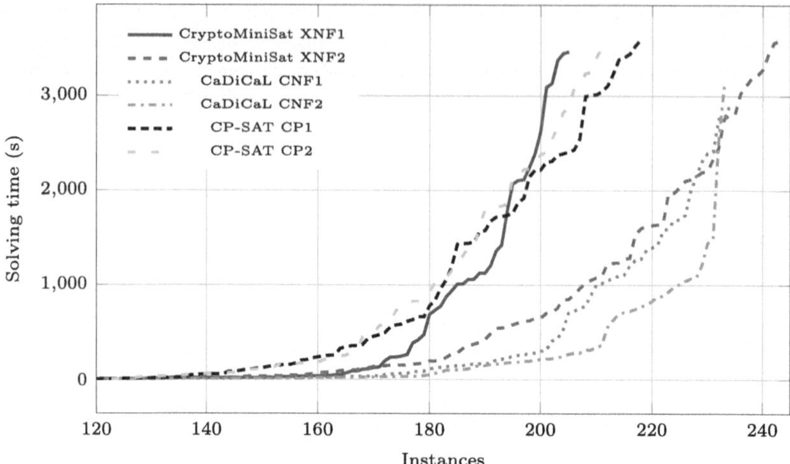

Fig. 1. Evolution of solving time for the different SDP models and solvers.

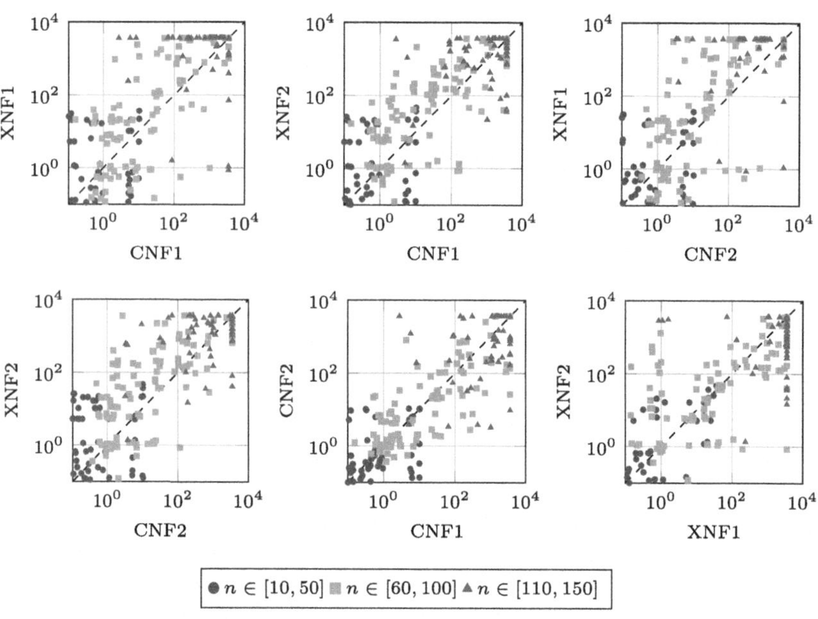

Fig. 2. Comparison of solving times in seconds per SDP instance.

However, while CNF2 is faster on easy and medium instances, XNF2 demonstrates slightly greater robustness by solving a higher total number of instances and showing a more gradual progression as it approaches the timeout limit.

We analyze in more detail the performance differences between the CNF and XNF models for SDP. Figure 2 illustrates a per-instance comparison of execution times between the different models. Among the XNF models, XNF1 is consistently the least efficient, being outperformed by the other models in the majority of cases. When comparing XNF2 to the CNF models, CNF1 is faster in 47% of cases versus 37% in favor of XNF2, and CNF2 also achieves better performance in 47% of cases compared to 38% for XNF2. This trend is particularly evident for intermediate-difficulty instances, where CNF1 and CNF2 outperform XNF2 in 64% and 62% of cases, respectively. Between the two CNF models, CNF2 proves slightly superior, being faster than CNF1 in 43% of cases compared to 36% in favor of CNF1. This dominance of CNF2 is especially visible on intermediate and hard instances. Overall, CNF models offer better performance than XNF representations in terms of solving time. Among them, CNF2 stands out as the most efficient, especially on intermediate and hard instances. In contrast, XNF1 consistently shows the weakest results. CNF1 and XNF2 perform better than XNF1 but still generally lag behind CNF2 in terms of solving time.

4.3 Performance on LWCP

Table 2 presents a detailed comparison of the performance of MaxSAT solvers on the LWCP instances using the two different CNF encodings. For each problem size n, the table reports the cumulative solving time (in seconds) required to reach an optimal solution across all corresponding instances. The last two rows provide the total solving time (SUM) with the total number of optimally solved instances, and the PSR score. When examining the results by encoding, CNF2 generally stands out. It performs best with RC2 for smaller instances, and with WMaxCDCL for larger instances. In particular, we observe that WMaxCDCL solves 90% of the instances for $n = 80$ with CNF1 and CNF2, compared to only 40% for the second best solver UWrMaxSAT using the same encodings. Overall, WMaxCDCL finds the optimal solution in approximately 99% of cases with both CNF1 and CNF2, but CNF2 is around 18% faster than CNF1 in terms of PSR score. The other solvers are able to solve fewer instances within the given time limit compared to WMaxCDCL, ranging from 14 to 77 fewer instances for MaxHS and GaussMaxHS, respectively. In particular, although GaussMaxHS is able to internally handle XOR reasoning, it shows poor performance, failing to solve instances with $n > 50$ and exhibiting sharply increasing solving times even for smaller instances.

Figure 3 shows, for each solver-model combination, the increasing solving times of the instances for which the optimal solution was found. In the first 120 instances, the curves are almost indistinguishable, making it difficult to draw any conclusions. However, beyond this point, we observe a sharp increase in solving times for all configurations. The two curves corresponding to WMax-CDCL are the least affected by this growth, with CNF2 being the lowest curve, confirming once again its robustness on the hardest solved instances. In contrast, the other curves show a similar upward trend, indicating a greater sensitivity to instance difficulty. The curves corresponding to GaussMaxHS, however, behave very differently: their solving times increase extremely rapidly, even for the first few instances, and remain well above all other curves throughout. This is particularly striking given that GaussMaxHS is capable of reasoning on XOR constraints using hard clauses and performing Gaussian elimination. One might have expected this solver to perform well on these cryptographic instances, but the curves clearly show that this is not the case, highlighting the limitations of XOR-reasoning and Gaussian elimination for our application.

Table 2. Sum of solving times in seconds for optimally solved instances for each n, LWCP model and solver. If some instances were not solved within the timeout, the number of optimally solved instances is shown in parentheses '()'. The best results in terms of number of solved instances, and total solving time in case of a tie, are highlighted in bold.

n	GaussMaxHS	RC2		MaxHS		UWrMaxSAT		WMaxCDCL		CP-SAT	
	XNF	CNF1	CNF2	CNF1	CNF2	CNF1	CNF2	CNF1	CNF2	CP1	CP2
10	0.8	**0.01**	**0.01**	89.1	84.2	4.6	5.4	117.5	127	0.3	0.3
20	5.3	0.05	**0.04**	103.5	45.8	14.5	14.1	139.6	110.8	0.23	0.2
30	60.3	**0.5**	**0.5**	107.3	117.7	3.9	4.1	40.4	54.8	0.8	0.6
40	17774.4	6.6	5.6	328.9	294.8	13	12.3	80.9	65.7	4.5	**2.5**
50	372.5 (1)	47.4	45.8	758.9	899.7	61.4	57.8	65.3	58.9	37.6	**28.3**
60	- (0)	580.3	495.3	1845.8	1842.7	461.7	500.2	478	416.9	**347.2**	567.7
70	- (0)	17857.9	20358.8	22882.2	18169.4	22364.2	18087.4	6613.4	**5428.8**	13032.1 (19)	19401.4
80	- (0)	11586.3 (3)	5021.8 (2)	5336.6 (2)	14548.1 (4)	46246.6 (8)	38922.2 (8)	57556.3 (18)	**44398.1 (18)**	3388.3 (2)	7064.9 (3)
SUM	18183.3 (81)	30079 (143)	25927.8 (142)	31452.3 (142)	36002.4 (144)	69170 (148)	57603.3 (148)	65091.4 (158)	**50661 (158)**	16811 (141)	27066 (143)
PSR	586983.3	152479	148327.8	161052.2	151202.4	155570	144003.4	79491.4	**65061**	153611	149465.9

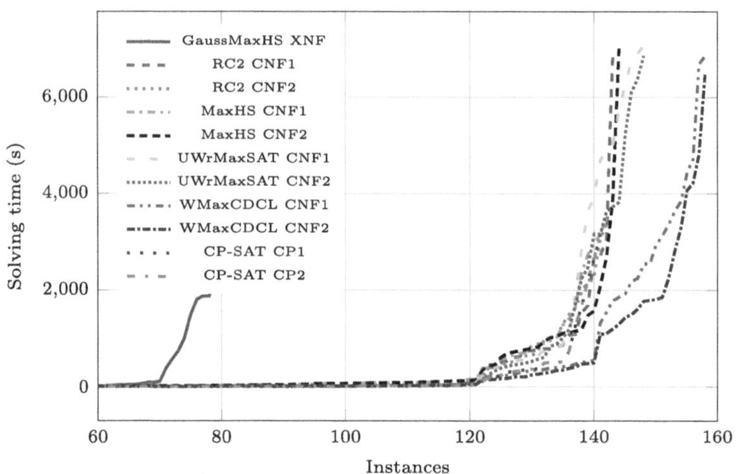

Fig. 3. Evolution of solving times for the different LWCP models and solvers.

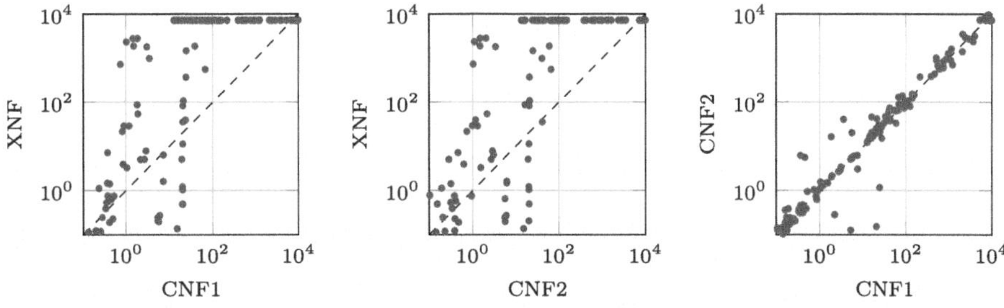

Fig. 4. Comparison of solving times per LWCP instance using the GaussMaxHS and MaxHS solvers.

In Fig. 4, we provide a more detailed comparison of the performance of the XNF model against the CNF models for LWCP, using the GaussMaxHS and MaxHS solvers. GaussMaxHS is based on the same architecture as MaxHS but adds a Gaussian elimination reasoning layer to efficiently handle XOR constraints, making the comparison between XNF and CNF particularly relevant. Regarding XNF versus the CNF models, it is visually clear that the CNF models generally outperform XNF, especially when considering the line of points corresponding to the time limit for reaching optimality. XNF failed to find the optimal solution within the allotted time in almost half of the cases (79 out of 160), particularly for larger instances. More specifically, CNF1 and CNF2 outperform XNF in approximately 62% and 60% of the cases, while XNF is better in about 31% and 33% of the cases. The XNF modeling only stands out compared to the CNF models for small instances ($n < 40$), where it shows better performance. Regarding the comparison between the two CNF models, the visual distinction is much less clear, as most points lie very close to the diagonal line. CNF1 is slightly more performant than CNF2 in about 56% of the cases, compared to 38% in favor of CNF2. However, CNF2 demonstrates better robustness, achieving optimality 144 times versus 142 for CNF1, with the difference primarily appearing on instances of size $n = 80$.

5 Conclusion

In this paper, we presented SAT-based approaches to solve the Syndrome Decoding Problem (SDP) and Low-Weight Codeword Problem (LWCP), taking advantage of state-of-the-art SAT and MaxSAT solvers. To this end, we introduced several encodings for SDP based on CNF and XNF, and we extended these encodings into partial MaxSAT formulations for LWCP. While XNF representations are typically regarded as more suitable for cryptographic problems, our results show that the CNF encodings we propose achieve comparable and often competitive performance. Furthermore, for LWCP, the proposed encodings, especially CNF2 combined with the WMaxCDCL solver, yield promising results.

As future work, it would be relevant to investigate more refined hybrid encodings that combine the strengths of CNF and XNF representations, particularly to tackle the most challenging instances. Additionally, experimenting with alternative encodings for PB constraints may further enhance solver performance. It could also be worthwhile to evaluate and potentially hybridize our encodings with incomplete solvers, as they may help address larger instances that remain challenging for complete approaches.

Acknowledgment. This work is supported by the projects ANR-24-CE23-6126 (BforSAT) and ANR-20-ASTR-0011 (POSTCRYPTUM), funded by the French National Research Agency. It was also granted access to HPC resources of "Plateforme MatriCS" within University of Picardie Jules Verne, co-funded by the European Union with the European Regional Development Fund (FEDER) and the Hauts-De-France Regional Council.

References

1. Asín, R., Nieuwenhuis, R., Oliveras, A., Rodríguez-Carbonell, E.: Cardinality networks and their applications. In: Kullmann, O. (ed.) SAT 2009. LNCS, vol. 5584, pp. 167–180. Springer, Heidelberg (2009). https://doi.org/10.1007/978-3-642-02777-2_18
2. Bacchus, F., Järvisalo, M., Martins, R.: Maximum satisfiability. In: Biere, A., Heule, M., van Maaren, H., Walsh, T. (eds.) Handbook of Satisfiability - Second Edition, Frontiers in Artificial Intelligence and Applications, vol. 336, pp. 929–991. IOS Press (2021). https://doi.org/10.3233/FAIA201008
3. Becker, A., Joux, A., May, A., Meurer, A.: Decoding random binary linear codes in $2^{n/20}$: How 1+1=0 improves information set decoding. IACR Cryptol. ePrint Arch. p. 26 (2012). http://eprint.iacr.org/2012/026
4. Berlekamp, E.R.: Algebraic coding theory. In: McGraw-Hill Series in Systems Science. McGraw-Hill (1968). https://www.worldcat.org/oclc/00256659
5. Berlekamp, E.R., McEliece, R.J., van Tilborg, H.C.A.: On the inherent intractability of certain coding problems (corresp.). IEEE Trans. Inf. Theory **24**(3), 384–386 (1978). https://doi.org/10.1109/TIT.1978.1055873
6. Bernstein, D., et al.: Classic mceliece (2017)
7. Biere, A.: Pseudo-Boolean and cardinality constraints. In: Biere, A., Heule, M., van Maaren, H., Walsh, T. (eds.) Handbook of Satisfiability, chap. 22, pp. 695–730. IOS Press (2009)
8. Biere, A., Faller, T., Fazekas, K., Fleury, M., Froleyks, N., Pollitt, F.: Cadical 2.0. In: Gurfinkel, A., Ganesh, V. (eds.) CAV 2024, , Part I. LNCS, vol. 14681, pp. 133–152. Springer, Cham (2024). https://doi.org/10.1007/978-3-031-65627-9_7
9. Biere, A., Heule, M., van Maaren, H., Walsh, T. (eds.): Handbook of Satisfiability - Second Edition, Frontiers in Artificial Intelligence and Applications, vol. 336. IOS Press (2021). https://doi.org/10.3233/FAIA336
10. Blomme, A., Cherif, S., Ionica, S., Dequen, G.: ANF-based satisfiability for weil-descent cryptographic attacks. In: 11th-2025 International Conference on Control, Decision and Information Technologies (CoDIT), Split - Croatia, Croatia (2025). https://hal.science/hal-05176414
11. Chen, L., Chen, L., Jordan, S., Liu, Y.K., Moody, D., Peralta, R., Perlner, R.A., Smith-Tone, D.: Report on post-quantum cryptography, vol. 12. National Institute of Standards and Technology, US Department of Commerce (2016)

12. Chen, Y., Safarpour, S., Veneris, A.G., Marques-Silva, J.: Spatial and temporal design debug using partial maxsat. In: Lombardi, F., Bhanja, S., Massoud, Y., Bahar, R.I. (eds.) Proceedings of the 19th ACM Great Lakes Symposium on VLSI 2009, Boston Area, MA, USA, May 10-12 2009, pp. 345–350. ACM (2009). https://doi.org/10.1145/1531542.1531621
13. Cherif, S., Sattoutah, H., Li, C., Lucet, C., Devendeville, L.B.: Minimizing working-group conflicts in conference session scheduling through maximum satisfiability (short paper). In: Shaw, P. (ed.) CP 2024, September 2-6, 2024, Girona, Spain. LIPIcs, vol. 307, pp. 34:1–34:11. Schloss Dagstuhl - Leibniz-Zentrum für Informatik (2024). https://doi.org/10.4230/LIPICS.CP.2024.34
14. Cook, S.A.: The complexity of theorem-proving procedures. In: Harrison, M.A., Banerji, R.B., Ullman, J.D. (eds.) STOC 1971, pp. 151–158. ACM (1971). https://doi.org/10.1145/800157.805047
15. Courtois, N.T., Bard, G.V.: Algebraic cryptanalysis of the data encryption standard. In: Galbraith, S.D. (ed.) Cryptography and Coding 2007. LNCS, vol. 4887, pp. 152–169. Springer, Heidelberg (2007). https://doi.org/10.1007/978-3-540-77272-9_10
16. Daemen, J., Rijmen, V.: The Design of Rijndael: AES - The Advanced Encryption Standard. Information Security and Cryptography, Springer, Heidelberg (2002). https://doi.org/10.1007/978-3-662-04722-4
17. Demirovic, E., Musliu, N., Winter, F.: Modeling and solving staff scheduling with partial weighted maxsat. Ann. Oper. Res. **275**(1), 79–99 (2019). https://doi.org/10.1007/S10479-017-2693-Y
18. Dumer, I.: On minimum distance decoding of linear codes (1991)
19. Esser, A., Bellini, E.: Syndrome decoding estimator. In: Hanaoka, G., Shikata, J., Watanabe, Y. (eds.) IACR 2022. LNCS, vol. 13177, pp. 112–141. Springer, Cham (2022). https://doi.org/10.1007/978-3-030-97121-2_5,
20. Gupta, A., Ganai, M.K., Wang, C.: SAT-based verification methods and applications in hardware verification. In: Bernardo, M., Cimatti, A. (eds.) SFM 2006. LNCS, vol. 3965, pp. 108–143. Springer, Heidelberg (2006). https://doi.org/10.1007/11757283_5
21. Ignatiev, A., Morgado, A., Marques-Silva, J.: RC2: an efficient maxsat solver. J. Satisf. Boolean Model. Comput. **11**(1), 53–64 (2019). https://doi.org/10.3233/SAT190116
22. Jeroslow, R.G.: On defining sets of vertices of the hypercube by linear inequalities. Discret. Math. **11**(2), 119–124 (1975). https://doi.org/10.1016/0012-365X(75)90003-5
23. Lafitte, F., Jr., J.N., Heule, D.V.: Applications of SAT solvers in cryptanalysis: Finding weak keys and preimages. J. Satisf. Boolean Model. Comput. **9**(1), 1–25 (2014). https://doi.org/10.3233/SAT190099
24. Lee, P.J., Brickell, E.F.: An observation on the security of McEliece's public-key cryptosystem. In: Barstow, D., Brauer, W., Brinch Hansen, P., Gries, D., Luckham, D., Moler, C., Pnueli, A., Seegmüller, G., Stoer, J., Wirth, N., Günther, C.G. (eds.) EUROCRYPT 1988. LNCS, vol. 330, pp. 275–280. Springer, Heidelberg (1988). https://doi.org/10.1007/3-540-45961-8_25
25. Li, S., Li, C.M., Coll, J., Habet, D., Manyà, F., He, K.: WMaxCDCL in maxsat evaluation 2024. In: Berg, J., Järvisalo, M., Martins, R., Niskanen, A., Paxian, T. (eds.) MaxSAT Evaluation 2024: Solver and Benchmark Descriptions, Department of Computer Science Series B, vol. B-2024-2, pp. 17–18. Department of Computer Science, University of Helsinki (2024)

26. Manthey, N., Philipp, T., Steinke, P.: A more compact translation of pseudo-Boolean constraints into CNF such that generalized arc consistency is maintained. In: Lutz, C., Thielscher, M. (eds.) KI 2014. LNCS (LNAI), vol. 8736, pp. 123–134. Springer, Cham (2014). https://doi.org/10.1007/978-3-319-11206-0_13
27. May, A., Meurer, A., Thomae, E.: Decoding random linear codes in $\tilde{\mathcal{O}}(2^{0.054n})$. In: Lee, D.H., Wang, X. (eds.) ASIACRYPT 2011. LNCS, vol. 7073, pp. 107–124. Springer, Heidelberg (2011). https://doi.org/10.1007/978-3-642-25385-0_6
28. McEliece, R.J.: A public-key cryptosystem based on algebraic coding theory. Deep Space Network Progress Report **44**, 114–116 (1978)
29. Melchor, C.A., et al.: Hamming quasi-cyclic (HQC). NIST PQC Round **2**(4), 13 (2018)
30. Melchor, C.A., et al.: The syndrome decoding in the head (SD-in-the-head) signature scheme. Technical report, Technical report, National Institute of Standards and Technology (2023)
31. Mironov, I., Zhang, L.: Applications of SAT solvers to cryptanalysis of hash functions. In: Biere, A., Gomes, C.P. (eds.) SAT 2006. LNCS, vol. 4121, pp. 102–115. Springer, Heidelberg (2006). https://doi.org/10.1007/11814948_13
32. Narisada, S., Uemura, S., Okada, H., Furue, H., Aikawa, Y., Fukushima, K.: Solving mceliece-1409 in one day - cryptanalysis with the improved BJMM algorithm. In: Mouha, N., Nikiforakis, N. (eds.) ISC 2024. LNCS, vol. 15258, pp. 3–23. Springer (2024). https://doi.org/10.1007/978-3-031-75764-8_1
33. Nawrocki, W., Liu, Z., Fröhlich, A., Heule, M.J.H., Biere, A.: XOR local search for Boolean Brent equations. In: Li, C., Manyà, F. (eds.) SAT 2021. LNCS, vol. 12831, pp. 417–435. Springer (2021). https://doi.org/10.1007/978-3-030-80223-3_29
34. Niskanen, A., Berg, J., Järvisalo, M.: Maxhs in maxsat evaluation 2022. MaxSAT Eval. **2022**, 35 (2022)
35. Piotrów, M.: Uwrmaxsat: efficient solver for maxsat and pseudo-Boolean problems. In: 32nd IEEE International Conference on Tools with Artificial Intelligence, ICTAI 2020, Baltimore, MD, USA, November 9-11, 2020. pp. 132–136. IEEE (2020). https://doi.org/10.1109/ICTAI50040.2020.00031
36. Prange, E.: The use of information sets in decoding cyclic codes. IRE Trans. Inf. Theory **8**(5), 5–9 (1962). https://doi.org/10.1109/TIT.1962.1057777
37. Rintanen, J.: Planning and SAT. In: Biere, A., Heule, M., van Maaren, H., Walsh, T. (eds.) Handbook of Satisfiability - Second Edition, Frontiers in Artificial Intelligence and Applications, vol. 336, pp. 765–789. IOS Press (2021https://doi.org/10.3233/FAIA201003
38. Safarpour, S., Mangassarian, H., Veneris, A.G., Liffiton, M.H., Sakallah, K.A.: Improved design debugging using maximum satisfiability. In: Formal Methods in Computer-Aided Design, 7th International Conference, FMCAD 2007, Austin, Texas, USA, November 11-14, 2007, Proceedings. pp. 13–19. IEEE Computer Society (2007). https://doi.org/10.1109/FAMCAD.2007.26
39. Silva, J.P.M., Sakallah, K.A.: GRASP - a new search algorithm for satisfiability. In: Rutenbar, R.A., Otten, R.H.J.M. (eds.) ICCAD 1996, pp. 220–227. IEEE Computer Society / ACM (1996).https://doi.org/10.1109/ICCAD.1996.569607
40. Soos, M., Meel, K.S.: BIRD: engineering an efficient CNF-XOR SAT solver and its applications to approximate model counting. In: The Thirty-Third AAAI Conference on Artificial Intelligence, AAAI 2019, The Thirty-First Innovative Applications of Artificial Intelligence Conference, IAAI 2019, The Ninth AAAI Symposium on Educational Advances in Artificial Intelligence, EAAI 2019, Honolulu, Hawaii, USA, January 27 - February 1, 2019. pp. 1592–1599. AAAI Press (2019). https://doi.org/10.1609/AAAI.V33I01.33011592,

41. Soos, M., Meel, K.S.: Gaussian elimination meets maximum satisfiability. In: Proceedings of the 18th International Conference on Principles of Knowledge Representation and Reasoning. pp. 581–587 (2021). https://doi.org/10.24963/kr.2021/55
42. Soos, M., Nohl, K., Castelluccia, C.: Extending SAT solvers to cryptographic problems. In: Kullmann, O. (ed.) SAT 2009. LNCS, vol. 5584, pp. 244–257. Springer, Heidelberg (2009). https://doi.org/10.1007/978-3-642-02777-2_24
43. Stern, J.: A method for finding codewords of small weight. In: Cohen, G.D., Wolfmann, J. (eds.) Coding Theory and Applications. LNCS, vol. 388, pp. 106–113. Springer, Heidelberg (1988). https://doi.org/10.1007/BFB0019850
44. Trimoska, M., Dequen, G., Ionica, S.: Logical cryptanalysis with WDSat. In: Li, C.-M., Manyà, F. (eds.) SAT 2021. LNCS, vol. 12831, pp. 545–561. Springer, Cham (2021). https://doi.org/10.1007/978-3-030-80223-3_37

Accelerating Kind Realizability: A Multi-stage Incremental Realizability Checking Framework

Sirui Liu and Wei Dong(✉)

College of Computer Science and Technology, National University of Defense Technology, Changsha, Hunan, China
{liusirui,wdong}@nudt.edu.cn

Abstract. Non-well-separation is a common quality issue in reactive synthesis specifications, where the synthesized system can avoid satisfying its guarantees by preventing the environment from satisfying its assumptions. Kind realizability extends the usual GR(1) by additionally requiring the system to always enable the environment to satisfy its assumptions, thereby addressing this issue, and is expected to replace the usual GR(1) realizability checking. Kind realizability relies on a reduction and a 4-nested fixed-point algorithm, whose runtime typically exceeds that of the usual GR(1) realizability checking algorithm by more than 3 times, creating a significant performance bottleneck in specification development processes that require frequent realizability checks. This paper presents a framework designed to accelerate kind realizability checking, comprising: (1) a multi-level incremental checking framework that sequentially integrates approximate computation with the complete 4FP algorithm, reusing previously computed sound bounds at each stage to eliminate redundant state-space exploration; and (2) two accompanying approximation algorithms with lower asymptotic time complexity, which efficiently compute sound upper and lower bounds of the system winning region. Experiments on benchmarks comprising hundreds of specifications demonstrate significant performance improvements.

Keywords: GR(1) Synthesis · Kind Realizability · Incremental Computation

1 Introduction

Reactive synthesis is an automated procedure for constructing a correct-by-construction reactive system directly from its temporal logic specification [25]. Rather than relying on model checking to verify a manually constructed implementation, synthesis automatically derives a provably correct implementation from the given specification, provided that such an implementation exists.

GR(1) is a fragment of Linear Temporal Logic (LTL), which has an efficient symbolic synthesis algorithm [6,24], and whose expressive power covers most of

A. Sampaio and M. Stoelinga (Eds.): FM 2026, LNCS 16556, pp. 240–258, 2026.
https://doi.org/10.1007/978-3-032-26204-2_13

the well-known LTL specification patterns of Dwyer et al. [9,20]. In recent years, GR(1) synthesis has been implemented in several tools, including Spectra [22], RATSY [3], and Slugs [10]. Its balance of expressiveness and computational efficiency has made it suitable for a wide range of applications in reactive synthesis, including robotics [15], hardware synthesis [4], aspect languages [23], event-based behavioral models [8], and device drivers [26], to name a few.

Non-well-separation (NWS) is a known quality issue in reactive synthesis specifications [14]. The problem of NWS occurs when the synthesized system can avoid satisfying its guarantees by preventing the environment from satisfying its assumptions. Although such a solution correctly satisfies the specification's *assume* → *guarantee* logic, it is undesired, as it misses the purpose of the system and the intention of the engineer. NWS appears in many specifications in several benchmarks, in specifications written both by students and formal methods experts [21]. Furthermore, it was recently reported as one of the major challenges faced by software engineers who start using a reactive synthesizer [17].

To address this, *non-conflictingness* was proposed, using a 4-nested fixed-point (4FP) algorithm to ensure the system allows the environment to satisfy its justice assumptions [18]. This was subsequently extended to kind realizability, which also handles safety assumption violations via a reduction (4FP+R) [12]. While the 4FP algorithm shares the same asymptotic complexity as the usual 3-nested fixed-point (3FP) GR(1) algorithm ($O(mnQ^2)$, where Q denotes the state space size), its practical runtime is reported to be more than three times slower than the 3FP algorithm [12,18], creating a significant performance bottleneck.

Replacing usual GR(1) realizability checking with kind realizability checking is desirable, as the latter represents the more useful, engineer-intended notion of realizability. However, the high computational cost of 4FP+R relative to 3FP is significantly magnified by the frequent realizability checks required in iterative development workflows. This work focuses on reducing this computational cost to optimize the developer's workflow. We propose a multi-level incremental kind realizability checking framework with the following two core contributions:

- A multi-level incremental checking framework where each stage utilizes sound bounds from preceding stages as hot-start initial values. This incremental computation reduces redundant fixed-point iterations and lowers the overall checking time.
- Two new approximate algorithms, supporting this structure, to compute sound lower and upper bounds of the system winning region. Both algorithms possess lower asymptotic complexity and support early termination.

We evaluated our method on the SYNTECH and AMBA/GenBuf benchmark suites, demonstrating significant performance improvements. Our approach does not rely on any specific heuristics and is compatible with existing heuristics [11, 28].

2 Preliminaries

We provide a short background on Linear Temporal Logic, GR(1) synthesis, non-well-separation and kind realizability, with references to relevant papers for more details and complete formal definitions.

2.1 Linear Temporal Logic

We adopt the standard definition of Linear Temporal Logic (LTL) [6]. LTL includes temporal operators such as `X` (next), `U` (until), `F` (finally), `G` (globally), and `H` (historically). An LTL formula ϕ is satisfiable if and only if there exists a computation path σ such that $\sigma \models \phi$. LTL formulas can serve as specifications for reactive systems, where atomic propositions are interpreted as environment (input) and system (output) variables.

2.2 GR(1) Synthesis

Since LTL synthesis is computationally expensive [25], authors have suggested LTL fragments with more efficient synthesis algorithms, for example, GR(1) [6,24], whose expressive power covers most of the well-known LTL specification patterns [9,20]. GR(1) specifications include assumptions and guarantees about conditions that must hold on all initial states, on all states and transitions (safety), and infinitely often on every run (justice). A GR(1) synthesis problem consists of the following elements [24]:

- $\mathcal{X}$: input variables controlled by the environment.
- $\mathcal{Y}$: output variables controlled by the system.
- θ^e: assertion over $\mathcal{X}$ characterizing initial environment states.
- θ^s: assertion over $\mathcal{X} \cup \mathcal{Y}$ characterizing initial system states.
- $\rho^e(\mathcal{X} \cup \mathcal{Y}, \mathcal{X})$: transition relation of the environment.
- $\rho^s(\mathcal{X} \cup \mathcal{Y}, \mathcal{X} \cup \mathcal{Y})$: transition relation of the system.
- $\{J_i^e\}_{i=1}^m$: justice constraints of the environment that must be satisfied infinitely often.
- $\{J_j^s\}_{j=1}^n$: justice constraints of the system that must be satisfied infinitely often.

We denote the GR(1) game structure by $\langle H, \mathcal{F}_A, \mathcal{F}_G \rangle$, where H is the game graph composed of $\langle \theta^e, \theta^s, \rho^e, \rho^s \rangle$, $\mathcal{F}_A = \{J_1^e, \ldots, J_m^e\}$, and $\mathcal{F}_G = \{J_1^s, \ldots, J_n^s\}$. The GR(1) synthesis problem is to find a winning strategy for the system player for a given GR(1) game, or to determine that no such strategy exists. This can be expressed equivalently as the search for a system strategy f on H such that:

$$\emptyset \neq \mathcal{L}(H, f) \subseteq \overline{\mathcal{L}(H, \mathcal{F}_A)} \cup \mathcal{L}(H, \mathcal{F}_G). \quad (1)$$

Here, $\mathcal{L}(H, f)$ is the set of all infinite plays generated by the strategy f, while $\mathcal{L}(H, \mathcal{F}_A)$ and $\mathcal{L}(H, \mathcal{F}_G)$ are the sets of plays that infinitely often satisfy the environment justice assumptions and system justice guarantees, respectively. The existence of such a strategy is determined by checking for (strict) realizability, which is defined by the following LTL formula [6]:

$$\varphi^{sr} = (\theta^e \rightarrow \theta^s) \wedge (\theta^e \rightarrow \mathtt{G}((\mathtt{H}\rho^e) \rightarrow \rho^s)) \wedge (\theta^e \wedge \mathtt{G}\rho^e \rightarrow \ (\bigwedge_{i=1}^{m} \mathtt{GF}J_i^e \rightarrow \bigwedge_{j=1}^{n} \mathtt{GF}J_j^s))$$

2.3 Non-well-Separation and Kind Realizability

Klein and Pnueli [14] defined Well-Separation (WS) as a property of the environment specifications, ensuring that the environment can satisfy its assumptions from every reachable state. Definition 1 repeats the definition of WS.

Definition 1 (Well-Separation). *An environment specification $\langle\theta^e, \rho^e, J^e\rangle$ of GR(1) is well-separated iff φ^{sr} has no reachable system winning states for the system specification* $\langle\mathtt{true}, \mathtt{true}, \{\mathtt{false}\}\rangle$.

The system specification $\langle\mathtt{true}, \mathtt{true}, \{\mathtt{false}\}\rangle$ leaves system choices unconstrained ($\theta^s = \rho^s = \mathtt{true}$) while imposing an unsatisfiable justice guarantee ($J^s = \{\mathtt{false}\}$). System strategies for φ^{sr} cannot win, except by ensuring that the left-hand side of one of the three implications in φ^{sr} does not hold, forcing the environment to violate its assumptions. In non-well-separation (NWS) specifications, the system actively prevents the environment from satisfying its assumptions, thereby causing the overall specification to be vacuously satisfied.

To address NWS, Majumdar et al. [18] proposed the *non-conflictingness* requirement, requiring the system strategy to always allow the environment to satisfy its justice assumptions. This is achieved via a 4-nested fixed-point (4FP) computation shown in Algorithm 1 for the μ-calculus formula φ_4.

$$\varphi_4 = \nu \begin{bmatrix} Z_1 \\ Z_2 \\ \vdots \\ Z_n \end{bmatrix} \cdot \begin{bmatrix} \mu Y\,(\bigvee_{i=1}^{m} \nu X.\mu W\,(J_1^s \wedge \circledcirc Z_2 \vee \circledcirc Y \vee \neg J_i^e \wedge \bigcirc(W) \wedge \circledcirc(W \vee X \wedge \neg J_i^e))) \\ \mu Y\,(\bigvee_{i=1}^{m} \nu X.\mu W\,(J_2^s \wedge \circledcirc Z_3 \vee \circledcirc Y \vee \neg J_i^e \wedge \bigcirc(W) \wedge \circledcirc(W \vee X \wedge \neg J_i^e))) \\ \vdots \\ \mu Y\,(\bigvee_{i=1}^{m} \nu X.\mu W\,(J_n^s \wedge \circledcirc Z_1 \vee \circledcirc Y \vee \neg J_i^e \wedge \bigcirc(W) \wedge \circledcirc(W \vee X \wedge \neg J_i^e))) \end{bmatrix}$$

We denote the states from which the system can force the environment to visit a state in R by $\circledcirc(R)$, defined as:

$$\circledcirc(R) = \{q \in 2^{\mathcal{X} \cup \mathcal{Y}} \mid \forall x \in 2^{\mathcal{X}} : \neg\rho^e(q, x) \vee \exists y \in 2^{\mathcal{Y}} : (\rho^s(q, \langle x, y\rangle)) \wedge \langle x, y\rangle \in R)\}.$$

Similarly, we denote the states from which the system and the environment can cooperate to visit a state in R by $\bigcirc(R)$ defined as:

$$\bigcirc(R) = \{q \in 2^{\mathcal{X} \cup \mathcal{Y}} \mid \exists x \in 2^{\mathcal{X}} : \rho^e(q, x) \wedge \exists y \in 2^{\mathcal{Y}} : (\rho^s(q, \langle x, y\rangle)) \wedge \langle x, y\rangle \in R)\}.$$

The 4FP algorithm extends the 3-nested fixed-point (3FP) algorithm for GR(1) by replacing the innermost greatest fixed point with a 2-nested fixed-point computation. Leveraging the intermediate results stored during the 4FP computation, Majumdar et al. [18] proposed a method for synthesizing a non-conflicting system strategy, denoted f^1. The strategy f^1 satisfies the non-conflictingness constraint; specifically, for any state $q \in [\![\varphi_4]\!]$, the property stated in Theorem 1 holds under f^1 [18]. A complete proof can be found in [19].

Theorem 1. *Let f^1 be the system strategy synthesized from the intermediate results of the 4FP algorithm. Then for any state q in the set of system winning states computed by the 4FP algorithm, the following three properties hold:*

$$\mathcal{L}_q(H, f^1) \subseteq \overline{\mathcal{L}_q(H, \mathcal{F}_A)} \cup \mathcal{L}_q(H, \mathcal{F}_G), \tag{2}$$

$$\mathcal{L}_q(H, f^1) \cap \mathcal{L}_q(H, \mathcal{F}_G) \neq \emptyset, \tag{3}$$

$$\mathcal{L}_q(H, \mathcal{F}_G) \subseteq \mathcal{L}_q(H, \mathcal{F}_A) \Rightarrow \boldsymbol{pfx}(\mathcal{L}_q(H, f^1)) = \boldsymbol{pfx}(\mathcal{L}_q(H, f^1) \cap \mathcal{L}_q(H, \mathcal{F}_A)). \tag{4}$$

Here, `pfx` denotes the set of finite prefixes of a play. Equation 2 represents the condition satisfied by the 3FP algorithm, which is identical to Eq. 1. Equations 3 and 4 are the additional conditions required for *non-conflictingness.* Equation 3 demands that the system strategy can satisfy the system guarantees infinitely often. Equation 4 demands that, given $\mathcal{L}_q(H, \mathcal{F}_G) \subseteq \mathcal{L}_q(H, \mathcal{F}_A)$, any finite play prefix under strategy f^1 must be extendable by the environment into an infinite play that satisfies its justice assumptions. The premise $\mathcal{L}_q(H, \mathcal{F}_G) \subseteq \mathcal{L}_q(H, \mathcal{F}_A)$ in Eq. 4 is necessary for *non-conflictingness.* Although the 4FP algorithm does not validate this premise, its validity can be verified via an independent symbolic check.

Algorithm 1: 4FP algorithm to compute system winning states.

```
Z ← true;
while not reach fixed-point of Z do
    for j ← 1 to |F_G| do
        Y ← false;
        while not reach fixed-point of Y do
            start ← J_j^s ∧ ⭘Z ∨ ⭘Y, Y ← false;
            for i ← 1 to |F_A| do
                X ← Z;
                while not reach fixed-point of X do
                    W ← false;
                    while not fixed-point of W do
                        W ← ¬J_i^e ∧ ○(W) ∧ ⭘(W ∨ X ∧ ¬J_i^e) ∨ start;
                    end
                    X ← W;
                end
                Y ← Y ∨ X;
            end
        end
        Z ← Y;
    end
end
return Z;
```

Gorenstein et al. [12] extended 4FP via a reduction (4FP+R) to prevent violations of safety assumptions as well. This reduction is achieved by transforming the specification with auxiliary variables, without modifying the 4FP algorithm. They formally defined this requirement, which covers both safety and justice assumptions, as kind realizability [12]. Extending 4FP to support kind realizability requires modifications only at the reduction level. The upper and lower bounds derived in our subsequent algorithms are specific to the 4FP algorithm.

3 Multi-level Incremental Kind Realizability Checking

Algorithm 2 presents our multi-level incremental kind realizability checking framework, constructed as a sequential three-stage computational structure:

- **Stage 1 (Lines 1–3):** Compute the sound upper bound W_U of the system winning region. If the set of initial states is not contained in W_U, the algorithm terminates early, and the specification is deemed not kind-realizable.
- **Stage 2 (Lines 4–6):** Incrementally compute the sound lower bound W_L of the system winning region using W_U. If the set of initial states is a subset of W_L, the algorithm terminates early, determining the specification is kind-realizable.
- **Stage 3 (Lines 7–11):** If the preceding approximate computations do not terminate early, utilize the computed W_U and W_L to execute a full incremental kind realizability check based on the 4FP algorithm, yielding the exact system winning region W_C, and return the final determination accordingly.

The multi-level framework employs approximation algorithms of lower complexity than the standard 4FP algorithm, facilitating correct early termination via sound bounds. The framework proves particularly advantageous when full computation is required. In such cases, the precomputed upper (W_U) and lower (W_L) bounds serve to initialize the greatest (ν) and least (μ) fixed-point iterations, respectively. This incremental initialization prunes the state space and mitigates redundant computations. Consequently, the cumulative runtime outperforms a single 4FP execution even after accounting for approximation overhead. Figures 1 and 2 illustrate, using the 4FP algorithm as an example, how this approach yields performance improvements.

In the standard 4FP algorithm (Fig. 1), the outer fixed-point (νZ) iteration commences from the full state space (`True`) and monotonically refines the system winning states until convergence to the fixed point, Z_W. Crucially, the inner minimal fixed-point (μ) computation must restart from the empty set (`false`) during every outer iteration (Line 10 in Algorithm 1), as indicated by the green arrows in Fig. 1. Consequently, the final winning set Z_W is recomputed 4 times, and the set difference $Z_2 \setminus Z_W$ is recomputed 3 times, and so forth. This substantial redundant computation during the iterative refinement process constitutes a primary source of the 4FP algorithm's performance bottleneck.

Algorithm 2: Multi-level incremental kind realizability check.

Data: Game structure $G = \langle \theta^e, \theta^s, \rho^e, \rho^s, \mathcal{F}_A, \mathcal{F}_G \rangle$
Result: Kind realizability checking result `true` or `false`

$W_U \leftarrow$ **UpperBoundCal**$(\rho^e, \rho^s, \mathcal{F}_A, \mathcal{F}_G)$;
if not SystemWinAllIni$(\theta^e, \theta^s, W_U)$ **then**
  return `false`;
$W_L \leftarrow$ **LowerBoundCal**$(\rho^e, \rho^s, \mathcal{F}_G, W_U)$;
if SystemWinAllIni$(\theta^e, \theta^s, W_L)$ **then**
  return `true`;
$W_C \leftarrow$ **CompleteCal**$(\rho^e, \rho^s, \mathcal{F}_A, \mathcal{F}_G, W_U, W_L)$;
if SystemWinAllIni$(\theta^e, \theta^s, W_C)$ **then**
  return `true`;
else
  return `false`;

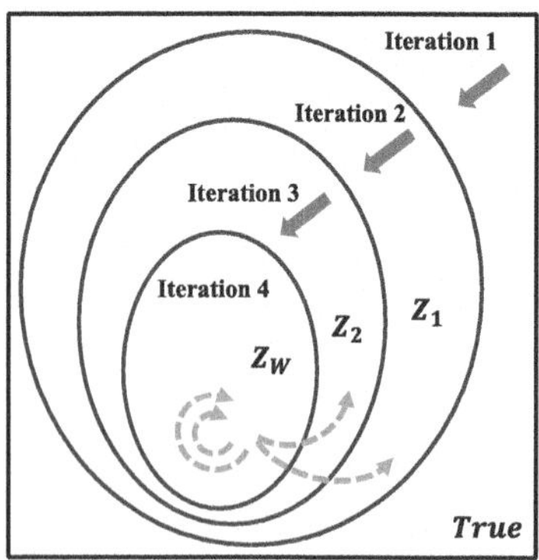

Fig. 1. Standard 4FP algorithm.

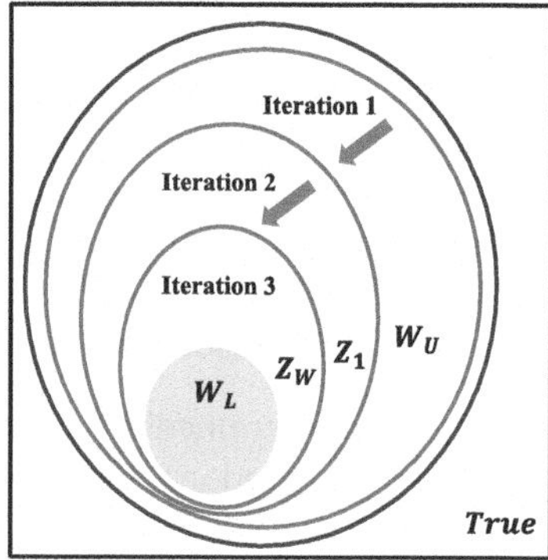

Fig. 2. Incremental 4FP algorithm.

In contrast, incremental computation significantly reduces this redundancy (see Fig. 2). The outer νZ loop is initialized with the precomputed upper bound W_U instead of `true`, leading to faster convergence and fewer iterations (e.g., 3 in Fig. 2, rather than 4 in Fig. 1). Furthermore, the inner μ loops are initialized with the lower bound W_L instead of `false`; consequently, the entire W_L region is spared from redundant recomputation during each outer fixed-point refinement. The incremental algorithm thus confines the state space to be processed to the region $W_U \setminus W_L$. This confinement reduces redundant computation during fixed-point iteration, lowering the number of required iterations and the size of the state space traversed in each step.

3.1 Sound Approximate Upper Bound Calculation

Algorithm 3 presents our algorithm for computing the sound upper bound, formally expressed by the μ-calculus formula:

$$\varphi_U = \nu Z(\bigwedge_{j=1}^{n} \mu Y(\nu X(J_j^s \wedge \bigcirc Z \vee \bigcirc Y \vee (\bigvee_{i=1}^{m} \neg J_i^e) \wedge \bigcirc X)))$$

This approximate upper bound computation constitutes a modified and simplified variant of the standard 3FP algorithm in [6]. The key modifications are detailed below:

- The initial stage (Lines 1–4) preprocesses environment justice guarantees by computing the disjunction of their negations, $\bigvee_{i=1}^{m} \neg J_i^e$. This set captures the states where at least one environment assumption is not satisfied.
- The nested fixed-point computation (Lines 5–18) bypasses the iteration over individual environment justice assumptions inherent in the standard 3FP algorithm. It substitutes the specific assumption negation $\neg J_i^e$ with the precomputed disjunction $\bigvee_{i=1}^{m} \neg J_i^e$. This substitution introduces a relaxed condition. Intuitively, while 3FP requires the system to guarantee the non-satisfaction of a specific J_i^e at the νX level, our approximation merely requires preventing at least one J_i^e from being satisfied.

By eliminating the iteration over the environment justice assumptions, our approximate upper bound algorithm reduces its asymptotic time complexity to $O(nQ^2)$, which is lower than that of the standard 3FP algorithm ($O(mnQ^2)$). Here, Q denotes the size of the state space, while n and m represent the number of system justice guarantees and environment justice assumptions, respectively.

Correctness. We now present the formal statement and proof of the sound approximate upper bound algorithm's correctness.

Theorem 2. *For a given specification, let W_{4fp} be the system winning region computed by the standard 4FP kind realizability algorithm (Alg. 1), and W_U be the region computed by our sound approximate upper bound algorithm (Alg. 3). The following inclusion holds: $W_{4fp} \subseteq W_U$.*

To establish Theorem 2, we first recall a foundational lemma linking the 4FP and standard 3FP algorithms.

Lemma 1. *Let W_{4fp} be the system winning region computed by the standard 4FP algorithm, and W_{3fp} be the system winning region computed by the standard 3FP algorithm [6]. Then, $W_{4fp} \subseteq W_{3fp}$ [19].*

By Lemma 1, it suffices to demonstrate $W_{3fp} \subseteq W_U$. The detailed proof follows:

Algorithm 3: Sound approximate upper bound calculation.

Data: $\langle \rho^e, \rho^s, \mathcal{F}_A, \mathcal{F}_G \rangle$ in game structure G
Result: Approximate upper bound W_U

$envNot \leftarrow$ `false`;
for $i \leftarrow 1$ **to** $|\mathcal{F}_A|$ **do**
  $envNot \leftarrow envNot \vee \neg J_i^e$;
end
$Z \leftarrow$ `true`;
while *not reach fixed-point of* Z **do**
  for $j \leftarrow 1$ **to** $|\mathcal{F}_G|$ **do**
    $Y \leftarrow$ `false`;
    while *not reach fixed-point of* Y **do**
      $start \leftarrow J_j^s \wedge \bigcirc Z \vee \bigcirc Y$, $Y \leftarrow$ `false`, $X \leftarrow Z$;
      while *not reach fixed-point of* X **do**
        $X \leftarrow start \vee (envNot \wedge \bigcirc X)$;
      end
      $Y \leftarrow Y \vee X$;
    end
    $Z \leftarrow Y$;
  end
end
return Z;

Proof. Recall $W_{3fp} = \nu Z. \bigwedge_{j=1}^{n} \mu Y. \bigvee_{i=1}^{m} \nu X.((J_j^s \wedge \bigcirc Z) \vee \bigcirc Y \vee (\neg J_i^e \wedge \bigcirc X))$. Our goal is to prove $W_{3fp} \subseteq W_U$. We will utilize the monotonicity property of fixed-point theory, propagating the subset relation from the innermost fixed-point outwards.

Let Z and Y be fixed arbitrary sets, and let j be a fixed index. We define two functions $f_i(X)$ and $g(X)$ for the innermost computations: $f_i(X) = (J_j^s \wedge \bigcirc Z) \vee \bigcirc Y \vee (\neg J_i^e \wedge \bigcirc X)$, and $g(X) = (J_j^s \wedge \bigcirc Z) \vee \bigcirc Y \vee ((\bigvee_{k=1}^{m} \neg J_k^e) \wedge \bigcirc X)$. For any $i \in \{1, \ldots, m\}$, the subset relation $\neg J_i^e \subseteq \bigvee_{k=1}^{m} \neg J_k^e$ holds. Since the $\bigcirc$, $\wedge$, and $\vee$ operators are all monotonic, this implies $(\neg J_i^e \wedge \bigcirc X) \subseteq ((\bigvee_{k=1}^{m} \neg J_k^e) \wedge \bigcirc X)$. Therefore, for any X and any i, we have $f_i(X) \subseteq g(X)$. By the Tarski-Knaster fixed-point theorem, if $f_i(X) \subseteq g(X)$ for all X, their respective greatest fixed points (νX) preserve this subset relationship: $\nu X.f_i(X) \subseteq \nu X.g(X)$. Since this holds for all $i \in \{1, \ldots, m\}$, the union of all $\nu X.f_i(X)$ must also be a subset of $\nu X.g(X)$: $\left(\bigvee_{i=1}^{m} \nu X.f_i(X)\right) \subseteq \left(\nu X.g(X)\right)$. By the property of monotonic fixed points, this subset relationship is preserved by the least fixed-point (μY) computation. Let $K_{3fp}(Y) = \bigvee_{i=1}^{m} \nu X.f_i(X)$ and $K_U(Y) = \nu X.g(X)$; we thus have $\mu Y.K_{3fp}(Y) \subseteq \mu Y.K_U(Y)$. This relation holds for all j, so the intersection ($\bigwedge_{j=1}^{n}$) also preserves the relation: $\left(\bigwedge_{j=1}^{n} \mu Y.K_{3fp}(Y)\right) \subseteq \left(\bigwedge_{j=1}^{n} \mu Y.K_U(Y)\right)$. W_{3fp} and W_U are the greatest fixed points (νZ) of these two functions. By the monotonicity property, we finally conclude: $W_{3fp} \subseteq W_U$.

3.2 Incremental Sound Approximate Lower Bound Calculation

Algorithm 4 presents our incremental computation algorithm for the sound approximate lower bound. In addition to $\rho^e, \rho^s, \mathcal{F}_G$, the algorithm's input includes the system winning region W_U computed by the sound approximate upper bound calculation (Algorithm 3). The core logic is defined by the μ-calculus formula:

$$\varphi_L = \nu Z(\bigwedge_{j=1}^{n} \mu Y(J_j^s \wedge \circledcirc Z \vee \circledcirc Y))$$

In Line 1 of Algorithm 4, the variable Z is initialized to the sound upper bound W_U, substituting the full state space `true`. This initialization confines the nested fixed-point iteration to the state space W_U, enabling incremental computation of the winning region. This algorithm utilizes two nested fixed points. Since it iterates only within the precomputed upper bound W_U rather than the entire state space, its asymptotic time complexity is $O(n|W_U|)$, which is lower than that of the standard 3FP and 4FP algorithms.

Algorithm 4: Sound approximate lower bound calculation.

Data: $\langle \rho^e, \rho^s, \mathcal{F}_G \rangle$ in game structure G, upper bound W_U
Result: Approximate lower bound W_L

```
1  Z ← W_U;
2  while not reach fixed-point of Z do
3      for j ← 1 to |F_G| do
4          Y ← J_j^s ∧ ⊚Z ;
5          while not reach fixed-point of Y do
6              Y ← Y ∨ ⊚Y;
7          end
8          Z ← Y;
9      end
10 end
11 return Z;
```

Correctness. We now present the formal statement and proof of the sound approximate lower bound algorithm's correctness.

Theorem 3. *Given a specification, let W_{4fp} be the system winning region computed by the standard 4FP algorithm, and let W_L be the system winning region computed by the lower bound algorithm (without using incremental computation). The following relation holds: $W_L \subseteq W_{4fp}$.*

Proof. We use a strategy-based argument to prove $W_L \subseteq W_{4fp}$. Our goal is to demonstrate that any strategy f_L originating from an arbitrary state $q \in W_L$ is also a non-conflicting strategy. Let $q \in W_L$. By the definition of W_L, there must exist a system strategy f_L such that the set of all infinite execution paths $\mathcal{L}_q(H, f_L)$ generated from q by f_L satisfies all system justice guarantees $\mathcal{F}_G$.

Formally, $\mathcal{L}_q(H, f_L) \subseteq \mathcal{L}_q(H, \mathcal{F}_G)$. We now prove $q \in W_{4fp}$ by showing that f_L satisfies all three sub-formulas (Eqs. 2–4) of Theorem 1.

- **Equation** 2: This is the standard GR(1) correctness requirement. As established, $\mathcal{L}_q(H, f_L) \subseteq \mathcal{L}_q(H, \mathcal{F}_G)$. By set theory, it follows that $\mathcal{L}_q(H, f_L) \subseteq \overline{\mathcal{L}_q(H, \mathcal{F}_A)} \cup \mathcal{L}_q(H, \mathcal{F}_G)$ must hold.
- **Equation** 3: This requires $\mathcal{L}_q(H, f_L) \cap \mathcal{L}_q(H, \mathcal{F}_G) \neq \emptyset$. We have $\mathcal{L}_q(H, f_L) \subseteq \mathcal{L}_q(H, \mathcal{F}_G)$. Assuming the set of plays is non-empty (i.e., $\mathcal{L}_q(H, f_L) \neq \emptyset$), the intersection of $\mathcal{L}_q(H, f_L)$ with its superset $\mathcal{L}_q(H, \mathcal{F}_G)$ is $\mathcal{L}_q(H, f_L)$ itself. Thus, $\mathcal{L}_q(H, f_L) \cap \mathcal{L}_q(H, \mathcal{F}_G) = \mathcal{L}_q(H, f_L)$, which is non-empty.
- **Equation** 4: This requires the implication $\mathcal{L}_q(H, \mathcal{F}_G) \subseteq \mathcal{L}_q(H, \mathcal{F}_A) \implies \texttt{pfx}(\mathcal{L}_q(H, f_L)) = \texttt{pfx}(\mathcal{L}_q(H, f_L) \cap \mathcal{L}_q(H, \mathcal{F}_A))$ to hold. We analyze this by cases. First, assume the premise $\mathcal{L}_q(H, \mathcal{F}_G) \subseteq \mathcal{L}_q(H, \mathcal{F}_A)$ is true. We know $\mathcal{L}_q(H, f_L) \subseteq \mathcal{L}_q(H, \mathcal{F}_G)$. By the transitivity of set inclusion, it follows that $\mathcal{L}_q(H, f_L) \subseteq \mathcal{L}_q(H, \mathcal{F}_A)$. Consequently, $\mathcal{L}_q(H, f_L) \cap \mathcal{L}_q(H, \mathcal{F}_A) = \mathcal{L}_q(H, f_L)$. Their sets of finite prefixes (`pfx`) must be equal. This proves the conclusion holds when the premise is `true`. Second, if the premise $\mathcal{L}_q(H, \mathcal{F}_G) \subseteq \mathcal{L}_q(H, \mathcal{F}_A)$ is `false`, the implication holds vacuously. In both cases, Eq. 4 is satisfied.

In summary, f_L satisfies all three properties defined in Theorem 1. Therefore, f_L is itself a non-conflicting strategy, and any state $q \in W_L$ is also a state in W_{4fp}. Thus, $W_L \subseteq W_{4fp}$.

The established relationship $W_L \subseteq W_{4fp}$ (Theorem 3) and $W_{4fp} \subseteq W_U$ (Theorem 2) yield the containment $W_L \subseteq W_U$. This confirms W_U functions as a valid upper bound for the lower bound calculation. Given the monotonic shrinking nature of the greatest fixed-point (νZ) iteration, and the necessary inclusion $W_L \subseteq W_U \subseteq \texttt{true}$, commencing the downward incremental iteration from the state set W_U is mathematically sound and obviates the need to begin from the complete state space `true`.

Theorem 4. $W_L \subseteq W_{4fp} \subseteq W_{3fp} \subseteq W_U$.

3.3 Incremental 4FP Algorithm

When the system winning region derived from approximate computation is insufficient to determine realizability, a complete computation of the winning region is unavoidable, as approximation cannot decide all cases. Moreover, during many stages of specification development, the full system winning region is required to support subsequent analysis steps, for which approximate results are not adequate substitutes. Instead of performing a complete computation from scratch, we leverage the already-computed sound bounds W_U and W_L to incrementally compute the full winning region, thereby mitigating redundant computations in the standard 4FP procedure (Algorithm 1).

Concretely, the incremental variant differs from the standard 4FP algorithm in the following modifications:

1. The outer greatest fixed-point Z is initialized with the sound upper bound, i.e., $Z \leftarrow W_U$ (replacing $Z \leftarrow$ `true`);
2. The intermediate least fixed-point Y is initialized with the sound lower bound, i.e., $Y \leftarrow W_L$ (replacing $Y \leftarrow$ `false`);
3. The innermost least fixed-point W is initialized with the sound lower bound, i.e., $W \leftarrow W_L$ (replacing $W \leftarrow$ `false`).

All other aspects of the nesting structure remain identical to Algorithm 1.

By initializing the greatest fixed-point (νZ) and least fixed-point ($\mu Y, \mu W$) iterations with the previously computed sound bounds W_U and W_L, the incremental procedure effectively restricts the nested fixed-point computation to the state space constrained by W_U and $\neg W_L$, which substantially reduces redundant recomputation.

The asymptotic time complexity of the standard 4FP algorithm is $O(mnQ^2)$, where Q denotes the size of the entire state space. In contrast, the incremental variant operates only over the reduced state space characterized by $W_U \setminus W_L$, yielding an improved asymptotic complexity of $O\big(mn \cdot |W_U \setminus W_L|^2\big)$. Consequently, as the sound approximations W_U and W_L become tighter with respect to the actual winning region, the asymptotic complexity of the incremental computation decreases accordingly.

4 Evaluation

We have implemented our algorithm within the Spectra GR(1) synthesizer [22]. To evaluate the efficacy of our multi-stage incremental framework, we conducted extensive evaluations using the SYNTECH, AMBA, and GenBuf benchmark suites. The experimental design addressed two research questions:

RQ1. What are the aggregate efficiency gains relative to the standard 4FP+R algorithm?
RQ2. What is the isolated contribution of the incremental computation architecture in the absence of early termination?

4.1 Benchmark Corpus, Implementation, and Experimental Setup

We employed two primary sources of specifications. The first is the SYNTECH benchmark suite, which comprises specifications written by computer science students between 2015 and 2023 as part of semester-long project courses. These specifications model a variety of robotic and other reactive systems and include not only final versions but also numerous intermediate drafts—many of which are unrealizable. The SYNTECH benchmarks have been widely used in prior evaluations [2,7,11,28]. The second source consists of the Spectra implementations of the parameterized AMBA [4] and GenBuf [5] specifications, which are standard benchmarks in GR(1)-based synthesis and form part of the SYNTCOMP benchmark suite [13].

To focus on cases where performance improvements are most valuable, we use the filtered specifications from [28], those for which the baseline realizability check in Spectra (augmented with the heuristics of [11]) required more than 60 s. This resulted in a dataset comprising 250 SYNTECH specifications and 12 from AMBA and GenBuf (denoted as **Diff-Spec**). Given that the realizability checking times for these specifications range from several minutes to hours, they constitute a computationally demanding benchmark suite, making this suite ideal for evaluating the efficacy of our method.

Additionally, we consider specification subsets from the SYNTECH benchmark suite that were employed in prior performance evaluations of incomplete heuristics for detecting NWS specifications [12]. These subsets include SYN15, SYN17, SYN20, and SYN23' (a subset of SYN23). Since the vast majority of specifications within these subsets can be processed within 60 s, we retained only those meeting this criterion to form the **Easy-Spec-60** dataset. This selection complements our evaluation by assessing performance on simpler instances.

Implementation. Our implementation extends the Spectra synthesizer [22], which already incorporates the heuristics from [11] and the reduction from [12]. The underlying symbolic engine uses a modified version of the CUDD BDD library [27].

Experimental Setup. All experiments were conducted on a server instance equipped with an Intel Xeon Gold 6330 CPU and 90 GB of RAM, running Ubuntu 22.04, using a single CPU core. Reported runtimes are averages over three independent runs (in milliseconds). Although the core algorithms are deterministic, we performed multiple runs to account for runtime variability introduced by JVM garbage collection and CUDD's dynamic variable reordering.

The baseline is the public version of Spectra (which also implements the 4FP algorithm with the heuristics from [11] and reduction from [12]). Heuristics from the recent work [28] were not included in either version, as their source code was not publicly available at the time of our implementation. However, our method is also compatible with these newer heuristics. Our approach focuses on structural reduction of the fixpoint nesting, which is orthogonal to low-level BDD optimizations and heuristics such as justice reordering proposed in [28]. Therefore, we expect our method to yield cumulative speedups when combined with these techniques.

Correctness Validation. To ensure correctness, we validated our multi-level incremental kind realizability algorithm. We disabled early termination in the approximation phase (i.e., lines 2,3 and 8,9 of Algorithm 2) and compared the resulting system winning regions computed by our method against those produced by the public version of Spectra. This comparison was performed across all specifications in our experimental corpus. In all cases, the computed winning regions were identical, confirming the correctness of our implementation.

4.2 Results

For our multi-level incremental approach, the reported runtime includes the execution time of all three sub-computation stages, and the iteration count represents the sum of innermost fixed-point iterations across these stages. The table columns and rows are defined as follows:

- *Analysis*: Indicates whether early termination was enabled.
- *Benchmark, Number*: The name of the benchmark and the number of specifications in the benchmark.
- *E-R, E-R<1*: *E-R* denotes the geometric mean of the ratio between the number of innermost fixed-point iterations of our method and the baseline. *E-R<1* reports the percentage of specifications where this ratio is below 1.0 (i.e., cases where our method required fewer iterations). Specifications that timed out were excluded from these calculations.
- *T-R, T-R<1*: *T-R* denotes the geometric mean of the ratio between the realizability checking time of our method and the baseline. *T-R<1* reports the percentage of specifications where this ratio is below 1.0. Specifications that timed out were excluded from these calculations.
- *B-TO, M-TO*: To manage experimental costs, a timeout limit of 30 minutes was imposed on all runs. *B-TO* and *M-TO* report the percentage of specifications that timed out for the baseline and our method, respectively.

Overall Performance (RQ1). Table 1 reports the experimental results on the **Diff-Spec** benchmark suite. The proposed approach delivers substantial speedups on computationally demanding specifications, with runtime reductions closely tracking iteration decreases. This alignment suggests that the gains primarily arise from eliminating redundant fixed-point iterations.

Table 1. Performance Comparison for **Diff-Spec**.

Analysis	Benchmark	Number	E-R	E-R<1	T-R	T-R<1	B-TO	M-TO
E	SYNTECH	250	0.19	71%	0.28	72%	27%	27%
	AMBA	6	0.15	100%	0.23	100%	50%	22%
	GenBuf	6	0.76	100%	0.83	67%	0%	0%
No E	SYNTECH	250	0.31	70%	0.32	71%	27%	26%
	AMBA	6	0.84	100%	0.67	50%	50%	28%
	GenBuf	6	0.76	100%	0.95	33%	0%	0%

On the SYNTECH benchmark suite comprising 250 specifications, our method achieves a pronounced acceleration over the baseline, with a time ratio of 0.28, corresponding to an average runtime reduction of approximately 72%. The iteration ratio is 0.19, meaning that the incremental approach requires only 19%

of the fixed-point iterations of the standard 4FP algorithm. The close agreement between these two ratios suggests that the reduction in iterations effectively translates into runtime improvements. Similar gains are observed on the AMBA benchmarks, where the time ratio reaches 0.23. In contrast, the improvements on **Easy-Spec-60** and GenBuf are more moderate, yet remain positive overall; the reasons are discussed in the subsequent analysis.

Contribution of the Incremental Structure (RQ2). To assess the impact of the incremental structure independent of the early-termination mechanism, we conducted a controlled evaluation under a configuration that enforces complete kind realizability checking. In this setting, the early-termination branch was disabled, and all three sub-computations were executed to obtain the full system winning region. This configuration reflects a common requirement in specification development workflows, where one often needs the complete winning region for subsequent analyses, such as incremental realizability checking.

In Table 1, under this configuration, the SYNTECH suite still exhibits a low time ratio of 0.32, indicating that the incremental structure alone can reduce the overall computational cost without early termination. These results demonstrate that the proposed method is effective not only for rapid decision scenarios but also for analysis settings that require computing the full winning region.

Limited Speedups on Easier Specifications. Table 2 shows that for **Easy-Spec-60** with short baseline runtimes, our method reduces fixed-point iterations, but the reduction does not yield a proportional runtime decrease. This is mainly due to inherent framework overheads, such as the potential impact of persisted BDDs on dynamic variable reordering. For short-running instances, the overheads account for a substantially larger fraction of total runtime, thereby weakening or even masking the runtime benefits brought by fewer iterations.

Table 2. Performance Comparison for **Easy-Spec-60**.

Analysis	Benchmark	Number	E-R	E-R<1	T-R	T-R<1
E	SYN15	61	0.42	97%	0.74	62%
	SYN17	95	0.62	81%	0.90	45%
	SYN20	53	0.52	85%	0.86	60%
	SYN23'	164	0.38	87%	0.90	55%
No E	SYN15	61	0.52	97%	0.81	61%
	SYN17	95	0.72	81%	0.94	52%
	SYN20	53	0.59	83%	0.94	57%
	SYN23'	164	0.63	79%	1.11	49%

This effect is captured by the gap between iteration and time ratios. In Table 2, with early termination on SYN23', the iteration ratio decreases to 0.38

while the time ratio remains 0.90, indicating that iteration savings do not proportionally translate into runtime reduction. In contrast, for the more time-consuming specifications in Table 1, the two ratios are typically closer, suggesting that when solving dominates overall cost, framework overhead becomes relatively minor and iteration reductions translate more directly into time savings.

Table 3. Geometric mean of time ratios for SYN23' in **Easy-Spec-60** across different baseline runtime intervals. Superscripts denote the number of test cases.

Analysis	<1 s	1–5 s	5–30 s	30–60 s
E	1.23^{111}	0.72^{34}	0.24^{15}	0.15^{4}
No E	1.55^{111}	0.84^{34}	0.28^{15}	0.16^{4}

Table 3 further substantiates this observation by partitioning SYN23' according to baseline execution time. For instances with baseline runtimes below 1 s, the method exhibits negative gains; as baseline runtime increases, speedups become positive and become more pronounced. This pattern indicates that inherent overhead dominates short-running cases but constitutes a smaller fraction of total time on slower instances.

GenBuf Shows Limited Gains. As reported in Table 1, the speedups on GenBuf are less pronounced, which can be attributed to two main factors. First, sound approximate upper and lower bounds that are tight enough to trigger early termination were not obtained on GenBuf, indicating that the proposed bounding algorithms yield comparatively weaker bound quality for this class of specifications. In contrast, on AMBA, early termination based on the computed sound lower bounds is triggered, leading to substantial acceleration, which indicates that the proposed lower-bound approximation is more effective on AMBA specifications than on GenBuf.

Second, GenBuf comprises parameterized variants of a single specification template, forming a highly homogeneous benchmark family. Consequently, if the approximate bound algorithms are not well aligned with the underlying template structure, the limitation persists consistently across the entire family, making the overall gains appear modest. This outcome should thus be interpreted as a reduced fit to a particular specification structure. Since sound approximations cannot be uniformly tight across all specification patterns, this behavior is expected and motivates future work on developing additional classes of sound approximation algorithms to broaden coverage.

5 Related Work

Approximate computation for general GR(1) realizability has been explored in prior work. Alur et al. [1] proposed a concurrent decision procedure that falls back to the full 3FP algorithm whenever the approximation fails. Consequently, this approach offers no improvement in the worst case. Our method differs fundamentally in two respects. First, we target kind realizability, whereas prior approximations were designed for standard GR(1) realizability and do not account for NWS specifications, making them inapplicable in our setting. Second, rather than relying on a concurrent fallback scheme, we introduce a sequential incremental computation framework. In this framework, sound over- and under-approximations are computed first and then used as warm-start initializations to incrementally constrain the subsequent full 4FP computation. By pruning irrelevant portions of the state space a priori, our approach reduces the number of fixed-point iterations.

Existing work on optimizing GR(1) performance has primarily focused on accelerating individual algorithm runs. Techniques such as early fixed-point detection, reuse of previously computed fixed points, early unrealizability checks, and reordering of justice assumptions have been shown to improve efficiency [11,28] and can be readily integrated into kind realizability checking.

6 Conclusion

Kind realizability checking is the ideal solution to the NWS quality issue in GR(1) synthesis, but its high computational cost hinders its adoption in iterative development. We propose a multi-level incremental 4FP algorithm featuring a two-stage pipeline: (1) compute low-cost over- and under-approximations; (2) use W_U and W_L as warm-start initializations and perform an incremental full 4FP computation constrained to the state space $W_U \setminus W_L$.

Implemented in the Spectra synthesizer and evaluated on SYNTECH and AMBA/GenBuf benchmarks, our method outperforms the baseline 4FP. Future work includes exploring faster and more precise approximation algorithms and more sophisticated incremental frameworks.

Acknowledgments. We thank the anonymous reviewers for the valuable comments. This research was supported by the National Natural Science Foundation of China (No. U2341212), Science Challenge Project (No. TZ2025002).

Data-Availability Statement. The artifact associated with this paper is available at Zenodo [16].

References

1. Alur, R., Moarref, S., Topcu, U.: Counter-strategy guided refinement of gr (1) temporal logic specifications. In: 2013 Formal Methods in Computer-Aided Design, pp. 26–33. IEEE (2013)
2. Amram, G., Ma'ayan, D., Maoz, S., Pistiner, O., Ringert, J.O.: Triggers for reactive synthesis specifications. In: 2023 IEEE/ACM 45th International Conference on Software Engineering (ICSE), pp. 729–741. IEEE (2023)

3. Bloem, R., et al.: RATSY – a new requirements analysis tool with synthesis. In: Touili, T., Cook, B., Jackson, P. (eds.) CAV 2010. LNCS, vol. 6174, pp. 425–429. Springer, Heidelberg (2010). https://doi.org/10.1007/978-3-642-14295-6_37
4. Bloem, R., Galler, S., Jobstmann, B., Piterman, N., Pnueli, A., Weiglhofer, M.: Automatic hardware synthesis from specifications: a case study. In: 2007 Design, Automation & Test in Europe Conference & Exhibition, pp. 1–6. IEEE (2007)
5. Bloem, R., Galler, S., Jobstmann, B., Piterman, N., Pnueli, A., Weiglhofer, M.: Specify, compile, run: hardware from PSL. Electron. Notes Theoret. Comput. Sci. **190**(4), 3–16 (2007)
6. Bloem, R., Jobstmann, B., Piterman, N., Pnueli, A., Sa'ar, Y.: Synthesis of reactive (1) designs. J. Comput. Syst. Sci. **78**(3), 911–938 (2012)
7. Cavezza, D.G., Alrajeh, D., György, A.: Minimal assumptions refinement for realizable specifications. In: Proceedings of the 8th International Conference on Formal Methods in Software Engineering, pp. 66–76 (2020)
8. D'ippolito, N., Braberman, V., Piterman, N., Uchitel, S.: Synthesizing nonanomalous event-based controllers for liveness goals. ACM Trans. Software Eng. Methodol. (TOSEM) **22**(1), 1–36 (2013)
9. Dwyer, M.B., Avrunin, G.S., Corbett, J.C.: Patterns in property specifications for finite-state verification. In: Proceedings of the 21st International Conference on Software Engineering, pp. 411–420 (1999)
10. Ehlers, R., Raman, V.: `Slugs`: extensible GR(1) synthesis. In: Chaudhuri, S., Farzan, A. (eds.) CAV 2016. LNCS, vol. 9780, pp. 333–330. Springer, Cham (2016). https://doi.org/10.1007/978-3-319-41540-6_18
11. Firman, E., Maoz, S., Ringert, J.O.: Performance heuristics for gr (1) synthesis and related algorithms. Acta Informatica **57**(1), 37–79 (2020)
12. Gorenstein, A., Maoz, S., Ringert, J.O.: Kind controllers and fast heuristics for non-well-separated gr (1) specifications. In: Proceedings of the 46th IEEE/ACM International Conference on Software Engineering, pp. 1–12 (2024)
13. Jacobs, S., et al.: The reactive synthesis competition (syntcomp): 2018–2021. Int. J. Softw. Tools Technol. Transfer **26**(5), 551–567 (2024)
14. Klein, U., Pnueli, A.: Revisiting synthesis of GR(1) specifications. In: Barner, S., Harris, I., Kroening, D., Raz, O. (eds.) HVC 2010. LNCS, vol. 6504, pp. 161–181. Springer, Heidelberg (2011). https://doi.org/10.1007/978-3-642-19583-9_16
15. Kress-Gazit, H., Fainekos, G.E., Pappas, G.J.: Temporal-logic-based reactive mission and motion planning. IEEE Trans. Rob. **25**(6), 1370–1381 (2009)
16. Liu, S.: Fm segsyn ae (2026). https://doi.org/10.5281/zenodo.18590272
17. Ma'Ayan, D., Maoz, S.: Using reactive synthesis: an end-to-end exploratory case study. In: 2023 IEEE/ACM 45th International Conference on Software Engineering (ICSE), pp. 742–754. IEEE (2023)
18. Majumdar, R., Piterman, N., Schmuck, A.-K.: Environmentally-friendly GR(1) synthesis. In: Vojnar, T., Zhang, L. (eds.) TACAS 2019. LNCS, vol. 11428, pp. 229–246. Springer, Cham (2019). https://doi.org/10.1007/978-3-030-17465-1_13
19. Majumdar, R., Piterman, N., Schmuck, A.: Environmentally-friendly GR(1) synthesis (2019). CoRR abs/1902.05629. http://arxiv.org/abs/1902.05629
20. Maoz, S., Ringert, J.O.: Gr (1) synthesis for LTL specification patterns. In: Proceedings of the 2015 10th Joint Meeting on Foundations of Software Engineering, pp. 96–106 (2015)
21. Maoz, S., Ringert, J.O.: On well-separation of gr (1) specifications. In: Proceedings of the 2016 24th ACM SIGSOFT International Symposium on Foundations of Software Engineering, pp. 362–372 (2016)

22. Maoz, S., Ringert, J.O.: Spectra: a specification language for reactive systems. Softw. Syst. Model. **20**(5), 1553–1586 (2021)
23. Maoz, S., Sa'ar, Y.: Aspectltl: an aspect language for LTL specifications. In: Proceedings of the tenth international conference on Aspect-oriented software development, pp. 19–30 (2011)
24. Piterman, N., Pnueli, A., Sa'ar, Y.: Synthesis of reactive(1) designs. In: Emerson, E.A., Namjoshi, K.S. (eds.) VMCAI 2006. LNCS, vol. 3855, pp. 364–380. Springer, Heidelberg (2005). https://doi.org/10.1007/11609773_24
25. Pnueli, A., Rosner, R.: On the synthesis of a reactive module. In: Proceedings of the 16th ACM SIGPLAN-SIGACT symposium on Principles of programming languages, pp. 179–190 (1989)
26. Ryzhyk, L., Walker, A.: Developing a practical reactive synthesis tool: experience and lessons learned. arXiv preprint arXiv:1611.07624 (2016)
27. Somenzi, F.: Cudd: Cu decision diagram package release 2.3. 0. University of Colorado at Boulder **621** (1998)
28. Yatskan, R., Shevrin, I., Maoz, S.: Performance heuristics for gr (1) realizability checking and related analyses. In: Gurfinkel, A., Heule, M. (eds.) TACAS 2025. LNCS, vol. 15696, pp. 40–59. Springer, Cham (2025). https://doi.org/10.1007/978-3-031-90643-5_3

Verifying Sampling Algorithms via Distributional Invariants

Daniel Zilken[1(✉)], Kevin Batz[2], Joost-Pieter Katoen[1], and Tobias Winkler[1]

[1] RWTH Aachen University, Aachen, Germany
daniel.zilken@cs.rwth-aachen.de
[2] University College London, London, UK

Abstract. This paper presents a Hoare-like verification framework for discrete probabilistic programs that we apply to two non-trivial sampling algorithms: Lumbroso's *Fast Dice Roller* and Saad et al.'s *Fast Loaded Dice Roller*. These algorithms have previously resisted formal verification due to their probabilistic nature, intricate loop structure, and parametric input. Our approach complements existing proof rules based on inductive distributional invariants, enabling us to verify both total and partial correctness of the two algorithms.

Keywords: Program Verification · Probabilistic Programs · Hoare Logic

1 Introduction

Sampling random numbers from prescribed probability distributions is fundamental to a growing number of applications in computer science and related fields. Examples include simulations of physical processes [13], randomized algorithms and data structures [32], and machine learning [18].

This paper addresses *functional correctness* verification of sampling algorithms encoded as *probabilistic programs*. The goal is to ensure that such a program generates a specified—possibly parameterized—target distribution. More precisely, the verification problem we address is as follows:

> *Given an imperative program C with coin flips and a distributional Hoare triple $\{\!|pre|\!\}\ C\ \{\!|post|\!\}$, prove that C, when executed on any input (distribution) satisfying pre, yields a (sub-)distribution satisfying post.*

In our framework, *pre* and *post* are *sets of (sub-)distributions* or predicates describing such sets; a (sub-)distribution μ *satisfies pre* or *post* if μ is an element of the respective set. Hoare triples enable reasoning about samplers for *parametric distributions*. For example, $\{\!|n \geq 0|\!\}\ C\ \{\!|y \sim \mathsf{unif}(0,\ldots,n)|\!\}$ asserts that, given input $n \geq 0$, program C outputs an integer y drawn uniformly at random from $\{0,\ldots,n\}$ (assuming C does not modify n).

Our problem statement poses three main challenges:

A. Sampaio and M. Stoelinga (Eds.): FM 2026, LNCS 16556, pp. 259–278, 2026.
https://doi.org/10.1007/978-3-032-26204-2_14

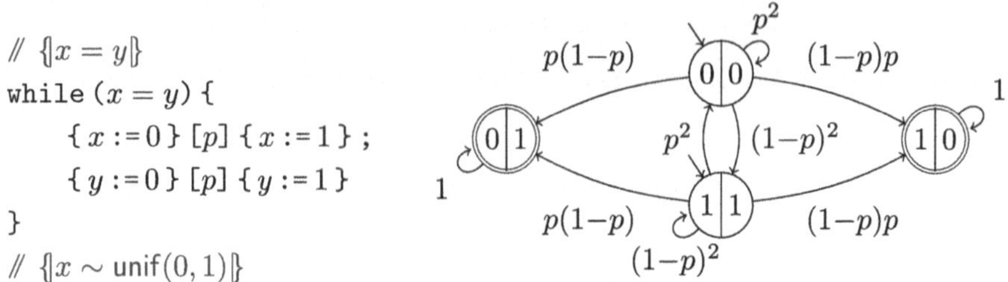

Fig. 1. *Left:* Probabilistic program modeling Von Neumann's algorithm [35], where $\{\,L\,\}\,[p]\,\{\,R\,\}$ executes sub-programs L and R with probability p and $1-p$, respectively. *Right:* The program's underlying Markov chain (Definition 8, Page 8). The terminal states (doubly circled) have a self-loop, which is important for our theory to work.

- (C1) The output distribution must be established *exactly*—approximations do not necessarily suffice.
- (C2) When coin flips occur inside *loops*, the target distribution may only be achieved *in the limit.*
- (C3) Sampling algorithms may take *parameters* as inputs, requiring verification over *infinite families of distributions.*

We tackle these challenges by adopting the *distributional paradigm* [1–4], which treats distributions over program states as first-class semantic objects. This point of view enables reasoning about *distributional invariant properties* such as "In every step, variable x is non-negative with probability ≥ 0.9". Such properties are inexpressible in the more conventional state-centric approach to probabilistic verification (e.g., [6, Chapter 10]). Distributional invariants turn out to be a natural fit for verifying sampling algorithms, as we illustrate next.

Sampler Verification with Distributional Invariants: Von Neumann's Fair Coin. Consider the problem of sampling a uniform random bit from a source of i.i.d. random bits with unknown bias $p \in (0, 1)$ towards, say, 0. The following solution is due to Von Neumann [35]: Extract two bits from the source; if they differ, return the first (or the second), otherwise discard the bits and start over. This is readily modeled as the program in Fig. 1. Albeit simple, the algorithm already presents challenges (C1) and (C2). Under the distributional paradigm, the program's dynamics is the following infinite trajectory of *reachable distributions*, illustrated here for $p = 0.4$ and the initial distribution satisfying $Pr[\text{00}] = 1$:[1]

$$\begin{matrix} \text{00} \\ \text{01} \\ \text{10} \\ \text{11} \end{matrix} \begin{pmatrix} 1 \\ 0 \\ 0 \\ 0 \end{pmatrix}_0 \rightsquigarrow \begin{pmatrix} 0.16 \\ 0.24 \\ 0.24 \\ 0.36 \end{pmatrix}_1 \rightsquigarrow \begin{pmatrix} 0.0832 \\ 0.3648 \\ 0.3648 \\ 0.1872 \end{pmatrix}_2 \rightsquigarrow \cdots \rightsquigarrow \begin{pmatrix} 0.0004 \\ 0.4993 \\ 0.4993 \\ 0.0010 \end{pmatrix}_{10} \rightsquigarrow \cdots \begin{pmatrix} 0.0 \\ 0.5 \\ 0.5 \\ 0.0 \end{pmatrix}_\omega \qquad (\dagger)$$

[1] Some numbers have been rounded. The rightmost vector is the limiting distribution.

```
// ⦃n > 0⦄
v := 1 ; c := 0 ;
while (v < n) {
    v := 2v ;
    {c := 2c} [0.5] {c := 2c + 1} ;
    if (c ≥ n) {
        v := v − n ; c := c − n
    }
}
// ⦃c ∼ unif(0, ..., n − 1)⦄
```

"Consider this statement, which is a loop invariant: c is uniformly distributed over $\{0, \ldots, v-1\}$" [27, p. 4]

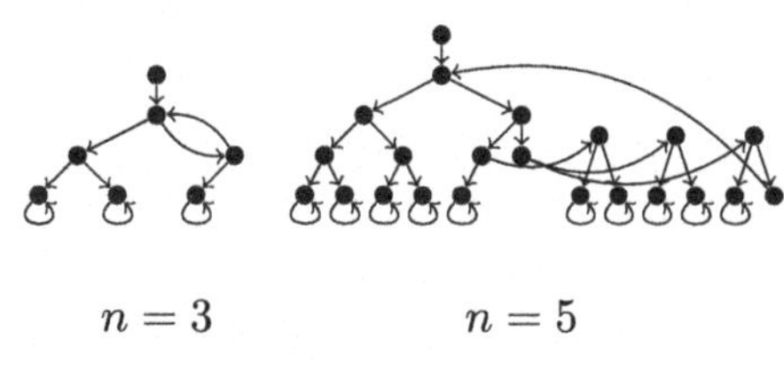

Fig. 2. *Left:* The Fast Dice Roller (FDR) algorithm adapted from [27] for discrete uniform sampling. *Right:* Lumbroso's distributional invariant [27] and two members of the FDR's infinite family of underlying Markov chains (Definition 8, Page 8).

As desired, the sequence converges (pointwise) to the uniform distribution over $\{\textcircled{01}, \textcircled{10}\}$. An elegant approach for proving this fact is to verify that the reachable distributions in (†) satisfy the following *distributional invariant*:

$$Pr[\textcircled{01}] \;=\; Pr[\textcircled{10}]\,, \qquad \text{i.e., \emph{the probability of being in} } \textcircled{01} \text{ \emph{is always equal to the probability of being in} } \textcircled{10}. \qquad (\star)$$

Notice that the 2nd and 3rd entries of the vectors in (†) are consistent with ($\star$). As we discuss in detail in Sect. 5, this invariant property restricted to terminal states still holds *in the limit.* Together with the fact that the program terminates *almost surely* (i.e., with probability 1), correctness follows.[2]

Efficient Discrete Uniform Sampling: A "Fast Dice Roller" [27]. Consider the program in Fig. 2 (left) for efficient generation of the discrete uniform distribution from unbiased i.i.d. random bits. The program depends on an integer input parameter $n > 0$ and thus poses all three challenges (C1)–(C3). Regarding (C3), we note that the FDR effectively describes an *infinite family* of finite Markov chains. Importantly, established *probabilistic model checking* techniques (e.g., [6, 21,22]) are not applicable to infinite families—these techniques can only verify the algorithm for finitely many values of n [31].

Lumbroso [27] has already sketched a surprisingly simple distributional invariant for the FDR (Fig. 2, right). In Sect. 6, we provide the remaining formal details and outline a proof of inductivity, establishing functional correctness of the FDR relative to a formal denotational semantics.

Contributions. In summary, this paper makes the following contributions:

Sampler verification: We formally verify two non-trivial sampling algorithms by means of distributional loop invariants: The FDR [27] (Fig. 2, left)

[2] Termination proofs are not in our scope. See, e.g., [28,30].

and a more recent, space-efficient variant for sampling from *arbitrary finite-support distributions*, the Fast *Loaded* Dice Roller (FLDR) [33].

Lifting the distributional paradigm from Markov chains to programs: We show that program-level *distributional loop invariants* coincide, in a precise sense, with a notion introduced in [2] for finite Markov chains (Theorem 2).

Extending the verification framework: We complement existing invariant-based proof rules for loops [7,20] and provide novel verification techniques for reasoning about injective state updates (Sect. 5).

An extended version of this paper containing all omitted proofs is available [8].

2 Preliminaries

$\mathbb{Z}$ is the set of integers, $[0,1] \subseteq \mathbb{R}$ are the *real* probabilities, and $\mathbb{B} = \{\mathsf{tt}, \mathsf{ff}\}$. A *predicate* on a set S is a function $\varphi\colon S \to \mathbb{B}$. We write $s \models \varphi$ iff $\varphi(s) = \mathsf{tt}$, otherwise $s \not\models \varphi$. We occasionally use λ-notation to define (unnamed) functions.

Probabilistic Programs. Throughout the paper we fix a finite set *Var* of (integer) *program variables* ranged over by x, y, etc. For $X \subseteq \mathit{Var}$ we define the (countable) set of *program states* over X as $\Sigma_X := \{\sigma \mid \sigma\colon X \to \mathbb{Z}\}$. We write Σ instead of Σ_{Var}. For $\sigma \in \Sigma$, $x \in \mathit{Var}$, and $c \in \mathbb{Z}$, we define the *updated program state* $\sigma[x/c] := \sigma'$, where $\sigma'(x) = c$ and $\sigma'(y) = \sigma(y)$ for all $y \in \mathit{Var} \setminus \{x\}$. $x_1 \mapsto c_1, \ldots, x_n \mapsto c_n$ denotes a program state in which, for all $i = 1, \ldots, n$, variable x_i has value $c_i \in \mathbb{Z}$, and all $x \notin \{x_1, \ldots, x_n\}$ have value 0.

Definition 1 (Syntax). *A probabilistic program C adheres to the grammar*

$$
\begin{array}{llll}
C & ::= \ \mathtt{skip} & \mid\ x := E & \text{(no-op | assignment)}\\
 & \mid\ \{C\}\,[p]\,\{C\} & \mid\ C\,;C & \text{(coin flip | sequential composition)}\\
 & \mid\ \mathtt{if}\,(\varphi)\,\{C\}\,\mathtt{else}\,\{C\} & \mid\ \mathtt{while}\,(\varphi)\,\{C\}\,, & \text{(conditional choice | loop)}
\end{array}
$$

where $x \in \mathit{Var}$, $p \in [0,1]$, $E\colon \Sigma \to \mathbb{Z}$, and $\varphi\colon \Sigma \to \mathbb{B}$ is a predicate.

We do not fix a concrete syntax for the *expressions* E and for the `if`- and `while`-*guards* φ in our programs. We abbreviate $\mathtt{if}\,(\varphi)\,\{C\}\,\mathtt{else}\,\{\mathtt{skip}\}$ to $\mathtt{if}\,(\varphi)\,\{C\}$. A program C is called *loop-free* if it does not contain `while`, and *deterministic* if it does not contain any coin flip constructs.

Distributions. Let S be a countable set (often Σ in the remainder). A function $\mu\colon S \to [0,1]$ with *mass* $|\mu| := \sum_{a \in S} \mu(a) \leq 1$ is called a *distribution*. We write $\Delta_{\sim\tau} S := \{\mu\colon S \to [0,1] \mid |\mu| \leq 1 \wedge |\mu| \sim \tau\}$ for the set of distributions with mass $\sim \tau$, where $\sim$ is a comparison relation and $\tau \in [0,1]$. For example, $\Delta_{<1} S$ is the set of *sub-distributions* on S. We define the shortcut $\Delta S := \Delta_{=1} S$ for the set of *proper* distributions on S. For $a \in S$, the *Dirac* (sometimes also called *point*) distribution $\delta_a \in \Delta S$ satisfies $\delta_a(a) = 1$. For a distribution $\mu \in \Delta_{\leq 1} S$ and a predicate $\varphi\colon S \to \mathbb{B}$, we define $\Pr_\mu[\varphi] := \sum_{s \models \varphi} \mu(s)$, the probability that φ is satisfied in μ. The *support* of $\mu \in \Delta_{\leq 1} S$ is $\mathrm{supp}(\mu) := \{s \in S \mid \mu(s) > 0\}$.

Program C	Denotational semantics $\mathsf{D}[\![C]\!](\mu)$ $\quad(\mu \in \Delta_{\leq 1}\Sigma)$
`skip`	μ
$x := E$	$\lambda\sigma.\sum_{\sigma'\colon \sigma'[x/E(\sigma')]=\sigma} \mu(\sigma')$
`{`C_1`} [`p`] {`C_2`}`	$\mathsf{D}[\![C_1]\!](p \cdot \mu) + \mathsf{D}[\![C_2]\!]((1-p)\cdot\mu)$
C_1 ; C_2	$\mathsf{D}[\![C_2]\!](\mathsf{D}[\![C_1]\!](\mu))$
`if (`φ`) {`C_1`} else {`C_2`}`	$\mathsf{D}[\![C_1]\!]([\varphi]\cdot\mu) + \mathsf{D}[\![C_2]\!]([\neg\varphi]\cdot\mu)$
`while (`φ`) {`B`}`	$(\mathsf{lfp}\,\Phi)(\mu)$, where $\Phi(f) = \lambda\eta.[\neg\varphi]\cdot\eta + f\big(\mathsf{D}[\![B]\!]([\varphi]\cdot\eta)\big)$

Fig. 3. Denotational semantics. $\mathsf{D}[\![C]\!](\mu)$ is the output distribution of C on input μ.

We endow the set of distributions $\Delta_{\leq 1} S$ with the (pointwise) partial order, i.e., for $\mu_1, \mu_2 \in \Delta_{\leq 1} S$, we write $\mu_1 \leq \mu_2$ iff for all $s \in S$, $\mu_1(s) \leq \mu_2(s)$. Note that every nondecreasing infinite sequence of distributions (ω-chain) has a supremum (least upper bound) in this order.

Addition $\mu_1 + \mu_2$ and multiplication $\mu_1 \cdot \mu_2$ of distributions $\mu_1, \mu_2 \in \Delta_{\leq 1} S$ are both defined componentwise (the result is not necessarily a distribution for $+$). For a predicate $\varphi\colon S \to \mathbb{B}$, the *Iverson bracket* $[\varphi]\colon S \to [0,1]$ casts truth values to numbers, i.e., for all $s \in S$, $[\varphi](s) = 1$ if $s \models \varphi$, and $[\varphi](s) = 0$ if $s \not\models \varphi$. Note that for $\mu \in \Delta_{\leq 1} S$, the product $[\varphi] \cdot \mu \in \Delta_{\leq 1} S$ is a *filtered* distribution which coincides with μ on all $s \models \varphi$, and is zero elsewhere. We also lift this notation to sets of distributions $M \subseteq \Delta_{\leq 1} S$: $[\varphi] \cdot M := \{[\varphi] \cdot \mu \mid \mu \in M\}$. Furthermore, we define $\langle\varphi\rangle := \{\mu \in \Delta_{\leq 1} S \mid \forall s \in \mathrm{supp}(\mu)\colon s \models \varphi\}$, the set of distributions that *only* assign probability mass to elements s with $s \models \varphi$.

The *marginal distribution* $\mathbb{M}_X(\mu) \in \Delta_{\leq 1}\Sigma_X$ of $\mu \in \Delta_{\leq 1}\Sigma$ in $X \subseteq \mathit{Var}$ is

$$\mathbb{M}_X(\mu) \;:=\; \lambda\sigma.\sum_{\tilde{\sigma}|_X = \sigma|_X} \mu(\tilde{\sigma}) \;.$$

We also write $\mathbb{M}_x(\mu)$ if $X = \{x\}$. Marginalization is mass-preserving.

3 Strongest Postconditions and Reachable Distributions

In this section, we first review a standard denotational semantics D for our programming language. We consider D as a *ground truth* relative to which we verify our sampling programs. Afterwards, we define *distributional strongest postconditions* (sp) and the notion of *reachable distributions* during execution of a loop.

Denotational Distribution Transformer Semantics. The denotational semantics we consider views probabilistic programs as transformers of input distributions to output distributions [25]. The definition given here closely follows [20].

Definition 2 (Denotational Semantics). *Let C be a probabilistic program. We define the* denotational semantics $\mathsf{D}[\![C]\!]\colon \Delta_{\leq 1}\Sigma \to \Delta_{\leq 1}\Sigma$ *by induction on the structure of C as in Fig. 3.*

```
// δ_{x↦0,c↦1}                                   (initial distribution μ_0)
while (c = 1) {
    {x := x + 1} [1/2] {c := 0}
} // Σ_{j=0}^{∞} 1/(2^{j+1}) δ_{x↦j,c↦0}   (denotational semantics μ_geo = D[[C_geo]](μ_0))
```

Fig. 4. Program C_{geo} generating a geometric distribution.

The semantics D satisfies the following (see, e.g., [24]): (1) For every program C and input distribution μ we have $|\mu| \geq |\mathsf{D}[\![C]\!](\mu)|$, i.e., programs do not generate probability mass. Further, $|\mu| > |\mathsf{D}[\![C]\!](\mu)|$ is only possible if C contains a loop; the missing probability mass accounts for the probability of non-termination. (2) $\mathsf{D}[\![C]\!]$ is *linear*, i.e., $\mathsf{D}[\![C]\!](\mu_1 + \mu_2) = \mathsf{D}[\![C]\!](\mu_1) + \mathsf{D}[\![C]\!](\mu_2)$, and $\mathsf{D}[\![C]\!](p \cdot \mu) = p \cdot \mathsf{D}[\![C]\!](\mu)$ for $p \in [0,1]$. (3) The least fixed point (lfp) occurring the `while`-case can be determined via fixed point iteration which, intuitively, corresponds to unfolding the loop to ever-increasing depth.

Distributional Strongest Postconditions. When verifying algorithms, we often have to consider an entire *set* of possible initial distributions and characterize the resulting set of output distributions.

Definition 3 (Distributional sp). *The* distributional strongest postcondition *transformer* $\mathsf{sp}[\![C]\!]$ *of probabilistic program C is defined as*

$$\mathsf{sp}[\![C]\!]\colon 2^{\Delta_{\leq 1}\Sigma} \to 2^{\Delta_{\leq 1}\Sigma}\,, \quad \mathsf{sp}[\![C]\!](M) \;:=\; \{\mathsf{D}[\![C]\!](\mu) \mid \mu \in M\}\,.$$

Reachable Distributions. Distributional invariants for probabilistic loops (to be defined in Sect. 4) overapproximate the set of distributions *reachable* during loop execution:

Definition 4 (Reachable Distributions). *Let $C = \texttt{while}\,(\varphi)\,\{B\}$ be a loop and $M \subseteq \Delta_{\leq 1}\Sigma$. The distributions* reachable *in C from M are defined as*

$$\mathsf{reach}[\![C]\!](M) \;:=\; \mathsf{lfp}\,X.\; M \,\cup\, \mathsf{sp}[\![\texttt{if}\,(\varphi)\,\{B\}]\!](X)\,.$$

Intuitively, reach collects all distributions encountered along the way, i.e., those reached from some initial distribution in M after any *finite* number of loop iterations. Unrolling the fixed point yields an equivalent characterization:

Corollary 1 *For every loop* $C = \mathtt{while}\,(\varphi)\,\{B\}$ *and* $M \subseteq \Delta_{\leq 1}\Sigma$ *it holds that*

$$\mathsf{reach}[\![C]\!](M) \quad = \quad \bigcup_{n\in\mathbb{N}} \mathsf{sp}[\![\mathtt{if}\,(\varphi)\,\{B\}]\!]^n(M)\ .$$

Since $\mathsf{sp}[\![C]\!]$ is monotonic with respect to $\subseteq$, so is $\mathsf{reach}[\![C]\!]$, as an immediate consequence of Corollary 1. Perhaps counter-intuitively, the output distribution $\mathsf{D}[\![C]\!](\mu_0)$ of a loop C on input μ_0 is *not* necessarily reachable in the sense of Definition 4:

Example 1 (Reachable Distributions) . Consider the program C_{geo} (Fig. 4) generating the geometric distribution μ_{geo} with parameter $1/2$. We have $\mu_{\text{geo}} \notin \mathsf{reach}[\![C_{\text{geo}}]\!](\{\mu_0\})$ because, intuitively, every reachable distribution assigns a strict positive probability to some program state σ with $\sigma(c) = 1$. More precisely, $\mathsf{reach}[\![C]\!](\{\mu_0\}) = \{\mu_i \mid i \in \mathbb{N}\}$, where $\mu_i(x \mapsto j, c \mapsto 0) = \frac{1}{2^{j+1}}$ for all $0 \leq j < i$ and, crucially, $\mu_i(x \mapsto i, c \mapsto 1) = \frac{1}{2^i}$.

Despite Example 1, the exact output distribution can be recovered from the reachable distributions by means of a supremum:

Theorem 1 (From reach to D). *Let* $C = \mathtt{while}\,(\varphi)\,\{B\}$ *and* $\mu_0 \in \Delta_{\leq 1}\Sigma$. *The distributions in the set* $[\neg\varphi] \cdot \mathsf{reach}[\![C]\!](\{\mu_0\})$ *form a nondecreasing sequence and*

$$\mathsf{D}[\![C]\!](\mu_0) \quad = \quad \sup\,[\neg\varphi] \cdot \mathsf{reach}[\![C]\!](\{\mu_0\})\ .$$

4 Distributional Invariants

While prior work [7,20] studied distributional invariants for probabilistic loops, we were inspired by distributional reasoning in probabilistic finite-state models such as (explicitly represented) Markov chains [2]. In the following, we first review the relevant notions on Markov chains, then define distributional invariants on program level, and then relate both notions.

Definition 5 (Markov Chain). *A* Markov chain *is a tuple* $\mathcal{M} = (S, P)$ *with* countable *state space* S, *and* transition probability[3] function $P\colon S \to \Delta_{\leq 1}S$.

Overloading notation, we view a Markov chain $\mathcal{M}$ as a distribution transformer similarly to the semantics D from Sect. 3; that is, for every distribution $\mu \in \Delta_{\leq 1}S$ we define its *successor distribution* as $\mathcal{M}(\mu) := \sum_{s\in S} \mu(s) \cdot P(s)$.

[3] Notice that $P(s)$ is allowed to be a *sub*-probability distribution. This is necessary for appropriate handling of loops that terminate with probability < 1; see Definition 8.

Definition 6 (Distributional Markov Chain Invariant [2]).[4] *A set* $I \subseteq \Delta_{\leq 1} S$ *is a* distributional invariant *w.r.t.* $\mathcal{M} = (S, P)$ *and* $\mu_0 \in \Delta_{\leq 1} S$ *if* $\mathcal{M}^n(\mu_0) \in I$ *for all* $n \in \mathbb{N}$. *We call* I inductive *(w.r.t.* $\mathcal{M}$*) if* $\forall \mu \in I \colon \mathcal{M}(\mu) \in I$.

Notice that every inductive set I is a distributional invariant w.r.t. every initial distribution $\mu_0 \in I$. Property ($\star$) in Sect. 1 is an informal example of a distributional Markov chain invariant.

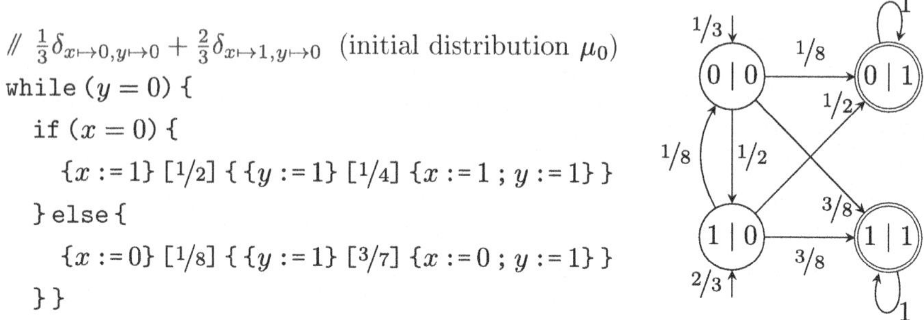

Fig. 5. *Left:* Probabilistic loop with initial distribution. *Right:* Reachable fragment of the loop's big-step operational Markov chain. Terminal states have a double boundary.

Distributional Invariants for Probabilistic Loops. Based on the reach-transformer (Definition 4), we now define distributional invariants for probabilistic loops. Our definition parallels—and is inspired by—the one for Markov chains (Definition 6).

Definition 7 (Distributional Loop Invariant). *Let* $C = \texttt{while}\,(\varphi)\,\{B\}$ *and* $M \subseteq \Delta_{\leq 1}\Sigma$. *A set* $I \subseteq \Delta_{\leq 1}\Sigma$ *such that* $\mathsf{reach}[\![C]\!](M) \subseteq I$ *is called* distributional loop invariant *w.r.t.* C *and* M. *Further,* I *is* inductive *if*

$$\forall \mu \in I \colon \mathsf{D}[\![\texttt{if}\,(\varphi)\,\{B\}]\!](\mu) \in I \quad \text{(i.e., } I \text{ is preserved by one guarded iteration).}$$

From Probabilistic Loops to Markov Chains. We now establish a relationship between distributional invariants in Markov chains (Definition 6) and distributional loop invariants (Definition 7). In a nutshell, loop invariants are invariants in a certain Markov chain defined in the spirit of a big-step operational semantics:

Definition 8 (Operational Markov Chain). *The* operational Markov chain *of a loop* $C = \texttt{while}\,(\varphi)\,\{B\}$ *is* $\mathcal{M}_C = (\Sigma, P)$, *where* $P(\sigma) := \mathsf{D}[\![\texttt{if}\,(\varphi)\,\{B\}]\!](\delta_\sigma)$.

[4] The definition in [2] is phrased for the *induced Markov chain* of a Markov decision process and excludes sub-distributions, i.e., applies only to proper distributions.

Intuitively, the operational Markov chain has a transition from every program state σ satisfying the loop guard to every state reachable from σ in *one guarded loop iteration*. Let us consider a more formal example next.

Example 2 (Invariants in Markov Chains) Figure 5 (right) depicts the fragment of the operational Markov chain of the program in Fig. 5 (left) that is reachable from the initial distribution μ_0. It can be verified that the Markov chain admits the following inductive invariant w.r.t. μ_0:

$$\begin{aligned} I \;:=\; \{\mu \in \Delta\Sigma \mid \mathrm{Pr}_\mu[x=1 \wedge y=0] \;&=\; 2 \cdot \mathrm{Pr}_\mu[x=0 \wedge y=0] \\ \wedge\; \mathrm{Pr}_\mu[x=1 \wedge y=1] \;&=\; \mathrm{Pr}_\mu[x=0 \wedge y=1]\;\} \end{aligned}$$

By Theorem 2 (stated below), I is thus also an inductive invariant for the program C in Fig. 5 (left).

Formally, the correspondence between distributional invariants in loops and Markov chains is as follows:

$$\frac{\{\!|I|\!\}\ \texttt{if}\ (\varphi)\ \{B\}\ \{\!|I|\!\}}{\{\!|I|\!\}\ \texttt{while}\ (\varphi)\ \{B\}\ \{\!|\mathcal{cl}([\neg\varphi]I)|\!\}} \qquad (\textsc{While-P})$$

$$\frac{\{\!|I|\!\}\ \texttt{if}\ (\varphi)\ \{B\}\ \{\!|I|\!\} \qquad C \text{ AST w.r.t. } I \qquad \tau = \inf_{\mu \in I} |\mu|}{\{\!|I|\!\}\ \texttt{while}\ (\varphi)\ \{B\}\ \{\!|\mathcal{cl}([\neg\varphi]I) \cap \Delta_{\geq\tau}\Sigma|\!\}} \qquad (\textsc{While-T})$$

Fig. 6. Proof rules for reasoning about loops.

Theorem 2 *Let* $C = \texttt{while}\,(\varphi)\,\{B\}$ *with operational Markov chain* $\mathcal{M}_C$. *Further, let* $\mu_0 \in \Delta_{\leq 1}\Sigma$ *and* $I \subseteq \Delta_{\leq 1}\Sigma$. *Then:*

I is a distributional invariant for C and $\{\mu_0\}$ (Def. 7)
if and only if *I is a distributional invariant for $\mathcal{M}_C$ and μ_0 (Def. 6).*

Furthermore, I is inductive w.r.t. C iff I is inductive w.r.t. $\mathcal{M}_C$.

Proof (sketch) The key observation is that the stream of distributions $\mathcal{M}_C^n(\mu_0)$, $n \in \mathbb{N}$, resulting from iterating $\mathcal{M}_C$ on μ_0 coincides with $\mathsf{reach}[\![C]\!](\{\mu_0\})$. The proof also exploits linearity of D.

5 Invariant Verification Framework

Proof Rules for Loops. Our framework uses proof rules for reasoning about loops. It is convenient to formulate these rules in Hoare triple notation.

Definition 9 (Hoare Triples [20]). *Let $M, N \subseteq \Delta_{\leq 1}\Sigma$ and C be a program. A* Hoare triple $\{\!|M|\!\}\ C\ \{\!|N|\!\}$ *is* valid *(denoted: $\models \{\!|M|\!\}\ C\ \{\!|N|\!\}$) if $\mathsf{sp}[\![C]\!](M) \subseteq N$.*

We provide one proof rule each for *partial* and *total* correctness in Fig. 6. Note that a program C is *almost surely terminating (AST)* w.r.t. $M \subseteq \Delta_{\leq 1}\Sigma$ if $\forall \mu \in M \colon |\mu| = |\mathsf{D}[\![C]\!](\mu)|$. Furthermore, the *ω-closure* of M is defined as

$$
cl(M) \;:=\; \left\{ \sup_{n\in\mathbb{N}} \mu_n \mid (\mu_n)_{n\in\mathbb{N}} \text{ is an } \omega\text{-chain in } M \right\} .
$$

Our proof rules are inspired by and complement existing Hoare logics [7,20] (see Sect. 8 for further discussion).

Injective Assignments. We now present a simplification technique that can be applied to assignments *injective in x*, i.e., assignments $x := E$ such that for any two program states $\sigma \neq \sigma'$, it holds that $\sigma[x/E(\sigma)] \neq \sigma'[x/E(\sigma')]$. Such assignments induce a *partial inverse* E_x^{-1} (see [8] for details)

Definition 10 (Substitution Operator for Distributions). *Let* $E \colon \Sigma \dashrightarrow \mathbb{Z}$ *be a partial function,* $x \in Var$*, and* $\mu \in \Delta_{\leq 1}\Sigma$*. We define the* substitution

$$
\mu[x/E] \;:=\; \lambda\sigma. \begin{cases} \mu(\sigma[x/E(\sigma)]) & \text{if} E(\sigma) \text{ is defined} \\ 0 & \text{otherwise.} \end{cases}
$$

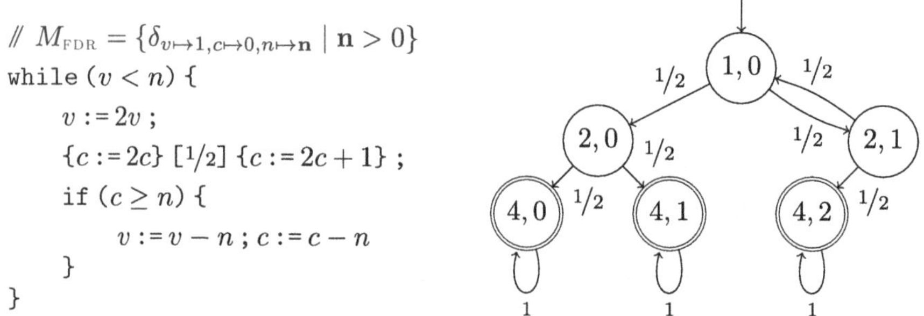

Fig. 7. *Left:* Program C_{FDR}. *Right:* Markov chain $\mathcal{M}_{C_{\text{FDR}}}$ (fragment; $\mathbf{n} = 3$). The state $(4, 3)$ is not reached, as it satisfies $c < n$.

For example, we have $\delta_{x\mapsto 1}[x/x+1] = \delta_{x\mapsto 0}$. Substitution is not mass preserving; e.g., $\delta_{x\mapsto 1}[x/2x] = 0$ because there does not exist $x \in \mathbb{Z}$ such that $2x = 1$.

Lemma 1 (Injective Assignments). *Let* $x := E$ *be an assignment where* E *is injective in* x *with partial inverse* E_x^{-1}*. Then it holds for all* $\mu \in \Delta_{\leq 1}\Sigma$ *that*

$$
\mathsf{D}[\![x := E]\!](\mu) \;=\; \mu[x/E_x^{-1}] .
$$

Unmodified Variables. The following is a useful observation:

Lemma 2 (Unmodified Variables). *Let C be a program with initial distribution $\mu_0 \in \Delta_{\leq 1}\Sigma$ and let $\mu = \mathsf{D}[\![C]\!](\mu_0)$. For all $x \in$ unmod(C) and $z \in \mathbb{Z}$,*

$$\Pr_{\mu}[x = z] \;\leq\; \Pr_{\mu_0}[x = z]\ ,$$

where unmod(C) *is the set of* unmodified variables *in C.*

In Lemma 2, we obtain an inequality due to potential non-termination of C. In the following two sections, we apply the techniques from this section to two non-trivial sampling algorithms.

6 The Fast Dice Roller

The *Fast Dice Roller* (FDR) [27] takes an integer $n > 0$ as input and outputs any integer $c \in \{0, \ldots, n-1\}$ with uniform probability $1/n$. We verify the FDR as stated in Fig. 7 (left), a slight adaptation of the original program [27] to suit our syntax. The FDR solves the uniform sampling problem using an optimal (expected) number of *fair* coin flips [27] (we do not verify optimality here).

The FDR operates on $Var_{\text{FDR}} = \{v, c, n\}$, where *values* are denoted $\mathbf{v}, \mathbf{c}, \mathbf{n} \in \mathbb{Z}$. The variables v and c are initialized with 1 and 0, respectively. The read-only variable $n \in$ unmod(C_{FDR}) is initialized with an arbitrary $\mathbf{n} > 0$. We thus consider the *infinite* set of initial (Dirac) distributions $M_{\text{FDR}} = \{\delta_{v\mapsto 1, c\mapsto 0, n\mapsto \mathbf{n}} \mid \mathbf{n} > 0\}$. As n is not modified, the operational Markov chain $\mathcal{M}_{C_{\text{FDR}}}$ consists of infinitely many disconnected fragments: one fragment for each value $\mathbf{n}$. The

```
// [v < n] · μ
v := 2v ;
// [v/2 < n] · μ[v/(v/2)]
{c := 2c} [1/2] {c := 2c + 1} ;
// 1/2 · [v/2 < n] · (μ[v/(v/2), c/(c/2)] + μ[v/(v/2), c/((c−1)/2)])
if (c ≥ n) {
    // 1/2 · [v/2 < n ∧ c ≥ n] · (μ[v/(v/2), c/(c/2)] + μ[v/(v/2), c/((c−1)/2)])
    v := v − n ;
    // 1/2 · [(v+n)/2 < n ∧ c ≥ n] · (μ[v/((v+n)/2), c/(c/2)] + μ[v/((v+n)/2), c/((c−1)/2)])
    c := c − n
    // 1/2 · [(v+n)/2 < n ∧ c ≥ 0] · (μ[v/((v+n)/2), c/((c+n)/2)] + μ[v/((v+n)/2), c/((c+n−1)/2)])
}
// 1/2 · [(v+n)/2 < n ∧ c ≥ 0] · (μ[v/((v+n)/2), c/((c+n)/2)] + μ[v/((v+n)/2), c/((c+n−1)/2)])
     + 1/2 · [v/2 < n ∧ c < n] · (μ[v/(v/2), c/(c/2)] + μ[v/(v/2), c/((c−1)/2)])
```

Fig. 8. Derivation of $\mathsf{D}[\![B]\!]([v < n]\mu)$, where B is the loop body of the FDR.

fragments reachable from state $n \mapsto \mathbf{n}, v \mapsto 1, c \mapsto 0$ for $\mathbf{n} = 3$, $\mathbf{n} = 5$, and $\mathbf{n} = 9$ are depicted in Fig. 7, Fig. 2, and [8, Appendix], respectively.

For $x \in \mathit{Var}$ and integer $m \geq 0$, let the (discrete) *uniform distribution* on $\{0, \ldots, m\}$ be defined as $\mathsf{unif}_x(0, \ldots, m) := \frac{1}{m+1} \cdot [0 \leq x \leq m]$. Formally, our goal is to prove validity of the Hoare triple $\{\!\!\{M_{\text{FDR}}\}\!\!\}\; C_{\text{FDR}}\; \{\!\!\{N_{\text{FDR}}\}\!\!\}$, where

$$N_{\text{FDR}} := \{\mu \in \Delta\Sigma \mid \exists \mathbf{n} > 0 \colon \Pr_\mu[n = \mathbf{n}] = 1 \wedge \mathbb{M}_c(\mu) = \mathsf{unif}_c(0, \ldots, \mathbf{n} - 1)\} \,.$$

Notice that the marginalization operator $\mathbb{M}_c$ operator (defined on page 5) discards the variables which are irrelevant for stating the correctness of the FDR.

We propose the following distributional loop invariant for C_{FDR} and M_{FDR}:

$$\begin{aligned} I_{\text{FDR}} = \Big\{\mu \in \Delta\Sigma \mid\ & \exists \mathbf{n} > 0 \colon \Pr_\mu[n = \mathbf{n}] = 1 && \text{(a)} \\ & \wedge\ \Pr_\mu[0 < v < 2n - 1] = 1 && \text{(b)} \\ & \wedge\ \Pr_\mu[0 \leq c < \min\{v, n\}] = 1 && \text{(c)} \\ & \wedge\ \forall \sigma, \sigma' \models 0 \leq c < \min\{v, n\} \wedge n = \mathbf{n} \colon \sigma(v) = \sigma'(v) \Longrightarrow \mu(\sigma) = \mu(\sigma')\Big\} && \text{(d)} \end{aligned}$$

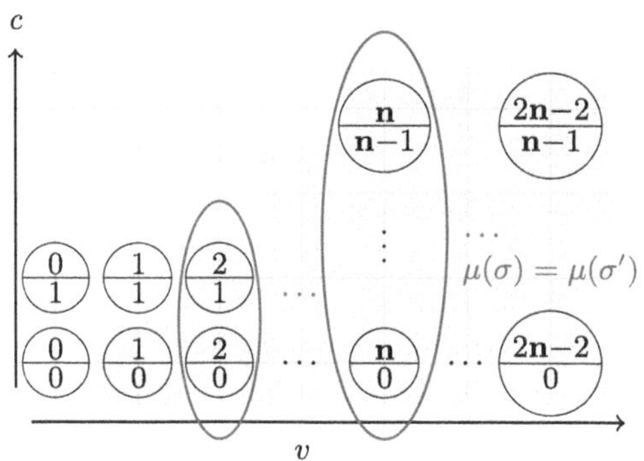

In I_{FDR}, condition (a) fixes $\mathbf{n} \in \mathbb{N}$, allowing us to focus on $(v, c) \in \mathbb{Z}^2$. Conditions (b)–(c) ensure that only finitely many states are reachable. By condition (d), the invariant assigns uniform probabilities per column for $c < \min\{v, n\}$ (red ellipses).

Fig. 9. Illustration of the invariant I_{FDR}.

The set I_{FDR} thus contains all *proper* distributions satisfying conditions (a) through (d); see Fig. 9. Intuitively, (a) ensures that the value of n is fixed in every $\mu \in I_{\text{FDR}}$. Conditions (b) and (c) ensure bounds on v and c, respectively. In fact, (a) through (c) altogether ensure that each $\mu \in I_{\text{FDR}}$ has *finite support* (Fig. 9). Finally, condition (d) formalizes Lumbroso's original correctness argument: "c is uniformly distributed over $\{0, \ldots, v - 1\}$" [27]. In our formulation of the FDR, variable c is at all times uniformly distributed between 0 and the *minimum* of $v - 1$ and $n - 1$. The uniform distribution is established by forcing the probability masses assigned to all the states σ with $\sigma \models 0 \leq c < \min\{v, n\}$ to be equal. The four conditions are illustrated in Fig. 9.

Lemma 3 (FDR Invariant). *I_{FDR} is an inductive distributional invariant for C_{FDR} and the set of initial distributions $M_{\text{FDR}} = \{\delta_{v\mapsto 1, c\mapsto 0, n\mapsto \mathbf{n}} \mid \mathbf{n} > 0\}$.*

Proof (sketch) The proof is split into two parts:

1. *Containment of the initial distributions:* We argue that $M_{\text{FDR}} \subseteq I_{\text{FDR}}$. Let $\mu \in M_{\text{FDR}}$. Since μ is a Dirac distribution, condition (a) is satisfied. Condition (d) is satisfied because, since μ is Dirac, there do not exist $\sigma \neq \sigma' \in \Sigma$ with $\mu(\sigma) > 0$ *and* $\mu(\sigma') > 0$. Conditions (b) and (c) are trivially satisfied.
2. *Inductivity:* We show that for all $\mu \in I_{\text{FDR}}$ it holds that $\mathsf{D}[\![\texttt{if}\,(\varphi)\,\{B\}]\!](\mu) \in I_{\text{FDR}}$ where $\varphi = [v < n]$ and B are the guard and the loop body of the FDR, respectively. We derive the sub-expression $\mathsf{D}[\![B]\!]([\varphi]\mu)$ in Fig. 8 by applying Lemma 1 repeatedly.

Using Lemma 3 and the proof rules WHILE-P and WHILE-T from Sect. 5, we can now derive the following partial and total correctness properties:

Theorem 3 (FDR Correctness). *Program C_{FDR} is partially correct, i.e., for all $\mu_0 \in M_{\text{FDR}}$ and $\mathbf{n} > 0$ such that $\Pr_{\mu_0}[n = \mathbf{n}] = 1$, the final distribution $\mu = \mathsf{D}[\![C_{\text{FDR}}]\!](\mu_0)$ satisfies:*

$$\exists r \in [0,1]: \quad \mathbb{M}_c(\mu) \;=\; r \cdot \mathsf{unif}_c(0, \ldots, \mathbf{n}-1)\ .$$

Moreover, if C_{FDR} is AST w.r.t. I_{FDR}, then program C_{FDR} is totally correct, i.e.,

$$\mathbb{M}_c(\mu) \;=\; \mathsf{unif}_c(0, \ldots, \mathbf{n}-1)\ .$$

```
// Inputs : a_1, ..., a_n
m := Σ_{i=1}^n a_i ; k := ⌈log(m)⌉ ;
a_{n+1} := 2^k − m ;
for j = 0, ..., k do {
  d := 2 · φ_h(j − 1) − 3
  for i = 1, ..., n+1 do {
    bool w := (a_i >> k − j) ;
    h[j] := h[j] + w ;
    if (w) {H[d, j] := i ; d := d − 1}
} }
```

```
// M_FLDR = {δ_{d↦0, c↦0, n↦n} | n > 0}
while ( d < φ_h(c) ) {
  c := c + 1 ;
  {d := 2d} [1/2] {d := 2d + 1} ;
  if ( H[d, c] = n + 1 ) {
    // reject and start over
    c := 0 ;
    d := 0
  }
}
```

Fig. 10. *Left:* Preprocessing for the FLDR. *Right:* The FLDR program C_{FLDR}. The output is given by the value of $H[d,c]$ upon program termination.

Notice that the partial correctness statement in Theorem 3 ensures equal probabilities for each final value of $0 \leq c < n$, but does not imply anything about the termination probability. We can prove that C_{FDR} is AST using existing techniques [28,30] (see [8, Appendix]). This establishes total correctness of the FDR.

7 The Fast Loaded Dice Roller

The *Fast Loaded Dice Roller* (FLDR) [33] samples a random integer from a given discrete probability distribution with finite support. Specifically, given positive integers $a_1, \dots, a_n$ as input, the algorithm outputs $i \in \{1, \dots, n\}$ with probability $\frac{a_i}{m}$, where $m := \sum_{i=1}^{n} a_i$. We use the tuple notation $(\frac{a_1}{m}, \dots, \frac{a_n}{m})$ for the resulting output distribution.

Like the FDR from Sect. 6, the FLDR relies on fair coin flips only. The high-level idea is to perform rejection sampling from the proposal distribution $(\frac{a_1}{2^k}, \dots, \frac{a_n}{2^k}, 1 - \frac{m}{2^k})$, where $k = \lceil \log_2 m \rceil$. Because the denominators are powers of 2, this distribution can be sampled efficiently using only unbiased random bits. While the FLDR does not achieve optimal runtime in terms of the number of coin flips, it can be implemented in a memory-efficient manner [33].

First, a preprocessing (Fig. 10, left) prepares suitable data structures: an array h and a matrix H (illustrated in Fig. 11). Then, the main program C_{FLDR} (Fig. 10, right) is executed. This program is a slight variant of the original FLDR from [33]: It is written in our syntax and contains less branches in the loop body. The short-hand notation $\phi_h(c) := 2^c - \sum_{j=0}^{c} h[j] \cdot 2^{c-j}$ denotes the first position in row c of matrix H that contains a number other than 0. Next, we provide an intuition for the data structures h and H, which encode a certain *binary tree.*

The Binary Tree Underlying a Distribution. Given a distribution $(p_1, \dots, p_n)$ with $n \geq 1$, its *underlying binary tree* is constructed as follows: For each i, a leaf labelled i appears in row $c \geq 0$ if and only if the binary expansion of p_i has a 1 at position c (e.g., the binary representation of $\frac{3}{8}$ is 0.011, which has 1s at positions 2 and 3). Within each row, the leaves are ordered by their labels in descending order, which uniquely determines the structure of the binary tree.

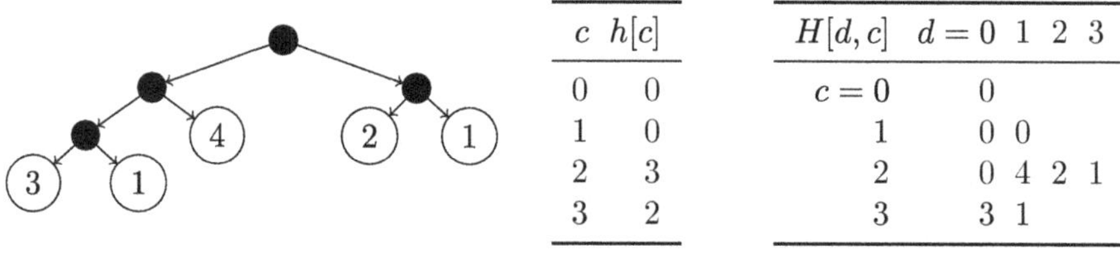

c	$h[c]$
0	0
1	0
2	3
3	2

$H[d,c]$	$d = 0$	1	2	3
$c = 0$	0			
1	0	0		
2	0	4	2	1
3	3	1		

Fig. 11. *Left:* Binary tree underlying the proposal distribution $(\frac{3}{8}, \frac{2}{8}, \frac{1}{8}, \frac{2}{8})$, which is $(0.011, 0.01, 0.001, 0.01)$ in binary. *Right:* Data structures h and H storing the binary tree. h determines the number of leaves in each row and H stores the leaf labels.

The FLDR preprocessing effectively determines the binary tree underlying its proposal distribution $(\frac{a_1}{2^k}, \dots, \frac{a_n}{2^k}, 1 - \frac{m}{2^k})$. The tree is stored in the data structures h and H in the following manner: $h[c]$ is the number of leaves in row c of the tree, and we have $H[d, c] = j$ if in the c-th row, the d-th node is labelled by j; otherwise, $H[d, c] = 0$.

Example 3 Consider the input $(a_1, a_2, a_3) = (3, 2, 1)$. The target output distribution is thus $(\frac{3}{6}, \frac{2}{6}, \frac{1}{6})$, and we have $m = 3 + 2 + 1 = 6$ and $k = \lceil \log_2 m \rceil = 3$. Since $2^k = 8$, the proposal distribution is $(\frac{3}{8}, \frac{2}{8}, \frac{1}{8}, \frac{2}{8})$ with binary encoding $(0.011, 0.01, 0.001, 0.01)$. Figure 11 shows the resulting binary tree for the proposal distribution as well as the data structures h and H.

Since h, H, k, and m remain fixed (unmodified) after the preprocessing, we formally consider the program C_{FLDR} to operate on $Var_{\text{FLDR}} = \{c, d, n\}$. The set of initial distributions is $M_{\text{FLDR}} = \{\delta_{d \mapsto 0, c \mapsto 0, n \mapsto \mathbf{n}} \mid \mathbf{n} > 0\}$.

A Distributional Invariant for the FLDR. We first define the following auxiliary notation: $\Theta_{n,h,H}(c) := [H[\phi_h(c), c] = n + 1]$ is a Boolean (0 or 1) indicating if row c contains a leaf labeled $n + 1$. The probability to draw $i \in \{1, \ldots, n\}$ with zero rejections is

$$\text{prob}_H(i) := \sum_{d,c\,:\,H[d,c]=i} 2^{-c}$$

and with any number of rejections, the probability is

$$\text{probt}_{n,H}(i) := \frac{\text{prob}_H(i)}{1 - \text{prob}_H(n+1)}.$$

Similarly, the probability to draw i without rejections starting at level j of the tree is

$$\text{prob}_H(i, j) := \sum_{d,c\,:\,H[d,c]=i,\ c>j} 2^{-(c-j)}$$

and $\text{probt}_{n,H}(i, j) := \text{prob}_H(i, j) + \text{prob}_H(n+1, j) \cdot \text{probt}_{n,H}(i)$ with rejections. Also recall that k has been defined above as $k = \lceil \log_2 m \rceil$. We propose the following distributional invariant I_{FLDR} for the FLDR:

$$I_{\text{FLDR}} := \Big\{\mu \in \Delta\Sigma \mid \exists \mathbf{n} > 0\colon \big(\Pr_\mu[n = \mathbf{n}] = 1 \qquad \text{(a)}$$

$$\wedge\ \Pr_\mu[0 \le d \le \mathbf{n}] = 1 \qquad \text{(b)}$$

$$\wedge\ \Pr_\mu[0 \le c \le k] = 1 \qquad \text{(c)}$$

$$\wedge\ \forall i \in \{1, \ldots, \mathbf{n}\}\colon$$

$$\sum_{\sigma\,:\,H[\sigma(d), \sigma(c)]=i} \Big(\mu(\sigma) + \textstyle\sum_{j=0}^{k-1} \mu(\sigma[d/0, c/j]) \cdot \text{probt}_{\mathbf{n},H}(i, j)\Big) \le \text{probt}_{\mathbf{n},H}(i) \qquad \text{(d)}$$

$$\wedge\ \forall \sigma, \sigma' \models (n = \mathbf{n} \wedge 0 \le d < \phi_h(c))\colon$$
$$\sigma(c) = \sigma'(c) \implies \mu(\sigma) = \mu(\sigma') \qquad \text{(e)}$$

$$\wedge\ \forall \sigma, \sigma' \models (n = \mathbf{n} \wedge \phi_h(c) + \Theta_{\mathbf{n},h,H}(c) \le d < \phi_h(c) + h[c])\colon$$
$$\sigma(c) = \sigma'(c) \implies \mu(\sigma) = \mu(\sigma') \qquad \big)\Big\} \qquad \text{(f)}$$

To provide some intuition for the invariant I_{FLDR}, let us briefly explain the role of each condition. As in the FDR invariant from Sect. 6, conditions (a)–(c) ensure that $\mathbf{n}$ is fixed, and that the variables c and d remain within the valid bounds determined by the number of rows and the width of the binary tree, respectively. Conditions (e) and (f) enforce uniformity of probabilities among program states that correspond to nodes in the same row of the binary tree: specifically, (e) ensures uniform probabilities for all internal nodes within a row, while (f) does the same for output nodes, except for those labelled with the rejection value $n+1$ (which always have probability 0 since the algorithm restarts upon reaching them). Condition (d) is unique to the FLDR invariant and is essential for inductiveness: it guarantees that, for each possible output $1 \leq i \leq n$, the total probability mass assigned to output nodes labelled i–both now and in all future loop iterations–never exceeds the desired output probability. See [8, Appendix] for further details.

Using our invariant, we obtain the following partial and total correctness results for the FLDR:

Theorem 4 (FLDR Correctness) . *Program C_{FLDR} is partially correct, i.e., for all $\mu_0 \in M_{\text{FLDR}}$ and $\mathbf{n} \in \mathbb{N}_{>0}$ with $\Pr_{\mu_0}[n = \mathbf{n}] = 1$, the output distribution $\mu = \mathsf{D}[\![C_{\text{FLDR}}]\!](\mu_0)$ satisfies:*

$$\forall 1 \leq i \leq \mathbf{n}\colon \quad \sum_{\sigma\colon H[\sigma(d),\sigma(c)]=i} \mu(\sigma) \;\leq\; \frac{a_i}{m}\,.$$

If C_{FLDR} is AST w.r.t. I_{FLDR}, then program C_{FLDR} is totally correct, i.e.,

$$\forall 1 \leq i \leq \mathbf{n}\colon \quad \sum_{\sigma\colon H[\sigma(d),\sigma(c)]=i} \mu(\sigma) \;=\; \frac{a_i}{m}\,.$$

As for the FDR, we have a proof that our FLDR encoding C_{FLDR} is in fact AST, using methods from [28,30] (see [8, Appendix]).

8 Related Work

This paper was inspired by recent work viewing explicit finite-state Markov models as distribution transformers [1–4]. The main difference to these works is that the programs we study naturally induce *infinite* Markov chains or *infinite families*. We also focus on *limiting* distributions rather than safety properties of the reachable distributions.

Hoare rules for loops based on distributional invariants have been studied in [7,20]. A technical difference to our rules (Fig. 6) is that we apply a closure operation to the *postcondition* rather than requiring the *invariant* to be already closed. We thus impose fewer constraints on the invariant. While this does not play a major role in our case studies, it could be beneficial in other examples. Similar proof rules with an extension to nondeterminism are provided by Zilberstein et al. [37,38]. Their (demonic) *outcome logic* enables reasoning about *sets* of inputs and outcomes of a program similar to our sp-transformer.

Several other theoretical frameworks exist that are—at least in principle—applicable to random sampler verification (i.e., they address challenges (C1)–(C3) from Page 2). A prominent example is the *weakest pre-expectation* (wp) calculus [23,26,29], a generalization of Dijkstra's classic weakest pre*condition* calculus [15,16]. Using wp, the correctness of e.g., a uniform sampling program C is expressed as $\mathsf{wp}[\![C]\!]([res = i]) = \frac{1}{n} \cdot [0 \leq i < n]$, where res stores the result and i does not occur in C. However, proving this equality requires guessing and verifying an *exact* least fixed point, which is notoriously difficult. To our knowledge, no published wp-based proof exists for either of our two case studies. A program analysis using *probability generating functions* was proposed in [24], but *comparisons* between program variables (e.g., $v < n$) were identified as a fundamental obstacle [12]. Recently, Haase et al. [19] provided a novel correctness proof for the FDR program from Sect. 6. Their proof uses a so-called *occupation invariant*—an approach orthogonal to our distributional invariants—which requires reasoning about the expected number of visits to each program state. The resulting invariant is arguably more complex and less intuitive than the distributional invariant we employ. Bagnall et al. [5] describe Zar, a tool that automatically generates formally verified executable samplers from high-level probabilistic program specifications. A *type system* for verifying sampling algorithms built from pre-defined deterministic samplers based on infinite streams was proposed in [14]. It appears promising to investigate whether the FDR could be verified assuming a pre-defined sampler for fair coin flips, though this would likely require extending their type system with unbounded iteration.

The related problem of inferring the *posterior distribution* of probabilistic programs with *conditioning* has also been studied extensively. The tool PSI [17] computes exact expressions for density functions but does not support unbounded while-loops [17, Sec. 3.6], which are required by the F(L)DR algorithms. Other approaches [9,36] support such loops, but provide only *approximations*.

Additional related work includes *testing* random samplers with statistical guarantees [10] and *equivalence refutation* for probabilistic programs, which can prove *incorrectness*, i.e., the presence of a bug in a given sampling algorithm [11]. Meel et al. [34] assess the quality of binomial samplers and verify the program code directly using a statistical distance framework.

9 Conclusion and Future Work

This paper provided formal correctness proofs for two efficient, non-trivial sampler algorithms: the FDR and the FLDR, which are key to a broad range of applications. We presented a framework to verify quantitative properties of probabilistic programs by viewing programs as distribution transformers.

For future work, we plan to investigate assertion languages for distributions, which would make reasoning with distributional invariants more syntactic and thus more amenable to automation. A particularly promising direction is to leverage the assertion language provided by Barthe et al. [7], who also provide a weakest precondition-style approach for reasoning about reachable distributions. Another opportunity for future work is to extend our verification framework toward probabilistic programs with non-determinism [29]—this appears feasible since the current approach already deals with sets of distributions.

Acknowledgments. The authors acknowledge support from the DFG RTG 2236 (UnRAVeL) and the European Union's Horizon 2020 research and innovation program under the Marie Skłodowska-Curie grant agreement No. 101008233 (MISSION).

Disclosure of Interests. The authors have no competing interests to declare that are relevant to the content of this article.

References

1. Aghamov, R., et al.: Model checking Markov Chains as distribution transformers. In: Principles of Verification (2). Lecture Notes in Computer Science, vol. 15261, pp. 293–313. Springer (2024)
2. Akshay, S., Chatterjee, K., Meggendorfer, T., Zikelic, D.: MDPs as Distribution Transformers: Affine Invariant Synthesis for Safety Objectives. In: Computer Aided Verification, Proceedings, Part III. Lecture Notes in Computer Science, vol. 13966, pp. 86–112. Springer (2023). https://doi.org/10.1007/978-3-031-37709-9_5,
3. Akshay, S., Chatterjee, K., Meggendorfer, T., Zikelic, D.: Certified policy verification and synthesis for MDPS under distributional reach-avoidance properties. In: IJCAI, pp. 3–12. ijcai.org (2024)
4. Akshay, S., Genest, B., Vyas, N.: Distribution-based objectives for Markov Decision Processes. In: LICS, pp. 36–45. ACM (2018)
5. Bagnall, A., Stewart, G., Banerjee, A.: Formally verified samplers from probabilistic programs with loops and conditioning. Proc. ACM Program. Lang. **7**(PLDI), 1–24 (2023). https://doi.org/10.1145/3591220,
6. Baier, C., Katoen, J.: Principles of model checking. MIT Press (2008)
7. Barthe, G., Espitau, T., Gaboardi, M., Grégoire, B., Hsu, J., Strub, P.: An assertion-based program logic for probabilistic programs. In: Programming Languages and Systems. Lecture Notes in Computer Science, vol. 10801, pp. 117–144. Springer (2018). https://doi.org/10.1007/978-3-319-89884-1_5,
8. Batz, K., Katoen, J., Winkler, T., Zilken, D.: Verifying sampling algorithms via distributional invariants. CoRR **abs/2509.06410** (2025). https://doi.org/10.48550/ARXIV.2509.06410,
9. Beutner, R., Ong, C.L., Zaiser, F.: Guaranteed bounds for posterior inference in universal probabilistic programming. In: PLDI, pp. 536–551 (2022). ACM (2022). https://doi.org/10.1145/3519939.3523721,
10. Chakraborty, S., Meel, K.S.: On testing of uniform samplers, pp. 7777–7784. AAAI Press (2019). https://doi.org/10.1609/AAAI.V33I01.33017777
11. Chatterjee, K., Goharshady, E.K., Novotný, P., Zikelic, D.: Equivalence and similarity refutation for probabilistic programs. Proc. ACM Program. Lang. **8**(PLDI), 2098–2122 (2024). https://doi.org/10.1145/3656462,
12. Chen, M., Katoen, J., Klinkenberg, L., Winkler, T.: Does a program yield the right distribution? - verifying probabilistic programs via generating functions. In: CAV (1). Lecture Notes in Computer Science, vol. 13371, pp. 79–101. Springer (2022)

13. Cranmer, K., Brehmer, J., Louppe, G.: The frontier of simulation-based inference. Proc. Natl. Acad. Sci. **117**(48), 30055–30062 (2020). https://doi.org/10.1073/pnas.1912789117
14. Dahlqvist, F., Silva, A., Smith, W.: Deterministic stream-sampling for probabilistic programming: semantics and verification. In: LICS, pp. 1–13. IEEE (2023)
15. Dijkstra, E.W.: Guarded commands, nondeterminacy and formal derivation of programs. Commun. ACM **18**(8), 453–457 (1975). https://doi.org/10.1145/360933.360975
16. Dijkstra, E.W.: A Discipline of Programming. Prentice-Hall (1976)
17. Gehr, T., Misailovic, S., Vechev, M.T.: PSI: exact symbolic inference for probabilistic programs. In: CAV (1). Lecture Notes in Computer Science, vol. 9779, pp. 62–83. Springer (2016). https://doi.org/10.1007/978-3-319-41528-4_4
18. Goodfellow, I., Bengio, Y., Courville, A.: Deep Learning. MIT Press (2016)
19. Haase, D., et al.: Generating functions meet occupation measures: Invariant synthesis for probabilistic loops (extended version) (2026). https://arxiv.org/abs/2601.13991, to appear at ESOP 2026
20. den Hartog, J., de Vink, E.P.: Verifying probabilistic programs using a hoare like logic. Int. J. Found. Comput. Sci. **13**(3), 315–340 (2002). https://doi.org/10.1142/S012905410200114X
21. Hensel, C., Junges, S., Katoen, J., Quatmann, T., Volk, M.: The probabilistic model checker storm. Int. J. Softw. Tools Technol. Transf. **24**(4), 589–610 (2022)
22. Junges, S., Katoen, J., Pérez, G.A., Winkler, T.: The complexity of reachability in parametric Markov decision processes. J. Comput. Syst. Sci. **119**, 183–210 (2021)
23. Kaminski, B.L.: Advanced weakest precondition calculi for probabilistic programs. Ph.D. thesis, RWTH Aachen University, Germany (2019). http://publications.rwth-aachen.de/record/755408
24. Klinkenberg, L., Batz, K., Kaminski, B.L., Katoen, J., Moerman, J., Winkler, T.: Generating functions for probabilistic programs. In: Logic-Based Program Synthesis and Transformation. Lecture Notes in Computer Science, vol. 12561, pp. 231–248. Springer (2020). https://doi.org/10.1007/978-3-030-68446-4_12,
25. Kozen, D.: Semantics of probabilistic programs. In: 20th Annual Symposium on Foundations of Computer Science, pp. 101–114. IEEE Computer Society (1979). https://doi.org/10.1109/SFCS.1979.38,
26. Kozen, D.: A probabilistic PDL. In: Proceedings of the 15th Annual ACM Symposium on Theory of Computing, pp. 291–297. ACM (1983). https://doi.org/10.1145/800061.808758
27. Lumbroso, J.O.: Optimal discrete uniform generation from coin flips, and applications. CoRR arXiv:abs/1304.1916 (2013)
28. Majumdar, R., Sathiyanarayana, V.R.: Sound and complete proof rules for probabilistic termination. Proc. ACM Program. Lang. **9**(POPL), 1871–1902 (2025)
29. McIver, A., Morgan, C.: Abstraction, Refinement and Proof for Probabilistic Systems. Monographs in Computer Science, Springer (2005).https://doi.org/10.1007/B138392
30. McIver, A., Morgan, C., Kaminski, B.L., Katoen, J.P.: A new proof rule for almost-sure termination. Proc. ACM Program. Lang. **2**(POPL) (Dec 2017). https://doi.org/10.1145/3158121
31. Mertens, H., Katoen, J., Quatmann, T., Winkler, T.: Computing expected visiting times and stationary distributions in Markov chains: fast and accurate. J. Autom. Reason. **69**(3), 23 (2025). https://doi.org/10.1007/S10817-025-09736-7
32. Pugh, W.W.: Skip lists: a probabilistic alternative to balanced trees. Commun. ACM **33**(6), 668–676 (1990). https://doi.org/10.1145/78973.78977

33. Saad, F., Freer, C.E., Rinard, M.C., Mansinghka, V.: The fast loaded dice roller: a near-optimal exact sampler for discrete probability distributions. In: The 23rd International Conference on Artificial Intelligence and Statistics, AISTATS 2020. Proceedings of Machine Learning Research, vol. 108, pp. 1036–1046. PMLR (2020). http://proceedings.mlr.press/v108/saad20a.html
34. Sarkar, U., Chakraborty, S., Meel, K.S.: Assessing the quality of binomial samplers: A statistical distance framework. In: Piskac, R., Rakamaric, Z. (eds.) Computer Aided Verification - 37th International Conference, CAV 2025, Zagreb, Croatia, July 23-25, 2025, Proceedings, Part II. Lecture Notes in Computer Science, vol. 15932, pp. 231–253. Springer (2025). https://doi.org/10.1007/978-3-031-98679-6_11,
35. Von Neumann, J.: Various techniques used in connection with random digits. Appl. Math Ser **12**(36–38), 5 (1951)
36. Wang, P., Yang, T., Fu, H., Li, G., Ong, C.H.L.: Static posterior inference of bayesian probabilistic programming via polynomial solving. Proc. ACM Programm. Lang. **8**(PLDI), 1361–1386 (2024). https://doi.org/10.1145/3656432
37. Zilberstein, N.: Outcome logic: A unified approach to the metatheory of program logics with branching effects. ACM Trans. Program. Lang. Syst. **47**(3) (Sept 2025). https://doi.org/10.1145/3743131,
38. Zilberstein, N., Kozen, D., Silva, A., Tassarotti, J.: A demonic outcome logic for randomized nondeterminism. Proc. ACM Programm. Lang. **9**(POPL), 539–568 (Jan 2025). https://doi.org/10.1145/3704855

Validating Formal Specifications with LLM-Generated Test Cases

Alcino Cunha and Nuno Macedo(✉)

INESC TEC and Universidade do Minho, Braga, Portugal
{alcino,nmacedo}@di.uminho.pt

Abstract. Validation is a central activity when developing formal specifications. Similarly to coding, a possible validation technique is to define upfront test cases or scenarios that a future specification should satisfy or not. Unfortunately, specifying such test cases is burdensome and error prone, which could cause users to skip this validation task. This paper reports the results of an empirical evaluation of using pre-trained large language models (LLMs) to automate the generation of test cases from natural language requirements. In particular, we focus on test cases for structural requirements of simple domain models formalized in the Alloy specification language. Our evaluation focuses on the state-of-the-art GPT-5 model, but results from other closed- and open-source LLMs are also reported. The results show that, in this context, GPT-5 is already quite effective at generating positive (and negative) test cases that are syntactically correct and that satisfy (or not) the given requirement, and that can detect many wrong specifications written by humans.

Keywords: Domain models · Formal specification · Validation · Test cases · Alloy · Large language models

1 Introduction

Formal methods practitioners mainly focus on verification ("did we build the software right?"), and tend to neglect the equally important validation ("did we build the right software?"). Validation aims to ensure that formal specifications are an accurate representation of the system and its requirements. Sitting at the border between the formal and the informal, and requiring the judgment of human stakeholders, validation cannot be fully automated and thus several, often complementary, techniques can be adopted. Simulation is popular in the validation of formal models of behavior, such as state machines, and is available in most model-checkers. Non-essential, even trivial, assertions can be verified to make sure the model is free of specific bugs ("check everything you can" [9]). Inspired by test-driven development for coding, *test-driven modeling* [26] can be adopted, where test cases and scenarios are defined before the formal specifications and later used to validate them. Some advocate that *validation obligations* [14] should be systematically incorporated in the development process, to be discharged as the specification evolves, likewise *proof obligations* for verification.

A. Sampaio and M. Stoelinga (Eds.): FM 2026, LNCS 16556, pp. 279–297, 2026.
https://doi.org/10.1007/978-3-032-26204-2_15

This paper focuses on the use of test cases for the validation of formal specifications of structural (non-behavioral) requirements of domain models. It focuses on the Alloy [6,7] specification language, since it is particularly well suited for *i*) the formalization of domain models due to its "everything is a relation" design principle; and *ii*) the employment of a test-driven approach. Alloy allows the automatic generation of examples satisfying (or not) a given formal specification, and their graphical depiction with user-customizable themes. This provides good support for validation, as examples can be shown to domain experts to help detect specification errors or clarify ambiguous requirements. However, this approach is not suitable for the iterative development of specifications, as it requires constant human intervention. In those contexts, it is preferable to adopt a test-driven modeling approach, where suites of executable (positive and negative) test cases are defined upfront with the help of domain experts, which can then be automatically run to validate specifications as they evolve. Alloy can support this methodology, since models can contain test cases as executable analysis commands. In fact, previous work has leveraged Alloy test cases for various tasks, such as AUnit [18], a test automation tool that provides coverage criteria, and can also generate tests suites or perform mutation testing [19], or ARepair [21], an automatic specification repair technique that uses test cases as oracle.

```
open util/ordering[Grade]
sig Person {
  teaches : set Course,
  enrolled : set Course,
  projects : set Project
}
sig Professor, Student in Person {}
sig Course {
  projects : set Project,
  grades : Person → Grade
}
sig Project {}
sig Grade {}

fact Enrollment {
  // Only students can be enrolled in courses

}
```

Fig. 1. Courses domain model in Alloy.

However, it is difficult to devise a good test suite with sufficiently diverse test cases, and despite the Alloy support for their specification and execution, it is still rather laborious and error-prone to encode them. Existing techniques for automatic test case generation (e.g., [19]), target the debugging phase and already require a (buggy) formal specification. These do not apply to our test-driven approach, where test cases are specified in early development phases from the natural language requirements. LLMs have been used successfully to generate unit tests for programs, as shown by various evaluation studies (e.g., [17,23]). Those experiments and their results do not directly transfer to our setting, where the input is a natural language requirement (instead of method implementations) and the quality of the generated test suite cannot be measured by code coverage. In this context, we devised a study to empirically evaluate whether LLMs could also be used to successfully generate test cases to validate formal specifications. Thus, our main contributions are:

- The design of the first study to evaluate the effectiveness of LLMs in generating test suites for the validation of formal specifications of structural requirements in domain modeling. It targets Alloy and GPT-5, a state-of-the-art LLM, using a public benchmark for domain models specified in Alloy.
- The execution of the study and an evaluation of the results under different aspects, namely: what is the influence of prompt design? what is the effect of non-determinism? how do competing LLMs perform? what characterizes invalid test cases? how diverse are the test suites?
- A summary of the major findings and implications for future research.

The scripts, raw data, and analysis results of our study are publicly available in the GitHub repository at https://github.com/haslab/Alloy-LLM-Testing.

2 Test-Driven Modeling with Alloy

Alloy [6,7] is a formal specification language initially focused on the design and specification of software structures[1]. In Alloy "everything is a relation", meaning all concepts in a domain are modeled with (mathematical) relations, sets of tuples of a given arity. Relations of arity 1 represent sets of elements and relations of higher arity represent associations between those elements. Declared sets are known as *signatures* (keyword **`sig`**). Top-level signatures partition the universe of discourse into disjoint types, but it is also possible to declare arbitrary or disjoint sub-set signatures (keywords **`in`** or **`extends`**, respectively). A signature can also be marked as **`abstract`**, forcing it to only contain elements that are contained in its extensions. Figure 1 presents the Alloy encoding of a domain model for a course management system, one of the examples used in our evaluation. In this model we have four top-level signatures (`Person`, `Course`, `Project`, and `Grade`), encoding the key concepts in the domain, and two sub-set signatures of `Person`, `Professor` and `Student`. These two signatures are arbitrary sub-sets because each person can simultaneously be a professor and a student (or neither). The automatic analysis of Alloy models (namely, checking assertions) is done via a bounded model finding procedure, so in analysis commands all top-level signatures have a *scope* that sets the maximum number of elements they can contain.

[1] Alloy 6 also allows the declarative specification of behavioral requirements using temporal logic [10]. However, our experiment focuses on structural assumptions, so the presentation is restricted to a subset of the language compatible with Alloy 5.

Fields are relations of arity higher than 1 declared inside a signature. Our example has five fields: `teaches`, `enrolled`, and `projects` associate each person with, respectively, the courses it teaches, the courses where it is enrolled, and the projects it is working on; (a different) `projects` and `grades` associate each course with, respectively, the projects proposed by it and the grades obtained by each person in it. Alloy supports overloading (there are two fields named `projects`) and fields of arity higher than 2 (`grades` is a ternary relation). Alloy has a module system, and the most frequently used among the pre-defined modules is `util/ordering`, a parametrized module that imposes a total order on a given signature. In particular, it declares a binary relation `next` that for each element gives the next element in the total order. The example uses it on signature `Grade`, so that grades can be compared to determine which one is higher. Relation `next` is also overloaded, since several total orders can co-exist in a model.

After declaring the relations that capture the entities and associations of a domain model, we proceed to specify additional requirements on those structures. Typically, these are elicited with domain experts using natural language prior to formalization. In Alloy, assumptions about the domain are specified inside **fact**s using relational logic, an extension of first-order logic with relational operators (such as dot-join composition or transitive closure), allowing a rather concise specification style. Additionally, **pred**icates and **fun**ctions can be declared for auxiliary formulas and expressions, respectively. Our example has one (empty) **fact** declared, `Enrollment`, annotated with a natural language assumption.

Besides analysis commands to check assertions, Alloy also supports so-called **run** commands, that can be used to search for model instances. This enables test-driven modeling in Alloy, since such commands allow for the specification of test cases to be used for validation. Figure 2 presents two such test cases, one positive that satisfies the assumption, and one negative, that does not satisfy it. It is important to specify both positive and negative test cases: the former allows the detection of over-specifications (if too restrictive, valid instances may be excluded), and the latter under-specifications (if too permissive, invalid instances may be accepted). Each **run** command encodes a specific test case, in the sense that it is a complete valuation of the declared signatures and fields, denoting one concrete instance of the model. They can be specified in relational logic using the well-known **some disj** pattern [4], where an outermost existential quantifier with the **disj** keyword denotes the different elements of each signature, followed by a formula that specifies the value of each signature and field using equality constraints. On the right-hand-side of each equality we have an expression that denotes a set of tuples, specified as a union (`+`) of singleton tuples, each specified with the cross product operator ($\rightarrow$). An empty signature is equal to **none** (a constant denoting an empty set of arity 1), and an empty field equal to an appropriate cross-product of **none** (although still denoting an empty set, to avoid an arity type error both sides of the equality must have the same arity). To disambiguate overloaded fields, the domain restriction operator (`<:`) is used. A **run** command should also specify the scope for each top-level signature after the **for** keyword, and the expectation about its satisfiability: for a positive test

```
run Positive {
// Only enrolled person is a Student
  some disj P1 : Person, disj C1 : Course, disj G1,G2 : Grade {
    Person = P1
    Professor = none
    Student = P1
    Course = C1
    Project = none
    Grade = G1 + G2
    teaches = none→none
    enrolled = P1→C1
    Person <: projects = none→none
    Course <: projects = none→none
    grades = none→none→none
    Grade <: next = G1→G2
  }
} for 1 Person, 1 Course, 0 Project, 2 Grade expect 1

run Negative {
// A professor (not a student) is enrolled in multiple courses
  some disj P1,S1 : Person, disj C1,C2 : Course, disj G1,G2 : Grade {
    Person = P1 + S1
    Professor = P1
    Student = S1
    Course = C1 + C2
    Project = none
    Grade = G1 + G2
    teaches = none→none
    enrolled = P1→C1 + P1→C2 + S1→C1
    Person <: projects = none→none
    Course <: projects = none→none
    grades = C1→S1→G1
    Grade <: next = G1→G2
  }
} for 2 Person, 2 Course, 0 Project, 2 Grade expect 0
```

Fig. 2. Example test cases for "Only students can be enrolled in courses".

case we should use **expect** 1 (it should yield an instance, i.e., be satisfiable); in negative test cases, **expect** 0 should be used.

Following a test-driven modeling approach, after specifying test cases we proceed to the formalization of the assumption in **fact** Enrollment. Let us suppose a (wrong) attempt at specifying the assumption was the following. The dot-join operator (.) is used to determine the set of courses where p is enrolled in.

```
all p : Person | p in Student implies some p.enrolled
```

The Alloy Analyzer has an option to run all analysis commands in sequence, reporting a summary of the respective results at the end. Running our two test cases would immediately report that our negative test case did not fail, contrary to expectation. The reason is that this specification still allows professors that are not students to also be enrolled in courses. If we change the specification to a correct one, for example by swapping both sides of the **implies**, both test cases would have the expected outcome. However, the following wrong specification would still pass the two test cases.

```
all p: Professor | no p.enrolled
```

This is the most common wrong specification written by our students for this requirement, because some incorrectly assume that professors cannot be simultaneously students. A test suite with diverse test cases is essential to help the specifier quickly rule out many wrong specifications. Nonetheless, note that the test-driven modeling approach alone might not be sufficient to ensure proper validation, since it is difficult to devise test cases that catch subtle errors. As such, it should be complemented by other validation tasks, such as checking expected (even apparently trivial) derived assertions.

3 Study Design

It should be now clear that, although Alloy can support test-driven modeling, it is rather laborious and error-prone to specify a diverse test suite manually. With this in mind, and following the recent successes in using LLMs for various software development and formal specification tasks, we devised an empirical evaluation study to assess the effectiveness of a state-of-the-art LLM for generating test suites for validating formal specifications. In particular, we studied version 2025-08-07 of GPT-5, one of the latest and most powerful models offered by OpenAI. In fact, the two test cases presented in the previous section were generated by GPT-5 in one of the experiments in our study. This section presents the research questions (RQs) and the design of the study, while the results are presented and discussed in the next section.

3.1 Research Questions

The proposed empirical evaluation study aims to answer the following RQs:

RQ1 How does prompt design influence the effectiveness of test case generation? In particular, what is the effect of including examples in the prompt, comparing zero-shot, one-shot, and few-shot prompts.

RQ2 What is the effect of non-determinism in test case generation? Even with low temperature settings, LLMs act non-deterministically, giving different responses to the same input, which may affect the outcomes.

RQ3 How do different LLMs compare in test case generation? Our evaluation focused mainly on GPT-5, but we also compared its effectiveness with other state-of-the-art LLMs, as well as cost-effective and open-source small models.

RQ4 What are the characteristics of invalid tests cases? Test cases can be invalid for different reasons (from invalid syntax to failure to comply with the requirement), so we studied the characteristics of invalid test cases to determine which factors are currently more challenging for LLMs.

RQ5 How good are the generated test suites at finding incorrect specifications? The previous RQs focus on the syntactic and semantic validity of generated test suites. This RQ aims to assess the diversity of the test cases through their ability to detect wrong formalizations of the natural language requirements.

3.2 Benchmark

For our evaluation we used four small domain models that are part of the Alloy4Fun dataset. Alloy4Fun [13] is a web-based version of Alloy that, among other features, enables the creation of small specification challenges whose correctness is checked against a hidden oracle. Alloy4Fun is used in some universities to help students study Alloy autonomously, including in our own formal methods courses, and over the years we collected thousands of correct and incorrect attempts at specifying several requirements. Most of this data is publicly available in a Zenodo data-set [12], and has been regularly used in the evaluation of Alloy-related techniques and tools.

An Alloy4Fun exercise usually consists of a simple model, declaring a few signatures and fields, and a set of specification challenges, each a predicate annotated with a natural language requirement that the student should specify. When specifying a requirement, the user can assume that all previous ones are valid. Table 1 describes the four exercises that we used for the evaluation, including the respective links to the Alloy4Fun web-application. Besides the number of requirements in each example, it also gives some statistics about the number of non-equivalent attempts at formalizing each requirement. To determine the latter, we ran a script over the data-set, to group all submissions to each requirement by logic equivalence [11]. In the paper GitHub repository we include the results of that analysis, including for each wrong specification of each requirement the syntactic formulation that occurred more frequently.

Table 1. Overview of the examples used for evaluation

Example	Reqs	Wrong specs		
		Min	Max	Mean
Social network	8	44	848	272
Production line	10	28	585	147
Train station	10	36	203	104
Courses	15	33	312	137
	43	28	848	157

For illustration purposes, consider the courses domain model already presented in the previous section. As we have seen, this example uses a few advanced

Table 2. Requirements of the courses domain model

Requirement	Wrong
Only students can be enrolled in courses	161
Only professors can teach courses	33
Courses must have teachers	82
Projects are proposed by one course	87
Only students work on projects and ...	
... projects must have someone working on them	248
Students only work on projects of courses they are enrolled in	168
Students work on at most one project per course	177
A professor cannot teach herself	79
A professor cannot teach colleagues	312
Only students have grades	80
Students only have grades in courses they are enrolled	87
Students have at most one grade per course	87
A student with the highest mark in a course must ...	
... have worked on a project on that course	291
A student cannot work with the same student in different projects	51
Students working on the same project in a course cannot ...	
... have marks differing by more than one unit	109

Alloy features, namely non-binary fields, overloading, and the `util/ordering` module. It contains 15 specification challenges, whose natural language description can be seen in Table 2. The table also shows the number of (semantically distinct) wrong specifications of each requirement, which vary between 33 for requirement "Only professors can teach courses", and 312 for requirement "A professor cannot teach colleagues", with an average of 137 per requirement. A higher number of wrong specifications can be a sign of both complexity and ambiguity. However, although some requirements may seem ambiguous, we argue that the one that is codified in the hidden oracle is always the most "correct" interpretation. Take, for example, the requirement with the most number of wrong specifications, "A professor cannot teach colleagues". At first, many students seem to interpret "colleagues" as any other professor. Under the previous requirements (which should be assumed to be true), that would forbid students that are also professors to be enrolled in any course. Since professors that are also students should be able to enroll, the reasonable interpretation of "colleagues" in this context is the one specified in the oracle: professors that teach some course together. The three other domain models are the following:

- A photo sharing social network model, where some users are influencers and some photos are ads. This is a simple example in terms of Alloy features (e.g.,

all fields are binary). However, it is the example with the highest average of wrong specifications per requirement. This could be either because it is the first example we give to students in our courses, so it is natural that they make more mistakes, or because some of the requirements are perhaps not standard in real social networks, which might confuse students.
- A production line model, that includes both human and robot workers, and that assembles complex, potentially dangerous, components that are made of other components and/or raw materials. This is the most complex example in terms of signature hierarchy, using both signature inclusion and extension, and signature multiplicities.
- A train station railway network model where tracks in the station can be entries, exits, or junctions, and where tracks can have signals attached. This is the simplest example.

The natural language requirements can be consulted by following the links in Table 1, and are also available in the GitHub repository, along with the oracles.

3.3 Prompt Design

Most LLMs nowadays distinguish between *system* and *user* prompts: the former clarify the instructions an LLM should follow in the subsequent interactions (for example, defining roles or formatting guidelines for the responses), while the latter contain task requests or questions to be answered according to the system instructions. We used both prompts in our evaluation. The user prompt is simple, asking for test cases for a given requirement and model. Let R_i be the natural language formulation of the i-th requirement of a domain model, and N be the number of positive and negative test cases to be generated. The user prompt starts as follows, after which the domain model in Alloy is provided.

Generate N positive and N negative instances for the requirement "R_i" for the following model. All instances must also satisfy the requirements "R_0", ..., and "R_{i-1}".

Minor adjustments are made for R_0 (removing the second sentence) and R_1 (adjusting the second sentence to a single requirement).

Since we want to measure the effect of including examples, we created three versions of the system prompt: *zero-shot*, *one-shot*, and *few-shot*. The three versions were iterated several times in the GPT-5 console until we reached a satisfactory result. These were then fixed and used for the whole evaluation with all LLMs, which was performed via remote calls to the respective APIs. All three system prompts start with a brief presentation of Alloy (a couple of sentences) and end with a definition of the LLM role and an itemized list of precise instructions. The main differences are the following:

Zero-shot Besides the mentioned Alloy introduction and final list of instructions, this version has no Alloy code, including only a paragraph in natural language explaining that test cases can be encoded using `run` commands with existential quantifiers and equality constraints.

One-shot Besides the content of the *zero-shot* prompt, this version includes an example of an Alloy domain model (different from the ones used in the evaluation) that uses all relevant features of the language, a paragraph explaining this model and the respective features, and a single example of a test case specified in Alloy using the `some disj` idiom.

Few-shot This version introduces Alloy features incrementally and provides examples of test cases along the way. It starts with a simple version of an Alloy domain model (just with two signatures and a binary field) along with a positive and a negative test case encoded with the `some disj` idiom, and a test case explaining how to specify that a field is empty. Then, signature extension and inclusion are introduced with a variant of the initial model, along with a test case example. Finally, ternary relations and the `util/ordering` module are introduced, along with a final test case example. In total, this prompt has three variants of a domain model and five examples of test cases.

The three variants of the system prompt can be found in the GitHub repository.

3.4 Metrics

For the first three RQs we evaluated the effectiveness in terms of syntactic and semantic correctness of the generated test suite. In particular, our result tables will present the following metrics:

Tests The number of test cases to be generated. We ask the LLM to generate N positive and N negative test cases for each requirement. As such, the full test suite should have $2 \times N \times 43$ test cases, since we have 43 requirements in total.

Syntax The number of test cases that are syntactically correct. To measure this, we attempt to parse each `run` command in isolation together with the respective Alloy model.

Consistent The number of syntactically correct test cases that produce an instance. A syntactically correct `run` command can be inconsistent for various reasons (e.g., wrongly specified scopes). To measure this, we execute each command in isolation together with the respective Alloy model and check if the result is satisfiable.

Previous The number of executable test cases that satisfy all previous requirements. To measure this we add to the model facts with the oracles of all previous requirements and check if each `run` command is still satisfiable.

Valid The number of test cases satisfying previous requirements that agree with the specified oracle. To measure this we add the oracle specification as a `fact` to the model, and check if the `run` command has the expected outcome (satisfiable/unsatisfiable for positive/negative tests). We also report this metric as a percentage of the total number of generated tests (%).

Cost The actual cost (at the date of the study) of using the LLM to generate the test suite. This is an indicator of the number of tokens used in total, including input, output, and reasoning tokens.

For RQ5 we evaluated the effectiveness in terms of the ability of the test suite to actually catch wrong specifications. To make fair comparisons, we focus only on the requirements for which the LLM generates a full test suite, with $2 \times N$ valid test cases. In the results for this RQ we present the following metrics:

Complete The number of requirements for which the LLM generates a complete valid test suite (out of the 43 possible).
Wrong The total number of incorrect specifications, considering only the requirements with a complete test suite.
Missed The total number of incorrect specifications that the test suite can detect. To measure this, we run all $2 \times N$ test cases of each requirement against each wrong specification and checked if the result was the expected.
Mean % The average of missed wrong specifications per requirement. Note that, since results are presented grouped by run, this is not the same as the ratio between **Missed** and **Wrong**.

Table 3. Influence of prompt design

Prompt	Tests	Syntax	Consistent	Previous	Valid	%	Cost
Few	258	255	255	252	247	96%	\$3.56
One	258	226	208	206	205	79%	\$3.69
Zero	258	137	120	119	118	46%	\$4.20

Table 4. Effect of non-determinism

Run	Tests	Syntax	Consistent	Previous	Valid	%	Cost
1st	258	255	255	252	247	96%	\$3.56
2nd	258	256	256	256	251	97%	\$3.50
3rd	258	252	252	250	246	95%	\$3.61

4 Results

This section presents a summary of the study results. The fully detailed results per example and per requirement can be found in the GitHub repository.

4.1 RQ1: Influence of Prompt Design

To assess the influence of prompt design we asked GPT-5 to generate test suites using the three different prompt versions described above with $N = 3$. The results are presented in Table 3. As can be seen, the *few-shot* prompt clearly outperforms the other two versions, being able to generate 247 valid tests out of the 258 requested (a success rate of 96%). Of the 11 test cases that were not valid, 3 failed the syntax check, 3 failed to satisfy the previous requirements, and 5 did not give the expected result according to the oracle. The 11 invalid test cases were distributed among 7 requirements, but all still had at least 3 valid test cases. The success rate drops to 79% for the *one-shot* prompt and 46% for the *zero-shot*. Most of this decrease is due to syntactic problems: among the test cases that are executable, 91% and 86% satisfy the previous requirements and the oracle with *one-shot* and *zero-shot* prompts, respectively. A possible explanation is the lack of Alloy test case examples in the training data, since most Alloy publications and educational material do not adopt a test-driven methodology. Interestingly, although the input size is much smaller for prompts with fewer examples, the total cost to generate the test suite is higher. The pricing structure for most commercial LLMs imposes a higher price on output tokens when compared to input tokens (sometimes 10× more), and reasoning tokens are charged as output tokens. Since the output is of comparable size, having less information and examples in the system prompt led to the need for more reasoning tokens, which alone justifies the higher cost.

Finding 1: GPT-5 with a *few-shot* system prompt is highly effective at generating Alloy test suites for structural requirements expressed in natural language. It is also more cost-effective due to less reasoning effort.

4.2 RQ2: Effect of Non-Determinism

LLMs are inherently non-deterministic, and can give different results for identical inputs. Some allow the user to set the so-called *temperature*, a parameter that affects the randomness of results, by adjusting the probability distribution of the next output token. However, even with temperature set to 0 (the most deterministic setting) determinism is not guaranteed due to hardware factors like GPU concurrency. GPT-5 in particular does not allow the user to set this parameter, so it is even more relevant to study the impact of non-determinism on the results. To assess that effect, we run GPT-5 three times with the same task ($N = 3$), and using the *few-shot* prompt that proved to be more effective. The results are presented in Table 4 (the **1st run** is the **Few-shot** run presented in Table 3). As can be seen, the overall results do not vary significantly, with a success rate always close to 96%. For 33 of the 43 requirements we always got the same number of valid, albeit possibly different, test cases.

Finding 2: The overall effectiveness of GPT-5 when using a *few-shot* prompt does not seem to be significantly affected by non-determinism.

4.3 RQ3: LLM Comparison

To answer this RQ, we compared the effectiveness of GPT-5, version 2025-08-07, with two other state-of-the-art models, Gemini 2.5 Pro from Google DeepMind and Claude Opus 4.1, version 2025-08-05, from Anthropic. We also compared with two less advanced models, namely GPT-5 Mini, version 2025-08-07, a cost-efficient and faster version of GPT-5, also from OpenAI, and the open-source smaller language model Llama 3.1 8B from Meta. Table 5 presents the results, again with $N = 3$ and the *few-shot* prompt. The results in **GPT-5** are the ones corresponding to the **Few-shot** run presented in Table 3. The results from Llama are omitted because this model performed quite badly, and was only able to generate a handful of syntactically correct test cases. Further research is needed to determine if small language models in general are unable to properly cope with this task, or if this result is specific to Llama. The two competing state-of-the-art models performed worse than GPT-5, although still with a success rate above 75%. Gemini 2.5 Pro struggled more with getting test cases that are executable (for example, forgetting to set the scope for a signature), while Claude Opus 4.1 always succeeded in that aspect but struggled to generate test cases that satisfied previous requirements. The main problem for the cost-efficient GPT-5 Mini was getting the syntax right, a pattern similar to the one obtained with GPT-5 for simpler the prompts.

Table 5. LLM comparison

Model	Tests	Syntax	Consistent	Previous	Valid	%	Cost
GPT-5	258	255	255	252	247	96%	$3.56
Gemini	258	248	220	212	210	81%	$2.78
Claude	258	258	258	202	197	76%	$5.55
Mini	258	188	183	179	174	67%	$0.53

Table 6. Wrong specification detection

N	Complete	Wrong	Missed	Mean %
1	41	5587	2204	38.10%
2	34	4623	814	17.02%
3	36	4395	525	9.90%
4	35	5129	446	7.45%
5	35	4816	348	6.43%

Finding 3: Different LLMs struggle with different aspects of test case generation, some struggle more with syntax while others with semantics.

4.4 RQ4: Characterization of Invalid Test Cases

To answer this RQ we manually analyzed all invalid test cases in the 3 runs of GPT-5 reported in Table 4. In total we had 30 invalid test cases, distributed as follows: 11 were syntactically incorrect, 5 failed to satisfy previous requirements, and 14 did not agree with the oracle.

All the 11 syntactically incorrect test cases were due to the same problem: to specify that a binary relation `R` is empty, formula `R = none` was used instead of `R = none→none`. This is a reasonable mistake to be made (often made by our students also), since the latter syntax is an Alloy specific notation needed to make the expression type-check. We actually noticed this problem in the initial experiments with the prompt design, and explored the viability of the alternative (uniform) syntax where to state that `R` is empty one just specifies `no R`. However, the LLM also struggled with this formulation, since it deviated from the standard equality constraint, sometimes generating the also syntactically incorrect `R = no R`. These are simple syntactic errors, that could easily be addressed with postprocessing the result.

> **Finding 4**: The syntactic errors made by GPT-5 are due to a peculiar feature of Alloy syntax and easily fixable by some post-processing.

Of the 5 test cases that failed previous requirements, one was because the test case was not fully specified and admitted multiple instances, some of them valid and some invalid. No pattern was detected in the remaining 4, all of them indeed failed in one of the previous requirements that were stated in the task prompt. Strangely, in 3 cases where the generated test cases for R_i failed to satisfy a previous requirement R_j for $j < i$, the LLM had been able to generate valid test cases directly for R_j.

Of the 14 test cases that did not agree with the oracle, 13 were negative test cases, which seems to suggest that the LLM struggles more with these. The only positive test case that was invalid was for the requirement "Components cannot be their own parts" in the production line example. The invalid test case had a component `A` that was a part of component `B` which in turn was part of `A`. Essentially, the requirement was interpreted literally, but obviously it is a wrong interpretation, as components cannot physically contain themselves direct or indirectly. The 13 invalid negative test cases were distributed among only 3 requirements: 1 for the requirement "Only students work on projects and projects must have someone working on them" in the courses example, because a student that is also a professor was wrongly assumed to not be able to work on a project; 3 for the requirement "Users can see ads posted by everyone, but only see non ads posted by followed users" in the social network example, due to a misinterpretation of the "can" as a "must" (all test cases had a user that did not see an ad, which was considered to be wrong); and 9 for the requirement "A professor cannot teach colleagues" because, likewise many of our students, it was incorrectly assumed that "colleagues" meant any other professor. Note that all 3 runs of GPT-5 made the last two mistakes, which is another indicator that the results are not significantly affected by non-determinism.

Finding 5: GPT-5 struggles more with negative test cases then with positive ones, but only on specific requirements that our anecdotal evidence suggests to be also ambiguous to humans.

4.5 RQ5: Effectiveness at Detecting Incorrect Specifications

For this RQ we asked GPT-5, using the *few-shot* system prompt, to generate test suites of increasing size, from $N = 1$ to $N = 5$. For the requirements where a complete valid test suite was obtained we computed the ratio of undetected wrong specifications in our benchmark. Table 6 presents the results, reporting for each test suite size the average of those ratios. As can be seen the ratio of missed wrong specifications decreases as the test suite size increases, with significant drops when N is increased from 1 to 2 and from 2 to 3. This is a clear indicator that GPT-5 is generating different scenarios in the test cases of each test suite. In the biggest test suite, in average only 6.43% of the wrong specifications went undetected, but only in 5 requirements were all of them detected. To put these results in context, we know (by using a brute-force exploration) that for most requirements it is possible to have a small test suite that catches all wrong specifications (in most cases it suffices to have $N = 2$ with a scope of 3 for top-level signatures). However, devising such a minimal test suite without knowing *a priori* the wrong specifications would be extremely difficult or even impossible for a human expert, so it is unrealistic to expect the LLM to do it.

Finding 6: GPT-5 generates diverse test cases for most requirements.

4.6 Threats to Validity

The threats to *internal validity* mainly lie in our experimental scripts. To minimize this threat both authors reviewed the code, and we also released all scripts and data in the GitHub repository for replication. The threats to *external validity* mainly lie in the used benchmark and LLMs. Unfortunately, we are not aware of any standard benchmark in this context. We acknowledge that the Alloy4Fun dataset mainly consists of educational examples, with domain models that are simpler than realistic ones. However, some of the requirements are already quite complex, and from our own consultancy experience, realistic cases have much more requirements, but they are not necessarily more complex, so we have some confidence that the results will generalize to that setting. As for the LLMs, we evaluated three of the most prominent commercial offerings so we are confident that the results are representative of the state of the art. For cost-efficient, open-source, and small language models, we only evaluated two offerings so we cannot generalize the results. We also acknowledge that our study focuses on Alloy (for the provided domain model and the test case specifications) and structural requirements, so we cannot generalize to other formal specification languages or other kinds of requirements.

The threats to *construct validity* lie mainly in the prompt design, non-determinism, and data leakage. When designing the study we iterated our prompt texts multiple times with GPT-5 until reasonable results were obtained, but we acknowledge that these may not be ideal for all configurations and other LLMs. Concerning non-determinism, ideally all experiments would have been run multiple times, but that would significantly raise the evaluation costs. We opted to study the effect of non-determinism effect in a dedicated RQ only with GPT-5 and a specific test suite size and considering only 3 different runs. This experiment showed that GPT-5 is rather consistent with the results, but we acknowledge that non-determinism is still a potential threat, in particular for the results of other models. As for data leakage, the Alloy4Fun dataset is publicly available for some time and may have been used in the training data of the LLMs. However, the dataset does not include test cases and we are also not aware of any other public dataset with test case examples for the Alloy4Fun domain model examples, so we are confident that data leakage is not a relevant threat.

5 Related Work

Alloy's support for test-driven methodologies has led to the development of techniques and tools for unit testing, such as the already mentioned AUnit framework [18]. AUnit automates the generation of unit tests [19]—specified using the same **`some disj`** pattern used in this study—but it does so by inspecting a formal specification and covering all its sub-expressions. In validation (our target) it is unknown whether the specification conforms to the requirements, so the user would have to manually classify all test cases. We propose instead to generate test cases from the natural language requirements before formalization starts. For the linked list example from [19] our technique easily generates a small test suite to validate the requirement "The list is acyclic" that detects the incorrect specification illustrated in the paper.

We are not aware of any research that uses LLMs to generate test suites for Alloy, but they have been used for other Alloy-related tasks. Hong et al. [5] explore using LLMs to generate Alloy specifications from simple requirements expressed in natural language, and conclude that they can be quite effective. Alhanahnah et al. [1] explore the effectiveness of LLMs at repairing buggy Alloy specifications, and conclude that a setup that pairs a repair agent with an instructor agent (that uses feedback from the Alloy Analyzer to generate repair prompts), can surpass state-of-the-art symbolic repair techniques. Similar autoformalization techniques have been developed for other formal specification languages and logics. For example, Zhao et al. [25] explored the viability of using LLMs to generate CTL specifications from natural language, and Zuo et al. [27] the generation of behavioral models specified in the PAT formal method [20].

The work by Pan et al. [16] on the generation of model instances using LLMs shares some similarity to ours, since it focuses on structural aspects. Given an XML description of a UML class diagram and a natural language description of a desired instance, LLMs are used to generate the corresponding XMI instance model. A key difference is that we do not expect natural language definitions of the test cases, but only of a high-level requirement. Moreover, their evaluation focuses only on syntactic correctness. To make the technique feasible with open-source, small LLMs, they use an abstract intermediate representation that is converted to XMI in post-processing. Our approach could employ a similar technique to reduce the rate of syntactic errors in the less advanced LLMs.

In the testing community there is some work on using LLMs to generate test cases from natural language requirements (rather than from code), that relate to our work (see, e.g., [24] for a comprehensive survey). For example, Korraprolu et al. [8] present an empirical study to compare the effectiveness of LLMs at generating test cases for Simulink from natural language requirements. Effectiveness was measured as coverage of the (executable) models implemented afterwards (the correctness of the test cases was not assessed). Test cases are simple input-output pairs of numerical or/and discrete values and generated in an tabular form (later translated manually to executable tests). A similar study was done by Xue et al. [22] for the concrete domain of FinTech software [22]. Our tests can also be seen as input-output pairs with a Boolean output but much more complex input (a graph of connected elements from the domain of discourse). Our tests are also directly executable without manual intervention and our evaluation focused on the correctness of the tests.

Several works attempted to generate high-level test cases from natural language requirements, in the sense that tests are themselves written in natural language, and thus potentially more accessible for LLMs. For example, Masuda et al. [15] use LLMs to extract not only high-level tests but also test design techniques from documents describing all application requirements. Arora et al. [2] use LLMs to generate test scenarios for an Austrian Post application for managing delivery and postage processes. There is also some work (e.g., [3]) on generating driving scenarios for autonomous driving applications using LLMs.

6 Conclusion and Future Work

Our experimental evaluation indicates that GPT-5 with a *few-shot* prompt is highly effective and consistent at generating test suites from natural language requirements, that can be used for the validation of structural requirements of domain models. Generated test cases are almost always syntactically correct, executable, and comply with the stated requirements. The generated test suite for each requirement is also diverse and is very effective at detecting incorrect specifications made by humans. Competing state-of-the-art LLMs are also effective, but less so, when compared with GPT-5. In the future we plan to experiment with alternative more targeted prompts (for example, task specific system prompts adapted for each domain model) and add a post-processing syntax repair procedure, that combined could increase the effectiveness of the technique with open source small language models, making the technique more accessible, namely in educational contexts. We also plan to evaluate the effectiveness of this approach for generating test suites for validating behavioral requirements, namely requirements to be specified with temporal logic. That would make the technique usable in a wider range of formal methods.

Acknowledgments. This work is funded by national funds through FCT – Fundação para a Ciência e a Tecnologia, I.P., under the support UID/50014/2025 (https://doi.org/10.54499/UID/50014/2025).

References

1. Alhanahnah, M., Rashedul Hasan, M., Xu, L., Bagheri, H.: An empirical evaluation of pre-trained large language models for repairing declarative formal specifications. Empir. Softw. Eng. **30**(5), 1–38 (2025)
2. Arora, C., Herda, T., Homm, V.: Generating test scenarios from NL requirements using retrieval-augmented LLMs: an industrial study. In: 32nd International Requirements Engineering Conference, pp. 240–251. IEEE (2024)
3. Chang, C., Wang, S., Zhang, J., Ge, J., Li, L.: LLMScenario: large language model driven scenario generation. IEEE Trans. Syst. Man Cybern. Syst. **54**(11), 6581–6594 (2024)
4. Cunha, A., Macedo, N., Brunel, J., Chemouil, D.: Practical Alloy: a hands-on guide to formal software design (2025). https://practicalalloy.github.io/
5. Hong, Y., Jiang, S., Fu, Y., Khurshid, S.: On the effectiveness of large language models in writing Alloy formulas. arXiv preprint arXiv:2502.15441 (2025)
6. Jackson, D.: Software Abstractions: Logic, Language, and Analysis. MIT Press (2012)
7. Jackson, D.: Alloy: a language and tool for exploring software designs. Commun. ACM **62**(9), 66–76 (2019)
8. Korraprolu, B.R., Pinninti, P., Reddy, Y.R.: Test case generation for requirements in natural language – an LLM comparison study. In: 18th Innovations in Software Engineering Conference, pp. 9:1–9:5. ACM (2025)
9. Lamport, L.: Specifying Systems, vol. 388. Addison-Wesley (2002)
10. Macedo, N., Brunel, J., Chemouil, D., Cunha, A., Kuperberg, D.: Lightweight specification and analysis of dynamic systems with rich configurations. In: 24th ACM SIGSOFT International Symposium on Foundations of Software Engineering, pp. 373–383. ACM (2016)
11. Macedo, N., Cunha, A.: Alloy4Fun semantic entries (2025). https://doi.org/10.5281/zenodo.17392203
12. Macedo, N., Cunha, A., Paiva, A.C.R.: Alloy4Fun dataset for 2024/25 (2025). https://doi.org/10.5281/zenodo.17390557
13. Macedo, N., et al.: Experiences on teaching Alloy with an automated assessment platform. Sci. Comput. Program. **211**, 102690 (2021)
14. Mashkoor, A., Leuschel, M., Egyed, A.: Validation obligations: a novel approach to check compliance between requirements and their formal specification. In: 43rd International Conference on Software Engineering: New Ideas and Emerging Results, pp. 1–5. IEEE (2021)
15. Masuda, S., Kouzawa, S., Sezai, K., Suhara, H., Hiruta, Y., Kudou, K.: Generating high-level test cases from requirements using LLM: an industry study. arXiv preprint arXiv:2510.03641 (2025)

16. Pan, F., Petrovic, N., Zolfaghari, V., Wen, L., Knoll, A.: LLM-enabled instance model generation. arXiv preprint arXiv:2503.22587 (2025)
17. Schäfer, M., Nadi, S., Eghbali, A., Tip, F.: An empirical evaluation of using large language models for automated unit test generation. IEEE Trans. Software Eng. **50**(1), 85–105 (2023)
18. Sullivan, A., Wang, K., Khurshid, S.: AUnit: a test automation tool for Alloy. In: 11th International Conference on Software Testing, Verification and Validation, pp. 398–403. IEEE (2018)
19. Sullivan, A., Wang, K., Zaeem, R.N., Khurshid, S.: Automated test generation and mutation testing for Alloy. In: 10th International Conference on Software Testing, Verification and Validation, pp. 264–275. IEEE (2017)
20. Sun, J., Liu, Y., Dong, J.S., Pang, J.: PAT: Towards flexible verification under fairness. In: 21st International Conference on Computer Aided Verification, LNCS, vol. 5643, pp. 709–714. Springer (2009)
21. Wang, K., Sullivan, A., Khurshid, S.: ARepair: a repair framework for Alloy. In: 41st International Conference on Software Engineering: Companion Proceedings, pp. 103–106. IEEE (2019)
22. Xue, Z., et al.: LLM4Fin: Fully automating LLM-powered test case generation for fintech software acceptance testing. In: 33rd ACM SIGSOFT International Symposium on Software Testing and Analysis, pp. 1643–1655. ACM (2024)
23. Yang, L., et al.: On the evaluation of large language models in unit test generation. In: 39th IEEE/ACM International Conference on Automated Software Engineering, pp. 1607–1619. ACM (2024)
24. Yang, Z., Huang, R., Cui, C., Niu, N., Towey, D.: Requirements-based test generation: a comprehensive survey. ACM Trans. Softw. Eng. Methodol. (2025), to appear
25. Zhao, M., Tao, R., Huang, Y., Shi, J., Qin, S., Yang, Y.: NL2CTL: automatic generation of formal requirements specifications via large language models. In: 25th International Conference on Formal Engineering Methods, LNCS, vol. 15394, pp. 1–17. Springer (2024)
26. Zugal, S., Pinggera, J., Weber, B.: Toward enhanced life-cycle support for declarative processes. J. Softw. Evol. Process **24**(3), 285–302 (2012)
27. Zuo, X., et al.: PAT-Agent: autoformalization for model checking. arXiv preprint arXiv:2509.23675 (2025)

BDD-Based Deadlock Avoidance for Automated Guided Vehicles in Warehouse Logistics (Case Study Paper)

Benjamin von Berg[1(✉)], Bernhard K. Aichernig[2], and Fabian Wedenik[3]

[1] Institute of Software Engineering and Artificial Intelligence, Graz University of Technology, Graz, Austria
benjamin.vonberg@tugraz.at
[2] Institute for Formal Models and Verification, Johannes Kepler University Linz, Linz, Austria
bernhard.aichernig@jku.at
[3] KNAPP Industry Solutions, Dobl, Austria
fabian.wedenik@knapp.com

Abstract. In this work, we present an industrial case study of deadlock avoidance in the context of automated warehouse logistics. In particular, we consider systems of Automated Guided Vehicles (AGVs) in which semi-autonomous robots move inside a facility along a predefined set of paths. The paper introduces a novel formalization of AGV systems that models the physical setup of the AGV system more accurately compared to previous approaches. In particular, our modeling approach captures movement restrictions due to physical proximity of vehicles regardless of the logical connectivity of the guide path network. The paper provides and compares three different encodings of such models as transition systems, which enable symbolic analysis of the system via Binary Decision Diagrams (BDDs). Based on these encodings we perform deadlock avoidance for warehouse layouts of both synthetic and real-world origin.

Keywords: deadlock avoidance · binary decision diagrams · automated guided vehicles · automated warehouse logistics

1 Introduction

Warehouse operations are an important aspect of the economy that has recently seen an increase in both scale and complexity exacerbated by the rise of e-commerce and flexible manufacturing. This requires a high degree of efficiency that is in part addressed by automation. A wide-spread case of warehouse automation is the usage of Automated Guided Vehicles (AGVs), where a fleet of semi-autonomous vehicles move along a predefined set of guide paths [9]. Ideally, this approach results in a reduction of manual labor while maintaining or even

A. Sampaio and M. Stoelinga (Eds.): FM 2026, LNCS 16556, pp. 298–316, 2026.
https://doi.org/10.1007/978-3-032-26204-2_16

increasing efficiency. However, coordinating a fleet of vehicles is a non-trivial task and wrong decisions during planning can lead to congestion or in the worst case deadlocks, i.e., an AGV becoming stuck, requiring human intervention. Overly conservative planning on the other hand can lead to suboptimal resource utilization and thus hamper efficiency.

In this case study, we investigate deadlock avoidance for a controller scheduling AGVs developed at KNAPP. However, we treat deadlock avoidance independently from planning. This allows for a shielding approach [1], where the set of actions that are available to the planning algorithm is restricted such that a deadlock can never occur. This approach can be combined with any planning method such as a classic planning algorithm or an agent trained with reinforcement learning. In particular, we are interested in a maximally permissive Deadlock Avoidance Policy (DAP) [5], i.e., a DAP that is both sound and complete. Existing approaches [2,17,22] for deadlock avoidance in AGV systems use a simple but well-established model of AGV movement. However, this model is not expressive enough to capture the complexity of modern AGV systems which often have to follow application-specific constraints that require finer granularity, e.g., regarding rotation maneuvers. We address this by providing a novel formalization of AGV systems that more accurately models the warehouse layout and the interaction between AGVs, which can easily be extended to include additional constraints. While the gain in expressiveness also comes with increased complexity, we show how the granularity of the model can be adapted locally, introducing complexity only where it is required. The proposed modeling method allows extracting a maximally permissive DAP based on Binary Decision Diagrams (BDDs).

The contributions of this paper are (1) a novel approach for modelling AGV systems catering to industry needs, (2) a simple abstraction method for reducing the complexity of the resulting models without interfering with the analysis of the system and (3) a case study of deadlock avoidance for AGV systems.

The remainder of this paper is structured as follows. In Sect. 2, we provide an overview of the presented case study. Section 3 covers the preliminaries on behavioral models and deadlocks required for Sect. 4, where we introduce our formalization of AGV systems with a focus on deadlock avoidance. An experimental evaluation based on synthetic and real-world scenarios is conducted in Sect. 5. Finally, Sect. 6 presents concluding remarks such as the relation to existing work and lessons learned.

2 Case Study Overview

KNAPP is a family owned business with roughly 8300 employees based in Austria from the domain of warehouse automation. They offer a wide range of goods and services ranging from robots to software solutions (see Fig. 1). In 2022, they launched a new product called KiSoft FCS, which is a fleet control system (FCS) for AGVs and Autonomous Mobile Robots (AMRs), collectively referred to as vehicles. The FCS obtains high-level tasks, also called orders, e.g., from

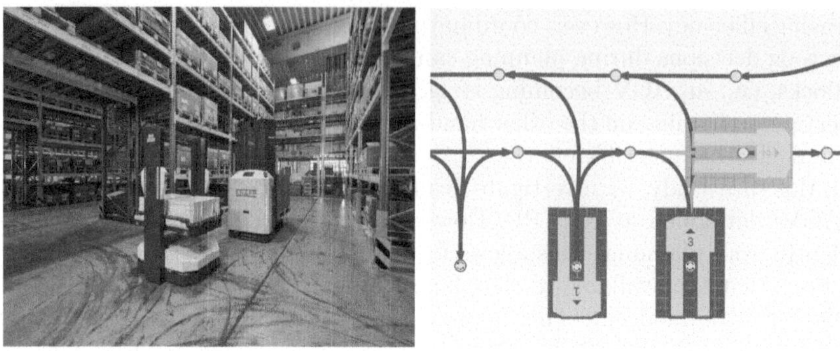

(a) Two AMRs in a warehouse (b) Lane map excerpt in KiSoft FCS

Fig. 1. Different aspects of automated warehouses covered by KNAPP © KNAPP/Niederwieser https://www.knapp.com/.

an operator or an automated system, potentially also provided by KNAPP. In this work, an order can be thought of as a request to pick up an object at some position and deliver it to another position. The FCS then assigns one of the vehicles to the task based on the capabilities of the vehicle and the current state of the warehouse, including pending orders. The FCS is also responsible for planning the routes of vehicles in an efficient way. This is done using predefined sets of locations and paths between them (also called lanes), along which vehicles can drive and which can be combined into routes. Collectively, these two sets form the guide path network. This network and other information regarding the warehouse layout and potential restrictions are aggregated in a data structure called *lane map*. An excerpt of a lane map with three forklift AMRs is shown in Fig. 1b. A formal definition of the part of the lane map that is relevant to this paper is provided later on. While the AMRs by KNAPP are capable of reversing at low speeds, this mode of movement is highly inefficient and not always safely possible, e.g., due to sensors being obstructed by a payload. Thus, the use of reversing can lead to significantly reduced throughput, comparable to downtime due to a deadlock. Consequently, reversing is disabled in normal operating conditions. Consider for example a narrow corridor in which vehicles can neither pass each other nor turn around. If two vehicles enter the corridor from opposite sides, neither can exit the corridor anymore. Such cases require intervention by a human operator resolving the deadlock by manually steering the vehicles in question to a non-blocking configuration from which the FCS can resume planning. This disrupts the normal operation of the system, which can incur costs, e.g., by causing downtime in a manufacturing plant that is supplied by the vehicles. This necessitates methods that mitigate deadlocks.

In the following, we describe our work in terms of established terminology in the field of AGV systems [20]. Although AMRs have more capabilities than AGVs, we refer to them as AGVs from now on, since we assume that routes follow a guide path network. In a *statically routed* AGV system, AGVs move between key points of interest on a fixed set of routes. We consider the more general case of *dynamically routed* systems, where routes are determined in real time according to the current state of the system. A system is considered *open* if AGVs are capable of entering and exiting the system at specific locations. This is in contrast to *closed* systems where all AGVs remain in the system. While this paper is concerned mainly with closed systems, parts of it generalize to open systems. Related approaches commonly assume that AGVs are point shaped or spherical and that AGV systems use a simple form of *zone control* where each path segment corresponds to a single zone to which an AGV accessing the path is guaranteed exclusive access. We use a more fine grained model that considers the actual footprint of AGVs and also covers dependencies between locations and lanes. Such dependencies can arise, e.g., as a consequence of physical proximity or application specific constraints. For example, our modeling approach can handle physically intersecting paths without assuming logical connectivity of the guide path network, the handover between lanes and constrained rotation at locations. Thus, our modeling approach supports a richer class of guide path designs, which provides more freedom and better supports compliance to regulations and efficient space utilization.

3 Preliminaries

In the following, we will discuss basic concepts used in the paper.

Definition 1. *A* Labeled Transition System *(LTS) is a tuple $\langle S, L, T\rangle$, where S is a set of states, L is a set of labels and $T \subseteq S \times L \times S$ is the transition relation.*

An LTS $\mathcal{S} = \langle S, L, T\rangle$ in state $s \in S$ can transition to a next state $s' \in S$ iff there exists a label $l \in L$ such that $\langle s, l, s'\rangle \in T$, in which case we also write $s \xrightarrow{l}_{\mathcal{S}} s'$. Moreover, we write $s \overset{\lambda}{\Longrightarrow}_{\mathcal{S}} s'$ for a conjunction of transitions according to the sequence of labels $\lambda = l_1, \ldots, l_n$. More formally, this is the case iff $\exists s_0, \ldots, s_n \in S : s_0 = s \wedge s_n = s' \wedge \forall i \in [1, n] : s_{i-1} \xrightarrow{l_i} s_i$. In both cases, $\mathcal{S}$ is omitted if it is unambiguously clear from the context. An LTS is deterministic iff for each state-label pair, there is at most one successor, which is formally described as $\forall s \in S, l \in L : \left|\left\{s' \in S : s \xrightarrow{l} s'\right\}\right| \leq 1$. In the following, LTSs are assumed deterministic unless stated otherwise. The *interleaving product* $\mathcal{S} = \mathcal{S}_1 \parallel \mathcal{S}_2$ of two LTSs $\mathcal{S}_1 = \langle S_1, L_1, T_1\rangle$ and $\mathcal{S}_2 = \langle S_2, L_2, T_2\rangle$ is given as $\mathcal{S} = \langle S, L, T\rangle$ with $S = S_1 \times S_2$, $L = L_1 \cup L_2$ and $T = \left\{\langle s_1, s_2\rangle \xrightarrow{l}_{\mathcal{S}} \langle s_1', s_2'\rangle \mid (s_1 \xrightarrow{l}_{\mathcal{S}_1} s_1' \wedge s_2 = s_2') \vee (s_1 = s_1' \wedge s_2 \xrightarrow{l}_{\mathcal{S}_2} s_2')\right\}$.

A state $s \in S$ of $\mathcal{S}$ is said to be a *deadlock* iff $\nexists l \in L, s' \in S : s \xrightarrow{l} s'$. In many cases, identifying deadlocks is easy and the difficulty of deadlock avoidance results from identifying states that may not be deadlocks themselves, but cannot sensibly avoid a deadlock in the future, which is also called a higher-order deadlock. Systems with several agents, such as AGV systems, require a compositional notion of deadlock, where the system is considered in a deadlock if any (non-empty) subset of its agents is indefinitely incapable of action. More specifically, if P_L denotes a partitioning of the set of labels of an LTS $\mathcal{S}$ into disjoint subsets L_i, each of which corresponds to a specific component of $\mathcal{S}$, a state $s \in S$ is said to deadlock with respect to P_L iff $\exists L_i \in P_L : \nexists \langle l_1, \ldots, l_n \rangle \in L^*, s' \in S : l_n \in L_i \wedge s \overset{l_1,\ldots,l_n}{\Longrightarrow} s'$. However, it is common in AGV research not to consider deadlocks directly, but the related concept based on a liveness property, which is simply referred to as *live* [20]. The basic idea behind this is that the system is assumed to start in an initial state s_0 that (ideally) enables all behavior required for normal operation. If it becomes impossible to restore s_0 after some action, the system is permanently deprived of some behavior available in s_0, which is undesirable in most cases. Note that this implicitly covers compositional higher-order deadlocks. Formally, the set of live states with respect to s_0 can be defined as the set of states $S_L(s_0)$ comprised of all (reachable) states that are co-reachable to s_0, i.e., all states that are in the same *Strongly Connected Component* (SCC) as s_0. Thus, we get $S_L(s_0) = \left\{ s \in S \mid \exists \lambda_1, \lambda_2 \in L^* : s_0 \overset{\lambda_1}{\Longrightarrow} s \wedge s \overset{\lambda_2}{\Longrightarrow} s_0 \right\}$. Determining liveness of a state is NP-complete even for statically routed systems [18]. This is because the state space of the corresponding LTSs grows exponentially with the size of the system.

One way to avoid enumerating large state spaces is the use of symbolic representations. This can be done using BDDs, which are data structures for propositional formulae [3]. In general, the construction of a BDD for a specific formula is an NP-complete problem in terms of the number of variables involved. However, in many cases, BDDs can efficiently represent formulae allowing for fast computation. Operations on BDDs include the common logic operators as well as variable substitution, existential hiding and universal specification. For a BDD f, the substitution of a variable p with an expression q is written $f[p := q]$. We use the same notation for collections of variables and expressions whenever the mapping between them is clear from context. Given a BDD f and an assignment σ to all variables of f, we write $f[\sigma]$ for the Boolean value of f under σ. This value can be obtained by traversing the BDD along a single path and, thus, has linear complexity in terms of the number of BDD variables n. BDDs can be used to symbolically encode an LTS $\mathcal{S} = \langle S, L, T \rangle$, e.g., via a binary encoding of the state space with $n = \lceil \mathrm{ld}(|S|) \rceil$ Boolean variables $p = p_1, \ldots, p_n$, where $\mathrm{ld}(x)$ denotes the binary logarithm. Each state $s \in S$ is encoded as an assignment to all variables, i.e., a minterm, denoted by $E(s)$. This notation is lifted to sets of states. The transition relation is then modeled using a second set of variables $p' = p'_1, \ldots, p'_n$ as a predicate equal to the disjunction of all possible transitions $\bigvee_{s \xrightarrow{l} d} E(s) \wedge (E(d)[p := p'])$. We omit the labels since they are only descriptive in our approach. The encoded transition relation $E(T)$ can be used to perform symbolic image computations $\texttt{img}(Q)$ for a set of states Q by computing $(\exists p : E(Q) \wedge E(T))[p' := p]$. The set of forward reachable states $\texttt{fwd}(Q)$ from a set of initial states Q corresponds to the least fixed point of the image that includes Q, which can be computed by value iteration. The preimage

$\mathtt{img}^{-1}(Q)$ and set of backward reachable states $\mathtt{bwd}(Q)$ can be computed in a similar fashion. The predicate for the set of live states with respect to the initial state s_0 can then be written as $\mathtt{scc}(s_0) = \mathtt{fwd}(E(s_0)) \wedge \mathtt{bwd}(E(s_0))$.

While forward reachability from s_0 is not strictly required, it does eliminate spurious unsafe states when enumerating live states. In a monitoring setting, forward reachability from s_0 holds by definition and only backward reachability has to be checked. Moreover, the expensive computation of $b = \mathtt{bwd}(E(s_0))$ can be performed offline. During planning, the system behavior can then be restricted to live states: a particular state s is live iff b evaluates to true under the minterm $E(s)$, i.e., iff $b[E(s)]$. This can be seen as an application of shielding [1] according to a maximally permissive DAP [5]. The maximally permissive DAP $f : S \rightarrow \mathbb{P}(L)$ maps states to sets of permissible actions and - assuming determinism - is given as $f(s) = \left\{ l \in L \mid \exists s' \in S : s \xrightarrow{l} s' \wedge b[E(s')] \right\}$.

4 System Specification

Lane Maps. In an AGV system, the individual AGVs are moving along predefined paths. We assume a planar layout which can be modeled as a *lane map*, a two-dimensional representation comprised of a set of locations (i.e. points) connected by lanes (i.e. curves). Lanes govern the trajectories along which AGVs travel between locations. An AGV taking a path through two lanes a and b meeting at location x may have to rotate at x to align its orientation with the angle at which b departs from x. Due to application specific restrictions, such rotation maneuvers may not be permitted at certain locations. We therefore distinguish between *turnable* and *non-turnable* locations. Figure 2a shows a visualization of an example lane map with six locations shown as yellow circles. Three of the locations are turnable, indicated by the circular arrows inside the locations.

The following provides a formal definition of lane maps. The spatial relation of an object to the global reference frame, i.e., the combination of its position and orientation, is commonly defined as a *pose*. In this case, the set of all poses is given as $P = \mathbb{R}^2 \times [0, 2\pi)$. For any pose p, we denote the position in 2D-space as p_x and the orientation as p_ϕ. The set of *motions* M is defined as the set of all functions $m : [0, 1] \rightarrow P$ mapping an abstract time parameter to poses.

Definition 2. *A* ***lane map*** *is a tuple* $\mathcal{L} = \langle X, X_{\circlearrowleft}, C \rangle$ *where*

- X *is a finite set of* ***locations*** *given as points in a plane, i.e.,* $X \subset \mathbb{R}^2$.
- $X_{\circlearrowleft} \subseteq X$ *is the set of* ***turnable*** *locations.*
- $C \subset M$ *is a finite set of* ***lanes*** *such that* $\forall c \in C : \exists x_0, x_1 \in X : c_x(0) = x_0 \wedge c_x(1) = x_1$.

Naturally, each lane in C has to conform the degrees of freedom of the AGVs and restrictions imposed by the warehouse geometry and regulatory norms. Apart from these restrictions, lanes are not further constrained. This means that lanes can intersect other lanes and pass through locations. While possible, we opted against incorporating turning actions into the concept of lanes to better reflect the model used at KNAPP.

At any point in time, each AGV holds a set of reservations that ensures exclusive access to a region within the facility, thus preventing collisions between AGVs. The set of reservations for each AGV has to contain at least the current location of the AGV and is therefore non-empty even if the AGV is not moving. Reservations are managed by a central controller with the aim of efficiently scheduling AGVs to fulfill a set of tasks. The concept of lane maps is motivated by a setting similar to fixed block signaling from the railway domain [21], where lanes are reserved atomically for an AGV to pass from one location to another. Turning in place is handled in a similar manner. The concept of fixed atomic reservation allows us to abstract from continuous-time motion to discrete events, i.e., AGVs departing from/arriving at locations or turning in place. Moreover, since this work considers deadlock avoidance rather than optimal planning, we

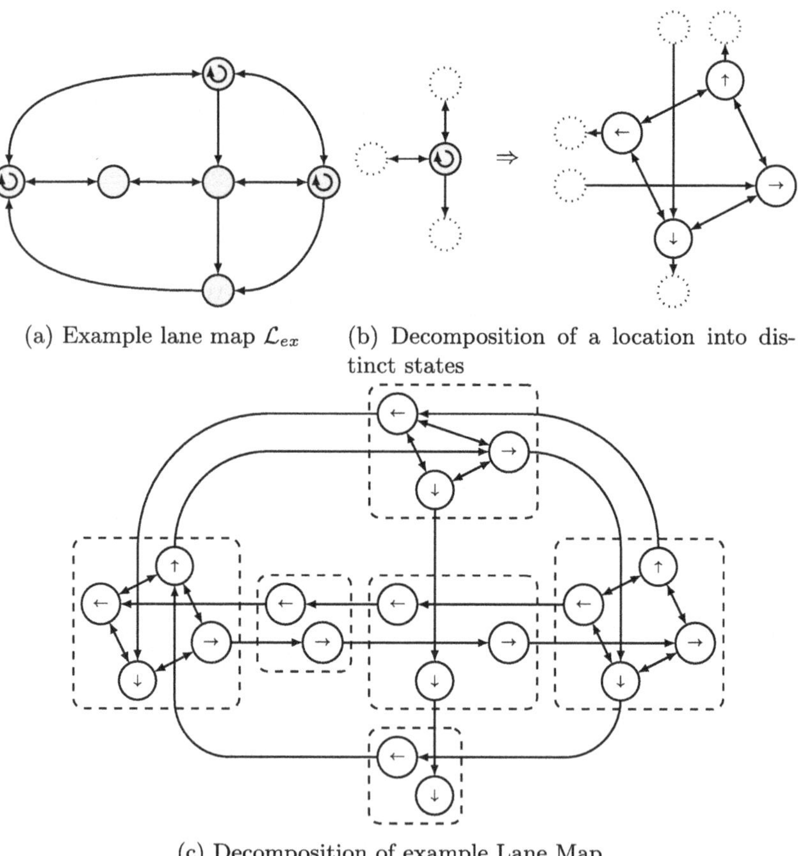

(a) Example lane map $\mathcal{L}_{ex}$ (b) Decomposition of a location into distinct states

(c) Decomposition of example Lane Map

Fig. 2. Decomposition of a Lane Map into a directed graph

need not consider simultaneous movement by several AGVs, thus further simplifying the system description from asynchronous to interleaving semantics. This is a common approach in deadlock avoidance.

Single-AGV LTS. To obtain a discrete abstraction from a given lane map $\langle X, X_{\circlearrowleft}, C\rangle$, we first extract a labeled transition system $\mathcal{S}_1$ that describes the movement of a single AGV as follows. The state space Q of $\mathcal{S}_1$ is given as a set of poses equal to all combinations of locations and possible orientations immediately before or after driving along a lane. For each location x, the finite set of possible orientations for an AGV at x is denoted as $O(x)$. This set is governed by the (finite) set of incoming and outgoing lanes, or formally $O(x) = \{\theta \in [0, 2\pi) \mid \exists c \in C, t \in \{0,1\} : c(t) = \langle x, \theta\rangle\}$. This gives us the finite state space $Q = \{\langle x, \theta\rangle \mid x \in X, \theta \in O(x)\}$.

Each transition t of the transition relation T of $\mathcal{S}_1$ has a unique label that corresponds to the continuous description of the motion that t abstracts. Two types of motion have to be considered for the transition relation: (1) movement along a lane $c \in C$ and (2) rotating in place at a turnable location. The set of turning motions $M_{\circlearrowleft}$ is defined as the subset of motions in M for which the position is constant and the orientation corresponds to a linear interpolation between two angles in a specific turning direction. For the discrete set of turning motions $C_{\circlearrowleft}(z)$ at a specific location z, we only consider motions that do not skip intermediate orientations, i.e., only the start and end orientation are in $O(z)$. More formally, $C_{\circlearrowleft}(z) = \{m \in M_{\circlearrowleft} \mid m_x(0) = z \wedge I(m_\phi) \cap O(z) = \{m_\phi(0), m_\phi(1)\}\}$, where $I(f)$ denotes the image of f. This allows us to define the transition relation as follows. A transition $\langle\langle x_0, \theta_0\rangle, m, \langle x_1, \theta_1\rangle\rangle \in Q \times M \times Q$ is part of the transition relation T iff the start- and end-poses of m coincide with the current and next state and the motion is either a lane or a valid turning action, i.e., $m(0) = \langle x_0, \theta_0\rangle \wedge m(1) = \langle x_1, \theta_1\rangle \wedge m \in C \cup C_{\circlearrowleft}(x_0)$. This process of decomposing a lane map into an LTS is illustrated in Fig. 3c using the lane map $\mathcal{L}_{ex}$. Figure 2b shows the decomposition of the rightmost location of $\mathcal{L}_{ex}$ into distinct states. The arrow inside each state indicates its orientation. The location has two incoming and three outgoing lanes. The orientation after the incoming lane from the north coincides with the starting orientation of the southbound outgoing lane, which results in four orientations. Figure 2c shows the decomposition of the whole lane map. The dashed boxes group states by their location.

Multi-AGV LTS. To model the joint system comprised of several AGVs we have to consider the restrictions due to conflicting reservations. To do so, it is necessary to account for the shape of the AGVs. We consider AGVs with a *footprint* $F \subset \mathbb{R}^2$, which covers a safety region around the area that the AGV physically occupies. The following assumes that the footprint (1) is time invariant, (2) is the same for all AGVs and (3) contains the origin, which corresponds to the rotation axis of the AGV. The transformation of the footprint to a specific pose is given as $A(F, p) = \{p_x + R(p_\phi)x \mid x \in F\}$, where $R(p_\phi)$ is the 2D-rotation matrix corresponding to p_ϕ. We lift A to motions such that $A(F, m) = \bigcup_{t \in [0,1]} A(F, m(t))$. Since we only consider sequential movement, it is sufficient to calculate restrictions between states and transitions. For each transition $t \in T$ with label m, we can obtain the subset of *conflicting poses* $Q_{\sharp}(t)$. This is defined as the set of poses in Q for which an AGV residing at one of said poses would disable t due to a safety violation: $Q_{\sharp}(t) = \{q \in Q \mid A(F, m) \cap A(F, q) \neq \varnothing\}$.

We consider three encodings of the joint system. While the first two encodings are conceptually centered around the occupation of locations and poses respectively, the last encoding focuses on the individual AGVs. All encodings use the same basic structure, where transitions correspond to a one-step motion of a single AGV. Thus, the transition relation is given as a conjunction of transitions such that (1) each transition corresponds to a transition in the single-AGV LTS $\mathcal{S}_1$, (2) all AGVs not involved in the transition remain standing and (3) the transition is not in conflict with any of the standing AGVs. While not covered in this paper, application specific constraints could also be encoded as BDDs and added to the transition relation or as a state invariant. For all encodings, s and s' denote the current and next state respectively and S denotes the state space.

In the *location-centric encoding* $\mathcal{E}_X$, states are modeled as the occupation status of each location. Each location $x \in X$ is either occupied with an AGV in one of the orientations $O(x)$ or free, which we denote with ϵ. Thus, the state space S corresponds to the set of all mappings from $x \in X$ to $O(x) \cup \{\epsilon\}$. In the BDD representation, the occupation status of each $x \in X$ can be binary encoded using $\lceil \mathrm{ld}(|O(x)| + 1) \rceil$ variables. If each location permits at most two orientations, the total number of variables degenerates to $|Q|$. The three conditions on the transition relation for any transition $t = \langle x, \theta \rangle \xrightarrow{m}_{\mathcal{S}_1} \langle x', \theta' \rangle$ are formalized as:

$$
\begin{aligned}
&(1)\ s(x) = \theta \wedge s'(x') = \theta' \wedge (x \neq x' \Rightarrow s'(x) = \epsilon \wedge s(x') = \epsilon) \\
&(2)\ \forall \hat{x} \in X \setminus \{x, x'\} : s(\hat{x}) = s'(\hat{x}) \\
&(3)\ \forall \langle \hat{x}, \hat{\theta} \rangle \in Q_{\sharp}(t) : \hat{x} \notin \{x, x'\} \Rightarrow s(\hat{x}) \neq \hat{\theta}
\end{aligned}
$$

In condition (1), the source and target orientations are enforced. If an AGV moves between locations, the source is empty after moving and the target was empty prior. Condition (2) states that the mapping is not updated for locations not involved in the transition. Condition (3) ensures that none of the conflicting poses are active, except for those involving the source or target location itself.

The *pose-centric encoding* $\mathcal{E}_P$ is defined in close analogy to the location-centric encoding. The main difference is that it directly encodes Q using a variable for each pose in Q. Consequently, each state s corresponds to a mapping from $q \in Q$ to $\{\top, \bot\}$, where $\top$ and $\bot$ signify that q is occupied or free respectively. For brevity, we omit the formal definition of the transition relation for this encoding as it differs only slightly from $\mathcal{E}_X$.

The *AGV-centric encoding* $\mathcal{E}_{AGV}$ explicitly models a fixed number N_{AGV} of AGVs in the system using an N_{AGV}-fold interleaving product of the single AGV LTS $\mathcal{S}_1$. This results in the state space $Q^{N_{AGV}}$, which requires $N_{AGV} \lceil \mathrm{ld}(|Q|) \rceil$ BDD variables when using a binary encoding of Q for each AGV. However, the interleaving product is too permissive, as it does not take into account the conflicts implied by $Q_{\sharp}$ and needs to be restricted accordingly. For any particular AGV with index $i \in [1, N_{AGV}]$, the conditions for the transition relation with respect to any transition $t = \langle x, \theta \rangle \xrightarrow{m}_{\mathcal{S}_1} \langle x', \theta' \rangle$ are given as follows, where s_k denotes the pose of the k-th AGV:

$$
\begin{aligned}
&(1)\ s_i = \langle x, \theta \rangle \wedge s_i' = \langle x', \theta' \rangle \\
&(2)\ \forall j \in [1, N_{AGV}] : i \neq j \Rightarrow s_j = s_j' \\
&(3)\ \forall \hat{s} \in Q_{\lightning}(t), j \in [1, N_{AGV}] : i \neq j \Rightarrow s_j \neq \hat{s}
\end{aligned}
$$

Condition (1) updates the state of the i-th AGV, (2) enforces inaction for all other AGVs and (3) ensures that no other AGV is in a conflicting pose.

Abstraction. While the distinction between different orientations at a location can be crucial to detect deadlocks, orientation specific deadlocks occur seldomly. Moreover, if a turnable location x is sufficiently far away from all other locations, its turning motions are unconstrained. In this case, modeling the different orientations at x only leads to a larger state space without contributing to deadlock avoidance. This can be avoided by simplifying the single-AGV LTS $\mathcal{S}_1$ and the corresponding set of conflicting poses $Q_{\lightning}$ accordingly. More formally, the set of locations that can be simplified is given as $\hat{X}_{\circlearrowleft} = \{z \in X_{\circlearrowleft} \mid \forall t \in T_{\circlearrowleft}(z), p \in Q_{\lightning}(t) : z = p_x\}$, where $T_{\circlearrowleft}(z)$ denotes the set of all transitions due to turning motions at z. Each location $z \in \hat{X}_{\circlearrowleft}$ can be modeled using a single pose $\langle z, \top \rangle$, where $\top$ is a special value denoting the set of all orientations. A transition t is in conflict with $\langle z, \top \rangle$ iff it is in conflict with each orientation at z, i.e., $\{\langle z, \theta \rangle \mid \theta \in O(z)\} \subseteq Q_{\lightning}(t)$. The simplified versions of $\mathcal{S}_1$ and $Q_{\lightning}$ can be obtained via a substitution process, which we do not formally define here for brevity. This simplification does not affect the liveness of states. We call such an abstraction a *liveness-preserving abstraction* of the original system.

To show that the proposed abstraction is indeed liveness-preserving, we need to consider the following two aspects: (1) the validity of subsuming several orientations at a specific location with respect to local behavior at that location and (2) the effect on the set of conflicting poses $Q_{\lightning}$ for lanes. Subsuming orientations for $z \in \hat{X}_{\circlearrowleft}$ allows the exact same behavior at z, since only a single AGV can occupy z and by definition any AGV at z is unconstrained in its ability to rotate without any dependence on the poses of other AGVs and can thus reach any desired orientation. For the reservation conflicts, consider a lane c. Either the lane is in conflict with each orientation at z or there is at least one orientation at z for which there is no conflict. In the former case, an AGV at z has to drive to another location to enable c. In the latter case, an AGV at z can assume one of the non-conflicting orientations without leading to a visible state change to enable c. Again, this is possible since the AGV at z can freely rotate. In both cases, the actual orientation of the AGV at z is irrelevant and the subsumption thus valid. While further study of liveness-preserving abstractions, in particular a more formal treatment thereof, is desirable, this is beyond the scope of the present paper.

5 Evaluation

Evaluated Lane Maps. The encodings introduced in the previous section are evaluated with respect to several different types of (parameterized) lane maps, which are in part illustrated in Fig. 3. For each combination of encoding, lane map and number of AGVs in the system, we pick a suitable starting configuration and report how long it takes to compute the BDD representation of the set of live states with respect to the chosen initial position.

The first type of lane map $\mathcal{L}_c(m, n)$ is shown in Fig. 3a and consists of two components: (1) m concentric rings divided into n sectors by spokes. Turnable locations are placed at each intersection of a spoke and a ring. Each of the $m \cdot n$ locations is bidirectionally connected to its neighbors. (2) An additional ring in the center consisting of n non-turnable locations that are pairwise connected. This design has a single deadlock that occurs when all locations of the innermost ring are occupied with AGVs facing inward.

The second type of lane map $\mathcal{L}_g(m)$ is illustrated in Fig. 3c. It consists of three parallel hallways of length m, comprised of turnable locations. The outer hallways have a single bidirectional track, whereas the middle hallway has two unidirectional tracks. The hallways are connected by bidirectional corridors with three non-turnable locations. A deadlock can occur in each corridor if it is accessed from both sides simultaneously.

Finally, we consider a set $\mathcal{L}_r$ of two lane maps that are fragments of lane maps extracted from real world settings. The lane maps $\mathcal{L}_{r,1}$ and $\mathcal{L}_{r,2}$ consist of 60 and 107 locations respectively. Figure 3d shows a part of $\mathcal{L}_{r,1}$ exhibiting reservation conflicts without logical connectivity, in particular with locations of the track in the middle. Figure 3b shows a small excerpt of $\mathcal{L}_{r,2}$ that models a corridor with two one-way tracks. Two reservation conflicts are indicated by red bolts. In particular, an AGV standing at $x_{l,2}$ is in conflict with the edge from $x_{r,1}$ to $x_{r,2}$ whereas an AGV at $x_{r,1}$ is in conflict with any rotation motion at $x_{l,2}$. This results in a deadlock if an AGV resides at $x_{l,2}$ facing northeast and another one resides at $x_{r,1}$.

The parameterized lane maps $\mathcal{L}_c$ and $\mathcal{L}_g$ leave sufficient space between locations such that the each transition is in conflict only with the poses involving the source and destination locations.

Results. Tables 1, 2 and 3 show the results for several instances of the lane maps $\mathcal{L}_c(m, n)$, $\mathcal{L}_g(m)$ and $\mathcal{L}_r$ respectively. The first line in the header groups the table into columns corresponding to the different encodings based on locations ($\mathcal{E}_X$), poses ($\mathcal{E}_P$) and AGVs ($\mathcal{E}_{AGV}$). For $\mathcal{L}_c$ and $\mathcal{L}_g$, we also investigated the effect of the abstraction of turnable goals, which is indicated in the second header line by $\mathcal{S}_A$ for the abstracted system and $\mathcal{S}_O$ for the original. The number of AGVs is denoted by N_{AGV}. For $\mathcal{L}_c(m, n)$, this is set to the number of spokes n, in order to obtain a deadlock. In all cases, the initial position of AGVs is chosen in a non-blocking manner. The column N_V refers to the number of variables used in the BDD encoding of the state space. The column t denotes the duration of the computation in seconds. A timeout of five minutes was used, which is indicated

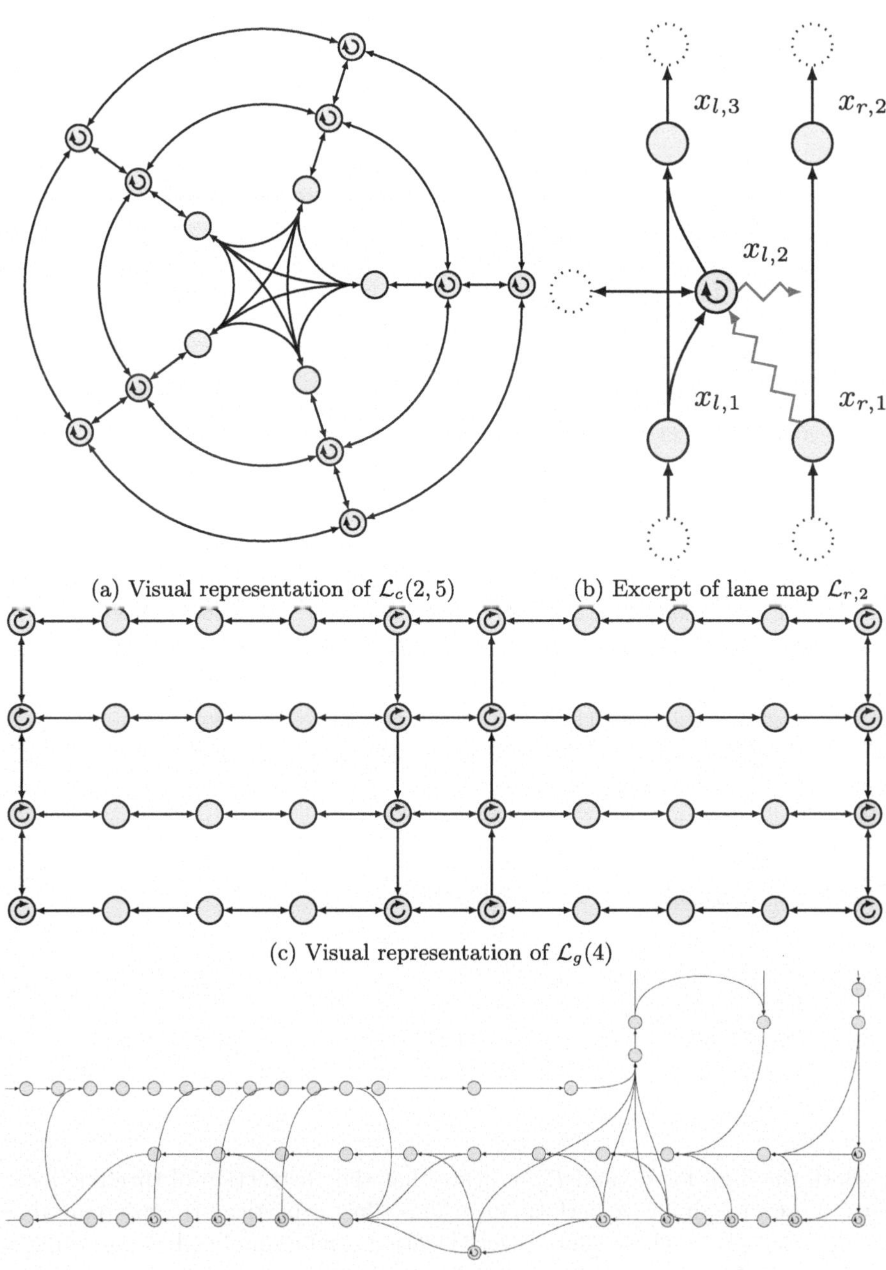

(a) Visual representation of $\mathcal{L}_c(2, 5)$

(b) Excerpt of lane map $\mathcal{L}_{r,2}$

(c) Visual representation of $\mathcal{L}_g(4)$

(d) Excerpt of lane map $\mathcal{L}_{r,1}$

Fig. 3. Examples of evaluated lane maps

by a dash in the tables. All experiments were run using a single core of a modern laptop with an intel i7-12700H CPU and 32 GB of RAM using the python BDD interface dd[1] with the CUDD library[2] under the hood. From the data shown in Tables 1, 2 and 3, the following observations can be made.

Table 1. Results for lane map $\mathcal{L}_c(m,n)$ with m rings, n sectors, and n AGVs, using the encodings $\mathcal{E}_X$, $\mathcal{E}_P$ and $\mathcal{E}_{AGV}$, with and without abstraction ($\mathcal{S}_A/\mathcal{S}_O$).

		$\mathcal{E}_X$				$\mathcal{E}_P$				$\mathcal{E}_{AGV}$			
		$\mathcal{S}_A$		$\mathcal{S}_O$		$\mathcal{S}_A$		$\mathcal{S}_O$		$\mathcal{S}_A$		$\mathcal{S}_O$	
m	n	N_V	t	N_V	t	N_V	t	N_V	t	N_V	t	N_V	t
5	3	21	0.03	51	1.06	21	0.03	66	1.54	15	0.12	21	0.60
10	3	36	0.79	96	11.68	36	0.44	126	20.37	18	0.58	21	2.93
20	3	66	7.29	186	139.81	66	6.51	-	-	21	4.90	24	19.78
40	3	126	92.36	-	-	126	56.09	-	-	21	32.32	27	126.43
2	4	16	0.02	32	1.77	16	0.02	40	2.19	16	0.18	24	3.64
3	4	20	0.06	44	8.29	20	0.06	56	6.54	20	0.61	24	11.01
4	4	24	0.26	56	5.57	24	0.16	72	19.24	20	1.40	28	30.22
5	4	28	0.60	68	12.94	28	0.61	88	20.95	20	3.36	28	58.06
6	4	32	1.34	80	28.54	32	1.18	104	70.97	20	6.46	28	92.40
10	4	48	4.99	128	126.89	48	7.20	168	-	24	43.29	32	-
2	5	20	0.21	40	11.79	20	0.25	50	26.66	25	6.86	-	-
3	5	25	0.91	-	-	25	0.59	70	139.03	25	24.23	-	-
4	5	30	1.43	-	-	30	1.60	-	-	25	76.63	-	-
5	5	35	6.51	-	-	35	3.12	-	-	-	-	-	-
6	5	40	9.56	-	-	40	9.64	-	-	-	-	-	-
10	5	60	240.51	-	-	60	127.69	-	-	-	-	-	-
2	6	24	1.82	-	-	24	1.08	-	-	-	-	-	-
3	6	30	4.88	-	-	30	4.61	-	-	-	-	-	-
4	6	36	11.70	-	-	36	35.61	-	-	-	-	-	-
5	6	42	50.89	-	-	42	34.21	-	-	-	-	-	-
6	6	48	136.58	-	-	48	241.40	-	-	-	-	-	-

Both the data for $\mathcal{L}_c$ and $\mathcal{L}_g$ indicate that the abstraction of turnable locations can severely improve performance. This effect is particularly pronounced in the ideal case of $\mathcal{L}_c$, where almost every location can be simplified. A particularly significant performance improvement of several orders of magnitude is observed for $\mathcal{L}_c(4,5)$. Here, the speedup factor for both $\mathcal{E}_X$ and $\mathcal{E}_P$ is lowerbounded by approximately 200 due to the timeout of $\mathcal{S}_O$. The effect is less pronounced for

[1] https://github.com/tulip-control/dd.

[2] https://github.com/cuddorg/cudd.

Table 2. Results for lane map $\mathcal{L}_g(m)$ with m locations per hallway, N_{AGV} AGVs, using the encodings $\mathcal{E}_X$, $\mathcal{E}_P$ and $\mathcal{E}_{AGV}$, with and without abstraction ($\mathcal{S}_A/\mathcal{S}_O$).

		$\mathcal{E}_X$				$\mathcal{E}_P$				$\mathcal{E}_{AGV}$			
		$\mathcal{S}_A$		$\mathcal{S}_O$		$\mathcal{S}_A$		$\mathcal{S}_O$		$\mathcal{S}_A$		$\mathcal{S}_O$	
m	N_{AGV}	N_V	t	N_V	t	N_V	t	N_V	t	N_V	t	N_V	t
4	2	64	0.51	88	5.19	64	0.40	104	2.99	12	0.07	14	0.17
4	3	64	1.65	88	24.84	64	1.97	104	14.06	18	2.18	21	4.53
4	4	64	9.36	88	254.25	64	7.25	104	154.29	24	125.46	28	-
5	2	80	1.06	110	5.01	80	1.04	130	6.49	14	0.10	16	0.28
5	3	80	4.19	110	17.48	80	4.68	130	22.82	21	4.51	24	9.13
5	4	80	16.34	110	174.47	80	35.67	130	184.28	28	-	32	-
5	5	80	67.78	110	-	80	-	130	-	35	-	40	-
6	2	96	2.40	132	9.02	96	1.80	156	6.08	14	0.14	16	0.37
6	3	96	7.83	132	37.06	96	9.23	156	52.00	21	6.76	24	14.91
6	4	96	22.04	132	-	96	45.58	156	-	28	-	32	-
6	5	96	77.04	-	-	96	-	-	-	-	-	-	-
6	6	96	-	-	-	-	-	-	-	-	-	-	-
7	2	112	4.56	154	45.03	112	3.35	182	20.30	14	0.18	16	0.4728
7	3	112	15.04	154	99.78	112	14.63	182	71.67	21	9.65	24	22.390
7	4	112	41.56	154	-	112	64.35	182	-	28	-	32	-
7	5	112	250.16	-	-	112	-	-	-	-	-	-	-

$\mathcal{E}_{AGV}$ due to the binary encoding of viable poses. The case of $\mathcal{L}_g$ provides a more realistic ratio of turnable locations with a speedup of approximately 6 for $\mathcal{E}_P$ and higher values reaching up to 100 at $m = 5$ and $N_{AGV} = 4$ for $\mathcal{E}_X$.

The encoding $\mathcal{E}_{AGV}$ outperforms $\mathcal{E}_X$ and $\mathcal{E}_P$ in case the number of AGVs N_{AGV} is small. This is expected due to the binary encoding of viable poses, which results in a lower number of BDD variables compared to the other encodings. However, the performance of $\mathcal{E}_{AGV}$ degrades faster than anticipated, breaking even with the other encodings when three or four AGVs are involved for all lane map types. For $\mathcal{L}_g$ and $\mathcal{L}_r$ in particular, this is far before $\mathcal{E}_{AGV}$ reaches a number of required BDD variables similar to $\mathcal{E}_X$ or $\mathcal{E}_P$. While performance of $\mathcal{E}_{AGV}$ quickly deteriorates with the number AGVs involved, this is not necessarily the case for the other two encodings, for which performance can stabilize even as N_{AGV} increases as can be seen for $\mathcal{L}_{r,2}$ in Table 3.

In a similar manner, we expected $\mathcal{E}_X$ to be superior to $\mathcal{E}_P$ as it uses at most as many variables as $\mathcal{E}_P$. While $\mathcal{E}_X$ is significantly faster on the lane map $\mathcal{L}_{r,2}$, none of the approaches is strictly better for the other lane maps. In particular, $\mathcal{E}_P$ outperforms $\mathcal{E}_X$ for $\mathcal{L}_g(4)$ with four AGVs even in the case without the abstraction of turnable locations, for which $\mathcal{E}_P$ uses significantly more variables than $\mathcal{E}_X$. With the abstraction of turnable goals, the encodings $\mathcal{E}_X$ and $\mathcal{E}_P$ require

Table 3. Results for lane maps $\mathcal{L}_{r,1}$ and $\mathcal{L}_{r,2}$ with N_{AGV} AGVs, using the encodings $\mathcal{E}_X$, $\mathcal{E}_P$ and $\mathcal{E}_{AGV}$.

	$\mathcal{L}_{r,1}$						$\mathcal{L}_{r,2}$					
	$\mathcal{E}_X$		$\mathcal{E}_P$		$\mathcal{E}_{AGV}$		$\mathcal{E}_X$		$\mathcal{E}_P$		$\mathcal{E}_{AGV}$	
N_{AGV}	N_V	t	N_V	t	N_V	t	N_V	t	N_V	t	N_V	t
2	73	1.225	73	0.863	14	0.140	119	5.262	121	4.323	14	0.380
3	73	2.317	73	2.183	21	5.028	119	8.793	121	8.656	21	24.752
4	73	7.242	73	5.295	28	264.438	119	29.890	121	38.683	28	-
5	73	18.345	73	11.622	35	-	119	62.259	121	76.356	-	-
6	73	24.381	73	23.794	-	-	119	145.109	121	265.760	-	-
7	73	29.306	73	27.528	-	-	119	135.892	121	262.977	-	-
8	73	51.569	73	59.489	-	-	119	136.415	121	249.977	-	-

the same number of variables for $\mathcal{L}_c$ and $\mathcal{L}_g$. However, the encodings still differ in their handling of non-turnable locations with two possible orientations, which requires two variables per location in both cases.

6 Conclusion

Summary. In this paper, we presented a case study on BDD-based deadlock avoidance for AGV systems with the aim of evaluating its feasibility. For this, we proposed a novel formalization of AGV systems that is more flexible than previously employed models and better reflects modeling approaches from industry. In particular, we employed a representation of AGV systems based on an LTS describing the movement patterns of a single AGV. We then provided several methods for encoding the LTS representation as a BDD, from which a maximally permissive DAP can be computed. While the increased flexibility of our approach leads to an increase in model complexity, we also provided an abstraction method that simplifies the model in areas where the increase in flexibility is not required. The subsequent evaluation showed that BDD-based deadlock avoidance is viable for mid-scale systems.

Related Work. A related and well studied problem is deadlock avoidance in Resource Allocation Systems (RAS), [16] a subset of Discrete Event Systems (DES) [14]. It covers resource allocation in a system with several resource types with limited availability and a fixed set of process types. Any number of processes can be executed in parallel with the restriction each process requires access to a multiset of resources in each of its steps. While this approach provides some flexibility by allowing processes to branch into different alternative paths, it does not permit a finite representation of dynamically routed AGVs. However, the RAS community has worked on statically routed AGV systems [2] and even provided a fast but suboptimal algorithm for deadlock avoidance based on finite state automata for dynamically routed systems [15]. A BDD-based approach for finding the maximally permissive DAP in the context of RAS with automata as an intermediate representation has been proposed by Fei et al. [5].

The shortcomings of RAS in the context of AGVs have led to the investigation of methods based on Partially Directed Graphs (PDG) [19,20]. The case of closed systems has been handled by Fanti et al. [4] and further improved by He et al. [6]. In the same vein, Reveliotis and Masopust [17] developed a polynomial algorithm for assessing liveness in open AGV systems based on irreversible, dynamically routed AGVs for a subset of possible configurations, which can also be employed for closed systems. An important difference between PDG-based approaches and our formalization is that the former assumes that there is a one to one correspondence between motions and reservations, i.e., there are no dependencies/restrictions between motions (and locations). This prevents turning motions to be modeled in PDGs which results in a coarser granularity and thus weaker modeling capabilities of PDG-based approaches. For example, PDG-based approaches are incapable of detecting orientation specific deadlocks such as the one depicted in Fig. 3b.

Another formalism that has seen extensive use in deadlock avoidance in automated manufacturing is Petri nets. An overview is given by Li et al. [7], which also covers the topic of AGVs, e.g., by Wu and Zhou [22]. However, to the best of our knowledge, existing approaches based on Petri nets make the same assumptions as PDG-based approaches. A BDD-based approach for flexible manufacturing systems is covered by Miremadi et al. [11]. Their benchmarks also contain a small AGV system from the literature based on a Petri net model.

A recent industrial case study by Pratissoli et al. [13] considers hierarchical traffic management in an AGV system using a finite horizon for deadlock avoidance, which is unsound if the horizon is not set correctly.

The issue of deadlocks has been studied in the related domain of railway systems [21]. However, approaches developed for the railway domain often make assumptions that are too strict for AGV systems such as static routing or restrictions on the structure of the guide path network [8,10,12].

Threats to Validity. The method presented in this paper computes a maximally permissive DAP for a discretized version of the AGV system with a finite set of possible reservations. However, this system description itself is not maximally permissive, since reservations could also be computed on the fly for partial motions. This results in a richer set of motions potentially allowing to resolve a system state that is considered a deadlock in the discretized system description. A parallel effort is currently undertaken in the domain of railway systems with the transition to moving block signaling [21].

The modeling approach outlined in this paper does not cover the whole complexity of AGV systems. For example, there could be (1) different types of AGVs with different footprints, (2) additional restrictions, such as constraints on how many AGVs are permitted in a specific area or (3) special reservations with a larger footprint for special actions such as picking up a pallet in a larger area. Those cases can be easily incorporated into our modeling approach. Different

AGV types could, for example, be modeled by extending the state space Q of poses in the single AGV system $\mathcal{S}_1$ with the AGV type and adapting the set of conflicts $Q_{\not\downarrow}$ accordingly. However, the influence of such modifications on the performance of BDD-based deadlock avoidance has not been studied in this work.

The evaluated lane maps were designed to mimic problematic cases in real world applications and included an example from industry. However, it is difficult to capture the domain of AGV systems with parametric approaches, since warehouse layouts can vary drastically from case to case, for example due to constraints imposed by preexisting infrastructure.

Lessons Learned. The results presented in this paper show that BDD-based deadlock avoidance can be employed for warehouse systems up to mid-scale. Even if a full analysis of large systems is infeasible, it can be used as a best-effort method using fewer AGVs and sub-regions of the whole warehouse. This applies in particular to the pose- and location-centric encodings. The AGV-centric encoding enables deadlock avoidance for large lane maps with a small number of AGVs. However, its performance degrades quickly even for small fleets.

In general, the problem of deadlock avoidance in dynamically routed AGV systems is NP-complete and the results for the parameterized lane maps discussed in Sect. 5 also suggest exponential patterns. Consequently, each gain in performance in orders of magnitude only allows us to analyze linearly bigger lane maps. However, liveness-preserving abstraction methods such as the abstraction of turnable goals work on the lane map as a whole and thus have the potential to significantly increase the feasibility of computing maximally permissive DAPs. This calls for the development of methods that perform liveness-preserving abstraction of lane maps in an at least semi-automatic manner, potentially reusing ideas from PDG literature.

Acknowledgements. The work in this paper was supported by the Austrian Science Fund (FWF) Cluster of Excellence Bilateral AI under contract number 10.55776/COE12 as well as the Transformative AI-Assisted Testing in Industrial Mobile Robotics (TASTE) project (project number FO999911053) funded by the Austrian Research Promotion Agency (FFG).

References

1. Bloem, R., Könighofer, B., Könighofer, R., Wang, C.: Shield Synthesis: runtime enforcement for reactive systems. In: Baier, C., Tinelli, C. (eds.) TACAS 2015. LNCS, vol. 9035, pp. 533–548. Springer, Heidelberg (2015). https://doi.org/10.1007/978-3-662-46681-0_51
2. Dotoli, M., Fanti, M.P.: Deadlock detection and avoidance strategies for automated storage and retrieval systems. IEEE Trans. Syst. Man Cybern. Part C **37**(4), 541–552 (2007). https://doi.org/10.1109/TSMCC.2007.897690
3. Drechsler, R., Becker, B.: Binary Decision Diagrams - Theory and Implementation. Springer, Cham (1998). http://www.springer.com/engineering/circuits+%26+systems/book/978-0-7923-8193-8

4. Fanti, M.P., Mangini, A.M., Pedroncelli, G., Ukovich, W.: Decentralized deadlock-free control for AGV systems. In: American Control Conference, ACC 2015, Chicago, IL, USA, 1–3 July 2015, pp. 2414–2419. IEEE (2015). https://doi.org/10.1109/ACC.2015.7171094
5. Fei, Z., Reveliotis, S.A., Miremadi, S., Åkesson, K.: A BDD-based approach for designing maximally permissive deadlock avoidance policies for complex resource allocation systems. IEEE Trans. Autom. Sci. Eng. **12**(3), 990–1006 (2015). https://doi.org/10.1109/TASE.2014.2369858
6. He, D., Ouyang, B., Fan, H., Hu, C., Zhang, K., Yan, Z.: Deadlock avoidance in closed guide-path based MultiAGV systems. IEEE Trans. Autom. Sci. Eng. **20**(3), 2088–2098 (2023). https://doi.org/10.1109/TASE.2022.3193946
7. Li, Z., Wu, N., Zhou, M.: Deadlock control of automated manufacturing systems based on Petri nets - a literature review. IEEE Trans. Syst. Man Cybern. Part C **42**(4), 437–462 (2012). https://doi.org/10.1109/TSMCC.2011.2160626
8. Luo, J., Zhou, M., Wang, J.: A place-timed Petri net-based method to avoid deadlock and conflict in railway networks. IEEE Trans. Intell. Transp. Syst. **23**(8), 10763–10772 (2022). https://doi.org/10.1109/TITS.2021.3095661
9. Maxwell, W.L., Muckstadt, J.A.: Design of automatic guided vehicle systems. A I I E Trans. **14**(2), 114–124 (1982). https://doi.org/10.1080/05695558208975046
10. Mazzanti, F., Spagnolo, G.O., Della Longa, S., Ferrari, A.: Deadlock avoidance in train scheduling: a model checking approach. In: Lang, F., Flammini, F. (eds.) FMICS 2014. LNCS, vol. 8718, pp. 109–123. Springer, Cham (2014). https://doi.org/10.1007/978-3-319-10702-8_8
11. Miremadi, S., Lennartson, B., Åkesson, K.: A BDD-based approach for modeling plant and supervisor by extended finite automata. IEEE Trans. Control. Syst. Technol. **20**(6), 1421–1435 (2012). https://doi.org/10.1109/TCST.2011.2167150
12. Pachl, J.: Avoiding deadlocks in synchronous railway simulations. In: 2nd International Seminar on Railway Operations Modelling and Analysis, vol. 2007 (2007)
13. Pratissoli, F., Brugioni, R., Battilani, N., Sabattini, L.: Hierarchical traffic management of multi-AGV systems with deadlock prevention applied to industrial environments. IEEE Trans. Autom. Sci. Eng. **21**(3), 3155–3169 (2024). https://doi.org/10.1109/TASE.2023.3276233
14. Ramadge, P.J., Wonham, W.M.: The control of discrete event systems. Proc. IEEE **77**(1), 81–98 (1989). https://doi.org/10.1109/5.21072
15. Reveliotis, S.A.: Conflict resolution in AGV systems. IIE Trans. **32**(7), 647–659 (2000). https://doi.org/10.1023/A:1007663100796
16. Reveliotis, S.A.: Real-time management of resource allocations systems: a discrete event systems approach. Springer (2005). https://doi.org/10.1007/b104057
17. Reveliotis, S.A., Masopust, T.: Efficient liveness assessment for traffic states in open, irreversible, dynamically routed, zone-controlled guidepath-based transport systems. IEEE Trans. Autom. Control. **65**(7), 2883–2898 (2020). https://doi.org/10.1109/TAC.2019.2934427
18. Reveliotis, S.A., Roszkowska, E.: On the complexity of maximally permissive deadlock avoidance in multi-vehicle traffic systems. IEEE Trans. Autom. Control. **55**(7), 1646–1651 (2010). https://doi.org/10.1109/TAC.2010.2046111
19. Roszkowska, E.: Liveness enforcing in closed AGV systems with dynamic routing. In: Proceedings of the 2004 IEEE International Conference on Robotics and Automation, ICRA 2004, 26 April–1 May 2004, New Orleans, LA, USA, pp. 5165–5170. IEEE (2004). https://doi.org/10.1109/ROBOT.2004.1302537

20. Roszkowska, E., Reveliotis, S.A.: On the liveness of guidepath-based, zone-controlled dynamically routed, closed traffic systems. IEEE Trans. Autom. Control. **53**(7), 1689–1695 (2008). https://doi.org/10.1109/TAC.2008.929375
21. Versluis, N.D., Quaglietta, E., Goverde, R.M., Pellegrini, P., Rodriguez, J.: Real-time railway traffic management under moving-block signalling: a literature review and research agenda. Transp. Res. Part C: Emerg. Technol. **158**, 104438 (2024). https://doi.org/10.1016/j.trc.2023.104438, https://www.sciencedirect.com/science/article/pii/S0968090X2300428X
22. Wu, N., Zhou, M.: Modeling and deadlock control of automated guided vehicle systems. IEEE/ASME Trans. Mechatron. **9**(1), 50–57 (2004). https://doi.org/10.1109/TMECH.2004.823875

Automatic Memory Management for Dataflows

Michael Lienhardt(✉)

DTIS, ONERA, Université Paris-Saclay, Palaiseau, France
michael.lienhardt@onera.fr

Abstract. Memory management in High Performance Computing (HPC) is a very important topic, as slow reads and writes can add an important overhead to the execution of an HPC application. In particular, to take advantage of the vectorization capabilities and cache capacities of the hardware, many of such applications are designed to align their data in a certain way or to perform some operations inplace. However, ensuring that the data are correctly aligned and that the inplace operations do not create data-races is a manual and difficult task. Moreover, many HPC applications are configurable and their data and computation may vary at every run: in this context, it is often impossible to manually ensure optimal memory management.

This paper proposes an approach that automatically generates a correct memory management with minimal overhead. Our approach is based on the *dataflow* computation model, and considers both data alignment constraints and inplace operations. We prove that the problem solved in this paper is NP-hard, and that our approach is sound and complete.

1 Introduction

High Performance Computing (HPC) applications are designed to run efficiently on highly parallel hardware architectures. This imposes several constraints on how their computation is executed, and on how their memory is allocated and managed. First, many HPC applications use *dataflows* to model their execution, either through HPC libraries [1,4,6,9,18,19,32] or with their own implementation, like the Computational Fluid Dynamics (CFD) simulation software SoNICS [14]. This model structures a computation using a Directed Acyclic Graph (DAG) where nodes are tasks or data and edges give the inputs and outputs of every tasks: the simple control flow of this model is well suited to be efficiently executed on many hardwares, including highly parallel ones. On the other hand, HPC applications must manage their memory in a way to ensure quick reads and writes. In particular, several physical simulators [14,23,33], structure their data into arrays instead of a complex graph of objects, and have two main dataflow-related constraints[1] on how these data are allocated and manipulated: a

This work was partially supported by the SONICE project, granted by the French Directorate General for Civil Aviation (DGAC).

[1] Other kind of memory constraints will be discussed in Sect. 5.

A. Sampaio and M. Stoelinga (Eds.): FM 2026, LNCS 16556, pp. 317–336, 2026.
https://doi.org/10.1007/978-3-032-26204-2_17

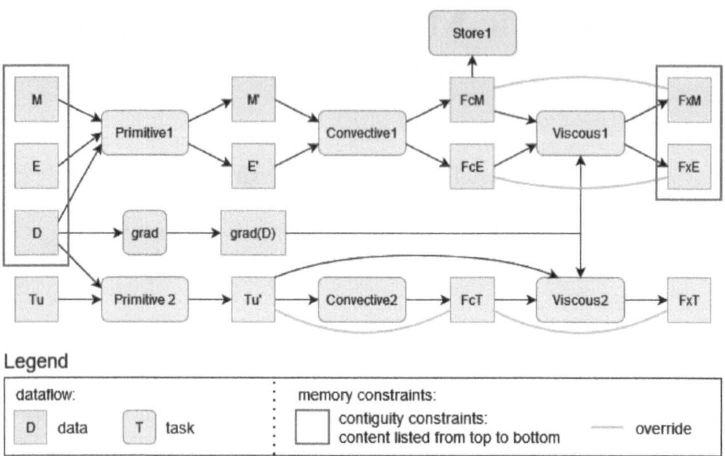

Fig. 1. Example of Dataflow with Memory Constraints.

contiguity constraint (CC) is when a task expects some of its inputs to be stored sequentially in memory, so its execution can be optimized with cache blocking and vectorization techniques; an *override constraint* (OC) is when a task writes one of its output in the array containing one of its input, again for efficiency purpose.

Example 1. Consider for instance Fig. 1 which presents a simple dataflow, inspired from a SoNICS's fluid flow simulation, that illustrates the core structure and memory constraints that could be encountered in many HPC applications.[2]

It starts on the left with input data `M` (the momentum of the fluid to simulate), `E` (its energy), `D` (its density), and `Tu` (its turbulent characteristics). The tasks `Primitive1` and `Primitive2` translate `M`, `E` and `Tu` into data that can be directly used to compute the fluid flow, `grad` computes the gradient of `D`, `Convective1` and `Convective2` compute the convective flux of the fluid (modeled with the data `FcM`, `FcE` and `FcT`) while `Viscous1` and `Viscous2` update the flux by considering the fluid's viscosity (the resulting flux being modeled with the data `FxM`, `FxE` and `FxT`). The task `Store1` stores the data `FcM` on disk. The memory constraints are as follows: `Primitive1` expects all its inputs to be contiguous in memory; `Viscous1` writes its outputs in sequence in one unique array; `Viscous1` overrides `FcM` into `FxM` and `FcE` into `FxE`; `Convective2` overrides `Tu'` into `FcT`; and `Viscous2` overrides `FcT` into `FxT`. □

Memory constraints can be solved in several ways. For instance in Example 1, the override on `FcM` performed by `Viscous1` (that creates a data race with `Store1`) can be solved by either copying `FcM` so that `Store1` will have in input a replica of `FcM` that will never be overwritten, or by adding a dependency stating

[2] While most HPC applications do not publish their internal structure, we believe that many of them, concerned with efficient memory management, face similar issues.

that Store1 must be executed before Viscous1. Similarly, CCs can be solved either by allocating data in the correct order right away, or it could be copied later on in an order that would satisfy the tasks requirements. In practice however, it is important to minimize the memory footprint of an application, and in particular the number of copies it performs.

Currently, solving memory constraints is a manual process performed by the dataflow developers, which is problematic for two reasons. First, memory constraints are difficult to solve due to the complex interactions between CCs, OCs, and the control flow of the dataflow. Consider for instance the three interactions in Example 1: *i*) the outputs of the task Viscous1 are aligned and overwriting FcM and FcE, which implies that these data must also be aligned; *ii*) the possible data-race between the tasks Viscous1 and Store1 on the data FcM can be solved by executing Store1 before Viscous1; *iii*) but this solution cannot be applied for the data-race between Convective2 and Viscous2 as it would introduce a deadlock in the dataflow. Indeed, since Convective2 computes the data FcT that is used by Viscous2, Convective2 must be executed before Viscous2; but since Convective2 overrides Tu', Viscous2 must be executed before it to ensure that it gets the correct data in input. Second, this manual process cannot be applied on automatically generated dataflows such as the ones used in the SoNICS simulator [24]. Indeed, such applications are highly configurable and every user input produces a different dataflow to execute: manually analysing and adapting that dataflow to obtain an efficient memory management is impossible, due to time and human limitations. The current solution for automatically generated dataflows is to use a generic memory management that works properly in most cases, but without any guarantee on efficiency. For instance, Devito [27] does not include any memory optimization.

This paper presents an approach to automatically solve such memory constraints. As discussed in [26], this approach has been implemented in the SoNICS simulator, but the approach's implementation and its formalization were never presented. More specifically, the contributions of the paper are: *i*) a formalization of *memory management* suited for the contiguity and override memory constraints; *ii*) a proof that solving CCs is linear and solving OCs is NP-hard; and *iii*) an algorithm that automatically computes, given a dataflow and a set of constraints, a memory management for the dataflow that satisfies the constraints and that performs the minimum number of copies possible.

This paper is structured as follows: Sect. 2 constructs a formal definition of the notion of *memory management* discussed in this paper; Sect. 3 presents an algorithm that solves CCs and proves that the problem is linear; Sect. 4 extends the previous algorithm to also solve OCs and proves that solving OCs is NP-hard; finally, Sects. 5 and 6 present the related work and conclude the paper.

2 Memory Management

Dataflow and Constraints. Before defining the notion of memory management, we first formalize the core notions that were discussed in the introduction:

dataflow and memory constraints. As previously discussed, a dataflow is a directed acyclic graph with two kinds of nodes, data and tasks, and two kind of edges: *input edges* which link data to tasks, stating which are the tasks' inputs; and *output edges* which link tasks to data, stating which are the tasks' outputs. Consequently, a dataflow is also a bipartite graph, where each data can have at most one incoming edge corresponding to the tasks producing it.

Definition 1. *A* dataflow *df is a bipartite directed acyclic graph* (T, D, E) *where:* T *is a set of tasks;* D *is a set of data;* $E \subseteq D \times T \cup T \times D$ *is the input/output relation such that for all* $d \in D$*, there exists at most one* $t \in T$ *such that* $(t, d) \in E$*.*

The first kind of memory constraints, *Contiguity constraints* (CCs), states how the different tasks in the dataflow expect their inputs and outputs to be aligned in memory. In principle, two tasks sharing some inputs could thus have incompatible CCs. Consider for instance the dataflow in Example 1: the task `Primitive1` requires that `D` is on the right of `E`, while the task `Primitive2` could additionally require that `D` is on the right of `Tu`. Solving incompatible CCs is possible using copies that creates an array specifically for each task's inputs and outputs. However, since the purpose of CCs is to speedup memory reads and writes, solving them by introducing additional copies is counter productive, and so any incompatible CCs is considered an error. The following definition formalizes CCs and introduces the notion of a *valid* set of CCs, i.e., where all CCs are compatible: informally, a set of CCs is valid if there exists a data alignment that validates every CC in the set.

Definition 2. *Given a dataflow* $df = (T, D, E)$*, a* contiguity constraint *(CC) is a sequence* $(d_1, \ldots, d_n)$ *for some* $n \in \mathbb{N}$ *such that* $d_i \in D$ *for all* $1 \leq i \leq n$*. A set of CCs* S *is* valid *iff there exists a sequence of distinct data* $(d_1, \ldots, d_n)$ *such that for all* $(d'_1, \ldots, d'_m) \in S$*, there exists* $0 \leq k \leq n - m$ *with* $d_{i+k} = d'_i$ *for all* $1 \leq i \leq m$*.*

Example 2. Example 1 contains two CCs: $(\mathtt{M}, \mathtt{E}, \mathtt{D})$ and $(\mathtt{FxM}, \mathtt{FxE})$. This set is valid, since the CCs do not share any data: the sequence $(\mathtt{M}, \mathtt{E}, \mathtt{D}, \mathtt{FxM}, \mathtt{FxE})$ trivially satisfies the definition. However, if we add for instance the CC $(\mathtt{Tu}, \mathtt{D})$, the set becomes invalid because it is impossible to build a sequence of data where `E` and `Tu` are both on the right of `D`. □

The second kind of memory constraints, *Override constraints* (OCs), models when a task uses the memory of one of its inputs to store one of its output. Additionally our definition forbids behaviors that are impossible: since a data is created by one task, for every data d, there can be at most one OC with output d; and since a memory space can hold only one data at a given time, a task can override its input at most once:

Definition 3. *Given a dataflow* $df = (T, D, E)$*, an* override *is a triplet* (d, t, d') *such that* $d \in D$ *and* $(d, t), (t, d') \in E$*. A set of overrides* O *is* valid *iff: i) for all* $d' \in D$*, there exists at most one* $(d, t) \in E$ *such that* $(d, t, d') \in O$*; and ii) for all* $(d, t) \in E$*, there exists at most one* $d' \in D$ *such that* $(d, t, d') \in O$*.*

Example 3. Example 1 contains four OCs: (FcM, Viscous1, FxM), (FcE, Viscous1, FxE), (Tu', Convective2, FcT), (FcT, Viscous2, FxT). This set is valid as every task overrides at most once its inputs and stores its outputs in either a new memory space or the memory space of exactly one input. □

Finally, the validity of a set of arbitrary memory constraints must consider the interaction between the CCs and OCs. Consider for instance the task Viscous1 in Example 1. The outputs of this task must be stored in a specific order, but these data are in the same memory space as the task's inputs: consequently, the inputs must be stored in the same order of the outputs. The following definition ensures that CCs and OCs contained in the same set of memory constraints are compatible:

Definition 4. *Let us suppose given a dataflow $df = (T, D, E)$ and a set of memory constraints $S = S_1 \cup S_2$ with $S_1 = \{(d_1^k, \dots, d_{n_k}^k) \mid k \in K\}$ and $S_2 = \{(d_i, t_i, d_i') \mid i \in I\}$ for some sets K and I. We write D_S the partition of D raised by the equivalence closure of the relation $\{(d_i, d_i') \mid i \in I\}$. We say that S is* valid *iff S_1 and S_2 are valid and $S_3 = \{(D_S[d_1^k], \dots D_S[d_{n_k}^k]) \mid k \in K\}$ is valid, where for any $d \in D$, $D_S[d]$ is the set in D_S containing d.*

Example 4. The set of memory constraints in Example 1 is valid. Indeed, we discussed in Example 2 and 3 that S_1 and S_2 are valid. Moreover, the non-singleton sets of its partition D_S are: {FcM, FxM}, {FcE, FxE}, and {Tu', FcT, FxT}. Consequently, the set of CCs S_3 of Definition 4 contains both ({M}, {E}, {D}) and ({FcM, FxM}, {FcE, FxE}): like S_1, this set is clearly valid. □

Memory Management. The main elements describing the memory management performed by an application are the allocations of the different arrays (with their given size) that will be used by the tasks to store their data, and the specification of where in this memory space every task fetches its inputs and stores its outputs. Additionally, as discussed in Sect. 1, data-races (caused by the OCs) can be avoided in two ways: either by forcing some tasks to be executed before their inputs are overwritten, or by copying the overwritten data.

The following definition formalizes the notion of memory management as follows. Allocations are encoded by simply stating which arrays must be allocated (given by a set A) with their size (given by a function α). Data access is encoded with a function $\mu_{\mathtt{in}}$ that gives, for every task t and every input d of t, the array cell (modeled with the pair (a, i), where a is an array and i is a valid index of a) from which t fetches d. Data storage is encoded with another function $\mu_{\mathtt{out}}$ that gives, for every task t and every output d of t, the array cells in which t stores d: note that $\mu_{\mathtt{out}}$ can give multiple cells to store one data, which encodes copies. And the ordering used to solve some data-races is directly encoded as a relation δ between tasks.

Definition 5. *Given a dataflow $df = (T, D, E)$, a* Memory Management *(MM) for df is a tuple $M = (A, \alpha, \mu_{in}, \mu_{out}, \delta)$ where: A is a set of arrays; $\alpha : A \to \mathbb{N}$ gives the size of each array; $\mu_{in} : (E \cap D \times T) \to A \times \mathbb{N}$ states for each task in*

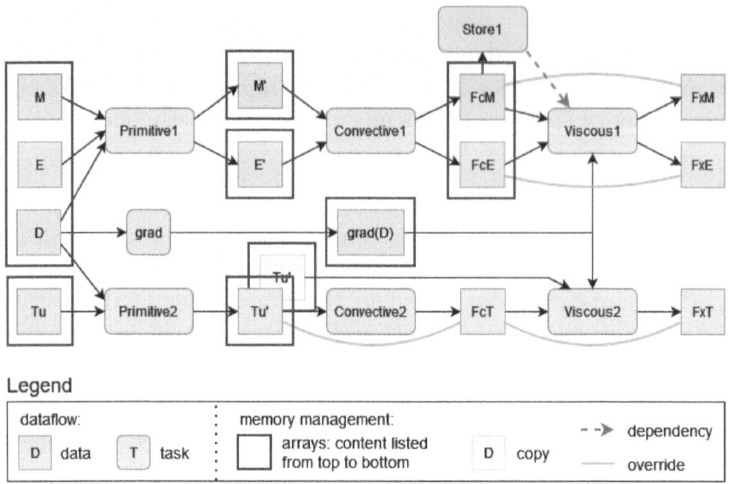

Fig. 2. Example of Dataflow with Memory Management.

which array cells it should fetch its input data; $\mu_{out} : (E \cap T \times D) \to 2^{A\times\mathbb{N}} \setminus \{\emptyset\}$ *states for each task in which array cells it should store its output data; and* $\delta \subseteq T \times T$ *is an additional ordering between tasks.*

Example 5. Figure 2 gives a graphical representation of a MM for Example 1. It allocates eight arrays: the first one stores the sequence (`M`, `E`, `D`); the second one stores `Tu`; the third, fourth and fifth arrays respectively store `M'`, `E'`, and `grad(D)`; the sixth array stores `Tu'`, which is then overwritten into `FcT` and then into `FxT`; the seventh array stores a copy of `Tu'` (to be used by the task `Viscous2`); and the last array stores the sequence (`FcM`, `FcE`), which will be overwritten into the sequence (`FxM`, `FxE`). Additionally, this MM forces the task `Store1` to be executed before `Viscous1`, to avoid a data-race over the data `FcM`. □

Finally, we define when a MM is valid w.r.t. a dataflow and a set of memory constraints. Informally, a MM is valid w.r.t. a dataflow if it stores all the inputs of the dataflow in different memory slots, its additional dependencies do not create a deadlock, and every task is sure to find the expected data when fetching their inputs. Moreover, it is valid w.r.t. a CC if every task have their inputs aligned in memory as specified in the CC, and it is valid w.r.t. an OC if the memory slots are consistent with the constraint and if there are no data-race.

Definition 6. *Let us suppose a dataflow* $df = (T, D, E)$*, a valid set of memory constraints* S *with CCs* S_1 *and OCs* S_2*, and a MM* $M = (A, \alpha, \mu_{in}, \mu_{out}, \delta)$ *for* df*. We write* $\mathtt{ins}(df)$ *the inputs of* df *and* $\mathtt{tdeps}(df)$ *the task dependencies of* df*:*

$$\mathtt{ins}(df) = \{d \in D \mid \forall t \in T,\ (t, d) \notin E\}$$
$$\mathtt{tdeps}(df) = \{(t, t') \in T \times T \mid \exists d \in D,\ (t, d), (d, t') \in E\}$$

We say that M validates df *iff the following conditions hold:*

1. *for all* $d_1 \neq d_2 \in \textbf{\textit{ins}}(df)$ *and all* $(d_1, t_1), (d_2, t_2) \in E$, $\mu_{in}(d_1, t_1) \neq \mu_{in}(d_2, t_2)$ *holds;*
2. *the graph* $G = (T, \texttt{tdeps}(df) \cup \delta)$ *is acyclic;*
3. *for all* $(t, d), (d, t') \in E$, *we have* $\mu_{in}(d, t') \in \mu_{out}(t, d)$*;*

We say that M validates *a CC* $(d_1, \ldots, d_n)$ *iff both conditions hold:*

1. *for all* $t \in T$ *and* $1 \leq i, j \leq n$ *such that* $(d_i, t), (d_j, t) \in E$, *we have* $\mu_{in}(d_j, t) = (a, k + (j - i))$ *with* $\mu_{in}(d_i, t) = (a, k)$*;*
2. *for all* $t \in T$ *and* $1 \leq i, j \leq n$ *such that* $(t, d_i), (t, d_j) \in E$, *and for all* $(a, k) \in \mu_{out}(t, d_i)$ *and* $(a', k') \in \mu_{out}(t, d_j)$ *with* $a = a'$, *we have* $k' = k + (j - i)$*;*

We say that M validates *an OC* (d, t, d') *iff both conditions hold:*

1. *we have* $\mu_{in}(d, t) \in \mu_{out}(t, d')$*;*
2. *for all* $(d, t') \in E$ *with* $\mu_{in}(d, t) = \mu_{in}(d, t')$, *we have* $(t', t) \in \delta$.

Finally, we say that M validates $(df, S_1 \cup S_2)$ *iff it validates* df *and all the constraints in* $S_1 \cup S_2$.

The rest of this paper presents our approach to produce a valid MM for a dataflow and a set of memory constraints. We prove our algorithm to be sound and complete, and that it produces a MM with the minimal possible number of copies. Section 3 introduces our algorithm by only solving CCs, and Sect. 4 extends this algorithm to also solve OCs.

3 Solving Contiguity Constraints

In principle, given a dataflow $df = (T, D, E)$, solving a set S of CCs can be reduced into a graph problem by interpreting individual constraints $(d_1, \ldots, d_n)$ as paths. We can merge all these paths to obtain a graph G where every edge (d, d') means that d must be placed on the left of d':

$$G = (D, E') \qquad \text{where} \qquad E' = \bigcup_{(d_1, \ldots, d_n) \in S} \ \bigcup_{1 \leq i < n} \{(d_i, d_{i+1})\}$$

Consequently, S is valid iff G does not contain any cycle and all data d has at most one predecessor and one successor. Finally, when S is valid, we can build a MM by stating that its arrays are the longest paths in G:

$$A = \{(d_1, \ldots, d_n) \mid \forall d \in D,\ (d, d_1), (d_n, d) \notin E' \wedge \forall 1 \leq i < n,\ (d_i, d_{i+1}) \in E'\}$$

In practice, we model the graph with an adjacency mapping that gives for every data $d \in D$ its left and right neighbors. This data structure is efficient and is well suited for this problem: the constraint that all data d has at most one predecessor and one successor is enforced by the data structure itself. The downside of this approach is that manually updating the adjacency mapping is

```
1  input: Data Set D
2  input: CC Set S
3  begin
4   Adj ← ∅
5   for((d_1, ..., d_n) ∈ S)
6    p ← ⊥
7    for(1 ≤ i ≤ n)
8     if(d_i ∉ dom(Adj))
9      Adj[d_i] ← (left = p, right = ⊥)
10     if(p ≠ ⊥)
11      if(Adj[p].right ≠ ⊥) error
12      else Adj[p].right ← d_i
13    elif(p ≠ ⊥)
14     if(Adj[d_i].left = ⊥)
15      if(Adj[p].right ≠ ⊥) error
16      Adj[d_i].left ← p
17      Adj[p].right ← d_i
18     elif((p ≠ Adj[d_i].left)) error
19    p ← d_i
20  for(d ∈ D)
21   if(d ∉ dom(Adj))
22    Adj[d] ← (left = ⊥, right = ⊥)
23  A ← ∅
24  for(d ∈ dom(Adj))
25   if(Adj[d].left = ⊥)
26    a = ()
27    while(d ≠ ⊥)
28     a.append(d)
29     d ← Adj[d].right
30    A.add(a)
31  if(⋃_{a∈A} a ≠ dom(Adj)) error
32  output: A
33 end
```

Fig. 3. The *ComputeArray* Algorithm

a bit tedious. Our algorithm to solve CCs is introduced in Figs. 3 and 4: the first figure presents the function *ComputeArray* that computes the arrays and their content, while the second one presents the full algorithm *MemoryGenCC* that translates these arrays into a MM.

The *ComputeArray* function in Fig. 3 takes a set of data D and a set of CCs S in input, and is structured in three loops. The first loop (Lines 5–19) iterates over the CCs $(d_1, \ldots, d_n)$, and translates them into the adjacency mapping `Adj` which maps each d_i to the pair of its neighbors on the left and on the right (the special value $\bot$ means that there are no known neighbors). That way, every time the algorithm encounters a data it already saw, it checks if the new constraint is compatible with the previous one. To perform this translation, the loop also iterates over every data d_i in $(d_1, \ldots, d_n)$ by also considering the data p placed on the left of d and initialized to $\bot$.

Then, we perform different operations depending on if d of p are already declared in `Adj` (since the constraint is traversed from left to right, $p \neq \bot$ is equivalent to $p \in \mathrm{dom}(\texttt{Adj})$: if neither d nor p are declared in `Adj`, we simply need to store the entry $d \mapsto (\texttt{left} = p, \texttt{right} = \bot)$ in `Adj`, stating that d's left neighbor is p and we don't know yet its right neighbor; if instead p is declared, its right neighbor can only be $\bot$ to not raise an error (since its actual right neighbor is d, which was never encountered until this iteration) and must be updated; if instead d is declared while p is not, nothing needs to be done; finally, if both d and p are declared, we check if their declarations are compatible and either raise an error or update them. Note that this loop does not ensure that the neigboring relation raised by the CCs does not form loops. Consider for instance the CC (d', d'): the first iteration of the loop, with $p = \bot$ and $d = d'$, creates the map $d' \mapsto (\texttt{left} = \bot, \texttt{right} = \bot)$, and the second iteration, with $p = d'$ and $d = d'$,

```
1  input: dataflow df = (T, D, E)
2  input: CC Set S
3  begin
4   A ← ComputeArray(D, S)
5   α ← {a ↦ len(a) | a ∈ A}
6   μin ← ∅; μout ← ∅; δ ← ∅
7   for(a ∈ A)
8    for(1 ≤ i ≤ len(a))
9     for((a[i], t) ∈ E)
10     μin(a[i], t) ← (a, i)
11    for((t, a[i]) ∈ E)
12     μout(t, a[i]) ← {(a, i)}
13  output: (A, α, μin, μout, δ)
14 end
```

Fig. 4. *MemoryGenCC* Algorithm.

sees that both p and d are already declared with no incompatibilities and updates the mapping to $d' \mapsto (\texttt{left} = d', \texttt{right} = d')$ that correctly encodes that d' is in a loop. We check for loops in *Adj* at the end of our algorithm, where it is simpler than performing a graph traversal of *Adj*.

The second loop (Lines 20–22) completes *Adj* with the data in D, by mapping every data $d \in D$ that is not already in *Adj* to the pair $(\texttt{left} = \bot, \texttt{right} = \bot)$, stating that this data has no neighbor.

The third loop (Lines 24–30) translates *Adj* into a set of arrays A by iterating over all entries in *Adj*: if a data d has no left neighbor, it is the starting point of a new array, and its builds that array by iterating over all the data on the right of d, until it reaches the end $\bot$.

Finally, Line 31 checks that the CCs do not contain loops. Since loops cannot contain a data with $\bot$ as left neighbor and that we start the construction of an array with such a data, an array in A cannot contain a data that is in a loop. Consequently, we just need to check that all data in *Adj* are placed in an array to ensure that the CCs do not contain loops.

The *MemoryGenCC* function in Fig. 4 takes a dataflow *df* and a set of CCs S in input, and produces a corresponding MM $(A, \alpha, \mu_{\texttt{in}}, \mu_{\texttt{out}}, \delta)$ as follows: A is the set of arrays produced by the *ComputeArray* algorithm; α maps all arrays in A to their size; $\mu_{\texttt{in}}$ and $\mu_{\texttt{out}}$ are computed in the loop in Lines 7–12 which iterates over all the arrays and all their cells and which simply states that every task that have the corresponding data in input should use that cell to fetch the data, and every task that outputs the corresponding data should store their output in that cell; and δ is empty as there are not data-races to solve.

Theorem 1. *MemoryGenCC has the following properties:*

- *it is complete, i.e., it only fails for invalid sets of CCs;*
- *it is sound, i.e., the produced MM validates the input dataflow and CCs;*
- *and its time and space complexity is linear.*

Proof (Sketch). Let us consider a dataflow $df = (T, D, E)$ and a valid set of CCs S. We first prove that *MemoryGenCC* is sound. Suppose that this function succeeds and produces a MM. This MM is valid w.r.t. *df* since: it gives a different array cell for every data; its set of dependencies is empty; and every task using and producing a data d fetches and stores that data from and in the same cell.

Moreover, this MM validates S since its arrays are build from `Adj` which capture the neighboring information in S. To prove that *MemoryGenCC* is complete and never raises an error, let us consider a sequence $(d_1, \dots, d_n)$ as described in Definition 2: all d_i are distincts and for all $(d'_1, \dots, d'_m) \in S$, there exists $0 \leq k \leq n - m$ such that $d_{i+k} = d'_i$ for all $1 \leq i \leq m$. This sequence ensures that all neighboring information in S is consistent and would not raise any error during the computation of `Adj`. Moreover, since all d_i are distincts, the CCs cannot specify any loop, and the last check of our algorithm succeeds. Finally, since *ComputeArray* iterates over S, and then three times over D (for the second and third loops, and for the last check), this function is linear. Moreover, *MemoryGenCC* builds its result by taking the arrays A produced by *ComputeArray*, iterates once over A, and once over E (in the loops, Lines 9 and 11), and so is also linear. □

4 Override Resolution

Considering OC constraints in additions to CCs raises three new issues that needs to be solved, as illustrated in Example 3: *i*) array cells may contain several data over the execution of the dataflow (like the cell initially containing `FcM` and then `FxM` after the execution of `Viscous1`); *ii*) some data must be copied (like `Tu'`); and *iii*) we need to avoid unnecessary copies by forcing some tasks to be executed before others (like `Store1`, forced to be executed before `Viscous1`). To illustrate how our approach solves these three issues, let us consider a dataflow $df = (T, D, E)$, a set of CCs S_1 and a set of OCs S_2.

The first issue can be easily solved with the *ComputeArray* algorithm. Indeed if we suppose that no copies are necessary, each data will be hosted in a single array cell, and the same cell will host all the data that override each other. Consequently, by applying *ComputeArray* not on D and S_1 directly, but on an abstraction that unifies overriding data, we would obtain a set of arrays A_{nc} that could host every data and that would use the same cell to host overriding data. More precisely, we apply *ComputeArray* on two constructions from Definition 4: D_S, the partition of D raised by the equivalence closure of the relation $\{(d, d') \mid (d, t, d') \in S_2\}$; and $S_3 = \{(D_S[d_1], \dots D_S[d_n]) \mid (d_1, \dots, d_n) \in S_1\}$ where $D_S[d]$ is the set in D_S containing d.

Example 6. Let us consider the dataflow and constraints presented in Example 1. As discussed in Example 4, we have:

$$D_S = \left\{ \begin{array}{c} \{\texttt{M}\}, \{\texttt{E}\}, \{\texttt{D}\}, \{\texttt{Tu}\}, \{\texttt{M'}\}, \{\texttt{E'}\}, \{\texttt{grad(D)}\}, \\ \{\texttt{FcM}, \texttt{FxM}\}, \{\texttt{FcE}, \texttt{FxE}\}, \{\texttt{Tu'}, \texttt{FcT}, \texttt{FxT}\} \end{array} \right\}$$

$$S_3 = \{(\{\texttt{M}\}, \{\texttt{E}\}, \{\texttt{D}\}), (\{\texttt{FcM}, \texttt{FxM}\}, \{\texttt{FcE}, \texttt{FxE}\})\}$$

By applying *ComputeArray* on D_S and S_3, we obtain the following set of arrays A_{nc} (where *nc* stands for *No Copy*):

$$A_{nc} = \left\{ \begin{array}{c} (\{\texttt{M}\}, \{\texttt{E}\}, \{\texttt{D}\}), (\{\texttt{Tu}\}), (\{\texttt{M'}\}), (\{\texttt{E'}\}), (\{\texttt{grad(D)}\}), \\ (\{\texttt{FcM}, \texttt{FxM}\}, \{\texttt{FcE}, \texttt{FxE}\}), (\{\texttt{Tu'}, \texttt{FcT}, \texttt{FxT}\}) \end{array} \right\}$$

```
1  input: dataflow df = (T, D, E)
2  input: CC Set S_1
3  input: OC Set S_2
4  begin
5    _ ← ComputeArray(D, S_1)
6    D_S, S_3 ← as in Definition 4
7    A_nc ← ComputeArray(D_S, S_3)
8    E' ← ∅; c ← ∅; o ← 0
9    for(d ∈ D)
10     a ← array in A_nc containing d
11     T_d ← {t | t ∈ T, (d, t) ∈ E}
12     T_d^o ← {t | (d, t, d') ∈ S_2}
13     T_d^s ← T_d \ dom(T_d^o)
14     for(t_1 ≠ t_2 ∈ dom(T_d^o))
15      c.add(V_a^{t_1} ≠ V_a^{t_2})
16     for(t_1 ∈ T_d^s, t_2 ∈ dom(T_d^o))
17      E'.add((t_1, t_2))
18      c.add(V_a^{t_1} = V_a^{t_2} ⇒ V_{t_1;t_2})
19     (t_1, ..., t_n) ← sq(T_d ∪ {t | (t, d) ∈ E})
20     for(1 ≤ i ≤ n)
21      o ← o + (⋁_{1≤j<i} V_a^{t_j} = V_a^{t_i}) ? 0 : 1
22    G = (T, tdeps(df) ∪ E')
23    for(p ∈ elementary_circuits(G))
24     c.add(⋁_{e∈p∩E'} ¬[e])
25    output: (A_nc, c, o)
26  end
```

Fig. 5. The *ConstraintGen* Algorithm.

The cells of these arrays are identified by sets of data, which describes all the data that will be hosted in that cell. For instance, `M` will not share its cell with any other data since it is not overwritten, but `FcM` and `FxM` do share the same cell. Note that since this process does not consider copies, `Tu'`, `FcT` and `FxT` also share the same cell which is not possible as discussed in Example 5: this problem will be solved later by introducing copies. □

Since the two other issues consist of choosing between adding costly copies, or introducing dependencies between tasks (with the risk of deadlocks), our approach translates them into an integer-based optimization problem that can be solved by an off-the-shelf solver[3], and then translates the provided solution into an MM $M = (A, \alpha, \mu_{\texttt{in}}, \mu_{\texttt{out}}, \delta)$. Because we now consider the possibility of copies, A cannot be A_{nc}, but like A_{nc}, every array in A must follow the constraints in S_3. We thus choose to model arrays in A as pairs (a, i) where $a \in A_{nc}$ and i is an integer distinguishing different replica of the array a. With this choice, all the elements in M can be thus encoded with two kinds of variables in the optimization problem. Our first kind of variable has the form $\texttt{V}_a^t$ where $a \in A_{nc}$ and $t \in T$, and corresponds to an integer capturing the main replica of a used by t. These variables are used to produce A (consisting of all replica of A_{nc}), $\mu_{\texttt{in}}$ and $\mu_{\texttt{out}}$. The second kind of variable has the form $\texttt{V}_{t;t'}$ where $t, t' \in T$, and corresponds to a boolean stating if t must be executed before t': these variables are used to produce δ.

The generation of the optimization problem is presented in Fig. 5. It consists of the function *ConstraintGen* that takes a dataflow *df*, a set of CCs S_1 and a set of OCs S_2 in input, and produces a triplet containing: a set of arrays A_{nc}, a constraint c and an objective o to minimize. This function is structured in three steps. The first step (Lines 5– 7) ensures in Line 5 that S_1 is valid, as stated in Definition 4; and then computes the set of array A_{nc} as previously described.

[3] Our implementation uses z3 [7], but cvc5 [3] or any minizinc [28] solver could work.

The second step (Lines 8–21) builds the constraint c and objective o. It starts by initializing the set E of task dependencies that might be included in δ to $\emptyset$, the constraint c to $\emptyset$, and the objective o to 0. Then, E, c and o are constructed iteratively in the loop in Lines 9–21 that iterates over every data d in D. This loop starts by getting the array a in which d is hosted, and by computing: the set T_d of tasks having d in input; the set T^o_d of tasks overriding d; and the set T^s_d of tasks that uses d without overriding it. The two following loops ensure data-race freedom: Lines 14–15 ensure that two tasks overriding d do not use the same replica (otherwise the data-race cannot be avoided); and Lines 16–18 state that if a task t_1 using d fetches it from the same array of an overriding task t_2, then t_1 must execute before t_2. The final part of this step (Lines 19–21) builds the objective o. The goal of this optimization problem is to minimize the number of copies, which corresponds to the following sum, where I is a solution of the optimization problem:

$$\sum_{d\in D} (\#\{I[\mathtt{V}^t_a] \mid ((d,t)\in E \vee (t,d)\in E) \wedge \mathtt{M_c}[d]=(a,i)\} - 1)$$

However, solvers do not accept such an optimization goal that aims to reduce the number of elements in a set. Instead, we use a trick to encode the cardinality of that set into a valid optimization expression: if we consider all tasks storing or fetching d and put them in a sequence $(t_1,\ldots,t_n)$, then, with $\mathtt{M_c}[d]=(a,i)$, the following equality holds

$$\#\{I[\mathtt{V}^{t_i}_a] \mid 1\le i\le n\} = \sum_{1\le i\le n} (\bigvee_{1\le j<i} \mathtt{V}^{t_j}_a = \mathtt{V}^{t_i}_a)?0:1$$

Informally, the right-hand side of the equality states that for every $1\le i\le n$, either t_i uses the same replica of a as a previous t_j in which case t_i does not need a new replica of d and we add 0 to o, either t_i uses a new replica of a, which implies that a fresh copy of d is needed and we add 1 to o.

Finally, the last step of the *ConstraintGen* function (Lines 22–24) ensures that no deadlocks are introduced in the dataflow. This is done by computing the graph G that includes all the tasks and their dependencies of the input dataflow, plus all the edges in E' that could be triggered by solving a data-race. Then, we iterate over all the elementary circuits of G, and forbid that this circuit could be closed by an edge in E'. This method to avoid deadlocks is based on techniques to solve the minimum feedback arc set problem [2,13,37].

Example 7. We illustrate the function *ConstraintGen* by applying it on the dataflow and constraints presented in Example 1. The first step of the function first checks if S_1 is valid and succeeds as discussed in Example 2, then compute the arrays A_{nc} as discussed in Example 6.

To ease the presentation of the second step, we use the following shortening notation for variables: we use initials to refer to tasks, and the initial of the first data of an array to refer to that array. For instance, $\mathtt{V}^{\mathtt{P1}}_{\mathtt{M}}$ is the variable capturing which replica of the array starting with `M` is used by `Primitive1`, and $\mathtt{V}_{\mathtt{V2;C2}}$ is the boolean variable stating if `Viscous2` must be executed before `Convective2`. Since this step iterates over the data in any order, let us suppose it starts with `M`: T_d^o for this data is empty and T_d^s is {`Primitive1`}; hence the loops in Lines 14–18 do not produce any edge in E' nor any constraint in c; and the last part of this step adds 1 to the objective o (stating that there is one instance of `M`). This step performs the same operation for the inputs `E` and `Tu` of the dataflow. Since `D` is used by several tasks, the last part of this step puts all the tasks using `D` in sequence, e.g., (`Primitive1`, `grad`, `Primitive2`), and adds the following expression to o:

$$1 + ((\mathtt{V}_{\mathtt{M}}^{\mathtt{P1}} = \mathtt{V}_{\mathtt{M}}^{\mathtt{g}})?0 : 1) + ((\mathtt{V}_{\mathtt{M}}^{\mathtt{P1}} = \mathtt{V}_{\mathtt{M}}^{\mathtt{P2}} \vee \mathtt{V}_{\mathtt{M}}^{\mathtt{g}} = \mathtt{V}_{\mathtt{M}}^{\mathtt{P2}})?0 : 1)$$

At that point of the execution of *ConstraintGen*, the constraint c is still empty, and the objective o is as follows:

$$o = 1 + 1 + 1 + 1 + ((\mathtt{V}_{\mathtt{M}}^{\mathtt{P1}} = \mathtt{V}_{\mathtt{M}}^{\mathtt{g}})?0 : 1) + ((\mathtt{V}_{\mathtt{M}}^{\mathtt{P1}} = \mathtt{V}_{\mathtt{M}}^{\mathtt{P2}} \vee \mathtt{V}_{\mathtt{M}}^{\mathtt{g}} = \mathtt{V}_{\mathtt{M}}^{\mathtt{P2}})?0 : 1)$$

For the data `M'`, `E'` and `grad(D)` that are not overwritten but have a generating task, the result of this step is identical as for the data `D`, extending the objective o with o_1:

$$\begin{aligned} o_1 = {} & 1 + ((\mathtt{V}_{\mathtt{M'}}^{\mathtt{P1}} = \mathtt{V}_{\mathtt{M'}}^{\mathtt{C1}})?0 : 1) + 1 + ((\mathtt{V}_{\mathtt{E'}}^{\mathtt{P1}} = \mathtt{V}_{\mathtt{E'}}^{\mathtt{C1}})?0 : 1) \\ & + 1 + ((\mathtt{V}_{\mathtt{g(D)}}^{\mathtt{g}} = \mathtt{V}_{\mathtt{g(D)}}^{\mathtt{V1}})?0 : 1) + ((\mathtt{V}_{\mathtt{g(D)}}^{\mathtt{g}} = \mathtt{V}_{\mathtt{g(D)}}^{\mathtt{V2}} \vee \mathtt{V}_{\mathtt{g(D)}}^{\mathtt{V1}} = \mathtt{V}_{\mathtt{g(D)}}^{\mathtt{V2}})?0 : 1) \end{aligned}$$

Let us now consider the overwritten data `FcM`. For this data, $T_d^o =$ {`Viscous1`} and $T_d^s =$ {`Store1`}. Consequently, the loops in Lines 14–18 store the edge (`S1`, `V1`) in E', produce the constraint $\mathtt{V}_{\mathtt{FcM}}^{\mathtt{S1}} = \mathtt{V}_{\mathtt{FcM}}^{\mathtt{V1}} \Rightarrow \mathtt{V}_{\mathtt{S1;V1}}$ stating that if the task `Store1` fetches `FcM` from the same array as `Viscous1` then it must execute before `Viscous1`, and extend o with o_2:

$$o_2 = 1 + ((\mathtt{V}_{\mathtt{FcM}}^{\mathtt{C1}} = \mathtt{V}_{\mathtt{FcM}}^{\mathtt{S1}})?0 : 1) + ((\mathtt{V}_{\mathtt{FcM}}^{\mathtt{C1}} = \mathtt{V}_{\mathtt{FcM}}^{\mathtt{V1}} \vee \mathtt{V}_{\mathtt{FcM}}^{\mathtt{S1}} = \mathtt{V}_{\mathtt{FcM}}^{\mathtt{V1}})?0 : 1)$$

This step performs the same operation for the other overwritten data `FcE`, `Tu'` and `FcT`, producing the set $E' = \{(\mathtt{S1}, \mathtt{V1}), (\mathtt{V2}, \mathtt{C2})\}$ and extending the constraint c and the objective o with c_1 and o_3 respectively:

$$\begin{aligned} c_1 &= (\mathtt{V}_{\mathtt{Tu'}}^{\mathtt{V2}} = \mathtt{V}_{\mathtt{Tu'}}^{\mathtt{C2}} \Rightarrow \mathtt{V}_{\mathtt{V2;C2}}) \\ o_3 &= 1 + ((\mathtt{V}_{\mathtt{FcE}}^{\mathtt{C1}} = \mathtt{V}_{\mathtt{FcE}}^{\mathtt{V1}})?0 : 1) \\ &\quad + 1 + ((\mathtt{V}_{\mathtt{Tu'}}^{\mathtt{P2}} = \mathtt{V}_{\mathtt{Tu'}}^{\mathtt{C2}})?0 : 1) + ((\mathtt{V}_{\mathtt{Tu'}}^{\mathtt{P2}} = \mathtt{V}_{\mathtt{Tu'}}^{\mathtt{V2}} \vee \mathtt{V}_{\mathtt{Tu'}}^{\mathtt{C2}} = \mathtt{V}_{\mathtt{Tu'}}^{\mathtt{V2}})?0 : 1) \\ &\quad + 1 + ((\mathtt{V}_{\mathtt{FcT}}^{\mathtt{C2}} = \mathtt{V}_{\mathtt{FcT}}^{\mathtt{V2}})?0 : 1) \end{aligned}$$

We conclude our illustration of the *ConstraintGen* function by discussing its last step: as we previously discussed, the set E' computed at the end of the third step contains the edges (`S1`, `V1`) and (`V2`, `C2`). Consequently, the graph G computed in Line 22 contains only one cycle: `Convective2` → `Viscous2` → `Convective2`. In this cycle, only the edge (`Viscous2`, `Convective2`) is in E', and it is thus forbidden by adding $\neg\mathtt{V}_{\mathtt{V2;C2}}$ to the constraint c. □

1 input: **dataflow** $df = (T, D, E)$
2 input: **CC Set** S_1
3 input: **OC Set** S_2
4 begin
5 $A_{nc}, c, o \leftarrow \mathit{ConstraintGen}(df, S_1, S_2)$
6 $\mathtt{M_c} \leftarrow \{d \mapsto (a, i) \mid a \in A_{nc} \wedge$
7 $1 \leq i \leq \mathtt{len}(a) \wedge d \in a[i]\}$
8 $I \leftarrow \mathtt{solution}(c,\ o)$
9 $A \leftarrow \bigcup_{a \in A_{nc}} \{(a, I[\mathtt{V}_a^t]) \mid \mathtt{V}_a^t \in \mathrm{dom}(I)\}$
10 $\alpha \leftarrow [(a, i) \mapsto \mathtt{len(a)} \mid (a, i) \in A]$
11 $\mu_{\mathtt{in}} \leftarrow \emptyset$; $\mu_{\mathtt{out}} \leftarrow \emptyset$
12 for$((d, t) \in E)$
13 $\mu_{\mathtt{in}}(d, t) \leftarrow ((a, I[\mathtt{V}_a^t]), i)$
14 **where** $\mathtt{M_c}[d] = (a, i)$
15 for$((t, d) \in E)$
16 $\mu_{\mathtt{out}}(t, d) \leftarrow \{\mu_{\mathtt{in}}(d, t') \mid (d, t') \in E\}$
17 $\cup \{(a, I[\mathtt{V}_a^t]), i)\}$ **where** $\mathtt{M_c}[d] = (a, i)$
18 $\delta \leftarrow \{(t, t') \mid \mathtt{V}_{t;t'} \in \mathrm{dom}(I) \wedge I[\mathtt{V}_{t;t'}]\}$
19 output: $(A, \alpha, \mu_{\mathtt{in}}, \mu_{\mathtt{out}}, \delta)$
20 end

Fig. 6. The *MemoryGen* Algorithm

The *MemoryGen* function in Fig. 6 wraps *ConstraintGen* and uses its result to produce a valid MM with an optimal number of copies. It takes a dataflow *df*, a set of CCs S_1 and a set of OCs S_2 in input, and produces its resulting MM $(A, \alpha, \mu_{\mathtt{in}}, \mu_{\mathtt{out}}, \delta)$ as follows. First, it executes *ConstraintGen* to get the set of arrays A_{nc}, the constraint c and the objective o; it produces the utilitary mapping $\mathtt{M_c}$ that gives, for every data $d \in D$, the cell (a, i) where d is stored in A_{nc}; and it uses a solver to get a model I of c that minimizes o. Lines 9–10 produce the actual arrays: A is produced as discussed before, by collecting every replica (a, i) of the arrays $a \in A_{nc}$, with $i \in \{I([\mathtt{V}_a^t]) \mid \mathtt{V}_a^t \in \mathrm{dom}(I)\}$; and α maps all arrays (a, i) in A to the size of a. Lines 11–17 compute the $\mu_{\mathtt{in}}$ and $\mu_{\mathtt{out}}$ mappings: for every input edge $(d, t) \in E$, t fetches d from the cell i of the array $(a, \mathtt{V}_a^t)$ where i is the cell of a containing d; and for every output edge $(t, d) \in E$, t stores d in all the cells where it is expected (i.e., $\{\mu_{\mathtt{in}}(d, t') \mid (d, t') \in E\}$), and also in the main storing cell i of the array $(a, \mathtt{V}_a^t)$ where i is the cell of a containing d. Note that since I minimizes o, $\mu_{\mathtt{out}}(t, d)$ is equal to $\{\mu_{\mathtt{in}}(d, t') \mid (d, t') \in E\}$ except when d is an output of the dataflow (in which case $\{\mu_{\mathtt{in}}(d, t') \mid (d, t') \in E\} = \emptyset$). Finally, Line 18 builds δ by including all the edges that were validated by I.

Example 8. The constraints generated in Example 7 have two optimal solutions. The first one is translated by *MemoryGen* into the MM presented in Example 5 that copies `Tu'` to be used by `Viscous2`. The second one performs the same copy but gives it in input to `Convective2` while the instance of `Tu'` stored by `Primitive2` is given to `Viscous2`. The two solutions have thus exactly the same overhead. □

Theorem 2. *MemoryGen has the following properties:*

- *it is complete, i.e., it only fails for invalid sets of constraints;*
- *it is sound, i.e., its output validates the input dataflow and constraints;*
- *the produced MM has a minimal number of copies.*

Proof (Sketch). Let us consider a dataflow $df = (T, D, E)$ and a valid set of memory constraints $S = S_1 \cup S_2$, with S_1 being a set of CCs and S_2 being a set of OCs. *MemoryGen* is complete: S is valid and so the steps 1 and 2 of *ConstraintGen* will not fail; it is easy to see that the model associating every variable $\mathtt{V}_a^t$ to a different integer and invalidating every edges in E' validates the constraint c. Let us now consider a result M of applying *MemoryGen* on *df*, S_1 and S_2. This result M validates *df*: all inputs of *df* are stored in different cells; δ does not create deadlocks; and $\mu_{\mathtt{out}}$ is constructed to store each data to a cell where it will be needed. Moreover, M validates S_1 as all replica of an array $a \in A_{nc}$ have exactly the same structure as a that, by Theorem 1, validates S_1: consequently, every data is stored and fetched with the right alignment. M also validates S_2 since both conditions in Definition 6 are enforced by constraints in c. Finally, M has an optimal number of copies since it is constructed by minimizing o. □

Theorem 3. *Producing an optimal MM is NP-hard.*

Proof (Sketch). To prove this result, we encode the NP-complete feedback arc set problem [20] into a dataflow with override constraints. Consider a graph $G = (V, E)$: we construct the corresponding dataflow by encoding all edges in E as dependencies triggered by overrides. More precisely, every node v corresponds to a task in the dataflow, and every edge e linking a node v to a node v' corresponds to two data: $(e, \top)$ is an input of both v and v'; and $(e, \bot)$ is an output of v' that overrides $(e, \top)$. Consequently, this encoding includes for every $(v, v') \in E$ a data-race between v and v': this data-race can only be solved by either introducing the edge (v, v') in δ or copying $(e, \top)$ to avoid a loop in δ. Formally, we construct the dataflow $df = (T, D, I \cup O)$ and the override constraints S_2 as follows:

$$
\begin{aligned}
T &= V \\
D &= \{(e, \top) \mid e \in E\} \cup \{(e, \bot) \mid e \in E\} \\
I &= \{(((v, v'), \top), v) \mid (v, v') \in E\} \cup \{(((v, v'), \top), v') \mid (v, v') \in E\} \\
O &= \{(v', ((v, v'), \bot)) \mid (v, v') \in E\} \\
S_2 &= \{(((v, v'), \top), v', ((v, v'), \bot)) \mid (v, v') \in E\}
\end{aligned}
$$

Let us now consider an optimal MM $(A, \alpha, \mu_{\mathtt{in}}, \mu_{\mathtt{out}}, \delta)$ for this problem. Since it minimizes the number of copies, this solution maximizes the number of edges in δ. Hence $E \setminus \delta$ is a minimal feedback arc set. □

5 Related Work

To the best of our knowledge, memory management for automatically generated dataflows and similar structures (e.g., statecharts [25] or transition systems [5,11]) was never investigated until now. These structures are used to model both middleware and embedded systems, and in both cases, data alignment and data-races must be managed by the programmer. This paper is thus complementary to many other works that focused on other topics of memory management: hardware designs and tools to improve the speed of data-access; tools and loop designs to help single tasks to efficiently use the underlying hardware; and data distribution to efficiently parallelize computation.

The first topic focuses on how the hardware can be designed or managed to improve memory access time. For instance, [16,36] discuss different cache technologies that improve speed and energy consumption of HPC applications; [12] proposes a data fetching policy to fill CPU caches with better performances; [15] discusses an allocation policy suited for GPU-like hardware; hwloc [8] is a library that gives programmers the possibility to query the hardware and to place their computation depending on the memory bandwidth; and [30] uses hwloc and a dedicated allocator to improve memory performance of distributed HPC applications.

The second topic focuses on how tasks manage their data so they can take advantage of the hardware capabilities. Many tasks manipulate collections of structured data, e.g., in Example 1, the Momentum `M` is a 3D vector implemented with three double. There are two different possibilities for handling such collections of structured data [17]: in the *Array of Structures* (AoS) approach, the collection is implemented as an array of structured data; while the *Structure of Array* (SoA) approach associates each attribute of the structure to its own array. AoS is intuitive to implement and easier to maintain, but SoA has better cache usage in many HPC applications. Moreover, to use the vectorization capabilities of the CPU, the elements in an array must be stored in a way that guarantees that all data in the vectorization loop are independent. ParaDiGM [31] is a library dedicated to the distributed management of meshes and is used by SoNICS to sort its arrays to enable vectorization.

The last topic focuses on the program's execution on a distributed architecture, and provides techniques to evenly distribute the computation load while introducing as little overhead as possible when copying the data between nodes. For instance, Chapel [9], DaCe [6,32] and Regent [34] are programming languages that automatically distribute the program specified by the developer. In particular, DaCe compiles a program into a distributed computation by using dataflow-based internal representation; and Regent is based on the Legion library [4] that introduces the concept of *region* to refer to a set of data that can be distributed and provides a high level mechanism [22] to control data distribution. HPX [18] is an HPC library that provides *co-arrays* [35], inspired by a similar mechanism in Fortran, to implement the automatic distribution of data. On the other hand, SoNICS uses tools like Scotch [10] and Metis [21] to compute how data should be distributed and performs the distribution using MPI [29].

6 Conclusion

Ensuring fast access to data is an important topic in High Performance Computing. While much work has been done on improving speed at the hardware level and on the distribution aspects of the computation, the problems of data contiguity and data-race are still manually managed by the programmers. In this paper, we presented an approach to automatically solve these two problems in a context where the computation is modeled by a dataflow. This approach is particularly useful for automatically generated dataflows which cannot be analysed and managed by programmers in reasonable time, as it is the case in the Computational Fluid Dynamics simulator SoNICS [14]. We moreover proved that our approach is sound and complete, and that the problem it solves is NP-hard. Finally, as noted in [26], this approach is implemented and used in practice in SoNICS.

In future work, we would like to extend our approach in four ways. First, we would like to include an additional constraint that we did not discuss in this paper: *partitions*. This constraint models the situation where some parts of a data (when that data is a collections of values) must be manipulated differently from the rest of the data. This constraint can encode the notion of *subregion* in Legion [4], which is used to implement the distribution of data, and is very useful in the context of SoNICS to model the limit of the simulation space (called *boundary conditions*). Second, we would like to improve the efficiency of the *ConstraintGen* algorithm. Indeed, the current version of this algorithm considers every array in building the constraint, while only the ones that could be used to close a cycle in the graph G (in Line 22 of the *ConstraintGen* algorithm) may have multiple replica and should be included in the constraint. Third, we would like to conclude the complexity analysis of our memory management problem. More precisely, we would like to check if this problem is NP-complete in general, and if there are some criteria that would make it linear in most practical cases. Finally, we would like to investigate the efficiency of our implementation in practice by performing some benchmarks.

References

1. Augonnet, C., Thibault, S., Namyst, R., Wacrenier, P.A.: StarPU: a unified platform for task scheduling on heterogeneous multicore architectures. Concurrency Computat.: Pract. Exp. **23**(2), 187–198 (2011). https://doi.org/10.1002/cpe.1631
2. Baharev, A., Schichl, H., Neumaier, A., Achterberg, T.: An exact method for the minimum feedback arc set problem. ACM J. Exp. Algorithmics **26** (2021). https://doi.org/10.1145/3446429
3. Barbosa, H., et al.: cvc5: A versatile and industrial-strength SMT solver. In: Fisman, D., Rosu, G. (eds.) TACAS 2022, ETAPS 2022, Part I. Lecture Notes in Computer Science, vol. 13243, pp. 415–442. Springer, Cham (2022). https://doi.org/10.1007/978-3-030-99524-9_24
4. Bauer, M.E.: Legion: Programming Distributed Heterogeneous Architectures with Logical Regions. Ph.D. thesis, Stanford University (2014)
5. ter Beek, M.H., Damiani, F., Lienhardt, M., Mazzanti, F., Paolini, L.: Efficient static analysis and verification of featured transition systems. Empir. Softw. Eng. **22**(1), 10:1–10:43 (2022). https://doi.org/10.1007/s10664-020-09930-8
6. Ben-Nun, T., de Fine Licht, J., Ziogas, A.N., Schneider, T., Hoefler, T.: Stateful dataflow multigraphs: a data-centric model for performance portability on heterogeneous architectures. In: Proceedings of the International Conference for High Performance Computing, Networking, Storage and Analysis (SC'19), pp. 81:1–81:14. ACM (2019). https://doi.org/10.1145/3295500.3356173

7. Bjørner, N., Phan, A.-D., Fleckenstein, L.: vz - An optimizing SMT solver. In: Baier, C., Tinelli, C. (eds.) TACAS 2015. LNCS, vol. 9035, pp. 194–199. Springer, Heidelberg (2015). https://doi.org/10.1007/978-3-662-46681-0_14
8. Broquedis, F., et al.: hwloc: A generic framework for managing hardware affinities in HPC applications. In: Danelutto, M., Bourgeois, J., Gross, T. (eds.) Proceedings of the 18th Euromicro Conference on Parallel, Distributed and Network-based Processing, PDP 2010, Pisa, Italy, 17–19 February 2010, pp. 180–186. IEEE Computer Society (2010). https://doi.org/10.1109/PDP.2010.67
9. Chamberlain, B.L., Callahan, D., Zima, H.P.: Parallel programmability and the Chapel language. Int. J. High Perform. Comput. Appl. **21**(3), 291–312 (2007). https://doi.org/10.1177/1094342007078442
10. Chevalier, C., Pellegrini, F.: Pt-scotch: a tool for efficient parallel graph ordering. Parallel Comput. **34**(6–8), 318–331 (2008). https://doi.org/10.1016/J.PARCO.2007.12.001
11. Classen, A., Cordy, M., Schobbens, P., Heymans, P., Legay, A., Raskin, J.: Featured transition systems: foundations for verifying variability-intensive systems and their application to LTL model checking. IEEE Trans. Softw. Eng. **39**(8), 1069–1089 (2013). https://doi.org/10.1109/TSE.2012.86
12. Fargo, F., et al.: Intelligent cache prefetchers in HPC architecture. Clust. Comput. **28**(3), 154 (2025). https://doi.org/10.1007/S10586-024-04854-0
13. Grötschel, M., Jünger, M., Reinelt, G.: Comments on "an exact method for the minimum feedback arc set problem. ACM J. Exp. Algorithmics **27** (2022). https://doi.org/10.1145/3545001
14. Gueyffier, D., Plot, S., Soismier, M.: Sonics: a new generation CFD software for satisfying industrial users needs. In: OTAN/STO/Workshop AVT-366, pp. 10–1–10–16. STO, Brussels, Belgium (2022)
15. Hayes, A.B., Zhang, E.Z.: Unified on-chip memory allocation for SIMT architecture. In: Bode, A., Gerndt, M., Stenström, P., Rauchwerger, L., Miller, B.P., Schulz, M. (eds.) 2014 International Conference on Supercomputing, ICS'14, Muenchen, Germany, 10–13 June 2014, pp. 293–302. ACM (2014). https://doi.org/10.1145/2597652.2597685
16. He, J., Callenes-Sloan, J.: Designing large hybrid cache for future HPC systems. In: Polok, L., Sosonkina, M., Thacker, W.I., Weinbub, J. (eds.) Proceedings of the 25th High Performance Computing Symposium, Virginia Beach, VA, USA, 23–26 April 2017, pp. 9:1–9:12. ACM (2017)
17. Homann, H., Laenen, F.: Soax: a generic C++ structure of arrays for handling particles in HPC codes. Comput. Phys. Commun. **224**, 325–332 (2018). https://doi.org/10.1016/j.cpc.2017.11.015
18. Kaiser, H., Heller, T., Adelstein-Lelbach, B., Serio, A., Fey, D.: HPX – a task based programming model in a global address space. In: Proceedings of the 8th International Conference on Partitioned Global Address Space Programming Models (PGAS'14), pp. 6:1–6:11. ACM (2014). https://doi.org/10.1145/2676870.2676883
19. Kale, L.V., Krishnan, S.: CHARM++: a portable concurrent object oriented system based on C++. In: Proceedings of the 8th Annual Conference on Object-Oriented Programming Systems, Languages, and Applications (OOPSLA'93), pp. 91–108. ACM (1993). https://doi.org/10.1145/165854.165874
20. Karp, R.M.: Reducibility among Combinatorial Problems, pp. 85–103. Springer, Boston (1972). https://doi.org/10.1007/978-1-4684-2001-2_9
21. Karypis, G.: METIS and parmetis. In: Padua, D.A. (ed.) Encyclopedia of Parallel Computing, pp. 1117–1124. Springer, Cham (2011). https://doi.org/10.1007/978-0-387-09766-4_500

22. Lee, W., Papadakis, M., Slaughter, E., Aiken, A.: A constraint-based approach to automatic data partitioning for distributed memory execution. In: Taufer, M., Balaji, P., Peña, A.J. (eds.) Proceedings of the International Conference for High Performance Computing, Networking, Storage and Analysis, SC 2019, Denver, Colorado, USA, 17–19 November 2019, pp. 45:1–45:24. ACM (2019). https://doi.org/10.1145/3295500.3356199
23. Leicht, T., et al.: Dlr-project digital-x - next generation CFD solver 'flucs'. In: Deutscher Luft- und Raumfahrtkongress 2016 (2016). https://elib.dlr.de/111205/
24. Lienhardt, M., ter Beek, M.H., Damiani, F.: Product lines of dataflows. J. Syst. Softw. **210**, 111928 (2024). https://doi.org/10.1016/J.JSS.2023.111928
25. Lienhardt, M., Damiani, F., Testa, L., Turin, G.: On checking delta-oriented product lines of statecharts. Sci. Comput. Program. **166**, 3–34 (2018). https://doi.org/10.1016/j.scico.2018.05.007
26. Lienhardt, M., Michel, B.: Sonics: design and workflow of a new CFD software. Comptes Rendus. Mécanique **353**, 1261–1287 (2025). https://doi.org/10.5802/crmeca.334
27. Luporini, F., et al.: Architecture and performance of devito, a system for automated stencil computation. ACM Trans. Math. Softw. **46**(1) (2020). https://doi.org/10.1145/3374916
28. Nethercote, N., Stuckey, P.J., Becket, R., Brand, S., Duck, G.J., Tack, G.: MiniZinc: towards a standard CP modelling language. In: Bessière, C. (ed.) CP 2007. LNCS, vol. 4741, pp. 529–543. Springer, Heidelberg (2007). https://doi.org/10.1007/978-3-540-74970-7_38
29. Nielsen, F.: Introduction to MPI: the message passing interface. In: Introduction to HPC with MPI for Data Science. UTCS, pp. 21–62. Springer, Cham (2016). https://doi.org/10.1007/978-3-319-21903-5_2
30. Pérache, M., Jourdren, H., Namyst, R.: MPC: a unified parallel runtime for clusters of NUMA machines. In: Luque, E., Margalef, T., Benítez, D. (eds.) Euro-Par 2008. LNCS, vol. 5168, pp. 78–88. Springer, Heidelberg (2008). https://doi.org/10.1007/978-3-540-85451-7_9
31. Quemerais, E., Maugars, B., Andrieu, B.: ParaDiGM: a library for parallel computational geometry (2024). https://github.com/onera/paradigm/
32. Rausch, O., Ben-Nun, T., Dryden, N., Ivanov, A., Li, S., Hoefler, T.: A data-centric optimization framework for machine learning. In: Proceedings of the International Conference on Supercomputing (ICS'22), pp. 36:1–36:13. ACM (2022). https://doi.org/10.1145/3524059.3532364
33. Refloch, A., et al.: CEDRE Software. Aerospace Lab (2), pp. 1–10 (2011). https://hal.science/hal-01182463
34. Slaughter, E., Lee, W., Treichler, S., Bauer, M., Aiken, A.: Regent: a high-productivity programming language for HPC with logical regions. In: Kern, J., Vetter, J.S. (eds.) Proceedings of the International Conference for High Performance Computing, Networking, Storage and Analysis, SC 2015, Austin, TX, USA, 15–20 November 2015, pp. 81:1–81:12. ACM (2015). https://doi.org/10.1145/2807591.2807629
35. Tan, A.T., Kaiser, H.: Extending C++ with co-array semantics. In: Elsman, M., Grelck, C., Klöckner, A., Padua, D.A. (eds.) Proceedings of the 3rd ACM SIGPLAN International Workshop on Libraries, Languages, and Compilers for Array Programming, ARRAY@PLDI 2016, Santa Barbara, CA, USA, 14 June 2016, pp. 63–68. ACM (2016). https://doi.org/10.1145/2935323.2935332

36. Ujaldon, M.: HPC accelerators with 3d memory. In: 2016 IEEE Intl Conference on Computational Science and Engineering, CSE 2016, and IEEE Intl Conference on Embedded and Ubiquitous Computing, EUC 2016, and 15th Intl Symposium on Distributed Computing and Applications for Business Engineering, DCABES 2016, Paris, France, 24–26 August 2016, pp. 320–328. IEEE Computer Society (2016). https://doi.org/10.1109/CSE-EUC-DCABES.2016.203
37. Younger, D.: Minimum feedback arc sets for a directed graph. IEEE Trans. Circuit Theory **10**(2), 238–245 (1963). https://doi.org/10.1109/TCT.1963.1082116

Hybrid Spatiotemporal Logic for Automotive Applications: Modeling and Model-Checking

Radu-Florin Tulcan[1], Rose Bohrer[2(✉)], Yoàv Montacute[3(✉)], Kevin Zhou[3], Yusuke Kawamoto[2], and Ichiro Hasuo[3]

[1] Theory and Logic Group, TU Wien, Vienna, Austria
[2] National Institute of Advanced Industrial Science and Technology (AIST), Tokyo, Japan
rose.bohrer@aist.go.jp
[3] National Institute of Informatics (NII), Tokyo, Japan
montacute@nii.ac.jp

Abstract. We introduce a hybrid spatiotemporal logic for automotive safety applications (HSTL), focused on highway driving. Spatiotemporal logic features specifications about vehicles throughout space and time, while hybrid logic enables precise references to individual vehicles and their historical positions. We define the semantics of HSTL and provide a baseline model-checking algorithm for it. We propose two optimized model-checking algorithms, which reduce the search space based on the reachable states and possible transitions from one state to another. All three model-checking algorithms are evaluated on a series of common driving scenarios such as safe following, safe crossings, overtaking, and platooning. An exponential performance improvement is observed for the optimized algorithms.

Keywords: Spatiotemporal logic · Hybrid logic · Autonomous vehicles

1 Introduction

Modern automotives are safety-critical cyber-physical systems (CPSs). From consumer cars to autonomous vehicles, software is a core component, responsible for protecting the safety of human passengers. For this reason, the formal verification of these systems' correctness has evolved into a mature field with diverse approaches such as monitoring [29], test generation [42], model-checking [14], and theorem-proving [19,32,43]. This diversity of approaches represents several fundamental tradeoffs: highly rigorous approaches are often less flexible, while highly expressive approaches are often require extensive user expertise. More subtly, different approaches are optimized for different components of an automotive software system. High-precision models such as hybrid-dynamical systems[1] are tuned to the precise low-level decision-making needed to safely

[1] Hybrid-dynamical systems, which combine discrete and continuous system dynamics, should not be confused with hybrid logic, which introduces names to modal logic.

A. Sampaio and M. Stoelinga (Eds.): FM 2026, LNCS 16556, pp. 337–356, 2026.
https://doi.org/10.1007/978-3-032-26204-2_18

control a vehicle's physical actuators. However, this precision can become a burden for high-level motion planning, which is more combinatorial in nature and values efficient search among possible paths. As automotive CPS increasingly enter real highways, it is essential to identify formal methods that can balance these tradeoffs, both to ensure that rigorous models can transfer into practice and to guarantee comprehensive safety from planning to control. Discrete model-checking approaches hold promise to achieve this balance: they combine a firm foundation in formal logic with high automation.

We introduce *Hybrid Spatiotemporal Logic for Automotive Safety* (*HSTL*), a new logic designed to balance rigor and expressiveness with ease of model-checking. Though the logic is quite general, its current emphasis is on highway driving. In planning for highway driving, a discrete grid-based model of space is natural: planning is more concerned with navigating between discrete lanes and comprehending finite relationships between vehicles (such as one vehicle being in front of another). Discrete grids enable efficient search among the many combinations of relationships between vehicles, long before precise coordinates in continuous space are ever considered.

As the name suggests, HSTL combines temporal, spatial, and hybrid logic features. Temporal operators are widespread in CPS formal methods because they allow us to specify safety properties that hold always, goals which are achieved eventually, and combinations thereof. Spatial operators allow specifying properties that hold at neighboring positions on a grid. Hybrid logic operators allow assigning and using names for positions on the grid. The resulting combination is greater than the sum of its parts, allowing complex specifications of vehicle motion over time, while maintaining a discrete model of motion that is amenable to search. We advocate that this makes HSTL an ideal interface between planning and control: HSTL model-checking effectively produces high-level motion plans, which can be consumed by following waypoint-based planning and eventually control stages.

We support this position by developing three increasingly sophisticated model-checking algorithms for HSTL and evaluating them on driving case studies such as following, intersection-crossing, overtaking, and platooning. In modeling the case studies, we show HSTL is flexible enough to model a diverse range of concrete scenarios. In evaluating algorithm performance, we show that fusing hybrid logic, spatial, and temporal operators does not increase the complexity of model-checking; on the contrary, it creates critical opportunities for optimization. When hybrid logic operators are used to precisely specify trajectories, the model-checker can identify these trajectories and commit to them, drastically reducing its search space and improving its scalability. We propose that the resulting algorithms are suitable for typical offline applications such as test case generation.

2 Related Work

We discuss related works in environment modeling, logic, and CPS verification.

Environment Modeling. The predominant model of driving environments is the scene graph (SG), which models objects' semantic relationships, including high-level spatial relationships [8,45] (SGs are not limited to driving applications). Machine learning plays a significant role both in generating SGs from raw visual data [27] and in processing existing SGs, e.g., to assess risk [46] or predict behavior [28]. Tool support for SGs is growing: the driving simulator CARLA [12] recently gained the SG generator CARLASGG [45] and the language Scenic [18] supports end-user SG and scenario generation. More closely related to this work, temporal correctness specifications on SGs have begun to receive attention as well [41]. We focus on enriching specifications to combine temporal, spatial, and hybrid reasoning, but conversely, we do not attempt to support the full SG data structures of modern SG tools like CARLASGG or Scenic. In reasoning about scene graphs, manipulating discrete spatial relationships between objects is an important challenge; the *grid-graph* structure in this paper is essentially a simplification of SGs that focuses on cardinal-direction spatial relationships amongst vehicles, lanes, and objects.

Hybrid and Spatiotemporal Logics. Hybrid logics extend modal logics with nominal formulas. In the simplest case, nominals give names to possible worlds. The origins of hybrid logic are generally attributed to Prior's hybrid tense logic [33] and the name attributed to Blackburn's work [5], though our work is inspired more directly by Braüner's presentation [7]. Though it is distinct from hybrid-dynamical systems, their combination has been explored, both to provide proof goal management [31] and to study information-flow security [6]. Our main deviation from traditional hybrid logic is that nominals do not name states, but positions. This approach is inspired by and refines that of Multi-Lane Spatial Logic [20] and its extensions [35,36], a hybrid spatial logic with more limited temporal features.

Spatiotemporal logics (e.g., [4,9,15,16,21]) combine both spatial and temporal reasoning, each of which come in many varieties, leading to many potential combinations. Topological approaches to space in applications, such as RCC8 reasoning [34], are common but computationally complex [4]. Advanced temporal logics like Signal Temporal Logic have been extended with spatial reasoning to provide practical formal methods like falsification [24,25]. We take inspiration from spatiotemporal logic on closure spaces [10,11] which, like us, explores practical model-checking algorithms, but differs in its operators because we are interested in grid-based vehicle motion, while it is interested in connectivity reasoning.

Verification of CPS. Verification of CPS is pursued both with logic and automata models such as hybrid automata [2,14]. In the automotive domain, automata have been successfully applied to runtime verification through model-checking [1,29]. For planning, temporal logics are widely-used [22,23,30,39]. The uncertainty of autonomous vehicles makes robustness [3,26,37,40,44,47] an important topic for control especially but planning as well; discretization often induces conservative over-approximation, which indirectly promotes robustness. Verification of control algorithms has seen success through program logics for hybrid systems, such as differential dynamic logic [32] and Hybrid Hoare Logic [43]. The more recent *differential Floyd-Hoare logic* [13,19] is a descendant of differential dynamic logic optimized for automotive safety in the *responsibility-sensitive safety framework* [38]. These program logics could potentially be combined with HSTL to verify that controllers safely implement the resulting plans.

3 Hybrid Spatiotemporal Logic for Automotive Safety

We introduce the syntax and semantics of *Hybrid Spatiotemporal Logic for Automotive Safety (HSTL)* and present non-trivial validities and non-validities.

3.1 Syntax

The language of HSTL contains temporal operations (which control the flow of time), spatial operations (which locally move the viewpoint in space), and hybrid operations (which allow us to name and jump between different points in space).

Definition 1 (Syntax). Given a set AP of atomic propositions and a set NP of nominals, the *formulas* of the logic are defined as follows:

$$\begin{aligned}\varphi ::= \top \mid \mathit{prop} \mid v \mid \neg\varphi \mid \varphi_1 \wedge \varphi_2 \mid \bigcirc\varphi \mid \varphi_1\, \mathcal{U}\, \varphi_2 \mid \\ \mathsf{Front}\,\varphi \mid \mathsf{Back}\,\varphi \mid \mathsf{Left}\,\varphi \mid \mathsf{Right}\,\varphi \mid @_v\varphi \mid {\downarrow} v\, \varphi\end{aligned}$$

with $\mathit{prop} \in AP$ atomic proposition and $v \in NP$ a nominal.

The *temporal operators* $\bigcirc$ and $\mathcal{U}$ for 'next' and 'until', as usual, representing moving along a (finite) trace. The *spatial modalities* Front, Back, Left, Right represent spatial movement in our representation of physical space (a grid-graph, which is defined in Sect. 3.2). The *hybrid operators* manipulate nominals v. In contrast to traditional hybrid logics (cf. [7]), our nominals v name the locations of vehicles within grid-graph G, rather than possible worlds. This leads to different design decisions: for example, the semantics of nominals v vary as a function of time. We use the binder ${\downarrow} v$ to store the current position in a fresh v for future use. By convention, the nominal SV means *subject vehicle* ("our vehicle") and the nominal POV means some *point-of-view vehicle* ("other vehicle").

3.2 Semantics

The semantics of HSTL give a formal specification of the meaning of each formula, which model-checking algorithms must faithfully implement. The HSTL semantics extend traditional trace-based semantics for temporal logic with an argument that tracks our *viewpoint* within some mathematical structure (cf. tracking the current world in traditional hybrid logic). Changing the viewpoint does not move any vehicle. The mathematical structures in which movement occurs are called *grid-graphs*. These are directed graphs in which each vertex corresponds to a cell of a grid, and each vertex has a directed edge to its four horizontal and vertical neighbors.

Definition 2 (Grid-graph). A *grid-graph* is a pair (Pos, E) where $Pos = \{p_{i,j} \mid 1 \leq i \leq m, 1 \leq j \leq n\}$ is a set of elements indexed by coordinates on an $m \times n$ grid, and E is a binary relation on Pos such that, for all $1 \leq i \leq m$ and $1 \leq j \leq n$, the pairs $(p_{i,j}, p_{i,j+1})$, $(p_{i,j}, p_{i,j-1})$, $(p_{i,j}, p_{i+1,j})$, and $(p_{i,j}, p_{i-1,j})$, whenever defined, are elements of E.

An example of a 3×4 grid-graph is shown in Fig. 1.

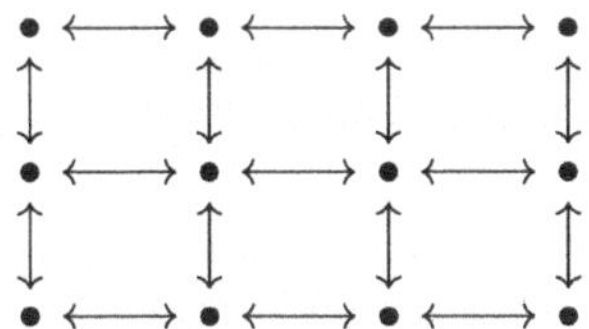

Fig. 1. A 3×4 grid-graph

The definition of a grid graph makes the underlying structure and adjacency relations entirely explicit. The formulation is intended to suggest a natural generalization to scene graphs [8]. In scene graphs, vertices and edges capture objects in the environment and relationships which hold between them.

We support temporal reasoning via traces: sequences in which each element is associated with a point in time. Each element of the sequence is a pair of functions assigning, at that time point, propositional variables and nominals to cells in the grid-graph.

Definition 3 (States & traces). Given a grid-graph $G = (Pos, E)$, a set AP of atomic propositions, a set NP of nominals, and a natural number $n \in \mathbb{N}$, a *state* $t = (x, y)$ is a pair of valuation maps, where $x : AP \rightarrow 2^{Pos}$ maps each proposition to a subset of points in G and $y : NP \rightarrow Pos$ maps each nominal to a unique point in G. A *trace* $\boldsymbol{t} = \big(t_0, \ldots, t_n\big)$ of length $n + 1$ consists of a finite sequence of states.

Let $\boldsymbol{t}^k \overset{\text{def}}{=} \big((x_k, y_k), (x_{k+1}, y_{k+1}), \ldots, (x_n, y_n)\big)$ denote the suffix of $\boldsymbol{t}$ starting at the k-th coordinate; and let $\boldsymbol{t}[v \mapsto p]$ be the element-wise substitution operation on the nominal component of the states, i.e.

$$\boldsymbol{t}[v \mapsto p] \overset{\text{def}}{=} \big((x_0, y_0[v \mapsto p]), \ldots, (x_n, y_n[v \mapsto p])\big).$$

Putting together grid-graphs and traces, we obtain our semantics for HSTL.

Definition 4 (Semantics). Given a grid-graph $G = (Pos, E)$, a trace $\boldsymbol{t} = ((x_0, y_0), \dots, (x_n, y_n))$ of length $n+1$ and a point $p_{i,j} \in Pos$, the satisfaction relation $\models$ is defined as follows:

- $G, \boldsymbol{t}, p_{i,j} \models \top$
- $G, \boldsymbol{t}, p_{i,j} \models a$ iff $p_{i,j} \in x_0(a)$, for $a \in AP$
- $G, \boldsymbol{t}, p_{i,j} \models v$ iff $p_{i,j} = y_0(v)$, for $v \in NP$
- $G, \boldsymbol{t}, p_{i,j} \models \neg\varphi$ iff $G, \boldsymbol{t}, p_{i,j} \not\models \varphi$
- $G, \boldsymbol{t}, p_{i,j} \models \varphi_1 \wedge \varphi_2$ iff $G, \boldsymbol{t}, p_{i,j} \models \varphi_1$ and $G, \boldsymbol{t}, p_{i,j} \models \varphi_2$

Temporal modalities

- $G, \boldsymbol{t}, p_{i,j} \models \bigcirc\varphi$ iff $\boldsymbol{t}^1$ is well-defined and $G, \boldsymbol{t}^1, p_{i,j} \models \varphi$
- $G, \boldsymbol{t}, p_{i,j} \models \varphi_1 \,\mathcal{U}\, \varphi_2$ iff $\exists k \in \{0, \dots, n\}$ s.t. $\boldsymbol{t}^k$ is well-defined, $G, \boldsymbol{t}^k, p_{i,j} \models \varphi_2$, and $G, \boldsymbol{t}^l, p_{i,j} \models \varphi_1$, for all $l < k$.

Spatial modalities

- $G, \boldsymbol{t}, p_{i,j} \models \mathsf{Front}\,\varphi$ iff $p_{i+1,j} \in Pos$ and $G, \boldsymbol{t}, p_{i+1,j} \models \varphi$
- $G, \boldsymbol{t}, p_{i,j} \models \mathsf{Back}\,\varphi$ iff $p_{i-1,j} \in Pos$ and $G, \boldsymbol{t}, p_{i-1,j} \models \varphi$
- $G, \boldsymbol{t}, p_{i,j} \models \mathsf{Left}\,\varphi$ iff $p_{i,j-1} \in Pos$ and $G, \boldsymbol{t}, p_{i,j-1} \models \varphi$
- $G, \boldsymbol{t}, p_{i,j} \models \mathsf{Right}\,\varphi$ iff $p_{i,j+1} \in Pos$ and $G, \boldsymbol{t}, p_{i,j+1} \models \varphi$

Hybrid modalities

- $G, \boldsymbol{t}, p_{i,j} \models @_v\varphi$ iff $G, \boldsymbol{t}, y_0(v) \models \varphi$
- $G, \boldsymbol{t}, p_{i,j} \models \downarrow v\,\varphi$ iff $G, \boldsymbol{t}[v \mapsto p_{i,j}], p_{i,j} \models \varphi$

We write $\models \varphi$ to denote the validity of a formula φ, i.e. $G, \boldsymbol{t}, p_{i,j} \models \varphi$ for all grid-graphs G, traces $\boldsymbol{t}$ and points $p_{i,j}$. We write $\not\models \varphi$ for φ that is not valid.

Derived Operators. Let $D \in \{\mathsf{Left}, \mathsf{Right}, \mathsf{Front}, \mathsf{Back}\}$ be any direction. We define $\langle D\rangle^n\psi \stackrel{\text{def}}{=} \bigvee_{i=1}^{n} D^i(\psi)$ and $[D]^n\psi \stackrel{\text{def}}{=} \bigwedge_{i=1}^{n}(D^i(\top) \rightarrow D^i(\psi))$, where D^i denotes i copies of nested D modalities. These respectively express that ψ is satisfied in some or every of the (extant) cells in direction D within distance n. When discussing a fixed grid-graph, we write $\langle D\rangle$ and $[D]$ to mean that the omitted superscript n is the number of rows in the grid-graph when $D \in \{\mathsf{Front}, \mathsf{Back}\}$ or the number of columns when $D \in \{\mathsf{Left}, \mathsf{Right}\}$.

Global and future modalities $\Box\varphi$ and $\Diamond\varphi$ respectively mean φ is true at all or some future (or current) times. Definitions $\Diamond\varphi \stackrel{\text{def}}{=} \top\,\mathcal{U}\,\varphi$ and $\Box\varphi \stackrel{\text{def}}{=} \neg\Diamond\neg\varphi$ are standard. We define a "weak next" modality $Ⓦ\varphi \stackrel{\text{def}}{=} (\bigcirc\top) \rightarrow (\bigcirc\varphi)$, which is like $\bigcirc$ but is true during the last timestep. Note, Ⓦ is the dual of $\bigcirc$.

Example 1 (Temporal modalities). Let $safe \in AP$, $POV \in NP$ and consider $(safe)\,\mathcal{U}\,(POV)$. Evaluated at $\boldsymbol{t}, p_{i,j}$, it expresses that the point $p_{i,j}$ is safe, until at some point in time POV occupies $p_{i,j}$.

Example 2 (Hybrid modalities). Let $SV, v \in NP$ and consider $@_{SV}\downarrow v\bigcirc @_{SV}v$. Evaluated at $\boldsymbol{t}, p_{i,j}$ it expresses that the next time step exists, and that SV remains in the same position at the next time step.

3.3 Nontrivial Validities

We explore the following valid formulas of HSTL to validate that HSTL semantics align with intuition as desired. Since our frames are rectangular $m \times n$ grids with temporal traces, the interaction between spatial modalities, temporal operators, and hybrid operators yields a number of nontrivial validities.

From a logical perspective, these validities serve as a sanity check that the operators behave according to the intended intuitions. Establishing validities ensures that the formal semantics aligns with the conceptual reading of the operators.

1. Commutation of orthogonal moves: horizontal and vertical moves commute on every grid point. Thus, for all formulas φ,

$$\mathsf{Front}\,\mathsf{Right}\,\varphi \leftrightarrow \mathsf{Right}\,\mathsf{Front}\,\varphi, \quad \mathsf{Front}\,\mathsf{Left}\,\varphi \leftrightarrow \mathsf{Left}\,\mathsf{Front}\,\varphi,$$

$$\mathsf{Back}\,\mathsf{Right}\,\varphi \leftrightarrow \mathsf{Right}\,\mathsf{Back}\,\varphi, \quad \mathsf{Back}\,\mathsf{Left}\,\varphi \leftrightarrow \mathsf{Left}\,\mathsf{Back}\,\varphi.$$

   These express that moving "up and then right" reaches the same point as "right and then up", and similarly for all orthogonal pairs.
2. Loops on the grid: traversing the four sides of a unit square and returning to the start yields the original truth value, whenever the entire cycle exists.

$$\mathsf{Front}\,\mathsf{Right}\,\mathsf{Back}\,\mathsf{Left}\,\varphi \rightarrow \varphi, \quad \mathsf{Right}\,\mathsf{Front}\,\mathsf{Left}\,\mathsf{Back}\,\varphi \rightarrow \varphi,$$

$$\mathsf{Front}\,\mathsf{Left}\,\mathsf{Back}\,\mathsf{Right}\,\varphi \rightarrow \varphi, \quad \mathsf{Back}\,\mathsf{Right}\,\mathsf{Front}\,\mathsf{Left}\,\varphi \rightarrow \varphi.$$

3. Space and time interaction: spatial modalities modify the grid coordinate while temporal modalities modify the trace index. Hence they commute.
   (a) Commutation of temporal with spatial moves: for all φ,

$$\bigcirc D\varphi \leftrightarrow D\bigcirc\varphi, \quad \Diamond D\varphi \leftrightarrow D\Diamond\varphi, \quad \Box D\varphi \leftrightarrow D\Box\varphi.$$

   (b) Distribution of spatial moves along until: for all φ and ψ,

$$D(\varphi\,\mathcal{U}\,\psi) \leftrightarrow (D\varphi)\,\mathcal{U}\,(D\psi).$$

4. Hybrid validities: The semantics of the hybrid modalities interacts nontrivially with space and time. The following standard [7] hybrid validities hold for $a, b, c \in NP$:

$$\downarrow a\, a, \quad @_a a, \quad @_a b \rightarrow @_b a, \quad @_a b \wedge @_a \varphi \rightarrow @_b \varphi$$

   As for binders, we have the following list of validities for all v, φ, ψ:

$$\downarrow v\,\varphi \leftrightarrow \downarrow v\, @_v \varphi, \quad \downarrow v \bigcirc \varphi \leftrightarrow \bigcirc \downarrow v\,\varphi, \quad \downarrow v\, \Diamond\varphi \leftrightarrow \Diamond \downarrow v\,\varphi,$$

$$\downarrow v\, \Box\varphi \leftrightarrow \Box \downarrow v\,\varphi, \quad \downarrow v(\varphi\,\mathcal{U}\,\psi) \leftrightarrow (\downarrow v\,\varphi)\,\mathcal{U}\,(\downarrow v\,\psi).$$

3.4 Nontrivial Non-validities

In contrast to the validities above, the following formulas fail on some model in the class of HSTL models. Each failure witnesses a different characteristic of the interaction between spatial, temporal and hybrid operations. Exploring these non-validities provides an awareness of where formal semantics may differ from intuition and helps establish the limits of HSTL expressiveness.

1. The hybrid operator @ is time sensitive, i.e. $\not\models @_v\varphi \rightarrow \bigcirc @_v\varphi$.
2. The hybrid operator @ and $\Diamond$ do not commute, i.e. $\not\models @_v\Diamond\varphi \leftrightarrow \Diamond @_v\varphi$.
3. Hybrid operators and D modalities do not commute, i.e. $\not\models @_v D\varphi \leftrightarrow D @_v\varphi$ and $\not\models \downarrow v\, D\varphi \leftrightarrow D \downarrow v\, \varphi$.

4 Modeling

The simple operators of HSTL combine to express rich specifications of how vehicle motion evolves over time in a dynamic road environment. We demonstrate how the HSTL operators work together to model an automotive scenario. Interactions are complex, but most practical models build on a few fixed idioms:

Definition 5 (Modeling idioms)

1. A *global state assumption* assumes a formula at all times for all initial viewpoints $p_{i,j}$. Specifically we support $\Box @_v\varphi$ where φ contains no temporal modalities other than $\Box$. Clearly $\Box$ captures all times, but $@_v$ capturing all initial viewpoints is more subtle: $@_v$ overwrites the viewpoint with v's position, so its truth value is viewpoint-independent. This detail simplifies model-checker soundness in certain edge cases.
2. A *static car assumption* consists of a single nominal. The assumption $v \in NP$ specifies that v is stationary for the whole trace, i.e., $y_k(v) = p_{i,j}$ for fixed values of i, j and any time k in the trace. It is expressed by the formula $@_v \downarrow v' \,\Box @_v v'$. We say that v is *static*.
3. A *relative motion assumption* consists of a pair of nominals v_1, v_2, and a sequence of spatial modalities $\boldsymbol{D}$. The assumption $(v_1, v_2, \boldsymbol{D})$ specifies that relative to v_1, v_2 is always in the position obtained by moving according to $\boldsymbol{D}$. It is expressed by the formula $\Box @_{v_1} \boldsymbol{D}\, v_2$. We say that v_1 is a *dependee* and that v_2 is *dependent* on v_1.
4. A *fixed motion assumption* consists of a nominal v and a set of sequences of spatial modalities M. The assumption (v, M) specifies that after one time step, v's original position relates to its new position by one of the directions in M. It is expressed by $\Box @_v \downarrow v' \,Ⓦ\, @_v \bigvee_{D \in M} \boldsymbol{D}\, v'$. We say that v has *fixed motion* from M.

The following examples, which use a grid-graph of size 5×3, build upon the idioms. Not all idioms appear directly in these examples, but all are supported in our model-checker (Sect. 5). In Figs. 2 and 3, the red car denotes SV, the blue car denotes POV, and the proposition h (road hazard) is illustrated by barricades. The yellow arrows are not part of the model; they merely indicate, for convenience, how the location of a nominal changes at the next time step.

Example 3 (Safe at all times). The *global state* formula $\varphi_1 = \Box @_{SV} \neg POV$ expresses that, at all points in time (i.e. at every state in $\boldsymbol{t}$), SV always occupies a different cell from POV, and is therefore safe.

Example 4 (Safe follow). The formula

$$\varphi_2 := @_{SV} \neg \,\mathsf{Back}\, \top \wedge \Box(@_{POV} \downarrow v' ⓦ @_{POV}(v' \vee \mathsf{Back}(v'))) \\ \wedge \Box\Big(@_{SV} \downarrow v ⓦ @_{SV}((\neg POV \wedge \mathsf{Back}(v)) \vee (v \wedge \mathsf{Front}(POV)))\Big)$$

expresses that SV follows POV safely. The first conjunct specifies that SV starts in the bottom row of the grid-graph, while the second conjunct, a *fixed motion assumption*, requires that at each time step POV either moves one cell forward or remains in place. To match this behavior, the third conjunct enforces that SV advances whenever the cell directly ahead is not occupied by POV, and otherwise stays in place. A model satisfying φ_2 is illustrated in Fig. 2.

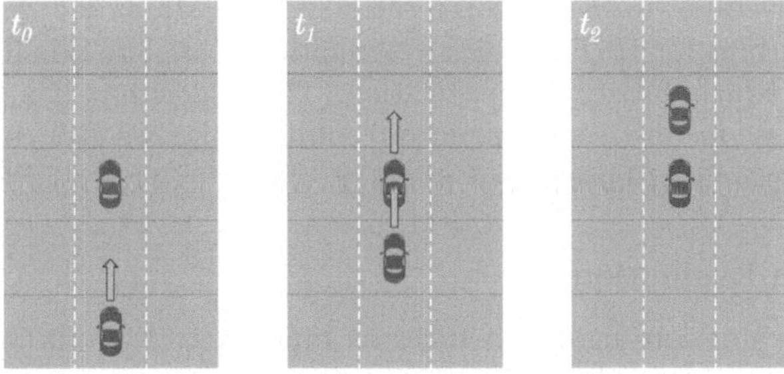

Fig. 2. A model satisfying the formula φ_2

Example 5 (Evading static hazard on an active road). The formula

$$\varphi_3 := @_{SV}\Big(\big(\mathsf{Right}(POV) \wedge \langle\mathsf{Front}\rangle\Box h\big) \wedge \\ (@_{SV} \downarrow v \bigcirc @_{SV}(\mathsf{Back}(v) \wedge \Box\neg h))\, \mathcal{U} \\ (@_{SV} \downarrow v \bigcirc @_{SV}(\mathsf{Left}(v) \wedge \langle\mathsf{Front}\rangle(POV) \wedge [\mathsf{Front}]\Box\neg h))\Big)$$

expresses the following behavior: POV is initially to the right of SV and there is a road hazard ahead whose position does not change over time. In addition, SV must eventually move to a position in the neighboring right-hand lane such that POV is in front of it and no road hazard lies ahead. Until that moment, SV remains in the lane of its initial position while avoiding collisions with road hazards. A model satisfying φ_3 is illustrated in Fig. 3.

Note that Fig. 3 is not the only model of φ_3. Line 2 allows POV to be anywhere, and the value of h is arbitrary everywhere except the current position and its front region. This under-specification reduces realism *and* makes the search space intractably large. Thus φ_3 showcases our motivations for nominals and motion assumptions: increased realism and reduced search space.

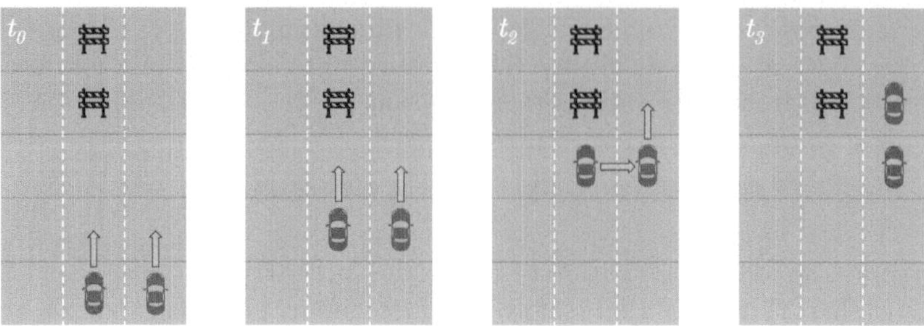

Fig. 3. A model satisfying the formula φ_3

5 Model-Checking

Model-checking is a broad set of verification techniques that systematically explore system states to verify correctness in each state. We develop model-checking algorithms for HSTL, which systematically explore possible traces and identify those which satisfy a specification. This algorithm is appropriate for offline usage, e.g., for test case generation. Additionally, we give correctness and complexity guarantees (Theorems 1 and 2).

5.1 Formula Evaluation

The formula evaluation algorithm takes as input a grid-graph G, a trace $\boldsymbol{t}$, a point $p_{i,j}$ in the grid-graph, and an HSTL formula φ, and outputs whether or not $G, \boldsymbol{t}, p_{i,j} \models \varphi$. Its pseudocode is given in Algorithm 1. It adapts a modern dynamic programming algorithm from LTL [17] to avoid an exponential dependence on the length of the formula that can arise from a naïve recursive evaluation of the Until operator.

Remark. In the implementation of the lookup table `memo`, distinct instances of a subformula φ' of φ result in distinct keys for the lookup table. That is, in the execution of EVAL_MEMO, if φ' and φ'' are syntactically identical formulas that arise separately in the parse tree of φ, the keys $(t, p_{i,j}, \varphi')$ and $(t, p_{i,j}, \varphi'')$ are considered distinct. This is necessary to ensure correctness of the spatial operators and the bind operator, since they alter the current position and the trace, respectively, on which the formula is evaluated.

Theorem 1 (Correctness and runtime of formula evaluator). *For every grid-graph G, trace $\boldsymbol{t}$, point $p_{i,j}$ in the grid-graph, and HSTL formula φ, Eval$(G, \boldsymbol{t}, p_{i,j}, \varphi)$ (as defined in Algorithm 1) returns True if and only if $G, \boldsymbol{t}, p_{i,j} \models \varphi$. Furthermore, Eval terminates within $O(|\boldsymbol{t}|^2 \cdot |\varphi|)$ steps.*

5.2 Model-Checkers

The model-checkers take as input a grid-graph G, a formula φ, a max trace length n, and optionally a list of assumptions A, in the form of the modeling

Algorithm 1. Formula evaluator

```
Function EVAL(G, t, p_{i,j}, φ)
    Input: Grid-graph G = (Pos, E), trace t = ((x_0, y_0), ..., (x_n, y_n)),
           point p_{i,j}, HSTL formula φ
    Output: Bool
    initialize lookup table memo
    return EVAL_MEMO(G, t, 0, p_{i,j}, φ)

Function EVAL_MEMO(G, t, k, p_{i,j}, φ)
    Input: Grid-graph G = (Pos, E), trace t = ((x_0, y_0), ..., (x_n, y_n)),
           time step k ≤ n, point p_{i,j}, HSTL formula φ
    Output: Bool
    if memo[(k, φ)] exists then return memo[(k, φ)]
    else
        match φ
            case ⊤: result ← True
            case a ∈ AP: result ← p_{i,j} ∈ x_0(a)
            case v ∈ NP: result ← p_{i,j} = y_0(v)
            case ¬φ_1: result ← not EVAL_MEMO(G, t, k, p_{i,j}, φ_1)
            case φ_1 ∧ φ_2:
                result ← EVAL_MEMO(G, t, k, p_{i,j}, φ_1) and EVAL_MEMO(G, t, k, p_{i,j}, φ_2)
            case ◯φ_1:
                result ← k < n and EVAL_MEMO(G, t, k + 1, p_{i,j}, φ_1)
            case φ_1 U φ_2:
                if EVAL_MEMO(G, t, k, p_{i,j}, φ_2) then result ← True
                else if k < n then
                    result ← EVAL_MEMO(G, t, k, p_{i,j}, φ_1) and
                             EVAL_MEMO(G, t, k + 1, p_{i,j}, φ)
                else result ← False
                end if
            case Front φ_1 / Back φ_1 / Right φ_1 / Left φ_1:
                if p_{i+1,j} / p_{i-1,j} / p_{i,j+1} / p_{i,j-1} ∈ Pos then
                    p' ← p_{i+1,j} / p_{i-1,j} / p_{i,j+1} / p_{i,j-1}
                    result ← EVAL_MEMO(G, t, k, p', φ_1)
                else result ← False
                end if
            case @_v φ_1: result ← EVAL_MEMO(G, t, k, x_0(v), φ_1)
            case ↓v φ_1:
                t' = ((x'_0, y'_0), ..., (x'_n, y'_n)) ← copy(t)
                for l = k, ..., n do
                    y'_l(v) ← p_{i,j}
                end for
                result ← EVAL_MEMO(G, t', k, p_{i,j}, φ_1)
        end match
        memo[(k, φ)] ← result
        return result
    end if
```

idioms (Definition 5). They output traces $\boldsymbol{t}$ of length up to n which satisfy the assumptions A, for which there are points $p_{i,j}$ such that $G, \boldsymbol{t}, p_{i,j} \models \varphi$. Three different model-checking algorithms are implemented:

1. The *baseline* algorithm generates all possible states on G (i.e., arbitrary assignments of atomic propositions and nominals), then generates all possible traces by arbitrarily assigning a state to each time step. Once generated, the specification is evaluated on each trace.
2. The *optimized* algorithm allows for global state assumptions, as formalized in Definition 5. The algorithm begins by identifying the set of states S that satisfy the given set of assumptions A. More precisely, it selects all states $t = (x, y)$ such that $G, t, p \models \alpha$ for every $p \in Pos$ and $\alpha \in A$. It then generates, similarly to the baseline algorithm, all possible traces composed exclusively of states in S. Once generated, the specification is evaluated on each trace.
3. The *motion* algorithm additionally allows motion assumptions. Traces are generated one step at a time, utilizing the motion assumptions to limit the number of assignments of nominals that need to be considered. For example, for a fixed motion assumption of the form (v, M), only states in which v has moved from its previous position according to M need to be considered. Once a candidate state for the next timestep is generated, it is evaluated against the global state assumptions, and kept iff it satisfies them. Traces generated this way are finally checked against the entire specification.

The pseudocode for the motion algorithm is given in Algorithm 2. See Definition 5 for the motion assumption templates, which are central to its design. Furthermore, we make these assumptions about the inputs:

Preconditions 1 (motion algorithm). We assume that the assumptions A given as input to the motion algorithm satisfy the following:

1. A is partitioned as $A = A_{static} \cup A_{rel} \cup A_{fixed} \cup A_{global}$ into static car, relative motion, fixed motion, and global state assumptions, respectively.
2. A_{static}, A_{rel}, and A_{fixed} are *consistent*, that is, contain no contradictions.
3. No nominal is both a dependee and dependent.
4. Any dependent nominal appears in exactly one relative motion assumption.

The last two conditions ensure that the positions of all dependent nominals can be determined precisely by (independently) choosing the positions of all dependee nominals. We also describe several helper functions at high level, omitting implementation details:

- `generate_initial_states`(G, A_{rel}, A_{global}) outputs the states which satisfy A_{rel} and A_{global}. That is, all dependent cars must be in the correct locations relative to their dependees, and every global assumption is satisfied.
- `valid_dependee_positions`(G, A_{rel}, v) outputs positions where dependee nominal v can be placed so all nominals dependent on v stay in G.
- `valid_prop_assignments`(G, A_{global}) outputs the collection of assignments of atomic propositions in a single state which satisfy A_{global}.

- `complete_state`$(G, A_{rel}, x, \tilde{y})$ takes as input an assignment of atomic propositions $x : AP \to 2^{Pos}$ and an assignment of all non-dependent nominals $\tilde{y} : NP \rightharpoonup Pos$, and outputs the state extending $(x, \tilde{y})$ in which all dependent nominals are assigned positions according to A_{rel}.
- `check_global_assumptions`$(G, \boldsymbol{t}, A_{global})$ checks that all global state assumptions are satisfied by $\boldsymbol{t}$.

The main bottleneck in model-checking lies in generating the large number of traces required to test against the specification. For simplicity of the analysis, suppose that the assignments of atomic propositions are empty at all times. If the grid has size $w \times h$, where n is the maximum trace length and $m = |NP|$, then naively generating all traces (as the baseline model-checker does) yields $\sum_{k=1}^{n}(w \times h)^{mk}$ traces: for each length k up to n, all m nominals must be assigned k times, from $w \times h$ possibilities. The optimized and motion algorithms improve on the baseline by limiting the number of traces that are generated based on the assumptions; therefore, it is necessary to show that these algorithms yield exactly those traces satisfying the assumptions and also give an upper bound on the number of traces generated.

Theorem 2 (Correctness and complexity of the motion algorithm). *Let G be a grid graph of size $w \times h$, and let $A = A_{static} \cup A_{rel} \cup A_{fixed} \cup A_{global}$ be a set of assumptions satisfying preconditions 1. Additionally suppose that the assignments of atomic propositions are empty at all times. Let s be the number of initial states which satisfy A_{global}. The branching factor b_v of each v is:*

- *$b_v = 1$ if v is static or dependent,*
- *$b_v = |M|$ if v has fixed motion from M,*
- *$b_v = |Pos| = w \times h$ otherwise.*

Then GENERATE_TRACES(G, A, n) *(defined in Algorithm 2) yields exactly the traces which satisfy the assumptions A, and the number of traces checked is at most*

$$O\left(s \cdot \sum_{k=0}^{n-1}\left(\prod_{v \in NP} b_v\right)^k\right).$$

The worst case for Algorithm 2 occurs when $s = (w \times h)^m$, i.e., there are no global state assumptions, and $b_v = w \times h$ for every $v \in NP$, i.e., there are no motion assumptions. This aligns with the number of traces generated by the baseline checker. The addition of static and relative position assumptions improves performance as much as elimination of a nominal. For k-direction fixed motion, the speedup factor vs. baseline is $(w \times h)/k$. Such motion is fundamental to vehicle dynamics and appears in every test scenario, and therefore we expect the motion algorithm to provide significant improvements over the baseline.

6 Evaluation

To demonstrate the effectiveness of our model-checking algorithms, we evaluate the implementations on a variety of test cases.

Algorithm 2. Model-checker: motion algorithm

```
Function SAT_TRACES(G, A, φ, n)
    Input: Grid-graph G = (Pos, E), assumptions A satisfying preconditions 1,
           specification φ, max trace length n
    Output: Stream of pairs (t, sat_points_t), where t is a trace and
            sat_points_t is a subset of Pos
    for t ∈ GENERATE_TRACES(G, A, n) do
        sat_points ← {p ∈ Pos | EVAL(G, t, p, φ) = True}
        if sat_points is not empty then yield (t, sat_points)
        end if
    end for

Function GENERATE_TRACES(G, A, n)
    Input: Grid-graph G = (Pos, E), assumptions A, max trace length n
    Output: Stream of traces satisfying A
    for initial_state ∈ generate_initial_states(G, A_rel, A_global) do
        yield from EXTEND_TRACE(G, A, 1, n, initial_state, [initial_state])
    end for

Function EXTEND_TRACE(G, A, k, n, t, t)
    Input: Grid-graph G = (Pos, E), assumptions A, current length k,
           max trace length n, previous state t = (x, y), current trace t
    (Note the font difference between t and t)
    Output: Stream of traces extending t and satisfying A
    yield t
    if k = n then return
    else
        for v ∈ NP do
            if v is static then
                C(v) ← {y(v)}
            else if v has fixed motion from M then
                C(v) ← {D y(v) ∈ Pos | D ∈ M}
            else if v is a dependee then
                C(v) ← valid_dependee_positions(G, A_rel, v)
            else if v is not dependent then
                C(v) ← Pos
            end if
        end for
        for ỹ ∈ ∏_v C(v) do
            for x' ∈ valid_prop_assignments(G, A_global) do
                y' ← complete_trace(G, A_rel, x', ỹ)
                t' ← (x', y')
                if check_global_assumptions(G, [t'], A_global) then
                    yield from EXTEND_TRACE(G, A, k + 1, n, t', t.append(t'))
                end if
            end for
        end for
    end if
```

Test Scenarios. We evaluate the model-checking algorithms on seven test cases: two basic formulas and five test scenarios. The first two are basic formulas of spatiotemporal and hybrid logics. The next five, in order, are: safe following (Fig. 2); hazard avoidance (Fig. 3); safe intersection crossing where one road has priority; safe overtaking, in which a vehicle accelerates in a separate lane before merging back; and safe joining a platoon of vehicles in a neighboring lane. These five scenarios are chosen because they are all fundamental and well-studied driving tasks; all except intersection crossing are focused on highway driving. In modeling these scenarios, we support the claim that HSTL is flexible enough to model a wide range of concrete driving scenarios. The test scenarios are designed for scalability: the grid size and trace duration can be increased to assess how well each algorithm handles increasing complexity. Platooning supports an arbitrary number of vehicles, allowing us to test scalability with respect to the number of nominals in a formula.

Table 1. Experimental results

Test	Noms.	Grid	Len	#Sat	#Trace1	#Trace2	#Trace3	Time1	Time2	Time3
1	1	(3,3)	3	819	819	819	819	0.0283	0.00417	0.0292
2	2	(3,3)	3	819	538083	819	538083	2.41	0.0118	3.42
3	2	(3,1)	3	9	819	258	270	0.0118	0.0151	0.00663
4	2	(6,1)	3	30	47988	27930	4752	0.923	2.16	0.0977
5	2	(9,1)	3	51	538083	378504	24786	14.7	11.9	0.686
6	2	(12, 1)	3	72	3006864	2317524	79488	184	88.5	2.79
7	2	(15, 1)	3	93	-	-	195750	-	-	8.38
8	2	(18, 1)	3	114	-	-	408240	-	-	20.5
9	2	(2,2)	2	32	65792	65792	65792	0.284	0.280	0.799
10	2	(2,2)	3	2080	16843008	16843008	16843008	65.4	96.1	109
11	2	(2,2)	4	-	-	-	-	-	-	-
12	2	(2,2)	2	6	272	156	48	0.0216	0.00663	0.00420
13	2	(3,3)	3	24	538083	378504	2754	15.9	18.4	0.121
14	2	(4,4)	4	60	-	-	298240	-	-	25.0
15	2	(4,2)	2	5	4160	812	480	0.203	0.0352	0.0206
16	2	(4,2)	3	17	266304	22764	6624	11.1	1.58	0.266
17	2	(4,2)	4	21	17043520	637420	88544	449	46.8	3.63
18	2	(4,2)	5	21	-	-	1137120	-	-	48.2
19	3	(5,2)	3	260	-	-	10850	-	-	1.75
20	4	(5,2)	3	1122	-	-	34650	-	-	6.66
21	5	(5,2)	3	4952	-	-	112850	-	-	25.5
22	6	(5,2)	3	22410	-	-	376650	-	-	101.45

Test Results. Experimental results are given in Table 1. Tests were run on a workstation with 32 GB of RAM and a i7-14700 processor at 2.1 GHz. A 10-min timeout is used; timeouts are indicated with a horizontal line –. This timeout is appropriate because our algorithms are intended for offline use and a 10-min timeout allows the test suite to complete within a day. For online use, in contrast, 10 Hz control loops are common, and planning timeouts would need to be consistent with such rates. All reported times are wall-clock times measured in a multitasking environment, so variance is expected.

The first two tests are simple and thus run only once. The test scenario parameters vary to explore scalability. Safe following is single-lane, enabling longer lanes. Safe crossing's grid size and crossing time are related, so we scale them in unison. Safe overtaking increases duration while keeping grid size fixed. Platooning's nominal count increases for fixed size and duration.

We assess the scaling behavior by observing the trends in running time as parameters increase. Since the optimized algorithms have higher cost per trace, they can be *slower* when little speedup is achievable, e.g., in tests 1,2,9,10,11. This is expected for 1,2 because they are not driving scenarios. Likewise, the hazard scenario (9,10,11) is designed to provide no optimization opportunity and to use an atomic proposition. By demonstrating the poor scalability of atomic propositions, it motivates the use of nominals. In the other test scenarios, the baseline algorithm times out on larger input sizes, while the optimized and especially motion algorithms continue to perform better. The motion algorithm performs particularly well for long durations, where its branching factor reductions relative to the optimized algorithm have the opportunity to compound, and in the platooning scenario where there is extensive fixed movement.

7 Conclusions

We developed Hybrid Spatiotemporal Logic (HSTL) for automotive safety, focused on highways. We modeled scenarios like following, passing, intersection-crossing, and platooning. We developed model-checking algorithms which exploit vehicle dynamics to minimize search space, proved them correct, and evaluated them on the scenarios.

Future work will explore using HSTL as a glue layer between planning and control. Motion plans can be expressed as traces. Likewise, a controller's resulting trajectory can be abstracted to a grid and monitored for plan compliance.

Acknowledgments. Radu-Florin Tulcan is funded by the Vienna Science and Technology Fund (WWTF) project ICT22-023, Grant No. 10.47379/ICT22023. Yoàv Montacute is supported by ACT-X, Grant No. JPMJAX24CR, JST, Japan. Radu-Florin Tulcan, Yoàv Montacute, Kevin Zhou and Ichiro Hasuo are supported by ASPIRE, Grant No. JPMJAP2301, JST, Japan. Yusuke Kawamoto is supported by FOREST, Grant No. JPMJFR242M, JST, Japan.

Disclosure of Interests. The authors have no competing interests to declare that are relevant to the content of this article.

References

1. Althoff, M., Dolan, J.M.: Online verification of automated road vehicles using reachability analysis. IEEE Trans. Rob. **30**(4), 903–918 (2014)
2. Alur, R., Courcoubetis, C., Henzinger, T.A., Ho, P.-H.: Hybrid automata: an algorithmic approach to the specification and verification of hybrid systems. In: Grossman, R.L., Nerode, A., Ravn, A.P., Rischel, H. (eds.) HS 1991-1992. LNCS, vol. 736, pp. 209–229. Springer, Heidelberg (1993). https://doi.org/10.1007/3-540-57318-6_30
3. Amini, A., et al.: Learning robust control policies for end-to-end autonomous driving from data-driven simulation. IEEE Rob. Autom. Lett. **5**(2), 1143–1150 (2020)
4. Bennett, B., Cohn, A.G., Wolter, F., Zakharyaschev, M.: Multi-dimensional modal logic as a framework for spatio-temporal reasoning. Appl. Intell. **17**(3), 239–251 (2002)
5. Blackburn, P.: Representation, reasoning, and relational structures: a hybrid logic manifesto. Logic J. IGPL **8**(3), 339–365 (2000)
6. Bohrer, R., Platzer, A.: A hybrid, dynamic logic for hybrid-dynamic information flow. In: Proceedings of the 33rd Annual ACM/IEEE Symposium on Logic in Computer Science, pp. 115–124 (2018)
7. Braüner, T.: Hybrid logic and Its Proof-Theory, vol. 37. Springer Science & Business Media (2010)
8. Chang, X., Ren, P., Xu, P., Li, Z., Chen, X., Hauptmann, A.: A comprehensive survey of scene graphs: generation and application. IEEE Trans. Pattern Anal. Mach. Intell. **45**(1), 1–26 (2021)
9. Cheng, H., Li, P., Wang, R., Xu, H.: Dynamic spatio-temporal logic based on RCC-8. Concurrency Comput. Pract. Experience **33**(22), e5900 (2021)
10. Ciancia, V., Grilletti, G., Latella, D., Loreti, M., Massink, M.: An experimental spatio-temporal model checker. In: Bianculli, D., Calinescu, R., Rumpe, B. (eds.) SEFM 2015. LNCS, vol. 9509, pp. 297–311. Springer, Heidelberg (2015). https://doi.org/10.1007/978-3-662-49224-6_24
11. Ciancia, V., Latella, D., Loreti, M., Massink, M.: Model checking spatial logics for closure spaces. Logical Methods Comput. Sci. **12** (2017)
12. Dosovitskiy, A., Ros, G., Codevilla, F., Lopez, A., Koltun, V.: CARLA: an open urban driving simulator. In: Conference on Robot Learning, pp. 1–16. PMLR (2017)
13. Eberhart, C., Dubut, J., Haydon, J., Hasuo, I.: Formal verification of safety architectures for automated driving. In: 2023 IEEE Intelligent Vehicles Symposium (IV), pp. 1–8. IEEE (2023)
14. Fan, C., Qi, B., Mitra, S., Viswanathan, M., Duggirala, P.S.: Automatic reachability analysis for nonlinear hybrid models with C2E2. In: Chaudhuri, S., Farzan, A. (eds.) CAV 2016. LNCS, vol. 9779, pp. 531–538. Springer, Cham (2016). https://doi.org/10.1007/978-3-319-41528-4_29
15. Fernández-Duque, D., Montacute, Y.: Untangled: a complete dynamic topological logic. In: Williams, B., Chen, Y., Neville, J. (eds.) Thirty-Seventh AAAI Conference on Artificial Intelligence, AAAI 2023, Thirty-Fifth Conference on Innovative Applications of Artificial Intelligence, IAAI 2023, Thirteenth Symposium on Educational Advances in Artificial Intelligence, EAAI 2023, Washington, DC, USA, 7–14 February 2023, pp. 6355–6362. AAAI Press (2023). https://doi.org/10.1609/AAAI.V37I5.25782

16. Fernández-Duque, D., Montacute, Y.: Dynamic tangled derivative logic of metric spaces. In: Wooldridge, M.J., Dy, J.G., Natarajan, S. (eds.) Thirty-Eighth AAAI Conference on Artificial Intelligence, AAAI 2024, Thirty-Sixth Conference on Innovative Applications of Artificial Intelligence, IAAI 2024, Fourteenth Symposium on Educational Advances in Artificial Intelligence, EAAI 2014, February 20-27, 2024, Vancouver, Canada, pp. 10509–10516. AAAI Press (2024). https://doi.org/10.1609/AAAI.V38I9.28920
17. Fionda, V., Greco, G.: LTL on finite and process traces: complexity results and a practical reasoner. J. Artif. Intell. Res. **63**, 557–623 (2018). https://doi.org/10.1613/JAIR.1.11256
18. Fremont, D.J., Dreossi, T., Ghosh, S., Yue, X., Sangiovanni-Vincentelli, A.L., Seshia, S.A.: Scenic: a language for scenario specification and scene generation. In: Proceedings of the 40th ACM SIGPLAN Conference on Programming Language Design and Implementation, pp. 63–78 (2019)
19. Hasuo, I., et al.: Goal-aware RSS for complex scenarios via program logic. IEEE Trans. Intell. Veh. **8**(4), 3040–3072 (2022)
20. Hilscher, M., Linker, S., Olderog, E.-R., Ravn, A.P.: An abstract model for proving safety of multi-lane traffic Manoeuvres. In: Qin, S., Qiu, Z. (eds.) ICFEM 2011. LNCS, vol. 6991, pp. 404–419. Springer, Heidelberg (2011). https://doi.org/10.1007/978-3-642-24559-6_28
21. Kontchakov, R., Kurucz, A., Wolter, F., Zakharyaschev, M.: Spatial logic+ temporal logic=? In: Handbook of Spatial Logics, pp. 497–564. Springer (2007)
22. Kress-Gazit, H., Fainekos, G.E., Pappas, G.J.: Temporal-logic-based reactive mission and motion planning. IEEE Trans. Rob. **25**(6), 1370–1381 (2009)
23. Kress-Gazit, H., Lahijanian, M., Raman, V.: Synthesis for robots: guarantees and feedback for robot behavior. Ann. Rev. Control Rob. Auton. Syst. **1**(1), 211–236 (2018)
24. Li, T., et al.: STSL: a novel spatio-temporal specification language for cyber-physical systems. In: 2020 IEEE 20th International Conference on Software Quality, Reliability and Security (QRS), pp. 309–319. IEEE (2020)
25. Li, T., et al.: Runtime verification of spatio-temporal specification language. Mob. Netw. Appl. **26**(6), 2392–2406 (2021)
26. Lygeros, J., Godbole, D.N., Sastry, S.: Verified hybrid controllers for automated vehicles. IEEE Trans. Autom. Control **43**(4), 522–539 (2002)
27. Malawade, A.V., Yu, S.Y., Hsu, B., Kaeley, H., Karra, A., Al Faruque, M.A.: ROADSCENE2VEC: a tool for extracting and embedding road scene-graphs. Knowl.-Based Syst. **242**, 108245 (2022)
28. Mylavarapu, S., Sandhu, M., Vijayan, P., Krishna, K.M., Ravindran, B., Namboodiri, A.: Towards accurate vehicle behaviour classification with multi-relational graph convolutional networks. In: 2020 IEEE Intelligent Vehicles Symposium (IV), pp. 321–327. IEEE (2020)
29. Pek, C., Manzinger, S., Koschi, M., Althoff, M.: Using online verification to prevent autonomous vehicles from causing accidents. Nat. Mach. Intell. **2**(9), 518–528 (2020)
30. Plaku, E., Karaman, S.: Motion planning with temporal-logic specifications: progress and challenges. AI Commun. **29**(1), 151–162 (2015)
31. Platzer, A.: Towards a hybrid dynamic logic for hybrid dynamic systems. Electron. Notes Theor. Comput. Sci. **174**(6), 63–77 (2007)
32. Platzer, A.: Logical Foundations of Cyber-Physical Systems. Springer (2018)
33. Prior, A.N.: Past, Present and Future. Oxford University Press (1967)

34. Randell, D.A., Cui, Z., Cohn, A.G., et al.: A spatial logic based on regions and connection. KR **92**(165-176), 40–40 (1992)
35. Schwammberger, M.: An abstract model for proving safety of autonomous urban traffic. Theoret. Comput. Sci. **744**, 143–169 (2018)
36. Schwammberger, M., Alves, G.V.: Extending urban multi-lane spatial logic to formalise road junction rules. arXiv preprint arXiv:2110.12583 (2021)
37. Schwarting, W., Alonso-Mora, J., Rus, D.: Planning and decision-making for autonomous vehicles. Ann. Rev. Control Rob. Auton. Syst. **1**(1), 187–210 (2018)
38. Shalev-Shwartz, S., Shammah, S., Shashua, A.: On a formal model of safe and scalable self-driving cars. arXiv preprint arXiv:1708.06374 (2017)
39. Smith, S.L., Tůmová, J., Belta, C., Rus, D.: Optimal path planning for surveillance with temporal-logic constraints. Int. J. Rob. Res. **30**(14), 1695–1708 (2011)
40. Sun, X., Khedr, H., Shoukry, Y.: Formal verification of neural network controlled autonomous systems. In: Proceedings of the 22nd ACM International Conference on Hybrid Systems: Computation and Control, pp. 147–156 (2019)
41. Toledo, F., Woodlief, T., Elbaum, S., Dwyer, M.B.: Specifying and monitoring safe driving properties with scene graphs. In: 2024 IEEE International Conference on Robotics and Automation (ICRA), pp. 15577–15584. IEEE (2024)
42. Tuncali, C.E., Fainekos, G., Ito, H., Kapinski, J.: Simulation-based adversarial test generation for autonomous vehicles with machine learning components. In: 2018 IEEE Intelligent Vehicles Symposium, IV 2018, Changshu, Suzhou, China, 26–30 June 2018, pp. 1555–1562. IEEE (2018). https://doi.org/10.1109/IVS.2018.8500421
43. Wang, S., Zhan, N., Zou, L.: An improved HHL prover: an interactive theorem prover for hybrid systems. In: Butler, M., Conchon, S., Zaïdi, F. (eds.) ICFEM 2015. LNCS, vol. 9407, pp. 382–399. Springer, Cham (2015). https://doi.org/10.1007/978-3-319-25423-4_25
44. Wang, X., Liang, A., Sprinkle, J., Johnson, T.T.: Robustness verification for knowledge-based logic of risky driving scenes. In: Future of Information and Communication Conference, pp. 572–585. Springer (2025)
45. Woodlief, T., Toledo, F., Elbaum, S., Dwyer, M.B.: Closing the gap between sensor inputs and driving properties: a scene graph generator for CARLA. In: 2025 IEEE/ACM 47th International Conference on Software Engineering: Companion Proceedings (ICSE-Companion), pp. 29–32. IEEE (2025)
46. Yu, S.Y., Malawade, A.V., Muthirayan, D., Khargonekar, P.P., Al Faruque, M.A.: Scene-graph augmented data-driven risk assessment of autonomous vehicle decisions. IEEE Trans. Intell. Transp. Syst. **23**(7), 7941–7951 (2021)
47. Yu, Y., Shan, D., Benderius, O., Berger, C., Kang, Y.: Formally robust and safe trajectory planning and tracking for autonomous vehicles. IEEE Trans. Intell. Transp. Syst. **23**(12), 22971–22987 (2022)

RustyDL: A Program Logic for Rust

Daniel Drodt(✉) and Reiner Hähnle

Technische Universität Darmstadt, Darmstadt, Germany
{daniel.drodt,reiner.haehnle}@tu-darmstadt.de

Abstract. Rust is a modern programming language that guarantees memory safety and the absence of data races with a strong type system. We present RustyDL, a program logic for Rust, as a foundation for an auto-interactive, deductive verification tool for Rust. RustyDL reasons about Rust programs directly on the source code level, in contrast to other tools that are all based on translation to an intermediate language. A source-level program logic for Rust is crucial for a human-in-the-loop (HIL) style of verification that permits proving highly complex functional properties. We discuss specific Rust challenges in designing a program logic and calculus for HIL-style verification and propose a solution in each case. We provide a proof-of-concept of our ideas in the form of a prototype of a Rust instance of the well-known deductive verification tool KeY.

Keywords: Deductive verification · Program logic · Rust verification

1 Introduction

Rust is a modern programming language with a strong type system, guaranteeing memory safety without garbage collection. For this, it relies on a type system for managing *ownership*, references, and borrowing, which prevents data races. Rust became highly popular and started being used in the Linux kernel [25,33]. In such safety-critical use cases, the correctness of programs is paramount, so formal verification plays an important role.

Over the last years, a variety of tools for formally verifying Rust code have been proposed. The general approach of most existing tools [4,9,12,23] is to translate Rust code and formal specifications into an intermediate language, such as Viper [27] or Why3 [16], which is supported by existing verification tools. This intermediate code is then used to generate first-order verification conditions to be discharged with SMT solvers.

This translation-based approach permits to implement a deductive verification tool with relative ease, because it is based on an existing tool chain. It also offers a high degree of automation. The downsides of the architecture are: first, one has to trust the (highly non-trivial) translation from Rust and its specification to an intermediate language; second, it is challenging to relate the output of an SMT solver to the code and specification under verification, in case a verification attempt fails: a verification engineer cannot directly interact with the proof or apply proof steps manually.

A. Sampaio and M. Stoelinga (Eds.): FM 2026, LNCS 16556, pp. 357–377, 2026.
https://doi.org/10.1007/978-3-032-26204-2_19

In the spectrum between full automation of proofs and full control over the verification process, existing Rust verification tools are trending towards the former. At the other end, verification tools such as KeY [7] or KIV [31] provide explicit proof objects and allow their users to inspect and apply any proof step, while retaining powerful automation capabilities. This is achieved with a program logic at the *source code* level, typically axiomatized in a sequent calculus. Such a "human-in-the-loop" (HIL), source code-level approach permits fine-grained control. Consequently, it was possible to verify (and find bugs in) highly complex, unaltered Java source code libraries [8,11]. This could so far not be replicated with systems based on translation to an intermediate language.

Right now, there is no HIL, source code-level deductive verifier for Rust. Therefore, a natural research question arises that we answer in the present paper: Can one transfer HIL, source code verification to the world of Rust? What are the necessary conditions? How can we model Rust's type system and behavior, including ownership and references, in a source code program logic? Accordingly, our main result is the program logic RustyDL for HIL, source code verification. We show that a Dynamic Logic with a few familiar extensions is a natural fit for Rust verification. As a proof-of-concept, we also provide a prototype of an implementation based on the KeY verifier, called *Rusty KeY*.

Section 2 provides background on Rust and introduces our program logic for Rust. In Sect. 3, we define the sequent calculus for RustyDL. Section 4 compares our approach with related work. We conclude the paper in Sect. 5.

2 The Rusty Program Logic

Rust is a complex language with a rich type system and support for concurrency. It is divided into two sub-languages: *safe Rust* limits the developer but provides strong memory safety guarantees, while *unsafe Rust* has weaker guarantees but offers more control. The latter must be marked with the keyword `unsafe`.

We focus on *safe* Rust because: (1) most Rust functions are safe; (2) modeling safe Rust provides opportunities (and challenges) for verification: mechanisms such as separation logic or dynamic frames are unnecessary in this setting; and (3) it can be assumed that unsafe Rust is encapsulated, i.e., it is confined to a part of the code that may be analyzed and verified separately [5]. Further, we focus here on a subset of Rust, mainly primitive values, shared and mutable references, and arrays. Structs and enums can be modeled similarly to arrays or references. We leave unions, smart pointers, and traits for future work.

2.1 The Rust Programming Language

We briefly review those features of Rust necessary to follow this paper. For details and the entirety of Rust, we refer to [22,29]. Rust applications and libraries are organized in units called *crates*, which can depend on other crates. Each crate is split into modules containing functions, type definitions, and implementations.

Listing 1. Shared and mutable references in Rust

```
1 let n: u32 = 1;
2 let x: &u32 = &n;
3 println!("{}", *x); // prints "1"
4
5 fn increase_lower(a: &mut u64, b: &mut u64, amount: u64) {
6   let lower = if a < b { a } else { b };
7   *lower = *lower + amount;
8 }
```

The Rust types important for this paper are bool, the integer types i8,..., i128 for signed integers, u8,..., u128 for unsigned integers, the empty tuple type (), and array types such as [i16; 10]. Rust arrays are of fixed length (here: 10) and their length is part of the type.

Rust's unique feature is the type system's enforcement of *ownership*, and *references*. Ownership means each value is *owned* by exactly one *owner* (e.g., a variable or an array field). The value is removed from memory, or *dropped*, once the owner goes out of scope. This feature is the basis of Rust's memory safety. Ownership of a value is *transferred* on assignment—one says the value is *moved*.

Example 1. Function increase_lower in Listing 1 takes two mutable references a, b as arguments, compares their values, stores the lower reference in lower, and increases that value by amount. Observe that in Rust, control structures such as conditionals, loops, and blocks are expressions. The assignment in line 6 moves either a or b to lower. Hence, one of a or b is *no longer initialized*, while lower now contains the moved value. Reading from a or b after line 6 is a compile-time error. This ensures that only initialized memory is read.

Types with a small memory footprint, e.g., integer types, do not follow the move semantics. Their value is *copied* rather than moved on assignment. In Rust terminology: They implement the Copy trait. The only types in this paper not implementing this trait are mutable references and arrays of mutable references.

Since accessing a value only through one owner is, in general, too limiting, Rust provides references. *Shared (or immutable) references* (&) permit read-only access to the *borrowed* value, while *mutable references* (&mut) permit read-and-write access. As seen in the first three lines of Listing 1, a shared reference of type u32 is of type &u32. The borrowed value 1 can be read from reference x using the *dereferencing* operator *x. While the borrow x is live, we say n is borrowed. In case of a mutable reference, the borrowed value cannot merely be read but also modified using the dereferencing operator, see the second to last line of the example.

The Rust compiler—more specifically, its *borrow checker*—ensures programs follow certain rules, which imply the absence of data races: (1) borrowed owners are not written to directly; (2) mutably borrowed owners are only read

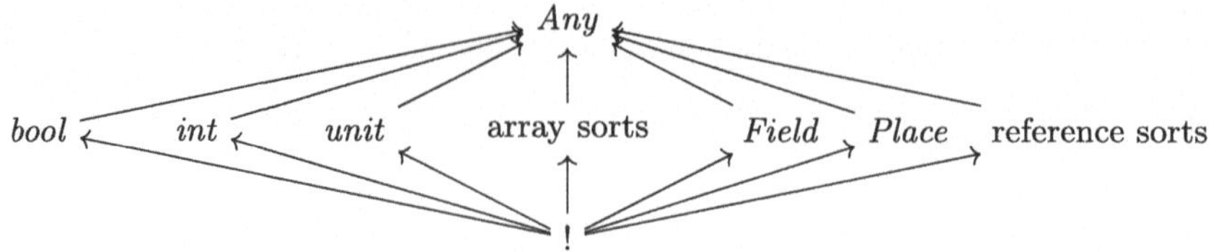

Fig. 1. The sort hierarchy of RustyDL.

through the reference; (3) at any point in the program, each owner is borrowed either mutably once or immutably arbitrarily often; (4) borrowed values are not dropped.

References in Rust have an associated *lifetime* which is necessary in complex programs. We do not consider lifetimes in our logic and omit them here.

In the following, we not only consider entire crates but also *fragments* of Rust programs. Definition 1 defines the set of legal program fragments, i.e., the Rust fragments our logic can deal with.

Definition 1 (Legal Program Fragment). *Let Crt be a valid, i.e., compiler approved, Rust crate. A* legal program fragment *is a sequence of Rust statements p in Crt (and an optional Rust expression at its end), with local variables* $\mathsf{a}_1, \ldots, \mathsf{a}_n$ *of Rust types* $\mathsf{T}_1, \ldots, \mathsf{T}_n$ *such that inserting the function*

$$\texttt{fn f(mut } \mathsf{a}_1\texttt{: } \mathsf{T}_1\texttt{, ..., mut } \mathsf{a}_n\texttt{: } \mathsf{T}_n\texttt{) \{ \{ } p \texttt{ \}; \}}$$

into the entry point of Crt yields a legal program according to the Rust compiler.

The fragment p is wrapped in a block expression. We add the semicolon to ensure that the function returns nothing, simplifying type checking.

2.2 Rusty Dynamic Logic

Dynamic logic is a program logic suggested in [28] and being highly suitable for program verification [2]. We present a version of dynamic logic tailored to Rust called RustyDL, which is an extension of typed first-order logic. Our definitions are based on those for JavaDL, a dynamic logic for Java, as presented in [1].

Figure 1 shows RustyDL's sort hierarchy, i.e., the hierarchy of logical types. *Any* is the super-sort of all sorts, while the "never sort" ! is the bottom sort no term can have. The type bool is mapped to *bool*, the unit type () to *unit*. Signed and unsigned integer types are mapped to mathematical integers *int* (see Sect. 3.4 for how we achieve an accurate model). For each array type [T;N] we create an array sort $[T; N]$. Further, for each sort A, we define a shared reference sort Ref^s_A and a mutable reference sort Ref^m_A. Rust types &T and &**mut** T map to the reference sorts in the expected way.

We demand of the signature that it contains the 0-ary predicates true and false, the binary predicate $\doteq(Any, Any)$ for equality, all usual integer functions and predicates such as $+, -, \cdot, >$, and the constants $TRUE, FALSE$ of sort *bool*.

We use both true and *TRUE* to differentiate between the tautology and the true boolean value, as the former is a formula and the latter a term; hence, they may appear in different scenarios. Analogous for false and *FALSE*.

RustyDL extends the set of classical first-order logic terms with *program variables*, e.g., $\mathsf{a} : int$, where *int* is a's sort. These are similar to constants, but their value is state-dependent. Unlike first-order logical variables, program variables may appear in programs, but one cannot quantify over program variables.

We extend the set of first-order formulas with the modal operators $\langle p\rangle\phi$ ("diamond") and $[p]\phi$ ("box"), for program fragment p and formula ϕ. Intuitively, for deterministic programs, $\langle p\rangle\phi$ expresses that p terminates, and, in the state resulting from this execution, ϕ holds, i.e. total correctness. Conversely, $[p]\phi$ holds iff p does not terminate, or ϕ holds in the resulting state, i.e. partial correctness.

A *Kripke structure* $\mathcal{K} = (\mathcal{D}, \mathcal{I}, \mathcal{S}, \rho)$ over domain $\mathcal{D}$ and interpretation $\mathcal{I}$ formalizes the state changes expressed by the modality formulas, ordering a set of states $\mathcal{S}$ according to possible state transitions ρ through programs. States in $\mathcal{S}$ map program variables to elements in $\mathcal{D}$. $\mathcal{I}$, as in FOL, evaluates functions and relations. For a program fragment p, $\rho(p)$ is a partial function from $\mathcal{S}$ to $\mathcal{S}$ that defines the state change caused by p. This change is only defined if p terminates normally, see Definition 2.

Definition 2 (RustyDL Kripke Structure). *Let Crt be a valid Rust crate. A* RustyDL Kripke structure *for a signature derived from Crt is a pair*

$$\mathcal{K} = (\mathcal{S}, \rho)$$

where

- $\mathcal{S}$ *is an infinite set of first-order structures* $s = (D, \mathcal{I})$*, called* states*, closed under the following property: all states coincide in their domain D and interpretation* $\mathcal{I}$ *of function and predicate symbols.*
- ρ *is a function mapping a legal program fragment* p *to a partial function* $\mathcal{S} \rightharpoonup \mathcal{S}$ *with* $\rho(\mathrm{p})(s_1) = s_2$ *iff evaluating* p *in state* s_1 *terminates normally in* s_2*. If* p *does not terminate normally starting in* s_1*,* $\rho(\mathrm{p})(s_1)$ *is undefined. Note that we assume Rust programs to be deterministic.*

For brevity, the transition function ρ is left undefined, as it depends on a formal semantics for Rust. Our calculus rules provide an axiomatic semantics of ρ. Definition 3 gives the semantics of terms and formulas, including program variables and modalities, relative to a Kripke structure $\mathcal{K}$.

Definition 3 (Semantics of RustyDL Terms and Formulas). *Let Crt be a valid Rust crate,* VSym *the set of logic variable symbols,* $\mathcal{K} = (\mathcal{D}, \mathcal{I}, \mathcal{S}, \rho)$ *a Kripke structure modeling Rust programs,* $s \in \mathcal{S}$ *a state, and* $\beta : \mathrm{VSym} \to \mathcal{D}$ *a variable assignment.*

For every RustyDL term t we define its evaluation inductively by the evaluation function $val_{\mathcal{K},s,\beta}$ *exactly as in first-order logic, with evaluation of program variables defined as* $val_{\mathcal{K},s,\beta}(\mathsf{a}) = s(\mathsf{a})$ *for each program variable* a.

For every RustyDL formula ϕ we define satisfaction, denoted $(\mathcal{K}, s, \beta) \models \phi$, exactly as in first-order logic with two new cases:

1. $(\mathcal{K}, s, \beta) \models [p]\phi$ *iff* $\rho(p)(s)$ *is undefined or* $\rho(p)(s) = s'$ *and* $(\mathcal{K}, s', \beta) \models \phi$,
2. $(\mathcal{K}, s, \beta) \models \langle p \rangle \phi$ *iff* $\rho(p)(s) = s'$ *exists and* $(\mathcal{K}, s', \beta) \models \phi$.

In RustyDL one can express a large variety of properties of Rust code. Partial correctness of program p w.r.t. pre- and post-conditions $pre, post$ is written as $pre \rightarrow [p]post$. This formula is equivalent to the Hoare triple $\{pre\}\, p\, \{post\}$ [19] and it is valid iff for every state s such that pre is satisfied in s, evaluating program p in s either does not terminate or in the resulting state s', $post$ is satisfied. In contrast, $pre \rightarrow \langle p \rangle post$ expresses total correctness. Unlike Hoare logic, dynamic logic is closed under all operations. Hence, e.g., $post$, may contain further modalities permitting to express program equivalence, refinement, etc. [2].

To obtain a usable RustyDL calculus that can model state changes efficiently, we provide a more fine-grained state transition mechanism than the modalities called *update*. Definition 4 extends JavaDL *updates* [1] with the *mutating updates.*

Definition 4 (Update, Update Application). *We define the set* Upd *inductively by (the second clause is new compared to [1]):*

1. $(\mathsf{a} := t) \in \mathrm{Upd}$ *for each program variable* $a : A$ *and each term* t *of sort* A,
2. $(t_1 \ast\!\!\rightarrow t_2) \in \mathrm{Upd}$ *for each term* t_1 *of sort* Ref^m_A *and* t_2 *of sort* A,
3. $\mathtt{skip} \in \mathrm{Upd}$,
4. $(u_1 \parallel u_2) \in \mathrm{Upd}$ *for all updates* $u_1, u_2 \in \mathrm{Upd}$,
5. $(\{u_1\}\, u_2) \in \mathrm{Upd}$ *for all updates* $u_1, u_2 \in \mathrm{Upd}$.

We extend the inductive definition of terms with term $\{u\}t$ *of sort* A *for all updates* $u \in \mathrm{Upd}$ *and terms* t *of sort* A. *The inductive definition of formulas is extended with formula* $\{u\}\,\phi$ *for all updates* $u \in \mathrm{Upd}$ *and formulas* ϕ.

Updates are *applied* syntactically to terms and formulas. Update application changes the state wherein a term (formula) is evaluated. Updates allow us to realize the decomposition of a large program fragment into a series of small, deterministic state changes (see Definition 5 below).

Example 2. Let x, y be program variables of type i32 and z of type **&mut** i32. We give examples of updates with their intuitive meaning:

- `skip` is an update expressing no state change.
- An elementary update $(\mathsf{x} := \mathsf{x} + 1)$ expresses a state change where program variable x is incremented by one. The update application $\{\mathsf{x} := \mathsf{x} + 1\}\,\mathsf{x}$ is semantically equivalent to the expression $\mathsf{x} + 1$.
- The *parallel* update $(\mathsf{x} := \mathsf{y} \parallel \mathsf{y} := \mathsf{x})$ expresses a state change where x and y swap values. Such parallel updates express state changes with no interference among them. Multiple updates to the same variable can occur in one parallel update; then, the last one overwrites the earlier ones.
- $(\mathsf{z} \ast\!\!\rightarrow \mathsf{y} - 1)$ is a *mutating* update, expressing that the location borrowed by z is set to $\mathsf{y} - 1$.

Mutating updates are crucial for representing mutable references in our logic. To model the latter in RustyDL, we need to involve not merely values, but also the borrowed location (the *lender*). To this end, we use the sort *Place* (the notion is taken from the Rust compiler [30]). For each program variable x, we define a unique constant $\llbracket \mathsf{x} \rrbracket : \mathit{Place}$. To model the location of an array field, we add a function $\mathit{arrPlc} : \mathrm{Ref}^m_{[A;n]} \times \mathit{int} \to \mathit{Place}$ for each sort A and $n \in \mathbb{N}$, intuitively, mapping each field to its place. We write $\llbracket t, t' \rrbracket$ for $\mathit{arrPlc}(t, t')$. Thus, the term $\mathit{mref}(\mathit{pl})$ is of sort Ref^m_A, where $\mathit{pl} : \mathit{Place}$ is the place of the lender of sort A. How these mutable references are used is shown in Sect. 3.5.

Example 3. Let $\mathsf{x} : \mathit{int}$ and $\mathsf{a} : [\mathit{int}; 4]$ be program variables. The mutable reference $\mathit{mref}(\llbracket \mathsf{x} \rrbracket)$ expresses that x is mutably borrowed and $\mathit{mref}(\llbracket \mathit{mref}(\llbracket \mathsf{a} \rrbracket), 1 \rrbracket)$ expresses that the field at index 1 of array a is mutably borrowed.

Mutating updates are the central extension of our logic. They fit naturally into our dynamic logic and allow for handling mutable references with little conceptual overhead. Alternatives, such as explicitly modeling memory or the set of active loans, rapidly become unwieldy and computationally complex when used in a logic.

Definition 5 formalizes the semantics of updates and their applications that was described above intuitively.

Definition 5 (Semantics of RustyDL Updates). *Let Crt be a valid Rust crate, $\mathcal{K} = (\mathcal{S}, \rho)$ a Kripke structure for Crt, $s \in \mathcal{S}$ a state, and $\beta : \mathrm{VSym} \to D$ a variable assignment. The valuation function $\mathit{val}_{\mathcal{K},s,\beta} : \mathit{Upd} \to (\mathcal{S} \to \mathcal{S})$ is defined as:*

$$\mathit{val}_{\mathcal{K},s,\beta}(\mathsf{a} := t)(s')(\mathsf{b}) = \begin{cases} \mathit{val}_{\mathcal{K},s,\beta}(t) & \text{if } \mathsf{b} = \mathsf{a} \\ s'(\mathsf{b}) & \text{otherwise} \end{cases} \quad \text{for all } s' \in \mathcal{S}, \mathsf{b} \in \mathrm{ProgVSym}$$

$$\mathit{val}_{\mathcal{K},s,\beta}(t_1 \twoheadleftarrow\!\!\!\!* \; t_2)(s')(\mathsf{b}) = \begin{cases} \mathit{val}_{\mathcal{K},s,\beta}(t_2) & \text{if } \mathit{val}_{\mathcal{K},s,\beta}(t_1) = \mathit{val}_{\mathcal{K},s,\beta}(\mathit{mref}(\llbracket \mathsf{b} \rrbracket)) \\ s'(\mathsf{b}) & \text{otherwise} \end{cases}$$

$$\text{for all } s' \in \mathcal{S}, \mathsf{b} \in \mathrm{ProgVSym}$$

$$\mathit{val}_{\mathcal{K},s,\beta}(\mathtt{skip})(s') = s' \quad \text{for all } s' \in \mathcal{S}$$

$$\mathit{val}_{\mathcal{K},s,\beta}(u_1 \parallel u_2)(s') = \mathit{val}_{\mathcal{K},s,\beta}(u_2)(\mathit{val}_{\mathcal{K},s,\beta}(u_1)(s')) \quad \text{for all } s' \in \mathcal{S}$$

$$\mathit{val}_{\mathcal{K},s,\beta}(\{u_1\}\, u_2) = \mathit{val}_{\mathcal{K},s',\beta}(u_2) \text{ where } s' = \mathit{val}_{\mathcal{K},s,\beta}(u_1)(s)$$

We extend the inductive definition of the semantics of RustyDL terms and formulas (Definition 3) with

$$\mathit{val}_{\mathcal{K},s,\beta}(\{u\}\, t) = \mathit{val}_{\mathcal{K},s',\beta}(t) \text{ where } s' = \mathit{val}_{\mathcal{K},s,\beta}(u)(s)$$

and

$$(\mathcal{K}, s, \beta) \models \{u\}\, \phi \text{ iff } (\mathcal{K}, s', \beta) \models \phi \text{ where } s' = \mathit{val}_{\mathcal{K},s,\beta}(u)(s) \ .$$

Example 4. Let x be a program variable of type i32. Clearly, $\mathsf{x} \doteq 0 \to \mathsf{x} > 0$ is unsatisfiable. However, applying the update $\mathsf{x} := \mathsf{x} + 1$ to the right-hand side makes the formula valid:

$$\models \mathsf{x} \doteq 0 \to \{\mathsf{x} := \mathsf{x} + 1\}\, (\mathsf{x} > 0).$$

Compare the update above with the following modality:

$$\mathsf{x} \doteq 0 \rightarrow \langle \mathsf{x} = \mathsf{x} + 1; \rangle (\mathsf{x} > 0).$$

It is instructive to observe the difference: Updates are *total* state changes, they are guaranteed to terminate normally. Hence, they are similar to explicit substitutions. Modalities, on the other hand, may not terminate. Addition may lead to an overflow, causing exceptional termination: $\rho(p)$ is partial.

3 RustyDL Calculus

Recall that functional total correctness of a program fragment p, relative to a precondition *pre* and postcondition *post*, is expressed by validity of the RustyDL formula $pre \rightarrow \langle p \rangle post$. This can be proven in a sequent calculus for RustyDL: Validity is shown by deriving the sequent "$\Longrightarrow pre \rightarrow \langle p \rangle post$".

The calculus given below is sound: All rules in this section have been proven sound relative to a formal semantics [14] in ongoing work.

3.1 Challenges in the Design of a Sequent Calculus for RustyDL

We model Rust's unique features and its semantics in terms of rules of a program logic, striving to retain a human-readable format to enable human interaction. For this, we work on the only slightly simplified and normalized high-level intermediate representation (HIR) used in the Rust compiler [30]. This representation is close to source-level Rust but with macros expanded and some structures like the different forms of loop normalized.

We identify five core features of Rust our logic must address: (1) ownership, (2) integer semantics, (3) data types, e.g., arrays, structs, (4) shared and mutable references, including references to array fields, and (5) the potentially unbounded behavior of function calls and loops. For space reasons, we only present an essential subset of the Rust fragment supported by our logic and implementation. The subset discussed in the following demonstrates how our logic and calculus models Rust's features while being the necessary minimum for complex problems.

3.2 Symbolic Execution Calculus

The sequent calculus contains the usual propositional and first-order rules, as well as a relatively complete rule set for mathematical integers. Since formulas may contain modalities, we require a way to simplify and decompose the program fragments contained in them until only first-order formulas remain. We follow [1,7] in the design of rule schemata that implement *symbolic execution*.

Consider an if-else expression. Its execution branches into two paths, depending on the value of its guard. Because we work with *symbolic* program variables, the calculus must cover all possible paths and split the current proof goal.

As seen in rule ifElseSplit below, the rules contain schematic variables: Γ, Δ stand for sets of RustyDL-formulas, ϕ for one RustyDL-formula, $\mathcal{U}$ for an optional update, se for a "simple expression" (a literal or program variable), $\{be_0\}$ and $\{be_1\}$ for block expressions. Additionally, the program modalities contain a *context* of the program fragment in focus, with *inactive program prefix* π and *remaining program* ω. Typically, π matches opening braces and ω the remaining statements and closing braces. This context allows the rule below to match any program fragment where the expression to be executed next is an if-else, even if further statements follow or it is the start of a block expression. All schematic variables are instantiated by concrete objects of the corresponding kind upon rule application.

$$\text{ifElseSplit}\ \frac{\begin{array}{c}\Gamma, \mathcal{U}(se \doteq TRUE) \Longrightarrow \mathcal{U}\langle \pi\ \{be_0\}\ \omega\rangle\phi, \Delta \\ \Gamma, \mathcal{U}(se \doteq FALSE) \Longrightarrow \mathcal{U}\langle \pi\ \{be_1\}\ \omega\rangle\phi, \Delta\end{array}}{\Gamma \Longrightarrow \mathcal{U}\langle \pi\ \mathsf{if}\ se\ \{be_0\}\ \mathsf{else}\ \{be_1\}\ \omega\rangle\phi, \Delta}$$

The rule models symbolic execution of a program starting with an if-else expression that has a simple (hence, side-effect free) guard. The proof goal in the conclusion is reduced to the two premises corresponding to each execution path. The sequents in the premises express that we know the value of the guard se in each branch: In the then-branch we know se to be $TRUE$, in the else-branch to be $FALSE$. Matching on expressions (in contrast to statements) allows us to handle assignments occurring in statements (x = y;) and, for example, as a block's value ({x = y}), with a single rule.

If the if's condition is a complex expression, i.e., neither a literal nor a program variable, we symbolically execute this condition by introducing a fresh auxiliary variable. In the rule unfoldIfElse, nse stands for a "non-simple expression" and x is a so far unused program variable.

$$\text{unfoldIfElse}\ \frac{\Gamma \Longrightarrow \mathcal{U}\langle \pi\ \{\mathsf{let\ x} = nse;\ \mathsf{if\ x}\ \{be_0\}\ \mathsf{else}\ \{be_1\}\}\ \omega\rangle\phi, \Delta}{\Gamma \Longrightarrow \mathcal{U}\langle \pi\ \mathsf{if}\ nse\ \{be_0\}\ \mathsf{else}\ \{be_1\}\ \omega\rangle\phi, \Delta}$$

To model state changes in the calculus, we employ updates. The rule copy below matches on any assignment of a simple expression to a program variable. Applying the rule adds an update in front of the modality that represents the assignment's state change and replaces the original expression of the assignment with the unit expression (). Unsurprisingly, the following rule only works for literals or variables of Copy type, i.e., without move semantics. Assignments causing a move need a separate rule.

$$\text{copy}\ \frac{\Gamma \Longrightarrow \mathcal{U}\{\mathsf{x} := se\}\langle \pi\ ()\ \omega\rangle\phi, \Delta}{\Gamma \Longrightarrow \mathcal{U}\langle \pi\ \mathsf{x} = se\ \omega\rangle\phi, \Delta}\quad se \text{ is a literal or implements Copy}$$

Subsequent applications of the copy rule accumulate updates in front of the modality that represent the state changes on one specific path through the control flow of a program fragment. The accumulated updates are simplified and ultimately applied to the postcondition. In consequence, the calculus contains *update simplification* rules. For instance, applying an elementary update $\mathsf{x} := t$, with a program variable x and a term t to the program variable x, corresponds to substituting x with t. In our notation:

$$\mathsf{applyOnPV} \quad (\{\mathsf{x} := t\}\,\mathsf{x}) \rightsquigarrow t$$

See [15] for the complete set of update simplification rules.

To get rid of the unit expressions left by rule copy and expressions like 2 in {2; a + b}, we use rule simpleExprStmt. This rule removes expression statements consisting of a simple expression, as these cannot affect the program state.

$$\mathsf{simpleExprStmt}\ \frac{\Gamma \Longrightarrow \mathcal{U}\langle \pi \quad \omega\rangle\phi, \Delta}{\Gamma \Longrightarrow \mathcal{U}\langle \pi\ se;\ \omega\rangle\phi, \Delta}$$

Example 5. Let x, y, z be program variables of type i32. Consider the sequent $\mathsf{x} \doteq \mathsf{z} \Longrightarrow \langle \mathsf{x = x + y;\ y = x - y;}\rangle(\mathsf{y} \doteq \mathsf{z})$. Applying copy and then simpleExprStmt twice yields the sequent $\mathsf{x} \doteq \mathsf{z} \Longrightarrow \{\mathsf{x} := \mathsf{x}+\mathsf{y}\}\,\{\mathsf{y} := \mathsf{x}-\mathsf{y}\}\,\langle\rangle(\mathsf{y} \doteq \mathsf{z})$ (ignoring overflow, to be discussed in Sect. 3.4). It can be simplified (rule not shown) to $\mathsf{x} \doteq \mathsf{z} \Longrightarrow \{\mathsf{x} := \mathsf{x}+\mathsf{y}\}\,\{\mathsf{y} := \mathsf{x}-\mathsf{y}\}\,(\mathsf{y} \doteq \mathsf{z})$, after update application and simplification it becomes $\mathsf{x} \doteq \mathsf{z} \Longrightarrow (\mathsf{x}+\mathsf{y}-\mathsf{y} \doteq \mathsf{z})$, a valid first-order sequent.

3.3 Ownership

Consider an assignment x = y, where y is not of a type implementing Copy, for example, a mutable reference. Then the value of y is moved out of y to x. We model this behavior in the logic: After the move, x's value should not be accessible via y in a formula. One way to model this in logic is with explicit *uninitialized values*. The downside is that then every variable on each access must be tested whether it contains such a special value. This is similar to the problems arising when using many-valued logic to model undefined values [17]. It is more efficient to rely instead on *underspecification* and simply use Skolemization (called anonymizing update in [1]). The rule move is similar to copy, but it updates y to a fresh constant c of matching type: While y still has *some* value, we know nothing about it besides its sort.

$$\mathsf{move}\ \frac{\Gamma \Longrightarrow \mathcal{U}\{\mathsf{x} := \mathsf{y} \,\|\, \mathsf{y} := c\}\langle \pi\ ()\ \omega\rangle\phi, \Delta}{\Gamma \Longrightarrow \mathcal{U}\langle \pi\ \mathsf{x = y}\ \omega\rangle\phi, \Delta}$$

$\mathsf{y} : A$, A is not Copy and $c : A$ a fresh constant

3.4 Handling Integers and Overflow

Rust provides multiple compilation modes with differing levels of optimization, the most prominent being called *debug* and *release*. The former contains more checks at the cost of performance. These modes also affect integer operations.

An expression like a + b may overflow which in Rust's semantics is unintended and causes a panic in debug mode [29]. In release mode, overflow checks are omitted and the value wraps around. For verification, we focus on the debug semantics, so RustyDL must show safety: the absence of overflows. Rule assignAddU32 matches on assigning the sum of two simple expressions to program variable x with Rust type u32. The rule splits a proof into two cases. If the result of the addition is in range of the u32 type, the sum is translated to an update. Otherwise, a panic is raised.

$$\text{assignAddU32}\quad \frac{\begin{array}{l}\Gamma, \mathcal{U}\, inU32(se_1 + se_2) \Longrightarrow \mathcal{U}\{\mathsf{x} := se_1 + se_2\}\langle \pi\ ()\ \omega\rangle\phi, \Delta \\ \Gamma, \mathcal{U} \neg inU32(se_1 + se_2) \Longrightarrow \mathcal{U}\langle \pi\ \mathsf{panic!}()\ \omega\rangle\phi, \Delta\end{array}}{\Gamma \Longrightarrow \mathcal{U}\langle \pi\ \mathsf{x} = se_1 + se_2\ \omega\rangle\phi, \Delta}$$

The semantics of the $inU32$ predicate is a bounds check between the constants u32::MIN $(= 0)$ and u32::MAX $(= 2^{32} - 1)$.

3.5 Rules for References

Recall that a program fragment p is only valid if the Rust compiler—including the borrow checker—accepts it. Thus, our calculus needs not to ensure that p adheres to the borrow checker's rules, instead, it can rely on its guarantees.

How to model references in RustyDL? One approach is to add a reserved program variable, or a ghost variable, call it loans, that stores which variables borrow from which others and whether these borrows are shared or mutable. Thus, loans represents the set of active loans at any moment. The reference rules may then be explicitly introduced, if necessary, as axioms or rules over loans. However, an explicit model of active loans must be kept up-to-date after *every state change*. If we encounter a statement as simple as x = y, we cannot use copy, because we also might have to update loans: What if x or y are borrowed? Then all active loans for these variables must be removed from loans. This approach does not benefit from Rust's borrow checker, but in effect re-implements it.

Therefore, we do not explicitly model the active loans, but express references as logical terms. For shared references, this is simple. On encountering x=&y, we know that the value x is borrowing cannot be changed while x is live. Hence, one disregards where the value is coming from and simply works with y's value:

$$\text{borrowShared}\quad \frac{\Gamma \Longrightarrow \mathcal{U}\{\mathsf{x} := sref(\mathsf{y})\}\langle \pi\ ()\ \omega\rangle\phi, \Delta}{\Gamma \Longrightarrow \mathcal{U}\langle \pi\ \mathsf{x} = \&\mathsf{y}\ \omega\rangle\phi, \Delta}$$

The current value of y is held by Γ, Δ, or $\mathcal{U}$. Any further change to y (which must necessarily come after x is dropped or re-assigned) does not affect x. Since x is not equivalent to y, we do not assign y to x but $sref(\mathsf{y})$, a shared reference term. Function $sref$ takes a term of type A and returns a term of type Ref^s_A.

Example 6. Consider the sequent $\Longrightarrow \langle \mathsf{y} = 2;\ \mathsf{x} = \&\mathsf{y}\rangle(\mathsf{x} \doteq sref(2))$. Applying first rule copy, then borrowShared results in

$$\Longrightarrow \{\mathsf{y} := 2\}\,\{\mathsf{x} := sref(\mathsf{y})\}\,\langle\rangle(\mathsf{x} \doteq sref(2))\ .$$

Reading values of shared references is done by function $*^s_A : \text{Ref}^s_A \to A$ for each sort A (omitted in the following for readability). Rule derefShared takes an assignment of the dereference of y to x and translates it to an update with $*^s$. The simplification rule derefOfSharedRef then translates the dereference of a shared reference of term t back to t.

$$\text{derefShared}\ \frac{\Gamma \Longrightarrow \mathcal{U}\{\mathsf{x} := *^s(\mathsf{y})\}\langle \pi\ ()\ \omega\rangle\phi, \Delta}{\Gamma \Longrightarrow \mathcal{U}\langle \pi\ \mathsf{x} = \mathsf{*y}\ \omega\rangle\phi, \Delta}\qquad \text{derefOfSharedRef}\quad *^s(\mathit{sref}(t)) \rightsquigarrow t$$

$\mathsf{x} : A, \mathsf{y} : \text{Ref}^s_A$, A is Copy

As shared references only consider the value, their treatment is exactly the same for shared references to arrays.

Mutable references differ in that we cannot treat them as the borrowed value at time of the borrow: If x is a mutable borrow of y, there might be an assignment such as $\mathsf{*x} = se$, which changes not x's value but y's. Thus, x's value contains the lender and we treat assignments to *x as assignments to this place.

Consider borrowing variables. When encountering a mutable borrow, for example, in x = &mut y, applying rule borrowMut adds an update for x with $\mathit{mref}(\llbracket \mathsf{y} \rrbracket)$, representing that x borrows y:

$$\text{borrowMut}\ \frac{\Gamma \Longrightarrow \mathcal{U}\{\mathsf{x} := \mathit{mref}(\llbracket \mathsf{y} \rrbracket)\}\langle \pi\ ()\ \omega\rangle\phi, \Delta}{\Gamma \Longrightarrow \mathcal{U}\langle \pi\ \mathsf{x} = \&\mathsf{mut}\ \mathsf{y}\ \omega\rangle\phi, \Delta}$$

To read the value borrowed by a mutable reference, we add the unary state-dependent operator $*^m_A$, which takes a term of sort Ref^m_A and is itself of sort A and declare a corresponding lookup rule derefOfMutReference $*^m(\mathit{mref}(\llbracket \mathsf{x} \rrbracket)) \rightsquigarrow \mathsf{x}$. The operator is state-dependent to reflect any update expressing a state change. This might be necessary when x was mutated. To update a variable x appearing in $*^m$ but keep other state changes possibly affecting the lender, we use the rule applyElemOnDeref $\{u_1 \parallel \mathsf{x} := t \parallel u_2\}\ *^m(\mathsf{x}) \rightsquigarrow \{u_1 \parallel u_2\}\ *^m(t)$.

Additionally, we require a rule for mutating a value through the mutable reference x. We want to update not the value of x, but the *place of the lender* $\llbracket \mathsf{y} \rrbracket$. This is why we introduced *mutating updates* $t_1 \ast\!\!\!\to t_2$, expressing that term t_2 is written to the place borrowed by t_1.

$$\text{mutate}\ \frac{\Gamma \Longrightarrow \mathcal{U}\{\mathsf{x} \ast\!\!\!\to se\}\langle \pi\ ()\ \omega\rangle\phi, \Delta}{\Gamma \Longrightarrow \mathcal{U}\langle \pi\ \mathsf{*x} = se\ \omega\rangle\phi, \Delta}$$

Example 7. Consider the sequent $\Longrightarrow \langle \mathsf{x} = 1;\ \mathsf{y} = \&\mathsf{mut}\ \mathsf{x};\ \mathsf{*y} = 3;\rangle\phi$ with program variables $\mathsf{x} : \mathit{int}$, $\mathsf{y} : \text{Ref}^m_{\mathit{int}}$. Applying rules copy, borrowMut, and mutate results in

$$\Longrightarrow \{\mathsf{x} := 1\}\ \{\mathsf{y} := \mathit{mref}(\llbracket \mathsf{x} \rrbracket)\}\ \{\mathsf{y} \ast\!\!\!\to 3\}\ \langle\rangle\phi\ .$$

To simplify such mutating updates, we declare two simplification rules. The first, applyOnMutating, applies an update u to a mutating update. Unlike for elementary updates (see [15] for details), u is applied to both sides of $\ast\!\!\rightarrow$. Rule mutatingToElementary transforms a mutating update, where the left-hand-side is known to be $mref(\mathsf{a})$ for some program variable a, to an elementary update $\mathsf{a} := t$.

applyOnMutating
$$\{u\}(t_1 \ast\!\!\rightarrow t_2) \rightsquigarrow \{u\}t_1 \ast\!\!\rightarrow \{u\}t_2$$

mutatingToElementary
$$mref(\llbracket \mathsf{a} \rrbracket) \ast\!\!\rightarrow t \rightsquigarrow \mathsf{a} := t$$

Example 8. Continuing Example 7, simplifying the first two updates leads to

$$\Longrightarrow \{\mathsf{x} := 1 \,\|\, \mathsf{y} := mref(\llbracket \mathsf{x} \rrbracket)\}\, \{\mathsf{y} \ast\!\!\rightarrow 3\}\, \langle\rangle\phi$$

Because the place $\llbracket \mathsf{x} \rrbracket$ is a *constant*, it is unaffected by updates. Further simplification yields $\Longrightarrow \{\mathsf{x} := 1 \,\|\, \mathsf{y} := mref(\llbracket \mathsf{x} \rrbracket) \,\|\, mref(\llbracket \mathsf{x} \rrbracket) \ast\!\!\rightarrow 3\}\, \langle\rangle\phi$. Using mutatingToElementary, we get $\Longrightarrow \{\mathsf{x} := 1 \,\|\, \mathsf{y} := mref(\llbracket \mathsf{x} \rrbracket) \,\|\, \mathsf{x} := 3\}\, \langle\rangle\phi$, where we see that $\mathsf{y} \ast\!\!\rightarrow 3$ is replaced by $\mathsf{x} := 3$. We finally simplify away the overridden update to $\Longrightarrow \{\mathsf{y} := mref(\llbracket \mathsf{x} \rrbracket) \,\|\, \mathsf{x} := 3\}\, \langle\rangle\phi$.

3.6 Modeling Array Access

To model array access we use two functions for each array type $[S; n]$: Function $get_{[S;n]} : [S; n] \times \mathit{Field} \to S$ takes an array and a term of type *Field* and evaluates it to the value of the array at the index represented by the field. Function $set_{[S;n]} : [S; n] \times \mathit{Field} \times S \to [S; n]$ takes an array, a field for index i, and a value t and creates a new array term with the value at the index i overwritten with t. The sort *Field* allows abstraction over indices: Function $idx : int \to \mathit{Field}$ turns an integer into a field. Sort *Field* is also used for tuple and struct fields. The present approach follows JavaDL and the theory of arrays [26]. The difference is that in RustyDL the only possible aliasing is over the array index, not the array entries. Array access in programs is symbolically executed: If the index is out of bounds, we continue with a panic; otherwise, we model the successful access with an update.

Example 9. Let $\mathsf{a} : [int; 4]$ and $\mathsf{i}, \mathsf{j} : int$ be program variables. The term

$$get_{[int;4]}(set_{[int;4]}(set_{[int;4]}(\mathsf{a}, idx(\mathsf{i}), 1), idx(\mathsf{j}), 2), idx(\mathsf{i}))$$

represents an access of a at index i after first setting the value at index i to 1, then writing 2 at index j. Assuming i and j are valid indices, the value of this term is 2 iff $\mathsf{i} \doteq \mathsf{j}$, and 1 otherwise.

We pretty-print a term like $get_{[S;n]}(t_0, idx(t_1))$ as $t_0[t_1]$ and omit the type of *set*. The term in Example 9 can be typeset as $set(set(\mathsf{a}, idx(\mathsf{i}), 1), idx(\mathsf{j}), 2)[\mathsf{i}]$.

For reading and writing to array indices, we use the functions above. Rule copyArrayIdx below models reading an array a at index i and storing the result

Listing 2. A program computing the product of a and b, storing it in n. Because we use **break** with a value, the result is also the loop's value.

```
let mut n = 0; let old_b = b;
loop {
  if b == 0 { break n; }
  n += a; b -= 1;
}
```

in x. We split the proof to check for possible out of bound errors which cause a panic. We omit the similar move version.

$$\text{copyArrayIdx}\ \frac{\begin{array}{c}\Gamma, \mathcal{U}(\mathsf{i} < 0 \lor \mathsf{i} \geq n) \Longrightarrow \mathcal{U}\langle \pi\ \mathsf{panic!()}\ \omega\rangle\phi, \Delta \\ \Gamma, \mathcal{U}(0 \leq \mathsf{i} \land \mathsf{i} < n) \Longrightarrow \mathcal{U}\{\mathsf{x} := \mathsf{a[i]}\}\langle \pi\ \mathsf{()}\ \omega\rangle\phi, \Delta\end{array}}{\begin{array}{c}\Gamma \Longrightarrow \mathcal{U}\langle \pi\ \mathsf{x} = \mathsf{a[i]}\ \omega\rangle\phi, \Delta \\ \mathsf{x} : S, \mathsf{a} : [S; n],\ S \text{ is } \mathsf{Copy}\end{array}}$$

Similarly, the rule writeArrayIdxCopy handles writing value x to an array a at index i. We add an update changing the value of a.

$$\text{writeArrayIdxCopy}\ \frac{\begin{array}{c}\Gamma, \mathcal{U}(\mathsf{i} < 0 \lor \mathsf{i} \geq n) \Longrightarrow \mathcal{U}\langle \pi\ \mathsf{panic!()}\ \omega\rangle\phi, \Delta \\ \Gamma, \mathcal{U}(0 \leq \mathsf{i} \land \mathsf{i} < n) \Longrightarrow \mathcal{U}\{\mathsf{a} := set(\mathsf{a}, idx(\mathsf{i}), se)\}\langle \pi\ \mathsf{()}\ \omega\rangle\phi, \Delta\end{array}}{\begin{array}{c}\Gamma \Longrightarrow \mathcal{U}\langle \pi\ \mathsf{a[i]} = se\ \omega\rangle\phi, \Delta \\ \mathsf{a} : [S; n],\ S \text{ is } \mathsf{Copy}\end{array}}$$

References of array fields follow the same general approach as in Sect. 3.5, but are more complex, because invalid array bounds may cause a panic which must be checked. Details are in [15].

3.7 Loop Invariants and Loop Scopes

Function calls and loops introduce potentially unbounded computation and, therefore, require some form of induction principle in deductive program verification to achieve relative completeness. Our approach is designed to handle function calls as well as loops in their full complexity, where treatment of the former closely follows [1]. For space reasons, we discuss it only in [15].

Instead, we discuss loops in some detail: While loop invariants are a standard concept, the rules become highly complex for loops that may terminate due to **break** or panic. We use the relatively recent concept of *loop scope* [32] to provide concise invariant rules that handle non-standard control flow. (For simplicity, we disregard labels, however, the presented approach is designed to handle them.)

Consider the program in Listing 2, where a, b, old_b are program variables of type u64. The loop is an expression and has a value: the value of n in the final iteration. To safely approximate the unknown number of loop iterations, we use a loop invariant: a RustyDL formula *inv* that holds before the first and after every subsequent iteration. Ignoring overflow, a sufficiently strong loop invariant *inv* to prove functional correctness of the loop in Listing 2 is the formula (we need not strengthen the invariant with $0 \leq \mathsf{b}$, as this is inferred from b's type):

$$\mathsf{n} \doteq \mathsf{a} \cdot (\mathsf{old\_b} - \mathsf{b}) \land \mathsf{b} \leq \mathsf{old\_b} \tag{1}$$

The Rust compiler translates all loops to unconditional loops as in Listing 2, so the invariant rules of Hoare [19], Dijkstra [13], or JavaDL [1], are unsuitable: All make a case distinction based on the guard's value. This is impossible here, as we are unable to extract a loop guard. To address this and to support statements redirecting control flow, such as **break** and **return**, we use an auxiliary control statement: A *loop scope* $\circlearrowleft_{\mathsf{x}} p \circlearrowright$ with *index variable* x and body p is a Rust expression, where x is a fresh program variable of type bool.

Intuitively, a loop scope represents a single generic loop iteration and records the reason for exiting the loop in the index variable x. For example, when exiting the loop through a **break**, x is set to true. When the loop is not exited this way, we set x to false. Like loops themselves, loop scopes in RustyDL are expressions and can have a value, namely the value of the loop they represent. We use loop scopes in the loop invariant rule to symbolically execute a generic loop iteration and to record how it was terminated. Rule loopScopeInvBox below matches on loops in the box modality. It splits a proof into two branches.

$$\text{loopScopeInvBox}\ \frac{\begin{array}{l}\Gamma \Longrightarrow \mathcal{U}\mathit{inv}, \Delta \\ \Gamma \Longrightarrow \mathcal{U}\mathcal{V}\Big(\mathit{inv} \rightarrow [\circlearrowleft_{\mathsf{x}}\, \mathit{body};\ \mathsf{continue};\ \circlearrowright]\big(\\ \quad (\mathsf{x} \doteq \mathit{TRUE} \rightarrow [\pi\omega]\phi) \land (\mathsf{x} \doteq \mathit{FALSE} \rightarrow \mathit{inv})\big)\Big), \Delta\end{array}}{\Gamma \Longrightarrow \mathcal{U}[\pi\ \mathsf{loop}\ \mathit{body}\ \omega]\phi, \Delta}$$

The first branch ensures that *inv* holds when entering the loop. The second branch puts the loop body into a loop scope with fresh index variable x and symbolically executes the loop body once, assuming the invariant holds. Then, the value of the index variable x is read to determine whether the loop exits ($\mathsf{x} \doteq \mathit{TRUE}$) or further iterations are executed ($\mathsf{x} \doteq \mathit{FALSE}$). In the first case, we must show that postcondition ϕ holds, in the second that *inv* remains valid.

The rule executes a *generic* loop iteration, where the value of program variables occurring in $\Gamma \cup \Delta$ is not known. Therefore, the value of such variables in $\Gamma \cup \Delta$ must be "forgotten." This is achieved by a so-called *anonymizing update* $\mathcal{V}$ [1] that assigns a fresh, unknown value to any variable written to in *body*.

The value of index variable x is set during symbolic execution of the loop scope by the rules handling **break**, **continue**, **return**, etc. We illustrate the mechanism with rules breakValue and continue and a trailing program p; see also [32]. Observe how breakValue returns the loop scope's value *se*.

$$\text{breakValue}\ \frac{\Gamma \Longrightarrow \mathcal{U}\langle\pi\ \{\mathsf{x} = \mathsf{true};\ \mathit{se}\}\ \omega\rangle\phi, \Delta}{\Gamma \Longrightarrow \mathcal{U}\langle\pi\ \circlearrowleft_{\mathsf{x}}\ \mathsf{break}\ \mathit{se};\ p \circlearrowright\ \omega\rangle\phi, \Delta}
\qquad
\text{continue}\ \frac{\Gamma \Longrightarrow \mathcal{U}\langle\pi\ \mathsf{x} = \mathsf{false}\ \omega\rangle\phi, \Delta}{\Gamma \Longrightarrow \mathcal{U}\langle\pi\ \circlearrowleft_{\mathsf{x}} \mathsf{continue};\ p \circlearrowright\ \omega\rangle\phi, \Delta}$$

Example 10. Consider the program in Listing 2. Let $\phi \equiv \mathsf{n} \doteq \mathsf{a} \cdot \mathsf{old\_b}$ and *inv* as in (1). After symbolically executing the assignments and simplifying, we have

$$\Longrightarrow \{\mathsf{n} := 0 \parallel \mathsf{old\_b} := \mathsf{b}\}\, [\mathtt{loop\ \{\ ...\ \}}]\phi.$$

Applying loopScopeInvBox yields two sequents: first, the "initially valid" case:

$$\Longrightarrow \{\mathsf{n} := 0 \parallel \mathsf{old\_b} := \mathsf{b}\}\, (\mathsf{n} \doteq \mathsf{a} \cdot (\mathsf{old\_b} - \mathsf{b}) \land \mathsf{b} \leq \mathsf{old\_b})$$

which is simplified to $\Longrightarrow 0 \doteq \mathsf{a} \cdot (\mathsf{b} - \mathsf{b}) \land \mathsf{b} \leq \mathsf{b}$. Integer simplification proves this branch. The second branch of loopScopeInvBox yields:

$$\Longrightarrow \{\mathsf{n} := 0 \parallel \mathsf{old\_b} := \mathsf{b}\}\, \{\mathsf{n} := c_n \parallel \mathsf{b} := c_b\} \Big(inv \rightarrow [\circlearrowleft_{\mathsf{x}} \mathtt{if\ b\ ==\ 0\ ...} \circlearrowright] \underbrace{((\mathsf{x} \doteq \mathit{TRUE} \rightarrow [\ ]\phi) \land (\mathsf{x} \doteq \mathit{FALSE} \rightarrow inv))}_{\psi} \Big) \quad (2)$$

Simplification and symbolically executing the if in (2) yields two branches (3), (4), where $u \equiv \mathsf{old\_b} := \mathsf{b} \parallel \mathsf{n} := c_n \parallel \mathsf{b} := c_b$ and $inv' \equiv \{u\}\, inv$:

$$inv', c_b \doteq 0 \Longrightarrow \{u\}\, [\circlearrowleft_{\mathsf{x}} \mathtt{break\ n;\ n+=a;\ b-=1;\ continue;} \circlearrowright]\psi \quad (3)$$

$$inv', c_b \not\doteq 0 \Longrightarrow \{u\}\, [\circlearrowleft_{\mathsf{x}} \mathtt{n+=a;\ b-=1;\ continue;} \circlearrowright]\psi \quad (4)$$

Applying breakValue to (3) drops the remaining loop body and the loop scope:

$$inv', c_b \doteq 0 \Longrightarrow \{u\}\, [\mathtt{\{x\ =\ true;\ n\}}]\psi \quad (5)$$

Hence, we know x is true in this branch, allowing us to simplify the sequent to

$$inv', c_b \doteq 0 \Longrightarrow \{u\}\, (\mathsf{n} \doteq \mathsf{a} \cdot \mathsf{old\_b}) \quad (6)$$

Applying the updates yields (7), easily proven by arithmetic simplification.

$$c_n \doteq \mathsf{a} \cdot (\mathsf{b} - c_b) \land c_b \leq \mathsf{b}, c_b \doteq 0 \Longrightarrow c_n \doteq \mathsf{a} \cdot \mathsf{b} \quad (7)$$

The proof steps for (4) follow similar lines.

3.8 Implementation of Calculus Rules

We implemented RustyDL and its calculus based on the KeY tool,[1] leveraging the general data structures and rule matching algorithm of that system. The proof system is not foundational; we rely on theories of integers, sequences, etc.

[1] See implementation and examples at https://github.com/Drodt/key/tree/rusty.

All rules are implemented in a domain specific language for writing schematic program logic rules in a sequent calculus called "taclets" [7]. They can be reviewed, checked, and partially, even mechanically proven independently from the remaining system. There has also been work to prove the rules sound relative to program semantics and to validate the transformation rules [3,34].

The KeY system is time-proven. Thus, we argue, the core is trustworthy and the implementation faithfully reflects the calculus rules above. At the moment, the implementation is a prototype able to manually and automatically prove a number of examples showcasing several Rust features, in particular, borrowing, loops, arrays, tuples, and (some) enums. Most instructive is a verification of binary search, creating a proof of 4260 rule applications in 2.1 seconds.

4 Related Work

Our approach to deductive verification was inspired by KeY [1]. Several other tools have been developed in the last years to verify Rust programs. *Creusot* [12] translates safe Rust programs to the intermediate language and verification tool *Why3* [16] which generates verification conditions that are discharged with SMT solvers. Mutable references are modeled using prophecies [21], in effect writing the value of the mutable reference back to the lender once the reference is dropped. The *Prusti* tool [4] is similar to Creusot, but based on separation logic, and translates to *Viper* [27]. *Aeneas* [18] translates safe Rust to several functional back ends, removing mutable references entirely. All these tools rely on translation to intermediate languages and allow no interaction, whereas our dynamic logic permits a HIL interaction pattern.

Verus [23] enables verification of unsafe Rust, based on verification condition generation and SMT solving. Presently, it is unclear how RustyDL might be extended to unsafe Rust, the "hybrid" approach of [6] being strong contender.

An alternative to logic modeling of references are *permissions* [10] to deal with read and read-and-write permissions to memory locations. Permissions were implemented in the KeY tool in [20], but here we chose mutable updates, because they cause less overhead and easily extend the existing update mechanism.

5 Conclusion and Future Work

We presented RustyDL, a dynamic logic for a subset of Rust, as well as a sequent calculus to prove validity of RustyDL formulas. We gave solutions for logic modeling of crucial Rust features with reasonable complexity. This demonstrates that the KeY approach to HIL program verification can be applied to Rust.

The RustyDL calculus presented here was implemented on top of the KeY verification tool as a proof-of-concept. We used that implementation to successfully verify several Rust functions, including ones containing loops and references, however, a fuller evaluation needs to wait until the degree of automation is sufficiently high.

Accordingly, future work can be divided into two directions: First, extending the subset of Rust to include Traits, iterators, pattern matching, and generic functions. This is time consuming, yet straightforward. Verification of unsafe Rust also should be considered, but one has to carefully weigh to which extent. It is likely that unsafe Rust requires a more explicit memory model than we introduced here; still, one would like this model to be minimal and refer to the safe version where possible. A thorough investigation remains to be done. Second, we are improving the implementation: flesh out the specification language, similar to JML [24] and implement a graphical user interface.

Acknowledgments. This work was supported by the DFG projects BU 2924/3-1 and HA 2617/9-1.

Disclosure of Interests. The authors have no competing interests to declare.

References

1. Ahrendt, W., Beckert, B., Bubel, R., Hähnle, R., Schmitt, P.H., Ulbrich, M. (eds.): Deductive Software Verification – the KeY Book: From Theory to Practice. No. 10001 in LNCS, Springer (2016). https://doi.org/10.1007/978-3-319-49812-6
2. Ahrendt, W., Beckert, B., Bubel, R., Hähnle, R., Ulbrich, M.: The many uses of dynamic logic. In: Ernst, G., et al., (eds.) Go Where the Bugs Are – Essays Dedicated to Wolfgang Reif on the Occasion of His 65th Birthday. LNCS, vol. 15765, pp. 56–82. Springer, Cham (2025). https://doi.org/10.1007/978-3-031-92196-4_4
3. Ahrendt, W., Roth, A., Sasse, R.: Automatic validation of transformation rules for Java verification against a rewriting semantics. In: Sutcliffe, G., Voronkov, A. (eds.) Logic for Programming, Artificial Intelligence, and Reasoning, pp. 412–426. Springer, Berlin, Heidelberg (2005). https://doi.org/10.1007/11591191_29
4. Astrauskas, V., et al.: The Prusti project: formal verification for Rust. In: Deshmukh, J.V., Havelund, K., Perez, I. (eds.) NASA Formal Methods – 14th International Symposium, NFM 2022, Pasadena, CA, USA, 24–27 May 2022, Proceedings, pp. 88–108. No. 13260 in LNCS, Springer (2022). https://doi.org/10.1007/978-3-031-06773-0_5
5. Astrauskas, V., Matheja, C., Poli, F., Müller, P., Summers, A.J.: How do programmers use unsafe Rust? Proc. ACM Program. Lang. **4**(OOPSLA), 136:1–136:27 (2020). https://doi.org/10.1145/3428204
6. Ayoun, S.É., Denis, X., Maksimović, P., Gardner, P.: A hybrid approach to semi-automated Rust verification. arXiv preprint arXiv:2403.15122 (2024)
7. Beckert, B., et al.: The Java verification tool KeY: a tutorial. In: Platzer, A., Rozier, K.Y., Pradella, M., Rossi, M. (eds.) Formal Methods, pp. 597–623. No. 14934 in LNCS, Springer Nature Switzerland, Cham (2025). https://doi.org/10.1007/978-3-031-71177-0_32
8. Beckert, B., Sanders, P., Ulbrich, M., Wiesler, J., Witt, S.: Formally verifying an efficient sorter. In: Finkbeiner, B., Kovács, L. (eds.) Tools and Algorithms for the Construction and Analysis of Systems – 30th International Conference, TACAS

2024, Held as Part of the European Joint Conferences on Theory and Practice of Software, ETAPS 2024, Luxembourg City, Luxembourg, 6–11 April 2024, Proceedings, Part I, pp. 268–287. No. 14570 in Lecture Notes in Computer Science, Springer (2024). https://doi.org/10.1007/978-3-031-57246-3_15
9. Blanc, A.L., Lam, P.: Surveying the Rust verification landscape. CoRR **abs/2410.01981** (2024). https://doi.org/10.48550/ARXIV.2410.01981
10. Boyland, J.: Fractional permissions. In: Clarke, D., Noble, J., Wrigstad, T. (eds.) Aliasing in Object-Oriented Programming. Types, Analysis and Verification, LNCS, vol. 7850, pp. 270–288. Springer (2013). https://doi.org/10.1007/978-3-642-36946-9_10
11. de Gouw, S., Rot, J., de Boer, F.S., Bubel, R., Hähnle, R.: OpenJDK's java.utils.Collection.sort() is broken: the good, the bad and the worst case. In: Kroening, D., Păsăreanu, C.S. (eds.) CAV 2015. LNCS, vol. 9206, pp. 273–289. Springer, Cham (2015). https://doi.org/10.1007/978-3-319-21690-4_16
12. Denis, X., Jourdan, J.H., Marché, C.: Creusot: a foundry for the deductive verification of Rust programs. In: Riesco, A., Zhang, M. (eds.) ICFEM 2022, Proceedings, pp. 90–105. No. 13478 in LNCS, Springer (2022). https://doi.org/10.1007/978-3-031-17244-1_6
13. Dijkstra, E.W., Scholten, C.S.: Predicate calculus and program semantics. Monographs in Computer Science. Springer, New York, NY, 1 edn. (1990). https://doi.org/10.1007/978-1-4612-3228-5
14. Din, C.C., Hähnle, R., Henrio, L., Johnsen, E.B., Pun, V.K.I., Tapia Tarifa, S.L.: Locally abstract, globally concrete semantics of concurrent programming languages. Trans. Program. Lang. Syst. **46**(1), 3:1–3:58 (2024). https://doi.org/10.1145/3648439
15. Drodt, D., Hähnle, R.: RustyDL: a program logic for Rust. Technical report (2026). https://doi.org/10.48550/arXiv.2602.22075
16. Filliâtre, J.C., Paskevich, A.: Why3 — where programs meet provers. In: Felleisen, M., Gardner, P. (eds.) Proceedings of the 22nd European Symposium on Programming. Lecture Notes in Computer Science, vol. 7792, pp. 125–128. Springer (2013). https://doi.org/10.1007/978-3-642-37036-6_8
17. Hähnle, R.: Many-valued logic, partiality, and abstraction in formal specification languages. Logic J. IGPL **13**(4), 415–433 (2005). https://doi.org/10.1093/jigpal/jzi032
18. Ho, S., Protzenko, J.: Aeneas: Rust verification by functional translation. Proc. ACM Program. Lang. **6**(ICFP), 711–741 (2022). https://doi.org/10.1145/3547647
19. Hoare, C.A.R.: An axiomatic basis for computer programming. Commun. ACM **12**(10), 576–580 (1969). https://doi.org/10.1145/363235.363259
20. Huisman, M., Mostowski, W.: A symbolic approach to permission accounting for concurrent reasoning. In: Grosu, D., Jin, H., Papadopoulos, G. (eds.) 14th International Symposium on Parallel and Distributed Computing, ISPDC 2015, Limassol, Cyprus, June 29 - July 2, 2015, pp. 165–174. IEEE Computer Society (2015). https://doi.org/10.1109/ISPDC.2015.26
21. Jung, R., et al.: The future is ours: Prophecy variables in separation logic. Proc. ACM Program. Lang. **4**(POPL), 45:1–45:32 (2020). https://doi.org/10.1145/3371113
22. Klabnik, S., Nichols, C.: The Rust programming language. No Starch Press, San Francisco, CA, 2 edn. (2022). https://doc.rust-lang.org/stable/book/
23. Lattuada, A., et al.: Verus: verifying Rust programs using linear ghost types. Proc. ACM Program. Lang. **7**(OOPSLA1), 286–315 (2023). https://doi.org/10.1145/3586037

24. Leavens, G.T., et al.: JML Reference Manual (2013). http://www.eecs.ucf.edu/~leavens/JML/OldReleases/jmlrefman.pdf
25. Li, H., Guo, L., Yang, Y., Wang, S., Xu, M.: An empirical study of Rust-for-Linux: The success, dissatisfaction, and compromise. In: Bagchi, S., Zhang, Y. (eds.) Proceedings of the 2024 USENIX Annual Technical Conference, USENIX ATC 2024, Santa Clara, CA, USA, 10–12 July 2024, pp. 425–443. USENIX Association (2024),.https://www.usenix.org/conference/atc24/presentation/li-hongyu
26. McCarthy, J.: Towards a mathematical science of computation. In: Information Processing, Proceedings of the 2nd IFIP Congress 1962, Munich, Germany, August 27 - September 1, 1962, pp. 21–28. North-Holland (1962). https://doi.org/10.1007/978-94-011-1793-7_2
27. Müller, P., Schwerhoff, M., Summers, A.J.: Viper: a verification infrastructure for permission-based reasoning. In: Jobstmann, B., Leino, K.R.M. (eds.) Verification, Model Checking, and Abstract Interpretation, pp. 41–62. Springer, Berlin, Heidelberg (2016). https://doi.org/10.1007/978-3-662-49122-5_2
28. Pratt, V.R.: Semantical considerations on Floyd-Hoare logic. In: 17th Annual Symposium on Foundations of Computer Science, Houston, TX, USA, pp. 109–121. IEEE, Los Alamitos, CA (1976). https://doi.org/10.1109/SFCS.1976.27
29. Rust Community: The Rust reference. Reference, Rust Foundation (2024). https://doc.rust-lang.org/stable/reference/introduction.html
30. Rust Community: Rust Compiler Development Guide (2025). https://rustc-dev-guide.rust-lang.org/
31. Schellhorn, G., Bodenmüller, S., Bitterlich, M., Reif, W.: Software & system verification with KIV. In: Ahrendt, W., Beckert, B., Bubel, R., Johnsen, E.B. (eds.) The Logic of Software. A Tasting Menu of Formal Methods – Essays Dedicated to Reiner Hähnle on the Occasion of His 60th Birthday. LNCS, vol. 13360, pp. 408–436. Springer (2022). https://doi.org/10.1007/978-3-031-08166-8_20
32. Steinhöfel, D., Wasser, N.: A new invariant rule for the analysis of loops with non-standard control flows. In: Polikarpova, N., Schneider, S.A. (eds.) Integrated Formal Methods - 13th International Conference, IFM 2017, Turin, Italy, 20-22 September 2017, Proceedings, pp. 279–294. No. 10510 in LNCS, Springer (2017). https://doi.org/10.1007/978-3-319-66845-1_18
33. Thompson, C.: How Rust went from a side project to the world's most-loved programming language. MIT Technol. Rev. **126**(2) (2023). https://www.technologyreview.com/2023/02/14/1067869/
34. Trentelman, K.: Proving correctness of JavaCard DL taclets using Bali. In: Proceedings of the Third IEEE International Conference on Software Engineering and Formal Methods, pp. 160–169. SEFM '05, IEEE Computer Society, USA (2005). https://doi.org/10.1109/SEFM.2005.37

Generating Rely-Guarantee Conditions with the Conditional-Writes Domain

James Tobler[1,2(✉)] and Graeme Smith[1,2]

[1] Defence Science and Technology Group, Brisbane, Australia
[2] School of Electrical Engineering and Computer Science, The University of Queensland, Brisbane, Australia
james.tobler@uq.edu.au

Abstract. Abstract interpretation has been shown to be a promising technique for the thread-modular verification of concurrent programs. Central to this is the generation of interferences, in the form of rely-guarantee conditions, conforming to a user-chosen structure. In this work, we introduce one such structure called the *conditional-writes* domain, designed for programs where it suffices to establish only the *conditions* under which particular variables are written to by each thread. We formalise our analysis within a novel abstract interpretation framework that is highly modular and can be easily extended to capture other structures for rely-guarantee conditions. We formalise two versions of our approach and evaluate their implementations on a simple programming language.

Keywords: Abstract interpretation · Concurrency · Rely-guarantee

1 Introduction

Abstract interpretation has been shown to be a scalable technique for automatically verifying sequential programs [2,12]. Its distinctive advantage lies in the provision of a simple parameter called an *abstract domain*, which constrains the structure of generated intermediary assertions over the program state. This allows proofs to be generated at a large scale, given a suitable abstract domain is provided for the target program. Unfortunately, these are not always easy for users to infer.

For concurrent programs, *interferences* between threads, captured by rely-guarantee conditions, must also be generated. Our work is based on the conjecture that, contrary to intermediary assertions (required for sequential programs), many of the interferences that suffice for verification (of concurrent programs) tend to take a similar structure across various concurrent programs. In this paper, we capture one of these structures in an abstract domain called the *conditional-writes* domain, which is designed for cases where it suffices to reason about thread interference in terms of only the *conditions* under which variables may be updated, rather than what they are updated to. For example, where it

A. Sampaio and M. Stoelinga (Eds.): FM 2026, LNCS 16556, pp. 378–396, 2026.
https://doi.org/10.1007/978-3-032-26204-2_20

suffices to establish: "Thread A can write to x when $z = 0$ and can write to y when $z = 1$ but never writes to z."

To precisely capture this structure in an abstract domain, we introduce a novel framework for applying abstract interpretation to concurrent programs. In current frameworks such as [13], thread interferences are abstracted into numeric abstract domains over the program variables and their primed counterparts, where a primed variable represents its value in the post-state of the interference. This approach is limited in that primed and unprimed variables are treated equally—that is, whether a variable is primed has no impact on where it may be placed within the structure of an abstract domain element. Consequently, they cannot represent structures that place different constraints on pre-states and post-states, such as our conditional-writes domain. This has motivated us to introduce a new class of abstract domain called an *interference domain*, of which the conditional-writes domain is one example.

In the abstract interpretation framework, a traditional abstract domain combines a lattice $\mathcal{D}$ over sets of states together with a *transfer function* that derives an element of $\mathcal{D}$ as a conservative pre- or post-condition of a program instruction. Conversely, an interference domain combines a lattice $\mathcal{I}$ over sets of *pairs of states* (representing rely and guarantee conditions) with two functions, both parameterised by an abstract domain with lattice $\mathcal{D}$. The first, which we call *transitions*, maps some $d \in \mathcal{D}$ and an assignment to an element of $\mathcal{I}$ that over-approximates the set of state transitions that may be induced by executing the given assignment under any state captured by d. The second, which we call *stabilise*, maps some $d \in \mathcal{D}$ and $i \in \mathcal{I}$ to an element of $\mathcal{D}$ that over-approximates the set of states reachable within one step of i from any initial state in d. Together, these two functions can be used to respectively derive and apply thread interferences (guarantee and rely conditions, respectively) during a thread-modular analysis.

In addition to these two functions, we equip our conditional-writes domain with a function *close* that over-approximates the transitive closure of thread interferences. Using this function to make some $i \in \mathcal{I}$ transitive allows us to account for the effect of one or more transitions in i with just one call to *stabilise*, thereby simplifying the process of applying interference at the cost of deriving this transitive closure. We determine whether this trade-off is worthwhile by implementing and evaluating two versions of our analysis: one where transitivity is enforced, and one where it is not.

We begin in Sect. 2 by introducing a simple programming language on which to evaluate our analyses. In Sect. 3, we define an abstract state domain which is used as a parameter to our analyses, and in Sect. 4, we define our interference domain including the functions *transitions*, *stabilise*, and *close*. The analyses with and without transitivity are formalised in Sect. 5 and evaluated on the simple programming language in Sect. 6. We discuss related work in Sect. 7 before concluding in Sect. 8.

2 Programming Language

We define $\mathcal{V}$ to be the set of program variables, $\mathcal{T}$ the identifiers of the threads comprising the program, and $\mathcal{S}$ the set of all states, where a state maps each variable in $\mathcal{V}$ to a constant. Each thread $t \in \mathcal{T}$ represents a sequential program in the language *inst*:

$$inst ::= inst \; ; \; inst \mid x_1, ..., x_n \texttt{ := } e_1, ..., e_n \mid \texttt{if } cond \texttt{ then } inst \texttt{ else } inst$$
$$\mid \texttt{while } cond \texttt{ do } inst \mid \texttt{skip}$$

where *cond* is the set of all boolean expressions, and for each $i \in \{1, ..., n\}$, we have $x_i \in \mathcal{V}$ and e_i is an expression. The concrete semantics of *inst* is denoted:

$$exec : inst \times \mathcal{S} \to \mathcal{S}$$

where $exec(c, s)$ is the program state reached by executing instruction c in the state s. In our simple language, all assignment statements are atomic, as are the evaluations of all branch conditions and loop guards.

For each thread $t \in \mathcal{T}$, we also let $\mathcal{V}_t \subseteq \mathcal{V}$ represent the set of variables over which the rely condition of t should be defined. Using $\mathcal{V}_t$, we can avoid complicating the intermediary assertions that are generated for t when accounting for interference specified by the rely. Typically, $\mathcal{V}_t$ is set to the union of the global variables and the local variables of t. However, in some cases, precision can be improved by including the local variables of other threads in $\mathcal{V}_t$[1], and conversely, efficiency can be improved by restricting $\mathcal{V}_t$ to only those variables that are relevant to our particular verification goals. Most existing abstract interpretation frameworks for concurrent programs do not distinguish between local and global variables [9,11,13] and therefore effectively have $\mathcal{V}_t = \mathcal{V}$ for all $t \in \mathcal{T}$.

3 Abstract State Domain

Our analysis is parameterised by an abstract domain with lattice $\mathcal{D}$, representing sets of states. To distinguish this from our interference domain, we call it the *state domain*, and call $\mathcal{D}$ the *state lattice*. For $d_1, d_2 \in \mathcal{D}$, we denote by $d_1 \sqsubseteq^\sharp d_2$ that d_1 is less than or equal to d_2 on the lattice, meaning it represents the same or fewer states. (From now on, we may say that d_1 is "stronger" than d_2, or that d_2 is "weaker" than d_1.) The lattice's top element $\top^\sharp$ represents the set of all states, and the bottom element $\bot^\sharp$ represents the empty set. In addition to the above, and the usual join $\sqcup^\sharp$ (least upper bound) and meet $\sqcap^\sharp$ (greatest lower bound) operators, our state domain is equipped with the following basic functions:

[1] In standard rely-guarantee approaches, this is akin to converting a local variable into an "auxiliary variable" [15,18].

$\gamma^\sharp : \mathcal{D} \rightarrow \mathcal{P}(\mathcal{S})$ where $\gamma^\sharp(d)$ is the set of states represented by d.

$\mathbb{S}^\sharp$: $inst \times \mathcal{D} \rightarrow \mathcal{D}$ where $\mathbb{S}^\sharp(c, d)$ is the abstract post-state of instruction c with respect to the abstract pre-state d.

$\mathbb{B}^\sharp$: $cond \times \mathcal{D} \rightarrow \mathcal{D}$ where $\mathbb{B}^\sharp(b, d)$ is the abstract state capturing all states in d that satisfy the condition b.

$\lightning : \mathcal{D} \times \mathcal{P}(\mathcal{V}) \rightarrow \mathcal{D}$ where $d \lightning V$ is an abstract state weaker than d which at least includes the set of states obtained from d when the value of all variables in V are unconstrained. Formally:

$$\gamma^\sharp(d \lightning V) \supseteq \{s \in \mathcal{S} \mid \exists s_0 \in \gamma^\sharp(d) : \forall v \in \mathcal{V} \setminus V : s(v) = s_0(v)\}.$$

Similar to the above functions, the precise definition of $\lightning$ is provided by the specific abstract state domain given to our analysis. However, soundness of our analysis requires that this definition satisfies the above inequality, in addition to the basic properties:

1. Havocing any variable set in $\perp^\sharp$ results in $\perp^\sharp$:

$$\forall V \in \mathcal{P}(\mathcal{V}) : \perp^\sharp \lightning V = \perp^\sharp.$$

2. Havocing additional variables that are not constrained has no effect:

$$\forall V_1, V_2 \in \mathcal{P}(\mathcal{V}), d \in \mathcal{D} : d \lightning V_1 = d \implies d \lightning V_1 \cup V_2 = d \lightning V_2.$$

3. The $\lightning$ operator is monotonic in that:

$$\forall V_1, V_2 \in \mathcal{P}(\mathcal{V}), d_1, d_2 \in \mathcal{D} : V_1 \subseteq V_2 \wedge d_1 \sqsubseteq^\sharp d_2 \implies d_1 \lightning V_1 \sqsubseteq^\sharp d_2 \lightning V_2.$$

We give $\lightning$ the highest precedence of all the state lattice operators.

4 Conditional-Writes Domain

To capture interference between threads, we introduce the notion of an *interference domain*. An interference domain is defined by a lattice $\mathcal{I}$ whose elements represent sets of pairs of states. It defines two functions over this lattice, both parameterised by a compatible state domain with lattice $\mathcal{D}$:

$$stabilise : \mathcal{I} \times \mathcal{D} \rightarrow \mathcal{D} \qquad\qquad transitions : \mathcal{D} \times Assign \rightarrow \mathcal{I}$$

where *Assign* are those elements of *inst* corresponding to assignment statements. We refer to a state domain as *compatible* if it defines on $\mathcal{D}$ all functions used in the definitions of *stabilise* and *transitions*.

In this work, we define an interference domain called the *conditional-writes domain*. It is parameterised by any state domain described by Sect. 3 and defines $\mathcal{I}$ to be a lattice over mappings from program variables to elements of the state lattice $\mathcal{D}$. Formally:

$$\mathcal{I} = \mathcal{V} \rightarrow \mathcal{D}.$$

Intuitively, an element $i \in \mathcal{I}$ of this domain maps each variable to an over-approximation of the set of states under which that variable may be written to, which we call its *write-condition*. For example, if i represents a valid guarantee condition of thread t, and takes the form $i = [v_1 \mapsto P_1, v_2 \mapsto P_2]$, then t only updates v_1 when the program is in a state captured by P_1, and only updates v_2 when the program is in a state captured by P_2. If the program is in a state captured by both P_1 and P_2, then t may change either variable, or both variables in one step. This is captured by the concretisation function $\gamma^\times : \mathcal{I} \to \mathcal{P}(\mathcal{S} \times \mathcal{S})$:

$$\gamma^\times(i) \mathrel{\widehat{=}} \left\{(s_1, s_2) \in \mathcal{S} \times \mathcal{S} \mid \forall v \in \mathcal{V} : s_2(v) \neq s_1(v) \implies s_1 \in \gamma^\sharp(i(v))\right\}.$$

That is, the pre-state of any transition in $\gamma^\times(i)$ which changes variable v must be a state in which i allows v to be updated.

Similar to our abstract state domain, for $i_1, i_2 \in \mathcal{I}$, we denote by $i_1 \sqsubseteq^\times i_2$ that i_1 is less than or equal to i_2 on the lattice, meaning it represents the same or fewer transitions. And likewise, we may say that i_1 is "stronger" than i_2, or that i_2 is "weaker" than i_1. The lattice's top element $\top^\times$ represents the set of all state transitions and the bottom element $\bot^\times$ represents the identity relation:

$$\top^\times \mathrel{\widehat{=}} \lambda v \in \mathcal{V} : \top^\sharp \qquad\qquad \bot^\times \mathrel{\widehat{=}} \lambda v \in \mathcal{V} : \bot^\sharp.$$

The join and meet operators, $\sqcup^\times$ and $\sqcap^\times$, are defined component-wise:

$$i_1 \sqcup^\times i_2 \mathrel{\widehat{=}} \lambda v \in \mathcal{V} : i_1(v) \sqcup^\sharp i_2(v) \qquad\qquad i_1 \sqcap^\times i_2 \mathrel{\widehat{=}} \lambda v \in \mathcal{V} : i_1(v) \sqcap^\sharp i_2(v).$$

4.1 Small Example

In this section, we provide a small example to demonstrate the mechanics of our analysis. The following program is comprised of threads T_0 and T_1, global variables x and z, and a variable r that is local to T_0. We aim to prove that $r = 0$ holds upon termination of the program, with respect to precondition *true*.

```
T0:
1: r := 0
2: if z == 0:
3:       x := 0
4:       r := x
```

```
T1:
1: if z == 1:
2:       x := 1
```

With a quick inspection of the program, we may infer that our postcondition is satisfied if $x = 0$ holds before the assignment at line 4 in T_0. Looking at T_1 now, we see that x may indeed be updated to 1, but crucially, only when $z = 1$. This constraint on the conditions under which x can be updated is the property that our analysis will infer in order to verify the program.

Our analysis is *thread-modular*. For each thread t, we derive an assertion over the program state at each instruction, which we call its *proof outline*. Our goal is for each of these assertions to over-approximate the states that are reachable at that location under any thread interleaving. Like many other thread-modular techniques [1,3,5,6,8,13], we accomplish this by generating a *guarantee condition* for each thread in t's environment, which is an over-approximation of its set of reachable state transitions. In our analysis, these guarantee conditions are represented as elements of the conditional-writes domain. By taking their join, we get a sound *rely condition* for t, which over-approximates the set of state transitions that may be executed in t's environment. To ensure that a given assertion in t's proof outline holds in all thread interleavings, we weaken it so as to include the post-states of any number of transitions allowed by this rely. We now demonstrate this process on the above example.

To initialise our analysis, we must provide the following arguments:

1. A state domain with lattice $\mathcal{D}$. We choose the *constant domain*, which is a partial mapping from variables to their constant values.
2. The variable sets $\mathcal{V}_0$ and $\mathcal{V}_1$ over which we would like the rely conditions of T_0 and T_1 to be defined respectively. We choose $\mathcal{V}_0 = \mathcal{V}_1 = \mathcal{V}$, thus effectively treating all program variables as global.
3. An integer N specifying the precision of the *stabilise* function, where $0 \leq N \leq |\mathcal{V}|$. In our case, $|\mathcal{V}| = 3$ and we choose $N = 3$ for maximum precision. We describe the precise meaning of this number in Sect. 4.2.

The analysis begins by deriving the reachable states for T_0 using our constant domain. We do not account for environment interference in this step. Elements of $\mathcal{D}$ are represented by mappings from variables to values; any variables not included are not constrained. For example, $[r \mapsto 0]$ denotes the set of states where $r = 0$ and x and z can have any value.

`T0:`

$\top^\sharp$

`1: r := 0`

$[r \mapsto 0]$

`2: if z == 0:`

$[r \mapsto 0,\ z \mapsto 0]$

`3: x := 0`

$[r \mapsto 0,\ z \mapsto 0,\ x \mapsto 0]$

`4: r := x`

$[r \mapsto 0,\ z \mapsto 0,\ x \mapsto 0]$

We now derive a guarantee condition that captures the states under which each variable may be written to in T_0. By inspecting the assertions in our proof outline, we observe that the assignment to r follows the assertion $\top^\sharp$ and thus r may be written to by T_0 while in any state. This fact is captured by the *transitions* function:

$$\textit{transitions}(\top^\sharp,\ r := 0) = \bot^\times[r \mapsto \top^\sharp]$$

where $f[x \mapsto y]$ denotes the function f with x mapped to y. For example, the above is equal to:

$$[r \mapsto \top^\sharp,\ x \mapsto \bot^\sharp,\ z \mapsto \bot^\sharp].$$

Likewise, we observe that x may only be written to when $r = 0 \wedge z = 0$, and that z is never written to. By applying the *transitions* function to each precondition-assignment pair and combining the results via $\sqcup^\times$, we derive a guarantee condition $G_0 \in \mathcal{I}$ which maps each variable to an over-approximation of the states (as elements of $\mathcal{D}$) under which they can be written to:

$$G_0 = [r \mapsto \top^\sharp,\ x \mapsto [r \mapsto 0,\ z \mapsto 0],\ z \mapsto \bot^\sharp].$$

We now convert this guarantee condition into a rely condition for T_1. We first map each variable not in $\mathcal{V}_1$ to $\top^\sharp$ and havoc them in each write-condition with $\lightning$, effectively removing them from the rely. Since $\mathcal{V}_1 = \mathcal{V}$, there is nothing to do here. To weaken our rely to capture any number of environment transitions, our next step is to derive its transitive closure. The analysis recognises that transitivity is not satisfied due to the following two-step transition allowed under G_0:

$$\begin{array}{|c|c|c|}\hline r & x & z \\ \hline 1 & 0 & 0 \\ \hline\end{array} \rightarrow \begin{array}{|c|c|c|}\hline r & x & z \\ \hline 0 & 0 & 0 \\ \hline\end{array} \rightarrow \begin{array}{|c|c|c|}\hline r & x & z \\ \hline 0 & 1 & 0 \\ \hline\end{array}$$

The first transition updates r and is permitted due to r being mapped to $\top^\sharp$. The second transition updates x and is permitted since the second state is captured by the write-condition $[r \mapsto 0,\ z \mapsto 0]$ of x. However, the transition from the first to the third state is not captured by our rely, since it involves an update to x, and the first state does not satisfy the write-condition of x since $r = 1$. To remedy this, our analysis weakens the write-condition of x using the *close* function:

$$R_1 = close(G_0) = [r \mapsto \top^\sharp,\ x \mapsto [z \mapsto 0],\ z \mapsto \bot^\sharp].$$

We now derive the reachable states for T_1. However, this time we must make sure to "stabilise" each generated intermediary assertion under R_1, which ensures our derived reachable states account for all possible interference from T_1's environment. Since R_1 is transitive, an assertion $d_1 \in \mathcal{D}$ can be stabilised by deriving some $d_2 \in \mathcal{D}$ that captures all states reachable within just one step captured by R_1 from any pre-state in d_1, and taking $d_1 \sqcup^\sharp d_2$. This is achieved by applying the *stabilise* function, where $stabilise(R_1, d_1)$ is a $\mathcal{D}$ element greater than d_1 that accounts for all one-step transitions captured by R_1. Our analysis performs this operation with a degree of precision specified by the parameter N that was provided upon initialisation (see Sect. 4.2). We derive the following reachable states which, in our small example, are already stable upon generation:

```
T1:
      ⊤♯
1: if z == 1:
         [z ↦ 1]
2:       x := 1
         [z ↦ 1, x ↦ 1]
```

We now generate a guarantee G_1 for T_1:

$$G_1 = [r \mapsto \bot^\sharp,\ x \mapsto [z \mapsto 1],\ z \mapsto \bot^\sharp].$$

Notice this guarantee captures our desired constraint: that x is only updated when $z = 1$. This guarantee is transitive as-is and since $\mathcal{V}_0 = \mathcal{V}$ we can immediately derive R_0 as G_1. We now reconstruct (from scratch) the proof outline for T_0 under this new rely. In our simple example, the stabilised assertions are identical to the last iteration and we have thus reached a fixpoint where we can return our current rely-guarantee conditions and proof outlines. The conjunction of the derived postconditions for T_0 and T_1 suffice to establish that $r = 0$ holds upon termination of the program.

The following subsections introduce the *stabilise*, *transitions*, and *close* functions that we use to respectively stabilise assertions under rely conditions, derive guarantee conditions from proof outlines, and derive transitive closures for interference domain elements.

4.2 The *stabilise* Function

In this section, we introduce the interference domain function:

$$\mathit{stabilise} : \mathcal{I} \times \mathcal{D} \to \mathcal{D}$$

and then define it for our conditional-writes domain. The purpose of this function is to capture the set of all post-states that are reachable within *one* transition of some $i \in \mathcal{I}$ (representing a rely) from any pre-state captured by some $d \in \mathcal{D}$:

$$\gamma^\sharp(\mathit{stabilise}(i, d)) \supseteq \gamma^\sharp(d) \cup \{s_2 \in \mathcal{S} \mid \exists s_1 \in \gamma^\sharp(d) : (s_1, s_2) \in \gamma^\times(i)\}. \quad (1)$$

When i is transitive, this is enough to ensure that $\mathit{stabilise}(i, d)$ captures all states reachable within any number of transitions in i from an initial state in d, thereby fully accounting for interference from an environment represented by i. The fact that $\mathit{stabilise}(i, d)$ also captures d accounts for the fact that the environment may not take any step, and thus accommodates non-reflexive interference domains which do not implicitly capture $\{(s_1, s_2) \in \mathcal{S} \times \mathcal{S} \mid s_1 = s_2\}$ as the conditional-writes domain does.

However, note that (1) is an over-approximation and hence there may exist a transition $(s_1, s_2) \in \gamma^{\times}(i)$ where $s_1 \notin \gamma^{\sharp}(d) \wedge s_1 \in \gamma^{\sharp}(stabilise(i, d))$ but $s_2 \notin \gamma^{\sharp}(stabilise(i, d))$. Consequently, although $stabilise(i, d)$ soundly captures the effects of interference by i on d, it may not be closed under transitions in i. The practical effect of this limitation on our analysis is that repeated applications of *stabilise* may yield increasingly weaker abstract states, and we may therefore expect the analysis to be more conservative for longer threads, where *stabilise* is invoked more often during the generation of proof outlines.

Most existing thread-modular analyses achieve this missing closure by repeatedly applying a rely condition until a fixpoint is reached. In our framework, this is equivalent to defining $stabilise(i, d)$ to be a fixpoint over some function that satisfies (1). That is, we iteratively weaken d until there are no longer any transitions in i with pre-states in d and post-states not in d. In addition to achieving this closure, this approach has the performance advantage that i does not need to be transitive for the sound capture of interference, which avoids the need to derive transitive closures for rely conditions. This raises an interesting question that we have not yet seen discussed in the literature: Is it more expensive to derive a fixpoint for every generated intermediary assertion than it is to derive a transitive closure for every generated rely condition? We investigate this problem by implementing two modes of our analysis: one where rely conditions are made to be transitive and *stabilise* is simply defined as a function that satisfies (1), and another where rely conditions are not made to be transitive and *stabilise* is defined as a fixpoint over the definition in the first mode. From now on, we use the notation f^* to denote the version of the function f that is used in the second (non-transitive) mode.

Let us now define $stabilise(i, d)$ in a way that satisfies (1). A naive definition is given by havocing in d every variable with a write-condition that intersects with d:

$$d \lightning \{v \in \mathcal{V} \mid d \sqcap^{\sharp} i(v) \neq \bot^{\sharp}\}.$$

Intuitively, if d does not intersect $i(v)$ then the environment cannot update v while the program is in any state captured by d. However, if d does intersect $i(v)$ then the environment may update v while in a state captured by d and, by adjusting d to $d \lightning \{v\}$, we capture all the possible post-states resulting from an arbitrary update to v from any state captured by d.

This definition is sound (in that it satisfies (1)), but also very conservative in that we are failing to account for the fact that, when v is updated in a state captured by d, we must also be in a state captured by $i(v)$. To improve precision, rather than havocing variables v in d we could havoc them in $d \sqcap^{\sharp} i(v)$ as follows.

$$d \sqcup^{\sharp} \bigsqcup_{v \in \mathcal{V}}^{\sharp} (d \sqcap^{\sharp} i(v)) \lightning \{v\}.$$

However, this definition is unsound! We are failing to account for those transitions in i that update multiple variables. To achieve soundness, we must capture the effects of transitions that update any combination $V \in \mathcal{P}(\mathcal{V})$ of variables. To do so, we first capture the set of states under which all variables $v \in V$ can be updated within one transition of i while in a state captured by d, which is the meet of d and all their write-conditions: $d \sqcap^\sharp \prod^\sharp_{v \in V} i(v)$. We then simulate the effect of variable updates by havocing V. Our new definition is thus:

$$d \sqcup^\sharp \bigsqcup^\sharp_{V \in \mathcal{P}(\mathcal{V})} \left(d \sqcap^\sharp \prod^\sharp_{v \in V} i(v) \right) \lightning V. \tag{2}$$

However, iterating over the powerset of $\mathcal{V}$ for every call to *stabilise* is infeasibly inefficient, so we must now decide whether to make our analysis conservative and fast, or precise and slow. Rather than providing a fixed definition, we accept a parameter N that allows the user to determine the appropriate trade-off. For all variable sets V with cardinality $|V| \leq N$, we consider the effects of transitions that update V precisely, as in (2). For the other, larger variable sets, we use a special technique to over-approximate their effects that only requires that we iterate over variable sets with cardinality $N + 1$.

To formalise our definition, let us first derive the set of states X that may be reached by executing any transition in i that updates N or fewer variables. This "precise" part of our definition is derived from (2):

$$X = \bigsqcup^\sharp_{V \in \mathcal{P}(\mathcal{V}), |V| \leq N} \left(d \sqcap^\sharp \prod^\sharp_{v \in V} \mathrm{i(v)} \right) \lightning \mathrm{V}.$$

The corresponding "conservative" part computes a coarse over-approximation of the set of states that are reachable from d via transitions in i that update more than N variables. The following technique can be used to derive this over-approximation efficiently by considering only those variable sets with cardinality $N + 1$, rather than all sets with cardinality $> N$. Let us first collect the set $\mathcal{V}_N$ of all of such sets $\{v_1, v_2, ..., v_{N+1}\}$ where the meet over the write conditions of $v_1, v_2, ..., v_{N+1}$ intersect with d. These are the variable sets with cardinality $N + 1$ in which all variables may be updated within one step of i from a state captured by d:

$$\mathcal{V}_N = \left\{ V \in \mathcal{P}(\mathcal{V}) \middle| |V| = N + 1 \land \left(d \sqcap^\sharp \prod^\sharp_{v \in V} i(v) \right) \neq \bot^\sharp \right\}.$$

We now collect an over-approximation of the set of states in d in which *any* of these variable combinations in $\mathcal{V}_N$ may be written to:

$$\bigsqcup^\sharp_{V \in \mathcal{V}_N} d \sqcap^\sharp \prod^\sharp_{v \in V} i(v).$$

Finally, we havoc in the above all variables that appear in $\mathcal{V}_N$:

$$Y = \left(\bigsqcup^\sharp_{V \in \mathcal{V}_N} d \sqcap^\sharp \prod^\sharp_{v \in V} i(v) \right) \lightning \bigcup_{V \in \mathcal{V}_N} V.$$

In Appendix A.1 of [16], we show that Y over-approximates the post-states of not only the transitions that update those variable sets in $\mathcal{V}_N$, but every subset of $\mathcal{V}$ with cardinality $> N$.

Our definition of $stabilise_N(i, d)$ is the join of d with the precise over-approximation X of post-states of transitions that update N or fewer variables, and the less precise over-approximation Y of post-states of transitions that update more than N variables:

$$stabilise_N(i, d) \mathrel{\widehat{=}} d \sqcup^\sharp X \sqcup^\sharp Y.$$

We prove that our definition satisfies (1) in Appendix A.1 of [16]. In the non-transitive mode of our analysis, we define the stabilisation function as the least fixpoint of the above:

$$stabilise^*_N(i, d) \mathrel{\widehat{=}} \mu d : stabilise_N(i, d).$$

As indicated above, the computation of $stabilise_N(i, d)$ may be slow for a large N due to the requirement to iterate over a large portion of $\mathcal{P}(\mathcal{V})$. In practice, we can implement a simple optimisation to reduce this domain. For any variable set $V_0 \in \mathcal{P}(\mathcal{V})$, if the meet over the write-conditions of the variables in V_0 is $\bot^\sharp$, we can ignore any superset of V_0. This is due to the fact that, since V is a superset of V_0, the meet over the write-conditions of the variables in V is also $\bot^\sharp$. This optimisation is formalised in Appendix B.1 of [16].

4.3 The *transitions* Function

In addition to the *stabilise* function, our analysis requires a method for generating guarantee conditions from proof outlines. Specifically, we require a definition of the function:

$$transitions : \mathcal{D} \times Assign \rightarrow \mathcal{I}$$

Intuitively, $transitions(d, A)$ captures all state transitions that may occur by executing the (local or global) assignment A under any state captured by d. Formally:

$$\gamma^\times(transitions(d, A)) \supseteq \left\{(s_1, s_2) \in \mathcal{S} \times \mathcal{S} \mid s_1 \in \gamma^\sharp(d) \wedge s_2 = exec(A, s_1)\right\}.$$

In our approach, we simply map each assigned variable to d and map the others to $\bot^\sharp$:

$$transitions(d, \langle x_1, ..., x_n := e_1, ..., e_n\rangle) \mathrel{\widehat{=}} \bot^\times[v \in \{x_1, ..., x_n\} \mapsto d].$$

where $f[x \in X \mapsto y]$ denotes the function f with each $x \in X$ mapped to y.

A guarantee for the whole thread can be derived by taking the join of $transitions(d, A)$ over each precondition-assignment pair (d, A) in its proof outline. We prove the soundness of our definition in Appendix A.2 of [16].

4.4 The *close* Function

Our analysis requires rely conditions to be transitive. In Appendix A.3 of [16], we prove that this property is violated if and only if $i \in \mathcal{I}$ captures a transition (s_1, s_2) from a state $s_1 \notin \gamma^\sharp(i(v))$ to a state $s_2 \in \gamma^\sharp(i(v))$ for some $v \in \mathcal{V}$. In this case, i contains a transition (s_2, s_3) that modifies v, but cannot contain (s_1, s_3) since s_1 is not in v's write-condition. Therefore, i is transitive if and only if, for all $v \in \mathcal{V}$:

$$\forall (s_1, s_2) \in \gamma^\times(i) : s_1 \notin i(v) \implies s_2 \notin i(v). \tag{3}$$

We therefore define a function:

$$close : \mathcal{I} \to \mathcal{I}$$

that satisfies (3) for all $v \in \mathcal{V}$.

To preserve the property that our rely captures all transitions of the other threads' guarantee conditions, we also require $i \sqsubseteq^\times close(i)$, i.e., in deriving $close(i)$ we are only able to *weaken* (that is, add states to) the write-conditions that variables are mapped to in i.

Now, let us imagine that i is not transitive and it therefore captures a transition (s_1, s_2) from a state $s_1 \notin \gamma^\sharp(i(v))$ to a state $s_2 \in \gamma^\sharp(i(v))$ for some $v \in \mathcal{V}$. The only means of rectifying such a counterexample via weakening a write-condition is to add s_1 to $\gamma^\sharp(i(v))$. A solution for deriving a transitive closure for i thus depends on a method for deriving, for some $v \in \mathcal{V}$, an over-approximation of all states $s_1 \notin \gamma^\sharp(i(v))$ where there exists a transition $(s_1, s_2) \in i$ for some $s_2 \in \gamma^\sharp(i(v))$.

A very coarse approach may be to simply collect all the states captured by the write-conditions of the variables that appear in $i(v)$. However, since we only invoke the transitive closure procedure once per derivation of a rely condition, and (especially due to the abstractions provided by $\mathcal{D}$ and $\mathcal{I}$) we do not expect to perform many of these derivations during our analysis, it may be useful to investigate more precise methods.

The intuition for our method is as follows: Suppose there exists a violating transition (s_1, s_2) as described above, that only modifies variable v'. Note that v' must be a different variable to v, since $s_1 \notin \gamma^\sharp(i(v))$ and thus v cannot be modified in the state s_1. Since our transition only modifies v', we must have that s_1 belongs to the set of states obtained by havocing v' in s_2:

$$s_1 \in \{s \in \mathcal{S} \mid \forall u \in \mathcal{V} \setminus \{v'\} : s(u) = s_2(u)\}$$

Since $s_2 \in \gamma^\sharp(i(v))$, we can obtain an over-approximation of this set with $i(v) \lightning v'$. Moreover, it should be obvious that s_1 is captured by $i(v')$, by virtue of i capturing (s_1, s_2) where $s_1(v') \neq s_2(v')$. Combining these two facts, we have:

$$s_1 \in \gamma^\sharp(i(v) \lightning \{v'\}) \cap \gamma^\sharp(i(v')).$$

In our analysis, we can derive an over-approximation of this set as a $\mathcal{D}$ element:

$$i(v) \lightning \{v'\} \sqcap^\sharp i(v').$$

Intuitively, this represents the subset of states in $i(v')$ that may result in a post-state in $i(v)$ when v' is updated. To account for the update of any other variable, we weaken $i(v)$ by taking the join of the above for every $v' \in \mathcal{V} \setminus \{v\}$:

$$i(v) \sqcup^\sharp \bigsqcup^\sharp_{v' \in \mathcal{V} \setminus \{v\}} i(v) \lightning \{v'\} \sqcap^\sharp i(v').$$

Since $i(v) \lightning \{v\} \sqcap^\sharp i(v) = i(v)$, we may simplify this definition by adding v to the domain of the join:

$$\bigsqcup^\sharp_{v' \in \mathcal{V}} i(v) \lightning \{v'\} \sqcap^\sharp i(v').$$

Now, recall that our reasoning above relied on v' being the only variable updated, whereas our conditional-writes domain captures transitions that modify multiple variables. For a true over-approximation of violating pre-states, we must actually iterate through the entire powerset of $\mathcal{V}$:

$$\bigsqcup^\sharp_{V \in \mathcal{P}(\mathcal{V})} i(v) \lightning V \sqcap^\sharp \bigsqcap^\sharp_{v' \in V} i(v'). \tag{4}$$

However, we discuss optimisations in Appendix B.2 of [16] that significantly reduce this search space.

We now have a method for weakening $i(v)$ so as to capture the pre-states of all transitions in i with post-states in $i(v)$. However, the new states added to $i(v)$ may themselves be post-states of other transitions captured by i, and thus we must derive a fixpoint on (4) to achieve (3) for v. Moreover, the new transitions added to i by weakening v's write-condition may invalidate (3) for the other variables, and thus to compute a transitive closure with this method, we must derive a fixpoint on (4) over *all* variables:

$$close(i) \mathrel{\widehat{=}} \mu i : \lambda v : \bigsqcup^\sharp_{V \in \mathcal{P}(\mathcal{V})} i(v) \lightning V \sqcap^\sharp \bigsqcap^\sharp_{v' \in V} i(v').$$

Let $i' = close(i)$. Upon termination of the fixpoint, we have:

$$\forall v \in \mathcal{V} : i'(v) \sqsupseteq^\sharp \bigsqcup^\sharp_{V \in \mathcal{P}(\mathcal{V})} i'(v) \lightning V \sqcap^\sharp \bigsqcap^\sharp_{v' \in V} i'(v')$$

which we prove to be sufficient for transitivity in Appendix A.3 of [16].

5 Rely-Guarantee Generation

A complete summary of the data structures and functions defined in the conditional-writes domain is provided in Appendix C of [16]. The purpose of this section is to formalise the process described in Sect. 4.1, thereby providing an example of integrating our domain into a complete program analysis, similar to the style of [12].

Our analysis involves iteratively building up rely conditions $R : \mathcal{T} \to \mathcal{I}$ and guarantee conditions $G : \mathcal{T} \to \mathcal{I}$ for each thread. Our rely conditions are directly computed from the generated guarantee conditions using the *rely* function:

$$\mathit{rely} : \mathcal{T} \times (\mathcal{T} \to \mathcal{I}) \to \mathcal{I}$$

which, in the transitive mode of our analysis, is defined as the transitive closure of the join over all environment guarantees:

$$\mathit{rely}(t, G) \mathrel{\widehat{=}} \mathit{close} \circ \mathit{reduce}_t \left(\bigsqcup_{t' \in \mathcal{T} \setminus \{t\}}^{\times} G(t') \right)$$

where $\mathit{reduce}_t(i)$ weakens i to eliminate all variables not in $\mathcal{V}_t$:

$$\mathit{reduce}_t(i) \mathrel{\widehat{=}} i \left[v \in \mathcal{V} \setminus \mathcal{V}_t \mapsto \top^\sharp\right] \left[v \in \mathcal{V}_t \mapsto i(v) \lightning \mathcal{V} \setminus \mathcal{V}_t\right].$$

When running in the non-transitive mode described in Sect. 4.2, we simply skip the transitive closure step:

$$\mathit{rely}^*(t, G) \mathrel{\widehat{=}} \mathit{reduce}_t \left(\bigsqcup_{t' \in \mathcal{T} \setminus \{t\}}^{\times} G(t') \right).$$

To derive a guarantee condition for a thread $t \in \mathcal{T}$, we generate a thread-local proof outline of t using a state domain with lattice $\mathcal{D}$, with intermediary assertions weakened to account for interference specified by t's rely. As reachable states are discovered, we use the *transitions* function to derive the state transitions they induce, and collect these transitions into a new guarantee for t. This analysis is formalised with the semantics $\mathbb{S}$ defined in Fig. 1, where $\mathbb{S}(c, (d, r, g))$ is a tuple of which the third element is a sound guarantee condition of program c with respect to precondition d and rely r. To provide a concise formalisation, we define a join operator $\sqcup$ on tuples of type $\mathcal{D} \times \mathcal{I} \times \mathcal{I}$:

$$\sqcup : (\mathcal{D} \times \mathcal{I} \times \mathcal{I}) \times (\mathcal{D} \times \mathcal{I} \times \mathcal{I}) \to (\mathcal{D} \times \mathcal{I} \times \mathcal{I})$$

$$(d_1, r_1, g_1) \sqcup (d_2, r_2, g_2) \mathrel{\widehat{=}} \left(d_1 \sqcup^\sharp d_2, r_1 \sqcup^\times r_2, g_1 \sqcup^\times g_2\right).$$

We define our entire analysis by the function *Analyse*, which takes a program precondition and returns a set of rely and guarantee conditions for the program:

$$\mathit{Analyse} : \mathcal{D} \to (\mathcal{T} \mapsto \mathcal{I}) \times (\mathcal{T} \mapsto \mathcal{I}).$$

$$\mathbb{S} : \textit{inst} \times (\mathcal{D} \times \mathcal{I} \times \mathcal{I}) \rightarrow \mathcal{D} \times \mathcal{I} \times \mathcal{I}$$

$$\mathbb{S}(c_1; c_2,\ X) \mathrel{\widehat{=}} \mathbb{S}(c_2,\ \mathbb{S}(c_1,\ X))$$

$$\begin{aligned}\mathbb{S}(c : \textit{Assign},\ (d,\ r,\ g)) \mathrel{\widehat{=}}\ & \text{let } d' = \textit{stabilise}_N(r,\ d) \text{ in} \\ & (\mathbb{S}^\sharp(c,\ d'),\ r,\ g \sqcup^\times \textit{transitions}(d',\ c))\end{aligned}$$

$$\begin{aligned}\mathbb{S}(\text{if } b \text{ then } c_1 \text{ else } c_2,\ X) \mathrel{\widehat{=}}\ & \text{let } X_1 = \mathbb{S}(c_1,\ \mathbb{B}(b,\ X)) \text{ in} \\ & \text{let } X_2 = \mathbb{S}(c_2,\ \mathbb{B}(\neg b,\ X)) \text{ in} \\ & X_1 \sqcup X_2\end{aligned}$$

$$\mathbb{S}(\text{while } b \text{ do } c,\ X) \mathrel{\widehat{=}} \mathbb{B}(\neg b,\ \mu X\ .\ X \sqcup \mathbb{S}(c,\ \mathbb{B}(b,\ X))$$

$$\mathbb{B}(b,\ (d,\ r,\ g)) \mathrel{\widehat{=}} (\mathbb{B}^\sharp(b,\ \textit{stabilise}_N(r,\ d)),\ r,\ g)$$

Fig. 1. Collective semantics for generating guarantee conditions.

It is defined as:

$$\begin{aligned}\textit{Analyse}(\textit{pre}) \mathrel{\widehat{=}}\ & \mu R, G : \\ & (\lambda t \in \mathcal{T} : \textit{rely}(t,\ G),\ \ \lambda t \in \mathcal{T} : \mathbb{S}(t,\ (\textit{pre},\ \textit{rely}(t,\ G),\ \bot^\times)).3)\end{aligned}$$

where $X.3$ refers to the third element of tuple X. In the non-transitive mode of our analysis, the functions $\textit{rely}^*$ and $\textit{stabilise}^*_N$ are used in place of $\textit{rely}$ and $\textit{stabilise}_N$ respectively.

6 Evaluation

We implemented both modes of our analysis in a simple Python prototype[2] and evaluated each mode using two state domains: the constant domain, and the powerset completion of the constant domain [12]. For all tests, we choose $N = |\mathcal{V}|$ and $\mathcal{V}_t = \mathcal{V}$ for each thread to attain maximum precision. We evaluated our analysis on five concurrent programs that are verifiable with the conditional-writes domain, and record our results in Table 1. All experiments were conducted on a 2019 MacBook Pro with a 2.3 GHz Intel Core i5 processor.

The program *spinlock* can be found in [17]. All other programs were crafted by the authors and can be found alongside the prototype implementation. We record whether the program was verified by our framework under *Ver.*, the number of $\sqcup^\sharp$ and $\sqcap^\sharp$ operations under *Ops*, and the performance time under *Time*.

Our preliminary results show that the transitive mode is nearly always slower and requires more state lattice operations than the non-transitive mode. Moreover, the transitive mode is less precise in that it fails to verify *reset* with the

[2] Available at https://doi.org/10.5281/zenodo.18589190.

Table 1. Verification results across different state domains and analysis modes.

Program	Constant Domain						Powerset Completion of Const. Dom.					
	Non-Transitive			Transitive			Non-Transitive			Transitive		
	Ver.	Ops	Time (s)	Ver.	Ops	Time (s)	Ver.	Ops	Time (s)	Ver.	Ops	Time (s)
reset	×	123	0.0004	×	168	0.0005	✓	533	0.0020	×	786	0.0067
circular	✓	620	0.0014	✓	836	0.0022	✓	1019	0.0053	✓	1235	0.0064
mutex1	✓	67	0.0004	✓	105	0.0006	✓	237	0.0013	✓	342	0.0021
mutex2	×	48	0.0006	×	51	0.0003	✓	318	0.0018	✓	339	0.0016
spinlock	×	336	0.0012	×	291	0.0009	✓	1291	0.0115	✓	2355	0.0116

powerset completion domain, whereas the non-transitive mode succeeds. This provides a degree of justification for the widely adopted fixpoint approach to stabilisation. However, we note that most of our benchmark programs are small algorithms, and these results may not generalise to programs with longer thread bodies, where the ratio of *stabilise* to *rely* calls is higher.

7 Related Work

Our work is inspired by the analyses introduced by Miné [9–11] and Monat and Miné [13] for generating rely-guarantee conditions with abstract interpretation. Of these, the framework presented in [13] is the most similar to ours in that it is defined over an abstract domain for representing states, another abstract domain for representing interferences, and their own versions of the *stabilise* and *transitions* functions for converting between the two. However, their analysis requires that interferences are represented by a standard numeric abstract domain over primed and unprimed variables, where primed variables represent their values in the post-state of the interference. This allows one to use existing abstract domains to represent interferences, and also allows for partially-defined *stabilise* and *transitions* functions that only require the user to define functions for adding and removing certain variables (for example, the primed variables) from the chosen abstract domains. However, we found that the conditional-writes domain cannot be neatly expressed as a numeric domain over primed and unprimed variables. One reason for this is that it imposes different structural constraints on the primed and the unprimed variables, such as the fact that a primed variable can only be constrained to be equal to its unprimed counterpart (when the write-condition for the variable is false) and is otherwise unconstrained. Moreover, our framework allows users to fully define the *stabilise* and *transitions* functions, which allows for more complex definitions such as that of our *stabilise* function. Finally, all of the analyses in the aforementioned works perform stabilisation by deriving a fixpoint over the rely condition, whereas we provide an additional analysis mode where rely conditions are made to be transitive and interference can therefore be accounted for by over-approximating just one step of the rely.

Our analysis is underpinned by the rely-guarantee proof method [7,18], which is known to be better suited to some classes of programs than other logics such as Concurrent Separation Logic [4,14]. Many techniques for generating rely-guarantee conditions do not use abstract interpretation and therefore do not enjoy the efficiency-precision trade-off afforded by an abstract domain [3,5,6,8]. To the authors' knowledge, the existing techniques that do are restricted to particular abstractions of interferences such as non-relational domains that map variables to sets of constant post-state values [1,10], or numeric domains over primed and unprimed variables [13]. In contrast, we abstract interferences into *interference domains* that can represent arbitrary structures of rely-guarantee conditions, and allow these to be paired with any *state domain* that implements the functions used in the definitions of *stabilise* and *transitions*.

8 Conclusion

In this work, we have introduced the notion of an *interference domain* for abstracting the set of state transitions that may be executed by a thread or its environment. An interference domain is parameterised by a compatible state domain, and is defined by a lattice over sets of pairs of states representing transitions, as well as the functions *stabilise* and *transitions* for respectively applying and deriving these transitions. We have then introduced a simple example of an interference domain, called the conditional-writes domain, for capturing rely-guarantee conditions that constrain only the conditions under which variables are updated, whilst disregarding what they are updated to. We have then described a simple analysis framework that demonstrates how interference domains can be used to generate sound rely-guarantee conditions for concurrent programs.

A significant limitation of this framework is the overly simple target language. In future, we would like to extend our framework to support common language features like procedure calls, dynamic thread creation, and mutexes. We would also like to create a suite of interference domains that are more suitable for sophisticated programs with complex data structures such as arrays and pointers. To this end, we intend to adopt an example-driven approach where we will identify useful interference domains by inspecting concurrent programs used in practice. Finally, we intend to explore existing static analysis tools in which to implement our framework, to improve performance and enable better comparison with existing analyses.

Acknowledgments. We would like to thank Kirsten Winter for her insightful comments and discussions on this paper.

Disclosure of Interests. The authors have no competing interests to declare that are relevant to the content of this article.

References

1. Carre, J., Hymans, C.: From single-thread to multithreaded: an efficient static analysis algorithm. CoRR **abs/0910.5833** (2009)
2. Cousot, P., Cousot, R.: Abstract interpretation: a unified lattice model for static analysis of programs by construction or approximation of fixpoints. In: POPL, pp. 238–252. ACM (1977)
3. Ezudheen, P., Neider, D., D'Souza, D., Garg, P., Madhusudan, P.: Horn-ice learning for synthesizing invariants and contracts. Proc. ACM Program. Lang. **2**(OOPSLA), 131:1–131:25 (2018)
4. Feng, X., Ferreira, R., Shao, Z.: On the relationship between concurrent separation logic and assume-guarantee reasoning. In: De Nicola, R. (ed.) ESOP 2007. LNCS, vol. 4421, pp. 173–188. Springer, Heidelberg (2007). https://doi.org/10.1007/978-3-540-71316-6_13
5. Flanagan, C., Qadeer, S.: Thread-modular model checking. In: Ball, T., Rajamani, S.K. (eds.) SPIN 2003. LNCS, vol. 2648, pp. 213–224. Springer, Heidelberg (2003). https://doi.org/10.1007/3-540-44829-2_14
6. Gupta, A., Popeea, C., Rybalchenko, A.: Threader: a constraint-based verifier for multi-threaded programs. In: Gopalakrishnan, G., Qadeer, S. (eds.) CAV 2011. LNCS, vol. 6806, pp. 412–417. Springer, Heidelberg (2011). https://doi.org/10.1007/978-3-642-22110-1_32
7. Jones, C.B.: Tentative steps toward a development method for interfering programs. ACM Trans. Program. Lang. Syst. **5**(4), 596–619 (1983)
8. Le, X., Sanán, D., Sun, J., Lin, S.: Automatic verification of multi-threaded programs by inference of rely-guarantee specifications. In: ICECCS, pp. 43–52. IEEE (2020)
9. Miné, A.: Static analysis by abstract interpretation of sequential and multi-thread programs. In: Reynier, P.A. (ed.) 10th School of Modelling and Verifying Parallel Processes. Marseille, France (2012). https://inria.hal.science/hal-00763076
10. Miné, A.: Static analysis of run-time errors in embedded real-time parallel C programs. Log. Methods Comput. Sci. **8**(1) (2012)
11. Miné, A.: Relational thread-modular static value analysis by abstract interpretation. In: McMillan, K.L., Rival, X. (eds.) VMCAI 2014. LNCS, vol. 8318, pp. 39–58. Springer, Heidelberg (2014). https://doi.org/10.1007/978-3-642-54013-4_3
12. Miné, A.: Tutorial on static inference of numeric invariants by abstract interpretation. Found. Trends Program. Lang. **4**(3–4), 120–372 (2017)
13. Monat, R., Miné, A.: Precise thread-modular abstract interpretation of concurrent programs using relational interference abstractions. In: Bouajjani, A., Monniaux, D. (eds.) VMCAI 2017. LNCS, vol. 10145, pp. 386–404. Springer, Cham (2017). https://doi.org/10.1007/978-3-319-52234-0_21
14. O'Hearn, P.W.: Resources, concurrency, and local reasoning. Theor. Comput. Sci. **375**(1–3), 271–307 (2007)
15. Stølen, K.: A method for the development of totally correct shared-state parallel programs. In: Baeten, J.C.M., Groote, J.F. (eds.) CONCUR 1991. LNCS, vol. 527, pp. 510–525. Springer, Heidelberg (1991). https://doi.org/10.1007/3-540-54430-5_110
16. Tobler, J., Smith, G.: Generating rely-guarantee conditions with the conditional-writes domain (2026). https://arxiv.org/abs/2602.17142

17. Winter, K., Coughlin, N., Smith, G.: Backwards-directed information flow analysis for concurrent programs. In: CSF, pp. 1–16. IEEE (2021)
18. Xu, Q., de Roever, W.P., He, J.: The rely-guarantee method for verifying shared variable concurrent programs. Formal Aspects Comput. **9**(2), 149–174 (1997)

Array-Carrying Symbolic Execution for Function Contract Generation

Weijie Lu[1], Jingyu Ke[1], Hongfei Fu[2(✉)], Zhouyue Sun[1], Yi Zhou[1], Guoqiang Li[1], and Haokun Li[3]

[1] Shanghai Jiao Tong University, Shanghai, China
[2] School of Computing and Artificial Intelligence, Shanghai University of Finance and Economics, Shanghai, China
hongfeifu1984@gmail.com
[3] Peking University, Beijing, China

Abstract. Function contract generation is a classical problem in program analysis that targets the automated analysis of functions in a program with multiple procedures. The problem is fundamental in interprocedural analysis where properties of functions are first obtained via the generation of function contracts and then the generated contracts are used as building blocks to analyze the whole program. Typical objectives in function contract generation include pre-/post-conditions and assigns information (that specifies the modification information over program variables and memory segments during function execution). In programs with array manipulations, a crucial point in function contract generation is the treatment of array segments that imposes challenges in inferring invariants and assigns information over such segments. To address this challenge, we propose a novel symbolic execution framework that carries invariants and assigns information over contiguous segments of arrays. We implement our framework as a prototype within LLVM, and further integrate our prototype with the ANSI/ISO C Specification Language (ACSL) assertion format and the Frama-C software verification platform. Experimental evaluation over a variety of benchmarks from the literature and functions from realistic libraries shows that our framework is capable of handling array manipulating functions that indeed involve the carry of array information and are beyond existing approaches.

1 Introduction

In program analysis, functional contract generation aims at the automated generation of contracts that specify the input-output relationship of an individual function. The input-output relationship typically involves preconditions and postconditions, and may also include assigns information (from the ANSI/ISO

W. Lu and J. Ke—These authors contributed equally to this work.
H. Fu—To join Shanghai University of Finance and Economics (formal procedures in process), leaving Shanghai Jiao Tong University.

A. Sampaio and M. Stoelinga (Eds.): FM 2026, LNCS 16556, pp. 397–418, 2026.
https://doi.org/10.1007/978-3-032-26204-2_21

C Specification Language (ACSL) assertion format) that specifies possible modifications over memory segments. The problem is fundamental in program analysis, as it facilitates interprocedural analysis by providing the basic information of functions. In this work, we focus on function contract generation for array-manipulating programs.

In the literature, various approaches have been proposed to address the automated generation of function contracts, including abstract interpretation [7,13–15,22,38,46], model checking/SMT solving [12,21,32], instrumentation [3], large language models (LLMs) [44,59], etc. Abstract interpretation chooses a suitable abstract domain for the abstraction of program states, and then performs a top-down analysis for each function. Existing abstract interpretation approaches accommodate contiguous array memory segments and support the inference of array invariants [15,22,38]. Model checking/SMT solving approaches [12,21] encode program execution as rules and leverage SMT solvers to verify whether an assertion in the function holds or not. The treatment of contiguous memory segments can be readily encoded by SMT constraints. Instrumentation [3] allows a user to specify rules to transform programs into a form with ghost variables that is easier to analyze, where specific array patterns (e.g., summation, maximum) are handled by special instrumentation rules. LLM-based approaches (e.g. [44,59]) perform supervised fine-tuning (SFT) using manually annotated programs as training data. The resulting fine-tuned model then infers function contracts using suitable prompts, often with possible guidance from static analysis and external experts.

While existing approaches tackle function contracts with array manipulations from different perspectives, they are limited in various aspects. For example, abstract interpretation has developed relational and segment-oriented domains that can reason about many array invariants [7,13,15,22,38]. However, for fully automated contract synthesis, preserving path-sensitive disjunctive loop-exit information and translating it into precise merged array-segment `assigns` information remains challenging. Model checking/SMT solving approaches can also infer summaries/contracts in multiple settings [2,12,19,21,32]. Nevertheless, depending on the encoding and property setup, many workflows are geared toward proving specific assertions, and may require additional summarization layers to produce reusable function-level contracts of the form $\langle Pre, Post, Assign\rangle$. Instrumentation focuses on manual specification of ghost variables, and hence does not have a dedicated treatment of contiguous array segments. LLM approaches usually require manual guidance from experts to avoid producing incorrect results caused by hallucinations. As a result, it remains a challenge to build a framework that handles array segments and invariants in function contract generation.

To address the aforementioned challenge, we propose a novel symbolic execution framework that carries array invariants and has a dedicated treatment of the contiguous array segments. Compared with previous results and existing symbolic execution techniques, our symbolic execution framework carries invariants generated from external invariant generators along the program statements, and carefully handles disjunction, splitting and merging of contiguous array segments. In our implementation, the invariant-generation back-end combines an affine/linear generator (the StInGX-style plugin based on Farkas-lemma reasoning [28,41]) with idiom-oriented generators for search and max/min loops. The full version on arXiv [43], appendix "Examples of Invariant Generators", gives concrete examples of these generators and the ACSL clauses they produce. The detailed contributions are as follows.

- Our symbolic execution is designed to receive numerical and array invariants from external invariant generators and propagate them along the execution of program statements. This allows our framework to leverage loop invariants to generate function contracts for general properties. Moreover, the propagation of invariants also produces tight preconditions for subsequent loop analysis.
- Our symbolic execution has a refined treatment of contiguous array segments. In detail, our framework handles disjunction of array segments resulting from different program execution paths (including different loop exit modes), and the merge/split of array segments during the symbolic execution. The merge and split of array segments allow precise tracking of information over these segments that is crucial to derive overall contracts related to array segments.
- We implement our symbolic execution technique as a prototype that comprises about 19000 lines in C++ within the LLVM platform [36,56]. We also integrate our prototype with the ACSL assertion format and the Frama-C software verification platform [9,17], so that the result of our symbolic execution can be fully verified by external verifiers.

Experimental evaluation over a wide range of benchmarks (including realistic benchmarks from active libraries) shows that our framework is capable of generating contracts that describe precise behavior of array-manipulating functions, while previous approaches fail to handle many of these benchmarks.

Limitations. Our symbolic execution has limited ability to handle pointers. Currently, we can only handle simple pointer arithmetic with base and offset arising from array addresses, and cannot handle recursive pointer structures such as linked lists and binary trees.

1.1 Related Works

Below we describe related works on function contract generation.

Abstract Interpretation. Abstract interpretation [13,16] generates function contracts by a top-down analysis that propagates elements from an abstract domain along the execution of the program, where functions are inlined upon procedure calls. Existing abstract interpretation methods handle arrays by abstract domains that express invariants over contiguous memory segments of arrays [15,38]. As we consider to extend symbolic execution with array segments and invariants, our result has a different focus from abstract interpretation methods.

Model Checking. Model checking approaches [12,21] often encode read/write operations of arrays by SMT rules and then solve target assertions with arrays. The most relevant works are by Tricera [2] and a SeaHorn-based verifier [20] that generate function contracts through a transformation into CHC solving (via e.g. the state-of-the-art CHC solver Eldarica [24]). A major disadvantage of existing model checking approaches is that they often follow top-down analysis, so the generated specification is often highly specific to the initial values of a program. Our approach circumvents this limitation by leveraging external invariant generators in our symbolic execution.

Large Language Models. In recent years, there has been a burgeoning focus on applying Large Language Models (LLMs) to support code specification generation [34,37,44,60]. A standard framework is AutoSpec [59] that leverages LLMs to synthesize ACSL-language specifications for C programs via a static analysis-guided bottom-up iterative approach, offering wider applicability than traditional works. Additionally, further studies [30,40,42,48,49] mainly focus on LLM-based invariant generation.

Symbolic Execution. Existing symbolic execution techniques analyze program with memory operations by symbolically encoding program states and maintaining a symbolic memory model that tracks heap and array updates across execution paths. For example, CLANG STATIC ANALYZER [33] performs a path-sensitive symbolic execution with a region-based memory model, but its reasoning over arrays and heap is local and non-relational. It propagates per-element constraints along each path, detecting out-of-bounds or null dereferences, yet lacks the ability to summarize iteration effects or infer relational properties over contiguous array regions across loop executions. KLEE [8] symbolically executes LLVM bitcode with SMT-based constraint solving, representing memory as byte-addressable symbolic objects and focusing on path exploration rather than invariant inference. While several extensions [27,50] enhance its handling of heap-allocated objects and symbolic pointers, KLEE and its variants still analyze memory at the level of individual allocations and lack the capability to infer relational or inductive invariants over contiguous array regions. The Gillian platform [45,55] provides a language-parametric symbolic execution architecture, and further integrates separation-logic-based verification with compositional memory models for JavaScript and C. Compared with Gillian, our work focuses on automatic contract synthesis for array-manipulating functions in C, where quantified array invariants are carried and merged along symbolic execution to synthesize ACSL `requires`/`ensures`/`assigns` clauses. Compared with existing results, our approach extends symbolic execution with contiguous memory segments of arrays.

Invariant Generation. Invariant generation can be addressed by abstract interpretation [7,13,15,22,38], constraint solving [10,11,28,35,41], instrumentation [3], recurrence analysis [29,58], etc. Low-level Bi-Abduction [25] is particularly relevant for compositional analysis of low-level pointer-intensive fragments, inferring function contracts through separation-logic bi-abduction with support for operations such as pointer arithmetic and block splitting/merging. In contrast, our target is contiguous array reasoning with carried quantified invariants and disjunctive segment summaries, which is tailored to postcondition and assigns synthesis in ACSL rather than low-level heap-shape reasoning over intrusive linked structures. Moreover, by integrating a Linear/Affine invariant generator plugin (in the style of StInGX/Farkas-lemma-based inference [28,41]) into our loop-analysis pipeline, our framework can effectively handle a broad class of numerical loops as well, including loops whose key properties are captured by affine index/value relations. Our approach utilizes these methods to generate numerical and array invariants to be carried during our symbolic execution.

2 Overview

Below we have an overview of our results via two illustrative examples.

```
/*@ requires size >= 1; */
uint SearchZero(const uint *data, int size)
{
    uint i = 0;
    while (i < size) {
        if (data[i] == 0)  break;
        i++;
    }

    if (i == size) return 0;
    else return 1;
}
```

(a) SearchZero function

```
#define ADD_ABC(carry, r, a, b, c)
    do {
        uint macroTmpS = (b) + (c);
        carry = (macroTmpS < (c)) ? 1 : 0;
        (r) = macroTmpS + (a);
        carry += ((r) < macroTmpS) ? 1 : 0;
    } while (0)
```

(b) ADD_ABC macro

```
uint BinAdd(uint *r, const uint *a, const uint *b, uint n)
{
    uint carry = 0; uint nn = n;
    const uint *aa = a; const uint *bb = b;
    uint *rr = r;

    while (nn >= 4) {  /* Process 4 groups in batches. */
        ADD_ABC(carry, rr[0], aa[0], bb[0], carry);  /* offset 0 */
        ADD_ABC(carry, rr[1], aa[1], bb[1], carry);  /* offset 1 */
        ADD_ABC(carry, rr[2], aa[2], bb[2], carry);  /* offset 2 */
        ADD_ABC(carry, rr[3], aa[3], bb[3], carry);  /* offset 3 */
        rr += 4;  /* a group of 4 */    aa += 4;  /* a group of 4 */
        bb += 4;  /* a group of 4 */    nn -= 4;  /* a group of 4 */
    }

    uint i = 0;
    for (; i < nn; i++) {
        ADD_ABC(carry, rr[i], aa[i], bb[i], carry);
    }

    return carry;
}
```

(c) BinAdd example

Fig. 1. Array program examples.

First Example. Consider the array manipulating function shown in Fig. 1(a), which is a function that searches whether there is a zero entry in the array data. The precondition of the function is size ≥ 1 which specifies that the size of the array should be positive. A notable feature of this function is that after the while loop, the function continues to check whether i equals size. If so, then the function returns 0, meaning that no zero entry is found. Otherwise, the function returns 1, meaning that a zero entry has been found.

To generate a complete contract for this function, our symbolic execution maintains both array invariants and contiguous array segments. For this example, our symbolic execution first calls an external invariant generator to generate loop invariant and summary for the while loop. By distinguishing different exit ways of the loop, our symbolic execution receives a disjunctive loop summary of two branching execution paths: one corresponds to the case when the loop exits upon encountering the conditional branch `data[i] != 0`, denoted as π_0, and the other corresponds to the case when the condition `data[i] == 0` consistently holds, denoted as π_1. Based on these execution paths, we extract the loop summary with information over the contiguous array segment with index from 0 to i as follows. Specifically, along the path π_0, our symbolic execution receives the assertion at the loop exit: $(\forall j.\ 0 \leq j < i \rightarrow \text{data}[j] = 0) \wedge \text{data}[i] \neq 0 \wedge i <$ size. On the other hand, along the path π_1, our symbolic execution receives $(\forall j.\ 0 \leq j < i \rightarrow \text{data}[j] = 0) \wedge i = \text{size}$. Note that the assertions of the two paths cannot be merged as they differ at whether `data[i] == 0` and `i == size`. Our symbolic execution maintains the disjunction of these two assertions, and carries it forward to the remaining part of the program so that the function contract below

$$\textbf{Pre}: \text{size} \geq 1 \qquad \textbf{Assigns}: \varnothing$$

$$\begin{aligned}\textbf{Post}: &\big[(i = \text{size}) \wedge (\forall j.\ 0 \leq j < \text{size} \rightarrow \text{data}[j] = 0) \wedge \text{res} = 0\big] \\ &\vee\ \big[(i < \text{size}) \wedge (\text{data}[i] \neq 0) \wedge (\forall j.\ 0 \leq j < i \rightarrow \text{data}[j] = 0) \wedge \text{res} = 1\big].\end{aligned}$$

is inferred, capturing precisely the behavior of the function. The main contribution of our symbolic execution here is the carry of (disjunctive) invariants and contiguous array segments.

Second Example. Consider the BnADD function extracted from the openHiTLS library [47], as shown in Fig. 1(c) (with macro given in Fig. 1(b)). To capture the overall memory modification in the execution of the function, one needs to merge the range of modified array segments in the two loops. Our symbolic execution detects changed array segments in each loop of the function, and merge the two segments into a single segment. In this example, the modified array range of the first loop is detected as $\text{rr}[0..4k)$, corresponding to the batched updates of four elements per iteration, where k is a ghost variable implicitly defined within the loop to represent the number of iterations executed so far. Informally, the term $\text{rr}[0..4k)$ means that the content from index 0 to index $4k$ of the array rr may be modified after k loop iterations. The counterpart of the second loop is detected as $\text{rr}[4k..\text{n})$, which handles the remaining elements after the batch processing. By merging the two modified ranges, our symbolic execution generates the overall modified range $\text{rr}[0..\text{n})$. The major contribution here is the merging of modified memory segments in our symbolic execution that allows us to generate the complete assigns information in the function contract.

3 Array-Carrying Symbolic Execution

In this section, we illustrate our symbolic execution framework over functions with integer and array variables that carries invariants and contiguous array segments, and aims at automatically synthesizing a function contract for a function in a given C program.

Due to the space constraints, we present the key concepts of invariants and function contracts in our symbolic execution informally, and defer the detailed definitions (over a simplified program model) to the full version on arXiv [43], appendices "A Basic Program Model" and "Invariants and Function Contracts". An *invariant* is a collection of formulas at certain program counters required to hold in every program state along every feasible execution path, thereby over-approximating the set of reachable program states. A *function contract* characterizes the intended behavior of a function by a *precondition* restricting admissible input program states, a *postcondition* describing the property that must hold upon termination, and an *assigns* information indicating possible memory locations whose content may be modified during function execution.

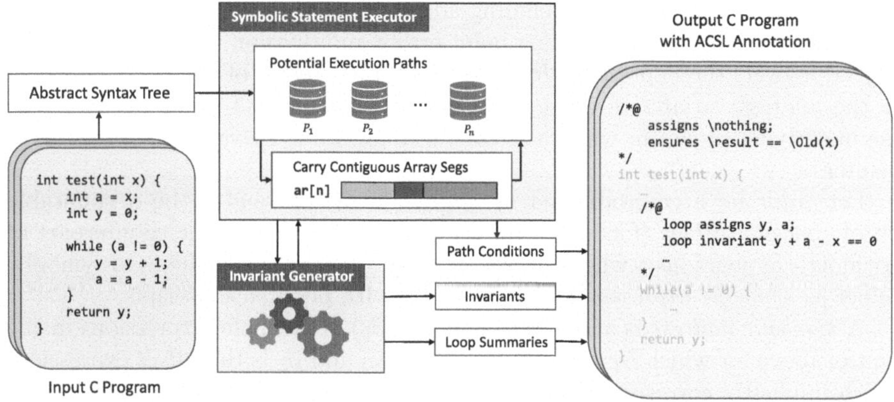

Fig. 2. General workflow of array-carrying symbolic execution.

Overview. Figure 2 demonstrates the workflow of our symbolic execution framework. The framework first takes as input an abstract syntax tree of the function body of the function to be analyzed. Then, a symbolic statement executor simulates the execution of the function body, producing multiple potential execution paths. During the simulation, the statement executor calls external invariant generators to generate invariants and summaries for loops. Moreover, the executor carefully maintains contiguous array segments of array contents and invariants, and carries them forward in the remaining execution. Finally, the execution paths with their path conditions, together with the carried invariants and contiguous array contents, are combined to obtain the function contract of the whole function. To maintain array segments and invariants, our symbolic statement executor incorporates an extended memory model to support constraint inference involving arrays and pointers.

Below we first present the high-level workflow of our framework, then the technical details on handling invariants and contiguous array segments, and finally a prototype implementation for our framework in LLVM.

3.1 Symbolic Execution Framework

In this section, we introduce our symbolic execution framework. We focus on the read and write aspects of arrays, and omit other technical aspects such as records and pointer arithmetic. A high-level program model is given in the full version on arXiv [43], appendix "A Basic Program Model".

As our symbolic execution handles array operations, we model array access and modification operations by direct read and write operations at memory addresses of array variables. In our framework, we consider arithmetic expressions γ with memory read operations by $\gamma ::= c \mid x \mid a \mid \gamma_1 \oplus \gamma_2 \mid R(a)$. In the syntax, we have integer variables x, integer constants c, address variables a and arithmetic operations $\oplus$ including addition, subtraction and multiplication (we omit division to avoid floating point errors and division by zero for simplicity). Moreover, the expression $R(a)$ represents the result of the read operation at the address variable a. Integer variables and constants are extracted from the underlying program, while address variables are fresh variables referring to pointers.

Let *Addr* be a countable set of *address constants* and V be a countable set of *symbolic values* (for undetermined values). We denote the counterpart of arithmetic expressions γ where the role of program variables switches to symbolic values as *symbolic expressions*, denoted by β with possible subscripts.

A *symbolic address* is an ordered pair (β_1, β_2) of symbolic expressions in the syntax above for which β_1 is the *base* expression and β_2 is the *offset* expression, which implicitly corresponds to the sum of the base and the offset (multiplied with the size of array entry). However, for the sake of clearly representing pointer arithmetic and intra-array offsets, we shall consistently use the pair notation (β_1, β_2) throughout the remainder of the paper to denote all address values. In our symbolic execution, we consider an intermediate program syntax as follows:

$$S ::= x := \gamma | a := \&x | W(a, \gamma) | \text{if } b \text{ then } S_1 \text{ else } S_2 | \text{while } b \text{ do } S | S_1; S_2 \ .$$

In the grammar, we have assignment statements for integer variables $x := \gamma$, conditional branches if b then S_1 else S_2, while loops while b do S, in which b represents the boolean expressions built from comparison of symbolic expressions and propositional logic connectives. In addition, we have a statement form $a :=\&x$ that assigns the symbolic address of x to an address variable a, corresponding to the address-of operation, and a statement form $W(a, \gamma)$ that writes the expression γ to the symbolic address of the address variable a.

Our symbolic execution works with symbolic states. Formally, a *symbolic state* Σ is an ordered pair (M, A) where M is a *memory map* that maps every symbolic address encountered so far to the symbolic expression held at the symbolic address, and A is an *address map* that maps each address and integer variable to its corresponding symbolic address where its concrete value lies. A symbolic state records the current symbolic addresses of the integer and array variables, and the current symbolic expressions at the symbolic addresses.

In our framework, read and write operations on addresses are realized by updating the corresponding maps in the current symbolic state. For example, the read expression $R(a)$ for a symbolic state (M, A) denotes the symbolic address $M(A(a))$ held in the address variable a.

The workflow of our symbolic execution is a traversal of program statements in the adapted program syntax S. During the traversal, we maintain a symbolic configuration *Conf*. Formally, a *symbolic configuration Conf* is a finite set of *symbolic paths*, where each symbolic path $P \in \mathit{Conf}$ is a tuple $(\ell, \Sigma, \mathit{Seg}, \mathit{pathCond})$ that specifies the current status after the execution of the path: ℓ is the current program counter, Σ is the current symbolic state, *Seg* is a structure that records the current information for contiguous array segments, and *pathCond* is a collection of path conditions resulting from the execution of the symbolic path. Invariants are treated as path conditions in *pathCond*.

Algorithm 1 presents the pseudocode of our queue-based symbolic execution procedure. The main workflow is an enumeration of all feasible execution paths under a program in the syntax of S. In this pseudocode, we require an input `PreCond` that corresponds to the input ACSL precondition (i.e., the `requires` clause of the target function). Here we focus on the update of ℓ, Σ and conditions in *pathCond* along the symbolic execution, and relegate the details for the update of *Seg* and invariants in *pathCond* to the next subsection.

The procedure begins by initializing the initial symbolic state $\Sigma_0 = (M_0, A_0)$ at the entry of a program, as shown in Algorithm 1, starting from line 1. The initialization works as follows.

- In the initial address map A_0, each program variable $x \in X$ is mapped to a symbolic address $\mathrm{addr}(x)$ drawn from the set *Addr*. As defined earlier, every $\mathrm{addr}(x)$ takes the form (β_1, β_2). The base address β_1 is a fresh address constant; for integer variables and pointers, the offset address β_2 is set to 0, whereas for an array element $arr[i]$, the offset is the symbolic expression $M_0(A_0(i))$.
- For each symbolic address $\mathrm{addr}(x)$ associated with a variable x in A_0, we insert into M_0 a mapping from $\mathrm{addr}(x)$ to an initial symbolic expression β_x. The expression β_x corresponds to the initial value assigned to x in the program. If such a value does not exist or cannot be statically determined, we instead assign a fresh symbolic value taken from V as the β_x. We also substitute program variables x in the given precondition by β_x.

Throughout this initialization procedure, all symbolic addresses $\mathrm{addr}(x)$ and symbolic values used for different variables are guaranteed to be distinct.

After the initialization, as shown in Algorithm 1 starting from line 6, the symbolic executor traverses the statements in the function. Suppose that S is the current statement in the traversal. To symbolically execute S, the algorithm dequeues existing symbolic paths from the path queue, and for each path P, invokes the `Exec` procedure. The `Exec` procedure serves as the *symbolic transfer function*: it interprets the semantics of S to compute the successor symbolic state and update the path conditions. Depending on the specific type of the

Algorithm 1: Symbolic Execution and Contract Synthesis Workflow

Input: *Func* as target function context, *PreCond* as the set of preconditions
Output: $Conf, \mathcal{I}_{all}, \mathcal{C}_{func}$ as symbolic configuration, loop invariants and synthesized function contracts

1 Extract variable set X from $Func$;
2 **foreach** $x \in X$ **do**
3 $\quad A_0(x) \leftarrow \text{addr}(x)$; $\texttt{Init}(M_0(addr(x)))$;
4 $\Sigma_0 = (M_0, A_0)$; $pathCond_0 \leftarrow \varnothing$;
5 $P_0 = (\Sigma_0, pathCond_0)$; Path.**enqueue**$(P_0)$; $\mathcal{I}_{all} \leftarrow \varnothing$;
6 **foreach** $S \in Func$ *in program order* **do**
7 $\quad$ Path$' \leftarrow \phi$;
8 $\quad$ **while** *Path is not empty* **do**
9 $\quad\quad$ Dequeue $P = (\Sigma, pathCond)$ from *Path*;
10 $\quad\quad$ **if** *S is* ***ifstmt*** **then**
11 $\quad\quad\quad P_1 \leftarrow (\Sigma,\ pathCond \wedge [b]_\Sigma)$;
12 $\quad\quad\quad (\Sigma'_1, pathCond'_1) \leftarrow \texttt{Exec}(S_1, P_1)$;
13 $\quad\quad\quad Path'$.**enqueue** $(\Sigma'_1, pathCond'_1)$;
14 $\quad\quad\quad P_2 \leftarrow (\Sigma,\ pathCond \wedge [\neg b]_\Sigma)$;
15 $\quad\quad\quad (\Sigma'_2, pathCond'_2) \leftarrow \texttt{Exec}(S_2, P_2)$;
16 $\quad\quad\quad Path'$.**enqueue** $(\Sigma'_2, pathCond'_2)$;
17 $\quad\quad$ **else if** *S is* ***whilestmt*** **then**
18 $\quad\quad\quad (M_{\text{loop}}, PC_{\text{loop}}, Inv) \leftarrow \texttt{LoopAnalyzer}(S, P)$;
19 $\quad\quad\quad \mathcal{I}_{all} \leftarrow \mathcal{I}_{all} \cup Inv$;
20 $\quad\quad\quad (\Sigma', pathCond') = \texttt{Update}((M_{\text{loop}}, PC_{\text{loop}}, Inv), P)$;
21 $\quad\quad\quad Path'$.**enqueue**$(\Sigma', pathCond')$;
22 $\quad\quad$ **else**
$\quad\quad\quad$ `// Handle assignment statements`
23 $\quad\quad\quad (\Sigma', pathCond') \leftarrow \texttt{Exec}(S, (\Sigma, pathCond))$;;
24 $\quad\quad\quad Path'$.**enqueue**$(\Sigma', pathCond')$;
25 $\quad Path \leftarrow Path'$;
26 $Conf \leftarrow Path$; $\mathcal{C}_{func} \leftarrow \texttt{ContractGen}(Conf)$;
27 **return** $(Conf, \mathcal{I}_{all}, \mathcal{C}_{func})$;

statement S, the symbolic path $P = (\Sigma = (M, A), pathCond)$ is updated by `Exec` as follows. (Here we omit the components ℓ, Seg in the path description as (i) the update of ℓ corresponds to the natural control flow successor of S and (ii) the update of Seg will be detailed in the next subsection.) Below, given a memory map M, we denote by $M[(\beta_1, \beta_2) \mapsto \beta]$ the memory map that maps the symbolic address (β_1, β_2) to the symbolic expression β, while maintaining the existing mappings for all other symbolic addresses.

- If S is a conditional statement with condition b, as shown in Algorithm 1 starting from line 10, then the symbolic executor splits the symbolic path P into two new symbolic paths $P_b, P_{\neg b}$. The symbolic path P_b equals

$(\Sigma, pathCond \cup \{[b]_\Sigma\})$, for which the condition $[b]_\Sigma$ is obtained by replacing every integer program variable x and read operation $R(a)$ in b by their corresponding symbolic expressions $M(A(x))$ and $M(A(a))$, respectively. The case for $P_{\neg b}$ is similar.

- If S is an assignment statement, as shown in Algorithm 1 starting from line 22, then the symbolic path is updated to $(\Sigma', pathCond)$ for which the updated symbolic state Σ' depends on the type of the assignment.
  1. If S is a variable assignment $x := \gamma$, we evaluate γ under Σ (by substituting each integer or address variable u into symbolic expressions stored at $A(u)$, namely $M(A(u))$, and each symbolic address (β_1, β_2) into the symbolic expression $M(\beta_1, \beta_2)$ held at the address) to obtain a symbolic expression $[\gamma]_\Sigma$, and then update the memory map at the address of x: $\Sigma' = (\, M[A(x) \mapsto [\gamma]_\Sigma],\ A\,)$.
  2. If S is an address-of statement $a := \&x$, we update the symbolic expression stored at $A(a)$ in the memory map with the address value $A(x)$: $\Sigma' = (\, M[A(a) \mapsto A(x)],\ A\,)$.
  3. If S is a write-back statement $W(a, \gamma)$, we evaluate γ to obtain $[\gamma]_\Sigma$, as described earlier. Then we update the corresponding memory entry at $M(A(a))$, i.e. the memory location at the address expression stored in a: $\Sigma' = (\, M[M(A(a)) \mapsto [\gamma]_\Sigma],\ A\,)$.
- If the next statement is the entry of a while loop, as shown in Algorithm 1 starting from line 17, the symbolic executor invokes an external loop analyzer. For each symbolic path in the current configuration, the executor sends the current symbolic state and path conditions, as the precondition for the loop), to the analyzer, which returns a set of inferred invariants and a loop summary. Let M_{loop} denote the modifications applied to the memory map during the loop execution, PC_{loop} the path conditions of the loop, and Inv the set of inferred loop invariants. The invariants Inv are added to the global collection $\mathcal{I}_{all}$ for contract synthesis. The executor then transfers control to PC_{loop} and updates the symbolic path accordingly. This update has two components: (1) conjoining the inferred invariants with the current path condition, and (2) updating the memory map to incorporate the loop effects. For post-loop variable states, the executor introduces fresh symbol values for the exit values of the program variables to facilitate subsequent symbolic execution when necessary—namely, for variables modified inside the loop whose final values cannot be precisely determined or summarized. Our current implementation uses a preliminary loop analyzer described in the full version on arXiv [43], appendix "Loop Analysis".

After the symbolic execution, the overall function contract $\mathcal{C}_{func}$ is inferred from the final symbolic configuration $Conf$. The `assigns` clause is derived by comparing the final memory map M of each path against the initial memory map M_0 from the function entry: any memory location whose final symbolic value differs from its initial value is recorded as modified. The logical components of the contract are then extracted from the accumulated path conditions $pathCond$ and the segment structural information in Seg. The projection step is performed by eliminating intermediate symbols introduced during execution and retaining only symbols associated with the function entry (for `requires`) and return state (for `ensures`/`assigns`). Concretely, we substitute each symbolic address with the corresponding source-level variable term, rewrite segment constraints into index-range predicates over arrays, and existentially quantify auxiliary symbols that do not correspond to user-visible program variables. The resulting formulas characterize the preconditions and postconditions under which the function is well-defined and the properties that must hold of its outcomes.

3.2 The Carrying of Invariants and Contiguous Array Segments

Invariant Carrying. The path-condition set *pathCond* records constraints over the symbolic expressions containing symbolic values which are generated during execution, rather than the program variables that may temporarily reference those expressions. When a loop invariant and its corresponding summary are obtained from the external invariant generator, the symbolic executor may introduce fresh symbolic values from V to represent the values of the integer variables upon loop termination. The loop summary is then instantiated by substituting these fresh symbolic values for the concrete integer variables, and the resulting condition is appended to *pathCond*. The symbolic execution of the remaining program proceeds using these newly introduced symbolic values as the initial values for their respective integer variables.

Representing Contiguous Array Segments. We formally define contiguous array segments using our address model. As mentioned earlier, each symbolic path carries a set of active segments, denoted as *Seg*. Unlike the memory map M which can only record independent symbolic expressions stored at discrete symbolic addresses, segments capture the relationship between the properties of a contiguous memory region and the symbolic expressions stored over that region. Based on this, one can derive different patterns of symbolic expressions that serve as constraint conditions associated with that memory segment.

We define a *segment* $s \in Seg$ as a triple $s := \langle(\beta_b, \beta_o),\ \beta_{len},\ \mathcal{C}\rangle$, where (β_b, β_o) denotes the starting symbolic address of the segment, β_{len} is a symbolic expression representing the number of elements in the segment, and $\mathcal{C}$ denotes the *content summary* of the segment, representing the pattern of invariants that hold over this segment.

Our framework employs a hybrid strategy to obtain the content summary $\mathcal{C}$:

1. *Directly-Indexed Invariants:* When the array content can be expressed as a function of the index, $\mathcal{C}$ is a symbolic expression $\phi(i_{off})$. Here, ϕ is a function representing the invariant pattern, and i_{off} is a placeholder variable representing the relative offset within the segment. For example, given the constraint $\forall 0 \leq i \leq n-1, arr[i] = i+2$ over the array *arr*, where n denotes the length of *arr*, one can derive the segment $s = \langle(A(arr), 0), n-1, \phi(i_{off}) := i_{off} + 2\rangle$.

2. *Aggregate Abstractions:* Certain program logic relies on reduction operations [3] (e.g., `sum`, `max`) over an array range. In such cases, we model $\mathcal{C}$ as a first-class arithmetic expression, denoted as $\beta_{agg} := \texttt{Agg}(\oplus, s)$. Here, $\oplus$ represents the reduction operator and s is the target segment. Unlike logical constraints which are restricted to *pathCond*, these aggregate expressions behave identically to standard symbolic expressions. Consequently, they can be inserted into the the memory map M as the symbolic expressions associated with the corresponding symbolic addresses and participate in subsequent arithmetic computations, enabling algebraic reasoning over array properties.

Certain loop-based properties require quantification over the actual iteration domain of the loop (i.e., the iterator k ranging over the loop bounds). Such invariants cannot be captured through simple index-pattern abstractions and therefore are not stored inside the segment tuple. Instead, they are represented explicitly as logical statements and added to the path condition set *pathCond*.

We formalize these complex invariants as *quantified constraints*. Formally, such a constraint is a tuple $\Phi := \langle \mathcal{Q}, \mathcal{R}, \psi \rangle$, representing the logical formula $\mathcal{Q}\, k \in \mathcal{R}.\psi(k)$, where $\mathcal{Q} \in \{\forall, \exists\}$ is the quantifier, $\mathcal{R}$ denotes the index range, typically defined by bounds $[\beta_{lower}, \beta_{upper})$, and $\psi(k)$ is the predicate over the loop iterator k. For instance, consider the `SearchZero` function presented in the overview, shown in Fig. 1(a). The loop iterates through the array to find the first non-zero element, effectively maintaining the invariant that all elements scanned so far are zero. Our framework captures this property as the tuple $\langle \forall, [0, i), \texttt{data}[k] = 0 \rangle$. Here, the quantifier $\forall$ applies to the index range $[0, i)$ (where i is the current loop variable), and the predicate $\texttt{data}[k] = 0$ asserts the specific constraint validated by the loop logic.

Updates on Segments and Invariants. During symbolic execution, the executor maintains and forwards the array-related information encoded in the segments, and performs the corresponding segment updates whenever a related array memory operation is executed.

- *Read* $R(a)$: Let $a = (\beta_{arr}, \beta_{len})$ be the symbolic address being read, where the offset address β_{len} is a symbolic expression evaluated under the current symbolic state. The executor first locates all segments $s = \langle (\beta_{arr}, \beta_o), \beta_l, \mathcal{C} \rangle \in Seg$ whose index range may overlap with β_{len}, i.e., all s satisfying $\beta_o \leq \beta_{len} < \beta_o + \beta_l$. For each such segment, the executor performs an index-based substitution, replacing the placeholder i_{idx} in its content summary $\mathcal{C}$ with the offset β_{len}, yielding the expression $\mathcal{C}(\beta_{len})$. If multiple segments are simultaneously feasible (e.g., due to symbolic index uncertainty), the executor constructs a disjunctive invariant of the form $\bigvee_{\mathcal{C} \in \mathsf{Cand}} \mathcal{C}(\beta_{len})$, where Cand is the set of all feasible segments.
- *Write* $W(a, \gamma)$: A write operation $W(a, \gamma)$ to an address a falling within a segment s may invalidate or split the segment. If a represents a concrete offset relative to the segment base, s is split into two or more new, smaller segments. For instance, writing to `arr[j]` may split a target segment $s = \langle (\beta_{arr}, 0), n, \mathcal{C} \rangle$ into a *prefix segment* $s_1 = \langle (\beta_p, 0), j, \mathcal{C}_1 \rangle$ and a *suffix segment*

$s_2 = \langle(\beta_p, j{+}1), n{-}j{-}1, \mathcal{C}_2\rangle$. The original content summary $\mathcal{C}$ is propagated to these new, smaller segments. In the current prototype, this splitting operation is implemented for segments with constant offset and length, while segments with symbolic offset or length remain a subject for future work.

- *Segment Merging:* The framework also merges segments to maintain coarse-grained array summaries. After a write operation or loop analysis, a syntactic merging strategy is applied. This procedure scans all segments sharing the same base address and identifies pairs of adjacent segments—e.g., $s_1 = \langle(\beta_b, \beta_o), \beta_{L1}, \mathcal{C}_1\rangle$ and $s_2 = \langle(\beta_b, \beta_o{+}\beta_{L1}), \beta_{L2}, \mathcal{C}_2\rangle$. If their content summaries are syntactically equivalent, the two are merged into a single, larger segment $s_{new} = \langle(\beta_b, \beta_o), \beta_{L1} + \beta_{L2}, \mathcal{C}_1\rangle$.

We provide an example for the carrying process as follows.

Example 1. Consider the first code example in Fig. 1(a). Starting from the input ACSL precondition $\mathsf{size} \geq 1$, symbolic execution initializes i and the symbolic state, then invokes the loop analyzer at the `while` entry. The analyzer returns a disjunctive summary: one branch exits with $(\forall 0 \leq j < i.\ \mathsf{data}[j] = 0) \land \mathsf{data}[i] \neq 0 \land i < \mathsf{size}$, while the other exits with $(\forall 0 \leq j < i.\ \mathsf{data}[j] = 0) \land i = \mathsf{size}$. We append these formulas to *pathCond*, carry the corresponding segment information in *Seg*, and continue symbolic execution through the final branch `if (i == size)`. The two resulting paths are finally merged into a disjunctive postcondition, while the `assigns` set remains empty for this read-only function.

Remark 1. As our symbolic execution framework relies on specific invariant generators, we describe the current state of the art on the invariant generation with numerical values and arrays. Numerical invariant generation (e.g., linear and polynomial invariants) has been extensively studied, including abstract interpretation [7,13], constraint solving [4,10,11,26,28,39,41,61], recurrence analysis [29,58], etc. Invariant generation with arrays is mostly tackled via contiguous array segments [15,22,35,38]. Array invariants can also be solved via CHC solving [19]. A recent result investigates instrumentation [3] to aid the generation of array invariants.

3.3 Prototype Implementation Detail

Our prototype is implemented on top of the Clang/LLVM toolchain [36] that comprises about 19000 lines in C++. We use the Clang front-end to obtain the abstract syntax tree of the input C program and traverse the AST to construct the intermediate program syntax S and the initial symbolic configuration described in Sect. 3.1. Our framework incorporates records and pointer arithmetic. For pointer arithmetic, the current implementation supports simple forms (e.g., linear base-plus-offset patterns), but does not yet handle complex shape analysis such as linked lists or binary trees. For each analyzed function, the framework generates corresponding ACSL annotations [5] that encode the synthesized function contract, including preconditions, postconditions, and `assigns` clauses. These annotations are then fed to Frama-C [31], where the WP plugin is used to automatically discharge the resulting proof obligations and thereby validate the soundness of the inferred contracts with respect to the original C code. Loop reasoning in the prototype is realized via the plugin-based `LoopAnalyzer` introduced in the full version on arXiv [43], appendix "Loop Analysis".

4 Evaluation

We evaluate our symbolic execution framework by comparing it against AutoDeduct [51], a state-of-the-art toolchain capable of generating ACSL annotations for C programs. The toolchain incorporates Saida [53], which requires TriCera [19,54,57], and the Interface Specification Propagator (ISP) [52] to manage, propagate, and emit specifications. We do not compare with popular software verification tools such as Seahorn [23] and CPAChecker [6] since they usually require assertions to verify, while our approach does not require assertions and instead tries to generate precise contracts without manually given assertions. We also do not compare with large language models as they follow a completely different principle (see the full version on arXiv [43], appendix "Rationale for Excluding LLM-based Baselines", for details). All experiments were conducted in a Docker container based on Ubuntu 24.04.3 LTS running on a WSL2 host (version 6.6.87.2-microsoft-standard-WSL2) on a machine with AMD Ryzen 7 8845H CPU and 8 GB RAM[1]

4.1 Experimental Setup

Benchmarks. We assembled a diverse dataset of 282 C programs comprising five distinct benchmark suites collected in [59], together with an additional set of real-world cryptographic routines, ranging from micro-benchmarks to realistic cryptographic modules:

1. **SyGuS** [1]: 133 C programs with single loops, adapted from the SyGuS competition.
2. **OOPSLA-13** [18]: 46 programs featuring various loop types, used in prior loop analysis research.
3. **Frama-C Problems:** 51 programs covering diverse logic patterns.
4. **SV-Comp:** 14 complex programs selected from the Software Verification Competition.
5. **X-509:** 6 programs derived from realistic PKI certificate processing code.
6. **openHiTLS:** 31 C functions extracted from the *openHiTLS* project, a modular high-performance TLS and cryptographic library, covering big-number arithmetic, low-level buffer operations, and certificate-processing related routines.

[1] We provide the source code, Docker environment, and benchmark scripts at: https://doi.org/10.5281/zenodo.18601854.

Table 1. Comparison of verification results. The reported runtime for our approach includes both symbolic execution and invariant-generation time. We additionally report partial-verification, timeout, and generation-failure counts to make unresolved cases explicit. **Full**: Fully verified; **Part.**: Partial verification (ACSL generated but verification failed); **T/O**: Timeout; **Fail**: Generation failed; **Time**: Average runtime for successfully generated cases; **AD**: AutoDeduct

		Full (#)		Part. (#)		T/O (#)		Fail (#)		Time (s)	
Suite	Total	Ours	AD	Ours	AD	Ours	AD	Ours	AD	Ours	AD
SyGuS	133	*53*	*0*	*78*	*131*	*0*	*0*	*2*	*2*	*0.140*	*2.23*
OOPSLA-13	46	*2*	*1*	*20*	*42*	*0*	*0*	*24*	*3*	*0.141*	*4.44*
Frama-C	51	*9*	*8*	*29*	*34*	*1*	*0*	*13*	*9*	*0.260*	*2.26*
SV-Comp	14	*3*	*0*	*5*	*13*	*0*	*0*	*6*	*1*	*0.065*	*3.48*
X-509	6	*1*	*1*	*2*	*5*	*0*	*0*	*3*	*0*	*0.090*	*1.98*
openHiTLS	31	*0*	*0*	*10*	*0*	*0*	*0*	*21*	*31*	*0.080*	-
Total	**281**	**68**	**10**	**143**	**225**	**1**	**0**	**69**	**46**	**0.148**	**2.703**

Baseline and Configuration. As mentioned previously, we compare our approach with AutoDeduct. To ensure a fair comparison regarding execution time, we account for the runtime characteristics of AutoDeduct, which is partially implemented in Scala and relies on the JVM. We execute AutoDeduct twice on the benchmarks without stopping the container; data from the second run is recorded to mitigate JVM warm-up and JIT compilation overheads.

Verification Workflow. For both tools, the evaluation follows a strictly automated pipeline: (1) The tool takes the C source code as input and generates an annotated file with ACSL contracts (preconditions, postconditions, loop invariants, and assigns clauses). (2) The annotated file is passed to the Frama-C WP plugin. (3) A verification is considered "Success" only if Frama-C WP can prove all generated verification goals.

4.2 Experimental Results

RQ1: Effectiveness and Precision. We assess effectiveness by the number of programs for which the tools generate sufficient invariants and contracts to satisfy Frama-C WP. Table 1 summarizes the results.

Our framework demonstrates significantly higher precision than the baseline. Out of the total 281 benchmarks, our tool successfully generated verifiable contracts for 68 programs. In contrast, AutoDeduct was only able to achieve complete verification for 10 programs. This disparity highlights the advantage of carrying segment-based array invariants and handling pointer arithmetic recursively, which allows our tool to prove complex properties that rely on precise memory information.

RQ2: Efficiency and Scalability. As shown in the "Avg. Time" column of Table 1, our framework demonstrates a substantial performance advantage. The weighted average execution time for our tool is 0.160 s per file, whereas AutoDeduct averages 2.706 s. This represents an approximate 17.1× speedup. While AutoDeduct incurs overhead from the JVM environment (even after accounting for warm-up phases), our tool's efficiency stems primarily from the lightweight design of the symbolic execution engine. By carrying array segments and invariants abstractly rather than unrolling loops or explicitly enumerating all array elements, our approach minimizes the symbolic state explosion, allowing for rapid analysis even on benchmarks with partial verification.

Analysis of Failed Cases. To better understand the limitations of both tools, we analyzed the cases classified as "**Fail**" (Generation Failed) and those that generated contracts but failed to fully verify ("**Part.**").

For our framework, **Fail** (69 cases) are primarily caused by syntax limitations in the current prototype. Specifically, the tool currently lacks support for certain bitwise and arithmetic operators (e.g., %, «, ») and does not yet handle nested loops. When these constructs are encountered, the analysis aborts to avoid unsoundness. The single **T/O** case is due to a program bug in our handling of recursive functions, which triggers unintended infinite recursion during analysis. The cases of **Part.** (where contracts are generated but not proven) are largely attributed to the loop invariant inference. While our plugin system captures many properties, some complex loops require stronger inductive invariants than our current plugins can synthesize. Moreover, another reason is that the current invariant generation methods have some compatibility issues with ACSL format and Frama-C WP. Nevertheless, the generated contracts remain semantically meaningful: manual inspection confirms that they accurately characterize the memory footprints and critical range constraints, providing a valuable descriptive summary of the function behaviour.

In contrast, AutoDeduct's failures are more structural. Its **Fail** cases often result from unsupported C syntax involving complex array initializers. More critically, its low verification success rate (only 10 fully verified) is due to its inability to incorporate loop invariants. For the vast majority of programs containing loops, AutoDeduct fails to synthesize the necessary loop invariant clauses, rendering the generated ACSL unverifiable by Frama-C WP.

5 Conclusion

In this work, we proposed a framework for symbolic execution that carries contiguous array segments and invariants to address the automated generation of function contracts with array manipulations. The main feature of our framework is the carry of contiguous array segments and array invariants (with merging and split operations) along the symbolic execution. A prototype is implemented in LLVM. Future works include a more thorough treatment of invariants into the splitting and merging of array segments, an extension in interprocedural analysis that utilizes contracts of lower level functions to generate contracts of higher level functions, and a deeper integration with existing invariant generation methods.

Acknowledgement. The authors would like to thank the anonymous reviewers for their valuable comments and constructive suggestions that helped improve the quality of this paper. This work is partially supported by the National Natural Science Foundation of China (NSFC) under Grant No. 62572297 and sponsored by the CCF-Huawei Populus Grove Fund.

References

1. Alur, R., Fisman, D., Padhi, S., Singh, R., Udupa, A.: Sygus-comp 2018: results and analysis (2019). https://arxiv.org/abs/1904.07146
2. Amilon, J.: Automated inference of ACSL function contracts using Tricera (2021)
3. Amilon, J., Esen, Z., Gurov, D., Lidström, C., Rümmer, P.: Automatic program instrumentation for automatic verification. In: Enea, C., Lal, A. (eds.) Computer Aided Verification - 35th International Conference, CAV 2023, Paris, France, 17-22 July 2023, Proceedings, Part III. Lecture Notes in Computer Science, vol. 13966, pp. 281–304. Springer (2023). https://doi.org/10.1007/978-3-031-37709-9_14
4. Asadi, A., Chatterjee, K., Fu, H., Goharshady, A.K., Mahdavi, M.: Polynomial reachability witnesses via stellensätze. In: Freund, S.N., Yahav, E. (eds.) PLDI '21: 42nd ACM SIGPLAN International Conference on Programming Language Design and Implementation, Virtual Event, Canada, 20-25 June 2021, pp. 772–787. ACM (2021). https://doi.org/10.1145/3453483.3454076
5. Baudin, P., Filliâtre, J.C., Marché, C., Monate, B., Moy, Y., Prevosto, V.: ACSL: ANSI/ISO C specification. https://frama-c.com/html/acsl.html (2021)
6. Beyer, D., Keremoglu, M.E.: CPAchecker: a tool for configurable software verification. In: Gopalakrishnan, G., Qadeer, S. (eds.) CAV 2011. LNCS, vol. 6806, pp. 184–190. Springer, Heidelberg (2011). https://doi.org/10.1007/978-3-642-22110-1_16
7. Boutonnet, R., Halbwachs, N.: Disjunctive relational abstract interpretation for interprocedural program analysis. In: Enea, C., Piskac, R. (eds.) VMCAI 2019. LNCS, vol. 11388, pp. 136–159. Springer, Cham (2019). https://doi.org/10.1007/978-3-030-11245-5_7
8. Cadar, C., Dunbar, D., Engler, D.R., et al.: Klee: unassisted and automatic generation of high-coverage tests for complex systems programs. In: OSDI. vol. 8, pp. 209–224 (2008)
9. CEA LIST: Frama-C: a software analysis platform (2024). https://frama-c.com
10. Chatterjee, K., Fu, H., Goharshady, A.K., Goharshady, E.K.: Polynomial invariant generation for non-deterministic recursive programs. In: Donaldson, A.F., Torlak, E. (eds.) Proceedings of the 41st ACM SIGPLAN International Conference on Programming Language Design and Implementation, PLDI 2020, London, UK, 15-20 June 2020, pp. 672–687. ACM (2020). https://doi.org/10.1145/3385412.3385969
11. Colón, M.A., Sankaranarayanan, S., Sipma, H.B.: Linear invariant generation using non-linear constraint solving. In: Hunt, W.A., Somenzi, F. (eds.) CAV 2003. LNCS, vol. 2725, pp. 420–432. Springer, Heidelberg (2003). https://doi.org/10.1007/978-3-540-45069-6_39

12. Cordeiro, L., Fischer, B., Marques-Silva, J.: SMT-based bounded model checking for embedded ANSI-c software. IEEE Trans. Softw. Eng. **38**(4), 957–974 (2011)
13. Cousot, P., Cousot, R.: Abstract interpretation: a unified lattice model for static analysis of programs by construction or approximation of fixpoints. In: Proceedings of the 4th ACM SIGACT-SIGPLAN Symposium on Principles of Programming Languages, pp. 238–252 (1977)
14. Cousot, P., Cousot, R., Fähndrich, M., Logozzo, F.: Automatic inference of necessary preconditions. In: Giacobazzi, R., Berdine, J., Mastroeni, I. (eds.) VMCAI 2013. LNCS, vol. 7737, pp. 128–148. Springer, Heidelberg (2013). https://doi.org/10.1007/978-3-642-35873-9_10
15. Cousot, P., Cousot, R., Logozzo, F.: A parametric segmentation functor for fully automatic and scalable array content analysis. In: Ball, T., Sagiv, M. (eds.) Proceedings of the 38th ACM SIGPLAN-SIGACT Symposium on Principles of Programming Languages, POPL 2011, Austin, TX, USA, 26-28 January 2011, pp. 105–118. ACM (2011). https://doi.org/10.1145/1926385.1926399
16. Cousot, P., Cousot, R., Logozzo, F.: Precondition inference from intermittent assertions and application to contracts on collections. In: International Workshop on Verification, Model Checking, and Abstract Interpretation, pp. 150–168. Springer (2011)
17. Cuoq, P., Kirchner, F., Kosmatov, N., Prevosto, V., Signoles, J., Yakobowski, B.: Frama-C. In: Eleftherakis, G., Hinchey, M., Holcombe, M. (eds.) SEFM 2012. LNCS, vol. 7504, pp. 233–247. Springer, Heidelberg (2012). https://doi.org/10.1007/978-3-642-33826-7_16
18. Dillig, I., Dillig, T., Li, B., McMillan, K.: Inductive invariant generation via abductive inference. SIGPLAN Not. **48**(10), 443–456 (2013). https://doi.org/10.1145/2544173.2509511
19. Esen, Z., Rümmer, P.: TriCera: verifying C programs using the theory of heaps. In: Proceedings of the 22nd Conference on Formal Methods in Computer-Aided Design (FMCAD 2022), pp. 360–367. TU Wien Academic Press (2022). https://doi.org/10.34727/2022/isbn.978-3-85448-053-2_45
20. Garcia-Contreras, I., Gurfinkel, A., Navas, J.A.: Efficient modular SMT-based model checking of pointer programs. In: International Static Analysis Symposium, pp. 227–246. Springer (2022)
21. Ghilardi, S., Nicolini, E., Ranise, S., Zucchelli, D.: Towards SMT model checking of array-based systems. In: International Joint Conference on Automated Reasoning, pp. 67–82. Springer (2008)
22. Gopan, D., Reps, T.W., Sagiv, S.: A framework for numeric analysis of array operations. In: Palsberg, J., Abadi, M. (eds.) Proceedings of the 32nd ACM SIGPLAN-SIGACT Symposium on Principles of Programming Languages, POPL 2005, Long Beach, California, USA, 12-14 January 2005, pp. 338–350. ACM (2005). https://doi.org/10.1145/1040305.1040333
23. Gurfinkel, A., Kahsai, T., Komuravelli, A., Navas, J.A.: The seahorn verification framework. In: Kroening, D., Pasareanu, C.S. (eds.) Computer Aided Verification - 27th International Conference, CAV 2015, San Francisco, CA, USA, 18-24 July 2015, Proceedings, Part I. Lecture Notes in Computer Science, vol. 9206, pp. 343–361. Springer (2015). https://doi.org/10.1007/978-3-319-21690-4_20
24. Hojjat, H., Rümmer, P.: The eldarica horn solver. In: 2018 Formal Methods in Computer Aided Design (FMCAD), pp. 1–7. IEEE (2018)
25. Holík, L., Peringer, P., Rogalewicz, A., Šoková, V., Vojnar, T., Zuleger, F.: Low-level Bi-abduction. In: 36th European Conference on Object-Oriented Programming (ECOOP 2022). LIPIcs (2022). arXiv:2205.02590

26. Ji, Y., Fu, H., Fang, B., Chen, H.: Affine loop invariant generation via matrix algebra. In: Shoham, S., Vizel, Y. (eds.) Computer Aided Verification - 34th International Conference, CAV 2022, Haifa, Israel, 7-10 August 2022, Proceedings, Part I. Lecture Notes in Computer Science, vol. 13371, pp. 257–281. Springer (2022). https://doi.org/10.1007/978-3-031-13185-1_13
27. Kapus, T., Cadar, C.: A segmented memory model for symbolic execution. In: ESEC/FSE, pp. 1002–1012. ACM (2019)
28. Ke, J., Fu, H., Liu, H., Sun, Z., Chen, L., Li, G.: Affine disjunctive invariant generation with Farkas' lemma. In: International Conference on Verification, Model Checking, and Abstract Interpretation, pp. 187–213. Springer (2025)
29. Kincaid, Z., Cyphert, J., Breck, J., Reps, T.: Non-linear reasoning for invariant synthesis. In: Proceedings of the ACM on Programming Languages, vol. 2(POPL), pp. 1–33 (2017)
30. King, D., Koutavas, V., Kovács, L.: LLM-Based generation of weakest preconditions and precise array invariants. In: Proceedings of the 13th IEEE/ACM International Conference on Formal Methods in Software Engineering, (FormaliSE@ICSE'25), pp. 1–5. IEEE (2025)
31. Kirchner, F., Kosmatov, N., Prevosto, V., Signoles, J., Yakobowski, B.: Frama-c: a software analysis perspective. Formal Aspects Comput. **27**(3), 573–609 (2015)
32. Komuravelli, A., Gurfinkel, A., Chaki, S.: SMT-based model checking for recursive programs. Formal Methods Syst. Des. **48**(3), 175–205 (2016). https://doi.org/10.1007/S10703-016-0249-4
33. Kremenek, T.: Finding software bugs with the clang static analyzer. Apple Inc **8**, 2008 (2008)
34. Krishna, M., Gaur, B., Verma, A., Jalote, P.: Using LLMs in software requirements specifications: an empirical evaluation. In: Preceedings of the 32nd IEEE International Requirements Engineering Conference (RE'24), pp. 475–483. IEEE (2024)
35. Larraz, D., Rodríguez-Carbonell, E., Rubio, A.: SMT-based array invariant generation. In: Giacobazzi, R., Berdine, J., Mastroeni, I. (eds.) Verification, Model Checking, and Abstract Interpretation, 14th International Conference, VMCAI 2013, Rome, Italy, 20-22 January 2013. Proceedings. Lecture Notes in Computer Science, vol. 7737, pp. 169–188. Springer (2013). https://doi.org/10.1007/978-3-642-35873-9_12
36. Lattner, C., Adve, V.: LLVM: A compilation framework for lifelong program analysis & transformation. In: Proceedings of the International Symposium on Code Generation and Optimization (CGO'04), pp. 75–86. IEEE Computer Society (2004)
37. Le-Cong, T., Le, B., Murray, T.: Can LLMs reason about program semantics? a comprehensive evaluation of LLMs on formal specification inference. In: Proceedings of the 63rd Annual Meeting of the Association for Computational Linguistics (ACL'25), pp. 21991–22014. Association for Computational Linguistics (2025)
38. Li, B., Tang, Z., Zhai, J., Zhao, J.: Automatic invariant synthesis for arrays in simple programs. In: 2016 IEEE International Conference on Software Quality, Reliability and Security (QRS), pp. 108–119. IEEE (2016)
39. Li, Y., Fu, H., Long, H., Li, G.: Constraint based invariant generation with modular operations. In: Bourke, T., Chen, L., Goharshady, A.K. (eds.) Dependable Software Engineering. Theories, Tools, and Applications - 10th International Symposium, SETTA 2024, Hong Kong, China, 26-28 November 2024, Proceedings. Lecture Notes in Computer Science, vol. 15469, pp. 64–84. Springer (2024). https://doi.org/10.1007/978-981-96-0602-3_4

40. Liu, C., Wu, X., Feng, Y., Cao, Q., Yan, J.: Towards general loop invariant generation: a benchmark of programs with memory manipulation. In: Annual Conference on Neural Information Processing Systems(NeurIPS'24). Advances in Neural Information Processing Systems, vol. 38 (2024)
41. Liu, H., Fu, H., Yu, Z., Song, J., Li, G.: Scalable linear invariant generation with Farkas' lemma. Proc. ACM Program. Lang. **6**(OOPSLA2), 204–232 (2022)
42. Liu, R., Chen, M., Wu, L., Ke, J., Li, G.: Enhancing automated loop invariant generation for complex programs with large language models. Sci. Comput. Program. **248**, 103387 (2026)
43. Lu, W., Ke, J., Fu, H., Sun, Z., Zhou, Y., Li, G., Li, H.: Array-carrying symbolic execution for function contract generation (2026). https://arxiv.org/abs/2602.23216
44. Ma, L., Liu, S., Li, Y., Xie, X., Bu, L.: SpecGen: automated generation of formal program specifications via large language models. In: Proceedings of the 47th IEEE/ACM International Conference on Software Engineering, (ICSE'25), pp. 16–28. IEEE (2025)
45. Maksimović, P., Ayoun, S.É., Santos, J.F., Gardner, P.: Gillian, part II: Real-world verification for javascript and c. In: Computer Aided Verification (CAV 2021), Proceedings, Part II. Lecture Notes in Computer Science, vol. 12760, pp. 827–850. Springer (2021). https://doi.org/10.1007/978-3-030-81688-9_38
46. McCloskey, B., Reps, T.W., Sagiv, M.: Statically inferring complex heap, array, and numeric invariants. In: Cousot, R., Martel, M. (eds.) Static Analysis - 17th International Symposium, SAS 2010, Perpignan, France, 14-16 September 2010. Proceedings. Lecture Notes in Computer Science, vol. 6337, pp. 71–99. Springer (2010). https://doi.org/10.1007/978-3-642-15769-1_6
47. openHiTLS Project: openhitls. https://github.com/openHiTLS/openHiTLS (2023), cryptography and TLS library, Accessed 27 Nov 2025
48. Pei, K., Bieber, D., Shi, K., Sutton, C., Yin, P.: Can large language models reason about program invariants? In: International Conference on Machine Learning (ICML'23). Proceedings of Machine Learning Research, vol. 202, pp. 27496–27520. PMLR (2023)
49. Pirzada, M.A.A., Reger, G., Bhayat, A., Cordeiro, L.C.: LLM-generated invariants for bounded model checking without loop unrolling. In: Proceedings of the 39th IEEE/ACM International Conference on Automated Software Engineering (ASE'24), pp. 1395–1407. ACM (2024)
50. Ramos, D.A., Engler, D.: Under-constrained symbolic execution: correctness checking for real code. In: USENIX Security (2015)
51. RSE-Verification: Auto-Deduct Toolchain: automated formal verification toolchain. https://github.com/rse-verification/auto-deduct-toolchain (2025), Accessed 30 Nov 2025 `cc41d5a602ab58dc997662530a8aa23efac36633`
52. RSE-Verification: Interface Specification Propagator (ISP): Frama-c plugin. https://github.com/rse-verification/interface-specification-propagator (2025), Accessed 30 Nov 2025
53. RSE-Verification: Saida: a frama-c plugin for ACSL contract verification. https://github.com/rse-verification/saida (2025), Accessed 30 Nov 2025
54. RSE-Verification: Tricera: A model checker for c programs (RSE-verification fork). https://github.com/rse-verification/tricera (2025), Accessed 30 Nov 2025
55. Santos, J.F., Maksimović, P., Ayoun, S.É., Gardner, P.: Gillian, part I: a multi-language platform for symbolic execution. In: Proceedings of the 41st ACM SIGPLAN International Conference on Programming Language Design and Implemen-

tation (PLDI 2020), pp. 927–942. ACM (2020). https://doi.org/10.1145/3385412.3386014
56. The LLVM Compiler Infrastructure: LLVM compiler infrastructure (2025). https://llvm.org, release 19.1.7
57. Uppsala University (uuverifiers): TriCera: a model checker for C programs. https://github.com/uuverifiers/tricera (2025), Accessed 30 Nov 2025
58. Wang, C., Lin, F.: Solving conditional linear recurrences for program verification: the periodic case. Proc. ACM Program. Lang. **7**(OOPSLA1), 28–55 (2023). https://doi.org/10.1145/3586028
59. Wen, C., et al.: Enchanting program specification synthesis by large language models using static analysis and program verification. In: Proceedings of the 36th International Conference on Computer Aided Verification (CAV'24) Part II. Lecture Notes in Computer Science, vol. 14682, pp. 302–328. Springer (2024)
60. Xie, D., et al.: How effective are large language models in generating software specifications? In: Proceedings of the 32nd IEEE International Conference on Software Analysis, Evolution and Reengineering (SANER'25), pp. 1–12. IEEE (2025)
61. Yao, P., Ke, J., Sun, J., Fu, H., Wu, R., Ren, K.: Demystifying template-based invariant generation for bit-vector programs. In: 38th IEEE/ACM International Conference on Automated Software Engineering, ASE 2023, Luxembourg, 11-15 September 2023, pp. 673–685. IEEE (2023). https://doi.org/10.1109/ASE56229.2023.00069

Incremental Synthesis of Safe Controller Guided by Learning-Enabled Barrier Certificates with Efficient LP Verification

Niuniu Qi[1], Hanrui Zhao[2], Zhengfeng Yang[1(✉)], Xia Zeng[3], Mengxin Ren[1], Chao Peng[1], and Zhiming Liu[3]

[1] Shanghai Key Lab of Trustworthy Computing, East China Normal University, Shanghai, China
jnaite@stu.ecnu.edu.cn, {zfyang,cpeng}@sei.ecnu.edu.cn

[2] College of Computer Science and Technology, National University of Defense Technology, Changsha, China
hrzhao@nudt.edu.cn

[3] School of Computer and Information Science, Southwest University, Chongqing, China
{xzeng0712,zhimingliu88}@swu.edu.cn

Abstract. Safe controller synthesis with formal guarantees is widely employed in safety-critical systems. However, existing controller synthesis methods are subject to significant limitations in scalability and efficiency. This paper presents a novel controller incremental synthesis framework guided by barrier certificates (BCs), thereby generating a safe controller with BC verification. To enhance verification efficiency, we construct a learning-enabled polynomial BC combined with efficient post-verification, which is transformed into smaller-scale linear Programming (LP) subproblems for feasibility determination. Furthermore, we have implemented a tool called *ISafeC* and evaluated its performance over a set of benchmark examples. The comparative experimental results demonstrate the effectiveness and efficiency of our approach.

Keywords: Formal verification · Controller synthesis · Reinforcement learning · Barrier certificate · Linear programming

1 Introduction

The design and synthesis of controllers for dynamical systems is a core challenge in control theory. Recent advances in deep learning have sparked significant research into applying Deep Neural Networks (DNNs) to control safety-critical systems, such as unmanned aerial vehicles, robotics and self-driving cars [2,20, 24]. In these applications, one of the most critical challenges is the synthesis of safety controllers with formal guarantees, that is, designing controllers to formally ensure that system trajectories avoid undesirable unsafe regions.

N. Qi and H. Zhao—These authors contributed equally to this work.

A. Sampaio and M. Stoelinga (Eds.): FM 2026, LNCS 16556, pp. 419–439, 2026.
https://doi.org/10.1007/978-3-032-26204-2_22

Many studies leverage the powerful simulation and representation capabilities of deep reinforcement learning (DRL) to define reward functions based on user-specified desired system behaviors, thereby enabling the learning of effective controllers [13,38]. However, controllers learned from a limited set of sampled trajectories fundamentally lack formal safety guarantees for the entire state space. To address this deficiency, especially for guaranteeing safety over infinite time horizons [21,25,29,45], Barrier Certificates (BCs) offer a powerful, formal verification approach [31]. Fundamentally, a BC is a state function that separates the reachable safe region from the unsafe region in the state space. As the existence of a BC serves as a formal witness to system safety, the synthesis of such a certificate is a prerequisite for verifying the controller [9,10,53].

Initial research explored joint synthesis methods, where the controller and the BC are learned simultaneously [10,53], followed by a formal verification step. However, these approaches suffer from poor convergence properties and high computational complexity, limiting their scalability to complex systems. Consequently, many researchers shifted to a phased training framework, first pre-training a controller, and then learning the BC in a separate stage [37,43,51,52]. While this partially alleviated convergence problems, the approach yields only modest success rates: a failure in BC generation or post-verification provides no actionable guidance for refining the initial, decoupled controller. To overcome these obstacles, verification-in-the-loop frameworks have been adopted due to their potential for better efficiency and guidance. These methods operate iteratively: they fix one component (either the BC or the controller) and then iteratively refine the other component based on the verification conditions to achieve a safe controller with formal guarantees. Although the framework represents progress, these methods universally face two fundamental challenges. First, the framework fails to consider the inherent co-existence requirements between the controller and the BC. Since the initial fixed component might not have a corresponding safe partner, iterative refinement is ineffective, leaving the design of a unified framework for co-synthesis as a significant challenge. Second, the framework's reliance on computationally expensive formal methods (e.g., Satisfiability Modulo Theories (SMT) or sum-of-squares (SOS) solvers) for verification in every iteration results in prohibitive computational overhead, limiting applicability to high-dimensional systems and mandating the urgent need for an efficient and scalable verification mechanism.

In this paper, we present a novel *Incremental Co-Synthesis* framework for safe controller synthesis refined by BCs. This framework achieves verifiable safety for nonlinear systems through the alternating refinement of the controller and the BC. The scheme operates in an iterative loop: it begins by deriving an easily verifiable initial polynomial controller, followed by formulating a learnable polynomial BC. Once the BC fails the verification, we construct a Quadratic Programming (QP) problem based on the BC conditions to incrementally refine the controller. This alternating process ensures that both the controller and the BC are actively refined toward a simultaneously feasible safe state, guaranteeing the synthesis of a provably safe controller. In the verification phase, we employ the theory of Krivine-Vasilescu-Handelman's (KVH) Positivstellensatz [26] to transform the verification conditions of the candidate BC into a tractable Linear Programming (LP) problem. Compared with SMT/SOS-based approaches, our LP-based method offers significantly lower computational complexity, enabling faster and more scalable verification. We have developed a prototype tool, *ISafeC*, for synthesizing safe controllers, and its efficiency, scalability, and practicability are demonstrated through extensive benchmark experiments.

The paper is organized as follows. Section 2 describes the connection between safety controller verification and BC generation. Section 3 introduces an Incremental safety controller synthesis approach guided by BCs. In Sect. 4, we present an experimental evaluation of our algorithm over a set of benchmark examples. We compare with related works in Sect. 5 before concluding in Sect. 6.

2 Preliminaries

Notations. Let $\mathbb{R}$ and $\mathbb{N}$ be the set of real number and natural number, respectively. The symbol $\mathbb{R}[\mathbf{x}] := \mathbb{R}[x_1, \ldots, x_n]$ represents the ring of polynomials with coefficients in $\mathbb{R}$ over variables $\mathbf{x} = [x_1, \ldots, x_n]^T$, and $\mathbb{R}[\mathbf{x}]^m$ denotes the polynomial ring over an m-dimensional vector space. $\mathbb{R}[\mathbf{x}]_d$ is the set consisting of all real polynomials in $\mathbf{x}$ with degree at most d. The degree of the polynomial $f(\mathbf{x})$ is denoted by $\deg(f(\mathbf{x}))$. $\mathbf{x}^\alpha = x_1^{\alpha_1} x_2^{\alpha_2} \cdots x_n^{\alpha_n}$ is a monomial, where $\deg(\alpha)$ denotes the degree of the monomial $\mathbf{x}^\alpha$.

A dynamical system is modeled by a first-order ordinary differential equation:

$$\dot{\mathbf{x}} = \mathbf{f}(\mathbf{x}, \mathbf{u}), \tag{1}$$

where $\mathbf{x} \in \mathcal{X} \subseteq \mathbb{R}^n$ is the state of the system, $\dot{\mathbf{x}}$ denotes the derivative of $\mathbf{x}$ with respect to time t, $\mathbf{f} = (f_1, \ldots, f_n)^T$ is the vector field on the state space $\mathcal{X} \subset \mathbb{R}^n$, and $\mathbf{u} \in \mathcal{U} \subseteq \mathbb{R}^m$ is the control input. We assume that $\mathbf{f}$ and $\mathbf{u}$ satisfy the local Lipschitz condition, so that (1) has a unique solution $\mathbf{x}(t, \mathbf{x}_0)$ for any initial state $\mathbf{x}_0 = \mathbf{x}(0) \in \mathcal{X}$ at time $t = 0$.

In many contexts, a *constrained continuous dynamical system* (CCDS) $\mathcal{C} \doteq (\mathbf{f}, \Theta, \Phi)$ is equipped with a domain $\Phi \subseteq \mathcal{X}$ and an initial region $\Theta \subseteq \Phi$. If all trajectories of the system $\mathcal{C}$ starting from the initial region Θ can not evolve into any prespecified unsafe region $\Xi \subseteq \mathcal{X}$, then the system $\mathcal{C}$ is safe. Next, we provide the formal definition of system safety as follows.

Definition 1 (Safety). *For a CCDS $\mathcal{C} \doteq (\mathbf{f}, \Theta, \Phi)$ with an unsafe region Ξ and control input $\mathbf{u} = \mathbf{k}(\mathbf{x})$, the system $\mathcal{C}$ is safe if each trajectory of $\mathcal{C}$ starting from Θ never reaches Ξ. Specifically, for all $\mathbf{x}_0 \in \Theta$, there exists no time $t_1 > 0$ such that $\forall t \in [0, t_1].\mathbf{x}(t, \mathbf{x}_0) \in \Phi$ and $\mathbf{x}(t_1, \mathbf{x}_0) \in \Xi$.*

According to Definition 1, the problem we considered in this paper is formulated as follows.

Problem 1 **(Safe Controller Synthesis).** For a controlled CCDS $\mathcal{C} \doteq (\mathbf{f}, \Theta, \Phi)$ with an unsafe region Ξ, design a locally Lipschitz continuous feedback control law $\mathbf{u} = \mathbf{k}(\mathbf{x})$ such that the system $\mathcal{C}$ with $\mathbf{f}(\mathbf{x}, \mathbf{k}(\mathbf{x}))$ is safe as per Definition 1.

The concept of barrier certificates (BCs) [31] plays an important role in safety verification of continuous systems. The basic idea is to identify a real-valued function $B(\mathbf{x})$ that maps all reachable states to non-negative real values and all states in the unsafe region to negative values. The BCs concept, derived from [31], can be utilized to ensure the safety of the given controlled CCDS.

Theorem 1 (Barrier Certificate [31]). *Given a controlled CCDS* $\mathcal{C} \doteq (\mathbf{f}, \Theta, \Phi)$ *with an unsafe region* Ξ *and feedback control law* $\mathbf{u} = \mathbf{k}(\mathbf{x})$, *if there exists a real-valued function* $B : \Phi \to \mathbb{R}$ *such that the following conditions hold:*

(i) $\forall \mathbf{x} \in \Theta. B(\mathbf{x}) \geq 0$;
(ii) $\forall \mathbf{x} \in \Xi. B(\mathbf{x}) < 0$;
(iii) $\forall \mathbf{x} \in \Phi. \mathcal{L}_f B(\mathbf{x}) - \lambda B(\mathbf{x}) > 0$, *where* $\mathcal{L}_f B(\mathbf{x})$ *represents the Lie-derivative of* $B(\mathbf{x})$ *along the vector field* $\mathbf{f}(\mathbf{x})$, *i.e.,* $\mathcal{L}_f B(\mathbf{x}) = \sum_{i=1}^{n} \frac{\partial B}{\partial x_i} \cdot f_i(\mathbf{x})$,

then the safety of $\mathcal{C}$ *is guaranteed. The* $B(\mathbf{x})$ *is called a barrier certificate of the system* $\mathcal{C}$ *with the control law* $\mathbf{k}(\mathbf{x})$.

For simplicity, the regions Θ, Φ, and Ξ in Problem 1 are assumed to be semi-algebraic sets, defined as:

$$\begin{aligned} \Theta &:= \{\mathbf{x} \in \mathbb{R}^n \mid \theta_1(\mathbf{x}) \geq 0, \ldots, \theta_\iota(\mathbf{x}) \geq 0\}, \\ \Phi &:= \{\mathbf{x} \in \mathbb{R}^n \mid \phi_1(\mathbf{x}) \geq 0, \ldots, \phi_\kappa(\mathbf{x}) \geq 0\}, \\ \Xi &:= \{\mathbf{x} \in \mathbb{R}^n \mid \xi_1(\mathbf{x}) \geq 0, \ldots, \xi_\nu(\mathbf{x}) \geq 0\}, \end{aligned}$$

where θ_i, ϕ_j and ξ_k are polynomials. In this work, we consider the control input $\mathbf{u}$ to be one-dimensional for ease of presentation without loss of generality.

3 An Incremental Scheme of Safe Controller Synthesis

For safe controller synthesis in safety-critical systems, learning-based techniques demonstrate significant advantages, but their application comes at the cost of lacking formal safety guarantees, necessitating complex post-verification. Conversely, utilizing polynomial networks directly for learning exhibits poor convergence in simulation and limited scalability for complex examples. Although one might attempt to inherit the benefits of learning by employing polynomial approximation to capture the control effect of the learned DNN—thereby enabling subsequent verification via polynomial optimization—this strategy faces significant drawbacks: the approximation cannot guarantee quantified precision, and simultaneously, the safety of the resulting polynomial controller does not guarantee the existence of a formal Barrier Certificate (BC). To address these issues, we design a special BC-guided incremental controller iteration method that simultaneously mitigates reliance on the initial polynomial approximation precision and leverages an efficient LP solver to obtain the BC for guiding the compensatory update of the current controller effect. We present an iterative framework called *ISafeC* for synthesizing controllers with safety guarantees for nonlinear dynamical systems, which establishes an inductive loop between a Controller Refiner and a BC Generator (See Fig. 1).

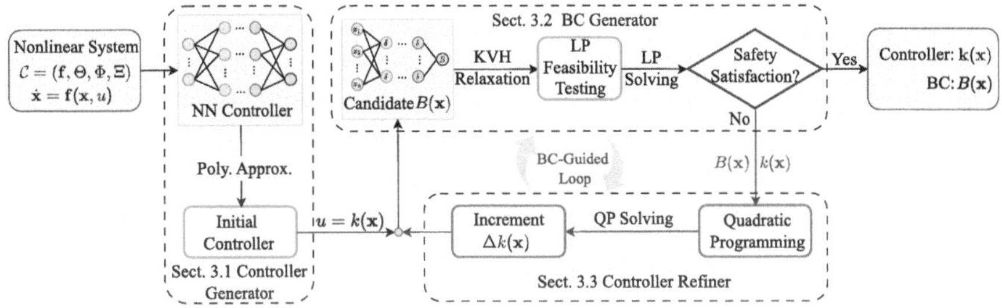

Fig. 1. ISafeC: the framework of incremental synthesis of safe controller.

- **Initial Controller Synthesis.** The mainstream PPO RL algorithm is employed to pretrain a well-performing DNN controller that satisfies the safety requirements of the closed-loop system underlying the DNN controller. Then, a low-degree polynomial is used to approximate the DNN controller by minimizing the squared error, thereby obtaining the polynomial controller $k(\mathbf{x})$.
- **Barrier Certificate Generation.** A specialized NN is employed to fit a polynomial $B(\mathbf{x})$ over a finite sample set. Leveraging the KVH Positivstellensatz, the validity of the $B(\mathbf{x})$ is transformed into three LP feasibility testing subproblems for solving, thereby enabling effective system safety verification.
- **Controller Refinement Guided by BC.** If the yield $B(\mathbf{x})$ fails to satisfy the BC conditions, the spurious $B(\mathbf{x})$ can be used to guide the refinement of the controller $k(\mathbf{x})$. Formally, the refinement of the controller is formulated as a quadratic programming problem based on current $B(\mathbf{x})$ and $k(\mathbf{x})$, which is then solved to incrementally update $k(\mathbf{x})$ by $k(\mathbf{x}) + \Delta k(\mathbf{x})$. The BC network is retrained under the updated controller for the next verification round.

3.1 Initial Polynomial Controller Synthesis

As illustrated in Fig. 1, the RL method is used to train a well-performing DNN controller, enabling the system to avoid obstacles. A low-degree polynomial is then employed to approximate the DNN controller, facilitating the formal verification of safety properties.

Pre-training DNN Controllers via Reinforcement Learning. In this part, we focus on the process of training a safe controller using the PPO algorithm, which is a popular reinforcement learning approach suited for continuous control systems. Specifically, the training process involves interaction with the environment using the current policy to collect samples of current states, actions, rewards, and next states, i.e., quadruples $(\mathbf{x}_t, k_t, reward(\mathbf{x}_t), \mathbf{x}_{t+1})$. By estimating the advantage function of the state-action pair through sampled data, a probability ratio clipping mechanism is introduced into the objective function to constrain the magnitude of policy updates, ensuring training stability. This process iteratively optimizes both the policy and value networks until the desired performance criteria are met or the specified number of iterations is reached.

To ensure good controller performance, the training objective is to prevent any trajectory that starts in the initial set Θ from entering the unsafe region Ξ. A reward function is defined by a joint Gaussian distribution on the system states to measure safety-compliant behaviors, that is, $reward_u(\mathbf{x}_t) = -\prod_{i=1}^{n} e^{-\frac{1}{2}(\frac{x_i(t)-x_{i_u}}{\rho_{i_u}})^2}$, where $\mathbf{x}_u = (x_{1_u}, \ldots, x_{n_u}) \in \Xi$ is the center of Ξ and $\rho_u = (\rho_{1_u}, \ldots, \rho_{n_u})$ is the radius of Ξ.

In the training phase, we first generate a set of initial states from Θ. For each sampled initial state $\mathbf{x}_0$, with the help of controller network, one may yield the corresponding trajectory as a discrete sequence of states $\{\mathbf{x}_0, \ldots, \mathbf{x}_t, \ldots, \mathbf{x}_m\}$ that avoids entering the unsafe region Ξ. Then, transition tuples $(\mathbf{x}_t, k_t, reward(\mathbf{x}_t),\ \mathbf{x}_{t+1})$ are collected and stored in a replay buffer. At regular intervals, a batch of data is sampled from the replay buffer to update the parameters of the policy and value networks. By simulating new trajectories with the updated controller, additional data is used to refine the policy iteratively until the controller achieves satisfactory performance.

Polynomial Approximation of DNN Controllers. Due to the difficulty of formally verifying DNN controllers, we adopt a verifiable polynomial controller as an alternative. Existing methods typically involve polynomial inclusion, where a polynomial is used to approximate the controller, and the Lipschitz constant is leveraged to achieve polynomial inclusion [11,51]. The focus of this paper is on the first step of this process, which involves obtaining an effective approximation of the DNN controller via Least-Squares (LS) method, and its error will be compensated through subsequent iterations.

Given sampling points, a polynomial controller $k(\mathbf{x}, \mathbf{c})$ of degree d can be obtained by solving the LS problem, i,e., $k(\mathbf{x}, \mathbf{c}) = \sum_j c_j \mathbf{x}^{\alpha_j}$, where $\mathbf{c}$ represents the vector composed of coefficients c_j. Due to the exponential growth in the number of terms in $k(\mathbf{x}, \mathbf{c})$ as d increases, we employ low-degree polynomials for fitting to mitigate computational overhead. Specifically, we generate a sufficient number of sample points chosen randomly from Θ, and further produce a series of discrete trajectories under the influence of the system $\mathcal{C}$ and the controller $k(\mathbf{x})$. To better fit the DNN controller, we construct a set $\mathcal{S}$ consisting of enough samples from these trajectories, namely, $|\mathcal{S}| \geq \binom{n+d}{d}$. At this point, by utilizing the sample points in $\mathcal{S}$, the optimal coefficients $\mathbf{c}^*$ can be obtained by solving the LS problem. Then we can obtain a polynomial controller $u = k(\mathbf{x})$.

3.2 Learning-Enabled Barrier Certificate Generation with LP Identification

For a learned controller, the verification of its safety typically relies on the synthesis of barrier certificates (BCs). The prevalent approach to generating BCs involves first learning a candidate BC, and subsequently performing a post-verification based on the prescribed BC conditions [10,50,51]. However, the use of methods like SMT or Sum-of-Squares (SOS) relaxations for this post-verification phase presents challenges in terms of efficiency and scalability. To address this issue, we propose a learning-enabled BC synthesis method with linear programming (LP) identification.

Candidate Barrier Certificate Generation. To facilitate the verification of learning BCs, we propose constructing a BC neural network with polynomial activation. Unlike the linear structure of skip connections in Residual Neural Networks (ResNet) (as shown in Fig. 2(a)), we adopt a variant of this structure, where the Hadamard product of the primary network $f(\mathbf{x})$ and the auxiliary network $g(\mathbf{x})$ is used as the input to the next layer. This effectively enhances the expressive capability of the BC network and allows for the generation of polynomial BC expressions of arbitrary degree (see Fig. 2(b)).

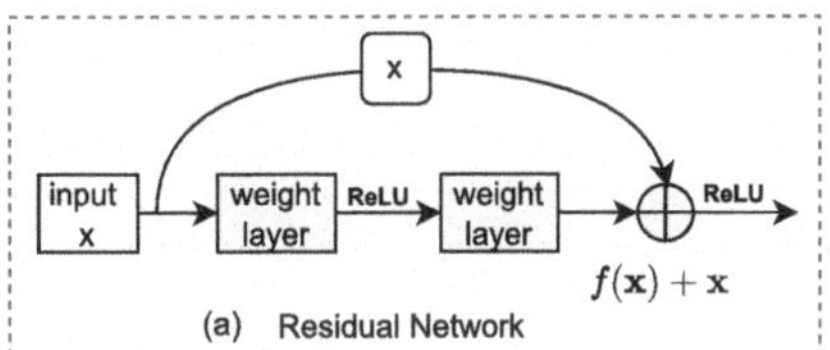

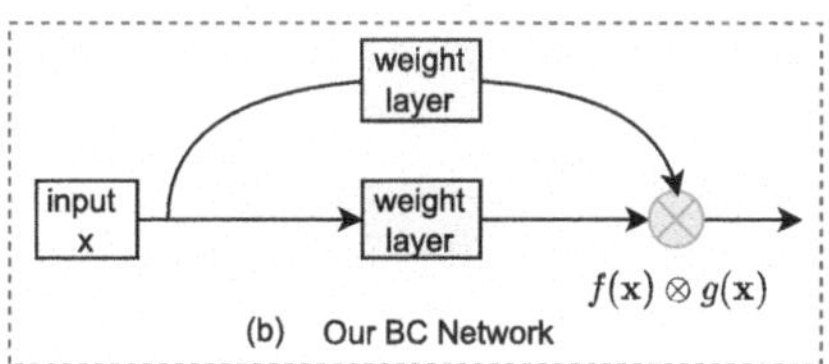

Fig. 2. Residual network structure and our barrier certificate network structure. $f(\mathbf{x})$ and $g(\mathbf{x})$ denote the primary network and the auxiliary network, respectively.

We consider the BC network as a feedforward NN consisting of an input layer $\mathbf{x}_{(0)} \in \mathbb{R}^n$, $l-1$ hidden layers, and a non-activated output layer $x_{(l)}$, where n denotes the dimension of the system $\mathcal{C}$. Let $\overline{W}_{(i)} \in \mathbb{R}^{k_i \times k_{i-1}}$ and $\bar{b}_{(i)} \in \mathbb{R}^{k_i}$ denote the weight matrix and the bias from the $(i-1)$-th layer to the i-th layer, respectively, where $k_i \in \mathbb{N}^+$ is the number of nodes in the i-th hidden layer. $\widetilde{W}_{(i)} \in \mathbb{R}^{k_i \times k_0}$ denotes the weight matrix multiplied by the input $\mathbf{x}_{(0)}$ of 1-th layer, and $\tilde{b}_{(i)} \in \mathbb{R}^{k_i}$ is the corresponding bias. Then the NN can be expressed as

$$\mathbf{x}_{(i)} = (\overline{W}_{(i)}\mathbf{x}_{(i-1)} + \bar{b}_{(i)}) \otimes (\widetilde{W}_{(i)}\mathbf{x}_{(0)} + \tilde{b}_{(i)}),\ 1 \le i \le l,$$

where $\otimes$ denotes the Hadamard product. This formulation yields a polynomial $B(\mathbf{x})$ as the output of the neural BC network.

During the training phase, datasets S_Θ, S_Ξ and S_Φ are constructed by randomly sampling points from the regions Θ, Ξ, and Φ, respectively. Following

Theorem 1, we construct an empirical loss function L_{BC} to measure the extent of violation of the three BC existence conditions, namely,

$$\begin{aligned} L_{BC} =& \frac{w_1}{|S_\Theta|} \sum_{s_\theta \in S_\Theta} \max\{\epsilon, -B(s_\theta)\} + \frac{w_2}{|S_\Xi|} \sum_{s_\xi \in S_\Xi} \max\{\epsilon, B(s_\xi)\} \\ &+ \frac{w_3}{|S_\Phi|} \sum_{s_\phi \in S_\Phi} \max\{\epsilon, -(\mathcal{L}_f B(s_\phi) - \lambda B(s_\phi))\}, \end{aligned}$$

where the positive tuning parameters w_1, w_2 and w_3 are introduced to balance the influence of the losses of the three conditions (i)-(iii) in Theorem 1. ϵ is a small positive constant introduced to enforce strict inequality satisfaction, enhancing the robustness of NN. During training, the loss function L_{BC} decreases gradually as the parameters are updated, which leads to improved satisfaction of the conditions and a more reliable candidate BC.

Barrier Certificate Identification by LP Solving. Since the previously trained BC is derived from a limited number of uniformly sampled points from the regions Θ, Ξ, and Φ, the candidate $B(\mathbf{x})$ may not strictly satisfy the three conditions (i)-(iii) in Theorem 1. Therefore, it is necessary to verify whether the candidate $B(\mathbf{x})$ satisfies these conditions. This paper replaces the SOS representation with the non-negativity conditions of polynomials on compact semi-algebraic sets, providing a computationally efficient alternative. This reformulation enables us to introduce new sufficient verification conditions for constructing BCs for dynamical systems and to transform the safety verification problem into a more tractable LP problem.

Let $\mathbb{S}$ be a compact semi-algebraic set defined by

$$\mathbb{S} = \{\mathbf{x} \in \mathbb{R}^n | h_1(\mathbf{x}) \geq 0, \ldots, h_m(\mathbf{x}) \geq 0\}, \tag{2}$$

where $h_j(\mathbf{x}) \in \mathbb{R}[\mathbf{x}]$, $j = 1, \ldots, m$. Define $\tilde{h}_j(\mathbf{x})$ as the normalized polynomial $h_j(\mathbf{x})$ with respect to $\mathbb{S}$, i.e.,

$$\tilde{h}_j(\mathbf{x}) = \begin{cases} h_j(\mathbf{x})/p_j^*, & \text{if } \ p_j^* > 0, \\ h_j(\mathbf{x}), & \text{otherwise}, \end{cases} \tag{3}$$

where $p_j^* = \max_{\mathbf{x} \in \mathbb{S}} h_j(\mathbf{x})$. For convenience, we denote the polynomial vector by $\tilde{\mathbf{h}} = [\tilde{h}_1(\mathbf{x}), \ldots, \tilde{h}_m(\mathbf{x}), 1 - \tilde{h}_1(\mathbf{x}), \ldots, 1 - \tilde{h}_m(\mathbf{x})]^T$, and $\tilde{\mathbf{h}}^\alpha = \prod_{j=1}^m \tilde{h}_j^{\alpha_j}(\mathbf{x})(1 - \tilde{h}_j(\mathbf{x}))^{\alpha_{j+m}}$ represents the polynomial product form. Now we can obtain another representation for non-negative polynomials on $\mathbb{S}$.

Lemma 1 *(KVH Positivstellensatz* [26]*). Let $\mathbb{S}$ be a compact semi-algebraic set defined as in (2). Suppose $\tilde{h}_j(\mathbf{x})$ is the normalized polynomial of $h_j(\mathbf{x})$ as in (3) for each j. Assume the family $\{\tilde{h}_j(\mathbf{x}), 1 - \tilde{h}_j(\mathbf{x})\}_{j=0}^m$ spans $\mathbb{R}[\mathbf{x}]$ with $\tilde{h}_0(\mathbf{x}) \equiv 1$. If $g(\mathbf{x}) > 0$ on $\mathbb{S}$, then $g(\mathbf{x})$ can be represented as:*

$$g(\mathbf{x}) = \sum_{\alpha \in \mathbb{N}^{2m}} c_\alpha \prod_{j=1}^m \tilde{h}_j^{\alpha_j}(\mathbf{x})(1 - \tilde{h}_j(\mathbf{x}))^{\alpha_{j+m}}, \quad c_\alpha \geq 0. \tag{4}$$

Lemma 1 provides a necessary and sufficient condition for $f(\mathbf{x}) > 0$ on the semi-algebraic set $\mathbb{S}$. However, generating this representation involves an infinite number of polynomial products in (4), making it computationally challenging. To address this, we introduce a degree bound D to provide sufficient conditions for polynomial non-negativity on $\mathbb{S}$.

Theorem 2. *Let $\mathbb{S}$ be a compact semi-algebraic set defined as in (2), and $\tilde{h}_j(\mathbf{x})$ be the normalized polynomial $h_j(\mathbf{x})$ as in (3) for each j. If there exists a positive integer D such that $f(\mathbf{x}) = \sum_{\deg(\tilde{\mathbf{h}}^\alpha)\leq D} c_\alpha \tilde{\mathbf{h}}^\alpha$, where $c_\alpha \geq 0$, then $f(\mathbf{x})$ is non-negative on $\mathbb{S}$.*

Proof. Due to $\tilde{h}_j(\mathbf{x})$ is the normalized polynomial with respect to $\mathbb{S}$, then $\tilde{h}_j(\mathbf{x})$ and $1 - \tilde{h}_j(\mathbf{x})$ are nonnegative on $\mathbb{S}$ for each j, then $\tilde{\mathbf{h}}^\alpha \geq 0$. If there exists a degree D such that the equation $f(\mathbf{x}) = \sum_{\deg(\tilde{\mathbf{h}}^\alpha)\leq D} c_\alpha \tilde{\mathbf{h}}^\alpha$ holds, it can be concluded that $f(\mathbf{x})$ is non-negative on $\mathbb{R}[\mathbf{x}]$.

According to Lemma 1 and Theorem 2, the safe verification conditions in Theorem 1 can be reformulated as the non-negativity conditions of polynomials on compact semi-algebraic sets. Now, let's illustrate with an example how to transform the verification condition into its corresponding nonnegative representation.

Example 1. Consider the first verification condition (i) in Theorem 1, $\forall \mathbf{x} \in \Theta. B(\mathbf{x}) \geq 0$. Let $\tilde{\theta}_i(\mathbf{x})$ be the normalized polynomial of $\theta_i(\mathbf{x})$ with respect to Θ for each $i, 1 \leq i \leq \iota$. Let $\tilde{\boldsymbol{\theta}}$ be the normalized polynomial vector

$$\tilde{\boldsymbol{\theta}} = [\tilde{\theta}_1, \ldots, \tilde{\theta}_\iota, 1 - \tilde{\theta}_1, \ldots, 1 - \tilde{\theta}_\iota]^T.$$

Following Theorem 2, $\forall \mathbf{x} \in \Theta. B(\mathbf{x}) \geq 0$ can beconverted into the conservative one with the given degree bound $D \in \mathbb{Z}_{>0}$, i.e.,

$$B(\mathbf{x}) = \sum_{\deg(\tilde{\boldsymbol{\theta}}^\alpha)\leq D} c_\alpha \tilde{\boldsymbol{\theta}}^\alpha, c_\alpha \in \mathbb{R}_{\geq 0} \Rightarrow \forall \mathbf{x} \in \Theta. B(\mathbf{x}) \geq 0.$$

Following Example 1, we next present a more manageable verification condition for the barrier certificates of controlled CCDS. For convenience, we use $\tilde{\boldsymbol{\theta}}$, $\tilde{\boldsymbol{\phi}}$, $\tilde{\boldsymbol{\xi}}$ to represent the normalized polynomial vectors with respect to Θ, Φ and Ξ, respectively.

Theorem 3. *Given a controlled $\mathcal{C} \doteq (\mathbf{f}, \Theta, \Phi)$ with an unsafe state set Ξ. Let $B(\mathbf{x})$ be a given polynomial and D be a positive integer. If there exist λ and non-negative scalars c_α, c_β, c_γ, along with positive constants ϵ_1 and ϵ_2, such that the following conditions hold:*

(i) $B(\mathbf{x}) = \sum_{\deg(\tilde{\boldsymbol{\theta}}^\alpha)\leq D} c_\alpha \tilde{\boldsymbol{\theta}}^\alpha$,
(ii) $-B(\mathbf{x}) - \epsilon_1 = \sum_{\deg(\tilde{\boldsymbol{\xi}}^\beta)\leq D} c_\beta \tilde{\boldsymbol{\xi}}^\beta$,
(iii) $\mathcal{L}_f B(\mathbf{x}) - \lambda B(\mathbf{x}) - \epsilon_2 = \sum_{\deg(\tilde{\boldsymbol{\phi}}^\gamma)\leq D} c_\gamma \tilde{\boldsymbol{\phi}}^\gamma$,

then $B(\mathbf{x})$ is a barrier certificate of system $\mathcal{C}$, and the safety of $\mathcal{C}$ is guaranteed.

Proof. Theorem 2 indicates that the conditions (i – iii) can imply the conditions (i – iii) in Theorem 1, respectively. Thus, the safety of the system $\mathcal{C}$ is proved.

Stated as above, $B(\mathbf{x})$ is a known polynomial yielded from learning, the conditions in Theorem 3 can be equivalently formulated as the following three subproblems, which can be solved in parallel:

$$\left.\begin{array}{ll}\text{find} & c_\alpha \\ \text{s.t.} & B(\mathbf{x}) = \sum_{\deg(\tilde{\theta}^\alpha)\le D} c_\alpha \tilde{\boldsymbol{\theta}}^\alpha, c_\alpha \ge 0\end{array}\right\}, \tag{5}$$

$$\left.\begin{array}{ll}\text{find} & c_\beta \\ \text{s.t.} & -B(\mathbf{x}) - \epsilon_1 = \sum_{\deg(\tilde{\xi}^\beta)\le D} c_\beta \tilde{\boldsymbol{\xi}}^\beta, c_\beta \ge 0\end{array}\right\}, \tag{6}$$

$$\left.\begin{array}{ll}\text{find} & c_\gamma, \lambda \\ \text{s.t.} & \mathcal{L}_f B(\mathbf{x}) - \lambda B(\mathbf{x}) - \epsilon_2 = \sum_{\deg(\tilde{\phi}^\gamma)\le D} c_\gamma \tilde{\boldsymbol{\phi}}^\gamma, c_\gamma \ge 0\end{array}\right\}, \tag{7}$$

where ϵ_1 and ϵ_2 are positive constants.

By examining the optimization problems (5), we can rewrite the equality constraints as a Linear Programming (LP) problems with variables $\mathbf{c}_\alpha$ by ordering the coefficients of variable $\mathbf{x}$:

$$\left.\begin{array}{ll}\text{find} & \mathbf{c}_\alpha \\ \text{s.t.} & A \cdot \mathbf{c}_\alpha \ge \mathbf{b}\end{array}\right\}, \tag{8}$$

where A and $\mathbf{b}$ represent a numerical matrix and a vector, respectively. Similarly, the feasibility problems of conditions (ii) and (iii) can also be transformed into LP problems in the form of (8).

The problem (8) can be solved using either the interior-point method or the Gurobi solver [17]. If problems (5) – (7) yield feasible solutions, $B(\mathbf{x})$ is confirmed as a real BC, thereby verifying the safety of the system $\mathcal{C}$. Otherwise, the candidate $B(\mathbf{x})$ is used to guide the refinement of the controller.

Complexity Analysis. We now analyze the complexity of the post-verification method based on LP solving. Let n denote the number of state variables of the system $\mathcal{C}$. The LP problem (8) has a predetermined degree bound D. Assume that the maximum number of polynomials defining the compact semi-algebraic sets in domains Θ, Ξ, and Φ of $\mathcal{C}$ is bounded by p_s. Therefore, the number of the decision variables in (8) is $\mathcal{V} = \binom{2p_s+D}{D}$. The number of constraints is $\mathcal{C} = \binom{n+D}{D} + \binom{2p_s+D}{D}$, where the first term is the number of equality constraints (5) associated with $\mathbf{c}_\alpha$, and the second one is the number of nonnegative constraints of $\mathbf{c}_\alpha$. The complexity of an LP solved by interior-point algorithms is well known to be approximately $O(\mathcal{V}^2\mathcal{C})$ [32]. Therefore, the complexity based on the LP solver is approximately $O(p_s^{2D}n^D)$. Similarly, the complexity of converting problems (6) and (7) into the corresponding LP problems for solution is also approximately $O(p_s^{2D}n^D)$. Therefore, the total time complexity of the post-verification process is approximately $O(p_s^{2D}n^D)$.

3.3 Controller Refinement Guided by Barrier Certificate

For the initial controller $\tilde{k}(\mathbf{x})$, if any of the LP problems in the form of (8) corresponding to conditions (i)–(iii) in Theorem 3 fail to yield a feasible solution, we cannot guarantee that the system $\mathcal{C}$ with the controller $\tilde{k}(\mathbf{x})$ is safe. Through extensive experiments, we have observed that conditions (i) and (ii) for generating the BC in Theorem 1 are relatively easy to verify, whereas condition (iii) is more stringent and challenging to satisfy. Therefore, we focus on how to use the current candidate $B(\mathbf{x})$ to guide the refinement of the controller $\tilde{k}(\mathbf{x}) + \Delta k(\mathbf{x})$ based on Lie derivative condition, aiming to satisfy the safety requirements. Here, we parametrize the unknown controller increment $\Delta k(\mathbf{x})$ by a polynomial, i.e., $\Delta k(\mathbf{x}, \mathbf{c}) = \sum_j c_j \mathbf{x}^{\alpha_j}$.

Specifically, the goal is to find a controller $k(\mathbf{x}) = \tilde{k}(\mathbf{x}) + \Delta k(\mathbf{x}, \mathbf{c})$ that satisfies $\sum_{i=1}^{n} \frac{\partial B}{\partial x_i} \cdot f_i(\mathbf{x}, k(\mathbf{x})) - \lambda B(\mathbf{x}) > 0$. Considering that the expected variation of $k(\mathbf{x})$ as small as possible, the refinement of the controller can be expressed as

$$\left.\begin{array}{ll} \min & \|\mathbf{c}\|_2 \\ \text{s.t.} & \sum\limits_{i=1}^{n} \frac{\partial B}{\partial x_i} \cdot f_i(\mathbf{x}, \tilde{k}(\mathbf{x}) + \Delta k(\mathbf{x}, \mathbf{c})) - \lambda B(\mathbf{x}) > 0 \qquad \forall \mathbf{x} \in \Phi \end{array}\right\}. \tag{9}$$

The constraints in (9) involve universal quantifiers, which makes the direct solution of the problem for a controller $k(\mathbf{x})$ that satisfies the Lie derivative condition with respect to the given $B(\mathbf{x})$ challenging. To avoid the direct elimination of these universal quantifiers, we propose a relaxation technique based on sampling points. Specifically, for Φ, let us first construct rectangular meshes in Φ with a mesh spacing $\gamma \in \mathbb{R}$ (say $\gamma = 0.05$). The resulting mesh point sets are denoted as Ω_Φ. It is known that for a continuously differentiable function $B(\mathbf{x})$ over a compact domain Φ, the mean value theorem yields that $|B(\mathbf{x} + \Delta \mathbf{x}) - B(\mathbf{x})| \leq n\eta |\Delta \mathbf{x}|_\infty$, where $\mathbf{x}, \Delta \mathbf{x} \in \Omega_\Phi$ are chosen randomly, $\eta = \sup_{\mathbf{x} \in \Phi} \|\nabla B(\mathbf{x})\|_\infty$. Then (9) can be relaxed as the following quadratic programming (QP) problem:

$$\left.\begin{array}{ll} \min & \|\mathbf{c}\|_2 \\ \text{s.t.} & \sum\limits_{i=1}^{n} \frac{\partial B}{\partial x_i} \cdot f_i(\mathbf{x}_j, \tilde{k}(\mathbf{x}_j) + \Delta k(\mathbf{x}_j, \mathbf{c})) - \lambda B(\mathbf{x}_j) + \epsilon > 0 \end{array}\right\}, \tag{10}$$

where $j = 1, \ldots, \Omega_\Phi$. To ensure that problem (10) has a feasible solution, we set $\epsilon = n\eta\gamma$. The matrix form of (10) can be represented as

$$\left.\begin{array}{ll} \min & \|\mathbf{c}\|_2 \\ \text{s.t.} & M \cdot [\lambda, \mathbf{c}^T]^T \succcurlyeq \mathbf{v} \end{array}\right\} \tag{11}$$

with variables λ and $\mathbf{c}$, where M and $\mathbf{v}$ represent the numerical matrix and vector, respectively. Therefore, we can efficiently solve problem (11) using Gurobi solver to obtain the refined controller $\tilde{k}(\mathbf{x})+\Delta k(\mathbf{x},\mathbf{c})$, and then continue training the BC to verify the safety of the updated controller.

The detailed procedure for the method is summarized in Algorithm 1.

Algorithm 1. ISafeC: Incremental Synthesis of Safe Controllers

Input: CCDS $\mathcal{C} := (\mathbf{f}, \Theta, \Phi)$; unsafe set Ξ; maximum number of iterations $maxIter$
Output: A real barrier certificate $B(\mathbf{x})$ and a controller u
1: Initialize $Iter \leftarrow 0$;
2: Train the DNN controller k_{NN} by the PPO RL algorithm;
3: Obtain the polynomial controller $k(\mathbf{x})$ by polynomial approximation of k_{NN};
4: **while** $Iter < maxIter$ **do**
5: Learn a $B(\mathbf{x})$ using Supervised Learning;
6: Set up the LP feasibility testing problems of the form (8) and call an LP solver to determine the feasibilities;
7: **if** the three LP subproblems in the form of (8) are feasible **then**
8: **return** barrier certificate $B(\mathbf{x})$ and controller $u = k(\mathbf{x})$;
9: **else**
10: Obtain $\Delta k(\mathbf{x})$ by constructing and solving the QP problem of the form (11) based on the candidate $B(\mathbf{x})$ and $k(\mathbf{x})$;
11: Update $k(\mathbf{x}) \leftarrow k(\mathbf{x}) + \Delta k(\mathbf{x})$;
12: Update $Iter \leftarrow Iter + 1$;
13: **end if**
14: **end while**
15: **return** ISafeC fails to find a safe controller.

The algorithm iteratively executes within a given maximum number of iterations. It begins by obtaining k_{NN} using RL, followed by polynomial approximation to derive an initial controller $k(\mathbf{x})$. Subsequently, supervised learning is employed to synthesize a candidate $B(\mathbf{x})$, and LP problems of the form (8) are solved to verify feasibility. If a feasible solution is not found, a QP problem (11) is solved to update $k(\mathbf{x})$, repeating this process until a safe controller is obtained or the program terminates.

Theorem 4 *(Soundness). If $B(\mathbf{x})$ and u are the function produced by Algorithm 1, then $B(\mathbf{x})$ satisfies all the BC conditions for the system $\mathcal{C}$ with controller u stated in Theorem 1.*

Proof. Consider a CCDS $\mathcal{C}$. By using RL and polynomial approximation, an verifiable initial controller is obtained. For the safety verification of the controller, a data-driven approach is used to model the BC as a polynomial network, which is then trained to obtain $B(\mathbf{x})$. The satisfiability of the candidate BC is then encoded as LP problems via the KVH Positivstellensatz. In Line 6 of Algorithm 1, we need to solve three LP problems of the form (8) to identify a real BC over the entire state space. If a feasible solution exists, it indicates that $B(\mathbf{x})$ is a real

BC, ensuring the safety of the controlled system. Otherwise, the current spurious-BC is used to guide refinement of the controller u in Line 10–12. Algorithm 1 will return a safe controller u with a real BC $B(\mathbf{x})$ within a finite number of iterations.

Remark 1. During the post-verification of the BC, if conditions (i) and (ii) in Theorem 3 are not satisfied, this indicates that the current BC is insufficiently trained. In this case, we retrain the BC network to generate a new candidate certificate and continue the safety verification. If only condition (iii) is violated, we utilize the candidate BC to guide the incremental refinement of the controller.

4 Experiments

We implemented a safe controller synthesis tool called *ISafeC* based on Algorithm 1. In this section, we first show our method by synthesizing a safety controller for the Van der Pol Oscillator system, and then compare *ISafeC* with other tools: *Fossil 2.0* [10], *NNcontroller* [53] and *SNBC* [51]. All experiments are conducted on a 2.5GHz AMD Ryzen 9 7945HX CPU under Windows 11 with 32GB RAM. The *ISafeC* code is available at https://github.com/mxrush129/ISafeC. The associated parameters necessary for the implementation of each example are also available in the aforementioned link.

Van der Pol Oscillator. [46] Consider the following nonlinear system:

$$\begin{bmatrix} \dot{x} \\ \dot{y} \end{bmatrix} = \begin{bmatrix} y \\ (1 - x^2)y - x + u \end{bmatrix}.$$

The system domain is defined as

$$\Phi = \{\mathbf{x} = [x, y]^T \in \mathbb{R}^2 | -1 \le x \le 0.5, -0.2 \le y \le 0.8\}.$$

Our goal is to design a control law $u = k(x, y)$ such that all system trajectories, starting from the initial region

$$\Theta = \{\mathbf{x} = [x, y]^T \in \mathbb{R}^2 | -0.51 \le x \le -0.49, 0.49 \le y \le 0.51\},$$

will never enter the unsafe region

$$\Xi = \{\mathbf{x} = [x, y]^T \in \mathbb{R}^2 | -0.4 \le x \le 0.1, 0.2 \le y \le 0.35\}.$$

We first apply the PPO algorithm to train a DNN controller and approximate it as a 2-degree initial polynomial controller $u_1 = 0.165x^2 - 0.171xy + 0.030x - 0.017y^2 - 0.678y$. Then, we learn a candidate BC for u_1 given by $B_1(x, y) = -9.121x^2 + 9.511xy - 5.915x - 10.117y^2 + 1.366y + 2.351$. However, $B_1(x, y)$ does not satisfy verification conditions. Therefore, we apply controller refinement guided by $B_1(x, y)$ to produce the updated controller $u_2 = 1.870x^2 - 1.863xy - 4.410x + 2.621y^2 + 3.225y - 0.146$. After two iterations, we finally identify u_2 as a safe controller with a real BC $B_2(x, y) = -9.115x^2 + 15.176xy - 6.150x -$

$7.039y^2 - 0.793y + 4.035$, which can provide the safety guarantee of the closed-loop system underlying the obtained controller u_2.

Comparison with Existing Approaches. Our *ISafeC* was implemented in Python, and was compared with three tools *Fossil 2.0*, *NNcontroller* and *SNBC* over a set of benchmarks from the literature on controller synthesis. Note that *Fossil 2.0* synthesis controllers using the CEGIS procedure with SMT post-verification. The tool *NNcontroller* jointly trains the controller network and the BC network, and uses iSAT3 for post-verification. *SNBC* performs a polynomial over-approximation of the DNN controller, trains a neural BC using the DDPG algorithm, and verifies the validity of the BC via LMI-based sum-of-squares (SOS) programming. Among these benchmark examples, $\mathrm{Ex1_{NP}}$-$\mathrm{Ex3_{NP}}$ are non-polynomial systems, and $\mathrm{Ex1_{P}}$-$\mathrm{Ex9_{P}}$ are polynomial systems. For $\mathrm{Ex1_{NP}}$-$\mathrm{Ex3_{NP}}$, we employ polynomial approximation with parameterization to enable verification using *ISafeC*. The results are shown in Table 1.

In Table 1, $n_{\mathbf{x}}$ denotes the number of system variables, $d_{\mathbf{f}}$ represents the maximum degree of polynomials in the vector field, and $Iters$ represents the number of iterations. ψ specifies the optimal activation function used for BC learning in *Fossil 2.0*, T denotes the total amount spent time. "OT" signifies failing to yield a safe controller after 600 s. The symbol "NA" denotes the impossibility of returning a safe controller.

Table 1. Performance Evaluation (time in seconds)

Ex.	$n_{\mathbf{x}}$	$d_{\mathbf{f}}$	*ISafeC*		*Fossil 2.0* [10]			*NNcontroller*	*SNBC*
			$Iters$	T	ψ	$Iters$	T		
$\mathrm{Ex1_{NP}}$ [37]	2	3	1	1.24	*Tanh*	2	**0.22**	25.34	NA
$\mathrm{Ex2_{NP}}$ [55]	2	2	2	**3.73**	*ReLU*	2	4.13	201.67	NA
$\mathrm{Ex3_{NP}}$ [43]	2	3	2	**0.64**	–	–	OT	3.47	NA
$\mathrm{Ex1_{P}}$ [46]	2	3	1	0.27	*ReLU*	1	**0.03**	9.07	0.29
$\mathrm{Ex2_{P}}$ [9]	3	2	1	0.21	*Tanh*	6	**0.18**	562.86	1.16
$\mathrm{Ex3_{P}}$ [6]	3	3	1	0.30	*Square*	2	**0.06**	OT	0.47
$\mathrm{Ex4_{P}}$ [7]	4	3	1	**0.67**	$Poly_2$	2	10.76	OT	0.84
$\mathrm{Ex5_{P}}$ [33]	5	2	2	**2.04**	$Poly_2$	2	16.50	OT	6.93
$\mathrm{Ex6_{P}}$ [46]	6	2	1	**1.09**	*ReLU*	2	22.77	OT	16.82
$\mathrm{Ex7_{P}}$ [22]	7	2	1	**1.58**	*Tanh*	4	178.08	OT	223.76
$\mathrm{Ex8_{P}}$ [22]	9	2	3	**11.82**	–	–	OT	OT	360.19
$\mathrm{Ex9_{P}}$ [12]	12	1	5	**92.75**	–	–	OT	OT	OT

Comparison with Joint Training Methods: Table 1 shows that *ISafeC* successfully handles all 12 examples, whereas *Fossil 2.0* succeeds on only 9 of them. In these 9 examples, *Fossil 2.0* takes an average of 25.86 seconds, whereas *ISafeC* completes the task in 1.24 seconds, making it 20.85 times faster than *Fossil*

2.0. The *NNcontroller* can only handle nonlinear systems with fewer than four dimensions. For the seven examples Ex3_P-Ex9_P, we were unable to synthesize a safe controller within the specified time limit despite multiple attempts with different network architectures. For systems with dimensions less than 4, *ISafeC* requires slightly more time than *Fossil 2.0*. However, for examples Ex4_P-Ex9_P, *Fossil 2.0* exhibits poor convergence, requiring significantly more iterations than our *ISafeC*. Therefore, for higher-dimensional systems (e.g., Ex4_P-Ex9_P), *ISafeC* demonstrates substantial performance improvements. In contrast, the method proposed in this paper demonstrates superior scalability and computational efficiency when dealing with high-dimensional systems.

Comparison with Pre-training and Post-Verification Method: As shown in Table 1, *SNBC* fails to handle non-polynomial systems but is capable of processing 8 polynomial systems (Ex1_P – Ex8_P) within the given time limit. To compare the efficiency of the *ISafeC* and *SNBC*, we consider the average time required to synthesize safe controllers for Ex1_P – Ex8_P. *SNBC* takes 76.31 seconds on average, whereas *ISafeC* accomplishes them in 2.25 seconds, achieving a 33.92 times faster than *SNBC*. The experimental results also show that, for most examples, *ISafeC* either obtains an almost-safe controller in the first iteration or refines the controller through the BC and converges in fewer than 5 iterations. This performance indicates that *ISafeC* is efficient and practical.

Evaluation for the Performance of the LP Post-verfication. To demonstrate the effectiveness of the proposed post-verification technique based on the KVH Positivstellensatz, we compare its performance with that of a verification scheme utilizing semidefinite programming (SDP) solvers [5]. The experimental results are presented in Table 2. BC_LP denotes the BC generation method proposed in this paper, which is based on learning and LP solvers, whereas BC_SDP refers to a BC generation method based on learning and SDP solvers.

Table 2. Performance Evaluation of Verification Technique (time in seconds)

Ex.	Ex1_NP	Ex2_NP	Ex3_NP	Ex1_P	Ex2_P	Ex3_P	Ex4_P	Ex5_P	Ex6_P	Ex7_P	Ex8_P	Ex9_P
BC_LP	0.92	2.29	0.02	0.02	0.07	0.09	0.50	0.19	0.35	0.43	6.58	88.16
BC_SDP	0.63	0.64	0.62	0.19	0.42	0.44	0.94	3.33	5.36	5.68	43.51	120.74

As evidenced by the experimental results in Table 2, our method exhibits longer computation times compared to BC_SDP for non-polynomial examples. Especially in Ex2_NP, the reason is that two rounds of iterative refinement are required, and a relatively large polynomial degree needs to be set for the post-verification. For polynomial systems, the proposed LP-based post-verification technique is more efficient, requiring less computation time than the SDP solution constructed via SOS relaxation. In particular, our method achieves a 17.53 speedup over BC_SDP in Ex5_P. Overall, the post-verification method based on LP solving demonstrates efficiency compared to the SDP-based solving method.

5 Related Work

Our work on synthesizing safe controllers for nonlinear systems guided by BCs is mainly related to two categories of research, i.e. safety verification of nonlinear systems and safety controller synthesis. There has been considerable research conducted on safety-critical systems in recent years.

Safety Verification of Nonlinear Systems. The safety requirements for nonlinear systems have been primarily addressed by existing works focused on reachability set computation, aiming to estimate the reachable region of the system through under-approximation or over-approximation techniques [14,15,35,40–42]. Recently, reachability set computation techniques have been further advanced, resulting in the development of a series of verification tools, including ReachNN [11], RINO [16], POLAR [18], Verisig 2.0 [19], CORA [23] and NNV 2.0 [27]. However, these methods are limited to state evolution within a finite time horizon. Another approach to verifying system safety properties is the synthesis of BCs, which can provide safety guarantees over an infinite time horizon. Theoretically, the generation of BCs presents a similarity to other problems involving the elimination of quantifiers. Existing methods typically employ relaxation techniques to formulate the BC generation problem as a convex optimization problem for solution [28,30,31]. In addition, combining NN learning with verification for BCs synthesis represents an emerging research direction [1,3,39,54]. However, the complexity of this SMT-based post-verification technique is relatively high, and its scalability is limited. Some researchers have proposed encoding the feasibility determination problem of BCs into an LMI problem using SOS relaxation techniques for post-verification, thereby improving verification efficiency and practicality [49,50]. However, for high-dimensional systems, the verification efficiency still requires further improvement. In this paper, we adopt an LP-based post-verification method.

Safety Controller Synthesis. In safe controller synthesis, a class of traditional approaches involves jointly training the controller and the BC to obtain a controller with safety guarantees [10,53]. For instance, Zhao et al. [53] proposed a method to ensure design correctness, which first applies supervised learning to simultaneously learn a DNN controller and a BC, followed by formal verification of the BC using an SMT solver. Unfortunately, this joint training approach exhibits poor convergence properties for neural networks. Therefore, many researchers have proposed using RL or supervised learning to construct an overall learning framework for synthesizing safety certificates [4,8,9,34,36,44]. Deshmukh et al. [9] presented a verification-in-the-loop DNN controller training algorithm, which integrates the RL framework with the reward function encoding of user-provided Control Barrier Functions (CBFs) and performs formal CBF verification based on SMT. Yang et al. [44] proposed an iterative method for sequentially synthesizing controllers and BCs, where the DNN controller and the corresponding BC are alternately synthesized, and the BC is updated during the iteration process to guide the retraining of the safe controller. Subsequently, many researchers have shifted towards a staged training framework, where a controller is first pre-trained, followed by the generation of a BC to verify the safety of the controlled system [43,47,48,51]. For example, Yang et al. [43] proposed a hybrid polynomial-DNN controller synthesis method combining RL, low-degree polynomial fitting, and knowledge distillation, with formal verification via BCs and Lyapunov-like functions. Zhao et al. [51] construct a polynomial inclusion of the DNN controller and propose a counterexample-guided BC synthesis procedure that provides formal safety guarantees. In this paper, our approach employs a learning-enabled BC to guide the incremental refinement of the controller, ultimately synthesizing a safe controller that is certified by a BC.

6 Conclusion

This paper proposes a BC-guided incremental controller synthesis framework, in which a high-performance DNN controller is first trained via RL algorithm, and then performs polynomial approximation of the controller to facilitate safety verification. Meanwhile, we propose an efficient LP-based verification method. This approach constructs a polynomial NN to generate candidate BCs, and then decomposes the feasibility testing problem of BCs into three LP subproblems for solution. If the BC satisfies the safety conditions, a controller with safety guarantees can be obtained. Otherwise, the controller is incrementally refined under the guidance of the candidate BC. Experimental results have confirmed the scalability and effectiveness of our approach.

Acknowledgments. This work was supported in part by the National Key Research and Development Program of China under Grant 2023YFA1009402; in part by the National Natural Science Foundation of China under Grant 62472362 and Grant 62272397; and in part by the Fundamental Research Funds for the Central Universities under Grant 40500-20104-222609.

References

1. Abate, A., Ahmed, D., Edwards, A., Giacobbe, M., Peruffo, A.: Fossil: a software tool for the formal synthesis of Lyapunov functions and barrier certificates using neural networks. In: Proceedings of the 24th HSCC, pp. 1–11 (2021)
2. Al-lQubaydhi, N., et al.: Deep learning for unmanned aerial vehicles detection: a review. Comput. Sci. Rev. **51**, 100614 (2024)
3. Alavi, A., Nadali, A., Zamani, M., Jafarpour, S.: Neural barrier certificates for monotone systems. IEEE Control. Syst. Lett. **9**, 1496–1501 (2025)
4. Ames, A.D., Coogan, S., Egerstedt, M., Notomista, G., Sreenath, K., Tabuada, P.: Control barrier functions: theory and applications. In: 17th European Control Conference, ECC 2019, Naples, Italy, June 25-28, 2019, pp. 3420–3431 (2019). https://doi.org/10.23919/ECC.2019.8796030
5. Andersen, E.D., Andersen, K.D.: The MOSEK interior point optimizer for linear programming: an implementation of the homogeneous algorithm. In: High Performance Optimization, pp. 197–232. Springer (2000)

6. Chen, X., Peng, C., Lin, W., Yang, Z., Zhang, Y., Li, X.: A novel approach for solving the BMI problem in barrier certificates generation. In: Lahiri, S.K., Wang, C. (eds.) CAV 2020. LNCS, vol. 12224, pp. 582–603. Springer, Cham (2020). https://doi.org/10.1007/978-3-030-53288-8_29
7. Chesi, G.: Computing output feedback controllers to enlarge the domain of attraction in polynomial systems. IEEE Trans. Autom. Control **49**(10), 1846–1853 (2004)
8. Compton, W.D., Cohen, M.H., Ames, A.D.: Learning for layered safety-critical control with predictive control barrier functions. In: 7th Annual Learning for Dynamics & Control Conference, Ann Arbor, MI, USA, 4-6 June 2025. vol. 283, pp. 153–165 (2025). https://proceedings.mlr.press/v283/compton25a.html
9. Deshmukh, J.V., Kapinski, J., Yamaguchi, T., Prokhorov, D.V.: Learning deep neural network controllers for dynamical systems with safety guarantees: Invited paper. In: Proceedings of the International Conference on Computer-Aided Design, ICCAD 2019, Westminster, CO, USA, November 4-7, 2019, pp. 1–7 (2019). https://doi.org/10.1109/ICCAD45719.2019.8942130
10. Edwards, A., Peruffo, A., Abate, A.: Fossil 2.0: Formal certificate synthesis for the verification and control of dynamical models. In: International Conference on Hybrid Systems: Computation and Control, HSCC, pp. 26:1–26:10 (2024)
11. Fan, J., Huang, C., Chen, X., Li, W., Zhu, Q.: ReachNN: a tool for reachability analysis of neural-network controlled systems. In: Automated Technology for Verification and Analysis - 18th International Symposium, ATVA. vol. 12302, pp. 537–542 (2020). https://doi.org/10.1007/978-3-030-59152-6_30
12. Gao, S.: Quadcopter model (2016). https://github.com/dreal/benchmarks
13. García, J., Fernández, F.: A comprehensive survey on safe reinforcement learning. J. Mach. Learn. Res. **16**, 1437–1480 (2015)
14. Goubault, E., Mullier, O., Putot, S., Kieffer, M.: Inner approximated reachability analysis. In: 17th International Conference on Hybrid Systems: Computation and Control (part of CPS Week), HSCC'14, Berlin, Germany, April 15-17, 2014, pp. 163–172 (2014). https://doi.org/10.1145/2562059.2562113
15. Goubault, E., Putot, S.: Forward inner-approximated reachability of non-linear continuous systems. In: Proceedings of the 20th International Conference on Hybrid Systems: Computation and Control, HSCC 2017, Pittsburgh, PA, USA, April 18-20, 2017, pp. 1–10 (2017). https://doi.org/10.1145/3049797.3049811
16. Goubault, E., Putot, S.: RINO: robust inner and outer approximated reachability of neural networks controlled systems. In: Computer Aided Verification - 34th International Conference, CAV, Haifa, Israel, August 7-10, 2022, Proceedings, Part I. vol. 13371, pp. 511–523 (2022). https://doi.org/10.1007/978-3-031-13185-1_25
17. Gurobi Optimization, LLC: Gurobi Optimizer Reference Manual (2023). https://www.gurobi.com/documentation/
18. Huang, C., Fan, J., Chen, X., Li, W., Zhu, Q.: POLAR: a polynomial arithmetic framework for verifying neural-network controlled systems. In: Automated Technology for Verification and Analysis - 20th International Symposium, ATVA 2022, Virtual Event, October 25-28, 2022, Proceedings. Lecture Notes in Computer Science, vol. 13505, pp. 414–430 (2022). https://doi.org/10.1007/978-3-031-19992-9_27
19. Ivanov, R., Carpenter, T., Weimer, J., Alur, R., Pappas, G., Lee, I.: Verisig 2.0: verification of neural network controllers using Taylor model preconditioning. In: Silva, A., Leino, K.R.M. (eds.) CAV 2021. LNCS, vol. 12759, pp. 249–262. Springer, Cham (2021). https://doi.org/10.1007/978-3-030-81685-8_11
20. Jiang, F., Wang, Z., Yue, G.: A novel cognitively inspired deep learning approach to detect drivable areas for self-driving cars. Cogn. Comput. **16**(2), 517–533 (2024)

21. Kamaldar, M., Hoagg, J.B.: Lyapunov-like functions for almost global convergence in discrete-time systems. Syst. Control Lett. **188**, 105807 (2024)
22. Kelley, R.: Systems biology in practice: concepts, implementation, and application. IEEE Eng. Med. Biol. Mag. **26**(6), 9–54 (2007)
23. Kochdumper, N., Schilling, C., Althoff, M., Bak, S.: Open- and closed-loop neural network verification using polynomial zonotopes. In: NASA Formal Methods - 15th International Symposium, NFM, Houston, TX, USA, May 16-18, 2023, Proceedings. vol. 13903, pp. 16–36 (2023). https://doi.org/10.1007/978-3-031-33170-1_2
24. Komoda, K., et al.: Hybrid-AI grasp planning system that integrates rule-based and DNN-based methods for throughput improvement of picking robots. In: IEEE International Conference on Advanced Intelligent Mechatronics, AIM, Boston, MA, USA, July 15-19, 2024, pp. 691–696 (2024). https://doi.org/10.1109/AIM55361.2024.10636988
25. Kumar, D., Raj, J., Raghuwaiya, K., Vanualailai, J.: Lyapunov-controlled quadrotor landings on dynamic mobile platforms. IEEE Access **13**, 60570–60588 (2025)
26. Lasserre, J.B.: Polynomial programming: LP-relaxations also converge. SIAM J. Optim. **15**(2), 383–393 (2005)
27. Lopez, D.M., Choi, S.W., Tran, H., Johnson, T.T.: NNV 2.0: the neural network verification tool. In: Computer Aided Verification - 35th International Conference, CAV 2023, Paris, France, July 17-22, 2023, Proceedings, Part II. Lecture Notes in Computer Science, vol. 13965, pp. 397–412 (2023). https://doi.org/10.1007/978-3-031-37703-7_19
28. Papachristodoulou, A., Anderson, J., Valmorbida, G., Prajna, S., Seiler, P., Parrilo, P.A.: SOSTOOLS version 3.00 sum of squares optimization toolbox for MATLAB. CoRR **abs/1310.4716** (2013). http://arxiv.org/abs/1310.4716
29. Patil, O.S., Le, D.M., Griffis, E.J., Dixon, W.E.: Lyapunov-based deep residual neural network (ResNet) adaptive control. IEEE Access **13**, 117943–117952 (2025)
30. Prajna, S., Jadbabaie, A.: Safety verification of hybrid systems using barrier certificates. In: Alur, R., Pappas, G.J. (eds.) HSCC 2004. LNCS, vol. 2993, pp. 477–492. Springer, Heidelberg (2004). https://doi.org/10.1007/978-3-540-24743-2_32
31. Prajna, S., Jadbabaie, A., Pappas, G.J.: A framework for worst-case and stochastic safety verification using barrier certificates. IEEE Trans. Autom. Control **52**(8), 1415–1428 (2007)
32. S. Boyd, L.V.: Convex optimization. Cambridge University Press (2004)
33. Sassi, M.A.B., Sankaranarayanan, S.: Stabilization of polynomial dynamical systems using linear programming based on Bernstein polynomials (2015)
34. Saveriano, M., Lee, D.: Learning barrier functions for constrained motion planning with dynamical systems. In: 2019 IEEE/RSJ International Conference on Intelligent Robots and Systems, IROS 2019, Macau, SAR, China, November 3-8, 2019, pp. 112–119 (2019). https://doi.org/10.1109/IROS40897.2019.8967981
35. Serry, M., Liu, J.: Underapproximating safe domains of attraction for discrete-time systems using implicit representations of backward reachable sets. IEEE Control. Syst. Lett. **8**, 2709–2714 (2024)
36. Srinivasan, M., Dabholkar, A., Coogan, S., Vela, P.A.: Synthesis of control barrier functions using a supervised machine learning approach. In: IEEE/RSJ International Conference on Intelligent Robots and Systems, IROS 2020, Las Vegas, NV, USA, October 24, 2020 - January 24, 2021, pp. 7139–7145 (2020). https://doi.org/10.1109/IROS45743.2020.9341190

37. Tuncali, C.E., Kapinski, J., Ito, H., Deshmukh, J.V.: Reasoning about safety of learning-enabled components in autonomous cyber-physical systems. In: Proceedings of the 55th Annual Design Automation Conference, DAC, San Francisco, CA, USA, June 24-29, 2018, pp. 30:1–30:6 (2018). https://doi.org/10.1145/3195970.3199852
38. Turchetta, M., Kolobov, A., Shah, S., Krause, A., Agarwal, A.: Safe reinforcement learning via curriculum induction. In: Advances in Neural Information Processing Systems 33: Annual Conference on Neural Information Processing Systems (2020)
39. Wang, Y., Chen, H., Lin, W., Ding, Z.: Formal synthesis of neural barrier certificates for dynamical systems via DC programming. IEEE Trans. Comput. Aided Des. Integr. Circuits Syst. **44**(10), 4038–4042 (2025)
40. Xiang, W., Tran, H., Johnson, T.T.: Reachable set computation and safety verification for neural networks with RELU activations. CoRR **abs/1712.08163** (2017). http://arxiv.org/abs/1712.08163
41. Xue, B., She, Z., Easwaran, A.: Under-approximating backward reachable sets by polytopes. In: Chaudhuri, S., Farzan, A. (eds.) CAV 2016. LNCS, vol. 9779, pp. 457–476. Springer, Cham (2016). https://doi.org/10.1007/978-3-319-41528-4_25
42. Xue, B., She, Z., Easwaran, A.: Underapproximating backward reachable sets by semialgebraic sets. IEEE Trans. Autom. Control **62**(10), 5185–5197 (2017)
43. Yang, Z., Zhang, L., Zeng, X., Tang, X., Peng, C., Zeng, Z.: Hybrid controller synthesis for nonlinear systems subject to reach-avoid constraints. In: Computer Aided Verification - 35th International Conference, CAV, Paris, France, July 17-22, 2023, Proceedings, Part I. vol. 13964, pp. 304–325 (2023). https://doi.org/10.1007/978-3-031-37706-8_16
44. Yang, Z., et al.: An iterative scheme of safe reinforcement learning for nonlinear systems via barrier certificate generation. In: Silva, A., Leino, K.R.M. (eds.) CAV 2021. LNCS, vol. 12759, pp. 467–490. Springer, Cham (2021). https://doi.org/10.1007/978-3-030-81685-8_22
45. Yao, J., Han, M., Yin, X.: Lyapunov-based distributed reinforcement learning control with stability guarantee. Comput. Chem. Eng. **195**, 108979 (2025)
46. Zeng, X., Lin, W., Yang, Z., Chen, X., Wang, L.: Darboux-type barrier certificates for safety verification of nonlinear hybrid systems. In: 2016 International Conference on Embedded Software, EMSOFT 2016, Pittsburgh, Pennsylvania, USA, October 1-7, 2016, pp. 11:1–11:10 (2016). https://doi.org/10.1145/2968478.2968484
47. Zeng, X., Liu, B., Zeng, Z., Liu, Z., Yang, Z.: Safe controller synthesis for nonlinear systems via reinforcement learning and PAC approximation. In: Proceedings of the 61st ACM/IEEE Design Automation Conference, DAC, San Francisco, CA, USA, 23–27 June 2024, pp. 283:1–283:6 (2024). https://doi.org/10.1145/3649329.3657332
48. Zeng, X., Ren, M., Liu, Z., Yang, Z.: Learning-aided safe controller synthesis with formal guarantees via vector barrier certificates. In: 62nd ACM/IEEE Design Automation Conference, DAC, San Francisco, CA, USA, June 22-25, 2025, pp. 1–7 (2025). https://doi.org/10.1109/DAC63849.2025.11132490
49. Zhao, H., Liu, B., Dehbi, L., Xie, H., Yang, Z., Qian, H.: Polynomial neural barrier certificate synthesis of hybrid systems via counterexample guidance. IEEE Trans. Comput. Aided Des. Integr. Circuits Syst. **43**(11), 3756–3767 (2024)
50. Zhao, H., Qi, N., Dehbi, L., Zeng, X., Yang, Z.: Formal synthesis of neural barrier certificates for continuous systems via counterexample guided learning. ACM Trans. Embed. Comput. Syst. **22**(5s), 146:1–146:21 (2023)

51. Zhao, H., Qi, N., Ren, M., Zeng, X., Zeng, Z., Yang, Z.: Neural barrier certificates synthesis of NN-controlled continuous systems via counterexample-guided learning. In: Proceedings of the 61st ACM/IEEE Design Automation Conference, DAC. p. 6 (2024). https://doi.org/10.1145/3649329.3658256
52. Zhao, H., Zeng, X., Qi, N., Yang, Z., Zeng, Z.: Safe DNN-type controller synthesis for nonlinear systems via meta reinforcement learning. In: 60th ACM/IEEE Design Automation Conference, DAC, San Francisco, CA, USA, July 9-13, 2023, pp. 1–6 (2023). https://doi.org/10.1109/DAC56929.2023.10247837
53. Zhao, H., Zeng, X., Chen, T., Liu, Z., Woodcock, J.: Learning safe neural network controllers with barrier certificates. Formal Aspects Comput. **33**(3), 437–455 (2021). https://doi.org/10.1007/s00165-021-00544-5
54. Zhao, Q., Chen, X., Zhao, Z., Zhang, Y., Tang, E., Li, X.: Verifying neural network controlled systems using neural networks. In: HSCC '22: 25th ACM International Conference on Hybrid Systems: Computation and Control, Milan, Italy, May 4 - 6, 2022, pp. 3:1–3:11 (2022). https://doi.org/10.1145/3501710.3519511
55. Zhu, H., Xiong, Z., Magill, S., Jagannathan, S.: An inductive synthesis framework for verifiable reinforcement learning. In: Proceedings of the 40th ACM SIGPLAN Conference on Programming Language Design and Implementation, PLDI, Phoenix, AZ, USA, June 22-26, 2019, pp. 686–701 (2019). https://doi.org/10.1145/3314221.3314638

Specializing Anti-unification for Interaction Models Composition via Gate Connections

Joel Nguetoum[1,2,(✉)], Boutheina Bannour[1], Pascale Le Gall[2], and Erwan Mahe[1]

[1] Université Paris-Saclay, CEA, List, Palaiseau 91120, France
christian.nguetoumkenne@cea.fr
[2] Université Paris-Saclay, CentraleSupélec, MICS, Gif-sur-Yvette 91192, France

Abstract. Interaction models describe distributed systems as algebraic terms, with gates marking interaction points between local views. Composing local models into a coherent global one requires aligning these gates while respecting the algebraic laws of interaction operators. This is achieved via anti-unification techniques. We specialize anti-unification (or generalization) via a special constant-preserving variant, which preserves designated constants while generalizing the remaining structure. We develop a dedicated rule-based procedure, for computing these generalizations, prove its termination, soundness, and completeness, extend it modulo equational theories, and integrate it into a standard anti-unification framework. A prototype tool demonstrates the approach's ability to recompose global interactions from partial views.

1 Introduction

Context. Our goal is to use anti-unification to merge partial views of a distributed system into a coherent global view. The notion of *anti-unification* (or *generalization*) was introduced independently by Plotkin [31] and Reynolds [33] as the process of computing the most specific generalization of a set of terms. Given two terms s and t, the task is to find a term r and substitutions σ_s and σ_t such that $r\sigma_s = s$ and $r\sigma_t = t$. This contrasts with *unification* [25], which seeks a substitution σ such that $s\sigma = t\sigma$. While unification computes a common instance, anti-unification computes a *most specific/least general generalization* (lgg) from which the original terms can be recovered. Anti-unification has applications in recursion-scheme detection [16], inductive synthesis of recursive functions [37], and automated software repair [10,35]. However, most existing work focuses on *syntactic* generalization. *Semantics-driven* approaches [8,19] leverage semantic equivalences between terms to be able to anti-unify a wider class of terms.

Interactions [28] describe distributed systems via atomic *emission* and *reception* actions and the empty behavior $\varnothing$ which are structured by *weak-sequencing* (seq), *alternative* (alt) and *parallel* (par) composition, as well as *repetition* (loop). Interactions are related to *Multiparty Session Types* [22,36] and can be drawn

A. Sampaio and M. Stoelinga (Eds.): FM 2026, LNCS 16556, pp. 440–460, 2026.
https://doi.org/10.1007/978-3-032-26204-2_23

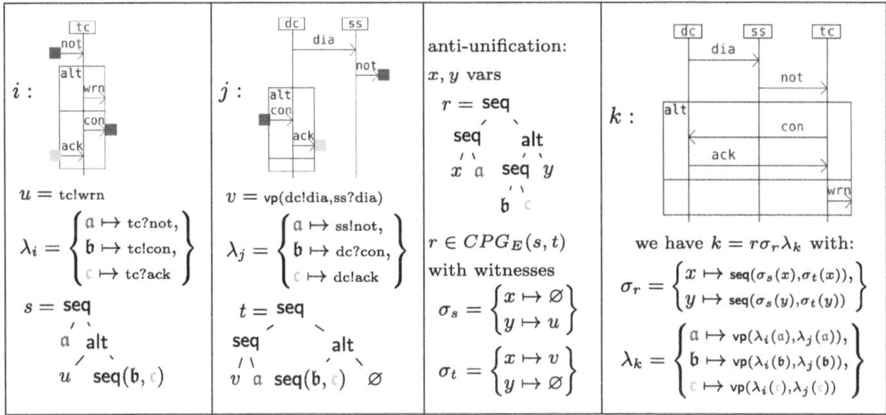

Fig. 1. Composing interactions i and j into k.

in the manner of *Message Sequence Charts* [1] or *UML sequence diagrams* [2]. The diagram on the right of Fig. 1 depicts an interaction k. Operators are represented by boxes, with seq being implicit and time flowing from top to bottom. Vertical lines, called *lifelines*, represent individual subsystems (here, a signaling server ss, a dialing client dc, and a target client tc). Horizontal arrows represent value passing (vp). Here, dc dials ss (via message dia), which then notifies tc (not). Finally, tc can either (represented by alt) refuse the connection and warn another system (wrn) not shown here, or accept it by sending con to dc, which is answered by an acknowledgment ack.

Method. Our objective is to build a global interaction k from partial views i and j defined over a partition of the lifelines (in Fig. 1, k is defined over $\{\text{dc}, \text{ss}, \text{tc}\}$, i over $\{\text{tc}\}$ and j over $\{\text{dc}, \text{ss}\}$).

We represent interactions as terms, which allows us to encode their composition as an anti-unification problem. As shown in Fig. 1, anti-unification allows the superimposition of the alt operator in i and j.

Our originality lies in identifying the communication channels connecting these partial views as special constants called *gates*. For example, in Fig. 1, the gate $\mathfrak{a}$ relates the reception tc?not in i and the emission ss!not in j. These two actions must be coupled in the resulting interaction k to form a value passing vp(tc?not, ss!not). Intermediate terms s and t are derived from i and j by substituting related actions by the gate that relates them ($\mathfrak{a}$, $\mathfrak{b}$, and $\mathfrak{c}$ in Fig. 1). This yields mappings λ_i and λ_j such that $s\lambda_i = i$ and $t\lambda_j = j$. Applying our *special constant-preserving anti-unification* modulo an equational theory E yields a generalization r of s and t with substitutions σ_s, σ_t such that $r\sigma_s =_E s$, $r\sigma_t =_E t$. As the generalization preserves the gates, r contains the three gates $\mathfrak{a}$, $\mathfrak{b}$, and $\mathfrak{c}$. Here, E includes $\mathsf{alt}(x, y) \approx \mathsf{alt}(y, x)$ (commutativity of alt) and $\mathsf{seq}(\varnothing, x) \approx x$ ($\varnothing$ neutral element for seq). The composed interaction k can then be built from

r, as illustrated in Fig. 1, by applying a substitution σ_r derived from σ_s and σ_t, along with a mapping λ_k derived from λ_i and λ_j.

Related Work. Compositionality for distributed systems is an active topic in Multi-party Session Types (MPST) [12,13,23,24,29,38]. Choreography-based languages, including MPST and our interaction language, represent systems as algebraic terms with equational laws defining operator semantics. MPSTs specify a global type and, via projection, derive local types that ensure safety and avoid deadlocks, at the cost of restrictive structural forms (e.g., "choice at sender"). [23] composes partial views expressed as CCS-like local types, while [29,38] consider partial MPSTs interacting with the environment, but remain constrained by operational assumptions. [12,13] introduce gateways relaying messages between sessions, enabling open-system composition. Similar ideas exist for Communicating Finite State Machines (CFSMs) [11,15,24], where composition relies on gateways or safe CFSM classes. Safety guarantees for communications after composition include preventing message loss (an emission not matched by a reception) and indefinite waiting for a reception (deadlock, in the dual case). Such guarantees are studied in e.g., [17], [14] and [24] for the composition of team automata, CFSM via synchronous buffers and CFSM into global graphs respectively. Our approach for composition cannot yield models in which deadlocks exist. It yields a process-algebra-like term in a language without a primitive for deadlock (like STOP in CSP) or explicit synchronisation operators. Moreover, it will not return a result if it cannot match all pairs of tagged emissions and receptions. Realizability [9,26] is an adjacent topic of interest. It consists in determining whether or not a global model can be implemented as a set of communicating automata. By construction, the approaches for composition from [14,17,24] yield a realizable global model because it is already obtained from a set of communicating automata. In our case, we might compose (sub-)interactions that are themselves not realizable and thus we do not have any claims w.r.t. the realizability of their composition. Still, realizability of interactions can be checked via complementary approaches (e.g., the local-choice property [20]). The soundness of our approach is related to trace-equivalence (projection of traces of the global model are accepted by the local models) and not bisimulation. From a practical perspective, interactions are high-level specifications that may abstract away implementation details and specify global wanted and unwanted scenarios. They need not be realizable and can be used to confront traces collected from an implementation (runtime verification [27]), for which we only need trace equivalence. In general, equational theories do not preserve bisimulation (e.g., distributivity of sequencing over non-deterministic choice).

Contributions and Paper Organization. In Sect. 2, we present standard concepts and notations related to term algebras and anti-unification. In Sect. 3, we introduce *special constant-preserving (sc-preserving) anti-unification*, which preserves designated constants while generalizing other subterms. We establish its relation to standard anti-unification, and characterize conditions for the existence and uniqueness of sc-preserving least general generalizations (lggs).

In Sect. 4, we prove termination, soundness, and completeness of our *rule-based algorithm* for computing sc-preserving lggs.

In Sect. 5, we extend sc-preserving anti-unification *modulo equational theories* [6,8]. In Sect. 6, we show that *interaction composition* reduces to sc-preserving anti-unification by encoding gates as special constants to align local views, proving preservation of local behaviors via projection. Finally, we present an experimental validation of a prototype tool that implements sc-preserving generalization modulo equations, demonstrating its ability to recombine interactions taken from the literature.

2 Preliminaries

Lists. For any set X, we denote by X^* (resp. X^n for $n \in \mathbb{N}$ and X^+) the set of all lists (resp. lists of length n and non-empty lists) of elements of X. ε denotes the empty list and for any list $\overline{x} \in X^*$ of length $|\overline{x}|$, $\forall i \in [1, |\overline{x}|]$, x_i denotes the element of $\overline{x}$ at index i. For any $p, q \in X^*$, we say that p is a strict prefix of q, denoted by $p \lhd q$, iff there exists some $p' \in X^+$ such that $q = p.p'$ where "." denotes list concatenation. This defines a strict partial order $\lhd$ on lists.

Terms. We adopt notations from [19]. Let $\mathcal{F} = (\mathcal{F}_n)_{n \in \mathbb{N}}$ be a family of function symbols indexed by their arity and $\mathcal{V}$ be a countable set of variables. The set of $\mathcal{F}$-terms over $\mathcal{V}$, denoted $\mathcal{T}(\mathcal{F}, \mathcal{V})$, is defined inductively by $t ::= x \mid f(t_1, \cdots, t_n)$ where $x \in \mathcal{V}$, $f \in \mathcal{F}_n$ and $t_1, \ldots, t_n \in \mathcal{T}(\mathcal{F}, \mathcal{V})^n$. For any $f \in \mathcal{F}_n$ and any list of n terms $\overline{t} \in \mathcal{T}(\mathcal{F}, \mathcal{V})^n$, we may denote the term $f(t_1, \cdots, t_n)$ by $f(\overline{t})$. Constants are function symbols in $\mathcal{F}_0$. The head symbol of a term is $\mathsf{head}(x) = x$ and $\mathsf{head}(f(\overline{t})) = f$. Given a term t, $\mathsf{Var}(t)$ is the set of variables occurring in it. If $\mathsf{Var}(t) = \emptyset$, t is said to be ground and $\mathcal{T}(\mathcal{F})$ denotes the set of all ground terms. The set of positions of t, denoted $\mathsf{pos}(t) \subset \mathbb{N}^*$, is defined by $\mathsf{pos}(x) = \{\varepsilon\}$ and $\mathsf{pos}(f(\overline{t})) = \{\varepsilon\} \cup \bigcup_{i=1}^{|\overline{t}|} \{i.p \mid p \in \mathsf{pos}(t_i)\}$, where the empty list ε identifies the root position. For $p \in \mathsf{pos}(t)$, the subterm at position p is denoted $t|_p$. The *size* of a term t is defined inductively as $\mathsf{size}(x) = 1$, and $\mathsf{size}(f(\overline{t})) = 1 + \sum_1^{|\overline{t}|} \mathsf{size}(t_i)$.

Substitutions. A *substitution* $\sigma : \mathcal{V} \to \mathcal{T}(\mathcal{F}, \mathcal{V})$ is a mapping which differs from the identity only on a finite number of variables. The application of σ to a term t, written $t\sigma$ using the usual postfix notation, is defined as $x\sigma$ if $t \in \mathcal{V}$, and $f(t_1\sigma, \ldots, t_n\sigma)$ if $t = f(t_1, \ldots, t_n)$, where $f \in \mathcal{F}_n$. The *domain*, *range* and *variable range* of σ are resp. defined as $\mathsf{Dom}(\sigma) = \{x \mid x\sigma \neq x\}$, $\mathsf{Ran}(\sigma) = \{x\sigma \mid x \in \mathsf{Dom}(\sigma)\}$, and $\mathsf{VRan}(\sigma) = \bigcup_{x \in \mathsf{Dom}(\sigma)} \mathsf{Var}(x\sigma)$. A substitution can be written as $\{x_1 \mapsto t_1, \ldots, x_n \mapsto t_n\}$, listing only the bindings for the variables in its domain. The identity substitution is denoted as $Id_{\mathcal{V}}$. The *composition* $\sigma\theta$ of substitutions σ and θ is defined by $t\sigma\theta = (t\sigma)\theta$ for any term t. A substitution σ is a *renaming* if there exists a substitution σ^{-1} such that $\sigma\sigma^{-1} = Id_{\mathcal{V}}$. Two terms t and t' are *renaming-equivalent* if there exists a renaming σ with $t\sigma = t'$.

Equational Theory. Terms of an algebra $\mathcal{T}(\mathcal{F},\mathcal{V})$ can be subject to properties expressed using equations. An equation is a couple (t,t') of terms in $\mathcal{T}(\mathcal{F},\mathcal{V})^2$, written as $t \approx t'$. Given a set of equations E, the equational theory $=_E$ is the least congruence on $\mathcal{T}(\mathcal{F},\mathcal{V})$ that contains E and is closed under substitutions.

E-generalization. For two terms $r,t \in \mathcal{T}(\mathcal{F},\mathcal{V})$, we say that r is *less specific* than t modulo a set of equations E, written $r \preceq_E t$, if there exists a substitution σ such that $r\sigma =_E t$. We also say that r is E-more general than t as it is possible to transform r, via the application of a substitution, into a term that is E-equivalent to the more specific t. The relation $\preceq_E$ is a *preorder*, i.e. is reflexive and transitive. We denote by $\prec_E$ and $\simeq_E$ the corresponding strict and equivalence relations, i.e. $r \prec_E t$ iff $(r \preceq_E t) \wedge (t \not\preceq_E r)$ and $r \simeq_E t$ iff $(r \preceq_E t) \wedge (t \preceq_E r)$.

A term r is an *E-generalization* of two terms s and t if there exist substitutions σ_s and σ_t such that $r\sigma_s =_E s$ and $r\sigma_t =_E t$, i.e., $r \preceq_E s$ and $r \preceq_E t$. The substitutions σ_s and σ_t are the *witnessing substitutions.* Intuitively, r captures a common structure of s and t modulo E, abstracting some differences by variables. For instance, given $E = \{f(x,f(y,z)) \approx f(f(x,y),z)\}$ an E-generalization of $s = f(f(a,u),u))$ and $t = f(a,f(v,v))$, is $r = f(a,f(x,x))$ with $\sigma_s = \{x \mapsto u\}$ and $\sigma_t = \{x \mapsto v\}$. The term $r' = f(a,f(x,y))$ is also an E-generalization of s and t but r' is strictly more general than r, i.e. $r' \prec_E r$, since $r'\{y \mapsto x\} = r$ and $r \not\preceq_E r'$.

A *least general E-generalization* (E-lgg) r is an E-generalization that is *maximal* with respect to $\preceq_E$, i.e., there exists no generalization r' such that $r \prec_E r'$. Dually, a *most general E-generalization* (E-mgg) reduces s and t to a single variable x (up to renaming), i.e., $r = x$. It does not capture any structure and is mainly of algorithmic interest.

When $E = \emptyset$ we will remove the E- prefix and use the wording lgg, mgg etc., as well as the notations $\preceq$, $\prec$, $\simeq$. The existence and uniqueness of lggs up to variable renaming has been established, for example, in [25].

3 Constant-Preserving Generalization

Let us introduce a set $\mathfrak{F}_0 \subseteq \mathcal{F}_0$ of *special constants.* In the following, we generically denote by $\mathfrak{a}, \mathfrak{b}, \mathfrak{c}, \ldots$ elements of $\mathfrak{F}_0$, and by $u, v, w, \ldots$ the *ordinary constants* in $\mathcal{F}_0 \setminus \mathfrak{F}_0$. For $t \in \mathcal{T}(\mathcal{F},\mathcal{V})$, let $SC(t)$ denote the set of special constants occurring in t, and extend this to sets by $SC(\{t_1,\ldots,t_n\}) = \bigcup_{i=1}^{n} SC(t_i)$.

For $r,s,t \in \mathcal{T}(\mathcal{F},\mathcal{V})$, r is a *special constant-preserving generalization (scpg)* of s and t if there exist witnessing substitutions σ_s and σ_t such that r is a generalization of s and t via σ_s and σ_t that do not introduce special constants:

Definition 1. *The set of* special constant-preserving (sc-preserving) generalizations *of two terms* $s,t \in \mathcal{T}(\mathcal{F},\mathcal{V})$ *is defined as:*

$$CPG(s,t) = \left\{ r \in \mathcal{T}(\mathcal{F},\mathcal{V}) \,\middle|\, \begin{array}{l} \exists\sigma_s,\ (r\sigma_s = s) \wedge (SC(\mathsf{Ran}(\sigma_s)) = \emptyset) \\ \exists\sigma_t,\ (r\sigma_t = t) \wedge (SC(\mathsf{Ran}(\sigma_t)) = \emptyset) \end{array} \right\}$$

Using the above notation, we observe that, since **(1)** σ_s and σ_t do not associate terms with special constants to variables, and that **(2)** the equalities $r\sigma_s = s$ and $r\sigma_t = t$ hold, this implies that all special constants appearing in s or in t are preserved in r:

Lemma 1. *For any two terms $s, t \in \mathcal{T}(\mathcal{F}, \mathcal{V})$ we have:*

$$CPG(s,t) \neq \emptyset \Rightarrow ((SC(s) = SC(t)) \wedge (\forall r \in CPG(s,t),\ SC(r) = SC(s)))$$

Proof. Assume $SC(s) \neq SC(t)$. Without loss of generality, let $\mathfrak{a} \in SC(s) \backslash SC(t)$. Suppose, for contradiction, that $r \in CPG(s,t)$ with witnessing substitutions σ_s and σ_t. Since $r\sigma_t = t$ and $\mathfrak{a} \notin SC(t)$, $\mathfrak{a}$ cannot occur in r. But $r\sigma_s = s$ requires $\mathfrak{a} \in SC(\mathsf{Ran}(\sigma_s))$, contradicting the sc-preserving condition.
Let r in $CPG(s,t)$ with witnessing substitutions σ_s and σ_t. As $s = r\sigma_s$, we have $SC(s) = SC(r\sigma_s) = SC(r) \cup SC(\mathsf{Ran}(\sigma_s)) = SC(r)$. □

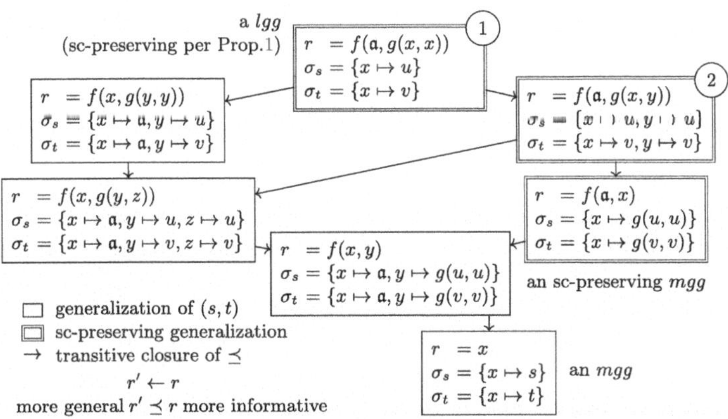

Fig. 2. Example illustrating generalizations and sc-preserving generalizations.

In Definition 2, we introduce sc-preserving lggs and mggs (scplgg and resp. scpmgg).

Definition 2. *For any $s, t \in \mathcal{T}(\mathcal{F}, \mathcal{V})$, we have that $r \in CPG(s,t)$ is an sc-preserving mgg (resp. lgg) of s and t if $\nexists\, r' \in CPG(s,t)$ s.t. $r' \prec r$ (resp. $r \prec r'$) i.e., r is minimal (resp. maximal) in $CPG(s,t)$ w.r.t. $\preceq$.*

It transpires that if an scplgg exists, then it is an lgg:

Property 1. An sc-preserving lgg of s and t in $\mathcal{T}(\mathcal{F}, \mathcal{V})$ is an lgg of s and t.

Proof. Let r be an scplgg of s and t with witnessing substitutions σ_s and σ_t. Suppose, for contradiction, that a generalization r' of s and t with witnessing substitutions σ'_s, σ'_t exists such that $r \prec r'$, i.e., $r\sigma = r'$ for some substitution σ. Then $r\sigma\sigma'_s = r\sigma_s = s$. Restricting domains of σ and σ_s to $\mathsf{Var}(r)$, we deduce $\sigma\sigma'_s = \sigma_s$. Hence, $SC(\mathsf{Ran}(\sigma'_s)) \subseteq SC(\mathsf{Ran}(\sigma_s))$. Since $r \in CPG(s,t)$, $SC(\mathsf{Ran}(\sigma_s)) = \emptyset$ and we get $SC(\mathsf{Ran}(\sigma'_s)) = \emptyset$. A similar reasoning holds by replacing the index s by t. Thus, r' is also sc-preserving, contradicting the maximality of r in $CPG(s,t)$. □

Consider the following example: $s = f(\mathfrak{a}, g(u,u))$ and $t = f(\mathfrak{a}, g(v,v))$. In Fig. 2, we provide several generalizations of (s,t) and how they are related via the $\preceq$ relation. Here, $r = f(\mathfrak{a}, g(x,x))$ (① in Fig. 2) is an lgg i.e., it minimally abstracts the differences between s and t and it is sc-preserving i.e., the special constant $\mathfrak{a}$ remains. As for $r' = f(\mathfrak{a}, g(x,y))$ (② in Fig. 2), it is also sc-preserving, but it is not least generalizing. Indeed, $r'\{y \mapsto x\} = r$.

Now consider a different example with $s = f(\mathfrak{a}, g(\mathfrak{b}, u))$ and $t = f(\mathfrak{a}, g(v, \mathfrak{b}))$. Here, any generalization would require a variable to map to a term with special constants: for instance, the candidate $r = f(\mathfrak{a}, g(x,y))$ would require $x\sigma_s = \mathfrak{b}$ and $y\sigma_t = \mathfrak{b}$, thus violating the sc-preservation.

Lemma 2. *If an sc-preserving lgg exists, it is unique up to renaming equivalence.*

Proof. Let r be a scplgg of s and t. By Property 1, r is an lgg, which is unique up to renaming by [25]. □

Conflict positions [6–8] are common positions in s and t at which a difference occurs. If there are no such positions then $s = t$. We distinguish in Definition 3 conflict positions in which the diverging subterms do or do not contain special constants.

Definition 3. *Let $s, t \in \mathcal{T}(\mathcal{F})$. A position $p \in \mathsf{pos}(s) \cap \mathsf{pos}(t)$ is a* conflict position *(cpos) iff $\mathsf{head}(s|_p) \neq \mathsf{head}(t|_p)$ and $\forall\ q \lhd p,\ \mathsf{head}(s|_q) = \mathsf{head}(t|_q)$. Moreover, it is a* failure cpos *(fcpos) iff $SC(s|_p) \neq \emptyset$ or $SC(t|_p) \neq \emptyset$ and a* solvable cpos *(scpos) otherwise.*

We denote by $cpos(s,t)$ (resp. $scpos(s,t)$, $fcpos(s,t)$) the set of $cpos$ (resp. $scpos$, $fcpos$) of any two terms s and t. The absence of failure conflict positions guarantees the existence of scpg, and conversely:

Lemma 3. *Given s and t in $\mathcal{T}(\mathcal{F})$, $(CPG(s,t) = \emptyset) \Leftrightarrow (fcpos(s,t) \neq \emptyset)$*

Proof. By induction on $N = \mathsf{size}(s) + \mathsf{size}(t)$.
– Base case: $N = 2$. Then s and t are both constant symbols. Let us reason according to whether they are equal or not. (a) If $s \neq t$, then the only generalization of s and t is a variable x (up to renaming). Case $CPG(s,t) = \emptyset$: then x is not sc-preserving. This implies that $SC(s) \neq \emptyset$ or $SC(t) \neq \emptyset$. Hence ε is a fcpos of s and t so $fcpos(s,t) \neq \emptyset$. Case $fcpos(s,t) \neq \emptyset$: let's consider one such $fcpos$. As s and t are constants, it can only be ε. We have that $SC(s|_\varepsilon) \neq \emptyset$ or $SC(t|_\varepsilon) \neq \emptyset$. We deduce that x is not an sc-preserving generalization. Hence $CPG(s,t) = \emptyset$. (b) If $s = t$, there is no fcpos, whether s is a special constant or

not. If s is (resp. is not) a special constant, then s (resp. x) is an sc-preserving generalization and $CPG(s,t) \neq \emptyset$.
– Induction case: $N > 2$. Then, s or t is not a constant. Let us assume that $s = f(s_1, \ldots, s_n)$ with $n \geq 1$ (the other case being equivalent) and let us reason according to whether s and t share the same head symbol or not. (a) If $head(t) \neq f$, then the only generalization of s and t (up to variable renaming) is a variable x. Let us suppose that there exists a fcpos, then it will be ε because $head(s) = f \neq head(t)$ and $SC(s)$ or $SC(t)$ will be not empty. It means that x is not sc-preserving. Hence $CPG(s,t) = \emptyset$. Conversely, if $CPG(s,t) = \emptyset$, then x is not an sc-preserving generalization. By definition, it means that $SC(s) \neq \emptyset$ or $SC(t) \neq \emptyset$. With $f \neq head(t)$, we deduce that ε is a fcpos of s and t. (b) If $head(t) = f$, let us introduce $t = f(t_1, \cdots, t_n)$. Then one of the following two possibilities applies: (1) either for all i, $CPG(s_i,t_i) \neq \emptyset$. By induction hypothesis, no subterm pairs (s_i,t_i) has a fcpos, thus there is no fcpos for s and t. For $r_i \in CPG(s_i,t_i)$, $f(r_1,\ldots,r_n)$ is in $CPG(s,t)$ and $CPG(s,t) \neq \emptyset$; or (2) for some i, $CPG(s_i,t_i) = \emptyset$. By induction, there exists a fcpos p_i for s_i and t_i. Then, $i.p_i$ is a fcpos of s and t with either $SC(s_{|i.p_i})$ or $SC(t_{|i.p_i})$ not empty. Let us suppose there exists $r \in CPG(s,t)$. Either r is a variable, and in this case, r is not sc-preserving since $SC(s_{|i.p_i})$ or $SC(t_{|i.p_i})$ is not empty; or r is of the form $f(r_1,\ldots,r_n)$, and in this case r_i would be in $CPG(s_i,t_i)$. Contradiction with the hypothesis $CPG(s_i,t_i) = \emptyset$. □

4 Algorithm for Sc-Preserving Generalizations

Following [3,19], generalization problems are represented as *anti-unification triples* (AUTs), written $x : s \triangleq t$ for ground terms $s,t \in \mathcal{T}(\mathcal{F})$. The variable x denotes an mgg of s and t, witnessed by the substitutions $\{x \mapsto s\}$ and $\{x \mapsto t\}$. The *size* of an AUT is $\mathsf{size}(x : s \triangleq t) = \mathsf{size}(s) + \mathsf{size}(t)$. Def. 4 introduces notations on sets of AUTs.

Definition 4. *Let A be a subset of the set $\mathcal{A} = \mathcal{V} \times \mathcal{T}(\mathcal{F})^2$ of all AUTs.*

$$\mathit{Index}(A) = \cup_{(x:s\triangleq t)\in A}\{x\} \qquad \mathit{Pairs}(A) = \cup_{(x:s\triangleq t)\in A}\{(s,t)\}$$
$$\mathit{Left}(A) = \cup_{(x:s\triangleq t)\in A}\{x \mapsto s\} \quad \mathit{Right}(A) = \cup_{(x:s\triangleq t)\in A}\{x \mapsto t\}$$

A *configuration* is a tuple $c = \langle A|S|\theta|x_0\rangle$, where $A \subset \mathcal{A}$ is a set of so-called *active* AUTs, $S \subset \mathcal{A}$ the store of so-called *solved* AUTs, θ the accumulated index-variable mappings, and x_0 the root variable. We denote by $\mathsf{Left}(c)$ and $\mathsf{Right}(c)$ the substitutions $\mathsf{Left}(A \cup S)$ and $\mathsf{Right}(A \cup S)$ respectively.

Starting from an initial configuration $c_0 = \langle\{x_0 : s_0 \triangleq t_0\}|\emptyset|Id_{\mathcal{V}}|x_0\rangle$ an anti-unification algorithm such as the ones from [8,19] computes a lgg of s_0 and t_0 by applying successive transformations from c_0 until reaching a configuration $c = \langle\emptyset|S|\theta|x_0\rangle$ in which the set of active AUTs is empty. Once this is done, the lgg is obtained by applying the substitution θ to the root variable x_0 i.e. $x_0\theta$ is a lgg of s_0 and t_0. The corresponding witnessing substitutions are $\sigma_L = \mathsf{Left}(c)$ and $\sigma_R = \mathsf{Right}(c)$, satisfying $x_0\theta\sigma_L = s_0$ and $x_0\theta\sigma_R = t_0$.

$$\text{(Decompose)}\ \frac{\langle \{x : f(\overline{s}) \triangleq f(\overline{t})\} \cup A \mid S \mid \theta \mid x_0\rangle}{\langle \bigcup_{i\in[1,n]}\{x_i : s_i \triangleq t_i\} \cup A \mid S \mid \theta\{x \mapsto f(\overline{x})\} \mid x_0\rangle}\ \begin{cases} f \in \mathcal{F}_n \\ \overline{s}, \overline{t} \in \mathcal{T}(\mathcal{F},\mathcal{V})^n \\ \overline{x} : n \text{ fresh vars}\end{cases}$$

$$\text{(Solve)}\ \frac{\langle \{x : s \triangleq t\} \cup A \mid S \mid \theta \mid x_0\rangle}{\langle A \mid \{x : s \triangleq t\} \cup S \mid \theta \mid x_0\rangle}\ \begin{cases} \mathsf{head}(s) \neq \mathsf{head}(t) \\ SC(s) = SC(t) = \emptyset \\ \nexists y \ s.t.\ (y : s \triangleq t) \in S\end{cases}$$

$$\text{(Recover)}\ \frac{\langle \{x : s \triangleq t\} \cup A \mid S \mid \theta \mid x_0\rangle}{\langle A \mid S \mid \theta\{x \mapsto y\} \mid x_0\rangle}\ \{\exists y \ s.t.\ (y : s \triangleq t) \in S$$

Fig. 3. sc-preserving generalization rules (no equations)

In Fig. 3, we introduce the inference rules of our sc-preserving anti-unification algorithm. The rule Decompose replaces in A an AUT $x : f(\overline{s}) \triangleq f(\overline{t})$ with a set of smaller AUTs $x_i : s_i \triangleq t_i$, introducing fresh variables $x_i \notin \mathsf{Index}(A \cup S) \cup \mathsf{Dom}(\theta)$, and extending θ with $\sigma = \{x \mapsto f(\overline{x})\}$. The rule Solve transfers an AUT from A to S when $\mathsf{head}(s) \neq \mathsf{head}(t)$, no duplicate $(y : s \triangleq t)$ exists in S, and both terms are free of special constants $(SC(s) = SC(t) = \emptyset)$. The rule Recover reuses a previously solved pair $(y : s \triangleq t) \in S$ by extending θ with $\{x \mapsto y\}$, enforcing variable sharing across identical subproblems. It should be noted that if we remove the condition $SC(s) = SC(t) = \emptyset$ in the Solve rule in Fig. 3, then these rules correspond to the usual anti-unification rules [8].

4.1 Examples and Relation to Conflict Positions

Example 1. We give below a derivation trace using the rules of Fig. 3 from the initial configuration $\langle \{x_0 : f(\mathfrak{a}, g(u,u)) \triangleq f(\mathfrak{a}, g(v,v))\} \mid \emptyset \mid Id_{\mathcal{V}} \mid x_0\rangle$, by using the first capital letter of the name of the rules to identify them.

$$\text{(D)}\ \frac{\langle \{x_0 : f(\mathfrak{a}, g(u,u)) \triangleq f(\mathfrak{a}, g(v,v))\} \mid \emptyset \mid Id_{\mathcal{V}} \mid x_0\rangle}{\langle \{x_1 : \mathfrak{a} \triangleq \mathfrak{a}, x_2 : g(u,u) \triangleq g(v,v)\} \mid \emptyset \mid \{x_0 \mapsto f(x_1,x_2)\} \mid x_0\rangle}$$

$$\text{(D)}\ \frac{\langle \{x_1 : \mathfrak{a} \triangleq \mathfrak{a}, x_2 : g(u,u) \triangleq g(v,v)\} \mid \emptyset \mid \{x_0 \mapsto f(x_1,x_2)\} \mid x_0\rangle}{\langle \{x_2 : g(u,u) \triangleq g(v,v)\} \mid \emptyset \mid \{x_0 \mapsto f(x_1,x_2)\}\{x_1 \mapsto \mathfrak{a}\} \mid x_0\rangle}$$

$$\text{(D)}\ \frac{\langle \{x_2 : g(u,u) \triangleq g(v,v)\} \mid \emptyset \mid \{x_0 \mapsto f(x_1,x_2)\}\{x_1 \mapsto \mathfrak{a}\} \mid x_0\rangle}{\langle \{x_3 : u \triangleq v, x_4 : u \triangleq v\} \mid \emptyset \mid \{x_0 \mapsto f(\mathfrak{a},x_2)\}\{x_2 \mapsto g(x_3,x_4)\} \mid x_0\rangle}$$

$$\text{(S)}\ \frac{\langle \{x_3 : u \triangleq v, x_4 : u \triangleq v\} \mid \emptyset \mid \{x_0 \mapsto f(\mathfrak{a},x_2)\}\{x_2 \mapsto g(x_3,x_4)\} \mid x_0\rangle}{\langle \{x_4 : u \triangleq v\} \mid \{x_3 : u \triangleq v\} \mid \{x_0 \mapsto f(\mathfrak{a}, g(x_3,x_4))\} \mid x_0\rangle}$$

$$\text{(R)}\ \frac{\langle \{x_4 : u \triangleq v\} \mid \{x_3 : u \triangleq v\} \mid \{x_0 \mapsto f(\mathfrak{a}, g(x_3,x_4))\} \mid x_0\rangle}{\langle \emptyset \mid \{x_3 : u \triangleq v\} \mid \{x_0 \mapsto f(\mathfrak{a}, g(x_3,x_4))\}\{x_4 \mapsto x_3\} \mid x_0\rangle}$$

In the last step, we have $x_0\theta = f(\mathfrak{a}, g(x_3,x_3))$ with $\{x_3 \mapsto u\}$ and $\{x_3 \mapsto v\}$ as left and right instantiations.

Example 2. Here, applying the rules of Fig. 3 does not allow us to empty the set of active AUT, as no sc-preserving generalization exists.

$$
\dfrac{\dfrac{\dfrac{\langle\{x_0 : f(\mathfrak{a}, g(\mathfrak{b}, u)) \triangleq f(\mathfrak{a}, g(v, \mathfrak{b}))\} \mid \emptyset \mid Id_{\mathcal{V}} \mid x_0\rangle}{\langle\{x_1 : \mathfrak{a} \triangleq \mathfrak{a}, x_2 : g(\mathfrak{b}, u) \triangleq g(v, \mathfrak{b})\} \mid \emptyset \mid \{x_0 \mapsto f(x_1, x_2)\} \mid x_0\rangle}\,(\mathsf{D})}{\langle\{x_2 : g(\mathfrak{b}, u) \triangleq g(v, \mathfrak{b})\} \mid \emptyset \mid \{x_0 \mapsto f(x_1, x_2)\}\{x_1 \mapsto \mathfrak{a}\} \mid x_0\rangle}\,(\mathsf{D})}{\langle\{x_3 : \mathfrak{b} \triangleq v, x_4 : u \triangleq \mathfrak{b}\} \mid \emptyset \mid \{x_0 \mapsto f(\mathfrak{a}, x_2)\}\{x_2 \mapsto g(x_3, x_4)\} \mid x_0\rangle}\,(\mathsf{D})
$$

The examples above illustrate that all introduced AUTs correspond to pairs of terms s, t located at the same position p in both s_0 and t_0 and which have the same parent symbols at any position q in s_0 and t_0 with $q \lhd p$.

Lemma 4. *There is a derivation from* c_0 *to* $c = \langle\{x : s \triangleq t\} \cup A|S|\theta|x_0\rangle$ *iff* $\exists\ p \in pos(s_0) \cap pos(t_0)$ *s.t.* $s_0|_p = s$, $t_0|_p = t$, *and for all* $q \lhd p$, $\mathsf{head}(s_0|_q) = \mathsf{head}(t_0|_q)$.

Sketch of proof. This trivially holds for $c = c_0$ with the position being the root ε. For any other AUT, we may simply remark that only Decompose introduces new AUTs, each step descending one level with identical heads. □

On Def. 5, we characterize final configurations of our algorithm as those which are irreducible by the rules of Fig. 3.

Definition 5. *Let* $c = \langle A|S|\theta|x_0\rangle$ *be a configuration reachable from* c_0. c *is said to be* final *if* c *is irreducible by the rules of Fig. 3. Moreover if* $A = \emptyset$, c *is said to be* solved *final configuration.*

In Lem. 5, we relate final configurations that are reachable from c_0 to the failure conflict positions of the initial terms s_0 and t_0.

Lemma 5. *For any final configuration* $c = \langle A|S|\theta|x_0\rangle$ *we have:*

$$
\mathit{Pairs}(A) \subseteq \bigcup_{p \in fcpos(s_0, t_0)} \{(s_0|_p, t_0|_p)\}
$$

Sketch of proof. Let $c = \langle A|S|\theta|x_0\rangle$ be a final configuration. For $x : s \triangleq t$ in A, $\mathsf{head}(s) \neq \mathsf{head}(t)$ (otherwise Decompose could be applied) and $SC(s) \neq \emptyset$ or $SC(t) \neq \emptyset$ (otherwise Solve or Recover could be applied). This combined with Lem. 4 implies that $\exists p \in fcpos(s_0, t_0)$ s.t. $s = s_0|_p$ and $t = t_0|_p$. □

4.2 Properties

Termination of our anti-unification algorithm can be directly proved via reasoning on a decreasing multiset measure.

Theorem 1 (Termination). *Derivations from* c_0 *applying the rules of Fig. 3 are finite.*

Proof. Let us first define, for a configuration $c = \langle A|S|\theta|x_0\rangle$, the multiset[1]

$$\mu(c) = \{\!\{\mathsf{size}(x : s \triangleq t) | x : s \triangleq t \in A\}\!\}$$

which cumulates the sizes of all AUTs in the active set A. Let $c = \langle A|S|\theta|x_0\rangle$ and $c' = \langle A'|S'|\theta'|x_0\rangle$ be configurations where c' is obtained from c by a single application of a rule of Fig. 3. We show that[2] $\mu(c) >_{mul} \mu(c')$ by case analysis. If Solve or $\mathsf{Recover}$ are applied, some $x : s \triangleq t$ is removed from A. As $A' \subsetneq A$, we directly obtain: $\mu(c') = \mu(c) \setminus \{\!\{\mathsf{size}(x : s \triangleq t)\}\!\}$. Therefore, $\mu(c) >_{mul} \mu(c')$. If $\mathsf{Decompose}$ is applied, given $f \in \mathcal{F}$ of arity $n \geq 0$, some $x : f(\overline{s}) \triangleq f(\overline{t}) \in A$ is replaced by $\bigcup_{i\in[1,n]}\{x_i : s_i \triangleq t_i\}$. This gives rise to the following equality:

$$\mu(c') = \left(\mu(c) \setminus \{\!\{\mathsf{size}(x : f(\overline{s}) \triangleq f(\overline{t}))\}\!\}\right) \cup \bigcup_{i\in[1..n]} \{\!\{\mathsf{size}(x_i : s_i \triangleq t_i)\}\!\}.$$

We get $\mu(c) >_{mul} \mu(c')$ as for each i, $\mathsf{size}(x_i : s_i \triangleq t_i) < \mathsf{size}(x : f(\overline{s}) \triangleq f(\overline{t}))$. As $>_{mul}$ is a well-founded order, any derivation under rules of Fig. 3 is finite. □

If we note $\langle A_0|S_0|\theta_0|x_0\rangle$ an initial configuration $c_0 = \langle x_0 : s_0 \triangleq t_0|\emptyset|Id_{\mathcal{V}}|x_0\rangle$ with ground terms s_0 and t_0, we have $\mathsf{Dom}(\mathsf{Left}(c_0)) = \mathsf{Dom}(\mathsf{Right}(c_0)) = \mathsf{Index}(A_0 \cup S_0) = \mathsf{Var}(x_0\theta_0)$, all equal to $\{x_0\}$. Moreover, $\mathsf{VRan}(\theta) = \mathsf{Var}(x_0\theta) \setminus \{x_0\}$. These properties are invariant on all the reachable configurations:

Lemma 6. *If $c = \langle A|S|\theta|x_0\rangle$ derives from c_0 via the rules of Fig. 3 then:*

- *$\mathsf{Dom}(\mathsf{Left}(c)) = \mathsf{Dom}(\mathsf{Right}(c)) = \mathsf{Index}(A \cup S) = \mathsf{Var}(x_0\theta)$;*
- *$\mathsf{VRan}(\theta) = \mathsf{Var}(x_0\theta) \setminus \{x_0\}$;*
- *$x_0\theta$ is a generalization of s_0 and t_0 with respective witnessing substitutions $\mathsf{Left}(c)$ and $\mathsf{Right}(c)$.*

Proofs of Lem. 6 are analogous to those of [8] established for syntactic anti-unification in the general case.

Lemma 7 (SC-preservation). *Let c be a solved configuration derived from c_0 by successive applications of the rules of Fig. 3, then $x_0\theta \in CPG(s_0, t_0)$.*

Proof. By Lem. 6, $x_0\theta$ is a generalization of s_0 and t_0 and $\mathsf{Dom}(\mathsf{Left}(c)) = \mathsf{Dom}(\mathsf{Right}(c)) = \mathsf{Index}(A \cup S) = \mathsf{Index}(S)$ since A is empty for a solved configuration. Each binding in $\mathsf{Left}(c)$ (resp. $\mathsf{Right}(c)$) is of the form $x \mapsto s$ (resp. $x \mapsto t$) with $x : s \triangleq t \in S$. As by construction, the set of solved AUTs only contains special-constant–free AUTs, we have $SC(\mathsf{Ran}(\mathsf{Left}(c))) = SC(\mathsf{Ran}(\mathsf{Right}(c))) = \emptyset$ so that $x_0\theta \in CPG(s_0, t_0)$. □

[1] Multisets are denoted $\{\!\{\cdots\}\!\}$ when explicitly listing elements by repeating them as many times as their multiplicity.

[2] For two multisets M and N, $M >_{mul} N$ iff N can be obtained from M by iteratively replacing one element of M by any number of smaller elements.

Theorem 2 (Soundness). *Let* $c = \langle \emptyset | S | \theta | x_0 \rangle$ *be a solved configuration derived from* c_0 *via the rules of Fig. 3, then* $x_0\theta$ *is a scplgg of* s_0 *and* t_0.

Proof. Let $c = \langle \emptyset | S | \theta | x_0 \rangle$ reached from c_0. By Lem. 7, $x_0\theta \in CPG(s_0, t_0)$. Assume that there is an sc-preserving lgg r and a substitution ρ with $x_0\theta\rho = r$ and ρ not a renaming. Take $\mathsf{Dom}(\rho) = \mathsf{Var}(x_0\theta)$. Since ρ is not a renaming, there exists y in $\mathsf{Dom}(\rho)$ that verifies either **(1)** $\exists y' \in \mathcal{V} \setminus \{y\}, y\rho = y'\rho \in \mathcal{V}$, i.e. ρ merges at least two variables occurring in $x_0\theta$ or **(2)** $y\rho \notin \mathcal{V}$.

Case **(1)**. By Lem. 6, the active set being empty, $\mathsf{Index}(S) = \mathsf{Var}(x_0\theta) = \mathsf{Dom}(\rho)$, so y and y' index solved AUTs in S: $y : s \triangleq t \in S$ and $y' : s' \triangleq t' \in S$. By Lem. 4 there are solvable positions p, p' with $s_0|_p = s, t_0|_p = t$ and $s_0|_{p'} = s', t_0|_{p'} = t'$. Now $r|_p = (x_0\theta\rho)|_p = (x_0\theta)|_p\rho = y\rho$ and similarly $r|_{p'} = y'\rho$. Given that we know that $y\rho = y'\rho$, this implies $r|_p = r|_{p'}$. Since $r \in CPG(s_0, t_0)$ there are witnesses σ_L, σ_R with $r\sigma_L = s_0$ and $r\sigma_R = t_0$, hence $s_0|_p = r|_p\sigma_L = r|_{p'}\sigma_L = s_0|_{p'}$ and similarly $t_0|_p = r|_p\sigma_R = r|_{'}\sigma_R = t_0|_{p'}$. We deduce $s = s'$ and $t = t'$. Thus S contains two solved AUTs with identical subproblems, which Recover forbids. Contradiction.

Case **(2)**. Again $\mathsf{Index}(S) = \mathsf{Var}(x_0\theta)$ so $y \in \mathsf{Index}(S)$ and $y : s \triangleq t \in S$. By Lem. 4 there is a solvable position p with $s_0|_p = s, t_0|_p = t$. Now $r|_p = (x_0\theta\rho)|_p = (x_0\theta)|_p\rho = y\rho$, which by hypothesis is a non-variable term. But $r \in CPG(s_0, t_0)$, so its witnessing substitutions σ_L, σ_R satisfy $r\sigma_L = s_0$ and $r\sigma_R = t_0$. Applying σ_L and σ_R to $r|_p = y\rho$ yields s and t, respectively; hence $\mathsf{head}(s) = \mathsf{head}(t) = \mathsf{head}(y\rho)$. Thus the solved AUT $y : s \triangleq t$ has identical root symbols which Solve forbids. Contradiction. □

Theorem 3 (Completeness). *For any* $r, s_0, t_0 \in \mathcal{T}(\mathcal{F})$, *if* r *is an sc-preserving lgg of* s_0 *and* t_0 *then there is a derivation from* c_0 *to a final configuration* $\langle \emptyset | S | \theta | x_0 \rangle$ *such that* $r \simeq x_0\theta$.

Proof. Let us suppose r is an scplgg of s_0 and t_0. Then $CPG(s_0, t_0) \neq \emptyset$ so by Lem. 3, we must have $fcpos(s_0, t_0) = \emptyset$. Then by Lem. 5, for any final configuration $c = \langle A | S | \theta | x_0 \rangle$ we must have $A = \emptyset$. Because the algorithm is terminating (Th. 1) one such configuration exists. Then by Th. 2, we must have that $x\theta$ is a sclgg of s_0 and t_0. Finally, by Lem. 2 we have $r \simeq x_0\theta$. □

Let us remark that, for any $c = \langle A | S | \theta | x_0 \rangle$, if $\exists x : s \triangleq t \in A$ s.t. $SC(s) \neq SC(t)$, then, in any c' reachable from c, A' cannot be empty. Indeed, if $\mathsf{head}(s) \neq \mathsf{head}(t)$, only Solve may remove $x : s \triangleq t$ from A and it cannot be applied. If $\mathsf{head}(s) = \mathsf{head}(t)$ with $s = f(\overline{s})$ and $t = f(\overline{t})$ then $\exists i \in [1, |\overline{s}|]$ s.t. $SC(s_i) \neq SC(t_i)$. Then, applying Decompose results in adding a $y : s_i \triangleq t_i$ with $SC(s_i) \neq SC(t_i)$ to A'. By induction, from c', no successor c'' can have $A'' = \emptyset$. As a result, one cannot find a scpg by exploring successors of c. Thus, we can pre-emptively prune the exploration of configurations by applying the higher priority Fail rule from Fig. 4. Its use will speed up the detection of failure cases (see Sect. 6).

$$\text{(Fail)}\ \frac{\langle\{x : s \triangleq t\} \cup A \mid S \mid \theta \mid x_0\rangle}{\bot}\ \{ SC(s) \neq SC(t)$$

Fig. 4. (Fail) a derived rule to complete rules ofs Fig. 3.

5 Equational Constant-Preserving Generalization

Sc-preserving anti-unification modulo an equational theory E requires E to be sc-preserving as per Def. 6. Otherwise, applying the equations could erase the special-constants (e.g., $f(a_f, x) \approx a_f$ with an absorbing element a_f of f).

Definition 6. *Given an equational theory E:*

- *E is* sc-preserving *if* $\forall s, t \in \mathcal{T}(\mathcal{F}, \mathcal{V}),\ s =_E t \Rightarrow SC(s) = SC(t)$
- *the* sc-preserving E-generalizations *(E-scpg) of terms $s, t \in \mathcal{T}(\mathcal{F}, \mathcal{V})$ are:*

$$CPG_E(s,t) = \left\{ r \in \mathcal{T}(\mathcal{F}, \mathcal{V}) \,\middle|\, \begin{array}{l} \exists\sigma_s,\ (r\sigma_s =_E s) \wedge (SC(\mathsf{Ran}(\sigma_s)) = \emptyset) \\ \exists\sigma_t,\ (r\sigma_t =_E t) \wedge (SC(\mathsf{Ran}(\sigma_t)) = \emptyset) \end{array} \right\}$$

Similarly as we did for CPG in Lem. 1, we characterize the preservation of special constants by CPG_E in Lem. 8.

Lemma 8. *For any sc-preserving theory E and $\forall s, t \in \mathcal{T}(\mathcal{F}, \mathcal{V})$ we have:*

$$CPG_E(s,t) \neq \emptyset \ \Rightarrow\ ((SC(s) = SC(t)) \ \wedge\ (\forall r \in CPG_E(s,t),\ SC(r) = SC(s)))$$

Proof. Assume that $r \in CPG_E(s,t)$ exists with witnessing substitutions σ_s and σ_t. Since E is sc-preserving, we have $SC(r\sigma_s) = SC(s)$ and $SC(r\sigma_t) = SC(t)$. But $SC(r\sigma_s) = SC(r\sigma_t) = SC(r)$ because σ_s and σ_t introduce no special constants. Hence, $SC(s) = SC(t)$. The second part is obvious. □

Unlike the scplgg of Def. 2, the E-scplgg of Def. 7 are not necessarily unique up to renaming. Consider for instance $s = f(\mathfrak{a}, g(u, u))$ and $t = f(g(v, v), \mathfrak{a})$ with $E = \{f(x, y) \approx f(y, x)\}$. Here both $r_1 = f(\mathfrak{a}, g(x, x))$ and $r_2 = f(g(x, x), \mathfrak{a})$ are E-scplggs of s and t. Yet, we may remark that we have $r_1 =_E r_2$.

Definition 7. *For any $s, t \in \mathcal{T}(\mathcal{F}, \mathcal{V})$, we have that $r \in CPG_E(s,t)$ is an E-scpmgg (resp. E-scplgg) of s and t if $\nexists\, r' \in CPG_E(s,t)$ s.t. $r' \prec_E r$ (resp. $r \prec_E r'$) i.e., r is minimal (resp. maximal) in $CPG_E(s,t)$ w.r.t. $\preceq_E$.*

With Prop. 2, we adapt Prop. 1 to the case modulo equations.

Property 2. An sc-preserving E-lgg of s and t in $\mathcal{T}(\mathcal{F}, \mathcal{V})$ is an E-lgg.

Proof. Let r be an sc-preserving E-lgg of s and t with witnessing substitutions σ_s and σ_t. Suppose, for contradiction, that an E-generalization r' of s and t with witnessing substitutions σ'_s, σ'_t exists such that $r \prec_E r'$, i.e., $r\sigma =_E r'$ for some substitution σ. Then $r\sigma\sigma'_s =_E r\sigma_s =_E s$ and $r\sigma\sigma'_t =_E r\sigma_t =_E t$.

Restricting domains of σ, σ_t and σ_s (resp. σ'_t and σ'_s) to $\mathsf{Var}(r)$ (resp. $\mathsf{Var}(r')$), we deduce $\sigma\sigma'_s = \sigma_s$ and $\sigma\sigma'_t = \sigma_t$. Hence, $SC(\mathsf{Ran}(\sigma'_t)) \subseteq SC(\mathsf{Ran}(\sigma_t))$ and $SC(\mathsf{Ran}(\sigma'_t)) \subseteq SC(\mathsf{Ran}(\sigma_t))$. Since r is an sc-preserving E-generalization, $SC(\mathsf{Ran}(\sigma_s)) = SC(\mathsf{Ran}(\sigma_t)) = \emptyset$, hence $SC(\mathsf{Ran}(\sigma'_s)) = \emptyset$ and $SC(\mathsf{Ran}(\sigma'_t)) = \emptyset$. Thus, r' is also sc-preserving, contradicting the maximality of r as an sc-preserving E-generalization. Therefore, r is an E-lgg of s and t. □

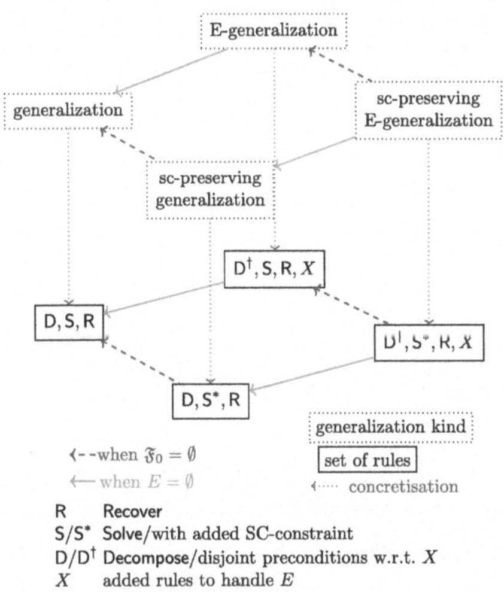

Fig. 5. Relating generalizations

Figure 5 illustrates the relationships between standard generalization [6–8] and our sc-preserving (E-)generalization. The dashed horizontal arrows indicate that our formulation naturally subsumes standard generalization when the set of special constants is empty. Similarly, the plain horizontal arrows show that in the absence of equational axioms, the problem reduces to syntactic generalization. The top and bottom layers respectively correspond to the problem definitions and the inference rules used to solve them.

We update the standard rules $\{\mathsf{D}, \mathsf{S}, \mathsf{R}\}$, substituting S with a S^* that enforces constant preservation[3]. E-generalization is implemented in [8,19] by introducing additional ad-hoc rules to handle specific theories (e.g. an operator f being associative, commutative, or having a neutral element, etc.) and combinations of theories (e.g. f being both associative and having a neutral element, etc.). In Fig. 5, we represent this via the set X of additional rules, and the use of $\mathsf{D}^\dagger$ instead of D as we do not apply the standard $\mathsf{Decompose}$ rule if a rule in X can be applied. To achieve sc-preserving E-generalization, we follow the same principle, the only difference being the use of the special S^* rule.

In Fig. 6, we propose one such ad-hoc rule. If we have $X = \{\mathsf{Decompose}_C\}$ as the X of Fig. 5 then the rule $\mathsf{Decompose}$ of Fig. 3 would not be applied if the shared head symbol f is commutative but $\mathsf{Decompose}_C$ would be applied instead.

Example 3. Reusing Ex. 2, we now assume that g is commutative and non-associative. By applying the rules of Fig. 3 together with rule of Fig. 6, an sc-preserving E-generalization exists: we have $x_0\theta = f(\mathfrak{a}, g(\mathfrak{b}, x_4))$ with $\{x_4 \mapsto u\}$

[3] Our Solve rule from Fig. 3 is denoted by S^* in Fig. 5 as it differs from the standard Solve rule from [8,19] by the added condition $SC(s) = SC(t) = \emptyset$.

$$(\mathsf{Decompose_C})\ \frac{\langle\{x : f(\overline{s}) \triangleq f(\overline{t})\} \cup A \mid S \mid \theta \mid x_0\rangle}{\langle\left\{\begin{array}{l} x_1 : s_1 \triangleq t_i, \\ x_2 : s_2 \triangleq t_{(i \bmod 2)+1} \end{array}\right\} \cup A \mid S \mid \theta\sigma \mid x_0\rangle}\ \begin{cases} f \in \mathcal{F}_2 \\ \overline{s}, \overline{t} \in \mathcal{T}(\mathcal{F}, \mathcal{V})^2 \\ \overline{x} : 2 \text{ fresh vars} \\ i \in [1, 2] \\ \sigma = \{x \mapsto f(\overline{x})\} \end{cases}$$

Fig. 6. Generalization rule for a commutative, non-associative function symbol [8]

and $\{x_4 \mapsto v\}$ as left and right instantiations.

$$\begin{array}{ll}
 & \langle\{x_0 : f(\mathfrak{a}, g(\mathfrak{b}, u)) \triangleq f(\mathfrak{a}, g(v, \mathfrak{b}))\} \mid \emptyset \mid Id_{\mathcal{V}} \mid x_0\rangle \\
(\mathsf{D}) & \overline{\langle\{x_1 : \mathfrak{a} \triangleq \mathfrak{a}, x_2 : g(\mathfrak{b}, u) \triangleq g(v, \mathfrak{b})\} \mid \emptyset \mid \{x_0 \mapsto f(x_1, x_2)\} \mid x_0\rangle} \\
(\mathsf{D}) & \overline{\langle\{x_2 : g(\mathfrak{b}, u) \triangleq g(v, \mathfrak{b})\} \mid \emptyset \mid \{x_0 \mapsto f(x_1, x_2)\}\{x_1 \mapsto \mathfrak{a}\} \mid x_0\rangle} \\
(\mathsf{D_C}) & \overline{\langle\{x_3 : \mathfrak{b} \triangleq \mathfrak{b}, x_4 : u \triangleq v\} \mid \emptyset \mid \{x_0 \mapsto f(\mathfrak{a}, x_2)\}\{x_2 \mapsto g(x_3, x_4)\} \mid x_0\rangle} \\
(\mathsf{D}) & \overline{\langle\{x_4 : u \triangleq v\} \mid \emptyset \mid \{x_0 \mapsto f(\mathfrak{a}, x_2)\}\{x_2 \mapsto g(x_3, x_4)\}\{x_3 \mapsto \mathfrak{b}\} \mid x_0\rangle} \\
(\mathsf{S}) & \overline{\langle\emptyset \mid \{x_4 : u \triangleq v\} \mid \{x_0 \mapsto f(\mathfrak{a}, x_2)\}\{x_2 \mapsto g(x_3, x_4)\}\{x_3 \mapsto \mathfrak{b}\} \mid x_0\rangle}
\end{array}$$

6 Application to the Composition of Interactions

Recall the interaction composition problem discussed in Fig. 1. Let $\mathcal{L}$ and $\mathcal{M}$ be the universes of lifelines and messages. Atomic actions are $\mathbb{A} = \{\, l!m,\ l?m \mid l \in \mathcal{L},\ m \in \mathcal{M}\,\}$, where for any $a \in \mathbb{A}$, $\Delta(a) \in \{!, ?\}$ and $\psi(a) \in \mathcal{M}$ denote its type and message. Value-passings form the set $\mathbb{VP} = \{\mathsf{vp}(l_1, m, l_2) \mid l_1, l_2 \in \mathcal{L}, m \in \mathcal{M},\ l_1 \neq l_2\}$. Two actions $u, v \in \mathbb{A}$ are *compatible* iff there exist $l_1, l_2 \in \mathcal{L}$ and $m \in \mathcal{M}$ with $l_1 \neq l_2$ such that $\{u, v\} = \{l_1!m, l_2?m\}$; for such actions, we may abusively write $\mathsf{vp}(u, v)$ (resp. $\mathsf{vp}(v, u)$) for $\mathsf{vp}(l_1, m, l_2)$. The set of interactions is $\mathbb{I} = \mathcal{T}(\mathcal{F})$, with signature $\mathcal{F} = (\mathcal{F}_n)_{n \in [0,2]}$ defined as:

$$\mathcal{F}_0 = \mathbb{A} \cup \mathbb{VP} \cup \{\varnothing\}, \quad \mathcal{F}_1 = \{\mathsf{loop}\}, \quad \mathcal{F}_2 = \{\mathsf{seq}, \mathsf{alt}, \mathsf{par}\}.$$

For any $i \in \mathbb{I}$, $\theta(i) \subset \mathcal{L}$ denotes the lifelines occurring in i, defined by $\theta(l!m) = \theta(l?m) = \{l\}$, $\theta(\mathsf{vp}(l_1, m, l_2)) = \{l_1, l_2\}$, $\theta(\mathsf{loop}(i)) = \theta(i)$, and $\theta(f(i, j)) = \theta(i) \cup \theta(j)$ for $f \in \{\mathsf{seq}, \mathsf{alt}, \mathsf{par}\}$. Semantically, seq, alt, and par are associative, alt and par commutative, and $\varnothing$ is the unit for seq and par. Let E denote the set of equations characterizing these properties.

Given a set $\mathfrak{F}_0$ of special constants called gates, a *tagging* γ of $i, j \in \mathbb{I}$ is a set such that: **(1)** each $g \in \gamma$ is a tuple $(p_i, p_j, \mathfrak{a})$ with $\mathfrak{a} \in \mathfrak{F}_0$, $p_i \in pos(i)$, $p_j \in pos(j)$, and $i|_{p_i}$, $j|_{p_j}$ are compatible actions; **(2)** for $g, g' \in \gamma$ with $g' = (p'_i, p'_j, \mathfrak{b})$, we have $\mathfrak{a} = \mathfrak{b}$ implies $(i|_{p_i} = i|_{p'_i}) \wedge (j|_{p_j} = j|_{p'_j})$. Condition **(1)** ensures each tag relates compatible actions via a gate, while **(2)** enforces the uniqueness of actions and gates. We denote by $\Gamma(i, j)$ the set of all taggings of i and j. For example, the tagging of the interactions i and j illustrated in Fig. 1 is $\gamma = \{(1, 12, \mathfrak{a}), (221, 211, \mathfrak{b}), (222, 212, \mathfrak{c})\}$.

Given interactions $i, j, k \in \mathbb{I}$, $(i,j) \overset{\gamma}{\propto} k$ means that k is obtained by composing i and j via a tagging $\gamma \in \Gamma(i,j)$ as defined in Def. 8. We use *mappings* to replace gate with actions or value-passings. A mapping is a partial function $\lambda : \mathfrak{F}_0 \rightharpoonup (\mathbb{A} \cup \mathbb{VP})$, written $\lambda = \{\mathfrak{a}_1 \mapsto u_1, \ldots, \mathfrak{a}_n \mapsto u_n\}$, so that $\mathsf{Dom}(\lambda) = \{\mathfrak{a}_1, \ldots, \mathfrak{a}_n\} \subseteq \mathfrak{F}_0$. For $t \in \mathcal{T}(\mathcal{F} \cup \mathfrak{F}_0)$, $t\lambda$ is defined by $t\lambda$ if $t \in \mathsf{Dom}(\lambda)$, $t\lambda = t$ if $t \in \mathfrak{F}_0 \setminus \mathsf{Dom}(\lambda)$, and $t\lambda = f(t_1\lambda, \ldots, t_m\lambda)$ if $t = f(t_1, \ldots, t_m)$ with $f \in \mathcal{F}_m$.

Definition 8. *For $i, j, k \in \mathbb{I}$ with $\theta(i) \cap \theta(j) = \emptyset$ and $\gamma \in \Gamma(i,j)$, we write $(i,j) \overset{\gamma}{\propto} k$ iff:*

- $\lambda_i = \{\mathfrak{a} \mapsto i|_{p_i} \mid (p_i, p_j, \mathfrak{a}) \in \gamma\}$ *and* $\lambda_j = \{\mathfrak{a} \mapsto j|_{p_j} \mid (p_i, p_j, \mathfrak{a}) \in \gamma\}$*;*
- $i = s\lambda_i$ *and* $j = t\lambda_j$ *for some* $s, t \in \mathcal{T}(\mathcal{F} \cup \mathfrak{F}_0)$*;*
- $r \in \mathcal{T}(\mathcal{F} \cup \mathfrak{F}_0, \mathcal{V})$ *is an E-scpg of s and t with witnesses* σ_s, σ_t*;*
- σ_r *satisfies* $\mathsf{Dom}(\sigma_r) = \mathsf{Dom}(\sigma_s)$ *and* $x\sigma_r = \mathsf{seq}(x\sigma_s, x\sigma_t)$ *for all* x*;*
- λ_k *satisfies* $\mathsf{Dom}(\lambda_k) = \mathsf{Dom}(\lambda_i)$ *and* $\mathfrak{a}\lambda_k = \mathsf{vp}(\mathfrak{a}\lambda_i, \mathfrak{a}\lambda_j)$ *for all* $\mathfrak{a}$*;*
- $k = r\sigma_r\lambda_k$.

To prove the soundness of our composition, we adapt the projection-based approach of [23], where a global type is inferred from local session types. Def. 9 introduces a projection operator π. In [27], we showed that π preserves interaction semantics, i.e., $\pi_L(i)$ gives the traces of i restricted to actions on L.

Definition 9. *The projection π_L onto a subset of lifelines $L \subset \mathcal{L}$ is defined by:*

$$\pi_L(l\Delta m) = \begin{cases} l\Delta m & \text{if } l \in L \\ \varnothing & \text{if } l \notin L \end{cases} \qquad \pi_L(\mathsf{vp}(l_1, m, l_2)) = \begin{cases} l_1!m & \text{if } l_1 \in L, l_2 \notin L \\ l_2?m & \text{if } l_1 \notin L, l_2 \in L \\ \mathsf{vp}(l_1, m, l_2) & \text{if } l_1 \in L, l_2 \in L \\ \varnothing & \text{if } l_1 \notin L, l_2 \notin L \end{cases}$$

$$\pi_L(\mathsf{loop}(i)) = \mathsf{loop}(\pi_L(i)) \qquad \forall f \in \{\mathsf{seq}, \mathsf{alt}, \mathsf{par}\}\ \pi_L(f(i,j)) = f(\pi_L(i), \pi_L(j))$$

With Th. 4, we show that whenever $(i,j) \overset{\gamma}{\propto} k$, projecting k on the lifelines of i (resp. j) yields an interaction semantically equivalent to i (resp. j). For this, we extend θ and π to $\mathcal{T}(\mathcal{F} \cup \mathfrak{F}_0, \mathcal{V})$ via $\theta(\mathfrak{a}) = \theta(x) = \emptyset$, $\pi_L(\mathfrak{a}) = \mathfrak{a}$, and $\pi_L(x) = x$.

Theorem 4. *For any $i, j, k \in \mathbb{I}$ with $\theta(i) \cap \theta(j) = \emptyset$ and any $\gamma \in \Gamma(i,j)$, if $(i,j) \overset{\gamma}{\propto} k$ then k is a sound E-γ-composition of i and j, meaning:*

$$\pi_{\theta(i)}(k) =_E i \qquad \textit{and} \qquad \pi_{\theta(j)}(k) =_E j.$$

Proof. We prove $\pi_{\theta(i)}(k) =_E i$ (the case $\pi_{\theta(j)}(k) =_E j$ is analogous). Let us introduce the terms s, t, r, mappings $\lambda_i, \lambda_j, \lambda_k$ and substitutions $\sigma_s, \sigma_t, \sigma_r$ such that the conditions of Def. 8 are satisfied.

First, note that $\theta(r) = \emptyset$. Indeed, r is a generalization of s and t (hence i and j), and cannot contain non-shared constants. As $\theta(i) \cap \theta(j) = \emptyset$, the only shared constants are $\varnothing$ or gate symbols in $\mathfrak{F}_0$, so $\pi_{\theta(i)}(r) = r$.

Then, consider that $\forall x \in \mathsf{Dom}(\sigma_r) = \mathsf{Dom}(\sigma_s)$, we have $x\sigma_r = \mathsf{seq}(x\sigma_s, x\sigma_t)$. Because σ_s is used to build s and then i from r, we must have $\theta(x\sigma_s) \subseteq \theta(i)$.

Similarly, $\theta(x\sigma_t) \subseteq \theta(j)$. Therefore, given $\theta(i) \cap \theta(i) = \emptyset$, we have $\pi_{\theta(i)}(x\sigma_r) = \pi_{\theta(i)}(\mathsf{seq}(x\sigma_s, x\sigma_t)) =_E x\sigma_s$. As a result, $\pi_{\theta(i)}(r\sigma_r) =_E \pi_{\theta(i)}(r)\sigma_s = r\sigma_s$.

Consider then that $\forall(\_,\_,\mathfrak{a}) \in \gamma$ we have $\mathfrak{a}\lambda_k = \mathsf{vp}(\mathfrak{a}\lambda_i, \mathfrak{a}\lambda_j)$. Via a similar reasoning, we have $\pi_{\theta(i)}(\mathfrak{a}\lambda_k) = \mathfrak{a}\lambda_i$. Therefore $\pi_{\theta(i)}(r\sigma_r\lambda_k) = \pi_{\theta(i)}(r\sigma_r)\lambda_i$.

Finally, as $k = r\sigma_r\lambda_k$, we have $\pi_{\theta(i)}(k) = \pi_{\theta(i)}(r\sigma_r)\lambda_i =_E r\sigma_s\lambda_i = s\lambda_i = i$. □

Experiments. We have implemented sc-preserving anti-unification modulo associativity, commutativity, and neutral elements in a Rust prototype tool, following the approach illustrated in Fig. 5 integrating the work of [6,8] with our concept of special constant preservation. The tool also supports interaction composition and integrates interaction manipulation facilities from an existing Rust-based tool [4]. Experiments were run on an Intel Core i7-13850HX (20-core, 2.1 GHz) with 32 GB RAM, using the Fail (abbreviated F) rule to improve performance, and a timeout threshold of 60 s. Figure 7 summarizes experiments on interactions adapted from the literature [18,22,24,34].

Interaction k	size(k)	Nb. Gates	Avg. composition Time (ms)			
			$(i_{\text{norm}}, j_{\text{norm}})$		$(i_{\text{mut}}, j_{\text{mut}})$	
			with F	without F	with F	without F
ATM[21]	33	[7, 17]	15.016(✓)	timeout	17.757(✓)	timeout
Alt3bit[24]	12	6	4.132(✓)	21.804(✓)	6.01(✓)	32.932(✓)
DistVoting[21]	23	8	8.243(✓)	timeout	10.955(✓)	timeout
FilterCo[24]	11	5	1.396(✓)	1.565(✓)	2.069(✓)	2.339(✓)
Game[24]	16	[5, 6]	2.525(✓)	3.179(✓)	3.163(✓)	4.283(✓)
HealthSys[24]	22	[4, 8]	5.978(✓)	18.496(✓)	7.495(✓)	22.786(✓)
Logistic[24]	26	[6, 11]	9.22(✓)	timeout	12.457(✓)	timeout
ProfOnline[34]	68	[14, 27]	59.567(✓)	timeout	75.474(✓)	timeout
Sanitary[24]	30	[6, 13]	11.491(✓)	40.242(✓)	14.795(✓)	51.265(✓)
TPM[24]	17	7	3.204(✓)	4.911(✓)	4.915(✓)	7.437(✓)
Travel[18]	26	[6, 11]	6.411(✓)	timeout	8.203(✓)	timeout
TwoBuyers[22]	22	[5, 11]	3.78(✓)	5.558(✓)	4.852(✓)	7.162(✓)

Fig. 7. Experiments on interaction composition using anti-unification.

For each interaction k with lifelines L, we randomly generate up to 5 partitions (L_1, L_2), each of size at least $\lfloor L/2 \rfloor$. For each partition we: (1) compute projections $(i = \pi_{L_1}(k), j = \pi_{L_2}(k))$ and their normal forms $(i_{\text{norm}}, j_{\text{norm}})$; (2) apply 7 random commutativity rewrites $\mathsf{par}(x,y) \approx \mathsf{par}(y,x)$ and $\mathsf{alt}(x,y) \approx \mathsf{alt}(y,x)$ using a rewriting tool [5] to produce mutated terms $(i_{\text{mut}}, j_{\text{mut}})$; (3) compose $(i_{\text{norm}}, j_{\text{norm}})$ and $(i_{\text{mut}}, j_{\text{mut}})$, and compare the normal forms of their compositions and that of k to determine success. Each row in Fig. 7 corresponds to an interaction: the second column shows its size, the third the range of gates in local partitions, and the last four columns report average composition durations with and without Fail, for $(i_{\text{norm}}, j_{\text{norm}})$ and $(i_{\text{mut}}, j_{\text{mut}})$. A global success

(✓) indicates that the result matches the original interaction. The corresponding experimental artifact can be accessed [30]. While anti-unification modulo equational theories may exhibit exponential worst-case behavior ([32] shows the number of linear generalizations - in which each variable occurs at most once - modulo AC increases exponentially with the size of the terms), it did not prevent our procedure to perform effectively on our benchmarks. Indeed, we do not compute the full set of sc-preserving least general generalizations modulo equations, but instead stop once the first is found. Moreover, the sc-preservation constraint restricts the search space, especially when the Fail rule is enabled. This results in our approach producing sc-preserving generalizations in tractable time which is sufficient to enable successful and practical composition of interactions.

7 Conclusion

In this paper, we introduced special-constant (sc-)preserving anti-unification, in a framework that extends the anti-unification modulo equational theories of [6,8]. We enrich the ground term language with special constants that may represent common sub-structures that need to be preserved and overlap in the generalization and its two instances. We propose an algorithm for sc-preserving anti-unification which upholds expected termination, soundness and completeness properties. Assuming this anti-unification approach can be extended to arbitrary equational theories (as in [6,8]), we apply it to the practical problem of composing sequence diagrams represented as interaction terms. Each partial view is represented as an interaction term tagged with gates that correspond to our special constants. The global view is obtained via sc-preserving anti-unification of the two partial views modulo associativity, commutativity and unit rules of relevant operators of the interaction language. Our approach for composition of interactions is supported by a prototype tool and experiments.

Future work includes providing a rigorous justification for the equational integration of associativity, commutativity and unit rules as well as exploring additional equations, such as idempotence, $\mathsf{alt}(x,x) \approx x$, and ad-hoc equations like $\mathsf{seq}(\mathsf{loop}(x), \mathsf{loop}(x)) \approx \mathsf{loop}(x)$, to further enhance anti-unification's ability to compose interactions.

Acknowledgements. The authors would like to acknowledge the support of the TWIN-LOOP Project (Grant Agreement No. 101192649), which is funded by the European Union. Views and opinions expressed are however those of the author(s) only and do not necessarily reflect those of the European Union or CINEA. Neither the European Union nor the granting authority can be held responsible for them.

References

1. Message Sequence Chart (MSC). https://www.itu.int/rec/T-REC-Z.120/
2. Unified Modeling Language (UML). https://www.omg.org/spec/UML/

3. https://github.com/Ermine516/UnitAU (2020), GitHub repository
4. https://github.com/erwanM974/hibou_label (2025), GitHub repository
5. https://github.com/maude-lang/Maude (2025), GitHub repository
6. Alpuente, M., Escobar, S., Meseguer, J., Sapiña, J.: Order-sorted equational generalization algorithm revisited. Ann. Math. Artif. Intell. 1–24 (2021). https://doi.org/10.1007/s10472-021-09771-1
7. Alpuente, M., Escobar, S., Meseguer, J., Ojeda, P.: A modular equational generalization algorithm. In: Logic-Based Program Synthesis and Transformation (2009). https://doi.org/10.1007/978-3-642-00515-2_3
8. Alpuente, M., Escobar, S., Espert, J., Meseguer, J.: A modular order-sorted equational generalization algorithm. Inf. Comput. (2014). https://doi.org/10.1016/j.ic.2014.01.006
9. Alur, R., Etessami, K., Yannakakis, M.: Inference of message sequence charts. In: Proceedings of the 2000 International Conference on Software Engineering. (ICSE) (2000). https://doi.org/10.1145/337180.337215
10. Bader, J., Scott, A., Pradel, M., Chandra, S.: Getafix: learning to fix bugs automatically. Proc. ACM Program. Lang. (2019). https://doi.org/10.1145/3360585
11. Barbanera, F., de'Liguoro, U., Hennicker, R.: Connecting open systems of communicating finite state machines. J. Logical Algebraic Methods Program. (2019). https://doi.org/10.1016/j.jlamp.2019.07.004
12. Barbanera, F., Dezani-Ciancaglini, M., Gheri, L., Yoshida, N.: Multicompatibility for multiparty-session composition. Assoc. Comput. Mach. (2023). https://doi.org/10.1145/3610612.3610614
13. Barbanera, F., Dezani-Ciancaglini, M., Lanese, I., Tuosto, E.: Composition and decomposition of multiparty sessions. J. Logical Algebraic Methods Program. (2021). https://doi.org/10.1016/j.jlamp.2020.100620
14. Barbanera, F., Lanese, I., Tuosto, E.: Composing communicating systems, synchronously. In: Leveraging Applications of Formal Methods, Verification and Validation: Verification Principles (2020). https://doi.org/10.1007/978-3-030-61362-4_3
15. Barbanera, F., Lanese, I., Tuosto, E.: Composition of synchronous communicating systems. J. Logical Algebraic Methods Program. (2023). https://doi.org/10.1016/j.jlamp.2023.100890
16. Barwell, A.D., Brown, C., Hammond, K.: Finding parallel functional pearls: Automatic parallel recursion scheme detection in Haskell functions via anti-unification. Futur. Gener. Comput. Syst. (2018). https://doi.org/10.1016/j.future.2017.07.024
17. ter Beek, M.H., Hennicker, R., Kleijn, J.: Compositionality of Safe Communication in Systems of Team Automata (2020). https://doi.org/10.1007/978-3-030-64276-1_11
18. Bouma, J., de Gouw, S., Jongmans, S.S.: Multiparty Session Typing in Java, Deductively. In: Tools and Algorithms for the Construction and Analysis of Systems (2023). https://doi.org/10.1007/978-3-031-30820-8_3
19. Cerna, D.M., Kutsia, T.: Unital Anti-Unification: Type and Algorithms. In: Leibniz International Proceedings in Informatics, LIPIcs, vol. 167 (2020). https://doi.org/10.4230/LIPIcs.FSCD.2020.26
20. Chmelík, M., Řehák, V.: Controllable-choice message sequence graphs. In: Mathematical and Engineering Methods in Computer Science (2013). https://doi.org/10.1007/978-3-642-36046-6_12
21. Edixhoven, L., Jongmans, S.S., Proença, J., Castellani, I.: Branching pomsets: Design, expressiveness and applications to choreographies. J. Logical Algebraic Methods Program. (2024). https://doi.org/10.1016/j.jlamp.2023.100919

22. Honda, K., Yoshida, N., Carbone, M.: Multiparty asynchronous session types. J. ACM (2016). https://doi.org/10.1145/2827695
23. Lange, J., Tuosto, E.: Synthesising choreographies from local session types. In: Concurrency Theory (2012). https://doi.org/10.1007/978-3-642-32940-1_17
24. Lange, J., Tuosto, E., Yoshida, N.: From communicating machines to graphical choreographies. In: Proceedings of the 42nd Annual ACM SIGPLAN-SIGACT Symposium on Principles of Programming Languages (POPL) (2015). https://doi.org/10.1145/2676726.2676964
25. Lassez, J.L., Maher, M.J., Marriott, K.: Unification revisited. In: Foundations of Logic and Functional Programming (1988). https://doi.org/10.1007/3-540-19129-1_4
26. Lohrey, M.: Realizability of high-level message sequence charts: closing the gaps. Theoret. Comput. Sci. (2003). https://doi.org/10.1016/j.tcs.2003.08.002
27. Mahe, E., Bannour, B., Gaston, C., Le Gall, P.: Efficient interaction-based offline runtime verification of distributed systems with lifeline removal. Sci. Comput. Program. (2025). https://doi.org/10.1016/j.scico.2024.103230
28. Mahe, E., Gaston, C., Le Gall, P.: Denotational and operational semantics for interaction languages: Application to trace analysis. Sci. Comput. Program. (2024). https://doi.org/10.1016/j.scico.2023.103034
29. Montesi, F., Yoshida, N.: Compositional choreographies. In: Concurrency Theory (2013). https://doi.org/10.1007/978-3-642-40184-8_30
30. Nguetoum, J., Bannour, B., Le Gall, P., Mahe, E.: Artifact for FM'26 paper: Specializing anti-unification for interaction models composition via gate connections (2026). https://doi.org/10.5281/zenodo.18636309
31. Plotkin, G.D.: A Note on Inductive Generalization. In: Machine Intelligence, Vol. 5 (1970)
32. Pottier, L.: Generalisation de termes en théorie équationnelle. cas associatif-commutatif. Rapport de Recherche RR-1056, INRIA Sophia Antipolis (1989). https://inria.hal.science/inria-00075503v1
33. Reynolds, J.: Transformational systems and the algebraic structure of atomic formulas. In: Machine Intelligence, Vol. 5 (1970)
34. Rocha, M., Simão, A., Sousa, T.: Model-based test case generation from UML sequence diagrams using extended finite state machines. Software Qual. J. **29**(3), 597–627 (2021). https://doi.org/10.1007/s11219-020-09531-0
35. Rolim, R., Soares, G., Gheyi, R., D'Antoni, L.: Learning quick fixes from code repositories. In: Proceedings of the XXXV Brazilian Symposium on Software Engineering (2018). https://doi.org/10.1145/3474624.3474650
36. Scalas, A., Yoshida, N.: Less is more: multiparty session types revisited. Proc. ACM Program. Lang. (2019). https://doi.org/10.1145/3290343
37. Schmid, U.: Inductive Synthesis of Functional Programs. LNCS (LNAI), vol. 2654. Springer, Heidelberg (2003). https://doi.org/10.1007/b12055
38. Stolze, C., Miculan, M., Di Gianantonio, P.: Composable partial multiparty session types for open systems. Softw. Syst. Model. (2023). https://doi.org/10.1007/s10270-022-01040-x

Differential Verification of Information Flow in SEAndroid Policies

Lorenzo Ceragioli(✉), Letterio Galletta, and Edoardo Lunati

IMT School for Advanced Studies Lucca, Lucca, Italy
{lorenzo.ceragioli,letterio.galletta,edoardo.lunati}@imtlucca.it
lorenzo.ceragioli@imtlucca.it, letterio.galletta@imtlucca.it,
edoardo.lunati@imtlucca.it

Abstract. SEAndroid is deployed on almost all modern Android devices to enforce mandatory access control. The Android Open Source Project regularly publishes a predefined SEAndroid policy that each vendor customises for its devices. These customisations and policy updates may cause security regressions: even small misconfigurations may introduce new information flows leading to exploitable vulnerabilities. We propose a differential verification framework that determines whether security relevant changes between two SEAndroid configurations affect information-flow properties as intended. Our verification framework is based on the novel comparative modal logic CML interpreted over pairs of Kripke structures. We formalise SEAndroid policies within this logic and define a suitable model-checking algorithm for differential reasoning. We implement our framework in the tool *Mordente*, and evaluate it on real-world SEAndroid policies.

Keywords: Comparative modal logic · Policy evolution analysis · Access control

1 Introduction

Android is currently the most widely used operating system for mobile devices, making it a frequent target of privilege escalation and code execution attacks [7, 16]. Typically, these attacks aim to compromise high-privileged system daemons, often bypassing the traditional discretionary access control of Linux systems [7]. To mitigate such threats, Security Enhancements for Android (SEAndroid), based on SELinux [2], introduces mandatory access control into the Android platform. SEAndroid is integrated into the kernel and checks every action performed by a subject (e.g., a process) over an object (e.g., a file or socket). In SEAndroid, subjects and objects are associated with abstract security labels as specified in a labelling policy. In addition, a permission policy lists the operations that a labelled subject may perform on a labelled object (all others being denied by default). The Android Open Source Project (AOSP) continuously updates a default SEAndroid policy, which the Android Original Equipment Manufacturers

A. Sampaio and M. Stoelinga (Eds.): FM 2026, LNCS 16556, pp. 461–479, 2026.
https://doi.org/10.1007/978-3-032-26204-2_24

(OEMs) further customise for their devices. Given the size and evolving nature of the Android codebase, ensuring that the SEAndroid configuration enforces the intended security properties is a challenging task [11]. Additionally, modifications to the permission and labelling policies affect the system's effective security posture, and both AOSP and OEMs have introduced misconfigurations and vulnerabilities in the past [14].

Previous work has investigated the security of SEAndroid and SELinux policies, proposing tools for visualisation, inspection, and static verification [5,9,10,12,15]. These tools formalise security in terms of information flow, a well-established approach for reasoning about integrity, confidentiality, and isolation. In practice, we say that there is an information flow from file f to file f' if some processes $p_1, p_2, \ldots, p_n$ and files $f_1, f_2, \ldots, f_{n+1}$ exist such that the process p_i reads from f_i and writes on f_{i+1}, with $f_1 = f$ and $f_{n+1} = f'$. Several important security properties for Android systems can be stated in terms of information flow. For example, to avoid privilege escalation, we can impose that low-privileged domains, such as `untrusted_app`, can never write to `system_file`, `exec_file`, or `shared_libs_file`. Moreover, to enforce cross-app isolation, we may prohibit `untrusted_app` or `platform_app` from interacting with `app_data_file` belonging to other applications. However, existing tools provide little support for comparing configurations across versions or vendors in terms of their security properties. Additionally, they do not help analysts preserve security properties when they are undocumented, which is often the case in real-world policies. While one could verify each version independently against a fixed security specification, this approach requires such a specification to be explicitly provided and fully documented. This situation is rarely met in practice, where security properties are often implicit and undocumented. Instead, directly comparing two configurations allows analysts to focus precisely on whether the changes introduced between versions have the intended security impact, without the need to reason about the entire policy from scratch.

To address this gap, we propose a differential verification framework that determines whether security-relevant changes between two SEAndroid configurations alter information-flow properties as intended. Our framework is based on the new *comparative modal logic* CML, interpreted over sets of Kripke structures representing different system versions. CML extends classical logic with three classes of operators: (*i*) two forward modalities $\Diamond$ ("for some next state") and $\Box$ ("for all next states"); (*ii*) two backward modalities $\blacklozenge$ ("for some previous state") and $\blacksquare$ ("for all previous states"); (*iii*) a version operator $\upharpoonright_i$ used to refer to the i-th version of the system, represented by the i-th Kripke structure. A peculiarity of CML is that, to decide the validity of a formula where two operators $\upharpoonright_i$ and $\upharpoonright_j$ occur (with $i \neq j$), the properties stated in terms of two different Kripke structures must be compared. We do this by enriching each of our Kripke structures with an interpretation over a common set Ω of concrete states.

To use CML for differential reasoning over SEAndroid policies, we first compute a relation describing the information flows between file labels permitted by each policy. The Kripke structure of a SEAndroid configuration consists of

```
(A/.*)|(.*/b)        a
C/a                  b
B/b                  c
C/b                  d
```

(a) File labeling policy of $\mathcal{C}_1$.

```
(A/.*)|(.*/b)        a
.*/a                 e
C/b                  d
```

(b) File labeling policy of $\mathcal{C}_2$.

```
allow p1 a : file { write };
allow p1 b : file { read };
allow p2 c : file { read write }
allow p2 a : file { setattr };
allow q1 b : file { read };
allow q1 d : file { write };
allow q2 d : file { write };
allow q2 c : file { getattr };
```

(c) Access control policy of $\mathcal{C}_1$.

```
allow p e : file { read };
allow p a : file { append };
allow q e : file { read };
allow q d : file { write };
```

(d) Access control policy of $\mathcal{C}_2$.

Fig. 1. Two examples of SEAndroid configurations.

file labels, the corresponding information-flow relation, and a state annotation capturing relevant security properties. In the context of SEAndroid, the set Ω of concrete states contains all the file paths, and the interpretation of Kripke structures derives from the labelling policy: file labels are assigned to file paths by matching regular expressions. This allows us to relate abstract labels to actual filesystem objects and reason about information flows in the system. Finally, we implement our framework in the tool *Mordente*, available at [1], and evaluate it on real-world SEAndroid policies of different vendors and versions.

To the best of our knowledge, our work is the first proposal comparing different versions of SEAndroid policies in terms of their information flow, taking into account the changes in the two labelling policies. A key advantage of our approach over other tools for regression verification is that it does not require the policy analyst to provide a complete specification of the desired security properties. When changing from one SEAndroid version to another, *Mordente* can verify that the update: (*i*) impacts the modified portion of the system as desired; (*ii*) preserves the needed permissions (these flows can only increase); (*iii*) does not add dangerous permissions (these flows can only decrease). Note that (*i*) allows expressing novel desired properties by stating them in terms of the problems of the previous version, whereas (*ii*) and (*iii*) encode the preservation of functional and security properties, including those not explicitly documented by the developers. Combining the last two points, one can verify that the update only impacts a portion of the system, leaving the remaining part unaltered.

***Mordente* at Work.** Consider the two SEAndroid configurations $\mathcal{C}_1$ and $\mathcal{C}_2$ of Fig. 1. Each configuration consists of two components: a *labelling policy* (above in the figure) and a *permission policy* (below in the figure).

The labelling policy is stored in a so-called *file-context* and consists of a sequence of rules mapping regular expressions of filesystem paths to the security context that labels them. Security contexts usually consist of a user, a role,

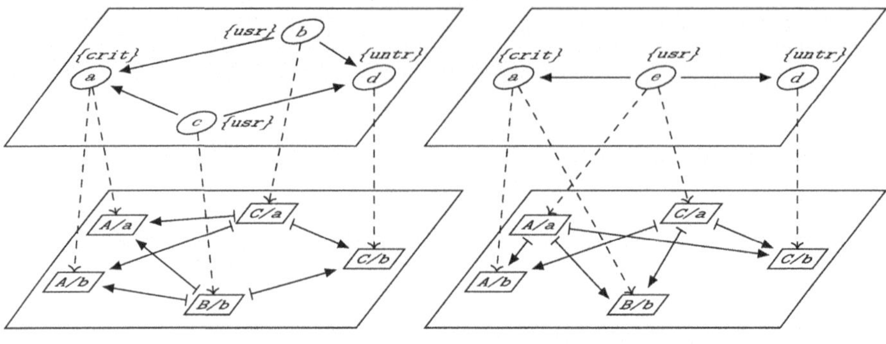

(a) File information flow in $\mathcal{C}_1$.

(b) File information flow in $\mathcal{C}_2$.

Fig. 2. Kripke structures of two SEAndroid configurations: solid arrows represent information flows, dashed arrows represent file labelling.

and a type, but for simplicity, we consider only the type component, which is the most relevant in Android (being type enforcement the primary access control mechanism in mobile devices); thus, hereafter, we treat labels as consisting solely of types. For example, in Fig. 1a the rule on line 1 assigns label `a` to all files in the directory `A` and to any file named `b`, while line 3 assigns `c` to just the file at path `B/b`. Note that the order of rules matters, and SEAndroid applies the last-matched one (regexes matching smaller languages are usually at the end of file contexts). Thus, `B/b` is associated with `c` (line 3) and not with `a` (line 1).

The permission policy specifies which operations labelled subjects are allowed to perform on labelled objects. Administrators typically specify configurations using SELinux's kernel policy language [4], which is then compiled to a kind of (kernel binary) access-control matrix. As illustrated in Fig. 1a, the permission policy is essentially a sequence of rules of the following form.

```
allow subject_type object_type : class {permissions}
```

For instance, the rule on line 1 permits subjects labelled `p1` writing files labeled `a`. Any operation not explicitly allowed is denied by default. Permission policies may also contain `neverallow` rules, attributes that group related types under shared behavioural constraints, and macros that expand into commonly used sets of permissions. The full policy language is outside the scope of this paper, as it is used only for examples, since our tool operates on compiled policies.

In order to compare the two configurations of Fig. 1, we first give them a semantics in terms of Kripke structures (see Fig. 2) where states represent file labels, and arcs the information flow between them induced by *read* and *write* operations (or similar ones like *getattr* and *setattr*). Then, we encode security properties using three atomic propositions: `crit` (i.e. *critical*, is associated with `a` both in $\mathcal{C}_1$ and $\mathcal{C}_2$), `untr` (i.e. *untrusted*, is associated with `d` both in $\mathcal{C}_1$ and $\mathcal{C}_2$) and `usr` (i.e. *user*, is associated with all the remaining labels). Note that label names differ in the two configurations, and the common ones may have a different meaning (like a). Therefore, in order to compare the semantics of the two configurations, their labels must be concretised in terms of actual file paths. This is achieved through the file labelling policies: for each policy, we evaluate the labels while preserving the edges, obtaining the graphs below in Fig. 2.

Using *Mordente*, the policy administrator can build these transition systems automatically, and can check the validity of the following CML proposition ϕ, stating that all the files that used to affect some untrusted file in $\mathcal{C}_1$ satisfy usr in $\mathcal{C}_2$, and they still influence the same files of the previous version.

$$\phi = \uparrow_1(\Diamond \mathtt{untr}) \Rightarrow \uparrow_2(\mathtt{usr} \wedge \Diamond \uparrow_1 \mathtt{untr})$$

The tool signals that ϕ is not satisfied by the version update, informing that the files labelled as c in $\mathcal{C}_1$ and as a in $\mathcal{C}_2$ contradict the property, e.g. the concrete file path B/b. Note indeed that in Fig. 2a, the file at path B/b accesses C/b, which is untrusted, while the same access is not possible in Fig. 2b.

Synopsis. In Sect. 2, we define CML and its model checking. Section 3 encodes SEAndroid using our logic. Section 4 presents *Mordente* and its experimental evaluation. In Sects. 5 and 6, we compare our approach with the literature and draw some conclusions.

2 A Comparative Modal Logic

We define Comparative Modal Logic (CML), a logic for comparing different versions of the same system, each represented as a transition system with states labelled by the properties of interest (a Kripke structure). In the following, we let $\mathbb{I}$ be the finite set of version names, and $\mathbb{P}$ the set of atomic propositions.

Definition 1 (CML **Proposition**). *A* CML *proposition $\phi \in \Phi$ is defined by the following grammar, with $i \in \mathbb{I}$ a version name and $p \in \mathbb{P}$ an atomic proposition.*

$$\phi :: \mathit{true} \mid p \mid \phi \wedge \phi \mid \neg\phi \mid \uparrow_i \phi \mid \Diamond\phi \mid \blacklozenge\phi$$

Intuitively: *true* is always satisfied; p tells that the atomic proposition p is satisfied; $\uparrow_i \phi$ is satisfied if ϕ is satisfied in the version i; $\Diamond\phi$ is satisfied if ϕ is satisfied in at least a next state; $\blacklozenge\phi$ is satisfied if ϕ is satisfied in at least a previous state; boolean conjunction and negation behaves as expected.

We derive other logical operators in the usual way.

$$\Box\phi = \neg\Diamond\neg\phi \qquad \blacksquare\phi = \neg\blacklozenge\neg\phi \qquad \phi \vee \psi = \neg(\neg\phi \wedge \neg\psi) \qquad \phi \Rightarrow \psi = \neg\phi \vee \psi$$

Example 1. Intuitively, the formula $\uparrow_1(\mathtt{a} \wedge \Diamond(\neg\mathtt{b} \wedge \uparrow_2 \mathtt{b}))$ is satisfied by a pair of versions of the same system if, in the first version, it is true that a is valid and we can access some state where b is valid only in the second version.

To give the CML semantics, we first define a model for versions in isolation.

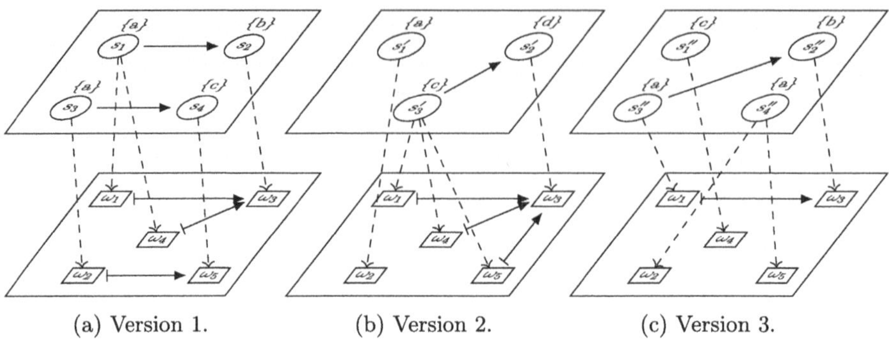

(a) Version 1. (b) Version 2. (c) Version 3.

Fig. 3. A CML model of example and the concretization its components.

Definition 2 (Kripke Structure). *A* Kripke structure $\mathcal{K} = (S, \twoheadrightarrow, \vdash)$ *is a triple with: S a set of states; $\twoheadrightarrow \subseteq S \times S$ the transition relation; and where $\vdash \subseteq S \times \mathbb{P}$ associates atomic propositions with states in which they hold.*

The purpose of CML is to compare different versions, and for that we need a common ground, which is represented by the special set of states $\Omega \ni \omega, \omega', \ldots$ that we assume to be *concrete states*. The states of each version can be thought of as abstract representations of classes of concrete states.

Definition 3 (State Evaluation). *A* state evaluation *for a set of states S is a function $\downarrow: S \longrightarrow 2^{\Omega}$ that associates each state with the concrete ones it represents, and it satisfies that $\downarrow(s) \cap \downarrow(s') = \emptyset$ if $s \neq s'$, and $\bigcup_{s \in S} \downarrow(s) = \Omega$.*

As a result of that, the Kripke structure of a version $\mathcal{K}$ can always be seen as an abstract representation of a Kripke structure over the set of concrete states: its concretisation is obtained by evaluating states according to the given function.

Definition 4 (Concretization). *Given a Kripke structure $\mathcal{K} = (S, \twoheadrightarrow, \vdash)$ and a state evaluation $\downarrow$ for S, the concretization of $\mathcal{K}$ with respect to $\downarrow$ is a Kripke structure $(\Omega, \mapsto, \Vdash)$ with*

- $\mapsto \subseteq \Omega \times \Omega$ *such that $\omega \mapsto \omega'$ if and only if $s \twoheadrightarrow s'$ for some s and s' in S with $\omega \in \downarrow(s)$ and $\omega' \in \downarrow(s')$;*
- $\Vdash \subseteq \Omega \times \mathbb{P}$ *such that $\omega \Vdash p$ if and only if $\omega \in \downarrow(s)$ and $s \vdash p$ for some $s \in S$.*

A CML model is a set of Kripke structures paired with state evaluations.

Definition 5 (Model). *A* CML *model* $\mathcal{M} = \{(\mathcal{K}_i, \downarrow_i)\}_{i \in \mathbb{I}}$ *is a collection of pairs indexed by the set $\mathbb{I}$ of versions, where $\mathcal{K}_i = (S_i, \twoheadrightarrow_i, \vdash_i)$ is the Kripke structure of the version i, and $\downarrow_i: S_i \longrightarrow 2^{\Omega}$ is its state evaluation.*

Example 2. Let $\Omega = \{\omega_1, \omega_2, \omega_3, \omega_4, \omega_5\}$. The CML model in Fig. 3 is $\mathcal{M} = \{(\mathcal{K}_1, \downarrow_1), (\mathcal{K}_2, \downarrow_2), (\mathcal{K}_3, \downarrow_3)\}$, where, e.g., the graph above in Fig. 3b represents $\mathcal{K}_2 = (\{s'_1, s'_2, s'_3\}, \{(s'_3, s'_2)\}, \{(s'_1, a), (s'_2, d), (s'_3, c)\})$, while the graph below is its concretisation with respect to the state evaluation represented by the vertical dashed arrows, $\downarrow_2 = \{(s'_1, \{\omega_2\}), (s'_2, \{\omega_3\}), (s'_3, \{\omega_1, \omega_4, \omega_5\})\}$.

We now define the validity of a formula according to a CML model. By expressing it in terms of concrete states, we allow for comparing different versions.

Definition 6. *Given a* CML *model* $\mathcal{M} = \{(\mathcal{K}_i, \downarrow_i)\}_{i \in I}$, *we define the validity of a* CML *proposition* $\phi \in \Phi$ *with respect to a concrete state* $\omega \in \Omega$ *and a version* $i \in I$ *though the following satisfaction relation* $\omega, i \models_{\mathcal{M}} \phi$*:*

$$\begin{array}{ll}
\omega, i \models_{\mathcal{M}} \mathit{true} & \\
\omega, i \models_{\mathcal{M}} p & \text{if } \omega \Vdash_i p \\
\omega, i \models_{\mathcal{M}} \phi \wedge \phi' & \text{if } \omega, i \models_{\mathcal{M}} \phi \text{ and } \omega, i \models_{\mathcal{M}} \phi' \\
\omega, i \models_{\mathcal{M}} \neg\phi & \text{if } \omega, i \not\models_{\mathcal{M}} \phi \\
\omega, i \models_{\mathcal{M}} \uparrow_j \phi & \text{if } \omega, j \models_{\mathcal{M}} \phi \\
\omega, i \models_{\mathcal{M}} \Diamond\phi & \text{if } \omega' \text{ exists such that } \omega \mapsto_i \omega' \text{ and } \omega', i \models_{\mathcal{M}} \phi \\
\omega, i \models_{\mathcal{M}} \blacklozenge\phi & \text{if } \omega' \text{ exists such that } \omega' \mapsto_i \omega \text{ and } \omega', i \models_{\mathcal{M}} \phi
\end{array}$$

where $(\Omega, \mapsto_i, \Vdash_i)$ *is the concretisation of* $\mathcal{K}_i$ *with respect to* $\downarrow_i$.

We say that a concrete state $\omega \in \Omega$ *satisfies a* CML *proposition* ϕ, *and we write* $\omega \models_{\mathcal{M}} \phi$, *if* $\omega, i \models_{\mathcal{M}} \phi$ *for any* $i \in \mathbb{I}$. *Finally, we say that the* CML *model* $\mathcal{M}$ *satisfies* ϕ, *and we write* $\mathcal{M} \models \phi$, *if* $\omega \models_{\mathcal{M}} \phi$ *for any* $\omega \in \Omega$.

Example 3. Consider the CML model $\mathcal{M}$ of Example 2 and assume that we want to preserve some property while passing from version i to j. The property encoded by the atomic predicate a is preserved if $\uparrow_i \mathsf{a} \Rightarrow \uparrow_j \mathsf{a}$, i.e. when all concrete states satisfying a in the first version also satisfy it in the second one. For example $\mathcal{M} \models \uparrow_2 \mathsf{a} \Rightarrow \uparrow_1 \mathsf{a}$, while $\mathcal{M} \not\models \uparrow_1 \mathsf{a} \Rightarrow \uparrow_3 \mathsf{a}$ (the state ω_4 is a counterexample).

The preservation of reachability is more involved: various CML propositions can be used, with different nuances in their meaning. Consider the following predicates, noting that $\uparrow_i(\mathsf{a} \wedge \Diamond\mathsf{b})$ is satisfied by concrete states that used to satisfy a and to access states that used to satisfy b in the old version i:

- $\phi_{i,j} = \uparrow_i(\mathsf{a} \wedge \Diamond\mathsf{b}) \Rightarrow \uparrow_j(\mathsf{a} \wedge \Diamond\mathsf{b})$ specifies that such states still satisfy a and can access states satisfying b now;
- $\psi_{i,j} = \uparrow_i(\mathsf{a} \wedge \Diamond\mathsf{b}) \Rightarrow \uparrow_j \Diamond \uparrow_i \mathsf{b}$ means that they replicate the accessibility of the previous version, but says nothing about satisfying atomic predicates;
- $\xi_{i,j} = \uparrow_i(\mathsf{a} \wedge \Diamond\mathsf{b}) \wedge \uparrow_j \mathsf{a} \Rightarrow \uparrow_j \Diamond\mathsf{b}$ requires only states that currently satisfy a to replicate the accessibility of the previous version.

Then, $\mathcal{M}$ satisfies $\psi_{1,2}$, $\xi_{1,2}$ and $\xi_{1,3}$ (see Fig. 3), but not $\phi_{1,2}$ nor $\phi_{1,3}$ (ω_4 does not satisfy a in $\mathcal{K}_2$ nor $\mathcal{K}_3$), and not $\psi_{1,3}$ (ω_4 does not access ω_3 in $\mathcal{K}_3$).

We now investigate the model-checking problem, namely, given a model $\mathcal{M}$ and a CML proposition ϕ, we want to check if $\omega \models_{\mathcal{M}} \phi$ for any $\omega \in \Omega$. Ideally, we want to compute the satisfaction set $\{\omega \in \Omega \mid \omega \models_{\mathcal{M}} \phi\}$, but Ω is often considerably large (even infinite in theory): we need a feasible way of computing a succinct representation of the satisfaction set in terms of the (finite and possibly small) sets of states S_i.

We start by defining a normal form for CML where $\uparrow_i$ appears only before modal operators and atomic propositions, and before each of them. Formally:

Definition 7 (Normal Form). CML *propositions in* normal form *are generated by the following grammar, with* $i \in \mathbb{I}$ *a version and* $p \in \mathbb{P}$ *atomic proposition.*

$$\phi :: \mathit{true} \mid \phi \wedge \phi \mid \neg\phi \mid \uparrow_i p \mid \uparrow_i \Diamond\phi \mid \uparrow_i \blacklozenge\phi$$

We let $\Phi^\bullet \subsetneq \Phi$ *be the set of* CML *propositions in normal form.*

Each CML proposition can be transformed into an equivalent normal form.

Theorem 1. *For each* CML *proposition* ϕ, *there exists a* CML *proposition in normal form* $\phi^\bullet$ *such that* $\omega \models_{\mathcal{M}} \phi$ *if and only if* $\omega \models_{\mathcal{M}} \phi^\bullet$ *for any* ω *and* $\mathcal{M}$.

We define compatible states, i.e. functions associating a state to each version i such that it is possible to be in all of the states at the same time. We write $\bar{s}$ for a function from versions to states, and $\bar{s}[i]$ for the state associated with $i \in \mathbb{I}$.

Definition 8 (Compatible State). *Given a* CML *model* $\mathcal{M} = \{(\mathcal{K}_i, \downarrow_i)\}_{i\in\mathbb{I}}$ *with* $\mathcal{K}_i = (S_i, \rightarrow_i, \vdash_i)$ *for all* $i \in \mathbb{I}$, *a* compatible state *of* $\mathcal{M}$ *is a function* $\bar{s}$ *associating a version* $i \in \mathbb{I}$ *with a state* $s \in S_i$ *such that* $\bigcap_{i\in I} \downarrow_i \bar{s}[i] \neq \emptyset$. *Let* $\mathbb{S}$ *be the set of all compatible states.*

Example 4 The compatible states of $\mathcal{M}$ of Example 2 follow, where we write each function from versions to states $\{(1, s), (2, s'), (3, s'')\}$ as the vector $[s, s', s'']$:

$$\bar{s}_1 = [s_1, s'_3, s''_1] \qquad \bar{s}_2 = [s_1, s'_3, s''_3] \qquad \bar{s}_3 = [s_2, s'_2, s''_2]$$
$$\bar{s}_4 = [s_3, s'_1, s''_4] \qquad \bar{s}_5 = [s_4, s'_3, s''_4]$$

We finally define the succinct representation for the satisfaction set of a CML proposition. More precisely, given ϕ, we compute the set of compatible states $\bar{s}$ that correspond to concrete states satisfying ϕ. The definition is given by recursion, immediately suggesting a model-checking procedure.

Definition 9 (Compatible Satisfaction Set). *Given a* CML *model* $\mathcal{M} = \{(\mathcal{K}_i, \downarrow_i)\}_{i\in I}$ *with* $\mathbb{S}$ *its set of compatible states and* $\mathcal{K}_i = (S_i, \rightarrow_i, \vdash_i)$ *for all* $i \in I$, *and given* $\phi \in \Phi^\bullet$, *we let the* compatible satisfaction set *of* ϕ *with respect to* $\mathcal{M}$ *be* $[\![\phi]\!] \subseteq \mathbb{S}$ *recursively defined as follows:*

$$[\![\mathit{true}]\!] = \mathbb{S} \qquad [\![\neg\phi]\!] = \mathbb{S} \setminus [\![\phi]\!] \qquad [\![\phi \wedge \phi']\!] = [\![\phi]\!] \cap [\![\phi']\!]$$
$$[\![\uparrow_i p]\!] = \{\bar{s} \in \mathbb{S} \mid \bar{s}[i] \vdash_i p\} \qquad [\![\uparrow_i \Diamond\phi]\!] = \{\bar{s} \mid \bar{s}' \in [\![\phi]\!] \text{ exists s.t. } \bar{s}[i] \rightarrow_i \bar{s}'[i]\}$$
$$[\![\uparrow_i \blacklozenge\phi]\!] = \{\bar{s} \mid \bar{s}' \in [\![\phi]\!] \text{ exists s.t. } \bar{s}'[i] \rightarrow_i \bar{s}[i]\}$$

Example 5. Consider $\psi_{1,3}$ of Example 3, and the compatible states of Example 4. The compatible satisfaction set for the normal form of $\psi_{1,3}$ is:

$$\begin{aligned}[\![\neg(\uparrow_1 \mathtt{a} \wedge \uparrow_1 \Diamond \uparrow_1 \mathtt{b} \wedge \neg \uparrow_3 \Diamond \uparrow_1 \mathtt{b})]\!] &= \mathbb{S} \setminus (\{\bar{s}_1, \bar{s}_2, \bar{s}_4\} \cap \{\bar{s}_1, \bar{s}_2\} \cap \{\bar{s}_1, \bar{s}_3, \bar{s}_4, \bar{s}_5\}) \\ &= \mathbb{S} \setminus \{\bar{s}_1\} = \{\bar{s}_2, \bar{s}_3, \bar{s}_4, \bar{s}_5\}\end{aligned}$$

Note that $\downarrow_1 \bar{s}_1[1] \cap \downarrow_2 \bar{s}_1[2] \cap \downarrow_3 \bar{s}_3[1] = \{\omega_4\}$, the only counterexample of $\psi_{1,3}$.

The following result guarantees the correctness of the compatible satisfaction set with respect to the satisfaction relation of CML.

Theorem 2. *Given a* CML *model* $\mathcal{M} = \{(\mathcal{K}_i, \downarrow_i)\}_{i \in I}$*, it holds for all* $\omega \in \Omega$ *and* $\phi \in \Phi^\bullet$ *that* $\omega \models_{\mathcal{M}} \phi$ *if and only if* $\omega \in \bigcup_{\bar{s} \in [\![\phi]\!]} \bigcap_{i \in I} \downarrow_i \bar{s}[i]$

3 Representing SEAndroid Policies

In the following, we let Ω be the set of legal file paths of Android devices. As it is clear from the notation, files will be the concrete states for our CML encoding. We also let $\Sigma \supsetneq \Omega$ be the set of all possible entities of an Android system: files, processes, ports. We denote with $\mathbb{L}$ and $\mathbb{L}_\mathtt{f} \subsetneq \mathbb{L}$ the sets of all SEAndroid labels and of those associated with files, respectively; $\ell_\perp \in \mathbb{L}_\mathtt{f}$ is the distinguished *default* file label used when no other labels can be associated (usually `default_t`). We assume O to be the set of operations controlled by SEAndroid (reading files, searching in directories, etc.). Finally, we let $\mathbb{P}$ be the set of properties appearing in security policies, which we will use as atomic propositions in the CML encoding.

A SEAndroid configuration has two main components: a set of permitted operations between labelled entities and a list of rules for associating files with labels. In addition, we consider a security policy annotating labels with their security properties, such as secrecy or trust level.

Definition 10 (SEAndroid Configuration). *A* SEAndroid configuration $\mathcal{C}$ *is a triple* $(\mathbb{A}, \mathbb{F}, \Gamma)$ *where*

- *the* access control policy $\mathbb{A}$ *is a finite set of triples* $(\ell, o, \ell') \in \mathbb{L} \times O \times \mathbb{L}$*;*
- *the* file labeling policy $\mathbb{F}$ *is a list of pairs* $(\mathcal{L}, \ell)$ *with* $\mathcal{L} \subseteq 2^\Omega$ *a regular language of file paths and* $\ell \in \mathbb{L}_\mathtt{f}$ *a file label;*
- *the* security policy $\Gamma \subseteq \mathbb{L}_\mathtt{f} \times \mathbb{P}$ *associates labels with predicates in* $\mathbb{P}$.

Example 6. Consider the configurations $\mathcal{C}_1 = (\mathbb{A}_1, \mathbb{F}_1, \Gamma_1)$ and $\mathcal{C}_2 = (\mathbb{A}_2, \mathbb{F}_2, \Gamma_2)$ of Fig. 1. We interpret each line `allow b a : file { write };` of the access control policies in Figs. 1c and 1d as a triple $(\mathtt{b}, \mathtt{file\ write}, \mathtt{a})$ in SELinux notation. The file labelling policies in Figs. 1a and 1b are lists of pairs, where languages are represented as regular expressions. In accordance with Android behaviour, we read the files bottom-up, thus taking a list in reverse order with respect to what is in Fig. 1. The security policies are:

$$\begin{aligned}\Gamma_1 &= \{(a, \mathtt{crit}), (b, \mathtt{usr}), (c, \mathtt{usr}), (d, \mathtt{untr})\} \\ \Gamma_2 &= \{(a, \mathtt{crit}), (e, \mathtt{usr}), (d, \mathtt{untr})\}.\end{aligned}$$

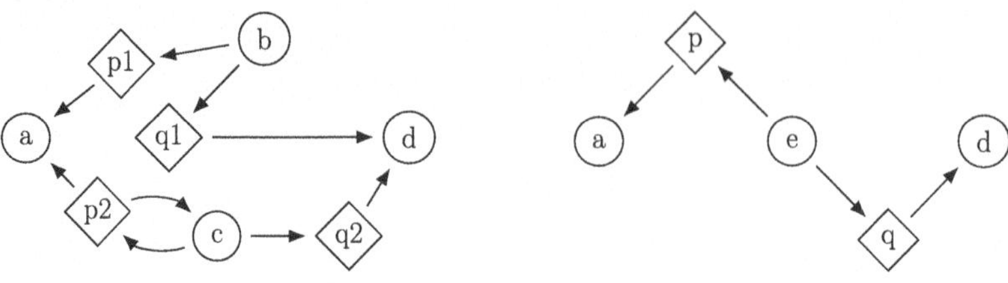

(a) Information flow relation of $\mathbb{A}_1$. (b) Information flow relation of $\mathbb{A}_2$.

Fig. 4. Information flow relation of two configurations: circles and diamonds are file and non-file labels respectively, we omit the arcs obtained by transitivity.

We assume an information flow evaluation function $\mathit{ife} : O \rightarrow 2^{\{\triangleright,\triangleleft\}}$ associating each operation o with the directions of the information flows it causes: $\triangleright \in \mathit{ife}(o)$ if o allows the process to send information to the object on which o is performed; $\triangleleft \in \mathit{ife}(o)$ if o allows the process to receive information from it. It is now possible to represent the information flow resulting from a policy.

Definition 11 (Information Flow Relation). *The* information flow relation *I of a SEAndroid access control policy $\mathbb{A}$ is the smallest subset of $\mathbb{L} \times \mathbb{L}$ such that:*

- *if $(\ell, o, \ell') \in \mathbb{A}$ for some o with $\triangleright \in \mathit{ife}(o)$ then $(\ell, \ell') \in I$;*
- *if $(\ell', o, \ell) \in \mathbb{A}$ for some o with $\triangleleft \in \mathit{ife}(o)$ then $(\ell, \ell') \in I$;*
- *if $(\ell, \ell'') \in I$ and $(\ell'', \ell') \in I$ then $(\ell, \ell') \in I$.*

Computing the Kripke structure of a SEAndorid configuration amounts to considering the information flow relation over file labels only, and to associate such labels with atomic propositions according to the security policy Γ.

Definition 12 (Kripke Encoding). *The Kripke structure of a SEAndroid configuration $(\mathbb{A}, \mathbb{F}, \Gamma)$ with information flow relation I is $(\mathbb{L}_\mathtt{f}, I \cap (\mathbb{L}_\mathtt{f} \times \mathbb{L}_\mathtt{f}), \Gamma)$.*

Example 7. The graphs above in Fig. 2 represent the Kripke structures of the two configurations $\mathcal{C}_1$ and $\mathcal{C}_2$ of Fig. 1. The transitions are obtained as the subset over file labels of the information flow relations depicted in Fig. 4; atomic propositions are associated according to the security policies Γ_1 and Γ_2.

Given $\mathbb{F}$, the file labelling policy of the SEAndroid configuration, we define $\lambda_\mathbb{F}$ to be the function used by the operating system to associate labels with files. Intuitively, given a file with path ω, the rules of $\mathbb{F}$ are processed sequentially (i.e. in reverse order with respect to the file context). For each pair $(\mathcal{L}, \ell)$, the regular expression representing $\mathcal{L}$ is considered: if $\omega \in \mathcal{L}$, the label ℓ is associated with ω, otherwise the process moves to the next pair.

Definition 13 (File Labeling Function). *Given a file labeling policy $\mathbb{F}$, its* file labeling function *$\lambda_\mathbb{F} : \Omega \longrightarrow \mathbb{L}_\mathtt{f}$ is defined as $\lambda_\mathbb{F}(\omega) = \ell$ if $(\mathcal{L}, \ell)$ is the first pair in $\mathbb{F}$ such that $\omega \in \mathcal{L}$, and $\lambda_\mathbb{F}(\omega) = \ell_\bot$ if no $\mathcal{L}$ of $\mathbb{F}$ contains ω.*

Example 8. The file labeling functions of $\mathcal{C}_1$ and $\mathcal{C}_2$ in Fig. 1 follow, where $\mathcal{L}_a$ and $\mathcal{L}_e$ are the languages recognized by `(A/.*)|(.*/b)` and `.*/a`, respectively.

$$\lambda_{\mathbb{F}_1}(\omega) = \begin{cases} b & \text{if } \omega = \texttt{C/a} \\ c & \text{if } \omega = \texttt{B/b} \\ d & \text{if } \omega = \texttt{C/b} \\ a & \text{if } \omega \in \mathcal{L}_a \setminus \{\texttt{C/a}, \texttt{B/b}, \texttt{C/b}\} \\ \ell_\perp & \text{otherwise} \end{cases} \qquad \lambda_{\mathbb{F}_2}(\omega) = \begin{cases} d & \text{if } \omega = \texttt{C/b} \\ e & \text{if } \omega \in \mathcal{L}_e \setminus \{\texttt{C/b}\} \\ a & \text{if } \omega \in \mathcal{L}_a \setminus (\mathcal{L}_e \cup \{\texttt{C/b}\}) \\ \ell_\perp & \text{otherwise} \end{cases}$$

The graphs below in Fig. 2 are pictorial representations of the concretisations of the Kripke structures of the two configurations above (see Example 7).

Finally, the CML model of a pair of SEAndroid configurations can be computed by associating their Kripke structures with the label evaluation obtained by inverting the file labelling function.

Definition 14 (CML **Encoding**). *The* CML *model of two SEAndroid configurations $\mathcal{C}_1$ and $\mathcal{C}_2$ is $\{(\mathcal{K}_1, \downarrow_1), (\mathcal{K}_2, \downarrow_2)\}$, where for $i = 1, 2$: $\mathcal{K}_i$ is the Kripke structure of $\mathcal{C}_i$; $\downarrow_i : \mathbb{L}_\mathtt{f} \longrightarrow 2^\Omega$ is such that $\downarrow_i(\ell) = \{\omega \mid \lambda_{\mathbb{F}_i}(\omega) = \ell\}$ for all $\ell \in \mathbb{L}_\mathtt{f}$, with $\mathbb{F}_i$ the file labeling policy of $\mathcal{C}_i$.*

We now use this encoding to compare two instances of SEAndroid in terms of their information flow through the procedure of Sect. 2.

Example 9. Consider the CML model for $\mathcal{C}_1$ and $\mathcal{C}_2$ of Fig. 1. We start by computing the set of compatible states $\mathbb{S}$. To simplify our notation, we represent compatible states as pairs $[\ell, \ell']$, with ℓ associated with the first configuration and ℓ' with the second. A pair of file labels $[\ell, \ell']$ is included in $\mathbb{S}$ if there exists at least a filepath that is associated with ℓ in the first policy and with ℓ' in the second one. For example, $[a, e] \in \mathbb{S}$ because of `A/a`, while $[c, e] \notin \mathbb{S}$ because c labels only `B/b` in $\mathbb{F}_1$ and e labels only filepaths ending with `a` in $\mathbb{F}_2$. Simple computations suffice for showing that $\mathbb{S} = \{[a, a], [a, e], [b, e], [c, a], [d, d]\}$.

Consider the CML formula $\phi = \uparrow_1(\Diamond\texttt{untr}) \Rightarrow \uparrow_2(\texttt{usr} \wedge \Diamond\uparrow_1\texttt{untr})$ of Sect. 1. To check the validity of ϕ in our model, we take $\neg\phi$ and normalise it (Theorem 1). The result is $\psi = \uparrow_1\Diamond\uparrow_1\texttt{untr} \wedge (\neg\uparrow_2\texttt{usr} \vee \neg\uparrow_2\Diamond\uparrow_1\texttt{untr})$. We compute the compatible satisfaction set of ψ according to Definition 9:

$$\begin{aligned} [\![\psi]\!] &= [\![\uparrow_1\Diamond\uparrow_1\texttt{untr}]\!] \setminus ([\![\uparrow_2\texttt{usr}]\!] \cup [\![\uparrow_2\Diamond\uparrow_1\texttt{untr}]\!]) \\ &= \{[b, e], [c, a]\} \setminus (\{[a, e], [b, e]\} \cup \{[a, e], [b, e]\}) = \{[c, a]\}. \end{aligned}$$

The property is not satisfied, and concrete counterexamples are those files labelled as c in $\mathcal{C}_1$ and as a in $\mathcal{C}_2$, i.e. $\downarrow_1(c) \cap \downarrow_2(a) = \{\texttt{B/b}\}$.

4 Implementation and Evaluation of *Mordente*

We implement our verification framework in the tool *Mordente*, available at [1]. Below, we discuss its internals and evaluate it on real-world policies.

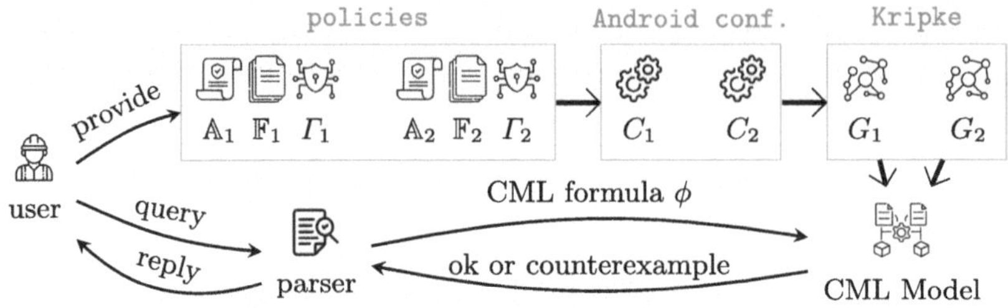

Fig. 5. Workflow of *Mordente*.

Algorithm 1. Compute the state evaluation $\downarrow_i$ of the i-th configuration.

Input: An ordered list $\mathbb{F}$ of pairs (ℓ, α) with ℓ a string and α an automaton
Output: A dictionary $\mathbb{D}$ from strings to automata

```
ζ ← ℒ(ϵ)                         ▷ ζ is the language of previously seen file paths
𝔻[ℓ] ← ∅ for all ℓ
for all pairs (ℓ, α) in 𝔽 do
    β ← α ∩ ζᶜ                    ▷ ζᶜ is the complement of ζ
    𝔻[ℓ] ← 𝔻[ℓ] ∪ β
    ζ ← ζ ∪ β
return 𝔻
```

***Mordente* Internals.** The workflow of *Mordente* is in Fig. 5. The user provides two compiled SEAndroid policies to be compared, each accompanied by its file context specification and its security policy Γ. For each policy, *Mordente* constructs a *SEAndroid configuration* $\mathcal{C} = (\mathbb{A}, \mathbb{F}, \Gamma)$ and then its *Kripke structure* $\mathcal{K}$. It then computes the *SEAndroid* CML *Model* for the pair of configurations, and waits for the user to submit CML queries for the differential verification.

More in detail, *Mordente* processes its input as follows. To build the access control policy $\mathbb{A}$, we extract all the *allow* rules from the compiled policy using setools [3]. Constructing the file labelling policy $\mathbb{F}$ requires additional work. We first process the file context entries in reverse order, as the Android system does. As a result, we obtain a list of pairs (`regex`, ℓ), where $\ell \in \mathbb{L}_\mathtt{f}$ is a label and `regex` a regular expression of file paths. We then translate each `regex` into an equivalent finite state automaton using *libmata* [6]. To compute $\downarrow_i(\ell)$, the regular language of file paths associated with ℓ, we apply Algorithm 1, which iteratively refines each automaton to remove paths already matched by earlier entries, resolving shadowing between overlapping file context regexes. More precisely, Algorithm 1 returns a dictionary $\mathbb{D}$ from labels to automata, such that the language of $\mathbb{D}[\ell]$ is disjoint from the one of $\mathbb{D}[\ell']$ if $\ell \neq \ell'$. Note that if the same label ℓ appears more than once in the file context, we take the union of the resulting automata.

For efficiency, *Mordente* does not explicitly construct the full information flow relation I of Definition11. Instead, it builds a graph G where nodes are SEAndroid labels and edges are a compact representation of I that omits transitive edges. More precisely, for each triple $(s, o, s') \in \mathbb{A}$, we add to G the edge (s, s')

Algorithm 2. Removes non-file labels from G while preserving connectivity.

Input: A graph $G = (N, E)$
Output: G where all the nodes are file labels

```
for all n ∈ N such that n is not a file label do
    for all (u, n) ∈ E with u ≠ n do
        for all (n, v) ∈ E with n ≠ v do                ▷ u and v are connected
            if not (u, v) ∈ E then E ← E ∪ {(u, v)}
    Remove n from G
return G
```

Table 1. *Mordente* experimental evaluation.

(a) Generation of the Kripke structures.

	file context lines	allow rules	build time (s)
① Pixel Comet (14)	1327	41296	436.24
② Pixel Comet (15)	1351	42744	454.74
③ Pixel Comet (16)	1397	45104	494.26
④ Xiaomi 11T	1940	52122	504.37
⑤ Xiaomi 14T	2264	63673	1188.80
⑥ Xiaomi 15T	2271	56784	1141.90

(b) Differential analysis.

	compatible states	build time (s)	query time (s)
① ↔ ②	769	17.52	2.18
② ↔ ③	814	17.51	2.39
① ↔ ④	1568	37.46	16.28
② ↔ ⑤	1592	38.11	13.96
② ↔ ⑥	1608	49.80	21.97

if $\triangleright \in \mathit{ife}(o)$ and (s', s) if $\triangleleft \in \mathit{ife}(o)$. We remove from G the non-file labels, i.e. those not in $\mathbb{D}$, while updating the edges to preserve connectivity: if two file labels were connected via a path possibly traversing non-file labels, the pruned graph maintains a path between them (see Algorithm 2). Formally, after this pruning of G, its edges compactly represent the relation $I \cap (\mathbb{L}_\mathtt{f} \times \mathbb{L}_\mathtt{f})$. Then, the Kripke structure $\mathcal{K}$ is obtained by considering the security policy Γ and associating atomic predicates to nodes of G accordingly.

After constructing both Kripke structures, *Mordente* computes the set of compatible states of the CML Model: these are pairs of labels (ℓ_1, ℓ_2) such that the intersection of their corresponding automata recognises a non-empty language. Finally, once the user submits a CML formula ϕ, the verification proceeds as follows. We take $\neg\phi$ and compute its normal form $\psi^\bullet$ (Theorem 1). A custom model-checking procedure, based on Definition 9, computes the set of compatible states $[\![\psi^\bullet]\!]$ that falsify ϕ (note in passing that the modalities $\uparrow_i\lozenge$ and $\uparrow_i\blacklozenge$ are interpreted as reachability over the graph G). If $[\![\psi^\bullet]\!]$ is empty, the property ϕ holds; otherwise, a counterexample is generated by instantiating the offending states in $[\![\psi^\bullet]\!]$ with concrete file paths.

Experimental Evaluation. We experimentally evaluated *Mordente* on a collection of policies from different vendors and Android versions. We automated the tests with a script, available at [1], which takes in input the Android firmware images of the systems to compare, it extracts the SEAndroid policy configuration

$$\phi_1 = \uparrow_j \texttt{critical} \Rightarrow \uparrow_i \texttt{critical}$$
$$\phi_2 = \uparrow_j \Diamond \texttt{critical} \Rightarrow \uparrow_i \Diamond \uparrow_j \texttt{critical}$$
$$\phi_3 = \uparrow_j (\texttt{untrusted} \wedge \Diamond \texttt{critical}) \Rightarrow \uparrow_i \Diamond \uparrow_j \texttt{critical}$$
$$\phi_4 = \uparrow_j (\texttt{untrusted} \wedge \Diamond \texttt{critical}) \Rightarrow \uparrow_i (\texttt{untrusted} \wedge \Diamond \texttt{critical})$$
$$\phi_5 = \uparrow_j (\texttt{untrusted} \wedge \Diamond \texttt{critical}) \wedge \uparrow_i \texttt{untrusted} \Rightarrow \uparrow_i \Diamond \texttt{critical}$$
$$\phi_6 = \uparrow_j (\texttt{critical} \wedge \blacklozenge \texttt{untrusted}) \Rightarrow \uparrow_i (\uparrow_j \texttt{critical} \wedge \blacklozenge \uparrow_j \texttt{untrusted})$$
$$\phi_7 = (\uparrow_j \Diamond \texttt{critical} \wedge \uparrow_i \texttt{untrusted}) \Rightarrow \uparrow_j \texttt{secure}$$

Fig. 6. CML formulas used for differential analysis of Sect. 4.

files (precompiled policy, file contexts, and information about the Android version). The user can choose to perform either a *vertical* or an *horizontal* analysis. In the first case, policies are from the same vendor but from different Android versions, and are compared incrementally, each version with the next one; in the second case, the policies are from different vendors (presumably of the same Android version) and are compared in every possible combination.

During the analysis, *Mordente* is first invoked once for each SEAndroid configuration to compute its Kripke structure, which is then saved for future use. Whereas the policies for access control and file labelling are extracted from the Android images, the security policy Γ of each version is defined according to the following heuristic: we considered the predicates *untrusted*, *secure*, and *critical*, and associated them with file labels that contain the predicate as a substring. In addition, we manually annotate well-known Android files with the most appropriate security properties. Then, the tool is applied to each pair of policies to compute their CML Model and compatible states, and finally to check the validity of some submitted queries.

We evaluated *Mordente* on 6 configurations as reported in Table 1: three are from major Android releases (14, 15, 16) of the firmware for a Pixel 9 Pro Fold (*Comet*) [8]; three others are from different Xiaomi devices (11T, 14T, 15T) [17], selected with a similar Android version (14, 15). These configurations were selected because they are released by two major OEMs: the Pixel devices are produced by Google, which leads Android development; while the Xiaomi devices are from one of the most widely used Android vendors worldwide. For any analyzed pair of versions i and j of SEAndroid configurations, we verified the seven CML formulas in Fig. 6, encoding the following intuitive properties: ϕ_1 says that critical files should not increase, encoding the desired minimality property of the trusted computing base of operating systems; ϕ_2 says that files influencing critical resources do not increase, as they can possibly lead to integrity violations; ϕ_3 checks that untrusted files influencing critical entities do not increase, thus weakening the previous formula; ϕ_4 and ϕ_5 are variations of the previous one discussed in Example 2; ϕ_6 checks that critical files influenced by some untrusted entity do not increase, limiting the impact of possibly malicious resources; ϕ_7 verifies that files that were once untrusted and can now influence critical entities must be labelled as secure, i.e. it allows declassification only when explicitly documented.

The experiments were conducted on a virtual machine with 4 cores of an Intel Core i7-10700 K processor (3.80 GHz) and 16GB of RAM, running Ubuntu 24.04. In more detail, Table 1a shows the size of each considered configuration (the number of file context lines and *allow* rules) as well as the time it takes on average over 10 executions to construct its Kripke structure. We analysed Pixel configurations vertically (comparing each version with the next one); whereas each Xiaomi configuration was assessed against the same Android major version of Pixel. Table 1b reports the results of our differential analysis over the selected pairs of configurations: the number of compatible states, the time to compute the resulting CML model, and the time to verify 7 formulas discussed above (average over 10 executions).

Overall, the time needed to compute the Kripke structure is acceptable for both vendors. Furthermore, the time required to compute a CML model is considerably smaller, and the queries are almost instant. In addition, *Mordente* is capable of storing the computed Kripke structure and reload it when needed, vastly reducing the expected loading times by a factor of 20 on average.

5 Related Work

The security of SEAndroid and SELinux has been extensively studied in the literature from various perspectives. Below, we first discuss proposals that examine how SEAndroid policies have evolved over the years and across various vendors. Then, we consider research on verifying information-flow properties in SELinux.

Im et al. [11] perform a historical analysis on the AOSP repository to understand the evolution of SEAndroid policy. In particular, the authors propose a metric for the complexity of policies and measure different commits of the main branch of the repository: the complexity of SEAndroid policies has been growing exponentially over time, confirming the necessity of specialised tools and techniques for their analysis. Yu et al. [18] investigate the status of SEAndroid policy customisation, namely, the differences in terms of permissions between the official AOSP policy and the versions of vendors. They propose the tool SEPAL to automatically predict whether the customised policy rules are potentially risky or unnecessary, using natural language processing techniques. Posemato et al. [14] perform a longitudinal study on Android OEM customisations with the goal of determining if these customisations lead to compatibility and security problems. They consider the various requirements imposed by Google to brand a device "Android", including some over SEAndroid. They highlighted that many customisations removed some `neverallow` rules from the AOSP policy, weakening the security of the resulting policy. The papers above compare SEAndroid policies using ad hoc algorithms that analyse individual rules and their granted permissions. In contrast, our work assigns a formal semantics to SEAndroid policies and verifies them not at the level of single rules, but in terms of the information flows induced by the permissions collectively granted across multiple rules. Moreover, our logic and model-checking procedure enable policy analysts to express and verify a variety of relational queries over pairs of policies, offering greater expressiveness than rule-by-rule comparison.

Some tools have been proposed to compare two SELinux policies. The `sediff` tool is a command-line utility, part of the SETools (SELinux Policy Analysis Tools) suite, used to compare and find the semantic differences between two SELinux policies. The tool operates at the entity level and highlights differences in various policy elements, including rules, types, and attributes. More precisely, given two policies, the tool can detect if an element exists only in one of the two policies or if it has been modified, namely, it exists in both policies, but the associated permissions have changed. The V3SPA [9] is a visualisation tool for SELinux policies that supports policy analysts in understanding the meaning of a policy and performing differential policy analysis, highlighting the changes between two policy versions. Policies are depicted as graphs, where nodes represent subjects and objects, and edges represent the permissions associated with them. These graphs can be manually inspected by analysts. These tools offer limited analysis capabilities because they either focus on individual permissions or require policy analysts to manually compare graph representations of the policies. In contrast, our approach supports the specification of more expressive information-flow properties and automatically checks them, thereby providing better scalability and generality. In addition, our work is the first to compare permissions in terms of concrete files, considering possibly different labelling policies, whereas previous approaches only reason at the level of labels.

Several papers target information flow in SELinux policies. Radika et al. [15] analyse SELinux configurations to identify potentially dangerous information flows, defined by the authors as those from some entity a to some b such that a `neverallow` rule prohibits a direct read access from b to a. They developed a tool to statically investigate such information flows, and applied it to the AOSP policy; Jaeger et al. [12] analyse the SELinux example policy for Linux 2.4.19, identifying the trusted computing base and studying its integrity. Hernandez et al. [10] investigate the Android policy environment, including SEAndroid, UNIX-style DAC, and Linux capabilities, and propose BigMAC, a framework that unifies all policy layers to produce a large, fine-grained attack graph. A logic-based query engine is then used to prune infeasible paths and unused types. Similarly, Lee et al. [13] describe PolyScope, a tool for analysing Android systems and identifying resources that attackers can modify, with and without policy manipulations. For each integrity violation detected, PolyScope characterises how attacks may be mounted. Ceragioli et al. [5] enriched the intermediate language CIL, used to specify SELinux configurations with a formal semantics and mechanisms to allow users to specify and verify information-flow requirements. All these papers analyse one policy at a time and therefore cannot detect differences in permitted information flow across different policies. In contrast, our proposal enables the specification and verification of information-flow properties over pairs of policies, thus supporting change-impact analysis of SEAndroid configurations.

6 Conclusion

We have presented a differential verification framework for SEAndroid that enables reasoning across multiple versions or vendor variants of a policy, capturing how changes in the permissions and labelling affect the information-flow properties. Our framework is built on CML, a modal logic that we designed explicitly to express comparative properties across pairs of Kripke structures. We have formalised SEAndroid policies as Kripke structures and have defined a suitable CML model-checking algorithm for differential reasoning on them. We have implemented our approach in the *Mordente* tool and evaluated its scalability on real-world SEAndroid policies from different vendors and Android releases. Our experiments show that differential verification is feasible in practice. To the best of our knowledge, *Mordente* is the first tool to compare SEAndroid configurations in a formally grounded way that simultaneously accounts for changes in both the permission and labelling policies. A key advantage of *Mordente* is that it allows proving the preservation of undocumented security properties.

Future work includes using *Mordente* to perform a large-scale security analysis of SEAndroid customisation to identify security-relevant deviations. Moreover, we plan to extend *Mordente* by integrating automated repair strategies for policy regressions.

Acknowledgements. Work supported by the project SERICS (PE00000014, PNRR M4C2 I1.3, CUP: D67G22000340001) under the MUR National Recovery and Resilience Plan funded by the European Union - NextGenerationEU.

References

1. Mordente: tool for differential verification of information flow in SEAndroid policies. https://doi.org/10.5281/zenodo.18606935. Repository: https://github.com/edoxthebest/Mordente
2. Selinux project. https://selinuxproject.org
3. Setools: policy analysis tools for selinux. https://github.com/SELinuxProject/setools
4. The SELinux Notebook - Kernel Policy Language. https://github.com/SELinuxProject/selinux-notebook/blob/main/src/kernel_policy_language.md#kernel-policy-language
5. Ceragioli, L., Galletta, L., Degano, P., Basin, D.: Specifying and verifying information flow control in selinux configurations. ACM Trans. Priv. Secur **27**(4), (2024)
6. Chocholatý, D., et al.: Mata: a fast and simple finite automata library. In: Finkbeiner, B., Kovács, L. (eds.) Tools and Algorithms for the Construction and Analysis of Systems, pp. 130–151. Springer Nature Switzerland, Cham (2024)
7. Drake, J.: Stagefright: scary code in the heart of android (2015). https://blackhat.com/docs/us-15/materials/us-15-Drake-Stagefright-Scary-Code-In-The-Heart-Of-Android.pdf. BlackHat USA

8. Google: full Ota images for nexus and pixel devices. https://developers.google.com/android/ota
9. Gove, R.: V3spa: a visual analysis, exploration, and diffing tool for selinux and seandroid security policies. In: 2016 IEEE Symposium on Visualization for Cyber Security (VizSec), pp. 1–8. (2016). https://doi.org/10.1109/VIZSEC.2016.7739580
10. Hernandez, G., Tian, D.J., Yadav, A.S., Williams, B.J., Butler, K.R.: BigMAC: fine-grained policy analysis of android firmware. In: 29th USENIX Security Symposium (USENIX Security 20), pp. 271–287. USENIX Association (2020). https://www.usenix.org/conference/usenixsecurity20/presentation/hernandez
11. Im, B., Chen, A., Wallach, D.S.: An historical analysis of the seandroid policy evolution. In: Proceedings of the 34th Annual Computer Security Applications Conference, pp. 629–640. ACSAC '18, Association for Computing Machinery, New York, NY, USA (2018). https://doi.org/10.1145/3274694.3274709
12. Jaeger, T., Sailer, R., Zhang, X.: Analyzing integrity protection in the selinux example policy. In: Procs 12th USENIX Security Symposium, USENIX Association, Washington, D.C., USA (2003)
13. Lee, Y.T., et al.: PolyScope: multi-policy access control analysis to compute authorized attack operations in Android systems. In: 30th USENIX Security Symposium (USENIX Security 21), pp. 2579–2596. USENIX Association (2021). https://www.usenix.org/conference/usenixsecurity21/presentation/lee-yu-tsung
14. Possemato, A., Aonzo, S., Balzarotti, D., Fratantonio, Y.: Trust, but verify: a longitudinal analysis of android OEM compliance and customization. In: 2021 IEEE Symposium on Security and Privacy (SP), pp. 87–102 (2021). https://doi.org/10.1109/SP40001.2021.00074
15. Radhika, B.S., Kumar, N.V.N., Shyamasundar, R.K., Vyas, P.: Consistency analysis and flow secure enforcement of selinux policies. Comput. Secur. **94**, 101816 (2020)
16. Seri, B., Vishnepolsky, G.: The dangers of bluetooth implementations: unveiling zero day vulnerabilities and security flaws in modern bluetooth stacks. Technical Report, Armis INC. White Paper (2023). https://info.armis.com/rs/645-PDC-047/images/BlueBorne
17. Xiaomi: Xiaomi community. https://c.mi.com/global/miuidownload/index
18. Yu, D., et al.: Sepal: towards a large-scale analysis of seandroid policy customization. In: Proceedings of the Web Conference 2021, pp. 2733–2744. WWW '21, Association for Computing Machinery, New York, NY, USA (2021). https://doi.org/10.1145/3442381.3450007

Formal Reasoning About Confidence and Automated Verification of Neural Networks

Mohammad Afzal[1,2(✉)], S. Akshay[1], Blaise Genest[3,4], and Ashutosh Gupta[1]

[1] Indian Institute of Technology Bombay, Mumbai, India
afzal.2@tcs.com
[2] TCS Research, Pune, India
[3] CNRS@CREATE & IPAL, Singapore, Singapore
[4] CNRS, IPAL, Paris, France

Abstract. In the last decade, a large body of work has emerged on robustness of neural networks, i.e., checking if the decision remains unchanged when the input is slightly perturbed. However, most of these approaches ignore the confidence of a neural network on its output. In this work, we aim to develop a generalized framework for formally reasoning about the confidence along with robustness in neural networks. We propose a simple yet expressive grammar that captures various confidence-based specifications. We develop a novel and unified technique to verify all instances of the grammar in a homogeneous way, viz., by adding a few additional layers to the neural network, which enables the use any state-of-the-art neural network verification tool. We perform an extensive experimental evaluation over a large suite of 8870 benchmarks, where the largest network has 138M parameters, and show that this outperforms ad-hoc encoding approaches by a significant margin.

1 Introduction

Neural networks are increasingly being used in safety-critical applications such as autonomous vehicles, medical diagnosis, and speech recognition [1–3]. However, as is well known e.g., in the image classification setting [4], a small perturbation in the input image may lead to misclassifying the output of the network, even if the perturbed image looks exactly like the original image. Such examples are called adversarial examples and there is a long line of work [5–7] that focuses on generating such examples. But failure to generate adversarial examples does not guarantee that they do not exist, and one often resorts to formal methods techniques for such guarantees.

One such paradigm has emerged around local (i.e., around a given input) robustness verification for image classification, where different techniques have been developed, including sound but incomplete techniques such as [8–11] as well as less scalable but complete techniques such as [12–16]. The success of these approaches can be judged by the VNN-COMP competition for robustness verification of neural networks [17], which has several competing solvers

A. Sampaio and M. Stoelinga (Eds.): FM 2026, LNCS 16556, pp. 480–499, 2026.
https://doi.org/10.1007/978-3-032-26204-2_25

working on neural networks of fairly large size, with the largest network having approximately 13.16 Million activations.

Different Robustness Variants. Different applications require different variants of robustness (e.g., see [18]). Further, many existing works on robustness verification regard answers returned by classifiers as binary, ignoring the fact that classifiers provide a confidence in the counterexample in terms of the classification probability, which is computed by the well known SOFTMAX function [19]. For instance, in Fig. 1(a-b) an image from the CIFAR-10 [20] dataset, is misclassified after an input perturbation, but with a very low confidence. If all misclassifications are low confidence ones, should such a network be called non-robust? This motivates a more *relaxed* notion of robustness which would allow such examples. At the other extreme, a *stronger* notion of robustness says that the network in Fig. 1(c-e) should be called non-robust since under minor input perturbations, the confidence in the classification has vastly changed, even if no misclassification is reported. Finally, we may consider top-k robustness [21] that requires the top-k predictions to remain within the top-k set under input perturbations, as illustrated in Fig. 1(f).

To handle variants such as those described above, the first step is to introduce a common specification mechanism for all of them. In this work, we use a simple grammar to provide a generalized way to reason about the confidence of neural network outputs. In brief, this grammar captures Boolean combinations of confidence-based and non-confidence-based conditions, and the variants introduced earlier are specific instances of this expressive framework. Since our grammar involved confidence, it becomes necessary to approximate the confidence (SOFTMAX) function to analyze these properties effectively, which we do, with formal guarantees on the error.

Difficulties in Encoding. The main difficulty that remains is whether such rich properties modeled as Boolean combinations of linear inequalities can directly be encoded in state-of-the-art tools. As standardized in VNN-COMP, robustness properties are specified in a special VNNLIB format as pre- and post-conditions that a neural network must satisfy. Although VNNLIB supports arbitrary Boolean combinations of linear constraints, most state-of-the-art neural network verifiers are optimized for simpler post-conditions which typically involve only disjunctions or conjunctions of linear atoms of over the outputs. Thus, verifying properties with multi-layered conjunctions, disjunctions, or combinations of both poses significant challenges: (i) Modifying the verifier's code to handle complex post-conditions requires a deep understanding of its implementation, which can be challenging for users unfamiliar with the codebase, i.e. $\alpha\beta$-CROWN [22] (ii) The source code for some commercial verifiers may not be publicly available, restricting the ability to make modifications. (iii) Even when access is available, adapting the code for each new property format is time-consuming and prone to errors. (iv) Constraint-based tools, i.e., MARABOU [23], allow such properties to be encoded directly as constraints, but users are then limited to a particular solver only. (v) Advanced techniques like Projected Gradient Descent (PGD) attacks, which are highly effective at finding counterexamples in neural networks, cannot always be applied directly due to the complexity of certain post-conditions.

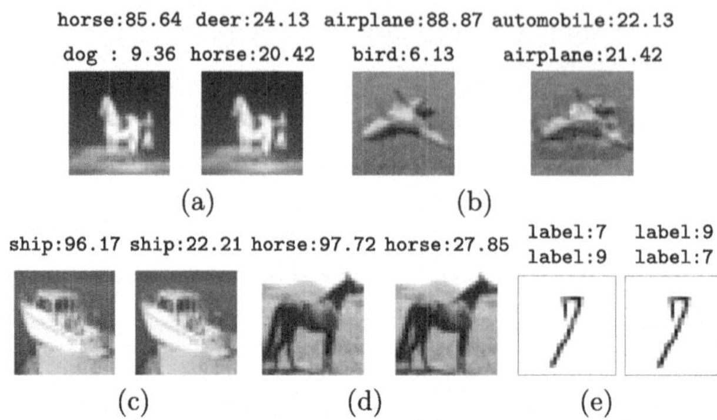

Fig. 1. Relaxed Robustness: (a-b) The network `convBigRELU-PGD.onnx` correctly classified the original image (left) as `horse` (and resp. `airplane`) with high confidence. With an input perturbation of 16/255, we can find misclassified images (right) but with low confidence. In fact, it turns out all counterexamples have low confidence and hence verification succeeds under the relaxed robustness criterion with an 80% confidence threshold, while state-of-the-art verifiers would have declared this network non-robust. **Strong robustness: (c-d)** The network `convBigRELU-PGD.onnx` classified the original image (left) of class `ship/horse/deer` with very high confidence and we found images (right) within perturbation of 16/255, such that the confidence drops drastically, although the class remains same. These images are robust with respect to the standard and relaxed robust criteria but not robust with respect to the strong robust criteria if confidence is allowed to fall upto 30%. **Top-k robustness: (e)** The network `mnist-net-256x6.onnx` correctly classifies the original input as label 7. With an input perturbation of 13/255, we obtain a counterexample classified as label 9. Top-k robustness requires that the top-k predictions remain unchanged under input perturbations. For $k = 2$, the top-2 predictions are labels 7 and 9, and this set is the same for both the original and perturbed images. Hence, the image shown above satisfies top-2 robustness but not local robustness.

Simplifying Post-conditions by Adding Layers. To overcome these challenges, we propose a technique that simplifies arbitrary postconditions by appending a few additional layers to the neural network. Intuitively, we encode an arbitrary postcondition as a sequence of layers and attach these layers to the original network. Our method is inspired by the NP-completeness proof in [24], where a reduction from 3-SAT formulas to neural networks is constructed. However, their encoding requires real variables to take values close to either 0 or 1, whereas our framework generalizes this idea to handle arbitrary formulas expressed in Linear Real Arithmetic (LRA) form. Our transformation converts the post-condition into a straightforward form, such as $y \geq 0$ or $y > 0$, where y is the output of an added node in the neural network, while maintaining low error bounds. This intricate transformation generates new layers that encode parts of the formulas and composes the outputs of these layers according to the Boolean operations in the formulas. Since most verifiers support the ReLU activation function, we employ ReLU to model Boolean operations in the post-conditions. The output of a sum of ReLUs can model conjunction or disjunction: if all inputs are negative, the output is zero; if any input is positive, the output is positive. Since we use ReLU operators to model all Boolean operations, conjunctions and disjunctions interpret input signals in opposite ways i.e., for a conjunction, a negative input yields 1 and a positive input yields 0, while for a disjunction, a positive input yields 0 and a negative input yields 1. To enable composition of conjunction outputs into disjunctions and vice versa, we introduce a novel technique that reverses the outputs using a flip operation, while maintaining low error bounds. These simplified post-conditions can be verified using any state-of-the-art verifier as a black box, eliminating the need for code modifications and ensuring seamless integration with existing tools. Summarizing, *our main contributions* are:

- We define a grammar that supports generalized reasoning on confidence of the outputs of the neural network. This grammar captures existing notions from the literature such as strong [18] and top-k robustness [21].
- Our framework allows us to define novel notions of relaxed robustness that incorporate confidence by distinguishing low-confidence counterexamples during robustness analysis.
- To encode the SOFTMAX function (characterizing the confidence) into Boolean combinations of linear constraints, we approximate it with formal guarantees on the error incurred by the approximation.
- We provide a new technique to verify any instance of the grammar, via a general encoding (for all properties that can be expressed using this grammar), which adds layers to the neural network. Our encoding enables the use of state-of-the-art neural network verifiers like $\alpha\beta$-CROWN, PyRAT.
- We perform a wide set of experiments over benchmarks ranging from 0.51K to 13.16M non-linear activation units. Our evaluation shows that this novel technique can efficiently verify several formulae definable in the grammar and it outperforms ad-hoc encodings from the literature [18,25].

Structure of the Paper. We define preliminaries in Sect. 2. Section 3 introduces different notions of confidence-based properties, the SOFTMAX approximation, and the grammar. In Sect. 4, we present our unifying technique to verify properties by encoding post-conditions as layers. Section 5 reports our experiments demonstrating the effectiveness of our translation, and we conclude in Sect. 6.

Related Work. In addition to the works already discussed, we discuss a few recent developments. The paper [25] recently introduced softmax-based confidence and its verification focusing on computing bounds on the output of the softmax function based on the bounds of its input. Our approximation is different, as explained in Sect. 3.3, and is fine-tunable with respect to the desired confidence level and usable with any neural network verified, not just constraint-based ones. [26] introduces convex bounds on the softmax function, providing both lower and upper bounds that are compatible with convex optimization. A case-study surveying different robustness variants is presented in [18] which includes strong and smooth robustness. The strong definition in [18] however, requires the logit value of the classified class should not drop below a certain threshold. We apply the same condition using confidence values, which are normalized between 0 and 100. Smoothness is an instance of Lipschitz continuity in neural networks [18,27–30], which bounds each class's logit values using a Lipschitz constant. Ours is a simplified version as we bound the confidence of the seed image's class by a threshold. The paper [31] performs robustness verification for cross-entropy loss functions, but there is a subtle difference, as we do not use the logarithm of the softmax output. Furthermore, the technique used in that paper is based on a *Satisfiability Modulo Convex Programming* [31] approach, whereas we use $\alpha\beta$-CROWN, which relies on a different suite of solver techniques, including PGD-attack [32], CROWN [33], α-CROWN [16], β-CROWN [15], among others. Other papers [34,35] have also explored encoding constraints into neural networks. The paper [34] appends a user-requirement as a layer to the neural network and trains the network to satisfy these requirements, however, their approach is limited to propositional formulae, and was not applied to post training robustness verification. The framework [35] simplifies neural networks by statically replacing unsupported operations with supported ones, enabling the underlying verifier to handle them. It also simplifies properties by decomposing them into smaller sub-properties that can be verified individually by the verifier. Finally, [36] introduced the concepts of top-k relaxed robustness and affinity robustness which we show can be captured in our approach.

2 Preliminaries

A neural network is composed of layers $l_0, l_1, \ldots, l_k$, where k represents the number of layers. Each layer contains an ordered set of neurons. A neuron n_{ij} represents the j-th neuron of layer l_i, and $|l_i|$ represents the number of neurons in layer l_i. Layers l_0 and l_k are the input and output layers, respectively; all other layers are hidden layers. We assume that input and output layers do not have any activation function, while each hidden layer l_i has an activation function σ_i. Some well-known non-linear activation functions include: ReLU: $\sigma_i(y) = \max(0, y)$; LeakyReLU: $\sigma_i(y) = \max(\alpha y, y)$, where α is the slope hyperparameter for the negative input region ($y \leq 0$); Sigmoid: $\sigma_i(y) = \frac{1}{1+e^{-y}}$; and Tanh: $\sigma_i(y) = \frac{e^y - e^{-y}}{e^y + e^{-y}}$. We consider any activation function as long as it is supported by state of the art verifiers. Each layer l_i, except the input layer, has a weight matrix $W_i \in \mathbb{R}^{|l_i| \times |l_{i-1}|}$ and a bias vector $B_i \in \mathbb{R}^{|l_i|}$. Let Φ_i denote the function representing the computation from layer l_0 to l_i. Then, $\Phi_i(x) = \boldsymbol{\sigma}_i(W_i \Phi_{i-1}(x) + B_i)$, where $\boldsymbol{\sigma}_i$ denotes the vectorized version of the scalar activation function σ_i, and $\Phi_0(x) = x$. For the output layer l_k, the network output is given by $N(x) = \Phi_k(x) = W_k \Phi_{k-1}(x) + B_k$. $N_i(x)$ represents the logits value of ith output neuron. The final decision $\hat{N}$ of a neural network is determined using the argmax [37] function, which returns the index/class of the maximum output value: $\hat{N}(x) = \text{argmax}(N(x))$. Thus, a neural network $N : \mathbb{R}^n \rightarrow \mathbb{R}^m$ is a function that takes an input of n dimensions and produces an output of m dimensions, i.e., $n = |l_0|$ and $m = |l_k|$.

To construct a verification query, we define predicates P and Q over the input and output layers, respectively. A *verification query* is defined as a triple $\langle N, P, Q\rangle$. We say that the query holds if, for every input x such that $x \models P$, it follows that $N(x) \models Q$, i.e., $\forall x, P(x) \implies Q(N(x))$. If the query does not hold, then there exists a counterexample x such that $x \models P$ and $N(x) \not\models Q$. For instance, the standard (local) robustness definition can be written as a verification query in the above form as follows.

Standard Local Robustness. For a given image x^* (sometimes called the seed image), a neural network N, and an input perturbation parameter ϵ, the local robustness property [11,33,38–40], states that for all images x close to x^*, the network's prediction for x should be the same as its prediction for x^*. We represent the closeness as $\texttt{dist}(x^*, x) = \|x^* - x\|_p$, where $p \in \{1, 2, \infty\}$. Formally:

$$\forall x \; \texttt{dist}(x^*, x) \leq \epsilon \implies \hat{N}(x^*) = \hat{N}(x) \tag{1}$$

This corresponds to the verification query $\langle N, P, Q\rangle$, where P is $\texttt{dist}(x^*, x) \leq \epsilon$ and Q is $\hat{N}(x^*) = \hat{N}(x)$. We call x a *misclassified* input if $\hat{N}(x^*) \neq \hat{N}(x)$.

Softmax-Based Confidence Computation in Neural Networks. In a neural network classifier, each output neuron is associated with a class, and the output of the neuron is the logit value for that class. The SOFTMAX function converts these logits into a probability distribution over the classes, which indicates the confidence of the network in its prediction. This is formally defined in Eq. 2 below, where t denotes the class for which we compute the confidence, and y_i denotes the logit value for the ith dimension (class i) of the output layer. The tuple $(y_1, .., y_m)$ is denoted by $\bar{y}$. This definition is adopted from [19,25,26].

$$\textsc{Conf}((y_1, .., y_m), t) = \textsc{Conf}(\bar{y}, t) = 100 \cdot \textsc{softmax}(\bar{y}, t) = \frac{100 \cdot e^{y_t}}{\sum_{i=1}^{m} e^{y_i}}. \tag{2}$$

3 Modeling Different Robustness Variants

Different robustness properties are required for different applications [18] and hence it is important to allow users to specify and verify new properties as needed. At the same time incorporating confidence into properties poses an additional challenge (as also noted in [18,25]), since confidence (as defined in Eq. 2) involves exponential functions. To integrate such properties with existing solver technologies, which primarily handle linear constraints or their Boolean combinations, one must approximate confidence in a suitable form. In this section, we present a grammar that captures a wide variety of robustness specifications, both with and without confidence. We then show our approximation of confidence and subsequently demonstrate how the confidence-based robustness variants discussed in the introduction are in this grammar.

3.1 Generalized Reasoning on Confidence

The following grammar describes the rules for the post-conditions considered in our analysis. *LE* denotes linear expressions. *CC* represents confidence constraints, and the final property is represented by PC (for PostCond), which denotes Boolean combinations of linear constraints and CC. Let $\bar{y} = (y_1, y_2, \ldots, y_m)$ represent the output logits of the neural network.

$$\begin{aligned}
\text{LE::} &= c_1y_1 + c_2y_2 + \cdots + c_my_m + b, \forall i \in [m], c_i, b \in \mathbb{R} \\
\text{CC::} &= \textsc{Conf}(\bar{y}, t) \bowtie b, t \in [m], b \in \mathbb{R}^+, \bowtie \in \{\leq, \geq, <, >\} \\
\text{PC::} &= \text{PC} \wedge \text{PC} \mid \text{PC} \vee \text{PC} \mid \text{CC} \mid \text{LE} > 0 \mid \text{LE} \geq 0
\end{aligned}$$

This grammar provides a unified representation for expressing a broad class of post-conditions that may combine logical constraints with confidence-based reasoning. Since the grammar involves expressions containing Conf, our first step is to approximate Conf in a way that yields linear constraints over rationals, also called linear rational arithmetic (or LRA for short). It is essential that the approximation produces only LRA constraints, because in the next section, we demonstrate that any constraint expressible in LRA form can be automatically verified using our layer-based encoding.

3.2 Approximation of *Conf*

As explained in Eq. 2, Conf, is derived from the well-known softmax function, which is highly non-linear, as it uses exponential terms. We approximate the Conf constraints by splitting into the following two cases:

Approximation of Conf $(\bar{y}, t) \leq b$ **and Conf**$(\bar{y}, t) < b$ **:** We consider the approximation of $\textsc{Conf}(\bar{y}, t) < b$, and the approximation of $\textsc{Conf}(\bar{y}, t) \leq b$ follows analogously. Recall that $\bar{y} = (y_1, \ldots, y_m) = N(x)$. Suppose the dimension for which we analyze the confidence is t, and y_t is the corresponding logit value. Consider the output dimension t' such that the corresponding logit value is $y_{t'} = \max_{i=1,\, i \neq t}^{m}(y_i)$. For any $b > 0$, we have the following. Let $\delta = -\ln\left(\frac{100}{b} - 1\right)$.

Claim 1. *If* $y_t < y_{t'} + \delta$ *holds, then* $\textsc{Conf}(\bar{y}, t) < b$, *else* $\textsc{Conf}(\bar{y}, t) \geq \frac{100}{1+(m-1)e^{-\delta}}$.

Proof. If $y_t < y_{t'} + \delta$, by removing all exponential terms from the denominator except for e^{y_t} and $e^{y_{t'}}$, we obtain $\textsc{Conf}(\bar{y}, t) \leq \frac{100e^{y_t}}{e^{y_t}+e^{y_{t'}}}$. After scaling the right-hand side by $\frac{1}{e^{y_t}}$, we get $\textsc{Conf}(\bar{y}, t) \leq \frac{100}{1+e^{-(y_t-y_{t'})}}$. Since $\delta > y_t - y_{t'}$, we have $\textsc{Conf}(\bar{y}, t) < \frac{100}{1+e^{-\delta}}$. Since $\delta = -\ln(\frac{100}{b} - 1)$, $\textsc{Conf}(\bar{y}, t) < b$. Suppose the assumption does not hold, then since $y_{t'}$ is the maximum among other logits, we can derive $\textsc{Conf}(\bar{y}, t) \geq \frac{100e^{y_t}}{e^{y_t}+(m-1)e^{y_{t'}}}$, replacing e^i by $e^{t'}$ for all $i, i \neq t$. After scaling the fraction in the RHS by e^{y_t}, we obtain $\textsc{Conf}(\bar{y}, t) \geq \frac{100}{1+(m-1)e^{y_{t'}-y_t}}$. Since $y_t \geq y_{t'} + \delta$, we obtain $\textsc{Conf}(\bar{y}, t) \geq \frac{100}{1+(m-1)e^{-\delta}}$. □

The first part of Claim 1 ensures that $\textsc{Conf}(\bar{y}, t) < b$ whenever $y_t < y_{t'} + \delta$ holds, establishing soundness, while the other provides the error bound, stating that if $y_t < y_{t'} + \delta$ does *not* hold, then we characterize the lower bound of

$\textsc{Conf}(\bar{y}, t)$. The relationship between τ and the error bound is illustrated in [41]. The condition $y_t < y_{t'} + \delta$ can be encoded in LRA:

$$\bigvee_{i=1,\, i \neq t}^{m} y_t < y_i + \delta. \tag{3}$$

Approximation of Conf $(\bar{y}, t) \geq b$ and Conf$(\bar{y}, t) > b$: Here also, we consider the approximation of $\textsc{Conf}(\bar{y}, t) > b$, and the approximation of $\textsc{Conf}(\bar{y}, t) \geq b$ follows analogously. Similar to the above approximations, let t' be such that $y_{t'} = \max_{i=1,\, i \neq t}^{m}(y_i)$. Let $\delta = -\ln\Big(\frac{1}{m-1}\left(\frac{100}{b} - 1\right)\Big)$. Then, for any $b > 0$, we have the following claim.

Claim 2. *If $y_t > y_{t'} + \delta$ holds, then $\textsc{Conf}(\bar{y}, t) > b$, else $\textsc{Conf}(\bar{y}, t) \leq \frac{100}{1+e^{-\delta}}$.*

Proof. The following proof is similar to the proof of part 2 of Claim 1. Let LHS of the claim be true. Since $y_{t'} = \max_{i=1, i \neq t}^{m}(y_i)$, we can derive $\textsc{Conf}(\bar{y}, t) \geq \frac{100 e^{y_t}}{e^{y_t} + (m-1) e^{y_{t'}}}$, replacing e^i by $e^{t'}$ for all $i, i \neq t$. After scaling the RHS by $\frac{1}{e^{y_t}}$, we obtain $\textsc{Conf}(\bar{y}, t) \geq \frac{100}{1+(m-1)e^{y_{t'} - y_t}}$. Since $y_t \geq y_{t'} + \delta$, we obtain $\textsc{Conf}(\bar{y}, t) \geq \frac{100}{1+(m-1)e^{-\delta}}$. Since $\delta = -\ln(\frac{1}{m-1}(\frac{100}{b} - 1))$, $\textsc{Conf}(\bar{y}, t) > b$. Suppose LHS does not hold. Since $y_{t'} = \max_{i=1, i \neq t}^{m}(y_i)$, we can derive $\textsc{Conf}(\bar{y}, t) \leq \frac{100 e^{y_t}}{e^{y_t} + e^{y_{t'}}}$, removing all e^{y_i} except e^{y_t} and $e^{y_{t'}}$. After scaling by $\frac{1}{e^{y_t}}$, we get $\textsc{Conf}(\bar{y}, t) \leq \frac{100}{1+e^{y_{t'} - y_t}}$, since $y_t \leq y_{t'} + \delta$, the expression reduced to $\textsc{Conf}(\bar{y}, t) \leq \frac{100}{1+e^{-\delta}}$. □

Again the first part of Claim 2 ensures soundness, and while the second provides the upper bound on the violation. Similar to Eq. 3, the condition $y_t > y_{t'} + \delta$ can also be written in LRA: $\bigwedge_{i=1,\, i \neq t}^{m} y_t > y_i + \delta$.

Suppose $CC^{\#}$ is the abstract constraint corresponding to a confidence constraint CC in our grammar. For example, $y_t < y_{t'} + \delta$ is the abstract constraint for the confidence constraint $\textsc{Conf}(\bar{y}, t) < b$ by Claim 1. By replacing CC with $CC^{\#}$ in our grammar, we obtain the abstract post-condition $PC^{\#}$. The following theorem establishes soundness. Moreover, since $CC^{\#}$ is in LRA form, it follows directly that $PC^{\#}$ is also expressible in LRA.

Theorem 1. *For any post-condition PC, the abstraction $PC^{\#}$ constitutes a sound abstraction of PC.*

Proof. We prove soundness by showing that whenever $PC^{\#}$ holds, the original post-condition PC also holds. The proof proceeds by induction on the length n of PC. If PC does not contain any confidence constraint CC, then PC and $PC^{\#}$ are identical. We therefore focus on cases where PC contains confidence constraints.

- **Base Case ($n = 1$):** In this case, $PC = CC$, which implies $PC^{\#} = CC^{\#}$. By Claims 1 and 2, we have $CC^{\#} \implies CC$, and thus $PC^{\#} \implies PC$.
- **Inductive Step:** Assume the theorem holds for all post-conditions of length n. Let PC_n be a post-condition of length n, and let $PC_n^{\#}$ be its corresponding abstraction. We now consider PC_{n+1} and its abstraction $PC_{n+1}^{\#}$, which form a post-condition of length $n+1$. The structure of PC_{n+1} must be one of the following:

1. $PC_{n+1} = PC_n \wedge CC$. Then $PC^{\#}_{n+1} = PC^{\#}_n \wedge CC^{\#}$. Since $CC^{\#} \implies CC$ (by Claims 1 and 2) and $PC^{\#}_n \implies PC_n$ (by the inductive hypothesis), we obtain $PC^{\#}_n \wedge CC^{\#} \implies PC_n \wedge CC$.
2. $PC_{n+1} = PC_n \vee CC$. Then $PC^{\#}_{n+1} = PC^{\#}_n \vee CC^{\#}$. Since $CC^{\#} \implies CC$ and $PC^{\#}_n \implies PC_n$, it follows that $PC^{\#}_n \vee CC^{\#} \implies PC_n \vee CC$.

□

3.3 Few Instances of Grammar

We now show how the notions of relaxed robustness, strong robustness, and smoothness are in our grammar as specific practical instances.

Relaxed Robustness: As discussed in Introduction, *relaxed robustness*, is a weaker notion where low-confidence counterexamples are ignored in determining robustness of the network, as shown in Fig. 1(a–b). For all images x close to given image x^*, their classification should be the same, unless the confidence of the network on x is less than a certain threshold. Incorporating the requirement in Eq. 1 gives us Eq. 4 which permits low-confidence counterexamples to bypass the strict robustness criteria. Let τ be the confidence level threshold, a tunable user specified parameter.

$$\forall x\ \texttt{dist}(x^*, x) \leq \epsilon \implies \Big(\textsc{Conf}(N(x), \hat{N}(x)) < \tau \vee \hat{N}(x^*) = \hat{N}(x)\Big) \tag{4}$$

Then in the verification query $\langle N, P, Q\rangle$, N and P remain same as in Eq. 1, while the post-condition Q now gets changed to $Q_{rel} = \textsc{Conf}(N(x), \hat{N}(x)) < \tau \vee \hat{N}(x^*) = \hat{N}(x)$. Letting $\bar{y} = N(x)$, $t = \hat{N}(x)$, $c = \hat{N}(x^*)$, we can rewrite Q_{rel} as: $\textsc{Conf}(\bar{y}, t) < \tau \vee \bigwedge_{i=1, i\neq c}^{m} y_c > y_i$, which is in our grammar. Applying Theorem 1 we get an approximation of Q_{rel}, which is $y_t < y_{t'} + \delta \vee \bigwedge_{j=1, j\neq t}^{m} y_c > y_j$, where $y_{t'}$ and δ are the same as in Claim 1. Further, by replacing $y_t < y_{t'} + \delta$ from Eq. 3, we get $\bigvee_{j=1, j\neq t}^{m} y_t < y_i + \delta \vee \bigwedge_{j=1, j\neq c}^{m} y_c > y_j$. Since $t = \hat{N}(x)$ means $y_t = \max_{i=1}^{m}(y_i)$, to encode the constraints for y_t, we just compare y_t with every other logits value, which finally gives:

$$Q'_{rel} = (\bigwedge_{i=1}^{m} \bigvee_{j=1, j\neq i}^{m} y_i < y_j + \delta) \vee \bigwedge_{i=1, i\neq c}^{m} y_i < y_c \tag{5}$$

Theorem 1 ensures soundness for Q'_{rel} i.e., $\langle N, P, Q'_{rel}\rangle \implies \langle N, P, Q_{rel}\rangle$. In fact, from Claim 1 we can also obtain a lower bound on the confidence of any counterexample as $\frac{100}{1+(m-1)e^{-\delta}}$.

Strong Robustness: The second variant of robustness, that we call *strong robustness*, aims to capture cases where the confidence on the seed image is high, but drops below a certain threshold within an ϵ-bounded perturbation, regardless of whether the classification label changes. In other words, a significant drop in confidence itself indicates a weakness in the underlying network. Recall that an example of such robustness was illustrated in Fig. 1(c-e), where the confidence for a seed image of class `ship` dropped from 96.17% to 22.21%. The definition of strong robustness, which generalizes the notion introduced in [18], can now be formally defined as follows. Let $\tau_1 > \tau_2$ be two threshold values.

$$\forall x\ \texttt{dist}(x^*, x) \leq \epsilon \implies \Big(\textsc{Conf}(N(x), \hat{N}(x^*)) > \tau_2 \land \hat{N}(x^*) = \hat{N}(x)\Big) \\ \lor \textsc{Conf}(N(x^*), \hat{N}(x^*)) < \tau_1 \quad (6)$$

The above equation asserts that for any x in the ϵ-neighborhood of x^*, if confidence of the network on x^* is at least τ_1, then x must be classified the same as x^* with a high confidence (above threshold τ_2). Thus, we get the query $\langle N, P, Q_{str}\rangle$ where P remains the same, while $Q_{str} = (\textsc{Conf}(N(x), \hat{N}(x^*)) > \tau_2 \land \hat{N}(x^*) = \hat{N}(x)) \lor \textsc{Conf}(N(x^*), \hat{N}(x^*)) < \tau_1$. Note that $\textsc{Conf}(N(x^*), \hat{N}(x^*)) < \tau_1$ can be computed beforehand since x^* is a given seed image. Thus, we will only need to show the condition $\textsc{Conf}(N(x), \hat{N}(x^*)) > \tau_2 \land \hat{N}(x^*) = \hat{N}(x)$. Let $t = \hat{N}(x^*)$ and $(y_1, .., y_m) = N(x)$. The condition $\hat{N}(x^*) = \hat{N}(x)$ can be represented as $\bigwedge_{i=1, i\neq t}^{m} y_t > y_i$, so, Q_{str} can be written as $\textsc{Conf}(N(x), t) > \tau_2 \land \bigwedge_{i=1, i\neq t}^{m} y_t > y_i$, which is in our grammar.

Smoothness: A third variant is smoothness, an instance of Lipschitz continuity in neural networks [27–29]. The work in [18] introduces the concept of Lipschitz robustness, which bounds each class's logit values using a Lipschitz constant. We propose a simplified instance of Lipschitz robustness, where we ask that, within an ϵ-perturbation, the confidence of network should not exhibit significant variations wrt the seed image. Let $t = \hat{N}(x^*)$, and $\tau > 0$ a threshold, then:

$$\forall x\ \texttt{dist}(x^*, x) \leq \epsilon \implies |\textsc{Conf}(N(x^*), t) - \textsc{Conf}(N(x), t)| < \tau \quad (7)$$

As before, $\textsc{Conf}(N(x^*), t)$ can be pre-computed as x^* is a given seed image; so we can fix $\textsc{Conf}(N(x^*), t) = C$, a constant. Substituting this, we obtain a verification query $\langle N, P, Q_{sm}\rangle$, where $Q_{sm} = C - \textsc{Conf}(N(x), t) > -\tau \land C - \textsc{Conf}(N(x), t) < \tau$, with P unchanged. Q_{sm} can be further simplified to $\textsc{Conf}(N(x), t) < C + \tau \land \textsc{Conf}(N(x), t) > C - \tau$, here $C + \tau$ and $C - \tau$ are constants. This simplified post-condition is again in our grammar.

Top-k Robustness: Till now, we have discussed robustness variants involving confidence, now we show that even other variants are also instances of our grammar. We consider the notion of top-k robustness introduced in [36]. Let $N(x, k)$ denote the k-th highest logit value of the network output, and define $N^k(x) = \{i \mid N_i(x) \geq N(x, k)\}$, the set of classes with the top-k highest logits. Top-k robustness is then defined as $\forall x'\ \text{dist}(x, x') \leq \epsilon \implies N^k(x) = N^k(x')$. The same paper [36] also defines a relaxed variant (*top-k-relaxed*) robustness: $\forall x'\ \text{dist}(x, x') \leq \epsilon \implies \exists k \leq K : N^k(x) = N^k(x')$. Another variant, *top-k-affinity*, permits the user to specify the set of classes in which misclassification is allowed. All three variants of top-k robustness are captured by our grammar, more details in [41].

4 Encoding Mechanism via Additional Layers

In this section, we provide an encoding for all robustness variants definable by the grammar, such that they can be integrated in state-of-the-art robustness verification engines. We begin by noting that the International Verification of Neural Networks Competition (VNN-COMP) [17] standardizes both the neural network format (ONNX) and the property format (VNNLIB). All neural network verifiers participating in VNN-COMP take as input a neural network in ONNX format and a property file in VNNLIB format. Importantly, the VNNLIB format encodes pre-condition P and negation of the post-condition Q of the neural network N, expressed as an arbitrary Boolean combination of linear constraints, i.e., exactly in the grammar that we described in the previous section. However, most state-of-the-art neural network verifiers are optimized for *simplified post-conditions*, typically involving only disjunctions or conjunctions of linear atoms over the outputs of the network. In what follows, we call a post-condition *simplified* if it is either atomic $y > 0$, $y \geq 0$, $y < 0$, or $y \leq 0$, where y is one of the outputs of N or conjunction/disjunction of the atomics.

In this section, we show how we can convert post-conditions into simplified ones *by just appending a few additional layers* to the neural network, without having to change the encoding within the verifiers. In doing so, we only add a linear number of neurons in the size of the post-condition and number of the layers added is at most the depth of the formula (represented as a Directed Acyclic Graph) in the post-condition. As we will see, while it is easy to do this for conjunctions, it is non-trivial when both conjunctions and disjunctions are present, and we achieve a solution with an approximation factor.

Translating Conjunctions. Translating conjunctions is relatively simple (as also done in [35]). Given $\bigwedge_{i=0}^{n} LE_i \leq 0$, where nodes $y_1, \ldots, y_m$ represent the original network's output nodes and $LE_i = \sum_{j=1}^{m} w_{ij} y_j + b_j$, defining a new output $y = \sum_{i=0}^{n} \text{ReLU}(LE_i)$ can be encoded as an additional layer as depicted in Fig. 2(a). Nodes $LE_1, LE_2, \ldots, LE_n$ represent actions of corresponding linear expressions followed by ReLU nodes. We immediately obtain the following lemma:

Lemma 1. $y \leq 0 \iff \bigwedge_{i=0}^{n} LE_i \leq 0$

Proof. ($\implies$) Since $y = \sum_{i=0}^{n} \text{ReLU}(LE_i)$, if $y \leq 0$ then $\forall i$, $\text{ReLU}(LE_i) = 0$, because ReLU's output is always ≥ 0. Therefore, $\forall i, LE_i \leq 0$ by the definition of ReLU. Therefore, $\bigwedge_{i=0}^{n} LE_i \leq 0$ holds. ($\impliedby$) Since $\bigwedge_{i=0}^{n} LE_i \leq 0$, we conclude $\bigwedge_{i=0}^{n} \text{ReLU}(LE_i) = 0$. Therefore, $\sum_{i=0}^{n} \text{ReLU}(LE_i) = 0$. Since $y = \sum_{i=0}^{n} \text{ReLU}(LE_i)$, $y \leq 0$. □

The number of ReLU nodes added is the number of clauses in the property, e.g., in Fig. 2(a), there are a total of n clauses; therefore, n ReLU nodes are added. We also deduce that $y > 0 \Leftrightarrow \bigvee_{i=0}^{n} LE_i > 0$, which encodes disjunction.

The General Translation. When we have both disjunctions and conjunctions in the post-condition, we cannot directly feed the output of conjunctions to the input of a disjunction, since for conjunction, $y = 0$ is interpreted as true and

$y > 0$ as false, while for disjunction, the roles are reversed. A straightforward approach to handle this asymmetry is to convert the post-condition into Disjunctive Normal Form (DNF) and execute each clause in parallel. However, this method suffers from several drawbacks: (i) the conversion to DNF may cause exponential blowup, (ii) information derived from one clause cannot be exploited by another, and (iii) the underlying verifier codebase may still need modifications to accommodate each clause. Another way to encode disjunctions is by using products, however, this introduces highly non-linear constraints, which are very inefficient to handle. Although some post conditions are expressible in DNF form, this is not always the case. For instance, for the top-k properties introduced in Sect. 3, the post-conditions are not in DNF, details are in [41].

Therefore, we take an alternate approach via a transformation $flip(b, v) = b - v$ of a signal v for some $b > 0$ (defined later), which allows us to feed output of disjunction to conjunction and vice-versa. Our translation will also introduce non-linear constraints but only as *Relu*'s which can be easily modeled in verifiers. In the following, let $\dagger \in \{\vee, \wedge\}$ and if $\dagger = \vee$, then $\bar{\dagger} = \wedge$, if $\dagger = \wedge$, then $\bar{\dagger} = \vee$. Wlog., we also assume that the post-condition is given in Negation Normal Form, with negations pushed inside the linear inequalities, with $\wedge$ and $\vee$ flattened (i.e., $\wedge$ and $\vee$ alternate when traversing the formula top-down). Then, $\dagger \in \{\vee, \wedge\}$, for any post-condition $Q \in \mathcal{PC}$ and a parameter $\eta \in \mathbb{R}$, we define the gadget $V(\dagger, Q, \eta)$ as an expression made up of $flips$, *Relu*, and summation functions. Hence for every such expression we can build a circuit $\mathfrak{C}_{V(\dagger,Q,\eta)}$ that can be integrated with the Neural network using additional layers (for $flip$ we use -1 weight on edges, while *Relu* and summation are standard operators in neural networks). Thus, given a set of input values to Q, $V(\dagger, Q, \eta)$ evaluates to a real output value y, satisfying some properties, as we shall describe below. Both V and its circuit are defined inductively based on the structure of the post-condition. For atomic formulas, we construct the gadgets V as given below, one for each value of $\dagger \in \{\wedge, \vee\}$:

$$V(\wedge, LE \leq 0, \eta) = LE + \eta \qquad V(\vee, LE \leq 0, \eta) = -LE + \eta \tag{8}$$

The following gives the gadget for $Q = Q_1 \dagger .. \dagger Q_k$ (where $\dagger \in \{\vee, \wedge\}$), whose circuit is pictorially illustrated in Fig. 2(b).

$$V(\dagger, Q, \eta) = \sum\nolimits_{i=1}^{k} Relu(flip(b(\dagger, k, \eta), V(\bar{\dagger}, Q_i, \eta))) \tag{9}$$

$$\text{where,} b(\dagger, k, \eta) = \begin{cases} \eta(1 + 1/k) & \text{if } \dagger = \wedge \\ 2 * \eta & \text{if } \dagger = \vee \end{cases} \tag{10}$$

The main intuition of the above construction is that after crossing every disjunct/conjunct, the direction of the bounds flip, i.e., upper bound on an output becomes a lower bound and vice versa. This allows us to propagate bounds when the circuit has disjuncts and conjuncts. Before formalizing this intuition and proving the properties of the translation, we present in Fig. 2(c), an illustrative example. In this example, the negation of the post-condition $\neg Q$ is

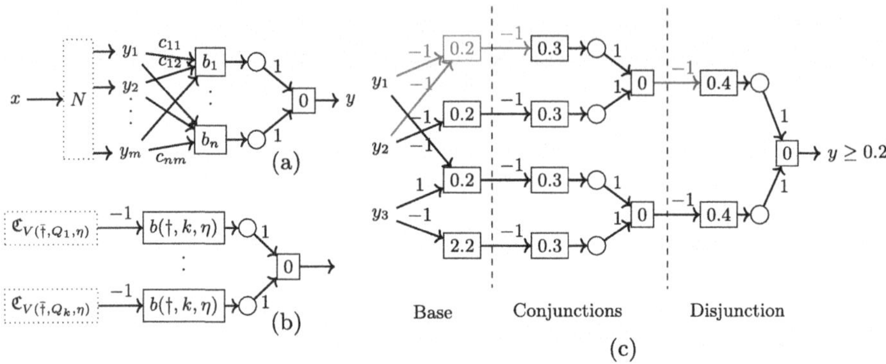

Fig. 2. (a) Neural network N appended with neural network layer that encodes either $\bigwedge_{i=0}^{n} LE_i \leq 0$ and its negation $\bigvee_{i=0}^{n} LE_i > 0$, where $LE_i = \sum_{j=1}^{m} c_{ij} y_j + b_i$. The circular nodes are ReLU and the square nodes are linear combinations. (b) The circuit for $\mathfrak{C}_{V(\dagger,Q,\eta)}$ (c) Translation of post-condition $\neg((y_1 + y_2 \leq 0 \wedge y_2 \leq 0) \vee (y_1 - y_3 \leq 0 \wedge y_3 \leq 2))$ using our scheme and $\eta = 0.2$.

$((y_1+y_2 \leq 0 \wedge y_2 \leq 0) \vee (y_1 - y_3 \leq 0 \wedge y_3 \leq 2))$, with atomic formulae $y_1+y_2 \leq 0$, $y_2 \leq 0$, and so on. The parameter η in the input constraint is set to 0.2 (user-defined). The part of circuit before the first dashed vertical line are the gadgets for atomic formulae. For instance, $y_1 + y_2 \leq 0$ is converted into $-y_1 - y_2 + 0.2$, which is represented by the red part of the circuit. Thus, the output at the red line satisfies $0.2 \leq -y_1 - y_2 + 0.2$ which is equivalent to $y_1 + y_2 \leq 0$. The reason to have this flipped representation is that $y_1 + y_2 \leq 0$ and $y_2 \leq 0$ are connected with conjunction, but the formulation of Eq. 9 expects the atomic formulae to be connected with disjunction, thus we apply the disjunctive rule in right had side of (8). The resulting outputs are connected with conjunctions, and the gadget between the two vertical lines corresponds to these conjunctions. Since this gadget represents conjunction, the value of b is determined by the conjunction case in Eq. 10, i.e., $b = \eta\left(1 + \frac{1}{k}\right) = 0.2\left(1 + \frac{1}{2}\right) = 0.3$. In other words, at the blue line the output will be less than or equal to 0.2 if $(y_1 + y_2 \leq 0 \wedge y_2 \leq 0)$ (as shown more generally in Lemma 2 below). Finally, the conjunctions are connected with disjunctions, represented by the gadget after the second vertical line, which is also constructed following Eq. 10, where $b = 2\eta = 0.2 \times 2 = 0.4$.

Our choice of $b(\dagger, k, \eta)$ is crucial for ensuring the desired properties of the gadget. The following technical lemma establishes how can we propagate the bounds on the signal $V(\dagger, Q, \eta)$ to the sub-formulas Q_i and vice-versa, which will help us relating bounds on the inputs of the gadget and the bounds on the output of the gadget.

Lemma 2. *For $\eta > 0$ and $\beta > 0$, the following holds for Q.*

1. $\forall i.\ \eta \leq V(\vee, Q_i, \eta) \Rightarrow V(\wedge, Q, \eta) \leq \eta$.
2. $\exists i.\ V(\wedge, Q_i, \eta) \leq \eta \Rightarrow \eta \leq V(\vee, Q, \eta)$.

Proof. The following is the proof of the above two parts.

1. We assume for each i, $\eta \leq V(\vee, Q_i, \eta)$. After a rewrite, $(1 + 1/k)\eta - V(\vee, Q_i, \eta) \leq \eta/k$. After applying definition of b and *flip*, $flip(b(\wedge, k, \eta), V(\vee, Q_i, \eta)) \leq \eta/k$ for each i. Due to the definition of V, we conclude $V(\wedge, Q, \eta) \leq \eta$.
2. We assume for some i, $V(\wedge, Q_i, \eta) \leq \eta$. After a rewrite, $\eta \leq 2\eta - V(\vee, Q_i, \eta)$. After applying definition of b and *flip*, $\eta \leq flip(b(\vee, k, \eta), V(\wedge, Q_i, \eta))$ for some i. Due to the definition of V, we conclude $\eta \leq V(\wedge, Q, \eta)$. □

Using the above lemma, we are now ready to state Lemma 3 that establishes the correctness of our translation scheme. The first two cases demonstrate correctness for atomic formulae, while Cases 3 and 4 establish correctness for general formulae.

Lemma 3. *For a given post condition Q and an $\eta > 0$, the following holds*

1. If $Q = LE \leq 0$, $V(\wedge, Q, \eta) \leq \eta \Leftrightarrow Q$
2. If $Q = LE \leq 0$, $V(\vee, Q, \eta) \geq \eta \Leftrightarrow Q$
3. If Q is conjunctive, i.e., $Q = Q_1 \wedge ... \wedge Q_k$, then $Q \Rightarrow V(\wedge, Q, \eta) \leq \eta$
4. If Q is disjunctive, i.e., $Q = Q_1 \vee ... \vee Q_k$, then $Q \Rightarrow V(\vee, Q, \eta) \geq \eta$

Proof. We prove this lemma by induction.

- **Base case:**
  1. If $Q = LE \leq 0$, then by definition, $V(\wedge, Q, \eta) = LE + \eta$. Given that $V(\wedge, Q, \eta) \leq \eta$, we derive: $LE + \eta \leq \eta \Leftrightarrow LE \leq 0$.
  2. If $Q = LE \leq 0$, then by definition, $V(\vee, Q, \eta) = -LE + \eta$. Given that $V(\vee, Q, \eta) \geq \eta$, we derive: $-LE + \eta \geq \eta \Leftrightarrow LE \leq 0$.
- **Inductive step:** Assume Lemma 3 holds for all formulae of depth d, denoted as Q^d. Consider a formula of depth $d + 1$, given by: $Q^{d+1} = Q^d_1 \dagger \cdots \dagger Q^d_k$.
  3. If $\dagger = \wedge$, Q^d_is are true. Due to the induction hypothesis, $\forall i,\ \eta \leq V(\vee, Q^d_i, \eta)$. By the part 1 of Lemma 2, we have: $\forall i,\ \eta \leq V(\vee, Q^d_i, \eta) \implies V(\wedge, Q^{d+1}, \eta) \leq \eta$. Therefore, $V(\wedge, Q^{d+1}, \eta) \leq \eta$ holds.
  4. If $\dagger = \vee$, Q^d_i is true for some i. Due to the induction hypothesis, $\exists i,\ V(\wedge, Q^d_i, \eta) \leq \eta$. By the part 2 of Lemma 2, we have: $\exists i,\ V(\wedge, Q^d_i, \eta) \leq \eta \implies \eta \leq V(\vee, Q^{d+1}, \eta)$. Therefore, $\eta \leq V(\vee, Q^{d+1}, \eta)$ holds. □

Using the above, we can finally define $N' = Append(N, V(\dagger, Q, \eta))$ to be the neural network obtained by attaching the circuit $\mathfrak{C}_{V(\dagger,Q,\eta)}$ after the neural network N with y being the final output. More precisely, the inputs of $V(\dagger, Q, \eta)$ are connected to the outputs of N and the output y of $V(\dagger, Q, \eta)$ is the only output of N'. Finally, from the above lemma, we can prove our theorem which justifies using it as a verification query.

Theorem 2. *Consider neural network N, pre-condition P, a post-condition Q, and $\eta > 0$. Let Z be the negation normal form of $\neg Q$. Let $N' = Append(N, V(\dagger, Z, \eta))$ be the neural network obtained by attaching $\mathfrak{C}_{V(\dagger,Q,\eta)}$ after neural network N and y be the final output.*

1. *If the top symbol of Z is disjunction,* $\langle N', P, y < \eta\rangle \Rightarrow \langle N, P, Q\rangle$
2. *If the top symbol of Z is conjunction,* $\langle N', P, y > \eta\rangle \Rightarrow \langle N, P, Q\rangle$

Proof. The following is the proof of the first part. Let us consider the successful query $\langle N', P, y < \eta\rangle$ to the solver. We know $\neg(y < \eta)$ is infeasible. Therefore, $\eta \leq V(\vee, Z, \eta)$ is infeasible. Due to the contrapositive of the fourth part of Lemma 3, we conclude that Z cannot be satisfied. Since Z is the negation normal form of $\neg Q$, Q always holds. Therefore, query $\langle N, P, Q\rangle$ holds. Similarly, we can prove the second part using the third part of Lemma 3. □

Integrating All Components: Soundness. We establish the soundness of our framework by integrating the two main components: confidence approximation (from Sect. 3) and the encoding mechanism (as defined in this section).

Theorem 3. *Let N be a neural network, P a pre-condition, Q any post-condition satisfied by grammar (specified in Sect. 3). Let N' be the appended neural network and Q' be the simplified post-condition obtained through the encoding (specified in this section). If the query $\langle N', P, Q'\rangle$ holds, then the original query $\langle N, P, Q\rangle$ also holds.*

Proof. Let Q'' denote an intermediate post-condition obtained after applying confidence approximations, but prior to encoding. From Theorems 1, we have: $\langle N, P, Q''\rangle \implies \langle N, P, Q\rangle$. Furthermore, from Theorem 2, we have: $\langle N', P, Q'\rangle \implies \langle N, P, Q''\rangle$. and hence together, we conclude $\langle N', P, Q'\rangle \implies \langle N, P, Q\rangle$. □

We also derive bounds on the error in the counterexamples incurred due to our encoding parameter η, see [41] for details. Therefore, η must be chosen as small as possible, but not smaller than the minimum precision supported by the underlying solver, as this may lead to numerical instability. Interestingly, we did not observe any counterexamples with such errors in our experiments. For simplicity of the presentation, we only considered non-strict inequalities above. We provide versions of the theorems that handle strict inequalities in [41].

5 Experiments

Our implementation encodes the post-conditions into additional neural network layers as described in the previous section and then invokes a Neural network verification engine. Our experiments are designed to address the following research questions: **RQ1:** How does our approach compare with an ad-hoc encoding of properties in a *constraint-based state-of-the-art solver*, e.g., MARABOU? **RQ2:** Does our layer-based approach work and scale for different variants of robustness on large VNN-COMP benchmarks, as it enables us to use $\alpha\beta$-CROWN, which has consistently ranked 1st in VNN-COMP 2021–2024, on top of Marabou. To demonstrate the empirical impact and meaningfulness of the different robustness variants introduced in Sect. 3, we provide illustrative images in [41].

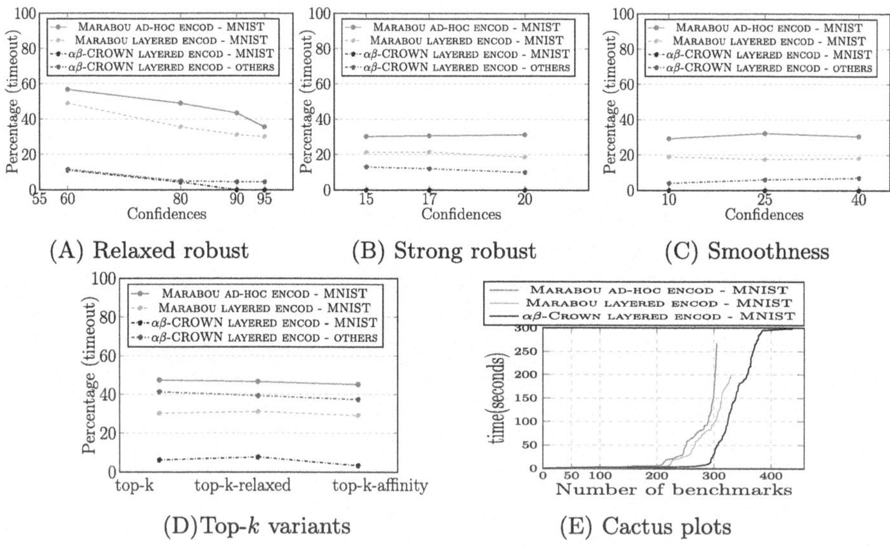

Fig. 3. (A)–(D) Comparison of the constraint-based solver MARABOU with ad-hoc encoding and our layered-based encoding, alongside $\alpha\beta$-CROWN with our layered-based encoding. "$\alpha\beta$-CROWN LAYERED ENCOD - OTHERS" represents the average of percentage of timeout on other datasets. (E) the x-axis shows the number of benchmarks solved, ordered by increasing solving time, and the y-axis shows the time taken to solve them.

Benchmarks: We conducted experiments on four different datasets: MNIST [42], CIFAR-10 [20], Traffic Sign Recognition (TSR) [43], and IMAGENET [44]. All networks used in the experiments, along with their properties (VNNLIB files), were taken from VNN-COMP 2021 to VNN-COMP 2024. The provided VNNLIB files correspond to standard robustness properties. We have listed our benchmarks in [41]. Our experiments covered a diverse set of benchmarks, ranging from fully connected networks to complex architectures, including convolutional layers, max-pooling layers, residual blocks, and ReLU activations, including standard and adversarially trained models. *Additionally, the network sizes ranged from small architectures with* 512 *ReLUs to large networks with* 11.16*M ReLUs leading to the largest network having* 138*M parameters. Each neural network, along with its corresponding property (VNNLIB) file, represents a single benchmark. In total, we evaluated 8,870 benchmarks in our experiments.* More details are provided in [41]. We set the value of our encoding parameter η to 1×10^{-4}.

Comparing with Ad-Hoc Encoding (RQ1): To compare our layer-based encoding with ad-hoc encodings, we directly encoded each property using the constraint-based solver MARABOU via its Python interface. We then compared this against our layer-based encoding evaluated with MARABOU (i.e., on the appended network with a simplified property) and with $\alpha\beta$-CROWN. Since $\alpha\beta$-CROWN does not provide an interface for directly expressing complex properties, we were unable to perform an ad-hoc encoding comparison for $\alpha\beta$-CROWN. However, our layer-based encoding enables $\alpha\beta$-CROWN to handle these properties. As MARABOU is a CPU-based solver [17], we ran the experiments on an Intel(R) Xeon(R) Gold 6314U CPU @ 2.30 GHz with 64 GB RAM. We observed that MARABOU ran out of memory on many CIFAR-10, GTSRB, and IMAGENET-1k benchmarks, so we restricted this comparison to MNIST. The blue, green and black lines in Figs. 3a–d summarize the comparison across all properties, and Fig. 3e presents the corresponding cactus plot. Our results show that $\alpha\beta$-CROWN with our layer-based encoding outperforms MARABOU with both the ad-hoc and the layer-based encodings, over varying confidence values. This is a direct result of our layer-based approach being amenable for integration with $\alpha\beta$-CROWN, a portfolio tool that incorporates efficient techniques such as PGD attacks [32] and CROWN [11]. However, we also see that our layer-based encoding on MARABOU performs better than MARABOU with the ad-hoc encoding. *This comparison demonstrates that our framework not only enables encoding of different properties, but also yields more efficient verification than direct encodings.*

Scalability Evaluation of Robustness Variants (RQ2): We conducted experiments on various robustness properties, as described in Sect. 3. The corresponding results are shown by the red dashed lines in Figs. 3a–3d itself. These curves report results on CIFAR-10, GTSRB, and IMAGENET-1k, which are considered challenging benchmarks in VNN-COMP. Accordingly, we used a GPU machine with a Tesla V100-SXM2-32GB, 9 vCPUs, and 32 GB RAM for these experiments. The red curves represent the percentage of timeout instances across different thresholds and remain relatively low, indicating that a large fraction of benchmarks are successfully solved. More experiments comparing our approach across *varying thresholds* for different variants are in [41]. Since we introduced an approximation of the SOFTMAX function, our SAFE results remain SAFE, while UNSAFE results may not satisfy the negation of the original confidence constraints, but rather the corresponding bounds induced by the SOFTMAX approximation.

6 Conclusion

In this paper, we considered different variants of robustness in neural networks that incorporate SOFTMAX-based confidence values. We introduced a grammar of post-conditions that captures all these variants and provided a unifying framework to transform them into a gadget that can be appended to an existing neural network, thereby simplifying arbitrary properties. This enables the use of verifiers such as $\alpha\beta$-CROWN. Our experiments demonstrate that our approach is more efficient than directly encoding the properties as constraints into state-of-the-art constraint-based solvers.

References

1. Bojarski, M., et al.: End to end learning for self-driving cars. volume arXiv:1604.07316 (2016)
2. Amato, F., et al.: Artificial neural networks in medical diagnosis. vol. 11, pp. 47–58. Elsevier (2013)
3. Hinton, G., et al.: et al.: Deep neural networks for acoustic modeling in speech recognition: The shared views of four research groups. IEEE Sig. Process. Mag. **29**(6), 82–97 (2012)
4. Goodfellow, I.J., Shlens, J., Szegedy, C.: Explaining and harnessing adversarial examples. In: Bengio, Y., LeCun, Y. (eds.) 3rd International Conference on Learning Representations, ICLR 2015, San Diego, CA, USA, 7–9 May 2015, Conference Track Proceedings (2015)
5. Dunn, I., Pouget, H., Kroening, D., Melham, T.: Exposing previously undetectable faults in deep neural networks. In: Proceedings of the 30th ACM SIGSOFT International Symposium on Software Testing and Analysis, pp. 56–66 (2021)
6. Hayes, J., Danezis, G.: Learning universal adversarial perturbations with generative models. In: 2018 IEEE Security and Privacy Workshops (SPW), pp. 43–49. IEEE (2018)
7. Baluja, S., Fischer, I.: Learning to attack: Adversarial transformation networks. In: Proceedings of the AAAI Conference on Artificial Intelligence, vol. 32 (2018)
8. Dvijotham, K., Stanforth, R., Gowal, S., Mann, T.A., Kohli, P.: A dual approach to scalable verification of deep networks. In: UAI, vol. 1, p. 3 (2018)
9. Singh, G., Gehr, T., Püschel, M., Vechev, M.T.: Boosting robustness certification of neural networks. In: 7th International Conference on Learning Representations, ICLR 2019, New Orleans, LA, USA, 6–9 May 2019. OpenReview.net (2019)
10. Weng, L., et al.: Towards fast computation of certified robustness for relu networks. In: International Conference on Machine Learning, pp. 5276–5285. PMLR (2018)
11. Zhang, H., Weng, T.W., Chen, P.Y., Hsieh, C.J., Daniel, L.: Efficient neural network robustness certification with general activation functions. In: Advances in Neural Information Processing Systems, vol. 31 (2018)
12. Katz, G., Barrett, C., Dill, D.L., Julian, K., Kochenderfer, M.J.: Reluplex: an efficient smt solver for verifying deep neural networks. In: International conference on computer aided verification, pp. 97–117. Springer (2017)
13. Ehlers, R.: Formal verification of piece-wise linear feed-forward neural networks. In: International Symposium on Automated Technology for Verification and Analysis, pp. 269–286. Springer (2017)
14. Huang, X., Kwiatkowska, M., Wang, S., Wu, M.: Safety verification of deep neural networks. In: International Conference on Computer Aided Verification, pp. 3–29. Springer (2017)
15. Wang, S., et al.: Beta-crown: efficient bound propagation with per-neuron split constraints for neural network robustness verification. Adv. Neural Inf. Process. Syst. **34**, 29909–29921 (2021)
16. Xu, K., et al.: Fast and complete: enabling complete neural network verification with rapid and massively parallel incomplete verifiers. *CoRR*, abs/2011.13824 (2020)
17. Brix, C., Bak, S., Johnson, T.T., Wu, H.: The fifth international verification of neural networks competition (vnn-comp 2024): summary and results. arXiv preprint arXiv:2412.19985 (2024)

18. Casadio, M., et al.: Neural network robustness as a verification property: a principled case study. In: International Conference on Computer Aided Verification, pp. 219–231. Springer (2022)
19. Goodfellow Ia. Deep learning/ian goodfellow, yoshua bengio and aaron courville (2016)
20. Krizhevsky, A., Hinton, G., et al.: Learning multiple layers of features from tiny images (2009)
21. Leino, K., Fredrikson, M.: Relaxing local robustness. Adv. Neural. Inf. Process. Syst. **34**, 17072–17083 (2021)
22. alpha-beta-crown. https://github.com/Verified-Intelligence/alpha-beta-CROWN (2025). Accessed 21 Jun 2025
23. Wu, H., et al.: Marabou 2.0: a versatile formal analyzer of neural networks. In: International Conference on Computer Aided Verification, pp. 249–264. Springer (2024)
24. Katz, G., Barrett, C., Dill, D.L., Julian, K., Kochenderfer, M.J.: Reluplex: a calculus for reasoning about deep neural networks. Formal Methods Syst. Des. 1–30 (2021). https://doi.org/10.1007/s10703-021-00363-7
25. Athavale, A., Bartocci, E., Christakis, M., Maffei, M., Nickovic, D., Weissenbacher, G.: Verifying global two-safety properties in neural networks with confidence. In: International Conference on Computer Aided Verification, pp. 329–351. Springer (2024)
26. Wei, D., Wu, H., Wu, M., Chen, P.Y., Barrett, C., Farchi, E.: Convex bounds on the softmax function with applications to robustness verification. In: International Conference on Artificial Intelligence and Statistics, pp. 6853–6878. PMLR (2023)
27. Wang, Z., Prakriya, G., Jha, S.: A quantitative geometric approach to neural-network smoothness. Adv. Neural. Inf. Process. Syst. **35**, 34201–34215 (2022)
28. Rosca, M., Weber, T., Gretton, A., Mohamed, S.: A case for new neural network smoothness constraints (2020)
29. Lindqvist, B.: A novel method for function smoothness in neural networks. IEEE Access **10**, 75354–75364 (2022)
30. Jordan, M., Dimakis, A.G.: Exactly computing the local lipschitz constant of relu networks. Adv. Neural Inf. Process. Syst. **33**, 7344–7353 (2020)
31. Naik, N., Nuzzo, P.: Robustness contracts for scalable verification of neural network-enabled cyber-physical systems. In: 2020 18th ACM-IEEE International Conference on Formal Methods and Models for System Design (MEMOCODE), pp. 1–12. IEEE (2020)
32. Dong, Y., Liao, F., Pang, T., Su, H., Zhu, J., Hu, X., Li, J.: Boosting adversarial attacks with momentum. In: Proceedings of the IEEE Conference on Computer Vision and Pattern Recognition, pp. 9185–9193 (2018)
33. Zhou, D., Brix, C., Hanasusanto, G.A., Zhang, H.: Scalable neural network verification with branch-and-bound inferred cutting planes. In: The Thirty-eighth Annual Conference on Neural Information Processing Systems (2024)
34. Giunchiglia, E., Tatomir, A., Stoian, M.C., Lukasiewicz, T.: Ccn+: a neuro-symbolic framework for deep learning with requirements. Int. J. Approximate Reasoning **171**, 109124 (2024). Synergies between Machine Learning and Reasoning
35. Shriver, D., Elbaum, S., Dwyer, M.B.: Dnnv: a framework for deep neural network verification. In: International Conference on Computer Aided Verification, pp. 137–150. Springer (2021)

36. Leino, K., Fredrikson, M.: Relaxing local robustness. In: Ranzato, M., Beygelzimer, A., Dauphin, Y., Liang, P.S., Wortman Vaughan, J. (eds.) Advances in Neural Information Processing Systems, vol. 34, pp. 17072–17083. Curran Associates, Inc. (2021)
37. Bishop, C.M., Nasrabadi, N.M.: Pattern recognition and machine learning, vol. 4. Springer (2006)
38. Singh, G., Gehr, T., Püschel, M., Vechev, M.: An abstract domain for certifying neural networks. Proc. ACM Program. Lang. **3**(POPL), 1–30 (2019)
39. Singh, G., Ganvir, R., Püschel, M., Vechev, M.: Beyond the single neuron convex barrier for neural network certification. In: Advances in Neural Information Processing Systems, vol. 32 (2019)
40. Xu, K., et al.: Fast and Complete: Enabling complete neural network verification with rapid and massively parallel incomplete verifiers. In: International Conference on Learning Representations (2021)
41. Afzal, M., Akshay, S., Genest, B., Gupta, A.: Formal reasoning about confidence and automated verification of neural networks. arXiv e-prints, page arXiv:2511.07293 (2025)
42. Deng, L.: The mnist database of handwritten digit images for machine learning research [best of the web]. IEEE Signal Process. Mag. **29**(6), 141–142 (2012)
43. Postovan, A., Eraşcu, M.: Architecturing binarized neural networks for traffic sign recognition. arXiv preprint arXiv:2303.15005 (2023)
44. Deng, J., Dong, W., Socher, R., Li, L.J., Li, K., Fei-Fei, L.: Imagenet: a large-scale hierarchical image database. In: 2009 IEEE Conference on Computer Vision and Pattern Recognition, pp. 248–255 (2009)

A Refined Ordering Consistency Theory: Full Sequential Consistency and Generalized Preventive Reasoning

Zhiheng Cai[1,2,3], Zhihang Sun[1,2,3], and Fei He[1,2,3](✉)

[1] School of Software, Tsinghua University, Beijing, China
{cai-zh24,sunzh20}@mails.tsinghua.edu.cn, hefei@tsinghua.edu.cn
[2] Key Laboratory for Information System Security, MoE, Beijing, China
[3] Beijing National Research Center for Information Science and Technology, Beijing, China

Abstract. SMT solving with ordering consistency theory achieves state-of-the-art efficiency in bounded model checking of concurrent programs. At its core is a dedicated theory solver that derives the write-serialization (WS) and from-read (FR) orders on the fly, thereby allowing their explicit encodings to be omitted. Additionally, the solver is equipped with *preventive propagation*, which proactively eliminates theory-level conflicts. This work presents a refined ordering consistency theory that overcomes two existing limitations. First, we address the *weak SC problem*, where the solver may fail to reconstruct a total WS order and thus admit executions weaker than Sequential Consistency. We identify the core reason as insufficient constraints on WS totality. As a solution, we restore the WS encodings to ensure its totality, while preserving WS derivation to curb the resulting growth in the search space. Second, the existing framework for preventive propagation does not support WS variables or atomicity constraints. We extend it to incorporate these elements, yielding a more general and principled propagation mechanism. Experiments show that our approach soundly prevents weak-SC behaviors, enables effective propagation, and maintains competitive overall performance.

Keywords: Verification · SMT · Sequential Consistency · Concurrency

1 Introduction

In bounded model checking of concurrent programs, executions are typically modeled using partial orders [4]. Under Sequential Consistency (SC) [30], an execution can be characterized by four relations: program order (`po`), read-from (`rf`), write-serialization (`ws`), and from-read (`fr`). An execution is *valid* if the happens-before relation – the transitive closure of their union – is acyclic. Traditional approaches encode all these relations, resulting in sizable formulas. To improve solving efficiency, Sun et al. [18,25,33] introduced the *ordering consistency theory* and developed a dedicated theory solver for compactly handling these ordering constraints. The theory solver performs saturated derivation to

A. Sampaio and M. Stoelinga (Eds.): FM 2026, LNCS 16556, pp. 500–519, 2026.
https://doi.org/10.1007/978-3-032-26204-2_26

reconstruct the `ws` and `fr` relations, allowing their explicit encoding to be omitted. In addition, they proposed a *preventive propagation* technique that identifies *fragile* variables – those whose assignment to *true* would lead to inconsistency – and proactively propagates their negations to the core solver (the SAT solver). These techniques enable DEAGLE, the corresponding tool, to achieve state-of-the-art performance, winning the `ConcurrencySafety` track of the software verification competition `SV-COMP` for three years [8–10].

However, DEAGLE still has several limitations. The most critical one is an unsoundness problem known as the *weak SC problem* [6]: DEAGLE may fail to reconstruct a total `ws` order in certain cases, thereby admitting behaviors that satisfy the weak SC memory model [40], rather than strict SC. Another limitation is that its underlying theoretical framework of preventive propagation does not support atomicity constraints, which limits the effectiveness of preventive propagation in the presence of atomic blocks.

In this work, we propose a refined ordering consistency theory to overcome these limitations. First, we address the weak SC problem. Through case analysis, we identify its core reason as insufficient constraints on `ws` totality. A natural idea is to directly check whether there exists a total `ws` that yields a valid execution. However, such a decision problem is known to be NP-complete [20,23,40]. As a solution, we restore the write-serialization encodings to impose those missing constraints, while retaining WS derivation to avoid exploring unproductive regions in the enlarged search space. The resulting approach is both sound and complete. Second, we extend the preventive propagation along two directions: (1) to the reintroduced write-serialization variables, mitigating the overhead of `ws` encodings, and (2) to settings with atomicity constraints, generalizing the overall framework. The key challenge is to efficiently identify fragile variables under atomic blocks, whose collective constraints induce more intricate dependencies than single events. We observe that although an atomic block may contain multiple events, its observable effect on any given location is simple: it behaves as a read, a write, or a read-modify-write. This block-level abstraction enables us to reason about atomic blocks in a uniform way. Building on this insight, we design an effective strategy that identifies four patterns of inconsistency – two inherited and adopted from the original framework and two newly introduced to capture conflicts arising from atomicity constraints. Our evaluations show that our approach effectively resolves the weak SC problem, extends preventive propagation, and achieves overall performance comparable to the state-of-the-art.

Contributions. In summary, this work proposes a refined ordering consistency theory that guarantees full sequential consistency and generalizes preventive propagation. Extensive experiments demonstrate the effectiveness of the proposed approaches and their overall efficiency.

2 Preliminaries

Relations. For a relation R over a set A, we interchangeably write $x \prec_R y$ and $(x, y) \in R$ to denote (x, y) belongs to R, where $x, y \in A$. Given an equivalence relation $\sim$ over A, we write $A/\!\sim$ to denote the set of equivalence classes induced by $\sim$. For any $x \in A$, we write $[x]_\sim$ to denote the equivalence class containing x (the subscript may be omitted when clear from context). We also write $R/\!\sim$ to denote the quotient relation $\{([x],[y]) \mid (x,y) \in R \wedge [x] \neq [y]\}$ over $A/\!\sim$.

Concurrent Executions. A *concurrent program* consists of multiple threads executing in parallel. It accesses a set of memory locations, which can be either *thread-local* or *shared*. We mainly focus on shared locations. An *event* (denoted by e) is a read or write operation on a shared location. We write $type(e) \in \{\mathsf{R}, \mathsf{W}\}$ to indicate that its type is either read (R) or write (W), and write $loc(e)$ to denote the location it accesses.

Let $\mathbb{E}$ be the set of events. An *execution* of a concurrent program can be characterized by the following relations over $\mathbb{E}$ [4]. The *program-order* relation ($\mathtt{po}$) is a total order of events within each thread, reflecting the order of program instructions. The *atomicity* relation ($\mathtt{atom}$) is an equivalence relation such that $(e_1, e_2) \in \mathtt{atom}$ if and only if e_1 and e_2 belong to the same atomic block. The *read-from* relation ($\mathtt{rf}$) links each read event to the write event from which it obtains its value. The *write-serialization* relation ($\mathtt{ws}$) is a total order of write events that access the same location. The *from-read* relation ($\mathtt{fr}$) is derived from $\mathtt{rf}$ and $\mathtt{ws}$, defined as $\mathtt{fr} = \mathtt{rf}^{-1} ; \mathtt{ws}$. Intuitively, if a read event e_1 reads from a write event e_2 and e_2 is later overwritten by e_3, then e_1 must happen before e_3; otherwise, e_1 would have read the more recent value written by e_3. Formally, an execution τ is defined as $\langle \mathbb{E}, \mathtt{po}, \mathtt{atom}, \mathtt{rf}, \mathtt{ws} \rangle$.

This work focuses on the correctness under Sequential Consistency (SC) [30]. Let $\mathtt{hb} = (\mathtt{po} \cup \mathtt{rf} \cup \mathtt{ws} \cup \mathtt{fr})^+$. An execution is *valid* if and only if both $\mathtt{hb} \cap \mathtt{atom}$ and $\mathtt{hb}/\mathtt{atom}$ are acyclic [32]. In particular, when $\mathtt{atom} = I_{\mathbb{E}}$ (i.e., $\{(e,e) \mid e \in \mathbb{E}\}$), the correctness condition reduces to the acyclicity of $\mathtt{hb}$.

Let a *history* h of a program, defined as $\langle \mathbb{E}, \mathtt{po}, \mathtt{atom}, \mathtt{rf} \rangle$, abstract a class of executions, i.e., executions can be obtained by extending h with a fixed $\mathtt{ws}$. A history h *satisfies* SC if there exists a valid execution extended by h. The *weak SC* memory model [40] is defined over histories, under which $\mathtt{ws}'$ and $\mathtt{hb}'$ are defined as relaxed versions of $\mathtt{ws}$ and $\mathtt{hb}$. Formally, $\mathtt{ws}'$ and $\mathtt{hb}'$ are the least fixed-points of

$$\mathtt{ws}' = ((\mathtt{hb}'|_{\mathsf{WR}} ; \mathtt{rf}^{-1}) \cup \mathtt{hb}'|_{\mathsf{WW}})^+ \text{ and } \mathtt{hb}' = (\mathtt{po} \cup \mathtt{rf} \cup \mathtt{ws}' \cup (\mathtt{rf}^{-1} ; \mathtt{ws}'))^+,$$

where $\mathtt{hb}'|_{\mathsf{WR}}$ (resp. $\mathtt{hb}'|_{\mathsf{WW}}$) denotes the projection of the relation $\mathtt{hb}'$ on pairs of write and read events (resp. pairs of write events) accessing the same location. A history satisfies weak SC if the resulting $\mathtt{hb}'$ satisfies the acyclicity condition. The concrete semantics of weak SC will be explained later.

Satisfiability Modulo Theory and DPLL(T). In first-order logic, a *term* is either a variable, a constant, or an n-ary function applied to n terms. An *atom* is either *true*, *false*, or an n-ary predicate applied to n terms. A *literal* is an atom or its negation. An *SMT formula* is built from literals using Boolean connectives and quantifiers. The *satisfiability modulo theories* (*SMT*) problem [7,17] asks the satisfiability of SMT formulas with background theories.

DPLL(T) [31] is a standard framework for solving SMT problems, which extends the classical DPLL algorithm [16] with theory solvers. It consists of a core solver (SAT solver) and one or more theory solvers. Given an input formula Ψ, DPLL(T) first constructs its *Boolean abstraction* $\mathcal{B}(\Psi)$ by replacing each atom with a fresh Boolean variable. $\mathcal{B}(\Psi)$ serves as an over-approximation of Ψ, meaning that a satisfying assignment of $\mathcal{B}(\Psi)$ may not necessarily be consistent with Ψ. Therefore, to determine the satisfiability of Ψ, the theory solvers check consistency of the current assignment with respect to their theory semantics. When an inconsistency is detected, the responsible theory solver reports it to the core solver as a *conflict clause*. The core solver then backtracks to resolve the conflict, and learns the clause to prevent revisiting the same conflict. If no inconsistency is found, the theory solver may perform theory propagation, inferring the values of unassigned literals based on the theory semantics so that the core solver can refine its decisions earlier.

3 Verification Based on Ordering Consistency Theory

In this section, we present the verification procedure based on the ordering consistency theory [18,25,33]. We first introduce the symbolic encoding of concurrent programs (Sect. 3.1) and then describe how SMT solving is performed using a dedicated theory solver for ordering constraints (Sect. 3.2).

3.1 Symbolic Encoding of Concurrent Programs

We use the three-thread program shown in Fig. 1 to introduce our encoding. The program is in the concurrent static single assignment (CSSA) form [37], where each event is labeled with a unique subscript identifier. We denote the read (resp. write) event on location x with identifier i by r_{x_i} (resp. w_{x_i}).

$x_0 := 0$

$x_1 := 1$	`if` $(x_2 = 0)$	`atomic {` $r_1 := x_4$
	$x_3 := 2$	$r_2 := x_5$ `}`
		`assert` $(r_1 + r_2 \neq 3)$

Fig. 1. An example program.

Due to branch conditions, some events may not be enabled. We introduce a Boolean expression $grd(e)$ for each event e, called the *guard condition* of e. $grd(e) = true$ indicates that e is enabled. In this example, $grd(w_{x_3}) := (x_2 = 0)$, while those of all other events are simply *true*.

Value Assignment. The *value assignment* (ρ_{va}) of the program is encoded as $\rho_{va} := (x_1 = 1) \land (grd(w_{x_3}) \rightarrow (x_3 = 2))$.

Error Condition. The negation of the correctness specification (stated in the assertion) is encoded as the *error condition* (ρ_{err}). Here, $\rho_{err} := (x_4 + x_5 = 3)$.

Program Order. The program-order constraint (ρ_{po}) is encoded as $\rho_{\mathsf{po}} := (w_{x_0} \prec_{\mathsf{po}} w_{x_1}) \land (w_{x_0} \prec_{\mathsf{po}} r_{x_2}) \land (w_{x_0} \prec_{\mathsf{po}} r_{x_4}) \land (r_{x_2} \prec_{\mathsf{po}} w_{x_3}) \land (r_{x_4} \prec_{\mathsf{po}} r_{x_5})$.

Atomicity. The atomicity constraint ($\rho_{\texttt{atom}}$) is encoded as $\rho_{\texttt{atom}} := (r_{x_4} \prec_{\texttt{atom}} r_{x_5}) \wedge (r_{x_5} \prec_{\texttt{atom}} r_{x_4})$, where the identity pairs (e, e) for $e \in \mathbb{E}$ are omitted.

Read-From. For each event pair (w_{x_i}, r_{x_j}) on location x, we introduce a Boolean variable $rf^x_{i,j}$ to specify whether r_{x_j} reads from w_{x_i} (i.e., whether $w_{x_i} \prec_{\texttt{rf}} r_{x_j}$). The read-from constraint ($\rho_{\texttt{rf}}$) conjoins the following three parts:

- *RF-Val* ($\rho_{\texttt{rf}\text{-}val}$). If $rf^x_{i,j}$ is *true*, then both w_{x_i} and r_{x_j} are enabled, and $x_j = x_i$, i.e., $rf^x_{i,j} \rightarrow grd(w_{x_i}) \wedge grd(r_{x_j}) \wedge (x_j = x_i)$.
- *RF-Ord* ($\rho_{\texttt{rf}\text{-}ord}$). If $rf^x_{i,j}$ is *true*, then $w_{x_i} \prec_{\texttt{rf}} r_{x_j}$, i.e., $rf^x_{i,j} \rightarrow w_{x_i} \prec_{\texttt{rf}} r_{x_j}$.
- *RF-Some* ($\rho_{\texttt{rf}\text{-}some}$). If r_{x_j} is enabled, then it must read from some w_{x_i}, i.e., $grd(r_{x_j}) \rightarrow \bigvee_{w_{x_i} \in \mathbb{E}} rf^x_{i,j}$.

Write-Serialization. Similar to $\texttt{rf}$, we introduce a Boolean variable $ws^x_{i,j}$ for each event pair (w_{x_i}, w_{x_j}) to specify whether $w_{x_i} \prec_{\texttt{ws}} w_{x_j}$. The write-serialization constraint ($\rho_{\texttt{ws}}$) conjoins the following three parts:

- *WS-Cond* ($\rho_{\texttt{ws}\text{-}cond}$). If $ws^x_{i,j}$ is *true*, then both w_{x_i} and w_{x_j} are enabled, i.e., $ws^x_{i,j} \rightarrow grd(w_{x_i}) \wedge grd(w_{x_j})$.
- *WS-Ord* ($\rho_{\texttt{ws}\text{-}ord}$). If $ws^x_{i,j}$ is *true*, then $w_{x_i} \prec_{\texttt{ws}} w_{x_j}$, i.e., $ws^x_{i,j} \rightarrow w_{x_i} \prec_{\texttt{ws}} w_{x_j}$.
- *WS-Some* ($\rho_{\texttt{ws}\text{-}some}$). If both w_{x_i} and w_{x_j} are enabled, then one must happen before the other, i.e., $grd(w_{x_i}) \wedge grd(w_{x_j}) \rightarrow ws^x_{i,j} \vee ws^x_{j,i}$.

From-Read. By the definition of $\texttt{fr}$, the from-read constraints ($\rho_{\texttt{fr}}$) encodes $rf^x_{i,j} \wedge ws^x_{i,k} \rightarrow r_{x_j} \prec_{\texttt{fr}} w_{x_k}$ for all events w_{x_i}, r_{x_j}, and w_{x_k}.

The Whole Encoding Formula. The whole encoding formula is

$$\Psi := \phi_{ssa} \wedge \phi_{ord},$$

where $\phi_{ssa} := \rho_{va} \wedge \rho_{err} \wedge \rho_{\texttt{rf}\text{-}val} \wedge \rho_{\texttt{rf}\text{-}some}$ encodes the control and data flow and $\phi_{ord} := \rho_{\texttt{po}} \wedge \rho_{\texttt{atom}} \wedge \rho_{\texttt{rf}\text{-}ord}$ encodes the ordering constraints.

Theorem 1. *$\Psi \wedge \rho_{\texttt{ws}} \wedge \rho_{fr}$ is satisfiable if and only if there is a valid counterexample of the program [18, Theorem 1].*

Note that ϕ_{ord} involves only ordering variables (i.e., *rf* variables) and ordering predicates (i.e., orders represented by $\prec$). A dedicated theory solver, called $\mathcal{T}_{ord}$-solver, is employed to handle ϕ_{ord}, while ϕ_{ssa} can be solved by off-the-shelf theory solvers. The underlying theory of $\mathcal{T}_{ord}$-solver is referred to as *ordering consistency theory*. $\mathcal{T}_{ord}$-solver is also responsible for deriving $\texttt{ws}$ and $\texttt{fr}$, allowing $\rho_{\texttt{ws}} \wedge \rho_{\texttt{fr}}$ to be removed from the encoding.

3.2 $\mathcal{T}_{ord}$-Solver

$\mathcal{T}_{ord}$-solver derives $\texttt{ws}$ and $\texttt{fr}$, computes the transitive closure of $\texttt{hb}$, and checks consistency according to the following theory axioms.

Axiom 1 (FR-Derivation). For any write events w, w' and any read event r such that $loc(w) = loc(w') = loc(r)$, $w \prec_{\texttt{rf}} r \wedge w \prec_{\texttt{hb}} w' \wedge grd(w') \rightarrow r \prec_{\texttt{hb}} w'$.

Axiom 2 (WS-Derivation). For any write events w, w' and any read event r such that $loc(w) = loc(w') = loc(r)$, $w \prec_{\texttt{rf}} r \wedge w' \prec_{\texttt{hb}} r \wedge grd(w') \rightarrow w' \prec_{\texttt{hb}} w$.

Axiom 3 (Transitivity). For any events e_1, e_2, and e_3, $e_1 \prec_{\texttt{hb}} e_2 \wedge e_2 \prec_{\texttt{hb}} e_3 \rightarrow e_1 \prec_{\texttt{hb}} e_3$.

Axiom 4 (Consistency). $\texttt{hb} \cap \texttt{atom}$ and $\texttt{hb}/\texttt{atom}$ are both acyclic.

To conclude, Axiom 1 derives `fr`, with the role of `ws` captured jointly by guard conditions and the hb relation, and with the resulting `fr` element reflected directly on hb; Axiom 2 derives `ws`, in a similar way [39]; Axiom 3 computes the transitive closure of hb; and Axiom 4 enforces the consistency requirement.

$\mathcal{T}_{ord}$-solver maintains two graph structures: $\langle \mathbb{E}, \texttt{rf} \rangle$ and $\langle \mathbb{E}, \texttt{hb} \rangle$. Accordingly, each event pair of a relation R is referred to as an *edge* of R. Before solving, rf is set to $\varnothing$, and hb is initialized to $(\texttt{po}^+)$[1]. Let X_{rf} and X_{grd} be the set of *rf* variables and guard conditions, respectively. During solving, when the core solver provides an assignment over $X_{rf} \cup X_{grd}$, $\mathcal{T}_{ord}$-solver is invoked to perform derivations according to Axioms 1, 2, and 3, and to check consistency according to Axiom 4. The derivations are performed in a *saturated* manner, i.e., Axioms 1, 2, and 3 are iteratively applied until no further derivation can be made. Solving terminates when either (1) the unsatisfiability of Ψ is proven, confirming the safety of the program; or (2) a satisfying assignment is found, witnessing the incorrectness.

Example. We reuse the example program in Fig. 1 to illustrate the theory solving process. Consider where r_{x_4} reads its value from. It cannot read from w_{x_0}, since that would leave no value of x_5 satisfying the error condition $x_4 + x_5 = 3$. Assume that r_{x_4} reads from w_{x_1}. Adding the rf edge (w_{x_1}, r_{x_4}) triggers the derivation of the hb edge (w_{x_1}, r_{x_5}) via transitivity. To satisfy the error condition, r_{x_5} must then read from w_{x_3}. The rf edge (w_{x_3}, r_{x_5}) derives (w_{x_1}, w_{x_3}) and subsequently (r_{x_4}, w_{x_3}), creating a cycle $[r_{x_4}] \prec_{\texttt{hba}} [w_{x_3}] \prec_{\texttt{hba}} [r_{x_5}]$ among atomic blocks, where **hba** denotes $\texttt{hb}/\texttt{atom}$ (shown in the left subfigure of Fig. 2). The theory solver reports this inconsistency with conflict clause $rf^x_{1,4} \wedge rf^x_{3,5}$. After resolving it, the only remaining case is that r_{x_4} reads from w_{x_3} and r_{x_5} reads from w_{x_1}, which leads to a similar cycle $[r_{x_4}] \prec_{\texttt{hba}} [w_{x_1}] \prec_{\texttt{hba}} [r_{x_5}]$ (shown in the right subfigure). Thus, regardless of where r_{x_4} reads from, the error condition cannot be satisfied. The SMT solver concludes that Ψ is unsatisfiable, proving the safety of the program.

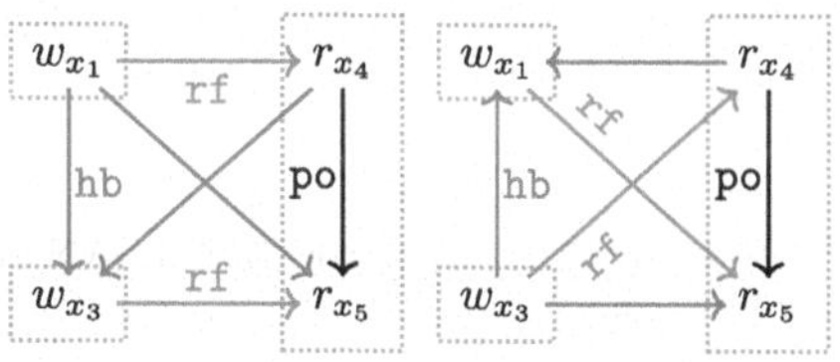

Fig. 2. Solving the example program. Irrelevant events are omitted, and atomic blocks are shown as orange dotted rectangles. (Color figure online)

[1] Consequently, it suffices to encode only adjacent po edges in $\rho_{\texttt{po}}$; see Sect. 3.1.

4 Addressing the Weak SC Problem

In this section, we describe the weak SC problem of $\mathcal{T}_{ord}$-solver [6], analyze the core reason and challenges behind it, and present our solution.

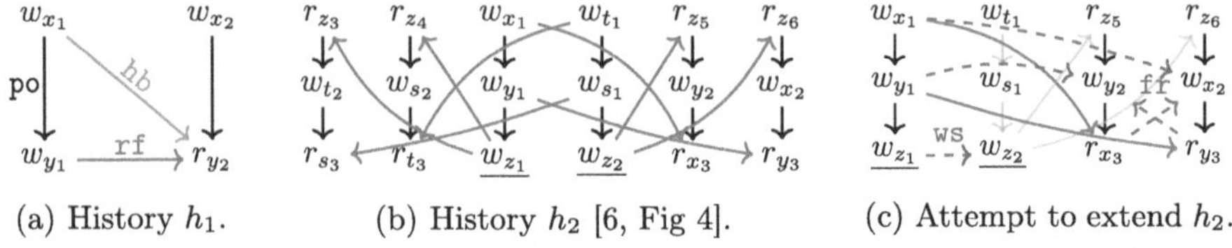

(a) History h_1. (b) History h_2 [6, Fig 4]. (c) Attempt to extend h_2.

Fig. 3. Histories that can be produced by $\mathcal{T}_{ord}$-solver.

4.1 The Weak SC Problem

Recall that $\mathcal{T}_{ord}$-solver runs under the encoding Ψ and Ψ involves only *rf* variables and guard conditions. Thus, when a satisfying assignment is found, it corresponds to a history of the program, rather than an execution.

Recall the definition of weak SC. Intuitively, weak SC imposes two requirements to enforce a ws$'$ edge:

(1) For any write events w and w', if $w \prec_{\mathtt{hb}'} w'$, then $w \prec_{\mathtt{ws}'} w'$; and
(2) For any write events w, w', and read event r, if $w \prec_{\mathtt{rf}} r$ and $w' \prec_{\mathtt{hb}'} r$, then $w' \prec_{\mathtt{ws}'} w$.

This process aligns with the WS-derivation in $\mathcal{T}_{ord}$-solver. A ws edge $w_1 \prec_{\mathtt{ws}} w_2$ is captured by $w_1 \prec_{\mathtt{hb}} w_2$ (together with guard conditions), corresponding to requirement (1); and the WS-derivation rule (i.e., Axiom 2) corresponds to requirement (2). Therefore, the produced histories of $\mathcal{T}_{ord}$-solver actually satisfy weak SC, rather than strict SC, which may compromise soundness.

We use two examples to illustrate the subtlety of the histories produced by $\mathcal{T}_{ord}$-solver, as shown in Fig. 3. For simplicity, we assume $\mathtt{atom} = I_{\mathbb{E}}$. Figure 3a presents a history h_1, where events of each thread are listed in columns, with black arrows denoting po and green arrows denoting rf. Consider the final produced hb relation of $\mathcal{T}_{ord}$-solver, besides the edges directly implied by rf or po, only one additional edge $w_{x_1} \prec_{\mathtt{hb}} r_{y_2}$ is derived (via transitivity, from $w_{x_1} \prec_{\mathtt{po}} w_{y_1} \prec_{\mathtt{rf}} r_{y_2}$). More importantly, $\mathcal{T}_{ord}$-solver leaves the write events w_{x_1} and w_{x_2} unordered, which violates the semantics of SC. To determine whether there is a genuine counterexample (i.e., a valid execution), one must extend h_1 by choosing either $w_{x_1} \prec_{\mathtt{ws}} w_{x_2}$ or $w_{x_2} \prec_{\mathtt{ws}} w_{x_1}$. Both choices lead to a valid execution, thus demonstrating the presence of a real counterexample.

However, not all produced histories can be extended to a valid execution. Figure 3b shows such a history h_2. The resulting hb (omitted in this Figure for simplicity) is acyclic, but the two underlined write events w_{z_1} and w_{z_2} remain unordered. We show its invalidity by attempting to extend it. Choosing $w_{z_1} \prec_{\texttt{ws}} w_{z_2}$ forces $w_{x_1} \prec_{\texttt{ws}} w_{x_2}$ and $w_{y_1} \prec_{\texttt{ws}} w_{y_2}$ by requirement (1). These edges derive $r_{x_3} \prec_{\texttt{fr}} w_{x_2}$ and $r_{y_3} \prec_{\texttt{fr}} w_{y_2}$ by the definition of fr, creating a cycle $w_{y_2} \prec_{\texttt{po}} r_{x_3} \prec_{\texttt{fr}} w_{x_2} \prec_{\texttt{po}} r_{y_3} \prec_{\texttt{fr}} w_{y_2}$, as shown in Fig. 3c (where newly added or derived edges are shown in dashed arrows). Choosing the opposite edge, $w_{z_2} \prec_{\texttt{ws}} w_{z_1}$, symmetrically creates another cycle involving w_{t_2}, r_{s_3}, w_{s_2}, and r_{t_3}.

In summary, the weak SC problem is that the history produced by $\mathcal{T}_{ord}$-solver may fail to be extended to a valid execution, leading the solver to report spurious counterexamples.

4.2 Understanding the Problem

In both examples, $\mathcal{T}_{ord}$-solver omits the ws ordering between certain writes. While the missing ws edges in h_1 still admit a valid extension, the absence of ws totality in h_2 inevitably leads to inconsistency. This contrast makes it clear that the lack of ws completeness is the core reason of the weak SC problem.

Recall that the WS-Some constraint enforces any enabled write events to be ordered. This constraint is removed from the encoding, and, more importantly, $\mathcal{T}_{ord}$-solver fails to enforce it. This naturally raises a question: can we refine the algorithm of the theory solver to decide whether there exists a total ws under which the produced history can be extended to a valid execution?

However, this decision problem is known to be NP-complete. When atom $= I_{\mathbb{E}}$, deciding whether a history satisfies SC is NP-complete [20,23,40], and allowing a general atom does not reduce this complexity[2]. Therefore, determining within the theory solver whether a weak-SC history can be extended to a valid execution essentially reruns the DPLL(T) decision procedure, offering little practical benefit.

4.3 Our Solution: Restoring $\rho_{\texttt{ws}}$ and Preserving WS-Derivation

As a solution, we restore the write-serialization encoding $\rho_{\texttt{ws}}$, yielding the final formula $\Psi' := \Psi \wedge \rho_{\texttt{ws}}$. Off-the-shelf theory solvers additionally process $\rho_{\texttt{ws-}cond} \wedge \rho_{\texttt{ws-}some}$, while $\mathcal{T}_{ord}$-solver processes $\rho_{\texttt{ws-}ord}$. When a *ws* variable $ws^x_{i,j}$ is assigned *true*, the corresponding hb edge $w_{x_i} \prec_{\text{hb}} w_{x_j}$ is added. Importantly, the axiom for deriving ws (i.e., Axiom 2) is still retained, allowing inconsistencies to be detected early. In addition, we extend the preventive propagation technique for those newly introduced *ws* variables, providing additional pruning and improving overall solving efficiency; see Sect. 5.

Although restoring $\rho_{\texttt{ws}}$ introduces a non-negligible increase in encoding size, the overall efficiency still remains comparable to that of other sound approaches, mainly for three reasons. First, the cost of enforcing ws totality is largely unavoidable once soundness is required, and modern DPLL engines, being highly optimized for NP-complete problems, generally deliver better performance. Second,

[2] Related results for histories with atomic blocks follow from the complexity of checking database transactional histories [11,13], which is also NP-complete.

incorporating these constraints imposes almost no additional burden on $\mathcal{T}_{ord}$-solver. Finally, integrating *ws* variables creates opportunities for domain-specific optimizations. Empirical evaluations also confirm the practical efficiency of this design; see Sect. 6.

Telbisz et al. [34] propose another solution to the weak SC problem: they introduce a second-stage solving after a candidate execution is found. In this stage, the total store order is explicitly encoded. However, this strategy requires an extra invocation of DPLL(T), which is undesirable. We also provide an empirical comparison between our approach and theirs; see Sect. 6.

4.4 Correctness

Theorem 2. *$\mathcal{T}_{ord}$-solver, under the encoding Ψ', does not suffer from the weak SC problem: if it accepts a satisfying assignment, there exists a valid execution.*

Proof Sketch. Let X_{ws} be the set of *ws* variables, and let an assignment α denote a set of literals over $X_{rf} \cup X_{ws} \cup X_{grd}$. From α, we define $\texttt{rf}(\alpha) = \bigcup_x \{(w_{x_i}, r_{y_j}) \mid rf^x_{i,j} \in \alpha\}$, $\texttt{ws}(\alpha) = \bigcup_x \{(w_{x_i}, w_{x_j}) \mid ws^x_{i,j} \in \alpha\}$. The components $\mathbb{E}$, $\texttt{po}$, and $\texttt{atom}$ of the program are fixed. Given a satisfying assignment α (which is complete), we obtain the execution $\tau = \langle \mathbb{E}, \texttt{po}, \texttt{atom}, \texttt{rf}(\alpha), \texttt{ws}(\alpha) \rangle$.

Let $\texttt{fr}(\alpha) = \texttt{rf}(\alpha)^{-1} ; \texttt{ws}(\alpha)$, $\texttt{hb}(\alpha) = (\texttt{po} \cup \texttt{rf}(\alpha) \cup \texttt{ws}(\alpha) \cup \texttt{fr}(\alpha))^+$. We write $\widehat{\texttt{rf}}(\alpha)$ and $\widehat{\texttt{hb}}(\alpha)$ for the $\texttt{rf}$ and $\texttt{hb}$ relations maintained internally by $\mathcal{T}_{ord}$-solver under assignment α. By construction, $\widehat{\texttt{rf}}(\alpha) = \texttt{rf}(\alpha)$ for all αs. Thus, the goal is to show that when α is complete, $\widehat{\texttt{hb}}(\alpha) = \texttt{hb}(\alpha)$. Once this holds, Axiom 4 ensures that $\texttt{hb}(\alpha)$ is acyclic, and therefore τ is valid.

Similar to the definition of weak SC, we have

Lemma 1. *For any α, let $\widehat{ws}(\alpha) = ((\widehat{hb}(\alpha)|_{\mathsf{WR}} ; \widehat{rf}(\alpha)^{-1}) \cup \widehat{hb}(\alpha)|_{\mathsf{WW}})^+$, then $\widehat{hb}(\alpha) = (po \cup \widehat{rf}(\alpha) \cup \widehat{ws}(\alpha) \cup (\widehat{rf}(\alpha)^{-1}; \widehat{ws}(\alpha)))^+$.*

Lemma 1 follows by induction on the sequence of assigned literals. We remark that this statement omits the effect of guard conditions, as accounting for them does not change the argument but would introduce unnecessary details.

Lemma 2. *For any α, $ws(\alpha) \subseteq \widehat{ws}(\alpha)$; when α is complete, $ws(\alpha) = \widehat{ws}(\alpha)$.*

Lemma 2 states that $\mathcal{T}_{ord}$-solver may derive additional $\texttt{ws}$ edges beyond those explicitly assigned in α. But when α is complete, the two relations are the same. This is because all edges directly implied by *ws* variables are included in $\widehat{\texttt{hb}}$, and Ψ' enforces the $\texttt{ws}$ to be total.

By Lemmas 1 and 2, for any complete assignment α, $\widehat{\texttt{hb}}(\alpha) = (\texttt{po} \cup \widehat{\texttt{rf}}(\alpha) \cup \widehat{\texttt{ws}}(\alpha) \cup (\widehat{\texttt{rf}}(\alpha)^{-1}; \widehat{\texttt{ws}}(\alpha)))^+ = (\texttt{po} \cup \texttt{rf}(\alpha) \cup \texttt{ws}(\alpha) \cup \texttt{fr}(\alpha)) = \texttt{hb}(\alpha)$. Thus, the constructed τ is valid. □

Moreover, we show that $\mathcal{T}_{ord}$-solver does not reject any valid execution.

Theorem 3. *If $\mathcal{T}_{ord}$-solver, under the encoding Ψ', deems a (partial) assignment α inconsistent, then there exists no complete assignment α' such that $\alpha \subseteq \alpha'$ and α' is a satisfying assignment.*

Proof Sketch. Theorem 3 follows from the monotonicity of acyclicity check. Since $\widehat{\mathtt{hb}}(\alpha) \subseteq \widehat{\mathtt{hb}}(\alpha')$, any cycle detected in $\widehat{\mathtt{hb}}(\alpha)$ must persist in $\widehat{\mathtt{hb}}(\alpha')$, implying that no complete α' corresponds to a valid execution. $\square$

5 Extending Preventive Propagation

Preventive propagation [33] effectively accelerates $\mathcal{T}_{ord}$-solver. The key idea is to propagate the negation of *fragile* variables [33, Definition 2] (i.e., variables whose assignment to *true* would immediately lead to theory inconsistency), thereby preventing the core solver from exploring invalid branches.

Since we reintroduced *ws* variables, it is natural to extend preventive propagation to these variables as well. Moreover, the original framework does not account for atomicity constraints. In practice, atomicity can introduce additional theory inconsistencies and thus create fragile variables that the original method cannot detect. Figure 4 illustrates such an example. Assume that, under a partial assignment in the SMT search, $w_{x_1} \prec_{\mathsf{po}} r_{y_2}$, $w_{y_1} \prec_{\mathsf{po}} r_{x_2}$, and $w_{x_1} \prec_{\mathtt{rf}} r_{x_2}$ hold. If atomicity constraints are not taken into account – even though $\{w_{x_1}, r_{y_2}\}$ and $\{w_{y_1}, r_{x_2}\}$ form two atomic blocks, respectively – then $rf^{y}_{1,2}$ is not fragile. Once $\mathtt{atom}$ is enforced, however, setting $rf^{y}_{1,2}$ to *true* introduces $w_{y_1} \prec_{\mathtt{rf}} r_{y_2}$ (dashed), violating the acyclicity of $\mathtt{hba}$; hence, $rf^{y}_{1,2}$ becomes fragile. Consequently, the original framework misses such atomicity-induced fragile variables, losing potential optimization opportunities.

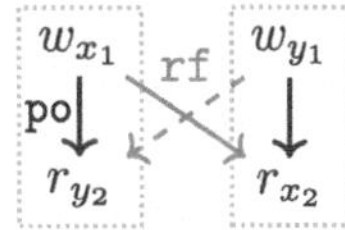

Fig. 4. Atomicity can introduce additional fragile variables.

In this section, we extend preventive propagation along both directions: supporting *ws* variables and incorporating atomicity constraints.

5.1 Revisiting the Original Framework

The original framework is designed for only *rf* variables and guard conditions, under the assumption that $\mathtt{atom} = I_{\mathbb{E}}$. The key to identify fragile variables lies in characteristic inconsistent subgraphs of $\langle \mathbb{E}, \mathtt{rf} \rangle$ and $\langle \mathbb{E}, \mathtt{hb} \rangle$, referred to as *inconsistency patterns*.

Figure 5 illustrates the two patterns adopted by the original framework [33]. The left pattern captures the case where an $\mathtt{rf}$ edge directly contradicts an existing $\mathtt{hb}$ edge, rendering the corresponding *rf* variable fragile. The right pattern involves write events w, w' and a read event r accessing the same location, where $w \prec_{\mathtt{hb}} w' \prec_{\mathtt{hb}} r$, $w \prec_{\mathtt{rf}} r$, and w' is enabled (i.e., $grd(w')$ is assigned *true*, shown in the red circle). In this situation, $r \prec_{\mathtt{hb}} w'$ can be derived via FR-derivation and $w' \prec_{\mathtt{hb}} w$ can be derived via WS-derivation, each producing a cycle. Thus, once $w \prec_{\mathtt{hb}} w' \prec_{\mathtt{hb}} r$ holds, the *rf* variable for (w, r) and $grd(w')$ cannot both be assigned *true*.

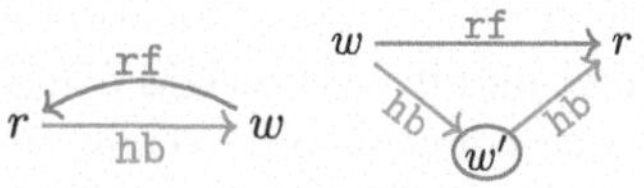

Fig. 5. Inconsistency patterns in the original framework.

5.2 Key Observations for Extending Preventive Propagation

The introduction of *ws* variables and atomicity constraints allows more intricate interactions among events. We present the key observations for supporting these elements, first for *ws* variables and then for atomicity constraints.

Identifying Fragile *ws* Variables. As before, we assume $\mathtt{atom} = I_{\mathbb{E}}$. The extension for identifying fragile *ws* variables is based on a simple observation.

Property 1. For any write events w and w', $w \prec_{\mathtt{ws}} w' \Leftrightarrow w \prec_{\mathtt{hb}} w'$.

By Property 1, if $w \prec_{\mathtt{hb}} w'$, then $\neg(w' \prec_{\mathtt{ws}} w)$. Motivated by this, we adopt a simple yet effective inconsistency pattern, shown in Fig. 6, in which the *ws* variable for (w', w) becomes fragile as soon as $w \prec_{\mathtt{hb}} w'$ holds.

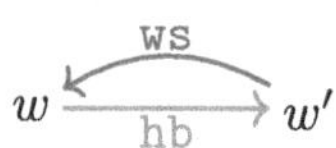

Fig. 6. The inconsistency pattern for *ws* variables.

Recall that any two enabled write events must be ordered. Let $ws_{w,w'}$ and $ws_{w',w}$ denote the corresponding variables for (w, w') and (w', w), respectively. Once $\neg ws_{w',w}$ is inferred, unit propagation immediately forces $ws_{w,w'}$. With the saturated derivation strategy, this pattern allows a large number of *ws* variables to be fixed early.

Incorporating Atomicity Constraints. Consider the case where $\mathtt{atom} \neq I_{\mathbb{E}}$. Under the consistency requirement, the acyclicity of $\mathtt{hb}$ decomposes into two parts: intra-block acyclicity (i.e., of $\mathtt{hb} \cap \mathtt{atom}$) and inter-block acyclicity (i.e., of $\mathtt{hb}/\mathtt{atom}$). For the intra-block acyclicity, we make the following observation.

Property 2. In any execution, $\mathtt{po}$ is a total order over enabled events within the same atomic block.

Proof Sketch. If two events e_1 and e_2 in the same atomic block are unordered by $\mathtt{po}$, they must lie on mutually exclusive control-flow branches (e.g., `if` e_1 `else` e_2), and thus cannot both be enabled. □

By Property 2, any intra-block cycle necessarily manifests as an edge that contradicts $\mathtt{po}$, and can therefore be detected directly. Thus, we focus on inter-block acyclicity. Our key observation is based on the observable effect of a whole atomic block.

Although an atomic block may contain many internal events, its observable effect on any given location is simple: it can behave only as a read, a write, or a read-modify-write (RMW). Specifically, for an atomic block and a location: if the block contains only reads, it must obtain its value externally and then behaves as a read; if it performs a write before any read, it behaves as a pure write (its reads, if any, obtain their values internally); if it first reads a value and later overwrites it, it exhibits RMW behavior.

This block-level abstraction allows us to reason about atomic blocks in a uniform way: on each location, their observable actions reduce to generalized read, write, or RMW behaviors, directly paralleling the event-level cases in the original framework.

5.3 Our Approach: Four Inconsistency Patterns

Building on these insights, we identify four inconsistency patterns: Self-Reversal, Stale-Read, RMW-Broadcast, and RF-Join, as shown in Fig. 7.

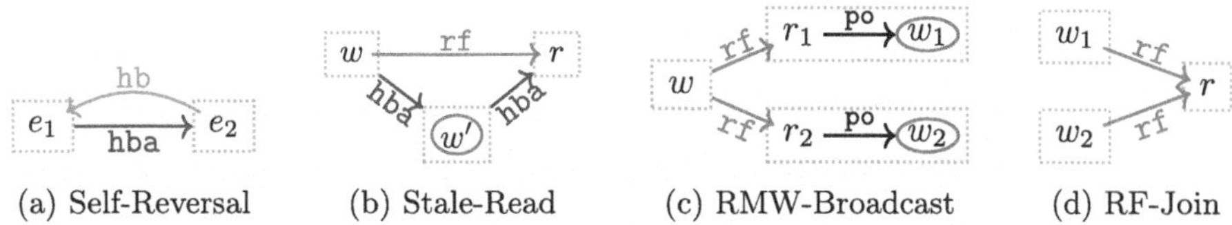

(a) Self-Reversal (b) Stale-Read (c) RMW-Broadcast (d) RF-Join

Fig. 7. Extended inconsistency patterns. Enabled events are shown in red circles, and events in a subgraph are assumed to access the same location. (Color figure online)

Let $\texttt{hba} = \texttt{hb}/\texttt{atom}$. Self-Reversal (Fig. 7a) generalizes the left pattern in Fig. 5 and the pattern in Fig. 6. Here, an hb edge (e_2, e_1) co-exists with $[e_1] \prec_{\texttt{hba}} [e_2]$, where (e_2, e_1) may correspond to an *rf* or *ws* variable. Such a variable becomes fragile once the hba edge $([e_1], [e_2])$ is derived. Stale-Read (Fig. 7b) generalizes the right pattern in Fig. 5. A read event r reads from a write event w, whose value is overwritten by w', i.e., $w \prec_{\texttt{rf}} r \wedge [w] \prec_{\texttt{hba}} [w'] \wedge [w'] \prec_{\texttt{hba}} [r] \wedge grd(w')$ holds. Under $[w] \prec_{\texttt{hba}} [w'] \prec_{\texttt{hba}} [r]$, the *rf* variable for (w, r) and $grd(w')$ cannot be both assigned *true*.

RMW-Broadcast (Fig. 7c) and RF-Join (Fig. 7d) are specialized forms of Stale-Read. In RMW-Broadcast, two atomic blocks read-modify-write from the same write w. Let $\{r_1, w_1\}$ and $\{r_2, w_2\}$ be the two RMW blocks. $grd(w_1)$ becomes fragile once $w \prec_{\texttt{rf}} r_1 \wedge w \prec_{\texttt{rf}} r_2 \wedge grd(w_2)$ holds; symmetrically, the *rf* variable for (w, r_1) becomes fragile under $grd(w_1) \wedge w \prec_{\texttt{rf}} r_2 \wedge grd(w_2)$. In RF-Join, a read event r appears to read from two writes w_1 and w_2. Although a single read cannot do so, Fig. 7d captures the case where r corresponds to two adjacent reads inside an atomic block, each reading from a different write. Thus, the *rf* variable for (w_1, r) becomes fragile once the rf edge (w_2, r) is derived.

Based on the four patterns, we design an algorithm to systematically detect fragile variables. After each assignment to the watched variables (i.e., $X_{rf} \cup X_{ws} \cup X_{grd}$), $\mathcal{T}_{ord}$-solver is invoked to perform saturation-based derivation while checking consistency; if saturation terminates without violating consistency, it then calls the algorithm to identify fragile variables by matching the inconsistency patterns. For any detected fragile variable that remains unassigned, we propagate its negation to the core solver. In this way, preventive propagation prunes invalid branches for the core solver, improving solving efficiency.

Example. We illustrate the effect of preventive propagation using the example program shown in Fig. 1. After $rf^{x}_{1,4}$ is assigned *true*, $\neg rf^{x}_{3,5}$ would be propagated because $\{w_{x_1}\}$, $\{w_{x_3}\}$, and $\{r_{x_4}, r_{x_5}\}$ match the RF-Join pattern, as shown in the left subfigure of Fig. 8. Similarly, once $rf^{x}_{1,5}$ is assigned *true*, $\neg rf^{x}_{3,4}$ would be propagated, as shown in the right subfigure. These preventive propagations allow the solver to reach unsatisfiability more efficiently.

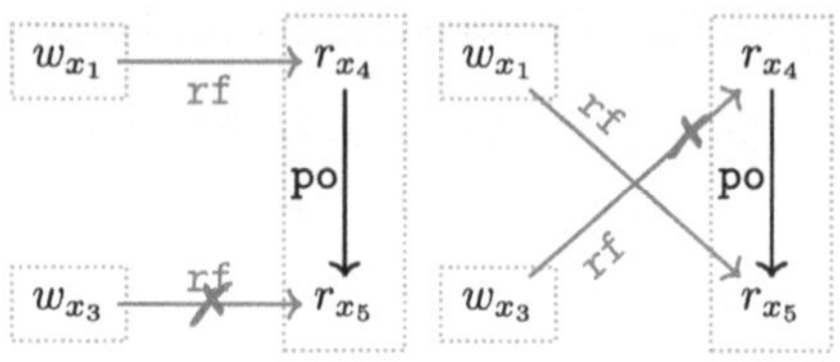

Fig. 8. Solving the example program with preventive propagation.

5.4 Correctness

Theorem 4. *The preventive propagation is sound; i.e., whenever the negation of a variable is propagated, the variable is fragile.*

Theorem 4 follows directly from the inherent inconsistency of the four patterns, and is therefore immediate.

On Completeness. The preventive propagation is incomplete, i.e., it cannot identify all fragile variables. We use an example to illustrate this limitation and explain why achieving completeness is generally impractical.

Consider the inconsistency pattern in Fig. 9. The atomic blocks $\{w_1\}$, $\{r_1, w_2\}$, $\cdots$, $\{r_{n-1}, w_n\}$, and $\{r_n\}$ form a RMW chain through consecutive `rf` edges. Assume there is another enabled write event w' such that $[w_1] \prec_{\texttt{hba}} [w'] \prec_{\texttt{hba}} [r_n]$. Intuitively, an RMW chain cannot be interrupted by an intervening write, so the happens-before order for these blocks cannot be linearized, indicating that the pattern is inconsistent. If $grd(w')$ is unassigned, however, w' cannot match any known pattern and thus cannot be identified as fragile.

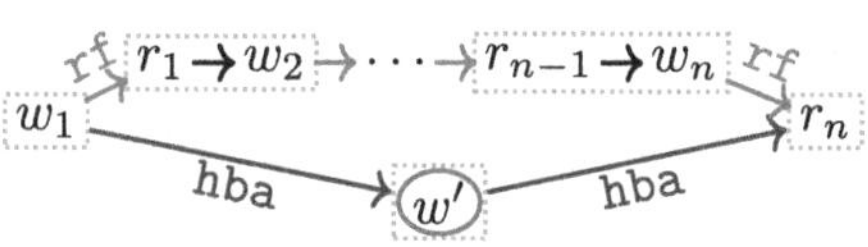

Fig. 9. A complex inconsistency pattern.

To show why completeness is impractical, consider the case where all *rf* variables are unassigned while w' remains enabled. From the inconsistency pattern, we know that the blocks $\{r_1, w_2\}, \cdots, \{r_{n-1}, w_n\}$ cannot form such a RMW chain under any ordering of their relative positions. This results in $(n-1)!$ possible arrangements. Achieving complete propagation would therefore require exhaustively enumerating and propagating these *rf* variables, which can in turn slow down the solving. For this reason, we adopt an effective but incomplete strategy and leave efficient handling of such patterns to future work. Our empirical results further confirm its effectiveness; see Sect. 6.

6 Evaluation

We implemented the proposed approaches (i.e., the weak SC solution and the extended preventive propagation) on top of Z3 user-propagator [12], called POCT (Propagator for refined Ordering Consistency Theory). CBMC [29] is adopted as the frontend to generate SMT formulas.

This section aims to answer the following questions:

(1) Can POCT and other tools address the weak SC problem?
(2) How effective is the preventive propagation in improving performance?
(3) How efficient is POCT compared with other tools?

We use the `Concurrency` category of the `SV-COMP` 2025 benchmarks [10], and compare POCT against DEAGLE [33] and THETA [34,35]. We primarily consider baselines that explicitly employ ordering-consistency reasoning, which is the focus of this paper. DEAGLE is an ordering-consistency-based solver equipped with preventive propagation, and thus provides the closest baseline to our setting. It also demonstrates top performance on `SV-COMP Concurrency` benchmarks. THETA employs ordering-consistency solving and introduces a second-stage check to address the weak SC problem (see Sect. 4.3). All experiments were conducted on a local server, equipped with an Intel 13th Gen i5 CPU and 32 GB of RAM. The timeout is set to 900 s and the memory limit is set to 24 GB.

6.1 Can Tools Address the Weak SC Problem?

Within the `SV-COMP` 2025 `Concurrency` benchmark suite, two benchmarks – `butterfly` and `wsc` – are specifically designed to expose the weak SC problem. Both contain a similar structure shown in Fig. 3b. A tool affected by this issue will incorrectly classify these programs as unsafe.

Table 1 presents the results, where ✓ and ✗ indicate the correctness of the tool. As expected, both POCT and THETA produce correct results. DEAGLE reports incorrect results but emits a warning indicating that the generated counterexample has an incomplete `ws`.

Table 1. Results for `butterfly` and `wsc`.

Benchmark	POCT	DEAGLE	THETA
`butterfly`	✓	✗	✓
`wsc`	✓	✗	✓

6.2 Ablation Analysis of Preventive Propagation

To investigate the effectiveness of preventive propagation, we conduct an ablation analysis by disabling it in POCT, producing a variant POCT (w/o prop). We run both versions on the entire set of 1063 benchmarks, with all loops unrolled twice.

POCT and POCT (w/o prop) produce identical outcomes: both solve 850 cases, time out on 2 cases, and report exceptions on 211 cases. Among the exceptions, 191 are caused by frontend errors, leaving only 20 solver-side failures (e.g., out-of-memory). On the 850 solved cases, POCT takes 907.442 s in total, whereas POCT (w/o prop) takes 2057.595 s, yielding an overall speedup of 2.27×. Since both versions process the same input formulas, all reported runtimes include only solver time and exclude frontend overhead.

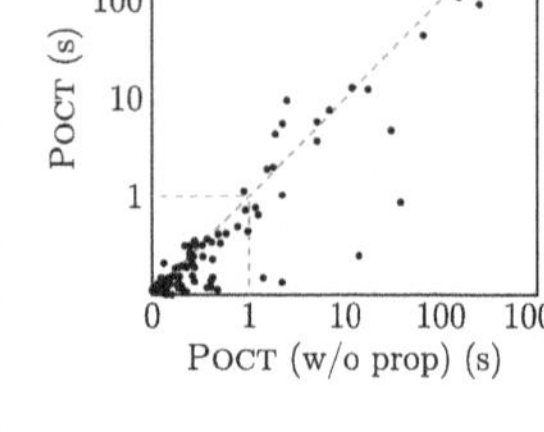

Fig. 10. Per-case runtime comparison between POCT and POCT (w/o prop).

Figure 10 shows the per-case runtime comparison. As illustrated, both versions verify 825 cases within one second, and preventive propagation accelerates 652 of them. Although 173 cases experience slowdown, these cases are generally very fast. In contrast, for harder cases taking more than one second to solve, the average speedup reaches 6.38×. These results together demonstrate the effectiveness of preventive propagation.

Table 2. Comparison of POCT, THETA, and DEAGLE.

Tool	Overall			On Non-Exception Cases [ii]	
	#Solved	#TO	#Exceptions (F. + S.) [i]	#	Runtime (s)
POCT	850	2	211 (191 + 20)	N/A	N/A
THETA	437	226	400 (391 + 9)	628	183107.785/2003.583
DEAGLE	1021	7	35	826	3490.145/3984.832

i F. and S. denote frontend and solver-side exceptions, respectively. For DEAGLE, we cannot distinguish frontend or solver-side exceptions.

ii Runtime is computed on benchmarks where neither tool reports an exception, with each timeout penalized by the 900 s limit (PAR-1). Values are reported as (competitor/POCT).

6.3 End-to-End Performance Comparison

We run DEAGLE and THETA on the entire benchmark set, and compare their performance with POCT. Table 2 summarizes the results.[3]

[3] Correctly solved tasks (`unreach-call` only, matching `SV-COMP` verdict): POCT 403, THETA 388, DEAGLE 650. This count closely depends on our setting (e.g., unwinding bound) and should not be interpreted as a `SV-COMP` capability measure.

Comparison with THETA. THETA solves 437 cases, times out on 226, and reports exceptions on 400. Among these exceptions, 391 have the return code 210, likely due to frontend limitations [6]. To compare overall performance, we consider benchmarks on which neither tool reports an exception and evaluate end-to-end runtime, penalizing each timeout with the 900 s threshold. Under this metric, THETA accumulates 50.86 h, while POCT takes 2003.583 s. Although part of this gap may be attributed to architectural and methodological differences, POCT still shows a clear advantage while strictly adhering to SC semantics.

Comparison with DEAGLE. DEAGLE solves 1021 cases, times out on 7, and reports exceptions on 35. Although DEAGLE appears to solve more cases, most of the discrepancies (185 of 198) arise from CBMC frontend limitations rather than the solver itself. Under the penalized metric, DEAGLE accumulates 3490.145 s, while POCT takes 3984.832 s, giving DEAGLE a slight advantage.

Figure 11 shows the per-case runtime comparison. Most points (779 of 826) fall within the sub-second $(0,0)$ – $(1,1)$ region, indicating that both tools are fast on most cases. Performance differences arise in the remaining 47 harder cases, where POCT is faster on 26, slower on 19, and both tools time out on the remaining 2. Although POCT wins more cases, DEAGLE's larger gains on its winning cases yield a lower overall runtime.

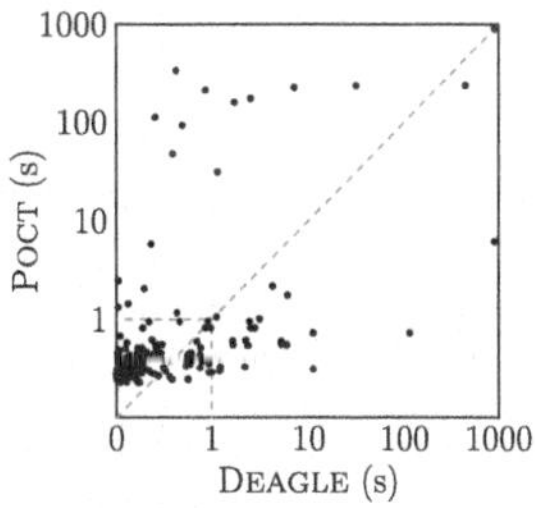

Fig. 11. Per-case runtime comparison between POCT and DEAGLE.

In summary, the two tools are broadly comparable: each outperforms the other on different subsets of benchmarks, and although DEAGLE is slightly faster overall, the gap is small and acceptable given that POCT fully enforces SC semantics.

7 Related Work

Ordering Consistency Theory. There are two mainstream approaches for verifying concurrent programs: bounded model checking (BMC) [15,21,22,36,38,39] and stateless model checking (SMC) [1,2,19,26–28]. Ordering consistency theory is based on BMC, following the partial-order-based framework of Alglave et al. [4,5]. ZORD [18,25] introduces the theory and designs a theory solver that derives `fr` and checks `hb` acyclicity, thus omitting $\rho_{\texttt{fr}}$. DEAGLE [33] further removes $\rho_{\texttt{ws}}$ and reconstructs `ws` via saturation, but this leads to the weak SC problem [6]. It also proposes preventive propagation, but does not handle *ws* variables or atomicity constraints. Our work resolves the weak SC problem and generalizes preventive propagation. THETA [34] applies this theory and adds a second-stage check for the weak SC problem. Inspired by the theory, DARTAGNAN [24] designs an offline solver configurable to memory models.

The Weak SC Problem. The weak SC memory model [40] is proposed to support a saturation algorithm for checking SC histories. A related weak-SC issue arises in the stateless model checker NIDHUGG [2] when using reads-from equivalence [3]. After detecting a violation, NIDHUGG performs a three-phase checking to determine whether a valid execution exists: the first phase applies the saturation algorithm [40], and the final phase serves as the decision procedure.

8 Conclusion and Future Work

We have presented a refined ordering consistency theory that guarantees full sequential consistency and generalizes preventive propagation. Our evaluation shows that our approach reliably eliminates weak-SC behaviors, enables effective propagation, and maintains competitive overall performance.

Our approach currently targets SC semantics. We are exploring how it can be generalized to weak memory models. Weak memory models are typically specified by base relations (e.g., `po`, `rf` and `ws`), derived relations, and consistency axioms. This structure aligns well with ordering-consistency solving: one can encode the base relations and build a theory solver that derives the derived relations on demand and checks the axioms. Our analysis of the weak SC problem can guide this encoding, and the preventive propagation can also be adopted to further accelerate solving.

Acknowledgements. We sincerely thank the anonymous reviewers for their valuable feedback on this paper. This work is supported by the National Natural Science Foundation of China (No. 62072267 and No. 62021002).

Data Availability. The artifact for this paper is available on Zenodo [14].

References

1. Abdulla, P., Aronis, S., Jonsson, B., Sagonas, K.: Optimal dynamic partial order reduction. In: Proceedings of the 41st ACM SIGPLAN-SIGACT Symposium on Principles of Programming Languages. POPL '14, New York, NY, USA, pp. 373–384. Association for Computing Machinery (2014). https://doi.org/10.1145/2535838.2535845
2. Abdulla, P.A., Aronis, S., Atig, M.F., Jonsson, B., Leonardsson, C., Sagonas, K.: Stateless model checking for TSO and PSO. In: Baier, C., Tinelli, C. (eds.) TACAS 2015. LNCS, vol. 9035, pp. 353–367. Springer, Heidelberg (2015). https://doi.org/10.1007/978-3-662-46681-0_28
3. Abdulla, P.A., Atig, M.F., Jonsson, B., Lång, M., Ngo, T.P., Sagonas, K.: Optimal stateless model checking for reads-from equivalence under sequential consistency. Proc. ACM Program. Lang. **3**(OOPSLA) (2019). https://doi.org/10.1145/3360576
4. Alglave, J., Kroening, D., Tautschnig, M.: Partial orders for efficient bounded model checking of concurrent software. In: Sharygina, N., Veith, H. (eds.) CAV 2013. LNCS, vol. 8044, pp. 141–157. Springer, Heidelberg (2013). https://doi.org/10.1007/978-3-642-39799-8_9
5. Alglave, J., Maranget, L., Sarkar, S., Sewell, P.: Fences in weak memory models. In: Touili, T., Cook, B., Jackson, P. (eds.) CAV 2010. LNCS, vol. 6174, pp. 258–272. Springer, Heidelberg (2010). https://doi.org/10.1007/978-3-642-14295-6_25

6. Bajczi, L., Telbisz, C., Szekeres, D., Vörös, A.: On stability in a happens-before propagator for concurrent programs (reproducibility study). In: Gurfinkel, A., Heule, M. (eds.) TACAS 2025. LNCS, vol. 15696, pp. 3–19. Springer, Cham (2025). https://doi.org/10.1007/978-3-031-90643-5_1
7. Barrett, C., Tinelli, C.: Satisfiability modulo theories. In: Handbook of Model Checking, pp. 305–343. Springer, Cham (2018). https://doi.org/10.1007/978-3-319-10575-8_11
8. Beyer, D.: Progress on software verification: SV-COMP 2022. In: TACAS 2022, Part II. LNCS, vol. 13244, pp. 375–402. Springer, Cham (2022). https://doi.org/10.1007/978-3-030-99527-0_20
9. Beyer, D.: Competition on software verification and witness validation: SV-COMP 2023. In: Sankaranarayanan, S., Sharygina, N. (eds.) TACAS 2023, Part II. LNCS, vol. 13994, pp. 495–522. Springer, Cham (2023). https://doi.org/10.1007/978-3-031-30820-8_29
10. Beyer, D., Strejček, J.: Improvements in software verification and witness validation: SV-COMP 2025. In: Gurfinkel, A., Heule, M. (eds.) TACAS 2025, Part III. LNCS, vol. 15698, pp. 151–186. Springer, Cham (2025). https://doi.org/10.1007/978-3-031-90660-2_9
11. Biswas, R., Enea, C.: On the complexity of checking transactional consistency. Proc. ACM Program. Lang. **3**(OOPSLA) (2019). https://doi.org/10.1145/3360591
12. Bjørner, N., Eisenhofer, C., Kovács, L.: Satisfiability modulo custom theories in Z3. In: Dragoi, C., Emmi, M., Wang, J. (eds.) VMCAI 2023. LNCS, vol. 13881, pp. 91–105. Springer, Cham (2023). https://doi.org/10.1007/978-3-031-24950-1_5
13. Bouajjani, A., Enea, C., Román-Calvo, E.: On the complexity of checking mixed isolation levels for SQL transactions. In: Piskac and Z. Rakamarić (Eds.) CAV 2025, Part IV. LNCS, vol. 15934, pp. 315–337. Springer, Cham (2025). https://doi.org/10.1007/978-3-031-98685-7_15
14. Cai, Z., Sun, Z., He, F.: Artifact for "a refined ordering consistency theory: full sequential consistency and generalized preventive reasoning" (2026). https://doi.org/10.5281/zenodo.18616443
15. Clarke, E., Biere, A., Raimi, R., Zhu, Y.: Bounded model checking using satisfiability solving. Form. Methods Syst. Des. **19**(1), 7–34 (2001). https://doi.org/10.1023/A:1011276507260
16. Davis, M., Logemann, G., Loveland, D.: A machine program for theorem-proving. Commun. ACM **5**(7), 394–397 (1962). https://doi.org/10.1145/368273.368557
17. De Moura, L., Bjørner, N.: Satisfiability modulo theories: introduction and applications. Commun. ACM **54**(9), 69–77 (2011). https://doi.org/10.1145/1995376.1995394
18. Fan, H., Sun, Z., He, F.: Satisfiability modulo ordering consistency theory for SC, TSO, and PSO memory models. ACM Trans. Program. Lang. Syst. **45**(1) (2023). https://doi.org/10.1145/3579835
19. Flanagan, C., Godefroid, P.: Dynamic partial-order reduction for model checking software. In: Proceedings of the 32nd ACM SIGPLAN-SIGACT Symposium on Principles of Programming Languages. POPL '05, New York, NY, USA, pp. 110–121. Association for Computing Machinery (2005). https://doi.org/10.1145/1040305.1040315
20. Furbach, F., Meyer, R., Schneider, K., Senftleben, M.: Memory-model-aware testing: a unified complexity analysis. ACM Trans. Embed. Comput. Syst. **14**(4) (2015). https://doi.org/10.1145/2753761

21. Ganai, M.K., Gupta, A.: Efficient modeling of concurrent systems in BMC. In: Havelund, K., Majumdar, R., Palsberg, J. (eds.) SPIN 2008. LNCS, vol. 5156, pp. 114–133. Springer, Heidelberg (2008). https://doi.org/10.1007/978-3-540-85114-1_10
22. Gavrilenko, N., Ponce-de-León, H., Furbach, F., Heljanko, K., Meyer, R.: BMC for weak memory models: relation analysis for compact SMT encodings. In: Dillig, I., Tasiran, S. (eds.) CAV 2019. LNCS, vol. 11561, pp. 355–365. Springer, Cham (2019). https://doi.org/10.1007/978-3-030-25540-4_19
23. Gibbons, P.B., Korach, E.: Testing shared memories. SIAM J. Comput. **26**(4), 1208–1244 (1997). https://doi.org/10.1137/S0097539794279614
24. Haas, T., Meyer, R., Ponce de León, H.: CAAT: consistency as a theory. Proc. ACM Program. Lang. **6**(OOPSLA2) (2022). https://doi.org/10.1145/3563292
25. He, F., Sun, Z., Fan, H.: Satisfiability modulo ordering consistency theory for multi-threaded program verification. In: Proceedings of the 42nd ACM SIGPLAN International Conference on Programming Language Design and Implementation. PLDI 2021, New York, NY, USA, pp. 1264–1279. Association for Computing Machinery (2021). https://doi.org/10.1145/3453483.3454108
26. Kokologiannakis, M., Marmanis, I., Gladstein, V., Vafeiadis, V.: Truly stateless, optimal dynamic partial order reduction. Proc. ACM Program. Lang. **6**(POPL) (2022). https://doi.org/10.1145/3498711
27. Kokologiannakis, M., Marmanis, I., Vafeiadis, V.: Spore: combining symmetry and partial order reduction. Proc. ACM Program. Lang. **8**(PLDI) (2024). https://doi.org/10.1145/3656449
28. Kokologiannakis, M., Raad, A., Vafeiadis, V.: Model checking for weakly consistent libraries. In: Proceedings of the 40th ACM SIGPLAN Conference on Programming Language Design and Implementation. PLDI 2019, New York, NY, USA, pp. 96–110. Association for Computing Machinery (2019). https://doi.org/10.1145/3314221.3314609
29. Kroening, D., Tautschnig, M.: CBMC – C bounded model checker. In: Ábrahám, E., Havelund, K. (eds.) TACAS 2014. LNCS, vol. 8413, pp. 389–391. Springer, Heidelberg (2014). https://doi.org/10.1007/978-3-642-54862-8_26
30. Lamport, L.: How to make a multiprocessor computer that correctly executes multiprocess programs. IEEE Trans. Comput. **28**(9), 690–691 (1979). https://doi.org/10.1109/TC.1979.1675439
31. Nieuwenhuis, R., Oliveras, A., Tinelli, C.: Solving sat and sat modulo theories: from an abstract davis-putnam-logemann-loveland procedure to dpll(t). J. ACM **53**(6), 937–977 (2006). https://doi.org/10.1145/1217856.1217859
32. Shasha, D., Snir, M.: Efficient and correct execution of parallel programs that share memory. ACM Trans. Program. Lang. Syst. **10**(2), 282–312 (1988). https://doi.org/10.1145/42190.42277
33. Sun, Z., Fan, H., He, F.: Consistency-preserving propagation for SMT solving of concurrent program verification. Proc. ACM Program. Lang. **6**(OOPSLA2) (2022). https://doi.org/10.1145/3563321
34. Telbisz, C., Bajczi, L., Szekeres, D., Vörös, A.: Theta: Various approaches for concurrent program verification (competition contribution). In: Gurfinkel, A., Heule, M. (eds.) TACAS 2025, Part III. LNCS, vol. 15698, pp. 260–265. Springer, Cham (2025). https://doi.org/10.1007/978-3-031-90660-2_22
35. Tóth, T., Hajdu, A., Vörös, A., Micskei, Z., Majzik, I.: Theta: a framework for abstraction refinement-based model checking. In: Stewart, D., Weissenbacher, G. (eds.) Proceedings of the 17th Conference on Formal Methods in Computer-Aided Design, pp. 176–179 (2017). https://doi.org/10.23919/FMCAD.2017.8102257

36. Wang, C., Jin, H., Hachtel, G.D., Somenzi, F.: Refining the sat decision ordering for bounded model checking. In: Proceedings of the 41st Annual Design Automation Conference. DAC '04, New York, NY, USA, pp. 535–538. Association for Computing Machinery (2004). https://doi.org/10.1145/996566.996713
37. Wang, C., Kundu, S., Limaye, R., Ganai, M., Gupta, A.: Symbolic predictive analysis for concurrent programs. Form. Asp. Comput. **23**(6), 781–805 (2011). https://doi.org/10.1007/s00165-011-0179-2
38. Yin, L., Dong, W., Liu, W., Li, Y., Wang, J.: YOGAR-CBMC: CBMC with scheduling constraint based abstraction refinement. In: Beyer, D., Huisman, M. (eds.) TACAS 2018. LNCS, vol. 10806, pp. 422–426. Springer, Cham (2018). https://doi.org/10.1007/978-3-319-89963-3_25
39. Yin, L., Dong, W., Liu, W., Wang, J.: Scheduling constraint based abstraction refinement for weak memory models. In: Proceedings of the 33rd ACM/IEEE International Conference on Automated Software Engineering.ASE '18, New York, NY, USA, pp. 645–655. Association for Computing Machinery (2018). https://doi.org/10.1145/3238147.3238223
40. Zennou, R., Atig, M.F., Biswas, R., Bouajjani, A., Enea, C., Erradi, M.: Boosting sequential consistency checking using saturation. In: Hung, D.V., Sokolsky, O. (eds.) ATVA 2020. LNCS, vol. 12302, pp. 360–376. Springer, Cham (2020). https://doi.org/10.1007/978-3-030-59152-6_20

Error-Awareness Accelerates Active Automata Learning

Loes Kruger(✉), Sebastian Junges, and Jurriaan Rot

Institute for Computing and Information Sciences, Radboud University, Nijmegen, The Netherlands
{loes.kruger,sebastian.junges,jurriaan.rot}@ru.nl

Abstract. Active automata learning (AAL) algorithms can learn a behavioral model of a system from interacting with it. The primary challenge remains scaling to larger models, in particular in the presence of many possible inputs to the system. Modern AAL algorithms fail to scale even if, in every state, most inputs lead to errors. In various challenging problems from the literature, these errors are observable, i.e., they emit a known error output. Motivated by these problems, we study learning these systems more efficiently. Further, we consider various degrees of knowledge about which inputs are non-error producing at which state. For each level of knowledge, we provide a matching adaptation of the state-of-the-art AAL algorithm $L^{\#}$ to make the most of this domain knowledge. Our empirical evaluation demonstrates that the methods accelerate learning by orders of magnitude with strong but realistic domain knowledge to a single order of magnitude with limited domain knowledge.

1 Introduction

Active Automata Learning (AAL) can be used to infer models by analyzing the input-output behavior of a given System Under Learning (SUL). AAL has been used to learn a wide variety of systems including network protocols [8,9,31], smart cards [3], legacy systems [32], neoVim [10] and Git version control [28]. Libraries such as AALpy [27] and Learnlib [30] implement common algorithms including L^* [1], TTT [15] and $L^{\#}$ [35] and support various types of automata.

Despite the significant progress in AAL, learning a complete model of a large real-world system is often not feasible within a day [33,39]. Systems with large input alphabets are particularly challenging [17,24,34]. Traditionally, learning algorithms study the system response to *every input* at *every state*, yet in many states, most inputs are invalid or practically impossible. Often, such inputs immediately yield error outputs, which indicate that the inputs were invalid and the system is now stuck. For example, network protocols often contain a handshake phase. During this phase, only handshake-related inputs are allowed; all other inputs lead to an error. We have observed that considering all these state-input

This research is partially supported by the NWO grant No. VI.Vidi.223.096.

A. Sampaio and M. Stoelinga (Eds.): FM 2026, LNCS 16556, pp. 520–540, 2026.
https://doi.org/10.1007/978-3-032-26204-2_27

pairs causes significant overhead. Therefore, we advocate using readily available domain knowledge about errors and error-producing inputs to reduce the overhead. Specifically, we show how to incorporate various degrees of knowledge about error-producing inputs in both the hypothesis learning and the hypothesis testing steps, accelerating the state of the art in AAL.

We consider *error-persistent* systems [38], i.e., systems where *known* error outputs are followed only by error outputs. Error persistence is common: Once a connection is closed in a network protocol, further messages yield a response indicating this. Error persistence also applies to fatal errors, shutdowns, and out-of-resource messages. Error persistence is also common when learning POMDP controllers [2] or runtime monitors [23], where some input sequences and their extensions are impossible. Intuitively, there is no need to learn the monitor response to teleporting cars, as long as cars cannot physically teleport.

Beyond error persistence, it is often reasonable to assume that some input words are known to lead to an error, cf. the teleporting cars. However, the *complete* set of error-inducing input words is not always known. For instance, network protocol specifications can underspecify certain input words, leaving it unclear whether they produce errors. We express domain knowledge as a regular language $\mathcal{L}$ describing the words that do *not* lead to errors. We call $\mathcal{L}$ the *reference* and distinguish three levels of knowledge, formalised as relations between $\mathcal{L}$ and the SUL $\mathcal{M}$: (1) *sound and complete*: a word is not in $\mathcal{L}$ if and only if it produces an error in $\mathcal{M}$, (2) *sound*: if a word is not in $\mathcal{L}$ then it produces an error in $\mathcal{M}$, and (3) *arbitrary*: no formal relation.

As standard in AAL, we assume the learning algorithm can ask two types of queries about the SUL [1]: Output queries (OQs, 'What is the output of this word?') and equivalence queries (EQs, 'Is the hypothesis equivalent to the SUL?'). Practically, we use EQs that are approximated using conformance testing [14,34]. Conformance testing techniques construct test suites from a hypothesis. Executing these tests requires the majority of the interactions with the SUL [34]. Given an error-persistent SUL, a reference, and an assumption about its relation to the SUL, our goal is to learn the model with few interactions.

Towards this goal, we adapt conformance testing and learning based on refined notions of equivalence which, intuitively, are parameterized by the reference $\mathcal{L}$. Specifically, in Sect. 3, we truncate test sequences to either before or after an error occurs, depending on the availability of a sound reference. We prove completeness of these new test suites, relative to a suitable fault domain. Further, in Sect. 4, we adapt the learning algorithm $L^{\#}$ [35]. First, we present a version tailored to learning error-persistent systems, without assuming any additional reference. Then, we provide new algorithms for learning with a reference, one for each assumption about this reference. In particular, if $\mathcal{L}$ is sound, certain states can be distinguished without queries, if $\mathcal{L}$ is additionally complete, the number of necessary EQs drops. For arbitrary references, we tailor adaptive AAL [18].

In summary, this paper contributes new test suites and variants of $L^{\#}$, summarised in Table 1. Each variant incorporates different forms of error-aware

Table 1. Overview of novel testing and learning algorithms.

Test suite	Sec.	Explanation	Alg.	Sec.	Explanation
T_e	3.1	Test suite w persistent errors	$L^\#_e$	4.1	$L^\#$ ([35]) w persistent errors
T_S	3.2	Sound test suite	$AL^\#_e$	4.2	$L^\#_e$ + $AL^\#$ ([18]) w arbitrary reference
$\mathsf{MoE}(T_e, T_S)$	3.2	Distribution over test suites ([17])	$L^\#_{e,S}$	4.3	$L^\#_e$ w sound reference
			$L^\#_{e,SC}$	4.4	$L^\#_e$ w sound and complete reference

domain knowledge to accelerate learning and testing of error-persistent systems. Our experimental evaluation shows that such domain knowledge is realistically obtainable and significantly reduces the interactions with the SUL. The full algorithms, proofs, benchmark details and results can be found in the appendix of the extended version of this paper [19].

2 Problem Statement

In this section, we introduce the problem statement and necessary preliminaries.

2.1 Automata

We refer to the i-th element of a word σ by σ_i and use $\sigma_{:i}$ to indicate $\sigma_0 \cdot \sigma_1 \cdots \sigma_i$. Function $\mathsf{last}\colon \Sigma^* \to \Sigma$ returns the last symbol of a word. Concatenation of languages $A, B \subseteq \Sigma^*$ is given by $A \cdot B = \{\sigma \cdot \mu \mid \sigma \in A, \mu \in B\}$. We write $f\colon X \rightharpoonup Y$ for a partial map, $f(x)\downarrow$ if f is defined for x, and $f(x)\uparrow$ otherwise.

Definition 2.1. *A* Mealy machine *is a tuple* $\mathcal{M} = (Q, q_0, I, O, \delta, \lambda)$ *with finite sets* Q *of* states, I *of inputs,* O *of outputs, an* initial state $q_0 \in Q$*, a* transition function $\delta\colon Q \times I \rightharpoonup Q$ *and an* output function $\lambda\colon Q \times I \rightharpoonup O$.

We lift the transition and output functions to words: for $i \in I$ and $\sigma \in I^*$, $\delta(q, i \cdot \sigma) = \delta(\delta(q, i), \sigma)$ and $\lambda(q, i \cdot \sigma) = \lambda(q, i) \cdot \lambda(\delta(q, i), \sigma)$. We define $|\mathcal{M}|$ to be the number of states in $\mathcal{M}$ and use superscript $\mathcal{M}$ to show to which Mealy machine we refer, e.g., $Q^{\mathcal{M}}$. We abbreviate $\delta(q_0, \sigma)$ by $\delta(\sigma)$. We assume that Mealy machines are complete and minimal, unless specified otherwise.

Definition 2.2. *Given a language* $\mathcal{L} \subseteq I^*$ *and Mealy machines* $\mathcal{M}$ *and* $\mathcal{N}$*, states* $p \in Q^{\mathcal{M}}$ *and* $q \in Q^{\mathcal{N}}$ *are* $\mathcal{L}$-equivalent, *written as* $p \sim_{\mathcal{L}} q$*, if* $\lambda^{\mathcal{M}}(p, \sigma) = \lambda^{\mathcal{N}}(q, \sigma)$ *for all* $\sigma \in \mathcal{L}$*. States* p, q *are* equivalent, *written* $p \sim q$*, if they are* I^**-equivalent. States* p, q *are* apart, *written* $p \# q$*, if there is some* $\sigma \in I^*$ *such that* $\lambda(q, \sigma)\downarrow$*,* $\lambda(p, \sigma)\downarrow$ *and* $\lambda(q, \sigma) \neq \lambda(p, \sigma)$.

Mealy machines $\mathcal{M}$ and $\mathcal{N}$ are $\mathcal{L}$-equivalent if $q_0^{\mathcal{M}} \sim_{\mathcal{L}} q_0^{\mathcal{N}}$. A prefix-closed language $P \subseteq I^*$ is a *state cover* for a Mealy machine $\mathcal{M}$ if, for every state $q \in Q^{\mathcal{M}}$, there exists $\sigma \in P$ s.t. $\delta(q_0, \sigma) = q$. A state cover P is *minimal* if $|P| = |Q^{\mathcal{M}}|$. A language $W_q \subseteq I^*$ is a *state identifier* for $q \in Q^{\mathcal{M}}$ if for all $p \in Q^{\mathcal{M}}$ with $p \# q$ there exists $\sigma \in W_q$ with $\sigma \vdash p \# q$. A *separating family* is a collection of state identifiers $\{W_q\}_{q \in Q^{\mathcal{M}}}$ s.t. for all $p \# q$, there exists $\sigma \in W_p \cap W_q$ with $\sigma \vdash p \# q$. We fix $\mathsf{sep}(W, p, q)$ to uniquely represent one such σ.

2.2 Learning and Testing

We assume our learning algorithm can perform output queries (OQs) on the System Under Learning (SUL) $\mathcal{M}$. This means that when the algorithm poses an OQ with $\sigma \in I^*$ on $\mathcal{M}$, $\mathcal{M}$ returns $\lambda^{\mathcal{M}}(q_0, \sigma)$. Traditionally, a learning algorithm can pose an equivalence query (EQ) to a teacher: the teacher replies yes if the provided hypothesis Mealy machine $\mathcal{H}$ is equivalent to the SUL, and no with a counterexample witnessing inequivalence otherwise. When no teacher is available, conformance testing can be used to approximate the EQ. Conformance testing constructs a test suite from a hypothesis Mealy machine $\mathcal{H}$ [14,34], and each sequence in the suite is posed as an OQ. Ideally, test suites contain a failing test for every alternative model of the SUL.

Definition 2.3. *A* fault domain *is a set of Mealy machines $\mathcal{C}$. A test suite $T \subseteq I^*$ is complete for $\mathcal{H}$ w.r.t. $\mathcal{C}$ if for all $\mathcal{M} \in \mathcal{C}$, $\mathcal{H} \sim_T \mathcal{M}$ implies $\mathcal{H} \sim \mathcal{M}$.*

Since equivalence is checked on output sequences, prefixes of test sequences add no additional information. Accordingly, all our examples use test suites with only maximal elements. For any finite test suite T a Mealy machine can be constructed that is inequivalent to $\mathcal{H}$ but produces the same outputs as $\mathcal{H}$ on every sequence in T. Therefore, test suites are constructed such that they provide guarantees such as k-completeness [26] or k-A-completeness [36]. For example, a test suite T is k-complete for $\mathcal{H}$ if it is complete w.r.t. all models with at most $|\mathcal{H}| + k$ states.

2.3 Problem Statement

In this paper, we focus on Mealy machines where after executing an input that produces an error, all following outputs are also errors.

Definition 2.4. *A Mealy machine $\mathcal{M}$ is* e-persistent *if there exists a special output $\mathsf{e} \in O$ such that for all $\sigma \in I^*$ and $i \in I$, $\mathit{last}(\lambda^{\mathcal{M}}(\sigma)) = \mathsf{e}$ implies $\mathit{last}(\lambda^{\mathcal{M}}(\sigma \cdot i)) = \mathsf{e}$. A language $\mathcal{L} \subseteq I^*$ is* e*-persistent if for all $\sigma \in I^*$ and $i \in I$, $\sigma \notin \mathcal{L}$ implies $\sigma \cdot i \notin \mathcal{L}$.*

Instead of a single output, e may be an alias for several outputs that are linked to erroneous behavior. We assume that the set of outputs representing e is given. Moreover, we may have domain knowledge in the form of an e-persistent DFA that rejects some or all words that produce errors and call such a reference DFA *sound*, respectively, *sound and complete.*

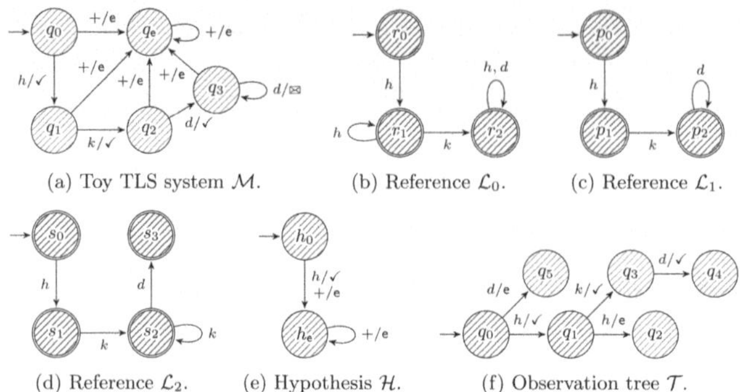

(a) Toy TLS system $\mathcal{M}$. (b) Reference $\mathcal{L}_0$. (c) Reference $\mathcal{L}_1$.

(d) Reference $\mathcal{L}_2$. (e) Hypothesis $\mathcal{H}$. (f) Observation tree $\mathcal{T}$.

Fig. 1. Mealy machine, DFA references and an observation tree related to a toy TLS system. Double circle states represent final states. Omitted DFA transitions lead to the (non-final) sink state. The +-symbol on transitions represents all inputs for which a transition is not explicitly drawn.

Definition 2.5. *Let $\mathcal{M}$ be a Mealy machine and $\mathcal{L} \subseteq I^*$ a regular language. $\mathcal{L}$ is* sound *for $\mathcal{M}$ if for all $\sigma \in I^*$, $\sigma \notin \mathcal{L}$ implies $\mathsf{last}(\lambda^{\mathcal{M}}(\sigma)) = \mathsf{e}$. $\mathcal{L}$ is* complete *for $\mathcal{M}$ if the implication holds the other way around.*

Example 2.6. Figure 1a shows a Mealy machine representing a toy version of the TLS protocol with $O = \{\checkmark, ⊠, \mathsf{e}\}$ and $I = \{h, k, d, c\}$ representing *hello*, *kex*, *data* and *close* respectively. The DFAs Fig. 1b, Fig. 1c, and Fig. 1d represent a sound, a sound and complete, and an unsound and incomplete reference, respectively. Figure 1b is not complete as $hh \in \mathcal{L}_0$. Figure 1d is neither sound nor complete as $hkdd \notin \mathcal{L}_2$ and $hkk \in \mathcal{L}_2$. Reference $\mathcal{L}_2$ can still be useful because most accepted words are non-error-producing.

In this paper, we focus on these *assumptions* and use them to learn a Mealy machine more efficiently, specifically. We solve the following problem:

Error-aware AAL with a Reference

Given an e-persistent SUL $\mathcal{M}$, a sound and complete/sound/arbitrary reference language $\mathcal{L}$, efficiently learn a Mealy machine $\mathcal{H}$ s.t. $\mathcal{M} \sim \mathcal{H}$.

3 Error-Aware Testing

In this section, we prune test suites using e-persistence and error-aware references.

3.1 Testing with Persistent Errors

We show that if an SUL $\mathcal{M}$ and a Mealy machine $\mathcal{H}$ are both e-persistent, test words can be truncated after the first e output without losing the power of the test suite. Let $\mathsf{first}_\mathsf{e}(\mathcal{H}, \sigma,)$ be the smallest i where $\lambda^\mathcal{H}(\sigma)_i \neq \mathsf{e} \wedge \lambda^\mathcal{H}(\sigma)_{i+1} = \mathsf{e}$ and ∞ if no such i exists. The *filter* f_e returns a truncated word:

$$f_\mathsf{e}(\mathcal{H}, \sigma) = \begin{cases} \sigma_{:i+1} & \text{if } i = \mathsf{first}_\mathsf{e}(\mathcal{H}, \sigma) < \infty. \\ \sigma & \text{otherwise.} \end{cases} \tag{1}$$

Definition 3.1. *Given a test suite T and a Mealy machine $\mathcal{H}$, the* e-persistent test suite *is $T_\mathsf{e}(\mathcal{H}) = \{f_\mathsf{e}(\mathcal{H}, \sigma) \mid \sigma \in T\}$.*

Example 3.2. For test suite $T = \{kh, dh, ch, hhh, hkh, hdh, hch\}$ and hypothesis $\mathcal{H}$ in Fig. 1e, the e-persistent test suite is $T_\mathsf{e}(\mathcal{H}) = \{k, d, c, hh, hk, hd, hc\}$.

We refer to $T_\mathsf{e}(\mathcal{H})$ by T_e, whenever possible. As we assume the SUL is e-persistent, we consider fault domains with only e-persistent Mealy machines.

Definition 3.3. *Let $\mathcal{C}$ be a fault domain. Then the* e-persistent fault (sub)domain *is $\mathcal{C}_\mathsf{e} = \mathcal{C} \cap \{\mathcal{M} \mid \mathcal{M}$ is e-persistent$\}$.*

Theorem 3.4. *Let $\mathcal{H}$ be an e-persistent Mealy machine and $\mathcal{C}$ a fault domain. If test suite T is complete for $\mathcal{H}$ w.r.t. $\mathcal{C}$, then T_e is complete for $\mathcal{H}$ w.r.t. $\mathcal{C}_\mathsf{e}$.*

When $\mathcal{C}$ is clear from the context, we may call T_e e-*complete.*

3.2 Testing with Reference Models

Given a reference that is sound for both the SUL and $\mathcal{H}$, a test word may be truncated to the longest prefix in $\mathcal{L}$. Unlike f_e, which truncates after observing e, a sound reference allows truncation to just before e is produced. Let $\mathsf{first}_\mathsf{e}(\mathcal{L}, \sigma)$ be the smallest i where $\sigma_{:i} \in \mathcal{L} \wedge \sigma_{:i+1} \notin \mathcal{L}$ and ∞ if no such i exists. If $\mathsf{first}_\mathsf{e}(\mathcal{L}, \sigma) < \infty$, then the filter f_S, defined below, cuts the word accordingly. If the resulting word ends with multiple error in $\mathcal{H}$, it is further cut by f_e.

$$f_\mathsf{S}(\mathcal{H}, \mathcal{L}, \sigma) = \begin{cases} \sigma_{:i} & \text{if } i = \mathsf{first}_\mathsf{e}(\mathcal{L}, \sigma) < \infty \wedge i \leq \mathsf{first}_\mathsf{e}(\mathcal{H}, \sigma). \\ f_\mathsf{e}(\sigma) & \text{otherwise.} \end{cases} \tag{2}$$

Definition 3.5. *Given a test suite T, a Mealy machine $\mathcal{H}$ and a reference $\mathcal{L}$, the* sound test suite *is $T_\mathsf{S}(\mathcal{H}, \mathcal{L}) = \{f_\mathsf{S}(\mathcal{H}, \mathcal{L}, \sigma) \mid \sigma \in T\}$.*

Example 3.6. Consider T and $\mathcal{H}$ from Example 3.2. For sound and complete reference $\mathcal{L}_1$ from Fig 1, the sound test suite is $T_\mathsf{S}(\mathcal{H}, \mathcal{L}_1) = \{hk\}$.

If the Mealy machine $\mathcal{M}$ and the hypothesis $\mathcal{H}$ are both e-persistent, the reference $\mathcal{L}$ is sound for both $\mathcal{M}$ and $\mathcal{H}$ and T is complete for some fault domain $\mathcal{C}$, then the sound test suite $T_\mathsf{S}(\mathcal{H}, \mathcal{L})$ is e-complete.

Theorem 3.7. *Let $\mathcal{H}$ be an e-persistent Mealy machine and $\mathcal{C}$ a fault domain. If a test suite T is complete for $\mathcal{H}$ w.r.t. $\mathcal{C}$ and reference $\mathcal{L}$ is sound for all $\mathcal{M} \in \mathcal{C} \cup \{\mathcal{H}\}$, then $T_\mathsf{S}(\mathcal{H}, \mathcal{L})$ is complete w.r.t. $\mathcal{C}_\mathsf{e}$.*

If the reference $\mathcal{L}$ is *not sound* for the SUL, performing only the tests in T_S does not guarantee e-completeness. However, the test suite T_S probably still contains counterexamples and is smaller than T_e. Therefore, we combine T_S and T_e using the Mixture of Experts (MoE) approach [17]. The MoE approach takes a set of test suites and maintains a confidence value for each test suite based on how often that test suite produced a counterexample during previous testing rounds. During testing, MoE selects the next test suite either at random or based on the confidence score, then generates the next test word from the chosen test suite. The algorithm terminates when all test suites have been fully executed or a counterexample has been found. We use $\mathsf{MoE}(T_\mathsf{e}(\mathcal{H}), T_\mathsf{S}(\mathcal{H}, \mathcal{L}))$ to refer to the MoE approach with the T_S and T_e test suites.

Lemma 3.8. *Let $\mathcal{H}$ be an* e*-persistent Mealy machine, $\mathcal{C}$ a fault domain, and $\mathcal{L}$ a reference. If test suite T is complete for $\mathcal{H}$ w.r.t. $\mathcal{C}$, then* $\mathsf{MoE}(T_\mathsf{e}(\mathcal{H}), T_\mathsf{S}(\mathcal{H}, \mathcal{L}))$ *is complete w.r.t. $\mathcal{C}_\mathsf{e}$.*

4 Error-Aware Learning

Below, we introduce four variations of the state-of-the-art AAL algorithm $L^{\#}$ [35]. Each variant matches an assumption about a reference or its absence (cf. Table 1).

4.1 $L^{\#}$ with Persistent Errors

We present $L^{\#}_\mathsf{e}$, a novel adaptation of $L^{\#}$ that assumes an e-persistent SUL. For readers familiar with $L^{\#}$, the main changes are: (1) the frontier excludes states with errors and (2) OQs are posed per symbol and stop after an error.

Definition 4.1. *A Mealy machine $\mathcal{T}$ is a* tree *if there is a unique word $\sigma \in I^*$ for each $q \in Q^\mathcal{T}$ such that $\delta^\mathcal{T}(q_0, \sigma) = q$. A tree $\mathcal{T}$ is an* observation tree *for a Mealy machine $\mathcal{M}$ if there exists mapping $m\colon Q^\mathcal{T} \to Q^\mathcal{M}$ such that $m(q_0^\mathcal{T}) = q_0^\mathcal{M}$ and if there is a transition $\delta^\mathcal{T}(q, i) = q'$, then there is a transition $\delta^\mathcal{M}(m(q), i) = m(q')$ and $\lambda^\mathcal{T}(q, i) = \lambda^\mathcal{M}(m(q), i)$.*

$L^{\#}_\mathsf{e}$ uses an observation tree to store the observed traces. In an observation tree $\mathcal{T}$, the basis B is a subtree of $\mathcal{T}$ consisting of distinct states of the hidden Mealy machine $\mathcal{M}$. All states in B are pairwise apart, i.e., for all $q \neq q' \in B$ it holds that $q \# q'$. Initially, B contains only the root state, i.e., $B = \{q_0\}$. For a fixed basis B, the frontier $F \subset Q^\mathcal{T}$ consists of all immediate successors of basis states which are not basis states themselves and are not reached by e-producing inputs, i.e., $F = \{r \mid \delta^\mathcal{T}(q, i) = r \wedge \lambda^\mathcal{T}(q, i) \neq \mathsf{e}$ for some $q \in B, r \notin B$ and $i \in I\}$.

Example 4.2. The tree $\mathcal{T}$ in Fig. 1 is an observation tree for $\mathcal{M}$ in Fig. 1a. Its basis B is $\{q_0, q_1\}$ as $h \vdash q_0 \# q_1$ and its frontier F is $\{q_3\}$. State q_2 is not in the frontier, as it is reached with an e-producing transition.

A frontier state $r \in F$ is *isolated* if it is apart from all $q \in B$ and *identified* with a basis state $q \in B$ if it is apart from all $q' \in B$ except q. The basis is *adequate* if $\delta(q,i)\downarrow$ for all $q \in B, i \in I$, and all states $r \in F$ are identified. When the basis is adequate, the observation tree may be folded into an e-persistent Mealy machine hypothesis using $\text{BUILDHYPOTHESIS}_{\mathsf{e}}$. This construction folds back frontier states to their identified basis state and directs transitions from basis states that produce e to a special sink state q_{e} if such transitions exist.

Definition 4.3. *Given an observation tree $\mathcal{T}$ with basis B and frontier F, $\text{BUILDHYPOTHESIS}_{\mathsf{e}}$ constructs a hypothesis Mealy machine $\mathcal{H} = (B \cup q_{\mathsf{e}}, q_0, I, O, \delta', \lambda')$*[1]*. Functions δ' and λ' are constructed as follows.*

$$\delta'(q,i), \lambda'(q,i) = \begin{cases} q_{\mathsf{e}}, \mathsf{e} & \text{if } \lambda^{\mathcal{T}}(q,i) = \mathsf{e} \vee \delta^{\mathcal{T}}(q,i)\uparrow \vee q = q_{\mathsf{e}} \\ b, \lambda^{\mathcal{T}}(q,i) & \text{if } \delta^{\mathcal{T}}(q,i) = b \in B \\ b, \lambda^{\mathcal{T}}(q,i) & \text{if } \delta^{\mathcal{T}}(q,i) = r \in F \wedge \exists b \in B \text{ s.t. } \neg(b \# r) \end{cases}$$

Moreover, we use OQ_{e} to pose inputs one by one and stop after an error e is observed. We write $\mathsf{access}(q)$ to indicate the word leading to q in $\mathcal{T}$. The $L^{\#}_{\mathsf{e}}$ algorithm repeatedly applies the following rules until the correct hypothesis is found:

- The *promotion rule* adds $q \in F$ to the basis B if q is isolated.
- The *extension rule* poses $\text{OQ}_{\mathsf{e}}(\mathsf{access}(q)i)$ for $q \in B$, $i \in I$ if $\delta(q,i)\uparrow$.
- The *separation rule* takes a state $r \in F$ that is not apart from $q, q' \in B$ and poses $\text{OQ}_{\mathsf{e}}(\mathsf{access}(r)\sigma)$ with $\sigma \vdash q \# q'$, resulting in $q \# r$ or $q \# r'$.
- The *equivalence rule* builds the hypothesis $\mathcal{H}$ if B is adequate. The procedure checks whether $\mathcal{T}$ and $\mathcal{H}$ agree on traces and then poses $\text{EQ}(\mathcal{H})$, handling a counterexample when necessary and terminating the algorithm if $\mathcal{H}$ is equivalent to $\mathcal{M}$. Only performing an EQ when B is adequate ensures each counterexample leads to a new basis state.

The equivalence rule ensures that the algorithm terminates only once the correct model is learned. A SUL $\mathcal{M}$ is considered *learned* if $\mathcal{H} \sim \mathcal{M}$, where $\mathcal{H}$ is the hypothesis produced by the algorithm. Correctness thus reduces to proving termination. Each rule application increases a norm, analogous to $L^{\#}$ [35].

Lemma 4.4. *Let $\mathcal{M}$ be an e-persistent SUL with n states and k inputs. $L^{\#}_{\mathsf{e}}$ learns $\mathcal{M}$ within $\mathcal{O}(kn^2 + n\log m)$ OQs and at most $n-1$ EQs, where m is the length of the longest counterexample returned by the EQs.*

4.2 Learning with a Reference

Next, we introduce $AL^{\#}_{\mathsf{e}}$, a so-called adaptive variant of $L^{\#}_{\mathsf{e}}$. Traditionally, adaptive AAL methods incorporate domain knowledge in the form of a reference *Mealy machine* via *rebuilding* [4,7] and *state matching* [18]. Instead, we assume

[1] If there exists some $b \in B$ such that $\delta(b,i) = b$ and $\lambda(b,i) = \mathsf{e}$ for all $i \in I$, we redirect all transitions from q_{e} to b and remove the afterwards unreachable q_{e}.

a minimal *DFA* representation $\mathcal{R}$ for the reference language $\mathcal{L}$, thereby explicitly relying on the regularity of $\mathcal{L}$. We borrow the notation from Mealy machines for DFAs. Compared to $AL^{\#}$ [18], we use tailored notions of rebuilding and matching and builds upon $L^{\#}_{\mathsf{e}}$. The main differences are clarified below.

Rebuilding. Let P be a state cover and W a separating family for $\mathcal{R}$. We introduce two rules that extend $L^{\#}_{\mathsf{e}}$ from Sect. 4.1. The *rebuilding rule* aims to show apartness between every $q \in B$ and some $r \in F$ to find a state in $\mathcal{R}$ that is not contained in B yet. The prioritized promotion rule ensures that $\mathsf{access}(q) \in P$ for every $q \in B$, which allows applying the rebuilding rule more often.

Example 4.5. Suppose we learn $\mathcal{M}$ using $\mathcal{L}_2$ (from Fig. 1). Initially, $Q^{\mathcal{T}} = \{q_0\}$. Let $q = q' = q_0$, $i = h$ and $k \vdash s_0 \# s_1$. Because $\varepsilon, h \in P$ and $\delta^{\mathcal{T}}(t_0, h)\uparrow$, the rebuilding rule is applied and poses $\mathrm{OQ}_{\mathsf{e}}(hk)$ and $\mathrm{OQ}_{\mathsf{e}}(k)$ to isolate $\delta^{\mathcal{T}}(q_0, h)$.

We formally define the rebuilding rules as follows:

- Consider states $q, q' \in B$ and $i \in I$. If ($\delta(q,i)\uparrow$ or $\delta(q,i) \in F$) and $\mathsf{access}(q')$, $\mathsf{access}(q)i \in P$, then the *rebuilding rule* poses queries $\mathrm{OQ}_{\mathsf{e}}(\mathsf{access}(q)i\sigma)$ with $\sigma = \mathsf{sep}(W, \delta^{\mathcal{R}}(\mathsf{access}(q')), \delta^{\mathcal{R}}(\mathsf{access}(q)i))$. We only apply this rule if *σ guarantees progress*. Some $\sigma \in I^*$ guarantees progress if there exists maximal prefixes ρ of $i\sigma$ and ρ' of σ such that $\delta^{\mathcal{T}}(q,\rho)\downarrow$, $\delta^{\mathcal{T}}(q',\rho')\downarrow$ and either $(\delta^{\mathcal{T}}(q,i\sigma)\uparrow \wedge \delta^{\mathcal{T}}(q,\rho) \neq \mathsf{e})$ or $(\delta^{\mathcal{T}}(q',\sigma)\uparrow \wedge \delta^{\mathcal{T}}(q',\rho') \neq \mathsf{e})$.
- If $q \in F$ is isolated and $\mathsf{access}(q) \in P$, *prioritized promotion* adds q to B.

Matching. Rebuilding heavily relies on the chosen P to discover states in $\mathcal{R}$. Thus, if $\mathcal{R}$ diverges from the SUL (only) in the initial state, rebuilding may fail to discover states. State matching, on the other hand, looks at the residual language of states in $\mathcal{R}$ and aims to match basis states with these languages. The matching relation $\mathsf{mdeg}\colon Q^{\mathcal{T}} \times Q^{\mathcal{R}} \to \mathbb{R}$ presented in [18] matches states based on the outputs of the words defined for the basis state. In contrast, our matching relation measures how often the basis state and $\mathcal{L}$ agree on whether a word yields an error. We define $\mathsf{WI}(q) = \{(w,i) \in I^* \times I \mid \delta^{\mathcal{T}}(q,wi)\downarrow\}$ as the defined words from state $q \in Q^{\mathcal{T}}$. We define

$$\mathsf{mdeg}(b,q) = \frac{|\{(w,i) \in \mathsf{WI}(b) \mid \lambda^{\mathcal{T}}(\delta^{\mathcal{T}}(b,w),i) = \mathsf{e} \leftrightarrow \delta^{\mathcal{R}}(q,wi) \notin Q^{\mathcal{R}}_F\}|}{|\mathsf{WI}(b)|},$$

using $0/0 = 0$. States $b \in B$ and $q \in Q^{\mathcal{R}}$ *match*, written $b \stackrel{\mathsf{e}}{=} q$, if for all $q' \in Q^{\mathcal{R}}$ with $q' \neq q$, $\mathsf{mdeg}(b,q) \geq \mathsf{mdeg}(b,q')$. We use this matching relation in the match separation and match refinement rules.[2]

[2] Prioritized separation, as used in $AL^{\#}$, is omitted here because it prioritizes witnesses in W which only concern e-production, $\mathcal{T}$ likely contains shorter witnesses.

Example 4.6. Consider state q_1 in $\mathcal{T}$ (Fig. 1f) and reference $\mathcal{L}_1$ (Fig. 1c). State q_1 matches p_1 as $\mathsf{mdeg}(q_1, p_1) = |\{k,h\}|/|\{k,h\}| = 1$, $\mathsf{mdeg}(q_1, p_0) = |\{h\}|/|\{k,h\}| = 1/2$ and $\mathsf{mdeg}(q_1, p_2) = |\emptyset|/|\{k,h\}| = 0$. Because $q_1 \stackrel{\mathsf{e}}{=} p_1$, $\delta^{\mathcal{T}}(q_1, k) \in F$ and $\delta^{\mathcal{R}}(p_1, k)$ does not match any $b \in B$, we apply match separation to try to show apartness between q_3 and q_1 with $\sigma = k$ as $\lambda^{\mathcal{T}}(q_1, k) \neq \mathsf{e} \wedge \delta^{\mathcal{R}}(hk, k) \notin Q^{\mathcal{R}}_F$. We pose $\mathrm{OQ}_{\mathsf{e}}(hkk)$ which leads to isolation of q_3.

We formally define the matching rules as follows:

- Consider basis states q, q', reference state p, p' and $i \in I$. If there exists $\delta^{\mathcal{T}}(q, i) = r \in F$, $\delta^{\mathcal{R}}(p, i) = p'$ such that $\neg(q' \# r)$, p matches q and p' has no matches, then the *match separation rule* poses $\mathrm{OQ}_{\mathsf{e}}(\mathsf{access}(q)i\sigma)$ where σ is chosen such that $\mathsf{last}(\lambda^{\mathcal{T}}(q', \sigma)) = \mathsf{e} \leftrightarrow \delta^{\mathcal{R}}(p', \sigma) \in Q^{\mathcal{R}}_F$.
- If frontier state q matches $p, p' \in Q^{\mathcal{R}}$, the *match refinement rule* poses $\mathrm{OQ}_{\mathsf{e}}(\mathsf{access}(q)i\sigma)$ with $\sigma = \mathsf{sep}(W, p, p')$.

The $AL^{\#}_{\mathsf{e}}$ algorithm consists of $L^{\#}_{\mathsf{e}}$ and the above-mentioned rules. Checking for undiscovered states in $\mathcal{R}$ increases complexity compared to $L^{\#}_{\mathsf{e}}$, but often reduces the number of EQs in practice.

Lemma 4.7. *Let $\mathcal{M}$ be an* e*-persistent SUL with n states and k inputs. Let $\mathcal{L}$ an* e*-persistent reference, canonically represented by a DFA with o states. $AL^{\#}_{\mathsf{e}}$ learns $\mathcal{M}$ within $\mathcal{O}(kn^2 + no^2 + n\log m)$ OQs and at most $n-1$ EQs, where m is the length of the longest counterexample returned by any EQ.*

4.3 Learning with a Sound Reference

Previously, we did not make any assumption about the quality of the reference. We now assume the reference is sound. In a nutshell, this assumption allows a stronger notion of apartness, relying on witnesses whose existence is implied by the reference instead of only relying on witnesses in the observation tree.

Definition 4.8. *Let $\mathcal{T}$ be an observation tree. States $q, p \in Q^{\mathcal{T}}$ are* S-apart *w.r.t. a sound reference $\mathcal{L}$, written $p \#_{\mathsf{S},\mathcal{L}} q$, if $\sigma \in I^*$ exists such that $\sigma \vdash p \# q$ or $\mathsf{last}(\lambda^{\mathcal{T}}(p, \sigma)) \neq \mathsf{e}$ and $\mathsf{access}^{\mathcal{T}}(q)\sigma \notin \mathcal{L}$ (or symmetrically with p and q swapped).*

The definitions of isolated and identified are lifted to $\#_{\mathsf{S},\mathcal{L}}$. The basis is S-adequate if all $r \in F$ are identified and $\delta(q, i)\downarrow$ for all $q \in B, i \in I$ with $\mathsf{access}^{\mathcal{T}}(q)i \in \mathcal{L}$.

Example 4.9. Consider reference $\mathcal{L}_1$ from Fig. 1b and $\mathcal{T}$ from Fig. 1f. States q_0, q_4 are S-apart with witness h, as $\lambda^{\mathcal{T}}(q_0, h) \neq \mathsf{e}$, while $\mathsf{access}^{\mathcal{T}}(q_4) \cdot h = hkdh \notin \mathcal{L}_1$.

We adapt $L^{\#}_{\mathsf{e}}$ in four main ways to take advantage of a sound reference:

1. We use OQ_{S} which poses inputs one by one and stops when the following input leads to a rejected state in $\mathcal{L}$ or after an error e is observed.
2. We use S-apartness in the $L^{\#}_{\mathsf{e}}$ rules.

3. We adopt the rebuilding procedure of $AL^{\#}_{\mathsf{e}}$ to rebuild the sound reference.
4. Theorem 3.7 and the correctness of the algorithm rely on $\mathcal{L}$ being sound for $\mathcal{H}$. We therefore check this assumption explicitly before posing an EQ restricted to language $\mathcal{L}$. If this check fails, then there must exist some counterexample $\sigma \in I^*$ such that $\sigma \notin \mathcal{L}$ and $\mathsf{last}(\lambda^{\mathcal{H}}(q_0, \sigma)) \neq \mathsf{e}$. We perform $\mathrm{OQ}_{\mathsf{S}}(\sigma, \mathcal{L})$ to add the counterexample to $\mathcal{T}$ and process it using ProcCounterEx$_{\mathsf{S}}$.

$L^{\#}_{\mathsf{e,S}}$, listed in Algorithm 1, has the same OQ and EQ complexity as $L^{\#}$ and learns a Mealy machine that is correct w.r.t. $\mathcal{L}$.

Theorem 4.10. *Let $\mathcal{M}$ be an* e*-persistent SUL and $\mathcal{L}$ an* e*-persistent reference. Let n, k and m be as in Lemma 4.4. $L^{\#}_{\mathsf{e,S}}$ requires $\mathcal{O}(kn^2 + n\ log\ m)$ OQs and at most $n-1$ EQs to learn the smallest Mealy machine $\mathcal{H}$ such that $\mathcal{H} \sim_{\mathcal{L}} \mathcal{M}$ and $\lambda^{\mathcal{M}}(\sigma) = q_{\mathsf{e}}$ for all $\sigma \notin \mathcal{L}$.*

When a reference is sound and the learned Mealy machine is consistent with the SUL on all non-error producing words, then $L^{\#}_{\mathsf{e,S}}$ learns the correct Mealy machine as all other words give output e.

Corollary 4.11. *If $\mathcal{L}$ is a sound reference for $\mathcal{M}$, then $L^{\#}_{\mathsf{e,S}}$ learns a Mealy machine $\mathcal{H}$ such that $\mathcal{H} \sim \mathcal{M}$.*

4.4 Learning with a Sound and Complete Reference

Next, we discuss optimising $L^{\#}_{\mathsf{e}}$ for utilising sound and complete references.

Definition 4.12. *Let $\mathcal{M}$ be an* e*-persistent Mealy machine. States $q, p \in Q^{\mathcal{T}}$ are* C-apart *w.r.t. a complete reference $\mathcal{L}$, written $p \#_{\mathsf{C},\mathcal{L}} q$, if $\sigma \in I^*$ exists such that $\sigma \vdash p \# q$ or $\mathsf{last}(\lambda^{\mathcal{T}}(p, \sigma)) = \mathsf{e}$ and $\mathsf{access}^{\mathcal{T}}(q)\sigma \in \mathcal{L}$ (or symmetrically with p and q swapped).*

Two states are SC-apart if they are S-apart or C-apart. We write $p \#_{\mathsf{SC},\mathcal{L}} q$ to indicate that states p and q are SC apart w.r.t. reference $\mathcal{L}$. We lift the definition of isolated and identified states to SC-apartness.

Contrary to $L^{\#}_{\mathsf{e,S}}$, we do not use the rebuilding procedure of $AL^{\#}_{\mathsf{e}}$. Because we assume references are minimized, the SUL must have at least as many distinct states as the sound and complete reference. Therefore, we construct the test suite $T_{\mathcal{L}}$ for $\mathcal{R}$ with P a minimal *accepting* state cover and W a separating family for $\mathcal{R}$. Here, an accepting state cover of a DFA is a state cover that contains a word σ such that $\delta(q_0, \sigma) = q$ for every reachable state $q \in Q_F$.

$$T_{\mathcal{L}} = \{piw \mid p \in P, i \in I^{\leq 1}, w \in W_{\delta^{\mathcal{R}}(pi)}\} \tag{3}$$

A test suite such as $T_{\mathcal{L}}$ is naturally contained in a k-complete test suite with $k \geq 0$ generated by the HSI-method [22,29]. After executing $T_{\mathcal{L}}$, we set the basis to $B = \{\delta^{\mathcal{T}}(p) \mid p \in P\}$ as all states reached by P are pairwise apart.

[3] Some $\sigma \in I^*$ guarantees progress w.r.t. soundness if there exists maximal prefixes ρ of $i\sigma$ and ρ' of σ such that $\delta^{\mathcal{T}}(q, \rho){\downarrow}$, $\delta^{\mathcal{T}}(q', \rho'){\downarrow}$ and either $(\mathsf{access}^{\mathcal{T}}(q)i\sigma \in \mathcal{L} \wedge \delta^{\mathcal{T}}(q, i\sigma){\uparrow} \wedge \delta^{\mathcal{T}}(q, \rho) \neq \mathsf{e})$ or $(\mathsf{access}^{\mathcal{T}}(q')\sigma \in \mathcal{L} \wedge \delta^{\mathcal{T}}(q', \sigma){\uparrow} \wedge \delta^{\mathcal{T}}(q', \rho') \neq \mathsf{e})$.

Algorithm 1. $L^{\#}_{\mathsf{e}}$ for a sound reference.

procedure $\mathrm{L}^{\#}_{\mathsf{e,s}}(\mathcal{L})$
  $\mathcal{R}_{\mathcal{L}} \leftarrow$ minimal DFA representation of $\mathcal{L}$
  $P \leftarrow$ minimal state cover of $\mathcal{R}_{\mathcal{L}}$
  $W \leftarrow$ separating family of $\mathcal{R}_{\mathcal{L}}$
  do either
  $[\!]$ $(\delta^{\mathcal{T}}(q,i) \in F \vee \delta^{\mathcal{T}}(q,i)\uparrow), \neg(q' \#_{\mathsf{s},\mathcal{L}} \delta^{\mathcal{T}}(q,i))$, $\mathsf{access}^{\mathcal{T}}(q)i, \mathsf{access}^{\mathcal{T}}(q') \in P$,
    $\sigma = \mathsf{sep}(W, \delta^{\mathcal{R}_{\mathcal{L}}}(\mathsf{access}^{\mathcal{T}}(q)i), \delta^{\mathcal{R}_{\mathcal{L}}}(\mathsf{access}^{\mathcal{T}}(q')))$,
    σ guarantees progress w.r.t. soundness[3]
    for some $q, q' \in B, i \in I \rightarrow$ ▷ rebuilding
   $\mathrm{OQ}_{\mathsf{s}}(\mathsf{access}^{\mathcal{T}}(q)i\sigma, \mathcal{L})$
   $\mathrm{OQ}_{\mathsf{s}}(\mathsf{access}^{\mathcal{T}}(q')\sigma, \mathcal{L})$
  $[\!]$ q isolated, for some $q \in F$ with $\mathsf{access}^{\mathcal{T}}(q) \in P \rightarrow$ ▷ prioritized promotion
   $B \leftarrow B \cup \{q\}$
  end do
  do either
  $[\!]$ q isolated, for some $q \in F \rightarrow$ ▷ promotion
   $B \leftarrow B \cup \{q\}$
  $[\!]$ $\delta^{\mathcal{T}}(q,i)\uparrow, \mathsf{access}^{\mathcal{T}}(q)i \subset \mathcal{L}$, for some $q \in B, i \in I \rightarrow$ ▷ extension
   $\mathrm{OQ}_{\mathsf{s}}(\mathsf{access}(q)\ i, \mathcal{L})$
  $[\!]$ $\neg(q \#_{\mathsf{s},\mathcal{L}}\ r), \neg(q \#_{\mathsf{s},\mathcal{L}}\ r'), r \neq r'$
    for some $q \in F$ and $r, r' \in B \rightarrow$ ▷ separation
   $\sigma \leftarrow$ witness of $r \#_{\mathsf{s},\mathcal{L}}\ r'$
   $\mathrm{OQ}_{\mathsf{s}}(\mathsf{access}(q)\ \sigma, \mathcal{L})$
  $[\!]$ B is S-adequate $\rightarrow$ ▷ equivalence
   $\mathcal{H} \leftarrow$ BuildHypothesis$_{\mathsf{e}}$
   $(b, \sigma) \leftarrow$ CheckConsistency$(\mathcal{H})$
   if $b =$ **yes then**
    $(b, \rho) \leftarrow$ CheckSoundness$(\mathcal{L}, \mathcal{H})$
    if $b =$ **yes then**
     $(b, \rho) \leftarrow$ EquivalenceQuery$(\mathcal{H})$ ▷ equivalence on $\mathcal{L}$
     if $b =$ **yes then**
      return $\mathcal{H}$
    $\mathrm{OQ}_{\mathsf{s}}(\rho, \mathcal{L})$
    $\sigma \leftarrow$ shortest prefix of ρ such that $\delta^{\mathcal{H}}(q_0^{\mathcal{H}}, \sigma) \#_{\mathsf{s},\mathcal{L}} \delta^{\mathcal{T}}(q_0^{\mathcal{T}}, \sigma)$ (in $\mathcal{T}$)
   ProcCounterExs$(\mathcal{H}, \sigma)$ ▷ using $\#_{\mathsf{s},\mathcal{L}}$
  end do

Lemma 4.13. *Let $\mathcal{M}$ be a Mealy machine, $\mathcal{L}$ a sound and complete reference for $\mathcal{M}$, P a minimal accepting state cover and $T_{\mathcal{L}}$ as in Eq. (3). Consider the observation tree $\mathcal{T}$ that arises when executing $T_{\mathcal{L}}$ using OQ_{S}, then P forms a basis, i.e., all states reached by $p \in P$ are pairwise* SC*-apart.*

We adapt $L^{\#}_{\mathsf{e}}$ in three main ways to exploit a sound and complete reference:

1. Similar to $L^{\#}_{\mathsf{e,S}}$, we use OQ_{S} instead of OQ_{e}.
2. We execute $T_{\mathcal{L}}$ and set B to the states reached by P before any of the rules.
3. We use SC-apartness in the $L^{\#}_{\mathsf{e}}$ rules.

The $L^{\#}_{\mathsf{e,SC}}$ algorithm has the same OQ complexity as $L^{\#}$ but requires fewer EQs whenever reference $\mathcal{L}$ has more than two states.

Theorem 4.14. *Let $\mathcal{M}$ be an* e*-persistent SUL and $\mathcal{L}$ an* e*-persistent reference. Let n, k and m be as in Lemma 4.4. If $\mathcal{L}$ is complete w.r.t. $\mathcal{M}$, then $L^{\#}_{\mathsf{e,SC}}$ requires $\mathcal{O}(kn^2+n \log m)$ OQs and at most $n-1$ EQs to learn the smallest Mealy machine $\mathcal{H}$ such that $\mathcal{H} \sim_{\mathcal{L}} \mathcal{M}$ and $\lambda^{\mathcal{H}}(\sigma) = q_{\mathsf{e}}$ for all $\sigma \notin \mathcal{L}$.*

Lemma 4.15. *If $\mathcal{L}$ is a sound and complete reference for $\mathcal{M}$, then $L^{\#}_{\mathsf{e,SC}}$ learns a Mealy machine $\mathcal{H}$ such that $\mathcal{H} \sim \mathcal{M}$ with at most $n - o$ EQs, with o as defined in Lemma 4.7.*

5 Experimental Evaluation

In this section, we empirically investigate the performance of the algorithms $L^{\#}_{\mathsf{e}}$, $AL^{\#}_{\mathsf{e}}$, $L^{\#}_{\mathsf{e,S}}$ and $L^{\#}_{\mathsf{e,SC}}$ proposed in Sect. 4 and compare it to the baseline $L^{\#}$ [35]. The source code and benchmarks are available online [20].[4] We investigate the following questions in three experiments:

RQ1 Do $L^{\#}_{\mathsf{e}}$ and $L^{\#}_{\mathsf{e,SC}}$ with a sound and complete reference improve over $L^{\#}$?
RQ2 Do $AL^{\#}_{\mathsf{e}}$ and $L^{\#}_{\mathsf{e,S}}$ with (sound) references improve over $L^{\#}_{\mathsf{e}}$?
RQ3 What happens when $L^{\#}_{\mathsf{e,S}}$ and $L^{\#}_{\mathsf{e,SC}}$ use unsound or incomplete references?

Additionally, we discuss whether the used references can be obtained realistically.

Benchmarks. We consider benchmarks from the literature representing network protocol implementations, lithograph systems or monitors:

TLS. Transport Layer Security (TLS) is a common security protocol of which several implementations have been learned by de Ruiter [31]. We use 18 models of this benchmark with between 6–16 states and 8–11 inputs. These models should adhere to the TLS1.2 specification [6].

ASML. The ASML benchmark contains 33 Mealy machines representing components in lithography systems for the semiconductor industry first released for the 2019 RERS challenge [16]. These models are hard to learn due to their size [17,39]. We limit ourselves to 11 models used in [17] with under 10000 transitions.

[4] https://gitlab.science.ru.nl/lkruger/errorawarelearningaalpy.

Monitors. We consider Mealy machine representations of runtime monitors for Hidden Markov Models (HMMs) used by [23]. These monitors flag potentially dangerous states when moving randomly through a partially observable state space. We restrict our analysis to the HMMs from [23] with the smallest environment parameters and select the two smallest or only horizon values, resulting in 14 models with between 21–75 states and 18–325 inputs.

Realistic References. For the TLS and ASML models, sound and complete references are not realistically obtainable as it is unlikely that precise enough specifications exist. However, for TLS or other non-proprietary network protocols, it is possible to create sound, but quite cautious, references by inspecting the open-source specifications. For the monitor benchmark, sound and complete references *are realistic* as they can be extracted from the underlying HMM.

Setup. We adapted the algorithms for $L^{\#}$ and $AL^{\#}$ implemented in learning library AALpy [27]. To test a hypothesis $\mathcal{H}$, we apply an adapted version of state-of-the-art randomized Wp-method [11,33] that truncates test words as in $T_{\mathsf{e}}(\mathcal{H})$ and $T_{\mathsf{S}}(\mathcal{H}, \mathcal{L})$. We run all experiments with 30 seeds. We measure the performance in the number of symbols (the sum of the length +1 of all OQs, including OQs asked in testing). We enforce a total symbol budget of 10^6. We omit the final EQ when the hypothesis and target are equivalent as standard. Finally, we cache OQs during learning and testing. Appendix C of the extended version of this paper [19] contains details on algorithm parameters, the references, and full benchmark results.

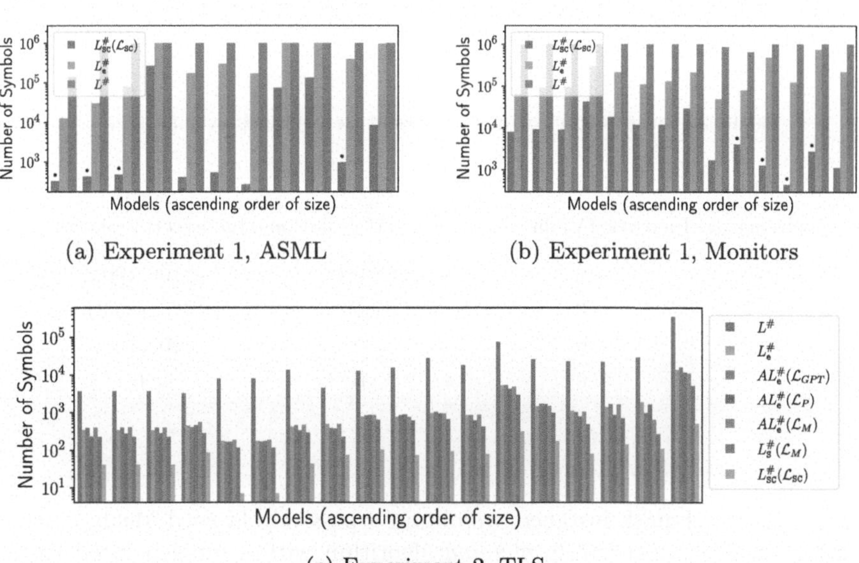

Fig. 2. Number of symbols (lower is better) for Experiment 1 and 2.

5.1 RQ1: Sound and Complete vs Error-Aware vs Baselines

We evaluate the performance of $L^{\#}_{\mathsf{e}}$ and $L^{\#}_{\mathsf{e,sc}}$ with a sound and complete against the baseline. We extract a sound and complete reference $\mathcal{L}$ for each (known) SUL.

Results. Figure 2a and 2b show the number of symbols (log scale) for learning and testing on the y-axis for the ASML and monitor benchmark, respectively. The results for TLS are included in Fig. 2c as the blue, orange and pink bars. The x-axis shows the models in ascending order of size $|\mathcal{M}| \times |I|$. The colors indicate the algorithms. Bars marked with * indicate the first hypothesis was correct.

Discussion. In every benchmark where $L^{\#}_{\mathsf{e}}$ remains within the budget, it achieves better performance than $L^{\#}$. Additionally, we observe that algorithm $L^{\#}_{\mathsf{e,sc}}$ significantly outperforms both $L^{\#}$ and $L^{\#}_{\mathsf{e}}$. For TLS (Fig. 2c), the sound and complete references are sufficiently informative to learn all states without EQs (as indicated by the *). For the ASML and monitor benchmark, even when EQs are required, $L^{\#}_{\mathsf{e,sc}}$ requires far fewer symbols. For example, to the 115 states of the largest ASML model, $L^{\#}_{\mathsf{e,sc}}$ requires 8368 symbols on average, while $L^{\#}_{\mathsf{e}}$ and $L^{\#}$ exceed the budget of 10^6 after learning only 73 and 27 states, respectively.

5.2 RQ2: Using Easy to Obtain References

Sound and complete reference models may not always be available. We investigate the performance on sound and arbitrary references on the TLS benchmark. We generate three types of references:

Table 2. Results RQ3, values represent percentages over all seeds.

Algorithm → Reference ↓	$AL^{\#}_{\mathsf{e}}(\mathcal{L})$ Incorrect(Violations)	$L^{\#}_{\mathsf{e,s}}(\mathcal{L})$ Incorrect(Violations)	$L^{\#}_{\mathsf{e,sc}}(\mathcal{L})$ Incorrect(Violations)
$\mathcal{L}_{MUT}$	0	55.6(0)	100(100)
$\mathcal{L}_{P}$	0	87.1(0)	95.1(85.3)
$\mathcal{L}_{M}$	0	0	100(100)
$\mathcal{L}_{\mathsf{SC}}$	0	0	0

1. For each benchmark instance, we obtain a passively learned Mealy machine using the *generalized state merging* algorithm with a pre-generated log file containing 10000 randomly generated traces. We then transform the Mealy machine into a minimal DFA with reference $\mathcal{L}_{P}$.

2. We prompt chatGPT-5 to use RFC 5246, the open-source specification of TLS1.2, to construct four DFAs with reference $\mathcal{L}_{GPT}$ using the alphabets from [31]: server-side with a full alphabet or reduced alphabet, client-side with a full alphabet or reduced alphabet.
3. We construct DFAs with reference $\mathcal{L}_M$ for the four specification cases by manually analyzing RFC 5246, leading to sound expert-based references.

We compare $AL^{\#}_{\mathsf{e}}(\mathcal{L})$ for $\mathcal{L} \in \{\mathcal{L}_P, \mathcal{L}_{GPT}, \mathcal{L}_M\}$, $L^{\#}_{\mathsf{e,s}}(\mathcal{L}_M)$ and $L^{\#}_{\mathsf{e}}$.

Results. Figure 2c shows the total number of symbols (log scale) as the height of the bar and the TLS models in ascending order of size on the x-axis.

Discussion. First, we observe that $L^{\#}_{\mathsf{e,s}}$ always outperforms the $L^{\#}_{\mathsf{e}}$ and $AL^{\#}_{\mathsf{e}}$, thus performance improves whenever sound references are available. When comparing $L^{\#}_{\mathsf{e}}$ and $AL^{\#}_{\mathsf{e}}$, we notice that the performance is usually quite similar. This may be explained by the fact that all models are relatively easy to learn or the references are too generic or not informative enough. Similar patterns were observed on limited tests with passively generated references for the ASML benchmark.

5.3 RQ3: Violated Reference Assumptions

We use the TLS benchmark to investigate whether the correct Mealy machine can be learned when the references violates the soundness or completeness assumption. We use the references $\mathcal{L}_P$ and $\mathcal{L}_M$ from RQ2, $\mathcal{L}_{\mathsf{sc}}$ from RQ1. The reference $\mathcal{L}_{MUT}$ is a mutation on $\mathcal{L}_{\mathsf{sc}}$ that redirects four transitions in the minimal DFA representation. For each run, we measure whether (1) the algorithm terminated with the correct model, (2) the algorithm terminated with an incorrect model, or (3) the algorithm detected that the assumptions were violated.

Results. Table 2 indicates per algorithm and reference combination how often a model was correctly learned, incorrectly learned or the completeness assumption was violated. The value is the percentage over all seeds and all TLS models.

Discussion. As expected, when a reference satisfies the assumption, the correct model is always learned. If a reference is incomplete, this is typically detected during the $L^{\#}_{\mathsf{e,sc}}$ algorithm, which reports an assumption violation. However, from $\mathcal{L}_{MUT}$ and $\mathcal{L}_P$ we observe that when references fail to meet the soundness assumption, the learned model is usually incorrect. This demonstrates that $L^{\#}_{\mathsf{e,s}}$ and $L^{\#}_{\mathsf{e,sc}}$ should only be applied when the assumption truly holds.

6 Related Work

Error-persistence and knowledge about inputs that lead to errors can be broadly categorized into using domain knowledge in AAL.

Domain knowledge in learning. Closest to our work is *adaptive AAL* [4,7,12,18]. Adaptive AAL tries to reduce the number of interactions required to learn the SUL by using a similar reference model. It assumes that the reference model is of the same type as the SUL. In contrast, this paper uses a reference language consisting of words that do not produce errors. We thus rely on less information as our references provides no details about non-error outputs. We believe that our references are easier to obtain from, e.g., specifications. Further, contrary to [4,7,12,18], we support additional assumptions on the relation between the reference and SUL. These assumptions, while realistic, prove to be very powerful.

Maler and Mens [24] tackle AAL with large alphabets by learning symbolic automata whose transitions are defined by predicates that group individual inputs. The correctness of their approach depends on the ability to find adequate predicates and finding such predicates is an open challenge. In contrast, we rely on knowledge about errors and prove correctness for varying levels of knowledge.

Wallner *et al.* [37] learn timed automata using an untimed skeleton of the target model, which may be incomplete or incorrect. Similar to our approach, they assume that domain knowledge in the form of a skeleton is often easy to obtain. Instead of embedding their skeleton within the MAT framework, they use the skeleton within a genetic programming approach to add timing information.

Dengler *et al.* [5] learn Mealy machines with stochastic delays by first deriving a behavioral Mealy machine and then extending it with distributions that represent probabilistic delay behavior. Their contribution lies in extending Mealy machines to capture stochastic delay behavior, whereas our approach uses error-aware domain knowledge to accelerate the learning of the (standard) Mealy machine.

Henry *et al.* [13] address the problem of large alphabets by assuming a concurrent component-based system in which certain inputs are disabled for specific components and can therefore be omitted. In contrast, we make no assumptions about component structure and operate at a different granularity, using the fact that certain input words (i.e., transitions) are not enabled.

Domain Knowledge in Testing. Yang *et al.* [39] test hypotheses on log traces before conducting the actual EQ when learning the ASML benchmark. To learn a model of embedded control software of a printer, related inputs were grouped into subalphabets to generate more effective test words by Smeenk *et al.* [33]. These two types of domain knowledge can be transformed into a reference language that our approach can use to avoid posing test queries that likely produce errors.

Yaacov *et al.* [38] use error persistence to adapt the EQ to learn informative bug descriptions. Their approach focuses on learning small DFAs that capture bugs, whereas we aim to learn the overall behavior of the SUL. Ruiter *et al.* [31] cuts off tests when *ConnectionClosed* is observed. Our adjustments to test suites build on these two methods but are more general, applying to any error-related outputs and enabling test truncation before an error-producing input is reached through domain knowledge.

Rather than relying on domain knowledge, Kruger *et al.* [17] infer assumptions about the SUL from the current hypothesis and use them to prioritize tests. Since tests are only prioritized but never discarded, the correct model is always learned. In contrast, when our assumptions hold, we can avoid posing certain queries altogether, leading to significantly fewer interactions.

Finally, Vaandrager and Melse [36] introduce k-A-complete fault domains where A typically represents the state cover of the specification of the SUL. If A is a state cover of some sound and complete reference $\mathcal{L}$, then $\mathcal{M}$ is guaranteed to be in the k-A-complete fault domain, if k is sufficiently large (proven in [19]).

Special Outputs. Several AAL algorithms consider teachers that answer *don't care* to an input when parts of the SUL are underspecified, unobservable, or irrelevant [2,21,25,38]. In some of these algorithms, a *don't care* may be replaced with any output that is consistent with the data. This approach leads to smaller models compared to using e when inputs are unobservable or irrelevant but the decision problem underlying finding a minimal model in the presence of don't-cares is NP-hard [21,25].

7 Conclusion

This paper presents learning and conformance testing techniques that effectively incorporate knowledge about error sources in systems. Our algorithms improve over standard AAL with several orders of magnitude by assuming the system is error persistent. Using knowledge about *which* inputs yield errors substantially lowers the cost of learning complex systems even further.

Future Work. This paper goes beyond the standard MAT framework by using a more fine-grained notion of equivalence that incorporates domain knowledge. This affects both the theory of testing and learning and required significant technical work. We therefore suggest to investigate a fundamental MAT framework for flexible notions of equivalence, thereby accommodating, e.g., more general domain knowledge. Further, we aim to investigate how we can broaden our notion of errors to include transient errors that quickly resolve themselves or recoverable errors that allow escape from an error state after acknowledging, and to examine whether a more fine-grained definition of errors can account for multiple sink states. On the practical side, we aim to investigate more applications and sources for error-aware references, such as sound references extracted from logs. Finally, we plan to compare our results, in terms of query complexity and runtime, with recent work using 'don't cares' instead of e-outputs [2,21,25].

References

1. Angluin, D.: Learning regular sets from queries and counterexamples. Inf. Comput. **75**(2), 87–106 (1987)

2. Bork, A., Chakraborty, D., Grover, K., Kretínský, J., Mohr, S.: Learning explainable and better performing representations of POMDP strategies. In: Finkbeiner, B., Kovács, L. (eds.) TACAS (2). LNCS, vol. 14571, pp. 299–319. Springer, Cham (2024). https://doi.org/10.1007/978-3-031-57249-4_15
3. Chalupar, G., Peherstorfer, S., Poll, E., de Ruiter, J.: Automated reverse engineering using lego®. In: WOOT. USENIX Association (2014)
4. Damasceno, C.D.N., Mousavi, M.R., da Silva Simao, A.: Learning to Reuse: Adaptive Model Learning for Evolving Systems. In: Ahrendt, W., Tapia Tarifa, S.L. (eds.) IFM 2019. LNCS, vol. 11918, pp. 138–156. Springer, Cham (2019). https://doi.org/10.1007/978-3-030-34968-4_8
5. Dengler, G., Apel, S., Hermanns, H.: Automata learning - expect delays! In: Damiani, F., Farrell, M. (eds.) iFM 2025. LNCS, vol. 16194, pp. 461–484. Springer, Cham (2025). https://doi.org/10.1007/978-3-032-10794-7_23
6. Dierks, T., Rescorla, E.: The transport layer security (tls) protocol version 1.2. Technical report (2008)
7. Ferreira, T., van Heerdt, G., Silva, A.: Tree-based adaptive model learning. In: A Journey from Process Algebra via Timed Automata to Model Learning. LNCS, vol. 13560, pp. 164–179. Springer (2022)
8. Fiterău-Broştean, P., Janssen, R., Vaandrager, F.: Combining model learning and model checking to analyze TCP implementations. In: Chaudhuri, S., Farzan, A. (eds.) CAV 2016. LNCS, vol. 9780, pp. 454–471. Springer, Cham (2016). https://doi.org/10.1007/978-3-319-41540-6_25
9. Fiterau-Brostean, P., Lenaerts, T., Poll, E., de Ruiter, J., Vaandrager, F.W., Verleg, P.: Model learning and model checking of SSH implementations. In: SPIN, pp. 142–151. ACM (2017)
10. Ganty, P.: Learning the state machine behind a modal text editor: The (neo)vim case study. In: Neele, T., Wijs, A. (eds.) SPIN 2024. LNCS, vol. 14624, pp. 167–175. Springer, Cham (2024). https://doi.org/10.1007/978-3-031-66149-5_9
11. Garhewal, B., Damasceno, C.D.N.: An experimental evaluation of conformance testing techniques in active automata learning. In: MODELS. pp. 217–227. IEEE (2023)
12. Groce, A., Peled, D.A., Yannakakis, M.: Adaptive model checking. Log. J. IGPL **14**(5), 729–744 (2006)
13. Henry, L., Mousavi, M.R., Neele, T., Sammartino, M.: Compositional active learning of synchronizing systems through automated alphabet refinement. In: CONCUR. LIPIcs, vol. 348, pp. 20:1–20:22. Schloss Dagstuhl - Leibniz-Zentrum für Informatik (2025)
14. Howar, F., Steffen, B.: Active automata learning in practice. In: Bennaceur, A., Hähnle, R., Meinke, K. (eds.) Machine Learning for Dynamic Software Analysis: Potentials and Limits. LNCS, vol. 11026, pp. 123–148. Springer, Cham (2018). https://doi.org/10.1007/978-3-319-96562-8_5
15. Isberner, M., Howar, F., Steffen, B.: The TTT algorithm: a redundancy-free approach to active automata learning. In: Bonakdarpour, B., Smolka, S.A. (eds.) RV 2014. LNCS, vol. 8734, pp. 307–322. Springer, Cham (2014). https://doi.org/10.1007/978-3-319-11164-3_26
16. Jasper, M., et al.: RERS 2019: combining synthesis with real-world models. In: Beyer, D., Huisman, M., Kordon, F., Steffen, B. (eds.) TACAS 2019. LNCS, vol. 11429, pp. 101–115. Springer, Cham (2019). https://doi.org/10.1007/978-3-030-17502-3_7

17. Kruger, L., Junges, S., Rot, J.: Small test suites for active automata learning. In: Finkbeiner, B., Kovács, L. (eds.) TACAS (2). LNCS, vol. 14571, pp. 109–129. Springer, Cham (2024). https://doi.org/10.1007/978-3-031-57249-4_6
18. Kruger, L., Junges, S., Rot, J.: State matching and multiple references in adaptive active automata learning. In: Platzer, A., Rozier, K.Y., Pradella, M., Rossi, M. (eds.) FM 2024. LNCS, vol. 14933, pp. 267–284. Springer, Cham (2024). https://doi.org/10.1007/978-3-031-71162-6_14
19. Kruger, L., Junges, S., Rot, J.: Error-awareness accelerates active automata learning (2026). https://arxiv.org/abs/2602.21674
20. Kruger, L., Junges, S., Rot, J.: Error-awareness accelerates active automata learning: supplementary material (2026). https://doi.org/10.5281/zenodo.18755292
21. Leucker, M., Neider, D.: Learning minimal deterministic automata from inexperienced teachers. In: Margaria, T., Steffen, B. (eds.) ISoLA 2012. LNCS, vol. 7609, pp. 524–538. Springer, Heidelberg (2012). https://doi.org/10.1007/978-3-642-34026-0_39
22. Luo, G., von Bochmann, G., Petrenko, A.: Test selection based on communicating nondeterministic finite-state machines using a generalized WP-method. IEEE Trans. Software Eng. **20**(2), 149–162 (1994)
23. van der Maas, L., Junges, S.: Learning verified monitors for hidden markov models. In: DÂťSouza, M., Komondoor, R., Srivathsan, B. (eds) ATVA 2025. LNCS, vol. 16145, pp. 180–203. Springer, Cham (2025). https://doi.org/10.1007/978-3-032-08707-2_9
24. Maler, O., Mens, I.-E.: Learning regular languages over large alphabets. In: Ábrahám, E., Havelund, K. (eds.) TACAS 2014. LNCS, vol. 8413, pp. 485–499. Springer, Heidelberg (2014). https://doi.org/10.1007/978-3-642-54862-8_41
25. Moeller, M., Wiener, T., Solko-Breslin, A., Koch, C., Foster, N., Silva, A.: Automata learning with an incomplete teacher. In: ECOOP. LIPIcs, vol. 263, pp. 21:1–21:30. Schloss Dagstuhl - Leibniz-Zentrum für Informatik (2023)
26. Moore, E.F., et al.: Gedanken-experiments on sequential machines. Autom. Stud. **34**, 129–153 (1956)
27. Muskardin, E., Aichernig, B.K., Pill, I., Pferscher, A., Tappler, M.: AALpy: an active automata learning library. Innov. Syst. Softw. Eng. **18**(3), 417–426 (2022)
28. Muskardin, E., Burgstaller, T., Tappler, M., Aichernig, B.K.: Active model learning of git version control system. In: ICSTW. pp. 78–82. IEEE (2024)
29. Petrenko, A., Yevtushenko, N., Lebedev, A., Das, A.: Nondeterministic state machines in protocol conformance testing. In: Protocol Test Systems. IFIP Transactions, vol. C-19, pp. 363–378. North-Holland (1993)
30. Raffelt, H., Steffen, B., Berg, T.: Learnlib: a library for automata learning and experimentation. In: FMICS, pp. 62–71. ACM (2005)
31. de Ruiter, J., Poll, E.: Protocol state fuzzing of TLS implementations. In: USENIX Security Symposium, pp. 193–206. USENIX Association (2015)
32. Schuts, M., Hooman, J., Vaandrager, F.: Refactoring of legacy software using model learning and equivalence checking: an industrial experience report. In: Ábrahám, E., Huisman, M. (eds.) IFM 2016. LNCS, vol. 9681, pp. 311–325. Springer, Cham (2016). https://doi.org/10.1007/978-3-319-33693-0_20
33. Smeenk, W., Moerman, J., Vaandrager, F., Jansen, D.N.: Applying automata learning to embedded control software. In: Butler, M., Conchon, S., Zaïdi, F. (eds.) ICFEM 2015. LNCS, vol. 9407, pp. 67–83. Springer, Cham (2015). https://doi.org/10.1007/978-3-319-25423-4_5
34. Vaandrager, F.W.: Model learning. Commun. ACM **60**(2), 86–95 (2017)

35. Vaandrager, F., Garhewal, B., Rot, J., Wißmann, T.: A new approach for active automata learning based on apartness. In: TACAS 2022. LNCS, vol. 13243, pp. 223–243. Springer, Cham (2022). https://doi.org/10.1007/978-3-030-99524-9_12
36. Vaandrager, F.W., Melse, I.: New fault domains for conformance testing of finite state machines. In: CONCUR. LIPIcs, vol. 348, pp. 34:1–34:22. Schloss Dagstuhl - Leibniz-Zentrum für Informatik (2025)
37. Wallner, F., Aichernig, B.K., Lorber, F., Tappler, M.: Mutating skeletons: learning timed automata via domain knowledge. In: ICSTW, pp. 67–77. IEEE (2025)
38. Yaacov, T., Weiss, G., Amram, G., Hayoun, A.: Automata models for effective bug pattern description. In: MODELS, pp. 119–129. IEEE (2025)
39. Yang, N., et al.: Improving model inference in industry by combining active and passive learning. In: SANER, pp. 253–263. IEEE (2019)

History-Constrained Systems

Louwe B. Kuijer[1], David Purser[1(✉)], Henry Sinclair-Banks[2,3], and Patrick Totzke[1]

[1] University of Liverpool, Liverpool, UK
D.Purser@liverpool.ac.uk
[2] University of Warsaw, Warsaw, Poland
[3] Max Planck Institute for Software Systems (MPI-SWS), Kaiserslautern, Germany

Abstract. We study verification problems for history-constrained systems (HCS), a model of guarded computation that uses nested systems. An outer system describes the process architecture in which a sequence of actions represents the communication between sub-systems through a global bus. Actions are either permitted or blocked locally by guards; these guards read and decide based on the sequence of actions so far in the global bus.

When HCS have both the outer systems and the local guard controllers modelled by finite automata, we show they have the same expressive power as regular languages and finite automata, but they are exponentially more succinct. We also analyse games on this model, representing the interaction between environment and controller, and show that solving such games is EXPTIME-complete, where the lower bound already holds for reachability/safety games and the upper bound holds for any ω-regular winning condition. Finally, we consider HCS with guards of greater expressive power, Vector Addition Systems with States (VASS). We show that with deterministic coverability-VASS guards the reachability problem is EXPSPACE-complete, while with reachability-VASS the problem is undecidable.

Keywords: Complexity · Distributed Computing · Reachability problems · Automata · Verification · Temporal Games · Logic

1 Introduction

We study distributed systems where independent components communicate using a global databus—a shared record of actions taking place in the system. The subsystems act and make decisions based on their own internal state and information from the global communication channel, but are isolated from the internal configuration of other subsystems. We introduce a model of guarded computation called history-constrained systems (HCS) that capture such distributed workflows. We then study the expressivity of this model as well as the computational cost of formally verifying such models.

Formally, HCS consist of an outer state-machine, whose transitions are labelled with global actions and which are guarded by languages over such actions whereby a transition is admissible if the whole sequence of prior actions is in

A. Sampaio and M. Stoelinga (Eds.): FM 2026, LNCS 16556, pp. 541–558, 2026.
https://doi.org/10.1007/978-3-032-26204-2_28

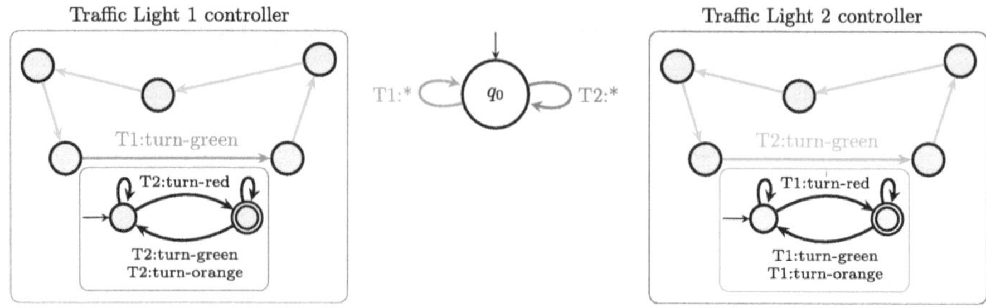

Fig. 1. Three layer HCS traffic light model. The outer system is a single state to hold each controller; "T1:*" represents all actions for traffic light 1. The middle layer represents the controller of each individual traffic light (the full mechanism of the traffic light controller (grey edges) is not depicted). The innermost system guards the "turn green" commands to ensure that the other set of lights have turned to red. The system enforces safety by ensuring that whenever a traffic light attempts to turn green, the other traffic light has turned to red. Unlabelled self-loops represent all actions other than those specified. (Colour figure online)

the (guard) language. For practical purposes, we will assume that the guard languages are themselves provided in the form of automata. Our systems can thus be seen as nested automata: an outer system and inner automata acting as guards on the transitions. The outer system models the overall architecture of the large-scale task, system, or process. Every action taken in the outer system is recorded in a global history (the bus). Each edge in the system may have a guard language, encoded by an automaton, which observes the event history so far and decides whether the transition is enabled at a given moment.

HCS are safe by construction: unsafe behaviour expressed as properties of the history are easily encoded into the guard conditions. As an example, consider a traffic-light controller that permits a "turn-green" action only after observing that perpendicular lights have executed a "turn-red" action, without requiring access to their internal states (see Fig. 1). Writing rules over event histories is usually simpler than writing imperative rules over joint states. Other examples which can easily be encoded include:

- Prerequisites/Cross-service dependencies "Service X may only perform action A if service Y has previously sent confirmation B",
- Rate limiting "Permit X only if 10 steps have passed since event Y", or
- Safety guards "Event X cannot happen if Event Y has happened".

Even with this "safe by construction" approach, it remains necessary to verify that the model can achieve its intended purpose under these guards: can the automaton still achieve its goal (reachability)? Is there a controller that can act against an adversarial environment? We investigate such questions for HCS.

The expressive power of the guard language determines the properties of the history upon which the decisions can be made (patterns, counts, timestamps, presence/absence of events) and the complexity or decidability of the verification

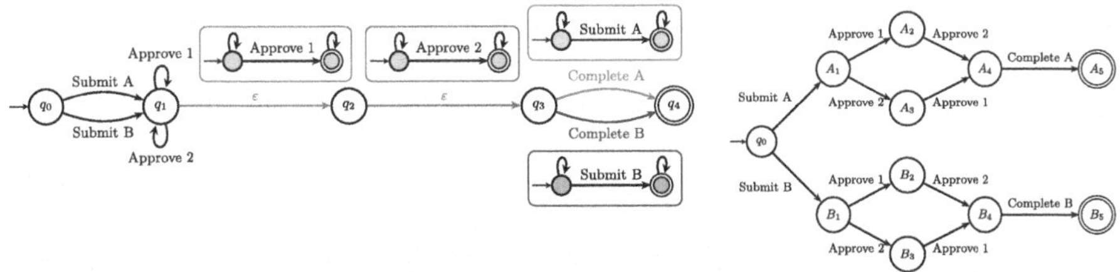

Fig. 2. Four-eyes approval workflow represented as both an HCS (left) and as a finite automaton (right). Approvals arrive in an unknown order, the finite automaton must explicitly encode this in the state, while the HCS can store this information on just the relevant edges. Three approvers would enlarge the finite automaton significantly, while the HCS needs just one more guarded transition. Unlabelled self-loops represent all actions other than those specified.

problems. For example, if we use context-free languages as guards, then these problems become undecidable (see Sect. 3.3).

Contributions. Besides introducing the model of history-constrained systems, we make contributions in two directions: when guards are regular languages and when guards are represented by automata with (limited) access to counters.

Regular Guards. HCS with regular guards have transitions that are each controlled by a deterministic finite automaton (DFA) or a non-deterministic finite automaton (NFA). We show that their expressivity is the same as that of DFAs (Sect. 3) but even deterministic HCS can be exponentially more succinct than NFAs (Sect. 4). To illustrate, consider the conditional workflow in Fig. 2: allowing conditions to be encoded locally avoids needing to encode information in the state space.

In Sect. 5 we consider games on HCS with regular guards and show that determining the existence of a winning strategy is EXPTIME-complete (Theorem 2). Note that this is a non-trivial bound, since such HCS are exponentially more succinct than DFAs, and games on the latter are PSPACE-complete (and hence we would trivially obtain an EXPSPACE upper bound). However, we are able to reduce this by carefully composing the parity game algorithm with the on-the-fly construction of the state space. The lower bound is one of our main contributions, by reducing from countdown games.

Guards with Counters. In Sect. 6 we consider the natural extension to allow guards to use counters. Such guards would be able to directly extend the example in Fig. 2 with "majority approval", where more people approve than reject. However, zero tests lead to undecidability, and so restrictions are needed.

We consider restricted guards with counters using Vector Addition Systems with States (VASS). VASS have one or more non-negative integer counters which can be incremented or decremented (but can neither be reset nor zero-tested).

VASS have two common acceptance conditions: Cover-VASS ask whether a final state is reachable but make no requirement on the final value of the counter (only that they remained non-negative), while Reach-VASS insist that the counters are finally exactly zero (or some other fixed choice).

Our results reveal an interesting subtlety depending on the acceptance conditions. HCS with deterministic Cover-VASS guards match exactly the expressive power of Cover-VASS, and the reachability problem is decidable in EXPSPACE.

However, HCS with deterministic Reach-VASS guards are more expressive than just Reach-VASS. While reachability in Reach-VASS is decidable (and recently shown to be Ackermann-complete [7,18]), it is undecidable in HCS with deterministic Reach-VASS guards.

Full Version. Omitted proofs are available in the extended version on arXiv [15].

Related Work. Distributed systems can broadly be classified by how individual components communicate: one-to-one (aka rendezvous) [25] and broadcasting (aka shared memory) [29]. Early automata models for broadcast communication include I/O automata [22] and team automata [5] where components communicate via shared actions but compared to our model, they do not expose the whole action history to guards like HCS allow.

Our work follows the canon of models with guarded computation, where the availability of local state changes depends on the history of the process so far. Examples of such models are Timed automata [2] which allow for inequality constraints on real-valued clocks; Petri Nets / Vector addition systems [1], where counters must remain non-negative. The structure of HCS as an outer system with inner ones representing the guards can be found in the *Nets in Nets* model [13,32], where Petri net tokens themselves represent identifiable Petri nets that can move and synchronise with the outer one in a rendez-vous fashion. That model is convenient for multi-agent systems, where it can model agent mobility. In HCS, individual components do not move but synchronise via broadcast, and we also consider different kinds of guard automata.

Our model can be used to succinctly model arenas for games on graphs, the mathematical foundation for model checking and reactive synthesis [8,9,27,28]. Related structures are *Temporal graphs*, [10,24] which extend graphs with discrete and global time and can specify for each edge at which times it can be traversed. Games on temporal graphs, succinctly encoded in existential Presburger Arithmetic, have recently been considered in [3,4]. Games on HCS, as done in Sect. 5 here, are essentially a generalisation of games on temporal graphs from linear to branching-time.

2 Preliminaries

Let X be a finite set, and $\mathcal{P}(X) := \{X' : X' \subseteq X\}$ be the power set of X. ε is the empty word of length 0. Let $\boldsymbol{v}_1 \in \mathbb{Z}^{d_1}$ and $\boldsymbol{v}_2 \in \mathbb{Z}^{d_2}$. We define the vector $(\boldsymbol{v}_1, \boldsymbol{v}_2) := (\boldsymbol{v}_1[1], \ldots, \boldsymbol{v}_1[d_1], \boldsymbol{v}_2[1], \ldots, \boldsymbol{v}_2[d_2]) \in \mathbb{Z}^{d_1+d_2}$.

2.1 History-Constrained Systems

A *History-constrained system* (HCS) is a tuple $A = (\Sigma, U, \mathcal{G})$ where Σ is a finite alphabet, U is a labelled transition system over the alphabet Σ with transitions T, and $\mathcal{G} = \{L_t \subseteq \Sigma^* : t \in T\}$ are the guards. A guard L_t is *trivial* if $L_t = \Sigma^*$.

We say that a sequence $(q_0, a_1, q_1, a_2, q_2, \ldots, q_{n-1}, a_n, q_n)$ is a run of A if

(1) q_0 is the starting state of U; and
(2) for every $1 \leq i \leq n$, $t = (q_{i-1}, a_i, q_i)$ is a transition in U and $a_1 a_2 \ldots a_{i-1} \in L_t$.

Note that the runs of A are a subset of the runs of U. When U is an automaton with an accepting condition, we say a run is accepting in A if the same run is accepting in U. In this case we say $w = a_1 a_2 \ldots a_n$ is accepted by A (i.e. $w \in L(A)$) if there is an accepting run on w, and $L(A)$ is the language of A.

In other words, while reading the word $w = a_1 a_2 \ldots a_n$, whenever a transition t is taken to read a_i (the i-th letter of w), it must be true that the current prefix read so far is accepted by the guard of the i-th transition, $a_1 a_2 \ldots a_{i-1} \in L_t$.

We say that an HCS $(\Sigma, U, \mathcal{G})$ is deterministic or non-deterministic if U is deterministic or non-deterministic, respectively.

2.2 Finite Automata

A *non-deterministic finite automaton* (NFA) is a 5-tuple $A = (\Sigma, Q, \delta, q_0, F)$ where Σ is a finite alphabet, Q is a finite set of states, $\delta : Q \times \Sigma \cup \{\epsilon\} \to \mathcal{P}(Q)$ is a transition function, $q_0 \in Q$ is an initial state and $F \subseteq Q$ is the set of accepting states. A is *deterministic* (DFA) if $|\delta(q, \sigma)| \leq 1$ for all $q \in Q$ and $\sigma \in \Sigma$ and $\delta(q, \epsilon) = \emptyset$. A accepts $w \in \Sigma^*$ if there is a run from q_0 to F labelled by w. The size of A is $\|A\| := |Q| + \sum_{q \in Q, \sigma \in \Sigma \cup \{\varepsilon\}} |\delta(q, \sigma)|$.

2.3 HCS Specified with Finite Automata

The languages guarding transitions can be specified however one wishes. As we alluded to in the introduction, we will consider the case that both the underlying automaton U and the transition guards are specified using finitely representable automata. Where the guard languages are regular languages we can specify the guards using DFAs or NFAs. We denote how the underlying automaton and guard languages are specified using X[Y] for an HCS whose underlying automaton is of type X and guard languages are specified as automata of type Y. The variants of HCS that we study include:

- DFA[DFA] are deterministic HCS with guards specified by DFAs,
- NFA[DFA] are non-deterministic HCS with guards specified by DFAs,
- DFA[VASS] are deterministic HCS with guards specified by vector addition systems with states, and
- DFA[PDA] are deterministic HCS with guards specified by pushdown automata.

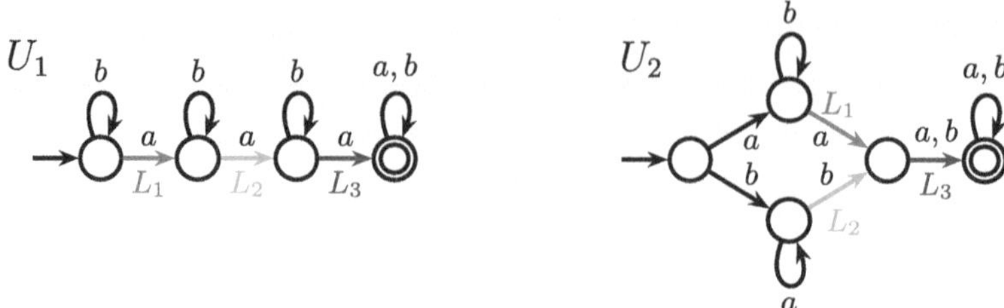

Fig. 3. Examples U_1 and U_2 sharing guards L_1, L_2, and L_3. Whenever we do not specify a guard, then one should assume we use the trivial guard $L_t = \Sigma^*$.

2.4 Emptiness and Reachability

Given an HCS $A = (\Sigma, U, \mathcal{G})$, the *emptiness* problem asks if $L(A) = \emptyset$. That is, no word has an *accepting* run from the initial state consistent with the guards on every transition.

Where the accepting condition of U is specified by accepting (or final) states F, we say F is *reachable* if $L \neq \emptyset$, and *unreachable* otherwise. For such systems, the emptiness problem and reachability problem coincide.

2.5 Examples

Consider the two examples of DFA[DFA] over $\Sigma = \{a, b\}$ depicted in Fig. 3 which share the guards L_1, L_2, and L_3 defined as:

- $L_1 = (ab)^* + a(ba)^*$ (Words of alternating 'a's and 'b's.)
- $L_2 = \{w \in \{a, b\}^* : |w| \in 3 \cdot \mathbb{N}\}$ (Words whose length is a multiple of three.)
- $L_3 = \{a, b\}^* aa \{a, b\}^*$ (Words containing two consecutive 'a's.)

The language of the DFA[DFA] with the underlying automaton U_1 is empty. In order to pass the first guard, zero 'b's have to be read. Thus, after the L_1 guard is passed, the prefix of the word is just 'a'. In order to pass the L_2 guard, at least two 'b' must be read using the second cycle. Hence, once the L_2 guard has been passed the prefix of the word cannot contain two consecutive 'a's. This means that the L_3 guard cannot be passed, and so the language is empty. The language of the DFA[DFA] with the underlying automaton U_2 is not empty. The word '$baaba$' is accepted. By traversing the lower branch, multiple 'a's can be read before passing the L_2 guard which allows for the later passing of the L_3 guard.

3 Expressivity of HCS

In this section we show that for finite automata, adding regular guards does not increase the expressivity (although in Sect. 4 we show they are more succinct). We then show that, in general, HCS can encode the intersection languages of their guard, with the consequence that context-free guards are too powerful.

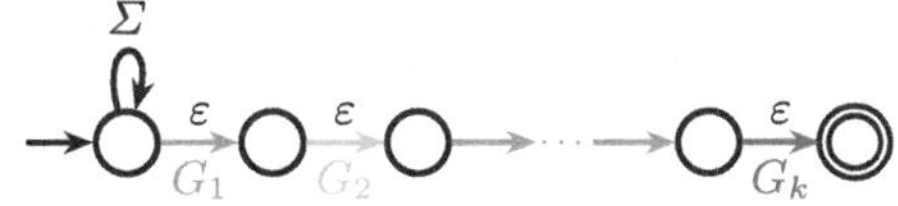

Fig. 4. NFA[X] for the intersection of $G_1, \ldots, G_k$.

3.1 The Expressivity of Regular Guards

We will first prove that finite automata with finite automata guards (NFA[NFA]) recognise the regular languages (Theorem 1). For this, we will construct a single DFA by converting each of the guard NFAs into equivalent DFAs and then convert the underlying NFA into a DFA whilst taking the product of the underlying NFA with the guard DFAs.

Theorem 1. *Given an NFA[NFA] A, we can construct an exponential size DFA D such that* $L(D) = L(A)$.

Proof Idea. The proof uses a careful mix of the powerset and product constructions. If A were a DFA[DFA] then we would just take the product of the underlying DFA with each of the guard DFAs (which are assumed to be complete), only keeping transitions if the relevant guard is in an accepting state.

Now, let A be an NFA[NFA] comprising an underlying NFA U with n states and NFA guards $G_1, \ldots, G_m$ with $n_1, \ldots, n_m$ states respectively; in total A has $n + n_1 + \cdots + n_m$ states. First, we directly transform $G_1, \ldots, G_m$ to DFAs using the standard powerset construction, each with at most 2^{n_i} states.

It remains to determinise the underlying automaton U. However, we must carefully avoid all possible products of guards. Instead, we compute a simultaneous powerset construction on U with a product construction on the guard DFAs. Each state of D takes the form $(Q', q_1, \ldots, q_m)$ where Q' is a subset of the states of the underlying automata and each q_i is a state of the i-th guard DFA. During this construction, we keep only transitions where an appropriate subset of the guards are in an accepting state. In total, D has at most $2^n \cdot 2^{n_1} \cdot \ldots \cdot 2^{n_m} = 2^{n+n_1+\cdots+n_m}$ states.

Corollary 1. *DFA[DFA], DFA[NFA], NFA[DFA], NFA[NFA] all recognise exactly the regular languages.*

3.2 Computing Intersections with HCS

Proposition 1. *Given automata $G_1, \ldots, G_k$ of type X over a common alphabet Σ, one can construct an HCS NFA[X] A of size $\mathcal{O}(k) + \sum_{i=1}^{k} |G_i|$ such that* $L(A) = \bigcap_{i=1}^{k} L(G_i)$.

Proof. We construct the NFA[X] $A = (\Sigma, U, \mathcal{G})$. Let $U = (\Sigma, Q, \delta, q_0, F)$ be the underlying NFA with $Q = \{q_0, q_1, \ldots, q_k, q_{k+1}\}$, $\delta = \{(q_0, \sigma, q_0) : \sigma \in \Sigma\} \cup \{(q_{i-1}, \varepsilon, q_i) : 1 \leq i \leq k\}$, and $F = \{q_{k+1}\}$ as depicted in Fig. 4. The NFA[X] $A = (\Sigma, U, \mathcal{G})$ has the guards: on the q_0-transitions there are no guards and, for every $1 \leq i \leq k$, the transition $(q_{i-1}, \varepsilon, q_i)$ has guard G_i. It is straightforward that, for every $w \in \Sigma^*$, w is accepted by A iff $w \in L(G_i)$ for every $1 \leq i \leq k$. □

Similarly, if we want a DFA we can replace the ε transitions in Fig. 4 with a new '\$ ' symbol (and update the guards to ignore them), entailing the following:

Proposition 2. *Given automata $G_1, \ldots, G_k$ of type X over a common alphabet Σ, one can construct a DFA[X] A of size $\mathcal{O}(k^2) + \sum_{i=1}^{k} |G_i|$ such that $L(A) = \{w\$^k : w \in \bigcap_{i=1}^{k} L(G_i)\}$ where '\$' is a symbol not in Σ.*

3.3 Context-Free Guards are Too Powerful

We now observe that context-free languages, recognised by pushdown automata (PDA), are too powerful to be used as guards. Recall that it is undecidable whether the intersection of two context-free languages is empty [11, Theorem 9.22]. Thus as a corollary of Proposition 2 we have:

Corollary 2. *Emptiness of DFA[PDA] is undecidable.*

In fact, in Sect. 6, we show that emptiness is already undecidable for a subcase of pushdown automata: vector addition systems with states with just one counter under reachability acceptance conditions.

4 Succinctness of HCS with Regular Guards

For any $\ell \in \mathbb{N}$, let C_ℓ be the ℓ-state DFA over the alphabet $\Sigma = \{a\}$ with the language $L(C_\ell) = \{a^{\ell n} : n \in \mathbb{N}\}$. In other words, C_ℓ is the DFA that is a simple cycle of a-transitions of length ℓ. We will use the pumping lemma for finite automata [11, Theorem 4.1] to prove the following claim.

Lemma 1. *Let $p_1, \ldots, p_k$ be the first k primes. Any NFA N with the language $L(N) = \{w\$^k : w \in \bigcap_{i=1}^{k} L(C_{p_i})\}$ has size at least 2^k.*

Proof Idea. The product of the first k primes is at least 2^k. Since the difference in length between any two accepting words is at least 2^k, there must be a cycle-free path of this length (or else a cycle could be depumped), entailing at least 2^k distinct states. □

We conclude this subsection by observing that DFA[DFA] can be exponentially more succinct than NFAs. Corollary 3 follows from Proposition 2 and Claim 1.

Corollary 3. *There exists an infinite family of DFA[DFA]s $\{A_k : k \in \mathbb{N}\}$ such that, for every $i \in \mathbb{N}$ and for every NFA N such that $L(N) = L(A)$, it is true that $|N| \geq 2^{C|A_k|^{\frac{1}{3}}}$ for some constant $C \leq 1$.*

4.1 Nesting HCS with Regular Guards

In principle, it is possible to use HCS as guards. So, for example, NFA[NFA[NFA]] is well-defined. Let $\mathcal{N}_k$ denote the class of automata that are NFAs with nested NFA guards of depth k; $\mathcal{N}_1 = \text{NFA[NFA]}$, $\mathcal{N}_2 = \text{NFA[NFA[NFA]]}$, and so on. By induction we can see that $\mathcal{N}_i$ recognise regular languages. However, by carefully applying Theorem 1 on the guard by induction, we can observe that the number of states in the DFA remains at most exponential.

Proposition 3. *Let $k \in \mathbb{N}$ and let $A \in \mathcal{N}_k$ be an NFA with nested NFA guards that contains n states in total (across the underlying NFA and all of its nested guard NFAs). There exists a DFA D such that $L(D) = L(A)$ and the number of states in D is at most 2^n.*

5 Games on HCS are EXPTIME-complete

We now consider games on history-constrained systems. Two-player zero-sum games played on graphs are common in formal verification, and formalise system correctness even in antagonistic environments. We refer to [8] for a comprehensive overview of games on graphs.

In this context, we will henceforth assume that the HCS under consideration is *non-blocking*, meaning that for every history $h = q_0a_1q_1a_2\dots q_k \in Q\times(\Sigma\times Q)^*$ there is at least one admissible continuation $h\,a_{k+1}q_{k+1}$ enabled via a transition that is from q_k, reads $a_{k+1} \in \Sigma$, leads to q_{k+1}, is guarded by L, and $a_1 \dots a_k \in L$. This is not a restriction because one can always make any HCS non-blocking by adding unguarded transitions to (winning or losing) sinks.

Definition 1. (Games on HCS). *Let $A = (\Sigma, U, \mathcal{G})$ be a non-blocking HCS and let Q denote the set of control states of the underlying automaton U.*

A game on A is played by two opposing players, 0 and 1, and determined by a predicate owner : $Q \to \{0, 1\}$, that associates with each state of U which player owns it, and a winning condition *$W \subseteq (Q \times \Sigma)^\omega$, that declares which outcomes are considered a win for player 0.*

The game is played in rounds, each of which extends the current history play $h \in Q \times (\Sigma \times Q)^*$, starting at the initial state $q_0 \in Q$. From history $h = q_0a_0 \dots q_k$, player owner(q_k) selects an admissible move $q_k \xrightarrow{a_k} q_{k+1}$ and the game continues with history $h\,a_kq_{k+1}$. In the limit, this describes an infinite sequence $\rho \in (Q \times \Sigma)^\omega$ called a play. *The play is won by Player 0 if $\rho \in W$, otherwise the play is won by Player 1. Player i* wins the game *if there is a strategy to select admissible moves for every history such that regardless of the opponent's choices, the resulting play is won by Player i.*

Solving a game refers to the decision question to verify whether a given game is won by Player 0. The decidability, and complexity, of game solving crucially depend on how the game is specified.

The main result of this section is the following theorem that concerns reachability games on finite-state HCS. Here, HCS are of the form NFA[DFA] and the winning condition W is defined by a subset $F \subseteq Q$ of target states that Player 0 aims to reach (i.e., $h \in W$ if and only if $q_i \in F$ for some $0 \leq i$).

Theorem 2. *Solving reachability games on NFA[DFA] is EXPTIME-complete.*

Before the proof, let's justify why these types of games are the most interesting and appropriate to study here.

Firstly, we argue that the dynamics of the game based on ownership of states is natural for modelling purposes, where one verifies robustness of protocols/programs against antagonistic environments. Conceivable alternatives where players take turns, or where one player picks an action in Σ and the other a such-labelled transition, can be easily encoded using the finite-state control.

Our choice to focus on NFA[DFA], in particular compared to more expressive guard automata, is natural because determinising NFA guards incurs negligible additional cost on top of having an NFA as the underlying automaton. Furthermore, allowing guards defined in terms of even more expressive models, like Vector Addition Systems with States (VASS) or PDA, quickly renders solving any kind of game on them undecidable. Indeed, even using guards defined as coverability languages for 1-VASS, a heavily restricted subclass of context-free languages, allows one to reduce the reachability problem for two-counter machines to solving games on 2-VASS [1] and completely analogously to games on HCS with VASS guards.

Finally, our subsequent focus on the reachability winning conditions is because more expressive alternatives commonly studied in formal verification/reactive synthesis can be solved using the same, naïve approach.

5.1 Exponential Time Upper Bound

To solve a game on NFA[DFA], we can employ a construction that is very similar to the construction presented in Theorem 1. We construct a finite-state game graph where the vertices represent configurations of the underlying NFA and all guard DFAs by using the product construction. Solving the original HCS game amounts to solving a game on the constructed graph, where a state's ownership, and other properties relevant to the winning condition like membership in F, are directly lifted to the game graph and its winning condition. Crucially, the size of this graph is exponential in the number of guards only. For Lemma 2, suppose that $\delta = \{t_1, \ldots, t_m\}$ are the transitions of the underlying NFA and the DFA guarding t_i has states Q_i and transitions δ_i.

Lemma 2. *Given an HCS game G one can in polynomial time construct a directed graph $G' = (V', E')$, a predicate $owner' : V' \to \{0, 1\}$, and an initial state $q_0' \in V'$ such that*

(i) Player 0 wins G iff Player 0 wins G';
(ii) $|V| \leq |Q| \cdot (|Q_1| + \ldots + |Q_m|)^m$ and $|E| \leq |\delta| \cdot (|\delta_1| + \ldots + |\delta_m|)^m$.

Solving the resulting reachability games can be done in polynomial time [8, Theorem 1.1] and therefore games on HCS can be solved in exponential time. The same construction allows one to solve history-constrained games with more expressive winning conditions, as long as solving their ordinary finite-state variants only depends polynomially on the number of control states. This applies to parity games (in $O(m \cdot n^k)$ [33]) as well as energy games and mean-payoff games (in $O(m \cdot n \cdot W)$ [6]). Since each of these subsumes reachability, the lower bound (to be proven next) also applies to them, entailing:

Corollary 4. *Solving parity, energy, and mean-payoff games on NFA[DFA] is EXPTIME-complete.*

5.2 Exponential Time Lower Bound

To conclude the proof of Theorem 2 we show the lower bound by reduction from solving *Countdown Games*, which is EXPTIME-complete [12, Theorem 4.5].

A countdown game is played on a weighted directed graph, where each edge has a weight in $\mathbb{N} \setminus \{0\}$, given in binary. A configuration is a pair (s, x), where s is a state and $x \in \mathbb{N}$ is the counter value. In any configuration (s, x), Player 0 chooses a number d such that there is at least one outgoing edge from s with weight d. Player 1 then chooses any edge (s, d, s') that starts in s and has weight d, and the game continues in configuration $(s', x - d)$. The goal of Player 0 is to make the counter reach 0, the goal of Player 1 is to prevent this. A countdown-game is therefore a concisely represented reachability game on $S \times \mathbb{N}$.

The above is the usual representation of countdown games. Here it is convenient to represent them slightly differently, however. Firstly, instead of counting down from x to 0, we will count up from 0 to x. Secondly, we "unravel" the choices of Players 0 and 1, meaning that we first have Player 0 choose an auxiliary successor state s_d by taking an edge (s, d, s_d), and then Player 1 choose a successor s' of s_d by taking an edge $(s_d, 0, s')$, see Fig. 6. Furthermore, we assume without loss of generality that all edge weights as well as the target number x are a power of 2 (or 0).

Lemma 3. *Let $\mathcal{C}$ be a countdown game. We can construct, in polynomial time, an NFA[DFA] reachability game $\mathcal{R}$ such that Player 0 has a winning strategy in $\mathcal{R}$ if and only if Player 0 has a winning strategy in $\mathcal{C}$.*

Proof. The main idea is to use the guarding DFAs to maintain the current counter value. Let 2^k be the target value and $x \leq 2^k$ denote the counter. We will have $k+1$ many DFA guards $D_0, D_1, \ldots, D_k$, which are shown in Fig. 5. The role of the i-th DFA guard D_i is to keep track of the i-th bit of x: state p_i represents 0, while q_i represents 1. The state a_i is used to force a *carry* operation when necessary, and r_i is a rejecting sink state.

The counter starts at $x = 0$, so the initial state of D_i is p_i, for $0 \leq i \leq k$. As 2^k is the target, the accepting states are p_i in D_i, for $0 \leq i < k$, and q_k in D_k.

Now, let us consider the game NFA, i.e., the outer automaton (see Fig. 6). Suppose that in the "countup" game, Player 0 chooses value 2^i. We represent

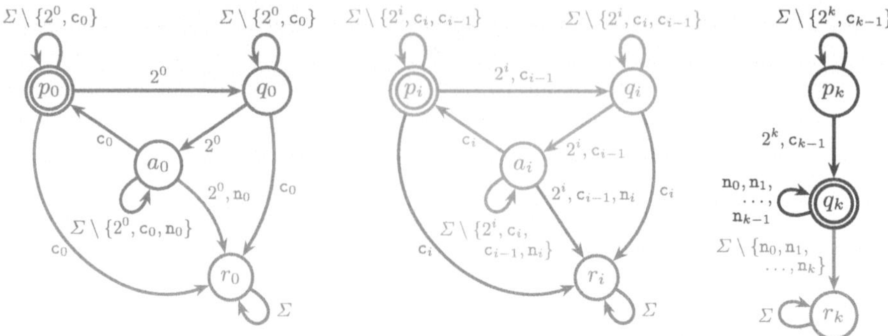

Fig. 5. The DFA guards; D_0 (left, red), D_i for all $1 \leq i \leq k-1$ (centre, green), and D_k (right, blue). Note that the sink states $r_0, \ldots, r_k$ and all transitions to/from sink states have been coloured grey to highlight the main function of the DFAs which occurs between states p_i, q_i, and a_i. (Colour figure online)

this using $k+1$ transitions in our NFA. The first transition is labelled 2^i. This symbol is also read by the guard automaton D_i, which increments from value 0 (state p_i) to value 1 (q_i), or from value 1 (q_i) to "preparing to carry" (a_i). All other guards D_j (for $j \neq i$) ignore the symbol 2^i, i.e., they loop and remain in the same state. Then, Player 0 chooses either $\mathtt{c}_0$ or $\mathtt{n}_0$, followed by $\mathtt{c}_1$ or $\mathtt{n}_1$, up to $\mathtt{c}_{k-1}$ or $\mathtt{n}_{k-1}$. After the final choice (between $\mathtt{c}_{k-1}$ or $\mathtt{n}_{k-1}$), we arrive in a state where Player 1 can choose a successor of s_0 among the ones where an edge with value 2^i exists in the countup game.

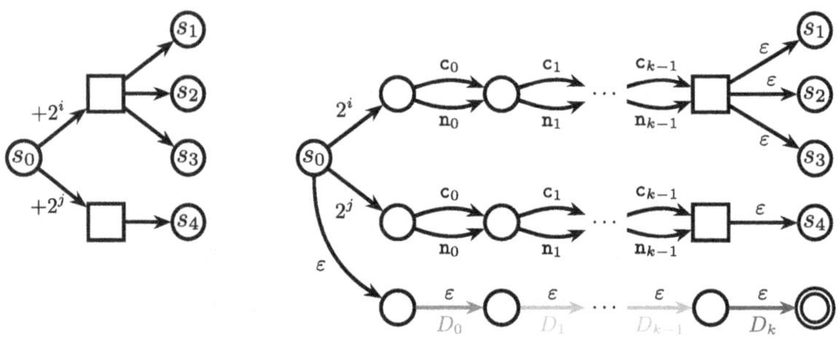

Fig. 6. Part of an example "countup" game with five circle states controlled by Player 0 and two square states controlled by Player 1 (left) and its corresponding part in the NFA[DFA] game (right). Outgoing edges of s_1, s_2, s_3, s_4 are omitted.

Additionally, in every state s, Player 0 may also choose to take an ε-transition that leads to a chain of ε-transitions guarded by $D_0, \ldots, D_k$ and terminating in (the only) accepting state. The eventual goal of Player 0 is to reach this accepting state, which requires all D_i, $0 \leq i \leq k$, to be in an accepting state. See Fig. 6.

When Player 0 chooses the action $\mathtt{c}_i$, this represents the i-th bit carrying over to the $(i+1)$-st bit. Hence the automaton D_i resets from state a_i ("preparing to carry") to p_i (value 0), while the automaton D_{i+1} increments from p_{i+1} to q_{i+1} or from q_{i+1} to a_{i+1}. If $\mathtt{c}_i$ is invoked when D_i is not in the carry state a_i, then the automaton moves into the sink state r_i. In order to reach the accepting state in the outer automaton, all D_i must be in an accepting state, so reaching r_i is immediately losing for Player 0. Hence if D_i is not preparing to carry, then playing $\mathtt{c}_i$ is a losing move. The action $\mathtt{n}_i$, conversely, represents no carry being required. This moves D_i to the sink state r_i if it is in the carry state a_i, so Player 0 must similarly not play $\mathtt{n}_i$ if D_i is in a_i.

Hence the only way for Player 0 to win is to correctly play $\mathtt{c}_i$ whenever the i-th bit needs to be carried and $\mathtt{n}_i$ otherwise, which means that $D_0, D_1, \ldots, D_k$ accurately track the value of the counter x. Then, once $x = 2^k$, all D_i will be in their accepting state, so Player 0 can take the chain of ε-transitions, guarded by $D_0, D_1, \ldots, D_k$ to finally reach the accepting state and win the game.

This NFA[DFA] therefore satisfies the requirements of the Lemma. □

6 HCS with VASS Guards

As a language recognition model, a d-dimensional VASS $V = (\Sigma, Q, T, q_0, F)$ consists of a finite alphabet Σ, a finite set of states Q, a finite set of transitions $T \subseteq Q \times \Sigma \times \mathbb{Z}^d \times Q$, an initial state $q_0 \in Q$, and a set of accepting states $F \subseteq Q$. A configuration of V is a pair $(q, \boldsymbol{x})$ where $q \in Q$ is the current state and $\boldsymbol{x} \in \mathbb{N}^d$ are the current counter values. Notice that the counter values are non-negative. To be clear, a transition $(q, \sigma, \boldsymbol{u}, q') \in T$ can be taken from $(q, \boldsymbol{x})$ if $\boldsymbol{x} + \boldsymbol{u} \geq \mathbf{0}$ (this inequality holds on all counters). A VASS is *deterministic*, denoted DVASS, if there is at most one transition for each outgoing state $q \in Q$ and character $\sigma \in \Sigma$.

The language defined by a given VASS depends on its acceptance condition. There are two acceptance conditions: reachability and coverability. The reachability acceptance condition necessitates that a word is accepted if it leads to a configuration $(q, \boldsymbol{x})$ such that $q \in F$ is an accepting state and $\boldsymbol{x} = \mathbf{0}$. The coverability acceptance condition is a relaxation that only requires that $q \in F$ and $\boldsymbol{x} \geq \mathbf{0}$ (i.e. only the control state matters). We use *Reach-VASS* to denote VASS with the reachability acceptance condition and *Cover-VASS* to denote VASS with the coverability acceptance condition. When the dimension d of the VASS is known, we write *Reach-d-VASS* and *Cover-d-VASS.*

This section is devoted to proving that language non-emptiness is undecidable for DFA[Reach-1-DVASS] (Theorem 3) and is EXPSPACE-complete for NFA[Cover-DVASS] (Theorem 4).

6.1 VASS Guards with Reachability Acceptance Conditions

Theorem 3. *Language emptiness for DFA[Reach-1-DVASS] is undecidable.*

To prove Theorem 3, we will reduce from reachability in two-counter machines (2CM), an undecidable problem [26]. We will construct an DFA[Reach-1-DVASS] that has a non-empty language if and only if reachability holds in a given 2CM.

A 2CM $M = (Q, T)$ consists of a finite set of states Q and a set of transitions $T \subseteq Q \times A \times Q$ where $A = \{\texttt{inc}_1, \texttt{dec}_1, \texttt{zero}_1, \texttt{inc}_2, \texttt{dec}_2, \texttt{zero}_2\}$ is the set of *counter actions*. A configuration of M is a pair $(q, (x, y))$ where $q \in Q$ is the current state and $(x, y) \geq (0, 0)$ are the current counter values. To be clear, a transition $(p, \texttt{dec}_1, q)$ can be taken from $(p, (x, y))$ to $(q, (x - 1, y))$ if $x - 1 \geq 0$ and a transition $(p, \texttt{zero}_2, q)$ can be taken from $(p, (x, y))$ to $(q, (x, y))$ if $y = 0$. We may also assume "action determinacy": for every state $p \in Q$ and for every action $\alpha \in A$, there is at most one transition from p of the form (p, α, q).

Proof Idea. We create a DFA[Reach-1-DVASS] D, operating over the alphabet $\{\texttt{inc}_1, \texttt{dec}_1, \texttt{zero}_1, \texttt{inc}_2, \texttt{dec}_2, \texttt{zero}_2\}$, where the underlying DFA U tracks the current state of the given 2CM M. There are two *distinct* Reach-1-DVASS guards G_1 and G_2, each consisting of only one state. The roles of G_1 and G_2 are to track the first and second counter of M, respectively. Whenever there is a transition $(p, \texttt{zero}_i, q)$, it is guarded by G_i; this equates to the i-th counter of M being zero. See Fig. 7 for an example of this construction. □

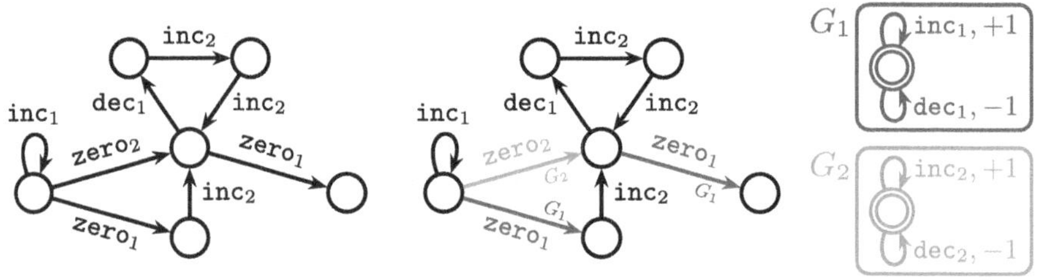

Fig. 7. A 2CM and its equivalent DFA[Reach-1-DVASS].

A key reason that non-emptiness in DFA[Reach-1-DVASS] is undecidable is that we can use the guards to simulate zero tests as many times as we like. When the number of zero tests of a 2-CM M is fixed, or even when it is not fixed but is bounded by some function of size of M, then reachability becomes decidable. This is because VASS can simulate counter machines with a bounded number of zero tests and reachability in VASS is decidable [14,17,19,20,23].

6.2 VASS Guards with Coverability Acceptance Conditions

This section observes that NFA[Cover-DVASS] are contained within the class of Cover-VASS (Proposition 4), but despite their succinct representation, the language emptiness problem is EXPSPACE-complete, matching the complexity for Cover-DVASS (Theorem 4).

Theorem 4. *Language emptiness for NFA[Cover-DVASS] is* EXPSPACE*-complete.*

Let us fix our attention on the NFA[Cover-DVASS] $A = (\Sigma, U, \mathcal{G})$ where $U = (\Sigma, Q, \delta, q_0, F)$ is the underlying NFA with transitions $\delta = \{t_1, \ldots, t_m\}$ and guards $\mathcal{G} = \{L_1, \ldots, L_m\}$. For every $i \in \{1, \ldots, m\}$, the guard is specified as a d_i-dimensional Cover-DVASS $G_i = (\Sigma, Q_i, T_i, q_{0,i}, F_i)$, so $L(G_i) = L_i$. We use $\|V\|$ to denote the size of a d-VASS encoded in unary.

Proposition 4. *Let $D = d_1 + \ldots + d_m$. There exists a D-dimensional Cover-VASS $V = (\Sigma, Q', T', q_0', F' = \{t\})$ such that $L(A) = L(V)$ and $\|V\| \leq 2(\|U\| + \|G_1\| + \ldots + \|G_m\|)^{m+2}$.*

Proof Idea. The construction takes the cross product of the underlying automaton U and the Cover-DVASS guards $G_1, \ldots, G_m$ simultaneously tracking the counters of all of the guards. We must be careful to show that a transition that would kill a run of a guard does not kill the whole run (the guard may not be used again). We also ensure that there is a single accepting state so we can apply arguments and algorithms for VASS coverability. □

Proposition 4 tells us that NFA[Cover-DVASS] are no more expressive than Cover-VASS. It remains to show that deciding non-emptiness (whether the state t is reachable in V) can be decided in EXPSPACE and that there is a matching lower bound.

Proof of Theorem 4. For this, we will use an exponential space algorithm for deciding coverability. Coverability in VASS is the following decision problem. Given a VASS V, an initial configuration $(s, \boldsymbol{x})$, and a target configuration $(t, \boldsymbol{y})$, decide whether there is a run in V from $(s, \boldsymbol{x})$ to $(t, \boldsymbol{y}')$ for some $\boldsymbol{y}' \geq \boldsymbol{y}$. In 1978, Rackoff proved that coverability in VASS can be decided in EXPSPACE [30]. We will use a more convenient formulation of Rackoff's Theorem from [16, Corollary 3.4] that states that coverability in a d-VASS V from an initial configuration $(s, \mathbf{0})$ and with a target configuration $(t, \mathbf{0})$ can be decided by a non-deterministic $\mathcal{O}(d^2 \cdot 2^d \cdot \log\|V\|)$-space algorithm.

For our purposes, we wish to decide coverability in the D-dimensional VASS $V = (\Sigma, Q', T', q_0, \{t\})$. If we prove that $\|V\|$ is at most exponential in the combined sizes of the underlying NFA and the Cover-DVASS guards, then we can use Rackoff's Theorem to conclude that language non-emptiness of A is decidable in NEXPSPACE. This is why, as per the statement of Theorem 4, we construct a VASS V with $\|V\| \leq 2(\|U\| + \|G_1\| + \ldots + \|G_m\|)^{m+2}$.

We conclude the upper bound by combining Proposition 4 and [16, Corollary 3.4]. There is a NEXPSPACE algorithm for deciding whether $(s, \mathbf{0})$ can cover $(t, \mathbf{0})$ in V. Precisely, the algorithm uses at most the following space:

$$\mathcal{O}(d^2 \cdot 2^D \cdot (m+2) \cdot \log(2(\|U\| + \|G_1\| + \ldots + \|G_m\|))).$$

Finally, by Savitch's Theorem [31], we know that NEXPSPACE = EXPSPACE.

As for the lower bound, language non-emptiness of DFA[Cover-DVASS] is EXPSPACE-hard because coverability in VASS is already EXPSPACE-hard [21]. Associate with each transition an alphabet character, so that the Cover-DVASS is deterministic, generating an alphabet Σ. Consider an DFA with two states p (the initial state) and q (the only accepting state) and transitions $t_1 = (p, \sigma, p)$ for each $\sigma \in \Sigma$, and $t_2 = (p, \$, q)$ for a new symbol $\$ \notin \Sigma$. There is just one guard, the Cover-DVASS in question which is allowed to update its configuration whenever t_1 is taken and which guards the transition t_2. This means that a word $w\$$ is accepted by the DFA[Cover-DVASS] if and only if the guard is able to achieve coverability on the word w. □

Acknowledgments. We gratefully acknowledge the TCS@Liverpool Open Problems Day for initiating the collaboration. This work is supported by the EPSRC project EP/X042596/1 and by the ERC grant INFSYS, agreement no. 950398.

Disclosure of Interests. The authors have no competing interests to declare.

References

1. Abdulla, P.A., Bouajjani, A., d'Orso, J.: Deciding monotonic games. In: Baaz, M., Makowsky, J.A. (eds.) CSL 2003. LNCS, vol. 2803, pp. 1–14. Springer, Heidelberg (2003). https://doi.org/10.1007/978-3-540-45220-1_1
2. Alur, R., Dill, D.L.: A theory of timed automata. Theor. Comput. Sci. **126**(2), 183–235 (1994). https://doi.org/10.1016/0304-3975(94)90010-8
3. Austin, P., Bose, S., Mazzocchi, N., Totzke, P.: Temporal explorability games. In: International Conference on Concurrency Theory (CONCUR). Leibniz International Proceedings in Informatics (LIPIcs), vol. 348, pp. 7:1–7:17. Schloss Dagstuhl – Leibniz-Zentrum für Informatik (2025). https://doi.org/10.4230/LIPIcs.CONCUR.2025.7
4. Austin, P., Bose, S., Totzke, P.: Parity games on temporal graphs. In: International Conference on Foundations of Software Science and Computational Structures (FoSSaCS). Lecture Notes in Computer Science, vol. 14574, pp. 79–98. Springer, Heidelberg (2024). https://doi.org/10.1007/978-3-031-57228-9_5
5. ter Beek, M.H., Ellis, C.A., Kleijn, J., Rozenberg, G.: Synchronizations in team automata for groupware systems. Comput. Support. Cooper. Work (CSCW) **12**(1), 21–69 (2003). https://doi.org/10.1023/A:1022407907596
6. Brim, L., Chaloupka, J., Doyen, L., Gentilini, R., Raskin, J.F.: Faster algorithms for mean-payoff games. Form. Methods Syst. Des. **38**(2), 97–118 (2011). https://doi.org/10.1007/s10703-010-0105-x
7. Czerwinski, W., Orlikowski, L.: Reachability in vector addition systems is Ackermann-complete. In: 2021 IEEE 62nd Annual Symposium on Foundations of Computer Science (FOCS), pp. 1229–1240 (2022)
8. Fijalkow, N., et al.: Games on graphs (2023)
9. Grädel, E., Thomas, W., Wilke, T. (eds.): Automata Logics, and Infinite Games: A Guide to Current Research. Springer, Cham (2002). https://doi.org/10.1007/3-540-36387-4
10. Holme, P., Saramäki, J.: Temporal Network Theory. Springer, Heidelberg (2019). https://doi.org/10.1007/978-3-030-23495-9

11. Hopcroft, J.E., Motwani, R., Ullman, J.D.: Introduction to automata theory, languages, and computation. ACM SIGACT News **32**(1), 60–65 (2001)
12. Jurdzinski, M., Sproston, J., Laroussinie, F.: Model checking probabilistic timed automata with one or two clocks. Log. Methods Comput. Sci. **4**(3) (2008). https://doi.org/10.2168/LMCS-4(3:12)2008
13. Köhler-Bußmeier, M.: Hornets: nets within nets combined with net algebra. In: Franceschinis, G., Wolf, K. (eds.) PETRI NETS 2009. LNCS, vol. 5606, pp. 243–262. Springer, Heidelberg (2009). https://doi.org/10.1007/978-3-642-02424-5_15
14. Kosaraju, S.R.: Decidability of reachability in vector addition systems (preliminary version). In: Proceedings of the 14th Annual ACM Symposium on Theory of Computing, San Francisco, California, USA, 5–7 May 1982, pp. 267–281. ACM (1982). https://doi.org/10.1145/800070.802201
15. Kuijer, L.B., Purser, D., Sinclair-Banks, H., Totzke, P.: History-constrained systems (2026). https://arxiv.org/abs/2602.18143
16. Künnemann, M., Mazowiecki, F., Schütze, L., Sinclair-Banks, H., Wegrzycki, K.: Coverability in VASS revisited: improving Rackoff's bounds to obtain conditional optimality. J. ACM **72**(5), 33:1–33:27 (2025). https://doi.org/10.1145/3762178
17. Lambert, J.: A structure to decide reachability in petri nets. Theor. Comput. Sci. **99**(1), 79–104 (1992). https://doi.org/10.1016/0304-3975(92)90173-D
18. Leroux, J.: The reachability problem for petri nets is not primitive recursive. In: 2021 IEEE 62nd Annual Symposium on Foundations of Computer Science (FOCS), pp. 1241–1252 (2022)
19. Leroux, J., Schmitz, S.: Demystifying reachability in vector addition systems. In: 30th Annual ACM/IEEE Symposium on Logic in Computer Science, LICS 2015, Kyoto, Japan, 6–10 July 2015, pp. 56–67. IEEE Computer Society (2015). https://doi.org/10.1109/LICS.2015.16
20. Leroux, J., Schmitz, S.: Reachability in vector addition systems is primitive-recursive in fixed dimension. In: 34th Annual ACM/IEEE Symposium on Logic in Computer Science, LICS 2019, Vancouver, BC, Canada, 24–27 June 2019, pp. 1–13. IEEE (2019). https://doi.org/10.1109/LICS.2019.8785796
21. Lipton, R.: The Reachability Problem Requires Exponential Space. Department of Computer Science. Yale University **62** (1976)
22. Lynch, N., Tuttle, M.: An introduction to input/output automata. CWI Q. **2**(3), 219–246 (1989)
23. Mayr, E.W.: An algorithm for the general petri net reachability problem. In: Proceedings of the 13th Annual ACM Symposium on Theory of Computing, Milwaukee, Wisconsin, USA, 11–13 May 1981, pp. 238–246. ACM (1981). https://doi.org/10.1145/800076.802477
24. Michail, O.: An introduction to temporal graphs: an algorithmic perspective. In: Zaroliagis, C., Pantziou, G., Kontogiannis, S. (eds.) Algorithms, Probability, Networks, and Games. LNCS, vol. 9295, pp. 308–343. Springer, Cham (2015). https://doi.org/10.1007/978-3-319-24024-4_18
25. Milner, R.: A Calculus of Communicating Systems, Lecture Notes in Computer Science, vol. 92. Springer, Heidelberg (1980).https://doi.org/10.1007/3-540-10235-3
26. Minsky, M.L.: Computation. Prentice-Hall, Englewood Cliffs (1967)
27. Pnueli, A., Rosner, R.: On the synthesis of a reactive module. In: Annual Symposium on Principles of Programming Languages, POPL '89, pp. 179–190. Association for Computing Machinery (1989). https://doi.org/10.1145/75277.75293

28. Pnueli, A.: The temporal logic of programs. In: Annual Symposium on Foundations of Computer Science, SFCS '77, pp. 46–57. IEEE Computer Society (1977). https://doi.org/10.1109/SFCS.1977.32
29. Prasad, K.V.S.: A calculus of broadcasting systems. Sci. Comput. Program. **25**(2–3), 285–327 (1995). https://doi.org/10.1016/0167-6423(95)00017-8
30. Rackoff, C.: The covering and boundedness problems for vector addition systems. Theor. Comput. Sci. **6**, 223–231 (1978). https://doi.org/10.1016/0304-3975(78)90036-1
31. Savitch, W.J.: Relationships between nondeterministic and deterministic tape complexities. J. Comput. Syst. Sci. **4**(2), 177–192 (1970). https://doi.org/10.1016/S0022-0000(70)80006-X
32. Valk, R.: Object petri nets: using the nets-within-nets paradigm. In: Desel, J., Reisig, W., Rozenberg, G. (eds.) ACPN 2003. LNCS, vol. 3098, pp. 819–848. Springer, Heidelberg (2004). https://doi.org/10.1007/978-3-540-27755-2_23
33. Zielonka, W.: Infinite games on finitely coloured graphs with applications to automata on infinite trees. Theor. Comput. Sci. **200**(1–2), 135–183 (1998)

Highly Incremental: A Simple Programmatic Approach for Many Objectives

Philipp Schröer(✉) and Joost-Pieter Katoen

RWTH Aachen University, Aachen, Germany
{phisch,katoen}@cs.rwth-aachen.de

Abstract. We present a one-fits-all programmatic approach to reason about a plethora of objectives on probabilistic programs. The first ingredient is to add a reward-statement to the language. We then define a program transformation applying a monotone function to the cumulative reward of the program. The key idea is that this transformation uses incremental differences in the reward. This simple, elegant approach enables to express e.g., higher moments, threshold probabilities of rewards, the expected excess over a budget, and moment-generating functions. All these objectives can now be analyzed using a single existing approach: probabilistic wp-reasoning. We automated verification using the Caesar deductive verifier and report on the application of the transformation to some examples.

1 Introduction

Probabilistic Programs. Probabilistic programs combine ordinary programming structures such as loops and conditionals with probabilistic choices. They are a powerful modeling tool for a wide range of applications, including randomized algorithms, security mechanisms, and probabilistic databases. Due to the intrinsic randomness, the runtime of a probabilistic program follows a probability distribution. Figure 1a models a web server retrying a database call until success. Variable `done` records success; each loop iteration yields a `reward` 1 (1 s). Each iteration succeeds with probability $1/2$ and the program terminates with probability one (*almost-sure termination*). Its expected runtime is 2 (*positive almost-sure termination*).

Same Expected Runtime, Different Variance. We add a cache (Fig. 1b) raising the success probability to $2/3$ at an initialization cost of $1/2$ seconds. The new program also terminates almost surely, and perhaps more surprisingly, its expected runtime is also 2. Despite identical expected runtimes, their runtime distributions differ (Fig. 2). The probability that Fig. 1a terminates earlier is higher, while Fig. 1b concentrates more tightly around 2 s. The variances are $2\,\mathrm{s}^2$ (no cache) versus $3/4\,\mathrm{s}^2$ (cache), making the runtime of the cached variant more predictable. The example shows that the expected value – an *average* – is not always sufficient to capture the behavior of a probabilistic program.

A. Sampaio and M. Stoelinga (Eds.): FM 2026, LNCS 16556, pp. 559–577, 2026.
https://doi.org/10.1007/978-3-032-26204-2_29

```
done := false;
while (¬done) {
  reward 1;
  {done := true} [1/2] {skip}
}                probabilistic choice
```

(a) Program modeling a web server which retries a database call, succeeding with probability 1/2. Each database call takes 1 second.

```
reward 1/2;
done := false;
while (¬done) {
  reward 1;
  {done := true} [2/3] {skip}
}                probabilistic choice
```

(b) Variant with a cache. It initializes a cache (taking 1/2 seconds) and then retries a database call which succeeds with probability 2/3. Each database call takes 1 second.

Fig. 1. Example programs modeling a web server retrying a database call.

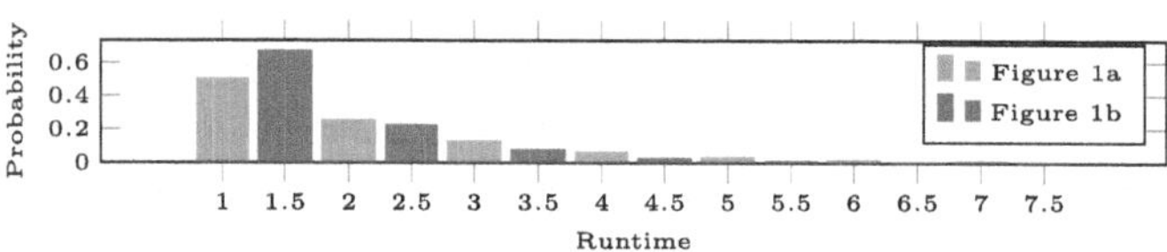

Fig. 2. Probability distribution of runtimes of the programs in Fig. 1.

Deductive Verification of Probabilistic Programs. Dedicated techniques have been developed to reason about different objectives of probabilistic programs. The weakest pre-expectation (wp) semantics [25] is a well-established formalism to reason about expected values on termination. An extensive catalog of proof rules has been developed, including [4,5,11,14,26]. The wp calculus has been extended for reasoning about expected runtimes [19,21] and general rewards [8]. Tool-assisted wp-based verification includes *HOL* mechanization [16] and the *Caesar* deductive verifier [33]. Tailored variations have been proposed for covariances [20], higher moments of rewards [23,36], and for amortized complexity analysis [7].

Programmatic Rewards as a Unifying Abstraction. Different objectives currently require separate wp-calculi, hindering reuse. We aim for a *one-fits-all* approach so that existing wp semantics, proof rules, and tools can be reused for a broad range of objectives. We do so by adding a `reward` statement to the programming language, inspired by [3,7], to collect (non-negative) *rewards* during program execution. The *expected cumulative reward* is then the expected sum of all rewards collected during a program run. We show how different objectives can be modeled using reward statements, including expected runtimes, expected visiting times, and discounted rewards.

Incremental Differences for Reward Transformations. To tackle objectives like higher moments of expected rewards, we need to reason about *transformed* expected rewards of program S such as $\mathsf{E}(\mathsf{rew}(S)^2)$. Our key idea is to make use of *incremental differences* of rewards, inspired by the aert calculus [7]. We define a simple program transformation that reduces reasoning about complex expected rewards to reasoning about standard expected rewards, allowing us to reuse existing wp theory, techniques, and tools.

Contributions and Outline. We provide one programming language and one weakest pre-expectation semantics to reason about a broad range of quantitative objectives of probabilistic programs in a unified way. Section 2 introduces the syntax and semantics for probabilistic programs. Our main contributions are:

1. A programmatic encoding for multiple quantitative objectives (Sect. 3),
2. A program transformation (Sect. 4.1) that is proven sound w.r.t. a Markov chain transformation (Sect. 4.2),
3. Application to different objectives, including higher moments. (Section 5),

Finally, we briefly touch on automation in Sect. 6, compare related work in Sect. 7 and conclude in Sect. 8.

2 Foundations: Semantics for Probabilistic Programs

In this section, we introduce the syntax and semantics of probabilistic programs with `reward` statements. Our presentation is based on [8], with two key adaptations: (1) we allow arbitrary expressions a in `reward` a statements instead of only constants, and (2) we allow program variables to take on values from the set $\mathbb{R}_{\geq 0}^{\infty} = \mathbb{R}_{\geq 0} \cup \{\infty\}$. We formally define the syntax of probabilistic guarded command language (pGCL) programs, describe their operational semantics via Markov chains, and present the weakest pre-expectation semantics.

2.1 Syntax of Probabilistic Programs

States and Expressions. We consider a finite set of variables Vars. A *program state* σ is a mapping from variables to values, i.e., $\sigma \in \mathsf{States} = \mathsf{Vars} \to \mathsf{Vals}$. In this work, we will use $\mathsf{Vals} = \mathbb{R}_{\geq 0}^{\infty}$. We write $\sigma[x \mapsto e]$ for the state σ updated so that x maps to the value of e in σ and all other variables are untouched, i.e. $\sigma[x \mapsto e](y) = e(\sigma)$ if $y = x$, and $\sigma(y)$ otherwise. An arithmetic expression $a \in \mathsf{AExp}$ is a mapping from program states to values, i.e. $\mathsf{AExp} = \mathsf{States} \to \mathsf{Vals}$. Boolean expressions $b \in \mathsf{BExp}$ map program states to $\{\mathtt{true},\ \mathtt{false}\}$.

Programs. The syntax of pGCL programs S is defined by the following grammar, where $x \in \mathsf{Vars}$, $a \in \mathsf{AExp}$, $p \in [0, 1]$, and $b \in \mathsf{BExp}$:

$$\begin{aligned} S = {} & \mathtt{skip} \mid x := a \mid \mathtt{reward}\ a \mid S_1\,;\ S_2 \\ & \mid \{S_1\}\ [p]\ \{S_2\} \mid \mathtt{if}\ (b)\ \{S_1\}\ \mathtt{else}\ \{S_2\} \mid \mathtt{while}\ (b)\ \{\ S\ \}\,. \end{aligned}$$

The `skip` statement does nothing. The assignment $x := a$ assigns the value of expression a to variable x. The `reward` a statement collects a non-negative reward a when executed. Note that a is an expression that may contain program variables. The sequential composition S_1; S_2 executes S_1 followed by S_2. The probabilistic choice $\{S_1\}$ $[p]$ $\{S_2\}$ executes S_1 with probability p and S_2 with probability $1 - p$. The conditional `if` (b) $\{S_1\}$ `else` $\{S_2\}$ executes S_1 if the boolean expression b evaluates to true, and S_2 otherwise. The loop `while` (b) $\{ S \}$ repeatedly executes S as long as the boolean expression b evaluates to true.

2.2 Operational Semantics

The operational semantics of programs is given by Markov chains with rewards, whose foundations we briefly recall.

A *Markov chain* is a tuple $\mathcal{M} = (\mathfrak{S}, \mathsf{Prob}, \sigma_1, \mathsf{rew})$, where $\mathfrak{S}$ is a (countable) set of configurations, $\mathsf{Prob}\colon \mathfrak{S} \to \mathsf{Dist}(\mathfrak{S})$ is the transition function, $\sigma_1 \in \mathfrak{S}$ is the initial configuration, and $\mathsf{rew}\colon \mathfrak{S} \to \mathbb{R}_{\geq 0}^{\infty}$ is the reward function.

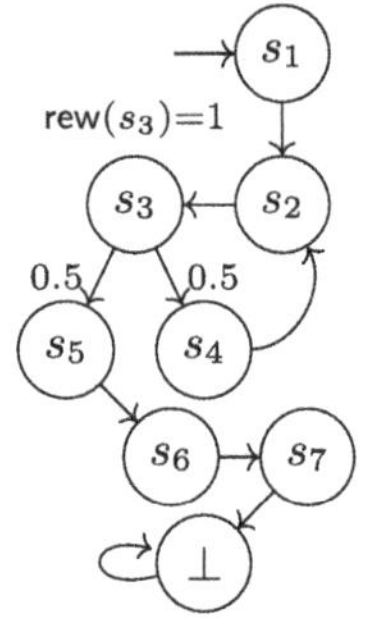

Fig. 3. Operational MC for Fig. 1a.

A (finite) *path* $\pi \in \mathsf{Paths}_{\mathcal{M}}^{=n}$ of length n in $\mathcal{M}$ is a sequence of configurations $\pi = s_1 s_2 \dots s_n$ with $\mathsf{Prob}(s_i)(s_{i+1}) > 0$ for all $1 \leq i < n$. We lift Prob and rew to finite paths by $\mathsf{Prob}(s_1 \dots s_n) = \prod_{1 \leq i < n} \mathsf{Prob}(s_i)(s_{i+1})$ and $\mathsf{rew}(s_1 \dots s_n) = \sum_{1 \leq i \leq n} \mathsf{rew}(s_i)$. Let $\mathsf{E}(\mathsf{rew}(\mathcal{M}))$ denote the expected cumulative reward of $\mathcal{M}$, given by $\sup_{n \in \mathbb{N}} \sum_{\pi \in \mathsf{Paths}_{\mathcal{M}}^{=n}(\sigma)} \mathsf{Prob}(\pi) \cdot \mathsf{rew}(\pi)$. More generally, the reward transformed by a function $f\colon \mathbb{R}_{\geq 0}^{\infty} \to \mathbb{R}_{\geq 0}^{\infty}$ is defined as $\mathsf{E}(f(\mathsf{rew}(\mathcal{M}))) = \sup_{n \in \mathbb{N}} \sum_{\pi \in \mathsf{Paths}_{\mathcal{M}}^{=n}(\sigma)} \mathsf{Prob}(\pi) \cdot f(\mathsf{rew}(\pi))$.

The *operational Markov chain* $\mathcal{M}_S^{\sigma_1} = (\mathfrak{S}, \mathsf{Prob}, s_1, \mathsf{rew})$ of program S is given by the reachable[1] configurations $\mathfrak{S} \subseteq (\mathsf{pGCL} \cup \{ \Downarrow \}) \times \mathsf{States} \cup \{ \bot \}$ with transition probabilities Prob (see [34]), initial configuration $s_1 = (S, \sigma_1)$, and reward function rew defined as follows:

$$\mathsf{rew}((S, \sigma)) = \begin{cases} r & \text{if } (\exists S' \in \mathsf{pGCL}.\ S = \texttt{reward}\ r;\ S') \vee (S = \texttt{reward}\ r) \\ 0 & \text{otherwise} \end{cases}$$

The operational Markov chain for the program in Fig. 1a is shown in Fig. 3. We write $\mathsf{E}(\mathsf{rew}^{\sigma_1}(S))$ to denote the expected cumulative reward of the operational Markov chain $\mathcal{M}_S^{\sigma_1}$, i.e., $\mathsf{E}(\mathsf{rew}(\mathcal{M}_S^{\sigma_1}))$. Let $\mathsf{E}(\mathsf{rew}(S)) = \lambda\sigma.\ \mathsf{E}(\mathsf{rew}^{\sigma}(S))$.

[1] The inference rules admit only finitely many transitions from each configuration, hence the set of reachable configurations is countable.

S	$\mathsf{wp}[\![S]\!](X)$	S	$\mathsf{wp}[\![S]\!](X)$
`skip`	X	$\{S_1\}\ [p]\ \{S_2\}$	$p \cdot \mathsf{wp}[\![S_1]\!](X) + (1-p) \cdot \mathsf{wp}[\![S_2]\!](X)$
$x := a$	$X[x \mapsto a]$	`if` (b) $\{ S_1 \}$ `else` $\{ S_2 \}$	$[b] \cdot \mathsf{wp}[\![S_1]\!](X) + [\neg b] \cdot \mathsf{wp}[\![S_2]\!](X)$
`reward` a	$a + X$		
$S_1;\ S_2$	$\mathsf{wp}[\![S_1]\!](\mathsf{wp}[\![S_2]\!](X))$	`while` (b) $\{ S' \}$	$\mathrm{lfp}\, Y.\ [b] \cdot \mathsf{wp}[\![S']\!](Y) + [\neg b] \cdot X$

Fig. 4. Inductive definition of the *weakest pre-expectation semantics* for program S, $\mathsf{wp}[\![S]\!] : \mathbb{E} \to \mathbb{E}$ where $X \in \mathbb{E}$ is the *post-expectation.*

2.3 Weakest Pre-expectation Semantics

An *expectation* is a function $f\colon \mathsf{States} \to \mathbb{R}^{\infty}_{\geq 0}$. Let $\mathbb{E}$ denote the set of all expectations. Expectations form a complete lattice $(\mathbb{E}, \preceq)$ with pointwise order $X \preceq Y$ iff $X(\sigma) \leq Y(\sigma)$ for all $\sigma \in \mathsf{States}$. Thus, all infima and suprema exist, and by Kleene's fixed-point theorem, least fixed points $\mathrm{lfp}\, Y.\ \Phi(Y)$ of monotone functions $\Phi\colon \mathbb{E} \to \mathbb{E}$ exist. Let $[b] \in \mathbb{E}$ map a Boolean expression b to $[b]\,(\sigma) = 1$ iff $b(\sigma) = \texttt{true}$, and to 0 otherwise. A substitution $X[x \mapsto a]$ of variable x by expression a in $X \in \mathbb{E}$ is given by $X[x \mapsto a](\sigma) = X(\sigma[x \mapsto a])$ for all $\sigma \in \mathsf{States}$. Arithmetic on expectations is lifted pointwise, e.g. $(X + Y)(\sigma) = X(\sigma) + Y(\sigma)$.

The *weakest pre-expectation* for a program S is a function $\mathsf{wp}[\![S]\!] : \mathbb{E} \to \mathbb{E}$ defined by structural induction on S; see Fig. 4. Intuitively, $\mathsf{wp}[\![S]\!](X)$ is the expected cumulative reward of the program S starting from the initial state σ, given that the reward earned on termination is X. The semantics is standard[2], but we highlight `reward` and while loops. For a reward statement `reward` a, we have $\mathsf{wp}[\![\texttt{reward}\ a]\!](X) = a + X$, i.e. the result of evaluating a in the current state is added to X. For a loop `while` (b) $\{ S \}$, the pre-expectation is given by the least fixed point of the functional $Y \mapsto [b] \cdot \mathsf{wp}[\![S]\!](Y) + [\neg b] \cdot X$, dubbed the *loop-characteristic functional w.r.t. post* X.

For example, the least fixed point for the loop in Fig. 1a with post $X = 0$ is given by $(\mathrm{lfp}\, Y.\ [\neg done] \cdot (1 + 0.5 \cdot Y[done \mapsto \texttt{true}] + 0.5 \cdot Y)) = [\neg done] \cdot 2$. For the full program S, we have $\mathsf{wp}[\![S]\!](0) = ([\neg done] \cdot 2)[done \mapsto \texttt{false}] = 2$.

Soundness. The expression $\mathsf{wp}[\![S]\!](X)(\sigma)$ evaluates to the expected cumulative reward in the Markov chain corresponding to the semantics of S starting in σ [8, Theorem 6], i.e. $\mathsf{wp}[\![S]\!](X)(\sigma) = \mathsf{E}(\mathsf{rew}^{\sigma}_{X}(S))$. Here, $\mathsf{rew}^{\sigma}_{X}(S)$ is the *reward function induced by* X on top of the operational Markov chain $\mathcal{M}^{\sigma}_{S}$, which collects the reward $X(\sigma)$ upon termination, and otherwise the reward defined for each statement S in configuration (S, σ) according to [34]. Formally, it is defined as $\mathsf{rew}_X((\Downarrow, \sigma)) = X(\sigma)$ and $\mathsf{rew}_X((S, \sigma)) = \mathsf{rew}((S, \sigma))$ otherwise. We use abbreviations $\mathsf{rew}^{\sigma}_{X}(S) = \mathsf{rew}_X(\mathcal{M}^{\sigma}_{S})$ and $\mathsf{E}(\mathsf{rew}_X(S)) = \lambda\sigma.\ \mathsf{E}(\mathsf{rew}^{\sigma}_{X}(S))$.

[2] The wp calculus was originally defined without `reward` statements [17,25]; we use the extended calculus of [8] with `reward` statements.

Healthiness Conditions. Corresponding to properties of expected values, wp satisfies several well-behavedness properties, often called *healthiness conditions* [8,17,25]. Let $S \in \mathsf{pGCL}$ be a program and $X, Y \in \mathbb{E}$ be expectations. Then, $\mathsf{wp}[\![S]\!]$ is monotonic, i.e. for $X \preceq Y$, we have $\mathsf{wp}[\![S]\!](X) \preceq \mathsf{wp}[\![S]\!](Y)$. Further, $\mathsf{wp}[\![S]\!]$ is linear for `reward`-free programs S, i.e. for all $X, Y \in \mathbb{E}$ and $a \in \mathbb{R}_{\geq 0}$, we have $\mathsf{wp}[\![S]\!](a \cdot X + Y) = a \cdot \mathsf{wp}[\![S]\!](X) + \mathsf{wp}[\![S]\!](Y)$.

3 Programmatic Reward Modeling

We introduce *programmatic reward modeling* for probabilistic programs via the program statement `reward`. By expressing rewards via `reward`, we can directly incorporate different reward structures into the program text.

3.1 Rewards on Termination

A common reward structure collects rewards only on termination, as considered by the original weakest pre-expectation semantics wp [13,17,25] (without `reward` statements). Here, for a program S and $f \in \mathbb{E}$, $\mathsf{wp}[\![S]\!](f)$ is the expected value of f on termination of S. Using wp, we can also easily query for transformed expected rewards on termination, e.g. $\mathsf{wp}[\![S]\!](x^2)$ to obtain the second moment of the value of x on termination of S.

For a more programmatic approach, we generalize the classical idea of embedding a post-condition into a program via an `assert` statement, which eliminates the need to specify the post-condition separately. Instead of specifying S explicitly with some post-expectation X, we can use the `reward` statement to collect rewards on termination, i.e. the sequence S`;` `reward` X, and use $X = 0$. The corresponding soundness statement is also simplified, replacing rew_X by rew. Here, it is essential that we allow arbitrary arithmetic functions X in the `reward` statement, including expectations $\mathbb{E}$ (c.f. Sect. 2).[3]

Lemma 1 (Programmatic Rewards on Termination). *Let $S \in \mathsf{pGCL}$ and $X \in \mathbb{E}$. Then, $\mathsf{wp}[\![S]\!](X) = \mathsf{wp}[\![S\texttt{; reward } X]\!](0) = \mathsf{E}(\mathsf{rew}(S\texttt{; reward } X))$.*

As the programmatic view indicates, this model only collects rewards on termination of the program. In particular, diverging executions collect no rewards.

3.2 Run-Times and Resource Consumption

The formal verification of expected run-times, and more generally resource consumption, is a well-studied topic in the literature [19,21–23,36]. The analysis is subtle. We already examined Fig. 1 which has a finite expected run-time despite having an infinite execution path (the database call never succeeding). In the following, we examine Fig. 5 which shows three different reward models for tracking runtimes for a schematic program consisting of a single while loop.

[3] Although not necessary for our setup, we conjecture that the assertion language from [6] can be extended to support `reward` statements while remaining *expressive*, i.e. for all syntactic $X \in \mathbb{E}$, one can syntactically express pre-expectation $\mathsf{wp}[\![S]\!](X)$.

```
τ := 0;
while (b) {
  τ := τ + 1;
  S'
}
reward τ
```

(a) Tracking runtimes via rewards on termination, corresponding to $\mathsf{wp}[\![S]\!](\tau)$.

```
τ := 0;
while (b) {
  τ := τ + 1;
  S'
}
reward τ²
```

(b) Tracking squared runtimes via rewards on termination, corresponding to $\mathsf{wp}[\![S]\!](\tau^2)$.

```
while (b) {
  reward 1;
  S'
}
```

(c) Tracking runtimes via incremental rewards, corresponding to $\mathsf{ert}[\![S]\!](0)$.

Fig. 5. Three different reward models for tracking runtimes for a schematic program consisting of a single while loop. The runtime of interest is the number of times the loop body S' is executed. Only Fig. 5c tracks the runtime correctly, whereas Fig. 5a and 5b have the result zero for a diverging loop ($b = \texttt{true}$).

Unsoundness with Counter Variables. In Fig. 5a, the runtime is tracked in variable τ and the reward of τ is collected on termination of the program. However, for e.g. the infinite loop ($b = \texttt{true}$), the reward is zero, because the execution never reaches the `reward` τ statement. This technique is unsound [22].

An adaptation to track the second moment of the runtime is similarly deficient. Figure 5b is a programmatic version of an approach of the rt calculus from [20], developed to analyze covariances of runtimes.[4] It collects the reward τ^2 on termination. But e.g. for the infinite loop, the reward is again zero.

A sufficient condition for the soundness of the counter variable approach (for the first moment of runtimes) was shown in [38]: *almost-sure termination* (AST), which is termination with probability 1. Proving AST is undecidable [18], and we therefore aim for an approach that avoids such a strong side-condition.

Incremental Runtime Collection. The ert calculus [21,22] is an extension of wp to reason about expected runtimes for all – including non-AST – programs.[5] The key idea is to collect the reward in each loop iteration incrementally. Therefore, the reward is always incremented and diverging paths will collect infinite rewards. To avoid using yet another calculus, we leverage programmatic reward modeling, as shown in Fig. 5c. The approach is sound without side-conditions on termination.

Lemma 2 (Incremental Runtime Collection). *Let loop-free $S' \in \mathsf{pGCL}$ and $b \in \mathsf{BExp}$. Then, $\mathsf{wp}[\![\texttt{while}\ (b)\ \{\ \texttt{reward}\ 1;\ S'\ \}]\!] = \mathsf{ert}[\![\texttt{while}\ (b)\ \{\ S'\ \}]\!]$.*

Thus, to correctly track the expected runtime of a program, one should avoid counter variables and instead use the `reward` statement to collect the

[4] The rt calculus from [20] is distinct from its successor, the ert calculus [21,22].

[5] For simplicity, we consider the runtime model which counts loop iterations.

reward incrementally. Extending this approach to other objectives such as higher moments of runtimes is the goal of Sect. 4.

3.3 Ghost Variables for Reward Modeling

We now illustrate how using *ghost variables*, we can encode a variety of reward structures via the `reward` statement. Ghost variables are program variables that do not affect the program's functional behavior, but are used to aid verification. The term *ghost variable* is standard in deductive verification; they are also called auxiliary (or observation) variables. The counter variable approach presented just before is one such example. We present several gadgets for different quantitative objectives, indicated as program transformations $S \rightsquigarrow S'$. Assuming that ghost variables are initialized to 0; the result of $\mathsf{wp}[\![S']\!](0)$ is the desired reward.

Discounted Rewards. In some applications, future rewards are considered less valuable than immediate rewards. This is known as *discounting* [32]. We encode discounting with a ghost variable τ to track program steps, collecting rewards discounted by a factor $\gamma \in [0, 1]$ at each time step.

$$\texttt{reward}\ a \quad \rightsquigarrow \quad \texttt{reward}\ \gamma^{\tau} \cdot a;\ \tau := \tau + 1\ .$$

Step-Indexed Expected Values. We obtain *step-indexed* expected values, considered by e.g. [28], using a ghost variable τ to track program steps and a logical variable N for the step of interest:

$$\texttt{reward}\ a \quad \rightsquigarrow \quad \texttt{if}\ (\tau = N)\ \{\ \texttt{reward}\ a\ \};\ \tau := \tau + 1\ .$$

When instead condition $\tau \leq N$ is used, we track cumulative expected values up to step N. This allows reasoning about *long-run average rewards*, i.e. the limit of the average reward up to step N as N goes to infinity: $\limsup_{N \to \infty} {}^{1}\!/\!{}_{N} \cdot \mathsf{wp}[\![S]\!](0)$.

Expected Visiting Times. The wp calculus allows symbolic conditions $b \in \mathsf{BExp}$. This enables reasoning about *expected visiting times* (a.k.a. *occupation measures*), i.e. the expected number of times states satisfying b are visited during program execution.

$$S \quad \rightsquigarrow \quad S;\ \texttt{if}\ (b)\ \{\ \texttt{reward}\ 1\ \}$$

Once computed, further expected values of random variable X reduce to simple multiplication of X by the expected visiting time [35]. This has been successfully used in probabilistic model checking [27].

First Visit and Return Times. Similarly, gadgets to track the first visit time and first return time of a state satisfying condition $b \in \mathsf{BExp}$ can be built. The ghost variable ϕ stores whether this is the first visit/return.

- *First Visit:* $S \rightsquigarrow S$; `if` (b) { `reward` $[\phi = 0]$; $\phi := 1$ }
- *First Return:* $S \rightsquigarrow S$; `if` (b) { `reward` $[\phi = 1]$; $\phi := \min(\phi + 1, 2)$ }

4 Reward Transformations

We now consider *f-transformed cumulative rewards*, i.e. the expected value of some function f applied to the cumulative reward. Whereas it is simple to apply f to expected rewards *on termination* using the weakest pre-expectation calculus (Sect. 3.1), this is not the case for cumulative expected rewards (Sect. 3.2). Instead of defining yet another variation of wp, we propose a program transformation $\mathcal{T}_f(S)$ for monotone functions $f\colon \mathbb{R}^{\infty}_{\geq 0} \to \mathbb{R}^{\infty}_{\geq 0}$. The program S with expected reward $\mathsf{E}(\mathsf{rew}(S))$ is transformed to program $\mathcal{T}_f(S)$ whose expected reward is the f-transformed expected reward, i.e. $\mathsf{E}(\mathsf{rew}(\mathcal{T}_f(S))) = \mathsf{E}(f(\mathsf{rew}(S)))$.

Incremental Reward Updates. At the heart of the reward transformation is the idea of collecting f-transformed rewards incrementally, an idea inspired by the aert calculus [7]. A `reward` a statement simply adds a to the cumulative reward; if the current cumulative reward is τ, the new cumulative reward is $\tau + a$. For f-transformed cumulative rewards, the collected reward equals $f(\tau)$ and the new cumulative reward equals $f(\tau{+}a)$. The key idea is to (1) *subtract* the previous cumulative reward $f(\tau)$ and (2) *add* the new cumulative reward $f(\tau{+}a)$.

Consider the modeling of expected runtimes, where 1 reward is collected at each step. Then, the sequence of rewards that starts with $f(\tau)$ has the telescoping property and collapses to the final cumulative reward $f(\tau + N)$:[6]

$$\underbrace{f(\tau)}_{(0)\text{ previous}} + \sum_{i=0}^{N-1} \underbrace{-f(\tau + i)}_{(1)\text{ reset}} + \underbrace{f(\tau + i + 1)}_{(2)\text{ set}} = f(\tau + N)\,. \tag{1}$$

Since f is monotone, the difference $f(\tau + a) - f(\tau)$ is non-negative, and we can encode this change in the program via a `reward` statement.

4.1 Program Transformation

The program transformation is simple: we introduce a ghost variable τ to track the cumulative reward of the original program S and transform every `reward` a statement to collect the difference $f(\tau{+}a) - f(\tau)$. In the following, we denote by $f\colon \mathbb{R}^{\infty}_{\geq 0} \to \mathbb{R}^{\infty}_{\geq 0}$ a monotone function to ensure non-negative reward differences.

[6] We define $\infty - x = \infty$ for all $x \in \mathbb{R}^{\infty}_{\geq 0}$ (in particular $\infty - \infty = \infty$) so that the sum is infinite if any $f(\tau + i)$ is infinite.

```
τ := 0;
reward 0;
done := false;
while (¬done) {
    reward 2·τ + 1;
    τ := τ + 1;
    {done := true} [1/2] {skip}
}
```

(a) Transformed version of Figure 1a.

```
τ := 0;
reward 1/4;
done := false;
while (¬done) {
    reward 2·τ + 1;
    τ := τ + 1;
    {done := true} [2/3] {skip}
}
```

(b) Transformed version of Figure 1b.

Fig. 6. Transformations $\mathcal{T}_f(S)$ of programs S in Fig. 1 with $f(x) = x^2$.

Definition 1 (Reward Program Transformation). *Let $S \in \mathsf{pGCL}$ and τ be a fresh variable not occurring in S. The f-transformed program $\mathcal{T}_f(S)$ is*

$$\mathcal{T}_f(S) \quad = \quad \tau := 0;\ \texttt{reward}\ f(0);\ \mathcal{T}'_f(S)\ ,$$

where the auxiliary transformation $\mathcal{T}'_f(S)$ replaces `reward` *statements:*

$$\mathcal{T}'_f(\texttt{reward}\ a) \quad = \quad \texttt{reward}\ (f(\tau + a) - f(\tau));\ \tau := \tau + a\ ,$$

and other statements are left unchanged.

Figure 6 shows the transformations of the example programs from Fig. 1 using $f(x) = x^2$, where the highlighted statements originate from the transformation. For example, the `reward` 1 statement in Fig. 1a is transformed to `reward` $((\tau + 1)^2 - \tau^2);\ \tau := \tau + 1$ in Fig. 6a.

The expected reward of the transformed program $\mathcal{T}_f(S)$ is equal to the expected value of f applied to the reward of the original program S.

Theorem 1 (Soundness). *For $S \in \mathsf{pGCL}$ and monotone $f\colon \mathbb{R}^{\infty}_{\geq 0} \to \mathbb{R}^{\infty}_{\geq 0}$:*

$$\mathsf{E}(\mathsf{rew}(\mathcal{T}_f(S))) = \mathsf{E}(f(\mathsf{rew}(S)))\ .$$

In terms of weakest pre-expectation semantics, we can express Theorem 1 as $\mathsf{E}(\mathsf{rew}(\mathcal{T}_f(S))) = \mathsf{wp}[\![\mathcal{T}_f(S)]\!](0) = \mathsf{E}(f(\mathsf{rew}(S)))$. In particular, the wp semantics of the (auxiliary) transformation of a `reward` statement reflects the telescoping idea from Eq. 1. For an expectation $X \in \mathbb{E}$, we have:

$$\mathsf{wp}[\![\mathcal{T}'_f(\texttt{reward}\ a)]\!](X) \quad = \quad \lambda\sigma.\ \underbrace{f(\sigma(\tau) + a(\sigma))}_{(2)\ \text{set}} - \underbrace{f(\sigma(\tau))}_{(1)\ \text{reset}} + \underbrace{X(\sigma[\tau \mapsto \tau + a])}_{\text{next}}\ .$$

The program transformation preserves healthiness conditions similar to wp.

Theorem 2 (Monotonicity). *Let $S \in \mathsf{pGCL}$ and let $f, g\colon \mathbb{R}^{\infty}_{\geq 0} \to \mathbb{R}^{\infty}_{\geq 0}$ be monotone with $f \preceq g$. For all $X \in \mathbb{E}$, we have $\mathsf{wp}[\![\mathcal{T}_f(S)]\!](X) \preceq \mathsf{wp}[\![\mathcal{T}_g(S)]\!](X)$.*

The transformation is linear with respect to scaling and shifting.

Theorem 3 (Linearity). *Let $S \in \mathsf{pGCL}$ and let $f\colon \mathbb{R}^{\infty}_{\geq 0} \to \mathbb{R}^{\infty}_{\geq 0}$ be monotone. Then, for all $\alpha, \beta \in \mathbb{R}_{\geq 0}$, we have $\mathsf{wp}[\![\mathcal{T}_{\alpha \cdot f + \beta}(S)]\!](0) = \alpha \cdot \mathsf{wp}[\![\mathcal{T}_f(S)]\!](0) + \beta$.*

For linear transformation functions, we can avoid the ghost variable τ from the transformed program $\mathcal{T}_f(S)$ entirely.

Theorem 4 (Ghost Buster). *Let $f\colon \mathbb{R}^{\infty}_{\geq 0} \to \mathbb{R}^{\infty}_{\geq 0}$ be of the form $f(x) = \alpha \cdot x + \beta$ for some $\alpha, \beta \in \mathbb{R}_{\geq 0}$. Then,*

$$\mathcal{T}_f(S) \;=\; \texttt{reward}\ \beta\texttt{;}\ \mathcal{T}'_f(S) \qquad \textit{and} \qquad \mathcal{T}'_f(\texttt{reward}\ a) \;=\; \texttt{reward}\ \alpha \cdot a\ .$$

The transformation is well-behaved with respect to composition of transformation functions. In essence: $\mathcal{T}'_g(\mathcal{T}'_f(S)) = \mathcal{T}'_{g \circ f}(S)$, where the equality is to be understood modulo the variables introduced by the transformations.

Theorem 5 (Composition of Transformations). *Let $S \in \mathsf{pGCL}$ and let $f, g\colon \mathbb{R}^{\infty}_{\geq 0} \to \mathbb{R}^{\infty}_{\geq 0}$ be monotone. Assume that $\mathcal{T}'_f(\cdot)$ and $\mathcal{T}'_{g \circ f}(\cdot)$ use the same variable τ and $\mathcal{T}'_g(\cdot)$ uses a different variable τ'. Then,*

$$\mathsf{wp}[\![\tau' := f(\tau)\texttt{;}\ \mathcal{T}'_g(\mathcal{T}'_f(S))]\!] = \mathsf{wp}[\![\mathcal{T}'_{g \circ f}(S)\texttt{;}\ \tau' := f(\tau)]\!]\ .$$

4.2 Transforming Rewards of Markov Chains

To prove soundness of the program transformation (Theorem 1), we define a reward transformation for Markov chains directly. The state space is augmented with a dimension $\mathbb{R}^{\infty}_{\geq 0}$ to track the accumulated reward of the original Markov chain, which is zero in the initial state σ'_1, and the reward function is adjusted to collect the incremental differences. Here, we restrict to monotone f with $f(0) = 0$ for simplicity.

Definition 2 (MC Transformation). *Let MC $\mathcal{M} = (\mathsf{States}, \mathsf{Prob}, \sigma_1, \mathsf{rew})$ and monotone $f\colon \mathbb{R}^{\infty}_{\geq 0} \to \mathbb{R}^{\infty}_{\geq 0}$ with $f(0) = 0$.*[7]
We define $\mathcal{T}_f(\mathcal{M}) = (\mathsf{States} \times \mathbb{R}^{\infty}_{\geq 0},\ \mathsf{Prob}',\ \sigma'_1,\ \mathsf{rew}')$ where

- $\sigma'_1 = (\sigma_1, 0)$,
- $\mathsf{Prob}'((\sigma, \alpha), (\sigma', \alpha')) = \begin{cases} \mathsf{Prob}(\sigma)(\sigma') & \textit{if } \alpha + \mathsf{rew}(\sigma) = \alpha', \\ 0 & \textit{otherwise} \end{cases}$

[7] The restriction $f(0) = 0$ in $\mathcal{T}_f(\mathcal{M})$ can be easily lifted by using the function $g(x) = f(x) - f(0)$ for $\mathcal{T}_g(\mathcal{M})$, and prepending a new initial state σ'_0 with reward $f(0)$. The full construction is presented in [34].

- $\mathsf{rew}'((\sigma, \alpha)) = f(\alpha + \mathsf{rew}(\sigma)) - f(\alpha)$.

Note that the transformation does not preserve the size of the reachable state space, because the added dimension $\mathbb{R}^{\infty}_{\geq 0}$ tracks the reward accumulation.

Example 1 (Reachable States Explosion). Let MC $\mathcal{M} = (\mathsf{States}, \mathsf{Prob}, \sigma_1, \mathsf{rew})$ with $\mathsf{States} = \{\sigma_1\}$, $\mathsf{Prob}(\sigma_1)(\sigma_1) = 1$, $\mathsf{rew}(\sigma_1) = 1$. Let $f(x) = x$. The transformed MC $\mathcal{T}_f(\mathcal{M})$ has an infinite path $(\sigma_1, 0), (\sigma_1, 1), (\sigma_1, 2), \ldots$ with probability one. The set of reachable states is $\{ (\sigma_1, \alpha) \mid \alpha \in \mathbb{N} \}$, which is infinite.

The paths of the transformed Markov chain $\mathcal{T}_f(\mathcal{M})$ correspond one-to-one to the paths of the original $\mathcal{M}$, from which the soundness theorem follows.

Lemma 3. *Let MC* $\mathcal{M} = (\mathsf{States}, \mathsf{Prob}, \sigma_1, \mathsf{rew})$ *and* $f : \mathbb{R}^{\infty}_{\geq 0} \to \mathbb{R}^{\infty}_{\geq 0}$ *be monotone with* $f(0) = 0$*. Let* $n \in \mathbb{N}$*. For every* $\sigma_1 \ldots \sigma_n \in \mathsf{Paths}^{=n}_{\mathcal{M}}$*, there is a one-to-one mapping to* $(\sigma_1, \alpha_1) \ldots (\sigma_n, \alpha_n) \in \mathsf{Paths}^{=n}_{\mathcal{T}_f(\mathcal{M})}$ *in* $\mathcal{T}_f(\mathcal{M})$ *such that:*

1. *same path probabilities:* $\mathsf{Prob}(\sigma_1 \ldots \sigma_n) = \mathsf{Prob}'((\sigma_1, \alpha_1) \ldots (\sigma_n, \alpha_n))$,
2. α_i *track previous untransformed rewards:* $\forall 1 \leq i \leq n.\ \sum_{j<i} \mathsf{rew}(\sigma_j) = \alpha_i$,
3. *transformed rewards:* $f(\mathsf{rew}(\sigma_1 \ldots \sigma_n)) = \mathsf{rew}'((\sigma_1, \alpha_1) \ldots (\sigma_n, \alpha_n))$.

It follows that the expected f-transformed reward of the original Markov chain $\mathcal{M}$ equals the expected reward of the transformed Markov chain $\mathcal{T}_f(\mathcal{M})$.

Theorem 6 (Soundness). *For each MC* $\mathcal{M}$ *and monotone* f*:*

$$\mathsf{E}(f(\mathsf{rew}(\mathcal{M}))) = \mathsf{E}(\mathsf{rew}'(\mathcal{T}_f(\mathcal{M}))) \ .$$

Note that one can lift the monotonicity requirement of function f. For the soundness of the transformation, it suffices that $f(\tau + a) - f(\tau) \geq 0$ holds for all actually occurring values τ and a in the Markov chain.

5 Reward Transformation Functions

We apply the program transformation with different transformation functions f.

5.1 Higher Moments of Rewards

The *k-th moment* of random variable X is the expected value $\mathsf{E}(X^k)$. Choosing the transformation function $f(x) = x^k$ for some $k \in \mathbb{N}_{>0}$ yields higher moments of cumulative rewards. By Theorem 1, we have $\mathsf{E}(\mathsf{rew}(S)^k) = \mathsf{wp}[\![\mathcal{T}_f(S)]\!](0)$.

Example 2 (Variance of Web Server Runtime). We return to Fig. 6, which shows the transformations of the web server examples from Fig. 1 using $f(x) = x^2$, to obtain the second moment of the expected runtime. To calculate the expected reward, i.e. $\mathsf{wp}[\![S]\!](0)$ of Fig. 6a, we first tackle the loop. The wp of the loop w.r.t. post 0 is given by

$$\mathrm{lfp}\, X.\ [\neg done] \cdot ((2 \cdot \tau + 1) + 0.5 \cdot X[done \mapsto \mathtt{true}] + 0.5 \cdot X) + [done] \cdot 0.$$

It evaluates to $[\neg done] \cdot (4 \cdot \tau + 6)$. Applying wp to the remaining first three lines yields $\mathsf{wp}[\![\mathcal{T}_f(S)]\!] = 6$. Thus, the second moment of the expected reward of Fig. 1a is 6. Since the first moment is 2 (c.f. Sect. 2.3), the variance is $\mathrm{Var}(\mathsf{rew}(S)) = \mathsf{E}(\mathsf{rew}(S)^2) - (\mathsf{E}(\mathsf{rew}(S)))^2 = 6 - 2^2 = 2$.

Similarly, one can show that $\mathsf{wp}[\![S_{\text{loop}}]\!](0)$ of the loop in Fig. 6b is equal to $[\neg done] \cdot (3 \cdot (\tau - 0.5) + 4.5)$. Applying wp to the first three lines, we obtain $\mathsf{wp}[\![\mathcal{T}_f(S)]\!](0) = 4.75$, the second moment of the expected reward of Fig. 1b. The variance of the expected reward is $\mathrm{Var}(\mathsf{rew}(S)) = 4.75 - 2^2 = 0.75$.

Example 3 (Biased Random Walk). Consider a random walk starting at position $x > 1$ that moves two steps to the left with probability 0.75 and two steps to the right with probability 0.25 until it reaches position $x \leq 1$. The second moment is upper-bounded by $x^2 + 3 \cdot x$, which we verified using the program transformation and wp reasoning.

5.2 Cumulative Distribution Functions

We can use $f(x) = [x \geq N]$ for some $N \in \mathbb{N}$ to compute the cumulative distribution function (CDF) of the expected rewards.

Example 4 (CDF of Web Server Runtime). To obtain the CDF for Fig. 1a, we transform it with $f(x) = [x \geq N]$:

$\tau := 0;$ `reward` $[0 \geq N]$; $done :=$ `false`;

`while` $(\neg done)$ {

`reward` $[\tau + 1 \geq N] - [\tau \geq N]$; $\tau := \tau + 1$; $\{done :=$ `true`$\}$ $[1/2]$ $\{$`skip`$\}$ }

Note that one may simplify the `reward` statement to `reward` $[\tau + 1 = N]$. For the CDF, we get $\mathsf{wp}[\![\mathcal{T}_f(S)]\!](0) = 0.5^{N \ominus 1}$, where $a \ominus b = \max(0, a - b)$.

5.3 Expected Excess

Consider a fixed budget $N \in \mathbb{R}_{\geq 0}$ and the objective is to determine how much the cumulative reward exceeds this budget in expectation. The following example shows that we can use our program transformation to compute the *expected excess* of a loop's runtime, i.e. $\mathsf{E}((\mathsf{rew}(S) \ominus N))$ for all $N \in \mathbb{R}_{\geq 0}$.

Example 5 Loop Splitting for Expected Excess. We compute the expected excess of the web server program from Fig. 1a, depending on a success probability $p \in [0, 1]$ of a database call and a budget $N \in \mathbb{N}$. Applying the transformation with $f(x) = x \ominus N$ yields, after simplification[8], the following:

$\tau := 0$; $done :=$ `false`;

`while` $(\neg done)$ { `reward` $[\tau \geq N]$; $\tau := \tau + 1$; $\{done :=$ `true`$\}$ $[p]$ $\{$`skip`$\}$ }

[8] We use that $(((\tau + 1) \ominus N) - (\tau \ominus N))$ is equal to $[\tau \geq N]$.

Now, it is not difficult to see that the loop runs in two phases. The first phase runs until the runtime is below N, collecting no reward, and the second phase collects the excess of the runtime. Splitting the loop in two loops yields:

$$\tau := 0;\ \mathit{done} := \texttt{false};$$
$$\texttt{while}\ (\neg \mathit{done} \wedge (\tau < N))\ \{\ \tau := \tau + 1;\ \{\mathit{done} := \texttt{true}\}\ [p]\ \{\texttt{skip}\}\ \};$$
$$\texttt{while}\ (\neg \mathit{done})\ \{\ \texttt{reward}\ 1;\ \tau := \tau + 1;\ \{\mathit{done} := \texttt{true}\}\ [p]\ \{\texttt{skip}\}\ \}$$

The second loop has an expected reward of $1/p$ if $\mathit{done} = \texttt{false}$, otherwise 0. Formally: $\mathsf{wp}[\![\mathit{loop2}]\!](0) = [\neg \mathit{done}] \cdot 1/p$. The probability that the first loop terminates with $\mathit{done} = \texttt{false}$ is $(1-p)^N$. Formally: $\mathsf{wp}[\![S]\!](0) = \mathsf{wp}[\![\mathit{loop1}]\!](\mathsf{wp}[\![\mathit{loop2}]\!](0)) = (1-p)^N/p$, which is the expected excess of the runtime over threshold N. For example, if $p = 0.1$ and $N = 10$, the expected excess is $(1-0.1)^{10}/0.1 \approx 3.486$.

5.4 Moment-Generating Functions

A *moment-generating function* of a random variable X is given by $\mathsf{E}(e^{t \cdot X})$ for $t \in \mathbb{R}_{\geq 0}$ [12]. They can be used to obtain *all* moments of X by differentiating the MGF at $t = 0$. With $f(x) = e^{t \cdot x}$, our reward transformation yields MGFs.[9]

Example 6 (MGF of a Randomized Assignment). Consider the program $S = \{x := 1\}\ [p]\ \{x := 0\};\ \texttt{reward}\ x$. Let $f(x) = e^{t \cdot x}$. One can show $\mathsf{wp}[\![\mathcal{T}_f(S)]\!](0) = (p \cdot (e^{t \cdot (\tau+1)} - e^{t \cdot \tau}) + e^{t \cdot \tau})[\tau \mapsto 0] = p \cdot e^t + (1-p)$. The n-th derivative at $t = 0$ yields the n-th moment: $\mathsf{E}(X^n) = p$ for all $n \in \mathbb{N}_{>0}$.

5.5 Multiple Rewards

Sometimes, it is useful to track multiple rewards simultaneously and aggregate them into a single reward. In some cloud computing platforms, for example, pricing is based on the product of the *runtime* and *memory consumption* [2].

Our transformation can be generalized to a multi-reward setting by introducing multiple reward variables τ_i. The generalized reward statements assign multiple rewards at once, e.g. $\texttt{reward}\ (a_1, a_2)$ assigns reward a_1 to reward 1 and reward a_2 to reward 2. The transformation $\mathcal{T}'_f(S)$ is generalized to $f\colon (\mathbb{R}^{\infty}_{\geq 0})^n \to \mathbb{R}^{\infty}_{\geq 0}$ that maps n rewards to a single reward:

$$\mathcal{T}'_f(\texttt{reward}\ (a_1, \ldots, a_n)) = \texttt{reward}\ f(\tau_1 + a_1, \ldots, \tau_n + a_n) - f(\tau_1, \ldots, \tau_n);$$
$$\tau_1 := \tau_1 + a_1;\ \ldots;\ \tau_n := \tau_n + a_n$$

[9] MGFs are similar to *probability-generating functions* (PGFs), recently used for inference in probabilistic programs [10,24,39]. However, $f(x) = X^x$ for PGFs is not monotone for $X < 1$ and our transformation is not applicable.

Example 7 (Expected Cost with Runtime and Memory Consumption). Consider a program starting with two units of memory and computation each. With probability p it needs more computation, for this, it requests an additional unit of memory with probability q. We can write this as a program, apply our transformation with $f(\tau_1, \tau_2) = \tau_1 \cdot \tau_2$ (modeling cost as product of runtime and memory), and compute the expected cost. The result is $\mathsf{wp}[\![\mathcal{T}_f(S)]\!](0) = 4 + (p \cdot (2 + (q \cdot 3)))$.

6 Automation

The off-the-shelf *Caesar* deductive verifier for probabilistic programs [33] was used, which supports `reward` statements and implements various proof rules for reasoning about lower and upper bounds of expected rewards. One example is the *induction proof rule* [17,31], to verify *upper bounds* $I \in X$ on $\mathsf{wp}[\![S]\!](X)$ for $S = \texttt{while}\ (b)\ \{\ S\ \}$ and $X \in \mathbb{E}$, where I is a user-provided loop invariant:

$$[b] \cdot \mathsf{wp}[\![S]\!](I) + [\neg b] \cdot X \sqsubseteq I \quad \text{implies} \quad \mathsf{wp}[\![\texttt{while}\ (b)\ \{\ S\ \}]\!](X) \sqsubseteq I\ .$$

We provide Caesar input files for examples in Sect. 5 in [34], verifying upper bounds on expected rewards using the induction proof rule. In addition, Caesar supports analysis of (finite) operational semantics with integer variables via the probabilistic model checker *Storm* [15]. For infinite-state operational semantics (c.f. Fig. 3), Storm can under-approximate the expected value.

7 Related Work

Expected Run-Time Analysis. In Sect. 3.2, we discussed the lack of support for e.g. higher moments of the ert calculus [21,22]. The same problems apply to the *amortized expected runtime calculus* [7], which extends the ert calculus to reason about potential functions, see [34] for details. Automated inference of ert-style run-times has been studied e.g. in [30]. We assume non-negative rewards; analyses for mixed-sign rewards include [9,37]. As a complimentary approach, [1] propose asymptotic bounds for run-time analysis instead of expected values.

Higher Moments. Kaminski et al. aim to reason about covariances of probabilistic programs [20]. They define a semantics called rt that increments a dedicated runtime variable τ by one for each statement executed and consider the expected value of τ^k on termination. However, as explained in Sect. 3.2, this approach is deficient for diverging programs. Kura et al. [23] focus on tail probabilities of run-times and make use of higher moments to obtain bounds on them. They synthesize upper bounds on the k-th moment via template-based invariants. In [36], Wang et al. present an automated approach for the inference of higher moments of expected runtimes of probabilistic programs. As for the previous approach, proof rules have to be proven specifically for their semantics. Lower bounds are also considered and used to derive central moments. Their approach is automated, and uses template-based invariant synthesis for interval bounds. Algebraic methods for higher moments of step-indexed expected value have been used in [28]. On programs with certain restrictions, e.g. acyclic non-linear variable dependencies and variables in conditions only assuming finitely many values, they can compute closed-form solutions for all moments. Hardness results for higher moments of step-indexed expected values are presented in [29].

8 Conclusion

We presented probabilistic programs with reward statements to obtain a one-fits-all approach for analyzing multiple objectives, e.g. expected runtimes, expected visiting times, higher moments of expected rewards, or the expected excess over a threshold. All reduce to the "classical" wp calculus, eliminating the need for dedicated calculi/semantics for each objective. Therefore, existing proof rules and tools for wp can be reused in our setting. Future work includes the incorporation of programs with non-determinism; programmatic reward modeling works in this setting as well, but the reward transformation introduces additional subtleties due to additional information introduced by the counter variable τ.

Acknowledgments. This work was partially supported by the ERC POC Grant VERIPROB (grant no. 101158076) and by the European Union's Horizon 2020 research and innovation programme under the Marie Skłodowska-Curie grant agreement MISSION (grant no. 101008233).

References

1. Ajdarów, M., Kučcera, A., Novotný, P.: Asymptotic analysis of probabilistic programs: when expectations do not meet our expectations. In: Jansen, N., et al. (eds) Principles of Verification: Cycling the Probabilistic Landscape: Essays Dedicated to Joost-Pieter Katoen on the Occasion of His 60th Birthday, Part I, pp. 85–97. Springer, Cham (2025). https://doi.org/10.1007/978-3-031-75783-9_4
2. Amazon Web Services: AWS Lambda Pricing. https://aws.amazon.com/lambda/pricing/. Accessed 1 Dec 2025
3. Avanzini, M., Moser, G., Schaper, M.: A modular cost analysis for probabilistic programs. Proc. ACM Program. Lang. **4**(OOPSLA), 172:1–172:30 (2020). https://doi.org/10.1145/3428240
4. Batz, K., Chen, M., Kaminski, B.L., Katoen, JP., Matheja, C., Schröer, P.: Latticed k-induction with an application to probabilistic programs. In: A. Silva and K.R.M. Leino. Computer Aided Verification - 33rd International Conference, CAV 2021, Virtual Event, July 20–23, 2021, Proceedings, Part II. LNCS, vol. 12760, pp. 524–549. Springer, Cham (2021). https://doi.org/10.1007/978-3-030-81688-9_25
5. Batz, K., Kaminski, B.L., Katoen, JP., Matheja, C.: How long, –O Bayesian network, will –I sample thee? –A program analysis perspective on expected sampling times. In: Ahmed, A. (ed.) Programming Languages and Systems - 27th European Symposium on Programming, ESOP 2018, Held as Part of the European Joint Conferences on Theory and Practice of Software, ETAPS 2018, Thessaloniki, Greece, April 14–20, 2018, Proceedings. LNCS, vol. 10801, pp. 186–213. Springer, Cham (2018). https://doi.org/10.1007/978-3-319-89884-1_7

6. Batz, K., Kaminski, B.L., Katoen, J., Matheja, C.: Relatively complete verification of probabilistic programs: an expressive language for expectation-based reasoning. Proc. ACM Program. Lang. **5**(POPL), 1–30 (2021). https://doi.org/10.1145/3434320
7. Batz, K., Kaminski, B.L., Katoen, J., Matheja, C., Verscht, L.: A calculus for amortized expected runtimes. Proc. ACM Program. Lang. **7**(POPL), 1957–1986 (2023). https://doi.org/10.1145/3571260
8. Batz, K., Kaminski, B.L., Matheja, C., Winkler, T.: J-P: MDP. FP. PP: characterizing total expected rewards in Markov decision processes as least fixed points with an application to operational semantics of probabilistic programs. In: Jansen, N., et al. (eds.) Principles of Verification: Cycling the Probabilistic Landscape - Essays Dedicated to Joost-Pieter Katoen on the Occasion of His 60th Birthday, Part I. LNCS, vol. 15260, pp. 255–302. Springer, Heidelberg (2024). https://doi.org/10.1007/978-3-031-75783-9_11
9. Chatterjee, K., Goharshady, A.K., Meggendorfer, T., Žikelić, U.: Quantitative bounds on resource usage of probabilistic programs. Proc. ACM Program. Lang. **8**(OOPSLA1) (2024). https://doi.org/10.1145/3649824
10. Chen, M., Katoen, J., Klinkenberg, L., Winkler, T.: Does a program yield the right distribution? - verifying probabilistic programs via generating functions. In: Shoham, S., Vizel, Y. (eds.) Computer Aided Verification - 34th International Conference, CAV 2022, Haifa, Israel, August 7–10, 2022, Proceedings, Part I. LNCS, vol. 13371, pp. 79–101. Springer, Heidelberg (2022). https://doi.org/10.1007/978-3-031-13185-1_5
11. Feng, S., Chen, M., Su, H., Kaminski, B.L., Katoen, J., Zhan, N.: Lower bounds for possibly divergent probabilistic programs. Proc. ACM Program. Lang. **7**(OOPSLA1), 696–726 (2023). https://doi.org/10.1145/3586051
12. Fristedt, B., and Gray, L.: A Modern Introduction to Probability Theory. In: Probability and Its Applications. Birkhauser Verlag AG, Basel, Switzerland (1996)
13. Gretz, F., Katoen, J., McIver, A.: Operational versus weakest pre-expectation semantics for the probabilistic guarded command language. Perform. Eval. **73**, 110–132 (2014). https://doi.org/10.1016/J.PEVA.2013.11.004
14. Hark, M., Kaminski, B.L., Giesl, J., Katoen, J.: Aiming low is harder: induction for lower bounds in probabilistic program verification. Proc. ACM Program. Lang. **4**(POPL), 37:1–37:28 (2020). https://doi.org/10.1145/3371105
15. Hensel, C., Junges, S., Katoen, J., Quatmann, T., Volk, M.: The probabilistic model checker Storm. Int. J. Softw. Tools Technol. Transf. **24**(4), 589–610 (2022). https://doi.org/10.1007/S10009-021-00633-Z
16. Hurd, J., McIver, A., Morgan, C.: Probabilistic guarded commands mechanized in HOL. Theor. Comput. Sci. **346**(1), 96–112 (2005). https://doi.org/10.1016/J.TCS.2005.08.005
17. Kaminski, B.L.: Advanced weakest precondition calculi for probabilistic programs. Ph. D. thesis, RWTH Aachen University, Germany (2019). https://doi.org/10.18154/RWTH-2019-01829
18. Kaminski, B.L., Katoen, J.: On the hardness of almost-sure termination. In: Italiano, G.F., Pighizzini, G., Sannella, D. (eds.) Mathematical Foundations of Computer Science 2015 - 40th International Symposium, MFCS 2015, Milan, Italy, August 24–28, 2015, Proceedings, Part I. LNCS, vol. 9234, pp. 307–318. Springer, Heidelberg (2015). https://doi.org/10.1007/978-3-662-48057-1_24

19. Kaminski, B.L., Katoen, J., Matheja, C.: Expected runtime analyis by program verification. In: Barthe, G., Katoen, J., Silva, A. (eds.) Foundations of Probabilistic Programming, pp. 185–220. Cambridge University Press (2020). https://doi.org/10.1017/9781108770750.007
20. Kaminski, B.L., Katoen, J. Matheja, C.: Inferring covariances for probabilistic programs. In: Agha, G., Houdt, B.V.(eds.) Quantitative Evaluation of Systems - 13th International Conference, QEST 2016, Quebec City, QC, Canada, August 23–25, 2016, Proceedings. LNCS, vol. 9826, pp. 191–206. Springer, Heidelberg (2016). https://doi.org/10.1007/978-3-319-43425-4_14
21. Kaminski, B.L., Katoen, J., Matheja, C., Olmedo, F.: Weakest precondition reasoning for expected run-times of probabilistic programs. In: Thiemann, P.(ed.) Programming Languages and Systems - 25th European Symposium on Programming, ESOP 2016, Held as Part of the European Joint Conferences on Theory and Practice of Software, ETAPS 2016, Eindhoven, The Netherlands, April 2–8, 2016, Proceedings. LNCS, vol. 9632, pp. 364–389. Springer, Heidelberg (2016). https://doi.org/10.1007/978-3-662-49498-1_15
22. Kaminski, B.L., Katoen, J., Matheja, C., Olmedo, F.: Weakest precondition reasoning for expected runtimes of randomized algorithms. J. ACM **65**(5), 30:1–30:68 (2018). https://doi.org/10.1145/3208102
23. Kura, S., Urabe, N., Hasuo, I.: Tail probabilities for randomized program runtimes via martingales for higher moments. In: Vojnar, T., Zhang, L. (eds.) Tools and Algorithms for the Construction and Analysis of Systems - 25th International Conference, TACAS 2019, Held as Part of the European Joint Conferences on Theory and Practice of Software, ETAPS 2019, Prague, Czech Republic, April 6–11, 2019, Proceedings, Part II. LNCS, vol. 11428, pp. 135–153. Springer, Heidelberg (2019). https://doi.org/10.1007/978-3-030-17465-1_8
24. Li, J., Zhang, Y.: Compiling with generating functions. Proc. ACM Program. Lang. **9**(ICFP) (2025). https://doi.org/10.1145/3747534
25. McIver, A., Morgan, C.: Abstraction, Refinement and Proof for Probabilistic Systems. Springer (2005). https://doi.org/10.1007/0-387-27006-X_2
26. McIver, A., Morgan, C., Kaminski, B.L., Katoen, J.: A new proof rule for almost-sure termination. Proc. ACM Program. Lang. **2**(POPL), 33:1–33:28 (2018). https://doi.org/10.1145/3158121
27. Mertens, H., Katoen, J., Quatmann, T., Winkler, T.: Computing expected visiting times and stationary distributions in markov chains: fast and accurate. J. Autom. Reason. **69**(3), 23 (2025). https://doi.org/10.1007/S10817-025-09736-7
28. Moosbrugger, M., Stankovic, M., Bartocci, E., Kovács, L.: This is the moment for probabilistic loops. Proc. ACM Program. Lang. **6**(OOPSLA2), 1497–1525 (2022). https://doi.org/10.1145/3563341
29. Müllner, J., Moosbrugger, M., Kovács, L.: Strong invariants are hard: on the hardness of strongest polynomial invariants for (probabilistic) Programs. Proc. ACM Program. Lang. **8**(POPL), 882–910 (2024). https://doi.org/10.1145/3632872
30. Ngo, V.C., Carbonneaux, Q., Hoffmann, J.: Bounded expectations: resource analysis for probabilistic programs. In: Foster, J.S., Grossman, D. (eds.) Proceedings of the 39th ACM SIGPLAN Conference on Programming Language Design and Implementation, PLDI 2018, Philadelphia, PA, USA, June 18–22, 2018, pp. 496–512. ACM (2018). https://doi.org/10.1145/3192366.3192394
31. Park, D.: Fixpoint induction and proofs of program properties. Mach. Intell. **5** (1969)

32. Puterman, M.L.: Markov Decision Processes: Discrete Stochastic Dynamic Programming. Wiley Series in Probability and Statistics. Wiley (1994). https://doi.org/10.1002/9780470316887
33. Schröer, P., Batz, K., Kaminski, B.L., Katoen, J., Matheja, C.: A deductive verification infrastructure for probabilistic programs. Proc. ACM Program. Lang. **7**(OOPSLA2), 2052–2082 (2023). https://doi.org/10.1145/3622870
34. Schröer, P., Katoen, J.-P.: Highly incremental: a simple programmatic approach for many objectives (extended version) (2026)
35. Sharir, M., Pnueli, A., Hart, S.: Verification of probabilistic programs. SIAM J. Comput. **13**(2), 292–314 (1984). https://doi.org/10.1137/0213021
36. Wang, D., Hoffmann, J., Reps, T.W.: Central moment analysis for cost accumulators in probabilistic programs. In: Freund, S.N., Yahav, E. (eds.) PLDI 2021: 42nd ACM SIGPLAN International Conference on Programming Language Design and Implementation, Virtual Event, Canada, June 20–25, 2021, pp. 559–573. ACM (2021). https://doi.org/10.1145/3453483.3454062
37. Wang, P., Fu, H., Goharshady, A.K., Chatterjee, K., Qin, X., Shi, W.: Cost analysis of nondeterministic probabilistic programs. In: Proceedings of the 40th ACM SIGPLAN Conference on Programming Language Design and Implementation. PLDI 2019, pp. 204–220. Association for Computing Machinery, Phoenix, AZ, USA (2019). https://doi.org/10.1145/3314221.3314581
38. Winkler, T.: A Note on the Expected Runtime of Discrete Probabilistic While Loops (Personal Note) (2023)
39. Zaiser, F., Murawski, A.S., Ong, C.L.: Exact bayesian inference on discrete models via probability generating functions: a probabilistic programming approach. In: Oh, A., Naumann, T., Globerson, A., Saenko, K., Hardt, M., Levine, S. (eds.) Advances in Neural Information Processing Systems 36: Annual Conference on Neural Information Processing Systems 2023, NeurIPS 2023, New Orleans, LA, USA, December 10 – 16, 2023 (2023)

QSeqSim: A Symbolic Simulator for Qiskit While Loops Using Sequential Quantum Circuits (Long Tool Paper)

Zihao Li[1,2], Ji Guan[1(✉)], and Mingsheng Ying[3]

[1] Key Laboratory of System Software (Chinese Academy of Sciences), Institute of Software, Chinese Academy of Sciences, Beijing 100190, China
{lizh,guanj}@ios.ac.cn
[2] University of Chinese Academy of Sciences, Beijing 101408, China
[3] Centre for Quantum Software and Information, University of Technology Sydney, Ultimo, NSW 2007, Australia
Mingsheng.Ying@uts.edu.au

Abstract. We present a tool *QSeqSim*, a Qiskit-integrated symbolic backend that fills the current gap of having no Qiskit-native support for simulating `while`-loop quantum programs and their induced sequential quantum circuits. *QSeqSim* takes Qiskit `QuantumCircuit` objects, translates them into OpenQASM 3 code, and organises the resulting program into a combination of combinational, dynamic, and sequential circuits, thereby assigning `while`-loops a precise sequential circuit semantics with explicit internal and external qubits. Building on this semantics, *QSeqSim* adopts a Binary Decision Diagram (BDD)-based symbolic representation and integrates weighted model counting to compute measurement probabilities efficiently by exploiting sharing in structured and sparse BDDs. On top of this Boolean backbone, it introduces dedicated symbolic operators for quantum state composition and state retention, thereby enabling efficient symbolic execution of sequential quantum circuits. Our experiments demonstrate that *QSeqSim* scales to substantial `while`-induced sequential circuits; in particular, in the quantum random walk benchmark we successfully simulate circuits with over 1000 qubits for more than 10 loop iterations.

QSeqSim is available at https://github.com/Veri-Q/QSeqSim.

Keywords: Quantum circuit simulation · Symbolic simulation · Sequential quantum circuits · Boolean operations · Formal methods

1 Introduction

The formal methods community has devoted substantial effort to the analysis and verification of quantum circuits and programs, both at the foundational level and in the form of automated tools. There is now a considerable body of work on quantum Hoare logic [26,40,44,48], as well as on other quantum program logics, deductive verification and semantics for languages with measurements and classical control [34,46]. On the circuit side, equivalence checking

A. Sampaio and M. Stoelinga (Eds.): FM 2026, LNCS 16556, pp. 578–598, 2026.
https://doi.org/10.1007/978-3-032-26204-2_30

and optimisation techniques based on decision diagrams [6,8,39,42,43,49], ZX-calculus [25,32], tree automata [9–11], and model counting [27,28,33] have been developed, and model checking and abstract-interpretation approaches for quantum and probabilistic systems have also been investigated [15,16,31,45].

In parallel with these developments, Qiskit [22], one of the most widely used quantum programming frameworks, has recently enriched the traditional circuit model with classical control, allowing users to express quantum algorithms with high-level constructs such as conditional branches (`if`/`else`, `switch`) and loops (`for`, `while`). In particular, the availability of `while`-loops makes it possible to encode measurement-controlled iteration patterns such as repeat-until-success (RUS) schemes [5,30], weakly measured variants of Grover's search [3], and quantum random walks with feedback [24]. At the level of abstract syntax, this brings mainstream quantum programming closer to the control-flow constructs long studied in quantum programming languages [34] and quantum Hoare logics [44].

On the execution side, however, the situation is markedly less mature:

At present, there is no Qiskit-native tool that can simulate Qiskit `while`*-loop programs.*

Qiskit-Aer, the default simulator in the Qiskit ecosystem, currently *does not* support the `while`-loop construct at all. In particular, attempting to run the official Qiskit API examples that use `QuantumCircuit.while_loop` through Aer results in parsing or compilation errors, indicating that such control flow cannot be lowered to a circuit that Aer is able to simulate. A similar limitation holds for the Qiskit cloud backends: when submitting circuits that contain `while`-loop constructs, the service explicitly reports that the available real-device backends *do not* support `while`-loop constructs. In other words, although Qiskit and OpenQASM 3 [13] expose `while`-loops at the programming and IR levels, neither the standard Qiskit simulator nor the current hardware backends can execute these constructs, and there is, at present, no Qiskit-native execution engine that realises the intended iterative semantics of non-trivial `while`-loop programs.

To bridge this gap, we present *QSeqSim*, a symbolic simulation backend for Qiskit programs with classical control, with a particular emphasis on `while`-loop–induced sequential behaviour. On the semantic side, we interpret Qiskit `while`-loops as *sequential quantum circuits (SQCs)* with an explicit partition into external and internal qubits, thereby making precise the notion of quantum state feedback across loop iterations. On the algorithmic side, we build on a BDD-based representation of quantum circuits [39] and extend it from purely combinational circuits to programs with structured control flow: `if`/`switch` constructs are treated as dynamic circuits with mid-circuit measurements, `for` loops with static bounds as repeated combinational circuits, and `while` loops as sequential circuits. At the Boolean level, we introduce new symbolic operators for *state composition* and *state retention*, which model how external inputs are combined with the current internal state and how the post-measurement internal state is fed back into the next iteration. These operators are integrated with existing Boolean gate update rules and a Boolean mid-circuit measurement operator into a unified BDD-based engine that executes mixed combinational, dynamic, and sequential fragments according to a small-step operational semantics, while systematically exploiting weighted model counting [7] techniques to carry out probability computation efficiently on structured and sparse BDDs.

Contributions. This paper makes the following main contributions.

1. *First Qiskit backend with direct* `while`*-loop support.* We present *QSeqSim*, to the best of our knowledge, the first backend that directly executes Qiskit programs containing `while`-loops, by lowering them to OpenQASM 3 and giving an executable small-step semantics for the resulting control flow.
2. *From combinational to sequential Boolean models. QSeqSim* extends a BDD-based encoding of combinational quantum circuits [39] with symbolic operators for state composition and retention, lifting the Boolean model from purely combinational to sequential circuits so as to support `while`-loops.
3. *Efficient and scalable symbolic simulation of* `while`*-loop programs (SQCs).* Leveraging mature BDD backends and model-counting techniques for efficient probability evaluation, *QSeqSim* symbolically simulates quantum circuits induced by `while`-loops, scaling beyond existing tools [9,41].

1.1 Related Work

Quantum Programming Backends. A rich ecosystem of quantum programming frameworks and simulators has emerged in recent years, including general-purpose stacks such as Qiskit [22], Cirq [12], ProjectQ [36], CUDA-Q [38], and Amazon Braket [17], as well as specialised high-performance simulators like QuEST [23], Qulacs [37], and Intel-QS (IQS) [20]. However, there remains a clear gap between the expressiveness of modern quantum programming models and the capabilities of current execution backends. On the language side, Qiskit has recently enriched its model with high-level classical control constructs such as `if_else`, `for_loop`, and in particular `while_loop`, enabling natural encodings of measurement-controlled iteration patterns. On the backend side, however, mainstream backends effectively lack native support for `while`-loops: Qiskit-Aer cannot currently execute `QuantumCircuit.while_loop`, and Qiskit's cloud hardware backends likewise report `while`-loops as unsupported. *QSeqSim* is designed to fill precisely this gap. Starting from `QuantumCircuit` objects, it translates circuits to OpenQASM 3, assigns the resulting programs a sequential-circuit semantics, and uses a BDD-based engine to execute `while`-loop programs at a scale that makes it suitable as an efficient backend.

Simulation Techniques for Quantum Circuits. There is also extensive work in the formal methods community on the simulation of quantum circuits [8,10,11,25,27,39,42,49]. However, these approaches remain essentially confined to combinational and very limited dynamic settings; they do not extend their models to *sequential quantum circuits* with explicit state feedback, and thus cannot support the Qiskit `while`-loop construct. *QSeqSim* builds directly on the Boolean framework of [39], and further integrates weighted model counting for probability queries, while also extending the framework with new symbolic operators for state composition and state retention. This yields a unified BDD-based engine that can simulate, within a single Qiskit program, combinational, dynamic, and sequential fragments and thereby natively support `while`-loop induced sequential behaviour.

2 Background

This section provides the necessary background on Qiskit, OpenQASM 3, and SQCs that underpins our semantics and implementation.

Figure 1 structures Qiskit `while`-loop programs into a three-stage pipeline that encompasses the programming language layer, intermediate representation layer, and circuit layer. It also maps each quantum stage to a well-known classical counterpart, allowing the quantum components to be understood through direct comparison with their classical equivalents.

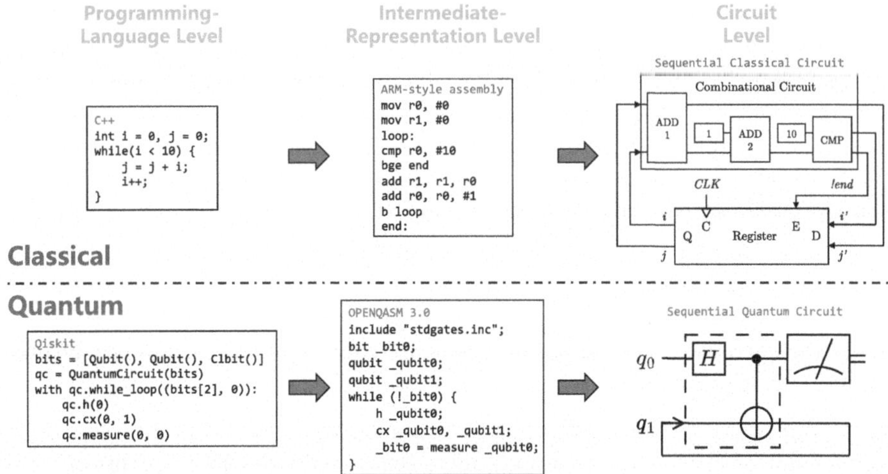

Fig. 1. Classical–quantum analogy from programs to IRs to circuits.

Programming-Language Level. In the top left of Fig. 1, a C++ `while` loop over integers (i, j) is the programmer-facing description of an iterative computation. In the bottom left, the Qiskit code shows a concrete quantum analogue: a RUS implementation of the X gate. Here, the `QuantumCircuit.while_loop` construct repeatedly invokes a small quantum subroutine and measures qubit q_0 to obtain a classical outcome; the loop terminates only when this measurement result is 1, at which point the target qubit q_1 has effectively been subjected to an X operation. This example illustrates how Qiskit `while`-loops are used in practice to express measurement-controlled iteration patterns.

Intermediate-Representation (IR) Level. The C++ `while` loop is then compiled to an ARM-style assembly fragment (top middle of Fig. 1). This assembly is a control-flow oriented IR that is easier to analyse and further compile than the original C++. Similarly, Qiskit compiles the Python-level program to an *internal* IR represented by a `QuantumCircuit` object. This object records the gates, measurements, and classical control structure in a uniform form. From there, Qiskit can export an *external* IR in the form of OpenQASM 3 code [13,29] (bottom middle of Fig. 1): a quantum assembly language with a formally defined syntax and semantics. In this work we treat OpenQASM 3, in the restricted fragment generated by Qiskit, as the semantic interface for `QuantumCircuit`.

Circuit Level. On the classical side (top right of Fig. 1), the ARM-style assembly fragment is implemented as a *sequential classical circuit*: a combinational logic block composed of standard components such as adders (ADD) and a comparator (CMP), together with a register and feedback wires. On the quantum side (bottom right of Fig. 1), we obtain the analogous notion of a *sequential quantum circuit*. The dashed box is the loop body: in this example it is a fixed subcircuit consisting of a Hadamard on q_0 followed by a controlled-X from q_0 to q_1, and one pass through this box corresponds to a single loop iteration. After the body, q_0 is measured and the outcome is used as the loop guard: a result of 0 triggers another iteration, whereas a result of 1 terminates the loop, exactly mirroring the role of the comparator in the sequential classical circuit. The wire for q_1 passes through the body and feeds back to its input, indicating that the quantum state on q_1 is preserved and updated across iterations, in direct analogy with the classical register that stores i and j.

3 Implementation Challenges

Filling the current gap of having no Qiskit-native tool that can simulate `while`-loop programs raises three main specific challenges.

Challenge 1: Matching Qiskit `while`*-loops with sequential semantics.* From the circuit point of view, a `while`-loop induces sequential behaviour: quantum state is fed back from one iteration to the next, and the guard is evaluated from intermediate measurement outcomes. The sequential quantum circuit (SQC) model of Wang et al. [41] captures this by iterating a fixed block over *external* and *internal* qubits, with only the external ones measured each round. Realistic Qiskit `while`-loops, however, both exceed and restrict this abstraction: their loop bodies may contain mid-circuit measurements and nested `if`/`else` branches not covered by the original SQC definition, yet they arise from concrete `QuantumCircuit` programs and do not exploit arbitrary per-iteration external inputs.

Our Approach. We adopt a Qiskit-oriented generalisation of SQCs with an explicit split between internal and external qubits and treat each `while`-loop body as a fixed dynamic subcircuit with mid-circuit measurements and classical control, executed unchanged in every iteration. This generalised SQC view is realised concretely by the CQC/DQC/SQC decomposition of the *Parser* and the small-step operational semantics implemented by the *Simulator* (Sect. 4, the *Parser* and Algorithm 1).

Challenge 2: *Symbolic simulation of sequential quantum circuits.* Even with a suitable semantics and IR, simulating `while`-loops with internal measurements and branches remains difficult. Sequential circuits involve feedback across iterations, entangled internal state, and dynamic bodies with nested `if`/`else` depending on mid-circuit outcomes. Naive statevector simulation scales poorly in both qubits and iterations, and existing decision-diagram-based techniques mostly target combinational or, at best, non-feedback dynamic circuits; they do not extend their models to general sequential behaviour with explicit state feedback.

Our Approach. Building on the BDD-based Boolean encoding of [39], we extend the symbolic model from purely combinational circuits to general SQCs by introducing operators for state composition and state retention, and by supporting external inputs and internal state feedback across iterations. The resulting SQC engine is implemented in the *Kernel* component `BDDSeqSim`, whose structure is detailed in Sect. 4 (Kernel and Algorithm 2).

Challenge 3: Probability computation for large-qubit, loop-heavy programs. Symbolic simulation of `while`-loop programs requires repeated evaluation of measurement probabilities, especially for mid-circuit measurements and loop guards, often over large yet structured decision diagrams. In existing BDD-based simulation techniques [39], such probabilities are obtained via a hyper-function construction over the decision diagrams; however, for circuits with large numbers of qubits and deep structure this approach becomes a major bottleneck and can dominate the overall runtime, even when the underlying BDDs remain compact. This raises a specific scalability challenge: how to obtain exact measurement probabilities while preserving and exploiting the sharing and sparsity structure of the BDDs generated by large quantum circuits.

Our Approach. We incorporate model counting techniques [7,27,28] from formal methods and adopt weighted model counting on structured and sparse BDDs as the core mechanism for evaluating measurement probabilities. This counting-based engine implements the GETPROB interface used by both the *Simulator* and the SQC *Kernel*, as detailed in Sect. 4 (Kernel, weighted model counting for probability evaluation).

4 Tool Architecture

This section describes the architecture of *QSeqSim* and explains how its components jointly address the challenges identified in Sect. 3.

Figure 2 presents the overall architecture of *QSeqSim*. Starting from a Qiskit program written in Python, *QSeqSim* operates over Qiskit's internal intermediate representation (IR), namely the `QuantumCircuit` object, and processes it through three core modules: a *Parser*, a *Simulator*, and a Boolean *Kernel*. At a high level, the *Parser* realises the compilation phase, whereas the Simulator and Kernel jointly implement the symbolic execution back-end. Together, the *Parser* and Simulator instantiate the generalised SQC semantics for Qiskit `while`-loops (Challenge 1), while the *Kernel* provides the symbolic machinery for SQCs (Challenge 2) and scalable probability computation (Challenge 3).

The end-to-end workflow, which corresponds to Fig. 2, is as follows.

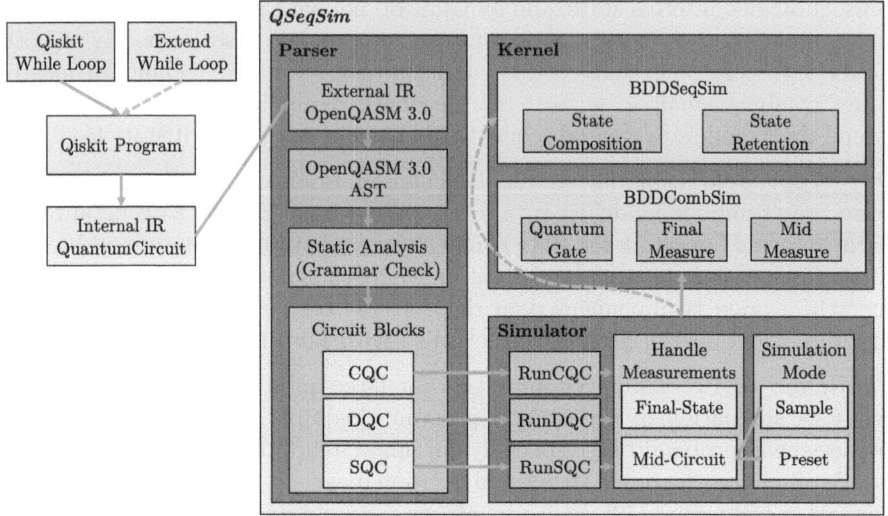

Fig. 2. *QSeqSim* workflow.

From Qiskit Program to Internal IR. The user specifies a circuit via the Qiskit Python API. Qiskit lowers it to a `QuantumCircuit` object, which is both its internal IR and the entry point to *QSeqSim*.

Parser (compile phase). Given a `QuantumCircuit`, the *Parser* performs the following steps:

1. *OpenQASM 3 export.* We invoke Qiskit's `qasm3.dumps` routine to obtain an *external* IR in the form of an OpenQASM 3 program.
2. *AST construction.* The resulting OpenQASM 3 code is parsed by the official OpenQASM 3 parser into an abstract syntax tree (AST).
3. *Static analysis.* On this AST, *QSeqSim* performs the following analyses: (i) it checks that all operations belong to the OpenQASM 3 fragment supported by the tool; (ii) it verifies that every unitary can be decomposed into the Clifford+T gate set implemented by the *Kernel*; (iii) it classifies each measurement as *mid-circuit* or *final*, depending on whether its outcome is used in any subsequent control condition; and (iv) it partitions the program into an ordered sequence of circuit blocks, each labelled as CQC, DQC or SQC. In particular, although we present the result as an ordered block sequence for simplicity, the *Parser* preserves the underlying *hierarchical* block structure induced by nested `if`/`switch`/`while` constructs.

The resulting block sequence preserves the original program order of the Qiskit circuit and constitutes the sole input to the symbolic backend. By explicitly identifying CQC, DQC, and in particular SQC blocks for loop bodies, the *Parser* provides exactly the structural interface required for the sequential semantics of Qiskit `while`-loops (Challenge 1).

Simulator (operational semantics). The *Simulator* provides an operational interpretation of the block sequence produced by the *Parser*. CQC blocks are treated as straight-line gate segments; DQC blocks implement branching controlled by measurement outcomes; and SQC blocks capture `while`-loops, which are unfolded by repeatedly executing their bodies until the loop guard, read from classical bits, evaluates to false. Algorithm 1 formalises this behaviour in high-level pseudo-code and instantiates the small-step semantics for mixed combinational, dynamic, and sequential fragments, completing the realisation of Challenge 1 on top of the *Parser*'s CQC/DQC/SQC decomposition.

Interfaces Used by the Simulator. Algorithm 1 relies on a small set of primitive operations provided by the BDD-based Kernel and the *Parser*:

- BDDCombSim(n, r): create an empty BDD-based symbolic simulator for n qubits with precision parameter r, i.e., the number of bit slices used to represent amplitudes in the encoding of [39].
- IsFinalMeas(G): return *true* iff measurement G is marked as *final* by the OpenQASM 3 static analysis in the *Parser*.
- GetProb(s, q): for a BDD-encoded state s, return the unnormalised probabilities $(p_0^{\text{joint}}, p_1^{\text{joint}})$ of outcomes 0 and 1 on qubit q (computed via weighted model counting in the *Kernel*; Challenge 3).
- MidMeasure(s, q, b): perform a symbolic mid-circuit measurement of qubit q with outcome $b \in \{0, 1\}$ on state s.

Kernel (Boolean engine). All quantum-state manipulation is delegated to the *Kernel*, which is implemented on top of BDDs. The *Kernel* provides the low-level symbolic operators used by the *Simulator* and is organised into two components, addressing Challenges 2 and 3.

- `BDDCombSim`, which implements Boolean gate-update rules for combinational circuits together with a mid-circuit measurement operator, following the BDD techniques of Tsai et al. [39]. Combined with CQC/DQC decomposition, this suffices to handle all combinational and dynamic fragments, as well as the mid-circuit and final measurements that arise in Qiskit programs.
- `BDDSeqSim`, which extends the *Kernel* to full sequential quantum circuits in the sense of Wang et al. [41]. Beyond Qiskit's current `while_loop` semantics, `BDDSeqSim` also supports an *extended* `while`-loop style, where each iteration injects a fresh external input state into a fixed SQC body, e.g.:

Algorithm 1. SIMULATOR($\mathcal{B}, n, r, m$)

Input: Parsed block sequence $\mathcal{B} = [B_1, \ldots, B_K]$; number of qubits n; BDD precision parameter r; measurement mode $m \in \{sample, preset\}$.
Output: BDD-encoded final quantum state s; path probability p_{global}.

```
s ← BDDCombSim(n, r)                                  ▷ initialise BDD kernel
initialise s to |0···0⟩
p_global ← 1
clbits ← empty map                                    ▷ classical store
ExecuteBlocks(B)
return [s, p_global]

procedure ExecuteBlocks(B')
    for each block B in B' in program order do
        if B is a CQC block then
            for each operation G in B in program order do
                if G is a measurement q → c then
                    HandleMeasure(q, c, IsFinalMeas(G))
                else
                    apply the Boolean gate update for G on s
                end if
            end for
        else if B is a DQC block then
            read guard bits from clbits and compute switch value v
            select branch B_sub of B according to v
            ExecuteBlocks(B_sub)
        else if B is an SQC block then                ▷ while loops
            while loop condition of B evaluated from clbits holds do
                let B_body be the body-block sequence of B
                ExecuteBlocks(B_body)
            end while
        end if
    end for
end procedure

procedure HandleMeasure(q, c, isFinal)
    if isFinal then
        record (q → c) as a deferred final measurement
    else
        (p_0^joint, p_1^joint) ← GetProb(s, q)        ▷ query prob. of q
        p_0 ← p_0^joint / (p_0^joint + p_1^joint); p_1 ← 1 − p_0
        if m = sample then
            sample b ∈ {0, 1} with Pr[b = 0] = p_0 and Pr[b = 1] = p_1
        else if m = preset then
            b ← next preset value for classical bit c
        end if
        p_global ← p_global × (b = 0 ? p_0 : p_1)
        s ← MidMeasure(s, q, b)                       ▷ symbolic collapse on q
        clbits[c] ← b
    end if
end procedure
```

```
q_internal = ... # internal qubits, persist across iterations
c = 0 # loop guard (classical bit)
while c == 0:
    p = new_qubit() # fresh external input with arbitrary state
    U(p, q_internal, ...) # body unitary using p and internal qubits
    c = measure(p) # update loop flag
```

To simulate such general SQCs, `BDDSeqSim` introduces two dedicated operators: *state composition*, which tensors the external input state with the current internal state, and *state retention*, which discards the measured external qubits while preserving the updated internal state (Challenge 2). Their pseudo-code is given in Algorithm 2.

Remark (internal vs. external qubits). For an SQC induced by a `while`-loop, *internal* qubits are the iteration-to-iteration state that is retained and fed back, whereas *external* qubits are iteration-scoped qubits that are measured and then discarded.

Algorithm 2. BDDSeqSim($|\psi_{\text{in}}\rangle, \mathcal{C}, \mathcal{I}, \mathcal{M}$)

Input: Initial internal quantum state $|\psi_{\text{in}}\rangle = (k, \{F^i_x\})$ (notation as in [39]); an SQC $\mathcal{C}$ whose body is a DQC $\mathcal{C}'$; a pair of sequences (or iterators) $\mathcal{I}$ and $\mathcal{M}$ providing, for each iteration, the external input state and the corresponding external measurement outcomes (given in *preset* mode or generated on the fly in *sample* mode).
Output: Final internal state $(\hat{k}, \{\hat{F}^i_x\})$; path probability p_{global} of $\mathcal{M}$.

$p_{\text{global}} \leftarrow 1$ ▷ accumulated probability of observing $\mathcal{M}$
$(k_{\text{in}}, \{F^i_{x,\text{in}}\}) \leftarrow (k, \{F^i_x\})$ ▷ initialise internal state
for each external input state $(0, \{F^i_{x,\text{ex}}\}) \in \mathcal{I}$ **do**
  $(k_{\text{total}}, \{F^i_{x,\text{total}}\}) \leftarrow (k_{\text{in}}, \{F^0_{d,\text{ex}} \wedge F^i_{x,\text{in}}\})$ ▷ state composition
  apply $\mathcal{C}'$ to $(k_{\text{total}}, \{F^i_{x,\text{total}}\})$ using Boolean gate transformations [39] and the HandleMeasure procedure of Algorithm 1
  $M[q_0], \ldots, M[q_{m-1}] \leftarrow \mathcal{M}$ ▷ get the corresponding measurement outcomes
  Construct assignment $\tilde{q}_0 \ldots \tilde{q}_{m-1}$ based on $M[q_0], \ldots, M[q_{m-1}]$.
  $(k_{\text{in}}, \{F^i_{x,\text{in}}\}) \leftarrow \left(k_{\text{total}}, \left\{ F^i_{x,\text{total}}\Big|_{\tilde{q}_0 \cdots \tilde{q}_{m-1}} \right\}\right)$ ▷ state retention
  compute probability p of observing $M[q_0], \ldots, M[q_{m-1}]$ via weighted model counting (see *Weighted model counting for probability evaluation*)
  $p_{\text{global}} \leftarrow p_{\text{global}} \cdot p$
end for
$(\hat{k}, \{\hat{F}^i_x\}) \leftarrow (k_{\text{in}}, \{F^i_{x,\text{in}}\})$
return $[(\hat{k}, \{\hat{F}^i_x\}), p_{\text{global}}]$

Remark (iterators for while loops). The `for`-loop in Algorithm 2 is conceptual: in the implementation, the SQC is unfolded by repeatedly consuming one element from $\mathcal{M}$ (and, if needed, $\mathcal{I}$) *while the loop guard holds.* In *sample* mode, $\mathcal{M}$ is an on-demand iterator whose next outcome is sampled when the guard is evaluated, and it stops producing values once the guard becomes false. In *preset* mode, the user provides a finite prefix of $\mathcal{M}$ (and $\mathcal{I}$), which fixes a bounded unrolling of the `while`-loop.

Weighted Model Counting for Probability Evaluation (Challenge 3). A central task of the *Kernel* is to evaluate measurement probabilities on BDD-encoded quantum states. Instead of using the hyper-function construction of [39], *QSeqSim* adopts a model counting view: probabilities are obtained via weighted model counting over structured and sparse BDDs representing the amplitude polynomials (see [7]). Because BDDs compactly encode large families of basis states with shared structure, weighted model counting can aggregate their contributions in time proportional to the size of the BDD representation (up to caching and arithmetic costs), avoiding explicit enumeration of exponentially many assignments. This does not imply polynomial-time counting in the worst case with respect to the original circuit; the gain comes from a compact BDD structure. This probability computation is tightly integrated into GetProb and into the SQC engine (Algorithm 2), and forms the main algorithmic ingredient in addressing the scalability issues highlighted in Challenge 3.

5 Functionalities

We summarise here the main functionalities offered to users by *QSeqSim*.

5.1 Simulation of Qiskit While Loop and Its Extensions

QSeqSim can be used as a backend to simulate a broad class of Qiskit `while`-loops, including patterns that are not yet natively supported by current Qiskit.

- **Qiskit `while_loop` programs.** Users can directly run Qiskit circuits containing `while_loop` constructs (possibly mixed with `if`/`else` and `for`). *QSeqSim* executes the loop semantics and returns the resulting quantum state together with the probability of a chosen measurement pattern.
- **Extended while loops.** Beyond standard Qiskit `while`-loop programs, users can also specify SQCs that admit an arbitrary external input state at each iteration. *QSeqSim* simulates such extended `while`-loops via `BDDSeqSim` and allows inspection of the state after any iteration.
- **General Qiskit programs with arbitrary control flow.** Qiskit programs with arbitrary combinations and nesting of `if`/`else`, `switch`, `for`, and `while` constructs are supported.

In all cases, users may either let *QSeqSim* randomly sample measurement outcomes (*sample* mode), or specify a concrete outcome pattern (*preset* mode) to fix a particular execution path.

5.2 Analysis of Quantum State Reachability

In formal methods, state reachability, namely deciding whether a given configuration can be reached and with what probability, is a central problem, from model checking of Markov chains and other probabilistic systems to the verification of (quantum) while loops [1,2,4,9,15,16,19,45].

QSeqSim supports such (bounded) *quantum state reachability* queries for while loops. A program point is fixed (for example, "after the k-th loop iteration") together with a target quantum state or basis configuration on some qubits. For a quantum random walk implemented with a `while`-loop, a reachability question of common interest is:

> "After the k-th iteration, is it possible for the walker to be at position i? If so, what is the probability of the execution paths that realise this?"

To answer such queries, candidate paths are encoded via the *preset* mode (fixing the sequence of measurement outcomes across iterations). *QSeqSim* then computes, for each path, the final quantum state and its probability, which allows users to check reachability and quantify the likelihood of reaching the target.

5.3 Analysis of Measurement Outcome Reachability

QSeqSim also supports queries about whether particular *measurement outcome patterns* can occur and with what probability, a central concern in the analysis of quantum protocols with repeated measurements and feedback, and in studying loop termination behaviour [14,41,47]. Given a sequence of measurement outcomes across iterations for a while loop, specified via the *preset* measurement mode, *QSeqSim* returns the probability of the corresponding execution. For a RUS circuit expressed as a `while`-loop that repeats until a measurement returns 0, a typical measurement outcome reachability question is:

> "What is the probability that the sequence of outcomes is `1111110` (that is, six times 1 followed by 0), and the loop terminates at that point?"

By varying such queries over families of patterns (for example, "eventually a 0 occurs"), one can empirically study whether a RUS or feedback-based protocol converges or may fail to terminate with non-zero probability.

6 Evaluation

We evaluate *QSeqSim* along three dimensions matching its intended uses: (i) simulation of Qiskit `while`-loops (Sect. 6.1), (ii) quantum state reachability (Sect. 6.2), and (iii) measurement outcome reachability (Sect. 6.3). All experiments were run on a MacBook Air 2023 (Apple M2, 16 GB unified memory) with Python 3.12.

6.1 Simulation of Qiskit While Loops

We consider three structured benchmarks (RUS [30], QRW [35], Grover [3,18]) and, separately, randomly generated `while`-loop programs. Unless stated otherwise, we use *preset* mode: a concrete sequence of mid-circuit measurement outcomes is fixed in advance, so that *QSeqSim* symbolically executes a single predetermined path.

For the RUS and random `while`-loop benchmarks, circuits are generated via the Qiskit Python API, exported to OpenQASM 3, and then passed to *QSeqSim* as in Sect. 3. In contrast, QRW and Grover rely in Qiskit on custom Python functions that repeatedly instantiate large static subcircuits (shift, oracle, diffusion), incurring significant OpenQASM parsing and construction overhead. To isolate the cost of symbolic simulation, we therefore bypass Qiskit for QRW and Grover and directly invoke the `BDDSeqSim` kernel on hand-specified sequential circuits, using the same BDD-based engine.

Repeat-Until-Success (RUS). We use the six two-qubit RUS circuits from Paetznick and Svore [30, Figures 7–10], where a common RUS pattern is instantiated with different single-qubit unitaries U and corresponding ancilla measurement rules. We implement these six RUS variants (RUS-1 to RUS-6) in the Qiskit API and invoke *QSeqSim* in *preset* mode. In each case the ancilla is measured every iteration and the loop terminates on a designated "success" outcome: for RUS-1–RUS-4 success is 0, while for RUS-5 and RUS-6 success is 1. Accordingly, we fix the ancilla outcome pattern to $0^{k-1}1$ for RUS-1–RUS-4 and to $1^{k-1}0$ for RUS-5/RUS-6, enforcing exactly k iterations.

Table 1 reports a representative configuration for six different RUS implementations U. The number of qubits and per-iteration gate count remain tiny (two qubits, 7–37 gates), so runtimes mainly reflect the symbolic cost of unfolding the loop. For short loops (10 iterations), all variants complete in under 1s.

Table 1. Performance of *QSeqSim* on Qiskit RUS `while`-loops (*preset* mode).

Benchmark	Implementation U	#Qubits	#Gates	#Iterations	Time (s)
RUS-1	$\frac{2X+\sqrt{2}Y+Z}{\sqrt{7}}$	2	7	10	0.300
				100	0.960
RUS-2	$\frac{I+2i\sqrt{2}X}{\sqrt{3}}$	2	13	10	0.673
				100	1.427
RUS-3	$\frac{I+2iZ}{\sqrt{5}}$	2	12	10	0.656
				100	11.081
RUS-4	$\frac{3I+2iZ}{\sqrt{13}}$	2	20	10	0.760
				100	20.807
RUS-5	$\frac{4I+iZ}{\sqrt{17}}$	2	37	10	0.963
				100	90.027
RUS-6	$\frac{5I+2iZ}{\sqrt{29}}$	2	33	10	0.994
				100	108.148

For 100 iterations, however, runtimes span nearly three orders of magnitude: from below 1.5s for RUS-1/RUS-2 to around 90–108s for RUS-5/RUS-6. This variability shows that *QSeqSim* is sensitive not only to loop depth but also to the specific unitary U, which affects BDD structure and sharing.

Quantum Random Walk (QRW). For QRW, we work directly with `BDDSeqSim`, following the experimental setup of Wang et al. [41, Figure 3]. Each iteration applies a Hadamard on the coin, a coin-controlled shift on an ℓ-qubit position register, and a multi-controlled X on a single flag qubit that flips when a fixed target basis state is reached, namely the internal all-ones configuration of the coin and the position register.

Table 2a shows runtimes as we scale the position register from $N = 16$ to $N = 1024$ sites and increase the number of iterations. For $N = 16$ (16 qubits, 31 gates per iteration), *QSeqSim* comfortably reaches hundreds of iterations, but the cost grows rapidly: going from 100 to 785 iterations increases the time from 5.3s to about 1800s. Larger walks are limited by qubit and gate counts rather than loop depth: for $N = 1024$ (1024 qubits, 2047 gates per iteration), only up to 13 iterations are feasible within a 30-minute timeout.

Grover's Search. The Grover benchmark follows the same pattern: a fixed number of data qubits plus a flag qubit, with each iteration consisting of an oracle phase flip on a single marked basis state followed by a diffusion operator. Again

Table 2. Performance of *QSeqSim* on different `while`-loops (`BDDSeqSim`).

(a) QRW `while`-loops

#Qubits	#Gates	#Iterations	Time (s)
16	31	3	0.041
		10	0.111
		100	5.303
		200	30.375
		785	1797.676
128	255	3	0.698
		10	2.861
		100	239.485
		200	1118.501
		244	1792.934
1024	2047	3	235.568
		5	438.156
		8	867.763
		10	1124.445
		13	1622.304

(b) Grover `while`-loops

#Qubits	#Gates	#Iterations	Time (s)
16	81	3	0.177
		10	2.354
		100	340.669
		150	866.182
		203	1781.141
128	641	2	3.115
		3	16.293
		6	135.108
		10	622.699
		15	1700.021
256	1281	2	256.593
		3	527.699
		4	840.786
		5	1156.052
		6	Timeout

we emulate a `while`-loop by enforcing a specific termination iteration via the mid-circuit measurement pattern.

Table 2b summarises the results. For 16 work qubits (81 gates per iteration), runtimes scale from 0.18s at 3 iterations to around 1780 s near 200 iterations. For 128 qubits, even 15 iterations already saturate our timeout. At 256 qubits and 1281 gates per iteration, *QSeqSim* handles up to 5 iterations (about 19 min) before timeout (30 min) at 6 iterations. These trends are consistent with QRW: BDD-based symbolic simulation can handle substantial gate counts and deep loops, but very large multi-qubit operators combine unfavourably with repeated iteration.

Random Quantum While Loops. To evaluate robustness under unstructured control flow, we generated random quantum circuits using the Qiskit API, which contain a `while`-loop with additional quantum gates placed outside the loop. We fixed the system size at 100 qubits and varied two key experimental parameters: computational density (defined as the total number of gates in the circuit, denoted G) and control complexity (defined as the total number of mid-circuit measurements, denoted M). These experiments were executed in *sample* mode: for each mid-circuit measurement performed within the loop, *QSeqSim* computes the exact outcome distribution over the current symbolic state, then samples the next execution branch, and proceeds until the loop terminates or reaches a predefined iteration bound of 1000.

As in *sample* mode the loop termination time is a random variable determined by the sampled measurement outcomes, the resulting runtime distribution is typically right-skewed; we therefore repeat each configuration 50 times and report the median and interquartile range (IQR $[Q_1, Q_3]$)[1]. Table 3 shows that *QSeqSim* remains tractable on 100-qubit circuits: across all tested settings, median runtimes stay within a minute. Runtime generally grows with circuit size, while

Table 3. Performance of *QSeqSim* on Qiskit random `while`-loops (*sample* mode).

Benchmark	Qubits	Gates	Mid-Meas	Total Time (s)
rqc_q100_g50_m5	100	50	5	0.218 [0.215, 0.915]
rqc_q100_g50_m10	100	50	10	0.273 [0.194, 1.158]
rqc_q100_g50_m20	100	50	20	0.214 [0.211, 0.367]
rqc_q100_g100_m5	100	100	5	0.971 [0.945, 3.053]
rqc_q100_g100_m10	100	100	10	0.949 [0.942, 2.789]
rqc_q100_g100_m20	100	100	20	1.149 [1.008, 6.092]
rqc_q100_g200_m5	100	200	5	2.235 [2.151, 5.910]
rqc_q100_g200_m10	100	200	10	15.978 [3.056, 22.853]
rqc_q100_g200_m20	100	200	20	2.116 [1.767, 10.228]

[1] The median is the 0.5 quantile of the sample distribution, and the interquartile range $[Q_1, Q_3]$ is the interval between the 0.25 and 0.75 quantiles; see [21].

mid-circuit measurements have a non-monotone, control-flow-dependent effect (e.g., G=200, M=10 vs. 20). As random `while`-loops may not terminate, our generator enforces almost termination; these results thus characterize robustness under terminating control flow.

6.2 Analysis of Quantum State Reachability

We next use the QRW benchmark to study quantum state reachability for a `while`-loop semantics. Each QRW step consists of a coin flip on a single qubit, a controlled shift on an ℓ-qubit position register, and a multi-controlled X that flips an external flag qubit q_0 precisely when the coin and position jointly equal a fixed target basis state (here, the all-ones internal configuration).

Reachability formulation. A reachability question of common interest is:

> *"After k QRW iterations, can the internal configuration (coin + position) reach the all-ones basis state, and if so, with what exact probability?"*

This reduces to the marginal state of the flag qubit q_0 after k steps: the all-ones state is reachable at iteration k iff q_0 can be in $|1\rangle$. Under *preset* mode, we fix the measurement outcomes controlling the loop guard to $0^{k-1}1$, so that the loop continues for $k-1$ iterations and terminates at step k. The branch probability of this classical pattern is then exactly the reachability probability of the all-ones internal configuration at step k.

Results. Table 4 reports results for a fixed system size of 256 qubits and iteration counts $k = 1, \ldots, 10$. For each k, `BDDSeqSim` symbolically executes the constrained path $0^{k-1}1$, checks whether measuring qubit q_0 in the computational basis can yield outcome 1, and returns the exact branch probability together with the runtime.

Table 4. Quantum state reachability of QRW `while`-loop.

#Qubits	k	Reachable?	Probability	Time (s)
256	1	Yes	0.5	1.264
	2	No	0	2.489
	3	Yes	0.125	3.808
	4	No	0	5.053
	5	No	0	6.399
	6	No	0	7.992
	7	Yes	0.0078125	9.729
	8	No	0	11.409
	9	No	0	13.453
	10	No	0	15.563

The non-zero rows reveal that the all-ones configuration is only reachable at specific iteration counts (here, $k = 1, 3, 7$), and the associated branch probabilities decay quickly. *QSeqSim* computes these probabilities exactly, without sampling noise, and the runtimes grow approximately linearly with k in this setting.

6.3 Analysis of Measurement Outcome Reachability

We finally evaluate how easily users can pose measurement-outcome reachability queries on the RUS-1 `while`-loop from Sect. 6.1. Each loop iteration applies the fixed two-qubit RUS-1 subcircuit and measures an ancilla; the loop continues while the ancilla is 1 and terminates on the first 0.

A typical measurement outcome reachability query is:

> *"What is the probability that the ancilla outcomes are* 1^k0*, so that the loop terminates exactly at iteration* $k + 1$*?"*

In *preset* mode, the user specifies the concrete pattern 1^k0; *QSeqSim* then symbolically follows this unique branch and returns: (i) the probability of that pattern, $p_{\text{path}}(k)$, and (ii) the probability that the loop has terminated by iteration $k + 1$, $p_{\text{term.}}(k)$. Here $p_{\text{term.}}(k)$ is obtained as the cumulative probability of all termination patterns up to iteration $k + 1$, i.e. $p_{\text{term.}}(k) = \sum_{i=0}^{k} p_{\text{path}}(i)$.

Table 5. Measurement-outcome reachability for the RUS-1 `while`-loop.

k	0	1	2	3	4	5	6	7	8
p_{path}	0.75000	0.18750	0.04688	0.01172	0.00293	0.00073	0.00018	0.00005	0.00001
$p_{\text{term.}}$	0.75000	0.93750	0.98438	0.99609	0.99902	0.99976	0.99994	0.99998	1.00000
Time (s)	0.02607	0.05073	0.04982	0.04946	0.07638	0.11201	0.15824	0.21086	0.29526

Table 5 shows the outputs for $k = 0, \ldots, 8$. The per-pattern probabilities p_{path} quickly become very small as k increases, while termination is already almost certain after a few iterations. All queries complete in well under one second, allowing interactive exploration of rare measurement patterns.

7 Conclusion

We have presented *QSeqSim*, a Qiskit-integrated symbolic backend that directly executes `while`-loop programs by interpreting them as sequential quantum circuits with explicit state feedback across iterations. Building on a BDD-based Boolean representation of quantum states and operations, *QSeqSim* provides symbolic operators tailored to this sequential setting and thus enables efficient exploration of loop-induced behaviours. Our experiments on RUS schemes, quantum random walks, and Grover's search on commodity hardware show that *QSeqSim* scales to substantial `while`-induced sequential circuits; in particular, in the quantum random walk benchmark we successfully simulate circuits with over 1000 qubits for more than 10 loop iterations, and we support both quantum state reachability and measurement outcome reachability queries for Qiskit `while`-loop programs. All experiments in this work are conducted on a PC. As future work, we plan to deploy *QSeqSim* on server-class machines and exploit parallelism to support larger-scale simulations and better serve subsequent formal verification of quantum programs with `while`-loops.

Acknowledgments. We sincerely thank the anonymous reviewers for their valuable comments and constructive suggestions. This work was partially supported by the Innovation Program for Quantum Science and Technology (Grant No. 2024ZD0300500), the Youth Innovation Promotion Association, Chinese Academy of Sciences (Grant No. 2023116), the National Natural Science Foundation of China (Grant No. 62402485), the Young Elite Scientists Sponsorship Program, China Association for Science and Technology, the CCF-QuantumCtek Superconducting Quantum Computing Special Cooperation Program (Grant No. CCF-QC2025007), and the International Partnership Program of the Chinese Academy of Sciences (Grant No. 096GJHZ2025013FN).

References

1. Agrawal, M., Akshay, S., Genest, B., Thiagarajan, P.: Approximate verification of the symbolic dynamics of Markov chains. J. ACM (JACM) **62**(1), 1–34 (2015)
2. Akshay, S., Antonopoulos, T., Ouaknine, J., Worrell, J.: Reachability problems for Markov chains. Inf. Process. Lett. **115**(2), 155–158 (2015)
3. Andrés-Martínez, P., Heunen, C.: Weakly measured while loops: peeking at quantum states. Quant. Sci. Technol. **7**(2), 025007 (2022)
4. Beauquier, D., Rabinovich, A., Slissenko, A.: A Logic of Probability with Decidable Model-Checking. In: Bradfield, J. (ed.) CSL 2002. LNCS, vol. 2471, pp. 306–321. Springer, Heidelberg (2002). https://doi.org/10.1007/3-540-45793-3_21
5. Bocharov, A., Roetteler, M., Svore, K.M.: Efficient synthesis of universal repeat-until-success quantum circuits. Phys. Rev. Lett. **114**(8), 080502 (2015)
6. Burgholzer, L., Wille, R.: Advanced equivalence checking for quantum circuits. IEEE Trans. Comput. Aided Des. Integr. Circuits Syst. **40**(9), 1810–1824 (2020)
7. Chavira, M., Darwiche, A.: On probabilistic inference by weighted model counting. Artif. Intell. **172**(6–7), 772–799 (2008)
8. Chen, T.F., Jiang, J.H.R.: SliQSim: A quantum circuit simulator and solver for probability and statistics queries. In: Gurfinkel, A., Heule, M. (eds.) TACAS 2025. LNCS, vol. 15698, pp. 129–138. Springer, Cham (2025). https://doi.org/10.1007/978-3-031-90660-2_7
9. Chen, Y.F.: AutoQ 2.0: from verification of quantum circuits to verification of quantum programs. In: Gurfinkel, A., Heule, M. (eds.) TACAS 2025. LNCS, vol. 15698, pp. 87–108. Springer, Cham (2025). https://doi.org/10.1007/978-3-031-90660-2_5

10. Chen, Y.F., Chung, K.M., Lengál, O., Lin, J.A., Tsai, W.L.: AutoQ: an automata-based quantum circuit verifier. In: Enea, C., Lal, A. (eds.) CAV 2023. LNCS, vol. 13966, pp. 139–153. Springer, Cham (2023). https://doi.org/10.1007/978-3-031-37709-9_7
11. Chen, Y.F., Chung, K.M., Lengál, O., Lin, J.A., Tsai, W.L., Yen, D.D.: An automata-based framework for verification and bug hunting in quantum circuits. Proc. ACM Program. Lang. 7(PLDI), 1218–1243 (2023)
12. Cirq Developers: Cirq (v1.6.1) (2025). doi: 10.5281/zenodo.16867504
13. Cross, A., et al.: OpenQASM 3: a broader and deeper quantum assembly language. ACM Trans. Quant. Comput. **3**(3), 1–50 (2022)
14. Eisert, J., Müller, M.P., Gogolin, C.: Quantum measurement occurrence is undecidable. Phys. Rev. Lett. **108**(26), 260501 (2012)
15. Feng, Y., Yu, N., Ying, M.: Model checking quantum Markov chains. J. Comput. Syst. Sci. **79**(7), 1181–1198 (2013)
16. Gay, S., Nagarajan, R., Papanikolaou, N.: Probabilistic model-checking of quantum protocols, (2005). arXiv preprint
17. Gonzalez, C.: Cloud based QC with Amazon Braket. Digitale Welt **5**(2), 14–17 (2021)
18. Grover, L.K.: A fast quantum mechanical algorithm for database search. In: Proceedings of the Twenty-Eighth Annual ACM Symposium on Theory of Computing, pp. 212–219. (1996)
19. Guan, J., Feng, Y., Turrini, A., Ying, M.: Measurement-based verification of quantum Markov chains. In: Gurfinkel, A., Ganesh, V. (eds.) CAV 2024. LNCS, vol. 14683, pp. 533–554. Springer, Cham (2024). https://doi.org/10.1007/978-3-031-65633-0_24
20. Guerreschi, G.G., Hogaboam, J., Baruffa, F., Sawaya, N.P.: Intel Quantum Simulator: a cloud-ready high-performance simulator of quantum circuits. Quant. Sci. Technol. **5**(3), 034007 (2020)
21. Hoaglin, D.C., Mosteller, F., Tukey, J.W.: Understanding Robust and Exploratory Data Analysis, Wiley (2000)
22. Javadi-Abhari, A.: Quantum computing with Qiskit, (2024). arXiv preprint
23. Jones, T., Brown, A., Bush, I., Benjamin, S.C.: QuEST and high performance simulation of quantum computers. Sci. Rep. **9**(1), 10736 (2019)
24. Kendon, V., Tregenna, B.: Decoherence can be useful in quantum walks. Phys. Rev. A **67**(4), 042315 (2003)
25. Kissinger, A., Van De Wetering, J.: PyZX: large scale automated diagrammatic reasoning, (2019). arXiv preprint
26. Liu, J., Zhan, B., Wang, S., Ying, S., Liu, T., Li, Y., Ying, M., Zhan, N.: Formal Verification of Quantum Algorithms Using Quantum Hoare Logic. In: Dillig, I., Tasiran, S. (eds.) CAV 2019. LNCS, vol. 11562, pp. 187–207. Springer, Cham (2019). https://doi.org/10.1007/978-3-030-25543-5_12
27. Mei, J., Bonsangue, M., Laarman, A.: Simulating quantum circuits by model counting. In: Gurfinkel, A., Ganesh, V. (eds.) CAV 2024. LNCS, vol. 14683, pp. 555–578. Springer, Cham (2024). https://doi.org/10.1007/978-3-031-65633-0_25
28. Mei, J., Coopmans, T., Bonsangue, M., Laarman, A.: Equivalence checking of quantum circuits by model counting. In: Benzmüller, C., Heule, M.J., Schmidt, R.A. (eds.) IJCAR 2024. LNCS, vol. 14740, pp. 401–421. Springer, Cham (2024). https://doi.org/10.1007/978-3-031-63501-4_21
29. OpenQASM Contributors: OpenQASM Live Specification (2025). https://openqasm.com/index.html. Accessed 02 Mar 2026

30. Paetznick, A., Svore, K.M.: Repeat-until-success: non-deterministic decomposition of single-qubit unitaries, (2013). arXiv preprint
31. Papanikolaou, N.K.: Model checking quantum protocols, University of Warwick (2009). Ph.D. thesis
32. Peham, T., Burgholzer, L., Wille, R.: Equivalence checking of quantum circuits with the ZX-calculus. IEEE J. Emerg. Sel. Top. Circuits Syst **12**(3), 662–675 (2022)
33. Quist, A.J., Mei, J., Coopmans, T., Laarman, A.: Advancing quantum computing with formal methods. In: Platzer, A., Rozier, K.Y., Pradella, M., Rossi, M. (eds.) FM 2024. LNCS, vol. 14934, pp. 420–446. Springer, Cham (2024). https://doi.org/10.1007/978-3-031-71177-0_25
34. Selinger, P.: Towards a quantum programming language. Math. Struct. Comput. Sci. **14**(4), 527–586 (2004)
35. Shenvi, N., Kempe, J., Whaley, K.B.: Quantum random-walk search algorithm. Phys. Rev. A **67**(5), 052307 (2003)
36. Steiger, D.S., Häner, T., Troyer, M.: ProjectQ: an open source software framework for quantum computing. Quantum **2**, 49 (2018)
37. Suzuki, Y., et al.: Qulacs: a fast and versatile quantum circuit simulator for research purpose. Quantum **5**, 559 (2021)
38. The CUDA Quantum development team: CUDA Quantum (0.11.0) (2025). doi: 10.5281/zenodo.15407754
39. Tsai, Y.H., Jiang, J.H.R., Jhang, C.S.: Bit-slicing the Hilbert space: scaling up accurate quantum circuit simulation. In: 2021 58th ACM/IEEE Design Automation Conference (DAC), pp. 439–444. IEEE (2021)
40. Unruh, D.: Quantum relational Hoare logic. Proc. ACM Program. Lang. 3(POPL), 1–31 (2019)
41. Wang, Q., Li, R., Ying, M.: Equivalence checking of sequential quantum circuits. IEEE Trans. Comput. Aided Des. Integr. Circuits Syst. **41**(9), 3143–3156 (2021)
42. Wang, Z., Cheng, B., Yuan, L., Ji, Z.: FeynmanDD: quantum circuit analysis with classical decision diagrams. In: Piskac, R., Rakamarić, Z. (eds.) CAV 2025. LNCS, vol. 15934, pp. 28–52. Springer, Cham (2025). https://doi.org/10.1007/978-3-031-98685-7_2
43. Wei, C.Y., Tsai, Y.H., Jhang, C.S., Jiang, J.H.R.: Accurate BDD-based unitary operator manipulation for scalable and robust quantum circuit verification. In: Proceedings of the 59th ACM/IEEE Design Automation Conference, pp. 523–528. (2022)
44. Ying, M.: Floyd-Hoare logic for quantum programs. ACM Trans. Program. Lang. Syst. (TOPLAS) **33**(6), 1–49 (2012)
45. Ying, M.: Model Checking for Verification of Quantum Circuits. In: Huisman, M., Păsăreanu, C., Zhan, N. (eds.) FM 2021. LNCS, vol. 13047, pp. 23–39. Springer, Cham (2021). https://doi.org/10.1007/978-3-030-90870-6_2
46. Ying, M.: Foundations of Quantum Programming, Elsevier (2024)
47. Ying, M., Feng, Y.: Quantum loop programs. Acta Informatica **47**(4), 221–250 (2010)
48. Zhou, L., Yu, N., Ying, M.: An applied quantum Hoare logic. In: Proceedings of the 40th ACM SIGPLAN Conference on Programming Language Design and Implementation, pp. 1149–1162. (2019)
49. Zulehner, A., Wille, R.: Advanced simulation of quantum computations. IEEE Trans. Comput. Aided Des. Integr. Circuits Syst. **38**(5), 848–859 (2018)

Reachability-Guided Abstraction Refinement

Pierre Ganty[1], Nicolas Manini[1,2(✉)], and Francesco Ranzato[3]

[1] IMDEA Software Institute, Madrid, Spain
pierre.ganty@imdea.org
[2] Universidad Politécnica de Madrid, Madrid, Spain
nicolas.manini@imdea.org
[3] Dipartimento di Matematica, University of Padova, Padova, Italy
francesco.ranzato@unipd.it

Abstract. To mitigate the state explosion problem in model checking, abstraction techniques provide sound but typically incomplete approximations of a system's behaviour. While complete abstractions eliminate false alarms, they are often impractical—or even uncomputable—due to their high computational cost. We introduce semi-completeness, a relaxed notion of completeness that retains sufficient precision to capture a system's behaviour over relevant regions of the domain. Building on this, we develop abstraction refinement algorithms that compute semi-complete abstractions without incurring the cost of full completeness. Furthermore, we present an algorithm that interleaves abstraction refinement with fixed-point computations—specifically reachability analysis. This achieves semi-completeness on-the-fly, without requiring prior knowledge of the region of interest, such as the reachable states. We demonstrate the effectiveness of our approach on fragments of the μ-calculus, showing that our abstractions preserve the validity of formulae over all reachable states.

Keywords: Abstract Model Checking · Reachable States · Abstraction Refinement · Complete Abstraction · Semi-Complete Abstraction

1 Introduction

Model checking is a fundamental technique for system verification, yet the well-known state explosion problem hampers its practical applicability to complex hardware and software systems. Abstraction techniques effectively address this issue by reducing the state space to a tractable size. However, while abstract model checking is sound-by-construction, it is typically incomplete. Ideally, abstractions should be complete to precisely capture the concrete system's behaviour; yet, such completeness is rarely achievable with standard abstract domains. In this paper, we address this limitation by investigating how to construct abstractions that, while not fully complete, preserve sufficient precision to enable effective verification.

A. Sampaio and M. Stoelinga (Eds.): FM 2026, LNCS 16556, pp. 599–618, 2026.
https://doi.org/10.1007/978-3-032-26204-2_31

Contributions. Section 3 introduces the notion of *semi-completeness*, a weakening of (forward) completeness for a concrete function f over a concrete domain C. The property ρ-semi f-completeness restricts the completeness of f to a semantically relevant region of C, determined by a parameter $\rho \subseteq C$ which is a lower closure operator specifying the extent to which completeness is required. To enforce ρ-semi f-completeness, we present Algorithm 1, an abstraction refinement procedure that requires as input a full specification R of the region where completeness must hold. In addition to proving its correctness, we show that the proposed algorithm performs strictly fewer refinement steps than the standard fully complete refinement procedure.

Section 4 introduces Algorithm 2, a refinement procedure that achieves semi-completeness without requiring a full specification R of the region in advance. Instead, this algorithm computes R on-the-fly; for instance, when R represents the reachable state subspace, the algorithm derives it from the initial states and the successor transformer. Notably, it achieves semi-completeness *without* constructing the fully complete refinement or generating the entire fixed-point R.

Section 5 applies these notions to μ-calculus model checking. We show that the computed semi-complete abstractions preserve the validity of formulas in the $\{\wedge, \exists\}$-free fragment over all reachable states: a reachable state s satisfies a formula φ in this abstraction if and only if it does so in the concrete model. Finally, we demonstrate how minor extensions of this algorithm cover both the universal fragment and the full μ-calculus.

Motivating Example. Figure 1 illustrates an example. The top-right inset depicts an extended finite state machine (FSM) with configurations $\langle s, x, y\rangle \in \{s_e, s_o\} \times \mathbb{Q} \times \mathbb{Z}$. This FSM induces a transition system where transitions follow the edges of the FSM; for instance, the system may move from $\langle s_e, 0, 0\rangle$ to $\langle s_o, 0, 1\rangle$ via the $y+1$ edge, or loop in $\langle s_e, 0, 0\rangle$ via the $2x$ edge. The main plot in Fig. 1 displays a fragment of this system for a fixed rational number $M \in \mathbb{Q}$. The vertical axis represents values of x and the horizontal axis represents y. System configurations with $s = s_e$ are marked as squares, while those with $s = s_o$ are circles. The initial configuration $\langle s_e, 0, 0\rangle$ is located at the origin of the axes. Reachable configurations are filled in black and lie entirely along the non-negative y-semiaxis.

We partition the configuration space into four blocks:

$$E_M^{>} \triangleq \{\langle s_e, x, y\rangle \mid x > M\}, \qquad E_M^{\leq} \triangleq \{\langle s_e, x, y\rangle \mid x \leq M\},$$
$$O_0^{\geq} \triangleq \{\langle s_o, x, y\rangle \mid x \geq 0\}, \qquad O_0^{<} \triangleq \{\langle s_o, x, y\rangle \mid x < 0\}.$$

In the figure, $E_M^{\leq}$ and $E_M^{>}$ are shown as gray blocks with continuous borders, while $O_0^{<}$ and $O_0^{\geq}$ appear as light gray blocks with dashed borders. Rounded corners indicate strict inequalities (open intervals), namely, $E_M^{>}$ and $O_0^{<}$.

Because the system has infinitely many reachable states and an infinite bisimilarity quotient, standard reduction techniques are infeasible. The key insight, however, is that combining reachability analysis with bisimilarity reveals a much

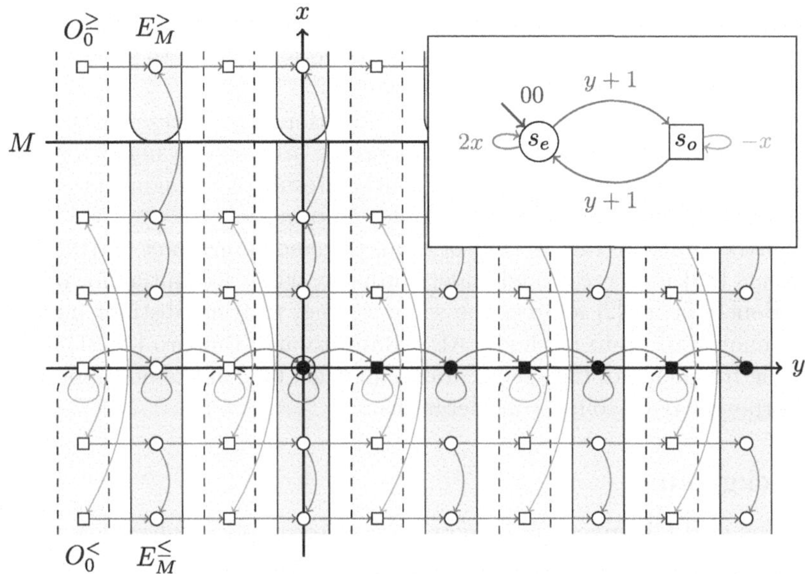

Fig. 1. The inset depicts an extended finite-state machine with variables x and y, together with its induced transition system. A partition of the state space into four blocks ($E_M^{>}$, $E_M^{\leq}$, $O_0^{\geq}$, $O_0^{<}$), parametrized by $M \in \mathbb{Q}$, is also shown: two gray blocks with solid borders and two light-gray blocks with dashed borders. (Color figure online)

simpler structure: among the infinitely many bisimilarity blocks, only two actually contain reachable configurations. Our approach leverages this observation to compute abstractions that preserve the relevant semantics (e.g., μ-calculus properties) over reachable states, without enumerating the entire reachable set or constructing the full bisimilarity quotient.

Related Work. System abstraction is a widely adopted and effective technique for mitigating the state-explosion problem in model checking. It shifts reasoning to a more tractable domain, at the cost of some loss of precision. To be sound and complete with respect to the properties of interest, an abstraction must preserve them: a property holds on the concrete system if and only if it holds on its abstraction. Due to space constraints, we focus on the most closely related works, classifying them along two dimensions: (i) whether refinement preserves a single property or an entire specification language, and (ii) whether reachability information is taken into account.

Counterexample-Guided Abstraction Refinement (CEGAR) [4,5] incrementally constructs abstractions that preserve a single ACTL* property, introducing just enough precision to eliminate spurious counterexamples. In contrast, our refinement is reachability-guided rather than counterexample-guided: reachability information determines where precision is required from a semantic standpoint, independently of any specific counterexample. In a similar manner,

Predicate-Directed Reachability (PDR) [3,15] takes as input a single safety property and aims to prove it; our approach, instead, is designed to model check all properties expressible in a given target logic.

Lee and Yannakakis [16] compute abstractions that preserve the full μ-calculus over reachable states, without enforcing precision on unreachable ones. Henzinger et al. [14] also study preservation results for fragments of the μ-calculus, but without exploiting reachability information.

In abstract interpretation, Cousot et al. [10] and Ranzato et al. [19] develop refinements that preserve a single safety property while accounting for reachable states. Bonchi et al. [2] address the same setting, relating abstract interpretation techniques to up-to methods. Also, Ranzato and Tapparo [20,21] focus on preserving fragments of the specification language, but, unlike our approach, do not incorporate reachability considerations.

2 Background

Functions and Closures. We denote by id_X (or simply id when clear from the context) the identity function on a set X. Given a function $f\colon X \to X$ and $i \in \mathbb{N}$, $f^i : X \to X$ denotes the usual i-th power of f (i.e., $f^0 \triangleq id_X$ and $f^{i+1} \triangleq f f^i$). For clarity, we sometimes omit parentheses in function application, writing $f\,x$ instead of $f(x)$. Complete lattices are denoted by $\langle C, \preceq_C, \curlywedge_C, \curlyvee_C, \top_C, \bot_C\rangle$, where subscripts are omitted when clear from the context. For $S \subseteq C$, $\downarrow S \triangleq \{c \in C \mid \exists s \in S.\, c \preceq s\}$ denotes the *downward closure* of S. A set S is *downward closed* iff $S = \downarrow S$ holds, and we write $\downarrow c$ as a shorthand for $\downarrow\{c\}$. We denote monotone (i.e., order-preserving) functions as $f\colon C \overset{m}{\to} D$. A function is *additive* (resp., *continuous*) when it preserves lubs of arbitrary subsets (resp., of chains). We denote with $\mathrm{lfp}_a(f)$ (resp., $\mathrm{gfp}_a(f)$) the least (resp., greatest) fixed point of $f\colon C \to C$ that is greater (resp., smaller) than $a \in C$, whenever it exists. Moreover, $\mathrm{lfp}(f) \triangleq \mathrm{lfp}_\bot(f)$ and $\mathrm{gfp}(f) \triangleq \mathrm{gfp}_\top(f)$. Defining $x_0 \triangleq a$ and $x_{n+1} \triangleq f(x_n)$ yields the *Kleene iterates* of f from a. For complete lattices and continuous functions, if $f(a) \preceq a$ then $\mathrm{lfp}_a(f) = \curlyvee\{x_n \mid n \in \mathbb{N}\}$.

We denote by $\mathrm{uco}(C)$ the set of *upper closure operators* (ucos) over a complete lattice C, that is, functions $\mu\colon C \to C$ that are monotone, idempotent, and extensive ($x \preceq_C \mu(x)$ for all x). Dually, $\mathrm{lco}(C)$ denotes the set of *lower closure operators* (lcos) $\rho\colon C \to C$, which are monotone, idempotent, and reductive ($\rho(x) \preceq_C x$). Both ucos and lcos are determined by their sets of fixed points, which coincide with their images $\mu(C)$ and $\rho(C)$, respectively. For $\mu \in \mathrm{uco}(C)$, this means that $\mu(C) = \{c \in C \mid \mu(c) = c\}$ and that, for all $c \in C$, $\mu(c) = \curlywedge_C\{x \in \mu(C) \mid c \preceq_C x\}$. Henceforth, we shorten the notation $\mu(C)$ for the set of fixed points of a closure operator by omitting the argument and writing simply μ. Viewing closure operators either as functions or as sets, depending on the context, provides a convenient and flexible notation. For instance, given $c \in C$, writing $c \in \mu$ means $c \in \mu(C)$, which is equivalent to $\mu(c) = c$. Similarly, $\mu \subseteq \nu$ stands for $\mu(C) \subseteq \nu(C)$, which in turn is equivalent to $\mu(c) = c$ implying $\nu(c) = c$ for all $c \in C$. We sometimes mix the two views, as in $\mu(\rho) \subseteq \rho$, which states that the fixed points of ρ, namely $\rho(C)$, include the images under μ of the fixed points of ρ. Upper and lower closures are compared using the pointwise order $\sqsubseteq$: If $\mu, \nu \in \mathrm{uco}(C)$ (or $\mu, \nu \in \mathrm{lco}(C)$), then $\mu \sqsubseteq \nu$ holds when for all $x \in C$, $\mu(x) \preceq_C \nu(x)$. For upper closures, $\mu \sqsubseteq \nu$ holds iff $\nu \subseteq \mu$, whereas for lower closures, $\mu \sqsubseteq \nu$ iff $\mu \subseteq \nu$. Accordingly, the intuition for upper closures is that if $\mu \sqsubseteq \nu$ then μ is a *refinement* of ν (or, equivalently, ν is an *abstraction* of μ), since the image of μ includes that of ν. Dually, for lower closures.

Complete Abstractions. Abstract domains are classically introduced either as Galois connections or as upper closure operators on a complete lattice C [8,9]; it is well known that the two formalisms are interchangeable [7, Chapter 11]. In this work we adopt the closure operator view, which in our setting provides significant advantages in terms of presentation. Thus, $\mu \in \mathrm{uco}(C)$ is regarded as an abstraction of C, so that $\mu(c)$ is the best abstract approximation of $c \in C$ in the abstract domain $\mu(C)$.

Given a function $f\colon C \to C$, an abstraction μ is *forward f-complete* when $f\mu = \mu f \mu$ holds; we write $\mathbb{C}^f(\mu)$ to denote this property. Intuitively, $\mathbb{C}^f(\mu)$ holds when the behaviour of f is fully preserved by the abstraction μ, since applying the concrete function f to abstract values in μ yields a result that is already an abstract value in μ. Forward complete abstractions are therefore ideal for model checking, as they introduce the least possible loss of precision. The *f-complete shell* (or simply *complete shell*) of μ [12]—the least refinement of μ that is forward f-complete, i.e., $f\text{-shell}(\mu) = \bigsqcap\{\nu \in \mathrm{uco}(C) \mid \mu \sqsubseteq \nu, \mathbb{C}^f(\nu)\}$—plays a key role in what follows. In this sense, forward completeness characterizes maximal precision, while complete shells are the coarsest abstractions (i.e., those that abstract as much as possible) achieving such precision.

Transition Systems. Let $G = (\Sigma_G, I_G, \to_G)$ be a transition system (TS), where Σ_G is a (possibly infinite) set of states, $I_G \subseteq \Sigma_G$ is the set of initial states, and $\to_G \subseteq \Sigma_G \times \Sigma_G$ is the transition relation. We write $x \to_G y$ to denote $(x, y) \in \to_G$. The successor transformer $\mathsf{post}_G\colon \wp(\Sigma_G) \to \wp(\Sigma_G)$ is defined as usual: $\mathsf{post}_G(X) \triangleq \{y \in \Sigma_G \mid \exists x \in X. x \to_G y\}$. Dually, the predecessor transformer $\mathsf{pre}_G\colon \wp(\Sigma_G) \to \wp(\Sigma_G)$ is defined by $\mathsf{pre}_G(Y) \triangleq \{x \in \Sigma_G \mid \exists y \in Y. x \to_G y\}$. The set of *reachable states* is $\mathsf{post}^*_G(I_G) \triangleq \mathrm{lfp}(\lambda X. I_G \cup \mathsf{post}_G(X))$. Subscripts are omitted when no ambiguity arises.

3 Semi-completeness

In this section we introduce *semi-completeness*, a weakening of forward completeness, together with its "operational" counterpart, *semi-stability*[1]. Recall that f-completeness requires an abstraction $\mu \in \mathrm{uco}(C)$ to capture the behaviour of $f\colon C \to C$ on *all elements* of C, thereby enforcing precision across the entire domain. Semi-completeness relaxes this requirement. The key idea is that many applications demand precision only in certain subspaces in which f is applied,

[1] The prefix "semi-" is inspired by Lee and Yannakakis [16, Definition 3.2].

rather than on the whole domain C. To express this, semi-completeness is parameterised by an additional lower closure $\rho \in \text{lco}(C)$, which specifies "to what extent" forward completeness should hold. This parameter function ρ should be seen as a "filter" that removes irrelevant information. Choosing ρ to be a lower closure operator is natural, since $\rho(c)$ represents the "region of c" relevant for achieving completeness, and therefore $\rho(c) \preceq c$ is an expected requirement. Moreover, monotonicity ensures that elements containing less information cannot retain more irrelevant information than elements containing more information, while idempotency guarantees that ρ removes all irrelevant information in a single step.

We introduce the *non-spilling* property to characterize how the "filter" ρ is expected to interact with the abstraction μ.

Definition 3.1 (Non-Spilling lco). Given an abstraction $\mu \in \text{uco}(C)$, we define $\text{NS}(\mu) \triangleq \{\rho \in \text{lco}(C) \mid \mu(\rho) \subseteq \rho\}$ as the set of lcos that are *non-spilling* for μ. Equivalently, $\text{NS}(\mu) = \{\rho \in \text{lco}(C) \mid \rho\mu\rho = \mu\rho\}$.

A non-spilling lower closure ρ ensures that ρ is "compatible" with μ: applying μ to a filtered element $\rho(x)$ does not reintroduce information that ρ removes, that is, formally, $\rho(\mu(\rho(x))) = \mu(\rho(x))$ holds.

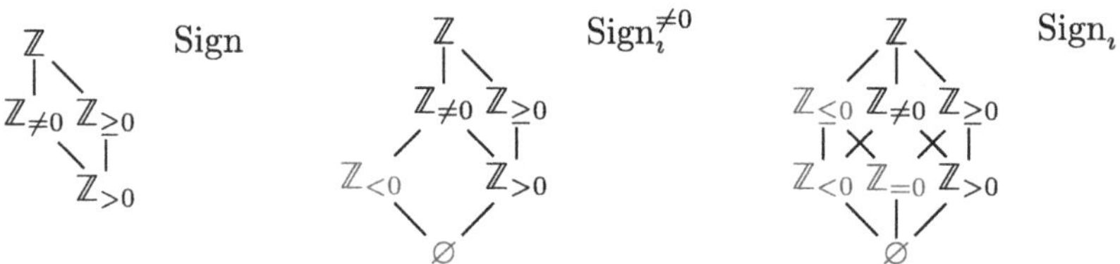

Fig. 2. Three Sign abstract domains. Elements represent subsets of $\mathbb{Z}$: $\mathbb{Z}_{\geq 0}$ denotes the set of non-negative integers, $\mathbb{Z}_{\neq 0}$ the set of non-zero integers, and so on.

Example 3.2 ((Non-)Spilling lco). Let $\mu \in \text{uco}(\wp(\mathbb{Z}))$ be the uco induced by $\text{Sign}_\imath^{\neq 0}$ in Fig. 2 (i.e., the fixed points of μ are the subsets of $\mathbb{Z}$ included in $\text{Sign}_\imath^{\neq 0}$). Consider the lco ρ' defined by $\rho' \triangleq \lambda X.\, X \cap \{-1, 1\}$. This lco is spilling for μ: for instance, $\{1\} \in \rho'$ (i.e., $\rho'(\{1\}) = \{1\}$), while $\mu(\{1\}) = \mathbb{Z}_{>0} \notin \rho'$, since $\rho'(\mathbb{Z}_{>0}) = \{1\} \neq \mathbb{Z}_{>0}$. On the other hand, the lco ρ defined by $\rho \triangleq \lambda X.\, X \smallsetminus \{0\}$ is non-spilling for μ. In fact, for any $X \in \rho$ (i.e., any X such that $0 \notin X$), we have $X \subseteq \mathbb{Z}_{\neq 0}$, and therefore $\mu(X) \in \{\mathbb{Z}_{\neq 0}, \mathbb{Z}_{<0}, \mathbb{Z}_{>0}, \varnothing\} \subseteq \rho$. $\Diamond$

Definition 3.3 (Forward Semi-Completeness). Given a concrete function $f \colon C \to C$, $\mu \in \text{uco}(C)$, and $\rho \in \text{lco}(C)$, μ is *forward ρ-semi f-complete* (or simply *ρ-semi f-complete*), denoted $\mathbf{fsc}_f^\rho(\mu)$, when $\rho\,\mu\,\rho\, f\,\mu = \rho\, f\,\mu$ holds[2].

[2] Note that $\mathbf{fsc}_f^\rho(\mu)$ holds when for all $x \in \mu$, $\rho f(x)$ is a fixed point of $\rho\mu$.

Sub/superscripts in $\mathbf{fsc}_f^\rho(\mu)$ may be omitted when they are clear from the context. Observe that semi-completeness $\mathbf{fsc}_f^\rho(\mu)$ is implied by $\mathbb{C}^{\rho f}(\mu)$, i.e. by forward ρf-completeness $\mu\rho f\mu = \rho f\mu$. In contrast, the semi-completeness equation $\rho\mu\rho f\mu = \rho f\mu$ requires this equality only up to the information selected by the filter lco ρ. Hence, $\mathbf{fsc}_f^\rho(\mu)$ can be viewed as a weakening of $\mathbb{C}^{\rho f}(\mu)$, enforcing completeness only on the portion of the domain retained by ρ. In particular, observe that when ρ is non-spilling, $\mathbf{fsc}_f^\rho(\mu)$ and $\mathbb{C}^{\rho f}(\mu)$ coincide:

$$\forall\mu \in \mathrm{uco}(C),\, \rho \in \mathrm{NS}(\mu).\ \mathbf{fsc}_f^\rho(\mu) \Leftrightarrow \mathbb{C}^{\rho f}(\mu)\ . \tag{1}$$

Moreover, even when ρ is spilling, decoupling ρ and f is advantageous. It allows one to reason independently about f, which determines the concrete behaviour for which completeness is sought, and ρ, which specifies where this completeness must hold. This separation also supports the refinement strategies developed in Sects. 3.2 and 4, where ρ is computed on-the-fly rather than assumed to be known in advance.

Example 3.4 (Semi-Completeness). Consider the sign abstractions in Fig. 2, the lcos ρ' and ρ from Example 3.2, and the inverse function $\imath : \wp(\mathbb{Z}) \to \wp(\mathbb{Z})$, i.e., $\imath(X) \triangleq \{-x \mid x \in X\}$. Let μ' be the uco induced by Sign. We first observe that the abstraction μ' is not ρ'-semi $\imath$-complete, since $\rho'\imath(\mathbb{Z}_{\geq 0}) = \{-1\}$ while $\rho'\mu'\rho'\imath(\mathbb{Z}_{\geq 0}) = \rho'\mu'(\{-1\}) = \rho'(\mathbb{Z}_{\neq 0}) = \{-1, 1\}$. The same example shows that μ' is not ρ-semi $\imath$-complete either. Let now μ be the uco induced by $\mathrm{Sign}_\imath^{\neq 0}$. We observe that μ is ρ'-semi $\imath$-complete. Indeed, for $X \in \{\mathbb{Z}, \mathbb{Z}_{\neq 0}\}$, we have $\rho'\imath(X) = \{-1, 1\}$ and $\rho'\mu(\{-1, 1\}) = \rho'(\mathbb{Z}_{\neq 0}) = \{-1, 1\}$. For $X \in \{\mathbb{Z}_{\geq 0}, \mathbb{Z}_{>0}\}$, we obtain $\rho'\imath(X) = \{-1\}$ with $\rho'\mu(\{-1\}) = \rho'(\mathbb{Z}_{<0}) = \{-1\}$. Finally, we have $\rho'\imath(\mathbb{Z}_{<0}) = \{1\} = \rho'\mu(\{1\})$, and $\rho'\imath(\varnothing) = \varnothing = \rho'\mu(\varnothing)$.

Observe that ρ' is a spilling lco for μ (as shown in Example 3.2), and indeed $\mathbb{C}^{\rho'\imath}(\mu)$ does not hold. For instance, $\rho'\imath(\mathbb{Z}_{<0}) = \rho'(\mathbb{Z}_{>0}) = \{1\} \notin \mu$. Consider now the non-spilling lco ρ. In this case, μ is ρ-semi $\imath$-complete. Indeed, $\rho\imath(\mathbb{Z}) = \rho\imath(\mathbb{Z}_{\neq 0}) = \mathbb{Z}_{\neq 0} = \rho\mu(\mathbb{Z}_{\neq 0})$ holds, along with $\rho\imath(\mathbb{Z}_{\geq 0}) = \rho\imath(\mathbb{Z}_{>0}) = \mathbb{Z}_{<0} = \rho\mu(\mathbb{Z}_{<0})$ and $\rho\imath(\mathbb{Z}_{<0}) = \mathbb{Z}_{>0} = \rho\mu(\mathbb{Z}_{>0})$. Finally, $\rho\imath(\varnothing) = \varnothing = \rho\mu(\varnothing)$ proves that ρ-semi $\imath$-completeness holds. By (1), this implies that $\mathbb{C}^{\rho\imath}(\mu)$ holds. ◊

As anticipated, semi-completeness is strictly weaker than forward completeness, meaning that: (I) $\mathbb{C}^f(\mu)$ is recovered as the special case of *id*-semi f-completeness, and (II) forward completeness strictly implies semi-completeness. In particular, given μ and f, the set $\{\rho \in \mathrm{lco}(C) \mid \mathbf{fsc}_f^\rho(\mu)\}$ is downward closed:

Lemma 3.5. *Let $f\colon C \to C$, $\mu \in uco(C)$, and $\rho \in lco(C)$. Then $\mathbf{fsc}_f^\rho(\mu)$ holds iff $\forall \rho' \in lco(C).\, \rho' \sqsubseteq \rho \Rightarrow \mathbf{fsc}_f^{\rho'}(\mu)$.*

Lemma 3.5 immediately yields point (II). Since $\rho \sqsubseteq id$ holds for every $\rho \in \mathrm{lco}(C)$, downward closure implies that $\mathbf{fsc}_f^{id}(\mu)$ (i.e., forward f-completeness) holds if and only if ρ-semi f-completeness holds for every $\rho \in \mathrm{lco}(C)$. The following example shows that semi-completeness is strictly weaker than forward completeness.

Example 3.6. Consider the domains in Fig. 2 and the lcos ρ' and ρ from Example 3.4, where we showed that $\text{Sign}_\imath^{\neq 0}$ is both ρ-semi $\imath$-complete and ρ'-semi $\imath$-complete. Note that $\text{Sign}_\imath$ is the $\imath$-complete shell of Sign. Moreover, $\text{Sign}_\imath^{\neq 0}$ is a strict abstraction of $\text{Sign}_\imath$. Therefore, forward semi-completeness may hold even when forward completeness does not. ◊

3.1 Semi-Stability

We now introduce *semi-stability*, a notion equivalent to semi-completeness that admits an "operational" formulation and underlies abstraction refinement algorithms aimed at achieving semi-completeness, such as Algorithms 1 and 2.

Definition 3.7 (Semi-Stability). Let $f\colon C \to C$, $\mu \in \text{uco}(C)$, and $\rho \in \text{NS}(\mu)$. Given a concrete value $x \in C$, μ is *ρ-semi f-stable on x* if

$$\forall y \in C.\, x \preceq \rho f y \Rightarrow \rho\mu x \preceq f\mu y \ .$$

A pair $\langle x, y\rangle \in C^2$ satisfying $x \preceq \rho f y$ and $\rho\mu x \not\preceq f\mu y$ is called *unstable*. Moreover, μ is ρ-semi f-stable if it is ρ-semi f-stable on every $x \in C$, denoted by $\mathbf{ssa}_f^\rho(\mu)$.

Sub/superscripts in $\mathbf{ssa}_f^\rho(\mu)$ may be omitted when clear from context. Semi-stability and semi-completeness are equivalent for monotone functions:

Lemma 3.8. *If* $f\colon C \overset{m}{\to} C$, $\mu \in$ *uco*(C), *and* $\rho \in$ *lco*(C), *then* $\mathbf{ssa}_f^\rho(\mu) \Leftrightarrow \mathbf{fsc}_f^\rho(\mu)$.

In particular, an unstable pair $\langle x, y\rangle$ witnesses non-semi-completeness: $\rho f\mu y \neq \rho\mu\rho f\mu y$, since $x \preceq \rho f y \Rightarrow \rho\mu x \preceq \rho\mu\rho f y \preceq \rho\mu\rho f \mu$ y, and $\rho\mu\rho f\mu y = \rho f\mu y$ would imply $\rho\mu x \preceq f\mu y$, contradicting instability.

Example 3.9. (Semi-stability). Consider the abstractions in Fig. 2, the lco ρ, and the ucos μ, μ' from Example 3.4, where μ' was shown to be not ρ-semi $\imath$-complete. By Lemma 3.8, μ' is therefore not ρ-semi $\imath$-stable: for example, the pair $\langle\{-1\}, \{0,1\}\rangle$ is unstable, since $\{-1\} \subseteq \{-1\} = \rho\imath(\{0,1\})$ and $\rho\mu'(\{-1\}) = \rho(\mathbb{Z}_{\neq 0}) = \mathbb{Z}_{\neq 0} \not\subseteq \mathbb{Z}_{\leq 0} = \imath\mu'(\{0,1\})$. On the other hand, μ is ρ-semi $\imath$-stable, since $\rho\mu(\{-1\}) = \rho(\mathbb{Z}_{<0})$, so the pair $\langle\{-1\}, \{0,1\}\rangle$ is not unstable in $\text{Sign}_\imath^{\neq 0}$. ◊

3.2 Ideal Semi-completion

We now exploit semi-stability (in particular its "operational" formulation) to design an algorithm for computing semi-stable abstractions, which, via Lemma 3.8, ensures semi-completeness. To this end, we introduce a class of lower closure operators, called *ideal closures*. Given a concrete value $c \in C$, define the function $\lfloor c\rfloor\colon C \to C$ as $\lfloor c\rfloor(x) \triangleq x \curlywedge c$. These functions are lower closures whose set of fixed points is the principal ideal $\downarrow c$ (see [9, § 6.4]). Intuitively, $\lfloor c\rfloor(x)$

returns the "portion" of x below c. In the context of $\lfloor c \rfloor$-semi f-completeness, the value c specifies the region of C on which we want f-completeness to hold, and $\lfloor c \rfloor(x)$ represents the portion of x where completeness is enforced. Observe that $c \preceq d \Rightarrow \downarrow c \subseteq \downarrow d \Rightarrow \lfloor c \rfloor \sqsubseteq \lfloor d \rfloor$.

We now define a procedure that, given a monotone function $f \colon C \xrightarrow{m} C$, an input abstraction $\mu_i \in \mathrm{uco}(C)$, and a value $c \in C$ specifying the region of interest, computes a refinement μ of μ_i that is $\lfloor \mu c \rfloor$-semi f-complete[3]. Moreover, the output μ is always coarser than the complete shell $\mu^* \triangleq f\text{-shell}(\mu_i)$ and is $\lfloor \mu^* c \rfloor$-semi f-complete. This procedure, called *ideal semi-completion*, achieves these guarantees without necessarily computing the full complete shell μ^*.

Algorithm 1: Ideal Semi-Completion

// **Input:** $f \colon C \xrightarrow{m} C$, $\mu_i \in \mathrm{uco}(C)$, $c \in C$.
1 $\mathrm{uco}(C) \ni \mu := \mu_i$;
2 **while** $\mathrm{UP} := \{\langle x, y \rangle \in C^2 \mid x \preceq \mu c,\ x \preceq fy,\ \mu x \not\preceq f \mu y\} \neq \varnothing$ **do**
  // Inv 1: $\mu \in \mathrm{uco}(C)$.
  // Inv 2: $\mu^* \sqsubseteq \mu$.
3 **choose**$\langle x, y \rangle \in \mathrm{UP}$;
4 $\mu := \mu \cup \{\mu z \curlywedge f \mu y \mid z \in C,\ \mu z \preceq \mu x\}$;
5 **end while**
6 **return** μ;

Algorithm 1 follows a "stabilization" approach: at each iteration, line 4 enforces $\lfloor \mu c \rfloor$-stability for a selected pair $\langle x, y \rangle$. The set UP of Unstable Pairs (line 2) is empty if and only if μ is $\lfloor \mu c \rfloor$-semi f-stable. Indeed, $x \preceq \mu c$ and $x \preceq fy$ hold if and only if $x \preceq \lfloor \mu c \rfloor fy$, and moreover, $x \preceq \mu c$ entails $\lfloor \mu c \rfloor \mu x = \mu x$, so that $\mu x \preceq f \mu y$ holds if and only if $\lfloor \mu c \rfloor \mu x \preceq f \mu y$. Upon termination, $\lfloor \mu c \rfloor$-semi f-stability, along with $\lfloor \mu c \rfloor \in \mathrm{NS}(\mu)$, and (1) guarantee that μ is $\lfloor \mu c \rfloor$-semi f-complete. A key aspect of the algorithm is that, while c is constant, the operator $\lfloor \mu c \rfloor$ is not: it depends on μ, which is updated at line 4. Thus, at each iteration, stabilization occurs with respect to a potentially different function $\lfloor \mu c \rfloor f$. In summary, Algorithm 1 computes $\lfloor \mu c \rfloor$-semi f-complete abstraction refinements while avoiding the full complete shell computation. This is particularly important because the resulting abstractions are precise in the domain region *below* $\mu(c)$, and the value of c can be chosen to encode the limit cases that the analysis should cover.

Theorem 3.10. (Correctness of Algorithm 1**).** *Upon termination, Algorithm 1 returns a refinement μ of μ_i such that both $\mathbf{fsc}_f^{\lfloor \mu^* c \rfloor}(\mu)$ and $\mathbf{fsc}_f^{\lfloor \mu c \rfloor}(\mu)$ hold, where $\mu^* \triangleq f\text{-shell}(\mu_i)$. Moreover, μ is refined at every iteration and remains coarser than μ^*.*

Notice that by instantiating Algorithm 1 with $c = \top$, we recover the standard stabilization approach, which computes the full f-complete shell.

[3] Considering $\lfloor \mu c \rfloor$ instead of $\lfloor c \rfloor$ yields abstractions coarser than f-shell(μ_i).

Example 3.11. (Execution of Algorithm 1*).* Consider the motivating example from Sect. 1. Note that, for any configuration s, $s = s_e$ holds iff y is even, so we represent configurations as pairs $\langle x, y\rangle$. Let $\mathbb{E}$ and $\mathbb{O}$ denote the set of even and odd integers, respectively. Given a set $S \subseteq \mathbb{Z}$, define $(a, b)_S \triangleq \{\langle x, y\rangle \in \mathbb{Q} \times \mathbb{Z} \mid a < x < b,\ y \in S\}$, the set of pairs $\langle x, y\rangle$ with x ranging in the open interval (a, b), and $y \in S$. This notation extends naturally to closed or mixed intervals. Let μ_i be the abstraction induced by the initial partition $\{[0, +\infty)_{\mathbb{O}}, (-\infty, 0)_{\mathbb{O}}, (M, +\infty)_{\mathbb{E}}, (-\infty, M]_{\mathbb{E}}\}$. That is, $\mu_i(X)$ is the union of all blocks intersecting X[4]. Moreover, let $c = [0, 0]_{\mathbb{Z}}$ (i.e., c is the horizontal axis). We execute Algorithm 1 on input $\langle \mathsf{pre}, \mu_i, c\rangle$.

At the *first iteration*, we have $\mu(c) = (-\infty, M]_{\mathbb{E}} \cup [0, +\infty)_{\mathbb{O}}$ and the pair $\langle c, [0, +\infty)_{\mathbb{O}}\rangle$ is unstable (i.e., it is in UP), since: $c \subseteq \mu(c)$ holds, along with $c \subseteq [0, +\infty)_{\mathbb{E}} \cup (-\infty, 0]_{\mathbb{O}} = \mathsf{pre}([0, +\infty)_{\mathbb{O}})$, and $\mu(c) \not\subseteq \mathsf{pre}\mu([0, +\infty)_{\mathbb{O}})$ holds (notice that the right hand side coincides with $\mathsf{pre}([0, +\infty)_{\mathbb{O}})$). Therefore, the algorithm refines μ by iterating over the abstract points $z \subseteq \mu(c)$ and adding the following new values to μ: for $z = \mu(c)$ we add $\mu(c) \cap \mathsf{pre}([0, +\infty)_{\mathbb{O}}) = [0, M]_{\mathbb{E}} \cup [0, 0]_{\mathbb{O}}$; for $z = (-\infty, M]_{\mathbb{E}}$ we add $(-\infty, M]_{\mathbb{E}} \cap \mathsf{pre}([0, +\infty)_{\mathbb{O}}) = [0, M]_{\mathbb{E}}$; for $z = [0, +\infty)_{\mathbb{O}}$ we add $[0, +\infty)_{\mathbb{O}} \cap \mathsf{pre}([0, +\infty)_{\mathbb{O}}) = [0, 0]_{\mathbb{O}}$; and for $z = \varnothing$ nothing is added to μ.

At the *second iteration*, we have $\mu(c) = [0, M]_{\mathbb{E}} \cup [0, 0]_{\mathbb{O}}$ and the pair $\langle c, [0, 0]_{\mathbb{O}}\rangle$ is unstable since: $c \subseteq \mu(c)$ holds, along with $c \subseteq c = \mathsf{pre}([0, 0]_{\mathbb{O}})$, and $\mu(c) \not\subseteq \mathsf{pre}\mu([0, 0]_{\mathbb{O}})$ (note that the right hand side coincides with $\mathsf{pre}([0, 0]_{\mathbb{O}})$). Therefore, the algorithm refines μ by iterating over the abstract points $z \subseteq \mu(c)$ and by adding the following new values to μ: for $z = \mu(c)$ we add $\mu(c) \cap \mathsf{pre}([0, 0]_{\mathbb{O}}) = \mu(c) \cap c = c$; for $z = [0, M]_{\mathbb{E}}$ we add $[0, M]_{\mathbb{E}} \cap c = [0, 0]_{\mathbb{E}}$; for $z = [0, 0]_{\mathbb{O}}$ we have that $[0, 0]_{\mathbb{O}} \cap c = [0, 0]_{\mathbb{O}}$ and no new element is added (same for $z = \varnothing$).

At the *third iteration*, $\mu(c) = c$ and UP $= \varnothing$ hold, since the abstraction is $\lfloor \mu c\rfloor$-semi pre-complete. In fact, $\mu = \mu_i \cup \{[0, 0]_{\mathbb{E}}, [0, 0]_{\mathbb{O}}, [0, 0]_{\mathbb{Z}}, [0, M]_{\mathbb{E}}\}$ holds. We now check that for all $x \in \mu$, $\lfloor \mu c\rfloor \mathsf{pre}(x) \in \mu$ holds. We first check the elements in μ_i: we have that $\lfloor \mu c\rfloor \mathsf{pre}((-\infty, M]_{\mathbb{E}}) = \lfloor \mu c\rfloor \mathsf{pre}([0, +\infty)_{\mathbb{O}}) = [0, 0]_{\mathbb{Z}} \in \mu$, and $\lfloor \mu c\rfloor \mathsf{pre}((M, +\infty)_{\mathbb{E}}) = \lfloor \mu c\rfloor \mathsf{pre}((-\infty, 0)_{\mathbb{O}}) = \varnothing \in \mu$. Moreover, for the remaining elements $x \in \mu_i$ (i.e., x is a union of blocks), we have that $\lfloor \mu c\rfloor \mathsf{pre}(x)$ coincides with $[0, 0]_{\mathbb{Z}}$ or $\varnothing$, depending on whether x intersects c or not. For the remaining points in μ, we have that $\lfloor \mu c\rfloor \mathsf{pre}([0, 0]_{\mathbb{E}}) = \lfloor \mu c\rfloor \mathsf{pre}([0, 0]_{\mathbb{O}}) = \lfloor \mu c\rfloor \mathsf{pre}([0, 0]_{\mathbb{Z}}) = \lfloor \mu c\rfloor \mathsf{pre}([0, M]_{\mathbb{E}}) = [0, 0]_{\mathbb{Z}} \in \mu$. We have thus shown that μ is $\lfloor \mu c\rfloor$-semi pre-complete, so that UP $= \varnothing$, i.e., Algorithm 1 terminates. $\Diamond$

To illustrate a practical application of Algorithm 1, consider a system modeling a machine whose behavior depends on temperature. Let t be a real-valued variable representing temperature in degrees Celsius. Since temperatures below absolute zero are physically impossible, we can exclude states with $t \leq 0$ K by defining $c = \{s \in \mathit{States} \mid t(s) > 0 \text{ K}\}$, where *States* denotes the state space.

[4] See Sect. 5 for a formal presentation of ucos induced by partitions.

This idea generalizes to constraints arising from design specifications rather than physical limitations. For instance, for machines intended to operate within a bounded temperature range, we can encode $c = \{s \in \mathit{States} \mid t(s) \in [t_{\min}, t_{\max}]\}$. Similarly, for systems with temporal constraints—such as airplane components operating for a limited time during flight—one can replace temperature with time and encode boundaries analogously.

4 Interleaving Fixed Point and Semi-completion Computations

Algorithm 1 computes semi-complete abstraction refinements μ with respect to the ideal lower closure $\lfloor \mu c \rfloor$, assuming that the concrete value c is given. We now consider a more general setting in which c is not known in advance and must be computed on-the-fly. Formally, given an initial abstraction $\mu_i \in \mathrm{uco}(C)$, and a pair of left- and right-adjoint functions $l, r \colon C \overset{m}{\to} C$, we aim to compute a refinement of μ_i that is $\lfloor \mu^*(c^*) \rfloor$-semi r-complete, where μ^* is the forward r-complete shell of μ_i and c^* is the least fixed point of l above some $a \in C$. Crucially, we show how to solve this problem without computing either $r\text{-shell}(\mu_i)$ or $c^* = \mathrm{lfp}_a(l)$. To motivate this general setting, consider the adjoint pair post and $\widetilde{\mathsf{pre}}$ of a transition system, where $\widetilde{\mathsf{pre}}(Y) \triangleq \{x \mid \forall y.\, x \to y \Rightarrow y \in Y\}$ is the weakest liberal precondition. Our approach then yields an abstraction μ that is $\lfloor \mu^*(\mathsf{post}^*(I)) \rfloor$-semi $\widetilde{\mathsf{pre}}$-complete. Intuitively, the lower closure $\lfloor \mu^*(\mathsf{post}^*(I)) \rfloor$ filters out unreachable states—which are irrelevant for model checking—thus allowing the abstraction μ to be effectively used in verification while remaining coarser than the entire complete shell μ^*. This application is developed in Sect. 5.

4.1 Interleaving Algorithm

We first recall that, given two complete lattices A and B, two functions $l \colon A \to B$ and $r \colon B \to A$ are respectively called *left* and *right adjoint* (or, together, an adjoint pair), if for all $a \in A$ and $b \in B$, $l(a) \preceq_B b \Leftrightarrow a \preceq_A r(b)$. We denote by $\mathrm{Adj}(C) \triangleq \{\langle l, r \rangle \mid l, r \colon C \to C \text{ form an adjoint pair}\}$ the set of adjoint pairs over the complete lattice C.

Given $\langle l, r \rangle \in \mathrm{Adj}(C)$, Algorithm 2 interleaves the computation of the fixed point $\mathrm{lfp}_a(l)$ with refinements of the abstraction μ in order to enforce $\lfloor \mu(c) \rfloor$-semi r-stability.

Algorithm 2: Fixed Point-based Ideal Semi-Completion

// **Input:** $\mu_i \in \text{uco}(C)$, $\langle l, r\rangle \in \text{Adj}(C)$, and $a \in C$.
1 $C \ni c := \bot$;
2 $\text{uco}(C) \ni \mu := \mu_i$;
3 **repeat**
    // `Inv 1:` $c \preceq \texttt{lfp}_a(l)$.
4   **while** $\mu(c) \neq \mu(a \curlyvee l(c))$ **do** $c := a \curlyvee l(c)$;
5   **if** $\text{UP} := \{\langle x, y\rangle \in C^2 \mid x \preceq \mu c,\ x \preceq ry,\ \mu x \npreceq r\mu y\} \neq \varnothing$ **then**
        // `Inv 2:` $\mu \in \texttt{uco}(C)$.
        // `Inv 3:` $\mu^* \sqsubseteq \mu$.
6   **choose**$\langle x, y\rangle \in \text{UP}$;
7         $\mu := \mu \cup \{\mu z \ \curlywedge\ r\mu y \mid \mu z \preceq \mu x\}$;
8   **end if**
9 **until** $\mu(c) = \mu(a \curlyvee l(c))\ \wedge\ \text{UP} = \varnothing$;
10 **return** $\langle \mu, c\rangle$;

In Algorithm 2 the concrete value c corresponds to the current Kleene iterate of $\lambda x.\, a \curlyvee l(x)$, while lines 5-8 follow the same stabilization strategy as Algorithm 1. In particular, the abstraction μ is refined at line 7 so as to stabilize a pair $\langle x, y\rangle$. Note that the value μc—and therefore the lco $\lfloor \mu c \rfloor$—is not constant during the repeat-until iterations of Algorithm 2: μ is refined at line 7, as in Algorithm 1, and additionally c is updated at line 4. In particular, the *concrete* fixed point iteration (line 4) updates the value of c to the next Kleene iterate of $\lambda x.\, a \curlyvee l(x)$ only when this results in a change of $\mu(c)$. Upon termination $\text{UP} = \varnothing$, and therefore the abstraction μ is $\lfloor \mu c\rfloor$-semi r-complete. This ensures that backward l-completeness holds on all the previously computed values of c. Consequently, $\mu(c)$ coincides with the abstract fixed point $\mu(\text{lfp}_a(l))$, and the resulting abstraction is $\lfloor \mu(\text{lfp}_a(l))\rfloor$-semi r-complete.

Theorem 4.1. (Correctness of Algorithm 2**).** *Upon termination, Algorithm 2 returns a pair* $\langle \mu, c\rangle$ *such that* $r\text{-}shell(\mu_i) = \mu^* \sqsubseteq \mu \sqsubseteq \mu_i$ *and* $\mu(c) = \mu(\mathit{lfp}_a(l))$*. Moreover, both* $\mathbf{fsc}_r^{\lfloor \mu(c)\rfloor}(\mu)$ *and* $\mathbf{fsc}_r^{\lfloor \mu^*\, \mathit{lfp}_a(l)\rfloor}(\mu)$ *hold, and* μ *is refined at every iteration.*

Example 4.2. (Execution of Algorithm 2*).* Consider the motivating example presented in Sect. 1, together with the notation introduced in Example 3.11. We execute Algorithm 2 on this TS with input $a = \{\langle 0, 0\rangle\}$, the adjoint pair $\langle \mathsf{post}, \widetilde{\mathsf{pre}}\rangle$, and the abstraction μ_i.

At the *first iteration*, the loop at line 4 first updates c to $[0, 0]_{\{0\}}$, since $\mu(\varnothing) = \varnothing \neq (-\infty, M]_{\mathbb{E}} = \mu([0, 0]_{\{0\}})$. It then updates c again so that $c = [0, 0]_{\{0,1\}}$, because $\mu([0, 0]_{\{0\}}) \neq (-\infty, M]_{\mathbb{E}} \cup [0, +\infty)_{\mathbb{O}} = \mu([0, 0]_{\{0,1\}})$. The loop terminates since $\mu([0, 0]_{\{0,1\}}) = \mu([0, 0]_{\{0,1,2\}})$, and therefore $\mu(c) = (-\infty, M]_{\mathbb{E}} \cup [0, +\infty)_{\mathbb{O}}$. The pair $\langle c, \mu(c)\rangle$ is unstable (i.e., it belongs to UP), since $c \subseteq \mu(c)$ and $c \subseteq [0, \frac{M}{2}]_{\mathbb{E}} \cup (-\infty, 0]_{\mathbb{O}} = \widetilde{\mathsf{pre}}((-\infty, M]_{\mathbb{E}} \cup [0, +\infty)_{\mathbb{O}}) = \widetilde{\mathsf{pre}}(\mu(c))$, while

$\mu(c) \not\subseteq \widetilde{\mathsf{pre}}(\mu(c))$. The abstraction μ is therefore refined by iterating over the abstract points $z \subseteq \mu(c)$ and adding the following new values: for $z = \mu(c)$ we add $\mu(c) \cap \widetilde{\mathsf{pre}}(\mu(c)) = [0, \frac{M}{2}]_{\mathbb{E}} \cup [0,0]_{\mathbb{O}}$; for $z = (-\infty, M]_{\mathbb{E}}$ we add $(-\infty, M]_{\mathbb{E}} \cap \widetilde{\mathsf{pre}}(\mu(c)) = [0, \frac{M}{2}]_{\mathbb{E}}$; for $z = [0, +\infty)_{\mathbb{O}}$ we add $[0,+\infty)_{\mathbb{O}} \cap \widetilde{\mathsf{pre}}(\mu(c)) = [0,0]_{\mathbb{O}}$; for $z = \varnothing$ nothing is added.

At the *second iteration*, line 4 does not update c, since $\mu([0,0]_{\{0,1\}}) = [0, \frac{M}{2}]_{\mathbb{E}} \cup [0,0]_{\mathbb{O}} = \mu([0,0]_{\{0,1,2\}})$. The pair $\langle c, \mu(c)\rangle$ remains unstable, since $c \subseteq \mu(c)$ and $c \subseteq [0,0]_{\mathbb{Z}} = \widetilde{\mathsf{pre}}([0, \frac{M}{2}]_{\mathbb{E}} \cup [0,0]_{\mathbb{O}}) = \widetilde{\mathsf{pre}}(\mu(c))$, while $\mu(c) \not\subseteq \widetilde{\mathsf{pre}}(\mu(c))$. The abstraction μ is refined again by considering $z \subseteq \mu(c)$ and adding to μ the following values: for $z = \mu(c)$ we add $\mu(c) \cap \widetilde{\mathsf{pre}}(\mu(c)) = [0,0]_{\mathbb{Z}}$; for $z = [0, \frac{M}{2}]_{\mathbb{E}}$ we add $[0, \frac{M}{2}]_{\mathbb{E}} \cap \widetilde{\mathsf{pre}}(\mu(c)) = [0,0]_{\mathbb{E}}$; for $z = [0,0]_{\mathbb{O}}$ no new element is added since $[0,0]_{\mathbb{O}} \cap \widetilde{\mathsf{pre}}(\mu(c)) = [0,0]_{\mathbb{O}} \in \mu$; for $z = \varnothing$ nothing is added.

At the *third iteration*, c is not updated and $\mu(c) = [0,0]_{\mathbb{Z}}$. We show that μ is $\lfloor \mu(c) \rfloor$-semi $\widetilde{\mathsf{pre}}$-complete. At this stage, we have $\mu = \mu_i \cup \{[0,0]_{\mathbb{E}}, [0,0]_{\mathbb{O}}, [0,0]_{\mathbb{Z}}, [0, \frac{M}{2}]_{\mathbb{E}}, [0, \frac{M}{2}]_{\mathbb{E}} \cup [0,0]_{\mathbb{O}}\}$. We verify that for every $x \in \mu$, $\lfloor \mu c \rfloor \widetilde{\mathsf{pre}}(x) \in \mu$ holds. First consider $x \in \mu_i$: for all $x \in \{\varnothing, (-\infty, M]_{\mathbb{E}}, [0,+\infty)_{\mathbb{O}}, (-\infty,0)_{\mathbb{O}}, (M,+\infty)_{\mathbb{E}} \cup (-\infty, M]_{\mathbb{E}}, [0,+\infty)_{\mathbb{O}} \cup (-\infty,0)_{\mathbb{O}}\}$, we have $\widetilde{\mathsf{pre}}(x) = \varnothing$, hence $\lfloor \mu c \rfloor \widetilde{\mathsf{pre}}(x) = \varnothing \in \mu$. Moreover, we have $\lfloor \mu c \rfloor \widetilde{\mathsf{pre}}((M,+\infty)_{\mathbb{E}} \cup [0,+\infty)_{\mathbb{O}}) = \lfloor \mu c \rfloor ((\frac{M}{2}, +\infty)_{\mathbb{E}}) = \varnothing \in \mu$, and $\lfloor \mu c \rfloor \widetilde{\mathsf{pre}}((M,+\infty)_{\mathbb{E}} \cup (-\infty,0)_{\mathbb{O}}) = \lfloor \mu c \rfloor ((M,+\infty)_{\mathbb{O}}) = \varnothing \in \mu$. Furthermore, $\lfloor \mu c \rfloor \widetilde{\mathsf{pre}}([0,+\infty)_{\mathbb{O}} \cup (-\infty, M]_{\mathbb{E}}) = \lfloor \mu c \rfloor ([0, \frac{M}{2})_{\mathbb{E}} \cup (-\infty, 0]_{\mathbb{O}}) = [0,0]_{\mathbb{Z}} \in \mu$, and $\lfloor \mu c \rfloor \widetilde{\mathsf{pre}}((-\infty, M]_{\mathbb{E}} \cup (-\infty,0)_{\mathbb{O}}) = \lfloor \mu c \rfloor ((-\infty,0)_{\mathbb{E}} \cup (0,M]_{\mathbb{O}}) = \varnothing \in \mu$. Similarly, $\lfloor \mu c \rfloor \widetilde{\mathsf{pre}}((M,+\infty)_{\mathbb{E}} \cup (-\infty, M]_{\mathbb{E}} \cup [0,+\infty)_{\mathbb{O}}) = \lfloor \mu c \rfloor \widetilde{\mathsf{pre}}((-\infty, M]_{\mathbb{E}} \cup [0,+\infty)_{\mathbb{O}} \cup (-\infty,0)_{\mathbb{O}}) = \lfloor \mu c \rfloor \widetilde{\mathsf{pre}}((M,+\infty)_{\mathbb{E}} \cup (-\infty, M]_{\mathbb{E}} \cup [0,+\infty)_{\mathbb{O}} \cup (-\infty,0)_{\mathbb{O}}) = [0,0]_{\mathbb{Z}} \in \mu$, and $\lfloor \mu c \rfloor \widetilde{\mathsf{pre}}((M,+\infty)_{\mathbb{E}} \cup [0,+\infty)_{\mathbb{O}} \cup (-\infty,0)_{\mathbb{O}}) = \lfloor \mu c \rfloor \widetilde{\mathsf{pre}}((M,+\infty)_{\mathbb{E}} \cup (-\infty, M]_{\mathbb{E}} \cup (-\infty,0)_{\mathbb{O}}) = \varnothing \in \mu$. This shows that $\lfloor \mu c \rfloor \widetilde{\mathsf{pre}}(x) \in \mu$ holds for every $x \in \mu_i$. Finally, for the elements $x \in \mu \setminus \mu_i$, we have $\lfloor \mu c \rfloor \widetilde{\mathsf{pre}}([0,0]_{\mathbb{E}}) = \lfloor \mu c \rfloor \widetilde{\mathsf{pre}}([0,0]_{\mathbb{O}}) = \varnothing \in \mu$, $\lfloor \mu c \rfloor \widetilde{\mathsf{pre}}([0,0]_{\mathbb{Z}}) = [0,0]_{\mathbb{Z}} \in \mu$, $\lfloor \mu c \rfloor \widetilde{\mathsf{pre}}([0, \frac{M}{2}]_{\mathbb{E}}) = \varnothing \in \mu$, and $\lfloor \mu c \rfloor \widetilde{\mathsf{pre}}([0, \frac{M}{2}]_{\mathbb{E}} \cup [0,0]_{\mathbb{O}}) = \varnothing \in \mu$. Thus, $\lfloor \mu c \rfloor \widetilde{\mathsf{pre}}(x) \in \mu$ for every $x \in \mu$, which proves that μ is $\lfloor \mu(c) \rfloor$-semi $\widetilde{\mathsf{pre}}$-complete. Consequently, $\mathrm{UP} = \varnothing$ and Algorithm 2 terminates. ◊

5 Abstract Model Checking

We apply our results in the context of model checking. We first discuss the role of unreachable states in the μ-calculus. Then, we recall the definition of abstract model checking and show how our refinement algorithm can be used to model check formulas over reachable states.

Given a finite set of atomic propositions $p \in \mathcal{P}$ and a set of variables $x \in \mathcal{X}$, μ-calculus formulas in $\mathscr{L}_1$ are defined as:

$$\mathscr{L}_1 \ni \varphi ::= p \mid \bar{p} \mid x \mid \varphi \vee \varphi \mid \varphi \wedge \varphi \mid \exists\bigcirc \varphi \mid \forall\bigcirc \varphi \mid \mu x\colon \varphi \mid \nu x\colon \varphi\ .$$

The semantics of a formula $\varphi \in \mathscr{L}_1$ is defined for a TS $G = \langle \Sigma, I, \rightarrow \rangle$, a context $\mathcal{E}\colon \mathcal{X} \rightarrow \wp(\Sigma)$, a state labeling function such that $p(\Sigma) \subseteq \Sigma$ is the set of states satisfying an atomic proposition $p \in \mathcal{P}$. The semantics $[\![\varphi]\!]^G_{\mathcal{E}}$ of φ over G and $\mathcal{E}$ is the set of states on which φ holds, defined as:

$$[\![p]\!]^G_{\mathcal{E}} \triangleq p(\Sigma) \qquad [\![\bar{p}]\!]^G_{\mathcal{E}} \triangleq \Sigma \setminus p(\Sigma) \qquad [\![x]\!]^G_{\mathcal{E}} \triangleq \mathcal{E}(x)$$

$$[\![\varphi_1 \left\{\begin{smallmatrix}\vee\\ \wedge\end{smallmatrix}\right\} \varphi_2]\!]^G_{\mathcal{E}} \triangleq [\![\varphi_1]\!]^G_{\mathcal{E}} \left\{\begin{smallmatrix}\cup\\ \cap\end{smallmatrix}\right\} [\![\varphi_2]\!]^G_{\mathcal{E}} \qquad [\![\left\{\begin{smallmatrix}\exists\\ \forall\end{smallmatrix}\right\} \bigcirc \varphi]\!]^G_{\mathcal{E}} \triangleq \left\{\begin{smallmatrix}\mathsf{pre}\\ \widetilde{\mathsf{pre}}\end{smallmatrix}\right\} [\![\varphi]\!]^G_{\mathcal{E}}$$

$$[\![\left\{\begin{smallmatrix}\mu\\ \nu\end{smallmatrix}\right\} x \colon \varphi]\!]^G_{\mathcal{E}} \triangleq \left\{\begin{smallmatrix}\mathrm{lfp}\\ \mathrm{gfp}\end{smallmatrix}\right\} \left(\lambda X.\, [\![\varphi]\!]^G_{\mathcal{E}[x\mapsto X]}\right) .$$

When clear from the context, superscripts will be omitted, and we define $[\![\varphi]\!]^G \triangleq [\![\varphi]\!]^G_{\mathcal{E}_\perp}$ where $\mathcal{E}_\perp$ is the empty context. For closed formulas (i.e., formulas where all variables are bound by a quantifier), and for any context $\mathcal{E}$, it holds that $[\![\varphi]\!]^G = [\![\varphi]\!]^G_{\mathcal{E}}$. Any subset, i.e. fragment, of $\mathscr{L}_1$ inherits the semantics $[\![\cdot]\!]^G_{\mathcal{E}}$.

We remark that removing unreachable states from a transition system has no effect on whether a reachable state r belongs to $[\![\varphi]\!]$. To formalize this, we introduce a modified semantics $(\!|\cdot|\!)^{G,S}_{\mathcal{E}}$ which is additionally parameterized by a set of states $S \subseteq \Sigma$. The semantics $(\!|\cdot|\!)^{G,S}_{\mathcal{E}}$ is defined inductively in the same way as $[\![\cdot]\!]^G$, except in the cases of $\forall\bigcirc$ and $\exists\bigcirc$, where we set:

$$(\!|\left\{\begin{smallmatrix}\exists\\ \forall\end{smallmatrix}\right\} \bigcirc \varphi|\!)^{G,S}_{\mathcal{E}} \triangleq \lfloor S \rfloor \left(\left\{\begin{smallmatrix}\mathsf{pre}\\ \widetilde{\mathsf{pre}}\end{smallmatrix}\right\} (\!|\varphi|\!)^{G,S}_{\mathcal{E}}\right) . \tag{2}$$

Intuitively, the definition in (2) ensures that only states in S are considered in the next-step semantics. In particular, if $\mathsf{post}^*(I) \subseteq S$, the operator $\lfloor S \rfloor$ effectively removes unreachable states from the semantics.

Theorem 5.1. (Model Checking for Reachable States). *Let $\varphi \in \mathscr{L}_1$ be a closed formula, $S \in \wp(\Sigma)$ satisfies $\mathsf{post}^*(I) \subseteq S$, and let $r \in \mathsf{post}^*(I)$. Then, $r \in [\![\varphi]\!]^G_{\mathcal{E}} \Leftrightarrow r \in (\!|\varphi|\!)^{G,S}_{\mathcal{E}}$.*

Hence, Theorem 5.1 shows that the validity of a formula φ on a reachable state r can be checked by testing whether $r \in (\!|\varphi|\!)^{G,S}$.

5.1 Abstract Semantics of μ-Calculus

Abstract domains can be equivalently defined as upper closures or as Galois connections [9]; in this section, where $C = \wp(\Sigma)$, we adopt Galois connections $\langle \alpha, C, A, \gamma \rangle$ for clarity of presentation, where $\alpha \colon C \to A$ maps concrete to abstract values, and $\gamma \colon A \to C$ is the corresponding concretization map. Abstract semantics for temporal logics play a central role in abstract model checking. This approach is well-studied (see, e.g., [1,5,6,11,13,17,18,21,23]), and relies on defining an abstract semantic function that assigns abstract values to formulas. We follow the framework of Ranzato and Tapparo [21], where the abstract semantic function $[\![\cdot]\!]^{\sharp A}_{\mathcal{E}} : \mathscr{L}_1 \to A$ is defined inductively by replacing each concrete semantic operator with its best correct approximation in A:

$$\llbracket p \rrbracket_{\mathcal{E}}^{\sharp A} \triangleq \alpha(p(\Sigma)) \qquad \llbracket \bar{p} \rrbracket_{\mathcal{E}}^{\sharp A} \triangleq \alpha(\Sigma \smallsetminus p(\Sigma)) \qquad \llbracket x \rrbracket_{\mathcal{E}}^{\sharp A} \triangleq \alpha(\mathcal{E}(x))$$
$$\llbracket \varphi_1 \left\{\begin{smallmatrix}\vee\\\wedge\end{smallmatrix}\right\} \varphi_2 \rrbracket_{\mathcal{E}}^{\sharp A} \triangleq \alpha(\gamma\llbracket \varphi_1 \rrbracket_{\mathcal{E}}^{\sharp A} \left\{\begin{smallmatrix}\cup\\\cap\end{smallmatrix}\right\} \gamma\llbracket \varphi_2 \rrbracket_{\mathcal{E}}^{\sharp A}) \quad \llbracket \left\{\begin{smallmatrix}\exists\\\forall\end{smallmatrix}\right\} \bigcirc \varphi \rrbracket_{\mathcal{E}}^{\sharp A} \triangleq \alpha(\left\{\begin{smallmatrix}\mathsf{pre}\\\widetilde{\mathsf{pre}}\end{smallmatrix}\right\} \gamma\llbracket \varphi \rrbracket_{\mathcal{E}}^{\sharp A}) \tag{3}$$
$$\llbracket \left\{\begin{smallmatrix}\mu\\\nu\end{smallmatrix}\right\} x \colon \varphi \rrbracket_{\mathcal{E}}^{\sharp A} \triangleq \left\{\begin{smallmatrix}\mathrm{lfp}\\\mathrm{gfp}\end{smallmatrix}\right\} \left(\lambda X.\, \llbracket \varphi \rrbracket_{\mathcal{E}[x \mapsto \gamma(X)]}^{\sharp A}\right) .$$

By construction, $\llbracket \varphi \rrbracket_{\mathcal{E}}^{\sharp A}$ soundly approximates the concrete semantics, i.e., $\alpha\llbracket \varphi \rrbracket_{\mathcal{E}}^{G} \preceq_A \llbracket \varphi \rrbracket_{\mathcal{E}}^{\sharp A}$, while the converse need not hold. An abstraction A is *strongly preserving* for a language $\mathscr{L} \subseteq \mathscr{L}_1$ if, for all $\varphi \in \mathscr{L}$ and $X \in \wp(\Sigma)$, $\alpha(X) \preceq \llbracket \varphi \rrbracket_{\mathcal{E}}^{\sharp A} \Leftrightarrow X \subseteq \llbracket \varphi \rrbracket_{\mathcal{E}}^{G}$ [17,21]. Strong preservation ensures equivalence between abstract and concrete validity for all formulas of $\mathscr{L}$. It is known [20,21] that strong preservation corresponds to forward completeness for the concrete semantic primitives defining the language.[5] In this work, we focus on a weaker notion, *reachable strong preservation* (r.s.p.), which requires strong preservation only over reachable states.

Definition 5.2. (Reachable Strong Preservation). Given a transition system G, an abstraction A, and $\mathscr{L} \subseteq \mathscr{L}_1$, an abstract semantics $\langle\!\langle \cdot \rangle\!\rangle^A \colon \mathscr{L} \to A$ (mapping closed formulas to their abstract semantics in A) satisfies the *r.s.p. property* for $\mathscr{L}$ if, for every $S \subseteq \mathsf{post}^*(I)$, $S \subseteq \llbracket \varphi \rrbracket^G \Leftrightarrow \alpha(S) \preceq \langle\!\langle \varphi \rangle\!\rangle^A$.

In the following, we show how our algorithms yield abstract semantics satisfying the r.s.p. property for increasingly expressive fragments of $\mathscr{L}_1$, by requiring more stringent assumptions on the abstractions: from general ucos to preorder-induced ucos and finally equivalence-induced ucos.

Challenge 1: Model Checking for Reachable States. Let us consider the disjunction-free universal fragment $\mathscr{L}_2$ of the μ-calculus:

$$\mathscr{L}_2 \ni \varphi \coloneqq p \mid \bar{p} \mid x \mid \varphi \wedge \varphi \mid \forall\bigcirc \varphi \mid \mu x \colon \varphi \mid \nu x \colon \varphi .$$

We show how Algorithm 2 can be used to produce an abstract semantics satisfying the r.s.p. property of Definition 5.2 for $\mathscr{L}_2$. To this end, given a set of states $S \subseteq \Sigma$, we consider an abstract semantic function $(\!|\cdot|\!)^{\sharp A,S} \colon \mathscr{L}_2 \to A$, which is the abstract counterpart of $(\!|\cdot|\!)^{G,S}$. More precisely, $(\!|\cdot|\!)^{\sharp A,S}$ is defined inductively as $\llbracket \cdot \rrbracket^{\sharp A}$ in (3), replacing every occurrence of $\llbracket \cdot \rrbracket^{\sharp A}$ with $(\!|\cdot|\!)^{\sharp A,S}$, except for the $\exists\bigcirc$ and $\forall\bigcirc$ connectives, for which we define:

$$(\!| \left\{\begin{smallmatrix}\exists\\\forall\end{smallmatrix}\right\} \bigcirc \varphi |\!)_{\mathcal{E}}^{\sharp A,S} \triangleq \alpha(\lfloor S \rfloor \left\{\begin{smallmatrix}\mathsf{pre}\\\widetilde{\mathsf{pre}}\end{smallmatrix}\right\} \gamma\llbracket \varphi \rrbracket_{\mathcal{E}}^{\sharp A}) . \tag{4}$$

Before proceeding, we recall some basic notions on relations. A relation $R \subseteq \Sigma \times \Sigma$ is a preorder if it is reflexive and transitive, and an equivalence if it is

[5] The continuity assumptions in [21] are satisfied here, since we work with finite abstractions.

also symmetric. It is known [22, § 5.2.1] that any preorder R (in particular, any equivalence) over Σ induces an additive uco $\mu \in \text{uco}(\langle \wp(\Sigma), \subseteq \rangle)$ defined for any $X \in \wp(\Sigma)$ by $\mu(X) \triangleq R(X)$, where $R(S) \triangleq \{s' \in \Sigma \mid \exists s \in S. (s, s') \in R\}$. For brevity, we write $R(x) \triangleq R(\{x\}) = \mu(\{x\})$. Any equivalence relation defines a partition (and vice versa), where the blocks of the partition and the equivalence classes coincide. We therefore write P both for a partition and its associated equivalence relation, and the map $\lambda X. P(X) = \cup\{P(s) \in P \mid s \in X\}$ defines an additive uco. Finally, let $\equiv_{\mathcal{P}}$ denote the equivalence induced by the atomic propositions $\mathcal{P}$, i.e., $s \equiv_{\mathcal{P}} s' \overset{\triangle}{\iff} \forall p \in \mathcal{P}. s \in p(\Sigma) \Leftrightarrow s' \in p(\Sigma)$, and let $P_{\mathcal{P}}$ be the corresponding partition.

Theorem 5.3. (Abstract Model Checking for Reachable States). *If Algorithm 2 terminates on input $\langle P_{\mathcal{P}}, \langle \mathsf{post}, \widetilde{\mathsf{pre}} \rangle, I \rangle$ and outputs $\langle \mu, c \rangle$, then $(\!|\cdot|\!)^{\sharp\mu,\mu(c)}$ satisfies the r.s.p. property for $\mathscr{L}_2$.*

Theorem 5.3 ensures that Algorithm 2 produces abstractions suitable for model checking every formula in $\mathscr{L}_2$ over the reachable states.

Challenge 2: Disjunctive Abstractions. Let us now consider the following universal fragment $\mathscr{L}_3$:

$$\mathscr{L}_3 \ni \varphi ::= p \mid \bar{p} \mid x \mid \varphi \vee \varphi \mid \varphi \wedge \varphi \mid \forall\bigcirc \varphi \mid \mu x \colon \varphi \mid \nu x \colon \varphi \ .$$

The fragment $\mathscr{L}_3$ is more expressive than $\mathscr{L}_2$, as it also allows disjunctions. Section 5.1 showed that Algorithm 2 supports abstract model checking of $\mathscr{L}_2$ formulas over reachable states. In order to achieve the same result for $\mathscr{L}_3$, we need to ensure that the resulting abstraction is additive (i.e., complete for unions), which is necessary for preserving disjunctions. To this end, we introduce a variant of Algorithm 2 where the uco μ is replaced by a preorder, thereby enforcing additivity. This modified procedure, Algorithm 2uni, is obtained from Algorithm 2 by substituting μ with a preorder R throughout the algorithm and by replacing lines (5–8) with the following primed lines:

5′ **if** UP $:= \{\langle x, y \rangle \in \Sigma^2 \mid x \in R(c), x \in r(\{y\}), R(x) \not\subseteq r(R(y))\} \neq \varnothing$ **then**
6′   **choose** $\langle x, y \rangle \in$ UP;
7′ $R := R \setminus \{(z, z') \in R \mid z \in R(x),\ z' \notin r(R(y))\}$;
8′ **end if**

Algorithm 2uni exploits the additivity of R and the distributivity of the lattice $\langle \wp(\Sigma), \subseteq \rangle$ to restrict the semi-completeness check at line 5′ to images of single states, rather than all abstract elements. The refinement step at line 7′ updates the underlying preorder[6]. Importantly, every refinement preserves reflexivity and transitivity, so that R remains a preorder throughout the execution.

[6] Each refinement might remove infinitely many pairs from R; however, with suitable symbolic representations of R, each update can be implemented in finitely many steps.

Theorem 5.4. *If Algorithm 2uni terminates on input* $\langle P_{\mathcal{P}}, \langle \mathsf{post}, \widetilde{\mathsf{pre}} \rangle, I \rangle$ *and outputs* $\langle R, c \rangle$, *then* $(\!|\cdot|\!)^{\sharp R, R(c)}$ *satisfies the r.s.p. property for* $\mathcal{L}_3$.

Challenge 3: Partitioning Abstractions. We now show how a further modification of Algorithm 2 achieves r.s.p. for the full language $\mathcal{L}_1$. Building on Sect. 5.1, we extend Algorithm 2uni so that semi-completeness is enforced also for pre, and not only $\widetilde{\mathsf{pre}}$, as above. As we previously replaced arbitrary ucos with preorders in order to guarantee additivity, we now further restrict the abstractions computed by the algorithm to those induced by *partitions*, that is, by symmetric preorders. The resulting procedure, Algorithm 2bis, is obtained from Algorithm 2 by replacing μ with a partition P and by substituting lines (5–8) with the following ones:

5′ **if** $\mathrm{UP} := \{\langle x, y \rangle \in \Sigma^2 \mid x \in P(c), x \in r(\{y\}), P(x) \nsubseteq r(P(y))\} \neq \varnothing$ **then**
6′   **choose** $\langle x, y \rangle \in \mathrm{UP}$;
7′ $P := (P \setminus \{P(x)\}) \cup \{P(x) \cap r(P(y)),\ P(x) \setminus r(P(y))\}$;
8′ **end if**

Algorithm 2bis exploits additivity in the same way as Algorithm 2uni, so that completeness is checked only on the blocks of the partition P, rather than on arbitrary abstract elements (i.e., unions of blocks). It enforces semi-completeness simultaneously for pre and $\widetilde{\mathsf{pre}}$, thus supporting the full $\mathcal{L}_1$ language.

Theorem 5.5. *If Algorithm 2bis terminates on input* $\langle P_{\mathcal{P}}, \langle \mathsf{post}, \widetilde{\mathsf{pre}} \rangle, I \rangle$ *and outputs* $\langle P, c \rangle$, *then* $(\!|\cdot|\!)^{\sharp P, P(c)}$ *satisfies the r.s.p. property for* $\mathcal{L}_1$.

Let us observe that Algorithm 2bis solves the problem addressed by Lee and Yannakakis [16]. However, our framework is more general and extends their approach in three directions: (i) it supports arbitrary abstractions, not only partitioning ones (cf. Challenge 1); (ii) completeness can be enforced for any concrete function, not only for $\widetilde{\mathsf{pre}}$; and (iii) the notion of reachable state space is generalized to any semantically relevant region, specified by the lco ρ.

The three constructions presented in Challenges 1–3 show how increasingly expressive fragments of the μ-calculus can be supported by progressively stronger classes of abstractions. Starting from arbitrary ucos, Algorithm 2 yields abstractions ensuring the r.s.p. property for the disjunction-free fragment $\mathcal{L}_2$. By restricting abstractions to preorder-induced ucos, Algorithm 2uni guarantees additivity, thereby enabling reachable-state model checking for the fragment $\mathcal{L}_3$ with disjunctions. Finally, by further restricting abstractions to partitions, Algorithm 2bis enforces semi-completeness for both $\widetilde{\mathsf{pre}}$ and pre, which suffices to obtain the r.s.p. property for the full μ-calculus $\mathcal{L}_1$.

6 Conclusion and Future Work

We addressed limitations of classical abstract model checking, where strong preservation typically requires globally complete abstractions. By introducing semi-completeness, we provide a principled relaxation of forward completeness that enables more practical refinements. Parameterized by lower closure operators, semi-completeness enforces completeness only over semantically relevant regions rather than globally. We presented two refinement procedures: one enforcing semi-completeness for a given region, and another interleaving refinement with the region's fixed point computation. Both avoid constructing fully complete abstractions and are especially effective when verifying reachable states. Applied to μ-calculus model checking, our framework yields reachability-aware abstract semantics for relevant fragments, reducing verification effort.

Several directions remain for future work. First, we plan to further investigate the algorithmic aspects of our approach, including complexity bounds, suitable symbolic representations, and the role of non-determinism in the refinement process. Second, integrating the proposed interleaving procedure into existing model checking frameworks would enable empirical evaluation and the development of practical optimizations. Finally, we aim to extend our framework to probabilistic and real-time systems, thereby broadening its applicability, and to further explore connections with related areas such as deductive verification.

Acknowledgements. Francesco Ranzato was partially supported by the *Italian MUR* under the PRIN 2022 PNRR project no. P2022HXNSC; by a *WhatsApp Research Award*; and by an *Amazon Research Award* for "AWS Automated Reasoning". This publication is also supported by grant PID2022-138072OB-I00, funded by MCIN/AEI/10.13039/501100011033/ FEDER, UE; by grant PIPF-2022/COM-24370, funded by the Madrid Regional Government; and by grant CEX2024-001471-M, funded by MICIU/AEI/10.13039/501100011033.

References

1. Banda, G., Gallagher, J.P.: Constraint-based abstract semantics for temporal logic: a direct approach to design and implementation. In: Clarke, E.M., Voronkov, A. (eds.) LPAR 2010. LNCS (LNAI), vol. 6355, pp. 27–45. Springer, Heidelberg (2010). https://doi.org/10.1007/978-3-642-17511-4_3
2. Bonchi, F., Ganty, P., Giacobazzi, R., Pavlovic, D.: Sound up-to techniques and complete abstract domains. In: Proceedings 33rd Annual ACM/IEEE Symposium on Logic in Computer Science, LICS 2018, pp. 175–184. ACM, New York, NY, USA (2018). https://doi.org/10.1145/3209108.3209169
3. Bradley, A.R.: SAT-based model checking without unrolling. In: Proceedings 12th International Conference on Verification, Model Checking, and Abstract Interpretation, VMCAI 2011. Lecture Notes in Computer Science, vol. 6538, pp. 70–87. Springer (2011). https://doi.org/10.1007/978-3-642-18275-4_7
4. Clarke, E., Grumberg, O., Jha, S., Lu, Y., Veith, H.: Counterexample-guided abstraction refinement. In: Emerson, E.A., Sistla, A.P. (eds.) CAV 2000. LNCS, vol. 1855, pp. 154–169. Springer, Heidelberg (2000). https://doi.org/10.1007/10722167_15

5. Clarke, E.M., Grumberg, O., Jha, S., Lu, Y., Veith, H.: Counterexample-guided abstraction refinement for symbolic model checking. J. ACM **50**(5), 752–794 (2003). https://doi.org/10.1145/876638.876643
6. Clarke, E.M., Grumberg, O., Long, D.E.: Model checking and abstraction. ACM Trans. Program. Lang. Syst. **16**(5), 1512–1542 (1994). https://doi.org/10.1145/186025.186051
7. Cousot, P.: Principles of Abstract Interpretation. MIT Press, Cambridge (2021)
8. Cousot, P., Cousot, R.: Abstract interpretation: a unified lattice model for static analysis of programs by construction or approximation of fixpoints. In: Proceedings ACM POPL 1977, pp. 238–252. ACM (1977). https://doi.org/10.1145/512950.512973
9. Cousot, P., Cousot, R.: Systematic design of program analysis frameworks. In: Proceedings ACM POPL 1979, pp. 269–282. ACM Press (1979). https://doi.org/10.1145/567752.567778
10. Cousot, P., Ganty, P., Raskin, J.-F.: Fixpoint-guided abstraction refinements. In: Nielson, H.R., Filé, G. (eds.) SAS 2007. LNCS, vol. 4634, pp. 333–348. Springer, Heidelberg (2007). https://doi.org/10.1007/978-3-540-74061-2_21
11. Dams, D., Grumberg, O.: Abstraction and abstraction refinement. In: Handbook of Model Checking, pp. 385–419. Springer, Cham (2018). https://doi.org/10.1007/978-3-319-10575-8_13
12. Filé, G., Giacobazzi, R., Ranzato, F.: A unifying view of abstract domain design. ACM Comput. Surv. **28**(2), 333–336 (1996). https://doi.org/10.1145/234528.234742
13. Giacobazzi, R., Ranzato, F.: Incompleteness of states w.r.t. traces in model checking. Inf. Comput. **204**(3), 376–407 (2006). https://doi.org/10.1016/J.IC.2006.01.001
14. Henzinger, T.A., Majumdar, R., Raskin, J.: A classification of symbolic transition systems. ACM Trans. Comput. Log. **6**(1), 1–32 (2005). https://doi.org/10.1145/1042038.1042039
15. Hoder, K., Bjørner, N.: Generalized property directed reachability. In: Cimatti, A., Sebastiani, R. (eds.) SAT 2012. LNCS, vol. 7317, pp. 157–171. Springer, Heidelberg (2012). https://doi.org/10.1007/978-3-642-31612-8_13
16. Lee, D., Yannakakis, M.: Online Minimization of Transition Systems. In: Proceedings of the 24th Annual ACM Symposium on Theory of Computing, STOC '92, pp. 264–274. ACM (1992). https://doi.org/10.1145/129712.129738
17. Loiseaux, C., Graf, S., Sifakis, J., Bouajjani, A., Bensalem, S., Probst, D.: Property preserving abstractions for the verification of concurrent systems. Formal Methods Syst. Design **6**(1), 11–44 (1995). https://doi.org/10.1007/bf01384313
18. Massé, D.: Semantics for abstract interpretation-based static analyzes of temporal properties. In: Hermenegildo, M.V., Puebla, G. (eds.) SAS 2002. LNCS, vol. 2477, pp. 428–443. Springer, Heidelberg (2002). https://doi.org/10.1007/3-540-45789-5_30
19. Ranzato, F., Doria, O.R., Tapparo, F.: A forward-backward abstraction refinement algorithm. In: Logozzo, F., Peled, D.A., Zuck, L.D. (eds.) VMCAI 2008. LNCS, vol. 4905, pp. 248–262. Springer, Heidelberg (2008). https://doi.org/10.1007/978-3-540-78163-9_22
20. Ranzato, F., Tapparo, F.: Making abstract model checking strongly preserving. In: Hermenegildo, M.V., Puebla, G. (eds.) SAS 2002. LNCS, vol. 2477, pp. 411–427. Springer, Heidelberg (2002). https://doi.org/10.1007/3-540-45789-5_29

21. Ranzato, F., Tapparo, F.: Generalized strong preservation by abstract interpretation. J. Log. Comput. **17**(1), 157–197 (2007). https://doi.org/10.1093/LOGCOM/EXL035
22. Ranzato, F., Tapparo, F.: Generalizing the Paige-Tarjan algorithm by abstract interpretation. Inf. Comput. **206**(5), 620–651 (2008). https://doi.org/10.1016/J.IC.2008.01.001
23. Shoham, S., Grumberg, O.: Monotonic abstraction-refinement for CTL. In: Jensen, K., Podelski, A. (eds.) TACAS 2004. LNCS, vol. 2988, pp. 546–560. Springer, Heidelberg (2004). https://doi.org/10.1007/978-3-540-24730-2_40

Towards Language Model Guided TLA$^+$ Proof Automation

Yuhao Zhou(✉) and Stavros Tripakis

Northeastern University, Boston, MA, USA
zhou.yuhao@northeastern.edu

Abstract. Formal theorem proving with TLA$^+$ provides rigorous guarantees for system specifications, but constructing proofs requires substantial expertise and effort. While large language models have shown promise in automating proofs for tactic-based theorem provers like Lean, applying these approaches directly to TLA$^+$ faces significant challenges due to the hierarchical proof structure of the TLA$^+$ proof system. We present a prompt-based approach that leverages LLMs to guide hierarchical decomposition of complex proof obligations into simpler sub-claims, while relying on symbolic provers for verification. Our key insight is to constrain LLMs to generate normalized claim decompositions rather than complete proofs, significantly reducing syntax errors. We also introduce a benchmark suite of 119 theorems adapted from (1) established mathematical collections and (2) inductive proofs of distributed protocols. Our approach consistently outperforms baseline methods across the benchmark suite.

Keywords: Formal Verification · Theorem Proving · Large Language Models · TLA$^+$

1 Introduction

Formal verification plays a crucial role in ensuring the correctness of critical systems, particularly distributed systems where subtle errors can have severe consequences. As systems grow in complexity and become more interconnected, the need for rigorous verification methods becomes increasingly vital. The TLA$^+$ specification language [26] has emerged as a powerful framework for modeling and verifying such systems, with significant adoption in companies like Amazon, Intel, and Microsoft [5,20,35,36]. Despite its effectiveness, constructing formal proofs in TLA$^+$ remains time-consuming and requires substantial expertise, creating a bottleneck in the verification process [45,47].

Proof automation is fundamentally challenging: the underlying problem of proving theorems in expressive logics is undecidable [10,56] and state-of-the-art provers still require substantial human guidance for complex proofs [33,51]. Therefore, any progress in techniques that assist or automate proof construction

A. Sampaio and M. Stoelinga (Eds.): FM 2026, LNCS 16556, pp. 619–640, 2026.
https://doi.org/10.1007/978-3-032-26204-2_32

represents a significant opportunity to lower the barrier to formal verification, by making it more practical and scalable.

Recent advances in Large Language Models (LLMs) have shown promise in automating formal theorem proving tasks, particularly in *tactic-based* theorem provers like Lean [65] and Rocq (previously known as Coq) [50]. These approaches leverage LLMs' capabilities to generate sequences of proof tactics that incrementally transform proof states toward the goal. However, TLA$^+$ employs a fundamentally different, *hierarchical* proof structure. Unlike Lean and Rocq, which sequentially transform proof states by tactics, TLA$^+$ proofs are organized as trees of claims and sub-claims. For example, while a tactic-based proof consists of a sequence of transformations (e.g., 'expand definition, apply distributive property, simplify'), a TLA$^+$ proof introduces intermediate claims that collectively establish the goal. This distinction is illustrated by the proofs of theorem T1 in Fig. 1 (TLA$^+$) and Fig. 2 (Lean).

```
-------- MODULE sums_even -------
EXTENDS Naturals, TLAPS

Even(x) == x % 2 = 0

THEOREM L0 == ASSUME NEW x ∈ Nat PROVE
      Even(x + x) = Even(x * 2)
OBVIOUS

THEOREM L1 == ASSUME NEW x ∈ Nat PROVE
      Even(x * 2) = ((x * 2) % 2 = 0)
BY DEF Even

THEOREM T1 == ASSUME NEW x ∈ Nat PROVE
      Even(x + x)
BY L0, L1 DEF Even
================================
```

Fig. 1. Theorem T1 proven in TLA$^+$.

```
1 import Mathlib.Tactic.Ring
2
3 def even (x : Nat) : Prop := x % 2 = 0
4
5 theorem T1 : ∀ x : Nat, even (x+x) := by
6     intro x
7     ring_nf
8     dsimp [even]
9     simp
```

Fig. 2. The same theorem T1 of Fig. 1, now proven in Lean. The Lean proof consists of a sequence of *tactics* (lines 6–9) that transform the proof state to solve the goal.

Additionally, while systems like Lean and Rocq have extensive libraries of formalized proofs that can serve as training data and benchmarks for machine learning approaches, TLA$^+$ lacks comparable datasets, creating a significant challenge for developing and evaluating learning-based proof automation.

In this paper, we present a language-model based approach to automating TLA$^+$ proof generation. Our method, called *Language Model Guided Proof Automation* (LMGPA), accommodates the hierarchical structure of TLA$^+$ proofs through a recursive decomposition strategy. This approach guides LLMs to recursively break down complex claims into simpler sub-claims that can be independently verified, mirroring the natural structure of TLA$^+$ proofs. Our system verifies each decomposition step, providing feedback to the LLM when necessary, and recursively applies the same process to each sub-claim until all claims can be verified by backend provers.

2 Preliminaries and Problem Statement

TLA+ and TLA+ Proof System. TLA+ is a formal specification language [26] designed for specifying and verifying properties of complex systems and algorithms, particularly distributed systems and concurrent algorithms. It has been adopted in both academia and industry, with companies such as Amazon, Microsoft, and Intel successfully applying it to verify critical systems and protocols [5,20,25,35]. TLA+ is supported by the TLA+ Foundation – see https://foundation.tlapl.us/.

As a language grounded in mathematical logic, TLA+ enables not only precise specification but also rigorous verification through model checking [67] and theorem proving. While model checking is an essential formal verification method [4,11,12], in the industry it is typically used for finding error traces quickly, and for verifying correctness of finite-state systems or bounded instances of infinite-state systems. In this paper, we focus on formal theorem proving, which allows to prove correctness of unbounded/infinite systems. Theorem proving for TLA+ is implemented in the TLA+ Proof System (TLAPS) [8], which serves as a bridge between human-written specifications and automated verification tools. TLAPS translates TLA+ specifications and proofs into forms supported by backend provers like Z3 [14], Zenon [6], and Isabelle [37,40].

The proving approach in TLA+ represents a distinct paradigm when compared to other prominent formal theorem provers, particularly in how proofs are structured and developed. In what follows, we discuss the most important differences.

TLAPS vs Tactic-based Interactive Theorem Provers. In the landscape of formal theorem proving, many popular *Interactive Theorem Provers* (ITPs) such as Lean [33], Rocq [51], and Isabelle/HOL [37] support a tactic-based approach to proof construction.[1] In the tactical style of proving, machine-checkable formal proofs are expressed as sequences of *tactics*—commands that systematically transform the proof state. Users guide the proof development by iteratively applying these tactics, effectively directing the prover through the proving process. The Lean proof in Fig. 2 illustrates this: the proof of `T1` is a sequence of tactics (lines 6–9) like `intro`, `ring_nf`, and `simp` that manipulate and solve the proof goal.

The proof methodology in TLA+, however, follows a fundamentally different structure. Rather than tactical transformations, TLA+ proofs are organized hierarchically—users establish complex claims by identifying and introducing intermediate sub-claims. For instance, the TLA+ proof in Fig. 1 demonstrates this structure, the explicit intermediate sub-claims `L0` and `L1` collectively establish the goal `T1`. This hierarchical proof continues growing until the entire proof

[1] Tactical proofs are not the only style these provers support. For example, Lean also supports calculational proofs. Isabelle also supports hierarchically structured proofs similar to TLAPS; in fact, Isabelle is one of the backend provers used by TLAPS.

```
1 -------- MODULE amc12a_2015_p10 -------
2 EXTENDS Integers, TLAPS
3
4 THEOREM Main ==
5     ∀ x, y ∈ Int: (0 < y) ∧ (y < x) ∧ (x
       + y + (x * y) = 80) ⇒ (x = 26)
6 =======================
```

Fig. 3. An example theorem represented in TLA$^+$ as input to our proof generation system.

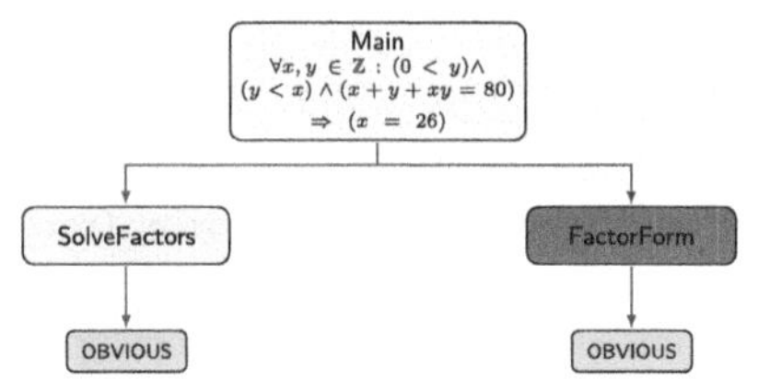

Fig. 4. Visualization of the proof tree for the proof in Fig. 5.

```
1  -------- MODULE amc12a_2015_p10 -------
2  EXTENDS Integers, TLAPS
3
4  THEOREM FactorForm ==
5      ASSUME  NEW x ∈ Int, NEW y ∈ Int,
6              0 < y, y < x,
7              x + y + (x * y) = 80
8      PROVE   (x + 1) * (y + 1) = 81
9  OBVIOUS
10
11 THEOREM SolveFactors ==
12     ASSUME  NEW x ∈ Int, NEW y ∈ Int,
13             0 < y, y < x,
14             (x + 1) * (y + 1) = 81
15     PROVE   x = 26
16 OBVIOUS
17
18 THEOREM Main ==
19     ∀ x, y ∈ Int: (0 < y) ∧ (y < x) ∧ (x
        + y + (x * y) = 80) ⇒ (x = 26)
20 BY FactorForm, SolveFactors
21 =======================
```

Fig. 5. Complete TLA$^+$ proof of the theorem in Fig. 3 (the entire proof was generated fully automatically by our system).

is directly machine-checkable by backend provers. This methodological distinction has significant implications for how proofs are developed, understood, and potentially automated within the TLAPS.

It is important to note that the proofs in Figs. 1 and 2 are presented purely for illustrative purposes to highlight this methodological difference. More direct or idiomatic proofs of T1 exist in both systems. While the theorem T1 is adapted from the TLA$^+$ example repository [54], the TLA$^+$ proof structure was intentionally modified to explicitly demonstrate the differences between hierarchical and tactic-based proving approaches.

TLA$^+$ Proof Structure. In TLA$^+$, a proof is a hierarchical arrangement of claims, where each claim represents a theorem to prove. To illustrate this structure, we refer to the examples in Figs. 3 and 5, which demonstrate a theorem and its corresponding proof in TLA$^+$. Using these examples as reference points, we now define the key terminology used throughout this paper:

- A *claim* is a boolean-valued expression written in TLA$^+$. For instance, line 5 in Fig. 3 (which is identical to line 19 in Fig. 5) is a claim. Lines 5–8 of Fig. 5 collectively form another claim.
- A *goal* is a specific claim that requires proof, representing the theorem or lemma of interest. In our example, the Main claim serves as the goal.
- *Context* is the collection of definitions and assumptions that provide the logical foundation for the goal. This includes imported modules such as the Integers module in Fig. 3, which provides the definition of Int.
- A *proof obligation* is a tuple of a context and a goal.

- A core construct in TLA$^+$ proofs is the `ASSUME-PROVE` structure, as seen in `FactorForm` and `SolveFactors` in Fig. 5. These are interpreted as logical implications where `ASSUME` F `PROVE` G means $\vdash F \Rightarrow G$, i.e., prove that F implies G.

While TLA$^+$ offers a rich and expressive proof language with multiple approaches to establishing claims, this paper focuses on a specific subset of proof structures for clarity and tractability. Specifically, we consider proofs that follow the pattern demonstrated in Fig. 5, where a claim may be associated with one of the following:

- An *auto proof*, where the claim can be directly verified by backend provers. In TLAPS, auto proofs use either the keyword `OBVIOUS` or the form `BY DEF` with a list of definitions to unfold. For example, the proofs of theorems `FactorForm` and `SolveFactors` in Fig. 5 use `OBVIOUS`, meaning they can be verified directly without unfolding any definitions. On the other hand, the proof of theorem `Main` is not an auto proof because it references other theorems.
- A proof by sub-claims, where the parent claim is established by a set of sub-claims. In TLAPS, this is expressed using the `BY` keyword followed by a list of the sub-claims. In Fig. 5, the parent claim `Main` is supported by two sub-claims: `FactorForm` and `SolveFactors`, which together provide a justification. Formally, if the parent claim asserts $F \Rightarrow G$, and it is supported by sub-claims A and B, then we are submitting to the solver the proof obligation $(A \wedge B) \Rightarrow (F \Rightarrow G)$, which is logically equivalent to $(A \wedge B \wedge F) \Rightarrow G$.
- No attached proof, as seen in Fig. 3 where the claim `Main` stands with no proof provided.

An important aspect of TLA$^+$ proof development, which is central to our work, is that appropriate sub-claims must be discovered to establish the parent claim. In Fig. 5, the sub-claims `FactorForm` and `SolveFactors` were not given in the original theorem statement (Fig. 3). They had to be formulated by the user with knowledge of quadratic equations. This discovery of effective intermediate steps represents a significant challenge in proof development. Human users must manually determine these sub-claims through mathematical insight and domain knowledge. Our system, however, attempts to automatically discover appropriate sub-claims.

TLA$^+$ provides several *proof directives* that instruct backend provers on how to prove the claims. These include `OBVIOUS` (indicating that the backend provers should verify the claim directly, as seen in line 9 of Fig. 5), `BY` (which proves the claim using specified facts and definitions, as demonstrated in line 20), `BY SMT` (restricting verification to only SMT solvers), and so on. These directives serve as an interface between the high-level proof structure and the specialized reasoning capabilities of various backend provers.

The status of a claim—whether it is considered *proved* or *unproved*—follows a recursive definition that reflects the hierarchical nature of TLA$^+$ proofs:

- A claim is *proved* if either:

  - It has an attached auto proof that is accepted by the backend provers, or
  - It is supported by a set of sub-claims that are themselves all *proved*, and the backend provers confirm that these sub-claims collectively establish the parent claim.
- Any claim not meeting these criteria remains *unproved*.

This hierarchical structure naturally gives rise to a tree representation of proofs, as visualized in Fig. 4 for the proof shown in Fig. 5. In this tree:

- Each node corresponds to a claim (`Main`, `FactorForm`, and `SolveFactors` in our example).
- The root node represents the primary goal (`Main` in our example).
- The edges capture the logical dependencies between claims, showing how sub-claims support their parent claims.

A proof achieves the status of a *complete proof* precisely when its root goal is *proved* according to the recursive definition above. This completion signifies that the entire proof has been successfully checked by backend solvers.

As constructing formal proofs manually requires significant expertise in both the problem domain and the formal prover itself, there exists a substantial barrier to the wider adoption of formal proving. Building on the framework outlined above, the central challenge addressed in this paper is the automated generation of complete proofs for TLA$^+$ proof obligations.

Problem Statement. Given a module containing an *unproved* claim (as in Fig. 3 where `Main` lacks a proof), our objective is to automatically construct a *complete proof* (like the one shown in Fig. 5).

3 Language Model Guided Proof Automation

Automated proof generation for TLA$^+$ presents unique challenges due to its hierarchical proof structure and rigorous verification requirements. In this section, we first describe the main challenges that naive methods face. We then introduce our approach, which leverages the reasoning capabilities of Large Language Models (LLMs) while addressing their limitations through a recursive claim decomposition strategy.

3.1 Challenges of Naive Methods

We consider two "naive" methods: (1) a symbolic method which simply attempts to use TLAPS to automatically prove the theorem; (2) an LLM-based method which prompts the LLM asking for a proof, up to a maximum of k times (this method is actually less naive when $k > 1$, as it uses feedback in subsequent prompts). We discuss each of these two naive methods next.

Naive Symbolic Method: `TLAPS OBVIOUS` The basic approach to automatically proving TLA$^+$ claims is to delegate them directly to TLAPS's backend provers

Algorithm 1 Direct LLM-Based Proof Generation

```
1: function DirectLLM-ProveObligation(context, goal)
2:     feedback ← null
3:     repeat
4:         proof ← LLMGenProof(context, goal, feedback)
5:         proved, feedback ← VerifyByTLAPS(proof)
6:     until proved or max retries reached
7:     return proved, proof
8: end function
```

without providing further information. In the TLA$^+$ proof language, this is done by asserting the claim as OBVIOUS. While this method works for simple claims, it often fails for more complex ones that require intermediate proof steps to be explicitly provided.

Direct LLM-Based Proof Generation. A straightforward approach to automated TLA$^+$ proof generation involves prompting LLMs to generate complete proofs in a single prompt. This method relies entirely on the LLM's ability to produce syntactically correct and logically sound proofs from the provided theorem statements and context.

Algorithm 1 outlines this direct approach. For a given proof obligation (*context*, *goal*), the algorithm repeatedly prompts the LLM to generate a complete proof (Line 4). After each generation, it verifies the proof using TLAPS (Line 5). If the proof is valid, the process terminates; otherwise, the algorithm incorporates feedback from the verification step (e.g., error messages) into subsequent prompts to guide the LLM's next attempt (Line 4). This loop continues until a valid proof is found or the maximum number of retries is reached.
Generating TLA$^+$ proofs directly presents several challenges:

- **Syntactic Correctness:** Our experimental results (Sect. 4.4) demonstrate that state-of-the-art general-purpose LLMs, including OpenAI o3-mini [39] and Google Gemini [18], frequently generate TLA$^+$ proofs containing syntax errors, even when provided with the prover's feedback. These errors prevent programmatic verification by TLAPS.
- **Monolithic Generation:** When generating complete proofs from a single prompt, LLMs may introduce errors at any point in the proof. Because verification occurs only after the entire proof is generated rather than after each individual step, early errors propagate through subsequent reasoning. This lack of incremental verification limits LLMs' ability to maintain sound reasoning throughout multi-step proofs.

Recent approaches such as ReProver [65] and COPRA [50] address similar challenges in tactic-based theorem provers by constraining LLMs to generate only tactics and premises for a given proof state, enabling step-by-step verification and eliminating syntactic correctness issues. However, as discussed in

Sect. 2, the proof structure and methodology of TLA$^+$ differ fundamentally from tactic-based provers, necessitating a specialized approach aligned with TLA$^+$ proof methodology. Recent studies [60,64] have demonstrated promising results with single-pass Lean proof generation by fine-tuning LLMs on extensive Lean proof corpora, but again are not applicable to TLA$^+$. In this paper, we propose a *hierarchical proof generation* approach tailored to TLA$^+$'s proof methodology.

3.2 System Architecture and Key Ideas

Our Language Model Guided Proof Automation system (LMGPA) leverages the complementary strengths of LLMs and symbolic methods: we use LLMs for their reasoning abilities to decompose complex claims into simpler sub-claims, while relying on symbolic provers for rigorous verification and for proving simple claims. The key components include:

- **Claim Decomposition:** LLMs guide the decomposition of complex goals into simpler, more manageable sub-claims.
- **Automated Proof Generation:** For sufficiently simple claims, the system attempts to generate *auto proofs* using TLA$^+$ directives (e.g., `OBVIOUS`) that can be directly verified by `TLAPS`.
- **Proof Validation:** The system uses `TLAPS` to verify that (1) sub-claims collectively establish their parent claim, and (2) auto proofs are valid.

Our hierarchical, recursive proof generation algorithm (detailed in Sect. 3.3) directly addresses the two challenges identified above. First, it mitigates *syntactic correctness* issues by (1) restricting LLMs to generating only claim decompositions rather than complete proofs, and (2) normalizing LLM-generated sub-claim structures (Sect. 3.4), which significantly reduces opportunities for syntax errors (Sect. 4.4). Second, it overcomes *monolithic generation* limitations through incremental verification at each recursive step, enabling localized error correction without discarding entire proof attempts.

3.3 Recursive Proof Generation Algorithm

Algorithm 2 presents our hierarchical proof generation approach. The algorithm recursively decomposes complex claims until reaching claims that can be directly verified by the backend provers, mirroring the hierarchical structure of TLA$^+$ proofs described in Sect. 2.

For a given proof obligation $(context, goal)$, the algorithm first attempts to generate an auto proof (Line 2). If this proof is successfully verified (Line 3), the algorithm returns it immediately. Otherwise, it leverages LLMs to decompose the goal into simpler sub-claims (Line 7) and verifies that these sub-claims collectively establish the original goal (Line 8). This verification-feedback loop continues until either a valid decomposition is found or the maximum number of retries is reached.

Once a valid decomposition is established, the algorithm recursively applies itself to each sub-claim (Lines 14–20), constructing a hierarchical proof structure consistent with `TLA+` proof conventions. If `ProveObligation` fails for any sub-claim (Lines 16–18), the entire proof attempt fails and the algorithm terminates without returning a valid proof, since all sub-claims must be discharged for the overall proof to be valid.

This recursive approach effectively combining the strengths of both symbolic provers (for rigorous verification) and LLMs (for non-trivial claim decomposition) to automate `TLA+` proof generation.

The final proof structure is assembled in Line 21, creating a complete `TLA+` proof that follows the hierarchical structure, with sub-claims serving as lemmas that collectively establish the parent claim.

Algorithm 2 Hierarchical Proof Generation

```
1: function ProveObligation(context, goal)
2:     autoProof ← GenerateAutoProof(context, goal)
3:     if VerifyProof(autoProof) then
4:         return autoProof
5:     end if
6:     repeat
7:         subClaims ← DecomposeIntoSubclaims(context, goal)
8:         decompositionValid ← VerifyDecomp(context, goal, subClaims)
9:     until decompositionValid or max retries reached
10:    if not decompositionValid then
11:        return failure
12:    end if
13:    proofs ← ∅
14:    for all claim ∈ subClaims do
15:        proof ← ProveObligation(context, claim)
16:        if proof is failure then
17:            return failure
18:        end if
19:        proofs ← proofs ∪ {(claim, proof)}
20:    end for
21:    return ConstructHierarchicalProof(goal, subClaims, proofs)
22: end function
```

In the following subsections, we delve deeper into the key components of our system, including LLM-guided claim decomposition, auto proof generation, and verification procedures. While developing this system, we explored various optimization techniques beyond those presented here. We focus on methods that demonstrated meaningful improvements in our experimental evaluation, while additional optimizations that did not yield significant benefits are documented in the Appendix of the extended version [73].

3.4 LLM-Guided Claim Decomposition

The `DecomposeIntoSubclaims` function forms the core of our approach, utilizing pretrained LLMs such as Claude [2] and o3-mini [39] to identify appropriate intermediate sub-claims that collectively establish a complex parent claim within the hierarchical proof structure. Notably, we use these models without any fine-tuning, relying instead on specialized prompting strategies to guide their reasoning toward valid claim decompositions.

To effectively leverage these models for claim decomposition and to overcome syntactic correctness challenges, we prompt the LLMs to generate normalized sub-claims that adhere to a specific structure (the complete prompt template is available in the Appendix of the extended version [73]).

Normalized Claim Structure. We constrain the generated sub-claims to follow a normalized format:

- Each LLM-generated sub-claim consists of a structured list containing assumptions (boolean expressions or definition references) and a single goal.
- Grammar constraints for expressions are embedded in the prompts, restricting output to ASCII characters and providing a table of acceptable notation.
- Our system parses these normalized claims and converts them into valid $\texttt{TLA}^+$ `ASSUME-PROVE` statements, eliminating a significant source of syntax errors.

Adaptive Feedback Loop. Although normalization substantially reduces syntax errors, complete correctness cannot be guaranteed. When `TLAPS` verification fails, our system feeds back the verifier's output to the LLM, allowing it to generate improved sub-claims in subsequent attempts.

3.5 Symbolic Auto Proof Generation

The `GenerateAutoProof` function employs a heuristic approach to efficiently handle simple claims without querying LLMs. This function first analyzes the parse tree of the given proof module to identify any definitions in the context that need to be explicitly unfolded in the goal claim. Based on this analysis, it generates appropriate auto proofs. If no definitions need unfolding, it applies the $\texttt{TLA}^+$ directive `OBVIOUS`, instructing backend provers to attempt verification directly. When the system determines that specific definitions must be unfolded to complete a proof, it generates a proof using the $\texttt{TLA}^+$ directive `BY` $l_1, l_2, ...$ `DEF` $d_1, d_2, ...$, where $l_1, l_2, ...$ are the assumptions and $d_1, d_2, ...$ are the definitions to be unfolded, both identified through syntax analysis.[2]

[2] We also explored a retrieval augmented [28] proof generation strategy but our preliminary results did not show sufficient improvements (c.f. the Appendix of the extended version [73]).

3.6 Verification Procedures

Our system includes two key verification procedures that ensure the correctness of both auto proofs and claim decompositions:

Auto Proof Verification. Function `VerifyProof` directly invokes `TLAPS` to determine whether a generated auto proof (e.g., `OBVIOUS`) is sufficient to justify a claim.

Decomposition Verification. Function `VerifyDecomp` validates that a set of sub-claims collectively establishes their parent claim. The system constructs a `TLA`$^+$ module that includes all sub-claims and the parent claim. `TLAPS` then verifies that the sub-claims collectively establish the parent claim.

4 Implementation and Evaluation

We present the implementation details of our system and evaluate its performance on the benchmark suite described in Sect. 4.2.

4.1 Implementation

We implemented the LMGPA system in Python 3.12, with components for parsing, verification, and LLM interactions. For syntax-level analysis in the auto proof generation phase (Sect. 3.5), we utilized the Tree-sitter `TLA`$^+$ parser [53], which enables efficient analysis of `TLA`$^+$ parse trees. LLM interactions are managed through LangChain [27], providing a unified interface to different language models.

The core verification pipeline integrates the `TLAPS` binary [55], with wrapper functions that handle the generation of temporary proof modules, execution of verification commands, and parsing of verification results. Our prompt templates include detailed instructions on the normalized claim format, examples of correct decompositions, and specific guidance on `TLA`$^+$ syntax constraints. Prompt templates are provided in the Appendix of the extended version of this paper [73]. The source code is available on GitHub [72] and the artifact on Zenodo [74].

4.2 Benchmarks

To evaluate our LMGPA system, we constructed a benchmark suite of `TLA`$^+$ theorems drawn from diverse sources to ensure variety in theorem types. The benchmark suite consists of: (a) 93 mathematical theorems adapted from the `miniF2F` [71] and `ProofNet` [3] collections; plus (b) 26 inductiveness proofs of candidate inductive invariants of distributed protocols, taken from [46] and its code repository [44]. `miniF2F` and `ProofNet` are standard benchmarks for evaluating AI-powered formal proof generation [65]. As these collections lack `TLA`$^+$ formalizations, we manually translated a curated subset of these theorems into

TLA$^+$ (for details, see the Appendix of the extended version of this paper [73]). Both the benchmark suite and our tool are publicly available, as an artifact [74] as well as in a GitHub repository [72].

We acknowledge the potential for data leakage in our benchmark. The mathematical theorems from miniF2F and ProofNet are commonly used benchmarks, and while our TLA$^+$ translations are new, the underlying proof strategies may have been encountered by the LLMs during pretraining in other formal languages such as Lean. Similarly, the inductiveness proofs from [46] are publicly available and could appear in pretraining corpora. Addressing potential data leakage issues can be done by constructing a leakage-free TLA$^+$ proof benchmark suite; this is beyond the scope of the current paper and part of future work.

4.3 Experimental Setup

We evaluated LMGPA on the benchmarks of Sect. 4.2. For our experiments, we selected state-of-the-art LLMs: Claude 3.7 Sonnet [2], Deepseek-V3.2-Exp [15], Gemini 2.0 Flash [18], Gemini 2.5 Flash [19], o3-mini-high [39], and GPT-5 [38]. This selection provides a diverse range of models, including both general language models (Claude and Gemini) and models optimized for reasoning tasks (o3-mini-high), as well as both open-source and proprietary models. We used all language models without any fine-tuning or additional training, relying solely on prompting strategies to guide these pretrained models.

For all experiments, we set consistent parameters across all models. We limited each model to a maximum of 4 decomposition attempts per claim (Algorithm 2, Line 9) and a maximum of 4 retries per proof obligation for direct LLM proof generation (Algorithm 1, Line 6). To ensure fair comparison and obtain results that are as deterministic as possible, we set the temperature to 0 for all LLM calls. All LLM requests were sent to the API provided by the LLM providers.

All experiments ran on a computer with a 16-core CPU and 64 GB RAM. We configured TLAPS to use 16 worker processes to fully utilize the available CPU capacity. We adhere to the default TLAPS timeouts. For each proof obligation, TLAPS attempts three backend provers in sequence: Z3 (5 s), Zenon (10 s), and Isabelle (30 s), resulting in a maximum total timeout of 45 s per obligation [1].

We evaluated our LMGPA system against the following baselines:

- Naive symbolic method (TLAPS OBVIOUS): see Sect. 3.1.
- Symbolic Auto Proof Generation (SAPG): see Sect. 3.5.
- Direct LLM Proof Generation (DLPG): see Sect. 3.1.

4.4 Results

Our evaluation focuses on three metrics: (1) the percentage of theorems successfully proved, which is our primary effectiveness measure, (2) the total number of LLM queries, and (3) the total time taken to process the entire benchmark suite.

Table 1. Evaluation results on the distributed protocol and mathematical benchmarks (c.f. Section 4.2). **Proved** is the percentage of theorems proved. **#Q** is the total number of queries made to the LLM. **Time** is the total execution time. The best result in each category is highlighted in **bold**.

	Distributed protocols			Mathematical		
Method	**Proved**	**#Q**	**Time**	**Proved**	**#Q**	**Time**
`TLAPS OBVIOUS`	0.0%	none	1m	44.1%	none	25m
SAPG	38.5%	none	14m	49.5%	none	34m
DLPG[Claude-3.7-Sonnet]	**15.4%**	98	4h 43m	17.2%	321	5h 14m
DLPG[Deepseek-V3.2-Exp]	0.0%	104	11h 27m	**29.0%**	336	39h 51m
DLPG[Gemini-2.0-Flash]	0.0%	104	41m	4.3%	359	39m
DLPG[Gemini-2.5-Flash]	0.0%	104	1h 30m	3.2%	364	3h 18m
DLPG[GPT-5]	3.8%	104	6h 36m	20.7%	307	24h 23m
DLPG[o3-mini-high]	0.0%	104	1h 5m	0.0%	372	8h 30m
LMGPA[Claude-3.7-Sonnet]	42.3%	83	1h 32m	53.8%	231	4h 49m
LMGPA[Deepseek-V3.2-Exp]	**50.0%**	73	9h 14m	**59.1%**	261	33h 17m
LMGPA[Gemini-2.0-Flash]	38.5%	54	39m	54.8%	251	1h 10m
LMGPA[Gemini-2.5-Flash]	46.2%	72	1h 25m	54.8%	224	5h 2m
LMGPA[GPT-5]	42.3%	89	4h 26m	58.1%	245	9h 58m
LMGPA[o3-mini-high]	42.3%	96	1h 44m	57.0%	241	5h 50m

The results are shown in Table 1. Across all benchmarks and all of the tested LLMs, our LMGPA system demonstrates consistent improvements in proof success rates compared to the baselines. The SAPG baseline itself consistently outperforms the `OBVIOUS`-only baseline, demonstrating the effectiveness of our heuristic-based symbolic proof generation component.

Timing Considerations. The timing differences are heavily influenced by factors unrelated to the models' capabilities. Network conditions, model architecture, caching strategies, and the hardware infrastructure of different model providers all significantly impact execution times—making raw timing comparisons between models less meaningful for evaluating proof generation effectiveness. The total time for evaluating the entire benchmark suite is thus reported for completeness.

Comparison with Combined Baselines. To further understand our approach, we compared it against a combined baseline that represents the best performance achievable by either baseline independently: see Table 2. Specifically, we consider a theorem as proved by the combined *SAPG+DLPG* baseline if either the SAPG or the DLPG successfully proves it. We also define a *total combined* approach, which considers a theorem as proved if it is successfully proved by any of the three methods, SAPG, or DLPG, or LMGPA.

Table 2. Comparison between combined baseline and our system

Model	Proved		
	SAPG+DLPG	*LMGPA*	*Total Combined*
Claude-3.7-Sonnet	52.9%	51.3%	54.6%
Deepseek-V3.2-Exp	52.9%	57.1%	61.3%
Gemini-2.0-Flash	49.6%	51.3%	52.9%
Gemini-2.5-Flash	49.6%	52.9%	55.5%
GPT-5	54.6%	54.6%	62.2%
o3-mini-high	47.1%	53.8%	53.8%

Syntax Errors in LLM-Generated Content. We also analyzed the syntactic validity of the content generated by LLMs in both DLPG and LMGPA systems. Because the generation targets differ, we aligned our evaluation with the specific output of each LLM query. For DLPG, we evaluated the full proofs, whereas for LMGPA, we evaluated the decompositions (sub-claims). We focused on decompositions for LMGPA because other proof structures are generated symbolically; thus, checking the decomposition isolates the LLM's actual contribution. Table 3 shows that while DLPG suffers from low syntactic validity, LMGPA achieves significantly higher syntactic validity rates. These results suggest that most of DLPG's failures stem from syntax errors, which aligns with our motivation for using normalized claim structure.

Table 3. Comparison of Syntactic Validity of LLM-Generated Proofs Between Approaches

Model	*DLPG*		*LMGPA*	
	Syn. Valid/#Queries	Percentage	Syn. Valid/#Queries	Percentage
Claude-3.7-Sonnet	88/434	20.3%	206/314	65.6%
Deepseek-V3.2-Exp	84/425	19.8%	287/334	85.9%
Gemini-2.0-Flash	27/463	5.8%	195/305	63.9%
Gemini-2.5-Flash	4/468	0.9%	228/296	77.0%
GPT-5	66/411	16.1%	290/334	86.8%
o3-mini-high	1/476	0.2%	252/337	74.8%

```
---- MODULE exercise_1_27 ----
EXTENDS Integers, TLAPS

Cube(x) == x * x * x

THEOREM L1 == ∃ x, y, z, w ∈ Int : Cube(x) + Cube(y) = 1729 ∧ Cube(z) + Cube(w) = 1729 ∧
        x ≠ z ∧ x ≠ w ∧ y ≠ z ∧ y ≠ w
THEOREM L2 == ∀ n ∈ Nat : (n < 1729) ⇒ ¬(∃ x, y, z, w ∈ Int : Cube(x) + Cube(y) = n ∧
        Cube(z) + Cube(w) = n ∧ x ≠ z ∧ x ≠ w ∧ y ≠ z ∧ y ≠ w)
THEOREM exercise_18_4 == ∀ n ∈ Nat : (∃ x, y, z, w ∈ Int : Cube(x) + Cube(y) = n
        ∧ Cube(z) + Cube(w) = n ∧ x ≠ z ∧ x ≠ w ∧ y ≠ z ∧ y ≠ w)  ⇒ n ≥ 1729
BY L1, L2 DEF Cube
======================
```

Fig. 6. An example of TLAPS limitation. Theorem L2 is the contrapositive of the target theorem, making the implication (L1 ∧ L2 ⇒ exercise_18_4) trivially valid. However, TLAPS fails to prove this within the timeout.

Failures Due to Prover Limitations. Beyond syntax errors and logically incorrect decompositions, another failure mode in LMGPA arises when LLMs generate mathematically valid decompositions that TLAPS fails to verify automatically. Figure 6 shows an LLM-generated decomposition attempt of theorem exercise_18_4 into sub-claims L1 and L2. Observe that L2 is the contrapositive of the target theorem. Thus, the decomposition is logically valid: (L1 ∧ L2) ⇒ exercise_18_4 holds (the assumption L1 is redundant, but this does not affect the validity of the implication). However, TLAPS cannot prove this implication within the default timeout.

Quality of Generated Proofs. We qualitatively analyzed the proofs generated by LMGPA. The generated proofs are generally well-structured, following TLA+ syntax with hierarchical organization of claims and sub-claims (e.g., Figs. 5 and 7). However, they do not yet match the quality of human-written proofs. Some proofs, while logically valid, do not correspond to the most concise and natural way to prove the theorem. For example, in the proof shown in Fig. 7, sub-claims CubeOf97_1 and SumIs16_4 are trivial calculations that are unnecessary in establishing the goal. We observed similar patterns elsewhere: decompositions that introduce more sub-claims than necessary or use intermediate claims uncommon in human proofs. Also, in some cases decompositions are not useful. For example, in Fig. 6, L2 is a restatement of the goal, so the LLM-generated decomposition does not meaningfully simplify the target theorem. These observations suggest room for improvement in generating more concise and natural proofs, as well as better decompositions. We nevertheless note that our system is capable of generating non-trivial proofs. For example, a distributed protocol inductiveness proof generated by our LMGPA system is 227 lines long (including 88 lines of definitions). This entire proof is listed in the Appendix of the extended version of this paper [73]. All proofs generated in our experiments can be found in the public repository [72] as well as in the artifact of this paper [74].

5 Related Work

LLM-assisted Theorem Proving. Recent years have seen significant advances in applying LLMs to formal reasoning tasks. In the domain of theorem proving, GPT-f [41] is a generative language model for automated theorem proving using Metamath [31]. Baldur [17] shows the LLMs' abilities on generating and repairing formal proofs in the Isabelle/HOL. Tahat et al. [49] present a case study on proof repair utilizing LLMs in Coq. LeanDojo [65] demonstrates the use of language models and retrieval-augmented generation for generating proof tactics and selecting premises in the Lean theorem prover, providing both tactical suggestions and a comprehensive benchmark suite for evaluating LLMs on formal proof tasks. COPRA [50] applies in-context learning to both Rocq and Lean provers, demonstrating how learning from existing examples can improve proof generation in these provers. Hilbert [57] leverages this idea and uses both general purpose and specialized LLMs for different levels of proof generation in Lean. Cobblestone [23] presents a divide-and-conquer approach for synthesizing Rocq proofs using off-the-shelf LLMs. Unlike these approaches, our method targets generating $\texttt{TLA}^+$ proofs.

Liang et al. [29] argue that general purpose LLMs perform well on high-level proof decomposition comparing to specialized models fine-tuned for theorem proving tasks. Zhang et al. [69] give a detailed analysis of LLMs' capabilities in formal theorem proving and proposes general suggestions to enhance their performance. Despite the successes in LLM-assisted reasoning, Mirzadeh et al. [32] discuss the limitations of LLMs in mathematical reasoning.

Fine-tuning approaches have also shown promise, with DeepSeek-Prover-V1.5 [64] and TheoremLlama [60] achieving notable results in single-pass Lean proof generation through specialized training on extensive Lean proof corpora. POETRY [58] generates Isabelle proofs recursively using a fine-tuned language model, whereas our approach leverages general-purpose LLMs to generate $\texttt{TLA}^+$ proofs. Rango [52] fine-tunes a language model to generate Rocq tactics step by step, augmenting the generation with retrieved similar proofs and relevant lemmas. Other approaches include LEGO-Prover [59], which employs a growing library of verified lemmas to augment LLMs' theorem proving capabilities, and work by Jiang et al. [22], which maps informal proofs to formal proof sketches that guide automated provers. DeepSeek-Prover-V2 [42] explores subgoal decomposition strategies via reinforcement learning to enhance formal reasoning capabilities for LLMs in Lean. Our work differs from these approaches by focusing on $\texttt{TLA}^+$, which employs a different proof structure.

These advances have been supported by standardized benchmarks such as miniF2F [71] and ProofNet [3], which provide diverse collections of mathematical problems for evaluating theorem provers across different formal systems.

LLMs for Software Verification. Beyond mathematical theorem proving, LLMs have shown promise in software verification tasks. Clover [48] leverages LLMs to generate Dafny code and annotations, while Chakraborty et al. [7] apply them to loop invariant generation. Wen et al. [62] combines LLMs with static analysis tools for program specification synthesis, and the Lemur system [63] demonstrates how LLMs can enhance traditional program verification frame-

```
---- MODULE mathd_numbertheory_234 ----
EXTENDS TLAPS, Integers

THEOREM CubeOf97_1 == 97 * 97 * 97 = 912673
OBVIOUS

THEOREM OnlySolution_2 ==
ASSUME NEW a ∈ Nat, NEW b ∈ Nat, a ≥ 1, a ≤ 9, b ≤ 9,
       (10 * a + b) * (10 * a + b) * (10 * a + b) = 912673
PROVE 10 * a + b = 97
OBVIOUS

THEOREM UniqueDigits_3 ==
ASSUME NEW a ∈ Nat, NEW b ∈ Nat, a ≥ 1, a ≤ 9, b ≤ 9, 10 * a + b = 97
PROVE a = 9 ∧ b = 7
OBVIOUS

THEOREM SumIs16_4 ==
ASSUME NEW a ∈ Nat, NEW b ∈ Nat, a = 9, b = 7
PROVE a + b = 16
OBVIOUS

THEOREM mathd_numbertheory_234 ==
∀ a, b ∈ Nat :
        (a ≥ 1) ∧ (a ≤ 9) ∧ (b ≤ 9) ∧
        ((10 * a + b) * (10 * a + b) * (10 * a + b) = 912673)
        ⇒ (a + b = 16)
BY CubeOf97_1, OnlySolution_2, UniqueDigits_3, SumIs16_4
==================================
```

Fig. 7. A valid but verbose proof generated by LMGPA: sub-claims `CubeOf97_1` and `SumIs16_4` are both trivial and redundant.

works. Laurel [34] provides a framework for using LLMs to generate and verify program specifications in Dafny and a benchmark extracted from real-world codebase. DafnyBench [30] provides a benchmark suite for evaluating LLMs in the context of Dafny program verification. Selene [68] proposes a benchmark for automated software verification, grounded in seL4 kernel [24].

Prompt Engineering and In-Context Learning. Research has explored LLMs' capabilities in general reasoning tasks [21, 70] and the role of prompt engineering in formal methods applications [9, 13]. Techniques such as in-context learning [16, 43] and dynamic prompt adjustment [61, 66] have proven effective in improving LLMs' performance on tasks requiring precise logical reasoning.

6 Conclusion

We present a language model-guided approach for automating `TLA`+ proof generation through hierarchical decomposition of complex proof obligations. Our key insight is that by constraining LLMs to generate normalized claim decompositions rather than complete proofs, we can leverage their reasoning capabilities while mitigating their tendency to produce syntactically incorrect formal proofs. Our evaluation shows substantial gains over direct LLM proof generation while highlighting the importance of combined LLM+symbolic tools.

Future work includes exploring specialized training methods, such as fine-tuning on TLA$^+$ proof corpora, to address persistent syntax errors, and to improve decomposition quality and the overall success rates. We also plan to investigate advanced prompting strategies and retrieval-augmented techniques. Another direction for future work is investigating how to guide LLMs to generate decompositions that are not only mathematically valid but also readily verifiable by automated provers. Training or guiding LLMs to understand the capabilities and limitations of symbolic provers could lead to more effective proof automation strategies.

Acknowledgments. We would like to thank William Schultz and Ian Dardik who provided the inductive invariant proofs that formed our distributed protocol benchmarks. This work has been supported by NSF's FMitF (Formal Methods in the Field) program, under awards 2319500 and 2525087.

References

1. TLA+ Proof System documentation: Tactics. https://proofs.tlapl.us/doc/web/content/Documentation/Tutorial/Tactics.html
2. Anthropic: Claude 3.7 Sonnet (2025). https://www.anthropic.com/news/claude-3-7-sonnet
3. Azerbayev, Z., Piotrowski, B., Schoelkopf, H., Ayers, E.W., Radev, D., Avigad, J.: ProofNet: autoformalizing and formally proving undergraduate-level mathematics. arXiv preprint arXiv:2302.12433 (2023)
4. Baier, C., Katoen, J.P.: Principles of Model Checking, MIT Press (2008)
5. Beers, R.: Pre-RTL formal verification: an Intel experience. In: Proceedings of the 45th ACM/IEEE Design Automation Conference, pp. 806–811 (2008)
6. Bonichon, R., Delahaye, D., Doligez, D.: Zenon: an extensible automated theorem prover producing checkable proofs. In: Dershowitz, N., Voronkov, A. (eds.) LPAR 2007. LNCS (LNAI), vol. 4790, pp. 151–165. Springer, Heidelberg (2007). https://doi.org/10.1007/978-3-540-75560-9_13
7. Chakraborty, S.: Ranking LLM-generated loop invariants for program verification. arXiv preprint arXiv:2310.09342 (2023)
8. Chaudhuri, K., Doligez, D., Lamport, L., Merz, S.: Verifying safety properties with the TLA$^{\text{âĂĽ+âĂĽ}}$ proof system. In: Giesl, J., Hähnle, R. (eds.) IJCAR 2010. LNCS (LNAI), vol. 6173, pp. 142–148. Springer, Heidelberg (2010). https://doi.org/10.1007/978-3-642-14203-1_12
9. Chen, Y., Gandhi, R., Zhang, Y., Fan, C.: NL2TL: transforming natural languages to temporal logics using large language models. arXiv preprint arXiv:2305.07766 (2023)
10. Church, A.: An unsolvable problem of elementary number theory. Am. J. Math. **58**(2), 345–363 (1936)
11. Clarke, E., Grumberg, O., Peled, D.: Model Checking, MIT Press (2000)
12. Clarke, E.M., Henzinger, T.A., Veith, H.: Handbook of Model Checking. Presented at the (2018). https://doi.org/10.1007/978-3-319-10575-8
13. Cosler, M., Hahn, C., Mendoza, D., Schmitt, F., Trippel, C.: NL2SPEC: interactively translating unstructured natural language to temporal logics with large language models. In: International Conference on Computer Aided Verification, pp. 383–396. Springer (2023). https://doi.org/10.1007/978-3-031-37703-7_18

14. de Moura, L., Bjørner, N.: Z3: An Efficient SMT Solver. In: Ramakrishnan, C.R., Rehof, J. (eds.) TACAS 2008. LNCS, vol. 4963, pp. 337–340. Springer, Heidelberg (2008). https://doi.org/10.1007/978-3-540-78800-3_24
15. DeepSeek-AI: Introducing DeepSeek-V3.2-Exp (2025). https://api-docs.deepseek.com/news/news250929
16. Dong, Q.: A survey on in-context learning. arXiv preprint arXiv:2301.00234 (2022)
17. First, E., Rabe, M.N., Ringer, T., Brun, Y.: Baldur: Whole-proof generation and repair with large language models. In: Proceedings of the 31st ACM Joint European Software Engineering Conference and Symposium on the Foundations of Software Engineering, pp. 1229–1241 (2023)
18. Google DeepMind: Gemini 2.0 flash: a powerful workhorse model with low latency and enhanced performance (2025). https://cloud.google.com/vertex-ai/generative-ai/docs/models/gemini/2-0-flash
19. Google DeepMind: Gemini 2.5 flash (2025). https://cloud.google.com/vertex-ai/generative-ai/docs/models/gemini/2-5-flash
20. Hackett, F., Rowe, J., Kuppe, M.A.: Understanding inconsistency in azure cosmos DB with TLA. In: 2023 IEEE/ACM 45th International Conference on Software Engineering: Software Engineering in Practice (ICSE-SEIP), pp. 1–12. IEEE (2023)
21. Ho, N., Schmid, L., Yun, S.Y.: Large language models are reasoning teachers. arXiv preprint arXiv:2212.10071 (2022)
22. Jiang, A.Q.: Draft, sketch, and prove: guiding formal theorem provers with informal proofs. arXiv preprint arXiv:2210.12283 (2022)
23. Kasibatla, S.R., Agarwal, A., Brun, Y., Lerner, S., Ringer, T., First, E.: Cobblestone: a divide-and-conquer approach for automating formal verification. arXiv preprint arXiv:2410.19940 (2024)
24. Klein, G.: seL4: formal verification of an OS kernel. In: Proceedings of the ACM SIGOPS 22nd Symposium on Operating Systems Principles, pp. 207–220 (2009)
25. Konnov, I., Kuppe, M., Merz, S.: Specification and verification with the TLA+ trifecta: TLC, Apalache, and TLAPS. In: International Symposium on Leveraging Applications of Formal Methods, pp. 88–105. Springer (2022). https://doi.org/10.1007/978-3-031-19849-6_6
26. Lamport, L.: Specifying systems: the TLA+ language and tools for hardware and software engineers (2002)
27. LangChain-AI: LangChain (2022). https://github.com/langchain-ai/langchain
28. Lewis, P.: Retrieval-augmented generation for knowledge-intensive NLP tasks. In: Advances in Neural Information Processing Systems, vol. 33, pp. 9459–9474 (2020)
29. Liang, Z.: Towards solving more challenging IMO problems via decoupled reasoning and proving. arXiv preprint arXiv:2507.06804 (2025)
30. Loughridge, C.: DafnyBench: a benchmark for formal software verification. arXiv preprint arXiv:2406.08467 (2024)
31. Megill, N., Wheeler, D.A.: Metamath: a computer language for mathematical proofs. Lulu. com, (2019)
32. Mirzadeh, I., Alizadeh, K., Shahrokhi, H., Tuzel, O., Bengio, S., Farajtabar, M.: GSM-symbolic: understanding the limitations of mathematical reasoning in large language models. arXiv preprint arXiv:2410.05229 (2024)
33. Moura, L., Ullrich, S.: The Lean 4 theorem prover and programming language. In: Platzer, A., Sutcliffe, G. (eds.) CADE 2021. LNCS (LNAI), vol. 12699, pp. 625–635. Springer, Cham (2021). https://doi.org/10.1007/978-3-030-79876-5_37
34. Mugnier, E., Gonzalez, E.A., Polikarpova, N., Jhala, R., Yuanyuan, Z.: Laurel: unblocking automated verification with large language models. Proc. ACM Program. Lang. **9**(OOPSLA1), 1519–1545 (2025)

35. Newcombe, C.: Why amazon chose TLA+. In: International Conference on Abstract State Machines, Alloy, B, TLA, VDM, and Z, pp. 25–39. Springer (2014). https://doi.org/10.1007/978-3-662-43652-3_3
36. Newcombe, C., Rath, T., Zhang, F., Munteanu, B., Brooker, M., Deardeuff, M.: How amazon web services uses formal methods. Commun. ACM **58**(4), 66–73 (2015). https://doi.org/10.1145/2699417
37. Nipkow, T., Paulson, L.C., Wenzel, M.: Isabelle/HOL – A Proof Assistant for Higher-Order Logic, LNCS, vol. 2283. Springer (2002). https://doi.org/10.1007/3-540-45949-9_5
38. OpenAI: OpenAI GPT-5 system card (2025). https://openai.com/index/gpt-5-system-card/
39. OpenAI: OpenAI o3-mini system card (2025). https://cdn.openai.com/o3-mini-system-card-feb10.pdf
40. Paulson, L.C.: Isabelle: A Generic Theorem Prover. Springer (1994). https://doi.org/10.1007/bfb0030558
41. Polu, S., Sutskever, I.: Generative language modeling for automated theorem proving. arXiv preprint arXiv:2009.03393 (2020)
42. Ren, Z.: DeepSeek-Prover-V2: advancing formal mathematical reasoning via reinforcement learning for subgoal decomposition. arXiv preprint arXiv:2504.21801 (2025)
43. Rubin, O., Herzig, J., Berant, J.: Learning to retrieve prompts for in-context learning. arXiv preprint arXiv:2112.08633 (2021)
44. Schultz, W.: GitHub repository for plain and simple inductive invariant inference for distributed protocols in TLA+. https://github.com/will62794/endive
45. Schultz, W., Dardik, I., Tripakis, S.: Formal verification of a distributed dynamic reconfiguration protocol. In: CPP 2022, Proceedings of the 11th ACM SIGPLAN International Conference on Certified Programs and Proofs, pp. 143–152. Association for Computing Machinery, New York, NY, USA (2022). https://doi.org/10.1145/3497775.3503688
46. Schultz, W., Dardik, I., Tripakis, S.: Plain and simple inductive invariant inference for distributed protocols in TLA. In: 2022 Formal Methods in Computer-Aided Design (FMCAD), pp. 273–283. IEEE (2022)
47. Schultz, W., Zhou, S., Dardik, I., Tripakis, S.: Design and analysis of a logless dynamic reconfiguration protocol. In: Bramas, Q., Gramoli, V., Milani, A. (eds.) 25th International Conference on Principles of Distributed Systems (OPODIS 2021). Leibniz International Proceedings in Informatics (LIPIcs), vol. 217, pp. 26:1–26:16. Schloss Dagstuhl - Leibniz-Zentrum für Informatik, Dagstuhl, Germany (2022). https://doi.org/10.4230/LIPIcs.OPODIS.2021.26, https://drops.dagstuhl.de/opus/volltexte/2022/15801
48. Sun, C., Sheng, Y., Padon, O., Barrett, C.: Clover: closed-loop verifiable code generation. arXiv preprint arXiv:2310.17807 (2023)
49. Tahat, A., Hardin, D., Petz, A., Alexander, P.: Proof repair utilizing large language models: a case study on the copland remote attestation proofbase. In: International Conference on Bridging the Gap between AI and Reality, pp. 145–166. Springer (2024). https://doi.org/10.1007/978-3-031-75434-0_10
50. Thakur, A., Tsoukalas, G., Wen, Y., Xin, J., Chaudhuri, S.: An in-context learning agent for formal theorem-proving. In: First Conference on Language Modeling (2023)
51. The Rocq Development Team: The Rocq reference manual - release 8.19.0 (2025). https://rocq-prover.org/doc/V9.0.0/refman

52. Thompson, K., et al.: Rango: adaptive retrieval-augmented proving for automated software verification. In: 47th IEEE/ACM International Conference on Software Engineering, ICSE 2025, Ottawa, ON, Canada, April 26 - May 6, 2025, pp. 347–359. IEEE (2025). https://doi.org/10.1109/ICSE55347.2025.00161
53. TLA+ Community: tree-sitter-tlaplus: TLA+ grammar for tree-sitter (2023). https://github.com/tlaplus-community/tree-sitter-tlaplus
54. TLA+ Foundation: Examples of TLA+ specifications (2025). https://github.com/tlaplus/Examples
55. TLA+ Foundation: The TLA+ proof system (2025). https://github.com/tlaplus/tlapm
56. Turing, A.M., et al.: On computable numbers, with an application to the Entscheidungsproblem. J. Math **58**(345–363), 5 (1936)
57. Varambally, S., Voice, T., Sun, Y., Chen, Z., Yu, R., Ye, K.: Hilbert: recursively building formal proofs with informal reasoning. arXiv preprint arXiv:2509.22819 (2025)
58. Wang, H.: Proving theorems recursively. In: Advances in Neural Information Processing Systems, vol. 37, pp. 86720–86748 (2024)
59. Wang, H.: LEGO-prover: neural theorem proving with growing libraries. arXiv preprint arXiv:2310.00656 (2023)
60. Wang, R.: TheoremLlama: transforming general-purpose LLMs into Lean4 experts. arXiv preprint arXiv:2407.03203 (2024)
61. Wei, J.: Chain-of-Thought prompting elicits reasoning in large language models. In: Advances in Neural Information Processing Systems, vol. 35, pp. 24824–24837 (2022)
62. Wen, C.: Enchanting program specification synthesis by large language models using static analysis and program verification. In: International Conference on Computer Aided Verification, pp. 302–328. Springer (2024). https://doi.org/10.1007/978-3-031-65630-9_16
63. Wu, H., Barrett, C., Narodytska, N.: Lemur: integrating large language models in automated program verification. arXiv preprint arXiv:2310.04870 (2023)
64. Xin, H.: DeepSeek-Prover-V1.5: harnessing proof assistant feedback for reinforcement learning and Monte-Carlo tree search. arXiv preprint arXiv:2408.08152 (2024)
65. Yang, K.: LeanDojo: theorem proving with retrieval-augmented language models. In: Advances in Neural Information Processing Systems, vol. 36 (2024)
66. Yao, S.: Tree of thoughts: deliberate problem solving with large language models. In: Advances in Neural Information Processing Systems, vol. 36 (2024)
67. Yu, Y., Manolios, P., Lamport, L.: Model checking TLA$^+$ specifications. In: Pierre, L., Kropf, T. (eds.) CHARME 1999. LNCS, vol. 1703, pp. 54–66. Springer, Heidelberg (1999). https://doi.org/10.1007/3-540-48153-2_6
68. Zhang, L., Lu, S., Duan, N.: Selene: pioneering automated proof in software verification. arXiv preprint arXiv:2401.07663 (2024)
69. Zhang, S.D., Ringer, T., First, E.: Getting more out of large language models for proofs. arXiv preprint arXiv:2305.04369 (2023)
70. Zhang, Y.: LLM as a mastermind: a survey of strategic reasoning with large language models. arXiv preprint arXiv:2404.01230 (2024)
71. Zheng, K., Han, J.M., Polu, S.: MiniF2F: a cross-system benchmark for formal olympiad-level mathematics. arXiv preprint arXiv:2109.00110 (2021)
72. Zhou, Y.: GitHub repository for language-model guided TLA+ proof automation (2026). https://github.com/YUH-Z/lmgpa

73. Zhou, Y., Tripakis, S.: Towards language model guided TLA+ proof automation. arXiv:2512.09758 (2025)
74. Zhou, Y., Tripakis, S.: Artifact for paper: language-model guided TLA+ proof automation (2026). https://doi.org/10.5281/zenodo.18637323

Exact Verification of Graph Neural Networks with Incremental Constraint Solving

Minghao Liu(✉), Chia-Hsuan Lu, and Marta Kwiatkowska

University of Oxford, Oxford, UK
{minghao.liu,chia-hsuan.lu,marta.kwiatkowska}@cs.ox.ac.uk

Abstract. Graph neural networks (GNNs) are increasingly often employed in high-stakes applications, such as fraud detection or healthcare, but are susceptible to adversarial attacks. A number of techniques have been proposed to provide adversarial robustness guarantees, but support for commonly used aggregation functions in message-passing GNNs is lacking. In this paper, we develop an exact (sound and complete) verification method for GNNs to compute guarantees against attribute and structural perturbations that involve edge addition or deletion, subject to budget constraints. Our method employs constraint solving with bound tightening, and iteratively solves a sequence of relaxed constraint satisfaction problems while relying on incremental solving capabilities of solvers to improve efficiency. We implement GNNEV, a versatile exact verifier for message-passing neural networks, which supports three aggregation functions – sum, max and mean – with the latter two considered here for the first time. Extensive experimental evaluation of GNNEV on real-world fraud datasets (Amazon and Yelp) and biochemical datasets (MUTAG and ENZYMES) demonstrates its usability and effectiveness, as well as superior performance on node classification and competitiveness on graph classification compared to existing exact verification tools on sum-aggregated GNNs.

Keywords: Formal verification · Constraint solving · Graph neural networks · Adversarial robustness

1 Introduction

Graph neural networks (GNNs) have been widely deployed in real-world applications, such as financial fraud detection [53,71], autonomous driving [14,15], healthcare treatment [27,45], and scientific discovery [36,58]. However, like all other neural network architectures, GNNs are vulnerable to adversarial attacks, where slight perturbations can cause a prediction change [21,67,87]. Therefore, it is desirable to ensure adversarial robustness of GNNs for high-stakes applications.

A. Sampaio and M. Stoelinga (Eds.): FM 2026, LNCS 16556, pp. 641–662, 2026.
https://doi.org/10.1007/978-3-032-26204-2_33

Formal verification is a rigorous methodology to mathematically prove that a system meets its specifications under all possible circumstances [5]. To evaluate the reliability and trustworthiness of neural networks, a number of approaches have been developed to verify the adversarial robustness of fully connected neural networks [11,38,72,74,81], convolutional neural networks (CNNs) [10,35,69], recurrent neural networks (RNNs) [1,24,40], and transformers [9,66]. Technically, these approaches can be classified into two categories. The first category is *exact* verification, also known as *complete* verification, where the verification task is formulated as a constraint satisfaction problem (CSP) [60] to deterministically prove whether the model is robust or not. The second category is *approximate* verification, also known as (sound but) *incomplete* verification, where the non-convex constraints are typically relaxed to convex ones, which admits efficient computation of a lower bound on the robust region. However, when the lower bound cannot be accurately computed, the outcome of the verification may be inconclusive, which does not offer strong robustness guarantees.

Recently, the concept of adversarial robustness has been extended to GNNs. Graph inputs present additional challenges, in that the perturbations can pertain to both node attributes [2,89] and graph structure, i.e., the addition and deletion of edges [7,37,41,90], or even node injection [42]. Since graph inputs are encoded using a combination of real-valued and discrete data, typical approaches to provide *deterministic* robustness guarantees are based on Mixed-Integer Programming (MIP) [33,82]. We also mention methods based on randomised smoothing [8,56,63], noting that their guarantees are *probabilistic* and thus not directly comparable.

Despite recent advances, existing exact verification approaches are still limited to GNNs with *sum* aggregation. However, other common aggregations, including *max* and *mean*, have been shown to be necessary and effective in both theory [20,59] and practice [23,80], and are supported as standard by the GraphSAGE library [32]. Existing methods also typically focus on graph classification problems in the context of structural perturbations, implemented only for edge deletion for tractability reasons. Node classification tasks have been under-explored, and yet are relied upon in high-stakes applications, for example, fraud detection in financial networks [71] and cyber attack localization in smart grids [31]. For such applications, in order to provide certified robustness guarantees, methods that yield conclusive outcomes are preferable.

We develop an exact verification method for GNNs to provide guarantees against both attribute and structural perturbations subject to local and global budget constraints. We support GNNs for both node- and graph-classification tasks with three commonly used aggregation functions, sum, max and mean, where the latter two are non-linear. We employ constraint solving with bound tightening and iteratively solve a sequence of relaxed CSPs while relying on incremental solving capabilities of solvers to improve efficiency. We implement GNNEv, a versatile and efficient exact verifier for GNNs, and conduct extensive experiments on two standard node-classification datasets, Cora and CiteSeer, two real-world fraud datasets, Amazon and Yelp, and two biochemical graph-classification datasets, MUTAG and ENZYMES. The results indicate that GNNEV outperforms SCIP-MPNN [33], the only MIP-based exact verifier known to us, on sum aggregation and edge deletion under different model sizes and perturbation budgets. On a range of aggregation functions, we show that GNNEV can provide useful insight into the susceptibility of GNNs to adversarial attacks, which is important for deployment in high-stakes applications.

Our novel contributions can be summarised as follows.

- We introduce the first exact verification method for GNNs with two common aggregation functions, max and mean, and design specialised tightened bound propagation strategies to reduce computational cost.
- We propose an algorithm that iteratively encodes GNN layers backwards and utilises incremental constraint solving to speed up performance while maintaining exact verification capability.
- We implement GNNEV, a versatile and efficient exact verifier for GNNs that supports new aggregation functions and edge addition, and show its usability on both structural and attribute perturbations through extensive experiments on real-world datasets.

Due to space constraints, additional details have been relegated to appendices in the full version of the paper [46].

2 Related Work

Adversarial Attacks Against GNNs. Several works [21,77,87,88] demonstrate that adversarial attacks can induce incorrect predictions by GNNs on node classification. Chang et al. [16], Mu et al. [54] propose black-box attack approaches without accessing any knowledge of the GNN classifiers. Li et al. [44], Zou et al. [86] further improve the efficiency and scalability of adversarial attack algorithms. Another direction is attacks on graph classification [84] and link prediction [17,85]. We emphasise that a failure to find an attack does not imply robustness. In contrast, we aim to verify that GNNs are not vulnerable to any admissible attack, which provides strong guarantees and can thus be used for robustness certification.

We further remark that, while most studies focus on undirected graphs and claim potential extensions to directed graphs, some works [17,28], along with our paper, consider both directed and undirected graphs.

Robustness Enhancement of GNNs. Adversarial training is a common technique applied to enhance the robustness of GNNs [22,25,30,43,77]. Wu et al. [75], Zhang and Zitnik [83] aim to enhance the robustness of GNNs by estimating potential adversarial perturbations and adjusting model weights to defend against these perturbations. Moreover, generalised randomised smoothing [8,70,84] and partition-ensemble [76] techniques have been developed for GNNs to provide defences against attacks with probabilistic guarantees. Instead, we develop a formal verification algorithm, which is complementary to robustness enhancement and offers deterministic guarantees.

Theoretical Analysis of GNN Verification. Expressiveness of sum-aggregated GNNs is studied in [4,6,55] and mean-aggregated in [64]. The adversarial robustness problem for node classification is shown decidable in Sälzer and Lange [62] under the assumption of bounded degree of input graphs. Benedikt et al. [6] (and Nunn et al. [55]) study verification of certain properties that quantify over all graph inputs proving PSPACE-completeness for GNNs with rational (resp. integer) coefficients, Boolean-attributed input graphs and truncated ReLU activation functions. We focus instead on a practical verification approach applicable to commonly used GNNs, with real-valued coefficients and attributes and ReLU activation functions. Our problem setting is clearly decidable because it only considers a finite and bounded input graph set.

Verification of Neural Networks. Adversarial robustness verification methods can be classified into complete (exact) methods, such as constraint solving [35,38,68], sound though incomplete methods, e.g., convex relaxation [61,79], which can be strengthened to completeness by employing branch-and-bound procedures [13,48], and probabilistic methods [19,49,73]. Katz et al. [38] prove that exact NN verification is generally NP-hard. More recent works move beyond fully-connected and convolutional architectures, and include MIP-based exact verification of recurrent networks [1] as well as approximate verification of transformers utilising the zonotope abstract domain [9] and linear bound propagation [34]. While some works focus on properties such as differential verification between models [51] and batched verification across inputs [3], we aim to verify the key property of adversarial robustness. Regarding GNN verification, existing approaches concern graph convolutional networks with respect to attribute [2,89] or structural [7,37,41,90] perturbations. Most are approximate, relying on optimisation [7,37,41,90] or zonotope-based relaxation [41]. Our approach is most similar to the exact MIP-based approach SCIP-MPNN [33] for sum-aggregated message-passing GNNs and edge deletion only. Their method supports static and dynamic (aggressive) bound tightening over the complete network encoding. In contrast, our method also supports max and mean, as well as edge addition, and proceeds by building the encoding incrementally layer by layer while statically tightening the bounds. For node classification tasks involving large numbers of neighbouring nodes, our exact method can greatly reduce the cost of encoding, thus enhancing performance. We also note a recent verifier RobLight [47], which supports structural perturbations only and references our work. Their method relies on a branch-and-bound approach with bound propagation, and is unable to generate certificates for verification that MIP-based methods permit [18].

3 Preliminaries

3.1 Graph Neural Networks

Let $G = \langle V, E, X \rangle$ be an *attributed directed graph*, where $V = \{v_1, v_2, \dots, v_n\}$ is a set of nodes, $E \subseteq V \times V$ is a set of edges with no self-loops, and $X =$

$\{\mathbf{x}_1, \mathbf{x}_2, \ldots, \mathbf{x}_n\}$ is a set of real *attribute vectors* for the nodes with the same dimension. For a node $v \in V$ and a natural number k, we denote the set of *k-hop incoming neighbours of v* by $\mathcal{N}_k(v)$. For simplicity, we write $\mathcal{N}(v)$ when $k = 1$. *Graph neural networks (GNNs)* are a class of neural network architectures designed to operate on graph data. In this paper, we consider node- and graph-classification tasks. Given a class set $C = \{c_1, c_2, \ldots, c_m\}$, for node classification, the goal is to classify a node $v \in V$ into a class within C; for graph classification, the goal is to classify a graph G into a class within C. More precisely, we view a GNN as a function f such that, given an attributed directed graph $G = \langle V, E, X\rangle$ and a node $v \in V$, $f(G, v) \in C$ for node classification, and $f(G) \in C$ for graph classification. The remainder of the formalisation focuses on the node classification case for simplicity. The variant for graph classification is similar, as discussed in Appendix A in the extended version [46].

There are a variety of GNN architectures. Existing formal verification works mostly focus on graph convolutional networks (GCNs) [39], which rely on a specific neighbourhood aggregation scheme and their expressiveness is restricted [78]. In this work, we consider *GraphSAGE* [32], also known as *Message-Passing Neural Networks (MPNNs)* [29], which are a more general GNN architecture because (i) they support the choice of multiple neighbourhood aggregation functions and (ii) the expressive power of MPNNs has been shown to encompass other popular variations such as GCNs and graph attention networks (GATs) [12].

A GNN consists of K layers. The dimension of a GNN is a $(K+1)$ tuple of positive integers $d_0, d_1, \ldots, d_K$. For an input attributed directed graph $G = \langle V, E, X\rangle$, for each node $v \in V$, its real-valued embedding vector $\mathbf{h}_v^{(0)}$ is a d_0-dimension vector initialised to its corresponding attribute vector $\mathbf{x}_v$. For the k-th layer, GNNs compute the d_k-dimensional embedding $\mathbf{h}_v^{(k)}$ by

$$\mathbf{h}_v^{(k)} = \sigma\left(\mathbf{W}_1^{(k)} \cdot \mathbf{h}_v^{(k-1)} + \mathbf{W}_2^{(k)} \cdot \mathbf{aggr}\left(\left\{\!\!\left\{\mathbf{h}_u^{(k-1)} \mid u \in \mathcal{N}(v)\right\}\!\!\right\}\right) + \mathbf{b}_1^{(k)}\right), \quad (1)$$

where $\mathbf{W}_1^{(k)}, \mathbf{W}_2^{(k)}$ are learnable parameter matrices with dimension $d_k \times d_{k-1}$ for the k-th layer, $\mathbf{b}_1^{(k)}$ is a learnable parameter vector, $\sigma(x) = \max(0, x)$ is the ReLU activation function, $\mathbf{aggr} \in \{\text{sum}, \text{max}, \text{mean}\}$ is the aggregation function, and $\{\!\!\{\}\!\!\}$ denotes a multiset. Finally, the last dimension d_K is exactly m, and the predicted class $\hat{c}_v$ of a node $v \in V$ is obtained by the Softmax function:

$$\hat{c}_v = \underset{c \in C}{\arg\max}\left(\text{Softmax}\left(\mathbf{h}_v^{(K)}\right)[c]\right). \quad (2)$$

3.2 Adversarial Robustness of GNNs

Node embeddings are directly affected by attribute perturbations and indirectly affected by structural perturbations through message passing, which may result in prediction instability. Changes in predictions caused by admissible perturbations indicate a lack of *adversarial robustness*. We slightly adapt the definition of adversarial robustness for GNNs in [7] by (i) allowing perturbations in both graph structure and node attributes, and (ii) removing the redundant fixed edge set. Given an attributed directed graph $G = \langle V, E, X\rangle$, the attacker typically has limited capabilities to perturb it. Let $F \subseteq V \times V$ be a set of *fragile edges*. Intuitively, an attacker can either remove edges in $F \cap E$ or insert edges in $F \backslash E$. For structural perturbations, we assume a global budget Δ and a local budget δ_v for each $v \in V$, both of which are non-negative integers. For attribute perturbations, we work with budgets $\epsilon^l_{v,i}, \epsilon^u_{v,i}$ ($\epsilon^l_{v,i} \leq \mathbf{x}_v[i] \leq \epsilon^u_{v,i}$) for each $v \in V$ and $i \in \{1, 2, \ldots, d_0\}$, which are real values representing the range of perturbation allowed for the i-th dimension of $\mathbf{x}_v \in X$. The admissible perturbation space is defined as follows.

Definition 1 (Admissible perturbation space of graph). *Given an attributed directed graph $G = \langle V, E, X\rangle$, a set of fragile edges $F \subseteq V \times V$, and perturbation budgets Δ, δ, ϵ, the* admissible perturbation space *$\mathcal{Q}(G)$ of G with respect to F and budgets is the set of attributed directed graphs $\tilde{G} = \langle V, \tilde{E}, \tilde{X}\rangle$ that satisfy*

1. *$E \backslash F \subseteq \tilde{E} \subseteq E \cup F$,*
2. *$|E \backslash \tilde{E}| + |\tilde{E} \backslash E| \leq \Delta$,*
3. *For every $v \in V$, $|\mathcal{N}(v) \backslash \tilde{\mathcal{N}}(v)| + |\tilde{\mathcal{N}}(v) \backslash \mathcal{N}(v)| \leq \delta_v$,*
4. *For every $v \in V$ and $1 \leq i \leq d_0$, $\epsilon^l_{v,i} \leq \tilde{\mathbf{x}}_v[i] \leq \epsilon^u_{v,i}$,*

where we denote the incoming neighbours of v in the graph $\tilde{G}$ by $\tilde{\mathcal{N}}(v)$. Note that this is a general formulation as F can be defined arbitrarily for different purposes, and allows us to consider edge addition when the size of F is moderate[1]. For example, if $F = E$, only edge deletion is allowed, and any existing edge can be deleted. If $F = V \times V$, edges can be added or deleted between any pair of nodes.

Finally, we introduce the formal definition of adversarial robustness of GNNs.

Definition 2 (Adversarial robustness of GNNs). *Given a node-classification GNN f, an attributed directed graph G with admissible perturbation space $\mathcal{Q}(G)$, a target node $t \in V$, and its predicted class $\hat{c}_t \in C$, we say that f is* adversarially robust *for t with class $\hat{c}_t$ if and only if, for every perturbed graph $\tilde{G} \in \mathcal{Q}(G)$, it holds that $f(\tilde{G}, t) = \hat{c}_t$.*

Adversarial robustness verification aims to guarantee that the prediction for a given node will not change under any admissible perturbations, subject to budget constraints, and can be reduced to computing the worst-case margin between the target class and other classes.

4 Exact Verification of GNNs

In this section, we introduce our method, which encodes the verification task as a constraint satisfaction problem (CSP). Next, the bound tightening strategies for max- and mean-aggregated GNNs are proposed. Finally, we illustrate an efficient exact verification algorithm based on incremental solving.

[1] The definition in Hojny et al. [33], Eq. (14) is a special case of ours when $F = E$.

4.1 Encoding

A CSP aims to determine whether there exists an assignment of variables that satisfies a given set of constraints. We encode the exact verification tasks as CSPs, which consist of three parts: input perturbation, GNN architecture, and verification objective. Following existing MIP encodings for GNNs [33,82], we extend them to accommodate max and mean aggregations, where for mean we use big-M encoding and for max we rely on the solver.

Input Perturbation. Consider an input attributed directed graph $G = \langle V, E, X\rangle$, where our goal is to verify the adversarial robustness for the target node $t \in V$. Note that, for K-layer GNNs, only perturbations to nodes in $\mathcal{N}_K(t)$ can affect the prediction of t. Two kinds of perturbations are allowed. The first is attribute perturbation, where the node attributes can be modified within a specified range. For each node $v \in \mathcal{N}_K(t)$, we set d_0 real variables $attr_{v,1}, attr_{v,2}, \ldots, attr_{v,d_0}$ as the attribute values after perturbations. Given the perturbation budgets $\epsilon^l_{v,i}, \epsilon^u_{v,i}$ for the i-th dimension of $\mathbf{x}_v$, the following constraint is applied:

$$\epsilon^l_{v,i} \leq attr_{v,i} \leq \epsilon^u_{v,i}. \tag{3}$$

The second type is structural perturbation, which can impact the message-passing mechanism. For each edge $(u, v) \in F$, we set a Boolean variable $pe_{u,v}$ to represent whether (u, v) is perturbed. Given the global budget Δ and the local budget δ_v for each $v \in \mathcal{N}_{K-1}(t)$, we have the constraints

$$\sum_{(u,v)\in F} pe_{u,v} \leq \Delta, \qquad \sum_{(u,v)\in F} pe_{u,v} \leq \delta_v. \tag{4}$$

GNN Architecture. We encode the architecture of GNNs as follows. For the k-th layer as shown in Eq. (1), the output embedding of node $v \in \mathcal{N}_{K-k}(t)$ is represented by d_k real variables $h^{(k)}_{v,1}, h^{(k)}_{v,2}, \ldots, h^{(k)}_{v,d_k}$. Let $h^{(0)}_{v,i} = attr_{v,i}$. The encoding for each layer consists of three parts.

First, the neighbours of node v are aggregated to produce the message. We set d_{k-1} real variables $msg^{(k)}_{v,1}, msg^{(k)}_{v,2}, \ldots, msg^{(k)}_{v,d_{k-1}}$ as the message vector. We support three common aggregation functions: sum, max, and mean. Note that the last two functions are non-linear, which accounts for higher computational complexity for verification. Before we give the encoding for the aggregation functions, we set the auxiliary variables $a^{(k)}_{v,i,u}$, which indicate the contribution of node u to $msg^{(k)}_{v,i}$ through the edge (u, v). The following constraints restrict the values of $a^{(k)}_{v,i,u}$: for every $(u, v) \in E\backslash F$,

$$a^{(k)}_{v,i,u} = h^{(k-1)}_{v,i}; \tag{5}$$

for every $(u, v) \in E \cap F$,

$$pe_{u,v} \rightarrow a^{(k)}_{v,i,u} = 0 \quad \text{and} \quad \neg pe_{u,v} \rightarrow a^{(k)}_{v,i,u} = h^{(k-1)}_{v,i}; \tag{6}$$

for every $(u,v) \in F \backslash E$,

$$pe_{u,v} \rightarrow a_{v,i,u}^{(k)} = h_{v,i}^{(k-1)} \quad \text{and} \quad \neg pe_{u,v} \rightarrow a_{v,i,u}^{(k)} = 0. \tag{7}$$

For sum and max aggregation, the constraints are shown in Eq. (8) and (9), respectively.

$$msg_{v,i}^{(k)} = \sum_{(u,v)\in F\cup E} a_{v,i,u}^{(k)}, \tag{8}$$

$$msg_{v,i}^{(k)} = \max_{(u,v)\in F\cup E} a_{v,i,u}^{(k)}. \tag{9}$$

For mean aggregation, the constraints are set as follows:

$$\begin{aligned} deg_v &= \sum_{(u,v)\in F\cap E} (1 - pe_{u,v}) + \sum_{(u,v)\in F\backslash E} pe_{u,v} + |E\backslash F|, \\ deg_v \cdot msg_{v,i}^{(k)} &= \sum_{(u,v)\in F\cup E} a_{v,i,u}^{(k)}, \\ -M \cdot deg_v &\leq msg_{v,i}^{(k)} \leq M \cdot deg_v, \end{aligned} \tag{10}$$

where M is a big real number[2]. Next, we introduce a constraint that represents the pre-ReLU embedding of node v as follows:

$$y_{v,i}^{(k)} = \sum_{j\in[1,d_{k-1}]} \mathbf{W}_1^{(k)}[i,j] \cdot h_{v,j}^{(k-1)} + \mathbf{W}_2^{(k)}[i,j] \cdot msg_{v,j}^{(k)} + \mathbf{b}_1^{(k)}. \tag{11}$$

Finally, we define the post-ReLU embedding, except the last GNN layer, as follows:

$$h_{v,i}^{(k)} = \max\left(y_{v,i}^{(k)}, 0\right). \tag{12}$$

Verification Objective. According to Definition 2, our objective is to verify that no admissible attribute or structural perturbation can make the prediction of the GNN inconsistent with the input attributed directed graph for a target node. Let the predicted class of target node t be $\hat{c}_t$, where the set of classes is denoted by C. Then we set the following constraint:

$$\left(\max_{c\in C\backslash\{\hat{c}_t\}} y_{t,c}^{(K)}\right) \geq y_{t,\hat{c}_t}^{(K)}, \tag{13}$$

which expresses the worst-case margin in the input of Softmax.

Let $\mathbf{y}_t^{(K)} = \left[y_{t,1}^{(K)}, y_{t,2}^{(K)}, \ldots, y_{t,|C|}^{(K)}\right]$. Since the Softmax function is monotonically increasing, Eq. (13) implies that there exists $c \in C$ with $c \neq \hat{c}_t$ such that

$$\text{Softmax}\left(\mathbf{y}_t^{(K)}\right)[c] \geq \text{Softmax}\left(\mathbf{y}_t^{(K)}\right)[\hat{c}_t].$$

[2] M is calculated by finding the maximum of the absolute values of the upper and lower bounds of all $a_{v,i,u}^{(k)}$ in Eq. (10).

If Eq. (13) is feasible, this means that a perturbed graph has been found that makes the GNN misclassify node t. Therefore, the robustness verification task is translated to deciding whether the above CSP is unsatisfiable.

Note that the encoding involves at most $5N^2D$ real variables, N^2 Boolean variables, and $8ND + 2$ constraints, where N is the number of nodes in $\mathcal{N}_K(t)$ and $D := \sum_{0 \leq i \leq K} d_i$. Furthermore, the encoding can be computed in time polynomial in the size of the GNN.

4.2 Bound Tightening for Aggregations

Tightening of variable bounds has been found to be critical to enhancing the efficiency of MIP solvers. Simultaneously, high-quality bounds form the basis of our incremental solving algorithm introduced in Sect. 4.3. Starting from the input variables (i.e., *attr*), whose bounds have been determined by Eq. (3), we propagate these bounds layer by layer to obtain tight bounds for other variables.

Since tightened bound propagation is straightforward for linear transformations and ReLU functions, our main focus is on tightening the bounds for aggregation functions. We formalise the problem as follows: given three finite sets of variables X_1, X_2, and X_3, the upper and lower bounds for each variable, and a non-negative integer s, compute the upper and lower bounds for the variable

$$z := \mathbf{aggr}(X_1 \cup X_2' \cup X_3'),$$

where $\mathbf{aggr} \in \{\text{sum}, \text{max}, \text{mean}\}$, $X_2' \subseteq X_2$, $X_3' \subseteq X_3$, and $|X_2 \backslash X_2'| + |X_3'| \leq s$. Let N be the total size of the sets X_1, X_2, and X_3. The intuition behind the formalisation is as follows: X_1, X_2, and X_3 represent the embedding vectors of nodes connected to the target node via non-fragile edges (E/F), fragile edges $(E \cap F)$, and fragile non-edges (F/E), respectively. The attacker can either delete fragile edges, that is, remove elements from X_2, or insert fragile non-edges, that is, select elements from X_3. The number of deletion and insertions is constrained by the budget s.

For a set of variables X and an integer k, let $hi(X, k)$ denote the k-th *largest upper bound* among the variables in X. If $k > |X|$, we define $hi(X, k) = -\infty$. Similarly, let $lo(X, k)$ denote the k-th *smallest lower bound* among the variables in X, with $lo(X, k) = \infty$ when $k \leq 0$. Note that $hi(X, k)$ and $lo(X, k)$ can be computed in $O(|X| \log k)$ time by maintaining a max- or min-heap. For multiple values $k_1, k_2, \ldots, k_\ell$, we can reuse the heap, resulting in an overall complexity of $O(|X| \log k)$, where k is the maximum value among $k_1, k_2, \ldots, k_\ell$.

For a variable x, its upper and lower bounds are denoted by $\overline{x}$ and $\underline{x}$ respectively. The case for sum aggregation has been shown by Hojny et al. [33]. We restate their bounds in the context of our formalisation for completeness:

$$\overline{z} = \sum_{x \in X_1 \cup X_2} \overline{x} + \sum_{1 \leq i \leq s} \max(hi(Y, i), 0),$$

$$\underline{z} = \sum_{x \in X_1 \cup X_2} \underline{x} + \sum_{1 \leq i \leq s} \min(lo(Y, i), 0),$$

where $Y = \{-x \mid x \in X_2\} \cup X_3$. The upper and lower bounds of z can be computed in time $O(N \log s)$.

Max Aggregation. The upper and lower bounds of z for max aggregation can be obtained by case analysis. For the corner case $s = 0$, $z = \max(X_1 \cup X_2)$. Note that, if $X_1 \cup X_2 = \emptyset$, then $\overline{z} = \underline{z} = 0$. We now focus on the case $s > 0$. For the upper bound:

$$\overline{z} = \begin{cases} \max(0, hi(X_2, 1), hi(X_3, 1)), & \text{if } X_1 = \emptyset, s \geq |X_2|, \\ \max(hi(X_1, 1), hi(X_2, 1), hi(X_3, 1)), & \text{otherwise.} \end{cases}$$

On the other hand, for the lower bound:

$$\underline{z} = \begin{cases} \min(0, lo(X_2, 1), lo(X_3, 1)), & \text{if } X_1 = \emptyset, s > |X_2|, \\ \min(0, lo(X_2, 1)), & \text{if } X_1 = \emptyset, s = |X_2|, \\ lo(X_2, |X_2| - s), & \text{if } X_1 = \emptyset, s < |X_2|, \\ lo(X_1, |X_1|), & \text{if } X_1 \neq \emptyset, s \geq |X_2|, \\ \max(lo(X_1, |X_1|), lo(X_2, |X_2| - s)), & \text{if } X_1 \neq \emptyset, s < |X_2|. \end{cases}$$

Note that the upper and lower bounds for z can be computed in time $O(N \log s)$.

Mean Aggregation. In this case, we reduce the original problem to a combination of subproblems. For non-negative integers s_2 and s_3, define the variable

$$z_{s_2,s_3} := \mathbf{mean}(X_1 \cup X_2' \cup X_3'),$$

where $X_2' \subseteq X_2$, $X_3' \subseteq X_3$, $|X_2 \backslash X_2'| = s_2$, and $|X_3'| = s_3$. The main difference is that we now explicitly fix separate budgets for deletions and insertions. The upper and lower bounds of the original problem z are given by

$$\overline{z} = \max_{\substack{s_2+s_3 \leq s \\ 0 \leq s_2 \leq |X_2| \\ 0 \leq s_3 \leq |X_3|}} \overline{z}_{s_2,s_3} \quad \text{and} \quad \underline{z} = \min_{\substack{s_2+s_3 \leq s \\ 0 \leq s_2 \leq |X_2| \\ 0 \leq s_3 \leq |X_3|}} \underline{z}_{s_2,s_3}.$$

For the subproblem z_{s_2,s_3}, since the budgets for deletion and insertion are separate, the upper and lower bounds can be obtained through greedy choices. In the corner case where X_1 is empty, $s_2 = |X_2|$, and $s_3 = 0$, $\overline{z}_{s_2,s_3} = \underline{z}_{s_2,s_3} = 0$. In all other cases, we have $\overline{z}_{s_2,s_3} = \overline{w}_{s_2,s_3}/n_{s_2,s_3}$ and $\underline{z}_{s_2,s_3} = \underline{w}_{s_2,s_3}/n_{s_2,s_3}$, where $n_{s_2,s_3} = |X_1| + |X_2| - s_2 + s_3$ and

$$\overline{w}_{s_2,s_3} = \sum_{x \in X_1} \overline{x} + \sum_{1 \leq i \leq |X_2| - s_2} hi(X_2, i) + \sum_{1 \leq i \leq s_3} hi(X_3, i),$$

$$\underline{w}_{s_2,s_3} = \sum_{x \in X_1} \underline{x} + \sum_{1 \leq i \leq |X_2| - s_2} lo(X_2, i) + \sum_{1 \leq i \leq s_3} lo(X_3, i).$$

Note that the summations over lo and hi can be computed incrementally among subproblems and, as there are at most $(s+1)^2$ subproblems, we can compute the upper and lower bounds for z in time $O(s^2 + N \log s)$ using a naïve approach. In fact, we can further improve this result by exploiting the unimodality of the sequence, reducing the computation time to $O((s+N)\log s)$. The detailed algorithm is provided in Appendix B in the extended version [46].

Theorem 1. *The upper and lower bounds provided in this section for max and mean aggregations are tight. That is, there exist sets $X_2' \subseteq X_2$ and $X_3' \subseteq X_3$ with $|X_2 \backslash X_2'| + |X_3'| \leq s$ that achieve these bounds exactly.*

The proof is included in Appendix C in the extended version [46].

Example 1. Consider sets of variables $X_1 = \{x_{1,1}\}$, $X_2 = \{x_{2,1}, x_{2,2}\}$, and $X_3 = \{x_{3,1}, x_{3,2}\}$. Each variable has upper and lower bounds as shown in Fig. 1. Let the budget $s = 1$. We now consider tightened bound propagation:

- For max aggregation, the upper bound is 5 by no operation, the same as the plain method[3]; the lower bound is 2 by deleting $x_{2,2}$, improved by 5 over the plain method.
- For mean aggregation, the upper bound is 3.25 by inserting $x_{3,1}$, improved by 0.08; the lower bound is 0.5 by inserting $x_{3,1}$, improved by 2.17.

For both aggregations, tightened bound propagation reduces the domain of the variable z.

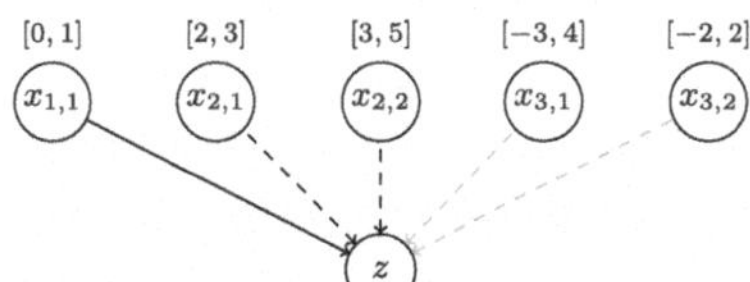

	Plain	Tightened
max (ub)	max(1, 3, 5, 4, 2) = **5**	max(1, 5, 4) = **5**
max (lb)	min(0, 2, 3, −3, −2) = −3	max(0, 2) = **2**
mean (ub)	$\frac{1+5+4}{3} = 3.33$	$\frac{1+5+3+4}{4} = \mathbf{3.25}$
mean (lb)	$\frac{0-3-2}{3} = -1.67$	$\frac{0+2+3-3}{4} = \mathbf{0.5}$

Fig. 1. An illustration of tightened bound propagation. Solid lines denote the non-fragile edges, black dashed lines denote fragile edges, and grey dashed lines denote fragile non-edges. The tighter bounds are shown in **bold** (Color figure online).

4.3 Verification with Incremental Solving

With tightened bound propagation, we can verify adversarial robustness of GNNs more efficiently. However, in node classification tasks, graphs are typically large in size, and for a node t we typically have that $|\mathcal{N}_{k+1}(t)| \gg |\mathcal{N}_k(t)|$ for the k-th

[3] The plain method computes the upper (lower) bounds for max aggregation as the maximum (minimum) bound of all the variables, and for mean aggregation by sorting variable bounds from $X_2 \cup X_3$ in ascending order and finding the maximum (minimum) mean value among all postfix (prefix) sequences.

Algorithm 1 Exact Verification of GNNs with Incremental Solving

Input: Trained GNN f with K layers, attributed directed graph $G = \langle V, E, X \rangle$, target node t (for node classification), fragile edge set F, perturbation budgets Δ, δ, ϵ.
Output: Verification result.

1: $Bounds \leftarrow \{\underline{attr}, \overline{attr}\}$;
2: **for** k from 1 to K **do**
3:     $\varphi_k \leftarrow \text{EncodeGNNLayer}(f, k, G, F, \Delta, \delta, \epsilon)$;
4:     $Bounds \leftarrow \text{BoundPropagation}(\varphi_k, Bounds)$;
5: **end for**
6: $\varphi_{obj} \leftarrow \text{EncodeObjective}(\varphi_K, t)$; //Also encode final layer for graph classification.
7: $S_\Theta \leftarrow \text{InitIncSolver}()$;
8: $\Phi \leftarrow \varphi_{obj}$;
9: **for** k from K to 1 **do**
10:     $\Phi \leftarrow \Phi \wedge \varphi_k$;
11:     $(result, \Theta) \leftarrow \text{IncSolve}(S_\Theta, \Phi, Bounds)$;
12:     **if** $result =$ **`unsat`** **then**
13:         **return** `robust`;
14:     **end if**
15: **end for**
16: **return** `non-robust`;

layer, leading to rapid expansion of the encoding and a decrease in efficiency. To improve performance while maintaining exactness of verification, we utilise *incremental solving*, an effective mechanism in existing CSP solvers, to iteratively solve a series of simplified relaxation problems compared to the original problem.

Algorithm 1 describes our verification method for GNNs that leverages incremental solving. First, the CSP is formulated and the bounds of variables are derived based on the rules of bound tightening of Sect. 4.2 and layer-by-layer propagation (lines 1–6). Next, we solve the formula Φ iteratively using an incremental solving mechanism (lines 7–15). Initially, $\Phi = \varphi_{obj}$. For node classification, φ_{obj} only contains the variables representing the final embeddings of the target node t. For graph classification, φ_{obj} contains the variables representing the sum of final embeddings of all nodes, along with the final summation and linear transformation layer. In each iteration, new variables and the corresponding constraints are added to Φ, and a MIP solver S_Θ is then called (line 11), where Θ represents the generated cuts, which are redundant constraints produced by the solver to prune the search space. If Φ is found to be unsatisfiable, then the GNN has been verified to be `robust`. Otherwise, the encoding of the previous layer is added to Φ. Finally, if the result of the last iteration remains satisfiable, then the GNN is verified as `non-robust`. Note that, when each additional layer is added in the graph, the number of neighbouring nodes can increase significantly. Therefore, our algorithm effectively reduces the size of the encoding in early iterations, which leads to a more efficient exact verification process.

Finally, we show the correctness of Algorithm 1 with the proof in Appendix D in the extended version [46].

Theorem 2. *Given a GNN f, an attributed directed graph G, and a perturbation space $\mathcal{Q}(G)$, f is adversarially robust (for a node t, if it is a node-classification GNN) if and only if Algorithm 1 returns* `robust`.

5 Experimental Evaluation

5.1 Implementation and Setup

We implement our method as GNNEv, a versatile and efficient exact[4] verifier specifically designed for message-passing GNNs[5]. GNNEv calls the underlying Gurobi 11.0.3 solver[6] for MIP solving. Compared to available exact GNN verifiers, GNNEv has three advantages: (i) it accepts three commonly used aggregation functions, sum, max, and mean, which broadens usability, (ii) it allows for both node attribute perturbation and edge addition/deletion, making it applicable to a wider range of attack scenarios, and (iii) it is designed as a Python library that accepts trained models built by the SAGEConv module in PyTorch Geometric [26], and thus can be used directly in the same environment as model implementation and training.

To evaluate performance, we trained a batch of GraphSAGE models on two citation network datasets, Cora and CiteSeer [65], two real-world fraud datasets, Amazon [50] and Yelp [57], and two biochemical datasets, MUTAG and ENZYMES [52]. The first four datasets are for node classification and the last two are for graph classification. We set the number of GNN layers $K = 3$ and aggregation functions $\mathbf{aggr} \in \{\text{mean}, \text{max}, \text{sum}\}$. We regard robustness verification for each node/graph as a task, which checks prediction stability for any set of admissible perturbations up to a given budget. For evaluation purposes, we run experiments with attribute and structural perturbation separately, but GNNEv supports their simultaneous use. All experiments were conducted on a server with Intel Xeon Gold 6252 @ 2.10 GHz CPU, 252 GB RAM, and Ubuntu 18.04 OS. A verifier, including both GNNEv and the baselines, ran each task on a single CPU core for fair comparison. The time limit for each task was set to 300s. More details of the datasets and experimental setups can be found in Appendix E in the extended version [46].

[4] For edge addition/deletion, GNNEv is a conditional exact verifier with respect to a given fragile edge set F.

[5] https://github.com/minghao-liu/GNNev.

[6] https://www.gurobi.com.

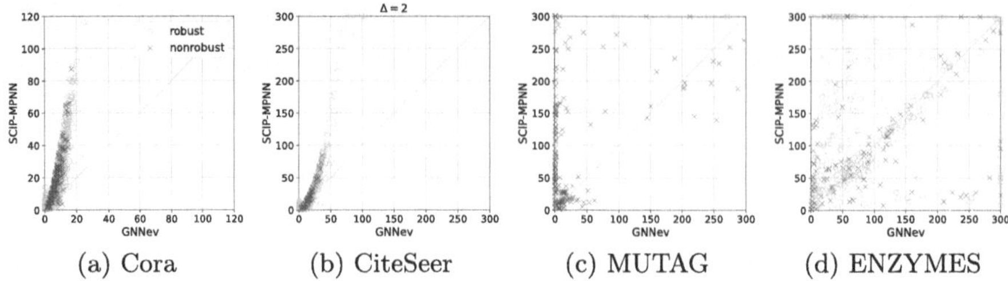

(a) Cora (b) CiteSeer (c) MUTAG (d) ENZYMES

Fig. 2. Comparison of runtime (in seconds) for sum-aggregated GNNs on node classification (a-b) and graph classification (c-d). Each data point represents a robustness verification task with $\Delta = 2$. A point above the diagonal line indicates that GNNEV outperforms SCIP-MPNN on that task.

5.2 Comparison with Baselines on Sum-Aggregation

We compare GNNEV to SCIP-MPNN [33] on edge deletion[7], the only MIP-based exact verifier immediately applicable to adversarial robustness of GNNs[8]. SCIP-MPNN includes five variants with different underlying solvers and bound tightening strategies. To make fair comparison, we use the two versions that also call Gurobi: GRBbasic and GRBsbt[9]. For each task, we ran these two versions separately and reported the shorter runtime as the result of SCIP-MPNN. To align with the restrictions of SCIP-MPNN, we utilised GNNs with sum aggregation, only allowed edge deletions (i.e., $F = E$), and adapted our verification objective[10].

Results. Figure 2 demonstrates the comparison of runtime between GNNEV and SCIP-MPNN with edge deletions. For node-classification datasets, Cora and CiteSeer, GNNEV solved all tasks within 40s and 120s, respectively, outperforming SCIP-MPNN on the vast majority of tasks. Note that GNNEV also solved 5 challenging tasks on which SCIP-MPNN failed within the time limit on CiteSeer. For graph-classification datasets, GNNEV demonstrated competitive performance. On MUTAG, GNNEV solved most tasks within seconds, likely due to the simpler and more efficient encoding produced through incremental solving. On ENZYMES, a highly challenging dataset, GNNEV also performed well

[7] We note that SCIP-MPNN does not implement edge addition and its interface does not support attribute perturbations.

[8] We remark that ROBLIGHT [47] outperforms our tool but it is not MIP-based, limited to structural perturbations only and does not allow certificate generation in the sense of [5].

[9] We excluded the three variants based on SCIP, noting that the experimental results in [33] showed that GRBbasic and GRBsbt have notably shorter runtime.

[10] According to Hojny et al. [33], Eq. (11) and Sect. 4.2, given the predicted class $\hat{c}_t$ for target node t, SCIP-MPNN aims to verify that $\mathbf{h}_t^{(K)}[\hat{c}_t] > \mathbf{h}_t^{(K)}[(\hat{c}_t + 1)\%|C|]$ holds for all perturbed graphs. This simpler objective, which provides weaker robustness guarantees than ours stated in Eq. (14), is used for tractability reasons.

compared to SCIP-MPNN by completing 6.1% of the solvable tasks that SCIP-MPNN could not complete within the time limit, and reducing runtime on 54.8% of the solvable tasks. Our experiments thus indicate that GNNEv is a highly promising approach for exact verification. See Appendix F in the extended version [46] for detailed comparison results on different perturbation budgets.

5.3 Performance on All Aggregation Functions

Next, we systematically evaluated the performance of GNNEv on sum-, max- and mean-aggregated GNNs with structural perturbations. For this experiment we set the strong verification objective as Eq. (13), which is more challenging to compute than Hojny et al. [33], Eq. (11). Due to the large number of nodes in Amazon and Yelp, we randomly selected 1,000 nodes for verification. Two fragile edge sets F were used: (i) *edge deletions* are allowed for all edges, i.e., $F = E$, and (ii) *edge additions* are allowed for selected set, i.e., for each node v, several sampled non-edges $(u, v) \notin E$ are added to F. See Appendix F in the extended version [46] for more details.

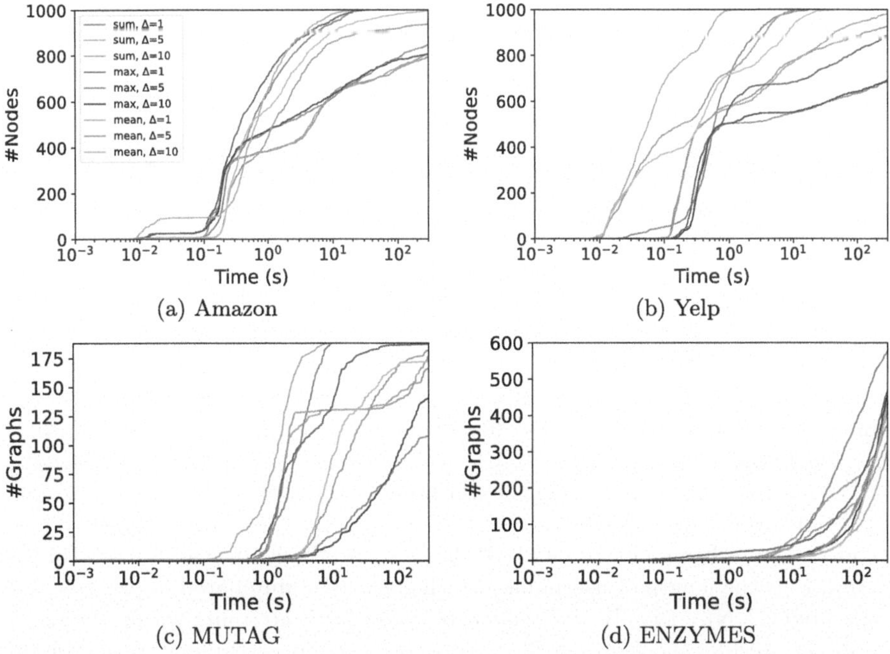

Fig. 3. The number of tasks solved by GNNEv on real-world node-classification (a-b) and graph-classification (c-d) datasets plotted against runtime under different aggregations and budgets. Only edge deletions are allowed ($F = E$). The verification objective is as defined in Sect. 4.1, Eq. (13). Full results are shown in Fig. 5 in Appendix F in the extended version [46].

Results. Figure 3 illustrates the runtime of GNNEV on real-world node- and graph-classification datasets under different aggregations and budgets Δ for edge deletion; results on additional datasets and for edge addition are in Fig. 5, 6 in Appendix F in the extended version [46]. First, MUTAG and ENZYMES are more challenging, as incremental solving can reduce the number of variables representing both nodes and layers for node classification, whereas it can only reduce the number of variables representing layers for graph classification. Second, across different aggregations, there was a performance drop for max aggregation when $\Delta \geq 5$, likely due to Gurobi struggling to efficiently process max constraints using internal big-M encoding. Moreover, for sum aggregation, the performance on Amazon and Yelp dropped compared to Cora and CiteSeer. This can be attributed to the much larger gap between upper and lower bounds of variables, which is most pronounced for sum aggregation in Table 5 in Appendix F in the extended version [46], where we see a significant increase in the gap after each layer. Finally, we conducted ablation experiments to show the effectiveness of bound tightening and incremental solving, with results detailed in Appendix F in the extended version [46].

5.4 Adversarial Robustness Case Study

We further use GNNEV to analyse the robustness of GNNs for both structural and attribute perturbations, especially in high-stakes domains such as fraud detection and scientific discovery. First, we performed evaluation of the number of (non-)robust tasks verified plotted against an increasing global structural perturbation budget, shown in Fig. 7, 8 in Appendix F in the extended version [46]. In most cases, instances were attacked successfully with a small budget. Some GNNs exhibited quite weak robustness. Specifically, we found that mean-aggregated GNNs were more vulnerable to adversarial perturbations than other types. Moreover, GNNEV was executed on Amazon and Yelp to verify mean-aggregated GNNs with attribute perturbation enabled. From the results shown in Fig. 9 in Appendix F in the extended version [46], even perturbing a single dimension of attributes can cause models to make wrong predictions in up to 75.8% of tasks.

Within these results, we identified a number of adversarial attacks on non-robust instances, which demonstrate the vulnerability of GNNs. Figure 4 illustrates two cases from Amazon and MUTAG, respectively. In Amazon, one of the attributes is the length of username, which is easily manipulated in practice. We configured GNNEV to only allow perturbations of this attribute within the range $[1, 10]$. The results showed that 29.1% of nodes were successfully attacked for the mean-aggregated GNN. In MUTAG, edge addition and deletion can easily lead to invalid structures, but GNNEV found that mean-aggregated GNNs reported 12.7% false positive results when $\Delta = 1$. These demonstrate that GNNEV is able to gain useful insight into the susceptibility of GNN models to adversarial attacks, which is important for pre-deployment analysis for high-stakes applications.

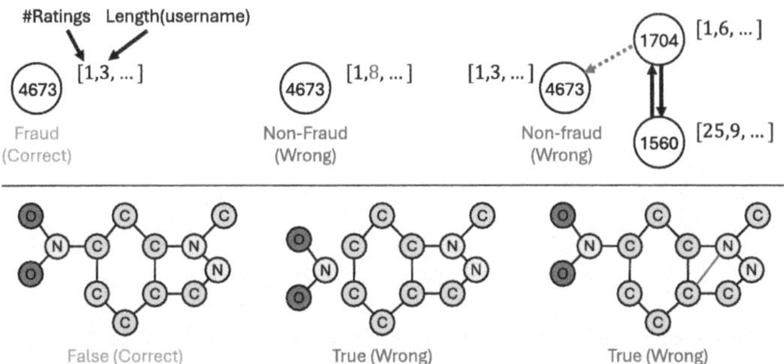

Fig. 4. Adversarial examples found by GNNEV. Top: Either modifying an attribute (here length of username) or adding an edge caused a node in the Amazon dataset to be misclassified as non-fraudulent. Bottom: Adding or deleting an edge on a graph in the MUTAG dataset leads to wrong prediction of having the given property even if the perturbed graphs are invalid.

6 Conclusion and Future Work

We have developed an exact robustness verification method for message-passing GNNs supporting a range of aggregation functions, which is implemented in GNNEV, a versatile and efficient verifier. Our approach is based on a reduction to a constraint satisfaction problem with bound tightening, solved incrementally. The support for two common aggregation functions, max and mean, is formulated here for the first time. Experiments on a range of datasets show that GNNEV can verify adversarial robustness of GNNs to attribute and structural perturbations. It outperforms state-of-the-art MIP-based baselines on node classification in both efficiency and functionality while remaining competitive on graph classification, and delivers strong performance on real-world fraud and biochemical datasets. One practical limitation of our approach is that the computational complexity grows quickly with the size of the fragile edge set. Future work will include mitigating the impact of the fragile edge sets on performance by combining heuristic search and distributed frameworks, and developing hybrid approaches to integrate probabilistic verification for improving scalability.

Acknowledgments. The authors would like to thank Michael Benedikt for the insightful comments and suggestions. This work was supported by the EPSRC Prosperity Partnership FAIR (grant number EP/V056883/1) and ELSA: European Lighthouse on Secure and Safe AI project (grant agreement No. 101070617 under UK guarantee). MK receives funding from the ERC under the European Union's Horizon 2020 research and innovation programme (FUN2MODEL, grant agreement No. 834115).

References

1. Akintunde, M.E., Kevorchian, A., Lomuscio, A., Pirovano, E.: Verification of RNN-based neural agent-environment systems. In: AAAI, pp. 6006–6013 (2019)
2. An, D., et al.: Graph convolutional network robustness verification algorithm based on dual approximation. In: ICFEM, pp. 146–161 (2024)
3. Banerjee, D., Xu, C., Singh, G.: Input-relational verification of deep neural networks. Proc. ACM Program. Lang. **8**(PLDI), 1–27 (2024)
4. Barceló, P., Kostylev, E.V., Monet, M., Pérez, J., Reutter, J.L., Silva, J.P.: The logical expressiveness of graph neural networks. In: ICLR (2020)
5. Barrett, C.W., Henzinger, T.A., Seshia, S.A.: Certificates in AI: learn but verify. Commun. ACM **69**(1), 66–75 (2026)
6. Benedikt, M., Lu, C., Motik, B., Tan, T.: Decidability of graph neural networks via logical characterizations. In: ICALP, pp. 127:1–127:20 (2024)
7. Bojchevski, A., Günnemann, S.: Certifiable robustness to graph perturbations. In: NeurIPS, pp. 8317–8328 (2019)
8. Bojchevski, A., Klicpera, J., Günnemann, S.: Efficient robustness certificates for discrete data: sparsity-aware randomized smoothing for graphs, images and more. In: ICML, pp. 1003–1013 (2020)
9. Bonaert, G., Dimitrov, D.I., Baader, M., Vechev, M.T.: Fast and precise certification of transformers. In: PLDI, pp. 466–481 (2021)
10. Boopathy, A., Weng, T., Chen, P., Liu, S., Daniel, L.: CNN-Cert: an efficient framework for certifying robustness of convolutional neural networks. In: AAAI, pp. 3240–3247 (2019)
11. Botoeva, E., Kouvaros, P., Kronqvist, J., Lomuscio, A., Misener, R.: Efficient verification of ReLU-based neural networks via dependency analysis. In: AAAI, pp. 3291–3299 (2020)
12. Bronstein, M.M., Bruna, J., Cohen, T., Velickovic, P.: Geometric deep learning: grids, groups, graphs, geodesics, and gauges. CoRR **abs/2104.13478** (2021)
13. Bunel, R., Turkaslan, I., Torr, P.H.S., Kohli, P., Mudigonda, P.K.: A unified view of piecewise linear neural network verification. In: NeurIPS, pp. 4795–4804 (2018)
14. Cai, P., Wang, H., Sun, Y., Liu, M.: DiGNet: learning scalable self-driving policies for generic traffic scenarios with graph neural networks. In: IROS, pp. 8979–8984 (2021)
15. Casas, S., Gulino, C., Liao, R., Urtasun, R.: SpAGNN: spatially-aware graph neural networks for relational behavior forecasting from sensor data. In: ICRA, pp. 9491–9497 (2020)
16. Chang, H., et al.: A restricted black-box adversarial framework towards attacking graph embedding models. In: AAAI, pp. 3389–3396 (2020)
17. Chen, J., Zhang, J., Chen, Z., Du, M., Xuan, Q.: Time-aware gradient attack on dynamic network link prediction. IEEE Trans. Knowl. Data Eng. **35**(2), 2091–2102 (2023)
18. Cheung, K.K.H., Gleixner, A.M., Steffy, D.E.: Verifying integer programming results. In: IPCO, pp. 148–160 (2017)
19. Cohen, J., Rosenfeld, E., Kolter, J.Z.: Certified adversarial robustness via randomized smoothing. In: ICML, pp. 1310–1320 (2019)
20. Corso, G., Cavalleri, L., Beaini, D., Liò, P., Velickovic, P.: Principal neighbourhood aggregation for graph nets. In: NeurIPS (2020)
21. Dai, H., et al.: Adversarial attack on graph structured data. In: ICML, pp. 1123–1132 (2018)

22. Dai, Q., Shen, X., Zhang, L., Li, Q., Wang, D.: Adversarial training methods for network embedding. In: WWW, pp. 329–339 (2019)
23. Dehmamy, N., Barabási, A., Yu, R.: Understanding the representation power of graph neural networks in learning graph topology. In: NeurIPS, pp. 15387–15397 (2019)
24. Du, T., et al.: Cert-RNN: towards certifying the robustness of recurrent neural networks. In: CCS, pp. 516–534 (2021)
25. Feng, F., He, X., Tang, J., Chua, T.: Graph adversarial training: dynamically regularizing based on graph structure. IEEE Trans. Knowl. Data Eng. **33**(6), 2493–2504 (2021)
26. Fey, M., Lenssen, J.E.: Fast graph representation learning with PyTorch Geometric. CoRR **abs/1903.02428** (2019)
27. Gao, C., Yin, S., Wang, H., Wang, Z., Du, Z., Li, X.: Medical-knowledge-based graph neural network for medication combination prediction. IEEE Trans. Neural Networks Learn. Syst. **35**(10), 13246–13257 (2024)
28. Geisler, S., Schmidt, T., Şirin, H., Zügner, D., Bojchevski, A., Günnemann, S.: Robustness of graph neural networks at scale. In: NeurIPS, pp. 7637–7649 (2021)
29. Gilmer, J., Schoenholz, S.S., Riley, P.F., Vinyals, O., Dahl, G.E.: Neural message passing for quantum chemistry. In: ICML, pp. 1263–1272 (2017)
30. Gosch, L., Geisler, S., Sturm, D., Charpentier, B., Zügner, D., Günnemann, S.: Adversarial training for graph neural networks: pitfalls, solutions, and new directions. In: NeurIPS (2023)
31. Haghshenas, S.H., Hasnat, A., Naeini, M.: A temporal graph neural network for cyber attack detection and localization in smart grids. In: ISGT, pp. 1–5 (2023)
32. Hamilton, W.L., Ying, Z., Leskovec, J.: Inductive representation learning on large graphs. In: NeurIPS, pp. 1024–1034 (2017)
33. Hojny, C., Zhang, S., Campos, J.S., Misener, R.: Verifying message-passing neural networks via topology-based bounds tightening. In: ICML (2024)
34. Huang, P., Wei, D., Isac, O., Wu, H., Wu, M., Barrett, C.: Parameterized abstract interpretation for transformer verification. In: AAAI (2026)
35. Huang, X., Kwiatkowska, M., Wang, S., Wu, M.: Safety verification of deep neural networks. In: CAV, pp. 3–29 (2017)
36. Jha, K., Saha, S., Singh, H.: Prediction of protein-protein interaction using graph neural networks. Sci. Rep. **12**(1), 8360 (2022)
37. Jin, H., Shi, Z., Peruri, V.J.S.A., Zhang, X.: Certified robustness of graph convolution networks for graph classification under topological attacks. In: NeurIPS (2020)
38. Katz, G., Barrett, C.W., Dill, D.L., Julian, K., Kochenderfer, M.J.: Reluplex: an efficient SMT solver for verifying deep neural networks. In: CAV, pp. 97–117 (2017)
39. Kipf, T.N., Welling, M.: Semi-supervised classification with graph convolutional networks. In: ICLR (2017)
40. Ko, C., Lyu, Z., Weng, L., Daniel, L., Wong, N., Lin, D.: POPQORN: quantifying robustness of recurrent neural networks. In: ICML, pp. 3468–3477 (2019)
41. Ladner, T., Eichelbeck, M., Althoff, M.: Formal verification of graph convolutional networks with uncertain node features and uncertain graph structure. Trans. Mach. Learn. Res. **2025** (2025)
42. Lai, Y., Zhu, Y., Pan, B., Zhou, K.: Node-aware bi-smoothing: certified robustness against graph injection attacks. In: IEEE SP, pp. 2958–2976 (2024)
43. Li, J., Peng, J., Chen, L., Zheng, Z., Liang, T., Ling, Q.: Spectral adversarial training for robust graph neural network. IEEE Trans. Knowl. Data Eng. **35**(9), 9240–9253 (2023)

44. Li, J., Xie, T., Chen, L., Xie, F., He, X., Zheng, Z.: Adversarial attack on large scale graph. IEEE Trans. Knowl. Data Eng. **35**(1), 82–95 (2023)
45. Li, M.M., Huang, K., Zitnik, M.: Graph representation learning in biomedicine and healthcare. Nat. Biomed. Eng. **6**(12), 1353–1369 (2022)
46. Liu, M., Lu, C., Kwiatkowska, M.: Exact verification of graph neural networks with incremental constraint solving. CoRR **abs/2508.09320** (2025)
47. Lu, C., Tan, T., Benedikt, M.: Robustness verification of graph neural networks via lightweight satisfiability testing. CoRR **abs/2510.18591** (2025)
48. Lu, J., Kumar, M.P.: Neural network branching for neural network verification. In: ICLR (2020)
49. Marzari, L., Cicalese, F., Farinelli, A.: Probabilistically tightened linear relaxation-based perturbation analysis for neural network verification. J. Artif. Intell. Res. **84** (2025)
50. McAuley, J.J., Leskovec, J.: From amateurs to connoisseurs: modeling the evolution of user expertise through online reviews. In: WWW, pp. 897–908 (2013)
51. Mohammadinejad, S., Paulsen, B., Deshmukh, J.V., Wang, C.: DiffRNN: differential verification of recurrent neural networks. In: FORMATS, pp. 117–134 (2021)
52. Morris, C., Kriege, N.M., Bause, F., Kersting, K., Mutzel, P., Neumann, M.: TUDataset: a collection of benchmark datasets for learning with graphs. In: ICML 2020 Workshop on Graph Representation Learning and Beyond (2020)
53. Motie, S., Raahemi, B.: Financial fraud detection using graph neural networks: a systematic review. Expert Syst. Appl. **240**, 122156 (2024)
54. Mu, J., Wang, B., Li, Q., Sun, K., Xu, M., Liu, Z.: A hard label black-box adversarial attack against graph neural networks. In: CCS, pp. 108–125 (2021)
55. Nunn, P., Sälzer, M., Schwarzentruber, F., Troquard, N.: A logic for reasoning about aggregate-combine graph neural networks. In: IJCAI, pp. 3532–3540 (2024)
56. Osselin, P., Kenlay, H., Dong, X.: Structure-aware robustness certificates for graph classification. In: UAI, pp. 1596–1605 (2023)
57. Rayana, S., Akoglu, L.: Collective opinion spam detection: bridging review networks and metadata. In: KDD, pp. 985–994 (2015)
58. Reiser, P., et al.: Graph neural networks for materials science and chemistry. Commun. Mater. **3**(1), 93 (2022)
59. Rosenbluth, E., Tönshoff, J., Grohe, M.: Some might say all you need is sum. In: IJCAI, pp. 4172–4179 (2023)
60. Rossi, F., Van Beek, P., Walsh, T.: Handbook of Constraint Programming. Elsevier (2006)
61. Salman, H., Yang, G., Zhang, H., Hsieh, C., Zhang, P.: A convex relaxation barrier to tight robustness verification of neural networks. In: NeurIPS, pp. 9832–9842 (2019)
62. Sälzer, M., Lange, M.: Fundamental limits in formal verification of message-passing neural networks. In: ICLR (2023)
63. Scholten, Y., Schuchardt, J., Geisler, S., Bojchevski, A., Günnemann, S.: Randomized message-interception smoothing: gray-box certificates for graph neural networks. In: NeurIPS (2022)
64. Schönherr, M., Lutz, C.: Logical characterizations of GNNs with mean aggregation. CoRR **abs/2507.18145** (2025)
65. Sen, P., Namata, G., Bilgic, M., Getoor, L., Gallagher, B., Eliassi-Rad, T.: Collective classification in network data. AI Mag. **29**(3), 93–106 (2008)
66. Shi, Z., Zhang, H., Chang, K., Huang, M., Hsieh, C.: Robustness verification for transformers. In: ICLR (2020)

67. Tao, S., Cao, Q., Shen, H., Huang, J., Wu, Y., Cheng, X.: Single node injection attack against graph neural networks. In: CIKM, pp. 1794–1803 (2021)
68. Tjeng, V., Xiao, K.Y., Tedrake, R.: Evaluating robustness of neural networks with mixed integer programming. In: ICLR (2019)
69. Tran, H., Bak, S., Xiang, W., Johnson, T.T.: Verification of deep convolutional neural networks using ImageStars. In: CAV, pp. 18–42 (2020)
70. Wang, B., Jia, J., Cao, X., Gong, N.Z.: Certified robustness of graph neural networks against adversarial structural perturbation. In: KDD, pp. 1645–1653 (2021)
71. Wang, D., et al.: A semi-supervised graph attentive network for financial fraud detection. In: ICDM, pp. 598–607 (2019)
72. Wang, S., Pei, K., Whitehouse, J., Yang, J., Jana, S.: Efficient formal safety analysis of neural networks. In: NeurIPS, pp. 6369–6379 (2018)
73. Weng, L., et al.: PROVEN: verifying robustness of neural networks with a probabilistic approach. In: ICML, pp. 6727–6736 (2019)
74. Weng, T., et al.: Towards fast computation of certified robustness for ReLU networks. In: ICML, pp. 5273–5282 (2018)
75. Wu, H., Wang, C., Tyshetskiy, Y., Docherty, A., Lu, K., Zhu, L.: Adversarial examples for graph data: deep insights into attack and defense. In: IJCAI, pp. 4816–4823 (2019)
76. Xia, Z., Yang, H., Wang, B., Jia, J.: GNNCert: deterministic certification of graph neural networks against adversarial perturbations. In: ICLR (2024)
77. Xu, K., et al.: Topology attack and defense for graph neural networks: an optimization perspective. In: IJCAI, pp. 3961–3967 (2019)
78. Xu, K., Hu, W., Leskovec, J., Jegelka, S.: How powerful are graph neural networks? In: ICLR (2019)
79. Xu, K., et al.: Automatic perturbation analysis for scalable certified robustness and beyond. In: NeurIPS (2020)
80. Ying, R., He, R., Chen, K., Eksombatchai, P., Hamilton, W.L., Leskovec, J.: Graph convolutional neural networks for web-scale recommender systems. In: KDD, pp. 974–983 (2018)
81. Zhang, H., Weng, T., Chen, P., Hsieh, C., Daniel, L.: Efficient neural network robustness certification with general activation functions. In: NeurIPS, pp. 4944–4953 (2018)
82. Zhang, S., et al.: Optimizing over trained GNNs via symmetry breaking. In: NeurIPS (2023)
83. Zhang, X., Zitnik, M.: GNNGuard: defending graph neural networks against adversarial attacks. In: NeurIPS (2020)
84. Zhang, Z., Jia, J., Wang, B., Gong, N.Z.: Backdoor attacks to graph neural networks. In: SACMAT, pp. 15–26 (2021)
85. Zhou, K., Michalak, T.P., Waniek, M., Rahwan, T., Vorobeychik, Y.: Attacking similarity-based link prediction in social networks. In: AAMAS, pp. 305–313 (2019)
86. Zou, X., et al.: TDGIA: effective injection attacks on graph neural networks. In: KDD, pp. 2461–2471 (2021)
87. Zügner, D., Akbarnejad, A., Günnemann, S.: Adversarial attacks on neural networks for graph data. In: KDD, pp. 2847–2856 (2018)
88. Zügner, D., Günnemann, S.: Adversarial attacks on graph neural networks via meta learning. In: ICLR (2019)
89. Zügner, D., Günnemann, S.: Certifiable robustness and robust training for graph convolutional networks. In: KDD, pp. 246–256 (2019)
90. Zügner, D., Günnemann, S.: Certifiable robustness of graph convolutional networks under structure perturbations. In: KDD, pp. 1656–1665 (2020)

Author Index

A
Afzal, Mohammad 480
Aichernig, Bernhard K. 298
Akshay, S. 480
An, Jie 3
Antonopoulos, Timos 21

B
Bannour, Boutheina 440
Bargmann, Lara 109
Batz, Kevin 259
Berton, Carl 220
Biere, Armin 170
Bohrer, Rose 337

C
Cai, Shaowei 89
Cai, Zhiheng 500
Cao, Jialun 211
Ceragioli, Lorenzo 461
Chen, Minrui 151
Chen, Zhihan 89
Chen, Zhiyong 211
Cherif, Sami 220
Cheung, Shing-Chi 211
Cunha, Alcino 279

D
Delaplace, Claire 220
Dong, Wei 240
Drodt, Daniel 357

F
Froleyks, Nils 170
Fu, Hongfei 397

G
Galletta, Letterio 461
Ganty, Pierre 599
Genest, Blaise 480
Guan, Ji 578
Gupta, Ashutosh 480

H
Hähnle, Reiner 357
Hartmanns, Arnd 189
Hasuo, Ichiro 3, 337
He, Fei 500
Heljanko, Keijo 170
Howar, Falk 130

J
Jiang, Huidong 151
Jouve-Genty, Martin 3
Junges, Sebastian 520

K
Katoen, Joost-Pieter 259, 559
Kawamoto, Yusuke 337
Ke, Jingyu 397
Kruger, Loes 520
Kuijer, Louwe B. 541
Kwiatkowska, Marta 641

L
Le Gall, Pascale 440
Li, Guoqiang 397
Li, Haokun 397
Li, Zihao 578
Lienhardt, Michael 317
Liu, Minghao 641
Liu, Si 47
Liu, Sirui 240
Liu, Zhiming 419
Lu, Chia-Hsuan 641
Lu, Weijie 397
Lunati, Edoardo 461
Luo, Ning 21

M
Macedo, Nuno 279
Mahe, Erwan 440
Manini, Nicolas 599
Montacute, Yoàv 337

A. Sampaio and M. Stoelinga (Eds.): FM 2026, LNCS 16556, pp. 663–664, 2026.
https://doi.org/10.1007/978-3-032-26204-2

N

Naujokat, Stefan 130
Neider, Daniel 130
Nguetoum, Joel 440

P

Peng, Chao 419
Piskac, Ruzica 21
Purser, David 541

Q

Qi, Niuniu 419
Quatmann, Tim 189

R

Ranzato, Francesco 599
Ren, Jiawei 67
Ren, Mengxin 419
Rot, Jurriaan 520

S

Saigo, Hiroto 151
Sato, Sota 3
Schallau, Till 130
Schmid, Dominik 130
Schröer, Philipp 559
Sinclair-Banks, Henry 541
Smith, Graeme 378
Su, Han 3
Sui, Yulei 67
Sun, Zhihang 500
Sun, Zhouyue 397

T

Tobler, James 378
Totzke, Patrick 541
Tripakis, Stavros 619
Tulcan, Radu-Florin 337

V

van Wijk, Mark 189
von Berg, Benjamin 298

W

Wang, Peixin 47
Wedenik, Fabian 298
Wehrheim, Heike 109
Westhofen, Lukas 130
Winkler, Tobias 259

X

Xu, Chang 211

Y

Yang, Zhengfeng 419
Ye, Furong 89
Ying, Mingsheng 578
Yu, Emily 170

Z

Zeng, Xia 419
Zhang, Guanqin 67
Zhang, Min 47
Zhang, Xindi 89
Zhang, Zhenya 3, 67
Zhao, Hanrui 419
Zhou, Kevin 337
Zhou, Yi 397
Zhou, Yuhao 619
Zhou, Zhou 47
Zhou, Ziwei 47
Zilken, Daniel 259

The manufacturer's authorised representative in the EU is Springer Nature Customer Service Centre GmbH, Europaplatz 3, 69115 Heidelberg, Germany. If you have any concerns regarding our products, please contact ProductSafety@springernature.com

Printed and bound by CPI Group (UK) Ltd, Croydon, CR0 4YY
16/07/2026
02169417-0001